CONTENTS

RESEARCHERS

Jorge Alvarez *Lisboa, Alentejo, Ribatejo, Estremadura, Northern Portugal*

Jorge got to the core of Portugal and rose above all challenges, from overzealous train authorities to the Portuguese wilderness. From encounters with Metallica to journeys through castles and cathedrals, Jorge's adventures, whether in fast-paced Lisboa or quiet Monsanto, never failed to liven up his editors' summers.

Gabriela Bortolomedi *Galicia, Asturias, Castilla y León*

Hailing from the warm shores of Puerto Rico, Gabi arrived in chilly Salamanca in June and promptly sought out a winter jacket and lots of *café con leche.* But when she hit the Atlantic coast, Gabi truly came alive. Whether writing about the islands of Vigo or the sunny streets of Santiago, her words brimmed with good humor, artistic joy, and a genuine love of the road. From shells to sardines, Gabi gave herself fully to the spirit of the Northwest.

Chimdimnma Esimai *Andalucía, Extremadura, the Algarve*

Chi-Chi's passion for all things Spanish led her to strap on a backpack for one blazing hot summer. Endlessly fascinated by cities like Córdoba and Cáceres, Chi-Chi took the time to talk to everyone from immigration workers to bartenders, sending back dispatches full of personal spark. We wish her all the best in graduate school, and eagerly await stories of her next jaunt through *al-Andalus.*

Charles Fisher-Post *Granada*

After a semester studying in the beautiful city of Granada, Charles was eager to bring his insider knowledge to *Let's Go* readers everywhere. And he did, with spirit and a smile. A two-time vet, Charles previously brought his professionalism to *Let's Go Greece 2008* and *Australia 2009.* We are the luckier for having had him join our team.

Jeffrey Phaneuf *Asturias and Cantabria, País Vasco, the Pyrenees*

Jeff's route was "hahd"—there's no denying it—but he took it by the horns with unbelievable determination. For Jeff, unforeseen snowstorms in the Pyrenees made Massachusetts winters seem like paradise. Buses failed to show up, and Phaneuf prevailed. Elderly female hostel owners got a little too friendly, and still Phaneuf prevailed. On top of it all, he stared down the bulls of Pamplona. Jeff Phaneuf was truly a champ of an RW—and that's no bull.

RESEARCHERS

Russell Rennie *Madrid and Morocco*

Part-time *aficionado* and full-time cultural voyeur, Russell hit the ground running in Madrid. Once in Morocco, he infiltrated markets and tanneries and kept his editors laughing, awestruck, all summer long. Expats, hippies, hustlers: no one was safe when Russell came to town. Whether scaling hostel roofs or Rif peaks, Russell was a tirelessly intrepid researcher. Yes, we are so glad he said yes.

Jessica Righthand *Valencia, Murcia, and Las Islas Baleares*

Jess island-hopped like a rockstar. Always on the lookout for artsy, hip coverage, Jess found her way into film festivals, hot nightclubs, and nudist colonies. She sunned on the white sands of Valencia and Murcia, jammed with the jazzy locals in an Ibizan nightclub, and met some unforgettable people along the way. Her most impressive feat? She managed to bring her guitar home in one piece.

Molly Strauss *Barcelona, Catalunya, Aragón, La Rioja, and Navarra*

Molly's enthusiasm was infectious. This easy-going Santa Monica girl brought her sunny ways to Spain, and despite a twisted ankle and a stolen pack, she powered through her research with unwavering commitment. From Gaudí's lizards to mooing dogs, her time in Barcelona was an adventure. She often told her editors that she fell in love with the city, and frankly, her editors fell in love with her.

Paul Katz *Paris, Nice*

Paul kept us laughing in the office all summer with his enthusiastically cheesy video blogs. Having traveled extensively in Latin America, this was his first extended trip to Europe, and he braved the language barrier and the hostile Parisian nightclub bouncers with admirable courage. Always going out of his way to improve our coverage and organization, we hope he'll remember us someday when he has his own travel show and turns those cheesy video blogs into hour-long films.

STAFF WRITERS

Sanders Bernstein   Billy Eck   Colleen O'Brien

CONTRIBUTING WRITERS

Antonio Córdoba was born in Sevilla, where he earned his B.A. in English Literature. He got his Ph.D. in Latin American literature from Harvard University in June of 2008, and is currently a lecturer in History and Literature at Harvard. Córdoba is completing a book on a 17th-century Andalusian poet.

Silvia Killingsworth was Editor-in-Chief of the 2008 *Let's Go* series. She graduated from Harvard in 2007 and now lives in New York City.

Victoria Norelid graduated from Harvard in 2007 with a degree in History. She has edited for *Let's Go Italy 2007, Let's Go Mexico 2008,* and *Let's Go London 2008,* and most recently was a Researcher-Writer for *Let's Go Australia 2009.* She is currently getting a Masters degree at Oxford University.

ACKNOWLEDGMENTS

TEAM SP&M THANKS: Our fabulous RWs. Dwight, for bustin' our chops. Nathaniel, for managing our tickets all summer long. Illiana, for seeing the world as it is. Ronan, for bringing S&P to the masses. Sam, Inés, and the Prod team, for making this book a reality.

ANNA THANKS: SPadThai. Meg for being shooptastic. Sr. Barbero for caravels and alfajores. Ashley for calming grace. Dwight for guiding brilliance. Nathaniel for outbursts and laughs. ROAD for Monday nights and the Garden of Life. Here's to RW love, sunlight, foreign muses, RadCrew, *Let's Go*, and my family.

MEAGAN THANKS: Our fantabulous RWs. Anna for her smiles and love of Lorca. DBarbs, a.k.a. "bro," for being silent but deadly. Dwight for being an honorary shoop, and shaking it like one. Ash for being a real person—and an amazing one. Nathaniel for his format prowess and coupons. Dube for Dunkin. Mapland for their dance parties. Mrs. O'Brien. Nicole. Hemingway. HRST 2009. *Let's Go.* Mom for being there through it all.

DANIEL THANKS: Anna, *para todo*, and for being the perfect foil to her crazy AEs; Meg, for singing to us (and more); Nathaniel and Ashley for completing wondrous SpadThai; my comrades at LG for making this a superb summer; as always, my family, for their support, understanding, and *pastafrola.*

ILLIANA THANKS: Anna for her constant smiles and hard work. Meg for her shoop-shoop dance moves. Dan for tolerating his split AE status with cheer. Mapland for all the laughs (most notably, Derek's Prince moments). All the SPaM RWs for bringing down the house. And Nemo for keeping me sane during the entire summer.

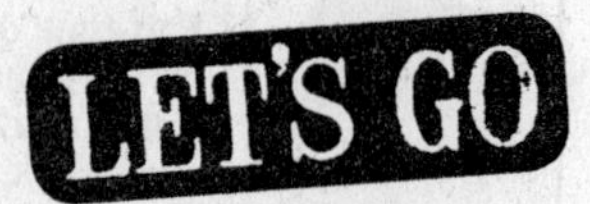

1 2 PRICE RANGES 3 4 SPAIN & PORTUGAL 5

Our Researchers list establishments in order of value from best to worst, honoring our favorites with the Let's Go thumbs-up (☒). Because the best *value* is not always the cheapest *price*, we have incorporated a system of price ranges based on a rough expectation of what you will spend. For **accommodations,** we base our range on the cheapest price for which a single traveler can stay for one night. For **restaurants** and other dining establishments, we estimate the average amount a traveler will spend in one sitting. The table below tells you what you'll typically find in Spain and Portugal at each price range, but keep in mind that no system can allow for the quirks of individual establishments.

ACCOMMODATIONS	RANGE	WHAT YOU'RE *LIKELY* TO FIND
❶	under €20	Campgrounds, HI hostels, basic dorm rooms, *albergues* or *refugios.* Expect bunk beds and a communal bath; you may have to provide or rent towels and sheets.
❷	€20-29	Upper-end hostels or lower-end *pensiones.* You may have a private bathroom, or there may be a sink in your room and a communal shower in the hall. Breakfast is often included, or meals may be available cheaply to hostel guests.
❸	€30-37	A small room with a private bath, probably in a budget hotel, *hostal,* or *pensión.* Should have decent amenities, like a phone and TV. Breakfast may be included.
❹	€38-50	Similar to ❸, but should have more amenities or be in a more highly-touristed or conveniently-located area. Breakfast is often included in the price of your room.
❺	above €50	Large hotels, upscale chains, or government-run luxury *paradores.* If it's a ❺ and it doesn't have the perks or service you're looking for, you've probably paid too much.

FOOD	RANGE	WHAT YOU'RE *LIKELY* TO FIND
❶	under €6	Probably a *kebap* or fast-food stand, *cafetería,* bar, or bakery. Rarely a sit-down meal, unless you're sitting at the bar feasting on free tapas with your drinks.
❷	€6-12	*Bocadillos* (sandwiches), salads, tapas, and some entrees and set *menús.* May be sit-down or take-out, but expect to be served by a waiter or bartender.
❸	€13-17	Typically a sit-down meal. Many set menús include a 3-course meal that includes wine and dessert.
❹	€18-25	Entrees are more expensive than ❸, but you're paying for quality service, ambience, and decor. Few restaurants in this range have a dress code, but you'll want to clean yourself up after a day of travel.
❺	over €25	Your meal might cost more than your hostel, but here's hoping it's something fabulous or famous. Just don't plan on wearing flip-flops.

DISCOVER SPAIN, PORTUGAL, AND MOROCCO

The Iberian Peninsula is a land apart. Cordoned from Europe and Africa by mountain and sea, Spain and Portugal are themselves cultural mosaics. Despite being fiercely proud of their individuality, Spain's regions share a common rhythm. Late-night parties segue into afternoon siestas, fast-paced cities shut down as citizens linger over lunch, and everything happens *mañana.* The dizzying Pyrenees and Picos de Europa exhilarate adventurers, while Spain's sands entice sun-lovers young and old. Pilgrims tread the path across northern Spain to the soaring cathedral of Santiago de Compostela, while other visitors make their pilgrimage to Madrid's famed art museums. Northeastern and central Spain are aesthetic wonders. Trendy, quirky Barcelona hugs a rugged coastline characterized by famed architecture like Antoni Gaudí's fantastical conjurings and Bilbao's shining Guggenheim Museum. The south, meanwhile, is the passionate Spain of popular imagination, home to bullfights, flamenco, tapas, and Moorish intricacies. The nocturnal energy of Madrid, Barcelona, and Ibiza could exhaust the most hardcore clubbers, but the Spanish tradition of *churros con chocolate* at dawn goes a long way to starting the next day off right. Spain is a paradise for partiers, a mecca for art lovers, a kick-start for thrill-seekers, and a rest stop for the restless.

Today, travelers will discover one of Europe's fastest-growing hotspots in Portugal. Lisboa, the capital and largest city, has the country's most impressive imperial monuments, while the southern Algarve, boasting spectacular beaches and wild nightlife, draws backpackers in droves. Northern Coimbra crackles with the energy of a university town, and Porto surpasses even Lisboa in elegance. Portugal's inland towns have a timeless feel, with medieval castles overlooking rushing rivers and peaceful town squares. The wild northern region, including the land in Trás-Os-Montes, is among the most pristine in all of Europe—some villages have remained unchanged for nearly a millennium.

While Morocco lies only 13 km from the southern tip of Spain, visitors will feel like they've stumbled into another world. Whether fascinated by the roots of Iberia's Muslim past, eager to experience the sounds and scents of bustling markets, or just longing to sit in a cafe with a steaming glass of mint tea, travelers consistently find that the bursting color and cultural hybridity of modern Morocco make a visit south from Iberia an unforgettable experience.

FACTS AND FIGURES

OFFICIAL NAMES: Kingdom of Spain, Portuguese Republic, Kingdom of Morocco

SPAIN POPULATION: 40.5 million

PORTUGAL POPULATION: 10.7 million

NUMBER OF PILGRIMS TO SANTIAGO DE COMPOSTELA IN 2007: 114,026

NUMBER OF CASTLES IN THE PORTUGUESE REPUBLIC: 101

NUMBER OF SPANISH SPEAKERS IN THE WORLD: 332 million

PORTUGAL'S MOST FAMOUS INVENTION: The hot air balloon, flown in Lisboa on August 8, 1709

HIGHEST PEAK IN IBERIA: 3478.6m (Mulhacén in Granada's Sierra Nevadas)

KILOMETERS SEPARATING SPAIN AND MOROCCO: 13

WHEN TO GO

Summer is **high season** *(temporada alta)* for coastal and interior regions in Spain and Portugal; winter is high season for ski resorts. In many areas, high season begins during **Semana Santa** (Holy Week; March 14-23 in 2008) and includes festival days. July and August see some of the hottest weather, especially in the central plains, where the mercury can creep up to 36°C (97°F). Tourism on the Iberian Peninsula peaks in August, when the coast overflows as inland cities empty out, leaving closed offices, restaurants, and lodgings. As a general rule, make **reservations** if you plan to travel in June, July, or August.

Traveling in the **low season** *(temporada baja)* has many advantages, most noticeably lighter crowds and lower prices. Many hostels cut their prices by at least 30%, and reservations are seldom necessary. While major cities and university towns may exude energy during these months, many smaller seaside spots are ghost towns, and tourist offices and sights cut their hours nearly everywhere. The weather is also ideal in spring and early summer, when temperatures are around 20-25°C (68-77°F). For a table of temperatures and rainfall, see **Climate,** p. 496. For a chart of **National Holidays** and **Festivals** in Spain, see p. 71; in Portugal, p. 369; and in Morocco, p. 455.

WHAT TO DO

Two millennia of invaders have swept over these countries, resulting in an edgy and eclectic culture ripe with custom, religion, history, and an irrepressible energy. You can see it in **Madrid's** famous nightlife (p. 110), in the sidewalk cafes of **Lisboa** (p. 384), and in extravagant festivals from small towns to big cities. There are countless ways to see Spain and Portugal: some choose to search out every Baroque chapel, while others spend weeks trekking on some of Europe's best trails. For those with time to spare, a trip down to Morocco adds more than a dash of spice to the Iberian experience.

IMAGES OF IBERIA

The insatiable frenzy of the **Queima das Fitas** in Coimbra (p. 439), **Las Fallas** in Valencia (p. 216), the **Feria de Abril** in Sevilla (p. 160), and the infamous **San Fermín** in Pamplona (p. 315) make it difficult to deny the overwhelming exuberance of the Iberian peninsula. But underneath Iberian fervor is a rich sonority of feeling—the poignant expressions of heartbreak are often as gripping and adrenaline-charged as the celebrations. The ritually tragic emotions of Portuguese **fado** would bring tears to the eyes of even the most macho bullfighters, who in turn create their own tragedies on Spanish sands. Meanwhile, art and architecture like Picasso's powerfully symbolic **Guernica** (p. 100) and the propagandistic **Valle de los Caídos** (p. 117) immortalize the real tragedies that scarred Spain during the last century. But ample opportunity exists for peace and quiet in the thin-aired reverence of **Santiago de Compostela** (p. 349) or the surreal calm of **Parc Güell** (p. 269).

CASAS TO CASTLES

From traditionally conservative to unconventionally decadent, the buildings and monuments of Iberia form a collage of architectural styles. The remains of ancient civilizations are everywhere—from the Celtiberian tower of **O Castro de Baroña** (p. 356) to Roman ruins like the aqueduct in **Segovia** (p. 127). Hundreds of years of Moorish rule left breathtaking monuments, including Granada's spectacular **Alhambra** (p. 201), Córdoba's **Mezquita** (p. 168), and Sintra's **Castelo dos Mouros** (p. 404). The Catholic church has spent immense sums of money to build some of the world's most ornate religious complexes, like the imposing **El Escorial** (p. 115). Spain's magnificent cathedrals are Gothic, Plateresque, or just plain bizarre, like Gaudí's unfinished *Modernista* **Sagrada Família** in Barcelona (p. 267). Recent additions to the architectural landscape include Lisboa's expansive **Parque das Nações** (p. 397), Bilbao's gleaming **Guggenheim Museum** (p. 332), and Valencia's huge **Ciudad de las Artes y las Ciencias** (p. 213). Casablanca's **Hassan II Mosque** (p. 483) provides a very different glimpse of the societies that have shaped these lands.

SUN AND SAND

Iberia's stunning shores deserve their reputation as Europe's playground. **San Sebastián's**) calm, voluptuous Playa de la Concha attracts young travelers from around the world, while **Santander** (p. 340) caters to an elite, refined crowd. The beaches of **Galicia** (p. 349) curve around crystal-green, misty inlets. On the **Islas Baleares** (p. 224), glistening bodies crowd the chic beaches, and southern Spain's infamous **Costa del Sol** (p. 184) draws tourists to its scorched Mediterranean bays by the plane-load. The eastern **Costa Blanca (p. 206)** mixes small-town charm with ocean expanses, while the looming cliffs and turquoise waters of Portugal's southern **Algarve** (p. 406) make for a relaxed vacation. Thrill-seekers will not be disappointed by the endless watersports opportunities—surfing, sailing, kiteboarding, scuba diving, and windsurfing are all popular. Morocco's **Essaouira** has a past of pirates and hippies, but today it's better known for music festivals and laid-back vibes.

WAYS TO SAVE IN SPAIN AND PORTUGAL

Exchange rate pinching your pocket? Travel in style while sticking to a budget with these tips for cheap eats, low-cost lodgings, and free entertainment.

1. Buy food in **open-air markets** and **grocery stores** instead of restaurants. If you do go out, try sharing a selection of tapas.

2. Stay in **alternative lodgings,** such as monasteries, university dorms, or *refugios.*

3. Be on the lookout for days when you can get into sights and museums for **free.**

4. Clubbing is pricey enough without depending on overpriced sangria; start the night off with **market-purchased booze.**

5. Keep an eye out for flyers and coupons (in weekly papers or from promoters) that offer heavy discounts at **clubs.**

6. Take **public transportation** or **walk** as much as possible.

7. Relax on one of the Iberian peninsula's many **beaches** or **parks,** where the scenery is worthwhile and your tan is free!

8. Bargain where appropriate, like in Madrid's El Rastro.

9. Get cheap tickets for flamenco and bullfighting shows by attending semi-professional events. They're less touristy, too.

10. Enjoy the **great outdoors;** hike in the Pyrenees, or enjoy the view of the Alhambra from the hills rising above Granada.

ALL NIGHT LONG

Nightlife in Spain and Portugal ranges from laid back to debaucherous. With countless bars and clubs and intoxicating energy, **Madrid** (p. 73) has earned international renown as one of the greatest party cities in the world. **Barcelona's** (p. 233) wild, edgy nightlife reflects the city's outrageous sense of style. Residents of **Sevilla** (p. 145) pack discotecas floating on the Río Guadalquivir, and on **Ibiza** (p. 226) you will find the world's largest club, filled with 10,000 decadent partiers. Student-packed **Salamanca** (p. 137) is a crazed, international frat party, and **Lagos,** in Portugal (p. 406), has more bars and backpackers per square meter than any town in the world. In **Morocco,** visitors channel expats of old by drinking espresso at outdoor cafes and lounging on open rooftops under the night sky.

LET'S GO PICKS

BEST PLACE TO STUPIDLY ENDANGER YOUR LIFE: Pamplona, during the infamous Running of the Bulls (p. 315).

BEST PLACE TO CRY LIKE A BABY: A fado house in Lisboa's Bairro Alto district, where melancholy music brings audiences to tears (p. 370).

BEST PLACE TO BUMP INTO MIRA SORVINO: Ibiza International Film Festival on the Islas Baleares (p. 226).

BEST PLACE TO HAVE A SURREALIST HALLUCINATION: Figueres at the Teatre-Museu Dalí (p. 309).

BEST MEDIEVAL RECYCLING PROJECT: The macabre Capela dos Ossos, in Évora, made from 5000 unwitting skeletons (p. 414).

BEST PLACE TO ATTACK UNSUSPECTING TOURISTS: Porto's Festa de São João, where for one evening in June townspeople beat each other over the head with plastic hammers (p. 439).

BEST PLACE TO BE LOUD AND PROUD: Madrid, during Orgullo Gay, one of the biggest gay festivals in the world, with parades and free concerts (p. 73).

BEST PLACE TO SIT ON THE THRONE: Sintra's Palácio da Pena, home of the Queen's golden toilet (p. 404).

BEST PLACE TO CHARM A SNAKE: Djemaa el-Fna, Marrakesh's bizarre bazaar. And when that's done, enjoy storytellers and magicians (p. 492).

AL-LOVIN' AL-ANDALUS (4 WEEKS)

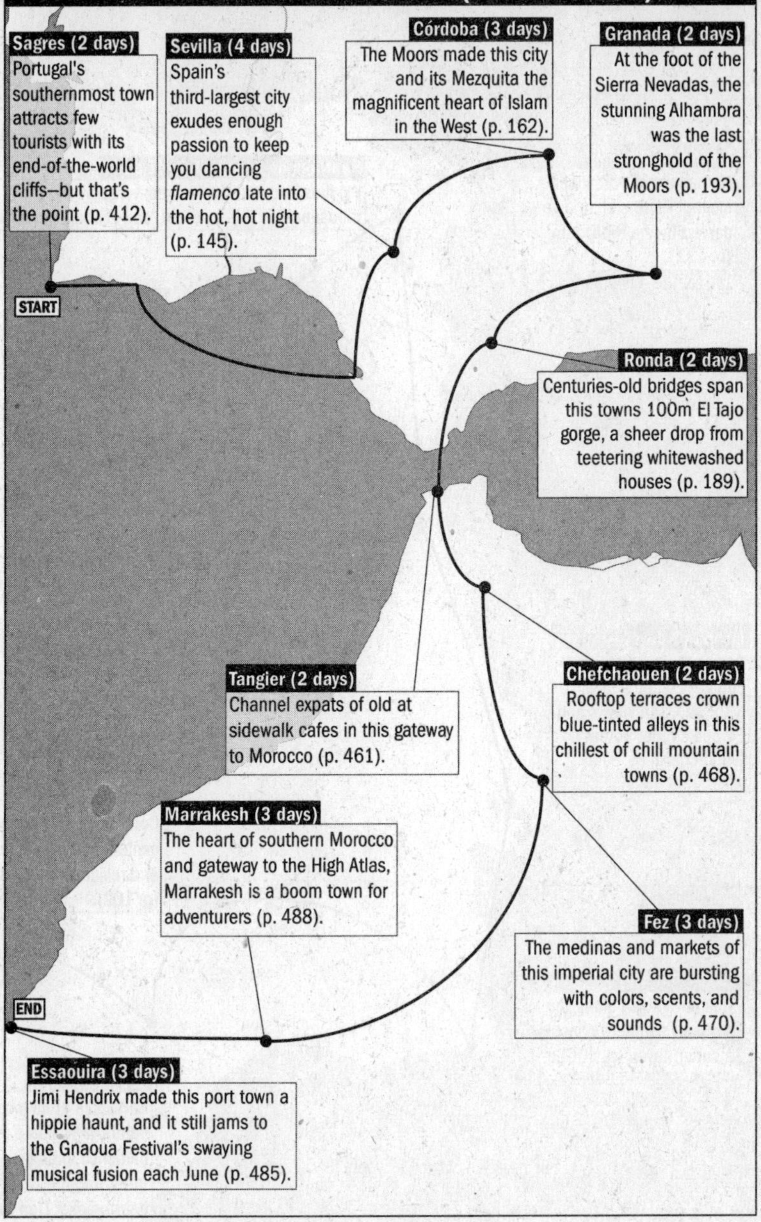

START

Sagres (2 days) Portugal's southernmost town attracts few tourists with its end-of-the-world cliffs—but that's the point (p. 412).

Sevilla (4 days) Spain's third-largest city exudes enough passion to keep you dancing *flamenco* late into the hot, hot night (p. 145).

Córdoba (3 days) The Moors made this city and its Mezquita the magnificent heart of Islam in the West (p. 162).

Granada (2 days) At the foot of the Sierra Nevadas, the stunning Alhambra was the last stronghold of the Moors (p. 193).

Ronda (2 days) Centuries-old bridges span this towns 100m El Tajo gorge, a sheer drop from teetering whitewashed houses (p. 189).

Tangier (2 days) Channel expats of old at sidewalk cafes in this gateway to Morocco (p. 461).

Chefchaouen (2 days) Rooftop terraces crown blue-tinted alleys in this chillest of chill mountain towns (p. 468).

Marrakesh (3 days) The heart of southern Morocco and gateway to the High Atlas, Marrakesh is a boom town for adventurers (p. 488).

Fez (3 days) The medinas and markets of this imperial city are bursting with colors, scents, and sounds (p. 470).

END

Essaouira (3 days) Jimi Hendrix made this port town a hippie haunt, and it still jams to the Gnaoua Festival's swaying musical fusion each June (p. 485).

BEST OF SPAIN AND PORTUGAL (6 WEEKS)

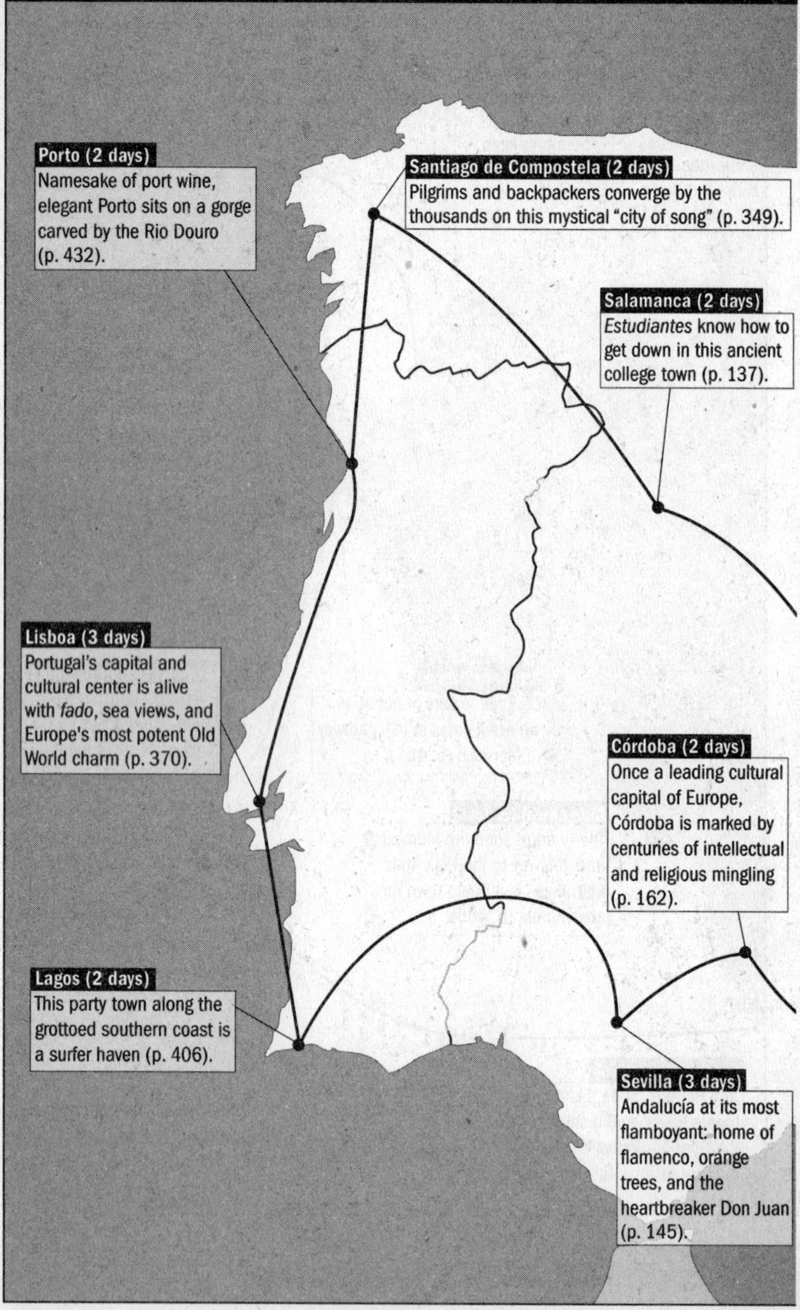

Porto (2 days)
Namesake of port wine, elegant Porto sits on a gorge carved by the Rio Douro (p. 432).

Santiago de Compostela (2 days)
Pilgrims and backpackers converge by the thousands on this mystical "city of song" (p. 349).

Salamanca (2 days)
Estudiantes know how to get down in this ancient college town (p. 137).

Lisboa (3 days)
Portugal's capital and cultural center is alive with *fado*, sea views, and Europe's most potent Old World charm (p. 370).

Córdoba (2 days)
Once a leading cultural capital of Europe, Córdoba is marked by centuries of intellectual and religious mingling (p. 162).

Lagos (2 days)
This party town along the grottoed southern coast is a surfer haven (p. 406).

Sevilla (3 days)
Andalucía at its most flamboyant: home of flamenco, orange trees, and the heartbreaker Don Juan (p. 145).

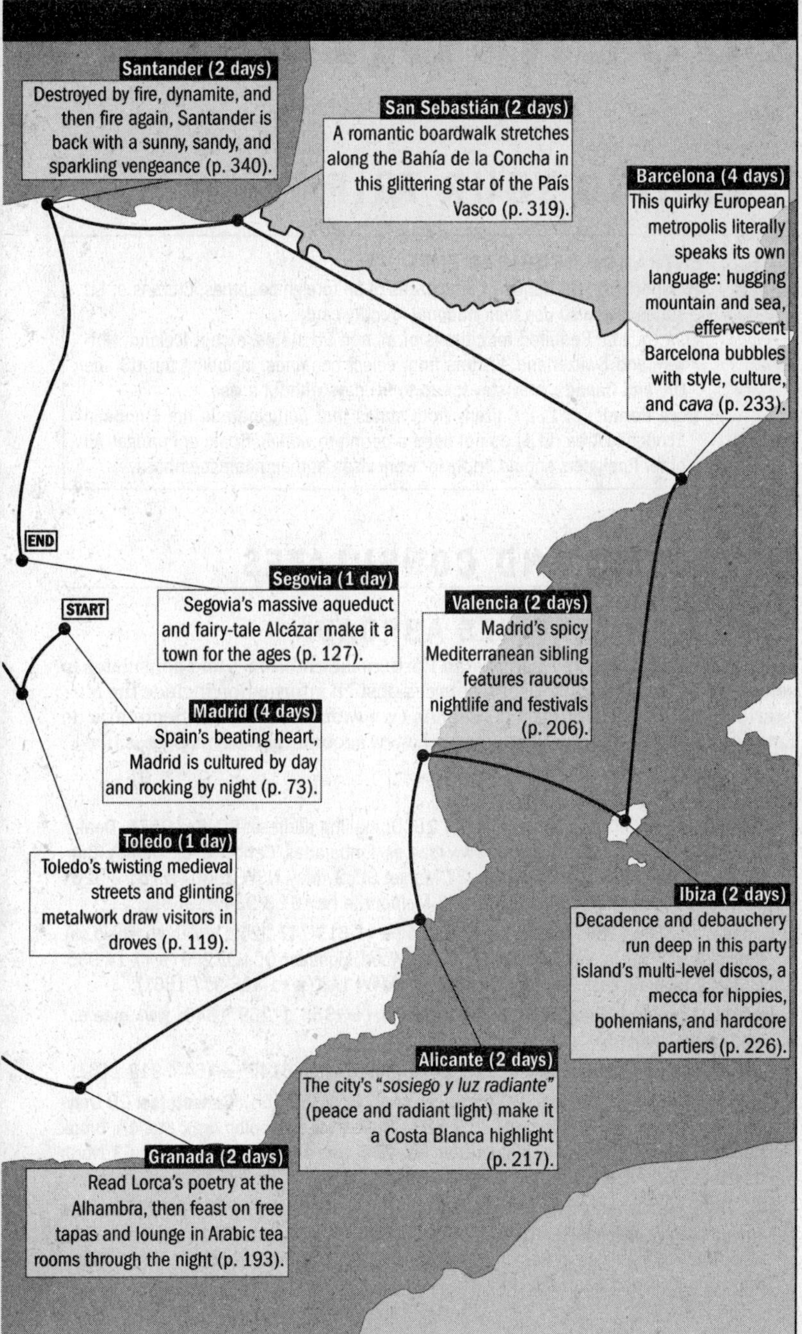
Santander (2 days)
Destroyed by fire, dynamite, and then fire again, Santander is back with a sunny, sandy, and sparkling vengeance (p. 340).
San Sebastián (2 days)
A romantic boardwalk stretches along the Bahía de la Concha in this glittering star of the País Vasco (p. 319).
Barcelona (4 days)
This quirky European metropolis literally speaks its own language: hugging mountain and sea, effervescent Barcelona bubbles with style, culture, and *cava* (p. 233).
END
Segovia (1 day)
Segovia's massive aqueduct and fairy-tale Alcázar make it a town for the ages (p. 127).
START
Valencia (2 days)
Madrid's spicy Mediterranean sibling features raucous nightlife and festivals (p. 206).
Madrid (4 days)
Spain's beating heart, Madrid is cultured by day and rocking by night (p. 73).
Toledo (1 day)
Toledo's twisting medieval streets and glinting metalwork draw visitors in droves (p. 119).
Ibiza (2 days)
Decadence and debauchery run deep in this party island's multi-level discos, a mecca for hippies, bohemians, and hardcore partiers (p. 226).
Alicante (2 days)
The city's "*sosiego y luz radiante*" (peace and radiant light) make it a Costa Blanca highlight (p. 217).
Granada (2 days)
Read Lorca's poetry at the Alhambra, then feast on free tapas and lounge in Arabic tea rooms through the night (p. 193).

ESSENTIALS

PLANNING YOUR TRIP

ENTRANCE REQUIREMENTS

Passport (p. 10). Required for citizens of all foreign countries. Citizens of EU states may also use their national identity card.

Visa (p. 11). Required for citizens of all non-EU states, except Iceland, Norway, and Switzerland. Visitors from select countries, including the US, the UK, and Canada, may stay for up to 90 days without a visa.

Work Permit (p. 11). Citizens from states that participate in the European Economic Area (EEA) do not need a permit to work in Spain or Portugal. All other foreigners should apply for work visas at their nearest embassy.

EMBASSIES AND CONSULATES

CONSULAR SERVICES ABROAD

The following listings are Spanish and Portuguese embassies and consulates in selected foreign countries. Useful sources of such information include the Ministerio de Asuntos Exteriores de España (www.mae.es) and the Secretaria de Estado das Comunidades Portuguesas (www.secomunidades.pt/postos.php).

SPANISH

Australia: 15 Arkana St., Yarralumla, ACT 2600; mailing address: P.O. Box 9076, Deakin ACT 2600 (☎+61 2 6273 3555; www.mae.es/Embajadas/Canberra/es/Home). **Consulates:** Level 24, St. Martin's Tower, 31 Market St., Sydney, NSW 2000 (☎+61 2 9261 24 33); 146 Elgin St., Carlton, VIC 3053 Melbourne (☎+61 3 9347 1966).

Canada: 74 Stanley Ave., Ottawa, ON K1M 1P4 (☎+1-613-747-2252; www.embaspain.ca). **Consulates:** 1 Westmount Sq., Ste. 1456, Ave. Wood, Montreal, QC H3Z 2P9 (☎+1 14-935-5235); 2 Bloor St. East. Ste. 1201, Toronto, ON M4W 1A8 (☎+1-416-977 1661).

Ireland: 17 Merlyn Park, Ballsbridge, Dublin 4 (☎+353 1 269 1640; www.mae.es/embajadas/dublin).

New Zealand: 56 Victoria Street, P.O.B. 24-150, Wellington 6142 (☎+64 4 913 1167).

UK: 39 Chesham Pl., London SW1X 8SB (☎ +44 207 235 5555). **Consulates:** 20 Draycott Pl., London SW3 2RZ (☎+44 207 589 8989; www.conspalon.org); Ste. 1A, Brook House, 70 Spring Gardens, Manchester M2 2BQ (☎+44 161 236 1262); 63 North Castle St., Edinburgh EH2 3LJ (☎+44 131 220 1843.)

US: 2375 Pennsylvania Ave. NW, Washington, D.C. 20037 (☎+1-202-728-2330; www.spainemb.org). **Consulates:** 150 E. 58th St., 30th fl., New York, NY 10155 (☎+1-212 355-4080s); branches in Boston, Chicago, Houston, Los Angeles, Miami, New Orleans, San Francisco, and San Juan (PR).

PORTUGUESE

Australia: 23 Culgoa Circuit, O'Malley, Canberra, ACT 2606; P.O. Box 92, Deakin, ACT 2600 (☎+61 2 6290 1733). **Consulate:** Level 9, 30 Clarence St., Sydney, NSW 2000; P.O. Box 3309, Sydney, NSW 2001 (☎+61 2 9262 2199; www.consulportugalsydney.org.au).

Canada: 645 Island Park Dr., Ottawa, ON K1Y 0B8 (☎+1-613-729-2270; www.embportugal-ottawa.org). **Consulates** in Toronto, Edmonton, Halifax, Kingston, Montreal, Quebec, Vancouver, and Winnipeg.

Ireland: Knocksinna House, Knocksinna, Foxrock, Dublin 18 (☎+353 1 289 4416).

New Zealand: See Australian embassy in Canberra. **Consulates:** 16 Fisher Crescent, Mt Wellington; PO Box 305, Auckland (☎+64 9 259 4014), Suite 1, 1st Fr, 21 Marion St., PO Box 1024 Wellington ☎+64 4 382 7655).

UK: 3 Portland Pl., London W1B-1HR (☎+44 20 7291 3770).

US: 2012 Massachusetts Ave. NW, Washington, D.C. 20036 (☎+1-202-350-5400). **Consulates:** 590 5th Ave., 3rd fl., New York, NY 10036 (☎+1-212-221-3165); branches in Boston, New Bedford, New Orleans, Newark, Providence, San Francisco.

ESSENTIALS

CONSULAR SERVICES IN SPAIN

Embassies and consulates are usually open Monday through Friday mornings and late afternoons, with siestas in between. Many consulates are only open mornings. Call ahead for exact hours.

Australia: Pl. del Descubridor Diego de Ordás, 3, Madrid 28003 (☎913 53 66 00; www.spain.embassy.gov.au). **Consulates:** Pl. Gala Placidia, 1-3, 1st fl., Barcelona 08006 (☎934 90 90 13); Federico Rubio, 14, Sevilla 41004 (☎954 22 09 71).

Canada: C. Núñez de Balboa, 35, Madrid 28001 (☎914 23 32 50; www.canada-es.org). **Consulates:** Elisenda de Pinós, 10 Barcelona 08034 (☎932 04 27 00); Pl. de la Malagueta, 2, 1st fl., Málaga 29016 (☎952 22 33 46).

Ireland: Po. de la Castellana, 46, 4th fl., Madrid, 28046 (☎914 36 40 93; www.dfa.ie). **Consulate:** Gran Vía de Carlos III, 94, 10th fl., Barcelona 08028 (☎934 91 50 21).

New Zealand: Pinar 7, 3rd fl., Madrid 28006 (☎915 23 02 26; www.nzembassy.com). **Consulate:** Tr. de Gràcia, 64, 4th fl., Barcelona 08006 (☎932 09 03 99).

UK: Po. de Recoletos, 7-9, 4th fl., Madrid 28004 (☎915 24 97 00; www.ukinspain.com). **Consulate-General:** Av. Diagonal, 477, 13th fl., Barcelona 08036 (☎933 66 62 00). **Consulates** in Alicante, Bilbao, Ibiza, Las Palmas, Málaga, Santa Cruz de Tenerife, and Palma de Mallorca.

US: C. de Serrano, 75, Madrid 28006 (☎915 87 22 40; www.embusa.es). **Consulate General:** Po. Reina Elisenda de Montcada, 23, Barcelona 08034 (☎932 80 22 27). **Consulates** in A Coruña, Las Palmas, Málaga, Palma de Mallorca, Sevilla, Valencia.

CONSULAR SERVICES IN PORTUGAL

Australia: Embassy: Av. da Liberdade, 200, 2nd fl., 1250-147 Lisboa (☎213 10 15 00; www.portugal.embassy.gov.au).

Canada: Av. da Liberdade, 198-200, 3rd fl., 1269-121 Lisboa (☎213 16 46 00; www.portugal.gc.ca. **Consulate:** R. Frei Lourenço de Santa Maria, 1, 1st fl., Apdo. 79, 8001 Faro (☎289 80 37 57).

Ireland: R. da Imprensa à Estrela, 1-4, 4th fl., 1200-684 Lisboa (☎213 92 94 40).

New Zealand: Contact New Zealand embassy in Rome: Via Zara 28, Rome 00198, Italy (☎396 441 7171; www.nzembassy.com). **Consulate:** Rua do Periquito, Lote A-13, Quinta da Bicuda, Cascais 2750-712 (☎213 705 779).

UK: R. de São Bernardo, 33, 1249-082 Lisboa (☎213 92 41 59; www.britishembassy.gov.uk). **Consulates** in Portimao (☎282 49 07 50) and Oporto (☎226 18 47 89).

United States: Av. das Forças Armadas, 1600-081 Lisboa (☎217 27 33 00; http://portugal.usembassy.gov).

TOURIST OFFICES

IN SPAIN

Spain's official tourist board provides information at www.tourspain.es.

Canada: Tourist Office of Spain, 2 Bloor St. West, 34th fl., Toronto, ON M4W 3E2 (☎+1 416 961 3131; www.tourspain.toronto.on.ca).

UK: Spanish National Tourist Office, 22-23 Manchester Sq., London W1M 5AP (☎+44 207 486 8077; http://www.spain.info/uk/TourSpain).

US: Tourist Office of Spain, 666 5th Ave., 35th fl., New York, NY 10103 (☎+1 212 265 8822; www.okspain.org). Additional offices in Beverly Hills, CA (☎+1-323-658-7188), Miami, FL (☎+1-305-358-1992), and Chicago, IL (☎+1-312-642-1992).

IN PORTUGAL

The official Portuguese tourism website is located at www.visitportugal.com.

Canada: Portuguese Trade and Tourism Commission, 60 Bloor St. West, Ste. 1005, Toronto, ON M4W 3B8 (☎+1-416-921-7376).

UK: Portuguese Trade and Tourism Office (ICEP), 11 Belgrave Sq., London SWIX 8PP (☎+44 207 201 6666; www.visitportugal.com).

US: Portuguese National Tourist Office, 590 5th Ave., 4th fl., New York, NY 10036 (☎+1-212-354-4403; www.portugal.com).

DOCUMENTS AND FORMALITIES

PASSPORTS

REQUIREMENTS

Citizens of Australia, Canada, Ireland, New Zealand, the UK, and the US need valid passports to enter **Spain** and to re-enter their home countries. To enter **Portugal,** citizens from EU states need only a national identity card and are not required to present a passport. Neither Spain nor Portugal allow entrance if the holder's passport expires in under 6 months; returning home with an expired passport is illegal and may result in a fine.

NEW PASSPORTS

Citizens of Australia, Canada, Ireland, New Zealand, the UK, and the US can apply at any passport office or at selected post offices and courts of law. Citizens of these countries may also download passport applications from the official website of their country's government or passport office. Any new passport or renewal applications must be filed well in advance of the departure date, though most passport offices offer rush services for a very steep fee. "Rushed" passports still take up to two weeks to arrive.

ONE EUROPE. European unity has come a long way since 1958, when the European Economic Community (EEC) was created to promote European solidarity and cooperation. Since then, the EEC has become the European Union (EU), a mighty political, legal, and economic institution. What does this have to do with the average non-EU tourist? The EU's policy of **freedom of movement** means that most border controls have been abolished and visa policies harmonized. Under this treaty, formally known as the **Schengen Agreement,** you're still required to carry a passport (or government-issued ID card for EU citizens) when crossing an internal border, but, once you've been admitted into one country, you're free to travel to other participating states. Britain and Ireland have also formed a **common travel area,** abolishing passport controls between the UK and the Republic of Ireland.

PASSPORT MAINTENANCE

Photocopy the page of your passport with your photo, as well as your visas, traveler's check serial numbers, and any other important documents. Carry one set of copies in a safe place and leave another set at home. Consulates also recommend that you carry an expired passport or an official copy of your birth certificate in a part of your baggage separate from other documents.

If you lose your passport, immediately notify the local police and nearest embassy or consulate of your home government. To expedite its replacement, you must show ID and proof of citizenship. Have a record of all information recorded in the passport. In some cases, a replacement may take weeks to process, and it may be valid only for a limited time. Any visas stamped in your old passport will be lost. In an emergency, ask for immediate temporary traveling papers that will permit you to re-enter your home country.

VISAS AND WORK PERMITS

VISAS

As of August 2008, EU citizens do not need a visa to enter Spain or Portugal. Citizens of Australia, Canada, New Zealand, and the US do not need a visa for stays of up to 90 days, though this three-month period begins upon entry into any of the countries that belong to the EU's freedom of movement zone. For more information, see **One Europe** (p. 11). Those staying longer than 90 days must apply for a visa in person at their local embassy or consulate. Double-check entrance requirements at the nearest embassy or consulate of Spain or Portugal (see **Embassies and Consulates, p. 8**) for up-to-date info before departure. US citizens can also consult http://travel.state.gov. Entering Spain or Portugal to study requires a visa (see **Beyond Tourism,** p. 44).

WORK PERMITS

Admission as a visitor does not include the right to work, which is authorized only by a work permit (see **Beyond Tourism,** p. 51).

IDENTIFICATION

When you travel, always carry at least two forms of identification on your person, including a photo ID. A passport and a driver's license or birth certificate should suffice. Never carry all of your IDs together; instead, split them up in case of theft or loss and keep photocopies in your luggage and at home.

STUDENT, TEACHER, AND YOUTH IDENTIFICATION

The **International Student Identity Card (ISIC)**, the most widely accepted form of student ID, provides discounts on some sights, accommodations, food, and transportation, access to a 24hr. emergency help line, and insurance benefits for US cardholders. In Spain, the ISIC can provide discounts like 20% off Alsa bus tickets. Applicants must be full-time secondary or post-secondary school students at least 12 years old. Because of the proliferation of fake ISICs, some services (particularly airlines) require additional proof of student identity.

The **International Teacher Identity Card (ITIC)** offers teachers the same insurance coverage as the ISIC and similar but limited discounts. To qualify for the card, teachers must be currently employed and have worked a minimum of 18hr. per week for at least one school year. For travelers who are under 26 years old but who are not students, the **International Youth Travel Card (IYTC)** also offers many of the same benefits as the ISIC does.

Each of these identity cards costs US$22. ISICs, ITICs, and IYTCs are valid for one year from the date of issue. To learn more about ISICs, ITICs, and IYTCs, visit www.myisic.com. Many student travel agencies (p. 23) issue the cards; for a list of issuing agencies or more information, see the **International Student Travel Confederation (ISTC)** website (www.istc.org).

The **International Student Exchange Card (ISE Card)** is a similar identification card available to students, faculty, and ages 12 to 26. The card provides discounts, medical benefits, access to a 24hr. emergency help line, and the ability to purchase student airfares. An ISE Card costs US$25. Call ☎+1-800-255-8000 in North America or ☎+1-480-951-1177 from all other continents for more info, or visit www.isecard.com.

CUSTOMS

CUSTOMS IN THE EU. As well as freedom of movement of people (p. 13), travelers in the European Union can also take advantage of the freedom of movement of goods. This means that there are no customs controls at internal EU borders (i.e., you can take the blue customs channel at the airport), and travelers are free to transport whatever legal substances they like as long as it is for their own personal (non-commercial) use—up to 800 cigarettes, 10L of spirits, 90L of wine (including up to 60L of sparkling wine), and 110L of beer. Duty-free allowances were abolished on June 30, 1999, for travel between the original 15 EU member states; this now also applies to Cyprus and Malta. However, travelers between the EU and the rest of the world still get a duty-free allowance when passing through customs.

Upon entering Spain or Portugal, you must declare certain items from abroad and pay a duty on the value of those articles if they exceed the allowance established by the Spanish or Portuguese customs service. Goods and gifts purchased at duty-free shops abroad are not exempt from duty or sales tax; "duty-free" only means that you won't pay tax in the country of purchase. Duty-free allowances were abolished for travel between EU member states on June 30, 1999, but still exist for those arriving from outside the EU. Upon returning home, you must likewise declare all articles acquired abroad and pay a duty on the value of articles in excess of your home country's allowance. In order to expedite your return, make a list of any valuables brought from home and register them with customs before traveling abroad. It's a good idea to keep receipts for all goods acquired abroad.

MONEY

CURRENCY AND EXCHANGE

CURRENCY

AUS$1 = EUR €0.59	EUR €1 = AUS$1.70
CDN$1 = EUR €0.62	EUR €1 = CDN$1.62
NZ€1 = EUR €0.47	EUR €1 = NZ$2.15
UK£1 = EUR €1.26	EUR €1 = UK£0.79
US$1 = EUR €0.65	EUR €1 = US$1.54

The currency chart above is based on August 2008 exchange rates between local currency and Australian dollars (AUS$), Canadian dollars (CDN$), European Union euro (EUR€), New Zealand dollars (NZ$), British pounds (UK£), and US dollars (US$). Check the currency converter on websites like www.xe.com or www.bloomberg.com for the latest exchange rates. As a general rule, it is cheaper to convert money in Spain or Portugal than at home. While currency exchange will probably be available in your arrival airport, it is wise to bring enough foreign currency to last for at least a few days.

When changing money abroad, try to go only to banks or *casas de cambio* that have at most a 5% margin between their buy and sell prices. Since you lose money with every transaction, it makes sense to convert large sums at one time (unless the currency is depreciating rapidly).

If you use traveler's checks or bills, carry some in small denominations (the equivalent of US$50 or fewer) for times when you are forced to exchange money at poor rates, but bring a range of denominations since charges may be applied per check cashed. Store your money in a variety of forms; ideally, at any given time you will be carrying some cash, some traveler's checks, and an ATM or credit card. All travelers should also consider carrying some US dollars (about US$50 worth), which are often preferred by local tellers.

TRAVELER'S CHECKS

Traveler's checks are one of the safest and most convenient means of carrying funds. American Express and Visa are the most recognized brands. Many banks and agencies sell them for a small commission. Check issuers provide refunds if the checks are lost or stolen, and many provide additional services, such as toll-free refund hotlines abroad, emergency message services and assistance with lost and stolen credit cards or passports. Traveler's checks are readily accepted in most parts of Spain and Portugal, though less convenient than ATMs or credit cards. Ask about toll-free refund hotlines and the location of refund centers when purchasing checks, and always carry emergency cash.

American Express: Checks available with commission at select banks, at all AmEx offices, and online (www.americanexpress.com; US residents only). AmEx cardholders can also purchase checks by phone (☎+1-800-528-4800). AmEx also offers the Travelers Cheque Card, a prepaid, reloadable card. Cheques for Two can be signed by either of 2 people traveling together. For purchase locations or more information, contact AmEx's service centers: in Australia ☎+61 2 9271 8666, in New Zealand +64 9 367 4567, in the UK +44 1273 696 933, in the US and Canada +1-800-221-7282; elsewhere, call the US collect at +1-336-393-1111. For emergency services in Spain, call ☎917 43 70 00, or in Portugal, ☎214 27 04 00/04 02.

Travelex: Visa TravelMoney prepaid cash card and Visa traveler's checks available. For information about Thomas Cook MasterCard in Canada and the US, call ☎+1-800-223-7373, in the UK +44 0800 622 101; from elsewhere, call the UK collect at +44 1733 318 950. For information about Interpayment Visa in the US and Canada, call ☎+1-800-732-1322, in the UK +44 0800 515 884; from elsewhere, call the UK collect at +44 1733 318 949. For more information, visit www.travelex.com.

Visa: Checks available (generally with commission) at banks worldwide. For the location of the nearest office, call the Visa Travelers Cheque Global Refund and Assistance Center: in the UK ☎+44 0800 895 078, in the US +1-800-227-6811; from elsewhere, call the UK collect at +44 2079 378 091. Checks available in British, Canadian, European, Japanese, and US currencies, among others. Visa also offers TravelMoney, a prepaid debit card that can be reloaded online or by phone. For more information on Visa travel services, see http://usa.visa.com/personal/using_visa/travel_with_visa.html.

CREDIT, DEBIT, AND ATM CARDS

PINS AND ATMS. To use a cash or credit card to withdraw money from a cash machine (ATM) in Europe, you must have a four-digit Personal Identification Number (PIN). If your PIN is longer than four digits, ask your bank whether you can use just the first four or whether you'll need a new one. Credit cards don't usually come with PINs, so, if you intend to hit up ATMs in Europe with a credit card to get cash advances, call your credit card company before leaving to request one.

Travelers with alphabetic rather than numerical PINs may also be thrown off by the lack of letters on European cash machines. The following are the corresponding numbers to use: 1 = QZ; 2 = ABC; 3 = DEF; 4 = GHI; 5 = JKL; 6 = MNO; 7 = PRS; 8 = TUV; 9 = WXY. If you mistakenly punch the wrong code into the machine three times, it will swallow your card for good.

Where they are accepted, credit cards often offer superior exchange rates—up to 5% better than the retail rate used by banks and other currency exchange establishments. Credit cards may also offer services like insurance or emergency help and are sometimes required to reserve hotel rooms or rental cars. **MasterCard** and **Visa** (a.k.a. Carte Bleue) are the most frequently accepted; **American Express** cards work at some ATMs and at AmEx offices and major airports.

ATM cards are widespread in Spain and Portugal. Depending on the system that your home bank uses, you can most likely access your personal bank account from abroad. ATMs get the same wholesale exchange rate as credit cards, but there is often a limit on the amount of money you can withdraw per day, usually around US$500. There is also typically a surcharge of US$1-5 per withdrawal. Debit cards are as convenient as credit cards but withdraw money directly from the holder's checking account. A debit card can be used wherever its associated credit card company (usually MasterCard or Visa) is accepted. Debit cards often also function as ATM cards and can be used to withdraw cash from associated banks and ATMs throughout Spain and Portugal.

The two major international money networks are **MasterCard/Maestro/Cirrus** (for ATM locations ☎+1-800-424-7787 or www.mastercard.com) and Visa/PLUS (for ATM locations ☎+1-800-847-2911 or www.visa.com). Most ATMs charge a transaction fee that is paid to the bank that owns the ATM.

GETTING MONEY FROM HOME

If you run out of money while traveling, the easiest and cheapest solution is to have someone back home make a deposit to your bank account. Otherwise, consider one of the following options.

WIRING MONEY

It is possible to arrange a **bank money transfer,** which means asking a bank back home to wire money to a bank in Spain or Portugal. This is the cheapest way to transfer cash, but it's also the slowest, often taking several days. Some banks may only release your funds in local currency, potentially sticking you with a poor exchange rate; inquire about this in advance. Money transfer services like **Western Union** are faster and more convenient than bank transfers—but also much pricier. Western Union has many locations worldwide. To find a local agent in Spain or Portugal, visit www.westernunion.com.

US STATE DEPARTMENT (US CITIZENS ONLY)

In serious emergencies only, the US State Department will forward money within hours to the nearest consular office, which will then disburse it according to instructions for a US$30 fee. If you wish to use this service, you must contact the Overseas Citizens Services division of the US State Department (☎+1-202-501-4444, from US 888-407-4747).

COSTS

The cost of your trip will vary considerably, depending on where you go, how you travel, and where you stay. The most significant expenses will probably be your round-trip (return) airfare (see **Getting to Spain and Portugal: By Plane,** p. 22) and your internal transport and accommodation costs. Before you go, spend some time calculating a reasonable daily budget.

STAYING ON A BUDGET

To give you a general idea, a bare-bones day in Spain or Portugal (camping or sleeping in hostels/guesthouses, buying food at supermarkets) would cost about €40 (US$62); a slightly more comfortable day (sleeping in hostels/guesthouses and the occasional budget hotel, eating one meal per day at a restaurant, going out at night) would cost closer to €60 (US$93); and, for a luxurious day, the sky's the limit. Don't forget to factor in emergency reserve funds (at least US$200) when planning how much money you'll need.

TIPS FOR SAVING MONEY

Some simpler ways include searching out opportunities for free entertainment, splitting accommodation and food costs with trustworthy fellow travelers, and buying food in supermarkets rather than eating out. Bring a sleepsack (p. 16) to save on sheet charges in hostels and do your laundry in the sink (unless you're explicitly prohibited from doing so). Museums often have certain days once a month or once a week when admission is free, so plan accordingly. If you are eligible, consider getting an ISIC or an IYTC card (p. 11) to reap the benefits of reduced admission at museums and sights. Bikes are a great way to get around, and renting a bike is cheaper than renting a moped or scooter. Don't forget about walking, though; you can learn a lot about a city by seeing it on foot. Drinking at bars and clubs quickly becomes expensive, so many Spanish youths continue the tradition of *botellón* (buying alcohol in the supermarket and partying in the street), though authorities tend to frown on public drunkenness.

TIPPING AND BARGAINING

IN SPAIN

Tipping is not widespread in Spain or Portugal. In restaurants, all prices include a service charge. Satisfied customers occasionally toss in some spare change and while it is purely optional, tipping is becoming customary in restaurants and other places that cater to tourists. Many people give train, airport, and hotel porters €1 per bag while taxi drivers sometimes get 5-10%. Bargaining is common at flea markets and with street vendors.

IN PORTUGAL

Tips are customary in fancy restaurants and hotels. Cheaper restaurants include a 10% service charge; if they don't and you'd like to leave a tip, round up and leave the change. Taxi drivers do not expect a tip unless the trip was especially long. Bargaining is not customary in shops, but give it a shot at the local *mercado* (market) or when looking for a private room.

TAXES

Both Spain and Portugal have a 7-8% **value added tax,** known as **IVA,** on all meals and accommodations. The prices listed in *Let's Go* include IVA unless otherwise mentioned. Retail goods bear a much higher 16% IVA, although listed prices are usually inclusive. Non-EU citizens who have stayed in the EU fewer than 180 days can claim back the tax paid on purchases at the airport. Ask the shop where you have made the purchase to supply you with a tax return form, though stores will often provide them only for purchases of more than €50-100. **Taxes,** presently 21%, are included in all prices in Portugal. Request a refund form, *Isenção de IVA,* which is presented to customs upon departure.

PACKING

Pack lightly: lay out only what you absolutely need, then take half the clothes and twice the money. The **Travelite FAQ** (www.travelite.org) is a good resource for tips on traveling light. The online **Universal Packing List** (http://upl.codeq.info) will generate a customized list of suggested items based on your trip length, the expected climate, your planned activities, and other factors. If you plan on doing a lot of hiking, also consult **The Great Outdoors,** p. 38.

Luggage: If you plan to cover most of your itinerary by foot, a sturdy internal-frame backpack is unbeatable. In addition, a smaller pack is useful for daily use.

Clothing: Depending on destination and season, pack rain gear and breathable, cotton or linen clothing, a warm jacket or wool sweater, sturdy shoes or hiking boots, and thick socks. Pack modest and respectful dress for visting religious sites. Flip-flops or waterproof sandals are useful for grubby hostel showers.

Sleepsack: Some hostels require that you either provide your own linen or rent sheets. Save cash by making your own sleepsack: fold a full-size sheet in half the long way, then sew it closed along the long side and one of the short sides.

Converters and Adapters: In Spain and Portugal, electricity is 230 volts AC, enough to fry any 120V North American appliance. 220/240V electrical appliances won't work with a 120V current, either. Americans and Canadians should buy an adapter and a converter. Don't make the mistake of using only an adapter (unless appliance instructions explicitly state otherwise). Australians and New Zealanders (who use 230V at home) won't need a converter, but will need a set of adapters.

Toiletries: Condoms, deodorant, tampons, and toothbrushes are readily available.

First-Aid Kit: Pack bandages, a pain reliever, antibiotic cream, a thermometer, a multifunction pocketknife, tweezers, moleskin, decongestant, motion-sickness remedy, diarrhea or upset-stomach medication (Pepto Bismol® or Imodium®), an antihistamine, sunscreen, insect repellent, and burn ointment.

Other Useful Items: Bring a money belt and a small padlock. Basic outdoors equipment (water bottle, compass, matches, pocketknife, sunglasses, sunscreen, hat) may also prove useful. Quick clothing repairs of torn garments can be done with a needle and thread or electrical tape. For laundry by hand, bring detergent and string for a makeshift clothes line. Consider packing an umbrella, alarm clock, flashlight, and earplugs. A cell phone can be a lifesaver on the road, and don't forget your camera.

Important Documents: Your passport, traveler's checks, ATM and/or credit cards, adequate ID, and photocopies of your documents are essential (p. 10). Other useful documents include a hosteling membership card (p. 11); driver's license (p. 31); travel insurance forms (p. 20); ISIC (p. 11), and/or rail or bus pass (p. 27).

SAFETY AND HEALTH

GENERAL ADVICE

In any type of crisis situation, the most important thing to do is stay calm. Your country's embassy abroad (p. 8) is usually your best resource when things go wrong. Register with that embassy upon arrival in the country. The government offices listed in the Travel Advisories box (p. 18) can provide a number of services to their citizens in the case of an emergency abroad.

LOCAL LAWS AND POLICE

Travelers are not likely to break major laws unintentionally while visiting Spain or Portugal. You can contact your embassy if arrested, although they often cannot do much to assist you beyond finding you legal counsel. You should feel comfortable approaching the police, although few officers speak English. There are three types of police in Spain. The **Policía Nacional** wear blue or black uniforms and white shirts; they deal with crime investigation (including theft), guard government buildings, and protect dignitaries. The **Policía Local** wear blue uniforms, deal with more local issues, and report to the mayor or town hall in each municipality. The **Guardia Civil** wear olive green uniforms and are responsible for issues more relevant to travelers: customs, crowd control, and national security. In Portugal, the **Polícia de Segurança Pública** is the police force in all major cities and towns. The **Guarda Nacional Republicana** polices more rural areas, while the **Brigada de Trânsito** is the traffic police, with red armbands. All three branches wear light blue uniforms.

DRUGS AND ALCOHOL

Recreational drugs are illegal in Spain and Portugal, and police take these laws seriously. The legal minimum drinking age in Spain and Portugal is 16. Spain and Portugal have the highest road mortality rates in Europe. Do not drive while intoxicated, and be cautious on the road.

SPECIFIC CONCERNS

TERRORISM

Basque terrorism concerns all travelers in Spain, with the active presence of a militant wing of Basque separatists called the Euskadi Ta Askatasuna (**ETA;** Basque Homeland and Freedom). March 2006, ETA declared a permanent cease-fire that officially ended in June 2007. ETA's attacks are typically targeted and are not considered random terrorist acts. The March 11, 2004 train bombings in Madrid were linked to **al-Qaeda,** and in June 2008, Spanish police arrested eight men in Barcelona, Pamplona, and Castellón under suspicion of involvement with an Algerian terrorist group linked to al-Qaeda. (See **Current Events, p. 61,** for more information.) While terrorism is rarely an issue in Portugal, Spain has experienced more than its fair share of troubles in recent years.

TRAVEL ADVISORIES. The following government offices provide travel information and advisories by telephone, by fax, or via the web:

Australian Department of Foreign Affairs and Trade: www.dfat.gov.au.

Canadian Department of Foreign Affairs and International Trade (DFAIT): www.dfait-maeci.gc.ca.

New Zealand Ministry of Foreign Affairs: www.mfat.govt.nz.

United Kingdom Foreign and Commonwealth Office: www.fco.gov.uk.

US Department of State: http://travel.state.gov.

PERSONAL SAFETY

EXPLORING AND TRAVELING

To avoid unwanted attention, try to blend in as much as possible. Respecting local customs (in many cases, dressing more conservatively than you would at home) may ward off would-be hecklers. Familiarize yourself with your surroundings before setting out and carry yourself with confidence. Check maps in shops and restaurants rather than on the street. If you are traveling alone, be sure someone at home knows your itinerary and never tell anyone you meet that you're by yourself. When walking at night, stick to busy, well-lit streets and if you ever feel uncomfortable, leave the area as quickly as you can. A good **self-defense course** will give you concrete ways to react to unwanted advances.

If you are using a **car,** learn local driving signals and wear a seatbelt. Study route maps before you hit the road and, if you plan on spending a lot of time driving, consider bringing spare parts. For long drives in desolate areas, invest in a cellular phone and a roadside assistance program, and do not sleep in your car. For info on the perils of **hitchhiking,** see p. 32.

POSSESSIONS AND VALUABLES

There are a few steps you can take to minimize the financial risk associated with traveling. First, bring as few valuables as possible. Second, buy a few padlocks to secure your belongings either in your pack or in a locker. Third, carry as little cash as possible. Keep your traveler's checks and ATM/credit cards in a money belt—not a "fanny pack"—along with your passport and ID cards. Fourth, keep a small cash reserve separate from your primary stash. This should be about US$50 (US dollars or euros are best) sewn into or stored in the depths of your pack, along with your traveler's check numbers, photocopies of your passport, your birth certificate, and other important documents.

Never let your passport or bags out of your sight. Hostel workers will sometimes stand at bus and train-station arrival points to recruit tired and disoriented travelers to their hostel; never believe strangers who tell you that theirs is the only hostel open. Beware of **pickpockets** in city crowds, especially on public transportation. Also, be alert in public telephone booths: if you must say your calling card number, do so very quietly; if you punch it in, make sure no one can look over your shoulder. If you will be traveling with electronic devices, such as a laptop computer or a PDA, check whether your homeowner's insurance covers loss, theft, or damage when you travel. If not, you might consider purchasing a low-cost separate insurance policy. **Safeware** (☎+1-800-800-1492; www.safeware.com) specializes in covering computers and charges $90 for 90-day comprehensive international travel coverage up to $4000.

IN SPAIN

Spain has a low crime rate, but visitors can always fall victim to tourist-related crimes. Tourists should take particular care in Madrid, especially in El Centro, and in Barcelona around Las Ramblas. If you happen to experience car problems, be careful about accepting help from anyone other than a uniformed Spanish police officer or Guardia Civil (Civil Guard). Travelers who accept unofficial assistance should keep their valuables secure. For those travelers using public transportation, be aware of your belongings and surroundings.

IN PORTUGAL

In Portugal, the highest rates of crime have been in the Lisboa area, especially on buses, in train stations, and in airports. Exercise the most caution in the Alfama district, the Santa Apolonia and Rossio train stations, Castelo de São Jorge, and in Belém. The towns around Lisboa with the most reported crimes in recent years are Cascais, Fátima, and Sintra. Thieves often try to distract people by staging loud arguments, passing a soccer ball back and forth on a crowded street, asking for directions, pretending to dance with their victim, or spilling something on their victim's clothing.

PRE-DEPARTURE HEALTH

In your passport, write the names of any people you wish to be contacted in case of a **medical emergency** and list any allergies or medical conditions. Matching a prescription to a foreign equivalent is not always easy, safe, or possible, so if you take **prescription drugs,** carry up-to-date prescriptions or a statement from your doctor. While traveling, keep all medication with you in your carry-on luggage. Spanish and Portuguese names for common drugs are quite similar to their English names (aspirina, ibuprofen, acetaminofén), and brand names are generally recognizable in both countries.

IMMUNIZATIONS AND PRECAUTIONS

Travelers over two years old should make sure that the following vaccines are up to date: MMR (for measles, mumps, and rubella), DTaP or Td (for diphtheria, tetanus, and pertussis), IPV (for polio), Hib (for *haemophilus influenzae* B), and HepB (for Hepatitis B).

USEFUL ORGANIZATIONS AND PUBLICATIONS

The American **Centers for Disease Control and Prevention** (**CDC;** ☎+1-877-FYI-TRIP; www.cdc.gov/travel) maintains an international travelers' hotline and an informative website. Consult the appropriate government agency of your home country for consular information sheets on health, entry requirements, and other issues for various countries (see the listings in the box on **Travel Advisories,** p. 18). For quick information on health and travel warnings, call the **Overseas Citizens Services** (From overseas +1-202-501-4444, from US 888-407-4747; line open M-F 8am-8pm EST). For information on medical evacuation services and travel insurance firms, see the US government's website at http://travel.state.gov/travel/abroad_health.html or the **British Foreign and Commonwealth Office** (www.fco.gov.uk). For general health information, contact the **American Red Cross** (☎+1-202-303-4498; www.redcross.org).

ONCE IN SPAIN OR PORTUGAL

ENVIRONMENTAL HAZARDS

Common sense is the simplest prescription for good health while you travel. Drink lots of fluids to prevent dehydration and constipation and wear sturdy, broken-in shoes and clean socks.

Heat exhaustion and dehydration: Summer temperatures in southern and central Spain can reach a scorching 36°C/97°F. Heat exhaustion leads to nausea, excessive thirst, headaches, and dizziness. Avoid it by drinking plenty of fluids, eating salty foods (e.g., crackers), avoiding excessive caffeine and alcohol, and wearing sunscreen.

Sunburn: Always wear sunscreen when spending excessive amounts of time outdoors. If you get sunburned, drink more fluids than usual and apply an aloe-based lotion.

Hypothermia and frostbite: A rapid drop in body temperature is the clearest sign of overexposure to cold. Victims may shiver, feel exhausted, have poor coordination or slurred speech, hallucinate, or suffer amnesia. To avoid hypothermia, keep dry, wear layers, and stay out of the wind. When the temperature is below freezing, watch out for frostbite. Drink warm beverages, stay dry, and slowly warm the area with dry fabric or steady body contact until a doctor can be found.

High altitude: Allow your body a couple of days to adjust to lower levels of oxygen before exerting yourself. Alcohol is more potent and UV rays are stronger at high elevations. You'll want to be careful in parts of the Pyrenees, the Picos de Europa, the Sierra Nevada, or in other high-altitude areas.

INSECT-BORNE DISEASES

Many diseases are transmitted by insects—mainly mosquitoes, fleas, ticks, and lice. Be careful of insects in wet or forested areas, especially while hiking and camping. Wear long pants and long sleeves, tuck your pants into your socks, and use a mosquito net. Use insect repellents with DEET and soak or spray your gear with permethrin (licensed in the US only for use on clothing). **Ticks**—which can carry Lyme and other diseases—can be particularly dangerous in rural and forested regions of Spain and Portugal.

Lyme disease: A bacterial infection carried by ticks and marked by a circular bull's-eye rash. Advanced symptoms include fever, headache, fatigue, and aches and pains. Antibiotics are effective if administered early. Left untreated, Lyme can cause problems in joints, the heart, and the nervous system. If you find a tick attached to your skin, grasp the head with tweezers as close to your skin as possible and apply slow, steady traction. Do not try to remove ticks with petroleum jelly, nail polish remover, or a hot match.

FOOD- AND WATER-BORNE DISEASES

Prevention is the best cure: be sure that your food is properly cooked and the water you drink is clean. Watch out for food from markets or street vendors that may have been cooked in unhygienic conditions. Other culprits are raw shellfish, unpasteurized milk, and sauces containing raw eggs. Salmonella bacteria, transmitted by raw eggs and egg shells, has been a prevalent problem in Spain in the past decade.

Traveler's diarrhea: Results from drinking fecally contaminated water or eating contaminated foods. Symptoms include nausea, bloating, and urgency. Try quick-energy, non-sugary foods with protein and carbohydrates to keep your strength up. Over-the-counter anti-diarrheals (e.g., Imodium®) may counteract the problem. The most dangerous side effect is dehydration; drink 8 oz. of water with tsp. of sugar or honey and a pinch of salt, try uncaffeinated soft drinks, or eat salted crackers. If you develop a fever or your symptoms don't go away after 4-5 days, consult a doctor.

Giardiasis: Transmitted through parasites and acquired by drinking untreated water from streams or lakes. Symptoms include diarrhea, cramps, bloating, fatigue, weight loss, and nausea. If untreated, it can lead to severe dehydration.

OTHER INFECTIOUS DISEASES

The following diseases exist all over the world. Travelers should know how to recognize them and what to do if they suspect they have been infected.

Hepatitis B: A viral infection of the liver transmitted via blood or other bodily fluids transmitted through unprotected sex and unclean needles. Symptoms may not surface until years after infection, but include jaundice, appetite loss, fever, and joint pain. A 3-shot vaccination sequence is recommended for sexually active travelers and anyone planning to seek medical treatment abroad; it must begin 6 months before traveling.

Hepatitis C: IV drug users, those exposured to blood, hemodialysis patients, and recipients of blood transfusions are at the highest risk, but the disease can also be spread through sexual contact or sharing items like razors and toothbrushes with traces of blood. No symptoms are usually exhibited. Hepatitis C can lead to liver failure.

AIDS and HIV: For detailed information on Acquired Immune Deficiency Syndrome (AIDS) in Spain or Portugal, call the 24hr. AIDS Hotline at ☎+1-800-342-2437 (USA).

Sexually transmitted infections (STIs): Gonorrhea, chlamydia, genital warts, syphilis, herpes, HPV, and other STIs are easier to catch than HIV and can be just as serious. Though condoms may protect you from some STIs, oral or even tactile contact can lead to transmission. If you think you may have contracted an STI, see a doctor immediately.

OTHER HEALTH CONCERNS

MEDICAL CARE ON THE ROAD

The public health-care system in Spain is very reliable; in case of emergency, seek out the *urgencias* (emergency) section of the nearest hospital. For smaller concerns, private clinics let you avoid long waits. Expect to pay cash up front (though most travel insurance will pick up the tab later, so request a receipt) and bring your passport and other forms of identification. *Farmacias* in Spain are also very helpful. A duty system has been set up so that at least one *farmacia* is open at all times in each town. Look for a flashing green cross. Spanish pharmacies are not the place to find your cheap summer flip-flops or greeting

ESSENTIALS

cards, but they sell contraceptives, common drugs, and many prescription drugs, answer simple medical questions, and can help you find a doctor. **Portugal's** public health system is equally good. A private clinic may be worth the money for quick, covenient service, and most travel insurance providers will cover the tab. Portuguese *farmacias* offer basic drugs and advice.

If you are concerned about obtaining medical assistance while traveling, you may wish to employ special support services. The **MedPass** from **GlobalCare, Inc.** (☎+1-800-860-1111; www.globalcare.net), provides 24hr. international medical assistance, support, and medical evacuation resources. The **International Association for Medical Assistance to Travelers** (**IAMAT**; US ☎+1-716-754-4883, Canada +1-519-836-0102; www.iamat.org) has free membership, lists English-speaking doctors worldwide, and offers information on immunization and sanitation.

Those with diabetes, allergies to antibiotics, epilepsy, heart conditions, or other health problems may want to obtain a **MedicAlert** membership (US$40 per year), which includes among other things a 24hr. collect-call number and ID tag. Contact the MedicAlert Foundation International (☎888-633-4298, outside US +1-209-668-3333; www.medicalert.org). If your regular insurance policy does not cover travel abroad, you may wish to purchase additional coverage.

WOMEN'S HEALTH

Vaginal yeast infections may flare up in hot and humid climates, but wearing loosely fitting trousers or a skirt and cotton underwear can help. Bring supplies from home if you are prone to infection, as they may be difficult to find on the road. Tampons, pads, and contraceptive devices are widely available, though your favorite brand may not be stocked. Abortion is illegal in Spain and Portugal, except in the first trimester for health reasons or in the case of rape. For sexual health information in Spain, contact the **Federación de Planificación Familiar de España (FPFE),** C. Ponce de Leon 8, 28010 Madrid (www.fpfe.org). In Portugal, contact the **Associação Para o Planeamento da Família (APF),** 38 Rua da Artilharia, 1250-040 Lisboa (www.apf.pt).

GETTING TO SPAIN OR PORTUGAL

BY PLANE

When it comes to airfare, a little research can save you a bundle. Courier fares are cheapest for those whose plans are flexible enough to deal with the restrictions. Tickets sold by consolidators and standby seating are also good deals, but last-minute specials, airfare wars, and charter flights often beat these fares. The key is to hunt around, be flexible, and ask about discounts. Students, seniors, and those under 26 should never have to pay full price for a ticket.

AIRFARES

Airfares to Spain and Portugal peak between the end of May and early September, and holiday periods are also expensive. The cheapest times to travel to the Iberian Peninsula are typically between December and February. Midweek (M-Th morning) round-trip flights run US$40-50 cheaper than weekend flights, but they are generally more crowded and less likely to permit frequent-flier upgrades. Not fixing a return date ("open return") or arriving in and departing from different cities ("open-jaw") can be pricier than round-trip flights. Patching one-way flights together is the most expensive way to travel. Flights between Spain and Portugal's capitals or regional hubs—Madrid, Barcelona, Lisboa—will tend to be cheaper.

If Spain or Portugal is only one stop on a more extensive globe-hop, consider a round-the-world (RTW) ticket. Tickets usually include at least five stops and are valid for about a year, and prices range US$1200-5000. Try **Northwest Airlines/KLM** (☎+1-800-225-2525; www.nwa.com) or **Star Alliance,** a consortium of 16 airlines including United Airlines (www.staralliance.com).

FLIGHT PLANNING ON THE INTERNET. The internet may be the budget traveler's dream when it comes to finding and booking bargain fares, but the array of options can be overwhelming. Many airline sites offer special last-minute deals on the web. Iberia Airlines (www.iberia.com) serves the entire peninsula, as well as other international destinations.

STA (www.statravel.com) and **StudentUniverse** (www.studentuniverse.com) provide quotes on student tickets, while **Orbitz** (www.orbitz.com), **Expedia** (www.expedia.com), and **Travelocity** (www.travelocity.com) offer full travel services. **Priceline** (www.priceline.com) lets you specify a price and obligates you to buy any ticket that meets or beats it. **Hotwire** (www.hotwire.com) offers bargain fares but won't reveal the airline or flight times until you buy. Other sites include www.bestfares.com, www.flights.com, www.lowestfare.com, www.onetravel.com, and www.travelzoo.com.

SideStep (www.sidestep.com) and **Booking Buddy** (www.bookingbuddy.com), and **Kayak** (www.kayak.com) help you sift through multiple offers; these let you enter your trip information once and search multiple sites.

BUDGET AND STUDENT TRAVEL AGENCIES

While knowledgeable agents specializing in flights to Spain and Portugal can make your life easy, they may not spend the time to find you the lowest possible fare—they get paid on commission. Travelers holding ISICs and IYTCs (p. 11) qualify for big discounts from student travel agencies. Most flights from budget agencies are on major airlines, but in peak season some may sell seats on less reliable chartered aircraft.

STA Travel, 5900 Wilshire Blvd., Ste. 900, Los Angeles, CA 90036, USA (24hr. reservations and info ☎+1-800-781-4040; www.statravel.com). A student and youth travel organization with over 150 offices worldwide.

Travel CUTS (Canadian Universities Travel Services Limited), 187 College St., Toronto, ON M5T 1P7, Canada (Toronto Toll Free ☎+1-888-359-2887, Toronto Office ☎+1-416-979-2406; www.travelcuts.com). Offices across Canada and the US including Los Angeles, New York, Seattle, and San Francisco.

USIT, 19-21 Aston Quay, Dublin 2, Ireland (☎+353 1 602 1906; www.usit.ie). Ireland's leading student/budget travel agency has 20 offices throughout Northern Ireland and the Republic of Ireland. Offers programs to work, study, and volunteer worldwide.

COMMERCIAL AIRLINES

The commercial airlines' lowest regular offer is the **APEX (Advance Purchase Excursion)** fare, which provides confirmed reservations and allows "open-jaw" tickets. Generally, reservations must be made seven to 21 days ahead of departure, with seven- to 14-day minimum-stay and up to 90-day maximum-stay restrictions. These fares carry hefty cancellation and change penalties. Book peak-season

APEX fares early. Use **Expedia** (www.expedia.com) or **Travelocity** (www.travelocity.com) to get an idea of the lowest published fares, then use the resources outlined here to try to beat those fares. Low-season fares should be appreciably cheaper than the high-season (mid-June to August) ones listed here.

TRAVELING FROM NORTH AMERICA

Basic round-trip fares to Spain and Portugal range from roughly US$200-750: to Barcelona, $450-1200; to Lisboa, $550-1200; to Madrid, $400-900; to Málaga, $400-800. Standard commercial carriers like American and United will probably offer the most convenient flights, but they may not be the cheapest, unless you snag a special promotion or airfare-war ticket. You will probably find flying one of the following "discount" airlines a better deal, if any of their limited departure points is convenient for you.

Iberia, USA (☎+1-800-772-4642; www.iberia.com). Extensive service from North America to major Spanish cities, as well as within Europe.

Spanair, (☎+1-888-545-5757; www.spanair.com). Flies out of New York, Boston, Houston, Los Angeles, Philadelphia, and other North American gateways to various cities in Spain and Portugal.

TRAVELING FROM IRELAND AND THE UK

Because of the many carriers flying from the British Isles to the continent, we only include discount airlines or those with cheap specials here. **ABTA, The Travel Association** in London (☎+44 020 7637 2444; www.abta.com) provides information on several participating travel agencies and tour operators in Spain and Portugal. **Cheapflights** (www.cheapflights.co.uk) publishes airfare bargains.

Aer Lingus, Ireland (☎+353 818 365 000; www.aerlingus.ie). Return tickets from Dublin, Cork, and Shannon to Madrid, Barcelona, and Málaga (EUR€16-280).

easyJet, UK (www.easyjet.com). London to Barcelona, Madrid, Majorca, Lisboa, and other Iberian destinations.

KLM Royal Dutch Airlines (☎+44 871 222 7474; www.klmuk.com). Cheap return tickets from London and elsewhere to many destinations in Spain and Portugal, including Madrid, Barcelona, and Lisboa.

Ryanair, Ireland (☎+353 818 303 030, UK +44 8712 460 000; www.ryanair.com). Many flights from Ireland and the UK to Spain and Portugal. From Dublin, Liverpool, and London to Madrid, Barcelona, and Porto, to name a few.

TRAVELING FROM AUSTRALIA AND NEW ZEALAND

Singapore Air, Australia (☎+61 13 10 11), New Zealand (+64 800 808 909; www.singaporeair.com). Auckland, Christchurch, Melbourne, Perth, and Sydney to Barcelona.

Thai Airways, Australia (☎+61 1300 651 960), New Zealand (☎+64 9 377 3886; www.thaiair.com). Auckland, Melbourne, Perth, and Sydney to Madrid.

AIR COURIER FLIGHTS

Those who travel light should consider courier flights. Couriers help transport cargo on international flights by using their checked luggage space for freight. Generally, couriers are limited to carry-ons and must deal with complex flight restrictions. Most flights are round-trip only, with short fixed-length stays (usually one week) and a limit of one ticket per issue. Most of these flights also operate only out of major gateway cities, mostly in North America. Generally, you must be over 18, in some cases 21. In summer, the most popular destinations usually require an advance reservation of about two weeks (you can usually book up to two months ahead). Super-discounted fares are common for "last-minute" flights (three to 14 days ahead).

Air Courier Association/CheapTrips, 1767 Denver West Blvd., Golden, CO 80401 (☎800-211-5119; www.aircourier.org). Several departure cities throughout US and Canada to Madrid and throughout Western Europe. One-year membership US$49.

International Association of Air Travel Couriers (IAATC; www.courier.org). Flights to Western Europe from Chicago, Los Angeles, Miami, Newark, San Francisco, and Washington, DC. One-year membership US$45.

Courier Travel (www.couriertravel.org). Searchable online database. Multiple departure points in the US to various European destinations.

STANDBY FLIGHTS

Traveling standby requires considerable flexibility in arrival and departure dates. Companies dealing in standby flights sell vouchers rather than tickets, along with the promise to get you to your destination (or nearby) within a certain window of time (typically 1-5 days). You call in before your specific window of time to hear your flight options and the probability that you will be able to board each flight. You can then decide which flights you want to try to catch, show up at the appropriate airport at the appropriate time, present your voucher, and board if space is available. Vouchers can usually be bought for both one-way and round-trip travel. You may receive a monetary refund only if every available flight within your date range is full; if you opt not to take an available (but perhaps less convenient) flight, you can only get credit toward future travel. To check on a company's service record in the US, contact the **Better Business Bureau** (☎+1-703-276-0100; www.bbb.org). It is difficult to receive refunds, and clients' vouchers will not be honored when an airline fails to receive payment in time.

TICKET CONSOLIDATORS

Ticket consolidators, or **"bucket shops,"** buy unsold tickets in bulk from commercial airlines and sell them at discounted rates. The best place to look is in the Sunday travel section of any major newspaper (try *The New York Times*), where many bucket shops place tiny ads. Call quickly, as availability is extremely limited. Not all bucket shops are reliable, so insist on a receipt that gives full details of restrictions, refunds, and tickets, and pay by credit card (in spite of the 2-5% fee) so you can stop payment if you never receive your tickets. For more info, see www.travel-library.com/air-travel/consolidators.html.

BY TRAIN

You can either buy a **railpass,** which allows you unlimited travel within a particular region for a given period of time, or rely on buying individual **point-to-point** tickets as you go. Almost all countries give students or youths (usually defined as anyone under 26) direct discounts on regular domestic rail tickets, and many also sell a student or youth card that provides 20-50% off of fares.

SHOULD YOU BUY A RAILPASS? Railpasses were conceived to allow you to jump on any train in Europe, go wherever you want whenever you want, and change your plans at will. In practice, it's not so simple. You still must stand in line to validate your pass, pay for supplements, and fork over cash for seat and couchette reservations. More importantly, railpasses don't always pay off. If you plan to spend extensive time on trains hopping between big cities, a railpass will probably be worth it. But in many cases, especially if you are under 26, point-to-point tickets may prove a cheaper option. It may be tough to make your railpass pay for itself in Spain and Portugal, where train fares are reasonable, distances short, and buses often preferable.

MULTINATIONAL RAILPASSES

EURAIL PASSES. Eurail is valid in much of Europe: Austria, Belgium, Bulgaria, Croatia, Czech Republic, Denmark, Finland, France, Germany, Greece, Hungary, Italy, Luxembourg, Montenegro, the Netherlands, Norway, Poland, Portugal, The Republic of Ireland, Romania, Serbia, Slovenia, Spain, Sweden, and Switzerland. It is not valid in the UK. **Eurail Global Passes,** valid for a given number of consecutive days, are best for those planning on spending extensive time on trains every few days. Global passes valid for any 10 or 15 (not necessarily consecutive) days within a two-month period are more cost-effective for those traveling longer distances less frequently. **Eurail Pass Saver** provides first-class travel for travelers in groups of two to five (prices are per person). **Eurail Pass Youth** provides parallel second-class perks for those under 26. Passholders receive a timetable for major routes and a map with details on possible bike rental, car rental, hotel, and museum discounts. Passholders often also receive reduced fares or free passage on many boat, bus, and private railroad lines. The **Eurail Select Pass** is a slimmed-down version of the Eurail Pass: it allows five, six, eight, 10, or 15 days of unlimited travel in any two-month period within three, four, or five bordering countries of 23 European nations.

SHOPPING AROUND FOR A EURAIL. Eurail Passes are designed by the EU itself and can be bought only by non-Europeans almost exclusively from non-European distributors. These passes must be sold at uniform prices determined by the EU. However, some travel agents tack on a handling fee, and others offer certain bonuses with purchase, so shop around. Also, keep in mind that pass prices usually go up each year, so save cash by purchasing before January 1 (you have 6 months from the purchase date to validate your pass in Europe). Because only a few places in major European cities sell them, and at a marked-up price, it is best to buy your pass before leaving. You can get a replacement for a lost pass only if you have purchased insurance under the Pass Security Plan (€10). Eurail Passes are available through travel agents, student travel agencies like **STA** (p. 23), as well as **Rail Europe** (www.raileurope.com) or directly from Eurail's website, www.eurail.com.

OTHER MULTINATIONAL PASSES. If your travels will be limited to one area, regional passes are often the best value. Visit www.raileurope.com and www.eurail.com for Portugal-Spain Pass options. If you have lived for at least six months in one of the European countries where **InterRail Passes** are valid, they prove an economical option. The InterRail Pass allows travel within 30 European countries excluding the passholder's country of residence. The **Global Pass** is valid for a given number of days (not necessarily consecutive) within a 10-day to one-month period. The **One Country Pass** limits travel to one European country. Passholders receive free admission to many museums as well as discounts on accommodations, food, and ferries. Passes are available at www.interrailnet.com as well as from travel agents, at major train stations throughout Europe, and through online vendors (like www.railpassdirect.co.uk).

GETTING AROUND SPAIN AND PORTUGAL

BY PLANE

Many national airlines offer multi-stop tickets for travel within Spain and Portugal. These tickets are particularly useful for travel between the Spanish mainland and the Islas Baleares and Islas Canarias. Outside of the peninsula, the recent emergence of no-frills airlines has made hopscotching around Europe by air increasingly affordable and convenient. Though these flights often feature inconvenient hours or serve less-popular regional airports, it's never been faster or easier to jetset across the Continent.

easyJet, UK (☎+44 871 244 2366; www.easyjet.com). Serves 78 destinations across Europe and northern Africa.

Ryanair, Ireland (☎+353 1 249 7791, UK 0871 246 0000; www.ryanair.com). Serves over 100 airports across Europe and northern Africa.

Vueling, Spain (☎902 33 39 33; www.vueling.com). Based in Barcelona, Vueling serves major cities in Spain and the rest of western Europe.

The Star Alliance European Airpass offers economy class fares for travel within Europe to more than 200 destinations in 44 countries. The pass is available to non-European passengers on Star Alliance carriers, including ANA, Austrian Airlines, BMI, LOT Polish Airlines, Lufthansa, Scandinavian Airlines, SWISS, TAP Portugal, Turkish Airlines, and US Airways. See www.staralliance.com for more information. In addition, a number of European airlines offer discount coupon packets. Most are only available as tack-ons for transatlantic passengers, but some are stand-alone offers. Most must be purchased before departure, so research in advance.

Europe by Air (☎+1-888-321-4737; www.europebyair.com). FlightPass allows you to country-hop to over 150 European cities. US$99 per flight.

Iberia (☎+1-800-772-4642; www.iberia.com). Offers discount airfare to and within Spain and Europe.

IN SPAIN

All major international airlines offer service to Madrid and Barcelona, most serve Las Islas Baleares and Canarias, and many serve Spain's smaller cities. **AirEuropa** (☎902 401 501; www.aireuropa.com) flies between major European cities. **Iberia** (Canada and US ☎+1-800-772-4642, Spain 902 40 05 00, UK +44 870 609 0500; www.iberia.com) serves all domestic locations and all major international cities. **SpanAir** (Spain ☎902 13 14 15 or 971 74 50 20, US +1-888-545-5757; www.spanair.com/en) offers international and domestic flights.

IN PORTUGAL

Most major international airlines serve Lisboa; some serve Faro, the Madeiras, and Porto. **TAP Air Portugal** (US and Canada ☎+1-800-221-7370, UK +44 845 601 0932, Lisboa 707 20 57 00; www.tap.pt) is Portugal's national airline, serving all domestic locations and many major international cities.

BY BUS

Though European trains and rail passes are popular, in some cases buses prove a better option. In Spain, the bus and train systems are on par; in Portugal, bus networks are more extensive, efficient, and often more comfortable. In the rest of Europe, bus travel is more of a gamble, and scattered offerings from private companies are often cheap but unreliable. Generally cheaper than rail passes, international bus passes allow unlimited travel on a hop-on, hop-off basis between major European cities. Prices below reflect high-season travel.

Eurolines, Estación Sur de Autobuses, Local 10, C. Méndez Álvaro 83, Madrid, Spain (☎+34 915 063 360; www.eurolines.com). The largest operator of Europe-wide coach services. Unlimited 15-day pass high season €329, under 26 €279, low season €199/169; 30-day pass high season €439/359, low season €299/229. Passes offer unlimited transit between hundreds of European cities and Morocco.

Busabout, 258 Vauxhall Bridge Rd., London SW1V 1BS, UK (☎+44 020 7950 1661; www.busabout.com). Offers 3 interconnecting bus circuits covering 60 cities and towns in Europe. Purchase a pass for the Western, Northern, or Southern loop starting at US$639, or for all of Europe starting at $549 (6 stops, additional stops $59). Also offers adventure tours throughout Europe, including Spain, Portugal, and Morocco.

IN SPAIN

Bus routes, far more comprehensive than the rail network, provide the only public transportation to many isolated areas, and almost always cost less than trains. They are generally quite comfortable, though leg room may be limited. For those traveling primarily within one region, buses are the best method of transport. We list below the major national companies, along with the phone number of their Madrid office; you will likely use many other companies. For more information, see the section for your transportation destination.

ALSA (☎913 27 05 40; www.alsa.es). Serves Madrid, Galicia, Asturias, and Castilla y León. Runs to many surrounding countries, including France, Germany, Italy, Morocco, the Netherlands, and Portugal.

Alosa (☎902 21 07 00; www.alosa.es). Operates primarily in northeastern Spain. Alosa serves a number of cities, including Barcelona, Huesca, Jaca, Pamplona, and Zaragoza.

Auto-Res (☎902 02 00 52; www.auto-res.net). Runs buses across much of central and western Spain.

Samar (☎917 23 05 06; www.samar.es). Serves Madrid, Zaragoza, and Sevilla, as well as international routes to Andorra, France, Italy, Morocco, Portugal, and Moscow.

IN PORTUGAL

Buses are cheap and frequent. They connect just about every town in Portugal. **Rodoviária** (☎212 94 71 00; www.rodotejo.pt), the national bus company, was recently privatized. Private regional companies also operate. Be wary of non-express buses in small regions like Estremadura and Alentejo, which stop every few minutes. Express coach service *(expressos)* between major cities is especially good; inexpensive city buses often run to nearby villages. Schedules *(horarios)* are usually printed and posted, but double-check with the ticket vendor to make sure they are accurate. Portugal's main Euroline affiliates are Intercentro, Internorte, and Intersul.

BY TRAIN

Trains in Spain and Portugal are generally comfortable, convenient, and reasonably swift. Almost all countries give students or youths (usually defined as anyone under 26) direct discounts on regular domestic rail tickets, and many also sell a student or youth card that provides 20-50% off for up to a year.

RESERVATIONS. While seat reservations are required only for selected trains (usually on major lines), you are not guaranteed a seat without one (usually US$5-30). You should strongly consider reserving in advance during peak holiday and tourist seasons (at the very latest, a few hours ahead). You will also have to purchase a supplement (US$10-50) or special fare for high-speed or high quality or trains such as Spain's AVE. Supplements are often unnecessary for Eurail pass and Europass holders.

OVERNIGHT TRAINS. Overnight trains can be one of the most time-efficient ways to travel, saving you valuable daylight hours and possibly even hotel fare. That efficiency, however, comes at the cost of comfort, scenery, and safety. Sleeping arrangements differ, but you can typically either sleep upright or in *couchettes* (berths), which typically have four to six seats per compartment (supplement about US$10-50 per person). Sleepers (beds) in private sleeping cars offer more privacy and comfort, but are considerably more expensive (supplement US$40-150). If you are using a railpass valid only for a restricted number of days, inspect train schedules to maximize the use of your pass: an overnight train or boat journey often uses up only one of your travel days if it departs after 7pm.

EURAIL PASSES

There is no reason to buy a Eurail Pass if you plan to travel only within Spain and Portugal. Trains are cheap, so a pass saves little money. Visit www.raileurope.com for more specific information on the passes below.

Spain Pass: Offers 3 days of unlimited travel over a 2-month period. 1st-class US$296, 2nd-class $231. Each additional rail-day (up to 10 days total) $40-50 for 1st-class, $30-40 for 2nd-class.

Portugal-Spain Pass: Good for 3 days of unlimited 1st-class travel in Spain and Portugal within a 2-month period. Travel may be on consecutive or non-consecutive days. US$341. Each additional rail-day (up to 10 days total) $40-50.

Spain Rail 'n Drive Pass: Good for 3 days of unlimited 1st-class train travel and 2 days of unlimited mileage in a Hertz rental car within a 2-month period in Spain. Prices US$316 and up, depending on number of travelers, type of car, and type of train ticket. Up to 7 additional rail-days and 7 additional car days available.

IN SPAIN

Spanish trains are clean, punctual, and reasonably priced, but tend to bypass many small towns. Spain's national railway is **RENFE** (☎902 24 02 02; www.renfe.es). Avoid *transvía*, *semidirecto*, or *correo* trains—they tend to be slow. **Alta Velocidad Española (AVE)** high-speed trains connect several major Spanish hubs, soaring above trains in comfort, price, and speed. Student discounts are available. Consult the RENFE website for complete listings and schedules of all train destinations, but for the most part, buses are an easier and more efficient means of traveling around Spain.

IN PORTUGAL

Caminhos de Ferro Portugueses (☎213 18 59 90; www.cp.pt) is Portugal's national railway, but for long-distance travel outside of the Braga-Porto-Coimbra-Lisboa line, the bus is better. The exception is around Lisboa, where local trains are fast and efficient. Most trains have first- and second-class cabins, except for local and suburban routes. Check the station ticket booth for the departure schedule; trains often run at irregular hours, and posted schedules *(horarios)* aren't always accurate. You can save 10% by buying a return ticket, but unless you own a Eurail pass the return on round-trip tickets must be used before 3am the following day. Keep your ticket with you; if you're caught without one, you'll be fined. Though there is a Portugal Flexipass, it is not worth buying.

BY CAR

Cars offer speed, freedom, access to the countryside, and an escape from the town-to-town mentality of trains. Although a solo traveler won't save by renting a car, four usually will. For a primer on European road signs and conventions, check out www.travlang.com/signs. The **Association for Safe International Road Travel** (**ASIRT;** www.asirt.org) can provide information on road conditions.

RENTING

You can rent a car from a US-based firm (Alamo, Avis, Budget, or Hertz) with European offices, from a European-based company with local representatives (Europcar), or from a tour operator (Auto Europe, Europe By Car, and Kemwel Holiday Autos) that will arrange a rental for you from a European company. Multinationals offer greater flexibility, but tour operators often strike better deals. Ask airlines about special fly-and-drive packages; you may get up to a week of free or discounted rental. Expect to pay US$80-400 per week, plus tax (5-25%), for a tiny car. Always check if prices quoted include tax and collision insurance. At most agencies, all that's needed to rent a car is a license from home and proof that you've had it for a year.

RENTAL AGENCIES

You can generally make reservations before you leave by calling major international offices in your home country. However, sometimes the price and availability information they give doesn't jive with what the local offices in Spain or Portugal will tell you, so try calling both numbers to make sure you get the best price. Local desk numbers are included in town listings; for home-country numbers, call your toll-free directory.

To rent a car from most establishments in Spain and Portugal, you need to be at least 21 years old. Some agencies require renters to be 25, and most charge those aged 21-24 an additional insurance fee. Policies and prices vary from agency to agency. Small local operations occasionally rent to people under 21, but be sure to ask about the insurance coverage and deductible, and always check the fine print. Rental agencies in Spain and Portugal include:

Auto Europe (US and Canada ☎+1-888-223-5555; www.autoeurope.com).

Avis (US ☎+1-800-331-1212, Spain 93 344 3700; www.avis.com).

Budget (US ☎+1-800-527-0700, international +1-800-472-3325; www.budget.com).

Europe by Car (US ☎+1-800-223-1516 or 212-581-3040; www.ebctravel.com).

Europcar (US ☎+1-877-940-6900, Spain 913 43 45 12; www.europcar.com).

Hertz (☎+1-800-654-3001; www.hertz.com).

Kemwel (US ☎+1-877-820-0668; www.kemwel.com).

COSTS AND INSURANCE

Renting a car in Spain is cheaper than in many other European countries. Prices start at around €50 per day from national companies, €25 from local agencies. In Portugal, prices start at around €50 per day from national companies, or €35 per day from local agencies. Expect to pay more for larger cars and for 4WD. Cars with automatic transmission can cost up to €30 per day more than standard manuals (stick shift), and in some places, automatic transmission is hard to find. It is virtually impossible, no matter where you are, to find an automatic with 4WD. Rental agencies are listed in the Practical Information at the start of each city.

Many rental packages offer unlimited kilometers, while others offer a limited number of kilometers per day with a surcharge per kilometer after that. Return the car with a full tank of gasoline (petrol) to avoid high fuel charges at the end. Insurance plans from rental companies almost always come with an excess charge for younger drivers and for 4WD. This means that the insurance bought from the rental company only applies to damages over the excess; damages up to that amount must be covered by your existing insurance plan. Many rental companies in Spain and Portugal encourage you to buy a Collision Damage Waiver (CDW), which will waive the excess in the case of a collision. Loss Damage Waivers (LDWs) do the same in the case of theft or vandalism.

National chains often allow one-way rentals (picking up in one city and dropping off in another). There is usually a minimum hire period and sometimes an extra drop-off charge of several hundred dollars.

ON THE ROAD

Spain's highway system connects major cities by four-lane *autopistas* (highways) with plenty of service stations. Traffic moves quickly and drivers can get annoyed if you don't; study your map before you leave. The speed limit in Spain is 31mph/50kph in cities, 55mph/90kph on open roads, and 74mph/120kph on highways. Speeders beware: police can "photograph" the speed and license plate of your car and issue a ticket without pulling you over. Purchase gas in both Spain and Portugal in super (97-octane), normal (92-octane), diesel, and unleaded. The average price for unleaded gas in Spain is approximately double the US price, and slightly higher in Portugal.Seatbelts are required in Spain, and drunk driving incurs hefty fines; be aware that allowed blood levels of alcohol are lower than in other countries in Europe.Portugal has the highest rate of car accidents per capita in Western Europe. The narrow, twisting roads are difficult to negotiate. Speed limits are ignored, recklessness is common, and lighting and road surfaces are often inadequate.

DRIVING PRECAUTIONS. When traveling in the summer or in the desert, bring substantial amounts of water (a suggested 5L of water per person per day) for drinking and for the radiator. You should always carry a spare tire and jack, jumper cables, extra oil, flares, a flashlight, and heavy blankets (in case your car breaks down at night or in the winter). If you don't know how to change a tire, learn before heading out, especially if you are planning on traveling in deserted areas. If your car breaks down, stay in your vehicle.

CAR ASSISTANCE

The Spanish automobile association is **Real Automóvil Club de España** (RACE, ☎902 40 45 45; www.race.es). It functions much like AAA, offering roadside assistance and general advice on driving in Spain. Portugal's automobile association, the **Automóvel Clube de Portugal,** or ACP (☎213 71 47 20; www.acp.pt) provides breakdown, towing, and first-aid services.

BY BICYCLE

With a mountain bike, you can also do some serious sightseeing. Some airlines will count your bike as your second piece of luggage, but others charge extra. The additional fee runs about US$50-150 each way. Airlines sell bike boxes at the airport, although it is easier and cheaper to get one from a local bike store. Most ferries let you take your bike for free or for a nominal fee. You can almost always ship your bike on trains, though the cost varies. Renting a bike beats bringing your own if your touring will be confined to one or two regions. *Let's Go* lists bike rental shops for larger cities and towns, when they exist. Some youth hostels rent bicycles for low prices. Some train stations rent bikes and often allow you to drop them off elsewhere.

BY MOPED AND MOTORCYCLE

In both Spain and Portugal, motorized bikes are a popular method of transportation for locals, and they can be a fun alternative for tourist daytrips. However, they're uncomfortable for long distances, dangerous in the rain, and unpredictable on rough roads and gravel. Always wear a helmet, and never ride with a backpack. If you've never been on a moped, the windy roads of the Pyrenees and the congested streets of Madrid are not the place to start. Before renting, ask if the quoted price includes tax and insurance, or you may be hit with an unexpected additional fee. Pay ahead of time instead—do not hand over your passport.

BY THUMB

LET'S NOT GO. *Let's Go* never recommends hitchhiking as a safe means of transportation, and none of the information here is intended to do so.

Let's Go strongly urges you to consider the risks before you choose to hitchhike. Hitching means entrusting your life to a stranger and risking assault, sexual harassment, theft, and unsafe driving. For women traveling alone (or even in pairs), hitching is a risky proposal. A man and a woman are a less dangerous combination; two men will have a harder time getting a lift. In Spain, hitchers report that Castilla and Andalucía are long, hot waits, and hitchhiking out of Madrid is virtually impossible. The Mediterranean Coast and the islands are more promising, and remote areas in Cataluña, Galicia, or the Pyrenees may be most accessible by hitching (if renting a car is not an option). In Portugal, hitchhikers are rare. Beach-bound locals occasionally hitch in summer, but otherwise stick to the inexpensive bus system.

KEEPING IN TOUCH

BY EMAIL AND INTERNET

Email is easy to access in Spain and Portugal. Internet costs only about €1-3 per hour in most cafes. Many hostels, libraries, and schools also provide free access. In small towns, if internet acess is not listed, check the library or the tourist office, where travelers occasionally get access for a small fee. These establishments are listed in the **Practical Information** sections of each city. Lucky travelers with wireless-enabled laptops may be able to take advantage of an increasing number of internet "hot spots," where they can get online for free or for a small fee, or at internet cafes with Wi-Fi. Newer computers can detect these hot spots automatically; otherwise, websites like www.jiwire.com, www.wififreespot.com, and www.wi-fihotspotlist.com can help you find them. For information on insuring your laptop while traveling, see p. 18.

WARY WI-FI. Wireless hot spots make internet access possible in public and remote places. Unfortunately, they also pose **security risks.** Hot spots are public, open networks that use unencrypted, unsecured connections. They are susceptible to hacks and "packet sniffing"—ways of stealing passwords and other private information. To prevent problems, disable "ad hoc" mode, turn off file sharing and network discovery, encrypt your email, turn on your firewall, beware of phony networks, and watch for over-the-shoulder creeps.

BY TELEPHONE

CALLING HOME FROM SPAIN AND PORTUGAL

Prepaid phone cards are a common and relatively inexpensive means of calling abroad. Each one comes with a Personal Identification Number (PIN) and a toll-free access number. You call the access number and then follow the directions for dialing your PIN. To purchase prepaid phone cards, check online for the best rates; www.callingcards.com is a good place to start. Online providers generally send your access number and PIN via email, with no actual "card" involved. Another option is to purchase a **calling card,** linked to a major national telecommunications service in your home country. Calls are billed collect or to your account. Placing a collect call through an international operator can be expensive, but may be necessary in case of an emergency. You can frequently call collect without a company's calling card just by calling its access number and following the instructions.

PLACING INTERNATIONAL CALLS. Dial:

1. Your **international dialing prefix.** From Australia, dial 0011; Canada or the US, 011; Ireland, New Zealand, Portugal, Spain, or the UK, 00.
2. The **country code** of the country you want to call. To call Australia, dial 61; Canada or the US, 1; Ireland, 353; New Zealand, 64; the UK, 44; Spain, 34; Portugal, 351; Morocco, 212.
3. The **city/area code.** *Let's Go* lists the city/area codes for cities and towns in opposite the city or town name, next to a ☎, as well as in every phone number. If the first digit is a zero (e.g., 020 for London), omit the zero when calling from abroad (e.g., dial 20 from Canada to reach London).
4. The **local number.**

CALLING WITHIN SPAIN AND PORTUGAL

The simplest way to call within the country is to use a coin-operated phone. **Prepaid phone cards** (available at newspaper kiosks and tobacco stores), which carry a certain amount of phone time depending on the card's denomination, may be more convenient, and usually save time and money in the long run.

Phone rates typically tend to be highest in the morning, lower in the evening, and lowest on Sunday and late at night.

CELLULAR PHONES

GSM PHONES. Having a GSM phone doesn't necessarily mean you're good to go when you travel abroad. The majority of GSM phones sold in the United States operate on a different frequency (1900) than international phones (900/1800) and will not work abroad. Tri-band phones work on all three frequencies (900/1800/1900) and will operate through out most of the world. Additionally, some GSM phones are SIM-locked and will only accept SIM cards from a single carrier. You'll need a SIM-unlocked phone to use a SIM card from a local carrier when you travel.

Some tourists find that the availability and usefulness of cell phones in Spain and Portugal make them worth their moderate cost. **Telefónica Movistar** (www.movistar.com) and **Vodafone** (www.vodafone.com) sell relatively inexpensive cell phones to travelers. The international standard for cell phones is **Global System for Mobile Communication (GSM)**. You will need a GSM-compatible phone and a **SIM (Subscriber Identity Module) card,** a country-specific, thumbnail-sized chip that gives you a local phone number and plugs you into the local network. Many SIM cards are prepaid, and incoming calls are frequently free. You can buy additional cards or vouchers (usually available at convenience stores) to "top up" your phone. For more information on GSM phones, check out www.telestial.com, www.orange.co.uk, www.roadpost.com, or www.planetomni.com. Companies like **Cellular Abroad** (www.cellularabroad.com) rent cell phones that work in a variety of destinations around the world.

TIME DIFFERENCES

Spain is one hour ahead of Greenwich Mean Time (GMT), while Portugal operates at GMT. Both countries observe Daylight Saving Time. The following table realtes Spain and Portugal's capitals to other localities at noon GMT.

BY MAIL

SENDING MAIL HOME FROM SPAIN AND PORTUGAL

Airmail is the best way to send mail home from Spain and Portugal. **Aerogrammes,** printed sheets that fold into envelopes and travel via airmail, are available at post offices. Write "airmail," *"par avion," "por avión," "por avião,"* or *"via aerea"* on the front. In Spain, airmail usually takes from five to 10 business days to reach the US or Canada. **Express mail** may be the most reliable way to send a letter or parcel, and takes four to seven business days. Be aware that Spain's **overnight mail** may not exactly be "overnight." For faster service, try companies like DHL, UPS, or SEUR, under *mensajerías* in the yellow pages. Stamps are sold at post offices and tobacconists (*estancos* or *tabacos*). Mail letters and postcards from the yellow mailboxes scattered throughout cities, or from the post office in small towns. Mail in Portugal can be inefficient—airmail can take from one to two weeks longer to reach the US. Again, stamps are available at post offices (which can have automatic stamp machines) and at central locations around cities. Fax machines are often available at post offices. **Surface mail** is by far the cheapest and slowest way to send mail. It takes one to two months to cross the Atlantic and one to three to cross the Pacific—good for heavy items you won't need for a while, such as souvenirs that you've acquired along the way.

SENDING MAIL TO SPAIN AND PORTUGAL

In addition to the standard postage system whose rates are listed below, **Federal Express** (www.fedex.com) handles express mail services from most countries to Spain and Portugal. Service tends to be best between major cities like Barcelóna, Lisboa, and Madrid. Rural areas often have slower service. There are several ways to arrange the pick up of letters sent to you while you are abroad. Mail can be sent via **Poste Restante** (General Delivery; **Lista de Correos (S); Lista de Correiros (P)**) to almost any city or town in Spain or Portugal with a post office, but it is not very reliable. Address **Poste Restante** letters like so:

Miguel de CERVANTES
Lista de Correos
Salamanca, España

The mail will go to a special desk in the central post office, unless you specify a post office by street address or postal code. Itiss best to use the largest post office, since mail may be sent there regardless. It is usually safer and quicker, though more expensive, to send mail express or registered. Bring your passport (or other photo ID) for pickup; there may be a small fee. If the clerks insist that there is nothing for you, ask them to check under your first name as well. *Let's Go* lists post offices in the **Practical Information** section for each city and most towns. **American Express's** travel offices throughout the world offer a free **Client Letter Service** (mail held up to 30 days and forwarded upon request) for cardholders who contact them in advance. Some offices provide these services to non-cardholders (especially AmEx Travelers Cheque holders), but call ahead to make sure. *Let's Go* lists AmEx locations for most large cities in **Practical Information** sections; for a complete list, call ☎+1-800-528-4800 or visit www.americanexpress.com/travel.

ACCOMMODATIONS

HOSTELS

Many hostels are laid out dorm-style, often with large single-sex rooms and bunk beds, with some private rooms that sleep two to four. They often have kitchens and utensils for your use, bike or moped rentals, storage areas, transportation to airports, breakfast and other meals, laundry facilities, and internet. There can, however, be drawbacks: some hostels close during certain daytime "lockout" hours, have a curfew, don't accept reservations, impose a maximum stay, or, less frequently, require that you do chores.

A HOSTELER'S BILL OF RIGHTS. There are certain standard features that we do not include in our hostel listings. Unless we state otherwise, you can expect that every hostel has no lockout, no curfew, free hot showers, some system of secure luggage storage, and no key deposit.

HOSTELLING INTERNATIONAL

Joining the youth hostel association in your own country (listed below) automatically grants you membership privileges in **Hostelling International (HI),** a federation of national hosteling associations. Non-HI members may be allowed to stay in some HI hostels, but will have to pay extra to do so. HI hostels are scattered throughout Spain and Portugal, and can be less expensive than private hostels. HI's umbrella website (www.hihostels.com), which lists the websites and phone numbers of all national associations, can be a great place to begin researching hosteling in a specific region. Other comprehensive hosteling websites include www.hostels.com and www.hostelplanet.com.

Most HI hostels also honor **guest memberships**—you'll get a blank card with space for six validation stamp, each night you'll pay a nonmember supplement (one-sixth the membership fee) and earn one guest stamp, and six stamps make you a member. Most student travel agencies (p. 23) sell HI cards, as do all of the national hosteling organizations listed below. All prices listed below are for one-year memberships unless otherwise noted.

Australian Youth Hostels Association (AYHA), 422 Kent St., Sydney, NSW 2000 (www.yha.com.au). AUS$52, under 18 $19.

Hostelling International-Canada (HI-C), 205 Catherine St., Ste. 400, Ottawa, ON K2P 1C3 (www.hihostels.ca). CDN$35, under 18 free.

Hostelling International Northern Ireland (HINI), 22-32 Donegall Rd., Belfast BT12 5JN (www.hini.org.uk). UK£15, under 25 UK£10.

Youth Hostels Association of New Zealand Inc. (YHANZ), Level 1, 166 Moorhouse Ave., P.O. Box 436, Christchurch (www.yha.org.nz). NZ$40, under 18 free.

Youth Hostels Association (England and Wales), Trevelyan House, Dimple Rd., Matlock, Derbyshire DE4 3YH (www.yha.org.uk). UK£16, under 26 UK£10.

Hostelling International (USA), 8401 Colesville Rd., Ste. 600, Silver Spring, MD 20910 (www.hiayh.org). US$28, under 18 free.

OTHER TYPES OF ACCOMMODATIONS

HOTELS, GUESTHOUSES, AND PENSIONS

Spanish accommodations have many aliases distinguished by the different grades of rooms. The cheapest and barest options are **casas de huéspedes** and **hospedajes.** While **pensiones** and **fondas** (like a B&B) tend to be a bit nicer, all are essentially just boarding houses; these establishments provide basic and well-used rooms with a shared bath, possibly a sink, but no A/C. Another relatively comfortable option is the **hostal,** which provides sheets and lockers. The government rates *hostales* on a two-star system, and even one-star establishments can be quite comfortable. *Hostal* owners tend to dip below official rates in the off season (Sept.-May), so bargain away.

The highest-priced accommodations are **hoteles,** which have a bathroom in each room but are usually on the pricey side, and rated with one to five stars. The top-notch hotels are the government **Paradores Nacionales**—castles, palaces, convents, and historic buildings that have been converted into luxurious hotels. They often are interesting sights in their own right.

In Portugal, **pensões,** also called **residencias,** are a budget traveler's mainstay. They are cheaper than hotels and only slightly more expensive than youth hostels. **Hotels** in Portugal tend to be pricey. Room prices typically include breakfast and showers, and most rooms that lack a bath or shower have a sink. When business is weak, try bargaining in advance. **Pousadas,** like Spanish *paradores*, outperform standard hotels, but are more expensive. Most are castles, palaces, or monasteries converted into luxurious, government-run hotels.

HOME EXCHANGES AND HOSPITALITY CLUBS

Home exchange offers travelers various types of homes (houses, apartments, condominiums, villas, even castles in some cases). For more information, contact **HomeExchange.com Inc.,** P.O. Box 787, Hermosa Beach, CA 90254, USA (☎+1-310-798-3864 or toll-free +1-800-877-8723; www.homeexchange.com) or **Intervac International Home Exchange** (☎934 53 31 71; www.intervac.com).

Hospitality clubs link their members with individuals or families abroad who are willing to host travelers for free or for a small fee to promote cultural exchange. In exchange, members must be willing to host travelers in their own homes, and a small fee may also be required. **The Hospitality Club** (www.hospitalityclub.org) is a good place to start. **Servas** (www.servas.org) requires a fee and an interview to join. An internet search will yield many similar organizations, some of which cater to special interests. Be sure to use common sense when planning to stay with or host someone you do not know.

LONG-TERM ACCOMMODATIONS

Travelers planning to stay in Spain or Portugal for extended periods of time may find it most cost-effective to rent an **apartment.** Many students spend time living in sublets, and there are plenty of places to be found. A basic one-bedroom (or studio) apartment in Madrid, Barcelona, or Lisboa will range €400-800 and beyond per month. In addition to the rent itself, prospective tenants usually are also required to front a security deposit (often one month's rent) and the last month's rent. Expatriates.com (www.expatriates.com) lists apartments for rent, with extensive entries for Spain and Portugal.

CAMPING

Campgrounds exist throughout Spain and Portugal, and their popularity varies by region. They are frequently located on the outskirts of cities and towns, making for inconvenient or extensive commutes. Campers heading to Europe should consider buying an **International Camping Carnet.** Similar to a hostel membership card, it is required at a few campgrounds and sometimes provides discounts. The card is available in North America from the **Family Campers and RVers Association** and in the UK from the **Caravan Club** (see below).

Most **campgrounds** charge separate fees per person, per tent, and per car; others charge for a *parcela*—a small plot of land—plus per-person fees. Be aware that although camping may seem like a budget option, prices can get high for lone travelers and even for pairs. Most tourist offices provide info on official areas, including the hefty *Guía de campings*. In Portugal, you will find many official campgrounds *(parques de campismo)* with amenities. Most have a supermarket or cafe, and many are even beach-accessible. Some may require reservations. Do not take the risk of illegal camping. A useful resource is *Portugal: Camping and Caravan Sites*, a free guide to official campgrounds. Otherwise, contact the **Federação de Campismo e Montanhismo de Portugal** (☎218 12 68 90/1; fcmportugal.com). For more information on outdoor activities in Spain and Portugal, see **The Great Outdoors,** below.

THE GREAT OUTDOORS

LEAVE NO TRACE. *Let's Go* encourages travelers to embrace the "Leave No Trace" ethic, minimizing their impact on natural environments and protecting them for future generations. Trekkers and wilderness enthusiasts should set up camp on durable surfaces, use cookstoves instead of campfires, bury human waste away from water supplies, bag trash and carry it out with them, and respect wildlife and natural objects. For more detailed information, contact the **Leave No Trace Center for Outdoor Ethics,** P.O. Box 997, Boulder, CO 80306 USA (☎+1-800-332-4100 or 303-442-8222; www.lnt.org).

USEFUL RESOURCES

A variety of publishing companies offer guidebooks to meet the educational needs of novicesor expert hikers. For information about camping, hiking, and biking, write or call the publishers listed below to receive a free catalog. The **Great Outdoor Recreation Page** (www.gorp.com) provides excellent general information for travelers planning on camping or enjoying the outdoors.

Automobile Association, Contact Centre, Lambert House, Stockport Rd., Cheadle SK8 2DY, UK (www.theAA.com). Publishes *Caravan and Camping Europe* and *Britain & Ireland* (UK£10) as well as road atlases for Europe, Britain, France, Germany, Ireland, Italy, Spain, and the US.

Sierra Club Books, 85 2nd St., 2nd fl., San Francisco, CA 94105, USA (☎+1-415-977-5500; www.sierraclub.org). Publishes general resources on hiking and camping.

The Mountaineers Books, 1001 SW Klickitat Way, Ste. 201, Seattle, WA 98134, USA (☎+1-206-223-6303; www.mountaineersbooks.org). Over 600 titles on hiking, biking, mountaineering, natural history, and conservation.

Vayacamping, (☎935 94 61; www.vayacamping.net). Publishes guides, maintains a website with resources for camping across Spain and Portugal. Also offers card-holding membership that gives discounts at participating establishments on the peninsula.

The Caravan Club, East Grinstead House, East Grinstead, West Sussex, RH19 1UA, UK (www.caravanclub.co.uk). For UK£34, members receive access to sites, insurance services, equipment discounts, maps, and a monthly magazine. Provides some European information covering Spain and Portugal.

NATIONAL PARKS

Spain and Portugal have extensive national park systems with opportunities for hiking, mountaineering, and other outdoor adventures. Camping within national park boundaries is usually illegal, but campgrounds can be found in most nearby towns. The general procedure is to stock up on equipment and supplies, stop by the visitor information center to pick up free maps, and head into the park. More detailed maps, with specific hiking or adventure information, can be purchased both at the visitors centers and in nearby towns.

The Spanish **Ministry of Natural Environment** operates a website (reddeparquesnacionales.mma.es/parques/index.htm) that provides information, mostly in Spanish but with some English, about the national park system, including trip-planning tools. The Spanish government's tourism portal also provides information, contact information, and listings for national parks at www.spain.info/TourSpain/Naturaleza. **Turismo de Portugal** (www.visitportugal.com), the official Portuguese tourist office website, offers some information in English and links to details about the parks, mostly in Portuguese.

WILDERNESS SAFETY

Staying warm, dry, and well hydrated is key to a happy wilderness experience. For any hike, prepare yourself for an emergency by packing a first-aid kit, a reflector, a whistle, high-energy food, extra water, rain gear, a hat, mittens, and extra socks. For warmth, wear wool or insulating synthetic materials designed for the outdoors. Check weather forecasts often and pay attention to the skies when hiking, as weather patterns can change suddenly. Always let someone—a friend, your hostel, or a park ranger—know when and where you are going. See **Safety and Health**, p. 17, for information on outdoor medical concerns.

ORGANIZED ADVENTURE TRIPS

Organized adventure tours offer another way of exploring the wild. Activities include hiking, biking, skiing, canoeing, kayaking, rafting, climbing, photo safaris, and archaeological digs. Tourism bureaus often can suggest parks, trails, and outfitters. Organizations that specialize in camping and outdoor equipment like REI and EMS are good sources for info, or contact the **Specialty Travel Index,** P.O. Box 458, San Anselmo, CA 94979, USA (www.specialtytravel.com).

SPECIFIC CONCERNS

SUSTAINABLE TRAVEL

As the number of travelers on the road rises, their detrimental effect on natural environments is an increasing concern. *Let's Go* promotes the philosophy of sustainable travel with this in mind. Through a sensitivity to issues of ecology and sustainability, today's travelers can be a powerful force in preserving and restoring the places they visit.

Ecotourism, a rising trend in sustainable travel, focuses on the conservation of natural habitats—mainly, on how to use them to build up the economy without exploitation or overdevelopment. Travelers can make a difference by doing advance research, by supporting organizations and establishments that pay attention to their carbon "footprint," and by patronizing establishments that strive to be environmentally friendly.

Staying at organic farms, campgrounds, or long-established monasteries and convents is one way to minimize your mark in fragile areas. Supporting local markets and shops instead of tourist restaurants and chains also helps. You can take part in more specialized conservation efforts, like preventing desertification in Spain (See **Beyond Tourism**, p. 44).

ECOTOURISM RESOURCES. For more information on environmentally responsible tourism, contact one of the organizations below:

Conservation International, 2011 Crystal Dr., Ste. 500, Arlington, VA 22202, USA (☎+1-800-406-2306 or 703 341 2400; www.conservation.org).

Green Globe 21, Green Globe vof, Verbenalaan 1, 2111 ZL Aerdenhout, the Netherlands (☎+31 23 544 0306; www.greenglobe.com).

International Ecotourism Society, 1333 H St. NW, Ste. 300E, Washington, DC 20005, USA (☎+1-202-347-9203; www.ecotourism.org).

United Nations Environment Program (UNEP), 39-43 Quai André Citroën, 75739 Paris Cedex 15, France (www.uneptie.org/pc/tourism).

RESPONSIBLE TRAVEL

Your tourist dollars can make a big impact on the destinations you visit. Travelers who care about the destinations and environments they explore should make themselves aware of the social and cultural implications of their choices. Simple decisions such as buying local products, paying fair prices for products or services, and attempting to speak the local language can have a strong, positive effect on the community.

Community-based tourism aims to channel tourist dollars into the local economy by emphasizing tours and cultural programs run by members of the host community. This type of tourism also benefits the tourists themselves, as it often takes them beyond traditional sightseeing in the region. *The Ethical Travel Guide* (UK£13), a project of Tourism Concern (☎+44 20 7133 3330; www.tourismconcern.org.uk), is an excellent resource for information on community-based travel, with a directory of 300 establishments in 60 countries.

TRAVELING ALONE

Traveling alone can provide a sense of independence and a greater opportunity to connect with locals. On the other hand, solo travelers are more vulnerable to harassment and street theft. If you are traveling alone, look confident, try not to stand out as a tourist, and be especially careful in deserted or very crowded areas. Stay away from areas that are not well lit. If questioned, never admit that you are traveling alone. Maintain regular contact with someone at home who knows your itinerary, and always research your destination before traveling. For more tips, pick up *Traveling Solo* by Eleanor Berman (Globe Pequot Press; US$18), visit www.travelaloneandloveit.com, or subscribe to **Connecting: Solo Travel Network,** 689 Park Rd., Unit 6, Gibsons, BC V0N 1V7, Canada (☎+1-604-886-9099; www.cstn.org; membership US$30-48).

WOMEN TRAVELERS

Women exploring on their own inevitably face some additional safety concerns. Single women can consider staying in hostels that offer single rooms that lock from the inside or in religious institutions with single-sex rooms. It's a good idea to stick to centrally located accommodations and to avoid solitary late-night treks or metro rides. Always carry extra cash for a phone call, bus, or taxi. Hitchhiking is never safe for lone women, or even for two women traveling together. Look as if you know where you're going and approach older women or couples for directions if you're lost or feeling uncomfortable. Dress conservatively, especially in rural areas. Wearing a conspicuous wedding band sometimes helps to prevent unwanted advances.

Your best answer to verbal harassment is no answer at all. Feigning deafness, sitting motionless, and staring straight ahead at nothing in particular will usually do the trick. Persistent aggressors sometimes be dissuaded by a firm, loud, and very public "go away!" in the appropriate language. Don't hesitate to seek out a police officer or a passerby if you are being harassed. Memorize the emergency numbers in places you visit, and consider carrying a whistle on your keychain. A self-defense course will both prepare you for a potential attack and raise your level of awareness of your surroundings (see **Personal Safety,** p. 18). Consider talking with your doctor about the health concerns that women face when traveling (See **Women's Heath,** p. 22).

GLBT TRAVELERS

Attitudes toward gay, lesbian, bisexual, and transgendered (GLBT) people in Spain and Portugal vary by region. GLBT travelers may feel out of place in the more traditional, rural areas of Spain and Portugal, given the countries' strong Catholic heritage, but overt homophobia is rare. In Spain, Sitges (p. 296) and Ibiza (p. 226) are internationally renowned as gay party destinations, and Madrid (see Chueca, p. 76) hosts the famous party *Orgullo Gay* (Gay Pride) party in June. The website www.guiagay.com has info about gay Spain, and www.portugalgay.pt offers listings in Portuguese and English.

Listed below are contact organizations, mail-order catalogs, and publishers that offer materials addressing some specific concerns. **Out and About** (www.planetout.com) offers a weekly newsletter addressing travel concerns and a comprehensive site addressing gay travel concerns. The online newspaper **365gay.com** has a travel section (www.365gay.com/travel/travelchannel.htm).

ADDITIONAL RESOURCES: GLBT

International Lesbian and Gay Association (ILGA), www.ilga.org.
Spartacus International Gay Guide 2008 (US$22).
Damron Travel Guides (US$18-24). www.damron.com.
The Gay Vacation Guide: The Best Trips and How to Plan Them, by Mark Chesnut. Kensington Books (US$15).
Gayellow Pages, by Frances Green. (US$20), http://gayellowpages.com.

TRAVELERS WITH DISABILITIES

Wheelchair accessibility varies widely in Iberia but is generally inferior to that in the US. Handicapped access is common in modern and big city museums. Some Spanish tourist offices abroad can provide useful listings of accessible (but often expensive) accommodations and sights.

Barcelona is particularly accessible to travelers with disabilities, having revamped much of its infrastructure in preparation for the 1992 Olympics. Other large cities may be amenable as well, but rural and small-town Iberia will be difficult to manage for the budget traveler with disabilities. Those with disabilities should inform airlines and hotels of their disabilities when making reservations, as some time may be needed to prepare special accommodations. Call ahead to restaurants, museums, and other facilities to find out if they are wheelchair-accessible. Guide-dog owners should inquire as to the quarantine policies of each destination country.

Trains are probably the easiest form of travel for disabled travelers in Europe: many stations have ramps, and some trains have wheelchair lifts, special seating areas, and specially equipped toilets. All Eurostar, some InterCity (IC), and some EuroCity (EC) trains are wheelchair-accessible, and CityNightLine trains and Conrail trains feature special compartments. Some car rental agencies (e.g., Hertz) offer hand-controlled vehicles.

USEFUL ORGANIZATIONS

Accessible Journeys, 35 W. Sellers Ave., Ridley Park, PA 19078, USA (☎+1-800-846-4537; www.disabilitytravel.com). Designs tours for wheelchair users and slow walkers. The site has tips and forums for all travelers.

Flying Wheels Travel, 143 W. Bridge St., Owatonna, MN 55060, USA (☎+1-507-451-5005; www.flyingwheelstravel.com). Specializes in escorted trips to Europe for people with physical disabilities; plans custom trips worldwide.

The Guided Tour, Inc., 7900 Old York Rd., Ste. 114B, Elkins Park, PA 19027, USA (☎+1-800-783-5841; www.guidedtour.com). Organizes travel programs for persons with developmental and physical challenges in Canada, Hawaii, Ireland, Italy, Mexico, Spain, the UK, and the US.

Mobility International USA (MIUSA), P.O. Box 10767, Eugene, OR 97440, USA (☎+1-541-343-1284; www.miusa.org). Provides a variety of books and other publications containing information for travelers with disabilities.

Society for Accessible Travel and Hospitality (SATH), 347 5th Ave., Ste. 610, New York, NY 10016, USA (☎+1-212-447-7284; www.sath.org). Advocacy group that publishes free online travel info. Annual membership US$49, students and seniors US$29.

MINORITY TRAVELERS

The cities of Spain are increasingly cosmopolitan due to immigration and tourism. The infrequent incidents of racism reported are rarely violent or threatening. However, after the arrest of Moroccans for the terrorist attack of 11-M (p. 61), travelers who appear Middle Eastern may face some harassment. Portugal, with its increasingly diverse ethnic composition and long history with Africa, Asia, and South America, is actively anti-racist, but travelers should always be aware of and sensitive to their surroundings.

DIETARY CONCERNS

The travel section of **The Vegetarian Resource Group's** website, at www.vrg.org/travel, has a comprehensive list of organizations and websites geared toward helping vegetarians and vegans traveling abroad. Vegetarians will also find numerous resources on the web; try www.vegdining.com, www.happycow.net, and www.vegetariansabroad.com, for starters.

Travelers who keep **kosher** should contact synagogues in larger cities for information. Your own synagogue or college Hillel should have access to lists of Jewish institutions across the nation. If you are strict in your observance, you may have to prepare your own food on the road. A good resource is the *Jewish Travel Guide* edited by Michael Zaidner (Vallentine Mitchell; US$18). Travelers looking for **halal** restaurants may find www.zabihah.com a useful resource. The database at http://shamash.org/kosher provides listings of Jewish centers and restaurants providing kosher food, mostly in Spain and Morocco.

OTHER RESOURCES

Let's Go tries to cover all aspects of budget travel, but we can't put everything in our guides. Listed below are books and websites that will help you conduct your own research.

WORLD WIDE WEB

Almost every aspect of budget travel is accessible via the web. In 10min. at the keyboard, you can make a hostel reservation, get advice on travel hot spots from other travelers, or find out how much a train from Lleida to Lisboa costs. Listed here are some regional and travel-related sites to start off your surfing; other relevant websites are listed throughout the book. Because website turnover is high, use search engines (like Google) to strike out on your own.

LET'S GO ONLINE. Plan your next trip on our newly redesigned website, **www.letsgo.com.** It features the latest travel info on your favorite destinations as well as tons of interactive features: make your own itinerary, read blogs from our trusty researcher-writers, browse our photo library, watch exclusive videos, check out our newsletter, find travel deals, and buy new guides. We're always updating and adding new features, so check back often!

THE ART OF TRAVEL

Backpacker's Ultimate Guide: www.bugeurope.com. Tips on packing, transportation, and where to go. Also tons of country-specific travel information.

BootsnAll.com: www.bootsnall.com. Numerous resources for independent travelers, from planning your trip to reporting on it when you get back.

How to See the World: www.artoftravel.com. A compendium of great travel tips, from cheap flights to self defense to interacting with local culture.

Travel Intelligence: www.travelintelligence.net. A large collection of works by distinguished travel writers.

INFORMATION ON SPAIN, PORTUGAL, AND MOROCCO

CIA World Factbook: www.odci.gov/cia/publications/factbook/index.html. Tons of vital statistics on geography, government, economy, and people.

Geographia: www.geographia.com. Highlights the culture and peoples of Spain, Portugal, and Morocco.

TravelPage: www.travelpage.com. Links to official tourist office sites.

PlanetRider: www.planetrider.com. A list of links to the "best" websites covering the culture and tourist attractions of Spain, Portugal, and Morocco.

World Travel Guide: www.travel-guides.com. Helpful practical info.

BEYOND TOURISM

A PHILOSOPHY FOR TRAVELERS

HIGHLIGHTS OF SPAIN, PORTUGAL, AND MOROCCO

SIMMER and slice with Basque chefs in San Sebastián (p. 319).

SPEAK Portuguese (almost) like the Portuguese in Lisboa (p. 370).

SWEAT as you plant cherry trees in the mountains of Morocco's High Atlas (p. 488).

FLIP to our "Giving Back" sidebar feature for more on Beyond Tourism (p. 44).

There comes a point when tourism and traveling diverge. Whether exploring Spain, Portugal, or Morocco, you will be surrounded by chances to immerse yourself in your environment. And as you do, certain realities around you become more obvious: environmental destruction, poverty, and discrimination, to name a few. Even as tourism plays a heavy role in the development of local economies, it contributes to some of the worst environmental and cultural erosion. Responsible and socially-conscious tourism, therefore, is not only essential but also one of the most rewarding ways to travel.

As a **volunteer** in Spain, Portugal, or Morocco, you can unleash that inner superhero with projects from fighting racism in Barcelona to painting murals in Marrakesh. This chapter is full of ideas to help get your search for NGOs and other relevent organizations started, whether you're hoping to pitch in for a few days or run away to a whole new life of Iberian activism.

The power of **studying** abroad is beyond comprehension. Thousands of students descend on Spain every year to take advantage of a broad array of language programs, and Portugal and Morocco offer equally incredible learning experiences. If you want to brush up your Arabic, birdwatch in the Pyrenees, or conquer the Spanish lisp, there is probably a course out there for you.

Working abroad can bring some of the most meaningful relationships and experiences of your life. (And it doesn't hurt that a job helps pay for more globetrotting.) High rates of unemployment in Spain, Portugal, and Morocco can make it difficult to find a job or obtain a work visa, and travelers should also realize that they could be taking away jobs from locals. That said, English speakers are always in high demand as teachers, au pairs, or workers in seasonal resort towns. In order to work abroad, you must meet the legal requirements for either short-term or long-term work (see **Working, p. 51**).

SHARE YOUR EXPERIENCE. Have you had a particularly enjoyable volunteer, study, or work experience that you'd like to share with other travelers? Post it to our website, www.letsgo.com.

VOLUNTEERING

Feel like saving the world this week? Volunteering can be a powerful and fulfilling experience, especially when combined with the thrill of traveling. While Spain, Portugal, and Morocco face very different realities, key problems unite them. Pressing issues like immigration, the environment, poverty, and women's rights make volunteering in these countries a compelling option.

Most people who volunteer do so on a short-term basis at organizations that make use of drop-in or once-a-week volunteers. The best way to find opportunities that match your interests and schedule may be to check with local or national volunteer centers. In Spain, contact the **Plataforma del Voluntariado de España,** C. Fuentes, 10, Madrid (☎902 12 05 12) in order to best match your interests to local needs. In Portugal, the **Plataforma Portuguesa das ONGD,** Rua da Madalena, 91, Lisboa (☎218 87 22 39) is a central coordinator of NGOs and volunteer opportunities. As always, read up before heading out.

Those looking for longer, more intensive volunteer opportunities usually choose to go through a parent organization that takes care of logistical details and often provides a group environment and support system—for a fee. There are two main types of organizations—religious and secular—although there are rarely restrictions on participation in either. Websites like **www.volunteerabroad.com, www.servenet.org,** and **www.idealist.org** allow you to search for volunteer openings both in your country and abroad. The following listings are just a starting point; local opportunities are endless.

BEYOND TOURISM

I HAVE TO PAY TO VOLUNTEER? Many volunteers are surprised to learn that some organizations require large fees or "donations," but don't go calling them scams just yet. While such fees may seem ridiculous at first, they often keep the organization afloat, covering airfare, room, board, and administrative expenses for the volunteers. (Other organizations must rely on private donations and government subsidies.) If you're concerned about how a program spends its fees, request an annual report or finance account. A reputable organization won't refuse to inform you of how volunteer money is spent. Pay-to-volunteer programs might be a good idea for young travelers who are looking for more support and structure (such as pre-arranged transportation and housing) or anyone who would rather not deal with the uncertainty of creating a volunteer experience from scratch.

SOCIAL ACTIVISM

Here's your chance to work toward goals of justice and equity, whether in Spain, Portugal, or Morocco. A diverse network of social organizations addresses all manner of problems, from homelessness to domestic abuse to human rights. Such volunteering can help you better understand the global scope of these issues and immerse you in a foreign environment with a community of like-minded individuals. The following is a brief selection of organizations to help you begin your search.

Abraço, Larco José Luis Champalimaud, 4a, 1600-110 Lisboa, Portugal (☎217 99 75 00; www.abraco.org.pt). With multiple offices in Portugal, this non-profit offers support services and fights HIV/AIDS discrimination.

Asociacion del Sur del Trabajo Voluntario y Social (ASTVS), N°480 Lot, Boutalamine 52000 Errachidia, Morocco (☎212 67 41 76 30; www.astvs.org). Works to further educational, cultural, and social goals in Morocco's southern region, organizing work camps with foreign and Moroccan volunteers. 2- to 4-week project €160.

Banco Alimentar, Av. de Ceuta, Estação C.P. Alcântara-Terra, Armazém 1, 1300-125 Lisboa, Portugal (☎213 64 96 55; www.bancoalimentar.pt). This federation of food banks operates branches throughout Portugal, providing much-needed food for the hungry.

Equanimal, Apdo. 14454, 28080 Madrid, spain (☎902 10 29 45; www.equanimal.org). Works for animal rights, including the abolition of bullfighting, through education. Volunteers can participate in demonstrations, distribute pamphlets, and organize events.

Fundación Triángulo, C. Eloy Gonzalo, 25, 28010 Madrid, Spain (☎915 93 05 40; www.fundaciontrangulo.es). Combats discrimination and promotes equality for gay, lesbian, bisexual, and transgendered people in Spain and around the world.

Stop SIDA, C. Muntaner, 121, Entresuelo 1, Barcelona, Spain (☎902 10 69 27; www.stopsida.org). A member of the federation Coordinadora GaiLesbiana, Stop SIDA helps combat the spread of AIDS by providing prevention information and support services.

IMMIGRATION

Today, Spain absorbs more immigrants than any other country in the European Union. Over the past decade, the number of immigrants has risen from 2 percent of the Spanish population to more than 10 percent, changing the face of Spanish cities and making booming economic growth possible. Though popular images suggest a flood of immigrants crossing the Strait of Gibraltar from Morocco, in reality only about 20 percent of Spain's immigrants come from Africa. The vast majority, in fact, emigrate from Europe and Latin America. Portuguese society has become just as multicultural and is now home to a huge number of immigrants, largely from former African colonies and Brazil.

Unlike both Spain and Portugal, Morocco's migration flows outward; thousands of workers attempt to reach Spanish shores each year. But with rising unemployment on the peninsula, attitudes toward foreign workers seem to be shifting as immigration policy becomes controversial for the first time. Below is a partial list of organizations that attempt to level social inequalities while alleviating the burdens placed on immigrants.

ARSIS, C General Weyler, 257, 08912 Barcelona, Spain (☎902 88 86 07; www.arsis.org). Opportunities to tutor underprivileged children, work in a women's center, or run food and clothing drives for recent immigrants.

Comisión Española de Ayuda al Refugiado (CEAR), Avda. General Perón 32, 2° 28020 Madrid, Spain (☎915 98 05 35; www.cear.es) Aims to protect the right to asylum with branches in Madrid, Barcelona, Bilbao, Sevilla, Gran Canarias, Mérida, and Valencia. Work in outreach, legal assistance, translation, and human rights.

Ecos do Sur, C. Ángel Senra, 25, 15007 La Coruña, Spain (☎981 15 01 18; www.ecosdosur.org). Works to ease recent immigrants' transitions into Galician society with English, Spanish, and Gallego classes and support services. Teach, assist with HIV/AIDS prevention programs, conduct tuberculosis tests, or do other community outreach.

Federació Catalana de Voluntariat Social, C. Grassot, 2, 3er, 08025 Barcelona, Spain (☎933 14 19 00; www.federacio.net). Umbrella organization of Catalan social service organizations. Volunteers can assist with projects to achieve better standards of living and equality for immigrants in the region.

SOS Racisme, C. Hospital, 49, 08001 Barcelona, Spain (☎934 12 00 34; www.sosracisme.org) and Quinta da Torrinha, Lote 11A, 1750 Ameixoeira, Lisboa, Portugal (☎217 55 27 00; www.sosracismo.pt). Volunteers strive to combat racism and achieve equal rights for non-citizens and migrant workers in Spain and Portugal.

ENVIRONMENTAL WORK

Development, abuse of natural resources, and rampant tourism all threaten the land and water of Spain, Portugal, and Morocco. Many tourists already make an effort to choose the most environmentally friendly travel possible, whether by using public transit or reducing their local consumption, but some go even further. Working with environmental conservation organizations can reduce the impact of your tourism, and working in the beauty of the landscapes you are helping to protect is its own reward.

Ecoforest, Apdo. 29, Coin 29100, Málaga, Spain (☎661 07 99 50; www.ecoforest.org). Fruit farm and vegan community in southern Spain that uses environmental education to develop a sustainable lifestyle for residents. Visitors are welcome to stay, contributing €5-15 per day toward operating costs.

High Atlas Foundation, Park West Station, P.O. Box 21081, New York, NY 10025, USA (☎+1-646-688-2946; http://highatlasfoundation.org). Formed by former Peace Corps volunteers in Morocco, this foundation works with community-based projects in rural areas of Morocco to plant fruit trees, ensure potable water, improve irrigation, and work for the rights of women and children. Contact the foundation for ways to contribute.

Sunseed Desert Technology, Apdo. 9, 04270, Sorbas, Almería, Spain (☎950 52 57 70; www.sunseed.org.uk). Researches methods of preventing desertification in the driest regions of Spain. Volunteers come for a mimimum of 2 weeks for a part-time position, or stay on with a full time residency. Costs range from €91-165 per week, room and board included. Student discounts available.

World Wide Opportunites on Organic Farms (WWOOF), Yainz 33, Casa 14, Cereceda, Cantabria, Spain (☎902 01 08 14; www.wwoof.es). Connects members with organic farms in Spain and Portugal, which offer work in exchange for food and board. Membership to the Spanish national organization costs €20 per year.

BEYOND TOURISM

FOR THE UNDECIDED ALTRUIST

The possibilities for meaningful volunteer work in Spain, Portugal, or Morocco are endless. These volunteer agencies are great resources; explore their options and find an opportunity that excites you and speaks to your talents.

Service Civil International, 5505 Walnut Level Road, Crozet, VA 22932, USA (☎+1-206-350-6585; www.sci-ivs.org). Organizes a huge variety of short- and long-term work camps in Spain, Portugal, and Morocco. All overseas camps cost $235, which includes simple shared housing and communal meals.

Volunteers for International Partnership, 70 Landmark Hill, Suite 204, Brattleboro, VT 05301 (☎802 246 1154; www.partnershipvolunteers.org) Coordinates 2- or 3-month volunteer programs in Morocco focusing on social welfare, the environment, teaching, and cultural tourism. Includes language courses and homestay. Must be 21 or older; 3-month program $2635 plus airfare.

Volunteers for Peace, 1034 Tiffany Road, Belmont, VT 05730, USA (☎+1-801-259-2759; www.vfp.org). Organizes 2-3 week group projects in Spain, Portugal, and Morocco on a wide range of social and environmental issues. Average project cost $300.

STUDYING

Study-abroad programs range from basic language and culture courses to university-level classes, often for college credit. In order to choose a program that best fits your needs, research as much as you can before making your decision—determine costs and duration, as well as what kind of students participate in the program and what sorts of accommodations are provided. Many American universities, as well as student travel organizations, provide international programs for undergraduates.

VISA INFORMATION. Most foreigners planning to study in Spain or Portugal must obtain a student visa, but those studying for fewer than three months in Spain need only a passport. Visa applications for study in Spain and Portugal can be completed in your home country, at your destination country's consulate (listed under **Consular Services Abroad,** p. 10). Obtaining a visa can be an arduous process; the consulate will often require you to apply in person and demands loads of paperwork (letter verifying enrollment, medical certificate, proof of health insurance, etc.) before they process your application. They are also likely to charge a processing fee of around $100. To study more than 90 days, you must obtain a student residency card (student visa) once in Spain for as long as you are enrolled in the university. For residents of most countries, a stay in Portugal or Morocco of less than three months requires a passport; beyond three months, a visa is necessary.

UNIVERSITIES

Most university-level study-abroad programs are conducted in the country's native language, although many programs offer classes in English as well as courses geared toward non-fluent speakers. Savvy linguists may find it cheaper to enroll directly in a university abroad, although getting college credit may be more difficult. You can search **www.studyabroad.com** for various semester- or summer-abroad programs that meet your criteria, including your desired location and focus of study. If you're a college student, your local study-abroad office is often the best place to start.

AMERICAN PROGRAMS

American Institute for Foreign Study (AIFS), College Division, River Plaza, 9 W. Broad St., Stamford, CT 06902, USA (☎+1-800-727-2437; www.aifsabroad.com). Organizes programs for high school and college study in universities in Spain. Offers study-abroad opportunities in Barcelona in the summer, and Granada and Salamanca in the summer and academic year.

Council on International Educational Exchange (CIEE), 300 Fore St., Portland, ME 04101, USA (☎+1-207-553-4000 or 800-40-STUDY/407-8839; www.ciee.org). One of the most comprehensive resources for work, academic, and internship programs around the world, including in Portugal. Students of all levels of Portuguese can study in Lisboa, where the curriculum focuses largely on the humanities and social sciences.

International Association for the Exchange of Students for Technical Experience (IAESTE; www.iaeste.org). IAESTE runs several branches across Spain and Portugal. Chances are that your home country has a local office, too: contact it to apply for hands-on technical internships abroad. You must be a college student studying science, technology, or engineering. Cost-of-living allowance is provided.

School for International Training (SIT) Study Abroad, 1 Kipling Rd., P.O. Box 676, Brattleboro, VT 05302, USA (☎+1-888-272-7881 or 802-258-3212; www.sit.edu/studyabroad). Semester-long programs in Spain run approximately US$23,000-24,000. In Morocco they run approximately US$18,300-19,300. Summer intensive language program in Morocco runs US$10,190. SIT also runs **The Experiment in International Living** (☎+1-800-345-2929; www.usexperiment.org), with its 3- to 5-week summer programs that offer high-school students cross-cultural homestays, community service, ecological adventure, and language training in Spain and Morocco (US$5300-6800).

SPANISH AND PORTUGUESE PROGRAMS

The European Union sponsors programs encouraging study abroad opportunities within Europe, and Spain and Portugal have not missed the train. From Valencia to Lisboa, Madrid to Coimbra, these countries are studded with dynamic university communities, and in less than a decade the number of foreign students in Barcelona alone has doubled. Information on Spanish study programs is provided by the **Organismo Autónomo de Programas Educativos Europeos** (www.oapee.es). For Portuguese programs, check out the **Programa de Aprendizagem ao Longo da Vida** (www.proalv.pt).

Agencia Nacional Erasmus, Vicesecretaría General del Consejo de Universidades, Juan del Rosal, 14, Ciudad Universitaria, 28040 Madrid, Spain (☎914 53 98 42; http://ec.europa.eu/education/index_en.html). Spanish branch of the European Union's study abroad program, which offers EU members the opportunity to study within Europe.

Agência Nacional para os Programas Comunitários Sócrates e Leonardo da Vinci, Av. Infate Santo, 2, Piso 1, 1350-178 Lisboa, Portugal (☎213 94 47 00; www.socleo.pt). Portuguese division of the European Union's study abroad program.

Universidad Complutense de Madrid, Vicerectorado de Relaciones Internacionales, C. Isaac Peral, 28040 Madrid, Spain (☎913 94 69 22/23; www.ucm.es/info/ucmp/index.php). The largest and one of the oldest universities in Spain. Hosts hundreds of foreign students annually. Opportunities for study in a variety of fields.

Universidade de Lisboa, Rectorate Al. da Universidade, Cidade Universitária, Campo Grande, 1649-004 Lisboa, Portugal (☎217 96 76 24; www.ul.pt). Allows foreign students to enroll directly.

MOROCCAN PROGRAMS

Morocco can be a great option for speakers of French or Arabic, or those with particular interests in subjects like development, religion, and contemporary politics in Africa and the Middle East.

Amideast, 35, Zanqat Oukaimeden, Agdal, Rabat Morocco (☎+212 2 225 9393; www.amideast.org). In partnership with Mohammed V University-Agdal in Rabat, offers a four-month-long program with classes in Arabic, French, humanities, and social sciences.

International Studies Abroad, 35, 1640-B E. 2nd St., Suite 200, Austin, TX 78702, USA (☎+1-800-580-8826; www.studiesabroad.com). Offers fall, winter, and summer programs in Meknès.

LANGUAGE SCHOOLS

Enrolling at a language school has two big perks: a slightly less rigorous course load and the promise that you'll learn exactly what those kids in Cadaqués are calling you under their breath. There is a great variety of language schools—independent, affiliated with a larger university, local, international—but one thing is constant: they rarely offer college credit. Their programs are best for younger high-school students who might not feel comfortable with older students in a university program. Some worthwhile organizations include:

Eurocentres, 56 Eccleston Sq., London SW1V 1PH, UK (☎+44 20 7963 8450; www.eurocentres.com). Language programs for beginning to advanced students with homestays in Barcelona and Valencia.

Language Immersion Institute, State University of New York at New Paltz, 1 Hawk Dr., New Paltz, NY 12561, USA (☎+1-845-257-3500; www.newpaltz.edu/lii). Short, intensive summer language courses and some overseas courses in Spanish, Portuguese, Arabic, and French. Program fees are around US$1000 for a 2-week course, not including accommodations.

Enforex, Alberto Aguilera, 26, 28015 Madrid, Spain (☎915 943 776; www.enforex.com). Offers 20 Spanish programs in Spain, ranging from 1 week to a year in duration. Opportunities in 12 Spanish cities, including Granada, Sevilla, Barcelona, and Madrid.

Amerispan Study Abroad, 1334 Walnut St, 6th Floor, Philadelphia, PA 19107, USA (☎+1-215-751-1100; www.amerispan.com). Offers language courses around the world, many including homestays. Arabic language programs in Fez, Rabat, and Tetouan. Also offers several programs in Spain and Portugal.

OTHER PROGRAMS

Associació per a Defensa i L'Estudì de la Natura (ADENC), Ca l'Estruch, C. Sant Isidre, 08208 Sabadell, Spain (☎937 17 18 87; www.adenc.org). Catalan conservation group offering short courses on bird-watching, landscape photography, and other ecotourism-related fields.

Escuela de Cocina Luis Irizar, C. Mari, 5, 20003 San Sebastián, Guipuzcoa, Spain (☎943 43 15 40; www.escuelairizar.com). Learn how to cook Basque cuisine at this culinary institute. Offers a 2-year diploma course. Professionals and amateurs alike can enroll in 1-week summer programs.

Taller Flamenco School, C. Peral, 49, E-41002 Sevilla, Spain (☎954 56 42 34; www.tallerflamenco.com). Offers courses in flamenco dance (€180-240 per week) and guitar (€225 per week) at varying levels of difficulty.

WORKING

As with volunteering, work opportunities tend to fall into two categories. Some travelers want long-term jobs that allow them to integrate into a community, while others seek out short-term jobs to finance the next leg of their travels. The most common form of long-term work in Spain and Portugal is teaching English, while short-term employment is centered on the tourist industry, whether it's bartending or giving tours of sherry bodegas. *Let's Go* discourages working in developing countries such as Morocco, as employment is scarce enough for locals; however, those with specialized skills may be able to make a positive contribution. **Transitions Abroad** (www.transitionsabroad.com) also offers updated online listings for work over any time span.

For Spain, begin your search at the **INEM (Instituto de Empleo).** The address and telephone number of regional employment offices *(Oficinas de Empleo)* can be found in any telephone guide or at www.inem.es. Many seasoned travelers, however, go straight to a particular town's Yellow Pages *(Páginas Amarillas)* or even go door-to-door. In Portugal, the English-language weekly **The News** (www.the-news.net) carries job listings. Note that working abroad often requires a special work visa.

MORE VISA INFORMATION. Travelers from within the European Union can work without a permit in Spain and Portugal, but those from outside the EU need a work permit. Obtaining a work permit requires extensive documentation, often including a passport, police background check, and medical records, and the cost varies. Contact your nearest consulate (p. 8) for a complete list of requirements. Any foreigner wishing to work in Morocco must obtain a residency permit, which requires a contract, passport, application forms, an AIDS test, and a fee. Again, contact your consulate for details.

LONG-TERM WORK

If you're planning on spending a substantial amount of time (more than three months) working in Spain, Portugal or Morocco, search for a job well in advance. International placement agencies are often the easiest way to find employment abroad, especially for those interested in teaching. Although they are often only available to college students, **internships** are a good way to ease into working abroad. Many say the interning experience is well worth it, despite low pay (if you're lucky enough to be paid at all). Be wary of advertisements for companies claiming to be able get you a job abroad for a fee—often the same listings are available online or in newspapers. Some reputable organizations include:

Council on International Educational Exchange (CIEE), 300 Fore St., Portland, ME 04101, USA (☎+1-207-553-4000 or 800-40-STUDY/407-8839; www.ciee.org). They assist with both studying and teaching abroad. Tucked among their study-abroad listings is a resource for international internships.

Career Journal (www.careerjournaleurope.com). The Wall Street Journal publishes this online journal listing thousands of jobs throughout Europe. There are both short- and long-term as well as part- and full-time jobs.

Escape Artist (www.escapeartist.com/jobs/overseas1). Offers information on living abroad, including job listings for Spain and Portugal.

Expat Exchange (www.expatexchange.com). Provides message boards where individuals seeking employment in Spain and Portugal can advertise.

Trabajos (www.trabajos.com). Contains job listings for all regions of Spain.

EURES (www.europa.eu.int/eures). EU agency providing job listings and opportunities across Europe, including Spain and Portugal.

TEACHING ENGLISH

As an English speaker, you have the chance to contribute your skills while forming lasting relationships with students and a community. In almost all cases, you must have at least a bachelor's degree to be a full-fledged teacher, although college undergraduates can often get summer positions teaching or tutoring. Many schools require teachers to have a **Teaching English as a Foreign Language (TEFL)** certificate. You may still be able to find a teaching job without one, but certified teachers often find higher-paying jobs. Teachers in public schools will likely work in both English and the local language, but private schools usually hire native English speakers for English-immersion classrooms where no Spanish, Portuguese, or Arabic is spoken. Placement agencies or university fellowship programs are the best resources for finding teaching jobs. The alternative is to contact schools directly or to try your luck once you arrive in the country. In the latter case, the best time to look is several weeks before the start of the school year. The following organizations are extremely helpful in placing teachers in Spain, Portugal, and Morocco.

International Schools Services (ISS), 15 Roszel Rd., P.O. Box 5910, Princeton, NJ 08543, USA (☎+1-609-452-0990; www.iss.edu). Hires teachers for more than 200 overseas schools. Candidates should have teaching experience and a bachelor's degree. 2-year commitment is the norm.

Teach Abroad (www.teach.studyabroad.com). Brings you to listings around the world for paid positions teaching English, including some in Spain and Portugal.

TESOL-Spain (www.tesol-spain.org). Non-profit association of English teachers in Spain. Site features a jobs board among its many resources.

TEFL Job Placement (www.tefljobplacement.com). Places teachers in countries across the world, including Morocco. Requirements and durations vary.

AU PAIR WORK

Au pairs are typically women aged 18-27 who work as live-in nannies, caring for children and doing light housework in foreign countries in exchange for room, board, and a small spending allowance or stipend. One perk of the job is that it allows you to get to know Spain or Portugal without the costs of traveling. An au pair can expect to make €50 and up per week. Drawbacks, however, can include mediocre pay and long hours. Much of the au pair experience depends on your relationship with the family with which you are placed. The agencies below are a good starting point for looking for employment.

InterExchange, 161 6th Ave., New York City, NY 10013, USA (☎+1-212-924-0446 or 800-AU-PAIRS/287-2477; www.interexchange.org). Families post messages seeking help. Organized by country for both Spain and Portugal.

Childcare International, Trafalgar House, Grenville Pl., London NW7 3SA, UK (☎+44 20 8906 3116; www.childint.co.uk). Offers opportunities in Spain.

International Au Pair Association (IAPA), Store Kongensgade 40 H, DK-1264 Copenhagen K, Denmark (☎+453 317 0066; www.iapa.org). Non-profit organization that connects to smaller au pair agencies in many nations, including Spain.

SHORT-TERM WORK

Many travelers try their hand at odd jobs to help pay for another few months of travel. However, obtaining a work permit is a long, complicated, and bureaucratic process, and requires a prior job contract, which can be difficult for short-term workers. It is illegal for non-EU citizens to work in Spain or Portugal without this work permit. However, many establishments hire travelers under-the-table for jobs like bartending, waiting tables, or promoting bars and clubs. Another popular option is to work several hours a day at a hostel in exchange for free or discounted room and/or board. Most often, these short-term jobs are found by word of mouth or by expressing interest to the owner of a hostel or restaurant. *Let's Go* lists temporary jobs of this nature whenever possible; look in a city's **Practical Information** listings or see below. *Let's Go* does not recommend working illegally.

EcoForest, Apdo. Correos, 29, 29100 Coin, Málaga, Spain (☎661 07 99 50; www.ecoforest.org). Exchanges free camping space for 3hr. of work per day. €20 initial fee.

Bodega Tour Guide, Jerez de la Frontera, Spain (p. 172).

Intern Jobs (www.internjobs.com). Lists not only internships, but also many ideal short-term jobs like camp counseling and bartending. Applies to Spain, not Portugal.

Transitions Abroad (www.transitionsabroad.com). Lists organizations in Spain and Portugal that hire short-term workers and provides links to articles about working abroad.

FURTHER READING ON BEYOND TOURISM

Alternatives to the Peace Corps: A Guide of Global Volunteer Opportunities, edited by Paul Backhurst. Food First, 2005 (US$12).

The Back Door Guide to Short-Term Job Adventures: Internships, Summer Jobs, Seasonal Work, Volunteer Vacations, and Transitions Abroad, by Michael Landes. Ten Speed Press, 2005 (US$22).

Green Volunteers: The World Guide to Voluntary Work in Nature Conservation, by Fabio Ausenda. Universe, 2007 (US$15).

How to Get a Job in Europe, by Cheryl Matherly and Robert Sanborn. Planning Communications, 2003 (US$23).

Live and Work Abroad: A Guide for Modern Nomads, by Huw Francis and Michelyne Callan. Vacation Work Publications, 2001 (US$20).

Work Abroad: The Complete Guide to Finding a Job Overseas, edited by Clayton A. Hubbs. Transitions Abroad, 2002 (US$16).

Work Your Way Around the World, by Susan Griffith. Vacation Work Publications, 2007 (US$22).

A DIFFERENT PATH

walking the walk

A Pilgrims' Path on the Camino de Santiago

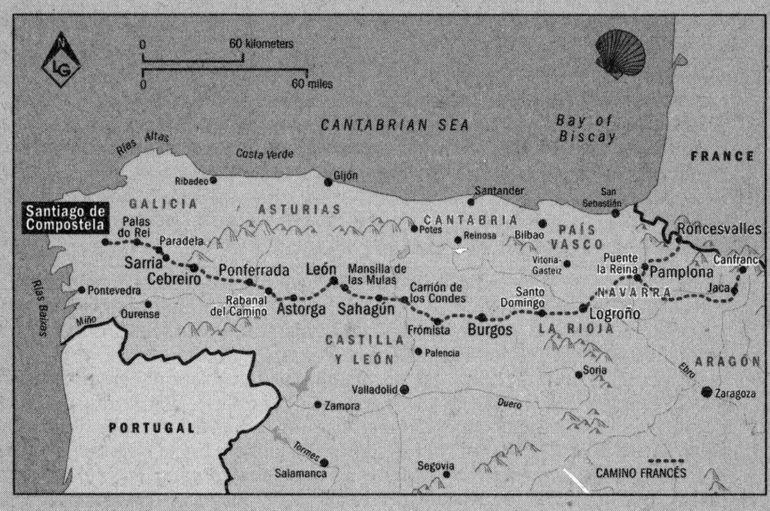

Any pilgrim would agree: the first day of the Camino de Santiago is the hardest. From St-Jean-Pied-de-Port, we hiked 23km uphill into the Pyrenees and then 4km downhill to the *albergue* (pilgrim hostel) in Roncesvalles. We faced drenching rain and impenetrable fog, blisters and scrapes, but we kept walking. And each day, we woke up a little less tired and sore than the day before. As the miles wore on and paths stretched to the horizon, we began to see the rolling wheat fields and *terra rossa* vineyards as calming. We appreciated the silence when our company was limited to grazing cows and the occasional roaming chicken. We encountered locals who offered us cake and cookies with our tea, apples for the road, and homemade *albóndigas* (meatballs). And we looked forward to each evening, when pilgrims from Australia, Italy, Japan, Germany, Venezuela, France, Spain, and a host of other nations would gather in the kitchen to cook and regale each other with stories of the road.

"We began to see the rolling wheat fields and *terra rossa* vineyards as calming

Thirty-four days after that painful first day, we found ourselves sitting in the pews at the Cathedral of St. James in Santiago, awaiting the pilgrims' daily mass. We completed all the traditional rituals, including hugging the golden statue of St. James in an awkward but oddly comforting metallic embrace. We were fumigated by the incense from the *botafumeiro*, a massive swinging contraption rigged to overpower the stench of sweaty pilgrims. Sitting there, we couldn't help but contemplate how many others had gone through the same motions days, months, and even centuries ago. And as we thought back to the first days of our journey, we took solace in the fact that that either we hadn't made a mistake after all, or we had done so in very good company.

Silvia Killingsworth was the Editor-in-Chief of the 2008 Let's Go series. She graduated from Harvard in 2007 and now lives in New York City. Victoria Norelid, a fellow Let's Go vet, graduated from Harvard with a degree in History. She is currently getting a Masters degree at Oxford University.

SPAIN (ESPAÑA)

Spain is colorful and playful, austere and refined. It is a place where medieval Moorish arches in Andalucía collide with wild *Modernista* spires in Cataluña, where classical royal paintings inspire flights of imagination by abstract artists, and where Celtic rock overlays flamenco beats. Three decades after the death of Franco and the country's rebirth as a liberated and politically significant player, Spain is still riding out its cultural and economic renaissance with style and flair. Today, whether travelers are making their pilgrimage to the cathedrals of León or to the pulsing nightlife of Madrid, they are bound to meet their fair share of hippies, nuns, shepherds, and mullet-sporting youth; speakers of Catalan, Gallego, and Basque; recent immigrants and seasoned expatriates; and all those in between. Blessed with cultural vitality and enviable geographic diversity, Spain is a land for the old, the young, and the truly young at heart.

HISTORY

Throughout its history, Spain has been both colony and colonizer. Under the rule of the Iberians, Celts, Romans, Visigoths, Arabs, and French, the country inherited an exotic mélange of influences. In the 16th century, it became a world superpower, ruling from Argentina to Austria. After the 1588 defeat of the Armada, Spain began a long and arduous descent from international empire to Pyrenean pauper, though artistic and literary achievements offset constant military defeats. In 1936, democracy disintegrated into civil war, bringing Generalissimo Francisco Franco to power. Now a thriving democracy with the ninth largest economy in the world, Spain surges into the 21st century with a glorious past and a promising future.

RULE HISPANIA (PREHISTORY-AD 711). Spain played host to a succession of civilizations—**Basque, Celtiberian,** and **Greek**—before the Romans came for an extended visit in the 3rd century BC. Over the next seven centuries, the Romans infused Spanish culture with their langauge, architecture, roads, and food (particularly grapes, olives, and wheat). Following the Romans, a slew of Germanic tribes swept through Iberia, and the **Visigoths**–newly converted Christians–emerged victorious. In AD 419 they established their court at Barcelona and ruled Spain for the next 300 years.

PLEASE, SIR, MAY I HAVE SOME MOORS? (711-1492). A small force of Arabs, Berbers, and Syrians invaded Spain in AD 711 following Muslim unification. The **Moors** encountered little resistance from the divided Visigoths, and the peninsula fell to the caliph of Damascus, the spiritual leader of Islam. The Moors established their Iberian capital at Córdoba (p. 162), which by the 10th century was the largest city in Western Europe with over 500,000 inhabitants. During Abderramán III's rule (929-961), many considered Spain the wealthiest and most cultivated country in the world. Abderramán III's successor, Al-Mansur, snuffed out opposition in his court and undertook a series of military campaigns that culminated with the destruction of Santiago de Compostela (p. 349) in AD 997 and the kidnapping of its bells. It took the Christians 240 years to get them back, and centuries more to retake Spain.

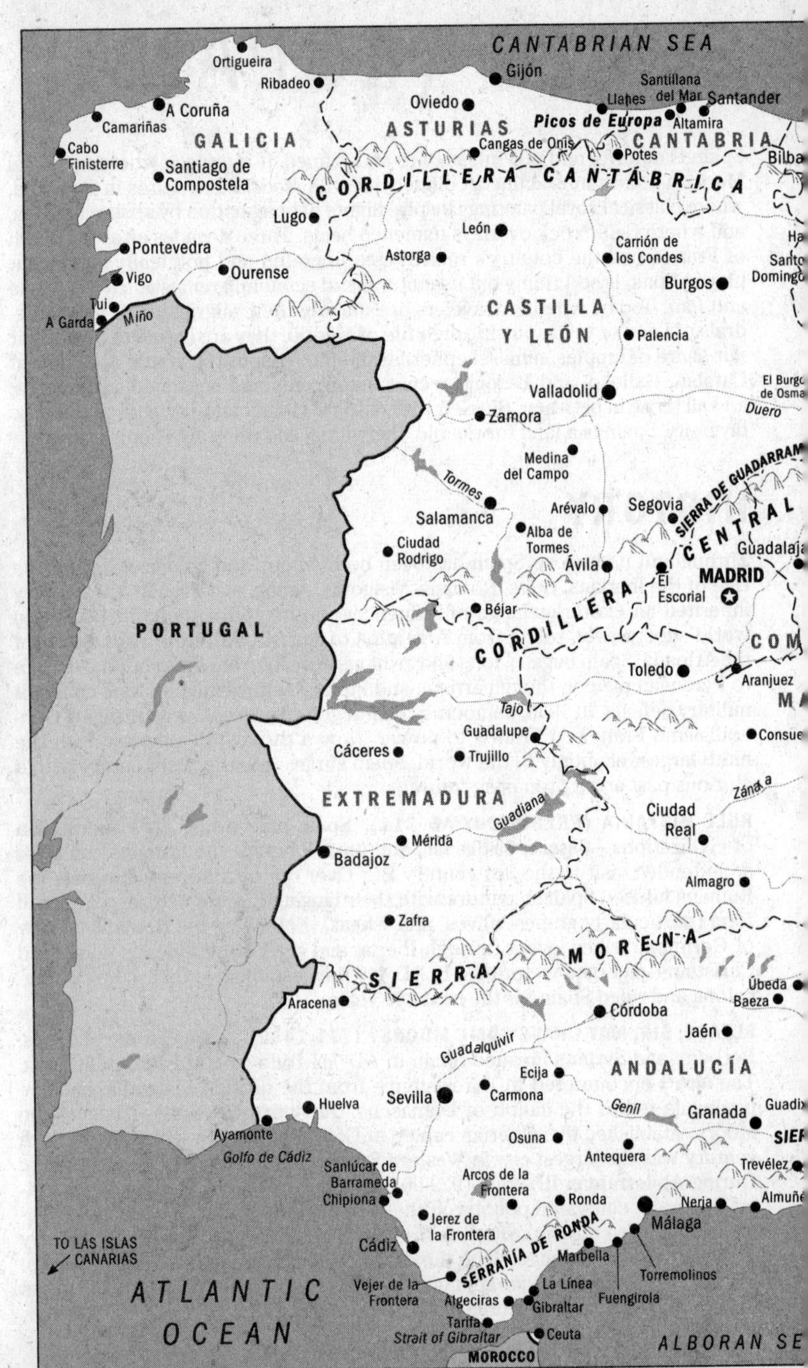

CANTABRIAN SEA
Ortigueira
Ribadeo
Gijón
Oviedo
Santillana del Mar
Llanes
Santander
Altamira
A Coruña
Camariñas
GALICIA
ASTURIAS
Picos de Europa
CANTABRIA
Bilba
Cabo Finisterre
Santiago de Compostela
Cangas de Onís
Potes
CORDILLERA CANTÁBRICA
Lugo
León
Carrión de los Condes
Pontevedra
Astorga
Vigo
Ourense
Burgos
Tui
A Garda
Miño
CASTILLA Y LEÓN
Palencia
Valladolid
El Burgo de Osma
Duero
Zamora
Medina del Campo
Tormes
Salamanca
Arévalo
Segovia
SIERRA DE GUADARRAMA
Alba de Tormes
Ciudad Rodrigo
Ávila
CENTRAL
Guadalaja
El Escorial
MADRID
Béjar
CORDILLERA
PORTUGAL
Toledo
Aranjuez
Tajo
Guadalupe
Consue
Cáceres
Trujillo
EXTREMADURA
Guadiana
Zána
Ciudad Real
Mérida
Badajoz
Almagro
Zafra
SIERRA MORENA
Úbeda
Baeza
Aracena
Córdoba
Jaén
Guadalquivir
ANDALUCÍA
Ecija
Sevilla
Carmona
Huelva
Genil
Granada
Guadix
Ayamonte
Osuna
Golfo de Cádiz
Antequera
Sanlúcar de Barrameda
Chipiona
Arcos de la Frontera
Ronda
Trevélez
Nerja
Almuñé
Málaga
Jerez de la Frontera
SERRANÍA DE RONDA
TO LAS ISLAS CANARIAS
Cádiz
Marbella
Torremolinos
Vejer de la Frontera
La Línea
Algeciras
Gibraltar
Fuengirola
ATLANTIC OCEAN
Tarifa
Strait of Gibraltar
Ceuta
MOROCCO
ALBORAN SE

SPAIN

Spain
BAY OF BISCAY
FRANCE
San Sebastián
Hondarribia
Irún
Guernica
PAÍS VASCO
Roncesvalles
NAVARRA
Pamplona
Vitoria-Gasteiz
Sangüesa
Estella
Olite
Logroño
RIOJA
PYRENEES
Torla
PIRINEOS
Jaca
Ainsa
Huesca
Vielha
ANDORRA
Andorra La Vela
La Seu d'Urgell
Puigcerdà
Núria
Ripoll
Figueres
Portbou
Cadaqués
Empúries
La Bisbal d'Empordà
Girona
Palafrugell
Tossa de Mar
Llobregat
CATALUÑA
ARAGÓN
Tudela
Tarazona
Ebro
Soria
CORDILLERA IBÉRICA
Zaragoza
Lleida
Montserrat
Mataró
Barcelona
Catalayud
Cariñera
Vilanova i la Geltrú
Valls
Sitges
Reus
Tarragona
Salou
Cambrils de Mar
Daroca
Sigüenza
SERRANÍA DE CUENCADOS
Tajo
TO MENORCA
Menorca
Ciutadella
Mahón
Morella
Henares
Albarracín
Teruel
Mora de Rubielos
Castellón
Cuenca
Golfo de Valencia
BALEARIC SEA
Alcúdia
Palma
Mallorca
Sagunt
Turia
Valencia
VALENCIA
CASTILLA LA MANCHA
Júcar
Cullera
LAS ISLAS BALEARES
San Antonio
Ibiza
Eivissa
Formentera
Albacete
Játiva
Gandía
Dénia
Calp
Benidorm
Alicante
Elx
Murcia
MURCIA
Lorca
Manga del Mar Menor
MEDITERRANEAN SEA
Águilas
NEVADA
Mojácar
Almería
Cabo de Gata
ALGERIA
N
LG
0
75 kilometers
0
75 miles

LOS REYES CATÓLICOS (1469-1516). The marriage of **Fernando de Aragón** and **Isabel de Castilla** in 1469 joined Iberia's two mightiest Christian kingdoms. During their half-century rule, these Catholic monarchs established Spain as the prime European exponent of Catholicism, and as an international power. They introduced the brutal **Inquisition** in 1478, which mandated execution or burning of heretics, principally Jews. The policy prompted a mass exodus, as Jews and Muslims who stayed faced conversion to Christianity or imprisonment and death. In 1492, the royal couple captured Granada from the Moors, victoriously ending the centuries-long *Reconquista* and uniting Spain under Catholic rule. This dominance continued to flourish with lucrative conquests in the Americas, beginning in 1492 when they agreed to finance **Christopher Columbus's** first adventure.

HABSBURGS TAKE THE STAGE (1516-1713). The daughter of Fernando and Isabel, **Juana la Loca** (the Mad) married **Felipe el Hermoso** (the Fair) of the powerful Habsburg family. When the young king died, La Loca, a possible schizophrenic, walked his coffin to Granada, opening it occasionally to kiss his corpse. Juana and Felipe secured their genetic legacy with the birth of **Carlos I,** better known as Holy Roman Emperor Charles V (1516-1556).

Under Carlos, the Spanish empire grew exponentially. Royal marriages placed the country in control of European territories in Sicily and Naples, while in the New World conquistadors plundered Mexico, Peru, and Chile, destroying the vast empires of the Aztec and Inca civilizations. They brought their booty back to Spain by the galleon, providing Carlos with funds for his battles and conquests. Gold and silver were complemented by the potatoes, corn, and exotic fruits that were introduced as new crops in Europe.

When Carlos retired to a monastery, **Felipe II** (1556-1598) inherited simmering rebellion in the Protestant Netherlands. His marriage to Mary Tudor, Queen of England, in 1554 created an international Catholic alliance, and Felipe made it his life's mission to create a true Catholic empire. In 1581, a year after Felipe II annexed Portugal, the Dutch declared their independence from Spain, starting a war and becoming embroiled with England's Elizabeth I. The conflict ground to a halt when Sir Francis Drake defeated Spain's "invincible" **Armada** in 1588. With much of his European empire lost and his wealth from the Americas sapped, Felipe retreated to **El Escorial** (p. 115) and sulked in its monastery until his death.

In 1609, **Felipe III** (1598-1621) expelled nearly 300,000 of Spain's remaining Moors. **Felipe IV** (1621-1665) painstakingly held the country together through his long, tumultuous reign while patronizing the arts (painter Diego Velázquez and playwright Lope de Vega both graced his court) and architecture (he commissioned the Parque del Buen Retiro in Madrid; p. 97). Defending Catholicism began to drain Spain's resources after the outbreak of the **Thirty Years' War** (1618-1648), which ended with the marriage of Felipe IV's

1100 BC
Phoenicians found the ports of Cádiz and Málaga.

500 BC
Celts cross the Pyrenees.

200 BC
The Roman Empire sets up camp.

409-711
Visigoths arrive in Iberia after sacking Rome, but fall to the Moors 300 years later.

900-1000
Córdoba claims the title of largest city in Western Europe.

1478
The Inquisition begins.

1492
Fernando and Isabel conquer Granada, the last Moorish holdout; Columbus sets sail with royal funding.

1519
Hernán Cortéz lands in Mexico in search of gold, silver, and chocolate.

1559
St. Teresa of Ávila has a vision of Christ that lasts for almost two years.

1588
Britain's Elizabeth I defeats Spain's "invincible" armada.

1605
Cervantes publishes *Don Quixote* in Madrid.

daughter María Teresa to Louis XIV of France. Felipe's successor **Carlos II el Hechizado** (the bewitched; 1665-1700), the product of generations of inbreeding, was known to fly into fits of rage and epileptic seizures. From then on, little went right: Carlos II left no heirs, Spain fell into an economic depression, and cultural bankruptcy ensued. Rulers from all over, particularly Habsburg Vienna, battled for the crown, and the **War of Spanish Succession** began.

THE REIGN IN SPAIN (1713-1931). The 1713 Treaty of Utrecht ended the ordeal (and Spain's possession of Gibraltar, which went to the English) and landed **Felipe V** (1713-1746), a Bourbon grandson of **Louis XIV,** on the Spanish throne. Though the new king cultivated a flamboyant, debaucherous court, he competently administered the Empire, at last regaining control of Spanish-American trade. The next century was dominated by the Bourbon effort to create a modern state, as the crown centralized power and stripped the different regions of their historical privileges. Finally, in 1808, **Napoleon** invaded Spain as part of his bid for world domination, inaugurating an occupation as short as the general himself. In the midst of the upheaval, most of Spain's Latin American empire threw off the colonial yoke, and those still beyond Napoleon's reach penned the progressive **Constitution of 1812**, which established Spain as a parliamentary monarchy. The violence ended when the Protestant Brits defeated the Corsican troops at Waterloo (1815), placing the reactionary **Fernando VII** (1814-1833) on the throne.

Parliamentary liberalism was restored in 1833 upon Fernando VII's death, and survived the conservative challenge of the first **Carlist War** (1833-1839), a dispute over the monarchy of **Queen Isabel II** (1843-1868). Her successor, **King Amadeo I** (1870-1873), enjoyed a short reign before the **First Spanish Republic** was proclaimed. After a coup d'etat in 1875, the monarchy was restored under **King Alfonso XII** (1875-1885), and the last two decades of the 19th century were marked by rapid industrialization. However, Spain's 1898 loss to the US in the **Spanish-American War** cost it the Philippines, Puerto Rico, Cuba, and any remaining dreams of colonial wealth.

Closer to home, Moroccan tribesmen rebelled against Spanish troops in northern Africa beginning in 1917, resulting in a series of embarrassing military defeats. These events further weakened Spanish morale and culminated in the massacre of 14,000 royal troops in 1921, threatening the very survival of the monarchy. The search for someone to blame for the disaster occupied aristocrats, bureaucrats, and generals for the next decade, throwing the country into chaos. In 1923, **General Miguel Primo de Rivera** sought to bring order to the situation in the form of Spain's first dictatorship.

REPUBLIC AND REBELLION (1931-1939). King Alfonso XIII (1902-1931) abdicated the throne in April 1931, giving rise to the **Second Spanish Republic** (1931-1939). Republican Liberals and Socialists established safeguards for farmers and industrial workers, granted women's suffrage, assured reli-

1701-1714
Europe jockeys for control of the Spanish monarchy in the War of Spanish Succession.

1808
Napoleon occupies Spain and rules for a short six years.

1873-1874
The first Spanish Republic forms and quickly dissolves.

1893
Anarchists bomb Barcelona's Liceu, killing 20 opera-goers.

1898
Spain loses the Spanish-American War and its last three colonies.

1921
14,000 Spanish troops are massacred in Morocco after their attempt to consolidate Spain's hold on its new protectorate.

1923
Spain's first dictator, General Primo de Rivera, rises to power in a coup.

1933-1936
The country is polarized by radical governments, the increased presence of the military, and the Fascist Falange.

1936-1939 Civil War engulfs Spain. Europe joins the fray.

1937 Nazi planes bomb the Basque town of Guernica; in response, Picasso paints *Guernica*.

1939 Franco begins his reign and the country enters a period later known as the "national tragedy."

1959 Twenty years into Franco's rule, the Euskadi Ta Askatasuna (ETA) forms.

1975 Franco dies, and "La Movida" begins: the nation explodes in a burst of creative expression.

1982 Felipe González is elected prime minister and works over the course of the next decade to expand the economy.

gious tolerance, and chipped away at traditional military dominance. National euphoria, however, faded fast. The 1933 elections split the Republican-Socialist coalition, increasing the power of right-wing and Catholic parties in parliament. Military dissatisfaction led to a heightened profile of the **Fascist Falange** (founded by Primo de Rivera's son José Antonio), which further polarized national politics. By 1936, radicals, anarchists, Socialists, and Republicans had formed a **Popular Front** coalition to win the February elections. Their victory, however, was short lived. After increasing polarization, **Generalísimo Francisco Franco** led a militarist uprising and the nation plunged into war, as the infectious ideology of **La Guerra Civil** (**The Spanish Civil War;** 1936-1939) diffused across the globe. Germany and Italy readily supplied Franco with troops and munitions, while the US and liberal European states instituted the Non-Intervention Treaty. The Soviet Union organized the **International Brigades,** an amalgamation of Communists and other leftist volunteers from all over Europe and the US, to battle Franco's fascism. Foreign aid waned as Stalin began to see the benefits of an alliance with Hitler. Bombings, executions, combat, starvation, and disease took nearly 600,000 lives and forced almost one million Spaniards to emigrate. In April 1939, Franco bid a "farewell to arms," marching into Madrid and ending the War.

FRANCO AND THE NATIONAL TRAGEDY (1939-1975). Franco's dictatorship was largely centered around the church, the army, and the Falange. Thousands of scientists, artists, intellectuals, and sympathizers were exiled, imprisoned, or executed in the name of order and purity. Franco initially pursued an isolationist economic policy, but stagnant conditions eventually forced him to adopt a more open policy. With prosperity came unrest. Dissatisfied workers and students engaged in protests, hoping to draw attention to the dark underside of Franco's reign. Groups like the Basque **ETA** also provided resistance throughout the dictatorship, often via terrorist acts, producing turmoil that undermined the legitimacy of the regime. In his old age, the general tried to smooth international relations by joining NATO, courting the Pope, and encouraging tourism. However, the **"national tragedy,"** as the tense period under Franco was later called, did not officially end until Franco's death in 1975. **King Juan Carlos I** (1975-), grandson of Alfonso XIII and nominally a Franco protégé, carefully set out to undo Franco's damage.

DEMOCRACY RISES (1975-2005). In 1978, under centrist Prime Minister **Adolfo Suárez,** Spain adopted a new constitution and restored parliamentary government and regional autonomy. The post-Franco years have been marked by progressive social change in the economic and political arenas. The period was also characterized by a movement known in Madrid as "La Movida," which saw an unprecedented outburst of artistic, cultural, and social expression after decades of censorship and inhibition. Suárez's resignation in early 1981 left the country ripe for an attempted coup on February

23rd of that year, when a group of rebels took over parliament in an effort to impose a military-backed government. King Juan Carlos I used his personal influence to convince the rebels to stand down, paving the way for the charismatic **Felipe González** to lead the PSOE (Spanish Socialist Worker's Party) to victory in the 1982 elections. González opened the Spanish economy and championed consensus policies, overseeing Spain's integration into the European Community (now the EU) four years later. Despite unpopular economic policies, González was reelected in 1986 and continued a program of massive public investment to rejuvenate the nation's economy. By the end of 1993, however, recession and revelations of large-scale corruption led to a resounding Socialist defeat at the hands of the Popular Party (PP) in the 1994 European parliamentary elections. The leader of the PP, **José María Aznar,** managed to maintain a fragile coalition with the support of the Catalan and Islas Canarias regional parties. He won an absolute majority in 2000. Since then Spain has moved in a more liberal direction. On July 1, 2005 it legalized gay marriage, eliminating all legal distinctions between same sex and heterosexual couples

GLOBAL TERRORISM. Under the conservative Aznar, Spain became one of the US's most prominent allies in the war on terror, but the relationship has since been strained. On **March 11, 2004,** days before the national elections, the country suffered its own grievous attack, often referred to as **11-M** *(el once eme)*. In an attack linked to Al-Qaeda, 10 bombs exploded on four trains heading to Madrid from the suburbs, killing 191 passengers and injuring more than 1800. Immediately thereafter, the conservatives lost the election to **José Luis Rodríguez Zapatero** of the PSOE. Many attributed the loss to the popular reaction against Aznar's attempt to shirk responsibility for the attacks. Under the new government, Spain withdrew its troops from Iraq in 2004.

CURRENT EVENTS

ETA TERRORISM. Spain has a long history of domestic terrorism, due to separatist movements, particularly in the Basque region in northwestern Spain. Since 1968, over 800 people have been killed in bombings planned by the movement's militant wing, the Euskadi Ta Askatasuna (**ETA**; Basque Homeland and Freedom). Violence continued into 2005 with a series of car bombings in Madrid. In March 2006, ETA declared a permanent cease-fire, promising to promote Basque separation through democratic means, but in December 2006 two bombs exploded in the Madrid airport. In June 2007, the cease-fire officially came to an end. In May 2008, Francisco Javier Lopez, the suspected leader of ETA, was arrested in France. While there may be some danger to travelers, the ETA's attacks are typically targeted and are not

1986
Spain joins the European Economic Community, later to become the European Union (EU).

1995
The Barcelona Process begins an EU effort to strengthen European ties with the Middle East and Maghreb.

1996-2004
Popular Party leader José Maria Aznar is elected prime minister and works to quell terrorism.

2004
Bombings linked to Al-Qaeda rock Madrid and kill 192 people. Days later, the Spanish elect José Luis Rodriquez Zapatero as prime minister.

2005
The Spanish parliament legalizes same-sex marriage.

2006
ETA announces the end of its terrorist attacks.

2007
ETA revokes the cease-fire, dashing hopes of peace.

2008
Francisco Javier Lopez, the suspected leader of ETA, is arrested in France.

considered random acts of terrorism. In more recent years, the organization has tended to provide advance warning.

WE WILL ROCK YOU. For the past 300 years, Spain has fought an uphill battle to regain control of **Gibraltar** (p. 181), a strategic 6km territory in the south currently under British rule. Britain's desire to improve relations with Spain paved the way for a 2002 proposal to share sovereignty of the rock between the two nations, but Gibraltar residents, who remain overwhelmingly loyal to the UK and enjoy salaries almost a third higher than the Spanish average, rejected the measure.

STRAITENED RELATIONS. In July 2002, a handful of Moroccan soldiers occupied **Perejil,** an island in Spanish territorial water known for its abundance of goats. The occurence sparked a minor international event. Amid much fanfare and grandstanding, the soldiers and their Moroccan flag were promptly removed. Its sovereignty and military prowess secured, Spain could once again direct its attention to pressing internal affairs, including increased **immigration** from northern Africa. The Canary Islands and Spain's outposts in Morocco, Ceuta, and Melilla are typical places of entry. In 2005, Spain granted amnesty to 700,000 of the illegal immigrants within its borders, and has continued to experiment with temporary worker programs.

FURTHER READING. These texts provide additional background on the history and culture of Spain.

Homage to Catalonia, by George Orwell (1938). A personal account of Orwell's time in uniform during the Spanish Civil War.

South from Granada, by Gerald Brenan (1957). A British writer's classic account of uprooting himself to a rural village life in Granada's Alpujarras.

Iberia, by James Michener (1968). A bestselling travelogue that captures Spain's past and present as they appeared in the 1960s.

The New Spaniards, by John Hooper (1995). An excellent introduction to contemporary, post-Francoist Spanish society.

The Ornament of the World, by María Rosa Menocal (2003). An insightful account of medieval Moorish, Christian, and Jewish coexistence in Toledo.

PEOPLE AND CULTURE

LANGUAGE

Castellano (Castilian) Spanish, spoken almost everywhere, is Spain's official language; other languages are official regionally. **Català** (Catalan) is spoken throughout Cataluña in the northeast and is the official language of Andorra. Permutations of català gave rise to the dialects **valencià** (Valencian), the regional tongue of Valencia, and **mallorquí,** the principal dialect of the Islas Baleares. Even tiny Asturias has its own dialect, **bable,** spoken mostly among older generations. The once-Celtic northwest corner of Iberia gabs in **gallego** (Galician), which is closely related to Portuguese and most prevalent in the countryside. **Euskera** (Basque), spoken in País Vasco and northern Navarra, is one of the oldest languages in Europe and known by only about 2% of the nation's population.

City and provincial names in this guide are listed in *castellano* first, followed by the regional language in parentheses where appropriate. Information within cities (e.g. street and plaza names) is listed in the regional language. For a **phrasebook, glossary,** and **pronunciation guide,** see p. 496.

RELIGION

The **Roman Catholic Church** has prevailed in Spain since 1492. In 2005 the Center for Sociological Investigation determined that almost 80 percent of the population still identified as Catholic. As a testament to the increasing secularism of the country, however, only 20% claimed to attend church regularly. Moreover, one need only look at Spanish art and architecture to see the influence of other religions, like **Islam** and **Judaism,** that once thrived in Spain. Before Fernando and Isabel's completion of the *Reconquista* in 1492, the Moors controlled the Iberian Peninsula for seven centuries, leaving buildings such as the 10th-century *mezquita* (mosque) in Córdoba to attest to their once dominant presence. The *Reyes Católicos* (Catholic kings) began the Spanish Inquisition in 1478, even before they had completely reclaimed the Iberian Peninsula from the Moors. Anyone who was suspected of practicing Judaism was tried, usually found guilty, and punished, often with death. The ultimate goal of the *Reyes Católicos* was the expulsion of all Jews and Moors from the peninsula. Many Jews converted to Catholicism or emigrated to North Africa to avoid persecution. In 1834 the Inquisition finally came to an end, after nearly 45,000 heresy trials and thousands of executions.

FOOD AND DRINK

Sometimes Spain's best cuisine is served not in expensive restaurants, but in private homes or steet-side bars. Many locals opt for tapas barhopping in lieu of a formal meal. Fresh, local ingredients play an integral part of every menu, varying according to each region's climate, geography, and history. Spanish fare is becomingly increasingly innovative, as the avant-guarde cuisine movement continues to gain prominence.

LOCAL FARE

ANDALUCÍA. Flavorful Andalusian cuisine boasts a rich past, as it maintains the cooking methods introduced by Islamic tribes in the first millennium AD. Centuries later, it was through **Sevilla** (p. 145) that New World products like corn, peppers, tomatoes, and potatoes first entered Europe. Andalusians have since mastered the art of *gazpacho*, a cold tomato-based soup perfectly suited to the hot southern climate. Andalucía is famous for its olive oil, which is found in a vast number of the region's dishes. The area is also known for its *pescadito frito* (fried fish), *rabo de toro* (bull's tail), egg yolk desserts, sherry wines, and tasty tapas. Spain's best cured ham, *jamón ibérico*, comes from the town of Jabugo, where black-footed pigs are pampered with daily oak acorn feasts.

THE CASTILLAS. Castilla La Mancha (p. 119) is famous for its sheep's milk *queso manchego*, the most widely eaten cheese in Spain, and the deliciously vegetarian *pisto manchego*, a mix of zucchini, tomatoes, and eggplant. Spain's most prized spice, *azafrán* (saffron), is also grown in La Mancha. Lamb and roasted game are essential menu items both here and in **Castilla y Léon** (p. 127). *Escabeche*, an Arab tradition of sautéing with vinegar, has become a specialty, as has *tortilla española* (potato omelette) and *menestra de verduras*, a succulent vegetable mix. **Madrid** (p. 73) rivals Andalucía with its tapas and renowned *cocido*, a heavy stew of meat, cabbage, carrots, and potatoes.

BEERS, BEERS, BEERS

Ordering in Spanish bars can be intimidating for an outsider. If you wish to partake of the fermented nectar, Spanish *cerveza*, it helps to talk like a local:

Quinto: This miniature bottle of beer, though non-existent in the States, maintains a distinct popularity in Spain. Normally taken straight from the bottle.

Caña (Can-ya): If you seek an inexpensive draft beer, ask for this cup-full of the house beer, usually marked with its logo on the tap at the bar.

Mediana (in Madrid and central Spain, *Tercio*): This is your standard bottled beer, often served with a glass, sometimes frosted. If you simply ask for a cerveza, this is what you will most likely receive.

Jarra: This large mug of beer is ordered more often by tourists than locals; it is your best bet for uninterrupted imbibing.

Lata: If you want cans of beer, ask for *latas*. These are normally sold in stores, but not in bars.

Para Llevar: Many Spanish bar owners will gladly pour your beer into a plastic cup to-go. Just ask for your drink *para llevar* (to carry out).

Litro: Those who really mean business stop by the supermarket and pick up a *litro* (liter) of *cerveza* and party in the streets with their *amigos*.

CANTABRIAN COAST. Farther north, the 800 miles of coastline in **Galicia** (p. 349) provide fresh ingredients for local shellfish dishes. Octopus, spider crab, and mussels are popular here, as is *empanada gallega*, a Galician pastry filled with anything from pork to chicken to fish. In **Asturias** (p. 334), dried beans rule the kitchen and *fabada asturiana*, a hearty bean and sausage stew, is the best way to refuel after a long day of work. Apples, *sidra* (cider), and cow's milk are also especially good here. **Cantabrian** (p. 340) sardines and tuna are among the best in Spain and are often included in a seafood stew. Food in the **País Vasco** (p. 319) rivals that of Cataluña in national prominence. The combination of coastal and mountain cultures has created a unique style of food in the Basque Country. Popular dishes include *bacalao* (salt cod), *angulas* (baby eels), *calamar en su tinta* (squid in its own ink), and suckling lamb.

THE PYRENEES. **Navarra** (p. 310) boasts the best red peppers in Spain, as well as the famous Roncal cheese. Game meats, sausages, and cauldron stews are popular here.

MEDITERRANEAN COAST. In **Cataluña** (p. 296), the Roman triumvirate of olives, grapes, and wheat prevails, and seafood, grilling, and even pasta play key roles in many meals. Cataluña is at the forefront of the avant-garde movement in cooking, led by innovative chef Ferran Adrià of El Bulli. On the Mediterranean coast, **Valencia** (p. 206) is renowned for its oranges and its *paella*—which has evolved profoundly since Arabic short-grained rice was first introduced to the area in the 8th century AD. It had matured from a simple dish into an increasingly elaborate mix of rice, vegetables, seafood, and meat.

DRINKS

VINO. When in doubt, the *vino de la casa* (house wine) is an economical and often delectable choice. Castilla y León's **Ribera del Dueros** are smooth and full-bodied reds, and Biezo has recently been unearthed as a red wine haven. Cataluña's whites and *cavas* (champagnes) and **Galicia's** *albariños* pack a refreshing punch, while the reds and whites of **La Rioja** are famous—and rightfully so. As the saying goes: *"El vino, para que sepa a vino, bébelo con un amigo"* (For wine to taste of wine, you must drink it with a friend). *Sidra* (cider) from Asturias and *sangria* (red-wine punch with fruit, seltzer, and sugar) are other delicious alcoholic options. *Jerez* (sherry), Spain's most famous libation, hails from **Jerez de la Frontera** (p. 172) in Andalucía. Try the dry *fino* and *amontillado* as aperitifs, or finish off a rich supper with the sweet *dulce*.

CERVEZAS. A normal-sized draft beer is a *caña de cerveza*, while a *tubo* is a little bigger. Small beers go by different names—*corto* in Castilian and *zurito* in Basque. Pros refer to mixed drinks as *copas:* beer and soda water make a *clara*, *calimocho* is a mix of Coca-Cola and red wine; another famous drink is *tinto de verano*, a mix of red wine and lemon soda. Spain whips up non-alcoholic quenchers as well, notably *horchata de chufa* (made by blending almonds and ice) and flavored crushed-ice *granizados*. *Café solo* means black coffee; add a touch of milk for a *nube;* a little more and it's a *café cortado;* half milk and half coffee makes a *café con leche*.

MEALS AND DINING HOURS

TYPICAL SPANISH MEALS. In Spain, mealtime is a social event. Spaniards start their day with *el desayuno*, a continental breakfast of coffee or thick, liquid chocolate accompanied by *bollos* (rolls), *churros*, or *porros* (dough fritters). Mid-morning they often have another coffee with a tapa to tide them over to the main meal of the day, *la comida*, which is eaten around 2 or 3pm. *La comida* consists of several courses: soup or salad, meat, fish, or, on special occasions, *paella*, and a dessert of fruit, cheese, or sweets. Supper at home, *la cena*, tends to be lighter—usually a sandwich or *tortilla española* anywhere from 8pm to midnight. Eating out starts anywhere between 9pm and midnight. Going out for tapas is part of the Spanish lifestyle; groups of friends will often spend several hours bar-hopping.

RESTAURANT DINING. While some restaurants are open from 8am to 1 or 2am, most serve meals from 1 or 2 to 4pm only and in the evening from 8pm until midnight. Some hints: eating at the bar is cheaper than at tables or on a terrace, and the check won't be brought to a table unless it is requested. Also, even though a server may bring bread to the table, it is often not free and the unwitting tourist falls prey to the "you touched it, you bought it" policy of most Spanish restaurants. Service is notoriously slow. Spaniards commonly choose the **menú del día**—two or three dishes, bread, a drink, and dessert—a good deal at roughly €7-12. *Raciones* are large tapas, comparable in size to entrees.

CUSTOMS AND ETIQUETTE

Spaniards are generally polite and courteous to foreigners and attempts to be culturally correct will not go unnoticed.

TABOOS. Spaniards are very proud and take offense to criticism about their country or customs. Foreigners should be careful when approaching Spanish women; fathers, husbands, or boyfriends can be aggressive. Be aware that shorts and short skirts are not common in most parts of Spain, save the coasts. Wearing these and other especially revealing clothing away from the beaches may garner unwanted attention, or at the very least, scream "I am a foreigner!" Women with bare shoulders should carry a shawl to tour churches and monasteries, and it is considered disrespectful to wear shorts in these places.

PUBLIC BEHAVIOR. The people of Spain are very polite in mannerisms and social behavior, so it's a good idea to be as formal as possible in first encounters. Be sure to address Spaniards as *Señor* (Mr.), *Señora* (Mrs.), or *Señorita* (Ms.), and don't be surprised if you get kissed on both cheeks, in place of a handshake. Machismo is very apparent, especially in Andalucía, and women may be the object of whistling and catcalling when walking alone or in groups without any men. The best response to this type of display is to ignore it.

TIPPING. Though a service charge is generally included in the check at bars and restaurants, an additional tip is common for good service: 5-10% will generally do the trick. Taxi drivers, theater ushers, and hotel porters will also expect small tips for their services.

THE ARTS

ARCHITECTURE

ANCIENT AND EARLY MODERN. A testament to six centuries of occupation, **Roman ruins** are scattered throughout the country, seen in the magnificent **aqueduct** in Segovia (p. 127), among others. Moorish rule began in 711 and left intricately-decorated mosques and palaces throughout the country's southern regions, rich in geometric designs, red-and-white horseshoe arches, and ornate tiles. The spectacular 14th-century **Alhambra** in Granada (p. 201) and the **Mezquita** in Córdoba (p. 168) epitomize the Moorish style. Periods of peaceful coexistence between Muslims and Christians inspired the synthetic **mudéjar** architectural movement, created by Moors living under Christian rule in the years between the Christian resurgence (11th century) and the *Reconquista* (1492). Sevilla's **Alcázar** (p. 153) is an exquisite example of this tradition.

The **Spanish Gothic** style (13th-16th centuries) fused *mudéjar* influences with European innovations of the Renaissance, including pointed arches, flying buttresses, airy spaces, and stained-glass windows. The cathedral in Toledo (p. 124) is one of the finest examples of the Spanish Gothic style, while Sevilla boasts the largest Gothic cathedral (p. 152) in the world. Spain also contains important **Romanesque** sculpture: Maestro Mateo's **Pórtico de la Gloria,** completed in 1188 in Santiago de Compostela (p. 349), is considered one of the finest examples.

RENAISSANCE AND BAROQUE. New World riches inspired the **Plateresque** ("silversmith") style, which brought ornamentation to shining new levels with the extravagant use of silver and gold. Intricate stonework and gleaming metals grace the facades of 15th- and 16th-century buildings like those of **La Universidad de Salamanca** (p. 141). In the late 16th century, Italian innovations in perspective and symmetry arrived in Spain and sobered the Plateresque style. These innovations influenced **Juan Bautista de Toledo** in his design for the austere **El Escorial** (p. 115), Felipe II's immense palace-cum-monastery. Opulence took center stage in 17th- and 18th-century **Baroque** Spain. The Churriguera family of Salamanca pioneered the new, aptly-named **Churrigueresque** style, whose elaborate ornamentation fused sculpture and architecture, giving buildings of this period a rich exuberance. Churrigueresque is perhaps most resonant in Salamanca's **Plaza Mayor** (p. 142).

MODERN AND POSTMODERN. In the late 19th and early 20th centuries, Cataluña's **Modernistas** burst on the scene in Barcelona, led by the eccentric geniuses **Antoni Gaudí, Lluís Domènech i Montaner,** and **Josep Puig i Cadafalch.** *Modernista* structures defied all precedents with their voluptuous curves, vibrant colors and striking textures. Unbridled imagination and organic forms inspired Gaudí's **La Sagrada Família** (p. 267) and the **Casa Milà** (p. 265), which stand as some of the most famous examples of Catalan *Modernisme.*

Spain's outstanding architectural tradition has continued through the 20th century. In the midst of Civil War, Catalan architect **Josep Lluís Sert** designed the Spanish Pavilion at the 1937 International Exposition in Paris. The pavilion played host to artistic protests against war and fascism, including Pablo Picasso's *Guernica* (p. 101) and works by **Joan Miró.** Today Spain boasts stars like **Rafael Moneo,** who designed the 2007 enlargement of the **Prado** in Madrid (p. 98), and **Santiago Calatrava,** who built elegant steel-and-crystal buildings in Valencia (p. 206) and unmistakable bridges in Sevilla, Mérida, and Bilbao. Spain has also acquired several new landmarks from foreign architects, most notably Frank Gehry's stunning **Guggenheim Museum** in Bilbao (p. 327).

PAINTING AND SCULPTURE

MEDIEVAL AND RENAISSANCE. The earliest art in Spain can be found at the caves at **Altamira** (p. 347), near Santander in Cantabria, which are home to some of the oldest Paleolithic cave paintings in the world. Frescoes and illuminated manuscripts from the 11th and 12th centuries adorn churches along the Camino de Santiago and in many Spanish cities.

During Spain's imperial ascent in the 16th century, Spanish painting reached its **Siglo de Oro** (Golden Age; roughly 1492-1650). Felipe II, one of the era's presiding monarchs, imported foreign art and artists to jump-start native production and embellish his palace, El Escorial. One hopeful artist, Crete-born Doménikos Theotokópoulos, a.k.a. **El Greco** (1541-1614), failed to earn the patronage of Felipe II, supposedly because of his daring use of bright, saturated colors and radical notions of form and space. El Greco's haunting, elongated figures and dramatic use of light have since garnered widespread appreciation. One of his most famous canvases, *El entierro del Conde de Orgaz* (*The Burial of Count Orgaz*, 1586) graces the Iglesia de Santo Tomé in Toledo (p. 124), the city whose landscape he painted so vividly.

Felipe IV's foremost court painter, **Diego Velázquez** (1599-1660), is considered one of the world's greatest artists. Whether depicting the family of Felipe IV or commoners buying water, Velázquez painted scenes with naturalistic precision and a virtually photographic quality. Nearly half of this Sevilla-born artist's works reside in the Prado, perhaps most notably his famous *Las Meninas* (1656; p. 99). Other distinguished Golden Age painters include **Francisco de Zurbarán** (1598-1664) and **Bartolomé Murillo** (1617-1682).

FROM MODERN TO AVANT-GARDE. While Spain's political power declined, its cultural capital flourished. **Francisco de Goya** (1746-1828) ushered European painting into the modern age. Hailing from provincial Aragón, Goya rose to the position of official court painter under Carlos IV. Goya cast flattery aside: his depictions of the royal family come close to caricature, as Queen María Luisa's haughty jaw line in Goya's famous *The Family of Carlos IV* (1800) can attest. His series of etchings, *The Disasters of War* (1810-1814), records the horrific Napoleonic invasion of 1808. Deaf and alone in his later years, Goya painted nightmarishly fantastic visions, inspiring expressionist and surrealist artists of the next century with his free and loose brushstrokes and dramatic presentation. His chilling **Black Paintings** (1820-1823) fill a room in the Prado.

Few artists influenced 20th-century painting as deeply as Málaga-born **Pablo Picasso** (1881-1973). During his Blue Period, characterized by somber depictions of society's outcasts, Picasso alternated between Barcelona and Paris. His permanent move to Paris in 1904 caused a shift in his artistic trajectory, and the Rose Period ushered in a new fascination with harlequins, clowns, and acrobats. With his French colleague Georges Braque, he founded **Cubism,** a method of abstraction in painting achieved by the geometric fragmentation of form. His 1937 mural *Guernica* portrays the bombing of the Basque city by Nazi planes during the Spanish Civil War. *Guernica* now resides in the Museo Nacional Centro de Arte Reina Sofía in Madrid (p. 101).

The chaotic, abstract lines and vivid colors of Catalan painter and sculptor **Joan Miró** (1893-1983) rebelled against the authoritarian society of post-Civil War years. **Salvador Dalí** (1904-1989), in contrast, scandalized society and leftist intellectuals in France and Spain by claiming to support the Fascists. His name has become synonymous with **Surrealism,** the artistic expression of the liberated, subconscious imagination. A self-congratulatory fellow, Dalí founded the Teatro-Museu Dalí in Figueres (p. 309), Spain's second-most visited museum after the Prado. A new generation of painters and sculptors has flourished with new museums as active platforms for their work. Today, **Antoni Tàpies** (1923-) constructs unorthodox collages and is a founding member of the self-proclaimed "Abstract Generation," while **Antonio López García** (1936-) paints hyperrealist works.

LITERATURE

A GOLDEN AGE. Spain's literary tradition first blossomed in the late Middle Ages (1000-1500). The 13th-century *El Cantar del Mío Cid* (Song of My Cid) is Spain's most important epic poem. It chronicles the life and military triumphs of national hero Rodrigo Díaz de Vivar, from his exile to his eventual return to grace in the king's court. At the end of the 15th century, **Fernando de Rojas** wrote the famous novel *La Celestina* (1499), a tragicomedy beloved for its witch-like matchmaker and star-crossed lovers Calixto and Melibea. The anonymous work *Lazarillo de Tormes* (1554) established the genre of the picaresque: a tale following the adventures of a roguish young rascal, in this case, an orphaned servant boy in Salamanca. Literature bloomed during Spain's literary **Siglo de Oro** (Golden Age; 16th and 17th centuries); some consider the sonnets of Garcilaso de la Vega (1503-1536) the most perfect ever written in *castellano.* The dense, difficult verse of **Luis de Góngora** (1561-1627) found a new following in the poets of the famed *Generación de 1927* years later. The Golden Age also produced outstanding dramatists, including **Pedro Calderón de la Barca** (1600-1681) and **Lope de Vega** (1562-1635), who collectively wrote over 2,300 plays. **Tirso de Molina's** (1584-1648) famed *El Burlador de Sevilla* (1630) introduced the character of Don Juan into the national psyche. **Miguel de Cervantes's** *Don Quixote* (1605-1615) is without a doubt the most famous work of Spanish literature. This humorous and satirical novel follows a hapless knight and his servant, Sancho Panza, as they undertake a chivalric quest to save the world.

ROMANTICS AND INNOVATORS. The 18th century brought a belated Enlightenment, while the 19th century inspired new heights of romanticism and realism. The lyrical verse of **Rosalía del Castro** (1837-1885) made her the most distinguished modern writer in Galician, while the naturalistic novels and bold critiques of **Leopoldo Alas** ("Clarín") made him one of Spain's most powerful voices. Essayist and philosopher **Míguel de Unamuno** and critic **José Ortega y Gasset** led the **Generación de 1898,** along with novelist **Pío Baroja,** playwright **Ramón del Valle Inclán,** and poets **Antonio Machado** and **Juan Ramón Jiménez.** Reacting to Spain's defeat in the Spanish-American War (1898), they contributed to reawakening Spain's culture of literary innovation and helped form a new national consciousness. This group, though not organized or unified, was a critical influence on the **Generación de 1927,** a group of experimental lyric poets including **Federico García Lorca** and **Rafael Alberti** that experimented with Surrealist and avant-garde poetry. This vibrant and cohesive group scattered at the onset of

Civil War, with several of its artists persecuted for Republican or communist leanings. Lorca was executed by the Nationalists in 1936, while **Miguel Hernández** was condemned to life imprisonment. Others such as **Jorge Guillén, Pedro Salinas,** and **Luis Cernuda** joined Spain's long history of intellectual and ideological exiles, writing and teaching in the United States, Mexico, and Europe.

MODERN MARVELS. Spanish Nobel Prize recipients include playwright and essayist **Jacinto Benavente y Martínez** (1922), poet **Vicente Aleixandre** (1977), and novelist **Camilo José Cela** (1989). Female writers, like **Mercè Rodoreda, Carmen Martín Gaite,** and **Almudena Grandes,** have likewise earned critical international acclaim. After the death of Franco, Spanish artists flocked to Madrid as they once did earlier in the century, and an avant-garde, liberated spirit—known as *La Movida*—was reborn. Writers like **Ana Rossetti** led a new generation of erotic poets into the 80s, placing women at the forefront of Spanish literature for the first time. Today, **Arturo Pérez-Reverte** is one of Spain's most translated and bestselling contemporary writers.

FICTION AND NONFICTION

The Sun Also Rises, by Ernest Hemingway (1926). Immortalizes bullfighting, machismo, and expatriates of the so-called Lost Generation.

San Manuel Bueno, Mártir, by Miguel de Unamuno (1933). Acclaimed novella of a saintly priest who has lost his faith.

The House of Bernarda Alba, by Federico García Lorca (1936). A drama about a family of repressed women stifled by Andalusian society.

Driving Over Lemons: An Optimist in Spain, by Chris Stewart (1999). A sunny read for those who dream of living amongst olive groves and oranges.

SPAIN

MUSIC

FLAMENCO. Spain's most famous art form combines *cante* (song), *baile* (dance), and *guitarra* (guitar). True flamenco artists are said to perform with *duende,* the soul or spirit behind any passionate performance. The music originated among Andalusian gypsies in the late 18th century and remains an extremely popular tradition that continues to engage audiences around the world. While it is possible to buy flamenco recordings, nothing compares to seeing a live performance. Flamenco heroes include **Andrés Segovia** (1893-1987), who was instrumental in giving the flamenco guitar the same renown as the violin and the cello, and singer **Antonio Mairena** (1909-1983). Today, bands like the **Gipsy Kings** mix flamenco with dance rhythms like salsa and rumba for a pop-oriented sound that has caught on across the globe.

CLASSICAL. Spain bred two of the world's greatest Renaissance composers in **Francisco Guerrero** and **Tomás Luis de Victoria,** who composed both sacred and secular masterpieces. Spain's classical tradition continued centuries later when **Pau (Pablo) Casals** (1876-1973), cellist, conductor, composer, pianist, and humanitarian, became one of the most influential classical musicians of the 20th century. Arguably the greatest Spanish composer of the last two centuries, Cádiz native **Manuel de Falla** (1876-1946) wrote the popular opera *El sombrero de tres picos (The Three-Cornered Hat),* which premiered in London in 1919 with stage design by Picasso. Spain also claims two of the world-famous "Three Tenors," Barcelona-born **José Carreras** and **Plácido Domingo,** who hails from Madrid.

FOLK MUSIC. While flamenco has come to epitomize Spanish music, every region adds its own rhythm. Accordion-based **trikitrixa** music defines Basque folk, while the **zambomba** drum, played by pulling on a rope inside the drum, is a staple of Extremadura. Valencia takes pride in its **brass bands,** and Cataluña celebrates with a hearty **sardana,** or circle dance.

CONTEMPORARY MUSIC. *Cantautores* (singer-songwriters) **Luis Eduardo Aute, Joaquin Sabina,** and **Joan Manuel Serrat** have been forces on the Spanish music scene since the 60s and 70s. Since Franco's demise, Spanish music has exploded. While the popular music scene is heavily influenced by American and Latin American artists, singers like **Julio** and **Enrique Iglesias,** as well as **Alejandro Sanz,** have gained international acclaim. Successful Spanish bands in recent years include the rock and pop groups **Mecano, Heroes del Silencio, Jarabe de Palo, La Oreja de Van Gogh,** the Celtic-infused **El Sueño de Morfeo,** and **Ojos de Brujo,** whose music is a socially conscious fusion of hip-hop and flamenco.

FILM

FILM UNDER FRANCO. Spain's first film, *Riña en un café* (directed by Fructuoso Gelabert), dates back to 1897, and technically-innovative director **Segundo de Chomón** is recognized worldwide as a pioneer of early cinema. **Luis Buñuel** produced several early classics, most notably his collaboration with **Salvador Dalí,** *Un Chien Andalou* (1929), a surrealist montage of startling and disturbing images. Buñuel followed up this controversial offering with the acclaimed *L'Âge d'or* (1930), banned for nearly 50 years for its perceived attack on Catholicism. Meanwhile, Franco's censors stifled most creativity, leaving the public with cheap westerns and innocuous spy flicks. As censorship waned in the early 1970s, Spanish cinema showed signs of life, led by **Carlos Saura's** dark, subversive hits such as *El jardín de las delicias* (1970) and *Cría cuervos* (1976).

CONTEMPORARY CINEMA. Domestic censorship laws were revoked in 1977. The move brought artistic freedom and financial hardship for Spanish filmmakers, who found their films shunned domestically in favor of newly permitted foreign films. Depictions of the exuberant fervor of a super-liberated Spain found increased attention and international respect. Basque director **Eloy de la Iglesia** portrays this radical shift in *El diputado* (1978). One of Spain's most highly acclaimed directors today, **Pedro Almodóvar**, is the creative force behind *Todo sobre mi madre* (1999) and *Hable con ella* (2002), and his *Volver* (2006) won Best Screenplay at the Cannes Film Festival. Chilean-born Spanish director **Alejandro Amenábar** received critical acclaim as well as the Best Foreign Language Film award at the 2004 Oscars for his poignant *Mar adentro (The Sea Inside)*. Most recently, Mexican writer/director Guillermo del Toro's *El laberinto del fauno (Pan's Labyrinth;* 2006) reached international audiences with its disturbing fantasy of post-Civil War Spain.

SPORTS

FÚTBOL

Soccer is a nationally unifying and locally divisive passion for Spaniards. Historically, Spanish national teams have underperformed at international tournaments, and for forty years their failure to punch their weight was both debated and lamented. Happily, Spanish fans' misery was ended in 2008, when **Fernando Torres** *et al* brought home the Euro 2008 trophy. Spanish club teams constantly bring back honors from European leagues, led by international icons like Brazilian **Ronaldinho,** Argentine **Lionel Messi,** and Cameroonian **Samuel Eto'o.** Squads

SPAIN

in the Spanish "La Liga" Premier League, like Real Madrid, FC Barcelona, and Valencia, bring Spaniards to their feet and into the street on game days. La Liga competition starts up every September.

BULLFIGHTING

The national spectacle of *la corrida* (bullfighting) derives from earlier Roman and Moorish practices, but its modern form dates to around 1726. A bullfight has three stages: first, *picadores* (lancers on horseback) pierce the bull's neck muscles to lower his head for the kill. Next, assistants on foot thrust *banderillas* (decorated darts) into the bull's back to provoke the tiring animal. Finally, the *matador* (bullfighter) has ten minutes to kill his opponent with a sword between the shoulder blades, executing artful passes with confidence and grace while daring the bull closer with agility and nerve. If the matador shows special skill and daring, the audience waves white *pañuelos* (handkerchiefs), imploring the bullfight's president to award the *matador* the coveted ears. The techniques of the modern *matador* were refined around 1914 by **Juan Belmonte,** considered one of the greatest *matadores* of all time (others include **Joselito, Manolete,** and **Cristina,** the first female *matadora*). Bullfighting has always had its critics: in the 17th century, it was the Church; more recently, the challenge comes from animal rights activists. Cataluña banned bullfighting in 2006, owing perhaps as much to Catalan nationalism as to cross-species sympathy.

JAI ALAI

Known as *pelota vasca* in Spanish, the Basque government promotes jai alai (meaning "Merry Game" in Basque) as the "fastest game on earth." Jai alai is a game played with a wicker *cesta* basket, used to hurl a ball against a *fronton* (open-walled arena). Points are awarded when the other team drops, misses, or sends the ball out of bounds. These deadly projectiles have been clocked in at incredible speeds of up to 188 mph.

OTHER SPORTS

Fans fondly remember five-time consecutive Tour de France champion **Miguel Indurain,** a Navarran hero and Spain's most decorated athlete. The Vuelta de España is a crucial piece of the European **cycling** circuit, along with the Tour de France and the Giro d'Italia. Spain is a contender on the international **rowing** circuit, with the 1992 Olympic course in Banyoles remaining a popular foreign training site. Old **tennis** favorites like **Arantxa Sánchez-Vicario** and **Carlos Moya** and up-and-comers like **Rafael Nadal,** one of the sport's top-ranked players, have all made names on the court.

NATIONAL HOLIDAYS

The following table lists the national holidays for 2009.

DATE	HOLIDAYS
January 1	Año Nuevo (New Year's Day)
January 6	Epifanía (Epiphany)
April 3-12	Semana Santa (Holy Week)
April 9	Jueves Santo (Maundy Thursday)
April 10	Viernes Santo (Good Friday)
April 12	Pascua (Easter)
May 1	Día del Trabajador (Labor Day)
August 15	La Asunción (Feast of the Assumption)

October 12	Día de la Hispanidad (National Day)
November 1	Día de Todos Santos (All Saints' Day)
December 6	Día de la Constitución (Constitution Day)
December 8	La Inmaculada Concepción (Feast of the Immaculate Conception)
December 25	Navidad (Christmas)
December 31	Noche Vieja (New Year's Eve)

SPANISH FESTIVALS IN 2010

The following table lists selected Spanish festivals for 2010.

DATE	HOLIDAYS
Mid-January to early February	Carnaval (Cadiz, Islas Canarias, Barcelona, and Sitges). Hedonism and frivolity at its best.
Late February to early March	Jerez Flamenco Festival (Jerez de la Frontera). A celebration with the nation's best singers and dancers.
March 12-19	Fallas de San José (Valencia). A pyromaniac's dream—fireworks and burning effigies.
April 3-12	Semana Santa (Sevilla). The city's Easter processions are justifiably famous. Join the crowd.
April 23	La Diada de Sant Jordi (Barcelona). Las Ramblas fills up with roses and booksellers for Cataluña's patron saint: a day for romantics and readers.
May 15	San Isidro (Madrid). Spain's biggest and most prestigious bullfighting exhibition.
June 20-29	Hogueras de San Juan (Alicante). Celebrate the summer solstice with fires and feasts.
June 22	Paso do Fuego (Soria). Fire walking: only the strong (and some say, only the locals) survive.
June 29	Wine Battle (Haro, La Rioja). Just what it sounds like: wet and wild.
Last week of June	Orgullo Gay (Madrid). One of Europe's biggest gay pride festivals.
July 6-14	San Fermín (Pamplona). Featuring the famous "running of the bulls," this festival was immortalized in Hemingway's *The Sun Also Rises*.
August 26	La Tomatina (Buñol). An organized food fight for those who really like tomatoes.
September 24	Festes de la Merce (Barcelona). Wood giants, human towers, and cava—all for a patron saint.
October 12	Día de la Hispanidad (nationwide). A celebration of the arrival of Christopher Columbus in the Americas.

MADRID

Welcome to Spain's political, intellectual, and cultural center—the country's wild, pulsing heart. While theoretically subject to the earth's rotations, Madrid seems to transcend traditional hours. In this city, morning commuters collide with stragglers leaving after-hour clubs at dawn. Tourists spend their time absorbed in its monuments, world-renowned museums, and raging nightlife, mingling with the 5.5 million *madrileños* sprawled in the city's plazas, tapas bars, and parks. Businessmen scoot along on mopeds, old women compare vegetables at the markets, and teens text furiously in search of the next hot club. Stock up on energy with a late afternoon siesta in the Parque del Buen Retiro or in your hostel; the city only truly comes awake after the sun has set.

Though Madrid witnessed the coronation of Fernando and Isabel, it did not achieve prominence until Hapsburg monarch Felipe II moved his court here in 1561. It served as Spain's artistic hub during the Siglo de Oro (Golden Age), becoming a seat of wealth, culture, and imperial glory, despite its considerable distance from vital ports and rivers. In the 18th century, Madrid experienced a Neoclassical rebirth when Carlos III embellished the city with wide, tree-lined boulevards and scores of imposing buildings. Things took a turn for the worse during the Peninsular wars (1808-14) against Napoleon, the bloody inspiration of some of Francisco de Goya's most famous paintings. During the Civil War, Madrid resisted Franco's troops until the spring of 1939. It was the second-to-last city in Spain to fall; immediately after, the Nationalists took Valencia and brought the four-year conflict to a close. For the next four decades, Madrid served as the seat of Franco's government. When the dictator died in 1975, Madrid, and the rest of Spain, came out in what is known today as *la movida* ("shift" or "movement") or *el destapeo* ("uncovering"). A 200,000-strong student population took to the streets and stayed there—and the city hasn't stopped moving yet.

HIGHLIGHTS OF MADRID

MUSE over world-famous museums along the **Avenida del Arte** (p. 98).

RELIVE royal dreams at the luxurious 18th-century **Palacio Real** (p. 95).

RETREAT in kingly fashion to the **Parque del Buen Retiro** (p. 97).

TRIP along the cobblestones in quirky **Malasaña** and **Chueca** (p. 102).

INTERCITY TRANSPORTATION

BY PLANE

All flights land at **Aeropuerto Internacional de Barajas** (☎902 404 704; www.aena.es.), 16km northeast of Madrid. The regional **tourist office** in Terminal 4 has maps and info. (☎915 881 636. Open daily 9am-8pm.) **Luggage storage** *(consigna)* is sometimes available. (☎913 936 805. 1 day €3.70; 2-15 days €4.78 per day. Max. storage 15 days. Open 24hr.)

The **Barajas metro stop** connects the airport to all of Madrid (€1 per metro ride plus €1 extra from the airport). From the airport arrivals area, follow signs to the metro, located in Terminals 2 and 4. Take Line 8 (pink) to Nuevos Ministerios and switch to Line 10 (dark blue, dir.: Puerta del Sur). At Tribunal, change to Line 1 (light blue, dir.: Valdecarros), and two stops later you'll find yourself at Sol, smack in the middle of Madrid's best accommodations and sights. The **Bus-Aeropuerto #200** leaves from the national terminal T2 and runs to the city center via the metro station Avenida de América. (☎902 50 78 50. Look for "EMT" signs just outside the airport doors. Daily every 10-15min. 5:20am-11:30pm. €1.) **Line 204** leaves from T4 and goes to Avenida de América as well. **Line 101** leaves from T1, 2, and 3 and goes to Canillejas. Fleets of **taxis** swarm the airport. Taxi fare to central Madrid should cost €35-40, including the €5.50 airport surcharge, depending on traffic and time of day.

BY TRAIN

Two largo *recorrido* (long-distance) **RENFE** stations, **Atocha** and **Chamartín,** connect Madrid to surrounding areas and the rest of Europe. Both stations are easily accessible by metro. Call RENFE (☎902 24 02 02; www.renfe.es) for reservations and info. Buy tickets at the station or online.

Estación Atocha, Av. Ciudad de Barcelona (☎915 066 137). M: Atocha Renfe. The cast-iron atrium of the original station has been turned into an urban rainforest, with lush plants, a small marsh with a colony of turtles, and the occasional bird. Galleries, boutiques, and restaurants provide more commercial diversions. There is a **tourist office** (☎913 15 99 76) in the station. Open M-Sa 8am-8pm, Su 9am-2pm. **RENFE information office** (☎902 24 02 02) located in the main terminal. Open daily 7am-11pm. **Luggage storage** (*consignas automáticas;* €2.40-4.50), at the back right corner of the atrium. Open daily 6:30am-10pm. Ticket windows open daily 6:30am-9pm; buy tickets at vending machines outside these hours. No international service. **AVE** (☎91 506 63 29) offers high-speed service to southern Spain, including **Barcelona** (3hr., 20-26 per day 5:45am-9pm, €110-130), **Sevilla** (2½hr., 24-20 per day 6:30am-11pm, €70-78) via **Córdoba** (1¾hr., €58-64), and **Valladolid** (1hr., 14-15 per day 6:35am-9pm, €21-34).

Estación Chamartín, C. Agustín de Foxa (☎913 00 69 69). M: Chamartín. Bus #5 runs to and from **Puerta del Sol** (45min.); the stop is just beyond the lockers. Alternatively, get off at M: Atocha Renfe and take a red Cercanías train (15min., every 5-10min., €1.20) to Chamartín. Be sure to keep your ticket, or you won't be able to exit the turnstiles. Chamartín is a mini-mall of useful services, including a **tourist office** (*Vestíbulo,* Puerta 14; ☎913 15 99 76; open M-Sa 8am-8pm, Su 9am-2pm), **currency exchange, accommodations service, post office, car rental, police,** and **luggage storage** (*consignas;* €2.40-4.50; open daily 7am-11pm). Call RENFE at ☎902 24 34 02 for international destinations and ☎902 24 02 02 (Spanish only) for domestic. Ticket windows open daily 6:30am-9pm; buy tickets at vending machines outside these hours. Chamartín serves both international and domestic destinations to the northeast and south. Most Cercanías (local) trains stop at both Chamartín and Atocha. Major destinations include: **Barcelona** (9½hr., daily 10pm, €41); **Bilbao** (5hr., 1-2 per day, €47); **Lisboa** (9hr., daily 10:25pm, €59); **Paris, FRA** (13½hr., 7pm, €115-130).

BY BUS

Numerous private companies serve Madrid, each with its own station and set of destinations. Most buses pass through **Estación Sur de Autobuses** or **Estación de Moncloa,** both easily accessible by metro. The Pl. Mayor tourist office and any other branch in the city has information on the most relevant intercity buses.

Estación Sur de Autobuses: C. Méndez Álvaro (☎914 68 42 00; www.estacionautobusesmadrid.com). M: Méndez Álvaro; inside station. Info booth open daily 6:30am-1am. **ATMs, food,** and **luggage storage** (€1.30 per bag per day; open M-F 6:30am-10:30pm, Sa 6:30am-3pm). Serves 40+ private bus companies. National destinations include:

Algeciras, Alicante, Aranjuez, Benidorm, Cartagena, A Coruña, Gijón, Lugo, Murcia, Oviedo, Santiago de Compostela, and **Toledo.** Check at the station or online or call for specific info on routes and schedules. Bus companies include:

AISA-Empresa Semar (☎915 271 294; www.aisa-grupo.com). Buses to **Aranjuez** (45min.; every 30-45min. 6:30am-11:30pm, €3.35).

ALSA (☎915 063 360; www.alsa.es). International destinations include: **Czech Republic, France, Germany, Holland, Italy, Poland, Portugal, Romania,** and **Switzerland,** but flying can actually be cheaper. Contact **Eurolines** for more information (reservations ☎902 405 040; www.eurolines.es). Open daily 7am-11pm.

Auto-Res (auto-res.net). Service to many domestic destinations. Prices and times are given with regular service first, then express service. To: **Badajoz** (4½-5½hr., 8 per day 7:30am-9pm, €27-39); **Cáceres** (3½-5hr., 7 per day 11:55am-11:50pm, €20-28); **Cuenca** (2-2½hr., 9 per day 9:15am-12:30pm, €11-18); **Mérida** (4-5hr., 7 per day 12:25pm-12:55am, €23-34); **Salamanca** (2½-3hr., 23 per day 7am-10:30pm, €12-19); **Trujillo** (2½-4hr., 12 per day 7:30am-9pm, €17-28); **Valencia** (3-4hr., 12 per day 1am-10:30pm, €23-29).

Empresa Larrea (☎913 983 805). To: **Ávila** (1hr.; 4-9 per day 7am-8:30pm, €7.54).

Empresa La Sepulvedana (www.lasepulvedana.es). Buses to **Segovia** (1hr., every 30min. 6:30am-11pm, €6.70).

Interurbanos: Consorcio Transportes Madrid (☎915 804 260; www.ctm-madrid.es) compiles information on *interurbanos,* buses run by independent companies that cover short-distance inter-urban routes. Companies and routes include the following:

Autocares Herranz: Headquarters located on C. Juan de Toledo, 5 (☎918 969 028), in the Intercambio de Moncloa. M: Moncloa. To **El Escorial** (20min., every 20-30min. 6:55am-12:30pm, €3.35).

Empresa Alacuber: Pl. del Caudillo, 2 (☎913 760 104). M: Moncloa. To **El Pardo** (25min., every 10-20min. 6am-12:30am, €1.10).

Empresa Continental Auto: Av. de América, 9 (☎902 422 242). M: Av. de América. To **Alcalá de Henares** (40min.; every 10-20min. M-F 5:30am-11pm, Sa-Su 6:30am-11pm; €1.25).

ORIENTATION

THE NEIGHBORHOODS OF MADRID

EL CENTRO: SOL, ÓPERA, AND PLAZA MAYOR

Puerta del Sol is the symbolic center of both Madrid and the whole of Spain. The "Kilómetro 0" sign in front of the police station marks the intersection of eight of Madrid's most celebrated streets and the starting point of the country's major highways. Tourist shops and fast-food restaurants mingle with ancient churches, gardens, and plazas. The heart of 16th- and 17th-century **Hapsburg Madrid** *(Madrid de los Austrias)* is vibrant **Plaza Mayor,** out of which radiate small, maze-like streets. Farther west of Sol by way of C. del Arenal lies the chief monument of Bourbon Madrid, the **Palacio Real,** with its gray facade rising above sprawling gardens.

STAYING SAFE IN MADRID. Madrid is just as safe as most major European cities, but Pta. del Sol, Pl. de España, Pl. Chueca, C. Gran Vía, and southern Malasaña can be intimidating late at night. As a general rule, avoid parks and quiet residential streets after dark and always watch out for thieves and pickpockets in crowds. .

LA LATINA AND LAVAPIÉS

South of Sol and west of Huertas are **La Latina** and **Lavapiés,** multicultural hot spots whose immigrant roots continue to show despite recent bohemian

MADRID

gentrification. Trendy *madrileños* socialize in the small markets that line the area's winding streets. Just a short walk (10min.) walk downhill from Huertas, the area is easily accessible and well worth the climb back up. **El Rastro,** an ancient, gargantuan flea market, is held here every Sunday morning.

HUERTAS

Huertas is the wedge carved out by C. de San Jerónimo and C. de Atocha, with C. de las Huertas running through the southern portion of the district. A seedy area in the not-too-distant past, Huertas has grown into a clean, popular cluster of theaters, restaurants, jazz clubs, and mojito joints. **Plaza Santa Ana, Calle del Príncipe,**and **Calle de Echegaray** contain some of the best bars in Madrid, but every hidden side street is worth investigating.

THE AVENIDA DEL ARTE AND RETIRO

East of Huertas, the **Avenida del Arte** is a symbolic line connecting Madrid's three finest and most unmissable museums: the Prado, the Reina Sofía, and the Thyssen-Bornemisza. Just behind the Prado, the lush **Parque del Buen Retiro** is Madrid's finest spot for a late afternoon nap or an evening stroll. The park stretches on for acres and houses a giant artificial lake, three exhibition spaces, and countless winding paths.

GRAN VÍA

North of Sol, busy **Gran Vía** is the commercial center of Madrid, called *"el broadway madrileño"* after its model in New York. Once an impressive feat of architectural ingenuity and determination, it has slowly given itself over to American fast food, crumbling theaters, sirens fighting their way through traffic, and designer apparel outlets. The parade of flashing cars, swishing skirts, and high-heeled shoes makes Gran Vía worth a quick look, but not much more.

CHUECA AND MALASAÑA

Across the Gran Vía to the north, and split down the middle by C. de Fuencarral, **Chueca** and **Malasaña** are Madrid's hub for all things alternative or funky. Small boutiques and unusual restaurants provide ample daytime activity; by night, Chueca's GLBT scene blooms into an outrageous, colorful universe of bars and clubs, while Malasaña's hip cafes and music venues keep the city's scenesters busy. Despite the alternative vibe, these two neighborhoods are diverse enough to offer something for nearly everybody. Traditional tapas bars and raging discos, old fruit markets, and sex shops sit in peaceful accord.

ARGÜELLES AND MONCLOA

Just outside the core of the city, north and northwest of the Palacio Real, the neighborhoods of **Argüelles** and **Moncloa,** along with the zone around **Calle San Bernardo,** form a cluttered mixture of middle-class homes, student apartments, tranquil parks, and bohemian hangouts. Located near the **Ciudad Universitaria,** the area is full of teenagers, university students, and an eclectic array of slower-paced sights and museums.

SALAMANCA

Madrid's most exclusive *barrio*, Salamanca is the capital's top destination for designer fashion. Tucked among the area's high-rise apartments and stately old homes are specialized museums focused on archaeology, science, and Renaissance-era sculpture.

MAPS

The free *Plano de Madrid* (street map) and *Plano de Transportes* (public transport map) are fantastic. Pick them up at any tourist office. Public transportation info is also available by phone (☎012) or on the web (www.ctm-madrid.es). **El Corte Inglés** (p. 109) offers a free one-page map of Madrid. For a comprehensive map with a street index, pick up an *Almax* map (€2-8 depending on level of detail) at any newsstand or bookstore.

LOCAL TRANSPORTATION

METRO

Safe, speedy, spotless, and almost always under *obras* (improvements), Madrid's Metro puts most major subway systems to shame. Trains run frequently; green timers above most platforms show increments of five minutes or less between trains. Free Metro maps (available at any ticket booth) and the wall maps showing surrounding streets are clear and helpful. Fare and schedule info is posted in every station; trains run daily 6am-2am, with the last inbound train leaving most terminal stations around 1:30am.

Twelve lines, totaling 284km, connect Madrid's 293 stations, making the city's metro the third most extensive in the world, after London and New York. Line 12 now extends coverage from Casa de Campo to the Puerta del Sur, Móstoles, and Getafe regions south of the city. An individual metro ticket costs €1, or €2 if you leave the city limits; children under the age of four travel free. Frequent riders opt for the **Metrobus** (10 rides valid for both the Metro and bus system; €7.40). Buy them at machines in Metro stops, *estancos* (tobacco shops), or newsstands. Remember to keep your ticket until you leave the metro—riding without one can subject you to outrageous fines. In addition, **abonos mensuales,** or monthly passes, grant unlimited travel within the city proper for €46, while **abonos turísticos** (tourist passes) come in various lengths (1, 2, 3, 5, or 7 days) and sell for €5-24. These are available at all metro stations or online. For information, call **Metro Info** (☎902 44 44 03) or visit www.metromadrid.es.

Violent crime in Metro stations is almost unheard of, and women usually feel safe traveling alone. Be advised, however, that crowded subway cars are a pickpocket's land of milk and honey. Though typically busy throughout the night, stations such as Tirso de Molina, La Latina, Lavapiés, Gran Vía, Pl. de España, Chueca, and Sol can be intimidating to solo travelers after midnight—use common sense.

BUS

While the Metro makes the most sense for trips across Madrid, buses cover areas inaccessible by Metro and are a great way to see the city. Most stops are clearly marked, but if you want extra guidance in finding routes and stops, try the handy *Plano de Transportes* or the English-language *Visiting the Downtown on Public Transport*, free at the tourist office or as a download from www.madrid.org.

Bus and Metro fares are equivalent, and tickets are interchangeable. Buses run 6am-11pm, generally every 10 to 15 minutes. From midnight-6am, the **Búho** (owl), or night bus, travels from Pl. de Cibeles and other marked routes to the outskirts of the city (M-Th and Sa every 30min. midnight-3am, every hr. 3-6am; F-Sa every 20min.) These buses, marked on the essential *Red de autobuses nocturnos*, available at any tourist office or from www.emtmadrid.es, run along 26 lines covering regular daytime routes. For info, call **Empresa Municipal de Transportes.** (☎902 50 78 50 or 914 06 88 10; www.emtmadrid.es. Open M-F 8am-2pm.)

MADRID

TRAIN

Renfe's rapidly expanding Cercanías (suburban train) network traverses Madrid and its surroundings, reaching areas inaccessible or impractical by Metro and bus. There are 10 lines, most of which connect directly to metro stations. Timetables are regular and posted at all stations. Fares follow a zone scheme; travel within the city itself costs €1.20, and prices increase up to €5 as you move outward. Trains run 5:30am-11:30pm every day.

TAXI

Taxis stream through Madrid around the clock. Call **Radio Taxi Madrid** (☎915 47 32 32), **Radio-Taxi Independiente** (☎914 05 55 00 or 914 05 12 13; www.radiotaxi-independiente.com), or **Teletaxi** (☎913 71 21 31; www.tele-taxi.es). A *"libre"* sign or a green light indicates availability. Base fare is €2.05 (or €2.20 M-F after 10pm and €3.10 Sa-Su after 10pm), plus €0.98 per km 6am-10pm and €1.15 10pm-6am. **Teletaxi** charges a flat rate of €1 per km. Fare supplements include airport (€5.50) and bus and train stations (€2.95). Official taxis are white with a red stripe on the door; avoid impostors.

Be sure to check that the driver starts the meter. If you have a complaint or think you've been overcharged, demand a *recibo oficial* (official receipt) and an *hoja de reclamaciones* (complaint form), which the driver is required to supply. Take down the license number, route taken, and fare charged. Take the forms and information to the **Oficina Municipal del Taxi,** C. Albarracín, 31 (☎914 80 46 23; M: García Noblejas; open M-F 9am-1pm) to request a refund. To request wheelchair-accessible taxi service, call ☎915 47 85 00 or 915 47 86 00. Rates are the same. If you leave belongings in a taxi, visit or call the **Negociado de Objetos Perdidos,** Paseo del Molino, 7. (☎915 27 95 90. M: Legazpi. Open M-F 9am-2pm.)

CAR RENTAL

There is no reason to rent a car in Madrid. If congested traffic and nightmarish parking don't drive you into hysterics, aggressive drivers, annoying mopeds, and sky-high gasoline prices will. If you do choose to drive, parking permits are available on the street from column-like machines with "P" signs. If you plan to drive to places outside of Madrid, a larger car rental chain is your best bet. See **By Car,** p. 30, for listings of multinational chains with offices in Spain.

MOPED AND BIKE RENTAL

Fortunately for pedestrians, Madrid has not descended into the moped mayhem that has consumed most European capitals. Though mopeds are swift, Madrid's stellar public transport system is more than sufficient for getting around. If you choose to ride, you'll need a lock and helmet. **Motocicletas Antonio Castro,** C. Clara del Rey, 17, rents mopeds from €23-95 per day, including unlimited mileage and insurance. (☎914 1300 47; www.blafermotos.com. M: Cartagena. Must be 25 or older and have a drivers' license valid for motorcycles. Open M-F 8am-6pm, Sa 10am-1:30pm.) **Alquiler de Motos A. Castro,** C. Conde Duque, 13, also rents motorcycles (☎915 42 06 57). For bike rental, try **Madrid Bike Rental and Tours,** C. Jardines, 12. (☎915 23 15 47; www.trixi.com. M: Gran Vía. Rental €8 for 4 hr., €12 for 8hr., €15 for 24hr., and €50 per week. Open M-F 10am-2pm and 4-8pm, Sa-Su 10am-8pm. Tours daily 11am; €22 for 3hr. tour with English-speaking guide, drink included. No reservations needed.)

PRACTICAL INFORMATION

TOURIST AND FINANCIAL SERVICES

Tourist Offices: English and French are spoken at most tourist offices. Those planning trips outside the Comunidad de Madrid can visit region-specific offices within the city; ask for their addresses at any tourist office.

Regional Office of the Comunidad de Madrid, C. del Duque de Medinaceli, 2 (☎914 29 49 51, info 902 10 00 07; www.turismomadrid.es). M: Banco de España. Brochures, transportation info, and maps for the Comunidad. Extremely helpful; if you are planning to travel beyond the city itself, make this your first stop. Open M-Sa 8am-8pm, Su 9am-2pm.

Madrid Tourism Centre, Pl. Mayor, 27 (☎915 88 16 36; www.esmadrid.com). M: Sol. Hands out indispensable city and transportation maps and a complete guide to accommodations as well as *In Madrid,* a monthly activity and information guide in English. Branches at Estación Chamartín (p. 74), Estación Puerta de Atocha (p. 74), and the airport (p. 73), also at Plaza de Cibeles, Plaza de Callao, and Plaza de Felipe II. All open daily 9:30am-8pm.

General Info Line: Linea Madrid (☎010). Info on all things Madrid, from police stations to zoo hours. Ask for *inglés* for an English-speaking operator.

Tours: Tours can be informative but pricey, so read the fine print before signing on. The *Ayuntamiento* offers walking tours in English and Spanish called **Descubre Madrid** (☎915 88 29 06. €3.90; students, children, and seniors €3.12); the tours leave from the municipal tourist office, where you can get more info. **Madrid Vision** (☎917 79 18 88; www.madridvision.es) operates double-decker bus tours. There are 2 routes (Madrid Histórico and Moderno) each of which makes 15-20 stops around the city, featuring monuments and museums. Get on and off the bus as you please. €19, ages 7-16 and seniors €10; discounts available online.

Budget Travel: TIVE, C. Fernando el Católico, 88 (☎915 43 74 12). M: Moncloa. Walk straight down C. Arcipreste de Hita (one street over, parallel to C. Princesa) and turn left on C. Fernando el Católico. A great resource for long-term visitors. Lodging, tourism, and student residence info. Organizes group excursions as well as language classes and cheap trips to other European cities. Some English spoken. Some services only for Spanish nationals. Sells cheap **ISIC** cards (€6) and **Hostelling International (HI)** memberships (€21), along with discount memberships for teachers and people above 26. Open M-F 9am-2pm. Arrive early to avoid lines. Another smaller branch is located at Paseo de Recoletos, 7 (☎917 20 13 24). M: Banco de España. Open M-F 9am-2pm.

Consulates: see **Embassies and Consulates,** p. 8.

Currency Exchange: The airport is the most convenient place to change your cash, but if you need to change more in the city later, head to **Banco Santander Central Hispano,** which does not charge commission on American Express Travelers Cheques, but will charge around €12-15 commission on all others. Max. exchange €300. Main branch, Po. Castellana, 7 (☎915 58 11 11). M: Sol. Follow C. San Jerónimo 100m to Pl. Canalejas. Open Apr.-Sept. M-F 8:30am-2pm; Oct.-Mar. M-F 8:30am-2pm, Sa 8:30am1pm. Other branches throughout the city with similar hours. Banks usually charge 1-2% commission (often with a minimum charge of €3). Booths in Sol and Gran Vía, though open as late as midnight and on weekends, have poor rates and are not a good deal. **ServiRed, ServiCaixa,** and **Telebanco** machines accept bank cards with Cirrus, PLUS, EuroCard, or NYCE logos. Check with your local bank about foreign withdrawal fees.

American Express: Currency exchange at 11 locations throughout the airport's 4 terminals. To report lost Travelers Cheques, call toll free ☎90 099 44 26.

LOCAL SERVICES

Luggage Storage: At the airport (€3.70 for the 1st day, €4.78 per day for the next 2 weeks) and bus and train stations (€2.40-4.50 per bag per day).

English-language Periodicals: International publications are available at kiosks everywhere, especially on Gran Vía, Paseos del Prado, Recoletos, Castellana, and around Pta. del Sol. *In Madrid* is an English-language guide to what's going on in the city, available at tourist offices. For books, try the sizeable English-language mezzanine at **Casa del Libro,** Gran Vía, 29. M: Gran Vía. Open M-Sa 9:30am-9:30pm, Su 11am-9pm.

Libraries: Madrid is home to two library networks throughout the area: one run by the region (**Bibliotecas Públicas**) and another by the city (**Bibliotecas Municipales**). Information about both is available at the municipal tourist office or online at gestiona.madrid.org/bpcm. The large **Biblioteca Centro-Pedro Salinas** (☎913 66 54 07) at M: Pta. de Toledo, has English-language periodicals. Open M-F 9am-9pm.

Women's Resources: For general information on women's services in Spain or to report an incident, call **Instituto de la Mujer,** C. Genova, 11 (24hr. information line ☎900 19 10 10; www.mtas.es/mujer). M: Colón or Alonso Martinez. Open M-F 9am-2pm.

GLBT Resources: Most establishments in Chueca carry *Shangay,* a free guides to gay nightlife in Spain, also available online at www.shangay.com. The guide also offers detailed listings and maps of the many gay establishments in and around Madrid. Alternatively, you can purchase *Zero* magazine (€5) at any kiosk, or check it out for free online at www.zero-web.com.

Colectivo de Gais y Lesbianas de Madrid (COGAM), C. Puebla, 9 (☎915 22 45 17; www.cogam.org). M: Callao. Provides a wide range of services and organizes activities; call or check the website for a schedule. Reception open M-Th 10am-2pm and 5-8pm, F 10am-2pm.

GAY-INFORM/Línea Lesbos (☎915 23 00 70). A gay info line and hotline provides counseling from 5-9pm every night. Th 7-9pm in English. F staffed by and for lesbians, but takes all calls. Also provides information about gay associations, activities, health issues, sports, and dinners.

Laundromat: Central Madrid is tragically devoid of self-service laundromats. Try to arrange for laundry service through your hotel, or call **Tintorería La Plancha Veloz,** C. Doctor Esquerdo, 96 (☎915 73 36 76; www.laplanchaveloz.com); they'll pick up and return your clothing right to your door for no additional charge. M: Conde de Casal. Open M-F 9am-2pm and 5-8pm, Sa 9am-2pm.

EMERGENCY AND COMMUNICATIONS

Police: C. de los Madrazo, 9 (☎913 22 11 60 or 900 15 00 00). M: Sevilla. Largely administrative. English forms available. Open daily 9am-2pm. **Policía Municipal,** C. Montera 18, has staff 24hr. **Servicio de Atención al Turista Extranjero (SATE),** C. Leganitos, 19, are police who deal exclusively with tourists; they help with administrative formalities, reporting crimes, canceling credit cards, contacting embassies and family members, finding lost objects, and finding counseling. (☎915 48 85 37 for the office or ☎902 102 112 to report a crime. M: Plaza de España. Open daily 9am-midnight.)

24hr. Pharmacy: Farmacia Ortopedia, C. Mayor, 13 (☎913 664 616), off Pta. del Sol. Dial ☎098 for additional rotating locations.

Hospitals: Emergency rooms are the best option for immediate attention. US insurance is not accepted, but if you get a receipt your insurance may pay. For non-emergency concerns, **Unidad Médica Angloamericana,** C. del Conde de Aranda, 1, 1st fl. (☎914 35 18 23; www.unidadmedica.com). M: Serrano or Retiro. Regular English-speaking personnel on duty M-F 9am-8pm, Sa 10am-1pm. English-speaking specialists in every branch of medicine do non-urgent consultations. Appointments required. AmEx/MC/V. Embassies and consulates keep lists of English-speaking doctors.

Emergency Clinics: In a medical emergency, dial ☎061 or 112. **Hospital de Madrid,** Pl. del Conde del Valle Suchil, 16 (☎914 47 66 00; www.hospitaldemadrid.com). M: Bilbao. **Hospital Ramón y Cajal,** Ctra. Colmenar Viejo, km 9100 (☎913 36 80 00). M: Begoña or Bus #135 from Pl. de Castilla. **Red Cross** (☎915 22 22 22, info 902 22 22 92). **Centro Sanitorio Sandoval,** C. Sandoval, 7 (☎914 48 57 58). M: Bilbao. Free, confidential government clinic specializing in HIV/AIDS and other STIs; call ahead to arrange a visit.

Telephones: Directory services ☎11822. (See **Keeping in Touch,** p. 32.)

Internet Access: Hundreds of internet cafes are spread across the city, and most hostels provide free internet access as well. Rates are generally consistent (roughly €1-1.50 per 30min. and €2 per hr.). **Kioscocity,** C. Montera 47. Internet and Wi-Fi €1 for 15min., €1.50 for 30min., €2 per hr. Domestic and international fax services available. Open daily 24hr.

Post Office: Palacio de Comunicaciones, C. Alcalá, 51, on Pl. de Cibeles (☎902 19 71 97). M: Banco de España. Enormous palace on the far side of the plaza from the metro. Info (main vestibule) open M-Sa 8:30am-9:30pm. Windows open M-Sa 8:30am9:30pm, Su 8:30am-2pm for stamp purchases. To find a more convenient location near you, check the website at www.correos.es. **Postal Code:** 28080.

ACCOMMODATIONS

The demand for rooms in Madrid is always high, and rises dramatically in summer. Although the city is filled with hostels, ones with good quality at good prices can be hard to find. Backpacker hostels are concentrated in the Centro and Huertas; they tend to be lively, have no curfew, and include linens, internet, and breakfast in the price of lodging. *Hostales* and *pensiones* offer inexpensive private rooms, sometimes have curfews, and often host guests staying for longer periods of time. Owners are accustomed to opening doors, albeit groggily, at all hours, or providing keys for guests, but be sure to check before you head out to make sure you won't be locked out. In winter, heating is standard; in summer, air-conditioning is not. Unless otherwise noted, communal bathrooms (toilet and shower) are the norm, although it is not unusual to get a private sink and/or shower in your room. Most of the *hostales* and *pensiones* listed below include linens, towels, toiletries, and Wi-Fi and offer laundry services, though few include breakfast. If these amenities aren't mentioned in a listing, don't expect to find them.

Prices for beds in shared dorms hover around €20, while individual rooms in *hostales* and *pensiones* are likely to run €25 to €60, depending on location, amenities, and season. Double rooms often cost only slightly more than singles; if you're traveling with a friend, sharing a double will likely be your cheapest option. As a general rule, higher prices don't necessarily indicate nicer accommodations; always ask to see your room before you pay, and try negotiating the price if you'll be staying for more than a week. Reservations are recommended in summer and on weekends, especially in the Puerta del Sol area and at the first few places we list in each neighborhood; on summer weekends reservations are essential. A "*completo*" sign indicates that there are no vacancies. Many tourist offices, including the one in the airport, have accommodations listings on hand; also check out www.hosteleriademadrid.com. Those staying in Madrid for long periods may want to check out *The Broadsheet* (€2.50), an English periodical with classifieds and events.

CAMPING

Tourist offices have the *Guía Oficial de Campings,* which provides info on the 22 campsites surrounding Madrid.

Camping Alpha (☎916 95 80 69; www.campingalpha.com). Site 12.4km down Ctra. de Andalucía in Getafe. M: Legazpi. From the metro, walk down Vado Santa Catalina, cross the bridge, and bear right. Take the green bus #447, which stops across from the Museo de Jamón (10min., every 20-30min. 6:45am-10pm, €1.25). Ask for the Camp Alpha stop. Cross the footbridge and walk 1½km back toward Madrid along the busy highway, following the signs. Welcoming reception, paved roads, pool, tennis courts, showers, laundry, and internet center. Oct-Mar €5.56 per person and per car, tents €5.68; Apr-Sept. €7 per person and per car, €7.10 per tent. Bungalows for 2-5 people €51-100. ❶

EL CENTRO: SOL, ÓPERA, AND PLAZA MAYOR

The following listings lie between the Sol and Ópera metro stops. For better deals in quieter spots, stray several blocks from Sol. Price and location in El Centro are ideal, especially if you are planning to brave its legendary nightlife. Buses #3, 25, 39, and 500 serve Ópera; buses #3, 5, 15, 20, 50, 51, 52, 53, and 150 serve Sol. Hotels here are largely indistinguishable, with the same pieces of furniture and pretty much the same rates, which are not the cheapest you'll find in Madrid, but the uniformity guarantees a good standard of cleanliness. M: Ópera or Sol.

Miguel Ángel Residencia Comunitaria, Pl. Celenque, 1, 4th fl. (☎915 22 23 55; www.hostelmiguelangel.com), 1 block up off C. Arenal. The cleanest, classiest "backpacker hostel" around and the best deal in the *centro.* Immaculate air-conditioned rooms have bright curtains and comforters. Communal bathrooms are big and

MADRID

very clean. English spoken. Breakfast included. Free internet and Wi-Fi. Reserve in advance. Dorms €17-21; triples €78. ❶

Hostal Oriente, C. de Arenal, 23, 1st fl. (☎915 48 03 14). Rooms have magnificently clean white tile and creamy peach walls and bedspreads. Balconies at this elegant *hostal* add breeze but unexciting views. 17 rooms have TV, phone, A/C, and bath. Free internet. Reserve ahead. Singles €45; doubles €65; triples €85. MC/V. ❹

Posada Real Valencia, Pl. del Oriente, 2, 3rd fl. (☎915 59 84 50; www.posadarealvalencia.com). Narrow glass elevator lifts you to 7 elegant (if slightly faded) rooms with the splendor of deep carpets and upholstered satin. All have TV, fan, and private, spacious bathrooms. Ask for a room with the Posada's unmatched view over beautiful Pl. del Oriente. Reserve ahead—the lone single can be booked weeks in advance. Single €45; doubles €72-92; triples €100-115. MC/V. ❹

Los Amigos Sol Backpackers Hostel, C. de Arenal, 26, 4th fl. (☎915 592 472). Hallways painted in bright orange lead past a small common room to tight but well-maintained 4- to 12-bed dorms. Breakfast included. Towels €2. Key deposit €5. Free internet and Wi-Fi. Dorms €16-24 depending on season and room size. AmEx/MC/V. ❶

Hostal Esparteros, C. de Esparteros, 12, 4th fl. (☎915 210 903; www.esparteros.com). M: Sol. Unbeatable price and location. Airy rooms with balconies or large windows are worth the 4-flight hike, as are the peace, quiet, and friendly family owners. Some rooms have private bath, TV, and fans. Laundry €9-10. Free internet and Wi-Fi. Singles €25; doubles €35; triples €50. Dicounts for stays over a month. Cash only. ❷

Hostal-Residencia Luz, C. de las Fuentes, 10, 3rd fl. (☎915 42 07 59; www.hostalluz.com). Modern rooms and bathrooms are bright and clean. Dorm-style rooms an excellent value for the area, if a bit cramped. Satellite TV, A/C, and free Wi-Fi. Breakfast €2. Laundry €5. 4-bed dorms €20 per person; doubles €50, with bath €65-70; triples €75. MC/V. ❷

HUERTAS

Smaller and quieter than nearby El Centro, Huertas is home to many of the city's finest backpacker hostels and other budget accommodations within walking distance of all of the city's sights, live music, and hundreds of bars as well as some of the world's finest art. The area's largest drawback is its lack of a centrally located Metro stop; the closest (Sol, Sevilla, Antón Martín, and Tirso de Molina) are a 5- to 15-minute stroll. The area's bus routes offer an alternative to the Metro: Sol-bound buses stop on C. del Príncipe, C. Núñez de Arce, and C. San Jerónimo; buses #10, 14, 27, 34, 37, and 45 run along Po. del Prado; and Buses #6, 26, and 32 run up C. Atocha—get off at C. San Sebastián for Pl. Santa Ana.

Way Hostel, C. Relatores 17 (☎914 20 05 83; reservas@wayhostel.com). M: Tirso de Molina. The sleek black-and-white lounge and inviting kitchen at this cozy, 70-bed hostel lend it a relaxed, friendly feel. Clean, spacious 6- to 10-bed dorms are a fantastic value; most come with A/C. Breakfast included. Towels €1. Free internet and Wi-Fi. Dorms €15-22. AmEx/MC/V. ❶

Cat's Hostel, C. Cañizares, 6 (☎913 69 28 07; www.catshostel.com). M: Antón Martín. This renovated 18th-century palace stands among Europe's most beautiful hostels, although some travelers complain that its size (200 beds) makes for an institutional vibe and its unfriendly staff make for a less than pleasant stay. Basic dorms (2-14 beds) and small doubles with private baths open onto a restored Moorish patio replete with plants, fountain, and luxurious cushions. Wood-paneled pub and cave-like basement bar draw crowds, especially after the courtyard closes at midnight. No kitchen. A/C and breakfast included. Laundry €5. Free internet and Wi-Fi. Reserve ahead, as it often fills quickly. Dorms M-Th and Su €17-20, F-Sa 18-22; doubles with bath €38-42. MC/V. ❶

Hostal Barrera, C. Alcalá, 96 (☎915 275 381, www.hostalbarrera.com). M: Atocha or Antón Martín. 19 hotel-style rooms thoughtfully decorated in earth tones. All come with TV, private granite-tiled bath, A/C, and classy chandeliers. Expensive, but the cozy elegance of this high-end *hostal* is worth the splurge. Safes €1 per use. Free Wi-Fi. Singles €50; doubles €68; triples €85. AmEx/MC/V. ❺

La Posada de Huertas, C. Huertas, 21 (☎914 29 55 26; www.posadadehuertas.com). M: Antón Martín or Sol. Neon-colored halls and 4- or 8-bed dorms are well kept, with comfortable beds and A/C. Spotless bathrooms. Kitchen and breakfast included.. Luggage storage available. Laundry €1 per 20min. of wash or dry. Free internet and Wi-Fi. Key deposit €15. Check-out 10:30am. Dorms from €18; singles €40; doubles €48. MC/V (3% surcharge). ❷

Mad Hostel, C. Cabeza, 24 (☎915 06 48 40; www.madhostel.com) M: Tirso de Molina. The Cat's crew's newest 190-bed hostel features standard but clean 4- to 6-bed dorms, 4-piece gym, shared kitchen, and small rooftop terrace. Lively scene in the spacious, welcoming bar with pool table. Breakfast, safe, and linens included. Towels available for €5 deposit. Laundry €5 wash and dry. Free internet and Wi-Fi. €10 key deposit. Reserve ahead. Dorms €20-22. MC/V. ❷

Hostal Plaza D'Ort, Pl. del Angel, 13 (☎914 29 90 41; www.plazadort.com). M: Antón Martín. Friendly staff and immaculate, pastel-colored rooms with bright blankets, A/C, and phone; some with TV and private bath. Safes €1 per use. Wi-Fi €5 per day. Singles €35-45; doubles €45-59; triples €70-90; spacious 3-person suite €130. MC/V. ❹

Musas Residence, C. Jesús y María, 12 (☎915 39 49 84). M: Tirso de Molina. Simple 2- to 14-bed dorms with metal bunk beds are supplemented by a small shared kitchen and living room. Dorms of 6 or more have A/C, others have fan. Doubles with shared bath also available. Breakfast included. Safes €1 per use. Towels €1. Laundry €10. Free internet and Wi-Fi. Addition with 30 beds and a new, larger common room, kitchen, and bar should be open by 2010. Dorms €15-18, F-Sa and in summer €19-20; doubles €38/42. AmEx/MC/V. ❶

Hostal Villar, C. del Príncipe, 18 (☎915 31 66 00; www.villar.es). M: Sol or Sevilla. Winding staircases and long corridors lead to quiet, faded rooms with old furniture and full baths, most with A/C. Small, bright common rooms with couches dot the floors. Singles €28, with bath €36; doubles €36/50; triples €50/60. MC/V. ❸

Pensión Magdalena, C. Magdalena, 26. M: Antón Martín. A no-frills *pensión* with small, unadorned, well-kept rooms. Some rooms have huge beds, balconies, A/C, and/or private bath; ask to see a few before you settle in. No phone or webpage, so you'll have to show up and hope for the best. Singles and doubles €25, with bath €35. Inquire about discounts for longer stays. Cash only. ❷

GRAN VÍA

The many *hostales* of Gran Vía put you right in the heart of Madrid's bustle (and its accompanying noise). Most are located on the upper floors of tall, elevator-equipped buildings a few decades past their prime; as you travel up, the view improves and the car horns and sirens grow (slightly) more distant.

Hostal Santillan, Gran Vía, 64, 8th fl. (☎915 48 23 28; www.hostalsantillan.com). M: Pl. de España. Take the glass elevator to the top of this gorgeous building. Leaf-patterned curtains and wooden furniture give rooms a homey feel. All have shower, sink, TV, and fan. A little more cash can you get you a bath and much bigger room; explore the options. Laundry €1-3 per piece. Free Wi-Fi. Singles €30-35; doubles €50-55; triples €70-75. MC/V. ❸

Hostal Concepción Arenal, C. Concepción Arenal, 6, 3rd fl. (☎915 22 68 83). M: Callao. Breezy and just far enough from Gran Vía to be tranquil. Brown decor. Quiet rooms have short but soft beds and well-scrubbed showers. Rooms come with shower and TV, some with full bath. Free Wi-Fi. Singles €29, with full bath €35; doubles €40/50; triples with ½-bath €60. MC/V. ❸

Hostal A. Nebrija, Gran Vía, 67, 8th fl., elevator A (☎915 47 73 19). M: Pl. de España. Knick-knacks from around the world and religious paintings in the lobby give way to spacious, unadorned rooms with terraces; many have spectacular views of the Palacio Real, cathedral, and gardens west. Rooms come with TV, fan, and shared bath. No smoking. Singles €28; doubles €36; triples €55. Cash only. ❸

Hostal Gran Vía 44, Gran Vía, 44, 8th fl. (☎915 21 00 51; www.hostalgranvia44.com). M: Callao. Cheerful rooms with high ceilings and bright, colorful bedspreads. Southward views over the city's red roofs. All rooms with TV, fan, shower, sink, and large exterior windows; some include full bathroom and balcony. Breakfast included. Lounge area and free Wi-Fi. Singles €40, with full bath 50; doubles €50/60; triples €75. MC/V. ❹

MALASAÑA AND CHUECA

Accommodations in Malasaña or Chueca may cost a bit more than in other neighborhoods, but staying here will put you right in the center of some of Madrid's funkiest, most nightlife-rich *barrios* without subjecting you to the tourist throngs of Huertas and the Centro. *Hostales* and *pensiones* here are usually located on the upper floors of older buildings, so be prepared to climb. Buses #3, 40, and 149 run along C. de Fuencarral and C. Hortaleza, and M: Chueca, Gran Vía, and Tribunal serve the area.

Hostal Don Juan, Pl. Vasquez de Mella, 1, 2nd fl. (☎915 22 31 01). M: Chueca. Luxury fit for the romancing namesake himself. Chinese vases, tapestries, and antique candlesticks fill the lobby and adjacent common room. Rooms come with beautiful wooden flooring and hand-carved furniture, A/C, TV, and gleaming bath; many have small balconies. Free internet and Wi-Fi. Singles €38; doubles €53; triples €71. AmEx/MC/V. ❹

Hostal Condestable, C. Puebla, 15, 2nd fl. (☎915 31 62 02; www.hostalcondestable.com). M: Callao. Pastel-hued, fully-carpeted lobby fronts tranquil rooms with tall ceilings, solid-wood furniture, TV, and A/C; some with full bath. Communal baths are clean and bright. Singles €30, with bath €38; doubles €40/48; triples with bath €60. ❸

Casa Chueca, C. de San Bartolomé 4, 2nd fl. (☎915 23 81 27; www.casachueca.com). M: Chueca. Colorful bed dressings, marine blue walls, and corrugated metal doors set this trendy, 7-room hostel apart. Serves primarily a gay clientele, but warmly welcomes all. Rooms have A/C, satellite TV, and private bath. "Mini-breakfast" included. Free Internet and Wi-Fi. Reservations strongly recommended. Singles €45; doubles €60; triples €85. MC/V. ❹

Hostal Corazón de Madrid, C. San Bartolomé, 7. 1st fl. M: Chueca. Dark wooden doors, laminate-wood-paneled walls, and brown leather in the lobby and along the hallways evoke a 70s-era professor's study. Many of the rooms with balconies and full baths. Singles €30-40; doubles €40-60. Cash only. ❸

ARGÜELLES AND MONCLOA

Accommodations are few here, and quite a hike from the sights in the *centro*. The only reason to stay here is the comfortable and wondrously cheap HI hostel located close to the Metro.

Albergue Juvenil Santa Cruz de Marcenado (HI), C. de Santa Cruz de Marcenado, 28 (☎915 47 45 32; fax 48 11 96). M: Argüelles. From the Metro, walk 1 block down C. de Alberto Aguilera away from C. de la Princesa, turn right onto C. de Serrano Jóver, then left onto C. de Santa Cruz de Marcenado. Smaller and with a bit more personality than your average HI hostel, the real appeal of this 72-bed *albergue* is its rock-bottom prices. Single-sex rooms available. Breakfast and linens included. Laundry €3.50. 6-day max. stay. Quiet hours after midnight. Reception daily 9am-9:45pm. 1:30am curfew. Reserve well in advance. Dorms €12, over 26 €16.34. €3.50 discount for HI members. Cash only. ❶

FOOD

Madrid prides itself on simple fare: bread, cheese, and every fathomable part of pig and cow that can be squeezed on a plate. Such traditional Spanish cuisine often comes in the form of tapas—small portions typically served alongside a *caña* of beer or a *copa* of wine. Trawling from bar to bar savoring tapas is a popular alternative to a full sit-down meal and a fun way to sample local food. Most tapas bars (*tascas* or *tabernas*) are open noon-4pm and 8pm-midnight or later. Some double as restaurants, and many are clustered around **Plaza Santa Ana** and **Plaza Mayor.** Enticing as the tapas crawl can be, even the greatest devotees of Spanish cuisine will need a break sooner or later. Fortunately, Madrid provides more excellent fusion, vegetarian, and ethnic restaurants than any other Spanish city; the culinary offerings in **Chueca** and **Malasaña** are as funky and diverse as anywhere else on the planet. Spread throughout the city, Madrid's cafes are rich in characer as well as caffeine, giving contemplative coffee drinkers a shot of historical ambience with their *café con leche.* For those on a shoestring budget, the absolute cheapest choices are *bocadillos de jamón* (ham sandwiches) or *kebaps* from Turkish or Middle Eastern joints. Wherever you eat, you won't be bothered with the check until you ask.

FOOD SHOPPING

In general, the bigger the market and the farther from the city center, the cheaper the groceries. Specialty items may require a visit to a pricey store, but *supermercados* are generally the best bet for cheap goods. Also look for shops labeled *"alimentaciones"* or *"frutos secos,"* small convenience stores that have a limited selection but generally low prices.

Groceries: Carrefour (www.carrefour.es) and **Día%** (www.dia.es) are the cheapest city-wide supermarket chains, though they tend to be far from the city center. There is, however, a **Día%,** C. Toledo, 32 (☎914 65 55 22), in La Latina at the corner of C. Toledo and C. de la Colegiata. M: La Latina. Open M-Sa 9:30am-9:30pm, Su 10am-6pm. MC/V.

Markets: Mercado de San Miguel, an upscale glass-enclosed market on Pl. de San Miguel, off the northwest corner of Pl. Mayor, sells fine seafood, produce, wine, and other goods, albeit at relatively high prices. Open M-W 10am-10pm, Th-Sa 10am-2am.

Pastry Shops: These are everywhere. **La Mallorquina,** C. Mayor, 2 (☎915 211 201) is the most famous in all Madrid, and their desserts live up to their reputation (€1-2 each, or €14-22 per kg). Open daily Sept.-July 9am-9:15pm. The sublime **Horno La Santiagüesa,** C. Mayor, 73 (☎915 596 214) sells everything from *roscones de reyes* (sweet bread for the Feast of the Epiphany) to *empanadas* (€18-23 per kg) and pastries doused in chocolate. Try the *tarta de Santiago* (almond bread). Open daily 8am-9pm.

Red-Eye Establishments: *Guía del Ocio* lists late-night eateries under *"La última hora."* Street vendors, some disguised as normal citizens, may catch you unawares offering beer and sandwiches at ungodly hours. You may see these sandwich-sellers fleeing into the darkness at the first hint of police presence. *Cervecerías* and *kebap* restaurants that stay open until 2am aren't hard to find, but nothing's open much past 3am.

EL CENTRO: SOL ÓPERA AND PLAZA MAYOR

Tourists flood the *centro*, which creates a neighborhood packed with over-priced places serving mediocre fare. Buried among them, however, are some of Madrid's most historically significant restaurants, old haunts of the literary crowd largely unchanged since the writers of the Siglo del Oro took their leave. Wandering into the streets just south of Sol and the *centro* moreover, leads to some cheaper food with character. M: Ópera or Sol.

El Mejillón de Madrid, Pasaje de Matheu, 4, just off Espoz y Mina. No-frills seafood under umbrellas right on Madrid's shellfish row. Try the heaping plate of mussels (€8), the restaurant's namesake, or the plate of paella (€25) for 2 or more. Order 4 *raciones* (€4-11) and you'll get a free jug of sangria for up to 4 people—the best deal in the *centro.* Open M-Th, Su 11:30am-12:30am, F-Sa 11:30am-1:30am. Cash only. ❷

Sobrino del Botín, C. Cuchilleros, 17 (☎913 66 42 17; www.botin.es), off Pl. Mayor. Advertising itself as the oldest restaurant in the world, Sobrino del Botín has seen its share of the famous since it opened in 1725. Goya washed dishes here when he was 19, and Hemingway, a regular customer, mentions it by name in *The Sun Also Rises* (as the sign out front won't let passers-by forget). Ancient wooden doors and patterned red walls with gold filigree lend the kind of class that only age can bring. Entrees €8-20. Suckling pig €22.50. Open daily 1-4pm and 8pm-midnight. AmEx/MC/V. ❹

Fast Good, C. de Teután, 3A (☎915 230 456; www.fast-good.com). Frustrated by the recent explosion of American-style burger joints, celebrity chef Ferran Adría posed a simple question: can't fast food be healthy? The innovative, fresh, and healhtful fare at Fast Good answers, "Yes!" Open M-Tu and Su 1-10pm, W-Th 1-11pm, F-Sa 1pm-midnight. MC/V. ❸

Inshala, C. de la Amnistía, 10 (☎915 48 26 32). Perfect for a fancy date, but cheap enough for a backpacker's meal. Moroccan decor and decidedly eclectic international fare, ranging from Japanese to Argentine. Dinner €12-20. Reservations strongly recommended. Open in summer M-Sa 5pm-2am, in winter M-Sa noon-2am. MC/V. ❸

TAPAS BARS AND CAFES

☒ **Chocolatería San Ginés,** Pl. San Ginés (☎913 66 54 31). M: Sol. Tucked into a small plaza behind Joy Eslava, this beautifully-tiled *chocolatería* is a legend among early-risers and clubgoers alike, both for its unbeatable *chocolate con churros* (€4) and for its steadfast refusal to close. Open daily 24hr. Cash only. ❶

Casa Labra, C. de Teután, 11 (☎915 310 081). A Madrid classic since the 19th century. No frills, just excellent tapas served at the small wood-paneled bar (*bocadillos* €4-6; *raciones* €8-16.50). *Cañas* €1.10. More elaborate (and expensive) dishes in the attached dining room. Open daily noon-11pm, dining room open daily 1:30-3:30pm and 8:30-11pm. Cash only. ❷

Cafe del Real, Pl. de Isabel II, 2 (☎915 472 124). Plant yourself in a leather chair in the cozy portrait-adorned main room and linger over a coffee or a slice of cake (€4.75). Open M-Th and Su 9am-1pm, F-Sa 10am-2am. MC/V. ❶

LA LATINA AND LAVAPIÉS

From the *centro*, a few narrow, mazy streets, chief among them ☒**Calle Almendro** and **La Cava Baja,** wind down toward Lavapiés and La Latina, which are quieter, more local, and brimming with exciting new restaurants, tapas bars, and terraces. The area is most alive in the evening, when many restaurants transform into bars and the streets fill with nocturnal revelers.

☒ **El Estragón Vegetariano,** Pl. de la Paja, 10 (☎913 65 89 82). M: La Latina. This unobtrusive restaurant, with its quiet decor and patio feel, would blush at any superlatives we might give it, but its vegetarian delights could convince even the most die-hard car-

MADRID

nivores to switch teams. Lunch *menús* M-F €8-12. Sa-Su special entrees €9. Open M-F 1:30-4pm and 8pm-midnight, Sa-Su 8pm-midnight. AmEx/MC/V. ❸

El Granero de Lavapiés, C. Argumosa, 10 (☎914 67 76 11). M: Lavapiés. For 2 decades, temporary art exhibits and inventive specials have kept this pale yellow hideaway packed with locals. Free-trade, organic food at low prices. *Plato granero* sampler €7. Dinner €6-9. Open daily 1-4pm and 8:30-11pm. Cash only. ❷

La Turuleta,C. Almendro, 25 (☎913 642 666; www.laturuleta.es). M: La Latina. Red bottom-lit walls and and old knotted wood floors mix traditional and contemporary in a sleek fusion reflected in the menu. *Raciones* €12.50-20. Open M-W noon-5pm and 8:30pm-2am, Th-Sa noon-2am. MC/V. ❹

DELIC, Costanilla de San Andrés, 25 (☎913 645 450). M: La Latina. Madrid's answer to 1950s-style retro, with old coke bottles in the window and a fashionable diner feel inside. International menu; entrees €8-20. Open M 8pm-2am, W-Sa 11am-2am, Su 11am-midnight. Cash only. ❸

TAPAS BARS AND CAFES

Almendro 13, C. Almendro, 13 (☎913 65 42 52). M: La Latina. Locals dive into plates of *huevos rotos* (eggs and ham over fried potatoes; €8.40) and the tomato salad (€5). Shout over the clamor to order *manzanilla alemondro* (almond liquer, €1.50). Open M-F 1-4pm and 7:30pm-12:30am, Sa-Su 1-5pm and 8pm-1am. Cash only. ❷

Casa Amadeo, Pl. de Cascorro, 18 (☎913 65 94 39). M: La Latina. The owner of 68 years supervises the preparation of his renowned *caracoles* (snails; €6). Good stop after a day at El Rastro. *Caña* €1.20. Open daily 8am-midnight. Cash only. ❷

HUERTAS

Huertas is, without a doubt, the best place to eat in the center of the city. The area is chock-full of seafood, salad, and vegetarian spots, a much-needed break from the heavy tapas fare that Madrid cherishes. Popular with locals, **Plaza de Santa Ana** is perfect for passing time with a drink and some good food. Quality is generally high, and if you head into the less-crowded streets, prices tend to drop by a few euro. As the evening progresses and the wine flows, the streets and squares of Huertas become the first stop of many a carousing *madrileño.*

La Finca de Susana, C. Arlaban, 4 (☎913 69 35 57; www.lafinca-restaurant.com). M: Sevilla. Simple, elegant dining at jaw-droppingly low prices. The beef and arugula sushi (€7.80) is one of countless top-notch plates. M-F lunch *menú* with wine an amazing €9.50. Arrive early to avoid the ever-present line down the street. Open daily 1-3:45pm and 8:30-11:45pm. AmEx/MC/V. ❷

Arrocería Gala, C. de Moratín, 22 (☎914 29 25 62; www.paellas-gala.com). M: Antón Martín. Pastoral Spanish scenes of bulls on hillsides are gracefully overlaid in vine and shadows from the gorgeous chandeliers. The specialty made-to-order paellas (€15-20 per person, minimum 2 people) are 2nd to none. Tasty sangria €10 per pitcher. Reserve ahead on weekends. Open Tu-Su 1-5pm and 9pm-1:30am. Cash only. ❸

Olsen, C. del Prado, 15 (☎914 29 36 59). M: Sevilla. Simple, stylish, and Scandinavian, with light wood, white lacquer, and enough handcrafted vodka to make a lush blush. After dinner, sample 3 desserts and 3 artisan vodkas for €18. Entrees €16-22. M-F lunch *menús* €10-15. Open M-Sa 1-4pm and 8pm-2am; kitchen open until midnight. MC/V. ❷

Al Natural, C. de Zorrilla, 11 (☎913 69 47 09; www.alnatural.biz). M: Sevilla. Dark ochre walls set a tranquil mood here, where fresh salads (€8) and light Mediterranean dishes (€9-12) rule the menu. An ideal break from crowded salty ham standing-room-only joints. M-F lunch *menú* €11.90; M-Th dinner *menú* €12.60. Open M-Sa 1-4pm and 9pm-midnight, Su 1-4pm. AmEx/MC/V. ❷

Restaurante El Basha, Plaza Matute, 7 (☎914 29 96 10). M: Antón Martín. A fountain at the center of the upstairs dining room is one of many exotic touches at this youthful Middle Eastern joint. The *baba ghanoush* (€5) perfectly complements flavored teas (€2.50). Come evening, a bohemian crowd gathers in the basement to smoke hookah (€8) on camel-hide stools. Open M-Th and Su 3pm-1:30am, F-Sa 1:30pm-2:30am. MC/V. ❶

Taberna Maceira, C. de Jesús, 7 (☎914 29 15 84). 2nd branch at C. Huertas, 66 (☎914 29 58 18). M: Antón Martín. Yellow-green walls and grog barrels make this funky seafood place feel like a psychedelic pirate ship. Try the *mejillones Maceira* (mussels in cream sauce; €5) or the specialty *arroz mariñera* lunch plate (seafood rice; €7). Open M 8:30pm--12:45am, Tu-Th 1:15-4:15pm and 8:30pm12:45am, F-Sa 1:15-4:45pm and 8:30pm-1:15am, Su 8:30pm-12:30am. Cash only. ❸

La Bio Tika, C. Amor de Dios, 3 (☎914 29 07 80). M: Antón Martín. An unobtrusive vegetarian/macrobiotic restaurant serving up a *menú* of wholesome food (healthy dessert included) in a simple setting, with a shop for all your macrobiotic grocery needs. Lunch *menú* €10; dinner *menú* €12.10 for dinner. Open M-Sa 1-4:30pm and 8-11:30pm, Su 1-4:30pm. MC/V. ❷

TAPAS BARS AND CAFES

Restaurante Casa Granada, C. Doctor Cortezo, 17, 6th fl. (☎914 20 08 25). The door (on the left side of C. Doctor Cortezo as you head downhill) is unmarked; ring the bell for the 6th fl. and then head up the elevators at the back of the modest lobby. Though easy to miss, the experience of a sunset meal on the rooftop terrace is hard to forget. Put your name on the outdoor seating list when you arrive; you'll be vying with lots of other *madrileños*-in-the-know for a table. *Cañas* of beer (€2.40) come with tapas. *Raciones* €6.50-14. Open daily noon-1am. MC/V. ❷

Casa Alberto, C. de las Huertas, 18 (☎914 29 93 56; www.casaalberto.es). M: Antón Martín. The manual-wash bar and shanks hanging from the walls are throwbacks to the early days of this bar, founded in 1827. Very popular; getting a table during bustling meal hours can be difficult. Sweet vermouth (€1.70) is served with original house tapas. Try the delicious cod and lamb omelette (€4) or the *patatas ali-oli* (garlic potatoes; €4.50). Open Tu-Sa noon-5:30pm and 8pm-1:30am. MC/V. ❷

Cervecería Alemana, Pl. de Santa Ana, 6 (☎914 29 70 33). M: Antón Martín. Food orders come out of the kitchen as fast as they go in, but the locals here linger over drinks from the massive bar selection for much longer, especially if they're lucky enough to nab a prime outdoor table on delightful Pl. Santa Ana. Spanish cider (€2.25) goes well with the exquisite *chorizo* (sausage; €9). *Bocadillos* €3.50-6. Open M, W-Th, Su 11am-12:30am; F-Sa 11am-2am. MC/V. ❷

El Imperfecto, Plaza Matute, 2 (☎913 66 72 11). M: Antón Martín. The potpourri of sombreros, birdcages, suspended globes, and sequined shawls work together in a surprisingly hip way in this diminutive bar, which offers up alcoholic coffees (€4) and flavored tea infusions (€2.50). Open M-Th and Su 3pm-2am, F-Sa 3pm-2:30am. Cash only. ❶

La Trucha, C. Manuel Fernández González, 3 (☎914 29 58 33). M: Sol. 2nd branch at C. Núñez de Arce, 6 (☎915 32 08 90), without terrace. Traditional *campesino* decor, with low arched ceilings and textured plaster walls covered in colorful plates. Grab the *rabo de toro* (bull's tail with potatoes; €11.80). Entrees €9-15. Open daily 12:304pm and 7:30pm-midnight. AmEx/MC/V. ❸

La Toscana, C. Manuel Fernández González, 10-12 (☎914 29 60 31). M: Sol or Sevilla. A local crowd hangs out over tapas of *morcillo asado* (€11.50). The more intrepid should try the *sezos rebozados* (fried brains; €5.50). Antique lettering and wrought-iron decor lend a medieval feel. Open M-Sa 1-4pm and 8pm--midnight. ❷

Heladeria Giuseppe Ricci, C. de las Huertas, 9 (☎914 29 33 45; www.heladeriaricci.com). M: Antón Martín. Forget tapas and *jamón;* this gelato is Madrid's best relief from a hot summer's day. Most patrons request 2 flavors, which still counts as 1 scoop. Small cones €2.30, large €3.20. Rich *batidos* (milkshakes) €3.10. Open daily 1pm-midnight. Cash only. ❶

GRAN VÍA

Good food is hard to find when American burger joints, overpriced tourist diners, and cheesy theme restaurants occupy every foot of real estate. Fear not—there are still some culinary diamonds in the rough, especially in the side streets just off of the colossus itself. Those in search of a broader array of quality choices can head to nearby Chueca, just northeast of the Gran Vía Metro stop.

Root, C. Virgen de los Peligros, 1 (☎912 75 81 18). M: Gran Vía. Sophisticated white leather mixes with soft light diffused through lots of glass walls to create a mellow environment. A professional crowd comes in for the lunch *menú* (M-F 1-3pm, €13.50) and the desserts. "Death by Chocolate" €5. Open M-Th and Su 1:30-4pm and 8:30-11:30pm, F-Sa 1:30-4pm and 9pm-12:30am. MC/V. ❸

El Jamonal, Mesonero Romanos, 7 (☎915 31 51 04). M: Gran Vía or Callao. Skip the metal bar that runs the perimeter of the cramped, littered interior and sit in the peaceful, tree-shaded area outside; it may be just a block from the heat and bustle of Gran Vía, but it feels like miles. *Menú* €10 on the terrace, €8.60 inside. Open daily 7am-midnight. Cash only. ❷

Gula Gula, Gran Vía, 1 (☎915 22 87 64; www.gulagula.net). M: Gran Vía. Nondescript buffet restaurant by day, outrageous drag show by night. Good variety of salad and vegetable dishes. Cold lunch buffet €9, hot €12. Dinner and show €25; performances M-Th and Su 10pm, F-Sa 10:30pm and midnight. Reserve 1 week ahead for weekend dinner. Open daily 1-5pm and 9pm-late. AmEx/MC/V. ❷

MADRID

CHUECA

Exceptional vegetarian, Middle Eastern, Italian, and fusion cuisine dominate the scene in Chueca. Don't worry about choice; you'll find something funky and worthwhile down any street. For seriously fresh fruit, try **Frutas Eloy,** C. Barbieri, 26. Right off the metro in Plaza de Chueca, this fruit stand makes you feel healthier just by walking in. (☎917 01 01 91. Open M-F 9am-9pm, Sa-Su 9am-3pm. Cash only.)

Bazaar, C. de la Libertad, 21 (☎915 23 39 05; www.restaurantbazaar.com). M: Chueca. Another fantastic and shockingly affordable bistro from the team behind La Fince de Susana. Bright dining room with white leather banquettes and funky wine glasses. Elegant entrees an amazing €6-9. M-F lunch *menú* €10. Open daily 1:15-4pm and 8:30-11:45pm. MC/V. ❷

Al-Jaima, Cocina del Desierto, C. de Barbieri, 3 (☎915 23 11 42). M: Gran Vía or Chueca. Ambience is a serious business here—waiters in Moroccan *djellabas* scurry through the heavily incensed air, bringing tea and Maghrebi dishes to patrons seated on cushions beside low tables. Try the *pollo con higos y miel* (chicken with figs and honey; €6.90). Dinner entrees €12-18. Couscous €6-9. Open daily 1:30-4pm and 9pm-midnight. Reserve ahead for dinner. MC/V. ❹

Il Pizzaiolo, C. de Hortaleza, 84 (☎913 19 29 64). M: Chueca. Authentic thin-crust Italian pizzas made with fresh ingredients. Friendly staff and bright, casual atmosphere. Pizzas €7.50-10. Tiramisu €4.50. Open M-Th and Su 1:30pm-midnight, F-Sa 1:30pm-12:30am. MC/V. ❷

El Inca, C. Gravina, 21 (☎915 32 77 45). M: Chueca. Colonial paintings, small tables, and soft music invite guests into this intimate Peruvian restaurant, which serves up massive seafood dishes along with other far-off favorites. Try the *solterito arequipeño* (vegetable and cheese dish; €10) or the *yucas fritas* (fried potatoes; €6.50). Lunch *menú* €11.50. Open daily 1:30-4pm and 8:30pm-1am. MC/V. ❹

Maoz, C. Hortaleza, 5. M: Gran Vía. Minimalist decor matches the simple menu, which offers filling falafel sandwiches and salads (each €4.20). Huge portions are a good break from salty ham, and service is quick. Several other locations in the city, including one at C. Mayor, 4. Open daily noon-2am. Cash only. ❶

Pizzeria Vesuvio, C. de Infantas, 32 (☎915 21 65 06). M: Gran Vía. Fresh pizza in 27 varieties. Artful exposed brick around the kitchen gives it a pleasant brick-oven feel. At lunch, counters are packed with a rowdy crowd. Pizzas €5-8. Extra ingredients €0.90 each. Open M-Th 1-4pm and 8pm-midnight, F-Sa 1-4pm and 8pm-1am. MC/V. ❷

TAPAS BARS AND CAFES

BAires Café, C. Gravina, 4 (☎915 32 98 79), corner of Pelayo. M: Chueca. What its ties are to Buenos Aires is unclear but this is a laid-back cafe with soft music playing and artwork covering the black-and-white walls. Sit down and take a load off with your *caña* (€2.20) or wine (€2-2.50), or try a traditional *café española* (coffee with aniseed liquor; €2.70). Open M-W and Su 3pm-1am, Th-Sa 3pm-2:30am. ❶

El Tigre, C. Infantas, 30 (☎915 32 00 72). Bursting with boars' heads, antlers, and other assorted animal parts, El Tigre Chueca's most happening *cañas* spot. The marvelous, salty tapas–included with your drink–get tastier with each sip. Beer €1.80. *Raciones* €4-7. Open daily 10:30am-1am or later. Cash only. ❶

Isolée, C. de las Infantas, 19 (☎915 22 81 38; www.isolee.com). White leather sets the hipster mood at this over-the-top cafe with 25+ varieties of bottled water. Don't miss the black and gold Moët and Chandon champagne lounge or the store selling handbags, soap, and pretentious home decor for all of your lifestyle needs. Sushi €7-10. Sandwiches €4. Free Wi-Fi. Takeout available. Open M-Th 10am-10pm, F-Sa 11am-1am, Su 4-10pm. MC/V. ❷

MALASAÑA

Once Madrid's capital of grunge, today's Malasaña draws a hip crowd to its trendy but affordable ethnic restaurants and cool cafes, which are concentrated along **Calle Espítiru Santo,Calle de San Andrés,** and **Calle Manuela Malasaña.** M: Tribunal or Bilbao.

La Granja de Said, C. de San Andrés, 11 (☎915 32 87 93). M: Tribunal or Bilbao. Moorish designs in the doorways, beautiful tiling, and the dim glow of light through lamps and tapestries bring the Middle East to Malasaña. Dine well, then puff peacefully on hookah (€8). *Tabouleh* salad €6. Delicious falafel plate €7. Open Tu-Su 1pm-5pm and 8pm-2am. MC/V. ❷

Olokun, C. Fuencarral, 105 (☎914 45 69 16). M: Bilbao. From the Gl. de Bilbao exit, walk south on Fuencarral. Beach scenes, tropical mixed drinks (€5-7), and delicacies like *tostones* (fried plantains; €6) served on wooden barrels bring Cuba to Malasaña. *Menú* €11.90. Salsa Th 5:30pm. Open daily noon-5pm and 9pm-2am; kitchen open until 1am. MC/V. ❷

Home Burger Bar, C. Espítiru Santo, 12 (☎915 22 97 28; www.homeburgerbar.com). M: Tribunal. In the US, it'd be hard to make a burger joint this hip, but in Madrid, anything is possible. Choose a gourmet "eco-friendly" burger from among the dozens of options included on the paper bag that will serve as your menu. Burgers and club sandwiches with fries and slaw €12; veggie burgers €10-11. Open M-Sa 1:30-4pm and 8:30pm-midnight, Su 1-4pm and 8:30-11pm. MC/V. ❷

Osteria Il Regno de Napoli, C. San Andrés, 21 (☎914 45 63 00). M: Bilbao. From the Gl. de Bilbao exit, head 1 block down C. Carranza and turn left onto C. San Andrés. Exquisite Neapolitan food arrives quickly. A quiet place to eat a calm lunch. The bruschetta (€4) is unbeatable. Lunch *menú* €10. Dinner entrees €9-15. Pizzas

€8-13. Reservations advisable on weekends. Open M-F 2-4pm and 9pm-midnight, Sa 9pm-midnight. AmEx/MC/V. ❸

TAPAS BARS AND CAFES

Lolina Vintage Cafe, C. Espíritu Santo, 9 (☎667 20 11 69; www.lolinacafe.com). This quirky cafe's mismatched armchairs, geometric wallpaper, and eccentric lamps could have come from a Brooklyn thrift store, but they fit perfectly into the trendy Malasaña scene. Great selection of teas (try the Green Earl Grey) in super-cool pots that detach to reveal cups hidden underneath (€2). Large salads €8. Hot dogs €5. Keeps bustling into the night, when mojitos are €6. Wi-Fi available. Open M-Tu and Su 9:30am-1am, W-Th 9:30am-2am, F-Sa 9:30-2:30am. MC/V. ❶

Café Comercial, Glorieta de Bilbao, 7 (☎915 21 56 55). M: Bilbao, just a few feet beyond C. Fuencarral beside the Gl. de Bilbao station exit. The marble and high mirrors of Madrid's oldest cafe have reflected the city's artists, politicians, journalists, and bullfighters since 1887, but they don't discriminate. Huge and open late. Coffee €1.90. Breakfast (€2-5) until 12:30pm. Internet €1 per 50min. Open M 7:30am-midnight, Tu-Th 7:30am-1am, F 7:30am-2am, Sa 8:30am-2am, Su 9am-midnight. ❶

La Musa, C. Manuela Malasaña, 18 (☎914 48 75 78; www.lamusa.com.es). M: Bilbao. From the Gl. de Bilbao exit, walk just a few feet down C. Fuencarral before turning right on C. Manuela Malasaña. Hip, chain bar-restaurant made hipper by a funky collection of shadowbox artwork. At night fills with couples sipping on the vast selection of reds and rosés. Wine €1.60-2.80 per glass. Mixed drinks €5-6. Wi-Fi available. Open M-Th and Su 1:30-5pm and 9pm-1am, F-Sa 1:30-5pm and 9pm-2am. MC/V. ❶

ARGÜELLES AND MONCLOA

Argüelles and Moncloa, modest residential areas just beyond Madrid's touristy center, brim with inexpensive markets and cheap *cafeterías.* If you're still in need of crowds and coffee, hit up the chic terraces on **Paseo del Pintor Rosales** overlooking the eminently picnicable Parque del Oeste.

Subiendo al Sur, C.Ponciano, 5 (☎915 48 11 47; www.subiendoalsur.org). M: Noviciado. From the colorful Central American decor to the warm, friendly waitstaff to the knowledge that 100% of proceeds from your meal will go to support development projects in the global South, it's hard not to feel good eating at this fair-trade cafe and restaurant. Lunch *menú* €9.50. *Caña* €1. Open M 1:45-4:30pm, Tu-Sa 1:45-4:30pm and 9pm-midnight. Cash only. ❷

Cáscaras, C. Ventura Rodríguez, 7 (☎915 42 83 36; www.restaurantescascaras.com). M: Ventura Rodríguez. A sprawling restaurant and cafe with panoramic city shots on the walls and shelves crammed with all manner of books to match the intellectual table talk. Well-dressed 30-somethings fill up on *pinchos* (€2.40-3.90) and specialty vegetarian dishes (€8-9). Open M-F 7am-1am, Sa-Su 10am-2pm. AmEx/MC/V. ❷

Pimiento Verde, C. Quintana, 1 (☎915 41 21 40), on the corner of Princesita just north of Ventura Rodríguez. The tall ceiling and wooden tables hold a little Basque soul and a lot of Basque cooking. The flowers and farm implements on the wall give a rustic feeling, but the prices are urban enough. For starters, try the cod omelette (€9.90). Seafood plates €19-22. Open daily 1:30-5pm and 9pm-midnight. MC/V. ❺

SIGHTS

Two dynasties, a dictatorship, and a cultural rebirth have bequeathed Madrid a broad, diverse, and fantastic collection of parks, palaces, plazas, cathedrals, and art museums. While Madrid is small enough to walk in a day, its sights are enough to keep you for weeks. Soak it all in, strolling from Sol to Cibeles and Pl. Mayor to the Palacio Real.

For hard-core visitors with a checklist of destinations, the municipal tourist office's *Plano de Transportes*, also available in English under the name *Visiting the Downtown on Public Transport*, is indispensable for mapping monuments and public transport (find it online at www.madrid.org). In this chapter, sights are arranged by neighborhood. If you are trying to design a walking tour of the entire city, it is best to begin in El Centro, the nucleus of Madrid. A good few days of sightseeing might move from historic central Madrid to the cafes of Huertas, through the city's celebrated *paseos*, and onto the relaxing Parque del Gran Retiro.

EL CENTRO

El Centro, Madrid's central neighborhood, is densely packed with monuments and tourists. Its principal sights radiate from the **Puerta del Sol** (Gate of the Sun), ultimately dividing into two adjacent sections named for the families that financed their famous monuments: **Hapsburg Madrid** *(Madrid de los Austrias)*, full of old plazas, convents, and churches, and **Bourbon Madrid** *(Madrid de los Borbones)*, with its immense palace and sculpted gardens. The directions for most of the sights in Hapsburg Madrid are given from Puerta del Sol, and directions for sights in Bourbon Madrid originate in Ópera.

PUERTA DEL SOL

Named for the Gate of the Sun that stood here in the 1500s, Puerta del Sol bustles day and night with taxis, performers, vendors hawking "designer" watches, and locals-in-transit trying to evade luggage-laden tourists. A web of pedestrian-only streets originating at **Gran Vía** funnels a rush of consumers into Sol, where today the sun shines over department stores, restaurants, and the ever-present tourist throng snapping photos with **El oso y el madroño,** a bronze statue of the bear and strawberry tree from the city's heraldic coat of arms. The "*kilométro cero*" (kilometer 0) sign on the pavement is the beginning of the national road system and marks the symbolic center of Spain. On New Year's Eve, citizens meet here to gobble one grape per clock chime at midnight, ensuring good luck in each month of the coming year.

HAPSBURG MADRID

In the 16th century, Hapsburgs of the Austrian dynasty funded the construction of **Plaza Mayor** and the **Catedral de San Isidro.** After moving the seat of Castilla from Toledo to Madrid (then only a town of 20,000) in 1561, Felipe II and his descendants commissioned the court architects (including **Juan de Herrera,** the master behind El Escorial) to update many of Madrid's buildings, creating a distinctive set of churches and palaces with wide central patios and scrawny black towers—the "Madrid style."

PLAZA MAYOR. In 1620, Juan de Herrera and his team finished work on the Pl. Mayor, a grand public square built to replace the cluttered, dirty area around the old Plaza del Arrabal. The plaza was commissioned by Felipe III; his statue, installed in 1847, stands at its center. Its elegant arcades, spindly towers, and pleasant verandas are defining elements of the aforementioned "Madrid style." In the 17th century, nobles on horseback spent Sunday afternoons chasing bulls in the plaza; bold citizens joined the fun on foot. The tradition came to be known as a *corrida*, from the verb *correr* (to run), and lives on in Pamplona's annual running of the bulls (p. 316). The Renaissance-era Pl. Mayor saw bloody spectacles of another kind, as it played host to the Inquisition's grand *autos-da-fé* (trials, or "acts of faith") and resulting public executions. The contemporary

Pl. Mayor bustles with commercial activity throughout the day, but it is in the evening, when siesta-fortified *madrileños* resurface, tourists multiply, and cafe tables fill with lively patrons, that Pl. Mayor truly awakens. Live performances of flamenco and music are a common treat. During the annual **Fiesta de San Isidro** (p. 108), held the Friday before May 15 through the following Sunday, the plaza explodes with celebration and dancing in traditional dress. *(From Pta. del Sol, walk 2 blocks down C. Mayor and turn left on Pasadillo de Sancines. M: Sol.)*

CATEDRAL DE SAN ISIDRO. Though Isidro, patron saint of crops, farmers, and Madrid, was humble, his final resting place is anything but. The church was designed in the Jesuit Baroque style in the 17th century, before San Isidro's remains were disinterred and brought here in 1769 at Carlos II's command. The cathedral, restored after it was razed to the ground during the Civil War, reigned as Madrid's principal church from the late 19th century until the **Catedral de la Almudena** (p. 95) was consecrated in 1993. The church's nine gilded chapels are the main draw—the chapel dedicated to San Isidro, third on the right, is made of marble with gold leaf inlay, and has a cupola dwarfed by the grand one in the center. *(From Pta. del Sol, take C. Mayor to Pl. Mayor, cross the plaza, and exit onto C. de Toledo. Cathedral is at the intersection of C. Toledo and C. de la Colegiata. M: Latina. Open daily in summer 7:30am-1:30pm and 7-9pm; in winter 7:30am-1pm and 5:30-8:30pm. Free.)*

MONASTERIO DE LAS DESCALZAS REALES. In 1559 Juana of Austria, Felipe II's sister, converted the former royal palace into a convent; today it is home to Franciscan nuns who watch over Juana's tomb. Claudio Coello's magnificent 17th-century frescoes line the staircase. The **Salón de Tapices** contains 11 renowned tapestries along with Santa Úrsula's jewel-encrusted bones. The highlights of the tour are in the final rooms, which include a portrait of Carlos II (the final, most terribly inbred Hapsburg monarch), an allegorical Flemish painting of demons assaulting society, a dark portrait of San Francisco by **Zurbarán,** and **Titian's** *Tributo de la Moneda al César.* Lines are long in the summer; arrive early to buy tickets, and enjoy the mandatory tour (1hr.) in Spanish. *(Pl. de las Descalzas, between Pl. de Callao and Pta. del Sol. ☎914 54 88 00; www.patrimonionacional.es; M: Callao, Ópera, or Sol. Open Tu-Th and Sa 10:30am-12:30pm and 4-5:30pm, F 10:30am-12:30pm, Su 11am-1:30pm. €5, students and children 5-16 €2.50, seniors and under 5 free.*

CONVENTO DE LA ENCARNACIÓN. The reliquary housed in this monastery, designed by Juan Gómez de Mora, stands among Europe's finest. It holds more than 1500 saintly relics, including a vial of San Pantaleón's blood believed to liquefy every year on July 27, his feast day. According to legend, disaster will strike Madrid if it fails to do so. Rumor has it that the blood didn't transform just before the outbreak of the Civil War, but the Church insists that it did. The ceiling in the reliquary, covered in intricately patterned tessellating figures separated by gold veins, was done by **Vicente Carducho,** as was the ominous painting of the Last Supper. The building can only be seen on a mandatory tour (1hr.) in Spanish. *(Pl. de la Encarnación. M: Ópera. From the Metro stop, facing the Ópera building, bear diagonally right up C. Arrieta. ☎915 47 53 50; www.patrimonionacional.es. Open Tu-Th and Sa 10:30am-12:45pm and 4-5:45pm, F 10:30am-12:45pm, Su 11am-1:45pm. €3.60; students, under 18, and over 65 €2; under 5 free. Joint visit with the Convento de las Descalzas Reales €6/3.40. EU citizens free W.)*

ALONG THE RÍO MANZANARES. Madrid's notoriously puny "river" snakes its way around the city past the **Puerta de Toledo.** The triumphal arch was commissioned by Joseph Bonaparte to celebrate his brother Napoleon, but was completed in honor of Fernando VII, the "exterminator of the French usurpers." The Baroque **Puente de Toledo** makes up for the river's inadequacies. Sandstone carvings by Juan Ron on both sides of the bridge depict the

€4/3.50; under 18 and over 65 free. Additional charge for certain temporary exhibitions. Free Tu-Sa 6-8pm, Su 5-8pm.

One of Europe's finest centers for 12th- to 17th-century art, the Prado is Spain's most prestigious museum and home to the world's greatest collection of Spanish paintings. Following Carlos III's order for a museum of natural history and sciences, architect **Juan de Villanueva** began construction of the Neoclassical building in 1785. In 1819, Fernando VII transformed it into the royal painting archive; the museum's 7000 pieces are the result of hundreds of years of collecting by the houses of Hapsburg and Bourbon. The walls are filled with Spanish and foreign masterpieces, including a comprehensive selection from the Flemish and Venetian schools. The museum is excellently organized: the ground floor houses Spanish painting from the 12th through 16th centuries along with 15th- to 16th-century Flemish, German, and Italian works. The first floor contains Spanish art from the 17th to the 19th centuries, with the *"Siglo de Oro"* painters concentrated here, along with French and Italian art from the Neoclassical and Baroque eras. The small second floor houses works by Goya and his contemporaries. The sheer quantity of paintings means you'll have to be selective. The museum provides a free and indispensable guide upon entry which describes each numbered room and points out the locations of some of the institution's most celebrated paintings. Audio guides in English are available for the best €3.50 you've spent in this city, and the museum's guidebooks (€10-25) offer extensive art history and criticism.

DIEGO VELÁZQUEZ. The first floor houses Spanish, French, Dutch, and Italian works. The most notable is its collection of works by Diego Velázquez (1599-1660). Known for his unforgiving realism and innovative use of light, Velázquez was the court painter and majordomo to Felipe IV (there are six portraits of the foppish monarch, on horseback, hunting, and doing other frivolously regal things). Many of Velázquez's most famous paintings are here, including *Las hilanderas* (The Spinners), *El Dios Marte* (Mars), and *Portait of the Count-Duke of Olivares on Horseback.* The painter's *magnum opus* and perhaps the museum's most famous work is **Las Meninas** (The Maids of Honor). Ostensibly depicting Velázquez at work painting a portrait of the king and queen, the painting places the viewer in the position of these royal subjects, who in fact only appear as a blurred reflection in a small mirror at the rear of the painting. Felipe's daughter stands at the center of the canvas, attended by her retinue. The painting's novel use of perspective and complex ambient lighting are Velázquez hallmarks.

FRANCISCO DE GOYA. In 1785, Francisco de Goya y Lucientes (1746-1828) became the court portraitist. Despite his controversial depictions of the royal family, Goya was never expelled from court. (He didn't escape punishment completely, however, and was hauled before the Inquisition in 1815.) His painting evolved as profound political changes—the French Revolution, the Napoleonic wars, and the Spanish defeat—shook Spain and Europe. Goya consciously imitated the techniques of his national predecessors, including a depiction of himself in the shadows of a royal portrait, *La Familia de Carlos IV*, in a nod to Velázquez's *Las Meninas.* The stark *2 de Mayo* and *Fusilamientos de 3 de Mayo* depict the terrors of the 1808 Napoleonic invasion, and may be Goya's most recognized works, along with the expressionless woman in *La maja vestida* and *La maja desnuda*, thought to be Goya's mistress, the Duchess of Alba. The *Pinturas Negras (Black Paintings)* are the most evocative; they feature grotesques on dark, obscure canvases. Goya painted them at the end of his life, when he was deaf and alone. *Saturno devorando a su hijo (Saturn Devouring His Son)* stands out; Goya captures the crazed eyes of Saturn as he bites off the head of his son after a prophecy that one of his children would overthrow him. The blurry *Perro semihundido (Half-Sunken Dog)* is unsettling in its obscurity. The greatest concentration of Goya's works are displayed on the museum's second floor.

ITALIAN, FLEMISH, AND OTHER SPANISH ARTISTS. The first floor of the Prado displays many of **El Greco's** (Doménikos Theotokópoulos, 1541-1614) religious paintings. *La Trinidad (The Holy Trinity)* and *San Andrés y San Francisco (St. Andrew and St. Francis)* are characterized by El Greco's luminous colors, elongated figures, and mystical subjects. El Greco's paintings are joined by works from Spanish artists like **Bartolomé Murillo, José de Ribera,** and **Francisco Zurbarán.**

The collection of Italian works spread over the museum's first two floors is formidable. The ground floor is particularly impressive, with massive collections by **Tintoretto, Veronese,** and **Titian,** whose *Danäe and the Shower of Gold* is emblematic of mythological themes that were typical during the Renaissance. Several enormous canvases by **Raphael,** including *The Transfiguration of the Lord,* are also on the ground floor. Some minor **Botticellis** and a slew of imitations are also on display. Among the works by **Rubens,** *The Adoration of the Magi* and *The Three Graces* best show his grand style. *The Annunciation,* **Fra Angelico's** symbolic work with gilt halos and sunbeams and mesmerizing blues, is equally striking.

As a result of the Spanish Hapsburgs' control of the Netherlands, the Flemish holdings are also top-notch. Striking works like **Albrecht Dürer's** Adam and Eve diptych, **Peter Brueghel the Elder's** terrifying *The Triumph of Death,* and **Hieronymus Bosch's** moralistic triptych **The Garden of Earthly Delights,** are displayed on the museum's ground floor.

LA AMPLIACIÓN. The Prado's newest expansion—the biggest in the museum's 200-year history—opened at the end of 2007. Designed by **Rafael Moneo,** the new building houses the cloisters of the former monastery of Los Jerónimos and a 440-seat auditorium, in addition to space for temporary exhibitions, restorations, and storage.

MUSEO NACIONAL CENTRO DE ARTE REINA SOFÍA

Pl. Santa Isabel, 52. ☎917 74 10 00; www.museoreinasofia.es. M: Atocha. Open M and W-Sa 10am-9pm, Su 10am-2:30pm. €6; students €3; Sa after 2:30pm, Su, holidays, under 18, over 65 free.

This public collection of 20th-century art, housed in a renovated hospital, has burgeoned since Juan Carlos I declared the building a national museum in 1988 and named it for his wife. The building is a work of art in itself, with two futuristic-looking glass elevators ferrying visitors up and down the museum as they look north over the skyline. The museum's 10,000-piece collection is amazing by anyone's standards, with impressive holdings of paintings, sculptures, installation pieces, and film. The second and fourth floors are mazes of permanent exhibits charting the Spanish avant-garde and contemporary movements. If that's not for you, head straight to the second-floor galleries dedicated to **Juan Gris, Joan Miró,** and **Salvador Dalí,** which display Spain's vital contributions to the Surrealist movement. Miró's works show spare, colorful abstraction, visible in the *Mujer y pájaro* (Woman and Bird) series, highlighting his love of both. Dalí's paintings, like *El gran masturbador (The Great Masturbator),* portray the artist's Freudian nightmares and sexual fantasies. Another must-see is surrealist Spanish film director **Luis Buñuel's** groundbreaking *Le chien andalou (The Andalusian Dog),*a project undertaken with Dalí and infamous for its unsettling images.

Pablo Picasso's masterpiece, **Guernica,** is the highlight of the Reina Sofía's permanent collection and the centerpiece of its knockout Gallery 206. Now freed from its restrictive glass cover and long exile in New York, it depicts the Basque town that was bombed by Nazi and Nationalist air forces during the Spanish Civil War (p. 60). Commissioned to produce a piece large enough for the main wall in the Spanish Pavilion at the Paris World's Fair in August 1937 (which itself is recreated in another room within the Gallery 206 suite), Picasso began work on the painting on May 1st and completed the mammoth work in just over a month. In this huge, colorless work of contorted, agonized figures, Picasso denounced the Nazi-supported attack unconditionally. When, at the fair, one German minister asked Picasso, "You did this?" he replied, "No, you did." While many have attempted to explain the allegories at work, Picasso himself refused to acknowledge its symbolism; still, most critics insist that the screaming horse symbolizes war while the twisted bull represents Spain. The contortions of the figures and the painful sharp points created by tongues and nipples are offset by more optimistic symbols: the dove, for peace; the horseshoe, for luck; and the flower, for rebirth. Picasso stipulated that the painting was not to return to Spain as long as a Fascist government was in place, and loaned the canvas to the Museum of Modern Art in New York on the condition that it be repatriated when democracy was restored. In 1981, six years after Franco's death, *Guernica* was delivered to the Prado and housed in El Casón del Buen Retiro (p. 97). The subsequent move to the Reina Sofía sparked an international controversy—Picasso's other request was that the painting hang only in the Prado, among the works of masters like El Greco, Goya, and Velázquez.

MUSEO THYSSEN-BORNEMISZA

Paseo del Prado, 8, on the corner of Po. del Prado and C. Manuel González. M: Banco de España or Atocha. ☎913 69 01 51; www.museothyssen.org. Open Tu-Su 10am-7pm. Last entry 6:30pm. Permanent collection €6, students and seniors €4; temporary exhibitions €5/3.50; both €9/5; under 12 free. Audio guides €4.

Unlike the Prado and the Reina Sofía, the Thyssen-Bornemisza covers international art from many periods; exhibits range from 14th-century canvases to 20th-century sculptures, and its collection encompasses periods of art overlooked by the other two. The museum is housed in the 18th-century **Palacio de Villahermosa** and contains the former collection of the late Baron Heinrich Thyssen-Bornemisza. The Spanish state acquired his collection in 1993, and today the museum is the world's most extensive private showcase. In June 2004, a new wing was opened to house the collection of his wife, Baroness Carmen, whose taste, if not her collection, rivals her husband's. More manageable than the Prado or Reina Sofía, the museum's collection is hung chronologically from the second floor down.

The top floor of the baron's collection is dedicated to the **Old Masters,** with stars like Hans Holbein's austere *Portrait of Henry VIII* and El Greco's *Anunciación.* You can chart the changing attitudes and representations of the body, from Lucas Cranach's *The Nymph of the Spring* to Titian's *Saint Jerome in the Desert* to Anthony van Dyck's *Portrait of Jacques Le Roy.* The Thyssen-Bornemisza's **Baroque** collection, with pieces by Caravaggio, Ribera, and Claude Lorraine, rivals that of the Prado. The baroness' collection on the second floor is eclectic, featuring both the old Italian masters and Rodin sculptures and moving toward early Impressionism, with work by Winslow Homer and John Constable. The museum's finest collection is down a floor, encompassing renowned works of **Impressionism, Fauvism,** and early **avant-garde** that paved the way to modern art. The Impressionist and **Post-Impressionist** works in the

Baroness' collections explode with texture and color—look for paintings by Sisley, Renoir, Manet, Degas, Monet, Cézanne, and Matisse. Van Gogh's brushstrokes make their mark here, as do the island scenes of Gauguin. Edvard Munch's strange contortions and pre-Cubist Picasso are also featured on this floor.

The conclusion of the tour is the museum's 20th-century collection, which reflects a diversity of styles and philosophies. You can trace the deconstruction of figurative painting, starting with Picasso, Georges Braque, and Juan Gris, moving toward the sterility of Piet Mondrian and the Constructivists. A cluster of pieces by Magritte, Chagall, and Kandinsky follows, and American Abstract Expressionism has its place here too; Jackson Pollock, Mark Rothko, Morris Louis, and Willem de Kooning are all represented. Look for Georgia O'Keefe's desert flowers and Rothko's enigmatic *Green on Maroon.* German Expressionism also make a strong showing. The second-to-last room holds Lucien Freud's disturbing work and some early Pop Art, but doubling back to the exit brings a bit of optimism amid modernist abstraction, as Maxim Gorky's *Hugging* and Dalí's *Dream Caused by the Flight of a Bumblebee around a Pomegranate* point the way to the gift shop.

MALASAÑA AND CHUECA

Devoid of the numerous historic monuments and palaces that characterize most of Madrid, the labyrinthine streets of Malasaña and Chueca house countless undocumented "sights," from street performers and sex shops to some of Madrid's best fashion. Chueca in particular is great for people-watching and boutique shopping. By night, both districts bustle with Madrid's alternative and gay scene. Although the area between **Calle de Fuencarral** and **Calle de San Bernardo** plays host to Madrid's avant-garde—architecture and art galleries included—the streets and the people are the real draw. These streets are a funky, colorful, and relaxing break for travelers weary of crucifixes and brushstrokes—though there are, of course, some of those, too. Visitors looking for a taste of traditional culture can supplement a relaxed day of wandering with a visit to one of Madrid's most beautiful churches, the Iglesia de las Salesas Reales.

MADRID

CONVENTO DE LAS SALESAS REALES. Bourbon King Fernando VI commissioned this convent and church in 1758 at the request of his wife. The Baroque/Neoclassical complex, with a facade of angels made of Carrera marble, towers over a lush rose garden and tall European cypresses. Inside is the massive sepulcher of the king, who died before the church's completion. The soaring dome is frescoed with various biblical scenes, among them the image of the dove returning to Noah after the Flood. The uncrowded church offers a quiet retreat in which to contemplate its treasures. *(C. Bárbara de Braganza, 1. M: Colón. From Pl. Colón, go down Po. de Recoletos and take a right onto C. de Bárbara de Braganza. ☎913 19 48 11; www.parroquiadesantabarbara.es. Open M-F 9:30am-1pm and 5:30-8pm, Sa 9:30am-2pm and 5-9pm, Su 9:30am-2pm and 6-9pm. Closed to tourists during Mass. Free.)*

MUSEO DE HISTORIA (ANTIGUO MUNICIPAL). An intricate facade welcomes visitors to explore Madrid's history through its art. Exhibits feature paintings, prints, and photographs, all of which document the changes and consistencies of this dynamic city over the past four centuries. Highlights include lithographs of the 1837 revolution and paintings of chivalric festivities in the Pl. Mayor. The 3D model of the city is a lifesaver for the disoriented tourist. *(The museum is currently closed for renovations through at least early 2010, although a sampling of its holdings is on display at the Centro Cultural Conde Duque (p. 104). C. de Fuencarral, 78, right outside M: Tribunal. ☎917 01 18 63. Call for hours.)*

GRAN VÍA

Urban planners paved Gran Vía in 1910 to link C. Princesa with Pl. de Cibeles, creating a cosmopolitan center of life in the city. The controversial project required the demolition of more than 300 buildings, several churches included, and the diversion or destruction of some 50 streets. After Madrid gained wealth as a neutral supplier during WWI, the city funneled much of its earnings into making Gran Vía one of the world's great thoroughfares. In its heyday, Hemingway described it as a cross between Broadway and Fifth Avenue. Today the lights, traffic, and tourist excess are much closer to New York's Times Square than anything else, and while it lacks much of historical note, it's worth a look.

Sol's shopping streets converge at Gran Vía's highest elevation in **Plaza del Callao** (M: Callao). C. Postigo San Martín splits off southward, where you'll find the famed **Convento de las Descalzas Reales** (p. 94). Westward from Pl. de Callao, Gran Vía heads up toward **Plaza de España** (M: Pl. de España). Locals relax on the shady grass, but you're better off going to the bottom of the park and turning left toward the **Jardines de Sabatini,** or right to **El Templo de Debod** (p. 103). Next to Pl. de España are two of Madrid's tallest skyscrapers, the **Telefónica building** (1929) and the **Edificio de España** (1953). Lewis S. Weeks of the Chicago School of Design made the plan for the Telefónica building, the tallest concrete building at the time (81m), which supposedly was used as a lookout by Republican forces during the Civil War. The best perspective of Gran Vía is from its eastern end, where it intersects with C. Alcalá. Walking a little bit from Pl. de Cibeles toward Gran Vía affords a long view up the thoroughfare past the dome of the Metropolis building and the statue of Victory on top of it. This distance hides the noise and commercialism and lends a little of the grandeur that must have been the vision of its architects.

ARGÜELLES AND MONCLOA

Wide-open spaces, eccentric sites, and small, distinctive museums are the hallmarks of Argüelles and Moncloa—where else in Madrid are you going to see a full-blown Egyptian temple or get lost in the woods?

TEMPLO DE DEBOD. In the 1960s, massive flooding created by Egypt's Aswan High Dam construction project threatened to destroy the ancient temple complex at Abu Simbel. Fortunately, a team of Spanish archaeologists helped to rescue the temples, and in appeciation, the Egyptian government shipped the Templo de Debod to Madrid's Parque de la Montaña, where it was reconstructed stone-by-stone in 1968. Built by King Adijalamani of Meröe 2200 years ago to honor Isis and Ammon, the structure was elaborated by Egyptian monarchs and later, by the Roman emperors Augustus and Tiberius, reliefs of whom accompany Egyptian gods performing offerings. Step inside the temple to see millenia-old hieroglyphs and, upstairs, a small archeological exhibit. A walk through the original archways outside dramatically juxtaposes the desert edifice with urban Madrid. After you've had your fill of ancient Egypt, step behind the temple to visit the adjacent *mirador* (lookout point), which commands views of the city. Or, facing away from the temple toward the *mirador*, walk 5min. along the ridge to the right to a tranquil rose garden with hundreds of species from around the world; a yearly competition determines which rosebush will be added to the permanent collection. *(M: Pl. de España or Ventura Rodríguez. From Ventura Rodríguez, walk down C. Ventura Rodríguez to Parque de la Montaña; the temple is on the right. ☎913 66 74 15; www.munimadrid.es/templodebod. Guided tours available. Open Apr.-Sept. Tu-F 10am-2pm and 6-8pm, Sa-Su 10am-2pm; Oct.-Mar. Tu-F 9:45am-1:45pm and 4:15-6:15pm, Sa-Su 10am-2pm. Free. Rose garden open daily 10am-8pm. Free.)*

MUSEO DE AMÉRICA. This museum houses an impressive collection of artifacts from Native American cultures, extending from Alaska to the tip of South America. Most comprehensive are the treasures from pre-Columbian cultures the Spanish conquered, including plumed Amazon headdresses, Mayan funerary urns and sculptures, and the remarkable Mayan *Códice de Madrid*, one of the four extant Mayan heiroglyphic documents in the entire world and an invaluable source of information about daily life in pre-historic southern Mexico. Colonial accounts and artwork provide a glimpse into the conquistadors' perspectives on the peoples they encountered. Especially compelling are period paintings depicting interracial families and the various ethnic identities assigned to their offspring, which help form a picture of the colonial mindset. *(Av. de los Reyes Católicos, 6, next to the Faro de Moncloa. M: Moncloa. ☎915 49 26 41; www.museodeamerica.mcu.es. Open Tu-Sa 9:30am-3pm, Su 10am-3pm. €3; EU citizens €1.50; under 18, over 65, and students free. Free Sa after 2:30pm and all day Su.)*

ERMITA DE SAN ANTONIO DE LA FLORIDA. Slightly off the beaten path, the Ermita (hermitage) is Goya's final resting place, and over his tomb is an elaborate fresco painted by the artist himself. On June 13th, single *madrileñas* offer their faith (and blood) to San Antonio in exchange for his help in the husband-hunt. The women line the baptismal fount with 30 pins and then press their hands into them. The number of resulting pin-pricks represents how many *novios* (boyfriends) they'll have in the next year. *(M: Príncipe Pío. From the metro, go right onto Po. de la Florida and walk to the 1st traffic circle; the Ermita is on the right. ☎915 42 07 22; www.munimadrid.es/ermita. Open Tu-F 9:30am-8pm, Sa-Su 10am-2pm. Free.)*

MADRID

CENTRO CULTURAL CONDE DUQUE. One of Madrid's finest cultural centers, Conde Duque hosts traveling exhibitions and is home to the **Museo Municipal de Arte Contemporáneo,** with an excellent collection of post-1960 contemporary art by Spanish painters, sculptors, and graphic designers. *(C. del Conde Duque, 9. Museum ☎915 88 59 28; www.munimadrid.es/museoartecontemporaneo. From M: San Bernardo, walk 4 very short blocks down C. de San Bernardino and turn left onto C. del Conde Duque; from M: Ventura Rodríguez, walk 2 blocks down C. de Alberto Aguilera and turn left on C. del Conde Duque. Open Tu-Sa 10am-2pm and 6-9pm, Su 10:30am-2:30pm. Free.)*

MUSEO CERRALBO. This museum displays the collections of the Marqués de Cerralbo in all their ornate, eclectic, *fin-de-siècle* glory. Highlights include El Greco's *Ecstasy of St. Francis* in the chapel, collections of battle-scarred European and Japanese arms, a quaint green garden, and a golden ballroom capped by a ceiling fresco of tumbling revelers. *(C. Ventura Rodríguez, 17. M: Ventura Rodríguez or Pl. de España. ☎915 47 36 46; www.museocerralbo.mcu.es. Closed indefinitely for renovation; call ahead or check the website before visiting.)*

CASA DE CAMPO. A universe unto itself, Madrid's largest park offers shaded areas, running and biking trails, and long walks around the lake, where you can rent a kayak or rowboat (€4.55 for 45min.). One of Madrid's largest outdoor pools, open June-August, is in the corner of the park, next to M: Lago. The Casa de Campo is also home to an expensive amusement park, the **Parque de Atracciones.***(M: Batán or bus #33 or 65. From the Metro, turn right walk up the paved street away from the lake. ☎914 63 29 00; www.parquedeatracciones.es. Open daily, but hours vary; check the website. €10.40, with unlimited rides €28.60.)* The **Zoo/Aquarium** (5min. away) is a more exciting—if still overpriced—prospect that features a panda, a rare Barbary lion, gorillas, and a dolphin show. *(☎915 12 37 70; www.zoomadrid.com. Open daily, but with frequent schedule changes; check website for hours. €18.50, under 7 and over 65 €15, under 3 free.)* To get to the park, you can take the **Teleférico from Po. del Pintor Rosales;** if you take it one-way, you'll need to make a 45-minute trek to exit the park. *(☎915 41 11 18. Open from mid-Mar. to mid-*

Sept. daily, from mid-Sept. to mid-Mar. F-Sa noon-1:45pm and 4-9:30pm. One-way €3.50, round-trip €5.10) Alternatively, M: Lago, Batán, and Casa de Campo are all within the park. Because much of the park is unattended, you'll want to be careful on unpaved, isolated trails and stick to daytime visits.

SALAMANCA

Madrid's highest-end residential district, Salamanca offers a window into the lives of Spain's modern-day aristocracy. The area surrounding the **Po. de los Recoletos** and the **Po. de la Castellana** is home to a number of specialized museums. Those with an interest in culture of the more wearable sort will find themselves drawn eastward to the luxury boutiques lining **Calle de Serrano** and **Calle José Ortega y Gasset;** the window shopping and people watching of this area makes for a pleasant afternoon, even without an AmEx Platinum burning a hole in your pocket.

MUSEO SOROLLA. Across the Po. de la Castellana from Salamanca, the former residence of the Valencian painter **Joaquín Sorolla Bastida** (1863-1923) displays the work of late 19th-century painters. The collection also includes centuries of colorful Spanish ceramics. Sorolla's vibrant works, known for their complex depiction of light, include *Mis Hijos* and *La Siesta.* His three-part garden, with fountains and myrtle taken from the Alhambra, is as fantastic as his art. *(Po. General Martínez Campos, 37. From M: Iglesia, turn right on Po. General Martínez Campos; from M: Rubén Darío, turn right on C. Miguel Ángel and left on Po. General Martínez Campos. ☎913 10 15 84; museosorolla.mcu.es. Open Tu-Sa 9:30am-8pm, Su 10am-3pm. €3, Su free.)*

MUSEO DE CIENCAS NATURALES. Paleontology (the study of pre-historic life), malacology (the study of mollusks), herpetology (the study of amphibians)—if it ends in "-ology," it's probably represented in this grand old monument to the sciences. Beautiful minerals, stuffed animals, and dinosaur bones aplenty are sure to engage visitors of all ages. *(C. José Gutiérrez Abascal, 2. ☎914 11 13 28; www.mncn.csic.es. From M: Gregorio Marañón, walk 2 blocks north on Po. de la Castellana. Open Tu-F 10am-6pm, Sa 10am-3pm, Su 10am-2:30pm. €5, under 14 and students €3, under 4 free.)*

MUSEO LÁZARO GALDIANO. This small palace displays a private collection of Italian Renaissance bronzes and Celtic and Visigoth brasses. Paintings include *Young Christ*, a painting unofficially attributed to Leonardo da Vinci, and Hieronymus Bosch's *Ecce Homo*, along with the classic Spanish trifecta: El Greco, Velázquez, and Goya. *(C. Serrano, 122. M: Gregorio Marañón. Turn right off Po. de la Castellana onto C. María de Molina. ☎915 61 60 84; www.flg.es. Open M and W-Su 10am-4:30pm. €4, students €3. EU citizens free W.)*

JARDINES DEL DESCUBRIMIENTO. Less a garden than a large, sculpture-rich urban plaza filled with monuments to Columbus and the "discovery" of America, the Jardines are most notable for what's next door: Spain's regal **Biblioteca Nacional** (National Library), which frequently hosts cultural performances and temporary exhibitons on literary or historical topics, and the attached **Museo Arqueológico Nacional,** brimming with artifacts from throughout the history of the Western world, including everything from pre-historic pottery to medieval European timepieces. *(Paseo de Recoletos, 20-22. M: Colón. Library ☎918 83 24 02; www.bne.es. Check website for a schedule of exhibitions and their hours. Free. Museum ☎915 77 79 12; man.mcu.es. Open Tu-Sa 9:30am-8pm, Su 9:30am-3pm. The museum is currently undergoing renovation, but a sampling of its artifacts is on view during regular opening hours. Free.)*

OUTSIDE THE CITY CENTER

EL PARDO. Built as a hunting lodge for Enrique IV in the 15th century, El Pardo was enlarged by generations of Hapsburgs and Bourbons. The palace attained its present form when Carlos III's architect, **Francisco Sabatini,** redesigned the building to resemble the Royal House of Austria. Though Spain's growing capital eventually extended into the old hunting grounds and enveloped the country retreat, the Pardo remains one of the nation's most compelling palaces. In 1940, centuries after its heyday as a hunting lodge, El Pardo opened its doors to its most trigger-happy resident when Franco, who fancied himself Felipe II reincarnate, decided to make the palace his permanent residence, remaining there until his death in 1975. Though the house's master has changed, the palace is still the official reception site for foreign dignitaries. Renowned for its collection of vivid pastoral tapestries—several of which were designed by Goya—the palace also holds a Velázquez painting and Ribera's *Techo de los Hombres Ilustres (Ceiling of the Illustrious Men).* You can also see Franco's bathroom, private prayer room, and the bedroom cabinet in which he kept Santa Teresa's silver-encrusted arm. Entrance to the palace's *capilla* (chapel) and gardens is free; the nearby **Casita del Príncipe,** created by Juan de Villanueva of Museo del Prado fame, can be visited F-Su for an additional fee. *(Take bus #601 from the underground bus station adjacent to M: Moncloa; every 15min., €1.10. ☎913 76 15 00. Palace open Apr.-Sept. M-Sa 10:30am-5:45pm, Su 9:30am-1:30pm; Oct.-Mar. M-Sa 10:30am-4:45pm, Su 10am-1:30pm. Mandatory 45min. guided tour in Spanish; last tour leaves 45min. before closing. €4, over 65 and students with ID €2.30. Citizens of the EU and Spanish-speaking countries free W. Casita del Príncipe open F-Sa 10:30am-5:45pm, Su 9:30am-1:30pm; mandatory tours leave every hr., €3.40/1.70.)*

MADRID

ENTERTAINMENT

Madrid's entertainment scene is an eclectic and exhilarating mix of traditional and avant-garde, with classic flamenco and contemporary acid jazz, orchestral music and modern dance, García Lorca and experimental Spanish theater playing out simultaneously at venues across the city. Anyone interested in live entertainment should stop by the **Círculo de Bellas Artes,** C. Alcalá, 42 (☎913 60 54 00) at M: Sevilla or Banco de España. The six-floor building houses performance venues and art exhibits, and is also an organizing center for events throughout Madrid, with current information on virtually all performances happening in the city. The *Guía del Ocio* (€1, comes out every F) is an indispensable guide to all entertainment in the city.

MUSIC

In summer, Madrid sponsors free concerts, ranging from classical and jazz to *bolero* and salsa, at **Plaza Mayor, Lavapiés, Oriente,** and **Villa de París;** check the *Guía del Ocio* for the current schedule. The city is undergoing a live music explosion in all genres; cover tends to be cheap and the venues intimate. Flamenco *tablaos* have music every week; call ahead to see who's playing. Most theaters suspend regular performances in July and August, but many participate in **Veranos en la Villa,** hosting special summer events or productions.

Huertas is a quiet capital of jazz and swing, with Europe's best acts in every week. In the darkened streets south of Gran Vía, a small rock enclave has sprouted up. **Costello,** Caballero de Gracia, 10, has 3-5 rock concerts per week in the long, fairly soundproof basement concealed under its bar. (☎915 23 01 74; www.costelloclub.com. Cover €7-20, depending on the band. Call for showtimes.) **El Sol,** Jardines, 3, showcases rock, salsa, ska—whatever's on the marquee—about 4 times per week. (☎915 32 64 90; www.elsolmad.com. Cover typically €9, includes one drink. Open Tu-Sa midnight-5:30am.) Madrid's major performance venues are listed below.

Auditorio Nacional, C. Príncipe de Vergara, 146 (☎913 37 01 40; www.auditorionacional.mcu.es). M: Cruz del Rayo. Home to the National Orchestra and features Madrid's best classical music performances. Tickets €6-100. Box office open M 4-6pm, Tu-F 10am-5pm, Sa 11am-1pm.

Fundación Juan March, C. Castelló, 77 (☎914 34 42 40; www.march.es). M: Núñez de Balboa. Hosts summer activities like lectures (usually Tu and Th 7:30pm; free), poetry readings, and concerts. No events June-Sept. Call ahead for details.

Teatro Monumental, C. Atocha, 65 (☎915 81 72 11, tickets 91 581 72 08). M: Antón Martín. Reinforced concrete–a Spanish invention–was first used in its construction in the 1920s, so be prepared for unusual acoustics. Tickets €6.50-18. Box office open Tu-F 11am-2pm and Th 5-7pm; July open mornings only. No regular concerts from mid-Apr. to mid-Oct.

Teatro de la Zarzuela, C. Jovellanos, 4 (☎915 24 54 10; teatrodelazarzuela.mcu.es.) M: Sevilla or Banco de España. The city's base for opera and *zarzuela* (light opera native to Madrid). Built in 1856, it was modeled on Milan's La Scala. No performances from late July to Aug. Box office open from noon until showtime on days with shows, noon-6pm on days without.

Teatro Real, Pl. de Oriente (☎915 16 06 60; www.teatro-real.es.) M: Ópera. The grande dame of Madrid's performance venues, featuring the city's best ballet and opera. Tickets sold M-Sa 10am-8pm. 50min. tours of the grand space are also available M and W-F 10:30am-1pm, Sa-Su 11am-1:30pm. €5, seniors and students under 26 €3, under 7 free.

FLAMENCO

Flamenco in Madrid is tourist-oriented and expensive, but a few nightlife spots are authentic (see **Cardamomo,** p. 114).

Las Tablas, Pl. de España, 9 (☎915 42 05 20; www.lastablasmadrid.com). M: Pl. de España. On the corner of C. Bailén and Cuesta San Vicente. Lower prices than most other clubs (€24, including one drink). Shows M-Th and Sa at 10:30pm, F-Sa at 8 and 10pm. Funk and jazz shows on occasion after the flamenco's over.

Casa Patas, C. Cañizares, 10 (☎914 29 84 71; www.casapatas.com). M: Antón Martín. Runs quality shows M-Th at 10:30 pm, F-Sa at 9pm and midnight, and teaches weekly lessons in conjunction with the Fundación Conservatorio Flamenco. Reserve by phone or online. Cover M-Th €25, F-Sa €30.

Teatro Albéniz, C. la Paz, 11 (☎915 47 69 79; www.certamenflamenco.com). M: Sol. Hosts the *Certamen de Coreografía de Danza Española* (Choreography Competition; 3-4 days in June) with original music and extraordinary flamenco.

THEATER

Theaters are scattered throughout the city, with older ones in Huertas and newer venues for musicals around Callao. In July and August, Pl. Mayor, Lavapiés, and Villa de París frequently host outdoor performances. Tickets range from €3-30; student and senior discounts are often available. Theatergoers should consult magazines published by state-sponsored theaters, like *TeatroMADRID*, available at most theaters. Some principal theaters are **Teatro Español,** C. del Príncipe, 25, in Pl. de Santa Ana (☎913 60 14 80; M: Sol or Sevilla); **Teatro Infanta Isabel,** C. Barquillo, 24 (☎915 19 47 69 or 915 21 02 12; M: Banco de España); **Teatro Fernán Gómez,** Pl. de Colón, 4 (☎914 80 03 00; M: Serrano or Colón); and the superb **Teatro María Guerrero,** C. Tamayo y Baus, 4 (☎913 10 15 00; M: Colón or Banco de España). Tickets can be purchased at theater box offices or at ticket agencies. (**El Corte Inglés** ☎902 40 02 22; **FNAC** 91 595 62 00; **Crisol** 902 11 83 12; **TelEntrada** 902 10 12 12; **Entradas.com** 902 48 84 88.)

FÚTBOL

Fútbol (soccer) festivities start hours before matches begin as fans with headphones congregate in the streets, listening to pre-game commentary and discussing it with other die-hard fans. If either **Real Madrid** (in all white) or **Atlético de Madrid** (in red and white stripes) wins a match, count on streets clogged with honking cars. Real, named the greatest club of the 20th century by FIFA, lost the much sought **La Liga** title to arch-rival Barcelona in 2009, but fans take solace in their team's historic dominance, with a total of 31 championships since the 1950s. Suburban **Getafe** doesn't quite have the same support, but only a few years ago won promotion to La Primera Liga, joining the other two. Every Sunday and some Saturdays between September and June, one of these three teams plays at home. Real Madrid plays at **Estadio Santiago Bernabéu,** Av. Cochina Espina, 1. (☎914 57 11 12. M: Santiago Bernabéu.) In the summer, the club offers tours of the stadium. (☎902 29 17 09; www.realmadrid.com. Tours on non-game days, M-Sa 10am-7pm, Su 10:30am-6:30pm. €15, under 14 €10.) Atlético de Madrid plays at **Estadio Vicente Calderón,** Po. de la Virgen del Puerto, 67. (☎913 64 22 34; www.clubatleticodemadrid.com. M: Pirámides or Marqués de Vadillos.) Getafe plays at **Coliseum Alfonso Pérez,** Av. Teresa de Calcuta s/n. (☎916 95 97 71. M: Los Espartales.) Tickets for Real games sell out well in advance and will probably run €50-100; tickets for Atlético are a little cheaper, and lower still for Getafe.

BULLFIGHTS

Some call it animal torture, others tradition; either way, bullfighting remains one of Spain's most cherished traditions, and it is at its brightest (or its darkest) at the **Plaza de las Ventas,** C. Alcalá, 237, the most important bullfighting arena in the world since its opening in 1931. (☎913 56 22 00; www.las-ventas.com or www.taquillatoros.com. M: Ventas.) The ring plays host to the real professionals; you can also catch a summer *Novillada* (beginner) show, when a younger and less experienced bullfighter takes on smaller bulls. Seats costs €2-115, depending on their location in the *sol* (sun) or *sombra* (shade). The cheap seats are in the boiling sun, but despite the heat they afford an exceptional view of the action and are the best value. Wherever you sit, bring a cushion—the concrete is not comfortable.

Tickets are available, in person only, the Friday and Saturday before and Sunday of a bullfight. There are bullfights every Sunday from March to October and less frequently during the rest of the year. From early May to early June, the **Fiestas de San Isidro** in Pl. de las Ventas stages a daily *corrida* (bullfight) with top *toreros* and the fiercest bulls. Look for posters in bars and cafes for upcoming *corridas* (especially on C. Victoria, off C. San Jerónimo). **Plaza de Toros Palacio de Vistalegre** also hosts bullfights and cultural events. (☎914 22 07 80. M: Vista Alegre. Call for schedule and prices.) To watch amateurs, head to the **Escuela de Tauromaquia de Madrid,** a training school with its own *corridas* on Saturdays at 7:30pm. (At the Casa de Campo, Avda. de Portugal Lago. ☎914 70 19 90. Open M-F 10am-2pm. €7, children €3.50.)

FESTIVALS

The city bursts with dancing and processions during **Carnaval** in February, which culminates on Ash Wednesday with the beginning of Lent and the *Entierro de la Sardina* (Burial of the Sardine). The latter festival which commemorates the arrival of a shipload of rotting sardines to Madrid during the reign of Carlos

III, who ordered them promptly buried. Goya's painting of the season's feasts and festivals hangs in the Real Academia de Bellas Artes. In March, the city gets dramatic for the renowned **International Theater Festival.** The Comunidad de Madrid celebrates its struggle against the French invasion of 1808 during the **Fiestas del 2 de Mayo** with bullfights and concerts. Starting May 15, the week-long **Fiestas de San Isidro** honor Madrid's patron saint with concerts, parades, and Spain's best bullfights. In the last week of May is the small but wonderful **Fería de la Tapa,** when restaurants and chefs put out their best for Madrid with fantastically cheap, exquisite tapas and beer. In the last week of June or the first week of July, Madrid goes mad with **Orgullo Gay** (Gay Pride; www.orgullogay.org). Outrageous floats filled with drag queens, muscle boys, and rambunctious lesbians shut down traffic between El Retiro and Puerta del Sol on the festival's first Saturday. Free concerts in Pl. Chueca and bar crawls among the congested streets of Chueca are popular weekend activities. Throughout the summer, the city sponsors the **Veranos de la Villa** (www.esmadrid.com/veranosdelavilla). Musical and theatrical performances occur throughout the city, while movies play nightly at 10:30pm in Parque de la Bombilla, Av. de Valladolid. (M: Príncipe Pío; June 2-Sept. 3. Ticket office opens at 9:30pm. Movies €5; schedule online and at tourist office.) The **Festivales de Otoño** (Autumn Festivals; www.madrid.org/fo), from September to November, offer more refined music, theater, and film events. In November, an **International Jazz Festival** (www.esmadrid.com/festivaljazzmadrid) entices great musicians to Madrid. On New Year's Eve, **El Fin del Año,** crowds gather at Puerta del Sol to count down to the new year. The brochure *Madrid en Fiestas*, available at tourist offices, contains comprehensive details on Spain's festivals. The *Guía de Fiestas* details all the festivals for the year around the Comunidad de Madrid.

SHOPPING

For upscale shopping, throw on your oversized Gucci sunglasses and sashay down the swanky **Calle Serrano** and **Calle Velázquez** in the famous **Salamanca** district (near Pl. de Colón), where fine boutiques and specialty shops like Pedro del Hierro line the streets next to designer labels like Mango, Zara, and Armani. Most major department stores can be found between Puerta del Sol and Callao, with smaller clothing stores scattered along Gran Vía. **El Corte Inglés,** Spain's unavoidable all-in-one store, has over 10 locations throughout the city. (www.corteingles.es. Some convenient locations include: C. Preciados, 3. ☎913 79 80 00. M: Sol. C. Goya, 76. ☎914 32 93 00. M: Goya. C. Princesa, 56 ☎ 914 54 60 00. M: Argüelles. All open daily 10am-10pm. AmEx/MC/V.)

Countless funky boutiques in Chueca display hot clubwear, tight jeans, and sexy street clothes. **Mercado Fuencarral,** C. Fuencarral, 45, specializes in off-beat attire and is home to many tattoo and piercing parlors. (☎915 21 41 52; www.mdf.es. Open M-Sa 11am9pm.) Many boutiques close in August, when almost everyone flees to the coast. Non-EU residents can shop tax-free at major stores, as long as they remember to ask for their VAT return form and spend more than €100. (☎900 43 54 82 for more info. Don't forget to bring your passport.) The municipal tourist office has the *Rutas de Compras en Areas y Centros Comerciales de la Comunidad de Madrid*, a map with shopping routes, along with coupon books and shopping suggestions.

EL RASTRO (FLEA MARKET)

For hundreds of years, **El Rastro** has been Madrid's premier Sunday-morning tradition. Come 9am, the streets of La Latina fill with *madrileños* of all sorts drinking beer and perusing the absurdly broad assortment of goods. The market begins at Pl. Cascorro off C. Toledo and ends at the bottom of C. Ribera de Cortidores. Its streets are lined with vendors selling everything from zebra hides and jeans to children's toys and hardware. As crazy as the market seems, it actually adheres to a rough sort of thematic organization: the main street is a labyrinth of clothing, cheap jewelry, leather goods, incense, and sunglasses, branching out into side streets, each with its own repertoire of at least tangentially related vendors and wares. As you descend further into the market, the typical shoestands disappear and more eclectic stalls appear, selling all manner of goods: back-issues of pornographic comic books, tarnished old silver tea services, and out-of-print editions of *Mein Kampf*. Fantastic collections of old books and LPs are sold in Pl. del Campillo del Mundo at the bottom of C. Carlos Arnides. Whatever price you're thinking (or being offered), it can probably be bargained down to half that. The flea market is a pickpocket's paradise, so ditch your camera, bust out the money belt, and turn that backpack into a frontpack. Take a cue from the locals and always keep your hand on your bag while walking. (Open Su and holidays 9am-3pm.)

BOOKS

Books in English tend to be outrageously expensive in Spain. If you read Spanish, however, it's worthwhile to buy books here and ship or carry them home. **The Rastro,** Paseo del Duque Fernán Nuñez, at the bottom of El Retiro and just across the Paseo del Prado from the Reina Sofia Museum, and the many little shops in Huertas, are great places to find antique and more recent books on the cheap. **Casa del Libro** is a chain of Spanish bookstores with a wide offering of books in every genre; the large store at Gran Vía, 29 has a broad selection, including many English titles. (☎902 02 64 02; www.casadellibro.com. Open M-Sa 9:30am-9:30pm, Su 11am-9pm. Also at C. Fuencarral, 119, and C. Alcalá, 96.) **Altair,** C. Gaztambide, 31, is a comprehensive travel bookstore with some excellent travel guides and a knowledgeable staff. (M: Moncloa or Argüelles. ☎915 43 53 00; www.altair.es. Open M-F 10am-2pm and 4:30-8:30pm, Sa 10:30am-2:30pm. AmEx/MC/V.) The **Berkana Librería Gay y Lesbiana,** C. Hortaleza, 64, a gay and lesbian bookstore in the heart of Chueca, hands out free map of gay Madrid and is an excellent source of information about GLBT happenings in the city. (M: Chueca. ☎915 22 55 99. Open M-F 10am-9pm, Sa 11:30am-9pm, Su noon-2pm and 5-9pm.)

NIGHTLIFE

Indulging in Madrid's world-renowned, mind-melting nightlife, especially in the summer months, is not an optional part of your visit—it's required. This city does nightlife bigger and better, later and harder, with more bars, clubs, and discos than nearly anywhere else on earth. People hit the streets around 10 or 11 when music and liquor begin pouring out of bars and *cervecerías*, and revelers don't go to bed until they've "killed the night" and, usually, a good part of the following morning. Proud of their nocturnal offerings, *madrileños* will tell you with a straight face that they were bored in Paris or New York—how can a city be truly exciting if the traffic isn't as heavy at 2am on a Saturday as it is at 5pm on a Monday?

Madrid's neighborhoods assume strikingly different characters after the sun drops down. La Latina and Lavapiés draw a relaxed, local bar-hopping crowd; Huertas entices with smooth jazz and the city's finest mojitos; El Centro and Gran Vía fill with stylish clubbers off to the city's flashiest *discotecas;* Malasaña swings to a beat half grunge-alternative and half hipster; and Chueca attracts a predominantly gay and lesbian crowd. Yet despite these divergent scenes, *madrileños* are loath to keep to just one neighborhood; in this city, mixing it up is at least half the fun. A typical *madrileño*'s night might start in the tapas bars of Huertas, move on to one of Malasaña's scenester cafes, and bottom out at a wild disco in Chueca or El Centro. While bars open their doors around dinner, most clubs and *discotecas* don't start raging until at least 1 or 2am; *"los afters,"* semi-mythical clubs that continue partying past the legal hour of 6am, constantly change and require an ear to the ground.

Except for the (relatively) quiet nights of Monday and Tuesday, Madrid parties hard every night—even if you've got the energy, your wallet may find it hard to keep up. The *entrada* (cover) at clubs and *discotecas* can run as high as €25; fortunately it nearly always includes a drink. Men may be charged up to €3 more than women, who may not be charged at all. Venues often change prices depending on the night; Saturdays are the most expensive. Keep an eye out for *invitaciones* and *oferta* cards—in stores, restaurants, tourist publications, and on the street—that offer a free *chupito* (shot) or discount to lure you in the door.

Walking home alone is obviously not as safe as walking with company, but if you must walk solo, avoid unlit areas like El Retiro, Salamanca, and some of the seedier metro stops around Sol, La Latina, and Lavapiés. Check a bus map for the best **Búho** (p. 74) home from Pl. de Cibeles, or take a registered taxi (white with a red diagonal stripe on the door).

NIGHT READING. For info on the latest hotspots, scan Madrid's entertainment guides. The *Guía del Ocio,* available behind the counter of any news kiosk, should be your first purchase in Madrid (€1). Although it's in Spanish, alphabetical listings of clubs and restaurants are invaluable even to non-speakers. The *Guía* comes out on Fridays; buy the latest issue. For an English magazine with articles on new finds in and around the city, pick up *In Madrid,* free at tourist offices and many restaurants. For articles as well as listings, do what the cool *madrileños* do and check out *Salir Salir Madrid* (€2) at any kiosk. Gay travelers can pick up the free magazine *Shangay,* which lists activities and nightspots, or buy *Zero* magazine at any kiosk (€5).

EL CENTRO AND GRAN VÍA

Bass beats pound well into the early morning in the boisterous *discotecas* on the neon-lit side streets of Gran Vía and the northern stretches of El Centro. Subtlety has never been a strong suit of this area, and clubs here tend to be packed and wild. A mix of seedy tourists and locals can make the area around Gran Vía intimidating late at night, especially for those traveling solo. Keep your wits about you, and remember that cabs are always an option (€3-5 from Pl. Cibeles). For a calmer night, head to the tapas bars and *cañas* joints southwest of Pl. Mayor, near M: La Latina.

▣ **Cool,** C. Isabel la Católica, 6 (☎902 49 99 94). M: Santo Domingo. Madrid's aptly named club-of-the-moment draws a beautiful, fashionable crowd of gay and straight people with its crisp design and pounding house beats. Small lounge and dance floor upstairs overlook the main room below. Men dominate "Royal Club" Sa, Madrid's best gay night. Lines can be long and the bouncers particularly difficult, so dress well and be polite. Cover €12-18, includes 1 drink. Call ahead to add yourself to the list for discounted entry. Open Th and Su midnight-5:30am, F-Sa midnight-6am. AmEx/MC/V.

▣ **Reinabruja,** C. Jacometrezo, 6 (☎915 42 81 93). M: Callao. A sinuous, subterranean jungle of stenciled pillars and curving, color-changing illuminated honeycombed walls surrounding a bumping central dance floor packed with trendy 20- to 30-year-olds. Come ready and raring to dance to house music—there's practically nowhere to sit down. Wine €7. Mixed drinks €9. Cover €12, includes 1 drink. Open Th-Sa 11pm-6am. MC/V.

Costello Club, C. Caballero de Gracia, 10 (☎915 23 01 74). M: Gran Vía. Packed spot with alternative rock for Madrid's scenesters. Concerts on weekends and some weekday evenings; usually €6. Beer €3-4. Mixed drinks €6-8. Happy hour. M-Tu 6-8pm. Open M-Th and Su 6pm-3am, F-Sa 6pm-3:30am. MC/V.

Shangai Club, C. Costanilla de los Ángeles, 20 (☎915 42 81 93). Done up in sleek reds and blacks, with elaborate LED displays and blue neon accent lights, classy Shangai Club is a cross between 21st-century New York and 1930s-era Hong Kong. Older 20- and 30-somethings fill the circular dance floor or lounge at surrounding tables (reserve in advance). Wine €7. Mixed drinks €9. Cover €12, includes 1 drink. Open Th-Sa 11pm-5:30am. MC/V.

Ocho y Medio/Dark Hole, C. Mesonero Romanos, 13 (☎91 541 35 00; www.tripfamily.com). M: Callao or Gran Vía. On F nights, hipsters pile onto Ocho y Medio's simple basement dance floor for their late-night indie-pop fix; the line will probably be long, so come early. Sa is Dark Hole, a goth extravaganza; if you're not wearing black, expect more than a few stares. Also hosts frequent parties and special events; check the website for schedule. Drinks €4-8. Cover €12, includes 1 drink. Look for flyers that give free entry before 2am. Open F-Sa 1-6am. Cash only.

Museo Chicote, C. Gran Vía, 12 (☎915 32 67 37; www.museo-chicote.com). M: Gran Vía. Recline in green leather chairs amid glamorous black-and-white pictures of silver screen celebrities. Share mixed drinks with Madrid's chic socialites after 11pm. Beer €4-5. Famous mixed drinks €9. Open M-Sa 4pm-4am; arrive by 3am at the latest. AmEx/MC/V.

Joy Eslava, C. Arenal, 11 (☎913 66 54 39; www.joy-madrid.com). M: Sol. There are three things you can count on in life: death, taxes, and Joy Eslava, which has been open every single day for the last 28 years. Number 1 among study-abroad students and foreign travelers, who are drawn to its eclectic mix of music (they play everything) and its classy setting in a converted old theater. International night Th. Live flamenco Sa at 2 and 2:30am, house music Su. Drinks €10-11. Cover M-W €12, Th €15, F-Su €18; all include 1 drink. 18+; bring ID. Open M-Th and Su 11:30pm-5:30am, F-Sa 11:30pm-6am. AmEx/MC/V.

Larios Café, C. Silva, 4 (☎915 47 93 94). M: Santo Domingo. Renowned designer Tomás Alía won a prestigious award for his work at this cafe-club, and it's no surprise—the upper-level restaurant and lounge looks more like an art gallery than a bar, with undulating sculptures suspended like stalactites from the soaring ceiling and columns decked out in translucent glass bubbles. Patrons in their 20s, 30s, and 40s sip mojitos upstairs (€7), while a lively crowd dances to house and commercial music downstairs. Cover after 11pm €10, includes 1 drink. Kitchen open daily 9pm-2am (June-Sept. closed M and Su); *discoteca* open Th 11pm-5am, F-Sa 11pm-6am. MC/V.

De Las Letras Restaurante, C. Gran Vía, 11 (☎915 23 79 80; www.hoteldelasletras.com). M: Sevilla or Gran Vía. Situated right on the border between El Centro, Chueca, and Gran Vía, this beautiful terrace atop the hotel fills with an urbane, champagne-sipping crowd. The view from the top is good enough to offset the drink prices. Wine €3.20. Mixed drinks €12. Open M-W and Su 8am-midnight, Th-Sa 8am-2am. MC/V.

LA LATINA AND LAVAPIÉS

Away from the clubs of the *centro* are the unpretentious and lively bars of La Latina and Lavapiés, which feature trusty fonts of beer and tapas. A diverse and decidedly local crowd takes to the street in search of these two things, packing the sidewalks around **Plaza de la Paja** and **Calle Cava Baja** in La Latina and **Calle de Argumosa** is Lavapiés come nightfall.

La Cabra en el Tejado, C. Santa Ana, 31, just off C. Toledo. M: La Latina. A funky place, packed as local acts stand on rickety wooden tables and sing Spanish favorites. Mediterranean tapas offers a break from the usual fare (hummus and *tzatziki;* €3.50). Beer €2.50. Cheap glass of *rioja* €1.30. Check the posters outside for concerts. Open M-Th 6pm-midnight, F-Sa 6pm-2am, Su 1pm-midnight. Cash only.

Eucalipto, C. Argumosa, 4 (☎629 33 49 98). M: Lavapiés. This tropical-themed cafe-bar serves up a wide range of *zumos tropicales* (fresh juice; €2.60-3.50) and *batidos* (shakes; €3.50). Lively sidewalk seating. At night it fills past capacity as *madrileños* spike up the night with daiquiris and caipirinhas (€6). Open daily 5pm-2am. Cash only. ❶

Taberna Vinoçola Mentridana, C. San Eugenio, 9 (☎915 278 760). M: Antón Martín. 1 block off C. Atocha as you head towards Atocha. A popular local tapas bar by day, at night this place revs up with locals thirsty for a glass of one of the countless reds, whites, and rosés lining the walls (€1.50-5). Open M-Th and Su 1:30pm-1am, F-Sa 1:30pm-2am. Cash only.

Achuri, C. Argumosa, 21 (☎914 687 856). M: Lavapiés. An alternative crowd—mohawks and Marxists—pile in and spill out onto the sidewalk for alcohol and huge sandwiches at proletarian prices. *Caña* of beer €1.10, liter €4.70. Wine €1-2 per glass. *Bocadillos* €4. Open daily 1:30pm-1:30am. Cash only.

HUERTAS

Huertas' variety makes the neighborhood one of Madrid's top places to party. **Plaza de Santa Ana** and the long **Calle Huertas** brim with *terrazas*, hookah bars, dancey dives, and jazz cafes. Many discobars convert to clubs as the night unfolds, spinning house and techno on intimate dance floors. **Calle del Príncipe** is lined with smaller spots, in contrast to the pricey, thumping discotecas of **Calle de Atocha.** Many locals begin their nights in Huertas and end them in El Centro or Chueca. If you do, skip the standard-issue bars offering the same five mixed drinks in favor of some of the area's more original offerings.

Cuevas de Sésamo, C. del Príncipe, 7 (☎914 296 524). M: Antón Martín. "Descend into these caves like Dante!" (Antonio Machado) is one of the many colorful literary tidbits that welcome you to this smoky, underground gem. Charming, worn plush seats, live jazz from an unassuming upright piano (Tu-Su), and strong sangria (large pitcher €10, small pitcher €6) bring in Madrid's bohemian youth. Open daily 7pm-2am. Cash only.

Teatro Kapital, C. de Atocha, 125 (☎91 420 29 06). M: Atocha. 7 fl. of justly famed *discoteca* insanity. From hip hop to house, cinemas to karaoke, Kapital offers countless ways to lose yourself, your dignity, and your money in the madness. Special-effects insanity on the massive main dance floor (converted from an old theater) include digital projections and a giant nitrogen-spray cannon. For a change of pace, ascend up through the surrounding 4-story maze of balconies to the palm- and fountain-filled rooftop *terraza,* where you can relax with a hookah (€30) or a game of pool under the open sky. Drinks €11. Cover Th €15, F €18, Sa €22, all with 1 drink included; keep your eyes peeled for flyers that will get you a 2nd drink free. Open Th midnight-5:30am, F-Sa midnight-6am. AmEx/MC/V.

El Café de Schérezad, C. Santa Maria, 18 (☎ 913 694 140). M: Antón Martín. Young *madrileños* lie on plush cushions smoking hookah and relaxing to soothing Moroccan music. Delicious herbal teas come with fresh fruit and small pastries. Tea €3.50; hookah €7-10. Open daily 5pm-3am. Cash only.

Trocha, C. Huertas, 55 (☎914 297 861; www.trochabar.com). M: Antón Martín. Watch the barman squeeze the lemons and limes into your caipirinha (€6-7), the house specialty, as you sit back and take in the smooth jazz and art prints on the walls. The ultimate place to relax. Other drinks €4-7. Open daily 4:30pm-2:30am. Cash only.

Dos Gardenias, C. Santa María, 13. M: Antón Martín. A diverse crowd packs this intimate, book-filled bar to chat about assorted intelligent things as jazz plays in the background. A few cozy couches, but mostly standing room. Wine €6-7; popular caipirinhas €6. Open daily in summer 8pm-2am, in winter 10pm-2am. Cash only.

Viva Madrid, C. Manuel Fernández González, 7 (☎914 293 640), off C. Echegaray. M: Sol or Sevilla. *Madrileños* young and old have been carousing here since 1870. It is worth the little extra for the breeze and ambience of an outdoor table, but there's plenty of room around the energetic bar and in the calmer, elegantly tiled seating area upstairs. Beer €3-4. Mixed drinks €8. Open M-Th and Su 1pm-2am, F-Sa 1pm-2:30am. Cash only.

Cardamomo, C. de Echegaray, 15 (☎913 690 757; www.cardamomo.net). M: Sevilla. Flamenco and Latin music spin all night. Live music at midnight on W nights brings out a dancing crowd, while mobs cram in to see professional dancing on Tu and Th at midnight—come early for a good spot. Weekends tend to see more dancing than lounging. Admission to shows €10-15, otherwise no cover. Beer €3.50. Mixed drinks €7-10. Open M-Tu and Su 9pm-3am, F-Sa 9pm-3:30am. MC/V.

The Penthouse, Pl. Santa Ana, 16 (☎917 016 020; www.gerberbars.com). M: Antón Martín or Sol. Directly across the lively Pl. Santa Ana from the Teatro Español, the Penthouse is a swanky hangout for an impeccably dressed elite. Atop the trendy ME Madrid hotel, the bar overlooks the Plaza for an expansive view of the city and its insomniac nightlife. The line can be long every night of the week, and the seating is limited, so arrive early. Drinks €10-14. Sushi €21. Open daily 9pm-3am. MC/V.

CHUECA

Chueca is one of the most exuberant gay neighborhoods in all of Europe; **Plaza Chueca** is its dynamic social hub. While it's safe to assume that any bar or club in this neighborhood is lesbian- and gay-friendly, straight partiers shouldn't worry that they'll feel out of place; unlike some gay ghettos, this is a neghborhood that welcomes visitors of all sorts. Many *madrileños* begin their nights by barhopping here until 2 or 3am, when they hit the clubs near Sol and Gran Vía. M: Chueca.

Why Not?, C. de San Bartolomé, 7. M: Chueca. A super-hip, wood-paneled underground bunker playing Europop and salsa. Well-dressed patrons sip drinks under a domed ceiling and the gazes of black-and-white Hollywood stars of olden days. Beer €7. Mixed drinks €10-15. Cover €10 when crowded, includes 1 drink. Open daily M-Th and Su 9pm-3:30am, F-Sa 9pm-6am. MC/V.

Bar Nike, C. Augusto Figueroa, 22 (☎915 21 07 51). M: Chueca. A colorless *cafetería* where half of Chueca comes to drink before clubbing. Absolutely packed from wall to wall. Fight your way to the bar for an enormous, sticky *calimocho* (red wine and cola; €4.50). Beer €4.80. Sangria €5. Open daily noon-3am. Cash only.

El Clandestino, C. del Barquillo, 34 (☎915 21 55 63). M: Chueca. Laid-back crowd nurses drinks under diffuse red light, then heads into the caves and dark corners downstairs to nod and dance to the DJ's acid jazz, fusion, and funk selections. Wine €2.50; beer €4. Mixed drinks €6-8. Live music most Th-Sa at 11:30pm. Open M-Sa 5pm-3am. MC/V.

El Truco, C. de Gravina, 10 (☎915 32 89 21). M: Chueca. It's a miracle that dancers find room to move in this packed disco-bar. Marvel at the feat or jockey for your own wiggle room. The line can be long, but outdoor seating on Pl. Chueca helps those not looking to dance avoid the wait and the cover (F-Sa after midnight €4). Beer €4. Same owners also run the popular **Escape,** also on the plaza. Open M-Th and Su 5:30pm-3am, F-Sa 5:30pm-3:30am or later. AmEx/D/MC/V.

I'levn, Pl. Vasquez de Mella, 11 (☎918 24 13 10). M: Chueca. A bar designed by dictionary aesthetes. Blue neon, wire mesh, and rockes piled behind metal grating vie martyrdom of San Isidro and his family. The **Puente de Segovia,** which spans the river along C. Segovia, conceived by Juan de Herrera and constructed in the late 16th century, is the oldest bridge in Madrid. The city may soon have a river worthy of recreation; the Madrid Río construction project currently underway will dam the river to create a small, elongated body of water surrounded by a planned series of parks and gardens. *(To reach Puente de Toledo from Pta. del Sol, take C. Mayor through the Pl. Mayor and onto C. Toledo; follow C. Toledo to the bridge; approx. 20min. away. M: Puerta de Toledo or Ópera.)*

BOURBON MADRID

Weakened by plagues and political losses, the Hapsburg era in Spain ended with the death of Carlos II in 1700. Felipe V, the first of Spain's Bourbon monarchs, ascended to the throne in 1714 after the 12-year War of the Spanish Succession. Bankruptcy, economic stagnation, and disillusionment compelled Felipe V to embark on a crusade of urban renewal, and his successors pursued the same ends with astounding results. Today, their lavish palaces, churches, and parks are the most spectacular (and touristed) in Madrid.

PALACIO REAL. The Palacio Real overlooks the Río Manzanares at the western tip of central Madrid. Felipe V commissioned Giovanni Sachetti to replace the Alcázar, which burned down in 1734, with a palace that would dwarf all others. When Sachetti died mid-construction, Filippo Juvara took over, basing his new facade on rejected designs for the Louvre. Decorating the palace's more than 2000 rooms with a vast collection of porcelain, tapestries, furniture, and art took over a century. Today the palace is used by the royal couple only on official occasions, but it continues to stand as one of Europe's most grandiose residences and a testament to the cultural wealth of Spain.

The palace's most impressive rooms are decorated in the Rococo style. The **Salón del Trono** (Throne Room) contains the two magnificent Spanish thrones, each supported by a golden lion. The **Salón de Columnas** (Column Room) is decked out in tapestries and an enormous royal carpet. This room was the scene of the official integration of Spain into the E.U. in 1985. The **Salón de Gasparini,** site of the king's ceremonial dressing before the court, houses one of **Goya's** many portraits of Carlos IV. The stunning **Porcelain Room** is composed of a wooden frame entirely covered in porcelain designs of fat cherubim; the edges are executed to perfection, with no roughness or inconsistency. The **Real Oficina de Farmacia** (Royal Pharmacy) has crystal and china receptacles used to hold royal medicine. Also open to the public is the **Real Armería** (Armory), which houses a substantial collection of knights' armor posed atop fully decorated horses. The palace also hosts temporary exhibitions of artwork from its collection, and often displays one of its most impressive holdings: the only complete Stradivarius quintet in the world, a complete set of the finest stringed instruments ever made. *(From Pl. de Isabel II, head toward the Teatro Real. M: Ópera. ☎ 914 54 87 88. Open Apr.-Sept. M-Sa 9am-6pm, Su 9am-3pm; Oct.-Mar. M-Sa 9:30am-5pm, Su 9am-2pm. Arrive early to avoid lines. Changing of the guard Sept.-May 1st W of every month at noon. €8, with tour €10; students, seniors, and children ages 5-16 €3.50/6; under 5 free. EU citizens free W.)*

PLAZA DEL ORIENTE. Between the Palacio and the **Teatro Real** (p. 107), the beautiful Pl. del Oriente is home to well-tended topiary and statues of Spanish kings and princes, from old Ataulfo (died AD 415) onward. The centerpiece is the imposing Felipe IV on horseback, a tribute to the monarch who cemented the decline of the Hapsburg monarchy. *(M: Ópera.)*

CATEDRAL DE NUESTRA SEÑORA DE LA ALMUDENA. Begun in 1879 and inaugurated more than a century later in 1993, this cathedral's simple forms and abstracted stained glass windows stand in stark contrast to the cherub-filled frescoes and gilded marble of most major Spanish churches. Even today, the building remains controversial, as gray stone walls clash with the ceiling panels of brilliant colors and sharp geometric shapes that verge on Art Deco. *(C. Bailén, 10. Left of the Palacio Real on C. Bailén. M: Ópera. ☎915 422 200. Open daily Sept.-June 9am-8:30pm,; July-Aug. 10am-2pm and 5-9pm. Closed during mass. €1 donation requested. Call ☎807 220 022 for a telephonic guided tour of the church.)* The blindingly white **crypt** below is worth a visit, but make sure you aren't interrupting any nuptials—oddly enough, it's a popular wedding spot. *(C. Mayor, 92; enter from the side facing away from the Palacio. Open daily 10am-1pm and 5-8pm. €2)* Visitors can also take in a **museum** that details the construction of the church; admission includes a trip up into the cupola, which affords spectacular views of the Campo del Moro, the Palace, and the city below. *(Behind the church, on the side facing the Palacio. ☎915 592 894; www.archimadrid.es. Open M-Sa 10am-2:30pm. €4.)*

MUSEO DE LA REAL ACADEMÍA DE BELLAS ARTES DE SAN FERNANDO. In 1752, Fernando VI established a royal academy to train the country's most talented artists. **Goya,** who was an early member of the *Academía*, is well-represented with two of his self-portraits and his *Niños (Children)* series. From time to time the Prado will loan some of his notable works to the collection. The **Calcografía Real** (Royal Print and Drawing Collection) contains Goya's studio and organizes exhibitions, along with an extensive collection of his engravings, many of them disturbing wartime scenes of hunger and execution. Other artists on display include Luca Giordano, Rubens, Ribera, and Archimboldo, whose delightful *La Primavera (Spring)*, a portrait of Maximilian II made entirely of flowers, is on the first floor. The top floor holds Picasso sketches. *(C. Alcalá, 13. M: Sol or Sevilla. ☎915 24 08 64; www.rabasf.insde.org. Free tours in Spanish Tu and Th-F 11am; no tours in Aug. Open July-Aug. Tu-F 9am-5pm and 7pm-9pm, Sa 9am-5pm, Su 9am-2:30pm; Sept.-June Tu-Sa 9am-5pm, Su 9am-2:30pm. €3, students €1.50. W free. Top 2 fl. often closed; call ahead.)*

PARKS. The **Campo del Moro,** visible from the west side of the Palacio, is worthy of the King, better than the Retiro, and worth the short hike to the entrance. Well-groomed trails lead through lush deciduous groves with the odd palm tree thrown in for good measure. The central lawn offers an unbroken view up to the Palacio. The secluded gardens are full of rosebushes and benches, and hide a small lake. Don't be afraid to stray from the path to check out the statues overgrown with vines, or to get a better glimpse of the rare and ostentatious **peacocks** haughtily preening themselves in the shade. *(From the palace, turn left onto C. Bailén, left again down Cuesta de San Vicente, and at the bottom of the hill turn left onto C. Puerto. From M: Príncipe Pío, cross the plaza to the entrance on C. del Puerto. Open in summer M-Sa 10am-8pm, Su 9am-8pm; in winter M-Sa 10am-6pm, Su 9am-6pm; last entry 30min. before closing.)* Lovers canoodling, poets dreaming, and the homeless sleeping all share the wading pool and manicured hedges of the **Jardines de Sabatini,** to the right when facing the Palacio. The high garden walls are among the best places to catch the sunset. *(Open daily 9am-9pm.)*

HUERTAS

Huertas is bordered by C. de Alcalá to the north, C. de Atocha to the south, and Po. del Prado to the east. Off C. San Jerónimo, streets slope downward, outward, and eastward toward various points along Po. del Prado and Pl. Cánovas de Castillo. Plaza de Santa Ana and its *terrazas* are the center of this old literary neighborhood, once home to Cervantes, Lope de Vega, and Quevedo during its heyday in the Siglo de Oro (see **Literature,** p. 68). Huertas's sights, from authors' houses to famous cafes, reflect its artistic past. A stroll down the neighborhood's namesake street, impressed in bronze with quotations and trivia related to its authors, gives a taste of their writing and time in Huertas.

CASA DE LOPE DE VEGA. A prolific playwright and poet of Spain's Golden Age, Lope de Vega spent the last 25 years of his life writing plays in this house. None of the objects here belonged to him, but they are all period pieces collected using a catalogue he left behind. Lope de Vega and Miguel de Cervantes were bitter rivals, but thanks to city planners, Cervantes is still enjoying the last laugh—Lope de Vega's 17th-century home is now officially located on C. Cervantes. *(C. Cervantes, 11. With your back to Pl. de Santa Ana, turn left onto C. del Prado, right onto C. León, and left onto C. de Cervantes. ☎91 429 92 16. Open Tu-Su 10am-3pm. Free.)*

CÍRCULO DE BELLAS ARTES. A statue of Minerva, Greek goddess of the arts, presides over this palatial home for artistic and those who love to flaunt their patronage of it. The Círculo is the hub of Madrid's performing arts scene, organizing performances and shows around the city and sponsoring **Radio Círculo,** 100.4 FM. Their quarterly magazine, *Minerva*, is available at the entrance (€15). Many facilities are for *socios* (members) only, but several galleries host rotating exhibits and are open to the public. Exhibitions range from photography to video art to abstract sculpture. An attached cinema shows student and art film (€3-4). Pick up a free program at the front desk. The attached **Cafe del Cícrculo de Bellas Artes,** with its high frescoed ceilings, crystal chandeliers, and leaded glass, is the hangout-of-the-moment for the city's illuminati. *(C. Alcalá, 42. From Pl. de Santa Ana, go up C. del Príncipe, cross C. San Jerónimo to C. Sevilla, and turn right onto C. Alcalá. ☎913 60 54 00; www.circulobellasartes.com. Open Tu-F 5-9pm, Sa 11am-2pm and 5-9pm, Su 11am-2pm. €1. Cafe open daily 10am-1am.)*

RETIRO

With the construction of the 300-acre **Parque del Buen Retiro** in the 1630s, Felipe IV intended to transform the former hunting grounds into a personal retreat, *un buen retiro*. Today, "the lungs of Madrid" are a menagerie of art exhibits and magicians, balloon twisters and beer vendors, all attending to the thousands of tourists and locals who've come to shake off the sweat and dirt of the city. The Medieval monastic ruins and waterfalls in the northeast corner of the park share space with the spectacular **Palacio de Cristal** and **Estanque Grande,** along with a running track, a sports complex with tennis courts and soccer pitches, a rose garden featuring the famous Milton-inspired **Fuente del Ángel Caído,** and myriad smaller garden plots and plazas.

On weekends, the promenades fill with musicians, families, and young lovers; on summer nights (when only the north gate remains open), the lively bars and cafes scattered around the park come alive with conversation and clinking glasses. Try to avoid the park after dark if you're alone—a slew of shady characters retire here by night, and the Retiro isn't well-signposted, making navigation difficult even during daylight. The park is accessible from the Retiro Metro stop. There are four entrances from the south, west, and north: C. Alfonso XII, C. Alcalá, Pl. de la Independencia, and Av. Menéndez y Pelayo. *(Park open Oct.-May 6am-10pm.; Apr.-Sept. 6am-midnight. Guided tours every Sa; check in the info kiosk near the Estanque or in the Jardín del Recuerdo.)*

ESTANQUE GRANDE. Amateur rowers young and old haphazardly maneuver their boats around this artificial lake, replacing the gondolas that used to glide across it. The colonnaded mausoleum of Alfonso XII, featuring a marble statue of the horsebacked *"Pacificador"* (the Peacemaker), is a popular gathering place and a prime spot for people-watching. Paddle away lazy afternoons in a **rowboat** on the lake or take in puppet shows and street performers on shore. Most Sundays from 5pm to midnight, over 100 percussionists gather for an immense drum circle by the monument beside the Estanque; synchronistic rhythms and hash smoke fill the air. *(The Estanque can be reached by following Av. de Méjico from the park's Pl. de la Independencia entrance. Boats for up to 4 people €4.55 per 45min.)*

PALACIO DE VELÁZQUEZ. Built in 1883, this Ricardo Velázquez creation has billowing ceilings, marble floors, and tiles by Daniel Zuloaga. The palace exhibits frequently changing contemporary and experimental works in conjunction with the **Reina Sofía** (p. 100). *(From the Estanque, walk straight to Pl. de Honduras and turn left onto Po. Venezuela; the palace will be on your right. ☎915 73 62 45. Closed for renovation as of 2009; call ahead for hours. Free.)*

PALACIO DE CRISTAL. A second Velázquez creation built to exhibit flowers from the Philippines in 1887, this exquisite steel-and-glass structure hosts a variety of art shows and exhibits, with subjects ranging from Bugs Bunny to the vocal recognition of bird calls. The little pond out front, with its rowdy family of ducks, has a beautiful reflection of the dome. *(From Palacio de Velázquez, head out the main door until you reach the lake and the palace. ☎915 74 66 14. Open Apr.-Sept. M and W-Sa 11am-8pm, Su 11am-6pm; Oct.-Mar. M and W-Sa 10am-6pm, Su 10am-4pm. Free.)*

PUERTA DE ALCALÁ AND CASÓN DEL BUEN RETIRO. Bullets from the 1921 assassination of Prime Minister Eduardo Dato permanently scarred the eastern face of the **Puerta de Alcalá** (1778), outside El Retiro's Puerta de la Independencia. To the south, facing the park, sits the **Casón del Buen Retiro,** home to the the Prado's library and a beautiful ceiling by Luca Giordano. *(☎902 10 70 77. Library open M-F 9am-2:30pm. Ceiling can be viewed by tour only, Sa-Su at 11am and 12:30pm. Register in advance with the Prado's Education Department, located inside the main building's Jerónimos entrance.)*

REAL JARDÍN BOTÁNICO. Located just outside the Parque del Buen Retiro, this garden dates from the 18th-century reign of Carlos III and showcases over 30,000 species of plants. The greenery ranges from traditional roses to delicate Japanese bonsai to medicinal herbs from the farthest reaches of the Americas. Pavilions within the garden house tropical, subtropical, and desert plants, along with rotating art exhibits. Horticulture courses are periodically offered; call for details. A perfect escape for both those with horticultural interests and those who just like gorgeous gardens. *(Pl. de Murillo, 2, next to the Prado's southern facade. ☎914 20 30 17; www.rjb.csic.es. Open daily May-Aug. 10am-9pm; Sept. and Apr. 10am-8pm; Oct. and Mar. 10am-7pm; Nov.-Feb. 10am-6pm. €2, students €1, under 10 and over 65 free.)*

AVENIDA DEL ARTE

If Madrid were reduced to a moonscape with nothing left but its art, it would still be worth a visit. Considered to be among the world's best art galleries individually, the Museo del Prado, Museo de Thyssen-Bornemisza, and the Museo Nacional Centro de Arte Reina Sofía together form Madrid's unparalleled "Avenida del Arte," a top destination on any tourist itinerary. While the Prado overshadows its smaller sisters, their collections of modern and avant-garde art pick up where it leaves off. From Goya in the Prado and Rothko in the Thyssen-Bornemisza to Picasso in the Reina Sofía, Madrid's museums form one of the most comprehensive collections in the world. The **Paseo del Arte,** available for €14.40 at all three museums, includes admission tickets to each of the three; they can be used together or on different days.

MUSEO DEL PRADO

Po. del Prado at Pl. Cánovas del Castillo. M: Banco de España or Atocha. ☎902 10 70 77; www.museodelprado.es. Open Tu-Su 9am-8pm. €8, by phone or online €7; students with artsy definitions of food, music, and sound on the front window. Jazz piano lends old-world class; shows at noon on Su. Beer €3. Mixed drinks €8-10. *Veuve Cliquot* €55. Open daily 2pm-2am. MC/V over €10.

MALASAÑA

Malasaña gained international fame as the anarchistic ground zero for *la movida*, the counter-cultural explosion that followed the collapse of Francisco Franco's moralistic regime in the 1970s. A few grungy alt-rock havens from the era continue to thrive here, especially in the blocks immediately to the east of bustling **Pl. del Dos de Mayo.** Since the '90s, however, Malasaña has gone a long way toward gentrification, and today, the area's nightlife is better known for the quirky hipster bars and stylish cafes packing **Calle Espíritu Santo, Calle San Andrés,** and **Calle Manuela Malasaña** than for a willingness to challenge authority. The neighborhood can still be a bit rough around the edges, especially as it approaches Gran Vía; solo travelers in particular should exercise caution walking here at night. Check out the cafes listed on p. 92; many stay open late and double as informal bars.

Café-Botillería Manuela, C. de San Vicente Ferrer, 29 (☎915 31 70 37). M: Tribunal. Gleaming marble, mirrors, and antique brass fixtures fill this Old World Parisian cafe. Player piano stacked high with classic board games. Enjoy conversation over a glass of *rioja* (€2.50). Tapas €3-8. Mixed drinks €6. Live music last Sa of every month at 9:30pm. Open June-Aug. daily 6pm-2am; Sept.-May daily 4pm-2am. Cash only.

El Sitio de Malasaña, C. Manuela Malasaña, 7 (☎914 46 68 76). M: Bilbao. From the Gl. de Bilbao exit, walk just a few feet down C. Fuencarral before turning right on C. Manuela Malasaña. Green and red-orange walls breathe life into this simple cafe offering cheap wine (from €1.90 per glass), Irish coffee (€5) and a wide selection of mixed drinks (€7). Delicious *tostas* (€4.90) include brie with fruit-infused honey. Open Tu-F 6:30pm-2am, Sa 1pm-2:30am, Su 1pm-1am. MC/V.

ARGÜELLES

The only reason to leave Madrid's better nighttime areas for Moncloa is **Los Bajos,** a concrete megaplex of diminutive bars serving incredibly cheap *chupitos*. Argüelles is about cheap drinks, not pretty decor. Bars are usually only open Fridays and Saturdays and close around 2-3am. From M: Moncloa, align yourself with the center of the imposing Ejército del Aire building on C. de la Princesa and cross the street under the double archway. Walk one block up C. de Hilarion Eslava and turn left onto C. de Fernando el Católico. Los Bajos is a few blocks down on the left.

DAYTRIPS FROM MADRID

SAN LORENZO DE EL ESCORIAL ☎918

El Escorial—half monastery and half mausoleum—is the most popular daytrip from Madrid. Although Felipe II constructed El Escorial for himself and God, the complex, with its magnificent library, palaces, and works of art, seems made for tourists. Visits are popular during August's Fiestas de San Lorenzo, when parades line the streets and fireworks fill the sky, and on Romería a la Ermita de la Virgen de Gracia, the second Sunday in September, when folk dancing contests fill the forests. The whole town shuts down on Mondays.

MADRID

TRANSPORTATION AND PRACTICAL INFORMATION

El Escorial's train station (☎918 90 00 15), on Ctra. Estación, is 2km outside of town. **Trains** run to Atocha and Chamartín stations in Madrid (1hr.; 30 per day M-F and Su 5:47am-10:15pm, Sa 19 per day 5:47am-10:15pm; €2.90). Autocares Herranz **buses** (☎918 96 90 28) run from Madrid's Moncloa metro station (bus #661, in the bus interchange just above the metro platform; 50min.; every 10-30min. M-F 6:15am-10pm, Sa 8am-8pm, Su 8am-10pm; €3.20) and back (every 15min. M-F 7:15am-10pm, Sa 9am-9:30pm, Su 9am-11pm; €3.20). **Shuttles** go between the bus and train stations (M-F every 20min. 7:23am-10:38pm, Sa-Su every 20min.-1hr. 9:44am-10:38pm; €1.15).

The **tourist office** is located at C. Grimaldi, 4. (☎918 90 53 13; www.sanlorenzoturismo.org. Open Tu-F 11am-6pm, Sa-Su 10am-3pm.) With your back to the bus station, turn right down C. Juan de Toledo, then make a right onto C. Floridablanca. Follow C. Floridablanca until the first archway on the left. From the train station, take the shuttle to the bus station or exit the train station, walk straight ahead, and follow the signs uphill (25min.). For a more peaceful walk, exit the train station and enter the Casita del Príncipe entrance directly in front of you. Start walking uphill and take the C. de los Tilos path, which leads to the monastery (25min.). The **police** are at Pl. de la Constitución, 3 (☎918 90 52 23). Many 24hr. **ATMs** can also be found along this street.

SIGHTS

MADRID

EL ESCORIAL

☎918 90 59 03. Complex open Tu-Su Apr.-Sept. 10am-7pm; Oct.-Mar. 10am-6pm. Last entry to palaces, pantheons, and museums 30min. before closing. Complete visit 2hr. Guided tour €10. Spanish tours every 15min.; English times vary. Monastery €8, students and seniors €4. Admission to tombs and library €8/4. EU citizens free W.

MONASTERIO. "*El escoria*" translates roughly to "scum." Indeed, the regal Escorial sits atop a mound that was once a refuse heap of bones and dung. Ironically, the pile of leftovers includes royal bones dating back to Charles V. Felipe II built the Monasterio de San Lorenzo de el Escorial as a gift to God and his people, and perhaps to alleviate his conscience for sacking a French church at the battle of San Quintín in 1557. In 1563, he commissioned Juan Bautista de Toledo to design the monastery-mausoleum complex on the side of Mt. Abantos, but Toledo died just four years into the project and the job fell to his pupil Juan de Herrera. With the exception of the Panteón Real and minor additions, the monastery was completed in just 21 years. Felipe oversaw the work from a chair-shaped rock, the Silla de Felipe II, 7km away.

What distinguishes El Escorial from other huge royal palaces is its utter simplicity. Four towers surround the central basilica in a perfect rectangle. Its "*herreriano*" style focuses on straight lines in preference to decorative pattern, which the architect thought distracted from the unity of the whole. Felipe himself described it as "majesty without ostentation." Majesty indeed, the complex has 16 patios, 88 fountains, 1200 doors, and some 2700 windows, an incredible number for a building used only during religious festivals.

GALLERIES AND LIVING QUARTERS. To avoid the worst of the crowds, enter El Escorial through the gateway on C. Floridablanca, where you'll find a collection of Flemish art. Though much of the work is standard religious fare, keep an eye out for some exceptions. Bosch's famous "Garden of Earthly Delights" hangs in replica on a tapestry in the first room. In the next room is El Greco's "El Martirio de San Mauricio,", which was apparently hidden away on a wall in the sacristy because it failed to please his majesty. Other works by Dürer, Zurbarán, Tintoretto, and Ribera also grace the walls of the galleries. The newly opened **Museum of Architecture,** after the art galleries, has plaster models of El Escorial, early building plans, and enormous 16th-century construction machinery that shows how the huge blocks of stone were lifted.

Azulejo tiles from Toledo line the Palacio Real, which includes the **Salón del Trono** (Throne Room) and two dwellings: Felipe II's spartan 16th-century apartments and the more luxurious 18th-century rooms of Carlos III and Carlos IV. Felipe II's rooms were designed so he could listen to and see masses from his own bed. The **Puertas de Marguetería,** crafted by German artist Jacob Weisshaupt, are doors inlaid with 18 kinds of wood in masterfully intricate patterns. The **Sala de Batallas** (Battle Room) features frescoes by Italian artists Grabelo and Castello. Look closer for comic details of the everyday; bowmen share a laugh during battle as two peasants look on, passing a wineskin.

LIBRARY. The *biblioteca* on the second floor holds over 40,000 priceless folios and manuscripts. Though several fires have reduced the collection, the extant volumes—some bound as early as 1500—are in remarkably good condition; the bindings, made of scraped hide, can last for hundreds of years. St. Agustin's *De Baptismo*, placed between the 5th and 6th centuries, Alfonso X's *Cantigas de Santa María*, Santa Teresa's manuscripts and diary, the gold-scrolled *Aureus Codex* of 1039 by German Emperor Conrad III, and an 11th-century *Commentary on the Apocalypse* by Beato de Liébana provide just a sampling.

BASÍLICA. Under the gigantic central dome is the basilica, which for years was seen as a direct link between the kings and God. Up the stairs are gilded statues of the entire royal family, genuflecting before Jesus and the more earthly retinue of Popes, saints, and clergymen. Felipe II's room overlooks Titian's ceiling fresco of the martyrdom of San Lorenzo.

PANTHEONS. The impressive—and creepy—**Panteón Real** contains the remains of Spanish kings since Charles V (and a lone queen, Isabel II); their stacked green marble tombs lie in a circular room. The nearby **Panteón de los Infantes** was built to house the remains of royal children.

VALLE DE LOS CAÍDOS

The Valle de los Caídos is accessible only via El Escorial. Autocares Herranz runs Bus #660 to the monument from the Pl. de la Virgen de Gracia (☎ 918 90 41 25 or 96 90 28. 20min.; Tu-Su 3:15pm, returns 5:30pm; round-trip plus admission €8.30.) Abadía Benedictina de Santa Cruz del Valle de los Caídos (☎ 918 90 56 11 or 918 90 13 98; patrimonionacional.es) holds mass M-Sa 11am; Su 11am, 12:30, 1, and 5:30pm. Entrance gate open Tu-Su 10am-6pm. €5.30. EU citizens free W.

In a valley 8km north of **El Escorial,** General Franco forced Republican prisoners to build the overpowering monument of **Santa Cruz del Valle de los Caídos** (Holy Cross of the Valley of the Fallen) as a memorial to those who gave their lives in the Spanish Civil War. As a historical wonder, this site should not be missed—but it also should not be misunderstood. Although ostensibly a monument to both sides, the inscription over the door to the crypt that reads "Caídos por Díos y España" (Fallen for God and Spain) suggests it is more a Nationalist memorial than anything else. Construction of the massive granite cross claimed the lives of at least 14 forced laborers. To climb to the base of the cross, follow the paved road up to the trailhead just past the monastery on the right (30min.), or take the **funicular.** Apocalyptic tapestries line the vast, austere, cave-like **basilica,** where the ghost of Fascist architecture rests. Muscular warrior monks watch the pews, while gigantic death-angels guard the crucified Jesus. Forty thousand dead Nationalists and many unidentified other soldiers are buried behind the chapel walls; **José Antonio Primo de Rivera** (godfather of Spanish fascism and the **Falange** party) and General Franco himself rest beside the high altar, underneath the imposing cross with its giant statues. While the monument could be seen as a testament to the glory of Franco's dictatorship, for most Spaniards it persists as a stain on the central Spanish landscape.

CASTILLA LA MANCHA

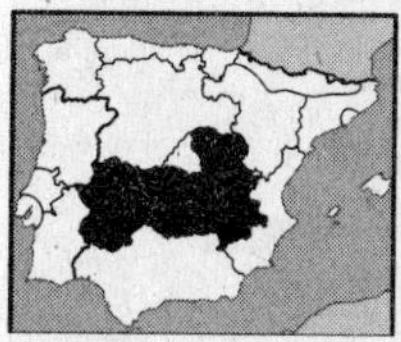

Castilla La Mancha is the Spanish Outback. Stark and barren compared to the rest of the country, these arid lands hardened New World conquistadors like Hernán Cortés and Francisco Pizarro and inspired some of Spain's greatest fictional characters, including the Man of La Mancha himself, Cervantes's Don Quixote. While much of Castilla La Mancha remains unexplored by tourists, Extremadura is undiscovered even by most Spaniards, despite the radiant beauty of its Roman ruins and traditional towns.

HIGHLIGHTS OF CASTILLA LA MANCHA AND EXTREMADURA

REMINISCE in **Toledo** about the days when everyone got along (see below).

EXPLORE the awe-inspiring cathedral in **Toledo** (p. 124).

CASTILLA LA MANCHA

Filled with sleepy medieval towns, cliffs, and—of course—windmills, Castilla La Mancha provokes the imagination with its solitary beauty. Drawing its name from the Arabic word *manza* (parched earth) and the Spanish *mancha* (stain), the province remains one of Spain's least-developed regions. Long ago, it was the epicenter of conflict between Christians and Muslims, and so became the domain of military orders modeled after crusading institutions like the Knights Templar, a society of powerful warrior-monks. In the 14th and 15th centuries, the region saw struggles between Castilla and Aragón before they were united in 1492 by the Reyes Católicos, Fernando and Isabel. Castilla La Mancha is Spain's largest wine-producing region, if not its best (Valdepeñas is a popular table wine), and the abundant olive groves and wild game influence local recipes, including Toledo's famed partridge dish. Stews, roast meats, and game are all *manchego* staples, as is *queso manchego*, Spain's beloved national cheese.

TOLEDO ☎925

Toledo (pop. 75,500), the pride of Castilla La Mancha, is, like any good medieval city, fraught with myth and legend. Cervantes called the hilltop town the "glory of Spain and light of her cities"; it is commonly called the "Ciudad de las Tres Culturas" (City of Three Cultures), at one time or another a flourishing capital of Muslims, Jews, and Christians. Locals will tell you the history has been a bit romanticized; still, with more monuments per cobblestone than almost any other city in the world, the hometown of El Greco holds a special mystique. With the Reconquista and the expulsion of the Jews and Muslims from Spain, the Christians reconsecrated the mosques and synagogues, creating the fusion of styles and faiths that makes Toledo so remarkable. On every twisting corner is a store selling Damascene swords (used on the set of *The Lord of the Rings*) or Toledo's famous marzipan, and you'll be lucky to get out of the city without having bought one or the other. In June, Toledo's movie-set-like facades come alive with costumed processions during the Corpus Cristi celebration.

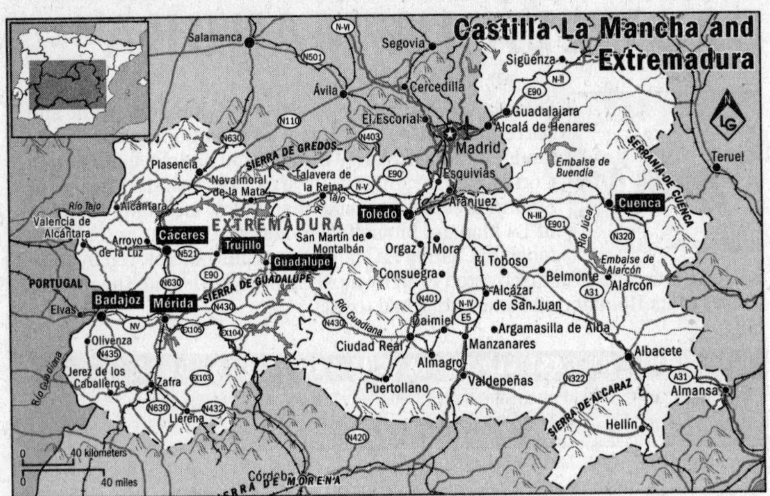

TRANSPORTATION

Trains: Po. de la Rosa, 2 (**RENFE** info ☎902 24 02 02), in an exquisite *neo-mudéjar* station just over Puente de Azarquiel. High speed AVE train to Atocha station in **Madrid.** (30min.; M-F 11 per day 6:55am-9:25pm, Sa-Su 9 per day 9:25am-9:25pm; €9)

Buses: Av. Castilla La Mancha (☎925 21 58 50), 10min. from Puerta de Bisagra. Open daily 7am-11pm. **Alsina Graells** (in Toledo ☎925 21 58 50, in Valencia 963 49 72 30) goes to **Valencia** (5hr., M-F 3pm, €25.05; buy ticket on board). **Continental Auto** (in Toledo ☎925 22 36 41, in Madrid 915 27 29 61) runs to Estación Sur in **Madrid** (1hr.; every 30min. M-F 6am-10:30pm, Sa 6:30am-10:30pm, Su 8am-11:30pm; €4.53).

Public Transportation: Buses 8.1 and 8.2 head from the bus station into the center of town. Buses 1-7 leave from Pl. de Zocodóver on various circular routes through town. Ask for routes at the tourist office. (€0.95, at night €1.25).

Taxis: Radio Taxi (☎925 22 70 70) and **Gruas de Toledo** (☎925 25 50 50).

Car Rental: Avis, in the train station (☎925 21 45 35). From €80 per day. 23+. Open M-F 9:30am-1:30pm and 4:30-7:30pm, Sa 9:30am-1pm.

ORIENTATION AND PRACTICAL INFORMATION

Consider yourself warned: the way in Toledo is uphill. To walk from the train station to the Plaza de Zocodóver (derived from the Arabic name for the market once held there, "Souk al Dawar") in the center, turn right and follow the left fork uphill to an incredible and ornate stone bridge, the Puente de Alcántara. Cross the bridge to the stone staircase; after climbing it, turn left and go up, veering right at C. Cervantes, which leads to Pl. de Zocodóver. The bus avoids the sidewalk-less uphill hike. To get to the Plaza from the bus station, exit via the cafeteria, head toward the traffic circle, and continue on the highway until you reach the bridge on your left. Then, turn right up the stone steps and continue up toward the city. A map is essential; the streets in Toledo fork deviously at every opportunity, and a wrong turn is just about inevitable.

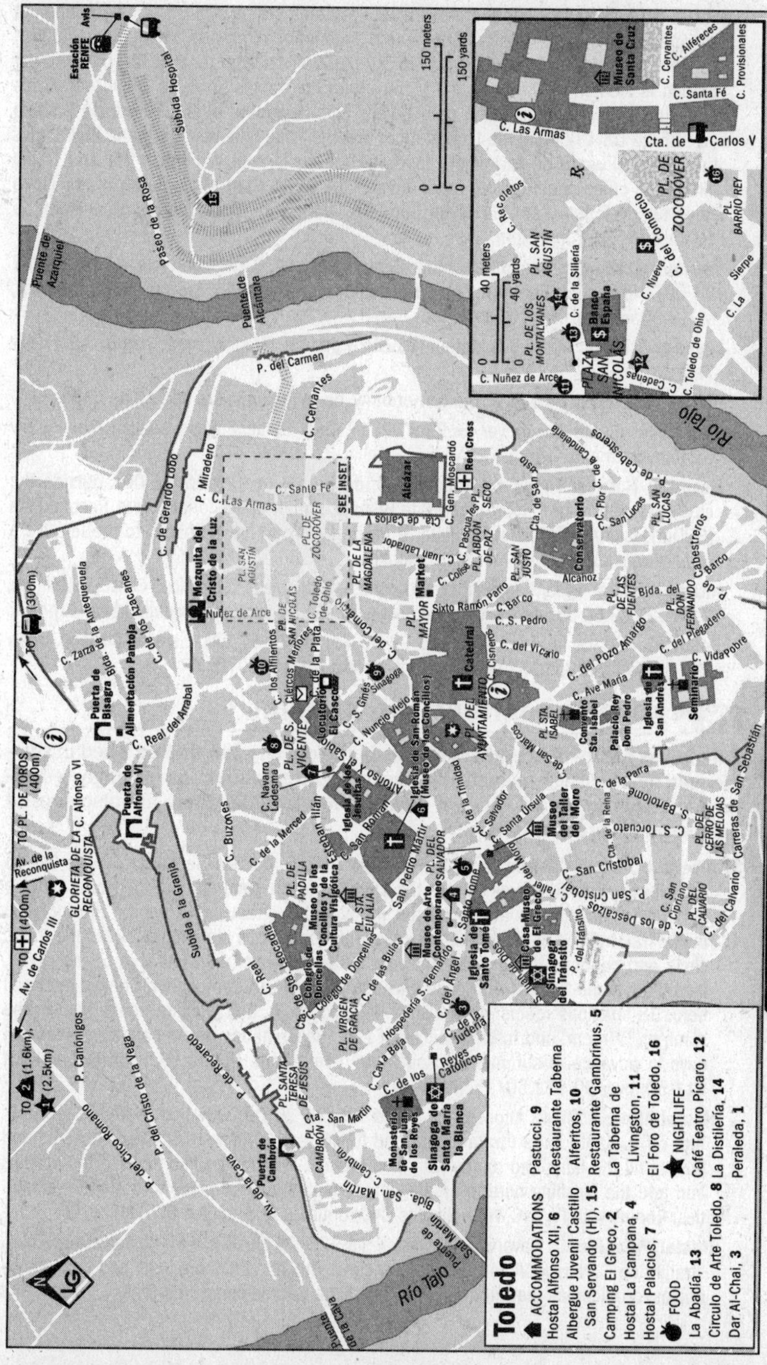
Toledo
ACCOMMODATIONS
Hostal Alfonso XII, 6
Albergue Juvenil Castillo San Servando (HI), 15
Camping El Greco, 2
Hostal La Campana, 4
Hostal Palacios, 7
FOOD
La Abadía, 13
Círculo de Arte Toledo, 8
Dar Al-Chai, 3
Pastucci, 9
Restaurante Taberna Alferitos, 10
Restaurante Gambrinus, 5
La Taberna de Livingston, 11
El Foro de Toledo, 16
NIGHTLIFE
Café Teatro Pícaro, 12
La Distilería, 14
Peraleda, 1
Río Tajo
Puente de Azarquiel
Puente de Alcántara
Estación RENFE
Avis
Alcázar
Red Cross
SEE INSET
Catedral
Market
Mezquita del Cristo de la Luz
Puerta de Bisagra
Puerta de Alfonso VI
Puerta de Cambrón
Alimentación Pantoja
Locutorio El Casco
Iglesia de los Jesuitas
Iglesia de San Román (Museo de los Concilios)
Museo de los Concilios y de la Cultura Visigótica
Colegio de Doncellas
Museo de Arte Contemporaneo
Iglesia de Santo Tomé
Casa Museo de El Greco
Sinagoga del Tránsito
Museo del Taller del Moro
Monasterio de San Juan de los Reyes
Sinagoga de Santa María la Blanca
Conservatorio
Convento Sta. Isabel
Palacio Rey Dom Pedro
Iglesia de San Andrés
Seminario
Museo de Santa Cruz
Banco España
PL. DE ZOCODOVER
150 meters
150 yards
40 meters
40 yards

Tourist Office: The **municipal** office, Pl. del Ayuntamiento (☎925 25 40 30) hands out indispensable maps and information about accommodations and eating. Some English spoken. Open M 10:30am-2:30pm, Tu-Su 10:30am-2:30pm and 4:30-7pm. Another branch is located at the Casa del Mapa under the arches in Pl. de Zocodóver. Maps and similar information. Open daily 11am-7pm. **Regional** office, Puerta de Bisagra (☎925 22 08 43). From the train station, turn right and take the right-hand fork across the bridge (Puente de Azarquiel), following the walls until you reach the 2nd traffic circle; the office is across the road, outside the walls. Staff offers handy maps. Open July-Sept. M-F 9am-7pm, Sa 10am-6pm, Su 10am-2pm; Oct.-June M-F 9am-6pm, Sa 10am-6pm, Su 10am-2pm.

Currency Exchange: Banco Santander Central Hispano, C. del Comercio, 47 (☎925 22 98 00). No commission and 24hr. **ATM.** Open Apr.-Sept. M-F 8:30am-2pm; Oct.-Mar. M-F 8:30am-2pm, Sa 8:30am-1pm.

Luggage Storage: At the bus station (€1.80/3 per day for small/large bags). Open daily 7am-11pm.

Police: (☎925 25 04 12). At the corner of Av. de la Reconquista and Av. de Carlos III.

Pharmacy: Pl. de Zocodóver (☎925 22 17 68). Some English spoken Open daily 9:30am-2pm and 5-8pm. MC/V.

Hospital: Hospital Virgen de la Salud, Av. de Barber (☎925 26 92 00), outside the city walls. With your back to Puerta de Bisagra, go left until Glorieta de la Reconquista (300m). Take Av. de la Reconquista to Pl. de Colón; Av. de Barber is to the left. It's a 10min walk up the road. No English spoken.

Internet Access: Options are limited, but access is available at Locutorio El Casco, C. La Plata, 2, (☎925 22 61 65), across from the post office. €1.50 per hr. Open daily 11am-11pm.

Post Office: C. de la Plata, 1 (☎925 22 36 11; fax 21 57 64). Lista de Correos. Open M-F 8:30am-8:30pm, Sa 9:30am-2pm. **Postal Code:** 45070.

ACCOMMODATIONS AND CAMPING

Toledo has plenty of accommodations in the old city, but finding a bed in summer can be a hassle, especially on weekends. Reservations are strongly recommended; try the tourist office if you run into trouble. There are also several campgrounds around Toledo.

Albergue Juvenil Castillo de San Servando (HI), C. de San Servando (☎925 22 45 54; albergueschm@jccm.es). Cross the street from the train station, then turn right up Subida del Hospital. Continue up the windy, uphill street past Hospital Provincial to the *hostal,* housed in a 14th-century castle. From the bus station, go toward the traffic circle and continue uphill; cross the footbridge to the left and head up to the castle. Incredible stone fortress that once gave refuge to El Cid Campeador, Spain's medieval hero. 38 spacious rooms, each with 2-4 bunks, bath, and wooden floors. Pool in the summer, TV room, and internet access €1/hr. Reservations recommended at least 15 days in advance in summer. Lockout from 11am-2pm. Dorms €9.50, with breakfast €11.50; over 30 €12.50/15. MC/V. ❶

Hostal Alfonso XII, C. Alfonso XII, 18 (☎925 25 25 09; www.hostal-alfonso12.com). Turn off C. Santo Tomé up Campana and follow it to C. Alfonso XII. Scented herbs and flowers fill the halls and rooms with nice aromas. Wooden beams traverse the ceilings and add the finishing note to an elegant, deceptively rustic place with modern amenities. Rooms with TV, A/C, WiFi. Singles €40; doubles €55; triples €70. MC/V. ❹

Hostal Palacios, C. Navarro Ledesma, 4 (☎925 28 00 83; www.hostalpalacios.net), straight up C. Nuncio Viejo from the cathedral. This hotel has big beds and long, glass-enclosed balconies that fill the rooms with light. Rooms come with TV, A/C, phone, and

WiFi. Singles €30, with breakfast/lunch/dinner at adjoining restaurant €32/40/45; doubles €50/54/65/80. AmEx/MC/V. ❸

Hostal La Campana, C. de la Campana, 10-12 (☎925 22 16 59 or 925 22 16 62; www.hostalcampana.com). The small, soft beds and wooden furniture feel like a country cottage, but for the balcony overlooking the narrow street. Great location—monuments at the doorstep. Rooms have bath, TV, phone, A/C, and Wi-Fi. Breakfast included. Reserve well in advance.Singles €36; doubles €60. MC/V. ❹

Camping El Greco, Ctra. CM-4000 km 0.7 (☎925 22 00 90; www.campingelgreco.es.vg), 1.5km from town. Take bus #7 from Pl. de Zocodóver. Clean, shady site between the Río Tajo and an olive grove. Restaurant, bar, supermarket, and pool. €5.94 per person, per tent, and per car. Pool €3.50. IVA not included. MC/V. ❶

FOOD

Many restaurants are a bit steep, but if you know where to look, reasonable eats are available. For those in a crunch, cheap *cafeterías* and the occasional kebab joint can be found in the streets snaking off Pl. de Zocodóver. Pastelería windows on every corner in Toledo beckon with *mazapán* (marzipan) of every shape and size, from colorful nuggets to half-moon cookies. For a wide array, stop by the market in Pl. Mayor, behind the cathedral. (Open M-Sa 9am-8pm.)

La Abadía, Pl. de San Nicolás, 3 (☎925 25 11 40; www.abadiatoledo.com). From Pl. de Zocodóver, bear left when C. de la Sillería splits; Pl. de San Nicolás is to the right. Dine on tapas (€3.25) or the delicious lunch *menú* (€11) in a maze of cave-like underground rooms. Excellent selection of German and American beers on tap (€2-2.50). Combo tapas plates €5-10. Open daily 8am-midnight. AmEx/MC/V. ❷

Restaurante Gambrinus, C. Santo Tomé, 10 (☎925 21 44 40). The shadiest outdoor seating in the old city is perfect for people-watching as you slowly conquer a hearty traditional Spanish plate. Has big soups (€6) as well as the whole partridge (€19.80) for the hungry. Meat dishes €10-11. Open daily 11am-4pm and 8pm-midnight. MC/V. ❸

Pastucci, C. Sinagoga, 10 (☎925 25 77 42; www.aplinet.com/pastucci). From Pl. de Zocodóver take C. del Comercio; turn right below the underpass just past the Rodier store. Pizza joint produces stunning array of gourmet hand-made pizzas. Pastas €5.60-7.50. Small pizzas €6.50-9.50. Open Tu-Su noon-4pm and 8pm-midnight. MC/V. ❷

Restaurante Taberna Alferitos, 24. C. Alferitos, 24 (☎902 10 65 77; www.alferitos24.com). Modern white decor meets old Toledo stone. Ground floor is a popular tapas stop (€5-8), while the levels above seat a dining crowd. Glass-roofed top floor. Woks €10-11. Entrees €12-15. Taberna *menú* €10.Open daily 8pm-midnight. AmEx/MC/V. ❸

El Foro de Toledo, Pl. de Zocodóver, 8 (☎925 28 95 55). Right in the middle of the action. Pay the extra €1 per plate to eat on red plush chairs outside, among tourists and guitar-strummers. Sells marzipan (bulk 250g pieces €7.80) for a sweet dessert. *Platos combinados* €4-7. *Bocadillos* €4-6. Open daily noon-midnight. AmEx/MC/V. ❶

La Taberna de Livingston, C. Alferitos, 4. Take C. Sillería from Pl. de Zocodóver and keep walking straight. Colonialism gone way overboard. Zebra-print stools and walls crammed with black and white pictures of big game and various native peoples set the mood, along with posters from British boys' schools. Look for the fake skull in the floor. Despite the aggressive decor, serves up regular *raciones* (€9-12) like meat *croquetas* (€9)—no rhino meat here. Mixed drinks €5. Open M-Th and Su 10am-2pm and 8-11pm, F-Sa 10am-2pm and 8pm-1:30am. Cash only. ❷

CAFES

Dar Al-Chai, Pl. de Barrio Nuevo, 6 (☎925 22 56 25; www.daralchai.com). Moorish arches straight from Alhambra and hilarious, squat little stools crowd this hip, busy tea joint, a favorite with local students. The crepes (€2.80-3.40) are sweet, fruity, and gigantic. Tea €2.30 per person or €10 for 6 people. Open M-Th and Su 9:30am-10pm, F-Sa 4pm-1am. MC/V. ❷

Circulo de Arte Toledo, Pl. de San Vicente, 2 (☎925 21 43 29; www.circuloartetoledo.org). A local university and hipster cafe that hosts regular concerts, exhibits, dance recitals, and theater. Gorgeously set in a 12th century *mudéjar* temple, the stage sits under a massive Moorish arch. Full bar. Tapas €5 and breakfast €1.90-2.30. Open daily,; hours and food availability change according to performance schedule. ❷

SIGHTS

Toledo is bursting with old churches, mosques, museums, and synagogues, all of which demand a visit and adequate time. Toledo's attractions wrap around its middle within the fortified 7th-century walls. An east-west tour beginning in Pl. de Zocodóver is largely downhill. Many sights are closed on Mondays.

CATEDRAL. Built between 1226 and 1498, Toledo's cathedral flaunts its architectural and artistic riches, coming from multiple periods and styles, with Gothic, Renassiance, and Baroque ornament all vying for attention. The cathedral consists of 5 naves, built around a central altarpiece and an adjacent courtyard, with chapels clustering around the sides. The **Capilla de San Ildefonso,** dedicated to Toledo's patron saint, portrays a scene replicated in various media all over town, of the Virgin descending to impose on Ildefonso a chasuble, the garment of a Catholic priest. Behind it is **Capilla de la Descensión,** which has a small red jasper box containing the stone the Virgin is rumored to have tread on when she descended. The newly restored **Capilla de San Blas,** beyond the courtyard, boasts bright, intricate designs. The treasury flaunts a 400 lb. 16th-century gold monstrosity that gets lugged through the streets during the annual Corpus Cristi procession on June 10th. The priestly vestments are hardly the main attraction in la Sacristía, which is practically a small art museum in itself. 18 of El Greco's portraits of the saints, along with works by Rafael, Titian, Caravaggio, Rubens, Goya, and Velásquez (to name a few) adorn the walls. *(☎925 22 22 41. Entrance down C. Chapinería. Open M-Sa 10am-6:30pm, Su 2-6:30pm. Audio tour in English, French, and Italian; €7, students €6. Tickets sold at the store opposite the entrance. Modest dress required.)*

EL GRECO SIGHTS. Greek painter Doménikos Theotokópoulos, better known as El Greco, spent most of his life in Toledo. Many works are displayed throughout town, but the majority of his masterpieces have been carted off to the Prado and other big-name museums. The best place to start is the **Casa Museo de El Greco,** the master's former home, which contains 19 of his paintings, among them glowing portraits of a sad-eyed Christ and a San Bartolomé who is poised to kill a *diablito* with a large knife. *(C. Samuel Leví, 2. ☎925 22 44 05. Open in summer Tu-Sa 10am-2pm and 4-9pm, Su 10am-2pm; in winter Tu-Sa 10am-2pm and 4-6pm, Su 10am-2pm. €2.40; students, under 18, and over 65 free. Sa-Su afternoons free. Closed due to renovation; call ahead to see if open.)* Up the hill and to the right is the **Iglesia de Santo Tomé,** which still houses one of his most famous and recognized works, *El Entierro del Conde de Orgaz (The Burial of Count Orgaz)*. The stark figure staring out from the back is El Greco himself, and the boy is his son, Jorge Manuel, architect of Toledo's city hall. Arrive early to beat out the tour groups. *(Pl. del Conde, 4. ☎925 25 60 98; www.santotome.org. Open daily Mar.-Oct. 15 10am-7pm; Oct.16-Feb. 10am-6pm. €2.30, students and over 65 €1.80.)* The **Hospital de Talavera,** built in 1541, also holds some of his paintings (C. Cardenal Tavera, 2, north of the city walls; ☎925 22 04 51; open daily 10am-1:30pm and 3-5:30pm; €4.50), as does the convent of **Santo Domingo el Antiguo,** along with his sepulcher. *(Pl. Santo Domingo el Antiguo. ☎925 22 29 30. Open daily 11am-1:30pm and 4-7pm. €2.30.)*

SYNAGOGUES. Only two of the many synagogues once in Toledo's *judería* (Jewish quarter) have been preserved. Samuel Ha Leví, diplomat and treasurer to Pedro el Cruel, built the Sinagoga del Tránsito in 1366, which now houses the **Museo Sefardí.** Stare up at the Hebrew letters carved into the *mudéjar* plasterwork and a stunning *artesonado* (coffered) wood ceiling. The museum documents the history of the Jews in Spain and Morocco and their diaspora abroad, with old relics and Hebrew bibles on display. *(Paseo del Tránsito, C. Samuel Leví. ☎925 22 36 65; www.museosefardi.net. Open Mar.-Nov. Tu-Sa 10am-2pm and 4-9pm, Su 10am-2pm; Dec.-Feb. Tu-Sa 10am-2pm and 4-6pm, Su 10am-2pm. €2.40; students, over 65, and under 18 free. Sa after 4pm and Su free.)* **Sinagoga de Santa María la Blanca,** built by Rabbi Joseph, one of Alfonso VIII's ministers, served as the principal synagogue in Toledo until 1405, when it was consecrated as a Christian temple, leaving the city's Jews to pray elsewhere until they were expelled entirely in 1492. The white Moorish arches and tracery along the ceiling betray its Islamic influences, harking back to the city's more multicultural days and the intolerant ones to follow. Now secular, its arches and tranquil garden are pleasant for any denomination.*(C. de los Reyes Católicos, 4. ☎925 22 72 57. Open daily June-Aug. 10am-7pm; Sept.-May 10am-6pm. €2.30.)*

IGLESIA DE LOS JESUITAS. This Jesuit church, former home of Juan de Mendoza, Count of Orgaz, and the birthplace of San Ildefonso, has **amazing views** of Toledo from its top towers. Completed in 1765, two years before the Jesuits were expelled from Spain, the interior is gleaming white and filled with art dating from the Counter-Reformation. Located at one of the highest points in the city, the roof offers a panorama of all the tower and tiled roofs in the old city and the hills for miles around. *(Pl. Padre Juan de Mariana, 1, up C. Nuncio Viejo from the Cathedral, and then a left on Alfonso X El Sabio. ☎925 25 15 07. Open daily Apr.-Sept. 10am-6:45pm, Oct.-March 10am-5:45pm. €2.30.)*

MONASTERIO DE SAN JUAN DE LOS REYES. At the far western edge of the city stands this Franciscan monastery, commissioned by Fernando and Isabel to commemorate their victory over the Portuguese in the Battle of Toro (1476). Over the church's entrance, a grinning skeleton awaits resurrection. The church is elegant but simple, with a single nave, and free of the gilded chapels that overwhelm other cathedrals. Better, though, is the cloister, with blossoming flowers and orange trees you can look down on from the upper level, largely by yourself; the monastery is relatively untouristed and the birdsong is the noisiest thing here. *(☎925 22 38 02. Ticket sales stop 20min. before closing. Open daily Apr.-Sept. 10am-7pm; Oct.-Mar. 10am-6pm. €2.30.)*

MEZQUITA DEL CRISTO DE LA LUZ. The only wholly preserved mosque remaining the city, La Mezquita has strangely syncretic name—meaning literally "Mosque of Christ of the Light"—of unknown origin. Legend has it that the monarch Alfonso VI's horse stumbled and would go no further as they approached the mosque, in those days called Bab al-Mardum. A strange light was observed, and hidden behind the wall was a cross illuminated continuously by a lamp for four centuries. The spot is marked on the paving in front of the mosque. The Arabic script on the facade is striking, as is the *qibla*, the wide arch that points toward Mecca. *(Cuesta de Carmelitas Descalzos, 10, just south of the Puerta de Sol. ☎925 25 41 91. Open daily May-Sept. 10am-7pm, Oct.-April 10am-6pm. €2.30.)*

MUSEUMS. Toledo was the seat of Visigoth rule and culture for three centuries prior to the Muslim invasion in 711. The exhibits at the **Museo de los Concilios y**

de la Cultura Visigótica pale in comparison to their beautiful setting, the **Iglesia de San Román.** The temple is an awesome fusion of Muslim and Christian elements, with painted images of saints fringed by inscriptions in Arabic and Christian martyrs decorating the underside of striped Moorish arches. The vivid artwork on the walls depicts heaven and hell, church elders, and saints battling dragons. *(C. San Román. ☎925 22 78 72. Open Tu-Sa 10am-2pm and 4-6:30pm, Su 10am-2pm. Free.)* The impressive and under-touristed **Museo de Santa Cruz** (1504) is an impressive example of ornate renaissance architectural embellishment. Inside, explore a handful of El Grecos, attributed El Grecos, and copies of El Grecos, along with temporary art exhibits. The basement is open intermittently but holds remains from local archaeological digs; check out the mastodon skull with tusks intact. Around the courtyard is a hodgepodge of marble slates from the Renaissance and older stone ones with Arabic inscriptions. *(C. Miguel de Cervantes, 3. ☎925 22 10 36; www.jccm.es. Open Tu-Sa 10am-6pm, Su 10am-2pm. Free.)*

NIGHTLIFE

Toledo's thick stone does a good job of concealing the nightlife, but if you keep an ear to the ground you'll find they can party, too. That said, the city doesn't really pull out the stops except on the weekends. Head downstairs into the dark at **La Destilería,** C. Sillería, 3, where local youth line the bar and cram into corners to listen to the mix and sip their cocktails (€6), getting up to dance when the salsa comes on. (☎925 25 47 74; www.casontoledo.com. Beer €2. Open Tu-Sa 10pm-3am.) Calle de la Sillería and Calle de los Alfileritos host a few upscale bars and clubs, including a bar at **La Abadía,** packed with locals, old, and young, with beers and *bocadillos* until late. (☎925 25 11 40. Open daily 1:30-4pm and 8pm-1am. For directions, see Food, p. 123.) To escape the raucous noise, check out the chill **Café Teatro Pícaro,** C. Cadenas, 6, where lights play on abstract art, and it's just as cool to be sipping on a *batido* (milkshake, €3, with Bailey's, €4) as a mixed drink. (☎925 22 13 01; www.picarocafeteatro.com. Mixed drinks €5. Beer €1.50-2.50. Open M-F 4pm-3am, Sa-Su 4pm-5am.) For die-hard partygoers, head past the hospital to the summer discos in **Peraleda** (Open Th-Sa, 11pm-4am). Inquire at the tourist office for more info.

CASTILLA Y LÉON

Culture and grandeur pervade the province of Castilla y León. Spanish icons like the fairy-tale Alcázar and Roman aqueduct of Segovia, the Gothic cathedrals of Burgos and León, the Romanesque belfries along the Camino de Santiago, the sandstone of Salamanca, and the city walls of Ávila all belong to this ancient region. Well before Fernando of Aragón and Isabel of Castilla were joined in a world-shaking matrimony, Castilla was the political and military powerhouse of Spain. During the High Middle Ages, it emerged from obscurity to lead the Christian charge against Islam. Its nobles, enriched by the spoils of combat, made their success official: *castellano* became the dominant language of the nation. Castilla's comrade in arms, León, though chagrined to be lumped with Castilla in a 1970s reorganization, shares many cultural similarities with its neighbor while bringing its own wealth of historical and natural beauty.

HIGHLIGHTS OF CASTILLA Y LEÓN

GUSH over the Roman aqueduct in **Segovia** (p. 131).

ROAM the ancient stone walls of **Ávila.**

LOSE yourself in the medieval library of the **Universidad de Salamanca** (p. 141)

SEGOVIA ☎921

Segovia's famous aqueduct and imposing castle, set high above lush green hills, make it feel like something out of a picture-book. Its beauty hasn't gone unnoticed, with tourists streaming in every day, cameras out, to try and capture a little of the magic. It was here, too, that Columbus charmed the crown into financing his journey to the New World. Though Segovia is a city of 60,000, you'd hardly notice—stay for a few days and you're sure to recognize a few faces by the end. If you do make it to this "stone ship" (so called because the stone aqueduct resembles a ship's helm), expect to shell out a little more cash; but trust us, Segovia should not be missed.

TRANSPORTATION

Trains: Po. Obispo Quesada (☎902 24 02 02). To **Madrid** (2hr.; 7-9 per day M-F 5:55am-8:55pm, Sa-Su 8:55am-8:55pm; €5.90) and **Villalba** (1hr., 7-9 per day M-F 5:55am-8:55pm, €3.90). Transfers to **Ávila, El Escorial, León,** and **Salamanca.**

Buses: Estación Municipal de Autobuses, Po. Ezequiel González, 12 (☎921 42 77 07). **Linecar** (☎921 42 77 06) to **Valladolid** (2hr.; M-F 12 per day, Sa 8 per day 6:45am-9pm, Su 6 per day 9am-9pm; €6.85). **La Sepulvedana** (☎921 42 77 07) to **Ávila** (1hr.; M-Sa 7:45am, 6pm; €4.25); **La Granja** (20min.; 9-15 per day M-Sa 7:40am-9:30pm, Su 10:30am-10:30pm; €1.05); **Madrid** (1hr.; 2 per hr. M-F 6:30am-10:30pm, Sa 8am-10:30pm, Su hourly 8am-10:30pm; €6.43).

Public Transportation: Transportes Urbanos de Segovia, C. Juan Bravo, in the Centro Comercial Almuzara (☎921 46 27 27). €0.80; discounted electronic passes available.

Taxis: Radio Taxi (24hr. ☎921 44 50 00). Taxis pull up by the train and bus stations. Stands in the Pl. Mayor and just beyond the Pl. Azoguejo.

ORIENTATION AND PRACTICAL INFORMATION

Take bus #8 from the train station to **Acueducto,** which drops off near **Plaza del Azoguejo** and the municipal **tourist office.** (M-F every 15-30min. 7:25am-10:03pm, Sa every 30-45min. 8:18am-10pm, Su 2 per hr. 8:50am-10pm). The office is just downhill in the plaza, at the foot of the aqueduct, along **Calle Real** (the main route from the Aqueduct to the Pl. Mayor, the city's historic center, composed of C. Cervantes, C. Juan Bravo, and C. Isabel la Católica). On foot from the train station (30min.), turn right, cross the street, and walk toward town along Po. Obispo Quesada, which becomes Av. Conde de Sepúlveda and then Po. Ezequiel González, before coming to the bus station. From there, (15min.) cross Po. Ezequiel González and follow Av. de Fernández Ladreda to Pl. del Azoguejo, or take bus #4 to the aqueduct. A taxi to the aqueduct is €3-4.

Tourist Office: Regional office, Pl. Mayor, 10 (☎921 46 03 34). Open July-Sept. 15 M-Th and Su 9am-8pm, F-Sa 9am-9pm; Sept. 16-June 9am-2pm and 5-8pm.

Municipal office (Centro de Recepción de Visitantes), Pl. del Azoguejo, 1 (☎921 46 67 20). Open M-F and Su 10am-7pm, Sa 10am-8pm.

Currency Exchange: Banco Santander Central Hispano, Av. de Fernández Ladreda, 12. Open Apr.-Sept. M-F 8:30am-2pm; Oct.-Mar. M-F 8:30am-2pm, Sa 8:30am-1pm. ATMs and other banks, which also change cash, line Av. de Fernández Ladreda.

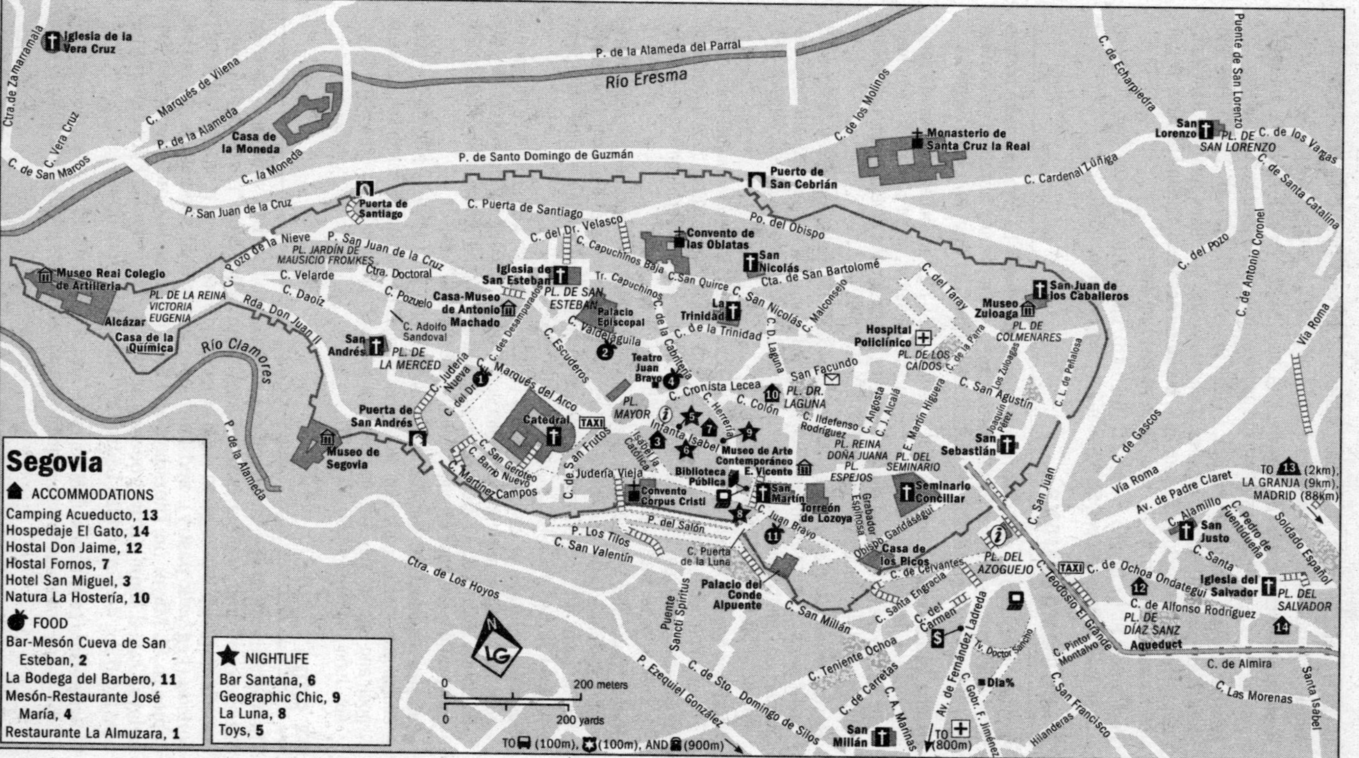
Segovia
ACCOMMODATIONS
Camping Acueducto, 13
Hospedaje El Gato, 14
Hostal Don Jaime, 12
Hostal Fornos, 7
Hotel San Miguel, 3
Natura La Hostería, 10
FOOD
Bar-Mesón Cueva de San Esteban, 2
La Bodega del Barbero, 11
Mesón-Restaurante José María, 4
Restaurante La Almuzara, 1
NIGHTLIFE
Bar Santana, 6
Geographic Chic, 9
La Luna, 8
Toys, 5
200 meters
200 yards
TO (100m), (100m), AND (900m)
TO (800m)
TO 13 (2km), LA GRANJA (9km), MADRID (88km)
Río Eresma
Río Clamores
Iglesia de la Vera Cruz
Museo Real Colegio de Artillería
Alcázar
Casa de la Química
PL. DE LA REINA VICTORIA EUGENIA
Casa de la Moneda
Puerta de Santiago
Monasterio de Santa Cruz la Real
Puerto de San Cebrián
Convento de las Oblatas
San Nicolás
La Trinidad
Iglesia de San Esteban
PL. DE SAN ESTEBAN
Palacio Episcopal
Casa-Museo de Antonio Machado
San Andrés
PL. DE LA MERCED
Puerta de San Andrés
Museo de Segovia
Catedral
PL. MAYOR
Teatro Juan Bravo
Museo de Arte Contemporáneo E. Vicente
Biblioteca Pública
Convento Corpus Cristi
San Martín
Torreón de Lozoya
Palacio del Conde Alpuente
Casa de los Picos
Seminario Concillar
Hospital Policlínico
Museo Zuloaga
San Juan de los Caballeros
San Sebastián
PL. DEL AZOGUEJO
Aqueduct
PL. DE DÍAZ SANZ
San Justo
Iglesia del Salvador
PL. DEL SALVADOR
San Lorenzo
PL. DE SAN LORENZO
Puente de San Lorenzo
San Millán
Puente Sancti Spiritus
Vía Roma
Av. de Padre Claret
Av. de Fernández Ladreda
C. de Sto. Domingo de Silos
P. Ezequiel González
Ctra. de Los Hoyos
P. de Santo Domingo de Guzmán
P. de la Alameda del Parral
P. de la Alameda
C. Cardenal Zúñiga
C. de Echarpiedra
C. de Antonio Coronel
C. de Gascos
C. San Juan
C. Cronista Lecea
C. Juan Bravo
C. de Cervantes
C. Teodosio El Grande
C. Marqués del Arco
C. Escuderos

Luggage Storage: Lockers at the train station (€3 per day). Open daily 6am-10:30pm.

Police: C. Guadarrama, 24 (☎921 43 12 12 or ☎091 for emergencies).

Hospital: Hospital General de Segovia, Crta. de Ávila s/n, (☎921 41 91 01, emergencies 41 91 00). A 10min. walk from the police station on the road to Ávila, on left.

Internet Access: Biblioteca Pública, C. Juan Bravo, 11 (☎ 921 46 35 33). Free and fast. Max. 30min. Passport required. Open July-Aug. M-F 9am-3pm, Sa 9am-2pm; Sept.-June M-F 9am-9pm, Sa 9am-2pm. **Locutorio Aceducto,** C. San Francisco, 6, just off Plaza de Azoguejo. €1 per hour. Open noon-11pm daily.

Post Office: Pl. Dr. Laguna, 5 (☎921 46 16 16), up C. Cronista Lecea from Pl. Mayor. Open M-F 8:30am-8:30pm, Sa 9:30am-2pm. **Postal Code:** 40001.

ACCOMMODATIONS

Segovia's many sights and its proximity to Madrid and La Granja make rooms scarce during the summer. Reservations are a must for any hotels in or around major plazas. *Pensiones* can be significantly cheaper than hotels in Segovia.

Natura La Hosteria, C. Colón, 5 and 7 (☎921 46 67 10; www.naturadesegovia.com), outside the Pl. Mayor. Every room is decorated in beautiful, bright solid colors, with huge soft beds. Free Wi-Fi. Prices change according to season and time of week–call ahead. Singles €35-40; doubles as low as €50-80. MC/V. ❸

Hostal Fornos, C. Infanta Isabel, 13 (☎921 46 01 98). Beige and green pastel walls and flowers make for a soothing feel. Well-maintained rooms with glass-enclosed balconies and pretty curtains. Rooms comes with TV, A/C, and large bath. Singles €41; doubles €55; triples €67. MC/V. ❹

Hotel San Miguel, C. Infanta Isabel, 6 (☎921 46 36 57; www.sanmiguel-hotel.com). Full of bright, modern amenities. Huge full bath is sparkling, and big beds have downy patchwork comforters. Balconies have good views over the street. Rooms come with TV, A/C, and phone. Singles €35; doubles €60. MC/V. ❸

Hostal "Don Jaime", C. Ochoa Ondátegui, 8 (☎921 44 47 87; hostaldonjaime@hotmail.com). A stone's throw from the aqueduct, visible from some of the room's balconies. Bright rooms with lots of space. Some rooms have bath for a higher price. July-Sept. singles €30, doubles €45; Oct.-June, €35/50. MC/V. ❸

Hospedaje El Gato, Pl. del Salvador, 10 (☎921 42 32 44; fax 43 80 47). Follow the aqueduct uphill to modern rooms with comfortable beds. The bar downstairs fills with locals day and night. All rooms have A/C, satellite TV, and private bath. Singles €25; doubles €40; extra bed for single/double €15/24. MC/V. ❷

Camping Acueducto, C. Borbón, 49/Highway CN-601, km 112 (☎921 42 50 00; www.campingacueducto.com), 2km toward La Granja. Restaurant, supermarket, showers, pool, and laundry. July-Aug. and *Semana Santa* €5 per person, per tent, and per car; Apr.-June and Sept. €4.50. MC/V. ❶

FOOD

The restaurants in the larger plazas all cater to tourists, and jack up their prices accordingly—steer clear of any menu printed on "parchment." *Sopa castellana* (soup with eggs and garlic), *cochinillo asado* (roast suckling pig), *ponche* (egg-yolk pastry), and lamb are all regional specialties. A market comes to Pl. Mayor on Thursdays and next to Av. de la Constitución on Saturdays (9am-2:30pm). Buy groceries at **Día%,** C. Gobernador Fernández Jiménez, 3, off Av. de Fernández Ladreda. (Open M-Sa 9am-9pm.)

Restaurante La Almuzara, C. Marqués del Arco, 3 (☎921 46 06 22), past the cathedral. The pastel flowers on the walls and the real ones in vases make for a pastoral meal.

Massive salads €9-12. Creative vegetarian plates €9.50. Open Tu 8-11:30pm, W-Su 12:45-4pm and 8-11:30pm. MC/V. ❷

Bar-Mesón Cueva de San Esteban, C. Valdeláguila, 15 (☎921 46 09 82). The owner knows his wines (he's still celebrating his 2002 victory in the national "nose of gold" competition), and with a prize-winning pork carver on his staff, food is excellent as well. *Menú* M-F €9, Sa-Su €10. Meat dishes €12-20. Open daily 11am-midnight. MC/V. ❸

Restaurante-Mesón José María, C. Cronista Lecea, 11 (☎921 46 11 11; www.rtejosemaria.com). With somber wood, yellow walls, and iron chandeliers, this restaurant is an ultra-typical Spanish *mesón,* but it distinguishes itself with succulent, if pricey, *cochinillo asado* (roast suckling pig; €21.35). Open M-W and Su 1-4pm and 8:30-11pm, Th-Sa 1-4pm and 8:30pm-12:30am. MC/V. ❹

La Bodega del Barbero, C. Alhóndiga, 2. (☎921 46 27 70), just off C. Juan Bravo. An easy-to-miss terrace that makes a perfect mid-day break. Technically a *"vinoteca"* (winery) with tastings and exhibitions, the bodega also keeps an inventive kitchen year-round. Glasses of wine €1.50-2.50. Mouth-watering salads €5.80-8.80 and lunch *menú* €10. Open Tu 11am-3:30pm, W-Su 11am-3:30pm and 7:30-11:30pm. MC/V. ❷

SIGHTS

Though dominated by its aqueduct and the romantic Alcázar, Segovia is packed with churches, convents, and palaces dating from medieval and Renaissance times, all worth exploring. When you tire of the cobblestones, head south out of the city into the massive hills and copses of the Pinarillo or explore one of the villages you can see from the city.

AQUEDUCT. The Romans built Segovia's aqueduct around 50 BC with 20,000 blocks of granite and not a drop of mortar. The two tiers of 166 arches supported by 128 pillars span 813m, reaching a height of 29m near Pl. del Azoguejo. This spectacular feat of engineering piped in water from the Río Fuenfría, 14km away, and was capable of transporting 30 liters of water per second to the Alcázar. It was in use until 60 years ago, but today the aqueduct primarily pipes in tourists from Madrid.

ALCÁZAR. Walt Disney reportedly modeled the Disney castle off the Alcázar's spiral towers and pointed turrets, and it does give a magical sense of *déjà vu.* Fortifications have commanded the site since Celtic occupation. Alfonso X beautified the original 11th-century fortress in the 13th century. Successive monarchs increased the grandeur; final touches were added for the coronation of Isabel I in 1474. In the Throne Room, the inscription above the throne reads *"Tanto Monta,"* a phrase meant to suggest that Fernando and Isabel had equal authority to rule. Process through various luxe royal bedrooms and halls. The **Tower of Juan II,** 152 steps up, offers incredible views of Segovia and the surrouding hills. *(Pl. de la Reina Victoria Eugenia. ☎921 46 07 59. Open daily Apr.-Sept. 10am-7pm; Oct.-Mar. 10am-6pm. Tower closed Tu. Buy tickets in the Real Laboratorio de Chimia, to the left of the Alcázar. Palace €4, seniors and students €2.50. Tower €2. Audio tours in English €3.)*

CASA-MUSEO DE ANTONIO MACHADO. Antonio Machado (1875-1939), literature professor, playwright, and, above all, poet, never made much money. The poet rented this small *pensión* from 1919 to 1932 for three *pesetas* per day while he taught French in the nearby university. A short, informative tour details major influences on Machado's poetry, including the 1909 death of his teenage wife and his affair with a married woman. The poet's room, filled with manuscripts and portraits (including a Picasso), has been left untouched. His last letter, written weeks before he died in France, is a poignant account of the hardships he would endure because of his flight from Spain in 1939. *(C. des*

Desamparados, 5. ☎921 46 03 77. Open M-Tu 4:30-7:30pm, W-Su 11am-2pm and 4:30-7:30pm. Mandatory guided tour in Spanish every 30min. €1.50, W free.)

CATHEDRAL. In 1525, Carlos V commissioned a cathedral in Pl. Mayor to replace the 12th-century edifice destroyed in the *Revuelta de las Comunidades*, a political uprising against the crown that lasted from 1520-1521. When the cathedral was finished 200 years later with an impressive 23 chapels topped with stained glass, it earned the nickname "The Lady of All Cathedrals." The altar was designed by Sabatini, creator of the gardens in Madrid, and features the four saints of Segovia. The **Sala Capitular,** hung with 17th-century tapestries, displays an ornate silver-and-gold chariot. Off the cloister (moved from the Alcázar) is the **Capilla de Santa Catalina,** filled with crosses, chalices, and candelabra. A framed coin collection on the cloister wall has currency from the royal mint going back 5 centuries. *(☎921 46 22 05. Open daily Apr.-Oct. 9am-6:30pm; Nov.-Mar. 9:30am-5:30pm; last entry 30min. before closing. Mass M-Sa 10am, Su 11am and 12:30pm. €3, under 14 free. Guided tours leave from the entrance at 11am, 4:30, 5:30pm.)*

NIGHTLIFE AND FESTIVALS

Plaza Mayor is the heart of Segovia's after-hours scene. Crowded **Calle Infanta Isabel,** toward the aqueduct, definitely earns its local nickname, *"calle de los barres,"* where locals fill the street sipping beers. The bars filling **Plaza del Azoguejo, Calle Fernandez de Ladreda,** and **Calle Carmen,** near the aqueduct, are frequented by a younger set, and club central is **C. Ruiz de Alda,** off **Pl. del Azoguejo.**

June 23rd-29th, Segovia holds a fiesta in honor of San Juan and San Pedro, with free open-air concerts on Pl. del Azoguejo, a pilgrimage to the hermitage of Juarrillos, 5km distant, and dances and fireworks on June 29. Zamarramala, 3km northwest of Segovia, hosts the **Fiestas de Santa Águeda** (the closest Su to Feb. 5). Women take over the town for a day and dress in period costumes to commemorate a **sneak attack** on the Alcázar in which women distracted the castle guards with wine and song. The all-female local council takes advantage of its authority to ridicule men and, at the festival's end, burns a male effigy.

Toys, C. Infanta Isabel, 13. *Copas* and childhood knick-knacks mix in the eclectic atmosphere of Toys. Techno music plays on a small dance floor as the crowd sips cocktails under red lights upstairs. Beer €1. Mixed drinks €4.50-5.50. Open daily 10pm-4am.

Geographic Chic, C. Infanta Isabel, 13 (☎921 46 30 38). Carries on Toys' doll fetish with mannequins lining the windows and cherubs smiling on the bar. A mixed crowd sips and dances as lights sweep the bar. Mixed drinks €5. Open W-Sa 10:30pm-4am.

Bar Santana, C. Infanta Isabel, 18 (☎921 46 35 64). Tasty tapas and rock music draw a casual older crowd, which loiters outside with drinks along the exterior bar. Photo and poetry exhibits line the back wall, but few are looking. Beer €1.10. Mixed drinks €4.50. Open Th-Sa 10:30pm-3:30am.

La Luna, C. Pta. de la Luna, 8 (☎921 46 26 51). From Pl. Mayor, head down C. Isabel la Católica onto C. Juan Bravo and take the first right. If you're looking for a club, this is the place. You can also count on a raucous American crowd and a lot of testosterone. Beer €1.50. *Chupitos* (shots) €3. Open daily 5pm-4am.

DAYTRIP FROM SEGOVIA

LA GRANJA DE SAN ILDEFONSO

La Sepulvedana buses (☎921 42 77 07) run from Segovia (20min.; 12-14 per day M-Sa 7:40am-9:30pm, Su 10:30am-10:30pm; return M-Sa 7:20am-9pm, Su 11am-10pm; €1.05). From the bus stop in La Granja, walk uphill through the gates and follow signs to the Palacio de La Granja. ☎921 47 00 19. Open Apr.-Sept. Tu-Su 10am-6pm; Oct.-Mar.

Tu-Sa 10am-1:30pm and 3-5pm, Su 10am-2pm. Tours, in Spanish, depart every 15min. €4.50, with guide €5; students and under 16 €3.

La Granja, a must-see located 11 km southeast of the city, is the most extravagant of Spain's royal summer retreats (the others being El Pardo, El Escorial, and Aranjuez). Felipe V, the first Bourbon King of Spain and grandson of Louis XIV, detested the Habsburgs' austere El Escorial. Nostalgic for Versailles, he commissioned La Granja in the early 18th century, choosing the site for its hunting and gardening potential. A fire destroyed the living quarters in 1918, but the structure was rebuilt in 1932. Today it houses the **Museo de Tapices,** one of the world's best collections of Flemish tapestries, which were popular in Spanish royal palaces. The usual marble clocks, oriental porcelain, and paintings by Luca Giordano round out the palace's decoration. French architect René Carlier designed the immense French **gardens** around the palace. Hedges surround impressive flowerbeds and lead to endless waterworks, including the decadent **Cascadas Nuevas,** an ensemble of illuminated fountains and pools representing the continents and seasons.The **Baños de Diana** is a massive pool with a bronze statue of the goddess, backed by a wall meticulously inlaid with hundreds of seashells. (Gardens open daily 10am-9pm. *Baños de Diana* July 22-Sept. 2 Sa from 10:30am-11:30pm. Other fountains suspended due to lack of water. Palace open June 17-Aug. 10am-9pm; May-June 16 and Sept. 10am-8pm; Apr. 10am-7pm; Mar. and Oct. 10am-6:30pm; Nov.-Feb. 10am-6pm.)

ÁVILA ☎920

Ávila (pop. 50,000) is a popular retreat from Madrid summer heat and winter bustle. The city makes its name with its incredible 12th-century stone walls and as the birthplace of the mystical Santa Teresa de Jesús (1515-1582). The old city, though, is full of beautiful buildings from Spain's glory days, and half the fun is stumbling upon half-hidden churches and palaces in a city almost totally untouched by urban grime and traffic.

TRANSPORTATION

Trains: Po. de la Estación (☎902 24 02 02). Info office open daily 7:30am-1:30pm and 3:30-9:30pm. To **El Escorial** (1hr.; 6-9 per day M-F 5:30am-8:15pm, Sa-Su 9:15am-10:15pm; €4.50); **Madrid** (1-2hr.; 15-23 per day M-F 5:30am-8:15pm, Sa-Su 7am-10:15pm; €7.55) via **Villalba** (1hr., €6.40); **Salamanca** (1½hr., 7-9 per day 7:10am-10:50pm, €8.35); **Valladolid** (1hr.; 5 per day 7:30am-9:30pm, €7.55).

Buses: Av. de Madrid, 2 (☎920 22 01 54). To **Madrid** (1hr.; 10-13 per day 6am-10:30pm, Su 6 per day 10am-10:15pm; €7.27) and **Segovia** (1hr.; M-F 5 per day 6:30am-7pm, Sa-Su 10:15am and 7:15pm; €4.25).

Taxis: Radio Taxis (☎920 35 35 45), in Pl. Sta. Teresa and the bus and train stations.

ORIENTATION AND PRACTICAL INFORMATION

The winding old city streets meet in the Plaza del Mercado Chico inside the walls and the recently revamped Plaza de Santa Teresa just outside. Bus #1 (€0.65) departs a block from the train station towards Pl. del Mercado Chico. To get from the bus station to Pl. Sta. Teresa, cross the intersection in front, follow the park, and turn left onto C. Duque de Alba.

Tourist Office: Pl. Pedro Dávila, 4 (☎920 21 13 87). English spoken. Open July-Aug. M-Th 9am-8pm, F-Sa 9am-9pm; Sept.-June M-Sa 9am-2pm and 5-8pm.

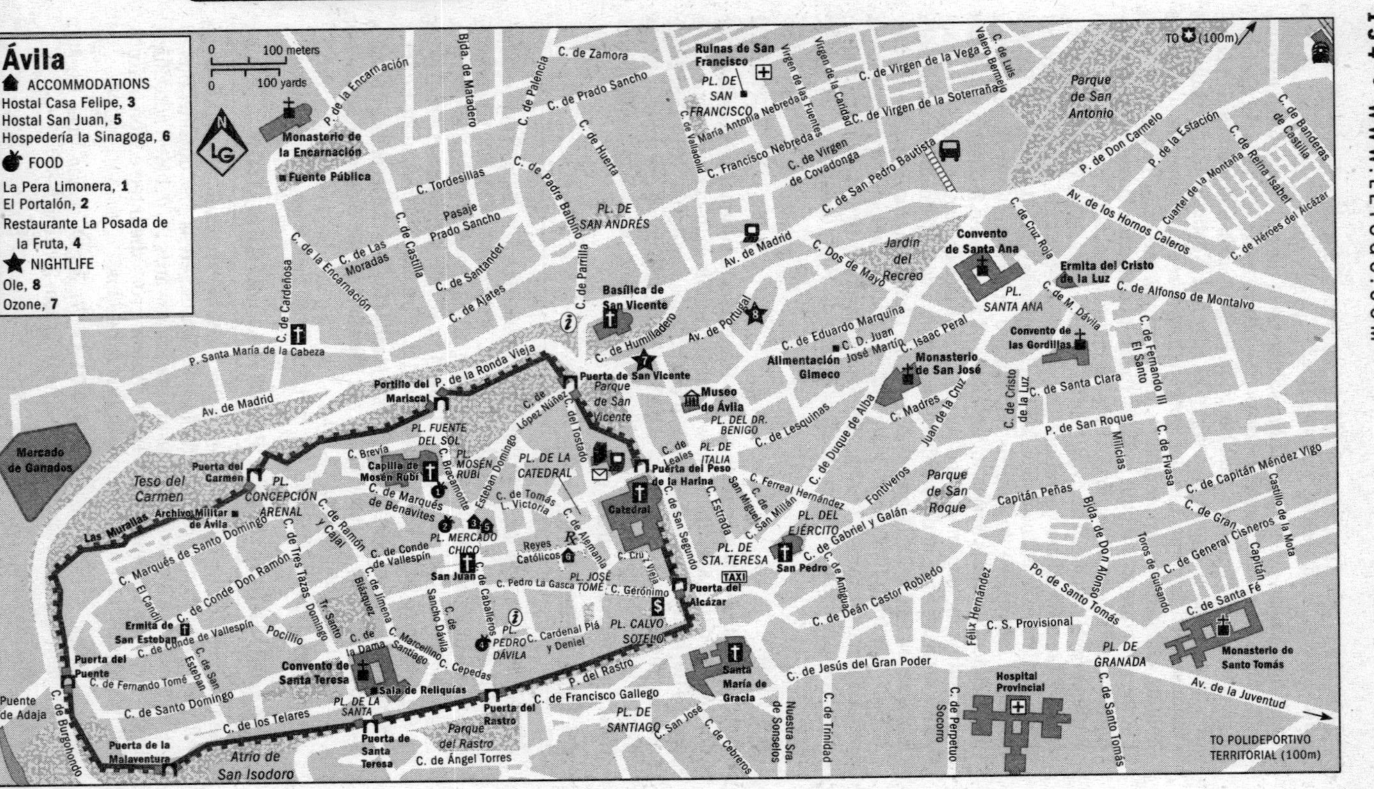

Ávila
ACCOMMODATIONS
Hostal Casa Felipe, 3
Hostal San Juan, 5
Hospedería la Sinagoga, 6
FOOD
La Pera Limonera, 1
El Portalón, 2
Restaurante La Posada de la Fruta, 4
NIGHTLIFE
Ole, 8
Ozone, 7
100 meters
100 yards
TO (100m)
TO POLIDEPORTIVO TERRITORIAL (100m)
Monasterio de la Encarnación
Fuente Pública
Rulnas de San Francisco
PL. DE SAN FRANCISCO
Parque de San Antonio
Jardín del Recreo
Convento de Santa Ana
PL. SANTA ANA
Ermita del Cristo de la Luz
Convento de las Gordillas
Monasterio de San José
Allmentación Gimeco
Basílica de San Vicente
PL. DE SAN ANDRÉS
Museo de Ávila
PL. DEL DR. BENIGO
Puerta de San Vicente
Parque de San Vicente
Portillo del Mariscal
PL. FUENTE DEL SOL
PL. MOSÉN RUBÍ
Capilla de Mosén Rubí
PL. DE LA CATEDRAL
Catedral
Puerta del Peso de la Harina
PL. DE ITALIA
PL. DEL EJÉRCITO
PL. DE STA. TERESA
San Pedro
Parque de San Roque
Puerta del Alcázar
PL. CALVO SOTELO
PL. MERCADO CHICO
San Juan
PL. JOSÉ TOMÉ
PL. PEDRO DÁVILA
Puerta del Carmen
Teso del Carmen
PL. CONCEPCIÓN ARENAL
Archivo Militar de Ávila
Las Murallas
Mercado de Ganados
Ermita de San Esteban
Puerta del Puente
Puente de Adaja
Puerta de la Malaventura
Atrio de San Isodoro
Convento de Santa Teresa
Sala de Reliquías
PL. DE LA SANTA
Puerta de Santa Teresa
Puerta del Rastro
Parque del Rastro
PL. DE SANTIAGO
Santa María de Gracia
Hospital Provincial
PL. DE GRANADA
Monasterio de Santo Tomás
Av. de Madrid
Av. de Portugal
Av. de los Hornos Caleros
Av. de la Juventud
P. de la Ronda Vieja
P. Santa María de la Cabeza
P. de Don Carmelo
P. de la Estación
P. de San Roque
Po. de Santo Tomás
C. de Jesús del Gran Poder
C. de Francisco Gallego
C. de Deán Castor Robledo
C. de Duque de Alba
C. de Eduardo Marquina
C. Dos de Mayo
C. de Humilladero
C. de Burgohondo
C. de Santo Domingo
C. de los Telares
C. de Ángel Torres
C. de Capitán Méndez Vigo
C. de Alfonso de Montalvo
C. de Fernando III El Santo
C. de Santa Clara
C. de Santa Fé
C. de Zamora
C. de Prado Sancho
C. de Padre Balbino
C. de Castilla
C. de la Encarnación
Bjda. de Matadero
Bjda. de Don Alonso

Centro de Recepción de Visitantes, Av. de Madrid, 39 (☎920 10 21 21), across the street from the northwest tower of the wall. Open summer 9am-8pm; winter 9am-6pm.

Currency Exchange: Banco Santander Central Hispano, C. Don Gerónimo, 8 (☎920 21 11 39). Open Apr.-Sept. M-F 8:30am-2pm; Oct.-May also Sa 8:30am-1pm.

Luggage Storage: At the train station (€3). Open daily 6am-11pm.

Police: Policía Municipal, C. Molino del Carril, 1 (☎920 35 24 24).

Pharmacy: Farmacia Vinuesa, C. Reyes Católicos, 31 (☎920 21 13 35). Open M-F 9:30am-2pm and 4:30-8pm, Sa 10am-2pm.

Hospital: Hospital Provincial, C. de Jesús del Gran Poder, 42 (☎920 35 72 00). Ambulance: ☎920 22 22 22. Open daily 9am-9pm.

Internet Access: Cybernet Locutorio DG, Av. de Madrid, 25 (☎920 253 800). €2 per hr., but you don't have to use all your time at once. Open daily 10am-3pm and 4-10:30pm. Also available at the **Biblioteca Municipal,** Pl. de la Catedral, 3 (☎920 25 46 38). max. 30 min., with passport. Open July-Aug. M-F 8:30am-2:45pm, Sa 9am-2pm, Sept.-June M-F 9am-9pm, Sa 9am-2pm.

Post Office: Pl. de la Catedral, 2 (☎920 35 31 06). Fax service available. Open M-F 8:30am-8:30pm, Sa 9:30am-2pm. **Postal Code:** 05001.

ACCOMMODATIONS

Comfortable, affordable accommodations can be found within the city walls. True budget options are a long march down the Av. de la Juventud, about 25min. outside of the old city. Those near the cathedral and Pl. de Sta. Teresa fill fast in summer, so call early. Many hotels double as restaurants, and breakfast can be had on the cheap with the price of a room; ask the receptionist or barman.

Hostal San Juan, C. Comuneros de Castilla, 3 (☎920 25 14 75). Excellent bargain hidden off the plaza. Huge full bath is sparkling. Bright green beds and yellow walls. Rooms with phone and TV. Oct.-May singles €24, doubles €38; June-Sept. €30/48. MC/V. ❷

Hostal Casa Felipe, Pl. Mercado Chico, 12 (☎920 21 39 24). Rooms with windows overlooking the plaza offer fresh air and light. All rooms have TV, phone, and sink. Singles €25; doubles €38, with bath €44. MC/V. ❷

Hospedería la Sinagoga, C. Reyes Católicos, 22 (☎920 35 23 21; www.lasinagoga.net). This former synagogue—now sharing space with a convent—offers tranquility and rooms with enormous full baths and balconies overlooking the quiet street. Beautiful central patio with couches and plants, brass-framed mirrors and old wooden beams. Great deal for groups and doubles. Singles €50; doubles €60. MC/V. ❺

FOOD

Ávila is filled with sober *mesones,* where vested waiters serve pricey meat dishes; variety is not Ávila's strong suit. Fridays, the **market** in Pl. Mercado Chico sells produce 10am-2pm. The supermarket, **Alimentación Gimeco,** C. Juan José Martín, 6, stocks basics. (Open in summer M 10:30am-2pm and 5:30-8:30pm, Tu-Su 9:45am-2pm and 5:30-8:30pm; winter M-Sa 9:45am-2pm and 5-8pm.)

El Portalón, Pl. del Mercado Chico, 4 (☎920 21 43 29). Nothing fancy, but big plates and a lively atmosphere right on the plaza. Cheapest terrace dining you'll find in town. The *platos combinados* (€9-11), combinations of meat, eggs, and fries, are a good bet. Hamburgers €5. *Menús* €12-18. Open daily noon-4pm and 8:30pm-1am. MC/V. ❷

Restaurante La Posada de la Fruta, Pl. Pedro Dávila, 8 (☎920 25 47 02; www.posadelafruta.com). Four seating locations at different prices—the shaded *terraza* is the most pleasant and cheapest. *Platos combinados* €6-8. *Menú* €9-11. Restaurant open daily 1-4:30pm and 8:30-11:30pm. Bar open 9am-midnight. MC/V. ❷

La Pera Limonera, Pl. Mosén Rubí, 5 (☎920 25 04 72) Cool lime-green walls and napkins, orchids, and black leather are a welcome break from endless "medieval-themed" fare. Style comes at a price, though: seafood and meat dishes €18-20. Smaller appetizers €13. Open Tu-Sa 1:30-4pm and 9pm-midnight, Su 1:30-4pm. MC/V. ❹

SIGHTS

LAS MURALLAS. These gigantic city walls were originally built to keep foreigners out. They now let thousands of them in each year for rampart-scaling and city views. Research dates the 2500 battlements, 88 towers, and 9 gates to the 12th century, though legend maintains that they are the oldest in Spain, dating back to 1090. **Cimorro,** the most imposing tower, doubles as the cathedral's apse. The walls can be reached from both **Puerta del Peso de la Harina** and **Puerta del Alcázar,** on either side of the cathedral. There are three walks along the ramparts, all included in the price of admission, but once you've done one, you've probably seen it all. **Tramo de la Carnicería** commands the best views of the city and its environs. *(☎920 25 50 88. Open Apr.-Oct. 15 M-W and Su 10am-8pm and 10pm-12:30am; Oct. 16-Mar. daily 11am-6pm. Theatrical tour June 16-Sept. 17 Th-Sa 10-11:30pm, last entry 45min. before closing. €4; students, groups, over 65, and under 8 €2.50; at night €6/4. 3-person theatrical tour €4.50.)* The best view of the walls and of Ávila is from the Cuatro Postes, past the Río Adaja, 1.5km along the highway to Salamanca. *(From Pl. de Sta. Teresa, walk out the Puerta del Puente. Cross the bridge and follow the road to the right for about 1km. The walk to Cuatro Postes takes approx. 25min.)*

CATEDRAL. Begun in the late 12th century, Ávila's is the oldest Spanish cathedral in the transitional style between Romanesque and Gothic. Look for the **Altar de La Virgen de la Caridad,** where 12-year-old Santa Teresa prostrated herself after the death of her mother. Behind the main altar is the alabaster tomb of Cardinal Alonso de Madrigal, a bishop of Ávila and prolific writer whose dark complexion won him the title "El Tostado" (The Swarthy, literally "Toasted"). The museum displays an El Greco portrait, enormous *libros de canti* (hymnals), and Juan de Arfe's silver, six-story Custodia de Asiento, complete with swiveling bells. *(Pl. de la Catedral. ☎920 21 16 41. Open July-Sept. M-F 10am-7:30pm, Sa 10am-8pm, Su noon-6pm; Nov.-Mar. M-F 10am-5pm, Sa 10am-6pm, Su noon-5pm; Apr.-June and Oct. M-F 10am-6pm, Sa 10am-7pm, Su noon-6pm. Last entry 45min. before closing. Front entrance only free; full cathedral and museum €4.)*

MONASTERIO DE LA ENCARNACIÓN. The monastery's museum holds items from Teresa's childhood in the lap of luxury, which she renounced for a life of asceticism. The mandatory tour visits Santa Teresa's tiny cell and the main staircase where she had a mystical encounter with the child Jesus; a mannequin on the stairs recreates the experience. Upstairs are personal effects given to the convent by wealthier nuns as bribes to procure entrance. *(Po. de la Encarnación. ☎920 21 12 12. Museum open in summer M-F 9:30am-1pm and 4-7pm, Sa-Su 10am-1pm and 4-7pm; in winter M-F 9:30am-1:30pm and 3:30-6pm, Sa-Su 10am-1:30pm and 3:30-6pm. Admission and tour €1.70.)*

EL MONASTERIO DE SANTO TOMÁS. One of the most strange and wonderful sights in the city is this untouristed Dominican monastery, built at the behest of Fernando and Isabel. Three cloisters hold various rooms and a church with the tomb of Prince Juan, a son of the monarchs, who died at 19. The Dominicans traveled widely as missionaries, and their souvenirs are on display in the **Museo de Arte Oriental,** off the third cloister, featuring kimonos, buddha statues, Chinese screens and paintings, and gorgeous calligraphy. Even stranger is the **Museo de Ciencias Naturales** (2nd cloister), which has all manner of exotic preserved animals, from birds to cattle to sharks and crocodiles; the **full-sized African lion** is the best. Take a break from Teresa and enjoy—it's the only church in Spain where you'll find an entombed prince and a snarling, mutant lamb. *(Pl. Granada, down Paseo de Santo Tomás. ☎920 35 22 37. Open daily 10am-1pm and 4-7pm. €3.*

OTHER SIGHTS. Santa Teresa's admirers built the 17th-century **Convento de Santa Teresa** at the site of her birth. *(Inside the city walls, near Puerta de Sta. Teresa. ☎920 21 10 30. Open daily 9:30am-1:30pm and 3:30-7:30pm. Free.)* If you see only one site related to Santa Teresa, visit **Sala de Reliquías,** near the convent, where you will find a small scrapbook of Santa Teresa relics, including her preserved ring finger, the sole of her sandal, and the cord she used to flagellate herself. Two bones of St. John of the Cross complete the collection. *(Open daily Apr.-Oct. 9:30am-1:30pm and 3:30-7:30pm; Nov.-Mar. Tu-Su 10am-1:30pm and 3:30-7pm. Free.)* For a larger display of items that Santa Teresa may have touched, looked at, or lived among, as well as artifacts of lesser-known Teresas, visit the **Museo de Santa Teresa,** built into a crypt. *(☎920 22 07 08. Open Apr.-Oct. daily 10am-2pm and 4-7pm; Nov.-Mar. Tu-Su 10am-1:30pm and 3:30-5:30pm. Last entry 30min. before closing. €2.)*

NIGHTLIFE

After nightfall, the Ávila's *centro* empties of its youth, as if St. Teresa's asceticism is still too strong within the city walls for late-night revelry. The **Parque San Vicente,** just to the left out of the Puerto del Peso de la Harina, is the gathering place of Ávila's teenagers, passing around 40s in paper bags, fighting, and flirting, occasionally relieving themselves on the city's sacrosanct 800-year-old walls. Across the street are the *terrazas* on **San Segundo,** where a more sedate crowd eats tapas and nurses drinks well into the night. The clubs and bars are just up the road and to the right on Av. de Portugal. Many only open on weekends. **Ozone,** Av. de Portugal, 4, is a lively place with a disco ball, Spanish alt-rock, and intense darts competitions in the corner. (Beer €2. Mixed drinks €5-6. Open F-Sa 11:30pm-5:30am.) Further down is **Ole,** Av. de Portugal, 18, a lively hive of conversation and European flags. (☎920 226 475. Beer €2-3. Mixed drinks €5-6. Open W-Sa 10pm-4am.)

SALAMANCA ☎923

Salamanca (pop. at term-time 363,000) is Spain's golden city. Once a battleground of Arabs and Christians, Salamanca has since become the home of the prestigious Universidad de Salamanca, in medieval times considered one of the four leading lights of the world. The city seems to radiate its own light, with massive buildings built of yellow Villamayor stone flaunting ornate facades that exemplify Spanish Plateresque architecture. Salamanca's location is also golden. While accessible from Spain's major transportation hubs, the city's mild summers make it a welcome retreat from the heat that the rest of Spain's interior can suffer. Salamanca remains steadfastly a university town; even in summer, thousands of students flood the streets, giving rise to a student scene that rivals those of major cities like Barcelona and Madrid.

TRANSPORTATION

Flights: Aeropuerto de Salamanca, Ctra. Madrid, km 14 (☎923 32 96 00).

Trains: Vialia Estación de Salamanca, Po.de la Estación (☎902 24 02 02). To: **Ávila** (65min., 7-8 per day 6am-7:53pm, €8.05); **Lisboa** (6hr., 4:51am, €47); **Madrid** (2hr., 6-7 per day 6am-7:53pm, €15); **Palencia** (2hr., 1:50pm, €9-21); **Valladolid** (2hr., 4-6 per day 7:35am-8:35pm, €6.05-13.40). The station offers **luggage storage,** a Carrefour supermarket, restaurants, and a movie theater.

Buses: Av. Filiberto Villalobos, 71-85 (☎923 23 67 17). Take C. Ramón y Cajal to Po. de San Vicente. Cross Po. de San Vicente, and C. Ramón y Cajal becomes Av. Filiberto Villalobos. Open M-F 8am-8:30pm, Sa 9am-2:30pm and 4:30-6:30pm, Su 10am-2pm and 4-7:30pm. **Avanza Grupo** (☎902 02 09 99) sends buses to: **Ávila** (1hr.; M-Th 4 per day 6:30am-8:30pm, F 6 per day 6:30am-8:30pm, Sa-Su 4 per day 8:30am-8:30pm; €5); **Alsa** (☎902 42 22 42, www.alsa.es) sends buses to **Barcelona** (11hr; M-Th and Sa 10am and 8pm, F 10am, 4:30, 8pm, Su 10am, 2:30, 8pm; €47, round-trip €73); **Linea Zamora** (☎923 223 587, www.zamorasalamanca.com) sends buses to **León** (2hr.; M-F 7 per day 7am-7:30pm, Sa 4 per day 10:15am-5pm, Su 4 per day 10:15-11pm, €12.80. **Avanza Grupo** to **Madrid** (2hr.; M-Sa 16 per day 6am-9:30pm, Su 16 per day 8am-11pm; €11.40-17); **Segovia** (2hr.; M-F 6:30am, 1:15pm, Sa-Su 8:30am, 5:30pm; €9.42, round-trip €17.29); **Valladolid** (1hr.; M-Sa 7-9 per day 7am-8pm, Su 6 per day 9am-10pm; €7, round-trip €13.20); **Linea Zamora** to **Zamora** (1hr.; M-F 21 per day 6:30am-9:40pm, Sa 10 per day 7:45am-8:30pm, Su 10 per day 8:45am-10:15pm; €4.25). **El Pilar** (☎923 22 26 08; www.elpilar-arribesbus.com) to **Ciudad Rodrigo** (1hr.; M-F 13 per day 7am-9:30pm, Sa 7 per day 8:30am-8pm, Su 4 per day 11am-9:30pm; €6).

Taxis: Radio Taxi (☎923 25 00 00). 24 hr.

Car Rental: Avis, Po. de Canalejas, 49 (☎923 26 97 53). Open M-F 9:30am-1:30pm and 4-7pm, Sa 9am-1:30pm. **Europcar,** C. Calzada de Medina 7-9 (☎923 25 02 70). Open M-F 9am-1:30pm and 4:30-8pm, Sa 9am-1:30pm.

ORIENTATION AND PRACTICAL INFORMATION

The majestic **Plaza Mayor** is the social and geographical center of Salamanca. Most hostels are to the south on **Rúa Mayor** and **Plaza de Anaya,** as are the **University** and most sights. From the train station, catch bus #1 (€0.80) to Gran Vía and get off at the Pl. Mayor (20min. from train station, 15min. from bus station).

Tourist Office: Municipal office, Pl. Mayor, 32 (☎923 21 83 42 or 923 27 24 08). Open June-Sept. M-F 9am-2pm and 4:30-8pm, Sa 10am-8pm, Su 10am-2pm; Oct.-May M-F 9am-2pm and 4-6:30pm, Sa 10am-6:30pm, Su 10am-2pm. **Regional office,** R. Mayor (☎923 26 85 71), in the Casa de las Conchas. Open July-Sept. M-Th and Su 9am-8pm, F-Sa 9am-9pm; Oct.-June daily 9am-2pm and 5-8pm. Look out for **DGratis,** a free listing of goings-on distributed every Friday available at tourist offices and distributors in Pl. Mayor. See www.salamanca.es for details.

Currency Exchange: EuroDivisas, R. Mayor, 2 (☎923 21 21 80). Open M-F 8:30am-10pm, Sa-Su 10am-7pm. ATMs can be found on every major street.

Luggage Storage: At the **train station** (24hr.; €3-4.50) and **bus station** (open daily 7am-7:45pm; €2).

Women's Resources: Office for the Assistance of Victims of Sexual Assault and Harassment, Gran Vía, 39-31, 4th fl. (☎923 12 68 75). **Association for the Assistance of Victims of Sexual Assault and Domestic Abuse,** Pl. Nueva de San Vincente, 5 (☎923 26 15 99).

Laundromat: Pasaje Azafranal, 18 (☎923 36 02 16), off C. Azafranal. Wash and dry €4. Open M-F 9:30am-2pm and 4-8pm, Sa 9:30am-2pm.

Police: In the Ayuntamiento, Pl. Mayor, 2 (☎923 19 44 40 or locally 923 27 91 00).

Red Cross: C. Cruz Roja, 1 (☎923 22 22 22).

Pharmacy: Amador Felipe, C. Toro, 25 (☎923 21 41 24). Open daily 9:30am-10pm.

Hospital: Hospital Clínico Universitario, Po. de San Vicente, 108 (☎923 29 11 00).

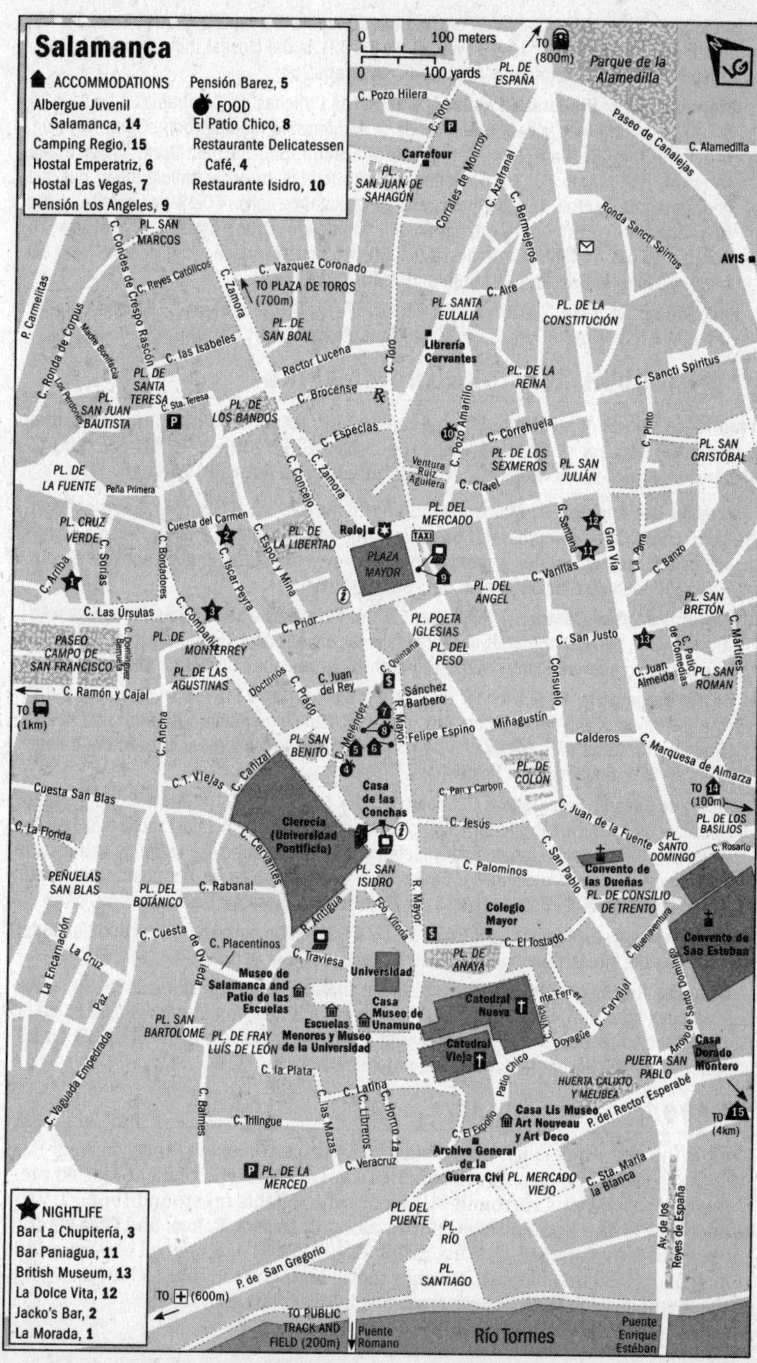
Salamanca
ACCOMMODATIONS
Albergue Juvenil Salamanca, 14
Camping Regio, 15
Hostal Emperatriz, 6
Hostal Las Vegas, 7
Pensión Los Angeles, 9
Pensión Barez, 5
FOOD
El Patio Chico, 8
Restaurante Delicatessen Café, 4
Restaurante Isidro, 10
NIGHTLIFE
Bar La Chupitería, 3
Bar Paniagua, 11
British Museum, 13
La Dolce Vita, 12
Jacko's Bar, 2
La Morada, 1
0 100 meters
0 100 yards
TO (800m)
PL. DE ESPAÑA
Parque de la Alamedilla
C. Pozo Hilera
C. Toro
Carrefour
PL. SAN JUAN DE SAHAGÚN
Corrales de Monroy
C. Azafranal
C. Bermejeros
Paseo de Canalejas
C. Alamedilla
Ronda Sancti Spiritus
AVIS
PL. SAN MARCOS
C. Condes de Crespo Rascón
C. Reyes Católicos
C. Zamora
C. Vazquez Coronado
TO PLAZA DE TOROS (700m)
P. Carmelitas
C. Ronda de Corpus
Madre Bonifacia
Los Perdones
PL. DE SAN BOAL
C. las Isabeles
Rector Lucena
PL. SANTA EULALIA
C. Aire
PL. DE LA CONSTITUCIÓN
Librería Cervantes
PL. DE LA REINA
C. Sancti Spiritus
PL. DE SANTA TERESA
PL. SAN JUAN BAUTISTA
C. Sta. Teresa
PL. DE LOS BANDOS
C. Brocense
C. Pozo Amarillo
C. Correhuela
C. Pinto
C. Especias
PL. DE LOS SEXMEROS
PL. SAN JULIÁN
PL. SAN CRISTÓBAL
PL. DE LA FUENTE
Peña Primera
Ventura Ruiz Aguilera
C. Clavel
C. Concejo
C. Zamora
PL. DEL MERCADO
G. Santana
Gran Vía
La Parra
C. Banzo
PL. CRUZ VERDE
C. Sorias
Cuesta del Carmen
C. Bordadores
C. Iscar Peyra
C. Espoz y Mina
PL. DE LA LIBERTAD
Reloj
TAXI
PLAZA MAYOR
C. Varillas
C. Arriba
PL. DEL ANGEL
PL. SAN BRETÓN
C. Las Úrsulas
C. Compañía
C. Prior
PL. POETA IGLESIAS
C. San Justo
C. Mártires
PASEO CAMPO DE SAN FRANCISCO
C. Domingo Beruela
PL. DE MONTERREY
PL. DEL PESO
C. Patio de Comedias
PL. SAN ROMAN
C. Juan Almeida
PL. DE LAS AGUSTINAS
Doctrinos
C. Quintana
C. Juan del Rey
Consuelo
C. Ramón y Cajal
TO (1km)
C. Prado
Sánchez Barbero
C. Ancha
C. Meléndez
R. Mayor
Felipe Espino
Miñagustín
Calderos
C. Marquesa de Almarza
PL. SAN BENITO
C. Cañizal
C.T. Viejas
PL. DE COLÓN
TO (100m)
Cuesta San Blas
C. Pan y Carbon
Casa de las Conchas
C. Juan de la Fuente
PL. DE LOS BASILIOS
C. La Florida
Clerecía (Universidad Pontificia)
C. Jesús
PL. SANTO DOMINGO
C. Rosario
C. Cervantes
C. San Pablo
PL. SAN ISIDRO
C. Palominos
Convento de las Dueñas
PL. DE CONSILIO DE TRENTO
PEÑUELAS SAN BLAS
PL. DEL BOTÁNICO
C. Rabanal
R. Antigua
Fco Vitoria
R. Mayor
Colegio Mayor
C. Buenaventura
Convento de San Esteban
C. Cuesta
C. Placentinos
C. El Tostado
La Encarnación
La Cruz
C. de Oviedo
C. Traviesa
PL. DE ANAYA
Museo de Salamanca and Patio de las Escuelas
Universidad
Paz
Casa Museo de Unamuno
Catedral Nueva
C. Carvajal
Arroyo de Santo Domingo
PL. SAN BARTOLOME
PL. DE FRAY LUÍS DE LEÓN
Escuelas Menores y Museo de la Universidad
Doyagüe
Casa Dorado Montero
C. Vaguada Empedrada
Catedral Vieja
Patio Chico
PUERTA SAN PABLO
HUERTA CALIXTO Y MELIBEA
C. la Plata
C. Latina
C. Horno 1a
C. Balmes
C. las Mazas
C. Libreros
C. Trilingue
C. El Expolio
Casa Lis Museo Art Nouveau y Art Deco
P. del Rector Esperabé
TO (4km)
Archivo General de la Guerra Civil
C. Veracruz
PL. DE LA MERCED
PL. MERCADO VIEJO
C. Sta. Maria la Blanca
Av. de los Reyes de España
PL. DEL PUENTE
PL. RÍO
PL. SANTIAGO
P. de San Gregorio
TO (600m)
TO PUBLIC TRACK AND FIELD (200m)
Puente Romano
Río Tormes
Puente Enrique Estéban

Bookstore: Spanning both sides of the street, Librería Cervantes, C. Azafranal, 11-13, and Pl. de Santa Eulalia, 13-19 (☎923 21 86 02), is the closest thing to a superstore. Open M-F 10am-1:30pm and 4:30-8pm, Sa 10am-2pm.

Internet Access: Biblioteca Pública, Casa de Las Conchas, C. Compañía, 2 (☎923 26 93 17). Free internet access and a modern, comfortable reading room. Open July-Aug. M-F 9am-3pm, Sa 9am-2pm; Sept.-June M-F 9am-9pm, Sa 9am-2pm. **Cyber Place Internet,** Pza. Mayor, 10, 1st fl., is flooded with foreign students calling mom, but has good rates on internet (€1 per hour) and long distance calls (€0.10 per minute to the US). Open M-F 11am-midnight, Sa-Su noon-midnight. **Cyber Anuario,** C. Traviesa 16 (☎923 26 13 54) offers internet at €1.50 per hour. Photocopying, printing, fax, CD burning. Open M-Sa 11am-2:30pm and 4:30-11pm.

Post Office: Gran Vía, 25-29 (☎923 28 14 57, fax 923 28 14 57). Lista de Correos. Open M-F 8:30am-8:30pm, Sa 9:30am-2pm. **Postal Code:** 37001.

ACCOMMODATIONS AND CAMPING

Thanks to floods of student visitors, reasonably priced *hostales* and pensiones pepper the streets of Salamanca, especially off Pl. Mayor, R. Mayor, and C. Meléndez. Make reservations a week in advance in July and August.

Pensión Los Ángeles, Pl. Mayor, 10, 2nd-3rd fl. (☎923 21 81 66; www.pensionlosangeles.com). Colorful rooms with balconies over the stunning Pl. Mayor. *Pensión* is very clean and well lit. Ask for a room with a view over the plaza. English spoken. Singles €15-25; doubles €25-60; triples €45-80. MC/V. ❷

Hostal Las Vegas Centro, C. Meléndez, 13, 1st fl. (☎923 21 87 49; www.lasvegascentro.com). TV, Wi-Fi, and friendly owners make for a great deal. Spotless rooms with white tile floor and shower. Singles €20, with bath €24; doubles €30. MC/V. ❷

Hostal Emperatriz, R. Mayor, 18 (☎923 21 91 56; fax 21 87 83). Operates out of the reception of the Hotel Emperatriz next door. Spacious rooms with bath and phone. Rooms with views of R. Mayor can be noisy, but rooms facing the courtyard are quieter. Singles €26; doubles €35. Cash only.

Albergue Juvenil Salamanca, C. Escoto 13-15 (☎923 26 91 41; www.alberguesalamanca.com). One of the least expensive student options in Salamanca, this friendly youth hostel is about a ten minute walk from Plaza Mayor but close to plenty of bars and nightclubs. Rooms are clean but basic. Storage of valuables €1 per night. Dorms with up to 20 beds €12.90; singles €25; doubles €36. Deposit for reservation. MC/V. ❶

Pensión Barez, C. Meléndez, 19 (☎923 21 74 95). Clean pink-and-yellow double rooms overlook the street. Common room with terrace. €14 per person. Cash only. ❶

Camping Regio, on Ctra. Salamanca, 4 km toward Madrid (☎923 13 88 88; www.campingregio.com). **Salmantino** buses leave every 30min. from Gran Vía near Pl. de la Constitución (€0.80). First-class sites with hot showers. Laundry €3. Pool €1.30. €3.20 per person; €2.80 per tent, per car, and for electricity. MC/V. ❶

FOOD

Pork is the city's speciality, with dishes ranging from *chorizo* (spicy sausage) to *cochinillo* (suckling pig). Try Salamanca's *hornazo*, a type of meat-stuffed pie. Cafes and restaurants surround Pl. Mayor, which lights up around 10pm. Try to branch out to the less-touristed north, along **C. Zamora, C. Toro,** and **Gran Vía** for more local fare. **Carrefour,** C. Toro, 82 (☎923 21 22 08), is a central supermarket (Open M-Sa 9:30am-9:30pm). Another tactic is to go from bar to bar, ordering drinks which come with *pinchos*, a more filling relative of tapas.

Restaurante Delicatessen Café, C. Meléndez, 25 (☎ 923 28 03 09). A dramatic departure from the traditional taverns that dominate the restaurant scene, this trendy locale serves up a wide variety of *platos combinados* (€11) and a lunch *menú* (€11) in a colorful solarium. Enjoy breakfast (€2.50) under the glass cupula, or enjoy the fresh air with the chatty, hip crowd sitting outside. Open daily 10am-midnight. MC/V. ❷

El Patio Chico, C. Meléndez, 13 (☎923 26 51 03). *Salmantinos* crowd this rustic joint, but the hefty portions of dishes like the *Farinato* are worth the wait. Try the *morcilla picante* (spicy blood sausage) and expect *pinchos* with your drink at the bar. Entrees €6-17. *Menú* €14. Open daily 1-4pm and 8pm-midnight. MC/V. ❷

Restaurante Isidro, C. Pozo Amarillo, 19 (☎923 26 28 48), a block from Pl. Mayor. Prompt and friendly service, big crowds, and generous portions. Numerous vegetable, seafood, and meat entrees (€4-15.50). You can't go wrong with the great *tortilla de chorizo*. *Menú* €10. Open M-Sa 1-3:30pm and 8-11:30pm. MC/V. ❷

SIGHTS

LA UNIVERSIDAD DE SALAMANCA. Salamanca's highlight is its renowned university, established in 1218. The entrance is one of the country's best examples of Spanish Plateresque, a 15th and 16th century architectural style named after the work of *plateros* (silversmiths) and characterized by the ornate motifs that cover the sandstone walls of Salamanca. Sculpted into the facade is a tiny frog atop a skull, now a mascot for Salamanca. Legend has it that if you find the croaker without assistance, good luck or marriage follow—but it's likely your chances will be spoiled by everyone else already pointing at it.

The old lecture halls inside the university are open to the public. The 15th-century classroom **Aula Fray Luis de León** has been left in more or less its original state; medieval students considered the hard benches luxurious, as most students then sat on the floor. Look for carved graffiti on the benches, an inheritance of 500 years of gossip and unrequited loves. The **Biblioteca Antigua,** one of Europe's oldest libraries, is the most spectacular room of all. The magnificent Plateresque staircase that ascends toward the library is said to represent the perilous path to true knowledge through youth, love, and adventure.

The University would administer its rigorous oral tests in front of the **chapel,** *La Capilla del Estudiante,* 800 years ago. That evening, the town would host a bullfight in honor of those who passed; the fresh blood of the bull was mixed with flour and used to paint the names of the new doctors on the university and cathedral walls. Look closely and you'll see faded red stamps and text on the sandstone. Across the street from the university and through the hall on the left corner of the patio is the **University Museum.** The reconstructed **Cielo de Salamanca,** Fernando Gallego's famous 15th-century fresco of the zodiac which used to crown the ceiling of the Capilla, is preserved here. *(From Pl. Mayor follow R. Mayor, veer right onto R. Antigua, then left onto C. Libreros; the University is on the left. University ☎923 29 45 00, ext. 1225, museum ext. 1150. Museum open M-Sa 10am-2pm and 4-8pm, Su 10am-2pm. University open M-F 9:30am-1:30pm and 4-7:30pm, Sa 9:30am-1:30pm and 4-7pm, Su 10am-1:30pm. €4, students and seniors €2.)*

CATEDRAL NUEVA. It took 220 years (1513-1733) to build this spectacular Gothic structure. Successive architects decided to retain the original late Gothic style but couldn't resist adding touches from later periods, particularly apparent in the Baroque tower. Modern renovators have left their marks too: look for an astronaut and a dragon eating ice cream on the left side of the main door. The church is best viewed first from the ground, but be sure to visit the **Ieronimus** exhibition in the heart of the tower, which offers a spectacular artifactual and architectural exhibition and an even more stunning **view** of the city and the New Cathedral. *(Pl. de Anaya. Cathedral open daily Apr.-Sept. 9am-8pm; Oct.-Mar. 9am-1pm and 4-6pm. Free. Ieronimus open daily 10am-8pm, last entry 7:15pm. €3.)*

CATEDRAL VIEJA. Constructed in 1140, the Romanesque **Catedral Vieja** has one of the most detailed cupolas in Spain, assembled from intricately carved pieces. The oldest part of the cathedral is the **Capilla de San Martín,** with frescoes dating from 1242. Look for the golden-hued statue of the Virgen de la Vega, Salamanca's patron saint. The **museum** features works by Renaissance artists Fernando Gallego and Pedro Bello. Visit the **Patio Chico** behind the cathedral, where students congregate and tourists head for a view of both cathedrals. *(Enter through the Catedral Nueva. Museum ☎923 21 74 76. Cathedral open daily Oct.-Mar. 10am-12:30pm and 4-5:30pm; Apr.-Sept. 10am-7:30pm. €4.25, students €3.50, children €2.75.)*

PLAZA MAYOR. Built on the orders of Bourbon King Philip V, the renowned Plaza Mayor owes its beauty to French architecture. Designed by Alberto Churriguera (see **Architecture**, p. 66) between 1729 and 1755, the plaza contains 88 towering arches, the **Ayuntamiento,** and three pavilions. The **Pabellón Real,** to the right of the *Ayuntamiento*, honors the Spanish monarchy (and, quite controversially, the 20th-century dictator Francisco Franco, behind the blue tarpaulin); the **Pabellón del Sur,** in front of the *Ayuntamiento*, is dedicated to famous Spanish conquistadors; and the **Pabellón del Oeste,** to the left of the *Ayuntamiento*, pays homage to important *salmantinos* like San Juan de Sahagún and Miguel de Unamuno. Additional spaces of honor were left intentionally blank for future generations. Plaza Mayor is a common meeting place for the young and old alike, right under the *reloj* (clock).

MUSEO DE SALAMANCA. Across from the university in the Patio de las Escuelas, the Museo de Salamanca occupies an astounding building that was once home to Álvarez Albarca, physician to Fernando and Isabel. Along with the Casa de las Conchas, this structure is among Spain's most important examples of 15th-century architecture. The museum has an intriguing collection of sculptures and paintings including *Mesa Alegre (Happy Table)* by Vincenzo Camp and *Viejo Bebedor (Old Drunk)* by Esteban March, Juan de Flandes's portrait of San Andrés, and Luis de Morales's *Llanto por Cristo muerto (Cry for the Dead Christ)*. *(Patio de las Escuelas, 2. ☎923 21 22 35. Open June-Sept. Tu-Sa 10am-2pm and 5-8pm, Su 10am-2pm; Oct.-May Tu-Sa 10am-2pm and 4-7pm, Su 10am-2pm. €1.20; students, children, and over 65 €0.60. Free Sa and Su.)*

CASA LIS MUSEO ART NOUVEAU Y ART DECO. This early 20th-century stained-glass palace houses an extensive collection of 19th- and 20th- century glassware, statues of **flappers** in various states of undress, and a set of bottles depicting curmudgeonly old Dickens characters. Walking through the *museo* feels like entering an F. Scott Fitzgerald parlor or Edith Wharton's most animated boudoir. *(C. El Explolio, 14. ☎923 27 10 89; www.museocasalis.org. Open Apr.-Oct. 15 Tu-F 11am-2pm and 5-9pm, Sa-Su 11am-9pm; Oct. 16-Mar 31 Tu-F 11am-2pm and 4-7pm, Sa-Su 11am-8pm. €3, students €2, under 14 free. Free Th 11am-2pm.)*

CASA MUSEO DE UNAMUNO. Miguel de Unamuno, a founding figure of the prolific Spanish literary movement known as the *Generación de 1898*, lived here as rector of the university in the early 20th century. His stand against General Miguel Primo de Rivera's 1923 coup led to his dismissal and exile, though he was triumphantly reinstated some years later. It is said that he began his first lecture back with the line, "As we were saying yesterday..." Poet, author, and intellectual badass, Unamuno's extensive library testifies to his fascination with religious philosophy and his ability to read in 14 different languages. *(C. Libreros, 25. To the right of the university's main entrance. Ring bell if house appears closed. ☎923*

29 44 00, ext. 1196. Open July-Sept. Tu-F 9:30am-1:30pm, Sa-Su 10am-1:30pm; Oct.-June Tu-F 9:30am-1pm and 4-6pm, Sa-Su 10am-1:30pm. Research room open M-F 9am-2pm. Mandatory tour in Spanish every 30min. €3, students €1.50.)

EL ARCHIVO GENERAL DE LA GUERRA CIVIL ESPAÑOLA. Once a vital organ in Franco's anti-Communist repression, this early 18th-century hospital now houses Spain's most extensive collection of Republican documents and rotating exhbitions. During the Spanish Civil War (1936-1939), Franco converted the building into a storage and work facility for the Office of Anti-Communist Investigation and Propaganda, which accumulated information on Republican forces. In 1938, the office was christened the State Delegation for the Recuperation of Documents. After Franco's death in 1975 and the end of his dictatorship, the collection of documents became a general archive, part of Spain's system of study and documentation centers. *(C. El Expolio, 2. ☎923 21 28 45; www.mcu.es/archivos/MC/AGC/index.html. Archive open M-Th 8am-8:30pm, F 8am-7:45pm. Museum on ground floor open Tu-Su 11am-2pm and 5-9pm. To consult documents, bring a passport and acquire a pass from the guards at the front door. Free.)*

CASA DE LAS CONCHAS. Follow R. Mayor from the Plaza Mayor until you reach a plaza with an organ-pipe fountain. On the right, you'll find the 15th-century Casa de las Conchas (House of Shells), with over 300 scallop halves on the facade, one of Salamanca's most famous landmarks. Pilgrims who journeyed to Santiago de Compostela (p. 349) traditionally wore shells to commemorate their visit to the tomb of Santiago. Legend has it that the Jesuits bought and leveled every house in the area to build their college—except the Casa de las Conchas, though they offered to pay one gold coin for every shell. Inquire about periodic *tertulias* (cultural or artistic social gatherings). *(C. Compañía, 2. Library ☎923 26 93 17. Open M-F 9am-9pm, Sa 9am-2pm. Casa open M-F 9am-9pm, Sa-Su 9am-2pm and 4-7pm, Su 10am-2pm and 4-7 pm. Free.)* Directly across from the Casa de las Conchas is **La Clerecía** (Royal College of the Holy Spirit), the main building of La Universidad Pontificia de Salamanca. *(☎923 27 71 00. Open Tu-F 10:30am-12:50pm and 5-7:30pm, Sa 10am-1:20pm and 5-8pm, Su 10am-1:20pm. €2.)*

PUENTE ROMANO. A 2000-year-old Roman bridge spans the scenic Río Tormes at the southern edge of the city. It was once part of the *Camino de la Plata* (Silver Way), a Roman trade route running from Mérida in Extremadura to Astorga. In medieval times, that was the route most Andalusian and Castilian Christians took to complete their pilgrimage to Santiago de Compostela. A headless granite bull called the **Toro Ibérico** guards one end of the bridge. Though it dates to pre-Roman times, the bull gained fame in the 16th century when it appeared in *Lazarillo de Tormes*, the prototype of the picaresque novel and a predecessor of *Don Quixote*. In one karmic episode, Lazarillo gets his head slammed into the bull's ear after cheating his blind employer. *(To reach the bridge, walk downhill toward the river.)*

NIGHTLIFE

Salmantinos claim Salamanca is the best place in Spain **para ir de marcha** (to go out on the town). With some 5,000 bars, Salamanca is not lacking in supplies. *Chupiterías* (bars selling mostly shots), *barres*, and discotecas line nearly every street, and the party doesn't wind down until it's time for *churros con chocolate* at dawn. For out-of-towners, the *marcha* starts in Pl. Mayor, where members of local *tunas* (medieval-style student troubadour groups) strut around the plaza dressed in traditional black capes, serenading women with mandolins and tambourines in hand. Student nightlife spreads out to **Gran Vía, Calle Bordadores,** and side streets, full of disco-bars. **Calle Prior** and **Rúa Mayor** are good bar spots; **Plaza de San Juan Bautista** fills with students kicking off their evening, date in one hand, infamous *litro* of beer in the other. On **C. Prior** and **C. Compañía,** tipsy young Americans and clubby *salmantinos* mix at **Niebla,** C. Bordadores, 14 (☎923 21 45 30) and **Gatsby,** C. Bordadores, 16 (☎923 21 73 62). Both host the same tight pants and free-flowing alcohol. Dress to impress; though none of the clubs have cover charges, bouncers can be picky. Club promoters are often in the streets handing out cards for free drinks.

Bar La Chupitería, Pl. de Monterrey. Make your way through the crowds and psychedelic Beatles posters to order from Los Exóticos, their extensive menu of specialty shots. Absinthe, anyone? *Chupitos* (shots) €1. Beer €2.50. Open daily 10pm-very late.

La Dolce Vita, Gran Vía, 48. Groove to salsa and pop in a Hollywood-themed disco. Unbeatable weeknight promotions on unlimited beer and sangria. Shots €1. Beer €3. Mixed drinks from €5. Open M-Th 10:30pm-3:30am, F-Sa 11pm-4:30am.

Jacko's Bar, C. Iscar Peyra, 22. Cheap shots and *litros* keep students—mostly American—coming to this Michael Jackson-inspired bar. *Litro* of beer, sangria, or *tinto de verano* €2. Specialty *litros* €3.90-7. *Chupitos* €1-1.50. Open daily 9:30pm-3am.

Bar Paniagua, C. Varillas, 1. Smartly dressed student crowd. Rumor has it that Paniagua is the place for foreigners to meet their *salmantino* mate. *Litro* of beer or *calimocho* (wine and Coke) €3.50. Open M-Th and Su 8pm-3am, F-Sa 8pm-5am.

British Museum, C. San Justo, 36. Despite the nerdy name, this bar attracts a laid-back, local student crowd who dig the Beatles, R.E.M., and American blues. Beer €1.50. Open M-Th 7pm-3am, F-Sa 7pm-4:30am.

ENTERTAINMENT AND FESTIVALS

Guia del Ocio, a free pamphlet distributed at the tourist office and at some bars, lists movies, special events, and bus schedules. Posters at the **Colegio Mayor,** Pl. de Anaya, advertise university events, free films, and student theater. On June 12, in honor of San Juan de Sahagún, the **Plaza de Toros** hosts a bullfight for charity. Take **C. Zamora** to **Po. Dr. Torres Villarroel;** the bullring is just beyond Pl. de la Glorieta. (Seats in the sun from €35.) A **Renaissance fair** runs until June 15. Between the end of July and September, Salamanca puts on **Verano en La Cueva,** a weekend music and theater festival in a cave in the Villena Antigua Muralla, across from the Convento de San Esteban. (Shows start at 9:15pm. For more info, visit www.salamanca.es.) Salamanca celebrates the week-long **Fiestas de Salamanca** in honor of their patroness the Virgen de la Vega; exhibitions abound, most honoring the bullfighting that has made the region's *ganaderías* (bull farms) the best in all of Spain. Salamanca goes all out during **Semana Santa,** with local traditions like *Lunes de Aguas.* In the 16th century, King Felipe II ordered all prostitutes to leave the city from Ash Wednesday until the end of Holy Week. A priest known as *El Padre Putas* would escort them across the Tormes and supervise their week of exile while the city put on its pious face. Then, on the Monday after Easter, jubilant students would ferry their Magdalene ladies back triumphantly as *salmantinos* drank and feasted on shore.

SEVILLA

Sevilla (pop. 700,000) embodies the *España* of popular imagination. The Andalusian arts of flamenco, bullfighting, and tapas are at their best in this famously romantic city, an amalgam of disparate political, culinary, and cultural influences. Once the official port for all goods passing in and out of the Americas, Sevilla has been shaped by the wealthiest and most powerful families in Spanish history—a fact to which the imposing Alcázar and grand Cathedral of Santa Cruz attest. But, as the one-time capital of the Moorish empire, many of Sevilla's most beloved buildings and traditions owe more to marginalized Gypsies, Jews, and North Africans than to any noblemen. The tourists who pack Sevilla's narrow, tangled streets in search of this diverse and beguiling cultural legacy join vivacious locals and an enormous student population that together infuse the city with an energy that is hard to match. The student traveler's experience here can be one of the best in Spain—with so many young people packed in during the academic year, the opportunities for things to do and see on a tight budget are almost overwhelming. For a taste of Sevilla fully unhinged, visit during its most prominent festivals—*Semana Santa* and the *Feria de Abril* are among the most lavish celebrations in Europe. No matter when you come, this exuberant and typically Andalusian city will deliver a colorful, multifaceted experience unlike any other to be had in Spain.

HIGHLIGHTS OF SEVILLA

FEEL the **duende** and see what the **flamenco** fuss is all about (p. 159).

SHOUT ¡OLÉ! and cover your eyes at a bullfight in the **Plaza de Toros** (p. 160).

SCREAM with a stadium full of crazed fans at a Betis-Sevilla **fútbol game** (p. 159).

WANDER the tangled, winding streets of Sevilla's bustling **Judería** (p. 147).

INTERCITY TRANSPORTATION

BY PLANE

All flights arrive at **Aeropuerto San Pablo,** Ctra. de Madrid (☎954 449 000; www.aena.es), 12km outside town. A taxi from the center costs about €25. **Los Amarillos** (☎954 989 184) runs a bus from outside the Prado de San Sebastián bus stop across from the university. (M-Sa every 15-30min. 5:15-12:15am; Su every 30min-1hr. 6:15am-11:15pm; €2.10. Also stops at the train station). **Iberia,** C. Guadaira, 8 (☎954 228 901, nationwide 902 400 500; open M-F 9am-1:30pm) runs daily flights to Barcelona (55min.) and Madrid (45min.). For student fares, head to **Barceló Viajes** (p. 148).

BY TRAIN

Estación Santa Justa, Av. de Kansas City. (☎902 240 202. Info and reservations open daily 4:30am-12:30am.) Services include **luggage storage, car rental,** and **ATM.** In town, the RENFE office, C. Zaragoza, 29, posts prices and schedules on the windows and also handles bookings. (☎954 54 02 02. Open in summer 9:30am-2pm and 5:30-8pm, in winter M-F 9am-1:15pm and 4-7pm.) To get to Santa Cruz from the station, take bus C-2 and transfer to C-3 at the Jardines del Valle; it will drop you off on

C. Menéndez Pelayo at the **Jardines de Murillo.** Turn right and walk 1 block past the gardens; C. Santa María la Blanca is on the left. Without the bus, it's a 15-20min. walk. To reach El Centro from the station, catch bus #32 to **Plaza de la Encarnación,** several blocks north of the cathedral.

Altaria and **Talgo** trains to: **Barcelona** (12½hr., 8:20am, €60); **Córdoba** (1hr., 8 per day 6:50am-9:35pm, €15); **Málaga** (2hr., 4-6 per day 6:05am-7:35pm, €35) and **Valencia** (9hr., 8:20am, €50).

AVE trains to **Barcelona** (5½hr., 4pm, €134), **Córdoba** (45min., 12-18 per day 6:15am-9:45pm, €26-30), **Madrid** (2½hr., 12-18 per day 6:15am-9:45pm, €70-78), and **Zaragoza** (3½hr, 4pm, €104)

Regionales trains to: **Almería** (5½hr., 4 per day 7am-5:40pm, €36); **Antequera** (2½hr., 6 per day 6:50am-7:35pm, €28); **Cádiz** (2hr., 11 per day 6:35am-9:35pm, €10); **Córdoba** (1½hr., 6 per day 7:50am-8:15pm, €8.60); **Granada** (3hr., 4 per day 7am-5:40pm, €23); **Huelva** (1hr.; 9:10am, 4:30, 8:40pm; €7.85); **Jaén** (2-3hr.; 1:25, 3, 7:52pm; €18-23); **Málaga** (2½hr., 5-6 per day 7:35am-8:10pm, €18).

BY BUS

Estación Prado de San Sebastián, C. Manuel Vázquez Sagastizábal (☎954 41 71 11), serves most of Andalucía and sits adjacent to its namesake. It's a five-minute walk (right on C. Diego Riaño, right on Av. Carlos V) to the Puerta de Jerez in Santa Cruz. (Open daily 5:30am-1am.) **Estación Plaza de Armas,** Av. Cristo de la Expiración (☎954 90 80 40), sends buses outside of Andalucía, including to many international destinations. (Open daily 5am-1:30am.) Bus C-4 connects the station to Prado de San Sebastián.

ESTACIÓN PRADO DE SAN SEBASTIÁN

Alsina Graells (☎913 270 540; www.alsa.es). Open daily 6:30am-11pm. To: **Almería** (7hr.; 7, 8am, 5pm; €32); **Córdoba** (2-3hr., 10 per day 7:30am-10pm, €10); **Granada** (3hr., 10 per day 8am-11pm, €19-25); **Jaén** (4hr., 1:30pm, €19); **Málaga** (2-3hr., 9 per day 7am-7:30pm, €16); **Murcia** (7½hr;, 3 per day 8, 11am, 11pm; €38).

Los Amarillos (☎902 210 317; www.touristbus.es). Open M-F 7:30am-2pm and 2:309pm, Sa-Su 7:30am-2pm and 2:30-8:30pm. To: **Arcos de la Frontera** (2½hr.; 8am, 2:30pm; €7); **Marbella** (3hr.; 8am, 4pm; €16); **Ronda** (2½hr., 8am, noon, 5pm; €11); **Sanlúcar de Barrameda** (2hr., 5-9 per day 8am-8pm, €7).

Transportes Comes (☎902 199 208; www.tgcomes.es). Open daily 6:30am-10pm. To: **Algeciras** (3½hr., 4 per day 9:30am-7:30pm, €18); **Cádiz** (1hr., 9 per day 7am-10pm, €11.40); **Jerez de la Frontera** (1½hr., 7 per day 10:45am-10pm, €7.50); **Tarifa** (3hr., 4 per day 9:30am-7:30pm, €17).

ESTACIÓN PLAZA DE ARMAS

ALSA (☎913 270 540; www.alsa.es). Open M-F 5:45am-10:30pm, Sa-Su 7:30am-10:45pm. To: **Cáceres** (4-4½hr., 7 per day 7am-8:30pm, €33); **León** (11hr.; 7, 11:30am, 8:30pm; €43); **Lisboa, POR** (6hr.; 3pm, midnight; €45); **Salamanca** (7hr., 6 per day 7am-8:30pm, €31); **Valencia** (9-11hr., 3 per day 9:30am, 4, 10pm, €50-57).

Damas (☎954 908 040; www.damas-sa.es). Open daily 6am-10pm. To: **Badajoz** (3hr., 5 per day 6:45am-8pm, €13.25); **Faro, POR** (4hr.; 4 per day 7:30am, 4:15pm; €16); **Lagos, POR** (7hr.; 7:30am, 6:15pm; €20); **Huelva** (1hr., 16-20 per day 7:30am-9:30pm, €7).

Socibus (☎902 229 292; www.socibus.es). Open daily 7:30-10:30am and 11-12:45am. To **Madrid** (6hr., 7 per day 8am-midnight, €19.40).

ORIENTATION

The **Río Guadalquivir** flows north to south through the city, bordered by Po. de Cristóbal, which becomes Po. de las Delicias by the municipal tourist office. Most of Sevilla's touristy areas, including **Santa Cruz** and **El Arenal,** are on the east bank. The historic *barrios* (neighborhoods) of **Triana, Santa Cecilia,** and **Los Remedios** lie on the western bank. **Avenida de la Constitución,** home of the *Andaluz* tourist office, runs along the cathedral. **El Centro,** a busy commercial pedestrian zone, starts at the intersection of Av. de la Constitución, **Plaza Nueva,** and **Plaza de San Francisco,** site of the *Ayuntamiento* (city hall). **Calle Tetuán** and **Calle Sierpes,** both popular shopping areas, run north from Pl. Nueva through El Centro.

THE NEIGHBORHOODS OF SEVILLA

SANTA CRUZ

In the very center of the city, Santa Cruz embodies Sevilla. The area is called the *Judería* because it was historically the city's Jewish neighborhood, but today its streets are home to more souvenir shops than synagogues. Home to world-class sites and the tourists that attend to them, Santa Cruz has a lively and surprisingly youthful vibe and is a great place to start exploring the city.

EL CENTRO

El Centro, a mess of narrow streets around Pl. de la Encarnación and Pl. del Duque de la Victoria, bustles with shoppers by day but is largely deserted at night. The area near Pl. Alfalfa, a prime tapas location, is more lively.

LA MACARENA

The area north of El Centro doesn't cater to tourists. Its character ranges from quirky to familiar—from tattoo parlors and punk boutiques to authentic bars—and many residents predict that it will be Sevilla's next hot spot.

TRIANA AND EL ARENAL

Immortalized by Siglo de Oro writers Lope de Vega, Francisco de Quevedo, and Miguel de Cervantes, Triana was Sevilla's chaotic 16th- and 17th-century mariners' district. Today, it is home to many of the city's best ethnic restaurants and retains a gritty feel, despite the elegant ceramics that are still manufactured in the local *talleres* (studios). Avoid overpriced C. del Betis and plunge down less expensive side streets. Between the river and Santa Cruz, El Arenal is the known as the "Plaza de Toros" district; it comes to life during the *Feria de Abril.*

LOCAL TRANSPORTATION

Public Transportation: TUSSAM (☎900 71 01 71; www.tussam.es). Most bus lines run daily every 10min. 6am-11:15pm and converge in Pl. Nueva, Pl. de la Encarnación, and at the cathedral. Night service departs from Pl. Nueva (every hr. M-Th and Su midnight-2am; F-Sa all night). C-3 and C-4 circle the center and #34 hits the HI-affiliated hostel, university, cathedral, and Pl. Nueva. €1.20. *Bonobús* (10 rides) €6. 30-day pass €30.

Taxis: TeleTaxi (☎954 622 222). **Radio Taxi** (☎954 580 000). Base rate €1.19 plus €0.83 per km; M-F after 9pm and all day Sa-Su €1.45 base plus €1.01 per km. Extra charge for luggage.

Car Rental: Hertz, at the airport (☎954 514 720; open daily 7am-midnight) and train station (☎954 538 331; open daily 8am-midnight). 25+. AmEx/MC/V.

Moped Rental: Alkimoto, C. Fernando Tirado, 5 (☎954 584 927; www.alkimoto.net). €23 per day. Open M-F 9am-1:30pm and 5-8pm.

Bike Share: Sevici (☎902 011 032; www.sevici.es). If you enjoy biking, this might be your best transportation option in Sevilla. A subscription fee (€5 per week., €10 per year) gains you access to an extensive self-service network of bike hire stations. Up to 30min. free; up to 1hr. €1 with weekly subscription, €0.50 with yearly subscription; each additional hr. €2/1. Subscribe at any Sevici kiosk; credit card required.

PRACTICAL INFORMATION

TOURIST AND FINANCIAL SERVICES

Tourist Offices: Municipal, provincial, and regional tourist agencies provide information on their respective domains:

Centro de Información de Sevilla Laredo, Pl. de San Francisco, 19 (☎954 592 915; www.turismo.Sevilla.org). Main municipal office. English spoken. Open M-F 9am-7:30pm, Sa-Su 10am-2pm.

Naves del Barranco, C. Aronja, 28 (☎954 221 714), near the bridge to Triana. Secondary municipal office. Open M-F 9am-7:30pm.

Turismo de la Provincia, Pl. del Triunfo, 1-3 (☎954 210 005; www.turismodeSevilla.org). Info on daytrips and specific themed itineraries. Open daily 10:30am-2:30pm and 3:30-7:30pm.

Turismo Andaluz, Av. de la Constitución, 21B (☎954 221 404; www.andalucia.org). English spoken. Info on all of Andalucía. Free maps of the region. Open M-F 9am-7:30pm, Sa-Su 9:30am-3pm.

Budget Travel: Barceló Viajes, C. de los Reyes Católicos, 11 (☎954 226 131; www.barceloviajes.com). Open June-Sept. M-F 9:30am-1:30pm and 5-8:30pm, Sa 10am-1pm; Oct.-May M-F 9:30am-1:30pm and 4:30-7:30pm, Sa 10am-1pm.

Currency Exchange: Banco Santander Central Hispano, C. Tetuán, 10, and C. Martín Villa, 4 (☎902 24 24 24). Open M-F 8:30am-2pm, Sa 8:30am-1pm;. Apr.-Sept. closed Sa. Banks and *casas de cambio* (currency exchange) crowd Av. de la Constitución, El Centro, and the sights in Santa Cruz.

LOCAL SERVICES

Luggage Storage: Estación Prado de San Sebastián. (€0.90 per bag per day; open 6:30am-10pm); **Estación Plaza de Armas** (€3.50 per day); **train station** (€3.50 per day).

English-Language Bookstore: Vertice International Bookstore, C. San Fernando, 33 (www.libreriavertice.com), in front of the university. Best selection of English-language books in Sevilla. Open July-Aug. M-F 9:30am-2pm and 5-8:30pm, Sa 11am-2pm. MC/V. **Trueque,** C. Pasaje de Vila, 2 (☎954 563 266). Used books in English and a smattering of other languages. Open M-F 10:30am-1:30pm and 5-8pm, Sa 10:30am-1:30pm. MC/V.

Laundromat: Lavandería Roma, C. Castelar, 2C (☎954 210 535). Wash, dry, and fold €6 per load. Open M-F 9:30am-2pm and 5:30-8:30pm, Sa 9am-2pm.

EMERGENCY AND COMMUNICATIONS

Police: Av. Paseo de las Delicias and Alameda de Hércules (☎091).

Medical Services: Cruz Roja (☎902 222 292). **Hospital Virgen Macarena,** Av. Dr. Fedriani, 56 (☎955 008 000).

Library: Av. María Luisa, 8 (☎954 712 205). Modern space with free internet access. Open from mid-June to mid-Sept. M-F 9am-8:30pm, from mid-Sept. to mid-June M-F 9am-9pm, Sa 9am-2pm.

Internet Access: It is substantially cheaper to use pre-paid minutes; most places offer internet *bonos*, which amount to wholesale bulk minutes (most come with a min. of 2hr. or more). Ask about *bonos* at the counter before using the computers. **Sevilla Internet Center,** Av. de la Constitucion at Almirantazgo (☎954 347 108; www.internetSevilla.com). €0.05 per min. Open daily 9am-10pm.

Post Office: Av. de la Constitución, 32 (☎954 21 64 76). **Lista de Correos** and fax. Have your mail addressed to the *Lista de Correos de la Constitución* (otherwise mail may end up at any of the Sevilla post offices). Open M-F 8:30am-8:30pm, Sa 9:30am2pm. **Postal Code:** 41080.

ACCOMMODATIONS

During *Semana Santa* and the *Feria de Abril*, vacant rooms vanish and prices double; reserve several months in advance. The tourist office has lists of *casas particulares* (private residences) that open for visitors on special occasions. Outside of these weeks, you should reserve a few days in advance and about a week ahead if you're staying for the weekend.

SANTA CRUZ

Santa Cruz's location is excellent, but many of its so-called *"hostales"* charge hotel prices. The narrow streets east of the cathedral around **Calle Santa María la Blanca** are full of less expensive, nearly identical *pensiones*, although the area's cheapest lodging rarely shares the neighborhood's charm. Because Santa Cruz is packed with tourists, it's best to reserve early, but last-minute rooms are not impossible to come by.

Pensión Vergara, C. Ximénez de Enciso, 11, 2nd fl. (☎954 215 668; www.pensionvergara.com). Above a souvenir shop at C. Mesón del Moro. Quirky, antique decor, colorful common spaces, and perfect location. Singles, doubles, triples, and quads, all with shared bath and A/C. No internet. €20 per person. Cash only. ❷

Samay Sevilla Hostel, Menéndez Pelayo, 13 (☎955 100 160; www.samayhostels.com). The lively rooftop terrace at this 2-year-old backpackers' hostel may be the finest in Santa Cruz. Free daily walking tours, internet, and Wi-Fi. Laundry €8. Key deposit €5. 8-bed dorms €15-19, 6-bed €16-20, 4-bed €17-22. MC/V. ❶

Pensión Bienvenido, C. Archeros, 14 (☎ 954 413 655; www.pensionbienvenido.com). 5 comfortable upstairs rooms surround a social patio; downstairs rooms overlook the inner atrium. Basic rooftop terrace with views of the cathedral. All rooms have A/C. Laundry €6. Free Wi-Fi coming soon; call to confirm. Singles €20; doubles €38, with bath €50; triples and quads €60-64. MC/V. ❷

EL CENTRO

Hostal Atenas, C. Caballerizas 1 (☎954 21 80 47; www.hostal-atenas.com), off Pl. de Pilatos. Everything about this hostel is appealing, from the *mudéjar*-style arches and traditional patio to the cheery rooms. All have A/C and baths Internet €1 per 30min. Singles M-Th and Su €43, F-Sa €48; doubles €55/70; triples €70/79; quads €79/86. Prices fall €5-10 in winter. MC/V. ❹

Oasis Sevilla, reception at Pl. Encarnación, 29 1/2 (☎954 29 37 77; www.hostelsoasis.com), rooms above reception and at C. Alonso el Sabio, 1A. Young, international crowd packs this energetic hostel. Co-ed dorms are centrally located above the guests-only **Hiro** lounge. On C. Alonso doubles and 4- to 6-person dorms share bathrooms and fridges and are roomier and quieter. All rooms with A/C. Terrace pool, weekly tapas tours, and free Wi-Fi, internet, and breakfast (served 8-11am). Towels €1. Key deposit €5. Reserve early. Dorms €20; doubles €46. MC/V. ❷

Casa Sol y Luna, C. Pérez Galdós, 1A (☎954 21 06 82 or 626 55 96 10; www.casasolyluna1.com). Magnificent arched doorway and marble staircase are a prelude to antique mirrors, a plush living room, and bright and spacious themed rooms. Friendly staff and quiet atmosphere. Laundry €10. Singles €22; doubles €38, with bath €45; triples €60; quads €80. Min. stay 2 nights. Cash only. ❷

Traveller's Inn Sevilla, C. Augusto Placéncia, 5 (☎954 216 724, www.Sevillabedandbreakfast.es), at Pl. de la Alfalfa. Small, simple, and remarkably affordable rooms surround a bright 3-story atrium with outdoor terrace. Free daily activities include walking tours and pub crawls. All rooms with A/C. Breakfast included. Towels €1. Laundy €4-10. Key deposit €10. 6- to 8-bed dorms €13-17. MC/V. ❶

LA MACARENA

Pensión Macarena, C. San Luis, 91 (☎954 37 01 41; www.hostalmacarena.es). Large yellow and green rooms with A/C surround a sunny inner atrium. Quiet, relaxed atmosphere and friendly staff. Singles €20; doubles €30, with bath and TV €40; triples €45/51. MC/V. ❷

Pensión Alameda, Alameda de Hércules, 31 (☎954 90 01 91; www.hostalalameda.es). Immaculate rooms with Wi-Fi, A/C, TVs, and small rooftop balconies. On the Alamada de Hercules, close to energetic nightlife (and the noise it entails). Singles €25-30; doubles with bath €45-50; triples with bath €60-70. MC/V. ❷

NEAR ESTACIÓN PLAZA DE ARMAS

Pensiones line **C. Gravina,** parallel to C. Marqués de las Paradas two blocks from the station. Hostels here tend to be less luxurious but cheaper than those in other neighborhoods and they're convenient for exploring **El Centro** (5min.) and **C. del Betis** and **Triana** on the west bank of the river (10-15min.).

Hostal Rio Sol, C. Marqués de Paradas, 25 (☎954 229 038; www.hostalriosol.com). Convenient location across from the bus station. A colorful yellow tiled staircase leads to basic rooms, all with TV, A/C, and private bath. Free Wi-Fi. Singles €18-25; doubles €45; triples €60; quads €70-75. AmEx/MC/V. ❷

Pensión Bailén, C. Bailén, 75 (☎954 221 635; www.pensionbailen.com). Small rooms are clean and include fan. Wi-Fi €5. No A/C. Singles €20; doubles €30, wth bathroom €40; triples €40/50; quads €65; quints €75. MC/V. ❷

OUTSIDE THE CENTER

Sevilla Youth Hostel (HI), C. Isaac Peral, 2 (☎955 056 500; inturjoven.com). Take bus #34 across from the tourist office on Av. de la Constitución; the 5th stop is the hostel. A large, institutional hostel popular with school groups. Doubles, triples, and quads, many with balcony and private bath. A/C and breakfast included. Other meals buffet-style for €8. Internet €1 per hr. Dorms €21.50, over 26 €27.50. Discount of €3.50 for HI members. ❶

Camping-Motel Club de Campo, Av. de la Libertad, 13 (☎954 720 250; www.terra.es/personal7/camping.motel), 7km from Sevilla in Dos Hermanas. Los Amarillos runs buses from Sevilla (45min., every 30min.); call ahead for exact directions. Showers and pool. Reception 7am-11pm. €3.65 per person, €3.65 per car; tent rental €3.65-4. MC/V. ❶

FOOD

Sevilla loves its tapas. Locals spend their evenings relaxing and socializing over plates of *caracoles* (snails) and fresh seafood, while sipping glasses of sangria and *tinto de verano* (red wine and lemon soda). For those on a tight budget, markets such as **Mercado de la Encarnación,** Pl. de la Encarnación (typically open M-Sa 8am-2pm; temporarily closed due to construction), and the more modern **Mercado del Arenal,** on C. Pastor y Landero (open M-Sa 9am-3pm), have fresh meat and produce. For a supermarket, try the mammoth basement of **El Corte Inglés** in Pl. del Duque de la Victoria (☎954 279 397), the **Mercadona** in the Centro Commercial Plaza de Armas next to the bus station, or any of the smaller grocery chains, like **%Día, Mas,** and **Super Sol.**

SANTA CRUZ

Restaurants near the cathedral cater almost exclusively to tourists. Food quality and prices improve as you walk down side streets and away from major attractions.

San Marco, C. Mesón del Moro, 6 (☎954 564 390). Branches at C. del Betis, 68 (☎954 28 03 10) and C. Santo Domingo de la Calzada, 5 (☎954 583 343). Entrees and Italian desserts in vaulted basement rooms that once housed Arab baths. A full menu of creative salads (€4.30-9.25), pizza (€7.50-8.90), and meat and fish entrees (€9.60-16.50). Open daily 1-4:15pm and 8pm-12:15am. MC/V. ❸

Bar Entrecalles, Ximenez de Enciso, 14 (☎617 86 77 52). Situated at the center of the tourist buzz, but the reggae music and relaxed atmosphere help maintain a local following. Tapas (only available inside, €2) and delicious gazpacho (meal-sized potion €6) are unusually generous. Open daily 1pm-2am. Kitchen closed 3:30-8pm. Cash only. ❶

Levíes Café-Bar, C. San José, 15 (☎954 215 308). The bar at this tapas restaurant predominates, pouring out deliciously liberal and refreshing glasses of *tinto de varano* (€1.45) and gazpacho (€3.30). Tapas €2.60-3.90. Entrees €6-12. Open M-F 7:30am2am, Sa-Su 11am-2am. ❶

Histórico Horno San Buenaventura, SA, Av. de la Constitución, 16 (☎954 221 819). A restaurant/bar/deli/pastry shop, Histórico Horno hosts a delightfully indulgent selection of everything from ice cream and pastries to stews and gourmet *jamón.* Breakfast until 12:45pm. Takeout available. Open M-Sa 8am-11pm, Su 9am-11pm. AmEx/D/MC/V. ❷

EL CENTRO

Plaza Alfalfa, Plaza de la Encarnación, and **Plaza San Pedro** frame a maze of tiny streets full of unassuming tapas bars and affordable international restaurants.

El Rinconcillo, C. Gerona, 40 (☎954 223 183). Founded in 1670 in an abandoned convent, this *bodega* is the epitome of a local hangout, teeming with gray-haired men deep in conversation and locals stopping in for a quick glass of wine or a delicious tapas spread. The bartender tallies up your tab in chalk on the wooden counter. Tapas €1.80-3.20. *Raciones* €6-14.50. Open daily 1:30pm-1:30am. AmEx/MC/V. ❶

Confitería La Campana, C. Sierpes 1 and 3 (☎954 223 570). Founded in 1885, Sevilla's most famous cafe has twice made an appearance in Spanish short stories, and it continues to serve up *granizadas de limón* (lemon-flavored crushed ice), ice cream (€2-2.50), and an astounding variety of homemade pastries (€1.50-3.40). Open daily 8am-11pm. AmEx/MC/V. ❶

Habanita Bar Restaurante, C. Golfo, 3 (☎606 716 456), off C. Pérez Galdós. Popular vegetarian/vegan-oriented cafe-restaurant serving Cuban fare, pastas, and salads; plenty of options for carnivores, too. Entrees €6.50-16; most available in ½-portions. Open M-Sa 12:30-4:30pm and 8pm-12:30am, Su 12:30-4:30pm. Reserve ahead for peak dinner hours. MC/V. ❷

Bar Europa, C. Siete Revueltas, 35 (☎954 221 354, www.bareuropa.info). Slightly pricier than average, but the award-winning tapas at this stylish, understated bar are worth the splurge. Tapas €2.50-4.50. Wine €1.80-3 per glass. Open M-Sa 8pm-1am, Su 8:30pm-1am. MC/V. ❸

Taberna Coloniales, Pl. Cristo de Burgos, 19 (☎954 229 137). A popular bar with shady outdoor seating on the plaza and a wide assortment of tapas. Most tapas €1.50-3.50. Restaurant open daily 11:30-12:15am. Kitchen closed 4:30-8:30pm. ❶

LA MACARENA

Contemporary cafes line the **Alameda de Hercules** in the east of La Macarena, while cheap, traditional, and undiscovered *cervecerías* fill the neighborhood's many side streets.

La Plazoleta Bodega, C. San Juan de la Palma (☎954 382 791), just past the church on the same side of the street. Serves generous potions of traditional Spanish fare with a contemporary twist. Try the tuna with chocolate sprinkles (€3)—it works. Tapas €2-4. Open daily 1-4pm and 7:30pm-midnight. MC/V over €10. ❷

El Samaritano, C Peris Mencheta, 42 (☎637 032 065). The simple yet creative dishes served at this cafe befit its modern white, red, and black interior. Set menu, including drink and dessert, €9.50. Open daily noon-4pm and 8:30-midnight. MC/V. ❷

TRIANA

Come to Triana for a break from traditional *cafeterías* and tapas joints. Of course, there are plenty of those here too, but this gritty neighborhood's main attraction is its delicious and varied international cuisine. You'll find restaurants serving cuisine from Japan, Argentina, Mexico, and the Middle East packed along **Calle Salado.**

Café-Bar Jerusalém, C. Salado, 6. Neighborhood kebab bar with falafel (€3.80) and chicken, lamb, pork, and cheese shawarma (€3-5.50). Open M, W-Th, and Su 8pm-2am; F-Sa 8pm-3am. AmEx/MC/V. ❶

Mingthao, C.Salado, 4 (☎954 458 046). This elegantly decorated pan-Asian restaurant serves food from Japan, China, Korea, and Thailand. Nationally themed set menus run €7.50-13, but it's the impressive €8 buffet that keeps the locals streaming in (served M-Th lunch and dinner, F lunch only). Limited vegetarian options. Open daily 12:30pm-midnight. MC/V. ❷

SIGHTS

While any visit to Sevilla should include the Catedral and Alcázar, there is much more to the city than Santa Cruz. Around these central icons are winding streets full of tapas joints, *artesanía*, and quirky finds. The **Plaza de Toros** is nestled on the riverbank to the east and serves as an ideal place to begin a scenic tour along the Guadalquivir. North of Santa Cruz, the bustling Centro, home to some of the city's finest museums, contrasts with the peaceful churches of La Macarena. Heading south toward the **Torre del Oro,** garden oases offer a breezy respite from the summer heat. There, the private gardens behind the Alcázar are flanked by the public **Jardines de Murillo,** near to the monumental **Plaza de España** and beautiful **Parque de María Luisa.**

SANTA CRUZ

CATEDRAL

Entrance by Pl. de la Virgen de los Reyes. ☎954 21 49 71; www.catedralSevilla.com. Open M-Sa 11am-5pm, Su 2:30-6pm. Last entry 1hr. before closing. €7.50, seniors and students under 26 €2, under 16 free. Audio tour €3. Mass held in the Capilla Real M-Sa 8:30, 10:30am, noon; Su 8:30, 10:30, 11am, noon, and 1pm. Free.

Legend has it that the *reconquistadores* wanted to demonstrate their religious fervor by constructing a church so great that "those who come after us will take us for madmen." Sevilla's immense cathedral does appear to be the work of an extravagant madman—with 44 individual chapels, it is the third largest in the world, after St. Peter's Basilica in Rome and St. Paul's Cathedral in London, and it is the biggest Gothic edifice ever constructed.

In 1402, a 12th-century Almohad mosque was destroyed to clear space for the cathedral. All that remains is the **Patio de Los Naranjos,** where the faithful washed before prayer, the **Puerta del Perdón** entryway from C. Alemanes, and **La Giralda** minaret, built in 1198. The tower and its twins in Marrakesh and Rabat are the oldest and longest-surviving Almohad minarets in the world. The 35 ramps leading to the tower's top were installed to replace the stairs that once stood there, allowing a disabled *muezzín* to ride his horse up to issue the call to prayer. Climbing the ramps will leave you breathless, as will the views from the top—the entire city of Sevilla lies just on the other side of the iron bells. (Be warned that these bells sound every 15min., and they are very loud.)

The 42m central **nave,** decorated with 3 tons of gold leaf, is considered one of the greatest in the Christian world—take a good look at its four tiers via a well-placed mirror on the nave's floor. In the center of the cathedral, the Renaissance-style **Capilla Real** stands opposite choir stalls made of mahogany recycled from a 19th-century Austrian railway. The **retablo mayor,** one of the largest in the world, is an intricately wrought portrayal of saints and disciples. Nearby, the bronze **Sepulcro de Cristóbal Colón** (Columbus's tomb) is supported by four heralds that represent the ancient kingdoms of Spain united by Fernando and Isabel. The coffin holds Columbus' remains, brought back to Sevilla from Cuba in 1898. Farther on stands the **Sacristía Mayor,** which holds works by Ribera, Zurbarán, Goya, and Murillo, and a glittering Corpus Cristi icon.

ALCÁZAR

Pl. del Triunfo, 7. ☎954 50 23 23. Open daily Apr.-Sept. 9:30am-7pm; Oct.-Mar. 9:30am5pm. Tours of private residence every 30min. Aug.-May 10am-1:30pm and 3:30-5:30pm; June-July 10am-1:30pm. Max. 15 people per tour, so buy tickets in advance. €7.50, students, over 65, and under 16 free. Tours €4.20. English audio tours €3.

The oldest European palace still used as a private residence for royals, Sevilla's Alcázar exudes extravagance. The palace, built by the Moors in the seventh century and embellished in the 17th century, is a mix of Moorish, Gothic, Renaissance, and Baroque architectural elements, but its intricacies are most prominently displayed in the *mudéjar* style of many of its many arches, tiles, and geometric ceiling designs. Fernando and Isabel, the Catholic monarchs of *reconquista* fame, are the palace's best known former residents; Carlos V also lived here after marrying his cousin Isabel of Portugal in the **Salón Techo Carlos V.**

The Alcázar is a network of splendid patios and courtyards, around which court life revolved. From the moment you step through the **Patio de la Montería,** the melange of cultures is apparent; an Arabic inscription praising Allah is carved in Gothic script. Through the archway is the **Patio del Yeso,** an exquisite geometric space first used by Moorish governors. The center of public life at the Alcázar, however, was the **Patio de las Doncellas** (Patio of the Maids), a colonnaded quadrangle encircled by tiled archways. The **Patio de las Muñecas** (Patio of the Dolls), served as a private area for Moorish kings; the room had an escape path so that the king would not have to cross a wide-open space during an attack. The columns are thought to have come from the devastated **Madinat Al-Zahra,** built at the height of the caliph period. Look for the little faces at the bottom of one column for a hint at how the patio got its name.

The palace's interior is a sumptuous labyrinth where even the walls are works of art. In the **Sala de los Azulejos del Alcázar,** history's stain is literally visible—the room was the stage of a bloody duel between 14th-century King Pedro I and his half-brother Fadrique, and even today the traces of unlucky Fadrique's blood can be seen on the floor. On a more peaceful note, the golden-domed **Salón de los Embajadores** (Ambassadors' Room) is rumored to be the site where Fernando and Isabel welcomed Columbus back from the New World. Their son, Juan, was born in the red-and-blue tiled **Cuarto del Príncipe.** The private residences upstairs, the official home of the King and Queen on their visits to Sevilla, have been renovated and redecorated throughout the years, and most of the furniture today dates from the 18th and 19th centuries. These rooms are accessible only by 25min. guided tours.

OTHER SIGHTS AROUND SANTA CRUZ

CASA LONJA. Between the cathedral and the Alcázar stands the 16th-century Casa Lonja, built as a commercial center for trade with the Americas. Today, it contains a collection of over 44,000 documents relating to the conquest of the New World and hosts temporary exhibitions. Highlights include Juan de la Costa's wildly inaccurate **Mapa Mundi** (world map) and letters from Columbus. *(Av. de la Constitución, 3, across from the post office. ☎954 50 05 28. Open M-Sa 9am-3:45pm, Su 10am-1:45pm. Free. Access to documents is limited to scholars.)*

TEMPLO ROMANO. Rising on C. Mármoles are the ruins of the Templo Romano. Its two columns ascend 15m from below street level and offer a glimpse of the depth of Sevilla's history; river sediment, accumulated after the construction of the temple, caused the ground level to rise.

OTHER SIGHTS. After Fernando III forced Jews who had been exiled from Toledo during the Inquisition to live in Santa Cruz, the area thrived as a lively **Jewish quarter,** and some locals still refer to it as the *judería*. Unfortunately, few sites of Jewish heritage remain. C. Gloria leads to the **Hospital de los Venerables,** a hospital-church adorned with art from the Sevillana School. The small garden and courtyard are calming respites from the city. *(Pl. de los Venerables. ☎954 56 26 96; www.focus.abengoa.es. Open daily for guided visits 10am-2pm and 4-8pm. €4.75, students €2.40. Children under 12 free. Free Su 4-8pm.)* **Calle Lope de Rueda,** off C. Ximénez de Enciso, is graced with two noble mansions, beyond which lies the fragrant **Plaza de Santa Cruz,** built on the former site of the neighborhood's main synagogue. South of the plaza are the **Jardines de Murillo,** a shady expanse of shrubbery, benches, and hidden water features.

SOUTH OF SANTA CRUZ. At the southern edge of the Jardines de Murillo, diagonally across Pl. Don Juan de Asturias, is the **Prado de San Sebastián,** a small manicured public park. Crossing the Av. de Portugal on the park's southern border will bring you to the **Plaza de España,** a 200m wonder of a building constructed for the 1929 Ibero-American Exposition. Designed by **Aníbal González,** one of Sevilla's most prominent 20th-century architects, the aristocratic-looking structure hugs a sweeping plaza, featuring tiled floors and a large marble fountain within the semicircle. Mosaics depicting every Spanish province line the colonnade, and balconies offer a view of the nearby **Parque de María Luisa,** a lush botanic garden filled with Moorish tiled fountains, a wide variety of bird species, and plants from across the world. *(Open in summer 8am-midnight, winter 8am-10pm.)* The park is also home to two adjacent museums: the **Museo de Artes y Costumbres Populares,** a small collection of Andalusian furniture and textiles housed in a beautiful Arabesque pavilion, and the **Museo Arqueológico,** with an extensive collection of Roman statuary and other artifacts. *(Pl. de América. Museo de Artes y Costumbres Populares ☎954 712 391. Museo Arqueológico ☎954 786 474; www.museosdeandalucia.es. Both museums open Tu-Sa 9am-8:30pm, Su 9am-2:30pm. €1.50 each; EU citizens free.)*

EL CENTRO

MUSEO PROVINCIAL DE BELLAS ARTES. This museum contains Spain's finest collection of works by painters of the Sevillana School, most notably Murillo, Valdés Leal, and Zurbarán, as well as El Greco and Dutch master Peter Brueghel. Much of the art was cobbled together from convents in the mid-1800s, finding a stately home amid the traditional tiles and courtyards of this impressive building. Not to be missed are **Gallery V** (formerly a church, it's a splendid setting for Baroque art) and José Villegas Cordro's somber 1913 canvas *La muerte del maestro* upstairs. *(Pl. del Museo, 9. ☎954 786 500; www.museosdeandalucia.es. Open Tu-Sa 9am-8:30pm, Su 9am-2:30pm. €1.50, students and EU citizens free.)*

MUSEO DEL BAILE FLAMENCO. See flamenco as you've never seen it before. Let life-size virtual dancers whisk you away to the heart of a gypsy camp, where screen after screen lights up with color and song to convey the history, music, and technique of this Andalusian art. The museum also features daily live performances and flamenco classes Monday through Thursday. *(C. Manuel Rojas Marcos, 3. ☎954 34 03 11; www.museoflamenco.com. Open daily 9am-7pm. €10, students and groups €8, children €6. 30min. performances M-Th 7pm, €12; 1hr. performances F-Sa 7:30pm, €25. Flamenco classes M-Th 6:30pm, €10. MC/V.)*

CASA DE PILATOS. This palatial residence has been inhabited continuously by Spanish aristocrats since the 15th century, and it effortlessly merges Andalusian architecture and art. On the ground floor, Roman artifacts coexist with tropical gardens in *mudéjar* patios. The second floor features rooms decorated over the centuries with oil portraits, sculptures, painted ceilings, and tapestries. *(Pl. de Pilatos, 1. ☎954 225 298. Open daily Apr.-Sept. 9am-7pm, Oct.-Mar. 9am-6pm. Guided tours every 30min. 10am-6pm. Ground level €5, with upper chambers €8; children under 10 free; EU citizens free Tu 1-5pm.)*

OTHER SIGHTS. Calle Sierpes, which starts in Pl. San Francisco, cuts through the Aristocratic Quarter. At the beginning of this street, a plaque marks the spot where the royal prison once loomed. Some scholars believe that Cervantes began writing *Don Quixote* here. Taste a sweet Spanish tradition at the **Convento de Santa Inés:** the nuns sell pastries and cakes through the courtyard's *torno* (revolving window). *(C. María Coronel. Sweets €2.50-7, sold by the kg. and dozen. Mixed box of pastries €10-12. Open M-Sa 9am-1pm and 5-6:45pm.)* The **Ayuntamiento,** Sevilla's city hall, has 16th-century Gothic and Renaissance interior halls, a domed ceiling, and a Plateresque facade. Art exhibitions take place here, framed by the building's beautiful stone work. *(Pl. de San Francisco; enter from Pl. Nueva. ☎954 590 107. Visits June Tu-Th at 6 and 6:30pm, from mid-Sept. to May at 5:30 and 6pm. Passport or other official documentation required. Free.)*

LA MACARENA

CONVENTO DE SANTA PAULA. The Convento de Santa Paula includes a church with Gothic, *mudéjar*, and Renaissance elements, as well as Montañés sculptures and Ribera's **San Jerónimo.** Nuns peddle **homemade marmalade** (300g, €2-3) and angel hair pastries. Knock if the door is closed. *(Pl. Santa Paula, 11. ☎954 536 330; www.santapaula.es. Museum open Tu-Su 10am-1pm. Church officially open Tu-Su 10am-1pm and 5-6:30pm, though often closes unpredictably during these hours. €2.)*

CHURCHES. A stretch of *murallas* (walls) built in the 12th century lines Ronda de Capuchinos near Pta. de Córdoba. Flanking the west end of the walls, the **Basílica de la Macarena** houses the venerated *Nuestra Señora de la Esperanza,* borne through the streets at the climax of the Semana Santa processions. *(C. Bécquer, 1. ☎954 90 18 00; www.esperanzamacarena.es. Basílica open M-Sa 9am-2pm and 5-9pm, Su 9:30am-2pm and 5-9pm. Basilica free. Museum €3.50, students €1.50. Mass M-F 9, 11:30am, 8, and 8:30pm; Sa 9am and 8pm; Su 10:30am, 12:30, and 8pm.)* Nearby, the Baroque **Iglesia de San Luis** has an unparalleled stained glass altar flanked by relics, including two skulls. *(C. San Luis. ☎954 55 02 07. Open Tu-Th 9am-2pm, F-Sa 9am-2pm and 5-8pm. Free.)* Toward the river is **Iglesia de San Lorenzo y Jesús del Gran Poder,** with Montañés's lifelike sculpture, *El Cristo del gran poder;* worshippers come to kiss Jesus's ankle. *(Pl. San Lorenzo. ☎954 915 672; www.gran-poder.es. Open M-Th 8am-1:30pm and 6-9pm, F 7:30am-10pm, Sa-Su 8am-2pm and 6-9pm. Free.)*

OTHER SIGHTS. A large garden beyond the *murallas* and the Basílica leads to the **Hospital de las Cinco Llagas,** a spectacular Renaissance building recently renovated to host the Andalusian parliament. Thursday mornings, a large flea market is held along **Calle Feria.** *(Th 9am-2pm.)* **Alameda de Hércules** is filled with outdoor cafes, and its side streets burgeon with funky restaurants.

EL ARENAL AND TRIANA

A riverside esplanade stretches along the banks of the Guadalquivir from the base of the Torre del Oro. Somewhat kitschy boat tours of Sevilla leave from in front of the tower (1hr., €15). To head out solo, look for **Lipasam Piragüismo** or head to **Pedalquivir Kayaking** (☎679 194 046. Open daily noon-9:30pm.)

PLAZA DE TOROS DE LA REAL MAESTRANZA. Bullfighting has been a staple of *Sevillano* culture for centuries, as evidenced by the city's beautiful and world-renowned Plaza de Toros. Home to one of the two great bullfighting schools (the other is in Ronda), the plaza fills to capacity (13,800) for the 13 *corridas* of the **Feria de Abril** (p. 160). Multilingual tours take visitors through a small museum, the chapel where *matadores* pray before fights, and the emergency room used when their prayers go unanswered—though only three matadors have died in the history of bullfighting in Sevilla. *(☎954 224 577; www.realmaestranza.com. Open May-Oct. 9:30am-8pm; Nov.-Apr. 9:30am-7pm. Mandatory tours every 20min. in English and Spanish. €6; students and seniors €2. See Bullfighting, p. 160, for ticket info.)*

TORRE DEL ORO Y MUSEO NAVAL. The 12-sided **Torre del Oro** (Tower of Gold), built by the Almohads in the early 13th century, overlooks the river from Po. de Cristóbal Colón. Today, a tiny yellow dome is the only remnant of the golden tiles that once covered the tower. Inside is the small **Museo Maritimo Naval,** a storehouse of maritime antiquities. Museum officers enthusiastically tend to visitors. *(☎954 222 419. Open Sept.-July Tu-F 10am-2pm, Sa-Su 11am-2pm. €2, students and seniors €1. Tu free.)*

OTHER SIGHTS. The **Torre de la Plata** (Tower of Silver) was once connected to the Torre del Oro by underwater chains designed to protect the city from river-borne trespassers. With old-fashioned piracy no longer a concern, the Torre is now a bank. One block farther inland, between Pte. de Isabel II and Pte. de San Telmo, is the **Iglesia de Santa Ana,** Sevilla's oldest church and the focal point of the fiestas that take over in July. *(C. Pelay Correa. Open M and W 7:30-8:30pm.)*

NEAR ESTACIÓN PLAZA DE ARMAS

CENTRO ANDALUZ DE ARTE CONTEMPORÁNEO. If you're interested in Spain's vibrant art scene, the 10-minute trek across the river from the Estación de

Armas is worth it. The interior of this repurposed monastery complex is a labyrinth of clean white spaces exhibiting everything from a collection of works inspired by writer Frederico García-Lorca to a room-sized late 20th-century take on the medieval tapestry. The monestary church at the center of the complex has been restored and is included in the cost of admission. The *centro* also frequently hosts special exhibitions and film viewings. *(Av. Américo Vespucio, 2. ☎955 037 070; www.caac.es. From the Plaza de Armas, walk 2 blocks to the left along Calle Torneo and cross the narrow Puente de la Cartuja; signs will direct you to the entrance. Open Tu-F 10am-9pm, Sa 11am-9pm, Su 10am-3pm. Last entry 30min. before closing. €3; €1.80 for monastery or art alone. Tu free.)*

NIGHTLIFE

Sevilla's nightlife is as hot as its scorching summer afternoons. During the school year, bars and *discotecas* throughout the city are packed regardless what day it is. Come summer, many indoor venues close as crowds head to breezy riverside *terrazas* and giant outdoor dance clubs. No matter the season, a typical night out on the town begins with tapas and drinks (in bars or in a giant mass of students on the city's major plazas), continues with dancing at *discotecas*, and ends with an early morning breakfast of *churros con chocolate*. Perennially energetic bars can be found around **Calle Mateos Gago** near the cathedral, **Calle Adriano** by the bullring, and **Calle del Betis** across the river in Triana; several popular summertime clubs lie along the river near **Puente de la Barqueta.** Gay establishments cluster around the **Plaza de Armas** and the **Alameda de Hercules** in La Macarena.

SANTA CRUZ AND SOUTH

La Carbonería, C. Levies, 18 (☎954 22 99 45). A gigantic cellar bar frequented by students and young summer travelers. Agua de Sevilla pitchers €20 (M-W and Su €15). Sangria pitchers €8.50. Free live flamenco shows nightly at 11pm. Open daily 8pm-3 or 4am. Cash only.

Terraza Chile, Po. de las Delicias at Av. de Chile. A 5min. walk from the Puente de San Telmo along the riverside Po. de las Delicias, away from the Torre del Oro. This popular, unpretentious bar-cafe transforms into a packed dance club Th-Sa, when loud salsa and pop bring together young *Sevillanos,* foreign students, and tourists. Beer from €2; mixed drinks from €5. Open June-Sept. M-W 9am-3am, Th-Sa 9am-5am; Oct.-May M-Th 9am-1am, F-Sa 9am-4am. MC/V.

LA MACARENA AND WEST

The **Alameda de Hercules,** a five-block plaza packed with bars and cafes, is transformed into a giant outdoor student party on Friday and Saturday nights, and is the perfect setting for an epic barhop. The area just across the river near the **Puente de la Barqueta** is the place to go for upscale summer clubbing. From the northern end of the Alameda, follow C. Calatrava for 5min. until you reach the bridge. (The A2 night bus runs at midnight, 1, and 2am from Pl. Nueva; ask to be let off near Pte. de la Barqueta. Taxi from Pl. Nueva €5-8.)

Antique (www.antiquetheatro.com), to the left of the Pte. de la Barqueta facing away from La Macarena. A monumental outdoor playground for Sevilla's rich and beautiful. Egyptian-stye columns preside over a lush outdoor dance space complete with VIP cabanas and a waterfall. Dress well and come before 2am to avoid a long line. Mixed drinks €8. No cover. Open in summer Tu-Su midnight-7am. MC/V.

Ritual (www.todounritoalacopa.com), to the right of the Pte. de la Barqueta facing away from La Macarena. Dancers in shimmering outfits and silky tents hung with North African lamps lend this upscale outdoor lounge and dance club a desert-oasis feel. Well-dressed 20-somethings dance to American hip hop, Latin favorites, and lots of reggaeton. Wine and mixed drinks from €6. Typically 21+. No cover. Open in summer daily 10pm-late. AmEx/MC/V.

Funclub, Alameda de Hercules (www.funclubSevilla.com). This chrome-accented performance space hosts regular pop, rock, funk, and hip-hop concerts that transition to dance parties after 2am. Cover typically €5, includes 1 drink. Closed July-Sept. Open Th 10pm-6am, F-Sa 10pm-7am. Cash only.

TRIANA

Puerto de Cuba, C. del Betis (www.riogrande-Sevilla.com), immediately to the right of the Pte. de San Telmo as you cross into Triana. Right on the bank of the river, it's hard to believe this palmy oasis has no cover charge. Recline in a wicker couch or curl up in a pillow-strewn beached dingy. Th-Sa dance parties. Dressy casual will get you past the bouncers and to the bar (beer €3.50; mixed drinks from €6.50). Open only in summer daily 10:30pm-4am.

Boss, C. del Betis, 67 (☎954 000 101; www.salaboss.es). In Sevilla, the night is always young, and Boss is...boss. Irresistible beats, a packed dance floor, and hazy blue lights make this a top nocturnal destination. Sa Boss Light for the under-18 crowd. Beer €3.50. Mixed drinks €6. Open W-Sa 9pm-5am. Closed in summer. MC/V.

GLBT NIGHTLIFE

Noveccento, C. Julio Cesar, 10 (☎954 229 102; www.noveccento.com). A predominantly lesbian crowd sips mojitos (€6) and chills in this cozy, relaxed bar. Open in summer M-Th and Su 8pm-3am, F-Sa 8pm-4am; in winter M-Th and Su 5pm-3am, F-Sa 5pm-4am. Cash only.

Hércules Mítico, Alameda de Hercules, 93 (☎954 375 992). This small, dancy bar attracts gay men and their admirers, especially during winter. House music. Beer €3. Wine €6. Open daily 4pm-4am. Cash only.

Itaca, C. Amor de Dios, 31 (☎954 907 733). 18- to 70-year-old men come to this dimly lit club to hit the dance floor, chill in the interior "sala de video," and take general advantage of the darkness. Fills around 3:30am. Mixed drinks €7. Drag and other performances Tu, Th, and Su. Cover €7, includes 1 drink. 18+. Open M-Th and Su 12:30pm-5am, F-Sa 10:30pm-7am. Cash only.

ENTERTAINMENT

The tourist office distributes *El Giraldillo* and its English counterpart, *The Tourist,* two free monthly magazines with listings on music, art exhibits, theater, dance, fairs, and film. It can also be found online at www.elgiraldillo.es.

THEATERS

Sevilla is a haven for the performing arts. The venerable **Teatro Lope de Vega** (☎954 590 867; www.teatrolopedevega.org), near Parque de María Luisa, has long been the city's leading stage. Ask about scheduled events at the tourist office or check the bulletin board in the university lobby on C. San Fernando. **Sala la Herrería** and **Sala la Imperdible** put on avant-garde productions in Pl. San Antonio de Padua. (Both ☎954 388 219; www.imperdible.org.) **Teatro de la Maestranza,** on the river between the Torre del Oro and the bullring, is a splendid concert hall that hosts orchestral performances, opera, and dance. (☎954 226 573; www.teatromaestranza.com. Box office open M-F 10am-2pm and 6-9pm.) On spring and summer evenings, neighborhood fairs are often accompanied by **free open-air concerts** in Santa Cruz and Triana. **Avenida 5 Cines,** C. Marqués de las Paradas, 15 (☎954 293 025), and **Corona Center,** in the mall between C. Salado and C. Paraíso in Triana (☎954 278 064), screen films from various countries subtitled in Spanish. For more theaters, look under "Cinema" in *El Giraldillo* or any local newspaper.

FLAMENCO

Sevilla would not be Sevilla without flamenco. Born of a *gitano* (gypsy) musical tradition, flamenco consists of dance, guitar, and songs characterized by spontaneity and passion. Rhythmic clapping, intricate fretwork on the guitar, throaty wailing, and rapid foot-tapping accompany the swirling dancers. Flamenco can be seen either in the touristy *tablaos,* where skilled professional dancers perform, or in *tabernas,* bars where locals dance *Sevillanas.* Both are good, but the *tabernas* tend to be free. In addition, the **Museo del Baile Flamenco** brings together a variety of top-notch performers for late-afternoon shows (p. 155). The tourist office provides a complete list of flamenco venues; ask about student discounts.

TABLAOS

Signs advertising *tablao* shows are everywhere, from souvenir shops to internet cafes, and the majority of flamenco *tablaos* in Sevilla cater to the tourist crowd rather than to true flamenco aficionados. Many *tablaos* are *tablao-restaurantes,* so you can eat while watching the show, but dinner tends to be very expensive. Less expensive alternatives are the impressive one-hour shows at the cultural center **Casa de la Memoria Al-Andalus,** C. Ximénez de Enciso, 28, in the middle of Santa Cruz. Ask at the tourist office or swing by their ticket office for a schedule of different themed performances, including traditional Sephardic Jewish concerts. (☎954 560 670; www.casadelamemoria.es. Shows nightly 9pm, in summer also 10:30pm; seating is very limited, so reserve your tickets a day or two ahead and up to four days in advance for weekend shows. €15, students €13, under 10 €9.) **Los Gallos,** Pl. de Santa Cruz, 11, is arguably the best tourist show in Sevilla. Buy tickets in advance and arrive early. (☎954 216 981; www.tablaolosgallos.com. 2hr. shows nightly 8 and 10:30pm. Cover €29, includes 1 drink.) **Casa Carmen Arte Flamenco,** C. Marqués de Paradas, 30, draws a student crowd. (☎954 21 28 89; www.casacarmenarteflamenco.com. Hour-long shows nightly 9:30 and 11pm. Reserve in advance. Cover €16, students €12.) Consult the tourist office or entertainment listings for more venues.

TABERNAS

La Carbonería, C. Levies, 18, fills with students and backpackers (p. 157). **El Tamboril,** Pl. de Santa Cruz, hosts a primarily middle-aged tourist crowd for midnight singing and dancing. (☎954 561 590. Open daily June-Sept. 5pm-3am; Oct.-May noon-3am.) Bar-filled Calle del Betis, across the river, houses several other *tabernas:* **Lo Nuestro, El Rejoneo,** and **Taberna Flamenca Triana.**

FÚTBOL

Sevilla has two professional teams, and soccer fever engulfs the city, especially when the cross-town rivals play each other. **Real Betis** wears green and white, **Sevilla FC** white and red. Sevilla FC plays at **Estadio Ramón Sánchez Pizjuán** (☎954 535 353) on Av. de Eduardo Dato, and Real Betis plays at **Estadio Manuel Ruiz de Lopera** (☎954 610 340) on Av. de la Palmera. Buy tickets at the stadium; price and availability depend on the quality of the match-up. Both teams struggle against the competitive **Barcelona** and **Real Madrid** clubs.

BULLFIGHTING

Sevilla's bullring hosts bullfights from *Semana Santa* through October. The cheapest place to buy tickets is at the ring on Po. Alcalde Marqués de Contadero. When there's a good *cartel* (line-up), buy tickets at booths on **Calle Sierpes, Calle Velázquez,** and **Plaza de Toros.** Prices can run from €20 for a *grada de sol* (nosebleed seat in the sun) to €75+ for a *barrera de sombra* (front-row seat in the shade). The two main options are *corridas de toros* (traditional bullfights) or *novilladas* (fights with apprentice bullfighters and younger bulls). During July and August, *corridas* occasionally occur on Thursday at 9pm; check posters around town. (Pl. de Toros ticket office ☎954 50 13 82; www.plazadetorosdelamaestranza.com. For more on bullfighting, see p. 71.)

SHOPPING

Sevilla is a great place to find Andalusian crafts, such as hand-embroidered silk, lace shawls, and traditional flamenco wear, albeit often at inflated tourist prices. **El Centro,** the area including C. las Sierpes, C. San Eloy, C. Velázquez, and C. Francos, offers a wide array of crafts, including ceramic shops, the most popular Spanish clothing chains, and hundreds of tiny shoe boutiques and jewelry stores. In **Santa Cruz,** the streets are packed with identical souvenir shops selling bullfighting and flamenco-themed clothing, trinkets, and postcards. A large, eclectic **flea market** is held Thursday 9am-2pm, extending along C. Feria. In February, July, and August, all of the stores hold huge **rebajas** (sales), during which everything is marked down 30-70%.

FESTIVALS

Sevilla swells with tourists during its fiestas, and with good reason: the parties are world-class. If you're in Spain during any major festivals, head straight to Sevilla—you won't regret it. Reserve a room a few months in advance, and expect to pay at least twice what you would normally.

Semana Santa, from Palm Sunday to Easter Sunday. In each neighborhood, thousands of penitents in hooded cassocks guide *pasos* (huge, extravagantly-decorated floats) through the streets, illuminated by hundreds of candles; the climax is Good Friday, when the entire city turns out for a procession along the bridges and through the oldest neighborhoods. Book rooms well in advance. The tourist office stocks a helpful booklet on accommodations and food during the festivities.

Feria De Abril, the final week in April. The city rewards itself for its Lenten piety with the *Feria de Abril,* held in the southern end of Los Remedios. Begun as part of a 19th-century revolt against foreign influence, the Feria has grown into a massive celebration of all things Andalusian, with circuses, bullfights, and flamenco. A spectacular array of flowers and lanterns decorates over 1000 kiosks, tents, and pavilions, known as *casetas,* which each have a small kitchen, bar, and dance floor. Most *casetas* are private, however, and the only way to get invited is by making friends with locals. The city holds bullfights daily during the festival; buy tickets in advance.

DAYTRIPS FROM SEVILLA

PARQUE DOÑANA

Doñana is accessible from almost any city in Andalucía. Bus schedules vary, but both Empresa Damas (☎954 90 77 37) and Los Amarillos (☎954 98 91 84) run to towns in the park's boundaries. Buses leave Sevilla's Pl. de Armas station 6 times per day. The easiest way to see Doñana is by car. Take A-483 off of A-92; 45min. ☎959 43 04 32; www.infodonana.com/donanavisitas. Open daily 9am-7pm. Trips through Parque Nacional leave Tu-Su from May to mid-Sept. 8:30am and 8pm; from mid-Sept. to Apr. 8:30am and 3pm. €23.

One of Europe's largest national parks, with everything from cork trees to wild buzzards, the immense and diverse Doñana park is both daunting and inspiring. The southern zone is the **Parque Nacional,** while the northern area is called the **Parque Natural,** a distinction that often proves confusing for visitors. The Parque Natural is more popular with long-term visitors and nature enthusiasts; there are ample opportunities for horseback-riding and hiking. Like the Marismas del Odiel, Doñana has its fair share of flamingos. The provincial tourist offices in Sevilla provide information on the park, including detailed driving directions, hiking suggestions, campsites, restaurants, and lodging in nearby towns. To visit the Parque Nacional, it's necessary to make a reservation for a tour (4hr., 80km) that includes a boat ride across the Río Guadalquivir and a trip in an all-terrain vehicle through the three ecosystems of the park—dunes, wetlands, and arid, coniferous forest.

ANDALUCÍA

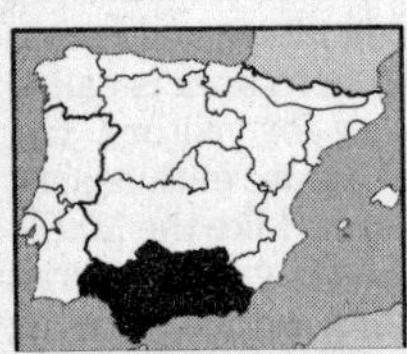

Situated at the crossroads between Western Europe and Africa, Andalucía is steeped in thousands of years of cultural heritage. Its intoxicating mix of Roman, Moorish, and *gitano* cultures can be found anywhere from the cities of Sevilla and Granada to the tiniest mountain villages of the Alpujarras. Andalucía has no single image: Roman ruins, monumental churches, medieval castles, sun-drenched beaches, snowy peaks, orange trees, and shimmering silver olive groves all have their place. But while Andalucía is far more than a stereotype, it is also home to Spain's most notorious icons. Bullfighting, sherry, and flamenco are all *andaluz*, and the region celebrates holidays and festivals like *Semana Santa* (Holy Week) and Carnaval with famously wild abandon.

The ancient kingdom of Tartessus grew wealthy off the Sierra Nevada's rich ore deposits, and the Greeks and Phoenicians established colonies and traded up and down the coast. The Romans cultivated wheat, olive oil, and wine from the fertile soil watered by the Guadalquivir, and in the AD 5th century, the Vandals passed through on their way to North Africa, leaving little more than a name—Vandalusia (House of the Vandals). The Moors, in control under various dynasties from 711 until 1492, had the most enduring influence, forming lasting ties to Africa and the Islamic world. They preserved and perfected Roman architecture (creating the distinctive Andalusian patio), furthered industry and technology, and developed the region's greatest cities. Sevilla and Granada reached the pinnacle of Islamic art and scholarship in these centuries, while Córdoba matured into the most culturally influential medieval Muslim city.

Through the turbulent 20th century, Andalucía retained its strength and solidarity—the region was one of the last strongholds against Franco during the Civil War. Many residents still describe themselves as Andalusian before Spanish and proudly draw from the melange of cultures that first made the region famous. As for visitors, whether they come to wander the medieval streets of the *juderías* (Jewish quarters) or clap along with a *Sevillana*, Andalucía will leave its golden light and vibrant colors warmly imprinted on the mind.

HIGHLIGHTS OF ANDALUCÍA

SCRUB like a sultan in the Arab baths of **Córdoba** (p. 162).

SAMPLE enough sherry to get sufficiently silly in **Jerez de la Frontera** (p. 172).

SIGH like the last of the royal Moors when you too must leave **Granada** (p. 193).

CÓRDOBA ☎957

Abundant courtyards, flowers dangling from balconies, and narrow, winding streets make Córdoba (pop. 323,600) a captivating and unhurried city. Perched on the southern bank of the Río Guadalquivir, it was once the largest city in Western Europe. For three centuries, Córdoba was the hub of the Moorish Empire and capital of the mighty Umayyad Caliphate, rivaled only by Baghdad and Cairo. Today's city preserves its past glory with monuments of Roman, Jewish, Islamic, and Christian origin. The *Judería* is one of Spain's oldest Jewish quarters, containing one of the three remaining synagogues on the Iberian

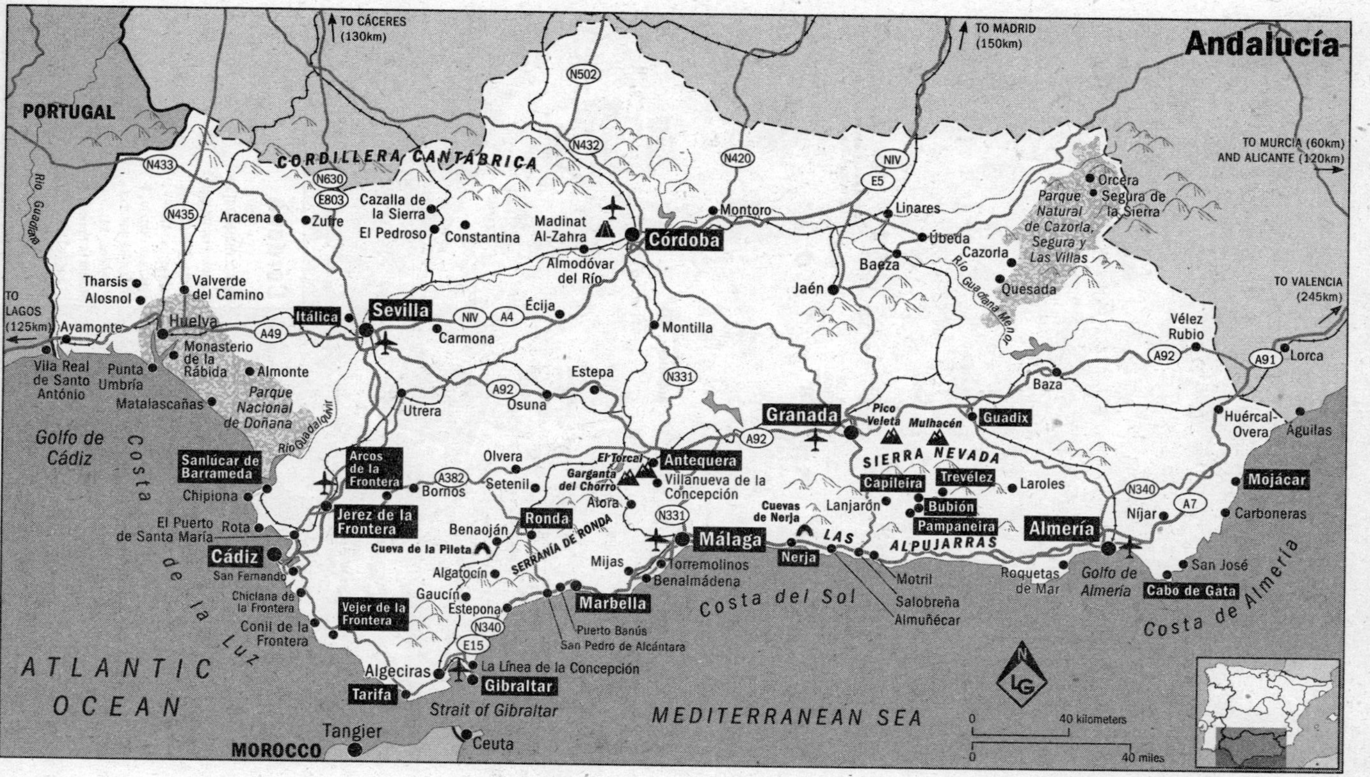
Andalucía
TO CÁCERES
(130km)
TO MADRID
(150km)
TO MURCIA (60km)
AND ALICANTE (120km)
TO VALENCIA
(245km)
TO
LAGOS
(125km)
PORTUGAL
MOROCCO
CORDILLERA CANTÁBRICA
SIERRA NEVADA
LAS ALPUJARRAS
SERRANÍA DE RONDA
Parque
Natural
de Cazorla,
Segura y
Las Villas
Parque
Nacional
de Doñana
Río Guadiana Menor
Río Guadiana
Río Guadalquivir
Córdoba
Sevilla
Granada
Málaga
Almería
Cádiz
Jaén
Huelva
Ronda
Antequera
Guadix
Mojácar
Nerja
Marbella
Gibraltar
Tarifa
Itálica
Capileira
Bubión
Pampaneira
Trevélez
Cabo de Gata
Sanlúcar de
Barrameda
Arcos
de la
Frontera
Jerez de la
Frontera
Vejer de la
Frontera
Linares
Úbeda
Baeza
Cazorla
Quesada
Orcera
Segura de
la Sierra
Vélez
Rubio
Lorca
Huércal-
Overa
Águilas
Carboneras
San José
Níjar
Baza
Laroles
Roquetas
de Mar
Motril
Salobreña
Almuñécar
Lanjarón
Pico
Veleta
Mulhacén
Cuevas
de Nerja
Torremolinos
Benalmádena
Mijas
Puerto Banús
San Pedro de Alcántara
La Línea de la Concepción
Estepona
Algeciras
Gaucín
Algatocín
Benaoján
Cueva de la Pileta
Setenil
Olvera
Bornos
Álora
Garganta
del Chorro
El Torcal
Villanueva de la
Concepción
Montilla
Montoro
Estepa
Osuna
Écija
Carmona
Utrera
Almodóvar
del Río
Madinat
Al-Zahra
Constantina
Cazalla de
la Sierra
El Pedroso
Zufre
Aracena
Valverde
del Camino
Monasterio
de la
Rábida
Almonte
Matalascañas
Tharsis
Alosnol
Ayamonte
Punta
Umbría
Vila Real
de Santo
António
Chipiona
Rota
El Puerto
de Santa María
San Fernando
Chiclana de
la Frontera
Conil de la
Frontera
Tangier
Ceuta
Strait of Gibraltar
Golfo de
Cádiz
Golfo de
Almería
Costa de la Luz
Costa del Sol
Costa de Almería
MEDITERRANEAN SEA
ATLANTIC
OCEAN
N433
N435
N630
E803
N502
N432
N420
NIV
E5
A49
A4
A92
N331
A382
N340
E15
A91
A7
0
40 kilometers
0
40 miles
LG

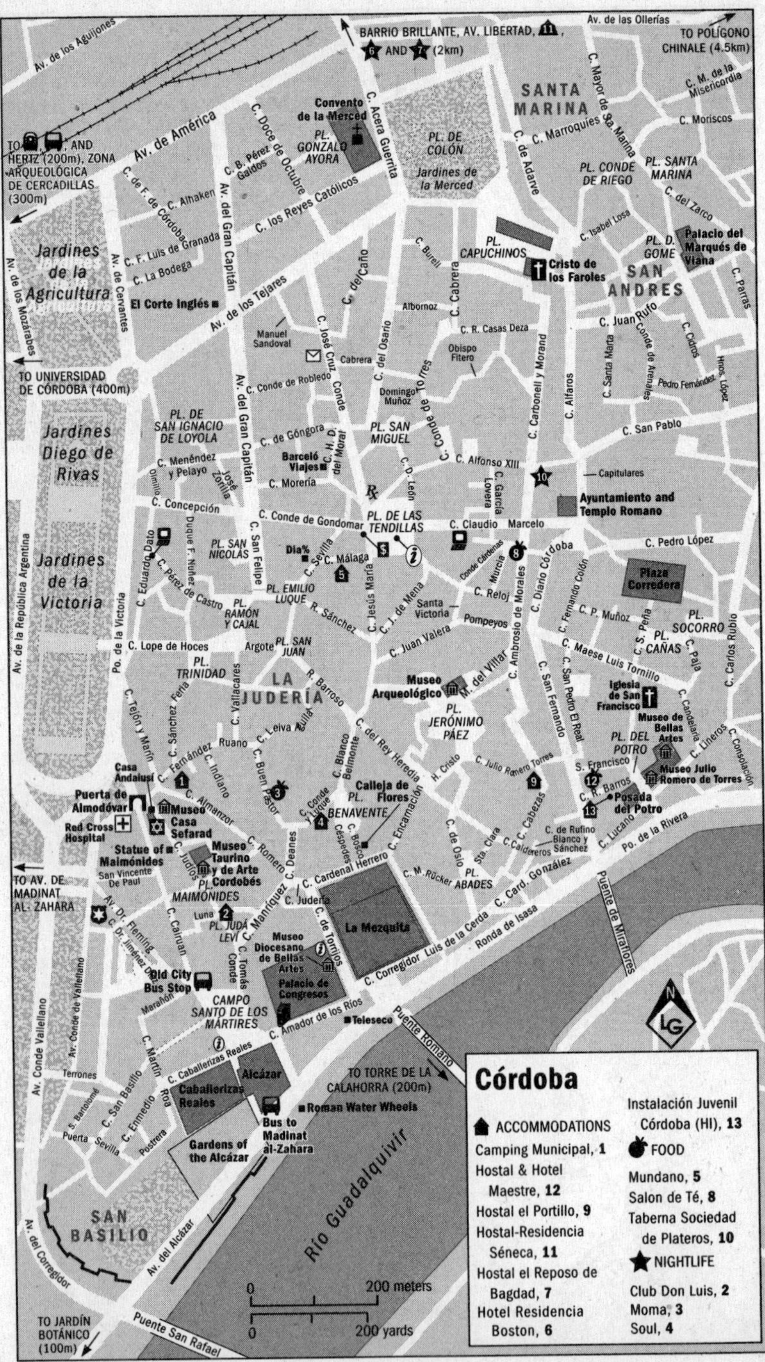
Córdoba
ACCOMMODATIONS
Camping Municipal, 1
Hostal & Hotel Maestre, 12
Hostal el Portillo, 9
Hostal-Residencia Séneca, 11
Hostal el Reposo de Bagdad, 7
Hotel Residencia Boston, 6
Instalación Juvenil Córdoba (HI), 13
FOOD
Mundano, 5
Salon de Té, 8
Taberna Sociedad de Plateros, 10
NIGHTLIFE
Club Don Luis, 2
Moma, 3
Soul, 4
BARRIO BRILLANTE, AV. LIBERTAD, 11, 6 AND 7 (2km)
TO POLÍGONO CHINALE (4.5km)
TO UNIVERSIDAD DE CÓRDOBA (400m)
HERTZ (200m), ZONA ARQUEOLÓGICA DE CERCADILLAS (300m)
TO AV. DE MADINAT AL-ZAHARA
TO TORRE DE LA CALAHORRA (200m)
TO JARDÍN BOTÁNICO (100m)
SANTA MARINA
SAN ANDRES
LA JUDERÍA
SAN BASILIO
Convento de la Merced
PL. DE COLÓN
Jardines de la Merced
Jardines de la Agricultura
Jardines Diego de Rivas
Jardines de la Victoria
El Corte Inglés
Palacio del Marqués de Viana
Cristo de los Faroles
PL. CAPUCHINOS
Ayuntamiento and Templo Romano
Plaza Corredera
PL. DE LAS TENDILLAS
Barceló Viajes
Dia%
Iglesia de San Francisco
Museo de Bellas Artes
Museo Julio Romero de Torres
Posada del Potro
Museo Arqueológico
PL. JERÓNIMO PÁEZ
Calleja de Flores
Casa Andalusí
Puerta de Almodóvar
Museo Casa Sefarad
Red Cross Hospital
Statue of Maimónides
Museo Taurino y de Arte Cordobés
La Mezquita
Museo Diocesano de Bellas Artes
Palacio de Congresos
Old City Bus Stop
CAMPO SANTO DE LOS MÁRTIRES
Teleseco
Alcázar
Caballerizas Reales
Roman Water Wheels
Bus to Madinat al-Zahara
Gardens of the Alcázar
Río Guadalquivir
Puente Romano
Puente de Miraflores
Puente San Rafael
Av. de América
Av. del Gran Capitán
Av. de los Tejares
C. Acera Guerrita
C. Claudio Marcelo
Av. de la República Argentina
Po. de la Victoria
Av. del Corregidor
Av. del Alcázar
Ronda de Isasa
Po. de la Rivera
C. Corregidor Luis de la Cerda
C. Cardenal Herrero
0 200 meters
0 200 yards

peninsula, and the decadent, visionary 14th-century Palacio del Marqués de Viana. A lively city today, Córdoba welcomes visitors with the same peaceful hospitality that gave the city its fame.

TRANSPORTATION

Trains: Pl. de las Tres Culturas (☎957 40 02 02, 902 24 02 02), off Av. de América. To: **Algeciras** via **Bobadilla** (2 per day 10:43am and 5:06pm, €35-54); **Barcelona** (10-11hr., 3 per day 10am-10:52pm, €55-91); **Cádiz** (2hr., 5 per day 7:20am-8:13pm, €18-55); **Madrid** (2-4hr., 21-33 per day 7:29am-10:28pm, €48-61); **Málaga** (2-3hr., 5 per day 7:12am-11:27pm, €19.05-40.70); **Sevilla** (45min., 4-8 per day 6:50am-9:30pm, €8-15). For tickets, visit the **RENFE** office, Av. Ronda de los Tejares, 10.

Buses: Estación de Autobuses (☎957 40 40 40), on Glorieta de las Tres Culturas across from the train station.

Alsina Graells Sur (☎957 27 81 00) to: **Algeciras** (5hr.; 8am, 3:15pm; €24); **Almería** (5hr., 8am, €23); **Antequera** (2hr.; 9am, 4pm; €9); **Cádiz** (4-5hr.; M-F 10am, 6pm; Sa-Su 10am; €21); **Granada** (3-4hr.; M-Sa 9-10 per day 8am-7pm, Su 11 per day 8am-8:30pm; €12); **Málaga** (3hr.; 5 per day 8am-7pm, more frequent June-Aug; €12).

Bacoma (☎902 42 22 42) to **Baeza** (3hr.; 12:20, 5:15pm; €9); **Barcelona** (10hr., 3 per day 5:15pm-12:35am, €64); and **Valencia** (4 per day 12:20pm-12:35am, €39-44).

Secorbus (☎902 22 92 92) runs cheap buses to **Madrid** (5hr., 6 per day 1am-6pm, €14.40).

Transportes Ureña (☎957 40 45 58) runs to **Jaén** (2hr.; M-Sa 7-8 per day 7:30am-8pm, Su 6 per day 7:30am-8pm; €8).

Autocares Priego (☎957 40 44 79), **Empresa Carrera** (☎957 40 44 14), and **Empresa Rafael Ramírez** (☎957 42 21 77) run buses to surrounding towns and campsites.

Local Transportation: 17 bus lines (☎957 25 57 00) cover the city, running from the wee hours until 11pm. **Bus #3** makes a loop from the bus and train stations through Pl. de las Tendillas, up to the Santuario, and back along the river and up C. Dr. Fleming. **Bus #10** runs from the train station to Barrio Brillante. €1.

Taxis: Radio Taxi (☎957 76 44 44). From bus and train stations to the *Judería* €4-5.

Car Rental: Hertz (☎957 40 20 61; www.hertz.com), in the bus station. 25+. Compact car €70 per day. Open M-F 8:30am-2pm and 5-9pm, Sa 9am-2pm.

ORIENTATION

Córdoba is divided into the new city and the old. The modern, commercial northern half extends from the train station on Av. de América down to **Plaza de las Tendillas,** the center of the city. The section in the south is a medieval maze known as the **Judería** (Jewish quarter). This tangle of disorienting streets extends from Pl. de las Tendillas to the banks of the Río Guadalquivir, winding past the **Mezquita** and **Alcázar.** The easiest way to reach the old city from the train or bus station is either the **#3** or **#4 bus** (€1) to the Pl. de Tendillas. Otherwise, it is a 20min. walk. From the train station, with your back to the platforms, exit through the left doors, then turn right and cross the parking lot. Continue right onto Av. de los Mozárabes. It is best to walk through the gardens, **Jardines de la Victoria,** in the middle of the boulevard. When the gardens end, the **Puerta Almodóvar,** one of the entrances into the *Judería*, will be on the left.

PRACTICAL INFORMATION

Tourist Offices: Andalucía Regional Office, C. Torrijos, 10 (☎957 35 51 79). From the train station, take bus #3 along the river until the Puente Romano. Walk under the stone arch and the office will be on your left. Open July-Aug. M-F 9:30am-7:30pm, Sa 10am-7:30pm, Su 10am-2pm; Sept.-June M-Sa 9am-7:30pm, Su 10am-2pm.

Turismo de Córdoba (☎902 20 17 74; www.turismodecordoba.org) has booths in the train station (open daily 9:30am-2pm and 5-8pm), on C. Caballerizas Reales (open daily 9:30am-2:30pm and 5-8pm), and in Pl. de Tendillas (open daily 10am-1:30pm and 6-9:30pm). Offers walking tours of the city at night (€15), a patio guide and an audioguide (€15).

Currency Exchange: Banco Santander Central Hispano, Pl. de las Tendillas, 1 (☎902 24 24 24). Open M-F 8:30am-2pm, Sa 8:30am-1pm.

Luggage Storage: At the bus station. €2 per day. Open 24hr. Library (see below) offers free locks for temporarily guarding purses and valuables while you sightsee.

Laundry: Teleseco, Ronda de Isasa, 10 (☎957 48 33 56), 1 block from La Mezquita, near the river. Coin service and dry cleaning. Washers €5, dryers €3. Full service with wash, dry, and fold €11.

Budget Travel Agency: Barceló Viajes, C. Historiador Díaz del Moral, 1 (☎957 48 55 55; www.barceloviajes.com), on the corner on C. Morería. Open M-F 9:30am-1:30pm and 5-8:30pm, Sa 10am-1:30pm.

Police: Av. Doctor Fleming, 2 (☎092 or 957 23 87 00).

Medical Services: Red Cross Hospital, Po. de la Victoria, near Puerta de Almodóvar (☎957 42 06 66, emergencies 22 22 22). English spoken.

Library: C. Amador de los Rios, a block from the Mezquita (☎957 35 54 92). Free internet access on 1st and 2nd floors. Open M-F 9am-9pm, Sa 9am-2pm.

Internet Access: Tele-Click, C. Eduardo Dato, 9 (☎957 94 06 15). New machines, A/C, and assorted refreshments. €1.80 per hr., €0.50 per 15min. Open M-F 10am-3pm and 5:30-10:30pm, Sa-Su noon-11pm. **Ch@t-is,** C. Claudio Marcelo, 15 (☎957 47 45 00). €1.80 per hr.; *bonos* from €9 per 10hr. Fax and copies available (€0.06-0.40, discount for students). Open M-F 10am-2pm and 5:30-9pm.

Post Office: C. José Cruz Conde, 15 (☎957 47 97 96). **Lista de Correos.** Open M-F 8:30am-8:30pm, Sa-Su 9:30am-2pm. **Postal Code:** 14070.

ACCOMMODATIONS

Hostels abound in the *Judería* and between La Mezquita and C. de San Fernando. Córdoba is especially crowded during *Semana Santa*, May, and June, and then dies down during the months of July and August. Still, it is generally a good idea to call in advance for reservations. Prices are higher in summer.

IN AND AROUND THE JUDERÍA

The *Judería*'s whitewashed walls and proximity to sights make it a great place to stay. During the day, souvenir booths and cafes keep the streets lively, but the area feels more deserted at night. Take bus #5 from the train station to the "Hotel Melia" stop across the street from the Puerta de Almodóvar. Go under the archway to reach the neighborhood.

Instalación Juvenil Córdoba (HI), Pl. Judá Levi, down C. Judios from Puerta Almodóvar (☎957 29 01 66). A mental asylum converted into a backpacker's paradise. Most rooms have bath and A/C. Courtyards surrounded by orange trees and graffiti art. Breakfast included. Lockers €1.80-2 per day. Towels €1.20. Laundry €2.50, dry €1.50. March-Oct. €19.50-€20.50; Nov.-Feb. €2.10 less. HI discount €3.50. MC/V. ❶

Hostal-Residencia Séneca, C. Conde y Luque, 7 (☎957 47 32 34). A beautiful Córdoba courtyard greets you at the entrance. Fans or A/C. Room size differs greatly, so ask to see one first. Breakfast included; special breakfast on Su. Singles €26, with bath €38; doubles €45/51; triples and 1 huge quad €89. MC/V. ❷

BETWEEN LA MEZQUITA AND CALLE DE SAN FERNANDO

Hostal El Reposo de Bagdad, Fernández Ruano, 11 (☎957 20 28 54). A beautiful Islamic-inspired hostel with large sunlit rooms with bathroom and fan. Pillow-strewn corner where you can eat breakfast in the morning (€3.50) and smoke hookah after dark. Singles €25; doubles €38. ❷

Hostal el Portillo, C. Cabezas, 2 (☎957 47 20 91; www.hostalelportillo.com). A traditional Andalusian house decorated with quirky flair in a quieter part of the neighborhood. Spacious rooms with wrought-iron beds, bath, Wi-Fi (ask for the code), and A/C; some have balconies. Singles €18-20; doubles €30-35. MC/V. ❶

Hostal and Hotel Maestre, C. Romero Barros, 6 (☎957 47 24 10; www.hotelmaestre.com), off C. de San Fernando. Both the hotel and *hostal* have similar royal-hued decor, but the *hostal's* corridors, a maze of Spanish trinkets, are more unique. All rooms with private bath and A/C, most with TV. Breakfast buffet €5. *Hostal* singles €23-28; doubles €30-40. Hotel singles €30-38; doubles €42-50. MC/V. ❷

ELSEWHERE

Hotel Residencia Boston, C. Málaga, 2 (☎957 47 41 76; www.hostel-boston.com), a 10min. walk from the *Judería.* Plain rooms equipped with A/C, TV, phone, safe, and bath. Breakfast in large dining room and lounge area €4. Internet €1 per 30min. Singles €32-35; doubles €50-57. AmEx/MC/V. ❸

Camping Municipal, Av. del Brillante, 50 (☎957 40 38 36). From the train station, turn left on Av. de América, left on Av. del Brillante, and walk uphill (20min.). Buses #10 and 11 from Av. Cervantes stop across the street. Supermarket, restaurant, hot showers. Laundry €3. 1-2 people and tent €18; 2 people, car, and tent €19.05; 2 people and camper €19. IVA not included. Cash only. ❷

FOOD

Touristy restaurants have taken over the Mezquita area, but a 5min. walk in any direction reveals good local spots. In the evenings, locals converge at the outdoor *terrazas* between **Calle Severo Ochoa** and **Calle Dr. Jiménez Díaz** for drinks and tapas. Cheap eateries are farther from the *Judería* in **Barrio Cruz Conde** and around **Avenida Menéndez Pidal** and **Plaza de las Tendillas.** Regional specialties include *salmorejo* (a gazpacho-like cream soup topped with hard-boiled egg and pieces of ham) and *rabo de toro* (bull's tail simmered in tomato sauce). For groceries, try **%Dia,** on C. Sevilla, 4, near Pl. de las Tendillas. (Open M-Sa 9am-3pm and 5:30-9pm.) **El Corte Inglés,** Av. Ronda de los Tejares, 30, has a supermarket on the bottom floor. (Open M-Sa 10am-10pm. AmEx/MC/V.)

Taberna Sociedad de Plateros, C. San Francisco, 6 (☎957 47 00 42). A mainstay since 1872, this place has the biggest *raciones* for the best prices (€4.80-14.80); a half-*ración* of salad can serve as a filling lunch. Open M-F 8am-3:45pm and 8-11:45pm, Sa 8am-3:45pm and 7:30-1:45pm. AmEx/MC/V. ❷

Mundano, C. Conde de Cárdenas, 3 (☎957 47 37 85). Back-alley locale combines homemade fare with funky style and art shows. Breakfast (€1.50-1.80), tapas (gazpacho €1.10), teas, and entrees (€3-5). Vegetarian options. Live music some weekends. Open M-F 10am-5pm and 10pm-2am, Sa noon-6pm and 10pm-2am. Cash only. ❶

Salon de Té, C. Buen Pastor (☎957 48 79 84). Lie back on satin pillows in this recreated 12th-century teahouse while savoring a huge selection of teas, juices, and Arab pastries. Try the mint lemonade for a refreshing variation on a summer favorite (€2.50). Open daily 11am-10:30pm. Cash only. ❶

SIGHTS

LA MEZQUITA

C. Cardenal Herrero, 1. ☎957 47 05 12. Open Mar.-Oct. M-Sa 8:30am-7pm, Su 8:30-10:30am and 2-7pm. €8, 10-14 €4, under 10 free. Wheelchair-accessible. Last ticket sold 30min. before closing. Mass M-Sa 8:30-10am, Su 11am and 1pm. Take advantage of the free admission M-Sa 8:30-10am (during mass). Silence is enforced; no groups.

Built in AD 785 on the site of a Visigoth basilica, this masterpiece is considered the most important Islamic monument in the Western world. Over the course of two centuries, La Mezquita was enlarged to cover an area the size of several city blocks. With more than 850 columns, it was the third-largest mosque in the Islamic world at the time, after only those of Mecca and Medina.

Visitors enter through the **Patio de los Naranjos,** an arcaded courtyard featuring carefully spaced orange trees, palms, and fountains, where the dutiful performed their ablutions before prayer. The **Torre del Alminar** encloses remains of the minaret from which the *muezzin* called the faithful to prayer. The grand entrances to the mosque were closed during its conversion to a Gothic cathedral, and today you must enter through the right corner of the facade.

Beginning in the oldest part of the mosque, built under Abd Al-Rahman I, the multiple pillars carved from granite and marble are capped by striped arches. Look for the rails that guard the remaining mosaic of the Visigothic basilica near the entrance. La Mezquita's most elaborate additions—the dazzling *mihrab* (prayer niche) and the triple *maksourah* (caliph's niche)—were created in the 10th century. Holy Roman Emperor Constantine VII gave the nearly 35 tons of intricate gold, pink, and blue marble Byzantine mosaics that shimmer across the arches of the *mihrab* to the caliphs. The *mihrab* formerly housed a gilt copy of the Qur'an and remains covered in Kufic inscriptions of the 99 names of Allah. To this day, historians remain stumped as to why the *mihrab* does not face Mecca, as Muslim architects had highly precise methods of calculation and would be unlikely to make such a mistake.

At the far end of the Mezquita lies the **Capilla Villaviciosa,** which in 1371 was the first Christian chapel to be built in the mosque, thus beginning the transition into a place of Christian worship. In 1523, Bishop Alonso Manriquez, an ally of Carlos V, proposed the construction of a cathedral in the center of the mosque. The town rallied violently against the idea, promising painful death to any worker who helped tear down La Mezquita. The bishop nevertheless erected a towering *crucero* (transept) and *coro* (choir stall), incongruously planting a richly adorned Baroque cathedral amid far more austere environs.

The cathedral's most noteworthy part is the **choir,** which depicts the entire Bible in mahogany panels. On one side of the transept, atop the church tower, the angel Raphael (the protector of Córdoba), watches over the faithful, proud that his is the most popular male name in the city.

IN AND AROUND THE JUDERÍA

ALCÁZAR DE LOS REYES CRISTIANOS. Along the river, to the left of La Mezquita, lies the Alcázar, built in 1328 during the *Reconquista* on the site of a strategic Roman trade and transport holding. Fernando and Isabel bade farewell to Columbus here (as seen by the towering statue in the gardens), and from 1490 to 1821, it served as a headquarters for the Inquisition. The reception hall directly above the hot rooms of the royal baths displays first-century Roman mosaics and a marble sarcophagus. Don't leave without visiting the endless gardens with hedges, flowers, dancing fountains, and fish pools. *Cor-*

dobeses come to cool down in this tranquil setting, which also serves as a stage for concerts. *(☎957 42 01 51. Open Tu-Sa 8:30am-2:30pm, Su and holidays 9:30am-2:30pm. €4, students €2; F free. Gardens open June 21-Sept. 8pm-midnight. €2, F Free.)*

SINAGOGA. Built in 1315, the synagogue, where famed philosopher Maimonides (1135-1204) once prayed, evokes the memory of Córdoba's once-vibrant Jewish community. Adorned with carved Mozárabe patterns and Hebrew inscriptions, the walls of the small temple have been restored to much of their original intricacy. The first floor is open to the public, but the upper hall, where women once prayed, is closed. *(C. Judíos, 20, just past the statue of Maimonides. ☎957 20 29 28. Open Tu-Sa 9:30am-2pm and 3:30-5:30pm, Su 9:30-1:30pm. €0.30, EU citizens free.)*

CASA DE SEFARAD. Located between the synagogue and Casa Andalusí, the permanent exhibition of the Casa de Sefarad, "Memories of Sefarad," explores the legacy of the Jewish presence in Spain and in Córdoba. It also highlights the men and women who were historic pillars of the Jewish community in Córdoba and throughout al-Andalus. *(From the synagogue, turn left on C. Judíos and make the first right at C. Averroes. ☎957 42 14 04; www.casadesefarad.com. Open M-Sa 10am-6pm, Su 11am-2pm. Free guided tours M-Sa noon and 5pm, Su noon. €4, students €3.*

CASA ANDALUSÍ. A restored 12th-century house, this private museum boasts a Visigothic basement with mosaic floors, a gorgeous flower-filled fountain, old Arabic texts and coins, and an interesting display on Córdoba's role in the rise of paper-making, complete with replicas of the old tools used in the process. Calligraphic posters (€2.50-7) and gorgeous paper samples are also on sale. *(C. Judíos, 12, next to the the synagogue. ☎957 29 06 42; www.lacasaandalusi.com. Open daily 10:30am-8pm. €2.50, students €2.)*

MUSEO TAURINO Y DE ARTE CORDOBÉS. Get ready for a lot of bull. Dedicated to the history and lore of the bullfight, rooms contain uniforms, posters, and artifacts from decades of bullfighting in Spain. The main exhibit includes a replica of the tomb of Spain's most famous matador, the dashing Manolete (1917-1947), and the hide of the bull that killed him. *(Pl. Maimónides. ☎957 20 10 56. The museum is currently undergoing renovations; call to confirm hours and prices).*

OTHER SIGHTS. El Jardín Botánico (Botanic Garden) is one of the Córdoba's best-kept secrets. Complete with an arboretum, glass houses, ethnobotanical museum, rose gardens, and a water wheel, the gardens offer a peaceful and educational retreat from the city. The gardens host many of the city's cultural and musical events at night. *(☎957 20 00 18; www.jardinbotanicodecordoba.com. Open Tu-Sa 10am-9pm, Su 10am-3pm. Museums open Tu-Sa 10am-2:30pm and 5-8pm, Su 10am-2:30pm. €2, students €1.30, groups of 20+ €1).* Townspeople take great pride in their traditional **patios.** Among the most beautiful streets are **Calleja del Indiano,** off C. Fernández Ruano at Pl. Ángel Torres, and the **Calleja de Flores,** off C. Blanco Belmonte, where geraniums cluster along the walls of the alley.

OUTSIDE THE JUDERÍA

MUSEO JULIO ROMERO DE TORRES. Romero (1874-1930) mastered the subtleties of mixing a dark palette and applied this talent to renditions of sensual *cordobesa* women. Exhibited here in the artist's former home is the lauded *Naranjas y limones* (Oranges and Lemons) and *La Chiquita Piconera* (The Little Coal Girl), along with dozens of other works. *(Pl. Potro, 5-10min. from La Mezquita. ☎957 49 19 09. Open Tu-Sa 8:30am-2:30pm, Su and holidays 9:30am-2:30pm. Last entry 30min. before closing. €4, students €2. F free.)*

MUSEO DE BELLAS ARTES. Across the courtyard from Museo Julio Romero de Torres, this art museum's building was a hospital during the reign of Fernando and Isabel. It hosts a vast collection of Renaissance religious art, works by the de Torres family, as well as works by more modern *cordobés* artists. *(Pl. del Potro. From la Mezquita, pass the Puento Romano, the Puente de Miraflores (the next bridge), and walk 5-10min to C. Torres. Pl. del Potro is next to the fountain. Alternately, Bus #3, 7, and 16 also pass by. ☎957 35 55 50; www.museosdeandalucia.es. Open Tu 2:30-8:30pm, W-Sa 9am-8:30pm, Su and holidays 9am-2:30pm. Last entry 30min. before closing. €1.50, EU citizens free.)*

PALACIO DEL MARQUÉS DE VIANA. An elegant 14th-century mansion, the palace displays 12 traditional patios complete with sprawling gardens, majestic fountains, tapestries, furniture, and porcelain. *(Pl. Don Gome, 2, a 20min. walk from La Mezquita. ☎957 49 67 41. Open July-Sept. M-Sa 9am-2pm; Oct.-June M-F 10am-1pm and 4-6pm, Sa 10am-1pm. Closed June 1-16. Complete tour €6, garden and courtyards only €3.)*

OTHER SIGHTS. Across the river on the Puente Romano is the Puerta del Puente, which houses the **Museo Torre de la Calahorra,** a lively and beautiful testament to the coexistence of the Muslim, Christian, and Jewish communities in Córdoba. *(☎ 957 29 39 29. Open daily 10am-2pm, 4:30-8:30pm. €4.50, groups and children €3. Price includes an 1½hr. audio guide and guidebook.)* Near the Palacio del Marqués de Viana in Pl. Capuchinos (also known as Pl. de los Dolores) and next to a monastery is the **Cristo de los Faroles** (Christ of the Lanterns), one of the most famous religious icons in Spain and the site of many all-night vigils. The eight lanterns symbolize the eight provinces of Andalucía. Remnants of second-century **Roman water wheels** line the sides of the Río Guadalquivir. Believed to have been used by Romans as mills, they were later used to bring water to the caliph's palace and the gardens around the city. The mills continued to function until Isabel la Católica demanded they be shut down—they disturbed her sleep.

NIGHTLIFE

Nightlife is tame in the old city, and hip bars and clubs tend to cluster together. Nearest to the old city, **Calle Alfonso XIII** and the adjacent **Calle Alfaros** host limited options. Farther away, the **Barrio Brillante** is a true nightlife hot spot, though its bars and clubs tend to open only on weekends. Bus #10 goes to Brillante from the train station until about 11pm, but the bars are empty until 1am and stay open until 4am. A taxi costs about €3-6, or it's a 45min. uphill hike. **Avenida Libertad,** close to the Brillante, offers a more chic (and costly) ambience with diverse and consistently gorgeous pubs.

In the winter, nightlife centers around the neighborhood where the Universidad de Córdoba used to be, especially in pubs on **Calle Los Alderetes** and **Calle Julio Pellicer,** and near the **Plaza de la Corredera.** An alternative to partying is a cool stroll along the **walk-through fountains** and falling sheets of water that line Av. de América between Pl. de Colón and the train station.

Soul, C. Alfonso XIII, 3 (☎957 49 15 80). Spontaneous dancing and a crazy young crowd. Bring earplugs or a fever for bass. Free Wi-Fi. Beer €2.10. Mixed drinks €4.50 and up. Open daily 9am-2pm and 4pm-3am, later on weekends. Cash only.

Moma, Av. Libertad, 4 (☎957 27 19 12). This ethnic-chic bar has African-styled stools and fake mosaic lamp shades. Beer €2-2.50. Mixed drinks from €5. Open M-Th and Su 9am-3am, F-Sa 10am-4am. AmEx/MC/V.

Club Don Luis, Av. del Brillante, 18. Trendy club draws local university students who dance to Spanish pop. Though there's a large outdoor terrace, most people pack inside. Beer €2.50. Mixed drinks €5. Open Th-Sa midnight-4:30am. Cash only.

ENTERTAINMENT

For the latest cultural events, pick up a free copy of the *Guía del Ocio* at the tourist office. Though *flamenco* is not cheap in Córdoba, the shows are high-quality and worth a visit for those not heading to Sevilla. Prize-winning dancers perform at **Tablao Cardenal**, C. Torrijos, 10, facing La Mezquita. Reserve seats there or at your hostel. (☎957 48 31 12; www.tablaocardenal.com. Shows M-Sa 10:30pm. Cover €18, includes one drink.) A cheaper but equally entertaining option is **La Bulería,** C. Pedro López, 3, with nightly shows also at 10:30pm. (☎957 48 38 39. €11, includes one drink.) Every July, Córdoba hosts a **guitar festival,** bringing talent from all over the world.

DAYTRIP FROM CÓRDOBA

MADINAT AL-ZAHRA

Bravo buses leave from Po. de la Victoria or in front of the Alcázar on Av. del Alcázar. A video with English subtitles plays on the ride. (30min.; Tu-Sa 11am and 6pm, Sa also 10am, Su 10, 11am; €6, reserve tickets at a Turismo de Córdoba office or at most accommodations.) Buses return to Córdoba 1hr. after arriving in al-Zahra. Visión Córdoba offers transportation and 1hr. tour in both Spanish and English (☎957 76 02 41, Tu-Su at 10:30am, €28). Alternatively, Bus #1 leaves from Po. de la Victoria; get off at Cruz de Madinat al-Zahra for a 3km walk to the ruins. (☎957 35 55 06/07; www.juntadeandalucia.es/cultura/madinatalzahra. Open May-Sept. 15 Tu-Sa 10am-8:30pm, Su 10am-2pm; Sept. 16-Apr. Tu-Sa 10am-6:30pm, Su 10am-2pm. €1.50, EU citizens free.)

In 940, the self-appointed caliph Abd al-Rahman III decided to move the region's seat of power 7km to the northwest of Córdoba. There, with the muscle of an estimated 10,000 workers and 3000 pack animals, the ruler constructed an indulgent 277-acre wonderland of courtyards, gardens, porticos, and salons in a symbolic effort to strengthen and reunify the steadily diminishing Moorish empire. Legend, on the other hand, attributes the grand palace-town to the caliph's desire to impress his favorite concubine, al-Zahra. Weakened by an internal power stuggle, the medina was soon ransacked by civilian mobs and foreign Berber armies; its precious colored marble, swirling columns, and jasper were looted. In less than 80 years, al-Zahra's glory faded completely, and looting continued into the 14th century.

The ruins are worth a visit for the historically inclined, but don't expect its dazzling former grandeur. The restoration process is ongoing; almost 90% of al-Zahra is still hidden underground. Once you enter through the gate, you'll be standing atop the town's third and highest terrace, offering a bird's-eye view of the medina and minuscule Córdoba below. Follow the city wall, reconstructed in 1920s, into the old town, keeping left until you reach the site where the mosque once stood. Although you can't reach the lower terrace, you can admire the excavated earthen foundation paved with flagstones in the caliph's prayer nave. A minaret once stood high above the sloping landscape, calling those in al-Zahra and Córdoba's Alcázar to prayer. The most striking part of the ruins is the caliph's royal reception hall. The High Garden, one terrace above the Lower Gardens, is a structural part of the hall and is a kind of organic red carpet for any worthy enough to be greeted by the ruler. Palm trees, hedges, and flowers were replanted in the 1920s to emphasize the geometrical mazes that once held murmuring fountains and an aviary. Inaccessible to the general public, the gardens are best viewed from the top terrace.

COSTA DE LA LUZ

While most of Andalucía is the domain of foreign tourists seeking wild nightlife and miles of beaches, the Costa de la Luz remains a destination populated primarily by Spanish vacationers looking for some fun in the sun. Beyond the *bodegas* of Jerez de la Frontera, the region offers picture-perfect *pueblos blancos* (white towns), opportunities to catch some wind or waves, and the golden light that is its namesake. Backed by dry pines and golden-hued dunes of fine sand, the expansive beaches of Costa de la Luz are home to strong winds and waves that make it a paradise for windsurfers and surfboarders. Less developed than other vacation destinations, this region is also known for its wealth of protected natural reserves.

JEREZ DE LA FRONTERA ☎956

Jerez de la Frontera (pop. 203,000) is the cradle of three staples of Andalusian culture: flamenco, Carthusian horses, and, of course, *jerez* (sherry). The sheer quantity and quality of the third staple draws hordes of tourists, most of whom are older Europeans. On the other end of the spectrum, the newest generations of flamenco performers take the stage throughout the city and give live rhythmic form to *el duende* (soul, emotion) itself. Jerez also makes a good departure point for the *ruta de los pueblos blancos* (white village route). Those not interested in *bodegas* or horses will still find flavor in Jerez: the local zest for flamenco, as well as a veritable list of historical sites, is worth a day or two.

TRANSPORTATION

Flights: Jerez Airport, Ctra. Jerez-Sevilla (☎956 15 00 00; www.aena.es), 7km from town. Taxi to the airport about €15. Airport shuttle (☎956 01 21 00; www.cmtbc.com). **Iberia** (☎956 18 43 94) has an office at the terminal. Most international flights connect to Jerez through Sevilla or Madrid.

Trains: Pl. de la Estación (☎956 34 23 19). **RENFE,** C. Larga, 34 (☎902 24 02 02). To: **Barcelona** (12hr.; 8:22am and 8:10pm; €95.80); **Cádiz** (45min.; M-F 18 per day 6:30am-10:25pm, Sa 4 per day 8:31am-5:29pm, Su 5 per day 8:31am-5:29pm; €3.65); **Madrid** (4hr.; 8:22am and 5:02pm; €62.30); **Sevilla** (1hr.; M-F 12 per day 7:39am-10:08pm, Sa 4 per day 7:39am-3:46pm, Su 5 per day 7:39am-3:46pm; €6.70).

Buses: Pl. de la Estación, next to the train station (☎956 33 96 66).

Linesur (☎956 34 10 63; www.linesur.com) to **Algeciras** (1hr.; M-F 9 per day 7:15am-9:45pm, Sa-Su 7 per day 8:30am-9:45pm; €10), **Sanlúcar** (45min.; M-F hourly 7am-9pm, Sa-Su every 2hr. 9am-9pm; €1.30), and **Sevilla** (1hr., 7-10 per day 6:30am-10:30pm, €7.

Secorbus (☎956 34 59 71; www.socibus.es) to **Madrid** (5hr., 6 per day 8:50am-11:50pm, €21.90).

Transportes Generales Comes (☎956 32 14 64 or 902 19 92 08; www.tgcomes.es) service to: **Cádiz** (50min.; M-F 22 per day 7am-11:15pm, Sa-Su 11 per day 7am-11:15pm; €2.90); **Granada** (4hr., 1pm, €25.77); **Ronda** (2hr., 3-6 per day 9:45am-7pm, €10.34); **Sevilla** (1hr.; M-Sa 5 per day 9am-11:30pm, Su 4 per day 10:30am-11:30pm; €7.20).

Transportes Los Amarillos (☎956 32 93 47 or 902 21 03 17; www.losamarillos.es) to **Arcos de la Frontera** (30min.; M-F 19 per day 7am-9pm, Sa 9 per day 7:45am-8:15pm, Su 11 per day 9am-9pm; €2.40).

Public Transportation: Most of the 17 bus lines run every 15-20min. (though less frequently at night). Most pass through Pl. del Arenal or next to Pl. Romero Martínez. Fare €1.10. Info office (☎956 34 34 46; www.cojetusa.com) in Pl. del Arenal. A *Jerez en tu bolsillo* guide, free from the tourist office, lists all the lines and schedules.

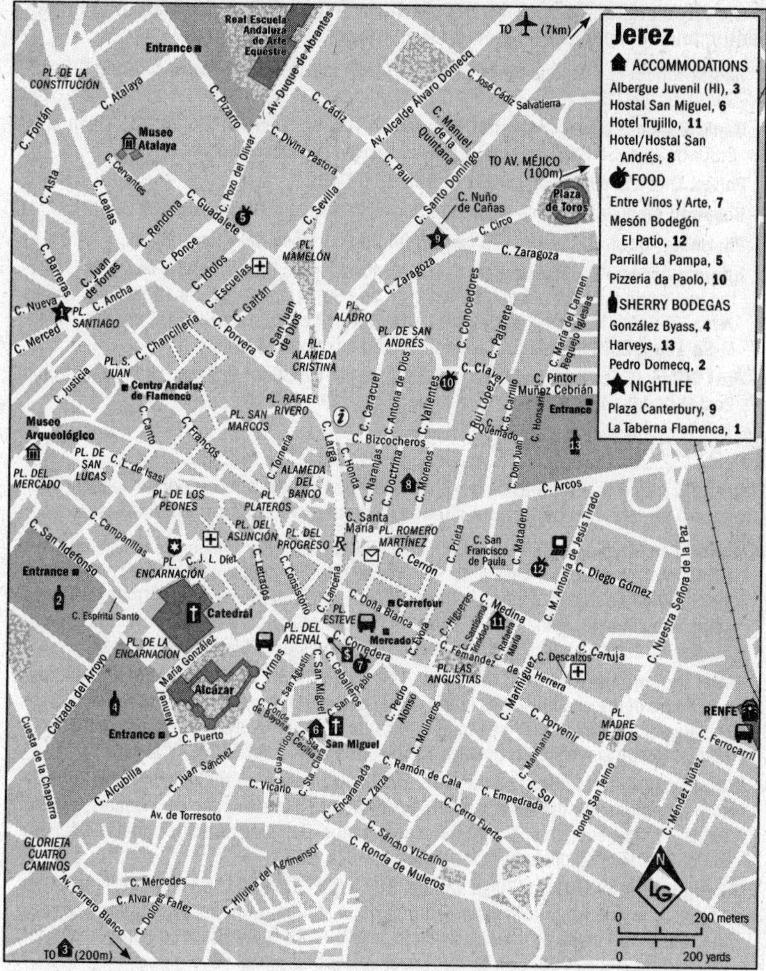

Car Rental: Niza, Ctra. N. IV Madrid-Cádiz, Km. 634 (☎956 30 28 60 or 956 18 15 75; www.nizacars.es). Take Av. Alcalde Álvaro Domecq to Hwy. N-IV toward Sevilla (next to El Corte Inglés). 21+ and must have had license for at least 1 yr. From €75 per day. Open daily 8:30am-8pm. AmEx/MC/V. **Bahía Rent A Car,** in the train station in Pl. de la Estación (☎956 32 25 92 or 669 86 17 89; www.bahiarentacar.com). Open M-F 9:30am-1:30pm and 5-8pm, Sa 9:30am-1:30pm. AmEx/MC/V. There are 7 car rental agencies at the airport.

Taxis: Teletaxi (☎956 34 48 60).

ORIENTATION AND PRACTICAL INFORMATION

The streets of Jerez are difficult to navigate without a map. Get a free one from the tourist office or at any of the major sights or *bodegas*. **Plaza Romero Martínez** is the city's center. **Calle Lancería/Calle Larga** is the main pedestrian road in the center, and *bodegas* are scattered along the outskirts of the old city.

Tourist Office: Pl. Alameda Cristina (☎956 34 17 11). Open M-F 10am-3pm and 5-7pm, Sa-Su 10am-2:30pm.

Bank: Banco Santander Central Hispano, Pl. Arenal, 5 (☎902 24 24 24). Open M-F 8:30am-2pm, Sa 8:30am-1pm. A slew of banks also lines C. Larga.

Police: On Pl. Encarnación (☎092 or 956 33 03 46).

Hospital: Ambulatorio de la Seguridad Social, C. José Luis Díaz (☎956 32 32 02).

Pharmacy: Central, C. Larga, 28 (☎956 34 28 93). Open daily 9am-10pm.

Internet Access: The Big Orange, C. M. Antonía de Jesús Tirado (☎956 35 01 01), near the bus station. €1.80 per hour. Open M-Th and Su 11am-1am, F-Sa 11am-3am. **Ciber Jerez,** C. Santa Maria, 3 (☎956 33 40 16; www.ciberjerez.com). €0.03 per min. Open M-Sa 10am-2:30pm and 5:30-11pm, Su and holidays 5-11pm.

Post Office: C. Cerrón, 2 (☎956 32 67 33). Open M-F 8:30am-8:30pm, Sa 9:30am-2pm. **Postal Code:** 11480.

ACCOMMODATIONS

Finding a place to crash in Jerez is as easy as finding a wine cork to sniff, but, like good sherry, it won't come cheap. Prices double during fall festivals.

Hostal San Miguel, Pl. San Miguel, 4 (☎956 34 85 62; http://galeon.com/hsanmiguel/Hostal.htm), behind the Iglesia de San Miguel. Marble details and statues surround a glass-roofed courtyard. Pleasant, colorful, and spacious rooms with A/C and TV, mere steps away from Pl. Arenal and C. Larga, in the center. Ask for a balcony over the church. Singles €22, with bath €33; doubles €37/43; triples €60/65. AmEx/MC/V. ❷

Hotel/Hostal San Andrés, C. Morenos, 12-14 (☎956 34 09 83; www.hotelsanandres.es). Some of the cheapest digs in the center of the city. Large rooms provide the basics; the adjacent hotel, with TV common room, offers pricier rooms with private baths, A/C, and TV. Hostal singles €22; doubles €30. Hotel €26/40. AmEx/MC/V. ❷

Hotel Trujillo, C. Medina, 36 (☎ 956 34 24 38; www.hoteltrujillo.com). The friendly staff complements the hotel's quiet locale. Rooms have wooden bed frames, private baths, TV, and enough space to flamenco in. Apr.-Oct. singles €30; doubles €42.80; triples €60. Prices cheaper in low season. MC/V. ❸

Albergue Juvenil (HI), Av. Blase Infante, 30 (☎856 81 40 01; www.inturjoven.com), a 15min. bus ride from downtown. From the bus station, walk past the train station to the rotary and cross at the crosswalk to take bus #9 to Av. Blase Infante. Closed for renovations until 2009. Call to verify availability and prices. ❶

FOOD

Food in Jerez rarely comes cheap. For deals, tapas-hoppers take on **Pl. del Arenal, C. Larga,** and **Pl. del Banco** in the old town. For fresh produce and the aroma of raw fish, head to **Mercado de Abastos,** Pl. Esteve. (Open M-Sa 8:30am-3pm.) For groceries, **Carrefour** is on C. Doña Blanca 13 (Open M-Sa 9:15am-9:30pm.)

Entre Vinos y Arte, C. Corredera, 30-32 (☎956 33 38 65), 3 blocks from Pl. del Arenal. Low on tourists, high on hospitality. Don't leave without sampling the bull's tail; a half-*ración* of this delicacy is enough to keep your stomach full. Vegetarian and meat tapas €1.50-2.50. *Raciones* €6. Open daily 8:30am-4pm and 7pm-midnight. MC/V. ❶

Parrilla La Pampa, C. Guadalete, 24 (☎956 34 17 49), near Pl. Mamelón. The hides dotting the walls hint at this spot's specialty—authentic, imported Argentine beef (€8.75-

19.70). Pork, chicken, veal, and ostrich (€16.20-17.70) round out the menu menagerie. Open M-Sa 12:30-4:30pm and 8:30pm-12:30am. AmEx/MC/V. ❸

Mesón Bodegón El Patio, C. San Francisco de Paula, 7 (☎956 34 07 36). Sumptuous traditional fare made with local produce in a refurbished sherry warehouse. Old portraits, antiques, and game heads fill the dining room. Tapas €1.50-4.25. *Raciones* €5-19. *Menú* €18. Open M-Sa 11:30am-4:30pm and 8pm-12:30am. MC/V. ❷

Pizzeria da Paolo, at the corner of C. Clavel and C. Valientes. Like a fancy Italian restaurant, but affordable. Tasty pizzas (€5-9) and pastas (€4.50-7.50). Plenty of vegetarian options. Open Tu-Su 1:15-4pm and 9pm-midnight. MC/V. ❷

SHERRY BODEGAS

People come to Jerez for the *bodegas* (wineries), and while many smaller *bodegas* offer tours, it's worth indulging your inner tourist and checking out the more famous ones. Tour guides explain the city's trademark *solera* (sherry-making process), leading visitors through heavenly-smelling barrel storage rooms and under grape-covered trellises before topping off the tour with free samples. The best time to visit is early September during the harvest; the worst is August, when many *bodegas* close down and wait for the grapes to ripen. Group reservations for tours must be made at least one week in advance. Looking for a job? Many *bodegas* hire English-speaking tour guides for two or three months, depending on need. *Bodegas* accept solicitations by mail, and if selected, workers undergo an intense training program before starting.

Pedro Domecq, C. San Ildefonso, 3 (☎956 15 15 00; www.bodegasfundadorpedrodomecq.com). Founded in 1730, Domecq is Jerez's oldest, most prestigious *bodega*. 1hr. tours include 20min. video. Unlimited sampling. Hourly tours in English and Spanish M-F 10am-1pm, Sa noon. Tour with tapas Tu, Th, Sa 2pm. Tour with tapas and flamenco May-Sept. Th 2pm. Regular tour €6, 2pm tour with tapas €11. AmEx/MC/V.

González Byass, C. Manuel María González, 12 (☎956 35 70 16 or 902 44 00 77; www.gonzalezbyass.es; www.bodegastiopepe.com). The makers of the popular Tío Pepe brand. The Disney World of *bodegas:* a bit commercial, but worth visiting and very kid-friendly. Trolleys whisk visitors past the world's largest weathervane and a storage room designed by Gustave Eiffel. June-Sept. tours in English M-Sa every hr. 11:30am-2pm and 4:30-6:30pm. Oct.-May tours in English M-Sa hourly 11:30am-5:30pm, Su 11:30am-1:30pm. €10, 2pm tour with tapas €15. AmEx/D/MC/V.

Harveys, C. Pintor Muñoz Cebrián (☎956 15 15 00 or 956 15 15 51; www.bodegasharveys.com). Makers of Harveys Bristol Cream, the best-selling sherry in the world. Reservations required; call in advance. 1hr. tours M-F 10am and noon. Tour and tasting Th 10am includes video and entrance to the Harveys museum. €8. MC/V.

SIGHTS

ALCÁZAR AND LA CÁMERA OSCURA. Along the southeastern axis of the city, the 12th century **Alcázar** of Jerez is one of the best preserved in the Iberian Peninsula. Visitors can also explore vestiges of the castle's renovations in the 15th and 18th centuries, including a Baroque palace and olive oil mill. The palace's tower houses the **Cámera Oscura,** the highest spot in Jerez, from which visitors can see live images of the city below. The Octagonal Tower, Torre del Homenaje, and Palacio de Doña Blanca are undergoing renovations until 2009. *(☎956 32 69 23. Open May-Sept. 15 M-Sa 10am-7:30pm, Su 10am-2:30pm; Sept. 16-Apr. daily 10am-7:30pm. Alcázar €3, students €1.80; Alcázar and Cámera Oscura €5.40/€4.20. Reservations for the guided tour are welcomed. €3. Visits to the Camera Oscura occur every 30min. with approx. 15 people per group.)*

REAL ESCUELA ANDALUZA DE ARTE EQUESTRE. Jerez's love for wine is almost matched by its passion for horses. During May, the Royal Andalusian School of Equestrian Art sponsors the **Feria del Caballo**—a horse fair with carriage competitions and races of Jerez-bred Carthusian horses. During the rest of the year, weekly shows feature a troupe of horses dancing in choreographed sequences. *(Av. Duque de Abrantes. ☎956 31 80 08; www.realescuela.org. Training sessions M and W 11am-2pm, July-Sept. also F. €6. Shows Tu and Th noon; Aug. also F noon. €13-21, depending on seat; children and seniors 40% off. Museum and training session €7, museum only €3. MC/V.)*

YEGUADA LA CARTUJA HIERRO DEL BOCADO. Every Saturday at 11am, the horses from the largest Carthusian thoroughbred stud farm in Spain strut their stuff for an appreciative audience. *(Ctra. Medina–El Portal, km 6.5. ☎956 16 28 09; www.yeguadacartuja.com. Sa 11am.)*

ENTERTAINMENT AND NIGHTLIFE

Rare footage of Spain's most talented flamenco singers, dancers, and guitarists is available for viewing at the **Centro Andaluz de Flamenco,** in Palacio Pemartín, on Pl. de San Juan. (☎956 34 92 65; www.centroandaluzdeflamenco.es. Open M-F 9am-2pm. Videos every hr. 10am-2pm. Free.) Most *peñas* and *tablaos* (clubs and bars that host flamenco) are in the old town and hold special performances in July and August. Occasionally there are free performances in some plazas, especially Pl. de Toros. For more frequent shows, walk over to Pl. Santiago to **La Taberna Flamenca,** Angostillo de Santiago, 3, which hosts some of Jerez's youngest flamenco dancers in an intimate setting reminiscent of the days of the gypsy camps. (☎956 32 36 93; www.latarbernaflamenca.com. Mid-May to Oct. shows daily 10:30pm, Tu-Th and Sa also 2:30pm. Nov. to mid-May shows Tu-Sa 10:30pm. Reservations recommended for dinner M-Sa noon-4pm and 8pm-midnight. Cover €15, includes 2 drinks; with dinner €30 min. AmEx/MC/V.)

Visitors to Jerez tend to be on the older side, and nightlife in the city center caters directly to them; to find a younger scene, head to the city outskirts. The Irish-themed bar and disco **Plaza Canterbury,** C. Nuño, is a hot spot for tourists and students alike, with two bars (O'Donoghue's and Gambrinus, the latter serving tapas), an outdoor patio, and a popular club. (Beer at bars €1.50-2, mixed drinks €4.50-5; at club €2.50/5. Club cover €8. **Gambrinus Bar** open M-Sa 9am-1:30pm, Su 4pm-1:30am. **O'Donoghue's** open daily 6pm-6am. Club open F-Sa 1:30-7am.) A slew of bars and clubs lines the well-lit **Avenida Méjico** between C. Santo Domingo and C. Salvatierra (a 25min. walk from Pl. del Arenal). Bars and pubs also cluster on the lively **Avenida Lola Flores** near the *fútbol* stadium.

Autumn, in addition to being grape harvest season, is festival season, when Jerez showcases its best equine and flamenco traditions. These festivals are collectively known as the **Fiestas de Otoño,** held from early September until the end of October. In September, the **Fiesta de la Bulería** and the **Festival de Teatro, Música y Baile** celebrate flamenco. The largest horse parade in the world, with races in Pl. del Arenal, is the highlight of the final week. Check at the tourist office for details; schedules are available in September for the upcoming year. And, for those with endless amounts of energy, the world-famous **Festival Internacional de Flamenco de Jerez** electrifies the city during February and March.

ARCOS DE LA FRONTERA ☎956

Arcos de la Frontera (pop. 33,000) has inspired many a poet, including Cristóbal Romero, who described it as a "Town extended in the sun/Winged, raised up in flight..." With whitewashed houses wrapped around a narrow ridge, Arcos is considered one of the most perfect *pueblos blancos* in Spain. Its plazas and churches, huddled in convoluted medieval streets flush with geraniums, make it a historical and romantic gem. The city comes alive in the evening after the heat dies down and locals congregate in the plazas and bars of the old city.

TRANSPORTATION

Buses: Station on C. Corregidores. Los Amarillos (☎956 32 93 47) runs buses to **Jerez** (30min.; M-F 19 per day 7am-8pm, Sa 9 per day 8am-8pm, Su 11 per day 8am-9pm; €2) and **Sevilla** (2hr.; 7am, 3pm; €7). Transportes Generales (☎ 956 70 49 77) to: **Cádiz** (1hr., 6 per day 7:20am-7:15pm, €4), **Costa del Sol** (3-4hr., 4pm, €10-13), and **Ronda** (1hr., 4 per day 8:15am-4pm, €6). Confirm times and prices at the tourist office, and buy tickets on the bus.

Taxis: C. Debajo del Corral. **Radio/Tele Taxi** (☎956 70 13 55/00 66). 24hr.

ORIENTATION AND PRACTICAL INFORMATION

To reach the town center from the bus station, exit left, follow the road, and turn left again. Continue uphill for two blocks on C. Josefa Moreno Seguro, taking a right onto C. Muñoz Vázquez. From there it's a 20min. walk uphill. Continue until reaching **Pl. de España,** then veer left onto C. Debajo del Coral, which quickly changes into C. Corredera; the old quarter is 500m ahead. **Manolo Blanco** minibuses run every 30min. from the bus station to C. Corredera (€0.80). A taxi costs around €4. If the tourist office is closed when you arrive, make your way to **Bar Hostal Zindicato,** a short climb uphill from the bus stop, where you'll find an invaluable tile map of the city complete with street key.

Tourist Office: Pl. del Cabildo (☎956 70 22 64). Runs **tours** of the old city, monuments, and patios M-F 11am, noon, and 6pm. €7, children under 12 free. Call ahead to reserve for Sa and 6pm tours. Open mid-Mar. to mid-Oct. M-Sa 10am-2pm and 4-8pm, Su 10am-2pm; mid-Oct. to mid-Mar. M-Sa 10am-2pm and 3:30-7:30pm, Su 10am-2pm. One computer with **Internet** access (€1 per 15min., €2.50 per hr.) and **printing** (€0.50 per page). An information kiosk with a more detailed street map is located on the island between C. Maldonado and C. Boticas near Pl. Boticas.

Bank and Currency Exchange: Banco Santander Central Hispano, C. Corredera, 63 (☎902 24 24 24). Open Oct.-Mar. M-F 8:30am-2pm, Sa 8:30am-1pm; Apr.-Sept. M-F 8:30am-2pm.

Laundry: Pressto, C. Debajo del Corral (☎914 48 58 61; www.pressto.com). Open M-F 9:30am-1:30pm and 5-8pm, Sa 9:30am-1:30pm.

Internet: Ciber-Locutorio "El Barrio," Pl. de las Aguas, 5 (☎956 70 45 69). €0.50 per 30min., €0.90 per hr. International phone service and phone credit recharging available. Snacks for sale. Open M-Sa 9:30am-2pm and 5:30-10pm, Su 10am-2pm.

Police: Av. Miguel Mancheño (☎092 or 956 70 16 52).

Medical Emergency: (☎061 or 956 51 15 53).

Hospital: Centro de Salud, C. Rafael Benot Rubio (☎956 70 07 87), in Barrio Bajo.

Pharmacy: Ldo. Ildefonso Guerrero Seijo, C. Corredera, 34 (☎956 70 02 13). Open M-F 9am-9pm. A list of doctors on call and available after hours is posted in the window.

Post Office: C. Murete, 24 (☎956 70 15 60). Open M-F 8:30am-2:30pm, Sa 9:30am-1pm. **Postal Code:** 11630.

ACCOMMODATIONS AND CAMPING

Arcos has a few budget hostels, but they are only slightly less expensive than classier hotels in town. Many restaurants on C. Corredera and in the old town have inexpensive rooms. Call ahead during Semana Santa and in the summer.

Hotel La Fonda, C. Corredera, 83 (☎956 70 00 57; www.hotelafonda.com), at the bottom of the hill leading to the old city. Originally a 19th-century inn, La Fonda retains a refined, old-fashioned feel. Plushly carpeted hallways lead to high-ceilinged rooms with A/C, full bath, TV, telephone, and balconies, some with terraces. Breakfast €1.70. Ask staff to use the computer downstairs for quick internet access. Singles €30; doubles €50; triples €65. Prices lower in winter. AmEx/MC/V. ❸

Pensión Callejon de las Monjas, C. Deán Espinosa, 4 (☎956 70 23 02). Rooms with incredible views, some with TV, bath, and A/C. Ask for the top floor, which has the best views, as well as a terrace. Singles €22, with bath €25; doubles €35, with terrace €40; triple €52; 4-person suite €66. MC/V, but cash preferred. ❷

Camping Lago de Arcos, Urbanización El Santiscal (☎956 70 83 33), at the foot of the hill by the lake. Has showers, pool, and electricity (€3). €3.95 per person, €3.30 per child, €4.70-4.95 per tent, €3.60 per car. ❶

FOOD

Cheap cafes and restaurants huddle at the bottom end of **C. Corredera,** while you can ascend to tapas nirvana in the old quarter uphill. Stock up on fresh fruit and produce at the small **market** on Pl. Boticas. (Open M-Sa 9am-3pm.)

Mabrouka, C. Debajo del Corral, 8 (☎956 70 06 12), downhill from C. Corredera. Enjoy authentic and filling Spanish fare in a Middle Eastern setting, complete with colorful cushions, soft music, and incense. Tapas €1.50-3.50, *montaditos* €2.50. Infusions and coffee €1-3. Extensive vegetarian *menú* €11; normal *menú* €9. Open Tu-Su 9am-5:30pm and 8pm-midnight. Cash only. ❷

Mesón "El Patio," C. Callejón de las Monjas, 4 (☎956 70 23 02; www.mesonelpatio.com). Located right next to the *pensíon,* this small establishment was originally a convent—it now specializes in *comida familiar* (local food) of all varieties. Salads €4.50-6. Tapas €2-3. *Raciones* €5-7.50. *Platos combinados* €8-10. Open daily noon-5pm and 7pm-midnight. AmEx/MC/V. ❷

SIGHTS AND FESTIVALS

The most beautiful sights in Arcos are the winding alleys, hanging flowers of the old quarter, and the stunning view from the **Plaza del Cabildo.** Festivals are spirited; on Easter Sunday is the **Toro de Aleluya,** in which two bulls run through the streets amid flamenco and general merriment. **Velada de San Pedro** is a celebration of the town's patron saint. Following a marching band processional and elaborate mass, 16 men provide the horsepower to move a larger-than-life icon of San Pedro out of the Iglesia de San Pedro and into the streets.

BASÍLICA DE SANTA MARÍA DE LA ASUNCIÓN. Built over an Arab mosque, the Basilica Baroque, Renaissance, and Gothic Plateresque styles. A symbol of the Inquisition—a circular design where exorcisms were once performed—is still etched into the ground outside on the church's left side. *(In the Plaza del Cabildo. Closed for repairs until 2009.)*

IGLESIA DE SAN PEDRO. This late-Gothic affair stands on the former site of an Arab fortress. Its gold altar is bookended by life-size icons, below which lie two saints removed from the Roman catacombs of St. Calixto. *(From Pl. Cabildo, follow C. Marqués Torresoto until Pl. Boticas. Follow C. Boticas, right on C. Núñez del Prado, which turns into C. San Pedro.Open daily 10am-2pm, 5-7pm. €1. Mass in winter 11:30am. Free.)*

EL SANTISCA. An artificial lake laps at Arcos' feet, and while it's not open to swimmers, the beach is a popular spot for a stroll. Ask about boat tours and rentals at the tourist office. *(Buses run from the bus station M-Sa 5 per day 9:15am-8:15pm, Su 2-4 per day 12:15-8:15pm; €0.90).*

TARIFA

☎956

Prepare for wind-blown hair—when the breezes pick up in the southernmost city of continental Europe, it becomes clear why Tarifa (pop. 20,000) is known as the Hawaii of Spain. World-renowned winds combined with kilometers of empty, white beaches bring some of the best kite and windsurfers from around the world, while the tropical, relaxed environment beckons divers and beach bums. Directly across the Strait of Gibraltar from Tangier, Morocco, Tarifa boasts incomparable views of Morocco to the south, the Atlantic to the east, and the Mediterranean to the west. From few other places in the world can you see two continents and two wide open seas at once.

TRANSPORTATION

Buses: Transportes Generales Comes buses go to the bus station, a trailer-like building on C. Batalla del Salado, 19. (☎956 68 40 38. Open M-F 7:30-9:30am, 10-11am, and 2:30-6:30pm, Sa-Su 3-7:45pm. Bus schedule posted on the window; if office is closed, buy tickets from driver.) Buses run to: **Algeciras** (30min., 7-11 per day 6:30am-8:15pm, €2); **Cádiz** (2hr., 7 per day 7:25am-8:55pm, €8); **La Línea** (1hr., 6 per day 12:05pm-11:15pm, €4); **Sevilla** (3hr., 4 per day 8am-5:15pm, €16).

Ferries: FRS boats (☎956 68 18 30; www.frs.es) leave from the port at the end of Po. de la Alameda for **Tangier** (35min.; daily every 2hr. 9am-11pm, F and Su last ferry at 9pm; return 9:30am-11:15pm, F and Su last return at 9:15pm Morocco time; €39, ages 3-12 €21. Small car €99).

Taxis: Parada Taxi can be reached at ☎956 68 42 41.

ORIENTATION

The **bus station** is on C. Batalla del Salado. Turn right toward the Repsol gas station and walk 10min. to the intersection with **Av. de Andalucía.** To reach the center of the old town, cross Av. de Andalucía and pass under the arch. To the left is C. Nuestra Señora de la Luz, which becomes **C. Sancho IV el Bravo,** home to many cafes and restaurants. To reach the tourist office, turn right on Av. de Andalucía before passing the arch. Take the first left onto Av. de la Constitución, then the first left into **Parque de la Alameda.**

PRACTICAL INFORMATION

Tourist Office: ☎956 68 09 93; www.tarifaweb.com. Located in Parque de la Alameda. Has detailed maps and information on adventure sports, including kite-surfing. (Open in summer M-F 10:30am-2pm and 6-8pm, Sa-Su 9am-2pm; in winter M-F 10am-2pm and 4-6pm, Sa-Su 9:30am-3pm.)

Currency Exchange: Banco Santander Central Hispano, C. Batalla del Salado, 17 and C. Sancho IV El Bravo in the walled town. (☎902 24 24 24. Open M-F 8:30am-2pm, Sa 8:30am-1pm.)

Police: Pl. Santa María, 3 (☎092 or 956 68 21 74).

Medical Services: Centro Salud, C. Amador de los Ríos, on the left after Punta de Europa when walking from the town center (☎956 02 77 00 or 956 02 77 01). **Pharmacy** on C. Batalla des Salado, 22, is nameless but conspicuous. (☎956 68 05 61. Open M-F 9:30am-10pm, Sa 9:30am-12:30pm.)

Laundry: Tarifa Top Clean, Av. Andalucía, 24 (☎956 68 03 03). A combination internet cafe, coffee bar, and laundry service. €11 for a large wash, dry, and fold. Internet €1.50 per 30min., €2.50 per hr. Open M-F 10am-2pm and 6pm-10pm.

Internet Access: Tarifa Top Clean (see Laundry, above). Cafes line Av. de Andalucía, but they aren't cheap; 1hr. of online access can cost you anywhere from €2-3. If you have a laptop, look for bars and cafes like **Bamboo** (see Food, below) which offer free Wi-Fi.

Post office: C. Coronel Moscardó, 9, is near Pl. San Mateo. (☎956 68 42 37. Open M-F 8:30am-2:30pm, Sa 9:30am-1pm.) **Postal Code:** 11380.

ACCOMMODATIONS

The cheapest rooms line C. Batalla del Salado and its side streets. Prices rise significantly in summer; those visiting in August and on weekends from June to September should call ahead and arrive early. Hard-core windsurfers often stay at one of the six campgrounds along the beach several kilometers from town; all have full bath and shower facilities, bars, and mini-supermarkets (see www.campingsdetarifa.com). Guests must bring their own tents. Cádiz-bound buses will drop you off if you ask, but flagging one down to get back is next to impossible; some surfers call for taxis or befriend fellow surfers with cars.

Hostal Facundo, C. Batalla del Salado, 47 (☎956 68 42 98; www.hostalfacundo.com). Draws the budget crowd with its "Welcome backpackers" sign. Common kitchen (8am-10pm), small TV room, and internet room provide a place to chat with your fellow travelers. Dorms €18-22; singles €25; doubles €38-45, with bath €42-50. Cash only. ❶

Hostal Villanueva, Av. de Andalucía, 11 (☎956 68 41 49). Villanueva has a restaurant and rooftop terrace with an ocean view. Spotless rooms all have bath and TV. Singles €25; doubles €45; triples €60. MC/V. ❶

Camping Río Jara, 4km from town on hightway CN-340 (☎956 68 05 70). A summer camp feel. €6.20 per person, €10 per site including tent, car, and electricity. ❶

FOOD

For cheap sandwiches (€1.50-3), try any one of the many *bagueterías* around C. Sancho IV el Bravo, or look for affordable options on C. San Francisco. To stock up for your beach trip, go to **Eroski Center** on C. San Jose, parallel to C. Batalla del Salado. (☎956 68 14 14. Open M-Sa 9:30am-9:30pm.)

Bamboo 1, Po. de la Alameda, 2 (☎956 62 73 04). A sensory wave of color, music, and both familiar and exotic tastes. Take off your shoes and lounge on eclectic, pillow-covered couches in the open-air seating area or log on for free Wi-Fi. The lounge becomes a bar at night. Teas €1.60-2. Fresh juices €3.50. Panini €2.80-4. Full breakfast €4. F-Sa Live DJ. Open M-Th 10am-2pm, F-Sa to 3am, Su to 2pm. AmEx/MC/V. ❶

Pizzería Horno de Leña, C. San Sebastián, 6, inside the Tarifa EcoCenter (☎956 62 72 20). Uses only organic local ingredients in its pizzas, staying true to its "Don't panic, it's organic" mantra. Free Wi-Fi, an organic and fair-trade shop, yoga and therapy room, bookstore, and local crafts make the EcoCenter a one-stop shop for healthy living. Live music Friday and Saturday. Pizzas €4.50-9. Tapas €2.50. Organic pastas €8-12. Open Su and M 9am-1:30pm, Tu-Sa 9am-2am. Cash only. ❷

Café Zumo, C. Sancho IV el Bravo, 26b (☎956 62 72 51). A small, lively nook that dishes out plates of vegetarian delights. Sip fresh-squeezed juice and read a book from the shelf or make an exchange. Meals from €3-9. Books €2 with an exchange, €6 without. Open M-F 10:30am-2pm and 6-8pm, Sa-Su 10am-2pm. Cash only. ❷

Vaca Loca 3, C. Cervantes, 6, is a rare steakhouse in the midst of Iberian ham country. Check the board for daily offerings (€11-23) and have your mind made up by the time you're seated. Open daily 11am-3am; food served until 1am. MC/V. ❷

SIGHTS AND OUTDOOR ACTIVITIES

Next to the port and just outside the old town are the facade and ruins of the **Castillo de Guzmán el Bueno,** built in AD 960. In the 13th century, the Moors kidnapped Guzmán's son and threatened his life if Guzmán didn't relinquish the castle. The father didn't surrender, even after his son's throat was slashed before his very eyes. (Open Apr.-Oct. Tu-Su 11am-2pm and 6-8pm; Nov.-May Tu-Su 11am-2pm and 4-6pm. €1.80.) Those with something less historical (or less gruesome) in mind can head 200m south to **Playa de los Lances** for 5km of the finest white sand on the Atlantic coast. Bathers should be aware of the occasional high winds and strong undertow. Adjacent to Playa de los Lances is **Playa Chica,** which is tiny but sheltered from the winds. **Tarifa Spin Out Surfbase,** 9km up the road toward Cádiz (ask the bus driver on the Cádiz route to stop, or take a taxi for €6), rents windsurfing and kitesurfing boards and instructs all levels. (☎956 23 63 52; www.tarifaspinout.com. Book ahead. Windsurf rental €26 per hr., €60 per day; 90min. lesson including all equipment €50. Kite and board rental €28 per hr., €58 per day; 2hr. lesson with all equipment €120.) Many campgrounds along CN-340 between km 70 and km 80 provide instruction and gear for outdoor sports. Ask at the tourist office for their list of kite- and windsurfing schools and rental shops.

NIGHTLIFE

At night, sunburned travelers mellow out in the old town's many bars, which range from jazz to psychedelic to Irish. People migrate to the clubs around 1 or 2am. The *terrazas* on C. Sancho IV el Bravo fill with locals and surfers chatting over beer or coffee. Almost every bar and club on **C. San Francisco** is a hot spot for backpackers and locals to meet, drink, and move to the music.

Moskito, C. San Francisco, 11, is a combination bar-club with a Caribbean motif, dance music, and tropical cocktails. Free salsa lessons W night 10:30pm. Beer €2.50. Mixed drinks €5-6. Open in summer daily 11pm-3am; in winter Th-Sa 11pm-later.

La Tribu, C. Nuestra Señora de la Luz, 7, a favorite among kite surfers, makes some of the most creative cocktails in town. Trance and techno pump energy into this otherwise mellow nightspot. Beer €2-3. Mixed drinks €6. Shots €1.50.

La Ruina, corner of C. San Francisco and C. Santísima Trinidad. This renovated hot spot is appropriately located in the ruins of a long-deserted Roman stronghold. Blasting house music amidst a funky surfboard-themed interior, La Ruina serves it up all night long. Beers €2-4. Mixed drinks €5-6. Open M-F 12am-3pm, Sa-Su 12am-4am. Cash only.

GIBRALTAR ☎350 OR 9567

Emerging from the morning mist, the Rock of Gibraltar's craggy face menaces those who pass by its shores. Ancient seafarers referred to the rock as one of the Pillars of Hercules, believing that it marked the end of the world. Today, it is known affectionately to locals as "Gib" and is home to more fish 'n' chips and pints of bitter per capita than anywhere in the Mediterranean. Though Gibraltar is a self-governing British colony, Spain continues to campaign for sovereignty. When a 1969 vote showed that Gibraltar's populace favored its colonial ties to Britain—at 12,138 to 44—Franco sealed the border. After 16 years of isolation and a decade of negotiations, the border re-opened on February 4,

1985. Tourists and residents cross with ease, but Gibraltar has a culture all its own, one that remains detached from Spain. While the mix of wild primates and Union Jacks makes Gibraltar worthwhile, it is also a tourist trap full of duty-free shops and pocket-burning prices. Cross the border and explore the Rock, then scurry back to España before nightfall.

TRANSPORTATION

Flights: Airport (☎730 26). **British Airways** (☎793 00) flies to London (2½hr., 2 per day, £168/€212) and Madrid (1hr., 2 per day, £142.60/€180).

Buses: From **La Línea,** on the Spanish border, to: **Algeciras** (40min.; M-F every 30min. 7:45am-11:15pm, Sa, Su, and holidays every 45min. 8:45am-11:15pm; €2); **Cádiz** (3hr., 4 per day 6:30am-8pm, €13); **Granada** (5hr., 7:15am and 2:15pm, €20); **Jerez de la Frontera** (4hr., 9:30am, €13); **Madrid** (7hr., 1:10 and 10:15pm, €26); **Málaga** (3hr.; 4 per day 7:15am-5:30pm, Su also 8:45pm; €11); **Marbella** (1hr., 4 per day 7:15am-5:30pm, €5); **Sevilla** (6hr., 4 per day 7am-4:15pm, €21); **Tarifa** (1hr., 7 per day 6:30am-8pm, €4).

Ferries: Turner & Co., 65/67 Irish Town St. (☎783 05; fax 720 06). Open M-F 8am-3pm. To **Tangier,** Morocco (1hr.; F 6pm, return Sa 5:30pm Moroccan time; £18/€32, under 12 £9/€16.20).

Public Transport: Most bus lines run from one end of the Rock base to the other. Buses #9 and #10 go between the border and the Rock for £0.60/€1. Round-trip £0.90/€1.50. Unlimited day pass £1.50/€2.50.

Taxis: Gibraltar Taxi Association (☎956 77 00 27).

EURO OR POUNDS? Although euro are accepted almost everywhere (except at pay phones and post offices), the pound sterling (£) is the preferred method of payment in Gibraltar. ATMs dispense money in pounds. Merchants and sights sometimes charge a higher price in euros than in pounds. Unless stated otherwise, however, assume that establishments accept euros; change is often given in British currency. The exchange rate fluctuates around £1 to €1.50. As of July 2008, £1 = €1.26.

ORIENTATION AND PRACTICAL INFORMATION

Make sure you have a valid passport before heading to Gibraltar, or you'll be turned away at the border. If you need a visa, the UK embassy in Madrid takes roughly a day to process them. Buses from Spain terminate in the nearby town of La Línea. From the bus station, walk directly toward the Rock (it's impossible to miss; the border is 5min. away). Once through customs and passport control, catch bus #9 or #10 or carefully walk across the airport tarmac into town (20min.); stay left on Winston Churchill Ave. when the road forks with Corral Ln. Cars take longer to enter and exit Gibraltar—often an hour or more.

Tourist Office: Duke of Kent House, Cathedral Sq. (☎450 00). Open M-F 9am-5:30pm, Sa 10am-3pm, Su 10am-1pm. Info booth at Spanish border in the immigration building. Open M-F 9am-4:30pm, Sa 10am-1pm.

Luggage Storage: Bus station in **La Línea.** €3 per day. Buy token for locker at a bus ticket booth. Open daily 7am-10pm.

Bookstore: Gibraltar Bookshop, 300 Main St. (☎718 94).

Emergency: ☎199.

Police: 120 Irish Town St. (☎725 00).

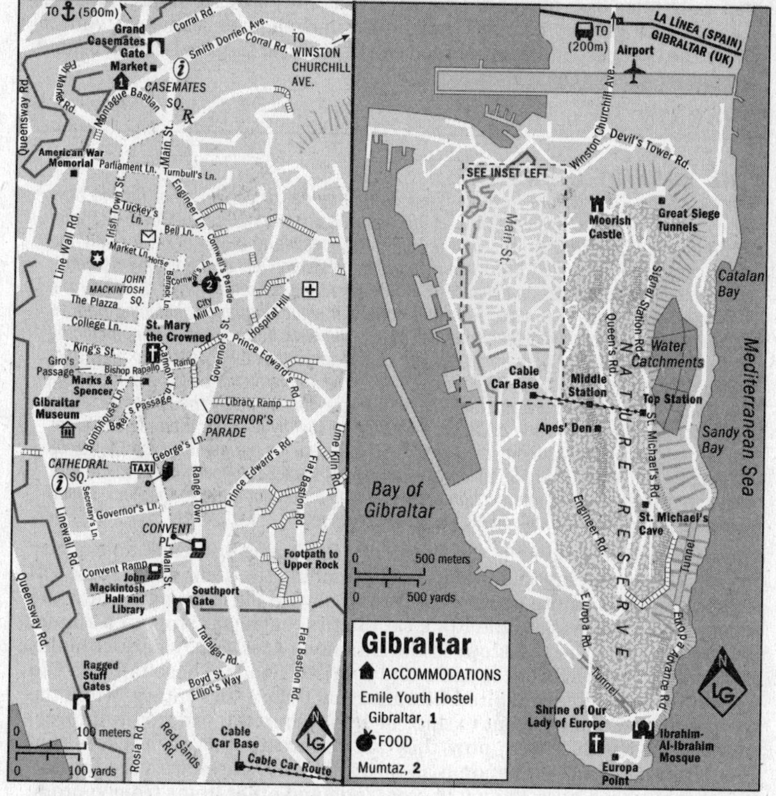

Pharmacy: Calpe Centre, Casemates Sq. (☎779 77). Open M-F 9am-7pm, Sa 10:30am-1:30pm.

Hospital: St. Bernard's Hospital, on Hospital Hill (☎797 00).

Internet Access: Call Shop, Main St., 293A (☎496 45). £2.50/€4 per hr. Accepts pounds, euros, and dollars; all change given in pounds. Open daily 9am-9pm.

Post Office: 104 Main St. (☎756 62). Open June to mid-Sept. M-F 9am-2:15pm, Sa 10am-1pm; mid-Sept. to May M-F 9am-4:30pm, Sa 10am-1pm. Pounds (£) only.

ACCOMMODATIONS AND FOOD

Gibraltar is best visited as a daytrip. The few accommodations in the area are pricey and often full, especially in the summer, and camping is illegal. At worst, you can crash across the border in La Línea. Back on the Rock, **Emile Youth Hostel Gibraltar ❷,** in Montague Bastian on Linewall Road, has bunk beds and clean communal baths. (☎511 06; www.emilehostel.com. Breakfast included. Lockout 10:30am-4:30pm. £1 for luggage storage or towels. Dorms £15/€20; doubles £34/€51. Cash only.) International restaurants are easy to find—try sampling the spices of Gibraltar's thriving Hindu community at **Mumtaz ❶,** 20 Cornwalls Ln., where authentic tastes and true *dhaba* style come at the lowest of prices. (☎442 57. Entrees £2.50-7, with ample vegetarian selection. Takeout available.

Open daily 11am-3pm and 6pm-12:30am. Cash only.) **Marks & Spencer** on Main St. has a small grocery/bakery. (Open M-F 9am-7pm, Sa 9:30am-5pm. AmEx/MC/V.) The cheapest and freshest food can be found at the local **market,** behind Casemates Square. (Open M-Sa 8am-2:30pm.)

SIGHTS

THE ROCK OF GIBRALTAR

The top of the Rock Nature Reserve is accessible by car or cable car, or for the truly adventurous, by foot. Cable cars (☎ 778 26) depart daily every 10min. 9:30am-5:15pm; last return 5:45pm. Tickets sold until 5:15pm. It's possible to buy a ticket for only the cable car (round-trip £8/€13.50), but if you plan on visiting any of the sights, it's better to buy a combined admission ticket (£16/€26.50). At the top, don't forget to ask for the interactive guided tour, an audio tour that comes in eight languages, including Hebrew and Swedish. Included with the cable car ticket. The walk down takes 2-3hr., including stops at the sights. Tour operators offer van or taxi tours that take visitors to all attractions in about 1hr. The official Taxi Tour booth is in the immigrations building across from the tourist booth; make sure you take the official tour sponsored by the Taxi Association. Prices for the Taxi Tour include all sights so it may be slightly cheaper than the cable car. For those traveling by car, there is a £8/€13.50 entrance fee per person, plus £1.50/€3 per car. On foot, take Library St. to Library Ramp from Main St., follow it uphill to the end, and turn right. At the next intersection there is a sign for the footpath to the Rock. Follow the footpath for 20min. until you hit a road, and turn left.

Gibraltar's claim to fame is the legendary Rock, and you can't do the city justice without seeing this titanic crag. Climbing the giant white rock will give you many a photo op to capture the severe cliffs plunging into the ocean. About halfway up the Rock (at the first cable car stop, or a 25min. walk down from the top stop) is the infamous **Apes' Den,** where colonies of **Barbary apes** cavort atop taxis and tourists' heads. These tail-less Old World monkeys have inhabited Gibraltar since the 18th century. When the ape population nearly went extinct in 1944, Churchill ordered reinforcements from North Africa; now they are procreating at such a rate that population control has become an issue. The monkeys are very tourist-friendly, but have been known to steal food and other items from visitors; keep all food hidden and bags closed to avoid unwanted confrontations with the animals. Although the monkeys are cute and friendly, tourists are advised not to touch them or their young. At the northern tip of the Rock, facing Spain, are the **Great Siege Tunnels.** Originally used to fend off a combined Franco-Spanish siege at the end of the American Revolution, the tunnels were expanded during WWII to span 33 miles underground. Nearby, on the way back to town, is the old Moorish castle, rebuilt several times, most recently in 1333. Although the castle is currently under renovation, the exterior still merits a quick look if you're already on the Rock. Thousands of years of water erosion carved the eerie chambers of **St. Michael's Cave.** Ask about a guided tour to the lower caves, which feature an underground lake and stalagmites.

COSTA DEL SOL

Artifice has replaced the once-natural charms of the Costa del Sol, as chic promenades, swanky hotels, and apartment buildings spring up between the small towns and the shoreline. The Costa del Sol extends from Tarifa in the southwest to Cabo de Gata, east of Almería; post-industrial Málaga lies directly between the two. To the northeast, hills dip straight into the ocean, and rocky beaches enhance the shore's natural beauty. To the southwest, however, waves seem to wash up onto more concrete than sand. Still, nothing detracts from the coast's major attraction: eight months of spring and four months of summer. News of the fantastic weather has spread, and July and August bring swarms of pale northern Europeans. Reservations are recommended in the summer anywhere on the coast, especially at hostels.

MÁLAGA ☎952

Málaga (pop. 561,250) is the busiest city on the coast, and while its beaches are better known for their bars than their natural beauty, the city has much to offer. The Alcazaba commands a hill to the west of the city, offering magnificent—and telling—views of Málaga: cranes and industrial ports in the distance contrast with the charming *casco antiguo* and verdant gardens. One of Málaga's most famous exports is the painter Pablo Picasso, whose hometown museum opened in 2003. As a critical transportation hub, Málaga is often seen as a stopover en route to other coastal cities, but the thriving city's bustle, beaches, palm trees, and dove-filled plazas are a worthy destination in their own right.

TRANSPORTATION

Flights: (☎952 04 88 04 or 902 40 47 04). From the airport, Bus #19 (2 per hr. 6:35am-11:35pm, €1) runs from the "City Bus" sign, stopping at the bus station and at the corner of C. Molina Lario and Postigo de los Abades. RENFE trains connect the city and the airport (12min., €1). **Iberia,** C. Molina Lario, 13 (☎952 13 61 66, 24hr. reservations 902 40 05 00), has daily international flights, mostly to England.

Trains: Estación de Málaga, Explanada de la Estación (☎952 12 80 79; www.renfe.es). Take bus #3 at Po. del Parque or #4 at Pl. de la Marina to the station. **RENFE** office, C. Strachan, 4 (☎902 24 02 02). To: **Barcelona** (13hr.; 7:20am, 8:35pm; €58); **Córdoba** (2hr., 9 per day 6:45am-8:20pm, €19); **Fuengirola** (30min., every 30min. 8am-10:30pm, €1); **Madrid** (5hr., 7 per day 6:35am-9pm, €71-79); **Sevilla** (3hr., 5-6 per day 7:40am-8:10pm, €17-33); **Torremolinos** (20min., every 30min. 5:45am-10:10pm, €2). Reservations for long-distance trains highly recommended.

Buses: Po. de los Tilos (☎952 35 00 61; **ALSA** 902 42 22 42; **Alsina Graells Sur** 952 31 82 95; **Casado** 952 31 59 08; **Daibus** 952 31 52 47; **Portillo** 902 14 31 44; www.ctsa-portillo.com), 1 block from the RENFE station along C. Roger de Flor, buses #3, 4, C1 and 19 stop at the station. To: **Algeciras** (3hr., 9-10 per day 5am-7:15pm, €10.82-11.39); **Almería** (6-9 per day 3:15am-7pm, €15.37); **Antequera** (1hr.; M-F 13 per day 7am-8:45pm, Sa 8 per day 9:30am-10pm, Su 9 per day 9:30am-11pm; €4.85); **Barcelona** (3.5hr., 6 per day 8:30am-12:31am, €75.17); **Cádiz** (4hr., 6 per day 6:45am-8pm, €21.59); **Córdoba** (3hr., 7 per day 9am-8pm, €12.21); **Granada** (2hr., 22 per day 7am-10pm, €9.38); **La Línea** (3hr., 5 per day 7am-7:15pm, €10.61); **Madrid** (7hr., 8-12 per day 8:30am-1am, €20.14 or 17.80 for youth); **Marbella** (1½hr.; M-F 25 per day 6:45am-9:45pm, Sa 22 per day 8:30am-9:45pm, Su 21 per day 9am-9:45pm; €4.64-4.97); **Murcia** (6hr., 5 per day 8:30am-9:45pm, €26); **Ronda** (3hr., 4-12 per day 8am-8:30pm, €9.57-9.90); **Salamanca** (9hr; daily 6pm, €42.41); **Sevilla** (3hr., 11-13 per day 7am-3:15am, €15.16).

Taxis: Radio Taxi (☎952 32 00 00). Town center to waterfront €6; to the airport €18-23; from the train and bus station to town center €5; from **Málaga** to **Balmádena** €20.

ORIENTATION AND PRACTICAL INFORMATION

The bus and train stations lie a block away from each other along C. Roger de Flor, on the other side of the **Río Guadalmedina** from the historical center and the majority of sights. To get to the town center from the **bus station,** exit right onto Callejones del Perchel, walk straight through the big intersection with Av. de la Aurora, take a right onto Av. de Andalucía, and cross Puente de Tetuán. From here, **Alameda Principal** leads into **Plaza de la Marina** (20min.). Alternatively, take bus #3, 4 or 21 along the same route (€1). From Pl. de la Marina, C. Molina Lario leads to the **cathedral** and the old town. C. Marqués de Larios, the main shopping and pedestrian street, connects Pl. de la Marina to **Plaza de la Constitución.** Behind the latter plaza, C. Granada leads to many good tapas bars and **Plaza de la Merced,** renowned for its *botellón.* Av. Cánovas del Castillo leads to **Playa de la Malagueta** (20min. walk), the closest beach worth visiting. After dark, be wary of the **Cruz del Molinillo** area (near the market) and desolate beaches.

Tourist Offices: Municipal, Av. de Cervantes, 1, Pl. de la Aduana (☎952 12 20 20; www.malagaturismo.com). Open daily 9am-7pm. **Branch:** Pl. de la Marina (☎952 12 20 20). Open M-F 9am-7pm. **Branch:** Pl. de la Aduana. Open M-F 9am-7pm, Sa 10am-7pm, Su 10am-2pm. **Junta de Andalucía,** Pje. de Chinitas, 4 (☎952 21 34 45). Open M-F 9am-8pm, Sa 10am-7pm, Su 10am-2pm. In winter offices may close earlier.

Currency Exchange: Banks (and **ATMs**) line most major roads and cluster around the intersection of Alameda Principal and C. Marqués de Larios.

Luggage Storage: Lockers at the train station (open daily 7am-10:45pm) and bus station (open daily 6:30am-11pm). Both €2.40-4.50 per day.

English-Language Bookstore: Rayuela Idiomas, Pl. de la Merced, 17 and C. Carcer, 1. (☎952 22 48 10). Open M-F 9:45am-1:30pm and 5-8:30pm, Sa 10am-2pm. MC/V.

Women's Center: Área de Igualdad de Opportunidades de la Mujer, C. Merced, 1 (☎952 13 47 56). Open M-F 9am-2pm.

Police: Policía Nacional, Plaza de la Aduana, 1 (☎952 04 62 00). **Policía Municipal,** Av. de la Rodaleda, 19 (☎952 12 65 00).

Pharmacy: Farmacia Caffarena, Alameda Principal, 2 (☎952 21 28 58), at the intersection with C. Marqués de Larios. Open 24hr.

Medical Services: ☎952 39 04 00, emergency ☎952 30 30 34. **Hospital Carlos Haya,** Av. Carlos Haya (☎951 29 00 00).

Internet Access: Across from the Picasso Foundation, **Telsat,** C. Gomez Pallete, 7 (☎952 21 28 22), offers access for €1 per hr., minimum €0.50. Open daily 9am-1am.

Post Office: Av. de Andalucía, 1 (☎902 19 71 97). **Lista de Correos.** Open M-F 8:30am-8:30pm, Sa 9:30am-2pm. **Postal Code:** 29080.

ACCOMMODATIONS

Budget accommodations in Málaga are just a little pricier than the Andalusian average—expect to pay about €18-30 for a single or dorm bed. Most *hostales* are in the old town between Pl. de la Marina and Pl. de la Constitución.

Picasso's Corner, C. San Juan de Letrán, 9, off of Pl. de la Merced (☎952 21 22 87; www.picassoscorner.com). This king of the hostels boasts a large DVD selection, free internet, large kitchen, and an elegant bathroom with massaging shower. Dorms are social, but staff enforces quiet hours for weary travelers looking to catch some winks.

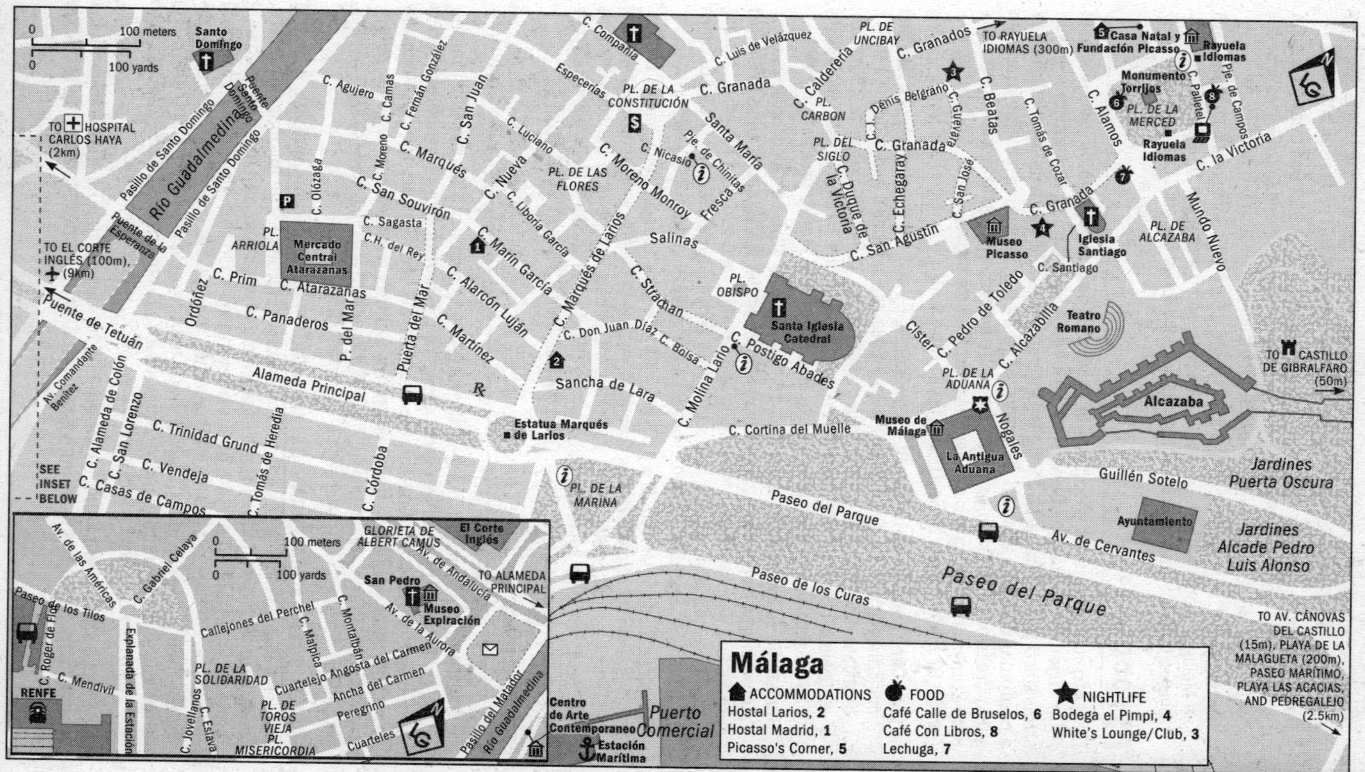
Málaga
ACCOMMODATIONS
Hostal Larios, 2
Hostal Madrid, 1
Picasso's Corner, 5
FOOD
Café Calle de Bruselos, 6
Café Con Libros, 8
Lechuga, 7
NIGHTLIFE
Bodega el Pimpi, 4
White's Lounge/Club, 3
Alcazaba
Teatro Romano
Santa Iglesia Catedral
Museo Picasso
Iglesia Santiago
La Antigua Aduana
Museo de Málaga
Ayuntamiento
Mercado Central Atarazanas
Estatua Marqués de Larios
Casa Natal y Fundación Picasso
Rayuela Idiomas
Monumento Torrijos
PL. DE LA MERCED
PL. DE LA CONSTITUCIÓN
PL. DE LAS FLORES
PL. OBISPO
PL. DE LA ADUANA
PL. DE LA MARINA
PL. DE ALCAZABA
PL. DE UNCIBAY
PL. ARRIOLA
Paseo del Parque
Paseo de los Curas
Av. de Cervantes
Guillén Sotelo
Jardines Puerta Oscura
Jardines Alcade Pedro Luis Alonso
Alameda Principal
Río Guadalmedina
Puerto Comercial
Estación Marítima
Centro de Arte Contemporaneo
TO CASTILLO DE GIBRALFARO (50m)
TO AV. CÁNOVAS DEL CASTILLO (15m), PLAYA DE LA MALAGUETA (200m), PASEO MARÍTIMO, PLAYA LAS ACACIAS, AND PEDREGALEJO (2.5km)
TO RAYUELA IDIOMAS (300m)
TO HOSPITAL CARLOS HAYA (2km)
TO EL CORTE INGLÉS (100m), (9km)
SEE INSET BELOW
TO ALAMEDA PRINCIPAL
El Corte Inglés
GLORIETA DE ALBERT CAMUS
San Pedro
Museo Expiración
Explanada de la Estación
RENFE
Santo Domingo
Puente Santo Domingo
Puente de la Esperanza
Puente de Tetuán
0 100 meters
0 100 yards

Breakfast and 24hr. coffee and tea included. Laundry €3 per wash/dry cycle. Roof-top hammocks €10. 4- to 6-bed dorms €18-19; doubles €22.50 per person. MC/V. ❶

Hostal Larios, C. Marqués de Larios, 9, 3rd fl. (☎952 22 54 90). Don't pay for a room with a private bath; the common ones are clean and new. TV and A/C. Singles €32-37, with bath €35-42; doubles €42-49/53-60; triples with bath €75-89. MC/V. ❸

Hostal Madrid, C. Marín García, 4, 2nd fl. (☎646 15 86 99). Some of the cheapest digs in Málaga. Rooms have showers and balconies, some with views of a peaceful street. Singles €30-40; doubles €30-60. During Aug. and *ferias* €40/60. Cash only. ❷

FOOD

Beachfront restaurants specialize in fresh seafood; *malagueños* love *pescaíto frito* (fried fish) and sardines roasted over open flames. Restaurants in the streets around C. Granada, Pl. de la Constitución, and Pl. de la Merced display a combination of classic and inventive salad menus. Try your hand at your own salad creation with fresh produce from the **market** on C. Ataranzas (open daily 8am-2pm). There is also a supermarket in **El Corte Inglés,** Av. de Andalucía, 4-6. (☎952 07 65 00. Open M-Sa 10am-10pm. AmEx/MC/V.)

Café Con Libros, Pl. de la Merced, 19 (☎952 21 51 89). Sit amid stacks of books and magazines as you sip on milkshakes, smoothies, tea, infusions, and coffee (€1.20-4), breakfast *menús* (€2.30-3.20), crepes and pastries (€2-3.40), tapas (€1.30-1.80), and salads (€6-7.50). The plush chairs, rotating paintings by local artists, and friendly English-speaking staff will tempt you to stay. Open daily 11am-2am. Cash only. ❶

Café Calle de Bruselas, Pl. de Merced, 16 (☎952 60 39 48; www.calledebruselas.com). Located right across from the information kiosk in the plaza, this Art Deco-influenced restaurant and bar offers a welcoming atmosphere, good fare, and free Wi-Fi. Thriving nightlife with live music and jazz, and a lively community feel. Breakfast €2.80. Lunch €5.50-7.50. Beer €2-3. Mixed drinks €5. Open daily 9am-3am. MC/V. ❶

Lechuga, Pl. de la Merced, 1(☎610 39 14 94). Despite its unassuming name, "Lettuce" offers a variety of creative concoctions of vegetarian delight, while the combination of airy interior and eclectic funky pop offers the perfect escape from the noisy Pl. de la Merced. Ten large salads (€8-9), starters (€4-8), and 3-course daily menu (€8) are tasty and quick. Wine €2.90-4. Open daily 1:30pm-12:30am. MC/V. ❷

SIGHTS

ALCAZABA. Towering high above the city, the Alcazaba is Málaga's most imposing sight. The fortress offers great views of the harbor from its medieval brick and stone walls. Guarding the east end of Po. del Parque, the 11th-century structure was originally used as both a military fortress and a royal palace by Moorish kings. *(Open June-Aug. Tu-Su 9:30am-8pm; Sept.-May Tu-Sa 8:30am-7pm. €2, students and seniors €0.60, under 7 free. Su free after 2pm.)*

SANTA IGLESIA CATEDRAL DE MÁLAGA. Málaga's commanding cathedral mixes a Renaissance aesthetic with a touch of Baroque. The intricate structure, complete with detailed columns, stained glass windows, and more than 15 side chapels, was built on the site of a former mosque. On the outside, the cathedral looks a bit off balance—it should have two towers, but one of them is only half-built—hence the cathedral's nickname *La Manquita* ("One-Armed Lady"). The small museum upstairs displays religious art. *(C. Molina Lario, 4. ☎952 22 03 45. Open M-F 10am-6pm, Sa 10am-5pm. Mass daily 9am. €3.50, includes audio tour.)*

CASTILLO DE GIBRALFARO. A Moorish lighthouse was built in this Phoenician castle, which offers sweeping vistas of Málaga and the Mediterranean. After admiring the cityscape, stop by the **Centro de Interpretación,** which has artifacts from the city's seafaring past. *(Bus #35 leaves every 20min. from the Alameda Principal; otherwise it's a shadeless 30min. uphill hike. Open daily Apr.-Oct. 9am-8pm; Nov.-March 9am-6pm. €1.95, students and seniors €0.60, combined with Alcazaba €3.20. Su free after 2pm.)*

CASA NATAL Y FUNDACIÓN PICASSO. Picasso left Málaga at a young age, but according to local officials, he always "felt himself to be a true *malagueño.*" The artist's birthplace now houses the **Picasso Foundation,** which organizes a series of exhibitions and lectures. The first floor is a seasonal gallery; upstairs is a permanent collection of photographs, drawings, and pottery by the artist. The Foundation also houses a Picasso Library on the 3rd floor. *(Pl. de la Merced, 15. ☎952 06 02 15; www.fundacionpicasso.es. Museum open daily 9:30am-8pm. Library open daily 9:30-2:30pm. €1, seniors, under 17, and students under 26 free.)*

MUSEO PICASSO. Though the collection isn't as impressive as those in Spain's larger museums, this relatively new exhibition dedicated to Málaga's most famous son traces his transition from child prodigy to renowned master. Visit the projection room, with its multilingual look at Picasso's methods, and the archaeological site in the basement, which explores Málaga's Phoenician, Roman, and Moorish roots through stone and ceramic arts. *(C. San Agustín, 8. ☎902 44 33 77; www.museopicassomalaga.org. Open Tu-Th, Su, and holidays 10am-8pm; F-Sa 10am-9pm. €6 permanent collection, €4.50 temporary, €8 combined; students, ages 11-16, and large groups €3; under 10 free. Free entrance last Su of each month 3-8pm. Free guided tours in Spanish Tu and Sa 6pm and 7pm, Th 6pm. Limit 20.)*

CENTRO DE ARTE CONTEMPORÁNEO. Some of today's foremost artists, such as Gerhard Richter and the controversial Chapman brothers, have exhibited in this renovated marketplace by the river. In addition to a hefty 400-piece permanent collection, which boasts a noteworthy selection of post-1950s American art, the museum's temporary exhibits uphold a fresh, avant-garde vibe. *(C. Alemania. ☎952 12 00 55; www.cacmalaga.org. Open Tu-Su 10am-2pm and 5-9pm. Free.)*

NIGHTLIFE

Many nightlife spots are only open Thursday through Saturday. **Bodega El Pimpi** is an ultra-popular traditional *bodega* with lots of little nooks and tiny rooms. The bar fills up early in the evening and stays crowded until about 1am. (Beer €1.70-3.40. Mixed drinks €4.30-6.50. Open Tu-Su 12pm-3am.) For a change in scenery, head to **Playa de la Malagueta,** a beach where young locals party by night at beachfront bars called *chiringuitos*. (30min. walk, but a quick and affordable taxi ride; buses don't run during late party hours.) When the city's bar scene is winding down, its clubs are just getting started. Head to **White's Lounge/Club,** C. José Denis Belgrano, 19, where small wall mirrors, bright fluorescent lights, and two semi-divided dance spaces serve as a backdrop to pulsing hip-hop and Spanish pop beats. (Beer €4. Mixed drinks €6. Open daily noon-6am.)

RONDA ☎952

When you first see Ronda (pop. 370,000), you'll think you've stumbled onto the pages of a fairy-tale. Centuries-old arches span the 100m El Tajo gorge, connecting the *casco antiguo* to the newer part of town, which is less romantic but full of life. The old city dates from Roman times, and the city earned fleeting political prominence under Moorish rule. The birthplace of modern bullfighting, Ronda has attracted such literary luminaries as Rainer Maria Rilke, who wrote his *Spanish Elegies* here, Ernest Hemingway, who based *For Whom the Bell Tolls* on the city, and Orson Welles, whose ashes are buried on a bull farm outside of town. While Ronda may hold you entranced for days, the city also makes an excellent base for exploring Andalucía's best *pueblos blancos* and the nearby Cuevas de la Pileta.

TRANSPORTATION

Train and bus stations are 3 blocks apart in the new city on Av. de Andalucía.

Trains: Av. Alférez Provisional (☎952 87 16 73 or 902 24 02 02). Ticket booth at C. Infantes, 20 (☎952 87 16 62). Open M-F 7am-10pm. To: **Algeciras** (2hr., 4 per day 7:10am-7:35pm, €6.70); **Granada** (3hr., 3 per day 8:57am-5:35pm, €12.25); **Madrid** (4hr., 10am and 4:46pm, €59.90); **Málaga** (2hr., M-Sa 7:12am, €8.85); or take the train to **Bobadilla** (1hr., 4 per day 7:52am-5:19pm, €4.40), which has more frequent trains to **Málaga** (1hr., 6 per day 8am-9:49pm, €4.40-13.70).

Buses: Pl. Concepción García Redondo, 2 (☎952 18 70 61). To: **Cádiz** (4hr.; 2-3 per day 9:30am-4:30pm, Sa-Su last bus 6pm; €12.61); **Málaga** (2hr., 8-11 per day 7am-7:45pm, €9.63); **Marbella** (1hr., 5-6 per day 6:30am-8:15pm, €5.02); **Sevilla** (3hr., 3-5 per day 7am-7pm, €10.17).

Taxis: (☎952 87 23 16 or 670 20 74 38). From the train station to Pl. de España €4.

ORIENTATION AND PRACTICAL INFORMATION

The 18th-century **Puente Nuevo** connects Ronda's old and new cities. On the new side, **Carrera Espinel** (the main street, which includes the pedestrian walkway known as La Bola) runs perpendicular to C. Virgen de la Paz, intersecting it between the bullring and **Plaza de España.** To reach the tourist office and town center, leave the train station and go straight on Av. Martínez Astein. Turn right when the road ends onto the pedestrian C. Espinel. From the bus station, turn left onto C. Naranja, walk four blocks, and then turn right onto pedestrian Carrera Espinel, which leads to the Pl. de España.

Tourist Office: Municipal, Po. Blas Infante (☎952 18 71 19), near the bullring. English spoken. Open June-Aug. M-F 10am-7:15pm, Sa-Su 10am-2pm and 3:30-6:30pm; Sept.-May M-F 9:30am-6:30pm, Sa-Su 10am-2pm and 3:30-6:30pm. **Regional** office, Pl. de España, 1 (☎952 87 12 72). English spoken. Open June-Aug. M-F 9am-8pm, Sa-Su 10am-2pm; Sept.-May M-F 9am-7pm, Sa-Su 10am-2pm. The tourist office also sells *bono* tickets for discounted entrance to Ronda's major sights.

Currency Exchange: Banco Santander Central Hispano, Carrera Espinel, 17 (☎902 24 24 24), near C. Virgen de los Remedios. Open M-F 8:30am-2pm; Oct.-May also Sa 8:30am-1pm. If banks are closed, try **Ronda Change,** C. Virgen de la Paz, 2 (☎952 87 96 04). Open M-F 10am-2pm and 4-8pm, Sa 10am-3pm.

Luggage Storage: At the bus station (€3 per day). Open daily 9am-8pm.

Police: Pl. Duquesa de Parcent (☎092), 3, near the town hall

Medical Emergency: ☎952 06 52 18 or 50 50 61. **Hospital de la Serranía** (☎951 06 50 01), en route to El Burgo.

Pharmacy: Farmacia Santos, Pl. de España, 5 (☎952 87 15 80). Open in summer M-F 9:30am-2pm and 5-8:30pm; winter M-F 9:30am-2pm and 5-8pm, Sa 9:30am-2pm.

Internet Access: Ciber Locutorio Rondatelecom, C. Jerez, 4-Bajo (☎952 87 25 57). Internet €1.40 per hr. Copies €0.20 per page. Public telephones available. Open M-Sa 11am-2pm and 5-10pm.

Laundry: Pressto, C. Mariano Soubirón, 17 (☎952 87 91 77; www.pressto.com). Open M-F 9:30am-2pm and 5-8:30pm, Sa 9:30am-2pm.

Post Office: C. Virgen de la Paz, 20 (☎952 87 25 57), across from Pl. de Toros. **Lista de Correos.** Open M-F 8:30am-8:30pm, Sa 9:30am-1pm. **Postal Code:** 29400.

ACCOMMODATIONS

Hotels in the old city are expensive, so you'll be better off staying in the new city. Most *pensiones* are concentrated around the bus station on side streets off Carrera Espinel—try C. Naranja, C. Lorenzo Borrego, or C. Sevilla. Expect room shortages in August and during the *Feria de Ronda* in September.

Hotel Arunda I, C. Espinel, 120 (☎952 19 01 02; www.hotelesarunda.com). Carved-wood-furnished rooms have bath, A/C, TV, and sunny windows. A little classier than its sister hotel. Internet access €2 per hr. **Arunda II,** C. José M.C. Madrid, 10-12 (☎952 87 25 19) has the same white-walled, dark-fixtured decor and internet prices but offers breakfast. Singles €27, with breakfast €29; doubles €44/47. AmEx/MC/V. ❸

Pensión La Purísima, C. Sevilla, 10 (☎952 87 10 50). Plant-filled hallways lead to bright rooms decorated with tasteful religious art. Some have private bath. Singles €17; doubles €30, with bath €35; triples with bath €50. Cash only. ❷

Hotel Morales, C. Sevilla, 51 (☎952 87 15 38; www.hotelmorales.es). A nature theme carries from the corridor into each room by way of wildlife posters and earth tone bedspreads; singles are small but cozy. All have private bath, A/C, and TV. Singles €23-25; doubles €39-42. MC/V. ❷

FOOD

Restaurants and cafes abound in Ronda, although many are geared to tourists and tend to be overpriced, especially those near Pl. de España. Rabbit and stewed bull's tail *(rabo de toro)* are local specialties.

El Pataton, C. San José, 8 (☎678 87 06 26), tucked between C. Molino and C. Sevilla. A popular takeout spot with locals. For only €3.50, the friendly chefs prepare a delicious variation on Spanish cuisine: tapas ingredients stuffed into potatoes. Choose from one of 11 options or try the €4.50 "El Pataton" for a giant potato with a filling of your choice. Open Tu-Su 8pm-midnight. Closed 1 month per year, usually July-early Aug. ❶

Casi Ke No, C. Molino, 6B. If choosing a sandwich is an existential struggle for you, beware of Casi Ke No. Serves 50 types of *montaditos* (€1.20), small but substantial sandwiches, as well as innovative tapas such as goat cheese topped with raspberry (€3). Open Tu-Su noon-4pm and 7pm-midnight. Cash only. ❶

Los Cántaros, C. Sevilla, 66 (☎952 87 63 23). A small local bar with big food. The bull's tail (€9) is heaping and melts off the bone. Soups (€2-6), fish (€6-11), and meat dishes (€6-15). Open Tu-Sa 9am-5pm and 8-11pm, Su and M 9am-5pm. ❷

Panadería Rondeña, C. Sevilla, 53 (☎952 87 52 82). Lines of sizable fresh pastries (€1-1.40). Pop in for a lemon *granizado* (small €0.70, large €1.40), a perfect refreshment after a day of sightseeing. Open Su and M 8am-8pm, Tu-Sa 7am-8:30pm. ❶

Chocolat, C. Sevilla, 16 (☎952 87 69 84) offers a gourmet chocolate experience in an airy, light cafe. Coffees (€2.25-2.50). Over forty varieties of green, black, white, and red teas (€1-3). Pastries and chocolate (€1-3.50). Open 8:30am-2pm and 4-8:30pm. ❶

SIGHTS

CASA DEL REY MORO. The name, "House of the Moorish King," is rather misleading. Despite its Moorish facade, the house dates from the 18th century and is not the main attraction; you enter it only to pay your admission. Descend the seemingly endless stairways—60m into the depths of a 14th-century mine, which has housed more than its share of prisoners and slaves over the centuries. A strategic defense point, the mine also has a room used to hold cauldrons of boiling oil and a "Room of Secrets," where whispers travel from one corner of the room to the other but are inaudible in the middle. The other main attractions are Forestier's serene gardens, high atop the cliffs and house, designed and constructed in the 1920s by the famous French landscape architect. *(Cuesta de Santo Domingo, 17. Take the first left after crossing the Puente Nuevo. ☎952 18 72 00. Open daily in summer 10am-7pm; in winter 10am-7pm. €4, children €2.)*

PLAZA DE TOROS AND MUSEO TAURINO. Bullfighting lies at the heart of Ronda's livelihood, as evidenced by the careful construction of this stunning bullring, the oldest in Spain (est. 1785). The attached museum traces the history of the sport, focusing largely on Ronda's native matadors. Ronda has had its share of famous bullfighters, including the Romero dynasty—three generations of fighters from the same family. Pedro, the most famous, killed his first bull at age 17 in 1771; over the course of his career, it is said he fought more than 5600 bulls without a single injury. The museum's hallways are filled with Goya prints of bullfights, authentic costumes, weapons, and the heads of the bravest bulls. Perhaps of greater interest are the actual bullring and stables. In early September, the Plaza de Toros hosts *corridas goyescas* (bullfights in traditional costumes) as part of the **Feria de Ronda.** *(☎952 87 41 32; www.rmcr.org. Open daily Apr. 16-Oct. 10am-8pm; Nov.-Feb. 10am-6pm; Mar.-Apr. 15 10am-7pm. €6, students €4. Museum audio tour €3. Wheelchair-accessible.)*

MUSEO DE LARA. The private collection of Juan Antonio Lara Jurado—who still lives above the museum—is a collection of, well, collections. He covers traditional Spanish culture with fans, bullfighting costumes, and a *bodega* room, and delves into the more bizarre with a guillotine and roomful of witchcraft and Inquisition torture devices. In the summer, the museum hosts weekend flamenco shows. *(C. Armiñán, 29. ☎952 87 12 63; www.museolara.org. Open daily 11am-8pm. €4, students and seniors €2, children free. Flamenco €23 at 10pm, includes museum admission. First floor wheelchair-accessible.)*

OTHER SIGHTS. Carved by the Río Guadalquivir, Ronda's **gorge** extends 100m below the Puente Nuevo, across from Pl. de España. Arrested highwaymen were once held in a prison cell beneath the bridge's center, and during the Civil War, political prisoners were thrown from the top. Supposedly, even as they faced certain death, they were told that if they were to survive the fall they would be free. Take a stroll through **Alameda del Tajo** for a cliffside walk. The **view** from the center is unparalleled. The innovative **Puente Viejo** was rebuilt in 1616 over an Arab bridge with the Arco de Felipe V, built in 1742, presiding over one end. Farther down, the **Puente San Miguel** (or Puente Árabe) is an Andalusian hybrid of a Roman base and Arabic arches. To reach them, walk on C. Santo Domingo past the Casa del Rey Moro. The tiny but informative **Museo del Bandolero,** C. Armiñán, 65, is dedicated to presenting "pillage, theft, and rebellion in Spain since Roman time," recounting the stories of bandits and the men who tracked them. *(☎952 87 77 85; www.museobandolero.com. Open daily in summer 10:30am-8pm; in winter 10am-6pm. €3, students and children €2.50, groups over 10 €2.)*

NIGHTLIFE

Locals congregate in the pubs and discotecas along C. Jerez and the streets behind Pl. del Socorro, and both local families and young people can be found in *heladerías* (ice cream parlors) along Carrera Espinel. With cheap drinks and hearty tapas, it's no surprise that **Bar Antonio,** C. San José, 1, is popular. (Beer €1. Mixed drinks €3.50. Tapas €1-2. Giant *bocadillos* €2-2.50. Open M-Sa 7:30am-2am.) A 20-something crowd heads to **Huskies Sport Bar-Café,** C. Molino, 1, for beer and sports. Taking its name from the UConn mascot, the bar is lined with posters of American sports teams—very popular with foreigners.

(www.huskiesbar.com. Beer €2. Mixed drinks €3.50. Open Tu-Su 4:30pm-3am, M 8:30pm-3am.) For a boisterous and ageless local scene, try **Bodeja-Bar 7,** C. Blas Infante, 7. Enjoy the moonlight at one of the outdoor tables on the patio. (☎952 87 60 97. Glass of sangria €1.70. Open noon-4pm and 8pm-late.)

DAYTRIP FROM RONDA

CUEVA DE LA PILETA

By car, take highway C-339 North (Ctra. Sevilla from the new city). The turnoff to Benaoján and the caves is about 22km out, in front of an abandoned restaurant. Taxis will go round-trip from Ronda for €50. A cheaper alternative is the train to Benaoján (20min.; 3 per day 7am-4:33pm, return 3 per day 1:39-8pm; round-trip €3.50). From the train station, it's a tough 1-2hr. climb to the caves, through the town of Benaoján, then along the highway. Ask locals for the way from Benaoján to the road, and don't stray off the highway or you might find yourself on an obscure mountainside path. ☎952 16 73 43. Caves open daily 10am-1pm and 4-6pm. Mandatory 1hr. tours begin on the hr., but call beforehand to hold your place. €8, groups of 10 or more €7 per person, student groups and under 12 €5.

The Cueva de la Pileta, 22km west of Ronda, is one of the few remaining privately owned caves in Spain, and as a national monument, one of the best preserved. The cave, which stretches over 2km underground, was discovered in 1905 by a local farmer looking for guano to use as fertilizer. Gas-lantern tours of this otherworldly expanse lead visitors along the 500m-long main gallery of the cave, past underground lakes, majestic mineral formations, and cathedral-like chambers. Inside, you'll find remarkably preserved Paleolithic and Neolithic paintings that represent a uniquely wide time frame, with some over 30,000 years old. Ceramics, animal bones, and human skeletons have also been discovered deep in the cave. The lamina formation nicknamed "the organ" is fascinating: years of falling water droplets carved its columns out of one giant sheet of rock, and each plays a different tone when struck. Visits are limited to 25 people, and reservations are accepted only in winter, so come early. Bring sturdy shoes and a sweatshirt—the caves are cool and slippery.

GRANADA ☎958

The splendors of the Alhambra, the magnificent fortress that crowns the city, have entranced princes, paupers, and poets for centuries. The golden hillsides, white rooftops, and vistas of the Sierra Nevada still bless Granada (pop. 238,000) today, but the city first blossomed into one of Europe's wealthiest, most culturally advanced cities after being conquered by Muslim armies in AD 711. As Christian armies turned back the tide of Moorish conquest in the 13th century, the city became the last Muslim outpost in Iberia. Fernando and Isabel capitalized on the chaos, capturing Boabdil—Granada's last Moorish ruler—and the Alhambra on the momentous night of January 1, 1492. As Boabdil fled, his mother berated him for casting a longing look back at the Alhambra, saying, "You do well to weep as a woman for what you could not defend as a man."

Although the Christians torched all the mosques and the lower city, embers of Granada's Muslim past still linger. The Albaicín, a maze of Moorish houses and twisting alleys, is Spain's best-preserved Arab quarter and the only part of the Muslim city to survive the Reconquista intact. Since then, Granada has grown into a university town, reveling in throngs of backpackers and Spanish youth. Granada's huge student population gives rise to spirited graffiti, lively tapas bars, and a thriving hippie subculture. A few days will give you a taste of Moorish Spain and Granada's vibrant nightlife, wonderfully rich in tapas and *teterías*—smoky, aromatic Arabic tea rooms. But do not be surprised if, like Boabdil, you leave longing for more days in this Andalusian gem.

TRANSPORTATION

Flights: Airport (☎958 24 52 00), 17km west of the city. **Autocares J. Gonzales** (☎958 49 01 64) runs a bus from Gran Vía, in front of the cathedral, to the airport (25min., 5 per day 6:50am-9:30pm, €3). A taxi costs about €25.

Trains: RENFE, Av. Andaluces (☎902 24 02 02. www.renfe.es). Take bus #3-6, 9, or 11 from Gran Vía to the Constitución 3 stops and turn left onto Av. Andaluces. To: **Algeciras** (4-5hr., 3 per day 7:15am-5pm, €18.35); **Almería** (2hr., 4 per day 10:03am-9:06pm, €14.45); **Barcelona** (12hr., 9:45pm, €52.10-57.40); **Madrid** (5-6hr.; 6:42am, 6pm; €61.80); **Sevilla** (4-5hr., 4 per day 8:18am-8:24pm, €21.65).

Buses: All major intercity bus routes start at the bus station (☎958 18 54 80) on the outskirts of Granada on Ctra. de Madrid, near C. Arzobispo Pedro de Castro. Take bus #3 or 33 from Gran Vía de Colón or a **taxi** (€6-7). Services reduced on Sundays.

ALSA (☎902 42 22 42 or 958 15 75 57; www.alsa.es.) to: **Alicante** (6hr., 6 per day 2:31am-11:30pm, €26.69); **Barcelona** (14hr., 5 per day 2:31am-11:30pm, €65.96); and **Valencia** (9hr., 5 per day 2:31am-11:30pm, €40.23). **Algeciras** (3hr., 6 per day 9am-8:15pm, €20.20); **Almería** (2hr., 8 per day 6:45am-7:30pm, €11.50); **Antequera** (1hr., 4 per day 9am-7pm, €7.20); **Cádiz** (5hr., 4 per day 3am-6:30pm, €29.52); **Córdoba** (3hr., 8 per day 7:30am-7pm, €12.04); Madrid (5-6hr., 15 per day 7am-1:30am, €15.66); **Málaga** (2hr., 16 per day 7am-9pm, €9.38); **Marbella** (2hr., 8 per day 8am-8:15pm, €14.35); **Sevilla** (3hr., 7 per day 8am-8pm, €18.57).

Public Transportation: Local buses (☎900 71 09 00). Pick up the bus map at the tourist office. Important buses include: "Bus Alhambra" #30 from Gran Vía de Cólon or Pl. Nueva to the Alhambra; #31 from Gran Vía or Pl. Nueva to the Albaicín; #10 from the bus station to the youth hostel, C. de Ronda, C. Recogidas, and C. Acera de Darro; #3 from the bus station to Av. de la Constitución, Gran Vía, and Pl. Isabel la Católica. €1.10, *bonobus* (9 tickets) €5.45.

Taxis: Teletaxi (☎958 28 06 54 or 958 13 23 23), with service throughout Granada and its environs. Taxi stands in Pl. Nueva and Pl. de la Trinidad 24hr.

Car Rental: Hertz, EuropCar, and **Avis** in the airport. Hertz has an office in the lobby of Hotel Central Granada, Av. Fuentenueva (☎902 40 24 05). Reservation line open 8am-11pm. Office open 9am-1:30pm and 3:30-8:30pm.)

ORIENTATION AND PRACTICAL INFORMATION

The center of Granada is small **Plaza Isabel la Católica,** at the intersection of the city's two main arteries, **Calle de los Reyes Católicos** and **Gran Vía de Colón.** Just off Gran Vía, you'll find the cathedral; farther down Gran Vía by Pl. de la Trinidad is the university area. Uphill from Pl. Isabel la Católica on C. Reyes Católicos sits **Plaza Nueva,** and the **Alhambra** rises on the hill above. From Pl. Nueva, **Calle Elvira,** lined with bars and eateries, runs parallel to Gran Vía. Downhill, the pedestrian streets off C. de los Reyes Católicos comprise the shopping district.

Tourist Offices: Junta de Andalucía, C. Santa Ana, 2 (☎958 57 52 02). Open M-F 9am-7:30pm, Sa 9:30am-3pm, Su 10am-2pm. Posts bus and train schedules and provides a list of accommodations. **Oficina Provincial,** Pl. Mariana Pineda, 10 (☎958 24 71 28). Walk up to the left past plaza Isabel and make a right on Pineda. Walk until the square. English spoken. Open M-F 9am-8pm, Sa 10am-7pm, Su 10am-3pm.

Currency Exchange: Banco Santander Central Hispano, Gran Vía, 3 (☎902 24 24 24). Open Apr.-Sept. M-F 8:30am-2pm.

Luggage Storage: 24hr. storage at the train and bus stations (€3). Frequently sold out.

English-Language Bookstore: Metro, C. Gracia, 31, off Veronica de la Magdalena, off C. Recogidas, which begins where Reyes Católicos hits Puerta Real. (☎958 26 15 65). Vast foreign language section. Open M-F 10am-2pm and 5-8:30pm, Sa 11am-2pm.

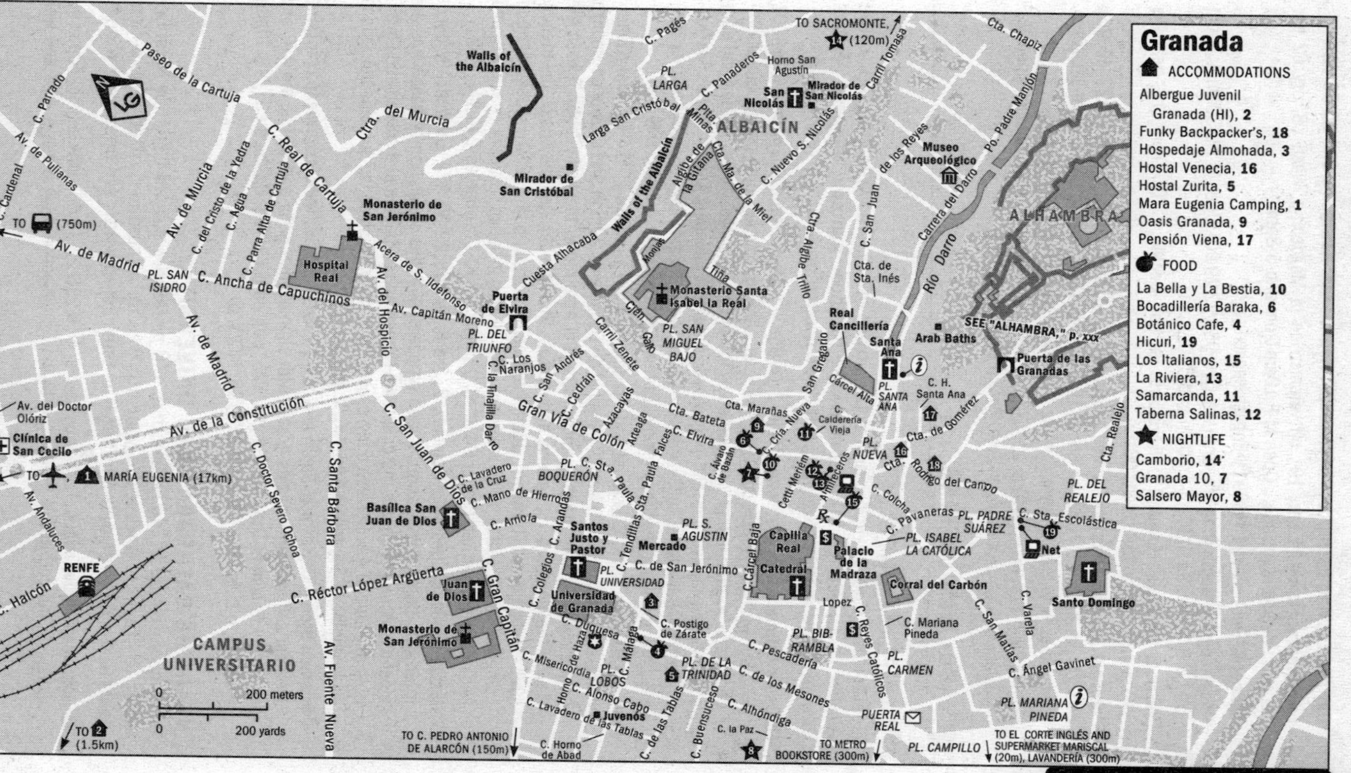
Granada
ACCOMMODATIONS
Albergue Juvenil Granada (HI), 2
Funky Backpacker's, 18
Hospedaje Almohada, 3
Hostal Venecia, 16
Hostal Zurita, 5
Mara Eugenia Camping, 1
Oasis Granada, 9
Pensión Viena, 17
FOOD
La Bella y La Bestia, 10
Bocadillería Baraka, 6
Botánico Cafe, 4
Hicuri, 19
Los Italianos, 15
La Riviera, 13
Samarcanda, 11
Taberna Salinas, 12
NIGHTLIFE
Camborio, 14
Granada 10, 7
Salsero Mayor, 8
SEE "ALHAMBRA," p. xxx
ALHAMBRA
ALBAICÍN
Walls of the Albaicín
Mirador de San Cristóbal
Monasterio de San Jerónimo
Hospital Real
Puerta de Elvira
Monasterio Santa Isabel la Real
Real Cancillería
Santa Ana
Arab Baths
Puerta de las Granadas
Museo Arqueológico
San Nicolás
Mirador de San Nicolás
Basílica San Juan de Dios
Santos Justo y Pastor
Mercado
Capilla Real
Catedral
Palacio de la Madraza
Corral del Carbón
Santo Domingo
Universidad de Granada
Juan de Dios
RENFE
Clínica de San Cecilio
CAMPUS UNIVERSITARIO
Gran Vía de Colón
Av. de la Constitución
C. Reyes Católicos
TO SACROMONTE, 14 (120m)
TO C. PEDRO ANTONIO DE ALARCÓN (150m)
TO METRO BOOKSTORE (300m)
TO EL CORTE INGLÉS AND SUPERMARKET MARISCAL (20m), LAVANDERÍA (300m)
TO 1 MARÍA EUGENIA (17km)
TO 2 (1.5km)
TO (750m)
200 meters
200 yards

Gay and Lesbian Resources: Información Homosexual Hotline (☎958 20 06 02).

Laundromat: C. de la Paz, 19., off Veronica de la Magdelena. Wash €8, dry €2 per 10min.; detergent included. Open M-F 10am-2pm and 5-8pm.

Police: C. Duquesa, 21 (☎091). English spoken.

Pharmacy: Farmacia Gran Vía, Gran Vía, 6 (☎958 22 29 90). Open M-F 9:30am-1:30pm and 5-8:30pm, Sa 9:30am-1:30pm and 5:30-9pm.

Medical Services: Hospital Universitario de San Cecilio, C. Dr. Olóriz, 16, near the Plaza de Toros (☎958 02 30 00).

Internet Access: Locutorio Cyber Alhambra, C. Joaquin Costa, 4 (☎958 22 43 96). €1.20 per hour; €5 *bono* for 6hr., €10 *bono* for 13hr. Open daily 9:30am-10:30pm. Second alley to left on Reyes Católicos walking away from Plaza Isabel.

Post Office: Pta. Real (☎958 22 48 35). Lista de Correos and fax service. Open M-F 8:30am-8:30pm, Sa 9:30am-2pm. **Postal Code:** 18009.

ACCOMMODATIONS

NEAR PLAZA NUEVA

Hostels line Cuesta de Gomérez, the street off Pl. Nueva leading up to the Alhambra. Crashing in this area is wise for those planning to spend serious time in the Alhambra complex, but these spots tend to fill up very quickly.

Oasis Granada, Placeta Correo Viejo, 3 (☎958 21 58 48; from Spain free at ☎9001 OASIS; www.hostelsoasis.com). Free internet, common kitchen, ping-pong table on outdoor patio, rooftop lounge. Frequented by the under-30 crowd. Weekly parties and daily activities like tapas tours and pub crawls. Breakfast included. Dinner *menús*, all-you-can-eat €4. If hostel is "full," try showing up early in the morning for a spot as they usually hold about 10 beds for walk-ins. Dorms €18; doubles €40. MC/V. ❷

Funky Backpacker's, Cuesta de Rodrigo del Campo, 13 (☎958 22 14 62; funky@alternativeacc.com). From Pl. Nueva, go uphill on Cuchilleros 20m to find Cuesta de Rodrigo on the right. Sizable dorms surround a central atrium over the funky lobby. Take in the view of the Alhambra, mountains, and rooftops from the bar atop the hostel. The friendly staff hangs out with travelers. Outings to nearby thermal baths (€10), tapas bars and *flamenco* shows (€21). A/C, breakfast, and lockers included. Laundry (wash, dry and fold) €7. Free internet. Dinner €4.50-6. Dorms €16.50-17; doubles €40. MC/V. ❶

Hostal Venecia, Cuesta de Gomérez, 2, 3rd fl. (☎958 22 39 87). Eccentrically decorated with bright colors and Granada paraphernalia, this small, homey hostel has the most character per square meter in town. Homemade herbal tea and conversation available any time of day. Reserve early, especially in summer, since the secret is out. Dorms €19; doubles €34; triples €45. MC/V. ❶

Pensión Viena, C. Hospital Santa Ana, 2 (☎958 22 18 59; www.hostalviena.com). The greatest selling points of this hostel, with simple white walls and blinds, are A/C and proximity to central Granada. Singles €25, with bath €30-38; doubles €37/48; triples €50/65; quads €60/75; quint €65/95. MC/V. ❷

NEAR THE CATHEDRAL AND UNIVERSITY

Hostels surround Pl. de la Trinidad, and *pensiones* around C. de los Mesones cater to students during the year but free up in summer, offering excellent deals to the diligent stair-climber. The ones listed below are open year-round.

Hospedaje Almohada, C. Postigo de Zárate, 4 (☎958 20 74 46; www.laalmohada.com). Follow C. Trinidad out of Pl. Trinidad to the T-intersection, then make a right and walk down the short street ahead. Look for double red doors with hand-shaped knockers. Lounge in the TV area, use the kitchen to cook your own meal, and peruse the communal music collection and travel guides. Laundry (wash and hang-dry) €5 for 8kg. 4-bed dorms €15; singles €19; doubles €35; triples €50. Cash only. ❶

Hostal Zurita, Pl. de la Trinidad, 7 (☎958 27 50 20; www.pensionzurita.com). Soundproof balcony doors are a blessing in this busy student-dominated neighborhood and above one of Granada's most pleasant plazas. Doubles are spacious, singles are small but adequate; all have TV and A/C. Notice some of the pieces of art are actually completed puzzles. Singles €21; doubles €34, with bath €42; triples €51/63. MC/V. ❷

ELSEWHERE

Hostels are sprinkled along Gran Vía de Colón, though many are expensive.

Albergue Juvenil Granada (HI), C. Ramón y Cajal, 2 (☎958 00 29 00). From the bus station, take bus #10; from the train station, #11. Ask the driver to stop at "El Estadio de la Juventud," across the field on the left. From the end of Gran Vía away from Pl. Isabela, continue down Ave. Constitución, make a left on Dr. Severo Ochoa, then eventually a right on Ronda, and look for a narrow street on the left just before a run-down sports complex. English-speaking staff available 24hr., but a trek from all of the sights. Dorm-style rooms and common baths. Dorms €19.5 for guests under 26, €23.5 over 26. HI discount €3.50 per night. ❶

CAMPING

Buses serve all campgrounds within 5km of Granada, albeit irregularly. Check schedules at the bus station or tourist office, and ask the driver to alert you at your stop. While camping is most convenient for those with their own transportation, the tourist office can provide a list of further camping options.

María Eugenia, Av. Andalucía (☎958 20 06 06; fax 20 94 10), at km 436 on the road to Málaga. Take the Santa Fé or Chauchina bus from the train station (every 30min.). Open year-round. Popular with families. €4.85 per person, €3.50 per child. ❶

FOOD

Though Granada offers a variety of traditional Spanish fare and ethnic restaurants, the best way to eat on a budget is to take advantage of the free tapas by ordering drinks. North African cuisine and vegetarian options can be found around the **Albaicín,** while more typical menus await in Pl. Nueva and Pl. de la Trinidad. The adventurous eat well in Granada—*tortilla sacromonte* (omelette with calf's brains and bull testicles) and *sesos a la romana* (batter-fried calf's brains) are traditional dishes. Picnickers can gather fresh fruit, vegetables, and meat at the large indoor **market** on Pl. San Agustín. (Open M-Sa 9am-3pm.)

NEAR PLAZA NUEVA

Pl. Nueva abounds with outdoor cafes. Those seeking more authentic fare would do better to comb the small side streets that lead out of the plaza.

GRANADA FOR POCKET CHANGE. Let's face it, you came to Granada for the Alhambra and complimentary tapas, so why not enjoy both for less than a train ride to Sevilla? Haggle vendors along **C. Cría Nueva** for souvenirs, clothing, and jewelry or get your name painted in Arabic. Refuel at **Oasis Granada** by chowing down at a weekly all-you-can-eat dinner for €4 with an €18 bed to match. If you're still feeling hungry, stock up on some late-night tapas at **La Riviera** and other bars around **C. Elvira** for the price of a drink, or grab a €1 treat at **Bocadillería Baraka.** Walk off the calories with a 15min. walk up to the *mirador* near Iglesia de San Nicolás for an unparalleled view of the Alhambra amidst the echoes of *flamenco.* Back in the city, dance away the night at **Salsero Mayor,** where the only cover is the timbered roof aglow with colored lights and undulating shadows.

La Riviera, C. Cetti Meriem, 7 (☎958 22 79 69), off C. Elvira. The best place to score delicious, free tapas. You can't go wrong with the extensive list of traditional fare. Beer or *tinto de verano* €1.80. Open daily 12:30-4pm and 8pm-midnight. ❶

Hicuri, C. Santa Escolástica, 12 (☎653 78 34 22), on corner of Pl. de los Girones. Walk uphill past Pl. Isabela about 200m. Your search for healthy, affordable cuisine stops here. This popular eatery's huge selection of vegetarian and vegan dishes will satisfy any tofu craving. Entrees €5.80-6.50. *Menú* €12. Open M-F 8:30am-4:30pm, Sa-Su 8:30am-4:30pm and 8:30-11:30pm. Cash only. ❷

La Bella y La Bestia, Carcel Bajo, 14. (☎958 32 55 69). Huge complimentary tapas proportionate to the number in your party, complete with fries, pasta salad, and *bocadillos.* Mixed drinks €1.40-2. Open M-Th and Su noon-2am, F-Su 11am-3am. ❶

ALBAICÍN

Wander the winding streets of the Albaicín and you'll discover many budget bars and restaurants above Pl. Nueva. This is a veritable paradise for fans of Middle Eastern cuisine; cheap falafel sandwiches abound. C. Calderería Nueva, off C. Elvira leading from the plaza, is crammed with teahouses and cafes.

Bocadillería Baraka, C. Elvira, 20 (☎958 22 97 60). Stands out among many Middle Eastern eateries for being the cheapest and the tastiest. Proud that their meat is home prepared and never frozen, Baraka serves delicious traditional pitas (€2.50-4) and addictive homemade lemonade infused with *hierba buena* (€1). Hedi, the owner and formerly in the travel business, also organizes week long, all-inclusive excursions through Morocco (☎649 11 41 71). Open daily 1pm-2am. Cash only. ❶

Taberna Salinas, C. Elvira, 13 (☎958 22 14 11). For a light but authentic dinner in this modern take on a rustic tavern, order a *tabla Salinas surtida* (plate of cheeses and *pâté;* €13.90) to complement a glass of wine. The menu also offers a wide selection of grilled meats and seafood (€11-24). Or enjoy tapas that vary with the day's *menú.* Wine €2.80. Beer €1.80. Open M-Th and F-Sa 12:30pm-2am, Su 12:30pm-1am. MC/V. ❸

Samarcanda, C. Calderería Vieja, 3 (☎958 21 00 04), walking away from Pl. Nueva down C. Elvira, up to the right where the road forks around a kiosk. Outdoor seating in a small, quiet plaza; interior is a calm Middle Eastern setting. For €43, you can order a huge *Mesa Libanesa* platter to share, complete with a bottle of Lebanese wine. English-language menu available. Entrees €8-12.50. Open M-Tu and Th-Su 1-4:30pm and 7:30pm-11:30pm. MC/V. ❸

GRAN VÍA AND ELSEWHERE

Filled with little bars and *pastelerías,* Gran Vía is great for breakfasts on a budget. Busy, student-filled cafes surround Pl. de la Trinidad and nearby Pl. Bib-Rambla. Restaurants right next to the cathedral tend to be overpriced; generally, the restaurants becomes less touristy farther down Gran Vía.

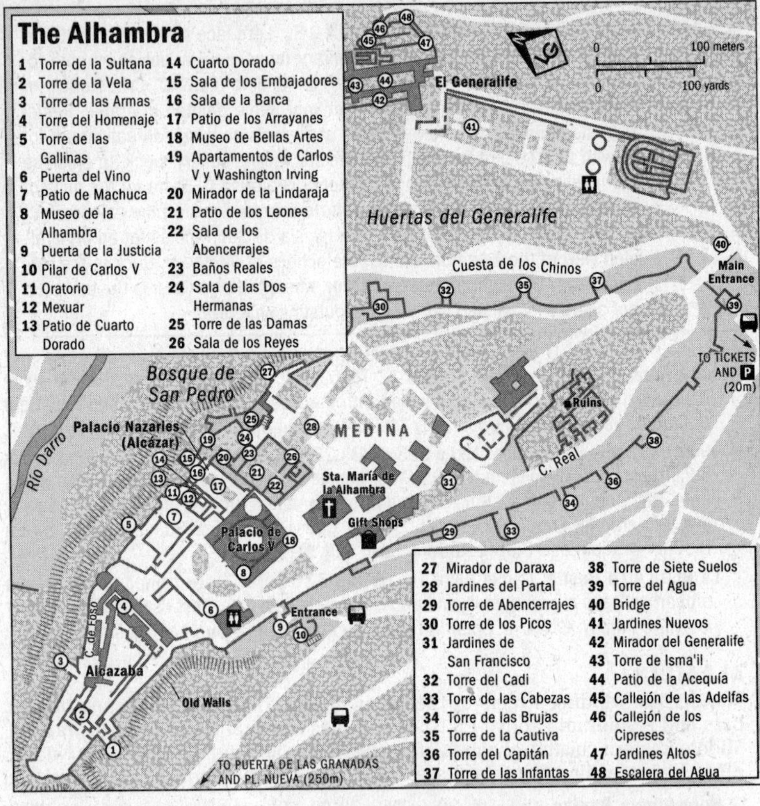

Botánico Café, C. Málaga, 3 (☎958 27 15 98), on the corner of Calle Trinidad. Serving self-described "fusion" cuisine, this trendy restaurant throws everything from Italian, Chinese, Spanish, and Mexican into the mix. Converts into a pub Sa-Su nights, but the kitchen stays open until midnight. Main dishes €8-16.95. *Menú* changes daily (served 1:30pm-4pm; €11.50); drink not included. Also serves tapas. Beer €1.75. Open Su-Th 1pm-1am, F-Sa 1pm-2am. MC/V. ❸

Los Italianos, Gran Vía, 4 (☎958 22 40 34). Don't just gape at the ridiculously cheap ice-cream prices; get in line and try another flavor. No seating. *Barquillos* (cones) €1-2; *tarrinas* (cups) from €1. Mar.-Oct. open daily 9am-2am. Cash only. ❶

SIGHTS

A *bono turístico* pass, which is good for one week and provides direct access to the Alhambra and several other sights throughout Granada, can be useful if you're going to be in the city for several days and are looking to tour the included monuments. The pass also includes nine free trips on local bus lines to destinations within the city. For reservations, call the **Caja Granada** information and booking office (☎902 10 00 95); tickets are available for direct sale at the Parque de las Ciencias. (€30. Cash only. Caja Granada also makes reservations in advance for €32.50. MC/V.)

THE ALHAMBRA

Take Cuesta de Gomérez off Pl. Nueva and be prepared to pant (20min.; no unauthorized cars 9am-9pm), or take the quick Alhambra minibus from Pl. Nueva (every 5min., €1.10). ☎902 44 12 21; www.alhambra-patronato.es; reservations for entrance ☎902 22 44 60; www.alhambra-tickets.es. Open daily Apr.-Sept. 8:30am-8pm; Oct.-Mar. 8:30am-6pm. Also open June-Sept. Tu-Sa 10-11:30pm; Oct.-May F-Sa 8-9:30pm. Audio tours are worth the expense and are available in English, French, German, Italian, and Spanish (€5). €12, under 12 and the handicapped free. €13 if purchased online. EU students with ID and EU seniors €9. Gardens only, €6. Limited to 7700 visitors per day, so get there early or reserve in advance. You must enter the Palace of the Nasrids (Alcázar) during the half-hour time slot specified on your ticket, but you can stay as long as desired. It is possible to reserve tickets in advance at banks for a €1 charge; recommended July-Aug. and Semana Santa. BBVA branches will also book tickets. Hotels can book tickets, but often take a larger commission.

From the streets of Granada, the Alhambra, meaning "the red one" in Arabic, appears blocky and purely practical—a military base planted in the foothills of the Sierra Nevada. This deceptive appearance conceals a universe of aesthetic and symbolic grandeur born of profound spirituality, artistic skill, and precision. The age-old saying holds true: *"Si mueres sin ver la Alhambra, no has vivido"* ("If you die without seeing the Alhambra, you have not lived").

ALCAZABA. The Christians drove the first Nasrid King Alhamar from the Albaicín to this more strategic hill, where he built the series of rust-colored brick towers that form the Alcazaba, or fortress. A dark, spiraling staircase leads to the **Torre de la Vela** (watchtower), where visitors can see all of Granada and the surrounding mountains. The tower's bells were rung to warn of impending danger and to coordinate the Moorish irrigation system. During the annual New Year commemoration of the Christian conquest of Granada, legend holds that local girls who scramble up the tower and ring the bell by hand before January 1st will receive a wedding proposal within a year. Compared to the rest of the Alhambra, the Alcazaba is the most utilitarian and bare-boned structure. Exit through the **Puerta del Vino,** the original entrance to the *medina* (city), where inhabitants of the Alhambra once bought tax-free wine (alas, no more).

ALCÁZAR. Follow signs to the Palacio Nazaríes to see the Alcázar, a royal palace finished by Moorish ruler Mohammed V (1354-1391) after his father, Yusuf I (1333-1354), was murdered by a political enemy in the palace's isolated basement. Throughout the palace, astonishingly intricate carvings and engravings mark every room. In the **Mexuar,** the first pillared council chamber after the entrance, the glazed tile arrangements reiterate the Nasrid dynasty mantra, "There is no victor but Allah," variations of which you'll see repeated throughout the entire palace. Attached to the Mexuar is a small prayer hall with an intricately decorated *mihrab*, marking the direction of prayer to Mecca. The Mexuar adjoins the **Patio del Cuarto Dorado** (Patio of the Gilded Room). The magnificently carved walls are topped by the shielded windows of the harem, so that the women could see out but no one could see in. The *hammams* (Arab baths) are behind an iron-grilled door but have been permanently closed for preservation. Off the far side of the patio, leafy horseshoe archways lead to the Cuarto Dorado, decorated by Mohammed V. Its carved wooden ceiling, inlaid with ivory and mother-of-pearl, displays colorful, geometric ceramic figures.

Next is the **Patio de los Arrayanes** (Courtyard of Myrtles), an expanse of water filled with goldfish. From there, glimpse the 14th-century **Fachada de Serallo,** the palace's elaborate facade. Flanking the courtyard is the **Sala de la Barca** (Hall of the Ship) named not for its inverted boat-hull ceiling, but for the Arabic word *"baraka,"* or blessing. The walls are covered with the 99 names of Allah.

Granada was formally surrendered to the Reyes Católicos in the elaborate **Sala de los Embajadores** (Hall of Ambassadors), adjoining the Sala de la Barca to the north. It was also here that Fernando and Columbus discussed his new route to India. The *mozárabe* dome, carved of more than 8000 pieces of wood and inlaid with cedar, forms its own system of constellations, and a section of the original floor remains in the center. From the **Patio de los Arrayanes,** the Sala de los Mozárabes leads to the **Patio de los Leones** (Courtyard of the Lions), the grandest display of Nasrid art in the palace. An arcade of marble columns borders the courtyard, which centers on a fountain supported by 12 marble lions (under restoration). Some believe that this fountain originally belonged to one of the sultan's Jewish advisors, but was later redecorated with Muslim motifs.

The adjoining **Sala de los Abencerrajes** tells one of the bloodiest chapters in the palace's history. Here, Boabdil, the last Arab king to rule from the Alhambra, slit the throats of 16 sons of the Abencerrajes family after one of them allegedly had amorous encounters with his concubine, Zorahayda. The rust-colored stains in the basin are said to mark the indelible traces of the butchery. Holy Roman Emperor Charles V was unfazed, however, dining here throughout the construction of his palace. Light filters in through the domed ceiling, which features an eight-pointed star representing terrestrial and celestial harmony.

Through archways at the far end of the Patio de los Leones lies the **Sala de los Reyes** (Hall of Kings). The only human figures in the entire palace—the 21 sultans who ruled from the Alhambra, important assemblies, and hunting parties—are depicted on detailed sheepskin paintings fixed to the walls with bamboo pins, but are currently covered for restoration. On the final side of the courtyard, the resplendent **Sala de las Dos Hermanas** (Chamber of the Two Sisters) is named for the matching slabs of marble that comprise most of the floor. It has a *muqarnas* (honeycombed) dome composed of thousands of tiny cells. This stalactite-like structure, typical of Islamic architecture, represents an ascension and the doors of heaven opening. From here, the secluded **Mirador de Daraxa** overlooks the **Jardines de Daraxa** (Gardens of the Sultana).

Passing the room where American author **Washington Irving** resided in 1829 and wrote the famous *Tales of the Alhambra* (1832), a courtyard leads to the Baños Reales, a less ornate 14th-century addition, toward the royal gardens and the exit. Do not leave the Nasrid Palace unless you are satisfied with your visit, because like Boabdil, you will not be allowed to return.

TOWERS AND GARDENS. Just outside the eastern wall of the Alcázar, lily-studded pools stand beside rose-laden terraces in the **Jardines del Partal**. The **Torre de las Damas** (Ladies' Tower) soars above it all. A series of six additional towers fills out the area between the Alcazaba and El Generalife.

EL GENERALIFE. Over a bridge, across the Callejón de los Cipreses and the shady Callejón de las Adelfas are the lively blossoms, towering cypresses, and streaming waterways of **El Generalife,** the sultan's vacation retreat. In 1313 Arab engineers changed the Darro's flow by 18km and employed dams and channels to prepare the soil for Aben Walid Ismail's design of El Generalife. Over the centuries, the estate passed through private hands until it was finally nationalized in 1931. The two buildings of El Generalife, the Palacio and the Sala Regia, connect across the **Patio de la Acequia** (Courtyard of the Irrigation Channel), embellished with a narrow pool fed by fountains that form an aquatic archway. Honeysuckle vines scale the back wall, and shady benches invite long rests. A dead cypress tree stands at the place where the sultana Zorahayda supposedly had amorous encounters with a nobleman from the Abencerrajes tribe.

PALACIO DE CARLOS V. Although Emperor Charles V's *palazzo* is incongruous with the surrounding Alhambra, scholars concede that it is one of the most beautiful Renaissance buildings in Spain. Designed by Michelangelo's disciple Pedro Machuca, the palace has a circular inner courtyard with two stories of Doric colonnades. Inside, the Museo de la Alhambra contains the only remaining original furnishings from the Alhambra, including old doors and the well-preserved *azulejo* tiles. *(☎958 22 75 27. Open Tu-Sa 9am-2:30pm. Free with admission to the Alhambra; free guided visits Tu-Sa 11am-1pm. €1.50. E.U. citizens free.)* Upstairs, the **Museo de Bellas Artes** has recently been renovated to better display its religious sculptures and paintings of the Granada School dating from the 16th century. *(☎958 22 48 43. Open Mar-Oct. Tu 2:30-8pm, W-Sa 9am-8pm, Su 9am-2:30pm.;Nov.-Feb. Tu 2:30-6pm, W-Sa 9am-6pm, Su 9am-2:30pm; €1.50. E.U. citizens free.)*

ALBAICÍN

Although generally safe, the Albaicín is disorienting, so use caution at night. Bus #32 runs from beside the cathedral to C. Pagés at the top of the Albaicín. Bus #31 goes from Gran Vía and Pl. Nueva through the neighborhood.

A labyrinth of steep, narrow alleys, the Albaicín was the only Moorish neighborhood to escape the torches of the Reconquista. After the fall of the Alhambra, a small Muslim population remained here until they were expelled in the 17th century. Today, the Albaicín attests to the persistence of Islamic influence in Andalucía—the mosque near Pl. San Nicolás and resurgence of North African cuisine, outdoor bazaars blasting Arabic music, and teahouses will leave you wondering if you're in Morocco. The best way to explore this maze is to proceed along **Carrera del Darro** off Pl. Santa Ana, climb the **Cuesta del Chapiz** on the left, then wander through the Moorish ramparts, cisterns, and gates. On Pl. Santa Ana, the 16th-century **Real Cancillería,** with its beautiful arcaded patio and stalactite ceiling, was the Christians' town hall. Farther uphill are the 11th-century Arab baths. *(Carrera del Darro, 31. ☎958 22 97 38. Call ☎958 22 56 03 to confirm hours. Free.)* The **Museo Arqueológico** showcases funerary urns, classical sculpture, Carthaginian vases, Muslim lamps, and ceramics. *(Carrera del Darro, 43. ☎958 22 56 03. Open Tu 2:30-8:30pm, W-Sa 9:30am-8:30pm, Su 9:30am-2:30pm. €1.50, EU citizens free.)* The **mirador** adjacent to **Iglesia de San Nicolás** affords the city's best view of the Alhambra. From C. de Elvira, go up C. Caldereria Nueva to C. San Gregorio and continue uphill past Pl. Algibe de Trillo, where it becomes Cta. Algibe de Trillo. At Pl. Camino, make a left onto Cta. Tomasa and another left onto Atarazana Cta. Cabras. The *mirador* is on the right.

SACROMONTE

If you're not up for the 20min. climb from Pl. Nueva, take bus #34 (€1.10). Ask at the tourist office for schedules and check with the driver that Sacromonte is the destination. Avoid isolated streets and corners in the neighborhood, as they are somewhat unsafe at night.

Above the Albaicín stands Sacromonte, home to a gypsy community ever since they took shelter here during the Inquisition. Cave dwellings plaster the hillside, still inhabited but updated with TVs and satellite dishes. The **Museo Cuevas del Sacromonte,** also called the Centro de Interpretación del Sacromonte, at the top of the hill, has an informative display of model caves, from a house and kitchen to a stable and caves for iron-working, basket-weaving, and pottery-making. The museum also enjoys an impressive view over the Sacromonte back towards the Alhambra and much of Granada. *(☎958 21 51 20; www.sacromontegranada.com. Open Apr.-Oct. Tu-F 10am-2pm and 5-9pm; Nov.-Mar. Tu-F 10am-2pm and 4-7pm. Museum €5.)* In summer, some caves host impromptu flamenco. Ask at the tourist office or the museum.

THE CATHEDRAL QUARTER

CAPILLA REAL. Downhill from the Alhambra, off Gran Vía de Colón on C. Oficios, stands Fernando and Isabel's private chapel. The Catholic monarchs funneled almost a quarter of their royal income into building a proper burial place. Intricate Gothic masonry and **La Reja,** the gilded grille of Maestro Bartolomé, grace the couple's resting place. Behind La Reja lie the lifelike marble figures of the storied royals themselves. Fernando and Isabel are on the right when facing the altar; beside them sleep their daughter, Juana la Loca, and her husband, Felipe el Hermoso. In the adjacent **Sacristía,** Isabel's private art collection favors Flemish and German artists of the 15th century. The glittering royal jewels—including the queen's golden crown and scepter and the king's sword—shine in the middle. *(☎958 22 92 39. Capilla Real and Sacristía both open Apr.-Sept M-Sa 10:30am-12:45pm and 4-7pm, Su 11am-12:45pm and 4-7pm; Oct.-May M-Sa 10:30am-12:45pm and 3:30-6:15pm, Su 11am-12:45pm and 3:30-6:15pm. Both sights €3.50.)*

CATEDRAL. Behind the Capilla Real and the Sacristía is Granada's cathedral. Construction began after the Reconquista, upon the smoldering embers of Granada's largest mosque, and was not completed until 1704. The first Renaissance cathedral in Spain, its massive Corinthian pillars support a 45m nave. While the eclectic side chapels and fanning pipes of its gilded organ are beautiful, this cathedral may not impress those who have seen a number of Spanish cathedrals. *(☎958 22 29 59. Open Apr.-Sept. M-Sa 10:45am-1:30pm and 4-8pm, Su 4-8pm; Oct.-Mar. M-Sa 10:30am-1:30pm and 4-7pm, Su 11am-1:30pm and 4-7pm. €3.50.)*

NIGHTLIFE

Granada's "free tapas with a drink" tradition lures crowds to its many pubs and bars. Some great tapas bars are found on the side streets off Pl. Nueva. The most boisterous crowds hang out on C. Pedro Antonio de Alarcón, between Pl. Albert Einstein and Ancha de Gracia, while hip new bars and clubs line C. de Elvira from C. Cárcel to C. Cedrán. Gay bars can be found by Carrera del Darro. Check the *Pocketguía* (€1), sold at newsstands and available for free at the Pineda Tourist Office; it lists clubs, pubs, and cafes. Clubs in Granada usually aren't lively until around 3am.

- **Camborio,** Camino del Sacromonte, 48 (☎958 22 12 15), a quick taxi ride or 20min. walk uphill from Pl. Nueva; bus #34 stops at midnight. DJ-spun pop music echoes through dance floors to the rooftop patio above. Striking view of the Alhambra. Beer €4. Mixed drinks €5. Cover €6, includes 1 drink. Open Tu-Sa midnight-7am. Cash only.
- **Salsero Mayor,** C. la Paz, 20 (☎958 52 27 41). An ageless group of locals and tourists alike flocks here for crowded nights of salsa, bachata, and merengue. Beer €2-3. Mixed drinks €5. Open M-Th and Su 10pm-3am, F-Sa 1pm-4am. Cash only.
- **Granada 10,** C. Cárcel Baja 3 (☎958 22 40 01). Movie theater by evening (shows Sept.-June at 8, 10pm), raging dance club by night. Flashy and opulent. No sneakers or sportswear. Open M-Th and Su 12:30-4am, F-Sa 12:30-6am. Cover €10. MC/V.

ENTERTAINMENT AND FESTIVALS

The daily paper, *Ideal*, lists entertainment venues in the back under *"Cine y Espectáculos;"* the Friday supplement highlights bars and special events.

FLAMENCO AND JAZZ. The most "authentic" flamenco performances change monthly; shows are advertised on posters around town. The tourist office also provides a list of nightly *tablaos* (flamenco shows), often more expensive and heavily touristed. A smoky, intimate setting awaits at **Eshavira,** C. Postigo de la

Cuna, in a secluded alley off C. Azacayas, between C. de Elvira and Gran Vía. This joint is the place to go for flamenco, jazz, or a fusion of the two. Photos of Nat King Cole and other jazz greats plaster the walls. Those with musical talent can pick up a guitar or sit right down at the piano to stage their own impromptu concert. *(☎958 29 41 25. Min. consumption €8. Su night flamenco. M-Th and Su 9 or 9:30pm-3:30am, F-Sa 9 or 9:30 pm-4am; call for schedule.)*

FESTIVALS. Parties sweep Granada in the summer. The **Corpus Cristi** celebrations and bullfights in May/June are world-famous. That same month, avant-garde theater groups from around the world make a pilgrimage to Granada for the **International Theater Festival** (☎958 22 93 44). The **Festival Internacional de Música y Danza** (mid-June to early July) sponsors performances of classical music, ballet, and flamenco in the Palacio de Carlos V and other venues. *(☎958 22 18 44; www.granadafestival.org. Prices vary. Senior and youth discounts available.)*

DAYTRIP FROM GRANADA

NERJA

ALSA buses leave from Granada (7 per day 7am-8pm, €8.84; return 6 per day 6:30am-7:15pm). All buses stop and depart on Av. de la Pescia, just before a roundabout and across the street from the ticket kiosk (☎952 52 15 04).

A 2hr. bus journey from Granada, Nerja is the most popular beach destination on the Costa Tropical. While the tourist presence is undeniable, the city more than makes up for it in sunny plazas, winding streets, palm trees, and dramatic Mediterranean vistas. Much of the town stands 15 to 20m above the water, allowing for brilliant ocean views from seaside cafes, while beaches are framed by rugged cliffs and outcroppings plunging down to clear, sparkling water. Three kilometers east of Nerja are the **Cuevas de Nerja,** Spain's third most popular tourist attraction after the Prado and the Alhambra. Featuring the world's widest column formed by a stalactite meeting a stalagmite, guests will also find the skeleton of an ancient Nerjan in caverns that go back at least 5 kilometers. Concerts are occasionally held in one of the cave's massive caverns. (Buses depart for the caves from the Av. de la Pescia stop. 12+ per day 8:30am-8pm, return 8:45am-7:30pm, €0.90 each way. Caves open daily Sept.-June 10am-2pm and 4pm-6:30pm; July-Aug. 10am-7:30pm. €7, ages 6-12 €3.50.)

Accommodations and eateries are found in abundance throughout town. If you're staying the night, **Nerjasol ❷**, Pintada, 54, is a great deal, with 21 elegant and comfortable rooms, all with A/C, TV, and bath, and a well-furnished terrace with mountain and ocean views. (☎952 52 21 21; www.hostalnerjasol.com. Singles €20-25; doubles €33-50.) To get to the **tourist office,** Puerta del Mar, 2, walk towards the circle, make a right into the triangular park and cross it to the far leg, C. Pintada, which runs down to the **Balcón de Europa,** a dramatic plaza looking over the Mediterranean. The tourist office is on the left just before the road meets the plaza. (☎95 252 15 31. Open daily in summer. English spoken.)

VALENCIA AND THE COSTA BLANCA

The whimsical southeast corner of Spain proudly boasts a little bit of everything. From the sun-drenched, silky beaches of the Costa Blanca to the cosmopolitan buzz of Valencia, this area is sure to enchant and impress. Its history is rife with power struggles among a cast of usual suspects: Phoenicians, Carthaginians, Greeks, Romans, and Moors, who all contributed to the region's varied architectural influences. The region first fell under Castilian control when El Cid expelled the Moors in 1094; he ruled in the name of Alfonso VI until his death in 1099. Without El Cid's powerful influence, Valencia and Murcia again fell to the Moors, remaining an Arab stronghold until 1238. After the expulsion of the Moors, Valencia established itself as a frontrunner in cultural and technological innovation; in 1492, the *valencianos* were the first bankers to lend funds to Queen Isabel for her patronage of Christopher Columbus. The region was besieged again in the 1930s, this time by Franco's troops. *Valencianos* resisted with strength—it was the last region incorporated into Franco's Spain and regained autonomy in 1977.

HIGHLIGHTS OF VALENCIA AND MURCIA

LIGHT 15 ft. puppets on fire in **Valencia** during the festival of **Las Fallas** (p. 216).

BURN the midnight oil in sleepless **Alicante** (p. 217).

VALENCIA

The region of Valencia is home to layers of history, each of which has left a visible cultural and aesthetic imprint on the region's development. Blue-roofed church domes battle new resort developments for skyline prominence, while pristine beaches, quaint coastal towns, and maze-like inland gardens offer a wealth of refuge for weary travelers. Crowded nightlife challenges even the most nocturnal adventurers on the hectic coastline, but it is worth venturing inland for a bit, if only for the unbeatable taste of local oranges. *Paella* also reaches culinary perfection here in its birthplace, especially the renowned *paella con mariscos* (seafood *paella*) and the hearty *paella valenciana* (chicken and rabbit). The commonly used regional dialect, *valencià*, is the legacy of Moorish invaders and Catalan crusaders who clashed in the northwest hundreds of years ago, and a recent mandate that all students enroll in one course of *valencià* reflects a resurgence of regional pride.

VALENCIA ☎963

Valencia (pop. 805,000) inherited the best genes of its sister cities: the clamoring energy of Madrid, the youthful and quirky sophistication of Barcelona, and the friendly warmth of Sevilla. Ancient traditions remain strong despite increasing modernity and commercialism. An evening glance around the central Pl. del Ajuntament reveals a merry mix of classic Spanish architecture, opulent 19th-century palaces, umbrella-crammed cafe patios, Art Deco movie theaters, and modern towers. After a deadly flood in 1957 drowned the streets in almost two meters of water, Valencia drained and diverted the Río Turia southward; now, the dry riverbed that surrounds the city is a lush, winding park that offers views of the city's standing fortifications. Beyond these older facades, toward the sea, the riverbed meets the Ciudad de las Artes y las Ciencias, a grandiose scientific complex and architectural marvel. The sudden transition from ancient to avant-garde reflects the city's eagerness to modernize competitively. The city's beaches and palm tree-studded plazas have fewer tourists than Spain's other large cities, so plan on using your Spanish here.

TRANSPORTATION

INTERCITY TRANSPORTATION

Flights: Aena, Aeropuerto de Manises/Airport of Valencia (☎961 59 85 00; www.aena.es), 8km from the city. **Aero-Bus** buses run between the airport and train station (35min. daily every 20min., €2.50). Stops: Airport, Av. del Cid, Bailén, Angel Guimerá. Subway line #3 or 5 goes straight to C. Xàtiva, on the outskirts of Valencia by the *Ajuntament* (€1.80). Taxis from airport to city about €15. **Iberia,** C. La Paz, 14 (☎963 52 05 00; www.iberia.com). Open M-F 9am-2pm and 4-7:30pm.

Trains: Estación del Norte, C. Xàtiva, 24 (☎963 52 02 02; www.renfe.es). Ticket windows open daily 7am-9pm. 1- to 6-zone distances range €1.15-3.95. **RENFE** (☎902 24 02 02) to: **Alicante** (2-3hr., 12 per day 7:04am-11pm, €23.60-31.30; Su differs by week); **Barcelona** (3hr., every 1-2hr. 5:50am-8:45pm, €29-37); **Madrid** (3hr., 12 per day 6:45am-9:15pm, €19.75-39; Su differs by week); **Sevilla** (8hr., 11:20am, €48.90). Cercanías trains run at least 2 per hr. to **Gandía** (1hr., €3.65), **Sagunt** (23min., €2.40), and **Xàtiva** (45min., €2.85). Allot time to go through security.

Buses: Estación Terminal d'Autobuses, Av. Menéndez Pidal, 11 (☎963 46 62 66), across the riverbed, a 20min. walk from the city center. Municipal bus #8 runs between Pl. del Ajuntament and the bus station (€1.10). **ALSA** (☎902 42 22 42) to: **Alicante** (4hr., 1-3 per hr. 4:45am-9:45pm, €17.70-18.20) via the **Costa Blanca; Barcelona** (4hr., 20 per day, 1-2 every 2hr., €25.14-33); **Granada** (8hr., 8 per day 2:45am-12:30am, €41.55-47.91); **Málaga** (11hr., 8 per day 2:45am-12:30am, €51.07-59.05); **Sevilla** (11hr., 10 per day 8am-4:45am, €49.86-74.69). **Auto Res** (☎963 49 22 30) goes to **Madrid** (4hr., 16-18 per day 1am-11pm, €23.64-25.15).

Ferries: Trasmediterránea, Muelle de Poniente (☎902 45 46 45; www.trasmediterranea.es). Take bus #4 from Pl. del Ajuntament or #1 or 2 from the bus station. To: **Mallorca** (5hr., 7:45pm, in summer €85) and **Ibiza** (3hr., 12:15pm, in summer €85). 1 13hr. ferry to **Menorca** per week. (Sa 11:30pm; in summer overnight €56.50, with cot €111.50.) Reserve through a travel agency or risk inconvenience by buying tickets at the port on the day of departure.

LOCAL TRANSPORTATION

EMT Office, Pl. Correo Viejo, 5 (☎963 15 85 15, handicapped hotline 963 15 85 25; www.emtvalencia.es). Open M-F 9am-2pm and 4:30-7:30pm. Bus schedules depend on route and day. Tourist routes 5, 5B, 35, 95. Bus #8 (every 9-11min. 6am-10:30pm) runs to the bus station. Buses #20, 21,and 22 (every 10-20min. 9am-8:40pm) go to Las Arenas and Malvarrosa along Pg. Marítim. Buy tickets (€1.50) on board; combination bus and metro monthly ticket (€35.60, student €26.70), or 1-day pass (€3.10) available at newsstands. No service 10:30-11:30pm. **Late-night buses** N1, N2, N3, N4, N5, N6, and N7 go through Pl. del Ajuntament (every 45min. M-W and Su 11pm-1am, Th-Sa 11pm-3am). **Metro,** P. de Xirivelleta (☎963 97 40 40; www.metrovalencia.com) service loops around the *casco antiguo* (old quarter) and into the outskirts. The most central stop is on C. Xàtiva across the street from the train station or C. Colón by El Corte Inglés. Buy tickets from machines in any station (€1.20-1.60 depending on distance, 10-ride pass €5.60-8).

Taxis: Onda Taxi (☎963 47 52 52), **Radio Taxi** (☎963 70 33 33), **Tele Taxi** (☎963 57 13 13), and **Buscataxi** (☎902 74 77 47).

Car Rental: C. Xàtiva, 24 (at the Estació del Nord train station). **Europcar** (☎963 51 90 55; www.europcar.es). Open M-Sa 8am-10pm, Su 8am-9pm. **Avis** (train station ☎963 52 42 64, airport 961 52 18 72; www.avis.es). **Hertz** (☎963 52 42 64; www.hertz.com) Car prices vary with season, type, and length of rental, but a medium-size car for 1 week costs around €200.

Bike Rental: Orange Bikes, C. Santa Teresa, 8 (☎963 91 75 51; www.orangebikes.net). From the main entrance of the Mercado Central, walk down Av. María Cristina away from Pl. *Ajuntamiento* and turn down the 2nd street, continuing on to the end. From Pl. de la Virgen,

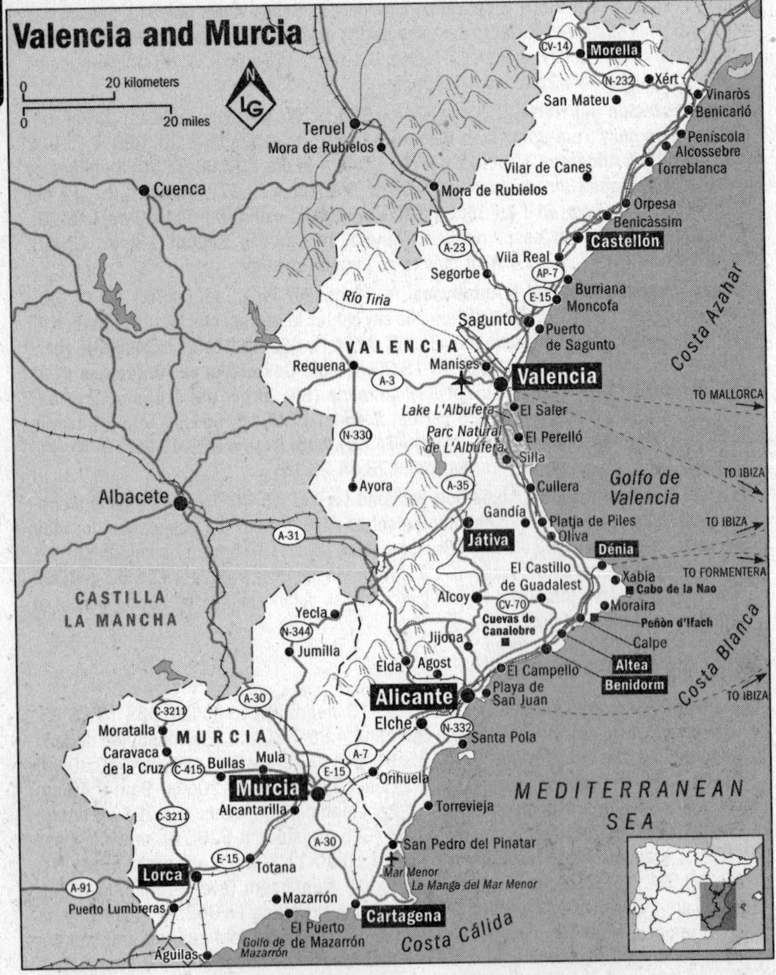

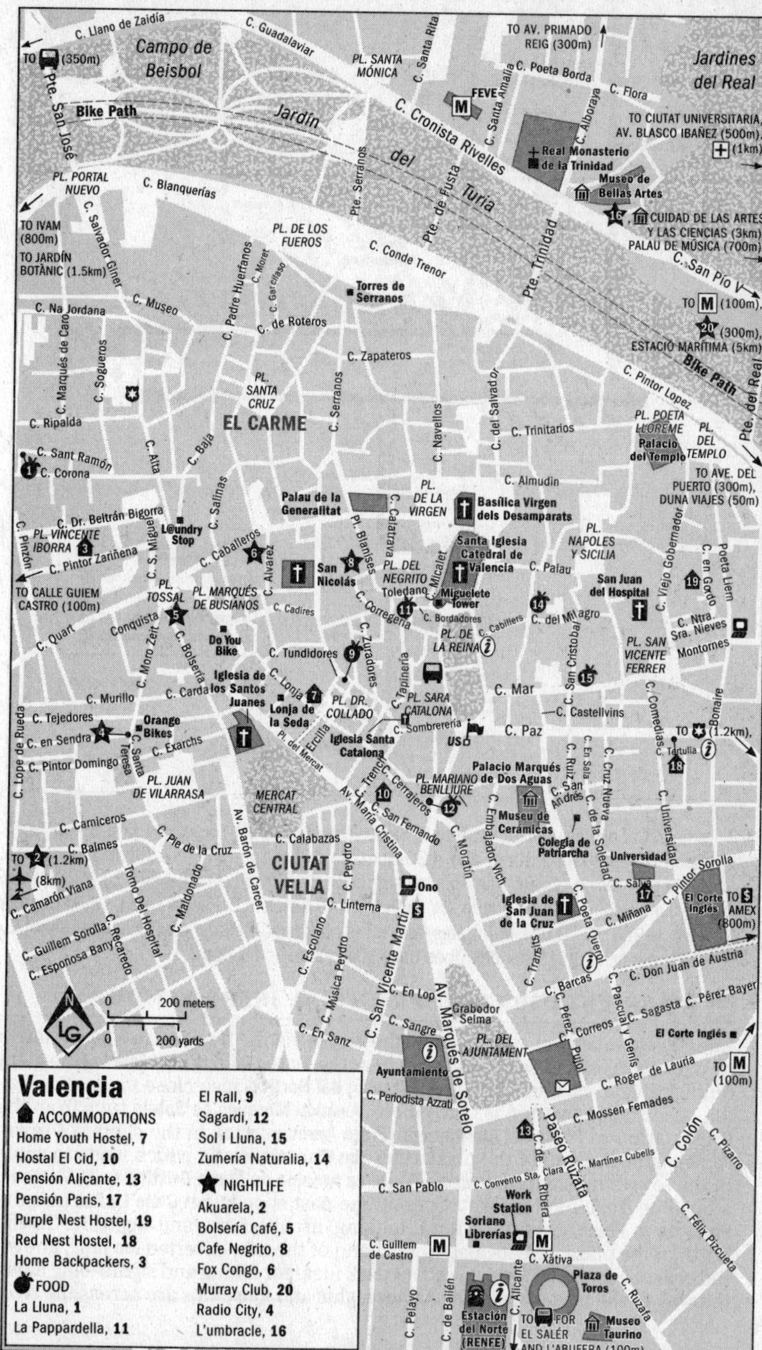

C. Llano de Zaidía
C. Guadalaviar
TO (350m)
Campo de Beisbol
Pte. San José
Bike Path
Jardín del Turia
PL. SANTA MÓNICA
C. Santa Rita
TO AV. PRIMADO REIG (300m)
C. Poeta Borda
C. Flora
Jardines del Real
FEVE
C. Santa Amalia
C. Alboraya
C. Cronista Rivelles
TO CIUTAT UNIVERSITARIA, AV. BLASCO IBAÑEZ (500m), (1km)
Real Monasterio de la Trinidad
Museo de Bellas Artes
CUIDAD DE LAS ARTES Y LAS CIENCIAS (3km), PALAU DE MÚSICA (700m)
C. San Pío V
PL. PORTAL NUEVO
C. Blanquerías
Pte. Serranos
Pte. de Fusta
Pte. Trinidad
TO IVAM (800m)
TO JARDÍN BOTÀNIC (1.5km)
C. Salvador Giner
PL. DE LOS FUEROS
C. Conde Trenor
C. Padre Huérfanos
C. Moret
C. Garcilaso
Torres de Serranos
TO (100m), (300m), ESTACIÓ MARÍTIMA (5km)
C. Na Jordana
C. Museo
C. de Roteros
C. Marqués de Caro
C. Sogueros
C. Zapateros
PL. SANTA CRUZ
C. Serranos
C. del Salvador
C. Pintor Lopez
Pte. del Real
C. Ripalda
EL CARME
C. Navellos
C. Trinitarios
PL. POETA LLOREME
Palacio del Templo
PL. DEL TEMPLO
C. Sant Ramón
C. Corona
C. Alta
C. Baja
C. Salinas
C. Almudín
TO AVE. DEL PUERTO (300m), DUNA VIAJES (50m)
Palau de la Generalitat
C. Calatrava
PL. DE LA VIRGEN
Basílica Virgen dels Desamparats
C. Dr. Beltrán Bigorra
L@undry Stop
C. Pinzón
PL. VINCENTE IBORRA
C. Pintor Zariñena
C. S. Miguel
C. Caballeros
Pl. Blanises
Santa Iglesia Catedral de Valencia
PL. NAPOLES Y SICILIA
C. Viejo Gobernador
C. en Gordo
Poeta Liem
TO CALLE GUIEM CASTRO (100m)
PL. TOSSAL
PL. MARQUÉS DE BUSIANOS
C. Alvarez
San Nicolás
PL. DEL NEGRITO
Toledano
C. Micalet
Miguelete Tower
C. Palau
San Juan del Hospital
C. Quart
Conquista
C. Cadires
C. Corregería
C. Bordadores
C. Cabillers
C. del Milagro
C. Ntra. Sra. Nieves
Montornes
C. Moro Zeit
C. Bolsería
Do You Bike
C. Tundidores
C. Zurradores
PL. DE LA REINA
C. San Cristobal
PL. SAN VICENTE FERRER
C. Murillo
C. Carda
Iglesia de los Santos Juanes
C. Lonja
Lonja de la Seda
PL. DR. COLLADO
C. Tapinería
PL. SARA CATALONA
C. Mar
C. Castellvins
C. Comedias
C. Bonaire
C. Tejedores
Orange Bikes
C. en Sendra
C. Santa Teresa
C. Exarchs
Pl. del Mercat
Ercilla
Iglesia Santa Cataloa
C. Sombrereria
US
C. Paz
TO (1.2km)
C. Tertulia
C. Lope de Rueda
C. Pintor Domingo
PL. JUAN DE VILARRASA
MERCAT CENTRAL
Av. María Cristina
C. Trench
C. Cerrajeros
PL. MARIANO BENLLIURE
Palacio Marqués de Dos Aguas
C. En Sala
C. Ruiz
C. Cruz Nueva
C. San Andrés
C. de la Soledad
C. Carniceros
C. San Fernando
C. Moratín
C. Embajador Vich
Museu de Ceràmicas
Colegia de Patriarcha
C. Universidad
C. Balmes
C. Pie de la Cruz
Av. Barón de Carcer
C. Calabazas
CIUTAT VELLA
C. Peydro
Universidad
C. Pintor Sorolla
TO (1.2km)
(8km)
C. Camarón Viana
Torno Del Hospital
C. Maldonado
Ono
C. Salva
El Corte Inglés
TO AMEX (800m)
C. Linterna
Iglesia de San Juan de la Cruz
C. Poeta Querol
C. Miñana
C. Guillem Sorolla
C. Recaredo
C. Esponosa Bany
C. Escolano
C. Música Peydro
C. San Vicente Martir
Av. Marques de Sotelo
C. Transits
C. Barcas
C. Don Juan de Austria
C. En Lop
C. Pérez Pujol
C. Pascual y Genis
C. Sagasta
C. Pérez Bayer
0 200 meters
0 200 yards
C. Sangre
Grabodor Selma
C. Correos
El Corte Inglés
C. En Sanz
PL. DEL AJUNTAMENT
Ayuntamiento
C. Roger de Lauria
TO (100m)
C. Periodista Azzati
C. Mossen Femades
Paseo Ruzafa
C. Colón
C. Pizarro
C. Convento Sta. Clara
C. Martínez Cubells
C. de Ribera
C. San Pablo
Work Station
Soriano Librerías
C. Félix Pizcueta
C. Guillem de Castro
C. Xàtiva
Plaza de Toros
C. Ruzafa
C. Pelayo
C. de Balién
C. Alicante
Estación del Norte (RENFE)
TO FOR EL SALÉR AND L'ABUFERA (100m)
Museo Taurino
Valencia
ACCOMMODATIONS
Home Youth Hostel, 7
Hostal El Cid, 10
Pensión Alicante, 13
Pensión Paris, 17
Purple Nest Hostel, 19
Red Nest Hostel, 18
Home Backpackers, 3
FOOD
La Lluna, 1
La Pappardella, 11
El Rall, 9
Sagardi, 12
Sol i Lluna, 15
Zumería Naturalia, 14
NIGHTLIFE
Akuarela, 2
Bolsería Café, 5
Cafe Negrito, 8
Fox Congo, 6
Murray Club, 20
Radio City, 4
L'umbracle, 16

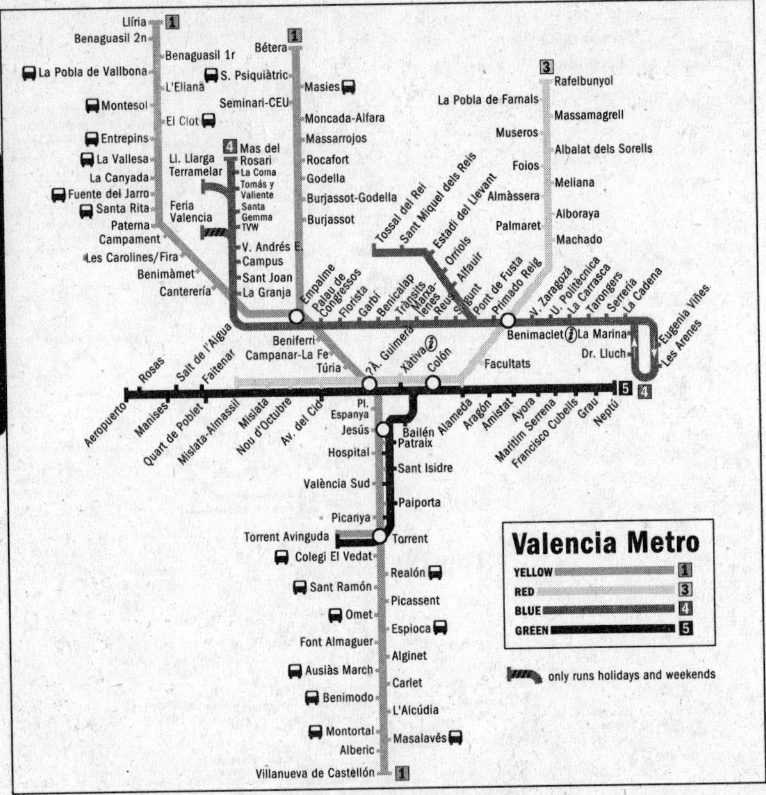

take C. Caballeros until it turns into C. Santa Teresa. Bikes €9-15 per day, €45-55 per week. Open M-F 9:30am-2:30pm and 4:30-8pm, Sa 10am-2pm and 7-7:30pm. **Douyoubike,** Corner C. Musico Magenti and Puebla Larga (☎963 15 55 51, Movil ☎675 73 02 18; www.doyoubike.com). Also Av. Puerto, 21 (☎963 37 40 24), and C. Puebla Larga, 13, at Guardia Civil (☎963 38 70 08). M-Th rates from €2 per hour and €10 per day; F-Su rates shoot up to €4 per hr. and €15 per day. Open daily 10am-2pm and 5-8pm.

ORIENTATION AND PRACTICAL INFORMATION

The most convenient way to enter the city is via the new metro line to Xàtiva or C. Colón. Xàtiva is a central stop near the **Museo Taurino de Valencia** (the giant bullfighting arena and museum). **Estación del Norte** is also close to the city center, so entrance by train is convenient. **Avenida Marqués de Sotelo** runs from the train station to **Plaça del Ajuntament (Plaza Ayuntamiento),** in the center of town. At the opposite end of the plaza runs **San Vincente Martir,** which leads to some of the town's most vibrant areas. Take **La Avenida de María Cristina** to **El Mercado,** a bustling fresh-food market, or continue past shop-laden **Calle La Paz** into the **Plaza de la Reina,** central to food, lodging, architecture, and nightlife. To the north of the plaza, streets lead to the bend of the now-diverted **Río Turia,** known today as the **Jardín del Turia,** a verdant park ideal for biking and sightseeing along the way to the port or beaches. Other sights and museums are across the river or on the outskirts of the city. The *casco antiguo* (old quarter) is best explored on foot, but the sidestreets can get confusing—keep a map handy.

Tourist Office: Regional office, C. de la Paz, 48 (☎963 98 64 22; www.comunitatvalenciana.com). Open M-F 9am-8pm, Sa 10am-8pm, Su 10am-2pm. Branches at **Estación del Nord,** C. Xàtiva, 24 (☎963 52 85 73; open M-Sa 9am-7pm, Su 10am-2pm), and Pl. de la Reina, 19 (☎963 15 39 31; www.turisvalencia.es; open M-Sa 9am-7pm, Su 10am-2pm).

Currency Exchange: Banks are easy to find. All have a min. commission of €6, and some will take a small percentage of any money exchanged. Banks are clustered around Pl. del Ajuntament and transportation hubs and are usually open 8am-2:30pm.

Luggage Storage: 24hr. storage at the **bus station** (€2.40-4.50) and **train station** (€2.40-4.50), depending on the size of your luggage. Open daily 5am-1am.

Bookstore: Librería Soriano, C. Xàtiva, 15 (☎963 51 03 78; www.libreriasoriano.com). Across the street from the train station. One of the most historic bookstores in Valencia. Small section of novels in English as well as maps and a few magazines. Open M-Sa 9:30am-9:30pm, Su 10:30am-12:30pm and 5:30-8:30pm. MC/V.

Laundromat: The L@undry Stop, C. Baja, 17 (☎963 91 35 28). This cyber laundromat offers internet while that laundry tumbles. Wash €4, dry €3, soap €0.50. Internet €0.50 for 20min. Wi-Fi available. Open daily 9:30am-10pm.

Emergency: ☎112.

Police: Po. de Alameda, 17 (☎963 60 03 50), or C. Maestre, 2 (☎963 15 56 90). Local police also reachable at ☎092.

Late-Night Pharmacy: Rotates daily, check listing in local paper *Levante* (€1) or the *farmacias de guardia* schedule posted outside any pharmacy around the Pl. de la Reina and Pl. de la Virgen (☎963 91 68 21). **Info Salud** (health info ☎900 20 22 02).

Hospital: Hospital Clínico Universitario, Av. Blasco Ibáñez, 17 (☎963 86 29 00). Take bus #81 from Pl. del Ajuntament or take the metro (line 3) at C. Xàtiva to Facultades. **Ambulance:** ☎112 or 96 152 51 59. **Red Cross Ambulances:** ☎96 367 73 75.

Internet Access: Ono, C. San Vicente Mártir, 22 (☎963 28 19 02; www.ono.com). Close to the *Ajuntament,* this 2-story complex is a high-ceilinged technological haven that was the 1st broadband internet center in Europe. Laptop stations, printing services, Skype, and more. 9am-2pm €2 per 45min., 2-10pm €2 per 30min., 10pm-1am €2 per hr. Cashier closes at 12:30am. Open M-F 9am-1am; Sa-Su and holidays 10am-1am. **Work Center,** C. Xàtiva, 19 (☎961 12 08 30; www.workcenter.es). 24hr. work station across the street from the train station offers office supplies, photocopying, and print services as well as DHL Express. €3 per hr. Open M-Th 24hr., F 7am-11pm, Sa 10am-2pm and 5-9pm, Su noon-2pm and 5-11pm. AmEx/MC/V.

Post Office: Pl. del Ajuntament, 24 (☎963 512 370; www.correos.es). This palatial building is a temple to the mail gods. **Western Union** and call center. Open M-F 8:30am-8:30pm, Sa 9:30am-2pm. **Postal Code:** Center: 46002; Renfe: 46007; Ruzafa: 46005.

ACCOMMODATIONS

Well-run youth hostels and *pensiones* for decent fares abound in Valencia, but finding a room can be a difficult task during travel-heavy summer months or the festival of Las Fallas (Mar. 12-19). The best deals are around **Plaça del Ajuntament** and **Plaça del Mercat,** both in the *casco antiguo.*

Red Nest Hostel, C. La Paz, 36 (☎963 42 71 68; www.nesthostelsvalencia.com). A classic, 16th-century Spanish building with a youthful, bright interior. Centrally located, with a busy atmosphere. Free luggage storage. Huge guest kitchen, lounge area, and terrace. Internet €1 per hr. Wash €2, dry €2. Open year-round. 12-person dorms in winter €14, in summer €18-20; 6-person dorm €16.50/20-22; 4-person dorm

€17.50/23-25; doubles €50/58, economy double €37/42; quad €84. In summer months, prices rise on F=Sa. **Purple Nest Hostel** branch with lounge and bar at P. Tetuan, 5 (☎963 53 25 61). AmEx/MC/V. ❶

Home Backpackers, at Pl. Vicente Iborra (☎963 91 37 97; www.likeathome.net). Though slightly farther from the center of the action, this branch of Home Youth Hostel has more beds per room and a more boisterous atmosphere. The bustling kitchen and roof terrace (closes at 11pm) are popular nightime hangouts. Open year-round. Beds in summer from €15 per night. MC/V. ❶

Home Youth Hostel, C. de la Lonja, 4 (☎963 91 62 29; www.likeathome.net). 20 rooms surround a lively, funky lobby. Reading room and kitchen. Hall baths co-ed, free towels. Internet €0.50 per 15min. Singles €23; doubles €40; triples in summer €63-69, in winter €45; qauds €84-92/60. 10% ISIC discount. ❷

Hostal El Cid, C. Cerrajeros, 13 (☎/fax 963 92 23 23). Off C. San Vicente Mártir near the Plaza de la Reina. In an unassuming, tiled building with 12 airy rooms. Antique artwork lines the hallways. Some rooms with balcony. English and French spoken. Book well in advance. Open year-round. Doubles with sink, shower, and TV €40-45. MC/V. ❹

Pensión Alicante, C. de Ribera, 8 (☎963 51 22 96). On a lively, cafe-lined street off the Pl. del Ajuntament in the direction of the train station. Rooms are clean; they vary in size, decoration, and amenities. Rooms facing the street are considerably brighter, with balcony. Common area and library. Open year-round. Singles €24, with bath and A/C €35; doubles for single use €30-35; doubles €35/45; triples €52 with bath. MC/V. ❷

Pensión Paris, C. Salvá, 12 (☎963 52 67 66; www.pensionparis.com). By Universidad de Valencia. 15 simple rooms, most with sink, minute balcony, and hall bath. Open year-round. Singles €22; doubles €32, with shower €38; triples €48. MC/V. ❷

FOOD

Valencia is renowned as the birthplace of *paella,* and a turn down any side-street will often reveal huge crowds of locals sharing this sticky dish from mammoth skillets. *Valencianos* buy heaps of fresh fish, produce, vegetables, snacks, and fruits in the bustling **Mercat Central,** the largest food market in Europe since 1928, located in an Art Nouveau building on Pl. del Mercat (☎963 82 91 00; open M-Sa 6am-2:30pm). For **groceries,** stop by **El Corte Inglés** on C. Pintor Sorolla (☎963 15 95 00). For a smaller market, try **Mercadona**, C. el Poeta, (open M-Sa 9:15am-9:15pm).

El Rall, C. Tundidores, 2 (☎963 92 20 90). This cheerful restaurant spills into an intimate, serene courtyard. Lucky customers may be serenaded by passing accordion players. *Paella* served in skillets according to party size. €12-21 per person, 2-person min. daily 1:30-3;30pm and 8:30-11:30pm. Reserve ahead. MC/V. ❸

Zumeria Naturalia, C. del Mar, 12 (☎963 91 12 11). This sherbet-colored gem is hidden steps below the cobblestone street outside. Hanging lamps dangle over low tables crammed with cushioned wicker chairs. Offers over 50 fruit drinks (€3.40-4.20 without alcohol, €5.50-6.50 smoothie mixed drinks). Delicious crepes and *bocadillos.* Open M-W 5pm-12:30am, Th 5pm-1am, F-Sa 5pm-2am, Su 5-10:30pm. Cash only. ❶

Sagardi, San Vincente Martir, 6 (☎963 91 06 68; www.sagardi.com). Basque-inspired tapas bar and restaurant with a bustling atmosphere. Lunchtime brings a steady stream of professionals to the tapas bar (tapas €1.60), while dinner and cocktails attract a varied crowd. Open daily, 11:30am-3:30pm and 7:30pm-1:30am. MC/V. ❶

Sol i Lluna, C. del Mar, 29 (☎963 92 22 16; www.solilluna.net). Relaxed bohemian hangout, with tapas bar, salads, and lighter entrees. Go for the set *menú* at midday or the inventive tapas served late into the night (€3.40-9). An eclectic ambience bar and ample open-air seating on a slow street just off Pl. de la Reina. Lots of regulars make for lively evenings. Open M 2-4pm, Tu-Sa 2-4pm and 9pm-last customer. MC/V. ❷

La Pappardella, C. Bordadores, 5 (☎963 91 89 15; www.viciositalianos.com). Chic and charismatic 2-story restaurant with some outdoor seating and a serene view of the plaza. Delicious Italian meals from pizza to spaghetti bolognese and vegetable dishes (€6-14). Ask to sit upstairs. Open daily 2-4pm and 9pm-midnight. AmEx/MC/V. ❷

La Lluna, C. Sant Ramón, 23 (☎963 92 21 46). Dark wood beams and low-hanging lamps characterize this quiet, tucked-away vegetarian restaurant. Serves a wide variety of traditional Valencian dishes, modified and embellished with fresh fruits and veggies. Appetizers and entrees €3.50-7. 4-course lunch *menú* (€6.50) on weekdays. Open M-Sa 1:30-3:30pm and 8:30-11pm. MC/V. ❶

SIGHTS

The older sights cluster around charming streets around **Plaza de la Reina** and **Plaza del Mercado.** Most museums, gardens, and notable landmarks are east along the Turia Riverbed. Though streets bordering the riverbed are high-speed thoroughfares, strolling through or above the riverbed is still a great way to take in the natural beauty and cultural activities that Valencia has to offer. EMT bus #5 drops off at most of the major sights, but, for a full informational tour, the double-decker **Bus Turístic** (☎963 41 44 00; www.valenciabusturistic.com) begins in Pl. de la Reina and loops around the old-town sights and along the riverbed toward the **Ciudad de las Artes y Ciencias** (€12 for a day pass).

CIUDAD DE LAS ARTES Y LAS CIENCIAS. This overwhelming urban citadel, dedicated to the arts and sciences, is a far cry from the blue-tiled church roofs that dominate most of the city skyline. This 350,000 sq. m. mini-city is Spain's largest museum, divided into four buildings covered with over 4000 panes of glass, all surrounding a vast reflecting pool. **L'Hemisfèric,** built to resemble an eye, hypnotizes onlookers with laser shows, a planetarium, and an IMAX theater. **L'Oceanogràfic** showcases 45,500 aquatic creatures in water channeled from the nearby Malvarossa beach. The enormous, glinting **Palau de les Arts** stages opera, theater, and dance performance. The **Museu de Les Ciències Príncipe Felipe,** the insect-like centerpiece, has hands-on exhibits. The garden running alongside L'Hemisfèric turns into a swanky club after dark. See **Nightlife, p. 214.** *(Bus #35 runs from Pl. del Ajuntament. ☎902 10 00 31; www.cac.es. Museum open daily 10am-7pm, high season 10am-9pm. €7.50, students and children €5.80. L'Oceanogràfic open high season daily 10am-midnight. Closed on certain holidays. €23.30, students and children €17.20. L'Hemisferic open M-Th 10am-7pm. €7.50, students and children €5.80. Combination tickets €19-30.50; can be bought at the train station through Cercanias trains.)*

INSTITUT VALENCIÀ D'ART MODERN (IVAM). This avant-garde museum features 20th- and 21st-century art. Its permanent collection on the first floor is famed for abstract works by 20th-century sculptor Julio González and artist Ignacio Pinazo. Temporary exhibits change frequently. *(C. Guillém de Castro, 118. Leaving the Basilica, take C. Caballeros until it turns into C. Quart. Walk under the Torres de Quart and take a right down C. Guiliem de Castro; the museum is on the right. Bus #5 from the Pl. del Ajuntament. ☎963 86 30 00; www.ivam.es. Open Tu-Su 10am-10pm. €2, students €1. Su free.)*

SANTA IGLESIA CATEDRAL DE VALENCIA. The original cathedral was replaced by a mosque during Muslim rule in the eighth century, but the first stone of the present cathedral was laid after the conquest of Valencia under James I in 1238. The steep 202-step climb up the **Miguelete** (cathedral tower) is worth the sweat; novelist Victor Hugo once counted 300 bell towers in the city from this vantage point. The Gothic **Capilla de Santo Cáliz** is home to a wealth of treasures, from the Crucifijo de Márfil statues, which depict "man's passions," to a chalice which was once claimed to be the Holy Grail used by Christ at the Last Supper. *(Pl. de la Reina. Cathedral ☎963 91 01 89. Open daily 7:30am-1pm and 4:30-8:30pm. Closes earlier in winter. Free. Tower open daily 10am-1pm and 4:30-7pm. €2. Museum ☎963 92 43 02. Open Mar.-Nov. M-Sa 10am-1pm and 4:30-7pm, Su 10am-1pm and 4:30-5:30pm. €4 includes multilingual audio tour. €2.70 for children and seniors. After 6:30pm free.)* Be certain to visit the grandiose gold altar at the neighboring **Basílica Virgen dels Desamparats.** *(In the Pl. de la Virgen, 6, right behind the Catedral. Open for mass M-F 7am-1pm and 4:45-8:30pm, Su 8:30am-1:30pm and 4:45-8:30pm. Free.)*

PARKS. On the other side of the river, next to the Museo de Bellas Artes, off C. Sant Pío, are the **Jardines del Real,** home to oddly shaped ponds, modern sculptures, a small aviary, and even a kitschy duck-shaped fountain dedicated to Walt Disney. Everyone can enjoy a stroll through these labyrinthine paths and ivy-covered arches. The garden also features an aviary and a small zoo. *(C. San Pío V. Walk to the river, take a left, pass the museum, and enter on C. Sant Pío V. Gardens open every day.)* You don't have to be a horticulturist to appreciate the **Jardín Botànic,** a botanical garden that cultivates 43,000 plants of 300 international species, including cacti and tropical palm trees. Benches and friendly felines line the winding paths. *(C. Quart, 80, on the western end of Río Turia near Gran Vía Fernando el Católico. M: Turia. Go left out of the Po. de Pechina, exit down Gran Vía, and take a left onto C. Quart. ☎963 15 68 17; www.uv.es/jardibotanic. Open Tu-Su May-Aug. 10am-9pm; Sept. and Apr. 10am-8pm; Oct. and Mar. 10am-7pm; Nov.-Feb. 10am-6pm. Closed Dec. 25 and Jan. 1. €0.60.)*

OTHER SIGHTS. The **Museo Taurino de Valencia** offers a permanent exhibition of Valencian *tauromachia* and a peek inside the formidable 13,000-seat bullfighting arena, the **Plaza de Toros.** *(C. Xàtiva, Open Tu-Su 10am-8pm.)* Valencia's **Palau de Música** is one of the world's premier concert halls, hosting local orchestras, national and international soloists, and jazz bands. *(Bus #35 runs from Pl. del Ajuntament. Po. de la Alameda, 30. ☎963 37 50 20; www.palauvalencia.com. Ticket window open daily 10:30am-1:30pm and 5:30-9pm.)*

NIGHTLIFE

Use your *siesta* wisely; Valencia's nightlife is rigorous. Bars, pubs, and courtyards start to fill up around midnight around **Plaza de la Virgen and Calle de Caballeros,** which hosts veritable tides of gung-ho club-hoppers into the wee hours. Follow the street to **Plazas Tossal** and **Collado,** where outdoor terraces, tall-windowed pubs, upbeat music, and *Agua de Valencia* (the region's famed alcoholic beverage) energize the masses. A lively local crowd frequents bars along C. Quart. The gay and lesbian scene centers on **Calle Quart** and **Plaza Vicente Iborra.**

Discotecas, which are quite empty until at least 1:30 or 2am, dominate the university area, particularly on **Avinguda Blasco Ibáñez.** There are a few calmer pubs with dancing around most of the main plazas. For more info, consult the *Qué y Dónde* weekly magazine (€0.50) or the weekly entertainment supplement, Valencia City (€0.50), both available at newsstands and tourist offices. Check out the free monthly *24/7 Valencia*, available in most internet cafes and tourist booths, for new hot spots.

L'umbracle Terraza, Av. de Saler, 5 (☎963 31 97 45; www.umbracleterraza.com). Located outside in the garden parallel to the Ciudad de las Artes y las Ciencias, this is the perfect setting to view Valencia's newest architectural gems in their illuminated splendor. Giant pink bubbles and couch-beds line the garden paths. 4 different bars, dancing, and hookah make this a truly luxe experience. If it gets chilly, head down to **Mya,** the discoteca below. Cover €15. Open April-Sept. M-Sa 11:30pm-late.

Akuarela, Pub: C. Juan Llorens, 49, disco: Eugenia Viñes, 152 (☎963 85 93 85), in Pl. Malvarossa; you'll probably need to take a moped, car, or taxi. Giant, but remarkably tasteful, discoteca. 4 rooms, each with own bar, and an enormous terrace replete with plush VIP seating. Salsa, top 40, and Valencia's own music from the 80s and 90s echo until dawn in these glam halls. Cover free with purchase of €7 or more at the pub; otherwise Th-Sa €13, 3am €16. Pub open daily 6pm-3:30am. Discoteca open daily midnight-7:30am.

Cafe Negrito, Pl. Negrito, 1 (☎963 91 42 33). A bold little cafe in a charming courtyard a few blocks from the Basilica. Dozens of silver tables, inside and out, fill quickly with revelers starting off the night right. Wide selection of reasonably priced drinks. Jar of *Agua de Valencia* €7. Open daily 3pm-3am. Cash only.

Radio City, C. Santa Teresa, 19 (☎963 91 41 51; www.radiocityvalencia.com). Popular bar and discoteca well suited for casual barhopping or wild dancing on the dark dance floor. Psychedelic lighting effects. Young, high-energy crowd. Order a beer (€2) or mixed drink (€6 and up) from 1 of 3 different bars. Tu flamenco at 11pm. New music and dance/theater performances M-F. Open daily 7:30pm-3:30am.

Bolsería Café, C. Bolsería, 41 (☎963 91 89 03; www.bolseriavalencia.com). Boisterous, beautiful people of all ages pack into this upscale, creatively constructed cafe-bar with floor-to-ceiling windows. Smaller terraces upstairs. Drinks €4-6. Free *Agua de Valencia* before 12:30am. M salsa, 1 drink minimum consumption; W "Americana." Cover Sa €8; includes 1 drink. Open daily 7:30pm-3:30am. MC/V.

Fox Congo, C. Caballeros, 35 (☎963 91 85 67). Walls and poles of welded metal glint under the light of the bar. Draws large crowds of hostel-dwellers and trendy locals. As in all places known to be frequented by travelers, stay alert for theft. T hip-hop nights. Beer €4. Mixed drinks €7. Cover Sa €10; includes 1 drink. Open Tu-Sa 8pm-3:30am.

Murray Club, Av. Blasco Ibáñez, 111 (☎963 71 65 96). An eclectic crowd of students and locals with impressive stamina rock out to a mix of house, 80s, and rock. Pop-art-decorated walls. Plan to stay a while if you make the trek. Festa Brasileira Tu night; Murray Rock Night Th. Cover M-Th and Su €6, F-Sa €9; includes 1 drink. Open daily 1:30-7am.

STRUMMING SAVVY

I am a musician, but it was not an easy decision to bring my guitar to Spain. Would it look like a Picasso by the end of the trip? But I decided to take my chances. If you too want to make a musical pilgrimage, here's how to travel like the minstrel you truly are.

Spare change? You know you're going to play anyway, so stake out a spot on the sidewalk and plop down a hat for tips. American pop and jazz standards are popular in Spain, and if you sing in English people will stop to listen.

Get help from hostels. Almost all hostels allow luggage storage after check-out—use it.

Buses. Several times, I could almost hear my guitar gently weeping under a mountain of carelessly heaped luggage in the underbelly of the bus. If there's an extra seat, see if the driver will let you bring it onboard. If not, wait until everyone else has loaded their heavy suitcases, then gently place your guitar on top for a safe ride.

Flamenco. While you're in Spain, learn about its musical traditions. Most major cities offer flamenco guitar lessons—take a little Spanish rhythm home with you.

I have spent eight weeks in Las Islas Baleares, the Costa Blanca, and the Costa del Sol, playing in clubs and on the street. Luckily, my guitar has survived like a champ—and the sounds of my spicy Spanish adventure have been incorporated into its strings.

—*Jessica Righthand*

BEACHES

On sunny weekends in Valencia, azure waters meet a sea of beach umbrellas planted in the fine, cream-colored sand. A wide boardwalk connecting the enormous beach is ideal for sun-drenched walks and bike rides. **Avenida del Puerto** has a direct bike path from the riverbed to the port, site of the 2007 America's Cup. From here, the beach is only a few blocks north. Buses #20, 21, and 22 all stop nearby and take about 15min. from the center of town. The boardwalk connects the most heavily populated beach, **Las Arenas,** to the popular **La Malvarossa.** Equally crowded but more attractive is Salér, a smooth stretch of pebbled beach 14km from the city that divides a lagoon from the sea. Cafeterias and snack bars line the shore. The **Autocares Herca** (☎963 49 12 50) bus goes to **Salér** (on the way to El Perello; 30min., every hr. 7am-9pm, €1-1.10 depending on destination) from the intersection of Gran Vía de Germanías and C. Sueca. To get to the bus stop, exit the train station and take a right down C. Xàtiva, then turn right onto C. Ruzafa to Gran Vía. Look for a yellow MetroBus post. The ride to Salér can be jammed on weekends. Plan on a day for a worthwhile trip.

FESTIVALS

Valencia's most famous festival is **Las Fallas** (Mar. 12-19), which features *ninots* (gigantic puppets), gunpowder, and bonfires. During **Semana Santa** in April, monks reenact biblical scenes and children perform the plays of Sant Vicent Ferrer. **Our Lady of the Forsaken** (May 11) entails masses of worshippers bearing a famous effigy of the Virgin Mary from the basilica to Valencia's main cathedral. **Corpus Christi,** usually held in June, is a week-long parade of *valencianos* dressing as religious characters to reenact scenes from the Old and New Testament. The **Festiu de Juliol,** in July, brings fireworks, concerts, bullfights, and a *batalla dels flors* (battle of flowers), when young girls in carriages blanket the streets with flowers. October 9 celebrates both lovers and the conquest of Valencia by James I in 1238. On that day, Valencia's coat of arms is paraded and hoisted outside the *Ajuntament.*

COSTA BLANCA

The "White Coast," named for the color of the fine sand and smooth pebbles that cover its shores, extends from Dénia to Alicante. Jagged mountains, jutting piers, pine forests, cactus-studded rock, and hills covered with cherry trees provide the backdrop for the towns of the Costa Blanca, all of which attract their fair share of tourists. The slower-paced towns of Altea and Dénia, visited primarily for sparkling beaches, each have a small *casco antiguo* surrounded by supermarkets, resort hotels, and construction sites. Nevertheless, they may offer relief from the disco droves that energize Alicante and Benidorm, making them ideal for families or travelers seeking more tranquil locales. These smaller towns are fast becoming havens for those seeking classy beach vacations, and waterfront hotels come at steep prices; many prefer to spend the night in Alicante or Benidorm and daytrip all over the coast. Fortunately, cheap, efficient modes of transportation make this an easy option.

TRANSPORTATION

Trains: Ferrocarrils de la Generalitat Valenciana (☎965 92 02 02, in Alicante 26 27 31), also known as the "Costa Blanca Express," hits almost every town and beach along the coast on its Alicante-Dénia line. Switch from train to tram (or vice versa) at the **El Campello** station. From the central TRAM Mercado stop in Alicante, trains run to: **Altea** (1½hr., every hr. 5:44am-8:44pm, €4.20); **Benidorm** (1¼hr.; every hr. 5:44am-8:44pm, €3.40); **Calpe** (1hr., every hr. 5:44am-7:44pm, €4.90); **Dénia** (2½hr., every hr. 5:44am-7:44pm, €7.30). Trains return to: **Alicante** from **Dénia** (every hr., 6:20am-8:20pm); **Calpe** (every hr., 6:59am-8:59pm); **Altea** (every hr., 6:16am-9:16pm); and **Benidorm** (every hr. 6:29am-9:29pm). **Tramsnochador** (☎965 26 27 31), the night train from Alicante, runs in July and Aug. to **Dénia** and **Benidorm.**

Buses: ALSA (☎902 42 22 42) runs between **Alicante** and **Valencia,** stopping in towns along the Costa Blanca. From Valencia buses run to: **Alicante** (2-4hr., 12-20 per day 4:45am-9:45pm, €17.15-20); **Benidorm** (2-4hr., 15-18 per day 4:45am-9:45pm, €13.35-15.75); **Calpe/Altea** (2-4hr., 8-10 per day 6am-5pm, €11); **Dénia** (2-3hr., 11-12 per day 6am-10:45pm, €10.10); **Gandía** (1hr., 9-15 per day 6am-9:45pm, €6.10); **Xàbia/Javea** (2-3hr., 6 per day 6:30am-8pm, €9.45). From Alicante buses run to: **Benidorm** (1hr., 1-4 per hr., €3.80); **Altea** (1hr.; 10 per day 7am-7pm, Sa 6 per day 7am-8pm, Su 8 per day 7am-7pm; €4.50); **Calpe** (1hr.; M-F 10 per day 7am-7pm, Sa 6 per day 7am-8pm, Su 8 per day 7am-7pm; €6); **Dénia** (2½-3hr.; M-F 12 per day 7am-8:10pm, Sa 9 per day 7am-9pm, Su 11 per day 7am-8pm, €9.35); **Valencia** (2½hr., 1-3 per hr. 6:30am-9pm, €17.15-20);

ALICANTE (ALACANT) ☎965

Alicante (pop. 322,000) is a city with verve. Though its wild bars, crowded beaches, and busy streets seem decidedly modern, the looming castle-topped crag, 14th-century churches, and marble esplanades declare otherwise. Alicante, once the Roman city Lucentum, is home to the remains of a fifth-century Iberian settlement. Though it is undoubtedly a traditional Spanish city, it has that extra spark of energy—the locals are friendly, and the nightlife is lively.

TRANSPORTATION

Flights: Aeroport Internacional de El Altet (☎966 91 91 00 or 966 91 94 00; www.aena.es), 11km south of the city center. **Iberia** (☎902 40 05 00) and **Air Europa** (☎902 40 15 01) have daily flights to **Madrid, Barcelona,** and the **Islas Baleares,** among other destinations. **British Midland Airways** (☎902 11 13 33) flies to **London. Alcoyana** (☎965 26 84 00) bus #C-6 runs to the airport from Pl. Luceros (every 40min., €1.10). Buses also leave from Pl. Puerta Mar.

Trains: RENFE, Estación Término (☎902 24 02 02; www.renfe.es), on Av. de Salamanca. Info open daily 7am-midnight. To: **Barcelona** (4-6hr., 5-6 per day 6:55am-6:20pm, €44.50-49.30); **Elx** (30min., every hr. 6:05am-10:05pm, €1.85); **Madrid** (4hr., 4-8 per day 7am-8pm, €39.90 and up); **Valencia** (1hr., 3-4 per day 6:55am-8:45pm, €12.25-25.60). **Cercanías** runs to **Murcia** (1hr., every hr. 6:05am-10:05pm, €4.30). **Ferrocarrils de la Generalitat Valenciana (TRAM),** Estació Marina, Av. Villajoyosa, 2 (☎900 72 04 72; www.fgvalicante.com), by the Mercado Central, has service along the Costa Blanca. In summer, the **Tramsnochador** runs to beaches including **Altea** and **Benidorm,** with some continuing to **Dénia** (every hr. 11:25pm-4:55am, €1.20-5.55).

Buses: C. Portugal, 17 (☎965 13 07 00; www.alicante-ayto.es/trafico). **ALSA** (☎902 42 22 42 or 965 98 50 03 for booking; www.alsa.es) sends buses to: **Altea** (1hr., 10 per day 7am-7pm, Sa 6 per day 7am-8pm, Su 8 per day 7am-7pm, €4.50); **Barcelona** (9hr., 8 per day 4:30am-11:30pm, €39.27-44.44); **Benidorm** (1hr., 1-4 per hr. 6:30am-10:30pm, €3.80); **Calp** (2-3hr.; M-F 10 per day 7am-7pm, Sa 6 per day 7am-8pm, Su 8 per day 7am-7pm; €6); **Dénia** (2½-3hr.; M-F 12 per day 7am-8:10pm, Sa 9 per day 7am-9pm, Su 11 per day 7am-8pm; €9.35);

Granada (6hr., 7 per day 11:36am-3am, €26.69-32.55); **Madrid** (5hr., 12-15 per day 8:45am-1:45am, €26.27-36); **Málaga** (7hr., 7 per day 2:20am-11:45pm, €35.90-43.60); **Sevilla** (10hr., 11:45pm, €46.49); **Valencia** (2½hr., 1-3 per hr. 6:30am-9pm, €17.15-20); **Xàbia/Javea** (2½hr., 5-8 per day 7am-8pm, €8.35). **Mollá** (☎965 26 84 00) runs buses to **Elx** (30min.; M-F 2 per hr. 6:45am-10:15pm, Sa every hr. 8am-10pm, Su 8 per day 9am-9:30pm; €1.70).

Public Transportation: TAM-Alicante Metropolitan Transport (☎965 14 09 36 or 900 72 04 72; www.subus.es). Buses #21 and 22 run from near the train station in Alicante to Playa San Juan (€1.10).

Taxis: Teletaxi (☎965 10 16 11), **RadioTaxi** (☎965 25 25 11).

ORIENTATION AND PRACTICAL INFORMATION

Trains to Alicante from the Costa Blanca arrive at the **TRAM station,** located next to the Mercado Central at the top of Rambla Méndez Núñez. This street, affectionately known as La Rambla, borders the *casco antiguo* and is full of **ATMs,** bus stops, and restaurants. All other trains arrive at the train station, which is toward the city outskirts at the end of **Avenida de la Estación,** which becomes Pl. Luceros. **Avenida Federico Soto** runs toward the beach, perpendicular to Pl. Luceros, which turns into Av. Doctor Gadea. Continuing through Pl. Luceros to **Avenida Alfonso X el Sabio** brings you to the TRAM station, and a right turn just beyond the market puts you on **La Rambla.** The *casco antiguo* is charming; its restaurant-filled plazas and quirky, hidden nooks provide a pleasant contrast to the city's expansive, crowded beaches. Nearly 2km in length and decorated with brilliant red marble only found near Alicante, the **Explanada d'Espanya** traverses the port and links the **Parque de las Canalejas** to the beach.

Tourist Office: Municipal office, C. Portugal, 17, by the bus station (☎965 92 98 02; www.alicanteturismo.com). English spoken. Open M-F 9am-2pm and 5-8pm, Sa 10am-2pm. **Regional office,** Rambla Méndez Núñez, 23 (☎965 20 00 00). Open M-F 9am-8pm, Sa 10am-8pm, Su 10am-2pm. **Branch** at Playa San Juan, on Av. de Niza, open in summer. **Airport branch** (☎965 28 50 11) open M 9am-3pm, Tu-F 9am-8pm, Sa 10am-8pm. Other branches by the train station and on the Explanada d'Espanya.

Budget Travel: IVAJ (Institut Valencia de la Juventud), Rambla Méndez Núñez, 41 (☎966 47 81 09; www.ivaj.es.) HI card €10.80. Open M-F 9am-2pm.

Luggage Storage: At the **bus station** €4-8 per bag. Open 8am-9pm).

English-Language Bookstore: FNAC (☎96 601 01 06), just by the train station on Ave. de la Estacion, 5. Open M-Sa 10am-10pm, Su noon-10pm.

Police: Av. Julian Bestero 15. Open 8am-3pm. **Comisaría,** C. Médico Pascual Pérez, 27 (☎965 10 72 00 or 092).

Hospital: Hospital General, C. Maestro Alonso, 109 (☎965 93 83 00).

Red Cross: ☎965 25 25 25.

Internet Access: Well-equipped internet centers are surprisingly hard to come by in Alicante. Though there are a few *locutorios* near Pl. Portal de Elche, one of the best options is the **Internet Cafe Xplorer,** C. San Vicente, 47, (☎965 21 46 24) with 30 computers, printing, fax, Skype, and breakfast. Internet €0.70 per 30min. 1hr. internet, *bocadillo,* and drink €2.90. Open daily 10am-2am. To get there, continue on La Rambla until it turns into San Vicente after the Mercado TRAM stop.

Post Office: Bono Guarner, 2 (☎965 22 78 71). Open M-F 8:30am-8:30pm, Sa 9:30am-1pm. **Branch** on the corner of C. Arzobispo Loaces and C. Alemania (☎965 13 18 87). Open M-F 8:30am-8:30pm, Sa 9:30am-1pm. **Postal Code:** 03002.

CULTURE COMES FREE. With the exception of Alicante's outstanding archaeological museum, the MARQ, all of the major sights in Alicante—the Castell de Santa Barbara, the Concatedral de San Nicolas, the *Ayuntamiento,* the Basilica de Santa Maria, and more—are free. So store your beach bag for an afternoon and check out the views from the castle or the ornate *Ayuntamiento* without putting a dent in your wallet.

ACCOMMODATIONS

The best budget accommodations in Alicante are in the *casco antiguo.* Though quality hostels abound in this area, ensuring a room requires an early arrival or reservation. If you're not particular, finding a cheap and safe room elsewhere in Alicante is fairly easy, except during **Fogueres de Sant Joan** (June 18-25), when accommodations are booked well in advance.

Hostal Les Monges Palace, corner of C. San Agustín, 4, and C. Monjas (☎965 21 50 46; www.lesmonges.es). Ornate green exterior, equally palatial interior. A/C €5. Breakfast €4. Internet €3 per hr. Singles €30, with bath €40, with hot tub €51; doubles €42/50/66; triples €53, with bath €64. AmEx/MC/V. ❸

Hostal-Pensión La Milagrosa, C. Villavieja, 8 (☎965 21 69 18; www.hostallamilagrosa.com). Soft-colored, spacious rooms in the center of the *casco antiguo* and easy walking distance from the beach and TRAM. Some rooms have balconies with amazing views of the castle or the Iglesia de Santa Maria. Shared baths and A/C. Internet €1.70 per 30min. Laundry €2. Communal kitchen on 3rd floor. Towels and room cleaning available upon request. June-Aug. singles from €20; doubles from €30. MC/V. ❷

Pensión Alicante San Nicolás, C. San Nicolás, 14 (☎965 21 70 39, www.alicante-sanicolas.com). A new, polished establishment. 7 elegant rooms in natural pinks and greens. Full English breakfast. A/C. In summer singles €30, with bath €35; doubles €42/48. In winter singles €25/30; doubles €35/42. Extra bed €15. MC/V. ❸

Pensión Versalles, C. Villavieja, 3 (☎965 21 47 93, 965 32 98 00). 12 small, quirky rooms. Fun, communal atmosphere encouraged by a casual outdoor courtyard/kitchen. Great for easygoing groups who want a place to crash. €18 per person. Cash only. ❶

FOOD

Restaurants and *kebap* stops are everywhere, though many are overpriced and on busy streets. Smaller bar/restaurants in the *casco antiguo* are often superior in atmosphere, authenticity, and value. On average, a four-course *menú del día* in the *casco antiguo* costs €9, though often a few extra euro will buy a meal of considerably higher quality. **Rambla Méndez Núñez** is full of chic, popular eateries. The port, which becomes a raucous nightlife hub as midnight nears, is littered with expensive *marisquerías,* generally of average quality. The enormous **central market** is on Av. Alfonso X el Sabio. (Open M-Sa 9am-2pm.) Buy groceries at **Mercadona,** C. Álvarez Sereix, 5 (☎965 21 58 94; open M-Sa 9am-9pm) or at **El Corte Inglés,** Av. Maisonnave, 53 (☎965 92 50 01; open daily 10am-10pm). There are smaller markets across from the **Playa de Postiguet. Deshoras** shops dot the city, a good option for late-night snacks and basic groceries; there's one at C. Bailén, 29. (☎965 21 11 42. Open 24hr.)

Restaurante Villahelmy, C. Mayor, 37 (☎965 21 25 29; www.villahelmy.com) With 2 lone tables amid a sea of patio seating in the Pl. Mayor, Villahelmy can easily go undetected. But its outrageous blue and orange interior, folkloric murals, and decorative birdcages are a far cry from ordinary. Mediterranean and Spanish cuisine, with

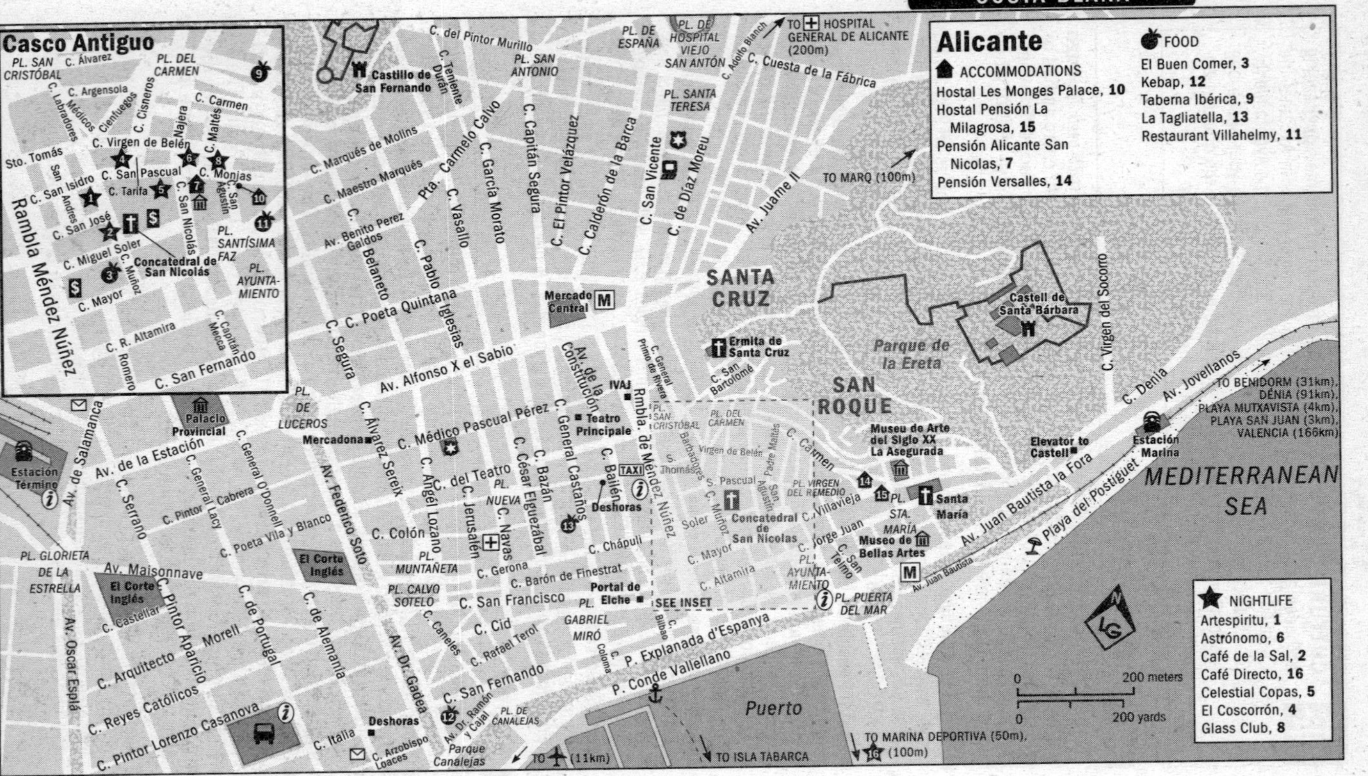
Alicante
ACCOMMODATIONS
Hostal Les Monges Palace, 10
Hostal Pensión La Milagrosa, 15
Pensión Alicante San Nicolas, 7
Pensión Versalles, 14
FOOD
El Buen Comer, 3
Kebap, 12
Taberna Ibérica, 9
La Tagliatella, 13
Restaurant Villahelmy, 11
NIGHTLIFE
Artespiritu, 1
Astrónomo, 6
Café de la Sal, 2
Café Directo, 16
Celestial Copas, 5
El Coscorrón, 4
Glass Club, 8
MEDITERRANEAN SEA
TO BENIDORM (31km), DÉNIA (91km), PLAYA MUTXAVISTA (4km), PLAYA SAN JUAN (3km), VALENCIA (166km)
Av. Jovellanos
C. Denia
Estación Marina
Playa del Postiguet
Av. Juan Bautista la Fora
Elevator to Castell
C. Virgen del Socorro
Castell de Santa Bárbara
Parque de la Ereta
SAN ROQUE
SANTA CRUZ
Ermita de Santa Cruz
TO MARQ (100m)
TO HOSPITAL GENERAL DE ALICANTE (200m)
C. Cuesta de la Fábrica
Av. Juame II
Museu de Arte del Siglo XX La Asegurada
Santa María
PL. STA. MARÍA
Museo de Bellas Artes
PL. PUERTA DEL MAR
PL. AYUNTAMIENTO
Concatedral de San Nicolas
SEE INSET
TO MARINA DEPORTIVA (50m), (100m)
TO ISLA TABARCA
TO (11km)
Puerto
P. Explanada d'Espanya
P. Conde Vallellano
Rmbla. de Méndez Núñez
C. San Vicente
C. de Díaz Moreu
C. Calderón de la Barca
C. El Pintor Velázquez
C. Capitán Segura
C. García Morato
C. Vasallo
PL. DE ESPAÑA
PL. DE HOSPITAL VIEJO SAN ANTÓN
PL. SAN ANTONIO
PL. SANTA TERESA
Mercado Central
Av. de la Constitución
Teatro Principale
IVAJ
C. General Castaños
C. Bailén
Deshoras
C. Bazán
C. César Elguezábal
PL. NUEVA
C. Navas
C. Jerusalén
C. Ángel Lozano
C. Colón
PL. MUNTAÑETA
PL. CALVO SOTELO
C. San Francisco
Portal de Elche
PL. GABRIEL MIRÓ
C. Cid
C. San Fernando
PL. DE CANALEJAS
Parque Canalejas
Av. Dr. Gadea
Av. Alfonso X el Sabio
C. Poeta Quintana
C. Pablo Iglesias
C. Segura
C. Álvarez Sereix
Mercadona
Av. Federico Soto
El Corte Inglés
C. de Alemania
C. de Portugal
Castillo de San Fernando
PL. DE LUCEROS
Palacio Provincial
Av. de la Estación
C. Serrano
Av. Maisonnave
C. Pintor Aparicio
C. Reyes Católicos
C. Pintor Lorenzo Casanova
Av. Oscar Esplá
PL. GLORIETA DE LA ESTRELLA
Estación Término
Av. de Salamanca
200 meters
200 yards
Casco Antiguo
PL. SAN CRISTÓBAL
PL. DEL CARMEN
C. Virgen de Belén
C. San Pascual
C. San Nicolás
C. San José
C. Miguel Soler
C. Muñoz
C. Mayor
C. R. Altamira
C. San Fernando
PL. SANTÍSIMA FAZ
PL. AYUNTAMIENTO
Concatedral de San Nicolás
Rambla Méndez Núñez

staples like *paella* and tapas. Salads €5-9, entrees €9-14. *Menú del día* €11. Open Tu-Sa 1-4pm and 8pm-midnight, Su 1-4pm. MC/V. ❷

Kebap, Av. Dr. Gadea, 5 (☎965 14 10 20). Not all *kebaps* are created equal. This shop uses fresh ingredients and is located next to a charming plaza. For lunch, take your food to go and eat outside—a cheap alternative to *bocadillos*. Mouthwatering pitas €3.50. Entrees €5.70-9. Open daily 1pm-1am. 2nd location at C. San Fernando, 12. MC/V. ❷

El Buen Comer, C. Mayor, 8 (☎965 21 31 03; www.elbuencomer.info). A tourist favorite with an old-town, traditional ambience and patio seating. Wide selection of tapas and fresh seafood. Tapas €3.75-9.10, entrees €7.80-30. *Menú del día* €9.50. Tapas fixed menu with drink €16.60 (min. 2 people). Open daily 10am-midnight. MC/V. ❸

La Taberna Ibérica, C. Toledo, 18, at Pedro Sebastia (☎965 21 62 58; www.tabernaiberica.com), 4 blocks behind the *Ayuntamiento* in the *casco antiguo*. Owned and run by an older local couple, this cozy *bodega* and restaurant allows you to sample some of the absolute best of traditional Spanish cooking. Though the menu is fairly standard, ingredients and preparation are top-notch. Tapas €4-10. *Menú del día* €14. Cash only. ❷

La Tagliatella, C. Castaños (☎965 20 87 97; www.latagliatella.es), parallels Rambla Méndez Núñez, a few blocks from the port. A romantically decorated Italian restaurant with warm colors and an upscale ambience; outdoor seating also available on the pedestrian C. Castaños. Serves exquisite variety of gourmet salads, pastas (€11-13), risottos, scallops, and pizza (€10-12). Open daily 1pm-midnight. MC/V. ❷

SIGHTS AND BEACHES

MUSEO ARQUEOLÓGICO PROVINCIAL DE ALICANTE. The ultramodern Museo Arqueológico Provincial de Alicante (MARQ), Pl. Dr. Gomez Ulla, won European Museum of the Year in 2004, and for good reason. Impeccably lit and arranged, the museum showcases remains from the Paleolithic, Iberian, Roman, Islamic, and modern periods. Be sure to ask for the audio tour, which provides a highly dramatic musical soundtrack to accompany your visit. There are always two seasonal exhibits in addition to the permanent collection, and a sizable portion of the museum is dedicated to archaeological methods and techniques. *(Take the TRAM to the Marq stop. ☎965 14 90 00; www.marqalicante.com. Open Tu-Sa 10am-7pm, Su and festivals 10am-2pm; July-Aug Tu-Sa 11am-2pm and 6pm-midnight, Su 11am-2pm. €3, students and seniors €1.50, children and handicapped free.)*

CASTELL DE SANTA BÁRBARA. The Castell de Santa Bárbara keeps guard over Alicante's shores and provides an awe-inspiring backdrop to the *casco antiguo* (old town). The castle's drawbridges, dark passageways, and hidden tunnels date from the ninth to 17th centuries, allowing a glimpse at the many layers of history that characterize the origins of the city. At 166m tall, Santa Barbara is one of Europe's most sizeable medieval fortresses, and it boasts a dry moat, dungeon, and ammunitions storeroom. The **Albacar Vell,** constructed during the Middle Ages, holds a sculpture garden with pieces by Spanish greats. A road from the northern border of the old section of Alicante provides a walk up that is much easier than it looks; otherwise, an elevator is accessible by a tunnel on Av. Jovellanos, across from Playa Postiguet near the white pedestrian overpass. *(☎965 16 21 28 or 26 31 31. Castle open daily until sunset. Free. Elevator €2.40, though the elevator has been in and out of service within the past year; the Turibus, which leaves from the elevator, serves as a €2 substitute.)*

BASÍLICA DE SANTA MARIA. In the old town, the Gothic-style Basílica de Santa Maria, Alicante's oldest church, stands over the ruins of an old mosque. The neighboring **Concatedral de San Nicolas de Bari** boasts a different flavor of Baroque architecture; a 45m dome allows light to flutter into the dim enclaves of this church. The **Ayuntamiento** on the edge of the *casco antiguo* (near the port) has a stunning 18th-century facade with twisted columns and stone sculptures. The interior, decorated originally to welcome the Queen to Alicante, is, well, palatial. Portraits of all former (and current) governors are displayed on the second floor, and at the bottom of the stairs, just next to the outrageous golden Gaudí sculpture is the official marker of sea level for the nation.

BEACHES. Alicante's **Playa del Postiguet,** near the *Ayuntamiento*, is a crowded stretch of sand. Sunbathers, ice-cream stands, and small cafes dot the wide adjacent boardwalk. For a more local scene and peaceful shores, the 6km of **Playa de Sant Joan** and **Playa del Mutxavista** are the nearest options, accessible by the tram station at the joint linking the Explanada and the Playa del Postiguet. *(The Alicante-Dénia train, TRAM, leaves the main station every 20min. in the summer, every hr. in winter, and stops at Playa del Muxtavista and Playa de San Juan; €0.95. To Sant Joan, take TAM bus #21, 22, or 31. For Mutxavista, take #21. Every 15min., €0.95.)*

NIGHTLIFE

Alicante's raucous nightlife can be somewhat capricious: bars that overflow one night are often closed or embarrassingly empty the next. Many of the hit locales are only open weekends. It's often best to follow the sound of chattering crowds. The most concentrated nightlife areas are the discotecas along the port and the bizarre pubs that spring to life in the *casco antiguo*.

PARTY ON. Given its long hours and disco destinations, the Tramsnochador is a godsend for all-night partiers. The bus runs to cities like Altea, Benidorm, and Dénia, with service until 5am.

CASCO ANTIGUO

The *casco antiguo* is the perfect place to start off the night while the dance floors along the port fill up. Though there are plenty of watering holes around **Plaza San Cristóbal** and **Calle Mayor,** the older part of town, referred to by most as *el barrio*, has the youngest crowd and the quirkiest bars. The cramped patios outside these hot spots accumulate crowds rapidly: the barhopping mentality in Alicante is unabashedly follow-the-leader.

Celestial Copas, C. San Pascual, 1 (☎663 50 26 32). Fills up later than surrounding bars, but the decor alone makes it worth a visit anytime. The garish bar drips with opulence and is sinfully offset by kitschy religious artwork. Red velvet curtains, decadent colors, and glinting gold chandeliers overwhelm tiny rooms. Spanish, flamenco, and Latin grooves. Outdoor seating also available. Beer €3, mixed drinks from €5. Open winter Th 10pm-3am, F-Sa 10pm-4am; summer daily 10pm-3am. Cash only.

Artespiritu, C. Labradores, 26 (☎675 01 99 94). As you walk along C. Labradores at night, you will inevitably stumble over the crowd at this corner bar, sitting outside, as a steady reggae-groove-electric mix provides the background for conversation and, later, dancing. Mixed drinks €5. Happy hour 10pm-midnight; €1 beer pints. Open daily 10am-4am, serves juices for breakfast. Cash only.

Astrónomo, C. Virgen de Belén, at C. Padre Maltés (☎965 14 35 22). 2 heavenly floors of dancing and drinking to Spanish pop, house, and everything in between. Escape across the street to their lush, gated outdoor terrace. Beer €3. Mixed drinks from €5. Happy hour midnight-2am. Open Th-Sa 11pm-4am. Cash only.

El Coscorrón, C. Tarifa, 2 (☎965 21 27 27). Named after the bump on the head you might receive from the 4 ft. door frame. Open since 1936, it claims to be the oldest bar in Alicante; from the looks of it, that just might be true. Beer €2. Mixed drinks €4-6. Open daily 7pm-last customer. Cash only.

Glass Club, C. de Montegon. Cool medical lab colors and blank mirrored walls let off icy steam in this large air-conditioned, space-age club. Techno and house music reverberate off of every shiny surface. Beer €4. Mixed drinks €5.50. Open 11pm-4am.

Directo, C. Virgen de Belén, 19. With 2 floors and popular international jams, this bar and dance club keeps everyone feeling good. Dark wood bars and plenty of space to salsa. Mixed drinks €6.50. Open Th-Sa 11:30pm-4am. Cash only.

Café de la Sal, C. Labradores, 5 (☎965 20 50 68; www.cafedelasal.com). You won't find locals here, but you will find great hiphop, crowds of expats and young people from all over the world, and great mixed drinks. Tu beer pong, Sa international guest DJs. Mixed drinks €6. Ask about special promotions/VIP cards, which give discounts on drinks. Open daily 8pm-4am. MC/V.

NEAR THE PORT

Alicante's main port houses a complex of cavernous bars and discotecas pumping music over the water. Though the music starts early, these bars fill up late, and some are only open on weekends. Revelers crowd the many huge discotecas on the port, to the left when facing the water. None of these has a cover charge, though there is sometimes a drink minimum. Beer is almost universally €3.50 and mixed drinks €6. The liveliest spots differ depending on the day of the week, but all have a fairly good crowd any night.

Havana Cafe, Rambla Méndez Núñez, 26 (☎965 21 69 26; www.havana.es). On the way from the old town to the port. Bohemian interior and huge crowds make for a lively feel. Open M-Th 7am-2:30am, F-Sa 3pm-4am. Beer €1.50, €2 outside. Cash only.

Coyote Ugly (☎618 38 00 09; coyoteuglypuerto.com). A popular, scandalous option, complete with poles on the bar. Early-morning breakfast served in the room next to the dance floor. Beer €2, mixed drinks from €6. Open daily 9:30am-6:30am. Cash only.

FESTIVALS

From June 20-24, the **Fogueres de Sant Joan** (Bonfires of St. John) and St. John's feast day celebrate the summer solstice in a hedonistic inferno. This rollicking, fire-worshipping blast kicks off with a citywide parade in traditional garb, and, by the third day, every district in the city has its incredible *foguera* (giant papier-mâché structure) on display. Temporary festival halls are erected and feasts take place in open air, punctuated by daily firework shows in the Plaza de los Luceros at 2pm. Parades, flower-offerings, and wild celebrations fill the hours until the festival culminates in a midnight display of fireworks atop Mt. Benacantil and a huge bonfire in the Pl. de Ayuntamiento. In June, the **Moors and Christians** festival pays costumed tribute to the Christian battles for Valencian reconquest. The city honors its patron saint, **La Virgen del Remedio,** from August 3 to 5 through choral concerts and processions. During late July and early August, Playa de San Juan becomes a stage for ballet and musical performances for the **Plataforma Cultural** series. (Events on Playa de San Juan free.) Monthly schedules for these festivals can be found on the tourist office website (www.alicanteturismo.com).

LAS ISLAS BALEARES

While all four islands—Mallorca, Menorca, Ibiza, and Formentera—share the crowds, each has a unique style and character that separates it from the rest. Mallorca, home to the bustling port city of Palma, absorbs the bulk of high-class, package-tour invaders and reigns as the commercial hub of the Baleares. Ibiza, a haven for counter-culture since the 1960s, entices bohemians and fashionistas alike with its outlandish parties, transforming crowds into glittering masses grooving to a deafening techno beat. Menorca, wrapped in green fields, staggering sandstone walls, and placid natural harbors, offers tranquility that the other islands do not, with secluded white beaches, fabulous hidden coves, and mysterious Bronze Age megaliths. Formentera, the smallest and most distant island, is sprinkled with a few fishing villages and boutique resorts, and boasts some of the calmest and most majestic beaches in the Mediterranean.

Summer, the best time to visit any of the islands, is hot, crowded, and fun, while winter tends to be chilly and slow, as nightlife does not hit full swing until around early July. Most hours, schedules, and prices listed are for summer only. Low-season prices at hostels and hotels can drop by up to half, and hours for sights and attractions are often limited.

HIGHLIGHTS OF LAS ISLAS BALEARES

BASK in the island sun on the beaches of **Ibiza** (p. 230).

GIGGLE in a laughing gas booth at a discoteca in party town **Ibiza City** (p. 226).

INTERCITY TRANSPORTATION

Flying to the islands is cheap and much faster than taking a ferry. Those under 26 can get discounts with **Iberia Airlines** (in Barcelona ☎902 40 05 00; www.iberia.com). Many travel agencies in Barcelona and Valencia book special airfare packages that include entrance to nightlife hot spots throughout the islands.

BY PLANE

Scheduled flights are the easiest to book, and flights from Spain to the islands won't break the bank as long as you reserve early. Frequent flights leave from cities throughout Spain and Europe (including Frankfurt, London, Paris, and Rome). Many daily Iberia flights connect Palma and Ibiza to Barcelona, Madrid, and Valencia. The cheapest way to get to Menorca is from Barcelona. Flights from the other cities are more expensive. Service from Alicante, Almería, and Bilbao also exists, but is less frequent and sometimes only available during peak summer months.

Iberia offers flights from Barcelona to Ibiza (55min.) and Madrid (1hr.). Prices for these flights can range from €30 to several hundred euro. **Air Europa** (☎902 40 15 01; www.air-europa.com), **Spanair** (☎902 13 14 15; www.spanair.com), and **Vueling** (☎902 33 39 33; www.vueling.com) also offer inexpensive flights to the islands through special *ofertas* if booked well in advance. Schedules and prices are highly variable and subject to change. Another option is a charter flight, sometimes offered as a division of scheduled airline companies. Most deals entail a stay in a hotel, but some companies (called *mayoristas*) sell

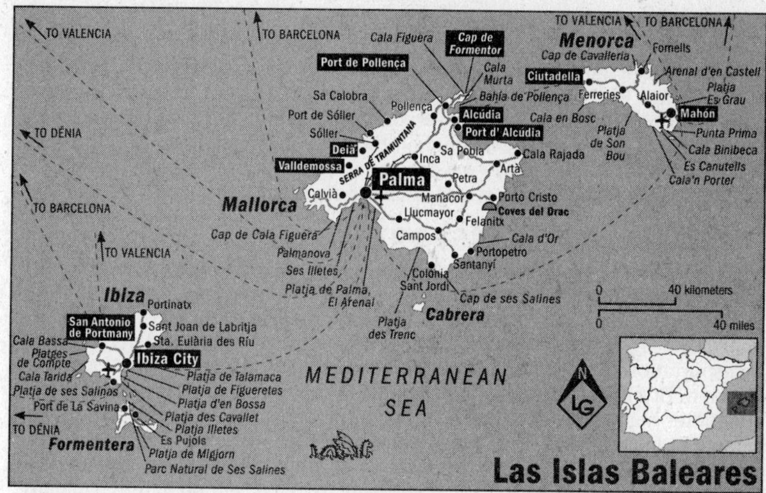

unoccupied seats on package-tour flights. Prices during summer, San Juan, and *Semana Santa* are higher than in low season (Oct.-May), when tickets are fairly easy to get not long before departure. Those traveling in July or August should reserve at least a month in advance, especially to Ibiza and Palma.

BY BOAT

Ferry service is not always cheaper than flying, and it takes longer. Discotecas and small swimming pools on some boats ease the ride, but beware that not all boats run at the same speed. Try to book the high-speed ferry options that take only 2-4hr. Ferries run from Barcelona and Valencia to Palma and Ibiza, and from Dénia (in Alicante) to Ibiza. Seats may be available up to an hour before departure, but reserve tickets a few days in advance to be sure.

Balearia (☎902 16 01 80; www.balearia.com) ferries run from **Dénia's** Estació Marítima, Valencia, or **Barcelona** to **Ibiza** (2-4hr., 2 per day, from €48), also with service to **Palma, Port d'Alcudia,** and **Formentera** (from €48).

Buquebus (☎902 41 42 42; www.buquebus.com) has super-fast catamaran service between **Barcelona** and **Palma** (3hr., 2 per day, €30-150).

Acciona Trasmediterránea (☎902 45 46 45; www.trasmediterranea.com) boats depart daily from **Barcelona's** Estació Marítima Moll, **Alicante,** and **Valencia's** Estació Marítima to **Ibiza, Mallorca,** and **Menorca.** Fares from the mainland are €30-150, depending on speed and distance. Fares between the islands range €28-75.

LOCAL TRANSPORTATION

INTER-ISLAND TRANSPORT

Iberia flies between Palma and Ibiza (40min., 11 per day, €72-85) and between Palma and Maó, Menorca (35min., 11 per day, from €84). **Air Europa, Spanair,** and **Vueling** (see **By Plane, p. 224**) connect the islands at similar prices.

Another viable option is to take the **ferry.** Prices and schedules change almost monthly, and can be infrequent depending on the season. It's best to consult with the tourist office or a travel agent. Ferries to and from Mahón can be lengthy (4hr.), but "fast ferries" now make the journey between the other three islands in under 2hr. **Trasmediterránea** (☎902 45 46 45) sails from Palma to Mahón (5hr., Su 8am, €41) and Ibiza (2hr., Su 8am and 8pm, €31-48). There is no direct Mahón-Ibiza connection. **Trasmapi** (☎902 16 01 80) links Ibiza and Formentera (25-35min., 6-10 per day depending on the season 7:10am-8pm, €15-21). **Iscomar Ferries** (☎902 11 91 28; www.iscomar.com) run between Menorca's Port de Ciutadella and Mallorca's Port d'Alcúdia for daytrips.

INTRA-ISLAND TRANSPORT

The three major islands have extensive bus systems, although in quieter areas (especially Menorca) transportation comes nearly to a halt on Sundays. Palma and Ibiza are especially easy to navigate by bus. Mallorca has two narrow-gauge train systems that are more of a tourist attraction than a major mode of transportation, although many recommend taking the train at least once for the view. Bus fares between cities range €1.20-7.50 each way. Cars and mopeds (the latter being substantially cheaper and riskier) are great ways to explore remote or inaccessible areas. On Mallorca and Menorca, roads can be confusing and dangerous, so cars are the best option, while in Ibiza and Formentera, a moped is adequate. Always ride mopeds with extreme caution. A tiny, standard transmission car costs around €45 per day, including insurance. Mopeds cost around €35, and bicycles a mere €8-15.

IBIZA (EIVISSA)

Nowhere on Earth are decadence, debauchery, and downright hedonism celebrated as religiously as on the turquoise shores of the island of Ibiza (pop. 84,000). Traces of Ibiza's 1960s hippie days still remain amongst the locals and expat populations. In many ways, however, the island has strayed from its bohemian roots towards an extravagant, techno-fueled party mecca. Disco fiends, movie stars, and party-hungry backpackers arrive in droves over the summer to be swept up in the island's outrageous party culture and to bake on its warm sands. Despite Ibiza's wild spirit, the island is a safe and accepting place, where anyone can come to let their hair down.

IBIZA CITY (EIVISSA) ☎971

During the day, Ibiza City (pop. 40,000) is a boutique-laden portside town beneath a 16th-century walled city; it would seem like any seaside village in Spain. At night, however, you couldn't possibly mistake this town for any other. Come sunset, flashy bars and a flashier crowd seem to appear out of nowhere, flooding the port with neon lights, drag queens, pumping music, street stands, and fast-talking promoters. At 3am the scene migrates to the colossal discotecas outside of town, where parties last until dawn (and often well beyond).

TRANSPORTATION

Flights: Airport (☎971 80 90 00), 7.5km southwest of the city, near Ses Salinas. Bus #10 runs between airport and Av. d'Isidor Macabich, 20 (30min.; summer 2 per hr. 6:50am-11:50pm, winter every hr. 7:30am-11:35pm; €1.35). Taxis cost around €14-15. **Iberia,** Pg. Vara de Rey, 15 (☎902 40 05 00), flies to **Alicante, Barcelona, Madrid, Palma,** and **Valencia. Air Europa** (☎902 40 15 01), **Vueling** (☎971 80 90

00), and **Spanair** (☎902 13 14 15) offer similar options. See **By Plane,** p. 224, or **Inter-Island Transport**, p. 225.

Ferries: Estació Marítima and **Estació Marítima Formentera.** Trasmediterránea (☎902 45 46 45) sells tickets for ferries to **Barcelona, Palma,** and **Valencia.** Office open M-F 9am-1pm and 4:30-7:30pm, and 2hr. before departures. **Trasmapi-Balearia** (☎971 31 07 11) runs daily to **Dénia,** near **Alicante, Palma,** and **Formentera.** Office open M-F 9am-2:15pm, 4:30-8pm, and midnight-1:15am; Sa 9am-2:15pm and 6-8pm; Su 9am-2:15pm and midnight-1:15am. **Umafisa Lines** (☎971 19 10 88) sends boats to **Barcelona** 3-4 times per week. For more info., see **Inter-Island Transport,** p. 225.

Buses: Ibiza City has an extensive bus system, but buses to remote areas run only a few times per day. The **bus station** is on Av. d'Isidor Macabich, past Pl. d'Enric Fajarnés i Tur walking away from the port. For an exact schedule, check the tourist office, though sometimes schedules posted at the bus stops themselves are more reliable. **Intercity buses** leave from Av. d'Isidor Macabich, 42 (☎971 31 21 17), to **Sant Antoni** (M-Sa every 15min., Su every 30min. 7:30am-midnight; €1.60) and **Santa Eulària des Riu** (#13 M-F 2 per hr., Sa-Su every hr.; €1.60). Buses to the beaches (☎971 34 03 82) cost €1.35 and leave from Av. d'Isidor Macabich, 20, and Av. d'Espanya to: **Cala Tarida** (5 per day 10:10am-6:45pm); **Cap Martinet** (in summer every hr. M-F 8:15am-11:15pm; in winter M-Sa 9 per day 8:15am-7:30pm); **Platja d'en Bossa** (7:45am and every 30min. 8:30am-11pm); **Ses Salinas** (#11; in summer 3:45 pm and every hr. 9:30am-1:30pm and 4:30pm-7:30pm, in winter M, W, F 10am and 1pm).

Taxis: ☎971 39 84 83 (listed in the *Diario de Ibiza*)

Car and Moped Rental: Casa Valentín, Av. B.V. Ramón, 19 (☎971 31 08 22 or 30 35 31 for the branch on C. Galicia 35; www.welcome.to/casavalentin). Mopeds €25-46 per day. Cars from €36-60 per day. Open daily 9am-1pm and 4-8pm.

LAS ISLAS BALEARES

ORIENTATION AND PRACTICAL INFORMATION

Ibiza City's energy flourishes in the three small districts clustered to the south of the port. **Sa Penya** and **La Marina** are situated side-by-side on the port and are crammed with bars, restaurants, boutiques, and trinket stands. Rising steeply behind this packed grid of streets is **D'alt Vila,** the historic walled town overlooking the sea. There are four available entrances to D'alt Vila, but the easiest and most central is **Portal de Ses Taules,** the cobblestone pedestrian ramp, just behind the Mercat Vell off Antoni Palau. **Pg. Vara de Rey** leads to La Marina and D'alt Vila from **Avinguda d'Espanya,** which runs to **Platja Figuretas** and boardwalk restaurants. The local paper, *Diario de Ibiza* (€1; www.diariodeibiza.es) has an *Agenda* page with essential information, including water and weather forecasts, and information on the island's 24hr. pharmacies and gas stations, hours for popular museums, and important phone numbers.

Tourist Office: Pg. Vara de Rey (☎971 30 19 00). Open M-F 9am-8pm, Sa 9am-7pm, Su 9am-3pm. Winter schedule subject to change. Second location at airport (☎971 19 43 93). Open May-Oct. Tu-Su 10am-2pm and 5-8pm.

Currency Exchange: *Casas de cambio* do exist in town, but banks and ATMs offer better rates. Major banks like **La Caixa, BBVA, Sa Nostra,** and **Deutsche Bank** huddle around the intersection of Av. d'Espanya and Av. D'Ignasi Wallis, at the end of Pg. Vara de Rey.

Laundromat: Wash and Dry, Av. d'Espanya, 53 (☎971 39 48 22). Self-service wash and dry €13, with service €15, ironing €1.50-3.50 per article.

Police: C. Vicent Serra (☎971 39 88 31 or 092).

Medical Services: Barrio Can Misses (☎971 39 70 00), a **hospital** west of town, and the large **Hospital Nuestra Señora del Rosario,** C. de Vía Romana, s/n (☎971 30 19 16), near the corner of C. Juan Ramón Jiménez. **Ambulance:** ☎971 39 32 32.

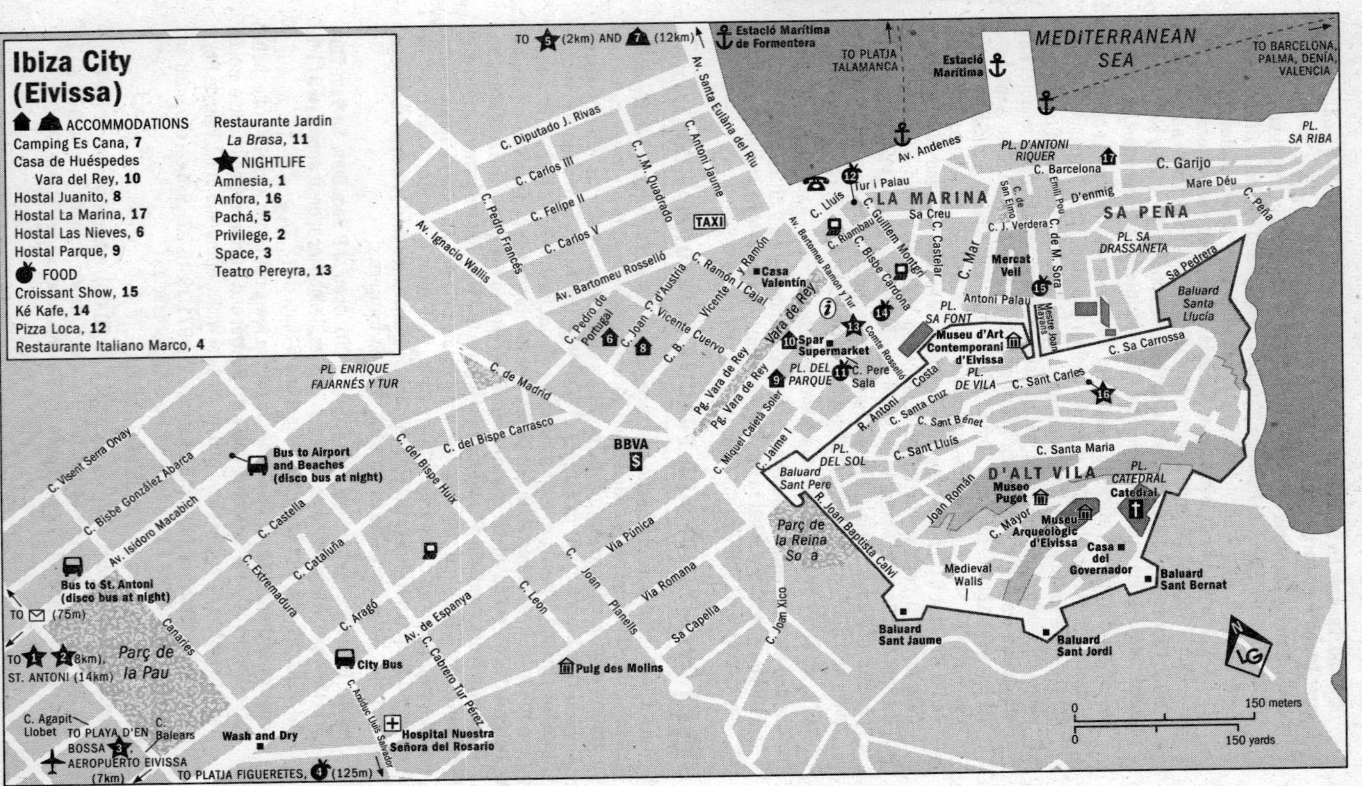
Ibiza City (Eivissa)
ACCOMMODATIONS
Camping Es Cana, 7
Casa de Huéspedes Vara del Rey, 10
Hostal Juanito, 8
Hostal La Marina, 17
Hostal Las Nieves, 6
Hostal Parque, 9
FOOD
Croissant Show, 15
Ké Kafe, 14
Pizza Loca, 12
Restaurante Italiano Marco, 4
Restaurante Jardin La Brasa, 11
NIGHTLIFE
Amnesia, 1
Anfora, 16
Pachá, 5
Privilege, 2
Space, 3
Teatro Pereyra, 13
TO (2km) AND (12km)
Estació Marítima de Formentera
TO PLATJA TALAMANCA
Estació Marítima
MEDITERRANEAN SEA
TO BARCELONA, PALMA, DENIA, VALENCIA
PL. SA RIBA
PL. D'ANTONI RIQUER
LA MARINA
SA PEÑA
PL. SA DRASSANETA
Mercat Vell
PL. SA FONT
Museu d'Art Contemporani d'Eivissa
Baluard Santa Llúcia
PL. DE VILA
PL. DEL PARQUE
PL. DEL SOL
D'ALT VILA
PL. CATEDRAL
Catedral
Museo Puget
Museu Arqueològic d'Eivissa
Casa del Governador
Baluard Sant Bernat
Baluard Sant Pere
Parç de la Reina Sofia
Medieval Walls
Baluard Sant Jaume
Baluard Sant Jordi
Casa Valentín
Spar Supermarket
BBVA
PL. ENRIQUE FAJARNÉS Y TUR
Bus to Airport and Beaches (disco bus at night)
Bus to St. Antoni (disco bus at night)
TO (75m)
TO (8km), ST. ANTONI (14km)
Parç de la Pau
City Bus
Puig des Molins
Hospital Nuestra Señora del Rosario
Wash and Dry
TO PLAYA D'EN BOSSA
AEROPUERTO EIVISSA (7km)
TO PLATJA FIGUERETES, (125m)
Av. Santa Eulària del Riu
Av. Andenes
Av. Ignacio Wallis
Av. Bartomeu Rosselló
Av. Bartomeu Ramon y Tur
Vara de Rey
Pg. Vara de Rey
Av. Isidoro Macabich
Av. de Espanya
Via Púnica
Via Romana
150 meters
150 yards

Internet Access: *Locutorios* abound by Platja Figueretes and among the streets behind the Estació Marítima de Formentera. Otherwise, try **Euro Ibiza Locutorio,** Av. Espanya, 91 (☎971 39 25 29). €.50 per 15min., €1 per hr. Open daily 10am-11pm. Also at **Touba Khelkom,** Av. Espanya, 32 (☎971 39 84 54). €0.50 per 15min., €2 per hr. Open daily 10am-midnight. Also at **Wash and Dry** (see above).

Post Office: (☎971 19 71 97). At the end of Av. d' Isidor Macabich away from the port. **Lista de Correos**. Open M-F 8:30am-8:30pm, Sa 9:30am-2pm. **Postal Code:** 07800.

ACCOMMODATIONS AND CAMPING

Hostels abound in the city, but few have it all. The best and safest accommodations are by the port, most off of Vara de Rey. The letters "CH" *(casa de huéspedes)* mark many doorways, and although these are often cheaper and have more character than *hostales*, prices still remain above €30 and reservations are often more difficult to make.

Hostel Parque, Pl. del Parque 4 (☎971 30 13 58; www.hostalparque.com). The most well-known hostel in town, ideally located below D'Alt Vila in the lively Plaza del Parque, where locals and tourists sip mojitos into the night. Large, airy rooms overlook the city. Mar.-June singles €45, doubles €110; July-Aug. singles €60, doubles €110. MC/V. ❹

Hostal La Marina/Los Caracoles, C. Barcelona 7 (☎971 31 01 72). Rooms are some of the best in town—each single, double, and mini suite has individual character, with royal blue walls and tidy, inviting beds. Rooms in La Marina (open year-round) have TV and A/C, but those across the street in Loc Caracoles (open Apr.-Oct.) are less expensive. All with private baths. €58 for basic single; €175 for mini suite. MC/V. ❺

Casa de Huespedes Vara de Rey, Pg. Vara e Rey, 7, 3rd fl. (☎971 30 13 76; www.hibiza.com). This bohemian hostel has truly unique rooms, decorated with everything from Tibetan prayer flags to fishing nets. The three flights of stairs can feel like a mile after a long night of partying, but the views of D'Alt Vila and the port are worth it. Also situated on Plaza del Parque, this establishment provides a less expensive alternative in a prime location. Reserve by phone or through the web site. Reception open M-Sa 9am-2pm and 7-10pm. Singles with shared bathroom €35; doubles, €70. MC/V. ❸

Hostal Juanito/Hostal Las Nieves, C. Joan d'Austria, 17-18 (☎971 19 03 19; www.hostalesibiza.com). Across the street from each other and under the same ownership, both hostels offer reasonably priced housing in a central area. All rooms come equipped with cheery yellow-and-blue tiled sinks and large windows. Juanito open year-round; Las Nieves (cheapest rooms with shared bath) open June-Sept. Singles €30; doubles €45, with bath €75. MC/V. ❸

Camping Es Cana (☎971 33 21 17; www.ibiza-spotlight.com/campescana). Pool and clubhouse. Close to restaurants and bars by the beach Des Canar, but a fair distance from Ibiza City. Reserve by phone. €6.50 per person, €7-12 per tent (depending on size). Bungalows €30-75, cabins €30. MC/V. ❶

FOOD

Ibizan dishes include *sofrit pagès*, a deep-fried lamb and chicken dish, *flao*, a lush lemon- and mint-tinged cheesecake, and *graxonera*, cinnamon-dusted pudding made from eggs and bits of *ensaimada* (sugar-coated bread). *Hierbas Ibicencas*, the island's strong, spicy favorite liqueur, often comes complimentary after restaurant meals. The small Mercat Vell, at the mouth of the Portal de ses Taules leading to D'Alt Vila, sells meat, fruit, and vegetables, among many other non-food products (open M-Sa 7am-7pm). For groceries, try **Spar Supermarket,** near Pl. del Parc (open M-Sa 9am-9pm).

Ke Kafe, C. Bisbe Azara, 5 (☎971 19 40 04; www.kekafe.com). Rough stone walls are decorated with local art, and orange globe lights bob from the ceilings of this new-age Middle Eastern restaurant. Try the 7 Pekados salad, with fresh strawberries, goat cheese, walnuts, and baby spinach (€7). MC/V. ❷

Croissant Show, Mercat Vell (☎971 31 76 65), on C. Antoni Palau. Bright cafe serves creative sandwiches (€4.50-6), quiches, salads, pastries, and *platos del dia* (€7.50). Popular for breakfast after a night of clubbing. Open daily 6am-2am (closes early for rain). MC/V. ❶

Pizza Loca, C. Lluís Tur i Palau, 15. Oven-heated pizza in all varieties is popular among young bar-hoppers at this happy hole-in-the-wall right on the port. Try the spinach, tomato, and mozzarella with a bit of cumin. Slices €2.70-4. Open daily 11am-4:30am. Cash only. ❶

Restaurante Jardin La Brasa, C. Pere Sala, 3 (☎971 30 12 02). Amongst a maze of candlelit white tables and walls covered with brilliant pink flowers, customers enjoy innovative food in an intimate atmosphere. Try the mussels in almond sauce (€10.50), or the rabbit (€18). Kitchen closes at 11pm, bar open later. MC/V. ❸

Restaurante Italiano Marco, Po. de ses Pitiuses (☎971 30 10 69). This elegant boardwalk establishment, especially popular among tourists, offers candlelit patio seating and friendly service above the sea on Platja Figuretas. Traditional *spaghetti bolognese* (€7.50), soups (€4.50), and pizzas (€5.50-12), with a separate vegetarian menu. Open 8pm-midnight. MC/V. ❷

SIGHTS

Ibiza City's best known sites are portside—the drag queens, disco publicity stunts, and vacationers-gone-wild make people-watching a competitive sport. Rising just behind is another group of sights, enclosed in the 16th-century walls of **D'alt Vila** (Old Town), declared a UNESCO World Heritage site in 1999.

14TH-CENTURY CATHEDRAL. Originally a Carthaginian temple, this cathedral is in the center of town near a small castle. *(Open M-Sa 9:30am-1:30pm).*

MUSEU ARQUELÒGIC D'EIVISSA. This museum houses a variety of artifacts dating from the Phoenician and Carthaginian days of the island. *(Across the small plaza before the cathedral. ☎971 30 12 31. Open Tu-Sa 10am-2pm and 6-8pm, Su 10am-2pm; in winter Tu-Sa 9am-3pm. €2.40, students €1.20, under 18 and 65+ free.)*

MUSEU D'ART CONTEMPORANI D'EIVISSA. The small museum displays art exhibitions ranging from video installations to photography, including a wide array of work by local artists and traveling international collections. *(Ronda de Narcís Puget, at the base of the old city. ☎971 30 27 23. Open Tu-F 10am-1:30pm and 5-8pm, Sa-Su 10am-1:30pm. €1.20, students free.)*

THE MUSEO PUGET. A building on the descent from the cathedral, this museum contains contemporary art by local artists like Antoni Pomar. *(☎971 39 21 47. Open Tu-F 10:30am-1:30pm and 4-6pm. Free.)*

PUIG DES MOLINS. This archaeological museum displays Punic, Roman, and Iberian artifacts. *(Vía Romana, 31 between Platja Figueretes and D'Alt Vila. ☎971 30 17 71. Open Tu-Sa 9am-3pm, Su 10am-2pm. €1.20.)*

BEACHES

In Ibiza City, if you're not at a disco, you're at the beach. Beaches feature satin sands, pale shores, and seas of shading umbrellas. More private coastal stretches lie along the northern and southwestern shores of the island and are accessible by car or moped. Still, there will be crowds everywhere you go. If you're looking for abandoned sands, you're better off heading to Formentera.

PLATJA DE SES SALINAS. A constant party, this beach is reflective of modern Ibiza. Masses of beautiful bodies groove to the New Age music pulsating from the Sa Trincha bar at the end of the beach. Reserve a beach chair for €6 in front of **The Jockey Club** (☎971 39 57 88; www.jockeyclubibiza.com) and receive full bar and restaurant service right from the sand as top DJs warm up for their club gigs. *(Bus #11 runs every hr. to Salinas from Av. d'Isidor Macabich, but not between 1:30pm and 4pm.)*

PLATJA FIGUERETES. This beach is just a short stretch of sand connected by a pedestrian boardwalk lined by large hotels, restaurants, and street-stands. *(Take a 15min. walk from Pl. Vera Rey down Av. d'Espanya and a left on Ramon Muntaner.)*

PLATJA D'EN BOSSA. The longest and liveliest of Ibiza's beaches, the Platja d'en Bossa has thumping bars and throngs of sun-seeking tourists. After tanning all day, take a dance break at the famous open club **Bora Bora** right on the beach. With an outside platform, a beachside bar, and blasting techno, this spot attracts half-naked dancers ready to party all day and into the night. *(Most efficiently reached by bus or ferry. Bus #14 runs every 30min. from Av. d'Isidor Macabich.)*

PLATJA DE TALAMANCA. This beach is a calm stretch of sand where a laid-back clientele enjoys the few bars and restaurants. *(On the opposite side of the port from town. 30min. walk or ferry from the port.)*

CALA DE SANT VINCENT. Among the more private coastal stretches, the German enclave at Cala de Sant Vincent offers white sands and breathtaking views. *(Past Santa Eulària des Riu on the road to St. Carles de Peralta.)*

CALA CARBÓ. This beach is small but beautiful, with awe-inspiring cliffs and a fantastic beachfront seafood restaurant. *(South of St. Antoni and west of St. Josep.)*

LAS ISLAS BALEARES

NIGHTLIFE

Bars in Ibiza City are crowded between 11pm and 3am and are the place to meet, greet, see, and be seen. The scene centers on **Carrer de Barcelona** and spills into the side streets, which can be jammed to the point of immobility, especially around midnight, when the area is flooded with discotecas promoters. All discos are outside of town, except for **Eden** and **Es Paradis** in St. Antoni which are accessible by foot. The **Discobus** runs to most of the hot spots but can be slow and unpredictable (leaves Ibiza City from Av. d'Isidor Macabich every hour in summer 12:30am-6:30am, schedule for other stops available at tourist office and hotels; €1.75). The main taxi line to the discos is at the end of the port on Av. Bartolome de Rosello—the line is usually long but moves quickly.

DON'T PANIC—GO TO THE DISCO! That's right—even the budget traveler can partake of the opulence that defines Ibiza's discos. By going down to C. Barcelona and talking up club promoters around midnight, you can often get a much better deal on club tickets. Stores and bars in town also sell tickets for cheaper than what you'll find at the door.

The island's **discos** are unbelievable, unequaled, and full of the unexpected; veterans claim that you will never experience anything half as wild. Drinks at Ibiza City's clubs are outrageously expensive—beers generally run €10 and mixed drinks €18, while cover runs €27-65. Most clubs open in early June.

Amnesia (☎971 19 80 41), on the road to Sant Antoni. This former warehouse has a phenomenal sound system, often accented by a live electric violinist. The central dance floor is flooded with psychedelic lights, vents spewing liquid nitrogen, acrobatic go-go dancers, and lasers. This club is also famous for its mobbed annual foam parties. Cover from €20-50. Opens daily 11pm-8am.

Space, Platja d'en Bossa (☎971 39 67 93; www.space-ibiza.es). Hopping party at virtually all hours. "We Love Space 08 Sundays" rocks out nonstop Su 4pm to M 6am, June 15-Sept. 28. Sa mornings "Matinee Group," W "La Troya," and Tu after-parties with Carl Cox are also popular. Cover €30-60. Open at midnight every night.

Pachá (☎971 31 36 00; www.pacha.com), 15min. from the port by foot. The most famous club chain in Spain, and the most elegant of Ibiza City's discos—complete with go-go dancers and all. Cocktails from €10. "Release Yourself" on M brings out the best up-and-coming DJs, and fabulous parties on F attract a rowdy crowd. Only club open year-round. Cover €35-60. Open daily midnight-7:30am.

Privilege (☎971 19 80 86; www.privilegeibiza.com), in the Urbanización San Rafael. On the Discobus to Sant Antoni, near Amnesia. There is a free Privilege bus that leaves from the Estació Marítima every 30min. Taxi €9. One of the world's largest clubs, filled with laughing gas booths and erotic dancers. The absence of a dress code translates to lots of bare skin. Cover from €30-50. Open June-Sept. daily midnight-7am. MC/V.

Anfora, C. Sant Carles, 7, in the D'alt Vila. A gay disco built into the hillside of the old city, the club's sunken dance floor sits beneath a small maze of bohemian lounges, tiled bars, and terraces. Don't miss Th "Night Fever" and Tu "Madonna." Cover €10, after 2am €15; includes 1 drink. Open daily midnight-6am.

Teatro Pereyra, C. Conde Rosello, 3 (☎871 30 44 32; www.teatropereyra.com). Despite Ibiza's roots in rock n' roll, this is the only true live music venue left in the city, where a smokin' blues band plays jaw-dropping solos. A converted theater lobby, Pereyra draws a somewhat older fun-loving crowd and many visiting musical artists. Music starts at 11pm every night and doesn't stop until late. Minimum consumption €7. MC/V.

BARCELONA

HIGHLIGHTS OF BARCELONA

RAMBLE along La Rambla and revel in the exuberant **Barri Gòtic** (p. 260).

CHILL at an outdoor jazz concert on the roof of the fantastical **Casa Milà** (p. 265).

IMAGINE what the future will bring to the unfinished **La Sagrada Família** (p. 267).

SIP to a speedy return at the **Font de les Canaletes** (p. 261).

INTERCITY TRANSPORTATION

Flights: Aeroport El Prat de Llobregat (**BCN;** ☎902 40 47 04; www.aena.es), 13km southwest of Barcelona. To get to Pl. Catalunya, take the **Aerobus** (☎934 15 60 20) in front of terminals A, B, or C (35-40min.; every 6-15min.; to Pl. Catalunya daily 6am--1am, to the airport 5:30am-12:15am; €4.05, round-trip €7.30). For early-morning flights, the Nitbus **N17** runs from Pl. Catalunya to all 3 terminals (from Pl. Catalunya every hr. 11pm-5am, from the airport every hr. 9:50pm-4:50am; €1.35). Cheaper, and usually a bit faster than the Aerobus is the **RENFE train** (C2; 20-25min. to Estació Sants, 25-30min. to Pg. de Gràcia; every 30min., from airport 6am-11:38pm, from Estació Sants to airport 5:35am-11:09pm; €2.80). To reach the train, take the pedestrian overpass in front of the airport (it's on the left when your back is to the entrance). **Taxis** (☎933 033 033) are in front of terminals A, B, and C; €25-30 to Pl. Espanya and Pl. Catalunya; €35 to Sagrada Familia.

Trains: Barcelona has 2 main train stations. **Estació Barcelona-Sants,** in Pl. Països Catalans (ⓂSants Estació), is the main terminal for domestic and international traffic. **Estació de França,** on Av. Marquès de l'Argentera (ⓂBarceloneta), services regional destinations, including Tarragona and Zaragoza, and a limited number of international locations. Note that trains often stop before the main stations; check the schedule. **RENFE** (reservations and info ☎902 24 02 02, international 24 34 02) to: **Bilbao** (6½-9hr., 12:30 and 11pm, €41-60); **Madrid** (3hr.; from mid-June to mid-Sept. 14-21 per day, from mid-Sept. to mid-June 4-7 per day; €44); **Sevilla** (5½-12hr., 3 per day 8am-10:05pm, €59-132); **Valencia** (3-4 hr., 14 per day, €34-41). International destinations include **Milan, ITA** (via **Figueres** and **Turin**) and **Montpellier, FRA,** with connections to Geneva, Paris, and the French Riviera. 20% discount on round-trip tickets.

Buses: Arrive at the **Barcelona Nord Estació d'Autobusos,** C. Alí-bei, 80 (☎902 26 06 06; www.barcelonanord.com). ⓂArc de Triomf or #54 bus. Info booth open 7am-9pm. Buses also depart from Estació Sants and the airport. **Sarfa** (☎902 30 20 25; www.sarfa.es). Bus stop and ticket office also at Ronda Sant Pere, 21 (☎933 02 62 23). To: **Cadaqués** (2¾hr.; M-F 2-4 per day 10:30am-7pm Sa-Su 2-4 per day 10:30am-8:45pm; €21); **Palafrugell** (2hr., 8-15 per day 8:15am-8:30pm, €16); **Tossa de Mar** via **Lloret de Mar** (1½hr., 7-13 per day 8am-8:30pm, €11). **Eurolines** (☎93 265 07 88; www.eurolines.es) goes to **Paris, FRA** via **Lyon** (15hr., M-Sa 9:30pm, €75-91); 10% discount under 26 or over 60. **ALSA/Enatcar** (☎902 42 22 42; www.alsa.es) goes to: **Alicante** (7-9hr., 8 per day, €41-46); **Bilbao** (7-8½hr., 4-7 per day, €42); **Madrid** (8hr., 18-21 per day 7am-1am, €29-41); **Sevilla** (15-20hr., 3 per day, €89); **Valencia** (4-5hr., 8 per day, €25-30); **Zaragoza** (4hr., 3-21 per day, €14-21).

Ferries: Transmediterránea (☎902 45 46 45; www.transmediterranea.es), in Terminal Drassanes, Moll Sant Bertran. **"Fast" ferry** (€51-69; round-trip €96-€103) June-Aug. to **Ibiza** (8-9hr., 1 per day Tu and Th-Su), **Mahón** (8½hr., M and W-Su 10:30pm), and **Palma de Mallorca** (8hr., 1-2 per day).

LOCAL TRANSPORTATION

METRO AND BUS

Barcelona's public transportation (info ☎010) is quick and cheap. If you plan to use public transportation extensively, there are several Autoritat del Transport Metropolità (ATM; www.atm.cat) *abonos* (passes) available, which work interchangeably for the Metro, bus, and urban lines of the FGC commuter trains, RENFE Cercanías, Trams, and Nitbus. The **T-10 pass** (€7.70) is valid for 10 rides and saves you nearly 50% off single tickets. The **T-Dia pass** (€5.80) is good for a full day of unlimited travel, and the **T-mes** (€48) is good for a month. If you just plan to use the Metro and daytime buses, there are 2-5 day passes at **Transports Metropolitans de Barcelona (TMB;** ☎933 18 70 74; www.tmb.net; 2 days €11, 5 days €24). These will save you money if you plan to ride the Metro more than three times per day.

Metro: (☎932 98 70 00; www.tmb.net). Vending machines and ticket windows sell passes. Red diamonds with the white letter "M" mark stations. Hold on to your ticket—riding without one can incur a €40 fine. Trains run M-Th, Su, and holidays 5am-midnight, F 5am-2am, Sa non-stop service. Extended holiday hours. €1.40 per *senzill/sencillo* (1-way ticket). Switching lines may involve a considerable walk.

Ferrocarrils de la Generalitat de Catalunya (FGC): (☎932 05 15 15; www.fgc.es). Commuter trains to local destinations with main stations at Pl. de Catalunya and Pl. d'Espanya. Note that some destinations within the city (parts of Gràcia and beyond) require taking the FGC. Blue symbols resembling 2 interlocking "V"s mark Metro connections. The commuter line costs the same as the Metro (€1.40) as far as Tibidabo. After that, rates go up by zone: Zone 2 €2.10, Zone 3 €2.90, etc. Metro passes are valid on FGC trains. Info office at the Pl. de Catalunya station open M-F 7am-9pm.

RENFE Cercanías (Rodalies): (☎902 24 02 02; www.renfe.es/cercanias). The C2 Nord to the **airport** (Zone 4; €2.80) is particularly useful. Destinations include **Blanes** (C1, Zone 6; €4.40) and **Sitges** (C2 Sud, Zone 4; €2.80). Main connections at Sants and Pg. de Gràcia, marked by either the RENFE double arrows or a funny-looking red circle with a backwards C.

Buses: Go almost anywhere, usually from 5am-10pm (many leave for the last round at 9:30pm). Most stops have maps, and you can easily figure out which bus to take. Many run on natural gas. Most buses come in central locations every 10-15min. €1.40.

Nitbus: (www.emt-amb.cat/links/cat/cnitbus.htm). 18 different lines run every 20-30min. 10:30pm-4:30am, depending on the line; a few run until 5:30am. All buses depart from around Pl. de Catalunya, stop in front of most club complexes, and work their way through Ciutat Vella and the Zona Alta. Maps are available at *estancos* (tobacco shops), at some bus stops, online, and in Metro stations.

Bus Turístic: Hop-on, hop-off tours of the city. Passes sold for 1-2 days (€21, €27).

TAXIS

About 11,000 taxis swarm the city. A *"lliure"* or *"libre"* sign or a green light on the roof means vacant; yellow means occupied. On weekend nights, you may wait up to 30min. for a ride; long lines form at popular spots like the Port

Olímpic. To call a cab, try **RadioTaxi033** (☎933 033 033; www.radiotaxi033.com; AmEx/MC/V) or **Servi Taxi** (☎933 30 03 00). **Taxi Amic** has wheelchair-accessible vehicles. (☎934 20 80 88).

CAR AND MOPED RENTAL

Avis, C. Corcega, 293-295 (☎932 37 56 80; www.avis.es). Open M-F 8am-9pm, Sa 8am-8pm, Su 8am-1pm. Branches at **airport** (☎932 98 36 00; open daily 7am-12:30am) and **Estació Sants,** Pl. dels Països Catalans, s/n. (☎933 30 41 93; open M-F 7:30am-11:30pm, Sa 8am-9pm, Su 9am-9pm).

Budget (☎932 98 36 00; www.budget.es), in the airport. Open M-Sa 7am-12:30am, Su 7am-midnight.

Cooltra, Pg. Joan de Borbo, 80-84 (☎93 221 40 70; www.cooltra.com). ⓂBarceloneta. Mopeds from €32 per day between 9:30am-8:30pm, €42 per 24hr., and €290 per month. Open daily from June to mid-Sept. 9am-8:30pm, from mid-Sept. to May 10am-8pm.

Europcar, Pl. Països Catalanes, s/n (☎902 10 50 55; www.europcar.es), near Sants. Open M-F 7am-12am, Sa-Su 8am-11pm. Branch at the airport (☎902 10 50 55). Open 24hr.

Hertz, Av. Diagonal, 3 (☎933 56 11 39; www.hertz.es). ⓂMareseme Fòrum. Open M-Sa 10am-10pm. Branch at the airport (☎932 98 36 37; open daily 7am-midnight) and by **Estació Sants,** C. Viriat, 45 (☎934 19 61 56; open M-F 8am-9:30pm, Sa-Su 8am-2:30pm).

BIKE RENTAL

Budget Bikes (☎933 04 18 85; www.budgetbikes.eu), C. Marquès de Barberà, 15 (ⓂLiceu); C. General Castaños, 6 (ⓂBarceloneta); C. Estruc, 38 (ⓂPl. Catalunya). €6 per 2hr., €16 per day, €26 per 2 days, each extra day after that €7. Themed tours €22-28. Open daily 10am-8pm.

Barcelona Bici, Mirador de Colom. (☎932 85 38 32). €4.50 per hr., €11 per 4hr., €15 per 8 hr., €21 per 2 days, €56per week. Open daily 10-8pm.

Fat Tire, C. Escudellers, 48 (☎933 01 36 12; www.fattirebiketoursbarcelona.com). €6 for 2hr., €10 for 2-4hr., €15 for 1 day, €25 for 2 days. Open daily from Mar. to mid-Dec. 10am-8pm. Famous bike tours include a break at the beach (€22 includes bike rental). Meet in Pl. St. Jaume. Tours from mid-Apr. to Oct. at 11am and 4pm, from Feb. to mid-Apr. and Nov. to mid-Dec. at 11am.

ORIENTATION AND PRACTICAL INFORMATION

Barcelona's layout is easy to visualize if you imagine yourself perched on Columbus's head at the **Monument a Colom** (on Pg. de Colom, along the shore), viewing the city with the sea at your back. From the harbor, the city slopes upward to the mountains. From the Columbus monument, **La Rambla,** the main thoroughfare, runs up to **Plaça de Catalunya** (M: Catalunya), the city center. The heavily touristed historic neighborhood, **Ciutat Vella,** is anchored by La Rambla and encompasses the Barri Gòtic, La Ribera, and El Raval. The **Barri Gòtic** is east of La Rambla (to the right, with your back to the sea), enclosed on the other side by **Via Laietana.** East of Via Laietana lies the maze-like neighborhood of **La Ribera,** bordered by Parc de la Ciutadella and Estació de França. To the west of La Rambla is **El Raval,** Barcelona's most multicultural neighborhood, with a growing number of museums and hip bars.

Beyond La Ribera—farther east, outside Ciutat Vella and curving out into the water—are **Poble Nou** and **Port Olímpic,**which boast the two tallest buildings in Barcelona, not to mention an assortment of discotecas and restaurants on the beach. To the west, beyond El Raval, rises **Montjuïc,** a hill crammed with sprawling gardens, museums, the 1992 Olympic grounds, and a fortress. Directly behind your perch on the Monument a Colom is the **Port Vell** (Old Port) development, where a wavy bridge leads to the ultra-modern (and tourist-packed) shopping and entertainment complexes **Moll d'Espanya** and **Maremàgnum.** North of Ciutat Vella is upscalel**'Eixample,** a gridded neighborhood created during the expansion of the 1860s that sprawls from Pl. de Catalunya toward the mountains. **Gran Via de les Corts Catalanes** defines its lower edge, and the **Passeig de Gràcia,** l'Eixample's main tree- and boutique-lined avenue, bisects this chic neighborhood. **Avinguda Diagonal,** the expansion's largest non-gridded street, marks the border between l'Eixample and the **Zona Alta** ("Uptown"), which includes Pedralbes, Gràcia, and other older neighborhoods in the foothills. The peak of **Tibidabo,** the northwest border of the city, offers the most comprehensive view of Barcelona.

TOURIST AND FINANCIAL SERVICES

Tourist Offices:

Plaça de Catalunya, Pl. de Catalunya, 17S, underground on the bottom left-hand corner facing south (toward La Rambla). ⓂCatalunya. The main office, along with Pl. de Sant Jaume, has free maps, brochures on sights and transportation, booking service for last-minute accommodations, a gift shop, money exchange, and a box office (Caixa de Catalunya). Open daily 9am-9pm.

Plaça de Sant Jaume, C. Ciutat, 2. ⓂJaume I. Open M-F 9am-8pm, Sa 10am-8pm, Su and holidays 10am-2pm.

Oficina de Turisme de Catalunya, Pg. de Gràcia, 107 (☎932 38 80 91; www.gencat.es/probert). ⓂDiagonal. Open M-Sa 10am-7pm, Su 10am-2pm.

Institut de Cultura de Barcelona (ICUB), Palau de la Virreina, La Rambla, 99 (☎933 16 10 00; www.bcn.cat/cultura). Info office open daily 10am-8pm.

Estació Barcelona-Sants, Pl. Països Catalans. (☎902 240 202) ⓂSants-Estació. Info and last-minute accommodation booking. Open June 24-Sept. 24 daily 8am-8pm; Sept. 25-June 23 M-F 8am-8pm, Sa-Su 8am-2pm.

Aeroport del Prat de Llobregat, terminals A and B. Info and last-minute accommodation booking. Open daily 9am-9pm

Tourist Office Representatives booths dot the city in the summer. Open daily July-Sept.; hours vary; many have shorter hours in winter.

Tours: In addition to the Bus Turístic (p. 234), the Pl. de Catalunya tourist office offers 2hr. **walking tours** of the Barri Gòtic daily at 10am (English) and Sa at noon (Catalan and Spanish). Group size limited; buy tickets in advance. (Info ☎932 85 38 32. €12, ages 4-12 €5.) 2hr. **Picasso tour** (☎932 85 38 32) of Barcelona Tu, Th, Sa, 4pm (English) and Sa at 4pm (Spanish or Catalan with pre-booking). €18, ages 4-12 €7, includes entrance to the **Museu Picasso.** 2hr. *Modernisme* tour through L'Eixample's Quadrat d'Or F-Sa 4pm (English) and Sa 4pm (Catalan and Spanish). €12, ages 4-12 €5. Self-guided tours of Gothic, Romanesque, *Modernista,* and Contemporary Barcelona available; pick up pamphlets with maps at the tourist office. **Bike tours** abound; see **Bike Rental** (p. 235). **Barcelona Segway Glides** offers 2hr. tours ("glides") for €60, Mar.-Nov. M-F 10am and 5pm, Dec.-Feb. 11am. Call for reservations. (☎678 77 73 71; www.barcelonasegwayglides.com. Cash only.)

Currency Exchange: ATMs give the best rates. The very best are those marked **Telebanco;** they report the exchange rate on the receipt and on-screen instead of leaving you guessing. Banks are your next best option. General banking hours M-F 8:30am-

2pm. La Rambla has many exchange stations open late, but the rates are not as good and they charge a commission.

American Express: La Rambla, 74 (☎933 42 73 11). Ⓜ Liceu. Open M-F 9am-11pm, Sa 11am-9pm.

LOCAL SERVICES

Luggage Storage: Estació Barcelona-Sants, Ⓜ Sants-Estació. Lockers €4.50 per day. Open daily 5:30am-11pm. **Estació Nord,** Ⓜ Arc de Triomf. Lockers €3.50-5 per day, 90-day limit. Also at the **El Prat Airport.** €5 per day.

Libraries: Visit www.bcn.es/biblioteques for info on Barcelona's libraries. **Biblioteca Francesca Bonnemaison,** C. Sant Pere més Baix, 7 (☎932 68 73 60). Ⓜ Urquinaona. Walk toward the water, then turn left past the Palau de Música Catalana and C. Sant Pere més Alt. Open M-Tu 4-9pm, W 10am-9pm, Th-F 10am-2pm and 4-9pm, Sa 10am-2pm. **Biblioteca Barceloneta-La Fraternitat,** C. Comte de Santa Clara, 8-10 (☎932 25 35 74), 2 blocks from the beach in Port Vell. Open M 4-9pm, Tu 10am-2pm, W 4-9pm, Th 10am-9pm, F 4-9pm. **Biblioteca Sant Pau-Santa Creu,** C. Hospital, 56 (☎933 02 07 97), in El Raval 1 block up C. Hospital from Las Ramblas. Ⓜ Liceu. Open M-Tu 3:30-8:30pm, W-Th 10am-2pm, F 3:30-8:30pm.

Gay and Lesbian Resources: Pick up the official **LGBT tourist guide** at tourist office in Pl. de Catalunya, 17S, which includes a section on LGBT bars, clubs, publications, and more. Barcelona's gay neighborhood is called L'Eixample or, colloquially, **Gaixample. GAYBARCELONA** (www.gaybarcelona.net) and **Infogai** (www.colectiugai.org) are useful websites in Catalan. Another such resource is the **Associació de Famílies Lésbianes i Gais,** Carrer Verdaguer i Callís, 10 (☎645 31 88 60; www.familiesig.org). Some info on the web site of **Barcelona Pride** (www.pridebarcelona.org/en) is seasonal, but the site is useful year-round in identifying gay-friendly businesses. **Antinous,** C. Josep Anselm Clavé, 6 (☎933 01 90 70; antinouslibros.com). Ⓜ Drassanes. Specializes in gay and lesbian books and films. Decent selection in English. Open M-F 10:30am-2pm and 5-8:30pm, Sa noon-2pm and 5-8:30pm. AmEx/MC/V. **Cómplices,** C. Cervantes, 4 (☎934 12 72 83; www.libreriacomplices.com). Ⓜ Liceu. A small gay-friendly bookstore with books in English and Spanish and an adequate selection of films. Also provides a map of Barcelona's gay bars and discotecas. Open M-F 10:30am-8pm, Sa noon-8pm. AmEx/MC/V.

Laundromats: Lavomatic, Pl. Joaquim Xirau, 1, a block off La Rambla and 1 block below C. Escudellers. Branch at C. Consolat del Mar, 43-45 (☎932 68 47 68), 1 block north of Pg. Colon and 2 blocks off Via Laietana. Wash €4.80. Dry €0.90 per 5min. Both open M-Sa 9am-9pm.

"HI. THIS IS BARCELONA." California native, 9-year Barcelona resident, and expert on local lore, Jordan Susselman offers a "Hi. This Is Barcelona" tour that shouldn't be missed. He and his team of passionate guides offer private tours and weekly student group tours (7-15 students, 2-3hr., €35 per person). Susselman promises to tell the truth—and only the truth—about a city he's come to know better than some of its locals. Email jordan@hithisisbarcelona.com well in advance for private or student tours, and check out www.hithisisbarcelona.com for more info.

EMERGENCY AND COMMUNICATIONS

Local police: ☎092. **National police:** ☎091.

Tourist Police: La Rambla, 43 (☎932 56 24 30). ⓂLiceu. Multilingual officers. This is where to go if you've been pickpocketed. Open 24hr.

Late-Night Pharmacy: Rotates. Check any pharmacy window for the nearest on duty, contact the police, or call **Información de Farmacias de Guardia** (☎93 481 00 60).

Hospital: Hospital Clínic i Provincal, C. Villarroel,170 (☎932 27 54 00). ⓂHospital Clínic. Main entrance at C. Roselló and C. Casanova. **Hospital de la Santa Creu i Sant Pau** (☎932 91 90 00; emergency ☎91 91 91). ⓂHospital de Sant Pau. **Hospital General de la Vall d'Hebron** (☎932 74 61 00). ⓂVall d'Hebron. **Hospital del Mar,** Pg. Marítim, 25-29 (☎932 48 30 00), before Port Olímpic. ⓂCiutadella or Vila Olímpica. **Medical Emergency:** ☎061.

Telephones: Buy phone cards at tobacco stores and newsstands; the lowest denomination is usually €6, which promises 45min. of international calling, though rates sometimes require you to use all your minutes in a single call. A much better option is to use **Locotorios** (international call centers), which dot the streets on either side of La Rambla. Purchase cell phones in **El Corte Inglés** in Pl. Catalunya; pre-pay phones with SIM card from €29.

Internet Access: Easy Internet Café, La Rambla, 31 (☎933 01 7507; www.easyinternetcafe.com). ⓂLiceu. Fairly reasonable prices and over 200 terminals in a bright, modern center. €2.10 per hr., min. €2. 1-day unlimited pass €7; 1 week €15; 1 month €30. Open 8am-2:30am. Branch at Ronda Universitat, 35. ⓂCatalunya. €2 per hour; 1-day pass €3; 1 week €7; 1 month €15. Open daily 8am-2:30am. **Navegaweb,** La Rambla, 88-94 (☎933 17 90 26; navegabarcelona@terra.es). ⓂLiceu. Good rates for international calls ($0.20 per min. to USA). Internet €2 per hr. Open M-Th 9am-midnight, F 9am-1am, Sa 9am-2am, Su 9am-midnight. **Bcnet (Internet Gallery Café),** C. Barra de Ferro, 3 (☎932 68 15 07; www.bornet-bcn.com), down the street from the Museu Picasso. ⓂJaume I. €1 for 15min; €3 per hr.; 10hr. ticket €19. Open M-F 10am-11pm, Sa-Su noon-11pm.

Post Office: Pl. d'Antoni López (☎902 197 197). ⓂJaume I or Barceloneta. Fax and **Lista de Correos.** Open M-F 8:30am-9:30pm, Su noon-10pm. Dozens of branches; consult www.correos.es. **Postal Code:** 08001.

ACCOMMODATIONS

While accommodations in Barcelona are easy to spot, finding an affordable bed or room can be more difficult. During one of the busier months (June-Sept. or Dec.), wandering up and down La Rambla looking for a place can be a recipe for anxiety and frustration. If you want to stay in a touristy area, reserve weeks ahead. Consider staying outside heavily trafficked Ciutat Vella; there are plenty of hostels in the Zona Alta, particularly in Gràcia, that have more vacancies. For the best rooms, l'Eixample has good deals and is also quiet at night. La Ribera and El Raval are smart alternatives to the hectic Barri Gòtic; they're just as close to the action and often cheaper. There are some less reputable parts of El Raval on the side streets farther from La Rambla, so choose wisely.

ALTERNATIVE ACCOMMODATIONS. Barcelona is not a cheap city, and a decent hostel will cost at least €23 a night. Those passing through for only a short time, and carrying no valuables, sometimes turn to another option: the so-called "illegal hostels" that offer rooms at significantly reduced prices (€15-18). Backpackers looking to stay illegally sometimes ask around at Travel Bar (C. Boqueria, 27). Illegal hostels can be dangerous and unpredictable, and Let's Go does not recommend them.

CAMPING

A handful of sites lie in the outskirts of the city, accessible by intercity buses (20-45min.; €1.50). The **Associació de Càmpings de Barcelona,** Gran Via de les Corts Catalanes, 608 (☎934 12 59 55; www.campingsbcn.com), has more info. A good choice is **Càmping Tres Estrellas ❶,** Autovía de Castelldefells, km 13.2. Take bus L95 (€1.40) from Pl. de Catalunya to the stop just 300m from the campsite, 13km south. (☎936 33 06 37; www.camping3estrellas.com. €6-8 per person. 2-person tents €7.50-9; cars €7.50-9. BBQ, pool, ATM, supermarket, and internet available. Open from mid-Mar. 15 to mid-Oct. MC/V.)

BARRI GÒTIC AND LA RAMBLA

LOWER BARRI GÒTIC

The following hostels lie between C. Ferran and the water. Backpackers flock here to be close to the late-night revelry at the popular, heavily touristed La Rambla. The cheapest accommodations tend to be cramped.

Hostal Levante, Baixada de San Miquel, 2 (☎933 17 95 65; www.hostallevante.com). ⓂLiceu. New rooms are large and tasteful, with light wood furnishings, exceptionally clean bathrooms, A/C, and fans; some have balconies. Ask for a newly renovated room. Apartments have kitchens, living rooms, and washing machines. Internet €1 per hr. Singles €35, with bath 45; doubles from €55/€65; 4-person apartments €30 per person. Credit card number required with reservation. MC/V. ❸

Pensión Mariluz, C. Palau, 4 (☎933 17 34 63; www.pensionmariluz.com), 3rd fl. ⓂLiceu or Jaume I. Gorgeous renovations turned this hostel into a warm, bright space around a classy old courtyard. Shared bathrooms are clean but a bit cramped. Offers short-term apartments nearby. A/C. Locker, sheets, and towels included. Free Wi-Fi in common area. Dorms €15-24; singles €30-41; doubles €40-60; triples €48-72; quads €65-90, with bath €94. MC/V. ❷

Hostal Fernando, C. Ferran, 31 (☎933 01 79 93; www.hfernando.com). ⓂLiceu. Clean rooms with a little more attention and care than most places in this price range. Dorms with A/C and lockers. Common kitchen with dining room and TV on 3rd fl. Private rooms have TV and bath. Towels €1.50. Internet €1 per 30min. Free Wi-Fi. Dorms €20-24; singles €45-55; doubles €65-77; triples €75-90. MC/V. ❷

Kabul Youth Hostel, Pl. Reial, 17 (☎933 18 51 90; www.kabul.es). ⓂLiceu. Legendary among backpackers—it's hosted nearly a million since its establishment in 1985. Rooms with balconies overlooking Pl. Reial available by request. Lounge and terrace. Breakfast and dinner included. Linens €2. Free Wi-Fi. Computers provided with 20min. of free use per day. Check-out 11am. Reservations available only on website with credit card. Dorms €20-30. MC/V. ❷

Pensión Canadiense, Bajada de San Miguel, 1 (☎933 01 74 61). ⓂLiceu, L3. Across the street from Hostal Levante. Spacious rooms with a slightly more romantic vibe than other hostels in the area. All rooms have bathrooms, A/C, and balconies. Free Wi-Fi. Doubles €68-75; triples €98-10. Discounts for stays over 5 nights. MC/V. ❺

Quartier Gothic, C. Avinyó, 42 (☎933 18 79 45; www.hotelquartiergothic.com). Attractive hostel in a bustling location. Dating back to 1859, it is the oldest Tuscan-style building in Barcelona. Large and comfortable common room. Rooms have TVs, fans, safes, and high ceilings. Free Wi-Fi. High-season singles €29; doubles €46, with bath €63; triples €63/€84. Cash only. ❷

Pensión Bienestar, C. Quintana, 3 (☎933 18 72 83; www.pensionbienestar.com). ⓂLiceu, L3. A left off C. Ferrán coming from Las Ramblas. The building on this small sidestreet may not look the most inviting, but inside you'll find plant-adorned hallways and a friendly staff. Rooms and shared bathrooms are clean and spacious. Singles €18-22; doubles €33-40, with bath €40-50. Cash only. ❶

UPPER BARRI GÒTIC

This section of the Barri Gòtic is between C. Fontanella and C. Ferran, and accommodations are closer to Pl. Catalunya and L'Eixample and a little farther from the rougher lower section of the neighborhood. Portal de l'Àngel, a chic pedestrian avenue, runs through the middle and is busy during the day but, unlike Las Ramblas, quiets down at night. Rooms are pricier here, though it may be worth it for a retreat from the continuous late-night revelry of lower Barri Gòtic.

Hostal Maldà, C. Pi, 5 (☎933 17 30 02). ⓂLiceu. Enter the small shopping center and follow the signs upstairs. Clean, no-frills rooms that would cost twice as much money at other places. All rooms have shared bath. Call for reservations. Singles €15; doubles €30; triples with shower €45. Cash only. ❶

Hostal-Residència Rembrandt, C. de la Portaferrissa, 23 (☎933 18 10 11; www.hostalrembrandt.com). ⓂLiceu. Range of unique rooms. Cheapest are fairly standardbut some have large baths, patios, and sitting areas. Breakfast €5. Reception 9am-11pm. Reservations require credit card or €50 deposit. Singles with shower around €30, with bath €40; doubles €50/65; triples €75/85. MC/V. ❷

Hostal Campi, C. Canuda, 4 (☎933 01 35 45; www.hostalcampi.com). Central location, warmly decorated rooms, and helpful staff. Most rooms have balconies, some have TVs. Internet €1 per hr. Singles €32; doubles €55, with bath €65; triples €75/85. Prices rise in high season. MC/V. ❸

Pensión Hostal Paris, C. del Cardenal Casañas, 4 (☎993 301 37 85). ⓂLiceu. Basic clean bedrooms but an exceptional common room with lavish gilt-framed paintings and a balcony overlooking La Rambla. Free Wi-Fi. Must pay one night with reservation. Singles €30; doubles €55, with bath 65; triples €85. MC/V. ❷

Hostal Residència Lausanne, Av. Portal de l'Àngel, 24 (☎933 02 11 39; www.hostalresidencialausanne.com). ⓂCatalunya. Up 2 fl. at the back of the entrance foyer. White walls, ornate marble staircase, and a lounge overlooking the busy Av. Portal de l'Àngel. Free internet and Wi-Fi. Doubles €54, with bath €64; triples €75-85. MC/V. ❹

Hostal Santa Anna, C. Santa Anna, 23 (☎933 01 22 46). ⓂCatalunya. Small but pretty rooms. Affordable rates given proximity to Pl. Catalunya. Doubles €50, with bath €60; triples €60. Cash only. ❹

BARCELONA

LA RIBERA

Fewer tourist attractions in La Ribera means fewer tourist accommodations. Still, the neighborhood is worth a look if you want a quieter, more authentic alternative.

Gothic Point Youth Hostel, C. dels Vigatans, 5 (☎932 68 78 08; www.gothicpoint.com). ⓂJaume I. Jungle-gym rooms with A/C. Most beds come with curtains and personal lockers. Highly social, with lots of events, including a weekly DJ jam and free concerts. Rooftop terrace and colorful lounge area with TV. Breakfast included. Lockers €3. Linens €2. Free internet. Refrigerator and kitchen access. Dorms €24. €1 credit card fee per night. AmEx/MC/V. ❶

Hostal de Ribagorza, C. de Trafalgar, 39 (☎933 19 19 68; www.hostalribagorza.com). ⓂUrquinaona. Ornate Modernista building with attractive rooms, homey decorations, and colorfully tiled floors. TV and A/C. Doubles €45-60; triples €60-75. MC/V. ❹

Pension Ciudadela, C. del Comerç, 33 (☎933 19 62 03; www.pension-ciudadela.com). ⓂBarceloneta. Climb 3 flights of stairs to this small hostel with big, brightly painted rooms. Rooms have TV and balcony; most have A/C. Doubles €50, with bath €56; triples from €66. MC/V. ❹

Hostal Nuevo Colón, Av. del Marquès de l'Argentera, 19 (☎933 19 50 77; www.hostalnuevocolon.com). ⓂBarceloneta. A modest *hostal* trapped in a gorgeous hotel's body. 26 modern rooms with balconies. Common area and TV. Reservations recommended. Singles €35, with bath €49; doubles €47/67; triples €67/87; quads with bath €87. 3- to 6-person apartments with bunk-beds and kitchenettes €90-155 per day. MC/V. ❸

Hostal Orleans, Av. del Marquès de l'Argentera, 13 (☎933 19 73 82; www.hostalorleans.com). Ⓜ︎Barceloneta. Follow Pg. de Joan de Borbó and turn right on Av. del Marqués de l'Argentera. Attractive rooms and a comfortable lounge. Internet €1 per 30min. Doubles €60-65; triples €75. AmEx/MC/V. ❺

Hostal Bresus, C. Sant Pere Més Alt, 61 (☎932 68 22 62). Ⓜ︎Arc de Triomf. Follow C. de Trafalgar, left on C. de Mendez Nuñez, right on C. Sant Pere Més Alt. Spacious rooms with TV, A/C, and balconies. Singles €40, with bath €50; doubles €40-65. Cash only. ❹

Hotel Triunfo, Pg. de Picasso, 22 (☎933 10 40 85; atriumhotels.com). Ⓜ︎Jaume I. Go west on C. de la Princesa and turn right on Pg. de Picasso. Sleek, modern rooms, each equipped with a private bathroom and TV. Doubles €70-80. MC/V. ❺

Pension Port-Bou, C. del Comerç, 29 (☎933 19 23 67). Ⓜ︎Barceloneta. Follow Pg. de Joan de Borbó, turn right on Av. del Marqués de l'Argentera, and make a left onto C. del Comerc. Simple, spotless rooms do the job. Singles €40; doubles €45, with bath €55. Cash only. ❹

EL RAVAL

Let's Go's favorite area of El Raval, by far, is the neighborhood around **Carrer Dr. Dou** and **Carrer Elisabets**—these student-dominated streets boast healthy restaurants and good shopping. (Even further toward M: Universitat, on C. Pelai, you'll find a number of chain stores, but these have less character and higher prices than the shops on C. Elisabet.) The lower part of El Raval is split roughly in half vertically by las Ramblas del Raval. The area between las Ramblas del Raval and Las Ramblas (M: Liceu) is well-traveled and feels perhaps deceptively safe (there are pickpockets aplenty here). Be careful on the far side of Las Ramblas del Raval, as streets can be eerily deserted late at night.

Hotel Peninsular, C. de Sant Pau, 34 (☎934 12 36 99; www.hpeninsular.com). M: Liceu. This *Modernista* building has 78 rooms with green doors, phones, and A/C around a beautiful 4-story interior courtyard festooned with hanging plants. Breakfast included. Safety deposit boxes €2 per day with €20 deposit. Free internet and Wi-Fi. Check-out 11am. Singles €55; doubles €78; triples €95; quads €120; quints €140. MC/V. ❺

Barcelona Mar Youth Hostel, C. de Sant Pau, 80 (☎933 24 85 30; www.barcelonamar.es). M: Paral·lel. This hostel hosts Spanish cooking classes (€18), a tapas-and-flamenco-night (€22), a pub crawl that includes cover and 1 drink per bar (€15), a free walking tour, and more. Shared bathrooms with separate rooms for toilets and new shower curtains. 125 dorm-style beds and ocean-themed decor. Breakfast and lockers included. Linens €2.50, towels €2.50; both €3.50. Self-service laundry €4.50. Free internet and Wi-Fi. 6- to 16-bed dorms in summer €26, in winter €16-19; Doubles €46-58, F-Sa add €2 per person. AmEx/MC/V. ❷

Ideal Youth Hostel, C. la Unió, 12 (☎933 42 61 77; www.idealhostel.com), off Las Ramblas, on the street next to the Gran Teatre Liceu. M: Liceu, L3. Located just a block off of Las Ramblas, this hostel feels like the most chic garage you'll ever step into. Entirely concrete 1st floor includes a mural, kitchen, and lounge space. 4- to 10-bed dorms are some of the best deals in the city. Vending machines. Linens €2.50. Laundry €4. Free internet and Wi-Fi. 4-bed dorms €23, 10-bed €20; private room with bath €30. ❶

Hostal Gat Xino, C. L'Hospital, 155 (☎933 24 88 33; www.gatrooms.com). M: Liceu. 2nd location at C. Joaquin Costa, 44 (☎934 81 66 70). This posh hostel's minimalist rooms are done up in black, white, and lime green and come with plasma TVs, phone, A/C, and bath. Breakfast room feels new, and rooftop terrace has a shady trellis, low wooden furniture, and brand-new-looking lounge pillows that encourage laziness. Singles €47, with bath €50; doubles €66/70. MC/V. ❹

Center Ramblas (HI), C. de l'Hospital, 63 (☎934 12 40 69; www.center-ramblas.com). M: Liceu. Young staff and 200 cheap beds in 4- to 10-bed dormitories. The ambience leaves something to be desired but feels well-kept and is in a great student district. Breakfast included. Lockers €2 per use. Linens included. Towels €2. Laundry €5. Free internet and Wi-Fi. Dorms in summer €24, in winter €17-21. MC/V. ❶

Hostal Ramos, C. L'Hospital, 36, (☎933 02 07 23). M: Liceu. This hostel has nicely carpeted hallways and 32 particularly clean rooms with windows that open either onto balconies or a peaceful interior courtyard. Rooms have TV, phone, and hairdryer. Internet in a *sala de estar* and Wi-Fi. The one suite has a small sitting area, a large bathroom with a jacuzzi, and a large outdoor terrace. Singles €55, in low season €35; doubles €72/45; suite €125. MC/V. ❹

L'EIXAMPLE

In this posh neighborhood, expect lodgings to be elegant, well appointed, and a bit pricier. That said, travelers on a budget will still find plenty of places to stay. Besides, it may be worth the extra euro to live among the multitude of nearby *Modernista* masterpieces.

AROUND PASSEIG DE GRÀCIA

By day, these accommodations lie securely within a busy stream of sight-seers and professionals. By night, the wide streets are much quieter than those of the Ciutat Vella.

Sant Jordi Hostel Aragó, C. Aragó, 268 (☎932 15 67 43; www.santjordihostels.com). ⓂPasseig de Gràcia. Walk 3 blocks up Pg. de Gràcia and make a left on C. Arago; it's on the left. Crash in this recently renovated hostel's sleek and homey common room and recuperate from a long day. They'll plan your night out for you if you so desire. Board games, DVDs, lockers, sheets, towels, TV, use of guitar all free. Laundry €5. Breakfast €3. Kitchen. Laundry €5. Internet and Wi-Fi. Parties and bar crawls organized regularly; call ahead. 4-bed dorms €14-17; 6-bed dorms €13-25. ❶

Somnio Hostel, C. Diputació 251. (☎932 72 53 08, www.somniohostels.com) ⓂPg. de Gràcia. Chic, clean, and neatly arranged rooms just blocks from Pl. de Catalunya. A/C throughout, free internet and Wi-Fi, TV in common area. Drinks available at the front desk. Breakfast €5. Single-sex dorms, complete with sheets and locker €25; singles €42; doubles €77, with bath €85. MC/V. ❷

Hostal Residència Oliva, Pg. de Gràcia, 32, 4th fl. (☎934 88 01 62; www.hostaloliva.com). ⓂPg. de Gràcia. Classy ambience—wooden bureaus, mirrors, and a light marble floor. Fragrant bouquets of flowers in the hallways are perhaps to be expected from a hostel that has been in operation since 1931. Rooms have TV, A/C, and Wi-Fi. Singles €38; doubles €66, with bath €85. Cash only. ❹

Hostal Qué Tal, C. Mallorca, 290 (☎934 59 23 66; www.quetalbarcelona.com), near C. Bruc. ⓂPg. de Gràcia or Verdaguer. Plants, both potted and painted, adorn the hallways of this *hostal*. Warm decorations make the spacious rooms feel cozy. Free internet. Singles €45; doubles €55-65, with bath €75-80. MC/V. ❺

BCN Hostal Central, Ronda Universitat, 11, 1st fl. (☎933 02 24 20; www.hostalcentral.net). ⓂUniversitat. Don't complain if the elevator to this *Modernista* building seems small or outdated; it's protected by the city and can't be replaced. Some rooms with balconies and inviting nooks. Free internet. Reception 24hr. Singles with shared bath €25-45; doubles €30-45, with bath €50-70; triples €65-75; quads €85-90. MC/V. ❹

Centric Point, Pg. de Gràcia, 33 (☎932 31 20 45; www.equity-point.com). ⓂPg. de Gràcia. The bunked bedrooms may be sparse but this large hostel is no bore, offering 2 bars, a terrace, and a rec room with TV, computers, Wii, and foosball to a host of young travelers. Breakfast included. Free lockers; bring a padlock. Linens €2. Free Wi-Fi. Wheelchair-accessible. 4- and 8- bed dorms €21-30; doubles €48-57. MC/V. ❸

Axel Hotel, C. Aribau, 33 (☎933 23 93 93; www.axelhotels.com). Ⓜ Universitat. Colorful, stylish, and plush rooms at this hotel catering to gay clientele. All guests have access to a pool, jacuzzi, and sauna. Room €70-250; book well in advance for lower rates. AmEx/MC/V. ❺

L'EIXAMPLE DRETA

In L'Eixample Dreta, it's best to find accommodations near a metro stop. The zone to the right of the Sagrada Familia is Barcelona's auto-shop district: you may find the number of restaurant and nightlife options here lacking. That said, **Barcelona Urbany Hostel** and **Sant Jordi's Apt. Sagrada Familia** are gems and only a quick metro ride from downtown bars and clubs. In short, stay here, but memorize this schedule: trains run until midnight on weekdays, until 2am on Fridays, and continuously on Saturdays.

Barcelona Urbany Hostel, Av. Meridiana, 97 (☎932 45 84 14; www.barcelonaurbany.com). Ⓜ Clot. Walk down Av. Meridiana. This sleek and modern hostel is perfect for those searching for a social experience. Large dining room, kitchen, and a terrace bar. Beer and sangria €1. Sa nights 8:30pm, the hostel serves paella (€2). Regular free walking tours. Access to new gym with swimming pool (next door) included. Towels €2. Free Wi-Fi. 8-room dorms €12-23; 6-room €14-25; 4-room €16-28; singles €50-82; doubles €25-41. MC/V. ❶

Sant Jordi Hostels: Apt. Sagrada Familia, C. Freser, 5 (☎934 46 05 17; www.santjordihostels.com). Ⓜ Hospital St. Pau. Walk down C. de Cartagena or C. del Dos de Maig until you reach C. Rossello. This street almost immediately forks; the upper street is C. Freser and the hostel is right at the fork. This 110-bed hostel is made up of 2- and 3-room apartments, each with a single room, a double room, and a 4-bed room (all individually locked) with a shared kitchen, bath, and free washing machine. Clean wood floors and balconies. Common room with TV and movie collection. Nightly excursions to bars and clubs. Towels €1. Free internet and Wi-Fi. Reception 8am-2am. 4-bed dorms €16-28 per person; singles €20-38; doubles €18-32 per person. MC/V. ❷

Hostal Gimon, C. Mallorca, 537 (☎934 55 44 32; gimon105@hotmail.com). Ⓜ Encants. Walk up C. del Dos de Maig and make a right on C. Mallorca. The 18 private rooms at Hostal Gimon are calm and tidy. TV. Reception 24hr. Singles €30; doubles €45, with bath €50; triples €65. ❷

Graffiti Hostal, C. Arago, 527 (☎932 65 09 74; graffiti.hostel@gmail.com). Ⓜ Clot. Walk down Av. Meridiana to C. Arago and make a right. The *hostal* looks like an apartment from the street; look for the buzzer. The establishment's appearance lives up to its name. That said, it's not far from the Sagrada Familia and the price is right. BYO padlock for lockers. Linens €2. Towels €1. Internet and Wi-Fi. Rooms €15-20. MC/V. ❶

L'EIXAMPLE ESQUERRA

L'Eixample, the spacious neighborhood known for its open, tree-lined avenues and significant gay population, is a great place to stay in a four- or five-star hotel. Translation: there are not many budget hotels, hostels, or *pensiones* in this peaceful, largely residential neighbhorhood. Also, long blocks make for long walks0151—if you do decide to stay here, be aware that it may take you awhile to get to dinner.

Hostal Residencia Neutral, Rambla de Catalunya, 42 (☎934 87 63 90). Ⓜ Passeig de Gràcia. Walk up the Passeig de Gràcia to the Carrer del Consell de Cent. Cozy upholstered chairs and mosaic tile floors make the antique but well-kept rooms feel immediately like home. The location can't be beat. Each room comes with TV, fan, and Wi-Fi; some have balconies that open onto La Rambla de Catalunya. Breakfast €8. Singles with shower €35; doubles with shower €60, with bath €65. MC/V. ❸

Pensión Aribau, C. Aribau, 37, 1st fl. (☎934 53 11 06; www.hostalaribau.com). ⓂPg. de Gràcia. Most of the hostel's 11 rooms have TVs and A/C. Ask for one with a balcony overlooking a terrace. Reserve at least 1 month ahead in summer. Singles and doubles €55, with bath €65; triples €70/80. AmEx/MC/V. ❹

Hostal Eden, C. Balmes, 55 (☎934 52 66 20; hostaleden@hotmail.com). ⓂPg. de Gràcia. From the Metro, walk down C. Aragó past Rambla de Catalunya to C. Balmes and turn left. Modern, well-kept rooms are equipped with TVs, lockboxes, and fans; most have large baths. Free internet and Wi-Fi. Singles €25-30, with bath €35-45; doubles €35-45/50-60. AmEx/MC/V. ❷

Pensión Cliper, C. Rosselló, 195 (☎932 18 21 88). ⓂDiagonal. Follow C. Rosselló for 3½ blocks. *Pensión* in Modernista building boasts large, antique rooms with high ceilings that have seen (much) better days. A step down from other listings in terms of quality. Also a step down in terms of price. Your call. €15-20 per person, €40 with shower. ❶

BARCELONETA

Lodging is not Barceloneta's forte, and rooms, especially cheap ones, are hard to come by. Hostels can be found in the area around Ⓜ**Barceloneta, L4.**

Pensión Francia, C. Rera Palau, 4 (☎933 19 03 76). ⓂBarceloneta, L4. Head right toward Pl. Palau, cross Pl. Palau, and turn right onto Av. Marqués de l'Argentera; C. Rera Palau is the 2nd left. Comfortable, airy rooms with balconies and TVs. The spotless shared bathrooms. Easy access to Barceloneta, La Ribera, and the Estació de França. Doubles with shower €50, with full bath €60; triples €65. MC/V. ❹

Hostal del Mar, Pl. del Palau, 19 (☎ 902 22 22 70; www.gargallo-hotels.com). ⓂBarceloneta, L4. From the station, head up the street away from the water toward Pl. de Palau, turn left and cross the plaza in front of the palace; it will be on the other side of the plaza. A popular, comfortable hostel. Singles €24; doubles €43, with shower €48, with full bath €58; triples €55/65/72; quads €71/85/85. MC/V. ❷

Pensión Palacio, Pg. Isabel II, 10 (☎933 19 36 09; www.pensionpalacio.com). ⓂBarceloneta. Cheerful, brightly colored rooms at some of the lowest prices around. Towels €1. Free internet. Singles €20-25; doubles €40-50; triples €60-75, with bath €75-90, quads €80-100/€100-120. MC/V with 7% fee. ❷

Sea Point, Pl. del Mar 1-4 (☎932 24 70 75; www.equity-point.com). ⓂBarceloneta. Follow Pg. Joan de Borbó until Pl. del Mar and enter the hostel through the cafe on the right side of the building. Not quite as sharp-looking as the other Barcelona equity-point hostels, but offers unbeatable beach access, just steps away from Platja Sant Sebastian. Kitchen access. Breakfast included. Extra linens, blankets, and towels €2 each. Free internet. Dorm-style beds in low season €15-20, in high season €21-25. MC/V. ❷

GRÀCIA

Gràcia is quickly growing in popularity, so it's best to reserve ahead, particularly in the high season (June through mid-September). Many hostels in Gràcia are on the second or third floor of an apartment building; just look for the buzzer on the ground floor, and the receptionist will ring you in.

Pensión Norma, C. Gran de Gràcia, 87 (☎932 37 44 78). ⓂFontana. Meticulously kept rooms with sinks and wardrobes. The spacious shared bath is clean with speckled tile floors. Free Wi-Fi. Singles €27-32; doubles €38-47, with bath €55-60. MC/V. ❷

Hostal Lesseps, C. Gran de Gràcia, 239 (☎932 18 44 34; www.hostallesseps.com). ⓂLesseps. 16 spotless rooms, each with a high ceiling, classy velvet walls, small desk, TV, and bath. A/C €5. Cats and dogs allowed. Free internet and Wi-Fi. Singles €40; doubles €65; triples €75; quads €90. MC/V. ❹

Pensión San Medín, C. Gran de Gràcia, 125 (☎932 17 30 68; www.sanmedin.com). ⓂFontana. Walking into this hostel is a psychedelic experience: the wallpaper has pink metallic floral swirls. 12 rooms with tiled sinks, TVs, and fans; some have balconies. Free Wi-Fi. Singles €30-38, with bath €39-48; doubles €45-60/€55-72. Special offers sometimes posted online. MC/V. ❸

Albergue Mare de Déu de Montserrat (HI), Pg. Mare de Déu del Coll, 41-51 (☎934 83 83 63; www.xanascat.cat), beyond Parc Güell. Buses #15, 28, and 92 stop across the street. From ⓂVallcarca, L3, walk up Av. República d'Argentina and take the stairs right before C. de Gomis (they're not far) to cross the bridge at C. Viaducte de Vallcarca; signs point the way up the hill. This huge government-sponsored hostel is gorgeous, complete with private grounds, stained-glass windows, and Alhambra-style tile work. Far from the city center, but the silver lining is a hilltop view of Barcelona and the chance to meet backpackers from all around the world. Multiple common spaces and restaurant. Breakfast included; lunch €7.50. Dinner €3-9. Laundry €4.50. Internet €0.90 per 30min. 6-night max. stay. Check-in 10am-3pm and 4:30-11pm. Check-out 10am. Midnight curfew, but doors open every 30min. Reservations suggested. Dorms €16-26. MC/V. ❶

Hostal Valls, C. Laforja, 82 (☎932 09 69 97). FGC: Muntaner. Walk 4 blocks downhill on C. Muntaner and turn left on C. Laforja. Though this hostel is not close to Gràcia's nightlife scene, the building compensates with Neoclassical Doric columns and Greek statues. Several large common spaces, including a TV lounge. Wi-Fi. Reservations suggested. Singles €40; doubles €45-70. MC/V. ❹

FOOD

Barcelona offers every kind of food and ambience imaginable. Whether Basque, Chinese, Indian, or American, restaurants here will exceed your culinary expectations. However, beware of touristy restaurants offering "traditional" dishes—good authentic food can be hard to find. Our best advice is to look to the Catalan option: *fideuà* unseats *paella*, *cava* champagne complements every meal, and *crema catalana* satisfies the local sweet tooth. Barcelona's tapas (sometimes called *pintxos*) bars, concentrated in La Ribera and Gràcia, often serve *montaditos*, thick slices of bread topped with all sorts of delectables from sausage to *tortilla* (omelette) to anchovies. Hopping from one tapas bar to another can be a fun, social, and often cheap way to pass the evening. Most tapas bars are self-serve and standing room only. Plates in hand, ravenous customers help themselves to the toothpick-skewered goodies that line the bars. The bartender calculates the bill by tallying up the toothpicks on the way out, and then it's on to another bar. Though vegetarian options in general have never been easier to find, vegetarians consult the extensive *Guía del Ocio*(€1) at newsstands for a list of available options.

BARRI GÒTIC AND LA RAMBLA

Barcelona's nucleus contains all types of eateries. Classic Catalan cuisine is juxtaposed with fast-food options and every species of bar imaginable. Choose carefully; anything along La Rambla is likely to be overpriced.

LAS RAMBLAS

Escribà, Las Ramblas, 83 (☎933 01 60 27). ⓂLiceu, L3 Gran Via, 546 (☎93 454 75 35) ⓂUrgell. This small, classy cafe is a gem, having been remodeled by Ros i Guell in 1902 back when it was a pasta shop known as Casa Figueras. Acquired by the Escribà family, it now offers cakes and sweets as exquisite as the ceramic exterior. Outside seating is available. Coffee €1.50. Pastries €1-4. Open daily 8:30am-9pm. ❶

Café de l'Opera, Las Ramblas, 74 (☎933 17 75 85; cafeoperabcn.com). ⓂLiceu, L3. Once an 18th-century inn and then a 19th-century chocolate shop. In 1929, this Barcelona institution adopted its current name, and was soon reincarnated as a post-opera tradition. Today the cafe retains the same upscale ambience while offering well-priced drinks and tapas. Hot chocolate €2. Churros €1.40. Tapas €2-5. Salads and cheeses €2-10. Open daily 8:30am-2:30am. MC/V over €20. ❷

LOWER BARRI GÒTIC

Les Quinze Nits, Pl. Reial, 6 (☎933 17 30 75; www.lesquinzenits.com). ⓂLiceu. Popular restaurant with lines halfway through the plaza every night; arrive early for excellent Catalan cuisine at unusually low prices. Sit in the classy interior or eat outside for no extra charge and keep an eye on your fellow tourists in Pl. Reial. Starters €4-7. Entrees €6-11. Wine €3. Sangria €4.70. Open daily 1-3:45pm and 8:30-11:30pm. AmEx/MC/V. ❷

L'Antic Bocoi del Gòtic, Baixada de Viladecols, 3 (☎933 10 50 67; www.bocoi.net). ⓂJaume I. Excellent salads (€7.20-9.20), *coques de recapte* (open-faced toasted sandwiches; €9), and cheese platters (€13-19) feature *jamón ibérico* and local produce. Look for the 1st-century Roman wall inside. Open M-Sa 8:30pm-midnight. Reserve in advance. AmEx/D/MC/V. ❸

Arc Café, C. Carabassa, 19 (☎933 02 52 04; www.arccafe.com). ⓂDrassanes. This secluded, handsome cafe serves curries (€9.50-12) and salads (€4-7). Entrees €8-17. *Menú del mediodía* €9.60. Breakfast until 1pm. Thai dinner menu Th-F. Open M-Th 10am-1am, F 10am-3am, Sa 11am-3am, Su 11am1am. MC/V. ❸

Juicy Jones, C. Cardenal Casañas, 7 (☎93 302 43 30; reservations 60 620 49 06). ⓂLiceu, L3. A vegan's haven, Juicy Jones is a refreshing touch of the psychedelic, with wildly decorated walls and a long bar spilling over with fresh fruit. The creative vegan *menú* (€8.50) features Spanish and Indian inspired dishes (after 1pm). They offer a full juice bar with every conceivable mixture of fresh juices and soy milkshakes (€3-5). Open daily 12:30pm-12am. Kitchen closes at 11:30pm. Cash only. ❷

Vegetalia, Escudellers, 54 (☎933 17 33 31; www.vegetalia.es). ⓂDrassanes. Laid-back establishment with hardcore veggie, protein, and organic options based on tofu, seitan, and tempeh, with 7 veggie burgers (€3.50 alone, €7.20 combo meal) that even meat-eaters can't resist. Also a small natural foods store in the back. Entrees €7-9. *Menú* €10. Open M-F and Su 1:30-11pm, F-Sa 12:30pm-midnight. AmEx/MC/V. ❷

Venus Delicatessen, C. Avinyó, 25 (☎93 301 15 85). ⓂLiceu, L3. Take a right off C. Ferran coming from Las Ramblas. With a black-and-white tiled floor and rotating exhibitions of local art on the stucco walls, this popular Mediterranean cafe fits in well with the funky scene on C. Avinyó right by Pl. Trippy. Unique and refreshing salads like the *ensalada erótica* (tuna, asparagus, and yogurt sauce) or *ensalada afrodita* (avocado, fruit, cheese, and mint). Coffee, wine, and pastries €3.50-4. Vegetarian dishes €8-10. Salads €6-8. *Menú* €10. Open M-Sa noon-midnight. Cash only. ❷

Maoz Vegetarian, C. Ferran, 13 and La Rambla, 95 (☎653 84 76 53; www.maozveg.com). If you don't have enough time, money, or room in your stomach for another enormous 3-course *menú*, this place is your best friend. Excellent, quick, and cheap falafel (€3.80-5.20) and fries (€2.20) served until late. Pile on sweet peppers, tahini, tabouleh, chickpeas, and hot sauce to taste. Open daily 11am-3am. MC/V. ❶

Irati, C. Cardenal Casañas, 17 (☎93 302 30 84; www.gruposagardi.com). ⓂLiceu, L3. Basque restaurant that attracts droves of hungry tapas-seekers. Once you've gorged on the *montaditos* offered on the long bar, the leftover toothpicks will cost you €1.80 apiece. Bartenders also pour Basque *sidra* (cider; €1.70) with the bottle high above your glass. Starters €10-16. Entrees €18-26. Open daily 11am-12:30am. AmEx/MC/V. ❹

El Salón, C. l'Hostal d'en Sol, 6-8 (☎93 315 21 59). Ⓜ Jaume I, L4. Follow Via Laietana toward the water, turn right on C. d'Angel Baixeras and then right on tiny C. l'Hostal d'en Sol; it's on the left. This mellow bar-bistro is perfect for unwinding after a day spent jostling fellow tourists. Sit on the terrace, nestled against a large section of 1st-century Roman wall, and feast on plates of bruschetta, risotto, chicken, pork, or fish (€13-16). Groups may call ahead to arrange lunch or Sunday meals. Open M-Sa 8:30pm-midnight. AmEx/MC/V. ❸

UPPER BARRI GÒTIC

Attic, La Rambla, 120 (☎933 02 48 66; www.angrup.com). Ⓜ Liceu. This chic restaurant promises high-class food at manageable prices. The modern, orange interior will feel like a refuge from touristy La Rambla. Mediterranean fusion cuisine, including fish (€10-14), meat (€8-15), and their specialty, ox burger (€11). Open daily 1-4:30pm and 7pm-12:30am. AmEx/MC/V. ❸

Xaloc, C. de la Palla, 13-17 (☎933 01 19 90). Ⓜ Liceu. Classy local favorite. A clean look complements the butcher counter where pig legs hang from the ceiling. Expect simple plates with high-quality ingredients. Tapas €3-7. *Cocas* €4-6. Open M-F 9am-midnight, Sa-Su 10am-midnight. AmEx/MC/V. ❷

The Bagel Shop, C. Canuda, 25 (☎93 302 41 61). Ⓜ Catalunya, L3. Walk down La Rambla and take the 1st left, and then bear right onto C. Canuda; it's on the left in Pl. Vila de Madrid. Bagels are rare in Spain, but here you'll find a diverse selection (€1, toasted €0.15 more) and a variety of spreads, from cream cheese to mango chutney. Good place to go for a tasty, inexpensive lunch with plenty of vegetarian options. Bagel sandwiches €4-6. Open M-Sa 9:30am-9:30pm, Su 11am-4pm. MC/V. ❶

Restaurante Self Naturista, C. Santa Anna, 11-17 (☎93 318 26 84). Ⓜ Catalunya, L4, on the left on C. Santa Anna off Las Ramblas. A self-service vegetarian cafeteria with a line of famished locals and an enormous selection of entrees (€3.30-€6.30) and desserts (€2-4). Lunch *menú* (3 dishes and a dessert) €8.80. Open M-Sa 11:30am-10pm. MC/V. ❶

Els 4 Gats, C. Montsió, 3 (☎933 02 41 40; www.4gats.com). Ⓜ Catalunya. Literally "the four cats," *els 4 gats* is actually a Catalan expression meaning "just a few guys," an ironically diminutive name considering the cafe's prestigious clientele. An old Modernista hangout of Picasso's with lots of Bohemian character; he loved it so much he created a personalized menu. The building itself was designed by Puig i Cadafalch in 1897. These days the restaurant tends to attract more tourists than artistic geniuses, but it's worth having one nice meal here. Food is expensive—entrees €12-20. M-F lunch *menú* 1-4pm (€13) is the best deal and comes with epic desserts; try the *crema catalana.* Live piano daily 9pm-1am. Open daily 10am-1am. AmEx/MC/V. ❹

Čaj Chai, Sant Domenic del Call, 12 (☎933 01 95 92). Ⓜ Jaume I, L4. With quality teas from around the globe, a mosaic-covered interior, and a clever assortment of mismatched chairs and sofas, this tea house attracts a pensive, international crowd, poetry notebooks in hand. Pronounced "chai chai." Tea €2-4. Small pastries €1-2. Open Tu-Su 10:30-10pm. Cash only. ❶

La Colmena, Pl. de l'Àngel, 12 (☎933 15 13 56). Ⓜ Jaume I. A busy dessert shop appropriately named "the Beehive" offering everything from bon-bons to fruit tarts to meringues. The chocolate and whiskey tartlet (€2) is a particularly indulgent treat. Small pastries €1-3. Open daily 9am-9pm. AmEx/MC/V. ❶

LA RIBERA

The eclectic gourmet restaurants of La Ribera cater to a young crowd. The neighborhood is home to a relatively high concentration of Asian restaurants, tapas bars, and wineries.

BARCELONA

La Llavor dels Origens, C. d'Enric Granados, 9 (☎934 53 11 20; www.lallavordelsorigens.com); C. de la Vidrieria, 6-8 (☎933 10 75 31); Pg. del Born, 4 (☎932 95 66 90); and C. de Ramón y Cajal, 12 (☎932 13 60 31). A hip dining room with a new-school twist. Delectable entrees include beef-stuffed onion (€6.40) and rabbit with chocolate and almonds (€6.40). Soups, meat dishes, and some vegetarian dishes €4.30-7. Open daily 12:30pm-1am. AmEx/MC/V. ❷

Petra, C. dels Sombrerers, 13 (☎933 19 99 99). ⓂJaume I. Some of the best food in the area at shockingly low prices. Clever decor—stained-glass windows, menus printed on wine glasses, and light fixtures made from silverware—give the place a charming bohemian feel. Try the duck with brie and apple or the rigatoni with *foie gras* sauce and peach. Salads and pasta €5. Entrees €8. Open Tu-Th 1:30-4pm and 9-11:30pm, F-Sa 1:30-4pm and 9pm-midnight, Su 1:30-4pm. MC/V. ❷

El Pebre Blau, C. dels Banys Vells, 21 (☎933 19 13 08). ⓂJaume I. A *nouveau gourmet* restaurant serving Mediterranean and Middle Eastern fusion dishes under starry lanterns. Throw in a cheeky menu (available in English) and an attentive waitstaff for the win. Most dishes €10-18. Open daily 8pm-midnight. Reserve ahead, especially for weekend. MC/V. ❸

El Xampanyet, C. de Montcada, 22 (☎933 19 70 03). ⓂJaume I. Near the Museu Picasso. Crowds spill onto the street, drinks in hand. The house special *xampanyet* (wine; €1.10) is served with *pa amb tomàquet* (bread with tomato) and anchovies (€4.20) or *jamon cerrano* (€1.50). Over 25 varieties of *cava*. *Sidra* (cider; €1.80). Bottles from €8. Open Sept.-July Tu-Sa noon-3:30pm and 7-11pm, Su noon-3:30pm. MC/V. ❷

La Pizza del Born, Pg. del Born, 22 (☎933 10 62 46). ⓂJaume I. The best of Argentine thick-crust pizza meets the best of Spain, with toppings like artichokes, jam *serrano*, and goat cheese. Lunch *menú* (€3.90) is 2 slices and a drink. Slices €1.80. Open M-Th and Su noon-1am, F-Sa noon-2am. Cash only. ❶

Tèxtil Cafè, Pl. Montcada, 12-14 (☎932 68 25 98; www.textilcafe.com). ⓂJaume I. A terrace cafe nestled in an old stone courtyard. Mediterranean salads (€7.50), tapas (€5.30), and a good vegetarian selection. Live jazz Su 9-11pm (cover €5). Lunch *menú* €11; dinner €18. Entrees €8.50-11. Wheelchair-accessible. Open from mid-Mar. to Nov. Tu-Th and Su 10am-midnight, F-Sa 10am-1am; from Nov to mid-Mar. Tu-W 10am-8-:30pm, Th and Su 10am-midnight, F-Sa 10am-1am. MC/V. ❷

Va de Vi, C. dels Banys Vells, 16 (☎933 19 29 00). ⓂJaume I. An inconspicuous but romantic spot for tapas and drinks in a candlelit 16th-century stone tavern. Choose from over 300 varieties of wine and *cava* (€1.90-7.70). Wide selection of cheeses €4.60-20. Tapas €1-19. Wheelchair-accessible. Open M-Th 7pm-1am, F-Sa 8pm-3am. Cash only. ❶

Bodega La Tinaja, C. d'Esparteria, 9 (☎933 10 22 50). ⓂJaume I. Walk down C. de la Princessa, make a right on C. de Montcada, take it to C. d'Esparteria, and make a left. Vaulted ceilings and stone walls hung with pots and pans, barrels of wine, and fresh flowers make this *bodega* rustic and charming, if slightly touristy. Serves Iberian comfort foods like ham-and-cheese plates and paella. Entrees €12-30. Occasionally hosts live flamenco guitar. Open M-Sa 8pm-midnight. AmEx/MC/V. ❸

Bubo, C. Caputxes 10 (☎932 68 72 24). ⓂJaume I. This artisanal sweet shop sells brightly colored, jewel-like chocolates, pastries, *petit fours*, and macaroons. Small sweets have big names: try the "light lychee cream and brilliance of strawberry and raspberry à la vanilla" or the "candied sunflower seeds with *fleur de salt*, candied orange-peel, and a sable coat of dark chocolate." Most sweets €1. Open M 4-10pm, Tu-Th 11am-10pm, F-Sa 10am-1am, Su 10am-10pm. MC/V. ❶

Gades Fondues, C. l'Esparteria, 10 (☎933 10 44 55; www.gadesfondues.com). ⓂJaume I. Walk down C. de la Princessa, make a right on C. de Montcada, take it to C. d'Esparteria, and make a left. Wearing your lederhosen and not sure what to do next? At

Gades, you'll find salads, carpaccio, and over 15 different fondues, including a cava and truffle cheese and melted-chocolate desert. The pots of melted cheese are served with chunks of bread or crudites such as small pickles and pickled onions. Exposed brick walls, vaulted ceilings, and geometric modern lights. Fondues €12 per person. Open M-Th 8:30pm-12:30am, F-Sa 8:30pm-1:30am. AmEx/MC/V. ❷

El Rovell, C. de l'Aregenteria, 6 (☎932 69 04 58; www.elrovelldelborn.com). ⓂJaume I. Walk down C. de l'Aregenteria. "Rovell" is the Catalan word for the yolk of an egg. Accordingly, while this restaurant serves tapas, bruschetta, grilled meat and more, its emphasis is on egg specials. Wine buckets hang at the end of the venue's tall, wood tables. Eclectic and fun. Try the salmon tartar and lettuce with anchovy vinaigrette (€7.50). Entrees €6-12. Open daily 1-4pm and 7pm-midnight. AmEx/MC/V. ❷

Lonja de Tapas, Plaça de les Olles, 6 (☎933 10 78 45; www.cellerdelaribera.com). Walk down C. de la Princessa, make a right on C. de Montcada, and another right on C. del Bonaire. This 2-tier restaurant has exposed brick walls, sleek black tables, and a long menu of fancy tapas. Try the deep fried camembert with red fruits sauce (€3.60) and the grilled oyster mushrooms with Catalan sausage and garlic dressing (€4.60). Tapas €3.60-13. Open M-Th noon-midnight, F-Sa noon-1am, Su midnight-1am. AmEx/MC/V. ❸

EL RAVAL

Authentic Catalan mainstays (found mostly on the side of El Raval farthest from Las Ramblas) and trendy fusion spots sit next to Middle Eastern restaurants and a growing number of student- and vegetarian-friendly juice/smoothie bars. There are several wholesome, tasty, self-service vegetarian eateries clustered around **Carrer Dr. Dou.** Near the MACBA, you'll find a few upscale restaurants catering to museum-goers.

Organic, C. Junta de Comerç, 11 (☎933 01 09 02; www.antoniaorganickitchen.com). This vegan-friendly eatery provides wholesome, healthy dishes—starting with the filtered water used to prepare the food. Vegan salad bar and lunch *menú* (M-F €10, Sa-Su €14) served under candlelight and exposed ceiling. Salad bar regulars include cheese-and-mushroom *croquetas* and cucumbers and yogurt. Dinner served a la carte. 2nd location in La Boqueria market also has a *menú* and *bocadillos;* takeout only. Open daily 12:30pm-midnight. MC/V. ❷

Rita Rouge, Pl. Gardunya (☎934 81 36 86; ritarouge@ritablue.com). M: Liceu. 2nd branch **Rita Blue,** Pl. Sant Augustí, 3 (☎933 42 40 86; www.ritablue.com). Savor a healthy, delicious, and high-quality lunch *menú* (€11; weekends €14) full of creative offerings and vegetarian choices on a shady, black-and-red terrace just behind La Boqueria, or come at night for a mixed drink (€6-8) on zebra-striped cushions or in the glittery bar's red and silver bucket seats. Entrees (€9.50-22) include chicken tandoori with yogurt and *basmati* rice. Salads and wok dishes €6-12. Open M-Sa noon-2am, Su 6pm-2am. ❸

Kasparo, Pl. Vicenç Martorell (☎933 02 20 72). ⓂCatalunya. Walk down Las Ramblas, make a left on C. Elisabets, and a first right onto C. de les Ramelleres. The plaza is on the right, and the restaurant is in the far right corner. Alternatively, walk down C. de Pelai and make a left onto C. de les Ramelleres. The plaza is 3min. down, on the left. Kasparo capitalizes on—and helps to create—the bustling atmosphere of the Raval plaza. Almost all of Kasparo's seating is outdoors; pull up a metal table under the building's vaulted overhang and people-watch to your heart's content. Perfect for an early-evening drink or a late-night *cortado*—but be warned, you might get comfortable and end up staying for dinner too. Luckily dishes (€5-8) include fresh soups, salads, and pasta, with some vegetarian options. Open daily 9am-midnight. Cash only. ❷

Restaurante Can Lluís, C. Cera, 49, and Reina Amalia, 1, (☎934 41 11 87). M: Sant Antoni, L2. From the metro, head down Ronda S. Pau and take the 2nd left on C. Cera.

For over 100 years, Can Lluís has been a defining force in Barcelona's cuisine—and politics. On Jan. 26, 1946, a grenade set off in the restaurant killed the owner and his son. Later, under Franco, artists used Can Lluís as a gathering place. Eschewing trendiness, the menu is filled with traditional Catalan favorites prepared home-style and always bursting with flavor, including succulent lamb ribs (€9.80), grilled squid (€10), and fresh grilled asparagus (€5.40). Dinner *menús* (€20-35) include wine. Entrees €6-20. Open M-Sa 1:30-4pm and 8:30-11:30pm. MC/V. ❸

Mendizabal, Junta de Comerç, 2. Try the *zumo del día* (juice of the day) at this colorful student favorite, right near the school of fine arts. Need something to wash down all that juice? No problem: beer is cheap (€2.50), as are the *bocadillos* (*serano* ham, brie, tomato; €3.50), freshly grilled behind the counter. Crayola-colored patio furniture beneath umbrellas in the plaza across the street. Open daily 8am-12:30am. Cash only. ❶

Shalimar, C. Carme, 71 (☎933 29 34 96). From M: Catalunya, L1/3, right on C. Carme. Indian and Pakistani cuisines make their peace at inexpensive prices. Walls sport blue-and-white tilework. Chicken, lamb, and seafood curries €6.50-9. Chicken tandoori €6.50. Open M and W-Su 1-4pm and 8pm-midnight, Tu 8pm-midnight. ❷

Hello Sushi, C. Junta de Comerç, 14 (☎934 12 08 30; www.hello-sushi.com). M: Universitat. Zen red-and-blue decor and small tea area with floor cushions. Lunch *menú* €9; dinner *menú* €15. Entrees €15-25. Open Tu-Sa 12:30-4:30pm and 8:30pm-12:30am, Su 8:30pm-12:30am. Reservations required F-Su nights. AmEx/MC/V. ❸

Madame Jasmine, Rbla. del Raval, 22. Eclectic decorations, a spirited staff, and an array of wonderfully mismatched chairs overlook Fernando Botero's fat cat sculpture in the middle of Rambla de Raval. Delicious *bocadillos* (€5.50) and salads (€7). Mixed drinks €6. Open M-F 5:30pm-2:30am, Sa-Su 1:30pm-2:30am. Kitchen open daily 1pm-midnight. ❷

Juicy Jones, C. Hospital, 74 (☎934 43 90 82; www.juicyjones.com). M: Liceu. Walk down C. L'Hospital. JJ is a DIY vegetarian juicebar where everything's made by hand, from the murals and graffiti on the walls to the menus on the tables. Offerings include a lunch *menù* (€8.50), *thalis* (mixed plates of Indian dishes), salads (€4.50-5.30), guacamole (€3.80), the house cookie (€1), and Pear-Celery-Lime juice (mixed juices with three fruits, €3.45; add spices like ginger for €0.50). Open daily 1-11:30pm. MC/V. ❷

Ultramarinos Bar, C. Sant Pau, 126 (☎635 14 47 26; www.ultramarinosbar.com). ⓂParal-lel. Walk down C. Sant Pau; the bar is on the left. By day, Ultramarinos serves up Iberian ham, cheese, and *pa amb tomaquet* (bread with tomato) as well as other traditional Catalan dishes. Showcases local artists' canvases. By night, the 2-tier bar has a DJ and a small but committed crowd of regulars. Entrees €5-10. Mixed drinks €5-7. Open daily 6pm-3am. Cash only. ❷

Elisabets, C. Elisabets, 2-4 (☎933 17 58 26). ⓂLiceu. Walk up Las Ramblas and make a left onto C. Elisabets. This welcoming, smoky old-school bar serves tapas (€1-8) and home-cooked dishes like lasagna to a young clientele. Popular during the day, but really buzzes on weekend nights. Lunch *menù* €8.50. Entrees €6-12. Open M-Th 8am-midnight, F-Sa until 2am. Cash only. ❷

Original Pizza-Bar, C. Joaquim Costa, 47 (☎933 17 20 89). ⓂUniversitat. Walk down Ronda de Sant Antoni and make a right on C. Joaquim Costa. This pizzeria has colorful red, orange, and black walls and serves greasy, delicious, and cheap slices, perhaps best enjoyed late at night. Try the eggplant, goat cheese and walnut pizza, or the ham-and-chili. Slices €2. *Empanadas* €2.90. Open daily 1pm-2am, F-Sa 1pm-3am. Cash only. ❶

Bar Invisible/Pizza Ravalo, Pl. d'Emili Vendrell, 1 (☎934 42 01 00), at the intersection of C. Joaquin Costa and C. del Peu de la Creu. ⓂLiceu. Walk up Las Ramblas and make a left onto C. del Carme. When you hit C. Joaquin Costa, make a right. The bar is on the left, just after the intersection. This bar is easy to miss, but a delight to find. Set back from C. del Peu de la Creu and obscured by shrubs in large terra-cotta pots, the burgundy-walled venue offers delicious mixed drinks. Try the specialty (cava, pineapple juice, peach, and cassis; €5). Pastas and pizzas €7.50-13. Be bold and try the "surprise" pizza (€13). Open daily 6pm-midnight. MC/V. ❷

Chelo, Pl. Vicenç Martorell (☎933 18 55 01). Ⓜ Catalunya. Walk down C. de Pelai and make a left onto C. de les Ramelleres. The plaza is about 3min. down, on the left. The beautifully stenciled plants and flowers on this restaurant's walls reflect its attention to detail and commitment to natural ingredients. Chelo has open-air seating on a popular plaza and serves excellent smoothies, milkshakes, and pastries (€3-6). Open 10am-midnight. Cash only. ❶

Cafe d'Annunzio, Pl. Vicenç Martorell (☎933 02 40 95). Ⓜ Catalunya. Walk down C. de Pelai and make a left onto C. de les Ramelleres. The plaza is about 3min. down, on the left. The decapitated heads of Greek statues stare at you from this cheerful eatery's red walls. Inside, 1 table is cozily tucked below the low-hanging ceiling in a sunken recess. The majority of the seating, however, is out in Pl. Vicenç Martorell—enjoy a full breakfast (rare in Barcelona) of coffee, eggs, ham, juice, and toast here for just €6. Entrees €6-12. Open 9:30am-1am. MC/V. ❷

Cafeterium, C. Tallers, 76 (☎667 64 01 11; www.cafetarium.com). Ⓜ Universitat. Walk down C. Tallers. This all-purpose cafeteria/restaurant/*cerveceria* has streamlined white tables by day and carmel-colored lighting by night. Tasty, elegantly presented dishes and a relaxing ambience explain why the venue is nearly always full. Tapas €3-12. Sandwiches €2-5. Happy hour 6pm-midnight; beer €1. Open M-Sa 8am-11:30pm. MC/V. ❷

Narin, C. Tallers, 80 (☎933 01 90 04). Ⓜ Universitat. Walk down C. Tallers. This shawarma restaurant sets itself apart from a thousand other similar venues with fresh ingredients, firey sauces, and a dining room with elaborately tiled walls and pine wood tables. You might even consider eating here sober. Hummus plate €3.40. Shawarma with chicken €3.90. Falafel combo plate €7. Open M-Th and Su 11am-2am, F-Sa 11am-3am. Cash only. ❶

L'Antic Forn, C. Pintor Fortuny, 28 (☎933 04 25 18; www.lanticforn.com). From Ⓜ Catalunya, C. Pintor Fortuny is 5min. down Las Ramblas. From Ⓜ Liceu, it's 5min. up Las Ramblas. It's rare to find lace curtains, white tablecloths, and gourmet dishes at prices this affordable. Try the risotto with shrimp and parmesan cheese (€6.50) or the grilled lamb chops with garlic salsa (€7.80). Selection of pizzas. Entrees €5.50-16. Open 9am-5pm and 8pm-midnight. MC/V. ❸

En Ville, C. Doctor Dou, 14 (☎933 02 84 67; www.envillebarcelona.es). From Ⓜ Catalunya, C. Pintor Fortuny is 5min. down Las Ramblas. From Ⓜ Liceu, it's 5min. up Las Ramblas. Make a right onto C. Doctor Dou; the restaurant is on the right. Although this restaurant is indoors, its terra-cotta floors, mirrored walls, and floral bouqets make it feel like an upscale, outdoor patio. Live music Tu and W nights after 9pm. Try the octopus carpaccio with arugula and citrus (€9.70) or the duck with polenta and carmelized apples (€15). Open M 1-4pm, Tu-Sa 1-4:30pm and 8pm-midnight. AmEx/MC/V. ❸

Tallers 76, C. Tallers, 76 (☎933 18 89 93; www.tallers76.com). Ⓜ Universitat. Walk down C. Tallers. This new restaurant serves Valencian-influenced tapas, sandwiches, paella, and a few meat dishes in a geometric, purple space with excellent natural lighting. Start with the tapa of paella (€5.50) and follow it up with a smoked salmon, fresh cheese, and lettuce sandwich (€4.80). Entrees €5-11. Open M-Su 9am-11:30pm. AmEx/MC/V. ❷

Olivia, C. Pintor Fortuny, 22 (☎933 18 63 80). From Ⓜ Catalunya, C. Pintor Fortuny is 5min. down Las Ramblas. From Ⓜ Liceu, it's 5min. up Las Ramblas. This white-walled cafe has light wood booths and an organic menu. Savor a perfect cup of coffee and a slice of carrot or apple cake (€3.50-4.50). Tranquil and newspaper-friendly. Open M-Sa 9am-9pm. MC/V. ❶

L'EIXAMPLE

With sidewalk cafes serving everything from fusion to traditional Catalan cuisine, wandering in l'Eixample easily induces rumbling stomachs, especially during a long day of shopping. These upper neighborhoods are full of good places to spend a long dinner (especially l'Eixample Esquerra), but the restaurants are scattered around and interspersed with plenty of nondescript corner bars serving the endless apartment buildings in the area. If you want to sample one of l'Eixample's trendy, high-quality restaurants, pick one ahead of time and put the blinders on as you walk past all the others. Be sure to make reservations on weekends and be prepared to pay a lot for the food and atmosphere.

AROUND PASSEIG DE GRÀCIA

Pg. de Gràcia is lined with nearly as many tapas bars and cafes as it is with shops and Modernista structures. Most are tourist-oriented, have sidewalk tables, and are on the expensive side. Eating outside is especially pricey; many establishments charge up to 15% extra. On the weekends, this neighborhood is a good choice for late-night food, as many places stay open until 2am. Sweet (and savory) deals on *bocadillos* and tapas are found on every corner.

La Rita, C. Aragó, 279 (☎934 87 23 76; www.laritarestaurant.com). A killer afternoon lunch *menú* has made Rita a local favorite for a cheap but quality midday meal. Bright red awnings draw crowds to enjoy everything from gazpacho to salmon carpaccio in orange-and-dill sauce. Lines frequently extend out the door; reservations recommended. *Menú* M-F €9. Entrees €6-10. Open daily 1-3:45pm and 8:30-11:30pm. AmEx/MC/V. ❷

Taktika Berri, C. Valencia, 169 (☎934 53 47 59). Ⓜ Universitat. Walk up C. d'Aribau and make a left onto C. Valencia. Many consider this Basque restaurant the best one in Barcelona. While you can always eat *pintxos* (skewered tapas) such as *monteditos* (small sandwiches) at the bar, you won't get a table unless you call weeks in advance. Entrees like battered cheek and cod omelette are delicious, but not cheap—expect to pay €35 for a full meal, whether of tapas or entrees. Good selection of Basque wines. Open M-F 1-4pm and 8:30-11pm, Sa 1-4pm. AmEx/MC/V. ❺

Kirin, C. Aragó, 231 (☎934 88 29 19) Rda. Universitat 20 (☎93318769). All-you-can-eat sushi, edamame, and other Asian delicacies roll by on a conveyor belt for you to choose from. While you're at it, grab some raw seafood and vegetables and have them grilled on the spot. Weekday lunch buffet €9.70. Dinner and weekend buffet €14, children €5.50. Open daily 1-4pm and 8pm-midnight. MC/V. ❷

Acalia, C. Rosselló, 197 (☎932 37 05 15). Sparkling French restaurant with an ambience as light and airy as its crepes (€4-7). Lunch *menú* €12. Dinner *menú* €16. Open Tu-Sa 1-4:30pm and 8:30-11:30pm. AmEx/MC/V. ❹

Thai Gardens, C. Diputació, 273 (☎93 487 98 98; www.thaigardensgroup.com). Ⓜ Catalunya, L1/3/5. The extravagant decor, complete with a wooden bridge entrance, lush greenery, and colorful silk pillows, makes for a romantic meal. Call ahead to reserve a traditional *kantok* table (cushions on the ground). If all you want is some Thai food, order take-out at reduced prices. Entrees €14-18. Dinner *menú* €31. Wheelchair-accessible. Open daily 1-4pm and 8-11:30pm. AmEx/MC/V. ❸

Txapela (Euskal Taberna), Pg. de Gràcia, 8-10 (☎93 412 02 89 www.angrup.com). Ⓜ Catalunya, L1/3/5. Decide between delicious offerings like eggplant with goat cheese or anchovy with mozzarella and cherry tomato. Tapas €1.40-2. Wheelchair-accessible. Open M-Th 8am-1:30am, F-Su 10am-2am. Tapas served starting at noon. ❶

Menjar Enrotllat, C. Valldonzella 33 (☎654 17 01 74). Ⓜ Universitat. Take Ronda Sant Antoni away from Pl. Universitat and take the 2nd left onto Valldonzella. Small, futuristic-looking joint boasts healthy and diverse food on the cheap. Maki from €1.50. Pasta €3.50. Lunch *menú* from €5. Open M-Sa 1-5pm and 8pm-midnight. Cash only. ❶

Elj apo nes, Passatge de la Concepció, 2 (☎93 487 25 92; www.grupotragaluz.com), 2nd location at C. Princesa, 35. Ⓜ Pg. de Gràcia, L2/3/4. Just off of Pg. de Gràcia. Serving all the Japanese cooking you could want: from tempura and skewers to noodles and

BARCELONA

sushi. Stylish red interior will leave you feeling chic as you fill your stomach with (and empty your wallet for) these tasty plates. Entrees €3.50-13. Wheelchair-accessible. Open M-W and Su 1:30-4pm and 8:30pm-midnight, Th-Sa 1:30-4pm and 8:30pm-1am. No reservations accepted. AmEx/MC/V. ❷

El Ultimo Agave, C. Aragó, 193 (☎934 54 93 43). Ⓜ Universitat. Walk up C. d'Aribau and make a left onto C. Arago. This popular Mexican restaurant, which shares its name with a brand of tequila, serves dishes like tacos with marinated pork, pineapple, onion, and coriander (€11). Try the special, *El Ultimo Agave* ("something better than fajitas"; €14). A real cantina: boisterous, fun, and often standing room only. Reservations are a must on weekends. Open daily 7pm-3am. MC/V. ❸

52, Valldonzella, 52. Ⓜ Universitat, L1/2. Take Ronda Sant Antoni away from Pl. Universitat and take the 2nd left onto Valldonzella. Learn directly from the students and have a late bite at this funky, orange-lit eatery. Order one of the healthy Asian-Mexican-Catalan fusion concoctions and wash it down with a beer (€1.5o). Tapas €4.10-7.10. Wheelchair-accessible. Open daily 7:30pm-1am, kitchen open 9pm-midnight. Cash only. ❷

Madrid-Barcelona (Pa Amb Tomàquet), C. Aragó, 282 (☎932 15 70 27). Ⓜ Pg. de Gràcia, L2/3/4. At the intersection of Pg. de Gràcia. Named for the railroad line that used to run here, this classy lunchtime hotspot attracts legions of native businessmen and shoppers. Waiters ladle soup and rice at your table straight from the stove. The classic Catalan dishes are tasty. Entrees €7-15. Wheelchair-accessible. Open daily 1-4pm and 8:30-11:30pm. AmEx/MC/V. ❸

Mauri, Rambla de Catalunya, 102 (☎93 215 10 20). Ⓜ Diagonal, L3/5. This *pastisseria* (pastry and sweet shop) has been turning out delicate sweets, mouth-watering bonbons, and gourmet *bocadillos* (€1.80-3) since 1929. Come to buy delectable gifts, have lunch in the delicatessen-style restaurant (lunch *menú;* €13), or simply to drool at the cake displays. A 2nd location (☎932 15 81 46) across the street specializes in candy and gift baskets. Open M-F 8am-9pm, Sa 9am-9pm, Su and holidays 9am-3pm. MC/V. ❶

Cervecería Catalana, C. Mallorca, 236 (☎93 216 03 68). Ⓜ Pg. de Gràcia, L2/3/4. All-in-one Catalan bar: they've got *flautas* (€3-7), tapas (€3-12), seafood, salads, burgers, and beers (€2.50). Crowded, noisy, friendly; you'll feel as at home as the locals who fill the place. Wheelchair-accessible. Open daily 8am-1am. AmEx/MC/V. ❷

Tapas 24, C. Diputació, 269 (☎934 88 09 77; www.carlesabellan.com). Ⓜ Pg. de Gràcia. Chef Carles Abellan, formerly of the legendary El Bulli, offers tapas at this less expensive alternative to his acclaimed Comerç 24. Sit at the pearl white bar if it's not too crowded and have a glass of wine (from €3) with your plate of *patatas bravas.* Tapas €2.50-8. *Raciones* €9-12. Open daily 8am-midnight. MC/V. ❷

Cata 1.81, C. Valençia, 181 (☎933 23 68 18; cata181@hotmail.com). Ⓜ Universitat. Walk up C. d'Aribau and make a left onto C. Valencia. This classy, modern wine bar has stainless-steel benches with orange seat cushions and matches its drinks with market-fresh food. Try a glass of cava (€2.50-3.50) and the black spaghetti with chicken and prawns (€6.60), or opt for bottles of high-end wine. Open M-F 1pm-midnight, Sa 1pm-1am. AmEx/MC/V. ❷

El Raim, C. Muntaner, 75 (☎934 53 59 53). Ⓜ Universitat. Wak to the left down C. Gran Via de les Corts Catalans. Make a right onto C. Muntaner and walk for 3 blocks; the cafe is on the left. Looking for the authentic Barcelona? This local cafe serves immensely satisfying yet inexpensive tapas like chicken leg with stewed plum and stuffed eggplant (€2-3). Salads €3.90. Combination plates €5.10-9.10. Open M-Sa 9am-1am. MC/V. ❷

L'EIXAMPLE DRETA

Laie Llibreria Cafe, C. Pau Claris, 85 (☎933 18 17 39; www.laie.es/cafe/PauClaris_prin_es.php). Ⓜ Urquinaona, L1/4. Additional locations at Marques de Camillas 6-8 (☎934 76 86 69) and Montcada 15-23 (☎932 68 43 92). An ultra-hip lunch spot for

BARCELONA

more than just bookworms. Cheap, fresh, and plentiful all-you-can-eat Catalan buffet lunch (M-F €14, Sa-Su €17) in an open, bamboo-draped room. Grab a praline cappuccino (€2.50) at the bar on the way out. Vegetarian options available. Internet €1 per 15min. Open M-F 9am-1am, Sa 10am-1am. AmEx/MC/V. ❸

La Muscleria, C. Mallorca, 290 (☎934 58 98 44; www.muscleria.com), on the corner with C. Bruc. ⓂVerdaguer, L4/5. In this bustling basement, you'll get a whole pot of mussels to yourself with fries on the side. The crustaceans come in any size, shape, and flavor (try "white wine") and are culled from Catalunya, France, Galicia, and The Netherlands. Entrees with fries from €9.50. Salads €7. *Cocas* €8. Reservations recommended F-Sa. Open M-Sa 1-4pm and 8:30-11:30pm, Su 1-4pm. MC/V. ❷

Can Cargol, C. València, 324 (☎934 58 96 31; www.cancargol.es), on the corner with C. Bruc. ⓂGirona, L4. Extremely popular—and thus noisy—Catalan restaurant with make-your-own *pan con tomate,* charcoal-grilled meats, and lots of snail options. *Platos del dia* €5-6. Reservations recommended F-Su. Open 1:30-4pm and 8:30pm-midnight. ❷

Blue Mandalay Café, C. Provença, 330 (☎93 458 60 17; www.mandalaycafe.net), between C. Roger de Llúria and C. Bruc. ⓂVerdaguer, L4/5. Exotic pan-Asian cuisine, including gourmet dim sum, Vietnamese noodles, seared fish, delicate meat, and elegant salads, served in a room so draped in color and sultanesque luxury (you can eat on a bed!) that it's been featured in books on interior design. F-Sa night trapeze artist around 11pm. Variable extra cover charge for show (around €2.50). Wheelchair-accessible. Entrees €9-13. Open Tu-Sa 8:30pm-midnight. AmEx/MC/V. ❷

Wok & Bol, C. Diputació, 294 (☎ 933 02 76 75), between C. Roger de Llúria and C. Bruc. ⓂGirona, L4. An elegant, colorful Chinese restaurant serving dim sum (€5-8 per small dish) and Peking duck (€18 per person) in addition to more common dishes like chow mein and veggie stir-fry (€6-8). Reservations recommended. Open M-Sa 1:30-3:30pm and 9:15-11:30pm. ❸

El Rodizio Grill, C. Consell de Cent, 403 (☎932 65 51 12), right next to ⓂGirona, L4. All-you-can-eat Brazilian and Mediterranean buffet *à la churrascaria:* grilled shish kebab-style chicken, salmon, and cod. Cold dishes include sushi, pasta, and salads. M-F lunch *menù* €19. Sa-Su lunch and dinner menù €21. Includes 1 drink and coffee. Rich desserts €3.30-5.50. Open M-Th 1-4pm and 9pm-midnight, F-Sa 1-4pm and 9pm-1am, Su 1-4pm. ❹

Campechano, C. València, 286 (☎932 15 62 33; campechanobarcelona.com), just to the right of Pg. de Gràcia when you're coming from Pl. de Catalunya. ⓂCatalunya, L1/3. This restaurant goes all out to recreate the atmosphere of a 1940s *merendero* (barbecue—picnic area) on the Barcelona mountainside, from a few real trees and a painted forest wall to train signs marking your progress "toward the mountain." Picnic tables make it perfect for large groups. Choose your favorite meat or poultry from their extensive list. French fries, salads, and a few other dishes serve as sides. *Menú* €10. Salads €4-6. Entrees €6-15. Open M 8am-2pm, Tu-Sa 8am-2am. ❸

A-Tipic, C. Bruc, 79 (☎932 15 51 06), between C. Aragó and C. Consell de Cent. ⓂGirona, L4. A lunchtime gem for vegetarians. A simple buffet (€10) that tastes more like home than a cafeteria, served in a relaxing blue and yellow dining room. Excellent choice of salad, rice, pasta, and veggie calzones. Open Sept.-July M-F 1-4pm. MC/V. ❷

Cafe Parc Belmont, C. Lepant, 256 (☎932 31 13 58). ⓂSagrada Familia. Walk downhill on C. Lepant. It's on the left. This tapas bar gets it right; it has both a better atmosphere (bright orange walls decorated with framed, old-fashioned photographs) and better food than most similar venues. Large, delicious salads €4-6. Tapas €1-8. Open M-Sa 9am-11pm. Closed Su. ❷

Frida's Restaurante Mexicana, C. Bruc, 115 (☎934 57 54 09). ⓂPasseig de Gracia. Walk down C. Arago until you hit C. Bruc; make a left. This fun, piñata-decorated restaurant is well up the block on the left. Your go-to for "real Mexican" (not Tex-Mex) from tacos (€1.90) to *pozole* (€7). Lunch *menú* €11, ½-*menú* €6.90. Margaritas €5-6. Open M-Tu 1-4pm, W-Sa 8:30am-2am, closed Su. ❷

L'EIXAMPLE ESQUERRA

Look around. Are you in l'Eixample Esquerra? On a corner? Chances are, you're only inches from a tapas bar, and probably a really good one. If you're looking to *picar* ("snack;" literally, "bite"), walk until one jumps out at you and then eat your fill of *croquetas* and *patatas bravas*. Those with heartier appetites will need heavier wallets—very little in l'Eixample comes cheap. If you do decide to hit up a nicer restaurant, your euro will be well spent.

Cerveceria Catalana, C. Mallorca, 236 (☎932 16 03 68). ⓂPg. de Gràcia, L2/3/4. If you want *the* Spanish experience, with locals to keep you company, head here. Noisy, friendly, energetic: the buzz of this restaurant-bar will make you want to return night after night. Pitchers of sangria and creative and fresh tapas €3-12. Wheelchair-accessible. Open daily 7:30am-1:30am. AmEx/MC/V. ❷

Racó d'en Baltá, C. Aribau, 125 (☎934 53 10 44; www.racodenbalta.com). ⓂHospital Clínic. Founded in 1900, this restaurant serves innovative Mediterranean dishes like fried camembert with blueberry sauce (€8.70) and veal sirloin with Bernaise (€18). Entrees €9-17. Lunch *menù* €11. Open M-Th 9am-11:30pm, Th-Sa 9am-3am. MC/V. ❸

La Flauta, C. Aribau, 23 (☎933 23 70 38). ⓂPg. de Gràcia, L2/3/4. 2nd branch at C. Balmes, 164-166 (☎934 15 51 86). The House specialties are hot or cold *flautas* (skinny, crusty bread sandwiches stuffed with veggies, cheeses, and meats; ½ €3.90-6.90, whole €5-8). Plenty of vegetarian options and a large selection of fresh *tapas del día.* Weekday lunch *menù* €10.50. Dishes €3-15. Open M-Sa 7am-1:30am. MC/V. ❷

Cafe Chapultepec, C. Comte Borrell, 152 (☎934 51 92 85; www.cafechapultepec.com). ⓂUrgell. Walk down Gran Via de les Corts Catalans to C. Comte Borrell and make a right. It's at the end of the 1st block, on the right. This Mexican cafe has Rubik's Cube-like tile floors and everything your Southwestern American heart may be longing for: *enchiladas verdes* or *rojas* (€5.90), pitchers of margaritas (€15), and even pancakes with maple syrup (€3.80). Open M-F 10am-4:30pm and 7-11pm, Sa 12:30-4:30pm and 7-11pm, Su 12:30-4:30pm. MC/V. ❷

La Pulpería, Consell de Cent, 329 (☎934 87 53 98; www.restaurantelapulperia.com). ⓂPasseig de Gràcia. Walk up Passeig de Gràcia to the Consell de Cent and make a left. The restaurant is on the right. This fun, classy establishment (think chalkboard menus and a bronze bar) serves a wide variety of Galician tapas and *raciones*, including, *el pulpo* (octopus). Plates €4.30-13. Kitchen closes at midnight. Open M-W and Su noon-4pm and 8-midnight, Th-F noon-2am, Sa noon-4pm and 8pm-1am. AmEx/MC/V. ❷

Ginza, C. Provença, 205 (☎934 51 71 93), between Balmes and Enric Granados. ⓂDiagonal, L3. Bamboo-filled restaurant serves delectable but affordable Japanese food. Eat in or take out. Sushi €5-15. Weekday 4 course lunch *menù* €8. Dinner and weekend *menù* €11. Wheelchair-accessible. Open M-Sa 1-4pm and 8pm-midnight, Su 1-4pm. D/MC/V. ❸

BARCELONETA

Barceloneta is mostly home to expensive seafood restaurants advertising paella *menús* (especially along Pg. Joan de Borbó). You have to go farther inside the neighborhood for smaller restaurants and grocery stores. There's a **Spar Express** on P. Juan de Borbó.

Jai-Ca Bar, C. Ginebra, 13 (☎932 68 32 65), 2 blocks down Pg. Joan de Borbó and 3 blocks toward the beach, on the corner with C. Baluard. Hugely popular tapas bar serv-

BARCELONA

ing all kinds of small seafood treats and plenty of beer (€1.70) to wash them down. Most tapas €3-6. Open Tu and Su 9am-10:30pm, W-Sa 9am-11:30pm. MC/V. ❶

La Bombeta, C. Maquinista, 3 (☎933 19 94 45). ⓂBarceloneta. Walk down Pg. Juan de Borbó (toward the beach) and take a left on C. Maquinista. A retro facade marks this tapas bar, which offers deep-fried *bombas* and a variety of seafood tapas. Appetizers €3-10. Entrees €9-12. Open M-Tu and Th-Su 9am-11:45pm. Cash only. ❷

Bar Bitacora, C. Balboa, 1 (☎933 19 11 10). ⓂBarceloneta. Walk down Pg. Juan de Borbó (towards the beach) and take the 1st left after Ronda del Litoral onto C. Balboa. Loud music and tapas (€4-10) draw young, hungry beachgoers. Open Tu-Su 9am-12am. Cash only. ❷

Can Maño, C. Baluard 12 (☎933193082). ⓂBarceloneta. Another busy restaurant serving fresh, simple seafood in a packed dining room. Meat and fish dishes €3-10. Combination plates €6-8. Open M-F 8am-5pm and 8-11pm, Sa 8am-5pm. Cash only. ❷

GRACIA

Without a doubt, Gràcia is the best place in Barcelona to find authentic cuisine from anywhere around the globe. Traditional markets and Catalan menus are popular, but the side streets of Gràcia are *the* place to find reasonably priced ethnic cuisine. Tapas bars dominate **Plaça del Sol** and **Plaça Virreina; Calle Verdi** is your go-to for culturally diverse (Egyptian, Japanese, Lebanese, Mexican, and Pakistani) food.

Gasterea, C. Verdi, 39 (☎932 37 23 43). ⓂFontana, L3. Follow C. Astúries for several blocks and make a right on C. Verdi. Yellow walls cast a warm glow in this table-less bar. Grab a seat at one of the counters and dig in to Gasterea's selection of excellent, fresh tapas (€1.10). Beer €2-3. Mixed drinks €5. Open daily 7pm-2am. Cash only. ❶

Ikastola, C. Perla, 22 (☎933 68 83 87), off C. Verdi. ⓂFontana, M3. Tired of being a grown-up? Then head to Ikastola (Basque for "nursery school") without letting go of the perks of adulthood (like alcohol). Ikastola has the best *bokatas* in the city, and all the locals know it. Every night, a young, hip crowd of would-be Picassos and Verdaguers overflows onto the small backroom terrace, eager to draw on Ikastola's chalkboards, play the upright piano, and eat sandwiches that would make any lunchbox proud. *Bokatas* €4.50, half portion €3. Salads €7. Beer and wine €2.50-5. Cash only. ❶

L'illa de Gracia, C. St. Domenec, 19 (☎932 38 02 29; www.illadegracia.com). ⓂFontana or Diagonal. Take C. Gran de Gràcia and turn on C. St. Domenec; the restaurant is 2 blocks down on the left. This spacious and brightly lit vegetarian restaurant has a long menu that will prove a relief to those who tire of persuading tapas-bar owners that ham isn't a vegetable. Salads €4.60-5.70. Crepes (sweet and savory) €4-6. Ice cream €3-4. Open M-Th 1-4pm and 9pm-midnight, F-Sa and Su 2-4pm and 9pm-midnight. MC/V. ❶

Sol y Lluna, C. Verdi, 50, (☎932 37 10 52). ⓂFontana. Walk up C. d'Asturies, make a right on Torrent de l'Olla, a left onto C. L'Or, and another left onto C. Verdi; Sol y Lluna is on the right. Locals rave about this understated gourmet restaurant, which has a marble bar, wood tables, and a giant hippopotamus statue. The menu includes large salads such as the *Perigord* (*foie gras*, duck, and caramelized apples; €8.30) and crepes (chocolate and banana, €3.80; Grand Marnier, €4.10). Open M-Th and Su 8-11:30pm, F and Sa 1-3:30pm and 8pm-12:30am. MC/V. ❷

La Gavina, C. Ros de Olano, 17 (☎934 15 74 50). ⓂFontana, L3. Walk down C. Gran de Gràcia and turn left on C. Ros de Olano. Enjoy delicious Italian food in this no-frills pizzeria, complete with a life-size patron saint and confessional candles. Try the *Catalana* (tomato, mozzarella, chorizo sausage, garlic, and artichokes; €16). Gigantic pizzas €8-16. Open Tu 8pm-1am, W-Th and Su 1:30pm-1am, F and Sa 1:20pm-2am. Cash only. ❸

Cantina Machito, C. Torrijos, 47 (☎932 17 34 14). ⓂFontana, L3. Take C. d'Asturies until you hit C. Torrijos and make a right. Mexican food is rare in Spain, but this cantina with colorful walls, straw-covered seats, and a few sombreros serves affordable and surprisingly authentic tacos, mole, guac, and margaritas. Well-known for its Cinco de Mayo celebration. Entrees €7.50-14. Open daily 1-5pm and 7pm-1am. MC/V. ❸

Lalla, C. d'Asturies, 17 (☎934 15 52 70). Ⓜ Fontana. Walk down C. d'Asturies. This Lebanese pizzeria's hip, red-and-black graphic decor and long, cushioned benches make you want to sit down and stay awhile. At any time of day, a young crowd lounges, eating gourmet pizzas (€7-11), drinking coffee, and socializing. Open daily 10am-midnight. Cash only. ❸

Niu Toc, Pl. Revolució de Setembre, 3 (☎932 13 74 61). Ⓜ Fontana. This restaurant, popular for business lunches and also with young people, serves a €10 *menù* of Catalan cuisine, day and night. Try the specialty—cod—or steak, or paella. The dinner menu is an especially good deal thanks to this restaurant's location on a plaza that is at the heart of Gràcia's young nightlife scene. Entrees €8-16. Open M-Th 1pm-midnight, F-Sa 1pm-1am. MC/V. ❷

Diamant, C. Asturies, 67 (☎932 17 02 18). Ⓜ Fontana. Walk down C. d'Asturies. This popular cafe and restaurant has cow-print coffee cups and a student-friendly atmosphere. Come in the morning for *cafe con leche* or at night to chew the cud with your friends. Sandwiches €3-5. Open daily 9am-3am. MC/V. ❶

Sushi Itto, C. Londres, 103 (☎932 41 21 99; www.sushi-itto.es). A classy sushi place fusing Japanese cuisine with Western flavors in eclectic rolls. Nigiri €2.20-4.40. Entrees €7-19. 8-piece rolls €14. Delivery €2. Open M-Su 7:30-11:30pm. MC/V. ❸

BARCELONA

Ugarit, C. Verdi, 11 (☎932 17 86 22; www.ugarit.es). Ⓜ Fontana. Walk down C. de Asturies to C. Verdi and make a right; the restaurant is on the right. Tired of *jamón* and *croquetas* and looking for a change of pace? This Syrian restaurant, named after an ancient city, offers *tabbuleh* salads (€8), *couscous* (€13) and more. Dishes €3.90-13. Open daily 1pm-1am. MC/V. ❷

La Llar de Foc, C. Ramon i Caja, 13 (☎932 84 10 25). Ⓜ Fontana. Walk down C. Gran de Gràcia to C. Montseny and make a left. This street turns into Ramón i Caja; the restaurant is on the left. Farm equipment on the walls and red-checkered tablecloths make this just the place to eat down-home, traditional dishes like *escalavida* (grilled vegetables) and *butifarra* (white sausage). Colorful chalkboard menus outside the restaurant advertise a wide selection of *carnes a la brasa.* Entrees €5.10-14. Open 1-4pm and 8:30pm-midnight. MC/V. ❷

Garda, C. Verdi, 15 (☎934 15 30 57). Ⓜ Fontana. Walk down C. de Asturies to C. Verdi and make a right; the restaurant is on the right. This romantic restaurant channels the decor and dishes of Provence in a uniquely Spanish way. Sip your wine at the bar or recline in a wicker chair and linger over a lamplit plate of camembert with small *chorizos* (€6.90). Entrees €6-15. Open daily 8:30pm-midnight. MC/V. ❸

NUT, C. Verdi, 2 (☎932 10 86 40), at Pl. Revolució de Setembre 1868. Ⓜ Fontana, L3. This stone-walled restaurant could well be in the center of a pyramid: statues of pharaohs and a precariously hanging mummy watch over you as you eat tasty Egyptian fare. Try some hummus (€6), the *ganog* (eggplant with vegetables and lemon; €6), or the *kuchari* (rice with lentils and spices; €7.90). Dinner *menú* €9.90. Open daily 1-4pm and 8am-1am. MC/V. ❷

SIGHTS

Barcelona has always been on the cutting edge of the art world. Visitors cross continents not only to see the paintings hanging in fantastic museums, but also to admire imaginative modern architecture and parks designed by world-renowned visionaries. The streets are the galleries for Barcelona's artistic spirit; intricate lampposts and murals light up even the most drab neighborhoods. You'll find the classics—Picasso, Miró, Mir, etc.—but also modern shows at museums like the Tàpies. Concentrated in l'Eixample, the *Modernista* treasures draw architecture aficionados from the far reaches of the world. Parc Güell and Parc Diagonal Mar allow for contemplation surrounded by innovative designs and sculptures. Sprinkled throughout the entire city lie plazas, tree-lined avenues, and corner parks, each with their own character to explore and discover.

RUTA DEL MODERNISME

For those with a few days in the city and an interest in seeing some of the most popular sights, the **Ruta del Modernisme** is the cheapest and most flexible option. The pass provides discount admission to dozens of *Modernista* buildings in the city, and comes with the purchase of a guidebook (€12); additional adult passes are €5, though an adult accompanying someone under 18 is free. Passes provide a 25-30% discount on the Palau de la Música Catalana, Fundació Antoni Tàpies, the Museu de Zoología, tours of l'Hospital de la Santa Creu i Sant Pau and the facades of La Manzana de la Discordia (Amatller, Lleó i Morera, and Batlló), and map tours of Gaudí, Domènech i Montaner, and Puig i Cadafalch buildings, among other attractions. The pass comes with a map and a pamphlet giving the history of different sights, which is helpful for prioritizing visits. Purchase passes at the Pl. Catalunya tourist office, the Modernisme Centre at **Hospital Santa Creu i Sant Pau,** C. Sant Antoni Maria Claret, 167, or **Pavellons Güell,** Av. de Pedralbes, 7. Centralized info can be found at ☎902 07 66 21, 933 17 76 52, and www.rutadelmodernisme.com. Many sights have tour times and length restrictions; visiting all of them on the same day is virtually impossible.

BARCELONA CARD

Another discount option is the **Barcelona Card.** The card is good for 2-5 days and includes free public transportation (on the Metro, daytime buses, and trains to the airport) and nearly 80 discounts (and sometimes free admission) at museums, cultural venues, theaters, and a few bars and clubs, shops, and restaurants. They are sold at tourist offices, Casa Batlló, El Corte Inglés, the Aquarium, and Poble Espanyol. Prices for 2-5 days range €24-36 for adults and €20-31 for ages 4-12. For students (usually with ISIC card; ISOS accepted less often), it may be cheaper to use student discounts to get into attractions.

BUS TURÍSTIC

Sit back and let the sights come to you. The Bus Turístic stops at 44 points of interest along three different routes (red for the north, blue for the south, and green for the eastern waterfront). Tickets come with an eight-language brochure with information on each sight. A full ride on the red or blue route takes about 2hr., green takes 40min., but the idea is to get off at any place of interest and use the bus (as many times as you want in your allotted days) as a convenient means of transportation. Multilingual guides stationed in every bus help orient travelers and answer questions. You can buy tickets once on board, or ahead of time at **Turisme de Catalunya,**Pl. de Catalunya, 17, in front of El Corte Inglés, and at www.barcelonaturisme.com. Many of the museums and sights covered by the bus offer discounts with the bus ticket; some are closed on Mondays. (Buses run daily every 5-25min. First departure 9-9:30am; no service Dec. 25 and Jan. 1. 1-day pass €20, ages 4-12 €12; 2-day pass €26.)

BARRI GÒTIC

The Barri Gòtic is the oldest part of Barcelona; it came into being well before the grid layout in the rest of the city. The Barri Gòtic was settled during Roman times and continued to develop during the Romanesque and Gothic periods. Be sure to set a day aside to wander around the Barri Gòtic and explore the layers of history that have accumulated here.

ESGLÉSIA CATEDRAL DE LA SANTA CREU I SANTA EULÀLIA (THE CATHEDRAL OF THE HOLY CROSS AND SAINT EULALIA). Three separate buildings have existed on this site: an AD fourth-century basilica, an 11th-century Romanesque church, and finally the present Gothic Cathedral, begun in 1298. The much-photographed facade comes from yet another era (1882), when it was added to the main structure by architect Josep Mestres. Mestres worked from a plan drawn up by Frenchman Carles Galtés de Ruán in 1408; this ensured a genuinely Gothic appearance.

In the cathedral's **plaça,** seven stylized letters crafted by Joan Brossa spell out "Barcino," commemorating the original Roman city settled on land that is now Barcelona. The Romans first marched through Spain in the third century BC in an effort to subdue North African powers in Carthage. They subjugated the resident Laietani and settled next to Montjuïc in 210 BC. In 15 BC, in honor of Augustus's rule, the Romans gave the small town the unwieldy name of Colonia Julia Augusta Faventia Paterna Barcino.

As you enter the church, the **cathedral choir** is directly in front of you. The backs of the stalls are painted with 46 coats of arms commemorating the Chapter of the Order of the Golden Fleece, an early United Nations of sorts, held in Barcelona in 1519. Behind the choir you'll find the most important liturgical elements of the Cathedral, including the marble *cathedra* (bishop's throne; thus "cathedral"), the altar with the bronze cross designed by Frederic Marès in 1976, and most notably the sunken **crypt** of Santa Eulalia, one of Barcelona's patron saints. Discovered in the Santa Maria del Mar in AD 877, Santa Eulalia's remains were transported here in 1339. The crypt holds a white marble sarcophagus that depicts scenes from the saint's martyrdom at age 13.

Behind the altar, the **Chapel of Sant Joan Baptista i Sant Josep** features one of the most famous pieces of artwork in the Cathedral, the *Transfiguration of the Lord* altarpiece created by Bernat Martorell in 1450. The elevator to the roof is to the left of the altar, through the Capella de les Animes del Purgatori; it will give you a close-up view of the Cathedral's spires, as well as a bird's-eye view of the entire city.

Just to the right of the tomb is the exit into the peaceful **cloister,** home to the Fountain of St. Jordi. Thirteen white geese occupy the cloister, serving as a reminder of St. Eulalia's age at the time of her death. The chapels in the cloister were once dedicated to the various guilds of Barcelona, and a few of them are still maintained today (including the shoe-makers' and electricians'). If you look back toward the interior of the Cathedral, you can see the only remaining piece of the Romanesque structure, the large, arched doorway leading back inside. The earlier fourth-century building was almost entirely destroyed by Muslim invaders in 985; what little is left is visible underground in the Museu d'Història de la Ciutat (see p. 271). Coming from the Cathedral, you'll find the Cathedral museum at the near right corner of the cloister. The museum's most notable holding is Bartolomé Bermejo's renowned oil painting *Pietà*, the image of Christ dying in the arms of the Virgin; it's in the Sala Capitular, to the left upon entrance. The museum also holds the famous monstrance (the receptacle used for holding the Host for communion), made of gold and silver and dripping with precious jewels. Legend has it that the monstrance was given to the cathedral by the last Catalan king, Martí, before he died childless in 1410.

The front of the Cathedral is also the place to catch an impromptu performance of the *sardana*, the traditional Catalan dance. Performances generally occur Sunday mornings and afternoons after mass. *(ⓂJaume I, L4. In Pl. Seu, up C. Bisbe from Pl. St. Jaume. Cathedral open daily 8:30am-12:30pm, 1-5pm, and 5:15-7:30pm. Museum open daily 10am-12:30pm, 1-5pm, and 5:15-7pm. Elevator to the roof open M-Sa 10am-12:30pm and 1-6pm. Services Su at noon and 6:30pm. From 1-5pm €5 (includes cathedral, elevator, and museum), otherwise free. Museum €2. Elevator €2.50.)*

PLAÇA DE L'ANGEL. Outside ⓂJaume I is the square where the main Roman gate into Barcelona (Barcino in antiquity) was once located. The *plaça* gets its name from the legend surrounding the transfer of St. Eulalia's remains from Santa Maria del Mar to the cathedral: supposedly the martyred saint's body suddenly became too heavy to carry, and an angel appeared in the *plaça* pointing a finger at one of the church officials, who, it turned out, had secretly broken off and stolen one of Eulalia's toes. The angel statue (facing Via Laietania) commemorates the event, pointing with one arm to her own toe and with her other arm to the culprit. *(ⓂJaume I, L4.)*

ROMAN WALLS. Several sections of the northeastern walls of Roman Barcino are still standing near the cathedral. **Carrer Tapineria,** which runs from Pl. de l'Angel (to the left when you are facing Via Laietana) to Pl. Ramon Berenguer, serves both as parking space for mopeds and a viewing area from which you can see a large stretch of an AD fourth-century barricade under the Palau Reial Major. Continuing along C. Tapineria and making a left onto Av. de la Catedral lands you in **Plaça Seu** (in front of the Cathedral), where you can see the only intact octagonal corner tower left today (part of the Museu Diocesà). To the right of the cathedral are several more Roman towers and a reconstruction of one of the two aqueducts which supplied water to Barcino. *(ⓂJaume I, L4.)*

LAS RAMBLAS

LA RAMBLA

La Rambla is a world-famous cornucopia of street performers, fortune-tellers, pet and flower stands, and artists. A glut of tourists has led to a ton of restaurants and shops that cater to them. Watch your wallet; this is a pickpocketer's paradise. The tree-lined thoroughfare consists of five distinct *ramblas* (promenades). Together, the Ramblas form one boulevard about one kilometer long, starting at Pl. de Catalunya and proceeding down to Rambla del Mar and the Mediterranean.

LA RAMBLA DE LES CANALETES. The portward journey along las Ramblas begins at the Font de les Canaletes, the glorified water pump for which la Rambla de les Canaletes is named; it is recognizable by the four faucets and the Catalan crests (red crosses next to red and yellow stripes) that adorn it. Legend has it that visitors who sample the water will fall in love with the city (if they haven't already) and are bound to return to Barcelona someday. Stationed around here are the first of many living statues that line Las Ramblas during the day. Because of its symbolic position at the top of Las Ramblas on the Pl. de Catalunya, La Rambla de les Canaletes also sees a fair number of political demonstrations and Barça victory celebrations.

LA RAMBLA DELS ESTUDIS. You'll hear the squawking of the caged residents of the next section of Las Ramblas before you see them. The next stretch of Las Ramblas, which extends to C. Carme and C. Portaferrissa, is often referred to as "La Rambla dels Ocells" ("Promenade of the Birds"). A number of stalls here sell birds of nearly every kind: roosters, parrots, ducks, and many, many parakeets. Guinea pigs, iguanas, fish, ferrets, tortoises, and pretty much every other kind of caged creature is also available. The official name of this stretch of rambla comes from the university that used to be located here; *estudis* is Catalan for "studies."

LA RAMBLA DE SANT JOSEP. Here the screeching birds give way to the sunflowers, roses, and tulips on the segment of Las Ramblas commonly known as "La Rambla de les Flors" ("Promenade of the Flowers"). Vendors here have offered a variety of fragrant bouquets since the mid-1800s. In April, the flower stands are joined by book vendors in preparation for the Día de Sant Jordi, a Catalan variation on Valentine's Day. On April 23, couples exchange gifts; women of all ages receive flowers while men receive books.

The hulking stone building at the corner of C. Carme is the Església de Betlem, a Baroque church whose interior never recovered from torching by anarchists during the Spanish Civil War. A bit farther down is the famous traditional Catalan market, Mercat de la Boqueria (p. 263), officially named El Mercat de Sant Josep, the oldest of the city's some 40 markets. At Pl. Boqueria, just before the Liceu metro stop, you'll walk across Joan Miró's circular pavement mosaic, created for the city in 1976 and now a popular meeting point.

LA RAMBLA DELS CAPUTXINS. Miró's street mosaic marks the beginning of La Rambla dels Caputxins, the most user-friendly of the five Ramblas and the first of Las Ramblas to be converted into an actual promenade. The pedestrian area widens, and the majestic trees provide a bit more shade. Across from the recently renovated opera house (the Liceu; see p. 262), a strip of restaurants with outdoor seating vie for tourist euro, offering unremarkable and fairly expensive food.

LA RAMBLA DE SANTA MONICA. Following the tradition of naming the parts of Las Ramblas after the goods sold there, this stretch would most likely be nicknamed La Rambla de las Prostitutas. At night, women of the oldest profession patrol this wide area leading up to the port, beckoning passersby with loud kissing noises and lots of cleavage. During the day, however, this rambla distinguishes itself with skilled practitioners of a different art. These virtuosos can whip up dead-on caricatures in just five minutes. Also along this stretch you are bound to see peoople playing *trile*, a shell game with three little boxes and a tiny ball. Careful—these guys know how to manipulate that little *bolita* and they often have accomplices in the audience to help rope people in. This part of the rambla will take you all the way down to the Monument A Colom, and beyond that is the short Rambla del Mar leading to Port Vell.

GRAN TEATRE DEL LICEU. After burning down for the second time in 1994, the Liceu was rebuilt and expanded dramatically; a tour of the building includes not just the original 1847 **Sala de Espejos** (Hall of Mirrors), but also the 1999 **Foyer** (a curvaceous bar/lecture hall/small theater). The five-level, 2292-seat **theater** is considered one of Europe's top stages, adorned with palatial ornamentation, gold facades, and sculptures. A brief visit will give you a worthwhile glimpse into the majesty of the theater, but to really experience the place, try to catch a performance. Discount tickets are often available (see p. 276). *(La Rambla, 51-59, by C. Sant Pau. Ⓜ Liceu, L3. ☎ 934 85 99 00; www.liceubarcelona.com. Box office open M-F 10am-1pm and 2-6pm or by ServiCaixa. Short 20min. non-guided visits daily 11:30am-1pm every 30min, €4. 1hr. tours 10am; €8.70, seniors and under 26 €6.70.)*

LA BOQUERIA (MERCAT DE SANT JOSEP). La Boqueria is just the place to pick up that hard-to-find animal part you've been looking for, plus any other delicacies you've been craving. A traditional Catalan *mercat*—and the largest outdoor market in Spain—located in a giant, all-steel *Modernista* structure, La Boqueria is a sight to behold. Specialized vendors sell produce, fish, organs, whole pigs, cheese, nuts, wine, and sweets from a seemingly infinite number of independent stands inside. A few excellent cafes have terraces outside and serve dishes incorporating fresh ingredients from the market. *(La Rambla, 89. Ⓜ Liceu. A plate of seafood will generally cost €6-15, mixed seafood platter €20-25, for two €30-37.Open M-Sa 8am-8pm.)*

LA RIBERA

PALAU DE LA MÚSICA CATALANA. This is the Graceland of Barcelona. The Orfeó Catalan choir society commissioned *Modernista* master Lluís Domènech i Montaner to design this must-see concert venue, built in 1903. By day, the music hall glows with tall stained-glass windows and a skylight; it comes alive again after dark with electric lights. Sculptures of winged horses and busts of the muses spring from the walls flanking the stage. An inverted glass dome, painted with 40 women dressed as angels, looms in the very center of the ceiling. When the Orféo choir was founded in 1891, it was the first to permit women and men to sing together. The angels on the ceiling were a welcome to those women and an affirmation of their rightful place in the choir. The muses in back, each with a different exotic instrument, are likewise meant to welcome and honor the music of foreign cultures. Back in 1908, foreign and exotic meant Beethoven and Wagner, but even today the Palau hosts a diverse range of musical guests, from high-profile orchestras to bossa nova and pop-rock. The Palau's 3,000-tube organ is finally back in service after a lengthy renovation. *(C. del Palau de la Música, 4-6. ☎ 902 44 28 82; www.palaumusica.org. Ⓜ Jaume I, Urinaona. Mandatory 50min. tours in English every hr. Open daily Sept.-July 10am-3:30pm, Semana Santa and Aug. 10am-6pm. €12, students and seniors €11. Check website for scheduled performances. Concert tickets €8-175. Box office open 9am-9pm. MC/V.)*

PARC DE LA CIUTADELLA. A quick walk from Barceloneta and Barri Gòtic and sandwiched between La Ribera and Poble Nou and, Parc de la Ciutadella is both a refreshing break from the speed of the city and a major cultural and historical site. Take a nap, take a stroll, take a lover—just keep an eye out for jamming musicians. Barcelona's military resistance to the Bourbon monarchy in the early 18th century convinced Felipe V to quarantine the city's influential citizens in a large citadel on the site of what is now Pg. de Picasso. An entire neighborhood was razed and its citizens evicted to make room for the *ciutadella*, which lorded threateningly over Barcelona. In a popular move, the city demolished the fortress in 1878 and replaced it with the peaceful promenades of Parc de la Ciutadella. Architect Josep Fontseré designed the new park, and brought with him newcomers Domènech i Montaner (of **Palau de la Música Catalana** fame, see p. 263) and Antoni Gaudí. Several Modernista buildings went up years later when Ciutadella hosted the Universal Exposition in 1888, including Montaner's stately Castell dels Tres Dragons, now the **Museu de Zoologia.** *(Ⓜ Ciutadella or Marina. Park open daily 8am-11pm).*

HIVERNACLE. Originally built to showcase unusual tropical plants not sturdy enough for the climate of Barcelona, Josep Amergós's iron and glass *hivernacle* (greenhouse) now houses white tablecloths and bow-tied waiters alongside a room of exotic fauna, the perfect spot for a tropical afternoon meal or drink. The park's public restrooms also lurk among the greenery. On Wednesday evenings from May through July, the Hivernacle holds jazz concerts (10:30pm, €4);

BARCELONA

in July, Thursday nights bring free classical music (10:15pm). Farther down the Pg. de Picasso on the other side of the Museu Geologia, the iron-tiered Umbracle, built in 1883 and renovated in 2001, offers a cooler, shadier escape than its brother greenhouse. *(On Pg. de Picasso, behind the Museu de Zoologia. Ⓜ Arc de Triomf, L1. ☎ 93 295 40 17. Currently closed for renovations.)*

ARC DE TRIOMF. Less famous than its French cousin, this monument, just north of the Parc de la Ciutadella, is no less magnificent: the palm-lined walkway at its feet makes it a charming photo-op. Rather than commemorating a military triumph, the Arc de Triomf was designed as the entrance to the 1888 Exposition. A stylistic nod to the Spanish Moors, the red bricks surround green and yellow ceramic tiles and sculpted bats, angels, and lions. The main facade is a friendly face smiling down at you, dear tourist—it represents the welcoming of foreign visitors to Barcelona. *(Ⓜ Arc de Triomf, L1.)*

EL RAVAL

PALAU GÜELL. Gaudí completed Palau Güell—a *Modernista* residence built for wealthy patron Eusebi Güell i Bacigalupi (the industrialist, landowner and politician of Parc Güell fame)—in 1890. Güell spared no expense on this house, which, as the only building that Gaudí actually completed that has not undergone any major modifications, is considered to be one of the first true representations of the architect's revolutionary style. Picasso, who famously wanted to "send Gaudí and the Sagrada Família to hell," painted his Blue Period work across the street. Palau Güell was a private residence for the Güell family until 1936. During the Spanish Civil War, the *palau* was turned into a barracks; this left it in such a state of disrepair that its then-owner (Eusebi's daughter) turned it over to the Barcelona city council. Because the building is currently under restoration, visitors can see only the main facade, the ground floor, and the basement—a detailed description of the chimneys that have been renovated, however, is available online. *(C. Nou de La Rambla, 3-5. M: Liceu. ☎ 933 17 39 74; www.palauguell.cat. Partial entrance only. Open Tu-Sa 10am-2:30pm. Free.)*

EL CALL (JEWISH QUARTER)

Records indicate that Jewish families started moving to Roman Barcino as early as the AD second century. The Jewish quarter sprang to life near the center of town, between present-day Pl. St. Jaume, C. Ferran, C. Banys Nous, and the Església Santa Maria del Pi. Although today there is little indicating its Jewish heritage, for centuries El Call was the most vibrant center of intellectual and financial activity in all of Barcelona; Jews even received a certain amount of governmental support and protection in return for their substantial economic and cultural contributions to the city.

Anti-Semitism spread throughout Europe in the 13th century, however, and Spain was no exception. In 1243, Jaume I ordered the complete isolation of the Jewish quarter from the rest of the city, and he forced all Jews to wear identifying red-and-yellow buttons. Anti-Semitism increased as citizens looked for scapegoats for the plagues and poverty of the 14th century, and in 1348, hundreds of Jews were blamed for the Black Death and tortured mercilessly until they "confessed" their crimes. In 1391, as harassment spread throughout Spain, a riot ended in the murder of nearly 1000 Jews in Barcelona's Call. By 1401, every single synagogue and Jewish cemetery was demolished, making the forced conversion law of 1492 an easy next step. To add insult to injury, Jewish tombstones were pilfered to construct other buildings around that time. If you keep an eye out you may be able to spot some still discernable Hebrew inscriptions on some of the old, 14th-century walls in Barri Gòtic, for example at Pl. de Sant Iu, above and to left of the gas lamp on the wall opposite the **Museu Frederico Marès.**

One Jewish synagogue was turned into a church, the **Església de Sant Jaume** (C. Ferran, 28) which is still in use today. Some of the only remaining tangible evidence of Jewish inhabitants in El Call is the ancient Hebrew plaque in tiny C. Marlet as well as at the **Associació Call de Barcelona,** which features a collection of relics and ruins from an old synagogue. To get there, take C. Call from Pl. St. Jaume and turn right onto C. Sant Domènech de Call and then left onto C. Marlet. The plaque is at the end of the block and the museum is at the beginning.

One of the best-known alleys in El Call has nothing to do with Jewish history: to the left off the end of C. Sant Domènech de Call (coming from C. Call) is the **Baixada de Santa Eulalia,** which is said to be the place where the city's patron saint was tortured to death, joining the ranks of Christian martyrs (see **Església Catedral de la Santa Creu,** p. 260). On the wall at the start of the street, a plaque written by Catalan poet Jacint Verdaguer commemorates the legend. *(Ⓜ Liceu, L3. Associació Call de Barcelona C. Marlet: ☎933 17 07 90; www.calldebarcelona.org. Open M-F 10:30am-2:30pm and 4-7pm, Sa-Su 10:30am-3pm. Tour €2.)*

L'EIXAMPLE

AROUND PASSEIG DE GRÀCIA

When **Ildefons Cerdà** drew up his designs for L'Eixample, he envisioned utopic, green, and well-ventilated city blocks where people from all social classes would live free of the congestion that plagued epidemic-prone old Barcelona. While he succeeded, to an extent—L'Eixample's avenues are indeed tree-lined and sunlit—the neighborhood has never quite realized Cerdà's vision of socio-economic integration (it was, and remains, posh). As Barcelona's bourgeoisie have increasingly moved uptown, the once-residential districts around Pg. de Gràcia have filled with offices and shops. Both in this zone and farther away, Cerdà's interminable blocks and wide-open plazas are broken up by architectural landmarks from every subsequent era. Make sure to look through the avenues' leafy ceilings; glimpses of *Modernista* casas and **Torre Agbar,** Jean Nouvel's spaceship-like, blue- and red-lit glass tower, will be your reward for doing so. Because l'Eixample is so large, the sights and museums in this neighborhood are grouped into three more manageable areas: l'Eixample Dreta, Pg. de Gràcia, and l'Eixample Esquerra.

CASA MILÀ (LA PEDRERA). Although innovative, Gaudí's unusual designs for Casa Milà were unpopular 100 years ago, and the name, La Pedrera (which means stone quarry in Spanish), came about as a result of popular jokes, critiques, and caricatures. The building's namesake, wealthy businessman Pere Milà, hired Gaudí because he liked his work on neighboring Casa Batlló (see p. 266). But as the project progressed between 1906 and 1910, Milà's wife, Rosario Segimon, became increasingly unhappy with the appearance and refused to pay the excessive building costs. Gaudí eventually filed a lawsuit against the couple over his fees (he won and promptly gave all of the money to the poor), and the Casa Milà ended up being the only residence he designed where he didn't also craft the furniture. Today, visitors have access to the main floor, the attic, the terrace, and a sample apartment equipped with period furniture. The rest of Casa Milà is inhabited by the lucky (read: wealthy) people who sat on the 20-year waiting list for an apartment as well as several offices of Caixa Catalunya, which acquired the building in 1986 (hence all the pamphlets that read "La Pedrera de Caixa Catalunya"). The attic, deemed the **Espai Gaudí,** is filled with displays about the construction of this and other Gaudí works, calling attention to the way Gaudí interpreted and expressed natural forms. Casa Milà in particular is built around two central courtyards, with an underground park in the basement and not a single flat wall in the entire space. For a great photo-op, climb to the roof of Casa Milà to get a picture of La Sagrada Família (see p. 267) framed by an arch. The summer concert series, *La Nit de Pedrera*, transforms the roof into a jazz cabaret on weekend nights. *(Pg. de Gràcia, 92. ☎902 40 09 73; www.lapedreraeducacio.org. Open daily Mar.-Oct. 9am-8pm, last admission 7:30pm; Nov.-Feb. 9am-6:30pm. €9.50, students and seniors €5.50. Free audio tour. Concerts last weekend of June-July F-Sa 9pm-midnight. €12, glass of cava included.)*

LA MANZANA DE LA DISCORDIA

According to Greek myth, a piece of fruit was responsible for the Trojan War: the goddess of Discord created a golden apple as a prize for the most beautiful, and divine disharmony ensued. Barcelona has its own competition for the golden apple on the block of Pg. de Gràcia between C. Consell de Cent and C. Aragó, where trademark houses by the three most important architects of Modernism stand side-by-side in proud competition: the Casa Lleó Morera by Domènech i Montaner, the Casa Amatller by Puig i Cadafalch, and the Casa Batlló by Gaudí. Even the most ardent Catalanists haven't wanted to give up the pun in the old name *la manzana*, which in Castilian means both "block" and "apple." The name "Block of Discord" is especially indicative of the contrast (and clash) between the styles and aesthetics of the three houses. All of these creations are renovations of older, pre-existing edifices. To see the architectural contrast most clearly, take a look from across the street.

BARCELONA

CASA BATLLÒ. The most fantastical member of the Block of Discord, Gaudí's Casa Batlló sees the most visitors. Gaudí was 52 when he reconstructed this house—one of his first works and completely "Gaudían" in style—after years of developing it. Shimmering and curving in shades of blue and green, the house looks slightly different at every hour of the day. Many see the building as a depiction of the legend of St. Jordi and the **dragon.** This interpretation incorporates all the major facets of the facade. The tall pinnacle on the left symbolizes the knight's lance after it has pierced the dragon's scaly back, which is represented by the warped, multi-colored, ceramic roof. The stairway supposedly represents the winding dragon's tail or the curves of his vertebrae, the outside balconies skulls, and the molded columns the bones of his unfortunate victims. Others see the house as having an underwater theme; walls and stained-glass windows are fluid and wavelike, and many of the ceilings spiral as if in a whirlpool. Particularly interesting is the way he tiled the central inner patio, dark blue on the top and lighter on the bottom, in order to distribute the light from above as evenly as possible. Of the many aspects of the building accessible by the tour, highlights include the mushroom-shaped fireplace, the house's dining room with two puzzlingly spaced pillars (only a few inches apart), the back porch decorated with colorful mosaics, and the roof, which allows for a closer look at the facade's scaly tiling as well as a decent view of the city. As you leave be sure to pay your respects to the Gaudí hologram, who salutes as you leave the upper level. *(Pg. de Gràcia, 43. ☎932 16 03 06; www.casabatllo.cat. Open daily 9am-8pm. €17, students, BCN card €13. Cash only. Call for group discounts for more than 20 people. Free multilingual audio tour.)*

CASA LLEÓ I MORERA. In 1902, textile tycoon Albert Lleó Morera hired **Domènech i Montaner** to add some pizzazz to his boring 1864 home on the corner of Pg. de Gràcia and C. Consell de Cent. Montaner responded by creating one of the most lavish examples of decorative architecture in Barcelona, for which he won the Ajuntament's annual prize for Best Building of the Year in 1905. Much of the street-level exterior was destroyed by the Loewe leather shop that now occupies the entry, but if you look up at the second-floor balconies on either side of the corner tribune, you can see two nymphs on each balcony, holding (from left to right) a gramophone, an electric light bulb, a telephone, and a camera, symbols of the new leisure technology available to the bourgeoisie of the early 1900s. There are carved lions on the balcony above the tribune. Mulberry leaves lace around the tops of the tribune's vertical columns. Together these refer to the family name: *lleó* in Catalan means "lion," and *morera* means "mulberry tree."

The mezzanine level of the interior, unfortunately closed to the public, boasts a stunning dining room with glimmering stained-glass windows and detailed ceramic mosaics of the Lleó Morera family picnicking outdoors. The famous furniture that Gaspar Homar originally designed for this room is permanently on display at the Museu d'Art Modern. *(Pg. de Gràcia, 35. Entrance not permitted.)*

CASA AMATLLER. Chocolate mogul Antoni Amatller planted the first seed for La Manzana de la Discordia in 1898, when he commissioned **Puig i Cadafalch** to redo the facade of his prominent home. Cadafalch turned out a mix of Catalan, neo-Gothic, Islamic, and Dutch architecture best known for its stylized, geometric, and multicolored upper facade. The lower exterior of the house also has character; look carefully and you can see the owner's personality inscribed in sculpture. Above the main door, the prominent carving of Catalan hero St. Jordi battling the **dragon** demonstrates Amatller's Catalan nationalism and the four figures engaged in painting, sculpture, architecture, and music represent Amatller's broad cultural interests. On either side of the main second-floor windows, there are caricatures of Amatller's favorite pastimes. On the left, small monkeys and rabbits busily mold iron (the main Catalan industry of Amatller's time), and a donkey with glasses reads while another plays with a camera; on the right side, frogs and pigs hold glass vases and pottery, a reference to Amatller's passion for vase-collecting. A huge "A" for Amatller adorns the outside of the entrance, intertwined with almond leaves (*amatller* means "almond" in Catalan). The long, single balcony with many doorways is also a traditional element of Catalan architecture.

Inside, the entrance foyer has original iron-and-glass lamps, bright, decorative tiles, and a stained-glass skylight just to the right of the main hallway. The small temporary art exhibit in the back room features various projects relevant to Modernist architecture—for example, miniature architectural models, stained-glass exhibitions, and collections of photographs from that period. Buy some Amatller chocolate to see for yourself whether he deserved his fortune. The apartment where the millionaire lived with his daughter is now home to the Institut Amatller d'Art Hispànic, open to students of the institute.

The Joieria Bagués, which holds a well-known collection of Modernist pieces from the Masriera tradition, occupies the right side of the entrance level. The mseum offers a tour of the store's sparkling dragonflies, nymphs, and flowers. *(Pg. de Gracià, 41. ☎934 877 217. House closed for renovations, expected to reopen 2012. Tours of film and temporary exhibition weekdays at noon, €5. More tours may be offered as renovations continue: call ahead.)*

L'EIXAMPLE DRETA

LA SAGRADA FAMÍLIA. Although Gaudí's unfinished masterpiece is barely a shell of the intended finished product, La Sagrada Família is without a doubt

BARCELONA

the world's most visited construction site. Despite the completion of only eight of the 18 planned towers (and those are the shortest), millions of people make the touristic pilgrimage to witness the work-in-progress. Its construction is entirely funded by popular donations; in the past, the Church told donors their patronage guaranteed them a place in heaven. (Luckily, visitors' entrance fees are considered just such "popular donations.") While it's questionable whether the price of admission will get you through the pearly gates, it will get you into an awe-inspiring world of nature, spirituality, and art. Finished or not, La Sagrada Família has become intertwined with the image of Barcelona.

An extremely pious right-wing organization called the **Spiritual Association for Devotion to St. Joseph (or the Josephines)** commissioned La Sagrada Família. Founded in 1866 in reaction to the liberal ideas spreading throughout Europe, the group was determined to build an Expiatory Temple for Barcelona, where the city could reaffirm its faith to the Holy Family of Jesus, Mary, and Joseph (hence the building's full name, Templo Expiatori de la Sagrada Família). The first architect they chose quit almost immediately when his ideas for the church strayed from those of the project's commissar. Gaudí replaced him in 1884, at the age of 31. For the first 15 or 20 years, private contributions kept the building process going, but as the mood and culture of the city changed with the onset of the modern age, construction slowed drastically, and the Civil War (see p. 60) brought it to a complete halt. The war years proved tragic for the temple. First Gaudí died after being hit by a tram just outside the church's walls in 1926, having overseen the completion of only the Nativity Facade. To make matters worse, in 1936, arsonists on the revolutionary side of the Civil War broke into the crypt, opened Gaudí's tomb, smashed his plaster models, and burned every single document in the workshop in a display of anti-establishment fury.

Today, the building remains under the auspices of the Josephines; architect Jordi Bonet, whose father worked directly with Gaudí, heads up the project with sculptor Josep Marià Subirachs, who finished the **Passion Facade** in 1998. Without Gaudí's exact calculations, the team works from ongoing reconstructions of his original plaster models. The computer models that engineers use to recreate his underlying mathematical logic are so complicated that they have earned an exhibit of their own. As today's workers slowly give shape to what they think Gaudí had in mind, they continue to achieve unprecedented architectural feats. Until now, it was nearly impossible to set a completion date because of the intricacies of the reconstructed models and the unsteady flow of donations. Most recent estimates predict that La Sagrada Família will be finished by 2030. Winged pigs may soar from the towers that same year.

When completed, the front of the temple—the **Glory Facade**—will feature four more bell towers; together the 12 towers will represent the 12 apostles. Above the center of the church will rise a massive 170m **Tower of Jesus,** with a shorter spire just behind it dedicated to Mary. The Jesus tower will in turn be surrounded by four more towers symbolizing the four Evangelists (the authors of the four gospels). As finishing touches, Gaudí envisioned an extravagant spouting fountain in front of the main Glory Facade and a tall purifying flame at the back. Gaudí's dedication to religious themes in his work on La Sagrada Família has even earned the attention of the Vatican. The continuation of Gaudí's greatest obsession has been fraught with fierce controversy. Some, like Salvador Dalí, have argued that the church should have been left incomplete as a monument to the architect.

Others believe that La Sagrada Família should be finished, but in a more "authentic" manner than has been the case so far. Critics usually attack most vehemently Josep Maria Subirachs i Sitjar's **Passion Facade.** The controversial Passion Facade, which faces the Pl. de la Sagrada Família, portrays Christ's Passion (Catholic lingo for his crucifixion, death, and resurrection). Its abstract, Cubist design contrasts starkly with the more traditional **Nativity Facade,** which depicts Christ's birth and faces the Pl. de Gaudí. Defenders of the facade argue that *Modernisme* has always been about celebrating the vision of individual Catalan artisans—and that this facade does precisely that.

Today's visitors can see detailed paintings of the projected church in the **Museu Gaudí.** Numerous pictures from the early years of the project, sketches by Gaudí, the glass-walled workshop where his models are still being restored, and various sculptures and decorative pieces from the temple are also on display. For a more somber experience, gaze down on Gaudí's crypt, where roses and tea lights line the grave as a statue of Mary watches over the man that lived and died for this church. *(C. Mallorca, 401. ☎932 08 04 14; www.sagradafamilia.org. Ⓜ Sagrada Família. Open daily Apr.-Sept. 9am-8pm, Oct.-Mar. 9am-6pm. Last elevator to the tower 15min. before close. Guided tours in English (€3) May-Oct. at 11am, 1, 3, 5pm; Nov.-Apr. at 11am and 1pm. €11, students €9, under 10 free. Elevator €2.50. Combined ticket with Casa-Museu Gaudí €13, students €11.)*

GRACIA

PARC GÜELL. On a hill at the northern edge of Gràcia lies Barcelona's most enchanting public park, designed entirely by **Gaudí,** and—in typical Gaudí fashion—not completed until after his death. After the pleasing results of his collaboration with Gaudí on Güell's Palau, Eusebi Güell, a Catalan industrialist and patron of the arts, commissioned the renowned architect to fashion a garden city in the tradition of Hampstead Heath and other parks in England, where Güell had spent many years. Güell was fascinated with rank and power (he longed to be granted a title by the king), and he envisioned a utopic community devoid of the lower classes (the turn-of-the-century Beverly Hills). Started in 1900, construction slowed to a halt in 1914 due to financial difficulties, and only three houses were completed. The citizens of Barcelona were put off both by Gaudí's shockingly bold designs and the park's then-great distance from the city. As a result, only two aristocrats signed on and as a housing development it was a complete failure.

As a park, Park Güell is fantastic. In 1918, the Barcelona City Council bought Park Güell, and in 1923 opened the multicolored, dwarfish buildings and mosaic stairways to the public. The park has since been honored as a UNESCO World Heritage Site. The park, with its Catalan themes, religious symbolism, and natural influences (read: beautiful flowers), is a symphony of color and form. The most eye-catching elements of the park—the surreal mosaics and fairy-tale fountains—are clustered around the main entrance on C. Olot. The entrance's Palmetto Gate, a replica of the iron work on Gaudí's *Casa Vicens,* is flanked by two small buildings originally meant to house the community's administrative offices. Visitors today can stop by the LAIE book and gift shop in the house on the left as you face the park entrance. These otherworldly houses were inspired by a Catalan production of Hansel and Gretel; the spire-topped construction belongs to the children, and the other, crowned with a bright red poisonous mushroom, belongs to the witch. Lavishly decorated with fan-shaped mosaics, the roofs resemble edible gingerbread and cream frosting. Behind

Hansel and Gretel's house, you'll find the park's restrooms and a popular cafe. (Coffee €1.50; tapas €1-3; bocadillos €3-6. Open during park hours.)

Facing the majestic double staircase, a cavernous stone area to the right, now under construction, was originally meant to house the carriages of park residents. When open, the structure, reminiscent of an elephant, serves as a shaded rest area for visitors. The staircase itself is divided into three sections, each with its own fountain. Tourists jostle to take pictures of their loved ones beside the gaping, multicolored **salamander fountain** as it drools into the basin below. The animal's sleek body is covered with a tightly woven mosaic of green, orange, and blue. Some believe it is a reference to the coat of arms of the French city of Nîmes, the northern boundary of Old Catalunya. At the next level, a curvaceous red mosaic fountain holds a stone interpreted to be either an oracle or the philosopher's stone. The mouth-like bench behind it is entirely protected from the wind and remains in the shade for three seasons (winter is the sunny one).

Stairs lead up to the **Hall of One Hundred Columns (Teatro Griego),** a Modernist masterpiece of 86 Doric columns (but who's counting?). A spectacular open space meant for the community's market, the hall's columns support a ceiling constructed of white-tiled domes. Toward the center, musicians often play classical music, and multicolored medallions are interspersed among the ceiling domes. **Josep Maria Jujol,** Gaudí's right-hand man, created every medallion, using scraps from discarded mirrors, plates, glasses, and even porcelain dolls.

Stairs on either side of the hall lead up to the **Plaça de la Naturalesa,** a barren open area partly supported by the columned hall below and surrounded by the **serpentine bench.** The shape of the bench is not only aesthetically pleasing, but also structurally necessary given the positioning of the columns below. It is also designed to cradle visitors' buttocks and is consequently incredibly comfortable. All of this thanks to the rumored "creative methods" of Jujol. He is said to have made one of the workers sit bare-assed in the wet cement to add that extra, anatomically correct touch. Pieced together from broken ceramic remnants from local pottery workshops, Gaudí and Jujol's multicolored bench is covered with brightly colored flowers, geometric patterns, and religious images. During the park's restoration in 1995, workers discovered that the 21 distinct tones of white are cast-offs from the **Casa Milà** (see p. 265) that had been cemented in the bench. The bench's abstract collage later became a great inspiration for Joan Miró's Surrealist work.

From here, sweeping paths supported by columns (meant to resemble palm trees) swerve through hedges and ascend to the park's summit, which commands tremendous views of the city. A pleasant walk through the grounds begins at the path directly to right when facing the salamander fountain. Follow the wide path past the sunny flower beds and open grassy area and veer right toward the shaded benches. As the path twists uphill, the turreted, pink **Casa-Museu Gaudí** (p. 271) appears on your left. Farther ahead, the **Pont dels Enamorats** offers views of the city all the way to the sea, and Gaudí's stone trees—tall columns topped with agave plants—are interspersed with curved benches. Around the next curve, **Casa Trías** (1905), the park's third house, purchased by the lawyer Trías Domènech and still owned by his family, is surrounded by less scenic walking paths that loop around to the left along Avenue del Coll del Portell. Farther along the wide, main path, past a grassy area with a small playground and plenty of benches, an upward slope spirals to **El Turo de Les Tres Creus.** Originally destined to be the park residents' church, the small tower is topped with a mere three crosses, which appear to form an arrow when you look toward the east. This peak is the park's highest point, offering a dazzling 360° view of the city below. To head back down, follow the twisting path that slopes toward the sea. Check out the views of the Hansel and Gretel houses and other park structures. At the Avenue Sant Josep de la Muntanya entrance, follow a narrow path to the right until it becomes El Viaducte de la Bugadera as it passes Güell's house (now a school) on the right. The irregularly shaped stone columns that support the covered passageway are composed of fascinating shapes. You'll find the statue of **La Bugadera** (the Washerwoman) on one of the last columns in the passageway. Stairs ahead lead back to the Pl. de la Naturalesa. *(Bus #24 from Pl. Catalunya stops at the upper entrance. Info center ☎ 93 284 62 00. Park and info center open daily 9am-dusk. Free.)*

CASA-MUSEU GAUDÍ. Designed by Gaudí's friend and colleague, **Fransesc Berenguer,** the Casa-Museu Gaudí was the celebrated architect's home from 1906 to 1926 when he moved into the Sagrada Família for the months leading up his death. Gaudí's leftover fence work from other projects was used to create the garden of metallic plant sculptures in front of the museum. The three-story house is a great place to examine Gaudí's anatomical furniture designs from the Casa Batlló, paintings of several of his works by notable artists, and his bronze-cast death mask from close-up. The ceilings, different in every room, highlight the otherwise sober spaces with touches of color and eye-catching patterns. Before leaving, peek into the Modernist bathroom where the toilet seat curves in Gaudí's trademark saddle-shape. *(☎ 93 219 38 11. Carretera del Carmel. Inside Park Güell, to the right of the Hall of One Hundred Columns when you are facing away from the sea. Open daily Apr.-Sept. 10am-8pm; Oct.-Mar. 10am-6pm. Last entrance 15min. before closing. €5.50, with ISIC or under 18 €4.50, under 10 free.)*

BARCELONA

OTHER HOUSES IN GRÀCIA

When in Gràcia, look up. The neighborhood's narrow, tree-lined streets are home to several of Modernism's lesser-known architectural masterpieces. Casting your eyes skyward can also prove rewarding: warped wrought-iron balconies and brightly patterned walls inform you that yes, you have stumbled upon a masterpiece. Because these buildings are private houses, their interiors are closed to the public. The houses are so distinctive, however, that even a good look at each exterior is well worth the (sometimes lengthy) walk.

CASA VICENS. Gaudi designed Vicens between 1883 and 1888 for a local tile manufacturer; it is fittingly decorated with blocks of cheerful green, white, and yellow ceramic tiles accented with red-painted brick. The famous architect studied Arabic design to come up with the casa's rigid angles. By contrast, the graceful, fluid ironwork of the balconies and the palm-leaf gate foreshadow the architect's style in later projects. In the summer, bougainvillea brims over the right hand corner of the house, adding a pleasing touch of purple. *(C. Carolines, 24-26.)*

MUSEUMS

BARRI GÒTIC AND LAS RAMBLAS

Barri Gòtic is not the place for contemporary art or halls full of the old masters; instead it is home to a smattering of quirky collections and historical exhibitions.

MUSEU D'HISTÒRIA DE LA CIUTAT. Buried some 20m below a seemingly innocuous old plaza lies one of the two components of the Museu d'Història de la Ciutat: the subterranean excavations of the Roman city of Barcino.

This **archaeological exhibit** displays incredibly well-preserved AD first- to sixth-century ruins; through glass sections, you can see huge ceramic wine casks, intricate Roman floor mosaics, and the reused cornerstones that form part of the Roman walls. The fourth-century wall fresco depicting a man on horseback is a particularly beautiful and well-preserved relic. Also accessible through the museum is the **Palau Reial Major,** which was built on top of the fourth-century ruins and served as the residence of the Catalan-Aragonese monarchs. The Gothic **Saló de Tinell** (Throne Room) is supposedly the place where Fernando and Isabel received Columbus after his journey to America, and now hosts exhibitions about contemporary Barcelona. *(Pl. del Rei. Ⓜ Jaume I. ☎ 932 56 21 00; www.museuhistoria.bcn.cat. Wheelchair-accessible. Open Apr.-Sept. Tu-Sa 10am-8pm, Su 10am-3pm; Oct.-Mar. Tu-Sa 10am-2pm and 4-7pm, Su 10am-3pm. Free multilingual audio guides. Pamphlets available in English. Museum €6, students €4. Exhibition €1.80/1.10. Museum and exhibition €6.80/5.10. Under 16 free.)*

CENTRE D'ART DE SANTA MÓNICA. Once a convent, this museum now houses temporary exhibitions and hosts artistic events. The provocative installations housed here are often interactive and tend to be quite elaborate. In April 2009, the museum turned heads by staging an "itinerant musical action" whereby a man played piano while being paraded down Las Ramblas with a man and a woman having passionate simulated sex atop his instrument. There are significant rebuilding phases between shows, so call and make sure the galleries are open before you visit. Just in front of the Museum is the **Punt d'Informació Cultural,** which has all the art-related programs and flyers you could ever want. *(La Rambla, 7. Ⓜ Drassanes. ☎ 933 16 28 10; www.artsantamonica.cat. Open Tu-Sa noon-10pm. Free. Punt d'Informació Cultural open M-F 9:30am-2pm and 3:30-7:30pm, Sa 10am-2pm.)*

BARCELONA

MUSEU DE L'ERÒTICA. This stimulating museum has an odd assortment of pictures, artwork, and artifacts that spans human history and depicts a variety of sexual acrobatics that seem to defy the limits of human flexibility. The 7 ft. wooden phallus is a classic photo-op. Be sure to catch the 1926 porno flick said to have been secretly commissioned by King Alfonso XIII. *(La Rambla, 96. Ⓜ Liceu, L1/3. ☎ 933 18 98 65; www.erotica-museum.com. Open daily 10am-9pm. €9, students €8.)*

MUSEU DE CERA (WAX MUSEUM). Over 300 wax figures form an endless parade of celebrities, fictional characters, and rather obscure European historical figures. The most recognizable ones have distinctive facial hair, like Fidel Castro and Chewbacca from Star Wars. If the celebrities upstairs are too banal, downstairs you'll find more gruesome depictions of famous martyrs, murderers, and monsters. For those dying to have their picture taken with a wax sculpture of Picasso mid-brush stroke, this is the place to go. *(La Rambla, 4-6 or Pg. de la Banca, 7. Ⓜ Drassanes. ☎ 933 17 26 49, www.museocerabcn.com. Open July-Sept. daily 10am-10pm; Oct.-June M-F 10am-1:30pm and 4-7:30pm, Sa-Su and holidays 11am-2pm and 4:30-8:30pm. Last entrance 30min. before closing. €10, ages 5-11 and seniors €6, under 5 free. Audioguide €3.50.)*

MUSEU PICASSO. This fascinating museum traces the development of Picasso as an artist with an exhibit of his early works organized chronologically. The large collection weaves through five connected mansions that were once occupied by Barcelona's nobility. Picasso's friend, Jaume Sabartés, made the museum's founding donation in 1963; the collection was later expanded by Picasso himself, and then by relatives after his death. Though you may not recognize Picasso the Cubist in this collection of his earlier works, the museum gives unsurpassed insight into his formative years as a painter in Barcelona. Visitors will also witness the artist's later experiences in Paris, where he first encountered the impressionists' experiments with light and Cézanne's technique of flatness.

The museum features several noteworthy works from Picasso's Blue and Rose periods, but most impressive of all is the display of the artist's 58 Cubist interpretations of Velázquez's *Las Meninas.* The original painting is a breathtaking, 7ft. portrait of the royal family. Hailed as the finest Spanish painting, *Las Meninas* is often re-interpreted by Spanish painters as a rite of passage of the great. Instead of simply transposing the picture, Picasso reinvents it, transforming the many vantage points of the original into the jarring fragments and lines of vision that would become the trademark of his Cubist technique.

Other exhibits of the museum showcase his early award-winning paintings and his later sculpture. Special temporary exhibitions highlight work by Picasso's contemporaries. As Barcelona's most popular museum, the Museu Picasso often has lines snaking a good way down C. de Montcada; the best times to avoid the museum-going masses are mornings and early evenings. *(C. de Montcada, 15-23. ⓂJaume I, L4. From the metro, head down C. de la Princesa and turn right on C. de Montcada. ☎932 56 30 00; www.museupicasso.bcn.es. Open Tu-Su 10am-8pm. Last entry 30min. before closing. Wheelchair-accessible. €9, students and seniors €6, under 16 free. Special exhibits €5.80. Free Su after 3pm. 1st Su of each month free.)*

MUSEU DE LA XOCOLATA. This unique and delectable museum is half educational journey through the history of chocolate, and half-impressive, if largely random, chocolate sculptures. Children will enjoy choco-versions of cartoon characters from Bambi to Homer Simpson. The cafe offers workshops on chocolate sculpting for children under 12, and chocolate tastings paired with wine and liquor for the rest of us. *(Pl. Pons i Clerch, C. del Comerç, 26. ⓂJaume I. ☎932 68 78 78; www.museudelaxocolata.com. Open M and W-Sa 10am-7pm, Su 10am-3pm. €4.30, students and seniors €3.70, with Barcelona Card €3, under 7 free. Alcohol and chocolate tasting €7.70; reservations required. Workshops for kids from €5.40; reservations required.)*

EL RAVAL

El Raval, home to the MACBA and the University of Barcelona, has "artsy" tattooed on its forehead. The streets below the University (in the direction of M: Liceu) tend towards a younger crowd; above the University (around M: Universitat and particularly on C. Consell de Cent) you'll find art galeries galore that host up-and-coming artists hoping to someday make it to MACBA's walls.

MUSEU D'ART CONTEMPORANI (MACBA). The gleaming white MACBA building, designed by American architect Richard Meier in 1995, was the final product of a collaboration between Barcelona's mayor and the Catalan government to restore El Raval by turning the neighborhood into a regional artistic and cultural center (14 years later: mission accomplished). The museum's modernity and scale, as well as sheer brightness, are a startling contrast with the narrow alleys and aging cobblestone streets of the surrounding neighborhood. The building's sparse decor was designed to allow the art to speak for itself, which it has—the MACBA has received worldwide acclaim for its focus on interwar avant-garde art. While the permanent collection provides a general overview of Western contemporary art, it is particularly successful in introducing the public to the works of some acclaimed artists from Barcelona. The main attractions are the highly innovative rotating exhibits and the "Nits de MACBA" (Th and F nights in the summer), when the museum stays open until midnight and the reduced price of admission (€3.50) includes a guided tour. Every year during Sonar (Barcelona's über-popular festival celebrating electronic and experimental music), the museum opens its exhibitions to festival-goers and hosts the Sonarcomplex stage, as well as other Sonar-related activities. To give a feel for what this means, on one Friday of the 2009 festival, there were live concerts at 1, 4:30, 7:30, and 9pm (as well as, of course, several "at night," or after 9pm). During Sonar, entry into the museum is limited exclusively to festival-goers, and the Museum's hours are the same as the Sonar's. *(Pl. Des Àngels, 1. M: Catalunya ☎934 12 08 10; www.macba.es. Open M and W-F 11am-8pm, Sa 10am-8pm, Su 10am-3pm. Tours in Catalan and English M and Th 6pm; Catalan and Spanish W and F 6pm, Su noon and 6pm. €7.50, students €6, under 14 free; temporary exhibitions €4. From mid-May to Sept. restaurant and bar service on 1st-fl. terrace. Restaurant and bar phone ☎672 20 73 89.)*

CENTRE DE CULTURA CONTEMPORANIA DE BARCELONA (CCCB). The center's striking architecture incorporates an early 20th-century theater with its 1994 addition, a sleek wing of black glass. CCCB hosts expositions, symposia, and courses having to do with its major themes (simple matters like the human condition, cosmopolitanism, public space, and creativity). It now has a cafe, gallery space, screening room, and bookstore. Along with MACBA, it is also a main daytime venue for the Sonar music festival. Check the center's exhaustive website or the *Guía del Ocio* for scheduled events. *(Casa de Caritat. C. Montalegre, 5. M: Catalunya or Universitat. ☎933 06 41 00; www.cccb.org. Open Tu-W and F-Su 11am-8pm, Th 11am-10pm. Expositions €4.70, students €3.60, under 16 free. 2 expositions for €6. 1st W of the month, Th 8-10pm and Su 3-8pm free.)*

L'EIXAMPLE

AROUND PASSEIG DE GRÁCIA

FUNDACIÓ FRANCISCO GODIA. This museum was created in 1998 by Godia's daughter in order to open his private art collection for public viewing. **Francisco Godia** (1921-1990) was a bizarre combination of astute businessman, accomplished Formula One race car driver, and passionate supporter of the arts. His collection boasts a huge variety of works and artists over the span of nearly a milennium. From an impressive collection of 12th-century religious sculptures and paintings to modern works by such names as Picasso and Tapiés. Highlights include Saragossa's stunning *Virgen de la Leche* (1374), Solana's bold, dark-lined *Bullfight at Ronda* (1927), Francesc Gimeno's life-like *Mother and Daughter* (1898), and the popular *At the Racecourse* (1905) by Ramon Casas. The Fundació also organizes exhibitions featuring private collections from throughout Spain. Be sure to check out the front room filled with Godia's racing trophies, proof that fast cars, engine grease, and art *can* go hand-in-hand. *(C. Diputació 250. ⓂPg. de Gràcia, L2/3/4. ☎932 72 31 80; www.fundacionfgodia.org. Open M, W-Sa, and Su 10am-8pm. Free guided tours Sa-Su noon in Spanish and Catalan; otherwise call ahead for a guided tour, €6. Wall descriptions and printed guides are in English, Catalan, and Spanish. Wheelchair-accessible. €6. MC/V.)*

L'EIXAMPLE ESQUERRA

FUNDACIÓ ANTONI TÀPIES. Antoni Tàpies's massive and bizarre wire sculpture, *Cloud with Chair*, atop Domènech i Montaner's red brick building announces this collection of contemporary abstract art. The top floor of the foundation is dedicated to famous Catalans, particularly Tàpies, while the other two floors feature temporary exhibits of other modern artists' work. Tàpies is one of Catalunya's best-known artists; his works often defy definition, springing from Surrealism and Magicism, and drawing inspiration from Picasso and Miró. Most of his pieces mix painting and sculpture, and are generally referred to as collage, although he also creates abstract sculptures. Most of his paintings include a "T" in some form, a symbol that has been variously interpreted (or misinterpreted) as a religious cross, sexual penetration, and the artist's own signature. In truth, no one knows the real meaning, if there is one. Tàpies's use of unorthodox materials—including objects found in the trash—and his dark, dirty colors are often construed as a protest against the dictatorship and the subsequent urban alienation pervading Spain's cities. Everyday materials, like sand, glue, wood, marble powder, dirt, and wire show the eloquence inherent in simplicity. The other highlights are the rotating exhibitions on the two lower floors—some of the best modern photography and video art in the city, as well as film screenings and lectures. In summer, check out DJ nights on the terrace, with free drinks and after-hours gallery access. *(C. Aragó, 255. ☎ 934 87 03 15. Ⓜ Pg. de Gràcia. Closed for renovation as of summer 2009. Call for more information.)*

BARCELONETA

MUSEU D'HISTÒRIA DE CATALUNYA. The last gasp of the old city before you hit the packed beaches of Barceloneta, the Museu provides a patriotic introduction to Catalan history, politics, and culture. The detailed displays, diagrams, and artifacts (all with English captions) all help thread together the centuries of background behind all the historical sights you've been marveling at in Barcelona. The city's entire history is here: Neolithic tools; artifacts of the Roman and Islamic rules of the AD first millennium; exhibits on the repression of Catalunya by Felipe V; the *Renaixença* and development of *Modernisme;* the Civil War; the rule of Franco, and the resurgence of culture and industry since Franco's death. (Whew.) Recreations of a 1930s Spanish bar, an AD eighth-century Islamic prayer tent, and other dioramas make the museum a full sensory experience. *(Pl. Pau Vila, 3. Near entrance to the Moll d'Espanya; left walk out toward Barceloneta. ☎ 932 25 47 00; www.mhcat.com. Open Tu and Th-Sa 10am-7pm, W 10am-8pm, Su 10am-2:30pm. €4; under 18 and students €3; university students, under 7, and over 65 free. Free 1st Su of the month.)*

MONTJUÏC AND POBLE SEC

MUSEU NACIONAL D'ART DE CATALUNYA (PALAU NACIONAL). Designed by Enric Catá and Pedro Cendoya for the 1929 International Exposition, the Palau Nacional has housed the Museu Nacional d'Art de Catalunya (MNAC) since 1934. The museum's main hall is a public event space that resembles of a wedding cake in its white, cream, and pink detailed splendor, while the ground-floor wings are home to the world's finest collection of Catalan Romanesque art (to your left as you walk in) and a wide variety of Gothic pieces (to your right). The Romanesque frescoes, now integrated as murals into dummy chapels, were salvaged in the 1920s from their original, less protected locations in northern Catalunya's churches. Their restoration creates a surprisingly spiritual tour through the medieval masterpieces. The museum's Gothic art corridor displays paintings on wood, the medium of choice during that period. The chronological tour of the galleries underlines the growing influence of Italy over Catalunya's artistic development, and ends with a breathtaking series of paintings by Gothic master **Bernat Martorell.**

Upstairs, you'll find MNAC's collections of Modern art (to the left), of Numismatics (coinage; slightly to the right), and of drawings, prints, and posters (farther to the right). The Modern Art collection comprises Catalan works of art that date from 1800 to the 1940s. Not surprisingly, the collection reflects the avant-garde movements that held sway in Catalonia at the time: *Modernisme* and *Noucentisme.* Its highlights include works by Fortuny, Casas, Rusinol, Gaudí, Jujol, Picasso, Gargallo, and Julio Gonzalez. Gaudi's 1907 "Confidant from the Batlló House" chair is one highlight. The Numismatics collection is a heist movie waiting to happen. It includes more than 134,000 pieces of money (Spanish coins, medals, and valuable papers) and walks the visitor through the history of Catalonia's coinage from Antiquity to today. The drawings, prints, and posters collection includes pieces that date from the 16th century to the beginning of the avant-garde. The museum's Fortuny collection is particularly acclaimed. *(From M: Espanya, walk up Av. Reina María Cristina, away from the twin brick towers, and take the escalators to the top. ☎936 22 03 76; www.mnac.es. Open Tu-Sa 10am-7pm, Su and holidays 10am-2:30pm. Wheelchair-accessible. €8.50, students and seniors €6, under 14 free. First Su of the month free. Audio tour included.)*

FUNDACIÓ MIRÓ. Miró's pieces are a personal and poignant tour through 20th-century Spanish history; the fundamental optimism of his later works, and the generosity he demonstrated throughout his life have made him one of Spain's—not just Catalunya's—most beloved artists. More than a museum, the Fundació Miró is a foundation to support contemporary art and young Catalan artists as well as a rotating collection of 11,000 of Miró's works and pieces by other artists inspired by Miró's unique style. Designed by Miró's friend Josep Luís Sert, the Fundació links interior and exterior spaces with massive windows and outdoor patios. Skylights illuminate an extensive collection of statues, paintings, and *sobreteixims* (paintings on tapestry) from Miró's career. The Fundació also sponsors music recitals in the summer months, and occasionally hosts film festivals (check the website for listings).

The first room of the permanent collection features the *Tapestry of the Foundation*, a colorful and wall-sized depiction of a woman. Outside, between rooms 11 and 12, The *Mercury Fountain* created by Miró's good friend Alexander Calder, commemorates the war-torn town of Almaden. Room 16 displays Miró's **Dream Paintings** (1925-1927), an eerie depiction of a world where "the pull of gravity" no longer exists. **The Constellation Series,** the more poetic of Miró's works, is on display in room 17. Pick up a headphone set from the ticket desk to guide you to some of the most famous pieces in the foundation. *(Take the funicular from M: Paral·lel or catch the Park Montjuïc bus from Pl. Espanya. ☎934 43 94 70; www.fundaciomiro-bcn.org. Library open M and Sa 10am-2pm, Tu-F 10am-2pm and 3-6pm. Fundació open July-Sept. Tu-W and F-Sa 10am-8pm, Th 10am-9:30pm, Su and holidays 10am-2:30pm; Oct.-June Tu-W and F-Sa 10am-7pm, Th 10am-9:30pm, Su and holidays 10am-2:30pm. Last entry 15min. before closing. €8, students and seniors €6, under 13 €4. Temporary exhibitions €4/3/4. Headphones €4. Concert tickets €10.)*

ENTERTAINMENT

MUSIC, THEATER, AND DANCE

Barcelona offers many options for theater aficionados, though most performances are in Catalan (*Guía del Ocio* lists the language of the performance). Reserve tickets through **TelEntrada** (24hr. ☎902 10 12 12; www.telentrada.com), **ServiCaixa** at any branch of the Caixa Catalunya bank (24hr. ☎902 33 22 11, for groups 88 80 90; www.servicaixa.com; open M-F 8am-2:30pm), or www.ticktackticket.com—the Spanish Ticketmaster. The **Grec** summer festival turns Barcelona into an international theater, music, and dance extravaganza. For information about the festival, ask at the tourist office, check out www.barcelonafestival.com, or, during the festival, stop by the booth at the bottom of Pl. de Catalunya, on Portal de Angel.

In the past decade, Barcelona has managed to establish itself as a major stop for touring bands—especially during summer music festivals. **Sónar,** the grandaddy of them all, comes to town in mid-June, attracting renowned DJs and electronica enthusiasts from all over the world for three days (and very long nights) of concerts and partying. Besides Sónar, major music festivals include **Summercase** (indie and pop), **Primavera Sound** (more indie and pop), and **Jazzaldia.** Check www.mondosonoro.com or pick up the *Mondo Sonoro* festival guide at hostels and bars. For info on cultural activities in the city, swing by the **Institut de Cultura de Barcelona (ICUB),** Palau de la Virreina, La Rambla, 99. (☎933 16 10 00; www.bcn.cat/cultura. Info office open daily 10am-8pm. Most performances around €18-30.) Check www.barcelonaturisme.com for occasional 10% discounts. **Palau de la Música Catalana,** C. Sant Francese de Paula, 2 (☎932 95 72 00; www.palaumusica.org; M: Urquinaona), to the right off Via Laietana near the level of Pl. Urquinaona, also sells concert tickets. (Concert tickets €8-175. Box office open M-Sa 9am-9pm, Su from 1hr. prior to the concert. No concerts in Aug.; check the *Guía del Ocio* for listings. MC/V.)

HIGH CULTURE, LOW BUDGET. The Gran Teatre del Liceu sells nosebleed seats at low prices. Beware of the cheapest tickets (€7-9) unless you want to sit behind an obstruction. Students with ID can arrive at the theater 2hr. before showtime (1hr. on weekends) and pick up remainder seats at a 30% discount. This is best attempted on weekdays, when seats more frequently go unsold.

Palau de la Música Catalana, C. Sant Francese de Paula, 2 (☎902 44 28 82; www.palaumusica.org) M: Jaume I, L4, in La Ribera, off Via Laietana near Pl. Urquinaona. Head up Via Laietana to the intersection of C. Ionqueres. Performances most often feature choirs and orchestras, but the venue also hosts pop and rock artists from time to time. Box office open M-Sa 10am-9pm, Su from 2hr. before show time. No concerts in Aug.; check website or the Guía del Ocio for listings. Concert tickets €8-175. MC/V.

Centre Artesà Tradicionàrius, Tr. de Sant Antoni, 6-8 (☎932 18 44 85; www.tradicionarius.com), in Gràcia. M: Fontana. Catalan folk music concerts Sept.-June. Tickets €6-12; frequent free concerts. Also dance, music workshops, and summer festivals; inquire for details. Open Sept.-July. M-F 11am-2pm and 5-9pm. Cash only.

Gran Teatre del Liceu, La Rambla, 51-59 (☎934 85 99 13; www.liceubarcelona.com). M: Liceu. Founded in 1847, destroyed by fire in 1994, and recently reopened, Liceu has regained its status as the city's premier venue for opera, ballet, and classical music. Reserve tickets in advance. Box office open M-F 1:30-8pm, Sa-Su and holidays 1hr. before showtime. 24hr. ticket sales at ServiCaixa. AmEx/MC/V.

L'Auditori, C. Lepanto, 150 (☎932 47 93 00; www.auditori.com), in L'Eixample between M: Marina and Glòries. Home to the city orchestra (the BOC) and host to visiting chamber, choral, and jazz groups. Concerts from late Sept. to mid-July. Tickets €6-50; special performances up to €120. Available by phone, through ServiCaixa or TelEntrada, or at ticket windows (open M-Sa noon-9pm, Su 1hr. before show starts). MC/V.

Teatre Lliure, C. Montseny, C. Montseny, 47 (☎932 18 92 51; www.teatrelliure.com), in Gràcia. M: Fontana. Showcases contemporary theater productions from summer festivals to Shakespeare. Call or check website for information. Tickets may be purchased at the theater or by calling Tel Entrada. Wheelchair-accessible. Shows May-Oct. Tu-Sa 9pm, Su 7pm; Nov.-Apr. Tu-Sa 9pm, Su 6pm. Tickets M-W balcony €12, orchestra €16; Th-Su €15/19. 20% discount for students.

Teatre Grec, 38 (Tel-Entrada ☎902 10 12 12; www.grec.bcn.es), across from the Museu d'Arqueològia. From M: Espanya, L1/L3 take bus #55 to Montjuïc. Located in the picturesque Jardins Amargós, the Teatre Grec was carved out of an old stone quarry in 1929 under the direction of Ramon Reventós. The open-air Grecian-style amphitheater is the namesake and occasional host of the Grec Barcelona Summer Theater Festival.

Most theater performances are in Spanish or Catalan, but there are plenty of music and dance shows. Outdoor cafe open July daily 8pm-3am.

FLAMENCO

Although Catalunya does not have a tradition of flamenco, a dance which originated with the gypsies in southern Spain's Andalucia, the tourist industry has fed the demand for flamenco venues. Though shows are geared toward tourists, in no way does that reflect poorly on their quality; some of the best flamenco musicians and dancers in Spain pass through these establishments.

El Patio Andaluz, C. Aribau, 242 (☎93 209 33 78), in Gràcia. M: Diagonal. From the Metro, take a left on Diagonal and turn right on C. Aribau. Lively Andalusian-themed restaurant showcases traditional Spanish flamenco. Show and 1 drink €30; show and *menú* from €54. Daily shows at 9:30pm and midnight. Call 9am-7pm for reservations. El Patio's red-paneled bar, **Las Sevillanas del Patio,** stays open until 3am for drinks and dancing.

Guasch Teatre, C. Aragó, 140 (☎93 323 39 50 or 93 451 34 62). M: Urgell, L1, in l'Eixample. Presents both children's theater, like Cinderella and Gulliver's Travel's, and adult theater. Often showcases flamenco; call for schedules. Tickets €6-18. Children's theater generally shown Th 6pm, F-Sa 12:30pm, Su 5:30pm; adult theater Th 9pm, F-Sa 10pm, Su 7:30pm. Ticket office opens 1hr. prior to performance.

JAZZ, POP, AND ROCK 'N' ROLL

Apolo, Nou de la Rambla, 113 (☎934 41 40 01; www.sala-apolo.com), M: Paral·lel. The first place to look for major indie acts to come through Barcelona (think people like Nouvelle Vague and Camera Obscura). Hosts its fair share of electronica and hip-hop artists as well, along with Flamenco shows the first W of every month (www.myspace.com/flamencoobsessions). Beer €4. Mixed drinks €8. Tickets €12-22, usually available online at www.sala-apolo.com. MC/V.

Jamboree, Plaça Reial, 17 (☎933 19 17 89; www.masimas.com), M: Liceu. Boasts a jazz series that's been active since the 60s and still brings relevant musicians (Elvin Jones and Art Farmer have appeared here). Also ventures into funk and hip hop with WTF Jam Sessions (M 9pm-1:30am, €4). Upstairs, **Tarantos** holds flamenco shows (daily 8:30, 9:30, 10:30pm; €7) Jazz performances Tu-Su 9 and 11pm. Tickets (€10-12) available through www.telentrada.com. AmEx/MC/V.

Sidecar, Plaça Reial, 7 (☎933 17 76 66; www.sidecarfactoryclub.com). M: Liceu. Hosts pop and rock shows. Tends to showcase more local acts and fewer internationally imported bands compared to other Barcelona concert venues. Check website for listings. Tickets (€6-14) often available through www.atrapalo.com. Cash only.

Razzmatazz, C. Pamplona, 88, and Almogàvers, 122 (☎932 72 09 10; www.salarazzmatazz.com). M: Marina. This massive converted warehouse now hosts a wide range of big name musical acts from reggae to metal to electro-pop (big name means big name: Gossip, Offspring, and so on). This is where Barack Obama goes when he's in Barcelona. Just kidding. Check website for upcoming concerts. Most tickets (€12-30) available online through Telentrada or Ticketmaster. AmEx/MC/V.

BEYOND THE GUÍA DEL OCIO. For the lowdown on both mainstream and underground shows in Barcelona, check out the following helpful sites: **www.infoconcerts.cat/ca** for concert listings from ASACC, an umbrella organization for Catalan venues; **www.maumaunderground.com** for local music news, reviews, and a daily agenda of shows and other happenings; and **www.lecool.com** to register to receive weekly arts updates. Butxaca (**www.butxaca.com**) publishes a thorough bimonthly agenda with film, music, theater, and art listings.

BEACHES

Barceloneses love their coast. The entire strip between Torre San Sebastiá and Parc de Diagonal-Mar is lined with public beaches. Due partially to strong riptides, few bathers swim more than a few meters from shore: the number one beach activity is tanning. Topless tanning is common on all the city beaches, and people begin to lose their suit bottoms toward the nether regions of **San Sebastià** although the only official nude beach is **Platja Mar Bella.** Barcelona's beaches are crowded at almost any time of day, but crowds tend to thin out on the eastern stretches. The beaches are cleaned every night by large sifting tractors. There are restaurants near practically all the beaches, although they become less frequent toward **Nova Mar Bella.** *(Beach info ☎932 21 03 48; www.bcn.cat/platges. Dogs, camping tents, motorcycles, soap, music, and trash are not allowed on the beaches. Shower stations, police, first aid, and info available on all beaches, June-Sept. 10am-7pm. All beaches have lifeguards June-Sept. daily 10am-7pm, Mar.-June Sa-Su 10am-7pm. Lockers at police stations. Nova Icaria, San Sebastiá, and Nova Mar Bella are fully wheelchair-accessible and provide bathing assistance services in July and Aug.)*

BARCELONETA. Barceloneta's two main beaches, **Platja San Sebastià** and **Platja Barceloneta** (adjacent to one another), are the neighborhood's biggest draws. These are the closest to Barceloneta and ⓂCiutadella as well as to Port Vell and Las Ramblas. Expect Platja Barceloneta to be the most crowded stretch of sand in Barcelona. The furthest tip of Platja San Sebastiá, near Torre San Sebastiá, offers more privacy, but with a summer-long public fiesta going on at the popular beaches next door, who needs it?

POBLE NOU. The beaches to the north of Port Olímpic (left, facing the water) include Platja Nova Icària, Platja del Bogatell, Platja Mar Bella, and Platja Nova Mar Bella. (From the port to Nova Mar Bella is about a 20min. walk.) Closest to the port Olímpic is the short **Platja Nova Icaria.** This beach is busy; it often fills up with families and volleyball players. Next is **Platja del Bogatell,** one of the most coveted tanning areas. Base Nàutica Mar Bella marks the end of Bogatell and the beginning of **Platja Mar Bella,** a section of which is designated nudist, secluded behind dunes. **Mar Bella** is the gay beach; a rainbow flag marks the spot. **Nova Mar Bella** and **Platja Llevant,** which lie just past Platja Mar Bella (the end of which is marked by the restaurant La Oca Mar) host mostly teenagers and 20-somethings. As they require the farthest walk to reach, fewer tourists find their way out to these beaches and there tends to be some space available even on weekends.

COSTA MARESME

For those who tire of the crowded beaches of Barcelona, there's plenty more coastline just a short train ride away. Some of the beaches below are worth a visit, though there's no need for too much planning in advance. Since the C-1

BARCELONA

RENFE line travels right along coastline with sand and surf in plain view, play it by eye and hop off at first stop that piques your interest.

BADALONA. This is the quickest way to escape the crowded Barcelona beaches (and many locals know it). The sand stretches for three kilometers, so you ought to be able to find a place of your own. Crowds begin to thin out as you walk north. *(RENFE stop: Badalona, C1. 20min. from Pl. Catalunya.)*

PLATJA D'OCATA. Right next to the train stop, this wide beach attracts a lot of daytrippers from Barcelona, but is large enough to provide plenty of space for volleyball nets and, of course, hours of tanning. *(RENFE stop: Ocata, C1. 30min. from Pl. Catalunya. Lifeguard on duty from June 24 to Sept 11 11:30am-7:30pm.)*

PLATJA DE MATARÓ. Technically made up of three smaller beaches (**Platja de Sant Simó, Platja del Callao** and **Platja del Varador**), Mataró is a spacious and sporty stretch of sand with kayak and wind-surfing rentals as well as goals set up for beach soccer. *(RENFE stop: Mataró, C1. 40min. from Pl. Catalunya. Facing the sea, Varador is just to the left of the train stop. Sant Simó and Callao are farther along in the same direction. Lifeguard on duty from mid-May to Aug. 10am-6pm.)*

PLATJA MUSCLERA. Musclera is a bit farther out of the way and more difficult to reach, but the pleasant and fairly secluded nude section on the left half of the beach (facing the sea) makes it worth it. *(RENFE stop: Caldes d'Estrac, C1. 50min. from Pl. Catalunya. Station is right across from Platja Pg. del Mar. Walk left (facing the sea) to reach Platja Musclera, which is the next beach over. Lifeguard on duty July-Aug. 10am-6pm.)*

SPECTATOR SPORTS

FÚTBOL CLUB BARCELONA

For the record, the lunatics covered from head to toe in red and blue stripes didn't just escape from an asylum—they are **F.C. Barcelona (Barça)** fans. A visit to Camp Nou, home of FCB, can be compared to a religious experience for many fans. The team, commonly referred to as El Barça, has the motto of "més que un club" (more than a club), and it's easy to see why. El Barça is a symbol of Catalunya and its proud people, and the team carries the political agendas of the entire region (see More than a Rivalry, p. 166). The club has a devoted worldwide following, and boasts more than 100,000 members. Even the Pope, while visiting Barcelona in 1982, signed the membership book and became an honorary member. The FCB also has teams in several other sports, including basketball, rugby, and roller hockey, who play in other buildings in the Camp Nou complex, which includes basketball courts, a mini-stadium and the Palau Blaugrana (Blue-Burgundy Palace).

Camp Nou,on C. Aristides Maillol. M: Collblanc. Head down C. Francese Layret and take the 2nd right onto Trav. de les Corts. A block later, turn left onto C. Aristides Maillol, which leads to the ticket office and museum entrance (see Sights & Museums, p. 114). ☎93 496 36 00; www.fcbarcelona.com. Tickets available for all club sport events. Ticket office open Sept.-June M-F (and the day before matches) 9:30am-1:30pm and 3:30-6pm; July-Aug. 8am-2:30pm.

GETTING TICKETS

Inaugurated in 1957, Camp Nou stadium was expanded in 1982 to hold 120,000 for the World Cup, and is today Europe's largest fútbol ground. However, getting tickets to a Barça match is not always easy; hardcore FCB fans already have tickets, leaving slim pickings for visitors. Matches usually take place on

Sunday evenings at 9pm, and the bigger the match, the harder it is to get in. Entradas (tickets) are available at the ticket office and usually go on sale to the public the Thursday before the match. A number of scalpers also try to unload tickets for copious amounts of cash in the days before the match. At the ticket office, expect to pay ^30-60, and bring your binoculars, as most available seats are on the third level. The seats may be in the nosebleed section, but even at that height, any Barça match is an incredible experience. The cheap seats offer a bird's eye view of the action and gorgeous views of the mountains of Tibidabo and Montjuïc. Even if you can't tell which player scored the goal, you'll have just as much fun celebrating it with 70,000 newfound friends.

BULLFIGHTING

Catalunya is not the stronghold of bullfighting in Spain; bullfights will typically not sell out and will be dominated by tourists. For more on the sport, see Museu Taurí (p. 88) and Bye-Bye Bully (p. 167).

Plaça de Toros Monumental, Gran Via de les Corts Catalans, 743 (☎93 245 58 02; www.torosbarcelona.com). M: Monumental. Built in 1915 by Ignasi i Morell, the bullring is one of the few prominent buildings in the city that draws overtly from Arabic architectural influences; it is a rare touch of Andalucia in Catalunya. The corrida (bullfighting) season runs Apr.-Sept., with fights every Su at 7pm. Tickets (^18-95) may be purchased at the bullring; ticket window open M-Sa 11am-2pm and 4-8pm; Su 11am-1pm. Tourist visits to the bull ring are also permitted during those hours; adults ^4, children ^3. Tickets may also be purchased at C. Muntanter, 24 (☎93 453 38 21; fax 93 451 69 98). Cash only.

FESTIVALS

While Barcelona works hard to distinguish itself from the rest of Spain, the city shares at least one thing in common with the rest of the country: it knows how to have fun. For information on all festivals, call the tourist office (☎933 01 77 75; open M-F 10am-2pm and 4-8pm) or check the "Agenda" or "Diary" on www.bcn.es. Double-check sight and museum hours during festival times, as well as during the Christmas season and *Semana Santa.* The streets fill with book vendors and rose sellers on the **Festa de Sant Jordi** (St. George; Apr. 23), the Catalan take on Valentine's Day; the day officially celebrates Cataluña's patron saint with a feast. Men give women roses, and women give men books. In the last two weeks of August, city folk jam at Gràcia's **Festa Mayor;** lights blaze in *plaças* and music plays all night as two dozen streets compete to be the best decorated. On September 11, the **Festa Nacional de Cataluña** brings out traditional costumes, dancing, and Catalan flags hanging from balconies. Barcelona's main festival, the **Festa de Sant Joan,** takes place the night of June 23. You might as well surrender to the all-night beachside partying (and erratic nightclub hours); ceaseless fireworks and bonfires in the street will keep your eyes wide open anyway. The largest Barcelona celebration, however, is the **Festa de Mercè,** the weeks before and after September 24. To honor the patron saint of the city, *barceloneses* revel with fireworks, *sardana* dancing, and concerts. **Santa Eulàlia,** the city's female patron saint, is celebrated February 12-13.

NIGHTLIFE

Barcelona truly lives by night (and all the way until early morning). Its wild and varied nightlife treads the precarious line between slick and kitschy. In many ways, the city is a tourist's clubbing heaven: things don't get going until late (don't bother showing up at a club before 1am) and keep going for as long as you can handle it—frequently 6am. Yet for every full-blown dance club, there are a hundred more relaxed bars, from Irish pubs to gay clubs to absinthe dens. Check the *Guía del Ocio*, available at newsstands, for even more up-to-date listings of nighttime fun, as the hot spots change often. *Barcelona Week*, the English arts weekly, also has listings.

BARRI GÒTIC AND LAS RAMBLAS

When night falls, the distinction between upper and lower Barri Gòtic becomes much clearer. The area above C. Ferran, dominated by shops, restaurants, and hostels, virtually shuts down by midnight, while **Carrer Ferran** and below becomes a human river of tourists and locals weaving their way from bar to bar. There are a few clubs and several hybrid bar-clubs in and around **Plaça Reial,** but overall the Barri Gòtic is more of a place for drinking and hanging out than for wild and crazy dance parties like the ones in Maremàgnum (p. 290) or Montjuïc (p. 291).

While Barri Gòtic has some nightlife, it is a favorite tourist spot and as such attracts drug dealers, pickpockets, and prostitutes. Prostitutes tend to stick to Las Ramblas, or other major streets (C. Ferran, C. Avinyó) and its best not to let them get a hold of your arm or clothing as they may soon try reaching for your pockets. Drug dealers tend to stick to sidestreets and alleys which come just off the main streets and plazas (i.e. Pl. Reial, Pl. Trippy, C. Avinyó) but generally leave passersby alone once they make it clear they're not interested. With its ancient, randomly arranged streets, Barri Gòtic is an easy place to get lost in. Get an idea of where you're going before you head down a street; you don't want to end up alone in the middle of one of the many narrow, empty sidestreets. When in doubt, you can always go back to Las Ramblas and work your way up and down the neighborhood from there. At night, the main drag is certainly host to its fair share of unsavory characters trying to sell beer, sex, and drugs, but it does offer light and the protection of crowds. Overall, the area is well-policed and whispers of "hashish" are probably the only indications of lawlessness that you'll encounter.

Just a short ways into the maze of Barri Gòtic is the infamous Plaça "Trippy." Located at the end of C. Escudellers from Las Ramblas, this square, officially named Plaça George Orwell, has long garnered a reputation for attracting an alternative crowd and the trade of illicit substances. It is rumored that the government removed all of the benches here to discourage loitering and drug dealing; how successful they were is debatable. More recently, a 24-hr. closed-circuit surveillance camera has been installed in the square, in a superbly ironic gesture (given the plaza's original name) meant to further curtail drug sales. Nowadays the trippiness of yore is gone, but you're sure to find a ready supply of smiley, rattily-clothed guitar players as well as some less smiley drug-dealers around the corner.

IT TAKES TWO. Of course traveling in groups at night is always a good idea but it can be especially helpful in Barri Gotìc. Even a single companion, especially of the opposite sex, can work wonders in decreasing the amount of attention you receive from unsavory characters. Women accompanied by men are sure to receive fewer catcalls by drunken tourists and locals, and men with a female companion will be spared a great deal of harassment by prostitutes.

BARS

El Bosq de les Fades, Pg. de la Banca, 16 (☎933 17 26 49), near the Wax Museum. ⓂDrassanes. This spooky cafe-bar used to be the horror section of the Wax Museum and retains a fairytale look, with gnarled trees, gourd-lanterns, and a wishing well. Fills up early, so it's a good place to start the night. Beer €3. *Cava* €3. Tequila Sunrise €7.20. Open M-Th and Su 10am-1am, F-Sa 10am-2am. MC/V.

Barcelona Pipa Club, Pl. Reial, 3 (☎933 02 47 32; www.bpipaclub.com). ⓂLiceu, L3. Unmarked—look for the small plaque on the door to the left of Glaciar Bar, on your left as you enter the square from Las Ramblas, and ring the doorbell. Don't let the pseudo-secrecy deter you. A welcoming place for late-night drinks. The decor is 100% Sherlock Holmes, the music mostly jazz and fusion, and the people are a mix of local bartenders, artists, and tourists in the know. An impressive collection of pipes from around the world is housed in a side-room along with a small pool table (€1.50 a game). Live music (often jazz) F 11pm. Mixed drinks €7, beer €4. Open daily 11pm-4:30am. Cash only.

Shangó, C. d'En Groch, 2 (☎662 10 51 65). ⓂJaume I. Walk down Via Laietana and take a right on C. d'Àngel Baixeras. Continue as it turns into C. Gignàs and take a right on the small C. d'en Groch. This colorful bar blasts Latin beats and attracts young locals with its delicious mojitos (€6). Free salsa classes Tu and W at 11pm. Beer from €2.20. Happy hour 9-11pm. Open daily 9pm-3am. Cash only.

Smoll Bar, C. Comtesa de Sobradiel, 9. ⓂLiceu, L3. Between Pl. Reial and Via Laietana. As promised, this chic, neon-lit bar is quite small, and fills up quickly and reliably. Be prepared to get cozy with a young, mostly gay crowd. Beer €3.50. Mixed drinks €6-7. Open M-Th 9:30pm-2:30am, F-Sa 9:30pm-3am. Cash only.

Sincopa, C. Avinyò, 35. ⓂLiceu, L3. Coming from Las Ramblas, take a right off C. Ferran. Bright, instrument-laden walls enclose a lively young crowd. Always blasting music, mostly Latin. When the upside-down musicians on the ceiling orient themselves you know you've had too much to drink. Wine €3. Mixed drinks €7. Open daily 6pm-3am. Cash only.

13 Bar, C. Lleona, 13. ⓂLiceu, L3. Coming from Las Ramblas, take a right off C. Ferran onto Avinyó and a left onto C. Lleona. At the end of this inconspicuous sidestreet lies a bar with a dark sense of humor and a crowd of locals. Presents a perfect mix of devilish music and fruity drinks. Beer €2.50. Wine €2.50. Mixed drinks €5. Happy hour 10:30-11pm. 2 for 1 drinks Su. Open M-Th and Su 8pm-2am, F-Sa 8pm-3am. Cash only.

La Ria, C. Milans, 4 (☎933 10 00 92). ⓂLiceu, L3. Coming from Las Ramblas, take a right off C. Ferran onto C. Avinyó and follow it until you see C. Milans on your left. Crowds pack into this tapas bar for the small array of cheap and tasty *montaditos* (€1.20) and beer (€2). Wine €3. Open M-Th noon-4pm and 6pm-1:30am, F-Sa noon-4pm and 6pm-3am. Cash only.

Andú, C. Correu Vell, 13 (☎646 55 39 30). ⓂSant Jaume I, L3. Coming from Pl. Sant Jaume, take a left off C. de la Ciutat. Stay on Avinyó. This cozy wine bar sports a well-executed antique look and attracts a young, sophisticated crowd. Good for an early glass of wine (€2.50-5) or a late bite to eat. Bottles €9-15. Sangria €5-15. Tapas €2.50-5. Meat and cheese platters €15. Open daily 8pm-3am. Kitchen closes at midnight. MC/V.

Oviso, C. Arai, 5 (☎www.barnawood.com). ⓂLiceu, L3. A youthful and colorful crowd to match the bright wall murals, befitting a bar right in the middle of Plaça Trippy. Serves food and fresh fruit juices during the day. Beer €2. Mixed drinks €6-7. Open M-Th and Su 10am-2:30am, F-Sa and holidays 10am-3am. Cash only.

Margarita Blue, C. J. A. Clavé, 6 (☎934 12 54 89). ⓂDrassanes, L3. Walk past the wax museum and take a left. It's off Las Ramblas, about 1 block from the port. This Mexican-themed bar draws a 20- and 30-something crowd with small blue margaritas, tropically painted walls, and a strangely arranged wall of mirrors behind the bar. Small Mexican dishes (€3.50-8) accompany the tequila. A wider array of mixed drinks (€7) than most. Open M-Th and Su 7pm-2:30am, F-Sa 7pm-3am. Kitchen closes at 1am.

Schilling, C. Ferran, 23 (☎933 17 67 87; www.cafeschilling.com). ⓂLiceu, L3. One of the more laid-back and spacious wine bars in the area, with dim lighting, velvet seat cushions, and bottles climbing the walls. Crowd gets younger as the night goes on. Excellent sangria (pitcher €18). Wine €3. Mixed drinks €8. Serves breakfast and sandwiches (€4-6) during the day. Open daily M-W 10am-2:30am. MC/V over €10.

CLUBS

Karma, Pl. Reial, 10 (☎933 02 56 80; www.karmadisco.com). ⓂLiceu. The club downstairs may look like a colorfully lit wind tunnel but it hosts a lively and fun atmosphere. DJ will not hesitate to play classic pop-rock throwbacks for all to sing along to. Beer €4. Mixed drinks €6-8. Club cover €10 includes 1 drink. Bar open Tu-Su 6pm-2:30am. Club open Tu-Su midnight-5am.

Harlem Jazz Club, C. Comtesa de Sobradiel, 8 (☎933 10 07 55). ⓂLiceu, L3. Between Pl. Reial and Via Laietana. Live music varies: blues, jazz, reggae, flamenco, and acoustic rock attract international musicians from as far away as Senegal, Kenya, Brazil, and Cuba. After the live music is over, plenty will stay and more will trickle in to dance late into the night. 2 sessions per night: Tu-Th and Su 10:30pm and midnight, F-Sa 11:30pm and 1am. The 2nd session is always much more crowded, especially on weekends. Beer €3.50. Admission €4-8, usually includes 1 drink. Cover F-Sa €7.50. Open Tu-Th 9pm-3am, F-Sa 9pm-5am, Su 9pm-5am during the summer. Get a schedule for the month at the front door. Cash only.

Jamboree, Pl. Reial, 17 (☎933 19 17 89; www.masimas.com). ⓂLiceu. A disorienting maze of stone arches and swirling lights thumps with hip hop; 2nd floor plays 80s and 90s pop. Dance floors fill up between 2-3am. Earlier in the night this popular venue hosts live jazz. Beer €5. Mixed drinks €9-10. Jazz 9 and 11pm €4-12. Cover €10; look for flyers with discounts. Difficult to get in on nights with lists. Open daily 9pm-1am; nightclub open M-Th and Su 12:30am-5am, F-Sa 12:30am-6am. Upstairs, Tarantos hosts flamenco shows (€6). Open daily 8-11pm.

New York, C. Escudellers, 5 (☎933 18 87 30). ⓂDrassanes, L3. Right off Las Ramblas. Once a strip joint, New York is now the biggest club in the Barri Gòtic; drink tables overlook the red and black, strobe-lit dance floor for your voyeuristic pleasure. Crowds don't arrive until after 3am; music includes reggae and Brit-pop. Cover 11:30pm-2am €6 includes 1 beer; 2-5am €13 includes 1 drink. Open Th-Sa midnight-5am. Cash only.

Soul Club, C. Nou de Sant Francesc, 7 (☎933 02 70 26; www.soulclub.es). ⓂDrassanes, L3. Take the 2nd right off C. Escudellers; it's on your left about 100 ft. down. The softly curved walls house a room of young jazz, funk, and soul aficionados. Dance floor is relatively small, but the expertly chosen tunes are sure to get people on their feet. Beer €3.50. Mixed drinks €7.50. Cover F-Sa €5 includes 1 cheap drink. Open M-Th and Su 11pm-2:30am, F-Sa 11pm-3am. Cash only.

Boulevard Culture Club, Las Ramblas, 27 (☎933 016289). ⓂLiceu, L3. Large, hi-tech club with bright pixelated lights raining upon the dance floor. Pumps electronica for a young, mostly tourist, crowd. Guys free until 1:30am, girls until 2:30am. Cover €13, with flyer €10. Beer €6. Mixed drinks €9-10. Open M-Th midnight-5am, F-Sa midnight-6am.

LA RIBERA

La Ribera's nightlife scene is more local and more varied than the scene on La Rambla. When the gas lantern goes on in front of Església de Santa Maria each night, people begin to migrate from small backstreet bars to second-floor sheesha lounges.

El Copetín, Pg. del Born, 19 (☎607 20 21 76). Ⓜ︎Jaume I. Cuban rhythms invade this casual, dimly lit nightspot. Copetín fills up before some places open, making it a good place to start the night. When the bartenders break out the maracas and cowbell, be ready to get down. Mojitos €7. Open M-Th and Su 6pm-2:30am, F-Sa 6pm-3am. Cash only.

Ribborn, C. Antic de Sant Joan, 3 (☎933 10 71 48; www.ribborn.com). Ⓜ︎Barceloneta. Deep crimson light and an eclectic music selection, from jazz to funk to soul. Beer €2.50. Mixed drinks €7. Jazz piano W 9pm. Happy hour Tu-Sa 7-10pm. Open Tu-Su 7pm-3am. MC/V.

El Born, Pg. del Born, 26 (☎933 19 53 33). Ⓜ︎Jaume I. Sit at the marble counter over the basins where they used to sell fish or follow the tiny spiral staircase for more casual seating. Free Wi-Fi. Beer €2. Open Tu-Su 10am-2:30am. MC/V over €10.

Pitin Bar, Pg. del Born, 34 (☎93 319 59 87; www.pitinbar.com). Ⓜ︎Jaume I. A shiny interior on the 1st floor and a cozy attic upstairs fill up nightly with the young and the young-at-heart. Start off with a beer (€2.50) and if that doesn't do enough for you, contemplate a shot of absinthe (€3.50). Or just skip right to the absinthe. Open Sept.-May Tu-Su 10am-2am, June-Aug. daily 10am-2am. Cash only.

Alma, C. de Sant Antoni dels Sombrerers, 7 (☎933 19 76 07). Ⓜ︎Jaume I. The tattoos and body piercings on display in this bar rival its dramatic red decor. Come during happy hour (8:30-9:30pm) to snag €4 mixed drinks and €8 pitchers of sangria. Open M-Th and Su 8:30pm-2:30am, F-Sa 8:30pm-3am. Cash only.

No Se, Pg. del Born, 29 (☎671 48 59 14). Ⓜ︎Jaume I. Walk down C. Princesa, make a right onto C. Montcada, and follow it until Pg. del Born. Perhaps in keeping with its laid-back name, this bar doesn't try as hard as some of its competitors on the busy Pg. del Born. The intimate space has a few canvases thrown up on the walls and a relaxing ambience. Mixed drinks €8-10. Open daily 8pm-2:30am. MC/V.

Kama, C. del Rec, 69 (☎932 68 10 29; www.kamabar.com). Ⓜ︎Barceloneta. Walk up Pl. del Palau, make a right on Av. del Marqués de l'Argentera, and a left on C. del Rec; the bar is on the right. Kama means "desire" in Sanskrit. At this fuschia-lit restaurant, you'll find what you desire—assuming that it's Indian dishes like *kheema mutter* and*palak paneer,* mixed drinks, and a sharp, cosmopolitan ambience. Lunch *menù* €10. Entrees €15-26. Mixed drinks €8-10. Open M 8:30pm-midnight, Tu-Sa 1-4pm and 8:30pm-midnight, Su 8:30pm-midnight. MC/V.

Cactus Bar, Pg. del Born, 30 (☎933 10 63 54; www.cactusbar.cat). Ⓜ︎Jaume I. Walk down C. Princesa, make a right onto C. Montcada, and continue until Pg. del Born. Walk toward the beach; the bar is a ways down, on the left. This corner bar has simple metal decor, windows ideal for people watching, and a prime location on a popular street. Come during the day to try the walnut-raisin bread with roquefort cheese (€3.80), or show up at night for a caipirinha (mixed drinks €8.50). Open M-Sa noon-2am, Su noon-midnight. MC/V.

Berimbau, Pg. del Born, 17 (☎933 19 53 78). Ⓜ︎Jaume I. Walk down C. Princesa and make a right onto C. Montcada. Turn on Pg. del Born; the bar is down the street, on the left. This Brazilian bar's low wicker chairs give it a beachy, laid-back feel. Brazilian music plays in the background. Mixed drinks €8-10. Open daily 6pm-2:30am. MC/V.

Princesa 23, C. Princesa, 23 (☎932 68 86 18; www.princesa23.es). Ⓜ︎Jaume I. Walk down C. Princesa. Shamelessly touristy and fun enough to get away with it. Princesa 23 serves mojitos and caipirinha cheap (€3.50) to an international crowd until 11pm and then keeps serving them for full price late into the night. Tasty food ranging from tapas and paella to wraps and hamburgers (€3.50-10). Large TVs, a quote by Kahlil Gibran scrawled across the walls, and late-night DJs spinning pop, R&B, and electronica mean that this restaurant has something for everyone. You may hate yourself for loving it here, but you're probably come back. Open M-Th 11am-2:30am, F-Sa 11am-3am, Su 11am-2:30am. MC/V.

EL RAVAL

If you stick to the Northern part of El Raval, you'll find yourself in hip, creatively decorated, colorful (literally) bars with a young, laid-back crowd—true to the artsy nature of the area. Be sure to check out **Calle Joaquim Costa,** near the MACBA, which packs in numerous distinctive and happening venues in just a few short blocks. As you move away from the University and MACBA, bars become more functional than artsy and cater more to tourists than to locals. Be aware that around Las Ramblas there are many wily pickpockets, around Las Ramblas del Raval prostitutes linger on the street corners, and in the depths of El Raval the streets can be eerily deserted late at night.

BARS

Marsella Bar, C. de Sant Pau, 65. M: Liceu. Don't be deterred by the tarnished mirrors and blackened bottles–they add to the cowboy charm of this oldest of Barcelona's bars (built in 1820). Religious figurines grace the walls of the bar, famous among locals for its *absenta* (absinthe; €5). Beer €3.20. Mixed drinks €5-6. Open M-Th 11pm-2am, F and Sa 11pm-3am. Cash only.

Betty Ford, Joaquin Costa, 56 (☎933 04 13 68). This local favorite is the place to see and be seen–amid chic and simple decor and raucous conversation. Happy hour 6-9pm offers fancy mixed drinks for €4; try a Manhattan or sugar-sweet mojito. Beer €2.50-4. Open M and Su 6pm-1:30am, Tu-Th 2pm-1:30am, F-Sa 2pm-2am.

Bar Almirall, C. Joaquín Costa, 33 (☎933 18 99 17, casalmirall@telefonica.net). M: Universitat. Marble floors and countertops, black chairs, dim lamps, and laid-back clientele. It's house policy to stop you after your 3rd absinthe (€5-7), but the staff is fond of saying that you won't make it there anyway. Beer €2-4. Mixed drinks €6-7. Free Wi-Fi. Open M-Th 5pm-2:30am, Sa until 3am, Su 7pm. Cash only.

Bar Ra, Pl. de la Garduña (☎933 01 41 63, reservations 61 595 98 72; www.ratown.com). M: Liceu, L3, just behind Las Ramblas's *Boqueria* market. Everything about Ra exudes cool, from its erotic Hindu mural to the individually painted tablecloths to the waiters themselves. Artfully prepared international food offerings use fresh ingredients from the nearby *Boqueria* market. Try the excellent vegetarian lasagna (€7.50) and duck magret with mango sauce (€9.50), or come for Sunday brunch in the sun. Entrees €6.50-13. Beer €2.50. Mixed drinks €6.50. Open M-Th 9am-midnight, F-Sa 9am-2:30am, Su noon-midnight. AmEx/MC/V.

L'Ovella Negra, C. Sitges, 5 (☎933 17 10 87; www.ovellanegra.com). M: Catalunya, L1/3. From Pl. de Catalunya, go down Las Ramblas and take the 1st right onto C. Tallers; C. Sitges is the 1st left. Young English-speaking tourists and some university students saddle up to a tavern that feels like a medieval stable. Cheap beer and sangria (huge pitcher of either €7.30) and Foosball tables. Lunch menu €6.10. Open M-Th 9am-2:30am, F 9am-3am, Sa 5pm-3am, Su 5pm-2:30am. Cash Only.

Sant Pau 68, C. de Sant Pau, 68 (☎934 41 31 15). M: Liceu. Floral wallpaper contrasts with painted black silhouettes and hanging bottle lights, perfectly mixing smooth and gritty. Beer €2. Mixed drinks €6. Open M-Th and Su 8pm-2:30am, F-Sa 8pm-3:30am. MC/V.

London Bar, C. Nou de la Rambla, 34 (☎933 01 25 40; www.londonbarbcn.com), off Las Ramblas. M: Liceu, L3. Locals and unruly expats rub shoulders at this smoky and always crowded Modernist tavern, which celebrated its 100th birthday on Día de Sant Joan (June 23) 2009. Beer €3. Wine €3. Mixed drinks €6.50-9. Absinthe €5. Open Tu-Th and Su 7:30pm-4:30am, F-Sa 7:30pm-5am. AmEx/MC/V.

Rita Blue, Placa Sant Agusti, 6 (☎933 42 40 86; www.ritablue.com), on C. Hospital off Las Ramblas. M: Liceu, L3. Sister to Rita Rouge. Live house music plays downstairs W-Su 11pm. DJs, poetry slams, other performances. Beer €2.20; mixed drinks €5.40-8. Call for dinner reservations. Open M-Th and Su 6pm-2am, F-Sa 6pm-3am.

Rambla Raval 10, Rambla del Raval, 10. ⓂLiceu or Paral.lel. Walk down C. Sant Pau until you reach the Rambla del Raval. When you walk into this bar, which is likely to be dark, packed with youth, and playing loud music, look up at the chandelier; it's made entirely of mini bottles of alcohol. Order a *piel de iguana* (iguana skin; 2 for €9) and lose yourself in the upbeat atmosphere. Mixed drinks €4.50-8. Open M-Th 8pm-2am, F-Sa 8pm-3am. Cash only.

La Masia, C. Elisabets, 16 (☎933 02 24 30). ⓂLiceu. Walk up Las Ramblas and make a left onto C. Elisabets. This bar, which maintains a charming traditional Spanish simplicity, has booze, cheap tapas (almonds €1.50; other dishes €1.50-8), and a great location right on the seam of the MACBA and El Raval districts. Happily chatting students fill the tables on weekend nights. Beer €2-3. Mixed drinks €5-6. Open M-Th 10am-2am, F-Sa 10pm-3am, Su 10pm-2am. MC/V.

Xhiwat Buen Cafe, C. Ramalleres, 26 (☎933 01 04 63). ⓂCatalunya. Walk down C. Pelai and make a left on C. de Jovellanos. This unpretentious and intimate shawarma, tea, and hookah restaurant has low tables, floor mats, and a friendly owner who will make you feel right at home. *Menù* includes bread, hummus, falafel salad, and shawarma (€8). Beer €2. Open M-Sa 1pm-2am. Cash only.

Manchester, C. Valldonzella, 40 (☎663 07 17 48; www.manchesterbar.com). ⓂUniversitat. Walk down the Ronda de Sant Antoni and make a left onto C. Joaquin Costa. Then make another left onto C. Valldonzella. This red-lit bar has old cassette tapes on the walls, ugly-chic artwork, and live music some nights. Check their Myspace for performance calendar. Mixed drinks €5-7. Open M-Th 7pm-2:30am, F-Sa 7pm-3am, Su 7pm-2:30am. Cash only.

Oddland, C. Joaquim Costa, 52 (☎934 12 00 49; oddland_bcn@hotmail.com). ⓂUniversitat. Walk down Ronda de Sant Antoni and make a right on C. Joaquim Costa. Tall green tables, funky walls with plaster and amoeba-shaped splotches, and a projected black-and-white movie on the back wall make this bar decidedly odd—but in a happy sort of way. Happy hour 6-10pm; mixed drinks €4. Serves snacks. Open M-Th 7pm-2am, F-Sa 7pm-3am. Cash only.

Café de les Delicies, Rambla del Raval, 47. ⓂLiceu or Paral.lel. Walk down C. Sant Pau until you reach the Rambla del Raval; the bar is on the right. Turquoise walls, wood tables, and fresh flowers make this bar feel like a trendy household kitchen—a great place to kick back for a quiet conversation with friends. At one end of the bar, you'll find leather sofas and books to read. Mixed drinks €6. Open M-Th 10am-2am, F-Sa 10am-3am. Cash only.

Tra.lers, C. Trallers, 39-41 (☎934 12 78 43). ⓂCatalunya. Walk down C. Pelai and make a left on C. de Jovellanos, then another left on C. Trallers. Restaurant by day and bar by night. No-frills black walls and L-shaped floorplan give it a grunge-chic feel. Convenient location near to the Pl. de Catalunya means that the venue gets rowdy at night. Lunch *menù* €10. Mixed drinks €5-7. Open M-Th 11am-2am, F-Sa 11am-3am, Su 11am-2am. MC/V.

Bar Centric, C. Ramelleres, 27 (☎933 01 81 35). ⓂCatalunya. Walk down C. Pelai and make a left on C. de Jovellanos. This historic-looking tapas bar has etched-glass windows, warm lighting, wooden booths, and a great location. Residents at the affiliated Hosteleria Grau and students come in the early evening. Beer €2-4. Open 8:30am-9pm. MC/V.

The Quiet Man, Marqués de Barbera, 11 (☎934 12 12 19). M: Liceu, L3. Take C. Unió off Las Ramblas; after 2 blocks it becomes Marqués Barbera. As authentic an Irish pub as you'll find in Barcelona, with homey decor, a good collection of Beleek (fine Irish china), and a friendly Irish staff. Late-night fish and chips (large, €7; small, €3.50), live music (pop or rock F-Sa midnight, Su 8:30pm), pool and foosball tables, and a private room available with reservation. Wi-Fi. Pints of imported drafts €4.40. Mixed drinks €7. Open M-W and Su6pm-2:30am, Th-Sa 6pm-3am. Cash only.

THE CLUB IN RAVAL

Moog, C. Arc del Teatre, 3 (☎933 01 72 82; www.masimas.com/moog). M: Liceu or Drassanes. Industrial metal walls and swirling green lights betray this as the techno headquarters of Barcelona, though the upstairs dance floor blasts music from the 80s and 90s. Look for discount flyers on Las Ramblas. Cover €10. Open daily midnight-5am, weekends until 6am. W especially popular. MC/V at bar.

THE OTHER CLUB IN RAVAL

Valhalla Rock Club, C. Tallers, 68 (www.myspace.com/valhallaclubderock). ⓂUniversitat. Walk down C. Tallers. A must-visit for rockers, goths, and death-metal enthusiasts. The club's 2009 summer lineup included artists such as Los Mercenarios and Riot of Violence. Check their Myspace page for upcoming shows and covers. Happy hour daily; kegs until 10pm. Open M-Th 6pm-2:30am, F-Sa 6pm-3am, Su 6pm-2:30am. Cash only.

L'EIXAMPLE

L'Eixample has upscale bars and some of the best—though not exclusively—gay nightlife in Europe. (Thus the area's nickname "Gaixample.") Some clubs can be difficult to get to, into, or back from; you may want to check out transportation ahead of time. Be sure to look up the NitBus schedule or the cost of a taxi home.

BARS

Zeltas, C. Casanova, 75 (☎934 50 84 69; www.zeltas.net). Complete with shimmering cloth hangings, feather boas, and low white couches, this exotic bar welcomes a classy clientele–usually gay–to sip a drink and enjoy the ambience. Wine €3. Beer €4.50. Mixed drinks €7. Open daily 10:30pm-3am. MC/V.

Les Gents que J'aime, C. València, 286, downstairs (☎932 15 68 79). ⓂPg. de Gràcia. You'll feel like Serge Gainsbourg at his hippest lounging in this dark, subterranean bar's velvet furniture. Background soul, funk, and jazz soothe patrons enjoying drinks like Les Gents (kiwi, lime, and pineapple juice; €7). Shotgun the chairs tucked beneath the staircase. Beer €4. Mixed drinks €6-7. Open daily 7pm-2:30am. AmEx/MC/V.

Espit Chupitos (Aribau), C. Aribau, 77 (www.espitchupitos.com). ⓂUniversitat. From Pl. de la Universitat, walk up C. Aribau. Colloquially known as "The Chupito Bar" (the bar has grown so popular that there are actually now three locations in Barcelona), this bar serves shots with flair. Servers perform when delivering so-called spectacle shots (€2): the Harry Potter shot involves lighting the bar on fire and the Monica Lewinsky shot...well, let's just say it's best ordered for an unsuspecting friend. Other locations at Carrer de la Unió 35 and Passeig de Colom 8. Open M-Th and Su 8pm-2:30am, F and Sa 8pm-3am. MC/V.

Dietrich Gay Teatro Cafe, C. Consell de Cent, 255 (☎934 51 77 07). ⓂUniversitat or Pg. de Gràcia. An unflattering caricature of a semi-nude Marlene Dietrich greets patrons at this inclusive gay bar. Beer €3.50. Mixed drinks €6. Drag shows, acrobatics, and dancing; check with the restaurant ahead of time. Open M-Th and Su 6pm-2am, F-Sa midnight-3am. MC/V.

La Chapelle, C. Mutaner, 67 (☎934 53 30 76). ⓂUniversitat. Walk up C. Mutaner. La Chapelle's decor juxtaposes antique devotional carvings with ultra-modern bubble lights. Gay-friendly. Beer €2.50. Mixed drinks €5. Open daily 4pm-2am. MC/V.

Atame, Consell de Cent, 257 (☎934 54 92 73). ⓂPg. de Gràcia or Universitat, L2/3/4. The door of this gay bar is draped in a rainbow flag, but otherwise the decor is sleek and minimalist. A mostly male, friendly, and energetic crowd shows up 7 nights a week for drag shows and more. Beer €2-3. Mixed drinks €6-7. Open M-Th and Su 6pm-2:30am, F-Sa 6pm-3am. MC/V.

Dow Jones, C. Bruc, 97 (☎932 07 63 75). ⓂPasseig de Gracia. Walk down C. Arago until you hit C. Bruc; make a left. At this stock-market themed bar, drinks (€2.50-7.50) are priced according to how frequently they're ordered, with the constantly-changing prices displayed on a TV screen. The best of i-banking (nice drinks) with the best of NASDAQ (large, lively crowds). The walls are papered in the *Financial Times.* Open M-F 7:30am-3am, Sa-Su noon-3am. MC/V.

Plata Bar, C. Consell de Cent, 233 (☎934 52 46 36). Stainless steel patio tables and a mostly male clientele spill from this corner bar onto the sidewalk. Colored lighting makes for a fun ambience. Open M-Th 6pm-2:30am, F-Sa 6pm-3am. MC/V.

Underground by Axel, C. Aribau, 33 (☎933 23 93 93). ⓂUniversitat. Walk up C. Aribau. Located in the "heterofriendly" (read: gay) Axel Hotel, this bar is all about steel, glass, and urbane animal magnetism. Happy hour M-F 8:30-11:30pm; 2-for-1 mixed drinks. Open daily 10:30am-2am. MC/V.

El Gato Negro, Consell de Cent, 268 (☎699 77 36 74). ⓂUniversitat. Walk up C. Aribau and make a right onto Consell de Cent. Part of the Espit Chupitos franchise (see p. 288). Both are usually bustling, so head to one if the other is full. Open Tu-Su 8pm-2:30am. MC/V.

Momo's Bar y Copas, Consell de Cent, 319 (☎934 87 33 14). ⓂUniversitat. Walk up C. Aribau and make a right onto Consell de Cent. Salsa, Merengue, and Bachata classes; call ahead for the season's schedule. Shots €2. Open daily 8pm-3am. MC/V.

Bar Snooker, C. Roger de Llúria, 42 (☎933 17 97 60; www.snookerbarcelona.com), between C. Gran Via and C. Diputació. ⓂTetuán, L2, or Pg. de Gràcia, L2/3/4. This large lounge bar has red velvet chairs, neon-green and blue lit pool tables, and an impressive list of scotches. Singles night W 8pm. Mixed drinks €8. Open daily 6pm-3am. AmEx/MC/V.

Topxi, C. València, 358 (☎932 07 01 20), just off Pg. St. Joan. ⓂVerdaguer, L4/5. A small, unpretentious bar-club that just happens to put on some of the most flamboyant drag and strip shows in the city—in intimate quarters. The orientation of the crowd varies by night and by show; call ahead to find out which way the evening swings. Cover €8-10; includes 1 drink. Open M-Th and Su 12:10am-5am, Sa 12:10am-6am. Cash only.

CLUBS

Mojito Club, C. Rosselló, 217 (☎654 20 10 06; www.mojitobcn.com). ⓂDiagonal. Buenavista salsa dance studio (☎932 37 65 28) by day and Mojito Club by night, this venue lures a fun-loving crowd with early-evening lessons and late-night Latin beats. Brazilian party W with free samba lessons at 11:30pm and R&B all night. Cover €10; includes 1 drink. For those taking regular lessons, cover may be waived. Open daily 11pm-5am. MC/V.

La Fira, C. Provença, 171 (☎650 85 53 84). ⓂHospital Clínic or FGC: Provença. A crowd swarms the circus-tent dance floor surrounded by carousel swings, carnival mirrors, and a fortune teller. The watchful sphinx perched atop the bar will make sure you don't go overboard with the wide selection of shots. Variety of shows and parties, often with entrance fee or 1 drink minimum. Open Th-Sa 11:30pm-3am. Cash only.

Luz de Gas, C. Muntaner, 246 (☎932 09 77 11; www.luzdegas.com). ⓂDiagonal, L3/5. Chandeliers, gilded mirrors, and deep red walls set the mood in this swanky uptown music venue. Concerts include the occasional big-name jazz, blues, or soul performer like Branford Marsalis, Bonnie Raitt, or Monica Green; thousands of performances have taken place here. After 1am, the chairs are folded up and the luxurious club becomes a high-class disco playing pop music. If you're looking to finish a conversation or talk about the show, head upstairs to the quieter glassed-in balcony. Beer €6. Mixed drinks €10. Cover €18; check the Guía del Ocio for specific show listings and times. Wheelchair-accessible. Open daily 11:30pm-5am. MC/V.

La Madame, Ronda de St. Pere, 23, between C. Bruc and Pl. Urquinaona. ⓂUrquinaona. A mixed gay-straight crowd fills the 2 huge dance floors of this popular club. Pounding house music by the Maintee Group's locally esteemed DJs. Beer €5. Mixed drinks €8. Wheelchair-accessible. Cover €15-20; includes 1 drink. Open F-Su midnight-6am. MC/V.

Zac Club, Av. Diagonal, 477 (☎933 21 09 22; www.zac-club.com). ⓂHospital Clìnic, L5. Big names, such as Lenny Kravitz and the Cindy Blackman Group, sometimes come to perform in this intimate disco setting. Live jazz, funk, and blues nightly midnight-2am. A smaller dance floor and plenty of bar room makes this a great place for people that shun the gyrating masses of larger venues. Drinks €4.20-7.20. Cover €10-15; includes 1 drink. Open Th-Sa 12:30am-dawn.

Aire, C. València, 236. (☎934 54 63 94; www.arenadisco.com) ⓂPg. de Gràcia, L2/3/4. One of Barcelona's biggest and most popular lesbian clubs. Throngs of women crowd the multicolored dance floor, grooving to pop, house, and 80s classics. Women-only strip show from 6-10pm 1st Su of every month. Cover €5-10; includes 1 drink. Open Th-Su 11:30pm-3am. Check out the Arena family's other gay discos, some of the most popular in the area: **Arena Classic** at C. Diputació, 233 plays 80s tunes; **Arena Dandy** at Gran Via, 593 pumps techno beats. The popular **Arena Madre** at C. Balmes, 32 is mostly for men, as is the more relaxed **Punto BCN** bar at C. Muntaner, 63. MC/V.

Roxy Blue, Consell de Cent, 294 (www.roxyblue.es). ⓂUniversitat. Walk up C. Aribau and make a right on Consell de Cent. Ubiquitous blue sparkling lights and 3 dance rooms make the new Roxy Blue Society Club a safe bet for a night of glamour. Music varies by night (check the web page) and includes R&B, soul, hip hop, minimal, electronica, and techno. Cover €12-18. Open W-Th midnight-5am, F-Sa midnight-6am. MC/V.

Antilla, C. Aragó, 141 (☎934 51 45 64; www.antillasalsa.com). ⓂUrgell. Walk up C. Comte de Urgell and make a left on C. Aragó. Wild neon lighting and a large, open dance floor make this salsa school and dance club a local favorite. Cover €10; includes 1 drink. Lessons for dancers of all levels Tu-Sa 5-11pm. Club open Tu-W 11pm-4am, Th 11pm-5am, F-Sa 11pm-6am. MC/V.

La Suite, C. Villarroel, 216 (☎658 31 45 03). Elegant and exclusive (Playboy has been known to throw its official parties here), La Suite plays R&B, hip hop, and rap in black-and-gold rooms. Cover €18. You may be able to get in for free before 2:30am if you visit their Facebook page (search "Suite Club Barcelona") and sign up. Open Th-Sa midnight-6am. MC/V.

Salvation, Ronda de St. Pere, 19-21, between C. Bruc and Pl. Urquinaona. ⓂUrquinaona. The place to come if you've sinned... and want to keep on sinning. A popular gay club with 2 huge dance floors and pounding house music. Beer €5. Mixed drinks €8. Wheelchair-accessible. Cover €11; includes 1 drink. Open F-Su midnight-6am.

BARCELONETA AND PORT VELL

Maremagnum, the one-time mecca of Barcelona nightlife, has shifted its focus toward being purely a daytime shopping mall, shutting down all but one of its clubs after a series of violent altercations took place on its premises at night. Today, beach nightlife has shifted toward Port Olímpic and Pg. Maritím, although a handful a worthwhile bars can be found in Barceloneta.

Absenta, C. Sant Carles, 36. ⓂBarceloneta. Walking down Pg. Joan de Borbó and take a left on C. Sant Carles. A green interior with vintage posters suits the star beverage at this absinthe bar, although most choose to sit out on the terrace during summer. Beer

€2.50. Wine €2.80. Absinthe €4-7. Open M, W-Th, and Su 11am-2am, Tu 6pm-2am, F-Sa 11am-3am. Cash only.

Ke?, C. del Beluart, 54. (☎932 24 15 88) ⓂBarceloneta. Walking down Pg. Joan de Borbó, take a left on C. Sant Carles and another left at the plaza onto C. del Beluart. Decor meanders between tropical surf, the American west, and Popeye the Sailor. Hosts an equally eclectic crowd, from rowdy beachgoers to locals using the Wi-Fi on the back sofa over a beer (€2). Open daily 11:30am-2:30am. Cash only.

PASSEIG MARITÍM DE PORT OLIMPÍC

If what you need is a crowded dance floor and loud music, this is the place to find it. The strip along the lower level of Port Olimpíc hosts a string of side-by-side clubs (with a few shisha bars and late-night fast-food joints sprinkled in between for good measure), each trying to drown out the music of the club next door. None of the clubs has a dress code, nor do they charge cover, so hop around until you find one you like. Though these clubs might not be quite as sleek as some of the more exclusive ones nearby, they attract plenty of young partiers looking for a good dance floor.

Opium Mar, Pg. Marítim de la Barceloneta, 34 (☎902 26 74 86; www.opiummar.com). The indoor-outdoor restaurant serves seafood until 1am, at which point the DJ starts blasting house music and the place turns into a glitzy, colorful club. When they aren't platform-dancing, bikini-clad waitresses serve drinks as chic patrons bust a move. Beer €8. Mixed drinks €10-15. Wheelchair-accessible. Cover €20 includes one drink. Restaurant open daily 1pm-1am. Club open M-Th and Su midnight-5am, F-Sa 1am-6am. AmEx/MC/V.

El Gran Casino, C. Marina, 19 (☎932 25 78 78; www.casino-barcelona.com), under the fish. Blackjack, American roulette, French roulette, slots, and *punto banco* are the action here. Attracts mostly an older crowd. Must be 18 to play. No sneakers or beach clothes; collared shirt recommended for men. Passport required. Wheelchair-accessible. Entrance fee €4.50. Open daily 1pm-5am. MC/V.

Shoko, Pg. Marítim de la Barceloneta, 34 (☎932 25 92 00; www.shoko.biz). Like its neighbor, Opium Mar, this is a terraced restaurant by day and exclusive club by night. It may appear mellow during dinner but by 2am it's packed with a crowd dancing to techno and house. Beer €6. Mixed drinks €10. Wheelchair-accessible. No cover, but look sharp: no sneakers, beach clothes, or lame shirts. Restaurant opens daily at noon. Club open daily noon-3am. AmEx/MC/V.

Catwalk, C. Ramón Trias Fargas, 2/4 (☎692 64 14 29; www.clubcatwalk.net). ⓂPort Olímpic. Sleek interior blasting house downstairs and hip hop and R&B upstairs. Attracts elite partiers from all over the world (even some from Barcelona itself), and during peak club hours you can expect to see a line running halfway down the block. Beer €7. Mixed drinks €12. Cover €20. Open Th and Su midnight-5am, F-Sa midnight-6am. MC/V.

MONTJUÏC AND POBLE SEC

Sala Apolo is the main nightlife draw in this neighborhood, but within its side-streets, Poble Sec offers some of the best off-the-beaten-path late-night hang-outs in the city. Lower Montjuïc is home to **Poble Espanyol** ("Spanish Village"), a recreation of famous buildings and sights from all over Spain, and a nightlife hotspot during the summer.

Tinta Roja, C. Creus dels Molers, 17 (☎934 43 32 43; www.tintaroja.net). Located just off Av. Paral·lel in a newly pedestrian section of Poble Sec. Red tinted lights, red velvet chairs. The dance floor gets serious, especially during tango classes W 9-10:30pm, (call for details). Specialties include tropical mixed drinks (€7) and Argentine *yerba-mate* (€4.80) Open Th 9:30pm-2:30am, F-Sa 9:30pm-3am. Cash only.

La Terrazza, Avda. Marquès de Comillas, s/n (☎932 72 49 80). On weekend summer nights, Poble Espanyol succumbs to the irrepressible revelry of La Terrazza, an outdoor dance club to one side of the village where you can sway along to techno with the masses. Get here after 2am and you may find yourself in a line of up to 100. Beer €6. Mixed drinks €9-10, although bars scattered in Poble Espanyol stay open late and serve cheaper alcohol. Cover €18, gets you into the village and club, plus 1 drink. Open June-Oct. Th midnight-5am, F-Sa midnight-6am. MC/V.

Mau Mau, C. d'En Fontrodona, 33 (☎60 686 06 17). M: Paral·lel, L2/L3. Follow C. d'En Fontrodona as it bends right, past C. Blai. Look for a gray door on the left as you walk up the street and ring the bell. Young locals sprawl out on sofas for drinks in this massive, inimitably cool hideout. Films screened Th-Sa at 10pm. Residents from Barcelona buy year-long memberships (€12), but out-of-towners need only sign in at the door. Beer €3. Mixed drinks €6. Open Th-Sa 10:30pm-3am. Cash Only.

Torres de Ávila (☎93 424 93 09), next to the main entrance of Poble Espanyol. M: Espanya, L1/3. A million-peseta construction that was at the height of club chic when it was built in the 80s. Torres is still going strong as one of the city's hottest night spots, complete with glass elevators, 7 bars, and a summertime rooftop terrace with gorgeous views of the city. DJs spin house and techno. Drinks €5-10. Dress to impress. Cover €18, includes 1 drink. Open Th-Sa midnight-6:30am.

Instinto, C. Mexic 7-9, (www.salainstinto.com) parallel to Av. Reina María Cristina and close to Poble Espanyol. M: Espanya, L1/3. Small warehouse converted into a nearly tourist-free dance club. Themed nights of music alternating between hip hop, drum 'n' bass, and latin rhythms. Strong mixed drinks €8-10. Cover €12, includes 1 drink. Open W-Th and Su midnight-5am, F-Sa midnight-6am. Cash only.

242, Carrer d'Entença, 37. M: Espanya. One of the longest running afters still operating within the city of Barcelona itself. Serious partiers trickle into this industrial setting once the clubs close for even more alcohol and electronica. Mixed drinks €10. Beer €5. €15 cover includes 1 drink. Open M and F-Su 6-11am. MC/V.

Rouge, C. Poeta Cabanyes, 21 (☎93 442 49 85). M: Paral·lel, L2/L3. From Av. Paral·lel, turn onto C. Peeta Cabanyes. Look for the door on your left and ring the bell. Distinguished, vintage decor bathed in warm red light make this a hip bar and lounge with a clientele and a cocktail menu to match. Try the BCN Rouge with vodka, berry liqueur and lime (€6.50). Beer €2.50. Open W-Th and Su 8pm-1am. F-Sa 8pm-3am. Cash only.

GRACIA

Gràcia is all about busy-but-intimate bars—the kind of venues where you run into friends and have to raise your voice to talk with them. Some of them have modern, relaxing decor, and colored lighting—Vinil is orange, Nictalia purple—while others, like Cafe del Sol and Blues Cafe, leave it to their clients and the drinks to make the ambience. If you feel a bit more adventurous, head to **Plaça de la Revolució de Septiembre 1868** or **Plaça del Sol** and take it from there; in this young, vibrant neighborhood, you really can't go wrong.

BARS

Vinil(), C. Matilde, 2 (☎669 17 79 45; www.vinilus.blogspot.com). This bar's dim orange lighting, mismatched pillows, mellow background music, and screened daily movies make you never want to leave. Beer and wine €2.70. Mojitos and *caipirinhas* (the only mixed drinks served) €6. Open in summer M-Th 8pm-2am, F-Sa 8pm-3am; in winter M-Th and Su 8pm-2am, F-Sa 8pm-3am.

Cafe del Sol, Pl. del Sol, 16 (☎932 37 14 48). Ⓜ Fontana. Walk down C. Gran de Gràcia, make a left on C. Ros de Olano and then a right on C. Cano/C.Leopoldo Alas. Locals pack the 8 tapas bars around Pl. del Sol every night and spill out into the plaza. This mainstay offers perfect tostadas (€3-5) and tapas (€1.70-5) as well as beer (€2-3), wine, and mixed drinks (€5-6). Come for lunch and take your tapas out into the plaza. Open M-Th and Su noon-2:30am, F and Sa noon-3am.

Nictalia, C. St. Domenec, 15 (☎932 37 23 23). Ⓜ Fontana. Walk down C. Gran de Gràcia to C. St. Domenec and make a left; Nictalia is 2 blocks down on the left. Step into this intimate bar and feel the magic—it's got blue fairy lights, purple walls, and colorful chalkboards (not to mention a buzzing crowd of locals and cheap shots). Beer €2-3. Mixed drinks €5. Shots €1.80. Open M-Th 6:30pm-2am, F and Sa 6pm-3am. Cash only.

Sol Soler, Pl. del Sol, 21-22 (☎932 17 44 40; www.myspace.com/solsolertapas). Ⓜ Fontana. Walk down C. Gran de Gràcia and make a left onto C. de Ros de Olano. Follow the noise and make a right onto Pl. del Sol. This beloved corner bar is on Pl. del Sol, the center of Gràcia's nightlife. Also open during the day, Sol Soler is a longtime local favorite and unquestionably the real deal. Crowd in with students around tables, shout to be heard, and feel like a local. Open M-W noon-1:30am, Th-Su noon-2:30am.

Bar Canigo, C. Verdi, 2 (☎932 13 30 49). Ⓜ Fontana. Walk down C. Gran de Gràcia and make a left on C. Ros de Olano. Keep walking (about 6 blocks) until you hit C. Verdi. A classic student haunt. Bar Canigo has cracked mirrors, pool tables, and a young, fun-loving clientele; noisy tables of friends jumble happily around long faux-marble tables to guzzle beers (€2-4). Mixed drinks €5-6. Open M-Th 8pm-2am, F-Sa 8pm-3am, Su 8pm-2am. MC/V.

Café del Teatre, C. Torrijos, 41 (☎934 16 06 51). Ⓜ Fontana. Walk down C. Gran de Gràcia and make a left onto C. Montseny. Walk 8 blocks; it's on the right. This corner bar has *Modernista* stained-glass accents, green lighting, alluring if slightly eerie statues of black cats behind the bar, and a prime location. The mojitos are especially good. Open M-Th 10pm-2am, F-Sa 10pm-3am. Cash only.

La Cervesera Artesana: Pub-Brewery, C. Sant Augusti, 14 (☎932 37 95 94). Ⓜ Diagonal. Walk down C. Corsega and then make a left onto C. Sant Agusti. It's up ahead, on the left. The only bar in Barcelona to brew its own beer, the Cervesera has long been making locals proud. Try the peppermint home brew (a pint €4.90); you might like it so much that you will take a case home with you. *Pica-pica* also served. Open M-Th 6pm-2am, F-Sa 6pm-3am, Su 6pm-2am. MC/V.

L'Astrolabi, C. Martinez de la Rosa, 14. Ⓜ Diagonal. Walk down C. Corsega and then make a left onto C. Sant Agusti. This street turns into C. Martinez de la Rosa. L'Astrolabi is shortly up, on the right. A crowd of intimate regulars gathers at this nautically-themed bar to listen to and play live music 7 nights a week. The scene is more campfire than rager. Beer €2-4. Mixed drinks €5-6. Live music from 10pm. Open 8pm-2am. Cash only.

El Otro Bar, Travessera de Gràcia, 167 (☎933 23 67 59). Ⓜ Fontana. Walk down C. Gran de Gràcia until you reach Trav. de Gràcia. Make a left. Even on weeknights, this Irish pub bustles. Colored chalk boards in the street advertise drink specials. Open M-Th 9pm-2am, F-Sa 9pm-3am, Su 9pm-2am. Cash only.

DeDues Cocktail & Bar, C. Torrent de l'Olla, 89 (☎934 16 14 96; www.dedues.es). Ⓜ Fontana. From the Metro, walk down C. Asturies until you hit C. Torrent de l'Olla. Walk 5½ blocks down C. Torrent de l'Olla. This posh *cocteleria* (the walls are bedecked with orange floral swirls) specializes in mojitos and caipirinha (€4). Open M-Th 8:30pm-2:30am, F 8:30pm-3am, Sa 6:30pm-3am. MC/V.

Mond Bar, Pl. del Sol, 21 (www.mondclub.com). Ⓜ Fontana. Walk down C. Gran de Gràcia and make a left onto C. Ros de Olano. Follow the crowds or the noise to Pl. del Sol. The sign above this bar's door reads "Pop Will Save Us." True to this, Mond Bar is your pop oasis in this happening but electronica-dominated plaza. iPod battles Th. Open M-Th 7pm-2:30am, F-Sa 7pm-3am, Su 7pm-2:30am. Beer €2-4. Mixed drinks €5-6. Cash only.

Mi Bar, C. de les Guilleries, 6. ⓂFontana. Walk down C. Gran de Gràcia and make a left on C. Montseny. Continue for 6 blocks, then make a right on C. de les Guilleries. This hideaway bar is glam-meets-graffiti; the walls are scrawled with red and black paint, but chandeliers and mirrors add a touch of class. Pool table in the back room. Drinks €3-8. Open M-Th, F-Sa until 3am, and Su 11pm-2:30am. Cash only.

Velcro Bar, C. Vallfogona, 10 (☎610 75 47 42). ⓂFontana. Follow C. de Asturies to C. Torrent de l'Olla and make a right. After 3 blocks on this street, make a left onto C. Vallfongona. White tables, lilac twinkle lights, and a location away from the madness of Gràcia's plazas makes this a favorite with young locals. Movies are played nightly on the back wall. Mixed drinks €5-8. Open nightly 7pm-2:30am. MC/V.

Stinger, C. Corcega, 338 (☎932 17 71 87). ⓂDiagonal. This bar, which is located between the student zone of Gràcia and the 5-star hotels on Pg. de Gràcia, straddles the line between cozy and classy. Convenient to the Metro, it's a good place to drink your 1st round. Mixed drinks €6.20-6.90. Open M-Th 6:30pm-2:30am, F-Sa 6:30pm-3am. Closed Aug. MC/V.

Enigma, C. Martinez de la Rosa, 27 (☎695 27 91 82). ⓂDiagonal. Walk down C. Corsega and make a left onto C. Sant Agusti. This street turns into C. Martinez de la Rosa; Enigma is on the left. Not much mystery here—this bar has a pool table, cheap drinks, and a clientele of would-be punks. Games of pool during the week free, weekends €2. Shots €2. Open in summer daily 8pm-2:30am; in winter daily 6pm-2:30am. Cash only.

Flann O'Brien's, C. Casanova, 264 (☎932 01 16 06; www.flannobrienbcn.com). ⓂDiagonal, L3/5. Authentic, boisterous Irish pub with barrels for tables and rugby shirts hanging from the ceiling. Popular with locals and Barcelona's English-speaking expats for almost 2 decades. Top off your evening with a Guinness or a mixed drink (€6). Live music Th-Sa 11:30pm. Open M-Th and Su 6pm-2:30am, F and Sa 6pm-3am.

La Baignoire, C. Verdi, 6, (☎606 33 04 60). ⓂFontana. From the Metro, walk down C. d'Asturies past Pl. del Diamante until you hit C. Verdi. Locals gather around busy La Baignoire's elegant, high tables to chat, drink cava, and sip mixed drinks (€6) before heading to more raucous venues. Open M-Th 6pm-1:30am, F and Sa 6pm-2am, Su 6pm-1am. MC/V.

CLUBS

Otto Zutz, C. Lincoln, 15 (☎932 38 07 22; www.ottozutz.com). FGC: Gràcia or ⓂFontana. Japanimation lighting and 3 dance floors make this one of Barcelona's most popular clubs. Named in honor of the legendary 70s club Autozut. Upstairs you'll find local DJs playing electronica; downstairs, you'll hear hip-hop and R&B. VIP access and private parties possible with reservation. Beer €6. Mixed drinks €6-12. Cover €10-15, includes 1 drink. Look for flyers at bars and hotels to get in free before 2am. Open W-Su midnight-6am. MC/V.

KGB, C. Alegre de Dalt, 55 (☎932 10 59 06; www.salakgb.net). ⓂJoanic, L4. Walk along C. Pi i Maragall and take the 1st left; to get a cab home, come back to Pi i Maragall. Techno and loud rock play to a mixed crowd of students and Soviet secret agents. Occasional live concerts 9pm. Beer €4-6. Mixed drinks €6-8. Cover €10, includes 1 drink. Open Th 1-5am, F-Sa and nights before public holidays 1-6am. Cash only.

Nick Havanna, C. Rosello, 208 (☎607 49 79 81; www.nickhavanna.com). FGC: Provenca. Spaniards and tourists looking *muy pijos* (very fly) dance beneath a metal, domed ceiling and rainbow lighting and grind to pop hits. Check out the rotating slide projections. Dress to impress (no sneakers). Drinks €6-8. Cover €10. Open Th-Sa, midnight-5am. MC/V.

Duvet, C. Córcega, 327 (☎93 237 43 22; www.duvet.es). ⓂDiagonal. It's right on C. Córcega, across the street from the Metro. This live music venue and club has nightly events that range from dance lessons to live music to DJs. Dance lessons Tu. Ladies' night W. The best of the 80s and 90s (with some modern hits) F and Sa. Ballroom Su. Open nightly. Cover and exact times vary by event, so check ahead online. MC/V.

TIBIDABO

Although pricey and hard to access, the few bars in Tibidabo offer fabulous, shimmering night views of Barcelona from on high. Unless you have really good shoes and willpower, getting here by taxi is the way to go. Ask the driver for the number of the taxi company to call on the way back.

Mirablau, Pl. Dr. Andreu (☎934 18 58 79). Next to Mirabé (see below). 2 terraces and the full window inside the bar afford spectacular views. On weekends, the crowd drifts downstairs to the nightclub. Open all day for those who care for an early drink and a view of Barcelona before nightfall. Mixed drinks €6-11. Wine and beer €4.70-6 (cheaper before 11pm). Sa-Su 1-drink min. Open M-Th 11am-4:30am, F and Sa 11am-5:45am. AmEx/MC/V.

Merbeyé (☎934 17 35 49), in Pl. Dr. Andreu. Set slightly back from the cliff, with a sultry interior that greets loungers for tapas and drinks. The outdoor canopy attracts easy-going crowds, with 80s pop tunes ablare. Creative drinks include the Merbeyé (Cointreau with cava and cherry brandy; €8.50). Open W 7pm-1am, Th and Su noon-2am, F-Sa noon-4am. MC/V.

Mirabé, Manuel Arnus, 2 (☎934 34 00 35; www.mirabe.es), in Pl. Dr. Andreu. A supremely elegant bar overlooking the Mediterranean shore. Potted palms and a small pond only heighten the luxury of the large terrace frequented by well-dressed professionals. Beers €4.50. Mixed drinks €9.50. Open Tu-Su 7pm-3am. MC/V.

Rosebud, Carrer d'Adrià Margarit, 27 (☎934 18 88 85; www.rosebud.es). Across from Museu de la Ciencia. Only the most elite, well-dressed revelers make it past the iron gate and up the red-carpeted stairs to the Xanadu-esque decadence that lies beyond. A list posted at the door bans (among other things) T-shirts, hair that is inappropriately long or unkempt (for men), and white socks. Cover €10 includes 1 drink. Open Th-Su midnight-6am. MC/V.

CATALUÑA (CATALUNYA)

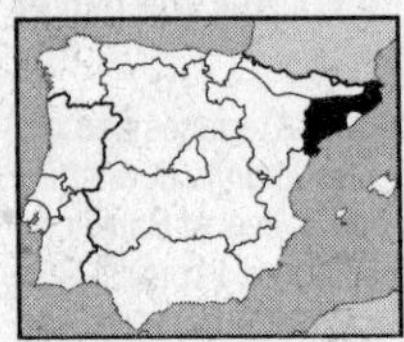

Cataluña is the most prosperous region in Iberia—and one of the proudest. The region's linguistic identity, rich natural resources, and cultural tradition have set it apart from the rest of Spain. Colonized first by the Greeks and then the Carthaginians, Cataluña later became one of Rome's favored provinces. It was briefly subdued by the Moors, and then fell into Charlemagne's domain for a short time. Cataluña declared independence in 989, growing more powerful after it united with the throne of Aragón in 1137. Still, while this pact allowed Cataluña to pursue her own empire for a time, it ultimately meant one thing: surrender to Spanish rule. The Catalan Nationalist Movement that resulted from the subjugation has been a contentious political issue for centuries.

Cataluña's achievements have lent credence to the region's fierce sense of autonomy. In the late 18th century, the region became one of Europe's premier textile manufacturers and pursued a robust trade with the Americas. Nineteenth-century industrial expansion nourished the arts and sciences, ushering in an age known as the Catalan *Renaixença* (Renaissance). The turn of the century gave birth to the *Modernista* movement and an all-star list of wildly innovative artists and architects including Picasso, Miró, Dalí, Gaudí, Domènech i Montaner, and Puig i Cadafalch. Despite all of its achievements, it was also the site of merciless persecution under Franco's dictatorship. Many *catalaneses* were imprisoned or killed, and dictatorship brought suppression of Catalan language instruction and publications, degrading the very foundation of the population's identity: its beloved tongue, a Romance language—not a dialect—closely related to Spanish and French. There is no "Spanish" here, only *castellano*, (literally, "language spoken in Castilla"), a distinction that allows *catalaneses* to differentiate themselves from a historically dominant culture. Since receiving full autonomy in 1979, Cataluña's media and arts have flourished; Catalan is once again the official language. After you've been to Cataluña, you may understand why many here call it "A Nation of Europe"—it isn't quite like anywhere else in Spain.

HIGHLIGHTS OF CATALUÑA

IMMERSE yourself in the Mediterranean on the **Costa Brava** (p. 301)

UNCOVER the secrets of the Kabbala at its birthplace in **Girona's** El Call (p. 305).

SURRENDER to Dalí's egotism at the Teatre-Museu Dalí in **Figueres** (p. 307).

COSTA DORADA

SITGES ☎938

Forty kilometers south of Barcelona, the beach town of Sitges (pop. 27,000) just might deserve its self-proclaimed title as the "jewel of the Mediterranean." Composed of crystalline water, sweeping bays, and beautiful tanning grounds baked by 300 sunny days per year, Sitges gained prominence in the late 19th century as one of the principal centers of the *Modernista* art movement. Today,

it's swarmed with young and fun-loving tourists who come for the thriving gay community and pulsating nightlife. Sitges makes an ideal daytrip along the coast, but it also merits a few nights' stay.

TRANSPORTATION

Trains: Cercanías trains (a.k.a. Rodalies; RENFE ☎902 24 02 02, www.renfe.es/cercanias) run from **Estació Barcelona-Sants** to **Sitges** (Line 2 toward St. Vicenç de Calders or Vilanova; 45min., every 15-30min. 5:40am-1:06am, €2.50). Trains also run from **Sitges** to **Cambrils** (1hr., €4.40) via **Tarragona** (€3.60).

Buses: Mon Bus (☎938 93 70 60; www.monbus.cat; info@monbus.org) connects the Barcelona **airport** to Pg. de Villafranca in **Sitges** (M-F every hr. from airport 7:40am-11:40pm, from Sitges 5:55am-11:55pm, Sa-Su every 2hr. from airport 8:40am-10:40pm, from Sitges 7:25am-8:55pm; €2.85). Late-night buses operate from Pg. de Villafranca to Rambla de Catalunya in Barcelona and back (12:11-4am, €2.85). **Bus Urbà** (☎938 14 49 89) runs 3 local bus lines (all leave from the train station; every 30min. M-F 8am-9pm, Sa-Su 9:30am-9pm; earlier in winter; €0.90-0.95).

Taxis: ☎938 94 13 29. Run between **Barcelona** and **Sitges** (€60-65).

Car Rental: ☎938 11 19 96. To reach the beaches and the *cales* (caves), rent a car in Barcelona or Sitges at **Europcar,** on the 1st fl. of the Mercat to the right from the train station. Open daily 7am-9pm. AmEx/MC/V.

ORIENTATION AND PRACTICAL INFORMATION

Most people arrive at the train station on **Carrer Carbonell** in the northern part of town. From there, the town center is 5min. by foot, and the beach 10min. To reach either, take a right as you leave the station and the third left onto **Carrer Sant Francesc.** This leads to the old town and intersects **Carrer de les Parellades,** the main strip of stores and restaurants running parallel to the ocean. Any street off Parellades will lead to the waterfront. **Passeig de la Ribera** runs along the central and most crowded beaches.

Tourist Office: C. Sinia Morera, 1 (☎938 10 93 40; www.sitgestur.com). From the station, turn right on C. Carbonell and take the next right at the roundabout, onto Pg. de Vilafranca. The office is 1 block up on the left. Free maps and monthly bulletin of events, **Sitges Agenda.** Open from mid-June to mid-Sept. M-Sa 9am-8pm; from late Sept. to early June M-F 9am-2pm and 4-6:30pm. **Branches** at the train station and near the beach, below the church. **Agis** offers **guided tours** of the city (☎619 79 31 99; www.sitges.com/agis; €8), while **Jafra Natura** takes visitors through the bordering Garraf Natural Park (☎938 96 84 65; www.jafranatura.com; €4, children €3).

Police: Pl. Ajuntament (☎704 10 10 92).

Medical Services: Hospital Sant Camil (☎938 96 00 25).

Internet Access: Cafe Cappuchino, C. Sant Francesc, 44. €1 per 15min. Open daily 9am-11pm.

Post Office: Pl. d'Espanya (☎938 94 12 47). Open M-F 8:30am-2:30pm, Sa 9:30am-1pm; no package pickup Sa. **Postal Code:** 08870.

CATALUÑA

ACCOMMODATIONS

Accommodations are difficult to find on summer weekends (especially F-Sa). Be sure to call well in advance for a room (although the nightlife is crazy enough that you may not need a bed of your own).

Hostal Parellades, C. de les Parellades, 11 (☎938 94 08 01; hostalparellades@hotmail.com), 1 block from the beach. Well-kept rooms, a terrace, and a piano. Easily accessible after late nights, as customers are given a key to the main door. Singles €30; doubles with bath €60; triples with bath €75. MC/V (but cash preferred). ❸

Hostal Bonaire, C. Bonaire, 31 (☎938 94 53 26 www.bonairehostalsitges.com). 12 cozy rooms a block from the beach. Ask for one of the rooms with a terrace overlooking party-prone C. Bonaire. Reception 24hr. All with TV, some with A/C. In summer singles with bath €40; doubles €55-65. In winter €35/45-50. MC/V. ❸

Hotel El Cid, C. Sant Joesp, 39 (☎938 94 18 42; www.hotelsitges.com). From the train station, take a right, pass the rotunda, and take the 4th left off C. Carbonell. One of the best deals in town and popular with young travelers. All rooms come with bath, safe, and fan. Small pool, bar, and garden in back. Reserve more than a month ahead. Breakfast included. Singles €48-82; doubles €71-107; triples €103-156, depending on season. Deals for stays of 6 nights or longer. Closed Nov.-Mar. MC/V. ❹

FOOD

Many of the restaurants in Sitges are tourist traps, especially on the beachfront, but the food here is world-class. Venture far down C. de les Parellades or on the pleasant side streets to escape the generic scene. Sitges isn't cheap by any means, however. You'll generally pay at least €20 for dinner, but expect to get your money's worth. Groceries are available at **Suma,** C. Carbonell, 24, across from the train station. (☎938 94 12 00. Open M-Sa 9am-9pm, Su 10am-2pm. MC/V.) Alternatively, swing by the **Mercat de Sitges,** C. Carbonell, 26, next door to the train station, which has fruit and vegetables, meat, fish, and cheese vendors as well as several cafes and bakeries and even a clothing store. (Open M-Th 8am-2pm, F-Sa 8am-2pm and 5-8:30pm.)

Izarra, C. Major, 24 (☎938 94 73 70), behind the museum area. Basque tapas bar good for a quick fix or a leisurely meal. Ask for a *plato* and grab whatever looks tasty, from Basque seafood concoctions to more traditional Spanish *croquetas*. Big entrees (€6.50-15) and great *sidra* (cider; €1.50). Bar open daily 8:30am-midnight, *menú* available 1:30-4pm and 8:30-11pm. MC/V. ❷

Ma Maison, C. Bonaire, 28 (☎938 94 60 54). This vast restaurant (which is gay-friendly) has outdoor seating and intricately detailed walls. It serves Mediterranean entrees from a different menu every 2 months. Su is *paella* day in winter. Dinner entrees €20. Open daily 8:30pm-midnight. MC/V. ❹

Alfresco Cafè, C. Mayor, 33 (☎938 11 33 07, www.alfrescorestaurante.com). Healthful, gourmet choices found on chalkboard menus that change regularly, with relaxing music and white, modern decor. Check out mouthwatering desserts in the glass case at the bar or admire the creative presentation of the mixed green salmon salad with sesame seeds, caramelized onions, and garnish (€10) or the pita filled with chicken, tomato, mango sauce and sweet chile (€7). Free Wi-Fi. Open daily 9am-11pm. MC/V. ❷

SIGHTS

Tourists flock to shop, eat, and drink on the pedestrian walkway Carrer de les Parellades, but wise locals stick to the side streets and the peaceful beaches that are located farther up the coast.

PALAU MARICEL. Across the street from the waterfront museums, fragments of Spanish artistic culture unite with *Modernista* ceramics here, on C. Fonollar, built in 1910 for the American millionaire Charles Deering. Prepare to be wowed by its sumptuous halls and rooftop terraces. Guided tours are available on some summer nights (July-Sept.) and include a glass of *cava* (sparkling wine) and a castanet concert in the rooftop *claustro*. *(☎938 94 03 64. Days and times vary; call ahead for reservations. €10.)*

MORELL'S MODERNISTA CLOCK TOWER. As soon as you come into the Plaça at the intersection of C. de les Parellades and C. Sant Francesc, stop and look high up above the Òptica store for this whimsical clock tower. It's easy to miss but worth ogling for a while. *(Pl. Cap de la Vila, 2.)*

MUSEUMS. Sitges has neatly united all of its museums under one consortium; they all have the same hours and prices, and combo tickets are available. Seven blocks from the clock on C. Fonollar, the **Museu Cau Ferrat** hangs high over the water's edge. Once the home of a driving force of *Modernista* architecture, Santiago Rusiñol (1861-1931), and a meeting place for the young Pablo Picasso and Ramón Casas, the building is a shrine to *Modernista* iron and glass work, sculpture, ceramics, and painting, featuring pieces by El Greco and Picasso. Farther into town, the **Museu Romàntic,** C. Sant Gaudenci, 1, off C. de les Parellades, is an immaculately preserved 19th-century house filled with period pieces like music boxes and two surprising collections: over 400 antique dolls from all over the world, and over 25 intricate dioramas of 19th-century life in Sitges. *(General info ☎938 94 03 64; www.diba.es/museus/sitges.asp. All museums open July-Sept. Tu-Sa 9:30am-2pm and 4-7pm, Su 10am-3pm; Oct.-June Tu-Sa 9:30am-2pm and*

3:30-6:30pm, Su 10am-3pm. Hourly guided tours in summer in Museu Romàntic €3.50, students and seniors €1.75; combo ticket for several museums €6.40/3.50.)

BEACHES

Sitges's sky-blue waters and proximity to Barcelona make it a viable alternative to the crowded sands of Barceloneta and Port Olímpic. At **Platja de la Fragata,** the main beach farthest to the left as you face the sea, sand sculptors create new masterpieces every summer day. By midday, the beaches close to downtown can become almost unbearably crowded; the best beaches, with calmer waters and more open space, like **Platja de la Barra** and **Platja de Terramar,** are a 1-2km walk away (or catch the L2 bus from the train station to the stop next to Hotel Terramar, and walk a bit back toward town; every 30min. 9am-9pm, €0.95). If you decide to walk, you will pass several small beaches, including **Platja de la Bassa Rodona,** popular with gay sunbathers. Rocks partly shield these beaches from waves, creating a shallow ocean swimming pool that extends far into the water and is ideal for children. Farther down, the water is bluer and there's more open sand to claim. Sitges is also well known for its peaceful nude beaches. **Platja de l'Home Mort** can be reached by walking past Terramar until you hit a golf course at the end of the sidewalk. Walk on the beach past the golf course, and **l'Home Mort** is in a small cove behind the hills where the train tracks run by the coast. Alternately, flaunt your birthday suit at **Cala Morisca,** on the opposite side of the city, past **Platja d'Alguadolç.** To reach **Platja del Balmins,** with clear water ideal for snorkeling, walk past the church and **Platja de Sant Sebastià,** go around the first restaurant you come to, and then take the dirt walkway between the coast and the high white walls of the cemetery. The path will go up and down a slope; the beach is a quiet cove before the port.

CATALUÑA

NIGHTLIFE

Sitges makes an easy daytrip and an (arguably) better night-trip. The wild clubs are the perfect escape from the confines of Barcelona's decidedly more cosmopolitan atmosphere. The places to be at sundown are **Carrer Primer de Maig** (which runs directly from the beach and Pg. de la Ribera) and its continuation, **Carrer Marquès Montroig,** off C. de les Parellades. Bars and clubs line both sides of the small streets, overflowing onto the roads and blasting pop and house music from 10pm until 3am. The clubs here are wide open and accepting, with a vibrant mixed crowd of people, gay and straight. Other popular spots can be found on C. Bonaire and C. Sant Pau, but most open only on weekends. The tourist office has copies of **Gay Life,** a gay map of Sitges including a guide to gay hotels, restaurants, bars, clubs, and sex shops.

Atlàntida, Platja les Coves, s/n (☎934 53 05 82; www.clubatlantida.com). For a crowded and sweaty (even shirtless) "disco-beach" scene, check out this club. It's about 3km from the city, and buses run from the Calipolis Hotel. On busier nights they may stop a 10min. walk from the club. Cover €10-20. Open Tu-Su midnight-6am. MC/V.

Pachá, C. de Sant Didac (☎938 94 22 98; www.pachasitges.com). A legendary club, the 1st of a chain in Spain. Cover €15-20; includes 1 drink.

Trailer, C. Àngel Vidal, 36 (☎693 55 94 40). Among the gay cafes and clubs of the town. Cover €15 with drink; flyer/invitation grants free admission. Open daily June-Sept. 1-6am; in winter only F, Sa, and holidays. MC/V.

Bar Perfil, C. Espalter, 7 (☎656 376 791). A gay-friendly discoteca with infamous W and Su foam parties, half a block from C. Sant Francesc. Open daily 10:30pm-3:30am.

FESTIVALS

When celebrating holidays, Sitges pushes the boundaries of style and spares no extravagance. During the **Festa de Corpus Cristi** (late May or early June), townspeople collaborate to create intricate carpets of fresh flowers in the **Concurs de Catifes de Flors.** To see papier-mâché dragons, devils, and giants dancing in the streets, visit during the **Festa Major,** held August 21-27 in honor of the town's patron saint, Bartolomé (fireworks on Aug. 23). Nothing compares to **Carnaval,** a preparation for fasting during the first week of Lent. Spaniards crash the town for a frenzy of parades, dancing, costumes, and vats of alcohol. Saturday and Tuesday nights are the wildest. A pistol shot starts the **Rallye de Coches de Época** in late March, an antique-car race from Barcelona to Sitges. July or August brings the **Festival Sitges Jazz Internacional** (part of the larger Sitges Music Festival; €10 per concert). In September, competitors tread on fresh grapes on the beach for the annual **Festa de la Verema,** or grape harvest, and September 22-23 brings the **Festivitat de Santa Tecla.** The famous **Festival Internacional de Cinema de Catalunya** runs through October and is perhaps Sitges's biggest event.

COSTA BRAVA ☎975

Skirting the Mediterranean Sea from Barcelona to the French border, the Costa Brava's cliffs and beaches draw throngs of European visitors—especially French—in July and August. Early June and late September can be remarkably peaceful; the water is warm and the beaches are much less crowded. In winter, the "Wild Coast" lives up to its name, as fierce winds batter quiet, practically empty beach towns. These rocky shores have long attracted romantics and artists like Marc Chagall and Salvador Dalí, a Costa Brava native. No wonder, then, that the Costa Brava is so distinctively Catalan—this is a region that prides itself on its history and on the architectural and artistic treasures it holds. Among these are Dalí's house in Port Lligat and his museum in Figueres. Certain towns have survived the summer-tourist onslaught better than others (Cadaqués has fared well), but there are still clear waters and pine-covered cliffs almost everywhere you turn.

GIRONA (GERONA) ☎972

Modern Girona (pop. 92,000) is Catalan through and through, but it's been almost everything else over the course of history. A Roman *municipium* and then an important medieval center, the "city of four rivers" was an exemplar of the Spanish settlements where Christians, Jews, and a small number of Arabs were able to coexist in peace. Girona was the home of the renowned *cabalistas de Girona*, a group of 12th-century rabbis credited with founding the school of mystic thought called the Kabbala. Although they, and other Jews, were banned from the city in 1492, you can still walk the streets (or, more accurately, the staircases) of El Call, the old Jewish quarter. In more recent years, the *Ajuntament* of Gerona returned to the city's roots by changing its name back to the original Catalan—Girona—in 1980. Now, this many-splendored metropolis enjoys international recognition as a cyclist's paradise—former Tour de France hero Lance Armstrong called the city home during training season.

TRANSPORTATION

Flights: Aeropuerto de Girona-Costa Brava, Termino Municipal de Vilobi d'Onyar (☎972 18 66 00; www.aena.es, choose Girona from the dropdown menu), is small and ser-

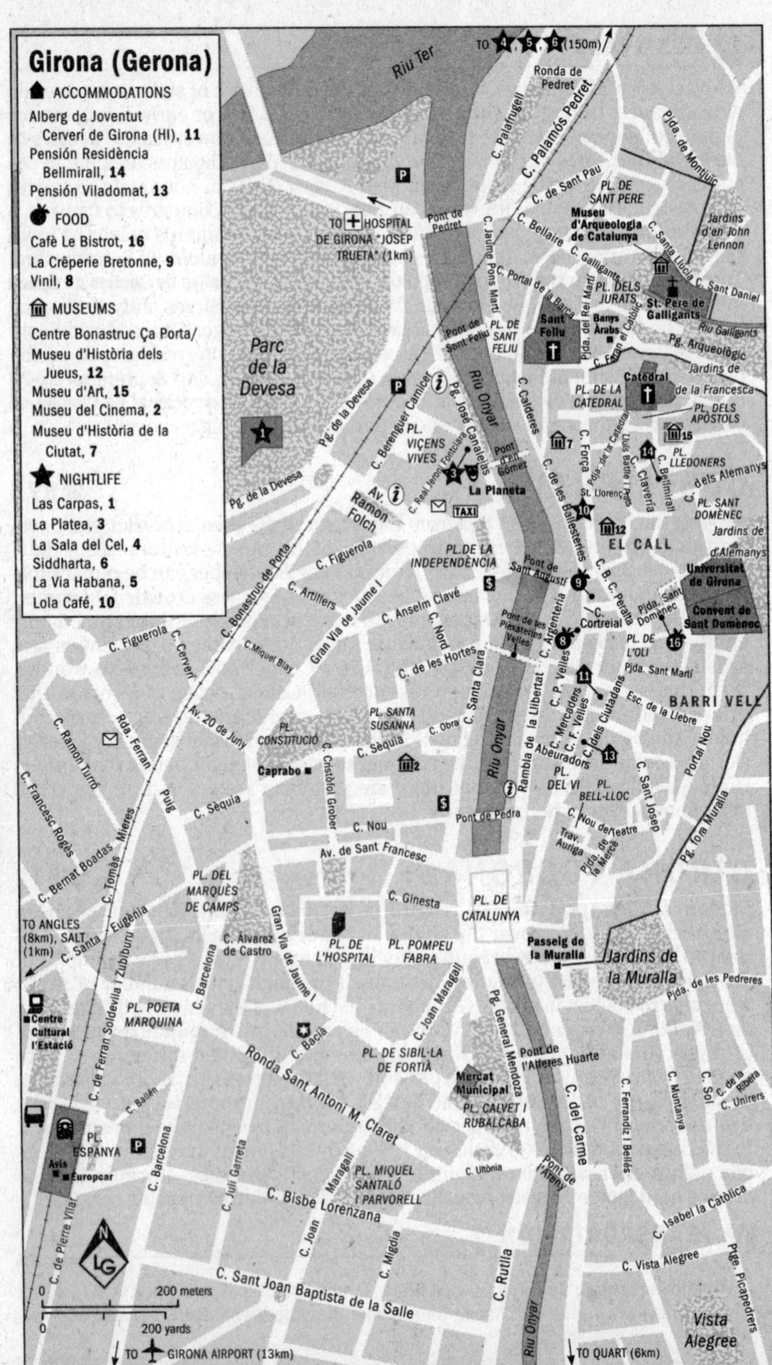
Girona (Gerona)
ACCOMMODATIONS
Alberg de Joventut Cerverí de Girona (HI), 11
Pensión Residència Bellmirall, 14
Pensión Viladomat, 13
FOOD
Cafè Le Bistrot, 16
La Crêperie Bretonne, 9
Vinil, 8
MUSEUMS
Centre Bonastruc Ça Porta/ Museu d'Història dels Jueus, 12
Museu d'Art, 15
Museu del Cinema, 2
Museu d'Història de la Ciutat, 7
NIGHTLIFE
Las Carpas, 1
La Platea, 3
La Sala del Cel, 4
Siddharta, 6
La Via Habana, 5
Lola Café, 10
TO 4, 5, 6 (150m)
Riu Ter
Ronda de Pedret
C. Palamós Pedret
C. Palafrugell
Pjda. de Montjuïc
C. de Sant Pau
PL. DE SANT PERE
Museu d'Arqueologia de Catalunya
Jardins d'en John Lennon
TO HOSPITAL DE GIRONA "JOSEP TRUETA" (1km)
Pont de Pedret
C. Jaume Pons Martí
C. Bellaire
C. Galligants
C. Santa Llúcia
C. Sant Daniel
C. Portal de la Barca
PL. DELS JURATS
St. Pere de Galligants
Riu Galligants
Pont de Sant Feliu
PL. DE SANT FELIU
Sant Feliu
Banys Àrabs
Pjda. del Rei Martí
C. Ferran el Catòlic
Pg. Arqueològic
Jardins de la Francesca
Parc de la Devesa
Pg. de la Devesa
C. Berenguer Carnicer
Pg. José Canalejas
Riu Onyar
C. Calderes
Catedral
PL. DE LA CATEDRAL
PL. DELS APÒSTOLS
PL. VIÇENS VIVES
C. Real Jeroni Fontciara
Pont d'en Gómez
C. Força
Pdja. de la Catedral
Lluís Batlle i Prats
C. Claveria
C. Bellmirall
PL. LLEDONERS
C. dels Alemanys
La Planeta
Av. Ramon Folch
TAXI
C. de les Ballesteries
St. Llorenç
PL. SANT DOMÈNEC
Jardins de d'Alemanys
EL CALL
C. Figuerola
PL. DE LA INDEPENDÈNCIA
Pont de Sant Agustí
Universitat de Girona
Convent de Sant Domènec
C. Bonastruc de Porta
C. Artillers
Gran Via de Jaume I
C. Anselm Clavé
C. Nord
C. Argenteria
C. Cortreial
C. B. C. Peralta
Pjda. Sant Domènec
PL. DE L'OLI
Pont de les Peixateries Velles
C. Cerverí
C. Miquel Blay
C. de les Hortes
C. Santa Clara
C. P. Velles
Pjda. Sant Martí
Esc. de la Llebre
BARRI VELL
Rda. Ferran
C. Ramon Turró
Av. 20 de Juny
PL. SANTA SUSANNA
C. Obra
PL. CONSTITUCIÓ
C. Sèquia
C. Mercaders
C. F. Velles
C. dels Ciutadans
Abeuradors
Portal Nou
Caprabo
C. Cristòfol Grober
Rambla de la Llibertat
PL. DEL VI
PL. BELL-LLOC
C. Sant Josep
C. Francesc Rogès
Puig
C. Sèquia
Pont de Pedra
C. Nou del Teatre
Trav. Auriga
Pjda. de la Mercè
Pg. Tora Muralla
C. Tomàs Mieres
C. Nou
Av. de Sant Francesc
C. Bernat Boadas
PL. DEL MARQUÈS DE CAMPS
Gran Via de Jaume I
C. Ginesta
PL. DE CATALUNYA
TO ANGLES (8km), SALT (1km)
C. Santa Eugènia
C. Àlvarez de Castro
PL. DE L'HOSPITAL
PL. POMPEU FABRA
Passeig de la Muralla
Jardins de la Muralla
C. Zubiburu
C. Barcelona
Pjda. de les Pedreres
Centre Cultural l'Estació
PL. POETA MARQUINA
C. Joan Maragall
Pg. General Mendoza
C. de Ferran Soldevila i
C. Bacià
PL. DE SIBIL·LA DE FORTIÀ
Pont de l'Alferes Huarte
Ronda Sant Antoni M. Claret
Mercat Municipal
PL. CALVET I RUBALCABA
C. del Carme
C. Ferrandiz I Bellés
C. Muntanya
C. Sol
C. de la Ribera
C. Unirers
C. Ballén
PL. ESPANYA
Avis
Europcar
C. Barcelona
C. Juli Garreta
C. Maragall
PL. MIQUEL SANTALÓ I PARVORELL
C. Ultònia
Pont de l'Areny
C. Bisbe Lorenzana
C. Isabel la Católica
C. de Pierre Vilar
C. Joan
C. Migdia
C. Vista Alegree
Pge. Picapedrers
C. Rutlla
C. Sant Joan Baptista de la Salle
0 200 meters
0 200 yards
Riu Onyar
Vista Alegree
TO GIRONA AIRPORT (13km)
TO QUART (6km)

CATALUÑA

vices a few regular flights on **Iberia** (☎902 40 05 00; www.iberia.com) and **Ryanair** (☎972 47 36 50; www.ryanair.com). **Barcelona Bus** (☎902 36 15 50; www.sagales.com) runs shuttles from Girona, Barcelona, and the Costa Brava to the airport (from the Girona bus station every hr. 5am-10pm, return every hr. 5:30am-12:30am; €2; from Barcelona 23+ per day 3:45am-7:30pm, return 28 per day 8:30am-12:10am; €12). A taxi to Girona's old city is roughly €35 (12km).

Trains: RENFE (☎902 24 02 02; www.renfe.es), in Pl. d'Espanya to the southwest of the city center. Open M-Sa 5:30am-11pm, Su 6:30am-11pm, info 6:30am-10pm. Trains to: **Barcelona** (1¼-1½hr.; M-F 23 per day 5:56am-9:40pm, Sa-Su 17 per day; €7), change at Maçanet for coastal train; **Figueres** (30-40min.; M-F 22 per day 7:25am-10:10pm, Sa 14 per day 8:28am-9:42pm, Su 15 per day 10:06am-10:10pm; €2.60) via **Flaçà** (15min., €1.70); **Milan,** ITA (11hr.; Tu, Th, Su 10:15pm, €168, under 26, over 60, and students with ISIC €118); **Zurich,** DEU (13 hr., Tu, Th, Sun 9:25pm, €170; under 26, over 60 and students with ISIC €119); and **Paris,** FRA (10½hr.; 10:17pm; €175, under 26, over 60, and students with ISIC €123).

Buses: Next to train station, 5min. from city center. **Sarfa** (☎902 30 20 25). Info open M-F 7:30am-8:30pm, Sa-Su 8:45am-noon and 4:30-8:30pm. Buses to: **Cadaqués** (2hr., M-F 6:30pm, €9); **Palafrugell** (1hr., M-F 14 per day 7:45am-8:30pm, €5) for connections to **Calella** and **Llafranc; Tossa de Mar** (40min., July-Aug. 6:30pm, €4.85). **Teisa** (☎972 20 02 75; www.teisa-bus.com) info open M-F 9am-7:15pm with 20min. breaks, Sa-Su 9am-1pm, Su 4:30-5:30pm. Buses to: **Lérida** (3hr.; M-F 3 per day 7:30am-7:15pm, Sa-Su 8:30am, 5:30pm; €20.05); **Ripoll** (2hr.; M-F 4:15pm, 8:15pm; €9.30). **Barcelona Bus** (☎902 36 15 50; www.barcelonabus.com). Express buses to **Barcelona** (1hr.; M-F 5 per day 7am-7:15pm, Sa-Su 3 per day; €11) and **Figueres** (50min.; M-F 4 per day 7:45am-6:15pm, Sa 2 per day, Su 3 per day; €4.65).

ORIENTATION AND PRACTICAL INFORMATION

The Riu Onyar divides the city into old and new sections. Eleven bridges, mostly pedestrian, connect the two banks. The **Pont de Pedra** leads into the **Barri Vell** (old quarter) by way of C. dels Ciutadans, one block off the bridge, which turns into C. Bonaventura Carreras i Peralta and then C. Força, leading to the cathedral and **El Call,** the historic Jewish neighborhood. The **train** and **bus terminals** are situated off **Calle Barcelona,** in the modern neighborhood. To get to the old city from a bus, walk through the terminal, across the parking lot and Pl. Espanya, turn left onto C. Barcelona and go straight (a bit more than three blocks) until you reach a plaza, then bear right on the plaza and right again onto the small C. Nou; it will take you across Pont de Pedra to the historic area. The iron bridge to your right was built by the Eiffel Company of Paris, France.

Tourist Offices: Rambla de la Llibertat, 1 (☎972 22 65 75; www.ajuntament.gi/turisme), by Pont de Pedra in the old town. English spoken. Pick up the biweekly *La Guia,* in Catalan but with clear listings of events. Also has listings of hotels, hostels, pharmacies, art galleries, theaters, libraries, and classes with addresses and phone numbers. Open M-F 8am-8pm, Sa 8am-2pm and 4-8pm, Su 9am-2pm. The **Punt de Benvinguda** office, C. Berenguer Carnicer, 3 (☎972 21 16 78) is 7 blocks up on the other side of the river. Open M-Sa 9am-2pm and 3-5pm, Su 9am-2pm.

Police: Policia Municipal, C. Bacià, 4 (☎972 41 90 92). To report a pickpocketing, contact the Mossos d'Esquadra, C. Vista Alegre (☎972 18 16 00).

Hospital: Hospital de Girona "Josep Trueta," Av. França, 60 (☎972 94 02 00).

Internet Access: Alberg de Joventut Cerverí de Girona (HI), C. dels Ciutadans, 9 (☎972 21 80 03; www.xanascat.net;alberg_girona@tujuca.com). This youth hostel offers unlimited internet access for €1 regardless of whether you choose to stay (see below). Cafes that line C. Coitadans often offer internet, many at reasonable prices.

Post Office: Av. Ramón Folch, 2 (☎902 19 71 97), a brick building with the golden dome. Open M-F 8:30am-8:30pm, Sa 9:30am-2pm. **Postal Code:** 17001.

ACCOMMODATIONS

There are enough hostels in Girona to find a room without much trouble, but some are no less expensive than the hotels in the new city. The best locations are within a couple of blocks of the river on either bank. If you have your heart set on a specific lodging, call ahead in the summer.

Pensión Residència Bellmirall, C. Bellmirall, 3 (☎972 20 40 09; email bellmirall1@telefonica.net for availability). To your right when facing the Museu d'Art. Pricey but well worth it. Delightful rooms, all with private bath, in a 14th-century house by the main cathedral. Included breakfast is served on the flowering garden patio. Closed Jan.-Feb. Singles €35; doubles €65; triples €80. €10 more in high season. Cash only. ❸

Pensión Viladomat, C. Ciutadans, 5 (☎972 20 31 76). Many rooms with balconies, some with high ceilings and large windows. Even if your room isn't the lap of luxury, the price is right. Quiet at night and at the center of the action during the day. All rooms have heaters. Singles with shared bath €22; doubles €40, with bath and TV €60; triples and small quads with bath and TV €85-100. Cash only. ❷

Alberg de Joventut Cerverí de Girona (HI), C. dels Ciutadans, 9 (☎972 21 80 03; www.xanascat.net; alberg_girona@tujuca.com). Plain walls and metal bunks, but good price, location, and amenities. Sitting rooms with TV/VCR, board games, videos, and ping-pong. Rooms of 2-8 or 10 beds with lockers (€2 each use). Breakfast included; lunch €5.90-7.75; dinner €7.50-10.55. Sheets included. Wash €2.50, dry €1.50. Unlimited internet access. Reception 8:30am-2:30pm, 3:30-9pm, and 10-11:30pm. Check-in 24hr. Dorms end of June-Sept. €19.25-21.90; Oct.-June €15.40-17.90. Non-HI members €2 more. AmEx/MC/V. ❷

FOOD

Girona boasts exciting local cuisine, both savory and sweet. Local specialties are *botifarra dolça* (sweet sausage made with pork, lemon, cinnamon, and sugar) and *xuixo* (sugar-sprinkled pastries filled with cream). A good place for moderately priced food is on **Calle Cort-Reial** at the top of C. Argenteria. **Rambla de la Llibertat** has several tourist cafes with terrace seating, and Pl. de la Independència, Girona's restaurant hub, offers both high-end and cheaper options, most of which have tables on the square. Join locals at the covered **mercat municipal** located in Pl. Salvador Espriu. (From the tourist office facing Pont de Pedra, walk left past Pl. Cataluña and cross the river at Pont de l'Areny. (☎972 20 19 00. Open M-Sa 6am-2pm. Cash only.) Get your **groceries** at **Caprabo,** C. Sèquia, 9, a block off the Gran Viade Juame 1. (☎972 21 45 16. Open M-Sa July-Aug. 9am-9pm; Sept.-June 9am-2pm and 5-9pm. MC/V.)

Cafè Le Bistrot, Pjda. Sant Domènec, 4 (☎972 21 88 03). Eat on the stone steps of the Convent de Sant Domènec, with a view of the old city below, or inside amidst Art Nouveau posters. Specialty creations are the *pizzas de pagès* (farmer's bread pizzas) made on typical Catalan round bread (€6-8, only offered for dinner). Lunch *menú* M-F €12-14, Sa-Su €17-20. Open daily 1-4pm and 8pm-1am. MC/V. ❸

La Crêperie Bretonne, C. Cort-Reial, 14 (☎972 21 81 20; www.creperiebretonne.com). Proof of Girona's proximity to France, this popular crepe joint brings a youthful atmosphere and tasty eats to the historic district. The food is cooked in a small bus bound for the town of Cerbère, but you can eat it on the cozy alley terrace or in the train-themed interior while it's fresh (never reheated). Lunch *menú* €8.50-11 Crepes

€2.75-8.60. Unusual salads (fig, duck) €9-10. Vegetarian options available. Open Tu-Sa 1:30-3:30pm and 8-11:30pm. MC/V. ❷

Vinil, C. Cort Reial, 17 (☎972 21 64 40). If you took Vinil's mantra, *"som el que mengem,"* (you are what you eat) to heart, then you'd be a salad with honey-soy dressing and thin slices of ham, a knockout hamburger, or a potato purée drizzled in raspberry sauce. Green chairs and walls, with renowned comics hanging from the walls. Lunch *menú* varies daily (€10.40). Open M-F 9am-1am, Sa 1pm-2am, Su 7pm-1am. MC/V. ❷

SIGHTS

Start your self-guided historical tour of the city at the **Pont de Pedra** and turn left down the tree-lined **Rambla de la Llibertat.** Continue on C. Argenteria, bearing right across C. Cort-Reial. C. Força begins on the left up a flight of stairs.

EL CALL. The part of the old town around C. Força and C. Sant Llorenç was once the center of Girona's thriving medieval Jewish community ("call" comes from *kahal,* Hebrew for "community"). The site of the last synagogue in Girona now serves as the Centre Bonastruc Ça Porta. The center includes the prominent **Museu d'Història dels Jueus,** with an excellent audio tour that explains the old Hebrew tombstones and text, as well as the story of the Jews in Girona before and after the Inquisition. Be sure to lose yourself (quite literally) in the narrow, winding stone staircases that surround the museum. *(C. Força, 8, halfway up the hill. ☎972 21 67 61; ajgirona.org/call. Center and museum open June-Oct. M-Sa 10am-8pm, Su 10am-3pm; Nov.-May M-Sa 10am-6pm, Su 10am-3pm. Wheelchair-accessible. Museum €2, students and over 65 €1.50, under 16 free. Guided walking tours of the Barri Vell, including El Call, are available through Ajuntament de Girona i Patronat Call de Girona (☎972 21 16 78; puntb@girona-net.com); tours leave from C. Berenguer Carnicer, 3, Tu-Su at 10:30am, June 15-Sept.15 €15, Sept. 16-June 14 €10, under 16 free. Tour price includes museum entrance.)*

CATHEDRAL COMPLEX. The breathtaking Gothic **Catedral de Girona** rises 90 steps from the *plaça.* Its tower, along with that of **Sant Feliu,** defines the Girona skyline. The **Torre de Charlemany** and **cloister** are the only structures left from the 11th and 12th centuries; the rest of the building dates from the 14th-17th centuries. Look at the keystone of the world's widest Gothic **nave** (23m); the builders eschewed solid stone in favor of a hollow rock with a wood "cork" for fear of weighing the structure down and collapsing it. A door on the left leads to the trapezoidal cloister and the **Tresor Capitular** museum, which holds some of Girona's most precious paintings, sculptures, and decorated Bibles. Its most famous piece is the **Tapis de la Creació**, an 11th-century tapestry depicting the events of Genesis. *(Museum ☎972 21 44 26; www.catedraldegirona.com. Open Apr.-Oct. M-F 10am-8pm, Sa 10am-4:30pm, Su 2-8pm; Nov.-Mar. M-F 10am-7pm, Sa 10am-4:30pm, Su 2-7pm. Wheelchair-accessible with advance notice. Cathedral, tresor, and cloister €5, students and over 65 €2, ages 7-16 €0.90, under 7 free. Free to all on Su.)*

SCENIC WALKS. Girona's renowned **Passeig de la Muralla,** a 2km trail along the fortified walls of the old city, can be accessed at several points: at the **Jardins de la Francesa** (behind the cathedral), the **Jardins d'Alemanys** (behind the Museu d'Art), and the main entrance at the bottom of the Rambla in Pl. de la Marvà. *(Open daily 8am-10pm.)* Behind the St. Pere de Galligants church (by the Museu d'Arqueologia), you can go up on a *mirador* for great views of the city. Behind the cathedral, the walk coincides with the equally beautiful **Passeig Arqueològic.** This path skirts the northeastern medieval wall and also overlooks the city. For the less athletically inclined, a small green train offers a 30min. guided tour of the main sights of the old town, including the town hall, cathedral, Església de Sant Feliu, El Call, and the walls. *(In summer tour leaves daily from the Pont de Pedra every 40-45min. 10am-1pm and 3-6pm. Less frequently in the winter; check at the tourist office.*

Available in English. €4, children under 10 €3.50.) Alternatively, relax in the flower-filled Jardins del la Francesa or the shady and tranquil Jardins d'Alemanys.

MUSEU DEL CINEMA. This unusual collection of artifacts, clips, and heavy machinery documents the rise of cinema from the mid-17th to 20th centuries, interspersed with a few Asian shadow theater pieces from as early as the 11th century. The exhibit chronicles the invention of the *camera obscura* (9th-12th centuries), the "magic lantern," and eventually daguerreotypes, 35mm, Edison, and TV, as well as the viewing culture that developed around each advance. A must for movie buffs, given Cataluña's central role in the early Spanish cinema. *(C. Sèquia, 1. ☎972 41 27 77; www.museudelcinema.org. Open May-Sept. Tu-Su 10am-8pm; Oct.-Apr. Tu-F 10am-6pm, Sa 10am-8pm, Su 11am-3pm. Wheelchair-accessible. €4, students and over 65 €2, under 16 free. AmEx/MC/V.)*

OTHER MUSEUMS. The **Museu d'Art** has enchanting pieces spanning the Romantic to the modern; look for the Saints' Day book, the pregnant virgin, and the temporary exhibition space in an old prison cell. *(Pujada de la Catedral, 12. ☎972 20 38 34; www.museuart.com. Open Mar.-Sept. Tu-Sa 10am-7pm, Su and holidays 10am-2pm; Oct.-Feb. Tu-Sa 10am-6pm, Su 10am-2pm. Wheelchair-accessible. €2, students, under 19, and over 65 €1.50.)* The **Museu d'Història de la Ciutat** showcases 2000 years of Girona's history and prominent figures. The exhibit on the *sardana*, Cataluña's national dance, features old musical instruments once used in a *cobla* (the band that traditionally plays for the *sardana*) and a how-to of *sardana* steps. *(C. La Força, 27. ☎972 22 22 29; www.ajuntament.gi/museuciutat/eng/index. Open Tu-Sa 10am-2pm and 5-7pm, Su and holidays 10am-2pm. Some descriptions in English. €3, students €2, under 16 free.)* The small **Banys Àrabs,** inspired by Muslim and Roman bathhouses, once contained saunas and baths of varying temperatures; now the graceful 12th-century structure hosts outdoor art exhibits in the summer. With no descriptive placards on the walls, you'll want to use an audio tour (€3) to appreciate the architecture and history of the space, or just rely on the free, basic pamphlet provided. *(C. Ferran el Catòlic, s/n ☎972 19 07 97; www.banysarabs.org. Open Apr.-Sept. M-Sa 10am-7pm, Su 10am-2pm; Oct.-Mar. daily 10am-2pm. €1.80, students €1.)*

NIGHTLIFE

Nightlife in Girona ranges from finger-snapping coffeehouses to rock bars and crowded discotecas. In the summer there is really only one nightlife alternative, and that is **Las Carpas** (the tents), an outdoor circus of dance floors, bars, and swirling lights in the middle of the **Parc de la Devesa.** Many clubs close in summer and operate only from their *carpa*, though some morph a bit and remain open in both guises. Las Carpas is so dazzling, though, that locals don't head inside until the park shuts down. (Drinks start at €4. Open May-Sept. 15 M-Th and Su 11pm-3:30am, F-Sa 11pm-4am.) The artsy bars and cafes in the old quarter are particularly mellow and a great place to start the evening.

Lola Café, C. Forca, 7 (☎972 22 88 24; www.lola-cafe.com). Patrons wait outside to crowd in and enjoy the sophisticated ambience (mood lighting, stone walls). Mixed drinks €6. Open daily 6pm-3am.

La Platea, C. Fontclara (☎972 22 72 88; www.localplatea.com), next to the Pont d'en Gomez. Flashing neon green stairs, white leather stools, mock-Gothic chandeliers, and pop music to boot. Mixed drinks €8-10. Open W-Sa midnight-6am.

La Sala del Cel, C. Pedret, 118 (☎972 21 46 64; www.lasaladelcel.cat). A 10min. walk down the Riu Ter, this popular nighttime destination is known as La Pedret. Its labyrinthine dance floors, massage parlor, game room, pool-side terrace, and, yes, **pool** are worth the walk. Cover €12 and up; drink included. Open F-Sa and nights before fiestas midnight-6am. Cash only.

Siddharta, C. Pedret, 116 (☎972 22 04 20). Siddharta specializes in pitchers of Tisane and fruity concoctions with cognac and other liquors, served in a maze of old stone arches. 1.5Lpitchers €16. Open daily 8pm-3am. Cash only.

La Via Habana, C. Pedret (www.viahabana.net). Drink mojitos (€7) and stumble your way to salsa prowess with a local crowd. Open Th-Su 11pm-5am. Cash only.

FESTIVALS

Starting on the second Saturday in May and lasting through the following two weeks, government-sponsored **Temps de Flors** (www.gironatempsdeflors.net) exhibitions spring up all over the city; local monuments and pedestrian streets swim in blossoms, and the courtyards of Girona's finest old buildings are open to the public (ask for the "*mapa de flors*" from the tourist office). Summer evenings often inspire spontaneous *sardana* dancing in the *plaça*. Girona, along with the rest of Cataluña, lights up for the **Focs de Sant Joan** on the night of June 23, featuring fireworks and bonfires. Try the traditional Coca de Sant Joan dessert with a glass of *cava*, of course. For *Viernes Santo*, the Friday of **Semana Santa,** *Cofrarías*, or church groups, dress up in Old World costumes. Keep an eye out for the men from San Luc decked out in full Roman soldier gear, including horses and weapons. From the end of June into July, the **Festival de Músiques Religioses del Món** (☎872 08 07 09; www.ajuntament.gi/musiques-religioses) draws choirs and artists from all over the world to perform in the cathedral and on its grand steps, while local restaurants cater from stands. The patron saint, **Sant Narcís,** is celebrated for five days at the end of October.

CATALUÑA

FIGUERAS (FIGUERES) ☎972

Sprawling Figueres (pop. 42,000) is functional, not beautiful. Outside of the touristed area, parts of the city seem to have fallen into disrepair. Nevertheless, it is the capital of Alt Empordà county and a major gateway city to France and the rest of Europe. In 1974, the mayor of Figueres asked native Salvador Dalí to donate a painting to an art museum the town was planning. Dalí saw his chance and ran with it, donating an entire museum. The construction of the Teatre-Museu Dalí in Figueres further catapulted the artist to international renown. To this day, a multilingual parade of Surrealism fans are entranced by Dalí's mind-bending and erotic works.

TRANSPORTATION AND PRACTICAL INFORMATION

Trains: Pl. de l'Estació (☎902 24 02 02). To **Barcelona** (2hr.; M-F 22 per day, Sa-Su 17 per day; €10) via **Girona** (30-40min., €2.60).

Buses: All buses leave from the **Estació d'Autobusos** (☎972 67 33 54), on the left side of Pl. de l'Estació if your back is to the train station. Sarfa (☎972 67 42 98; www.sarfa.com) is open 6am-9pm. If closed, buy tickets on bus. To: **Cadaqués** (1hr.; July-Aug. 7 per day 9am-8pm; Sept.-June M-F 3 per day, Sa-Su 4 per day; €4.50) and **Palafrugell** (1hr.; M-F 6 per day 8:30am-8pm, Sa 2 per day 12:15, 6pm, Su 12:30pm, 6pm; €7.50). Barcelona Bus (www.barcelonabus.com) runs to **Barcelona** (2hr.; M-F 4 per day 7:45am-8:15pm, Sa 2 per day 11am-4:15pm, Su 3 per day 7:45am-6:15pm; €15.50) via **Girona** (1hr., €5). Buy tickets on bus, platform 4.

Taxis: Taxis line La Rambla (☎972 50 00 08) and the train station (☎972 50 50 43).

Car Rental: Hertz, Pl. de l'Estació, 9 (☎972 67 02 39). 25+; must have had driver's license for 1 year. All-inclusive rental from €59 per day. Open M-F 9am-1pm and 4-7pm, Sa 9am-1pm. AmEx/MC/V. **Avis,** Pl. de l'Estació s/n (☎972 51 31 82), in the train station. 23+; credit card only. Rental from €50 per day (underage surcharge varies; approx. €30). Open M-Sa 9am-1:30pm and 4-7pm. AmEx/MC/V.

ORIENTATION AND PRACTICAL INFORMATION

From the tip of **Plaça de l'Estació** with your back to the train station, bear left on C. Sant Llàtzer, walk six blocks to C. Nou (the third main road), and take a right to get to Figueres's tree-lined **Rambla.** To reach the **tourist office,** walk all the way up La Rambla and continue on C. Lasauca straight out from the left corner. The blue, all-knowing "i" beckons across the rather treacherous intersection with Avinguda Salvador Dalí.

Tourist Offices: Main Office, Pl. Sol s/n. (☎972 50 31 55; www.figueresciutat.com, English spoken). Dalí-themed tours M-Sa 11am, noon, 2, 3, 5pm. €16; includes Teatre-Museu Dalí. Open July-Sept. M-Sa 8am-8pm, Su 10am-3pm; Oct. and Apr.-June M-F 8:30am-3pm and 4:30-7pm, Sa 9:30am-1:30pm and 3-6pm; Nov.-Mar. M-F 8am-3pm. 2 additional summer **branches**, in the train station (open July-Sept. 15 M-Sa 10am-2pm and 3-6pm) and in front of the Teatre-Museu Dalí (open July-Sept. 15 M-Sa 9am-7pm, Su 10am-3pm).

Currency Exchange: Banco Santander Central Hispano, La Rambla, 21. Open M-F 8:30am-2pm, Sa 8:30am-1pm. **ATMs** on La Rambla, Pl.

Police: Av. Salvador Dalí, 107 (☎972 51 01 11). To report a crime, contact the **Mossos d'Esquadra,** C. Ter s/n (☎972 54 18 00).

Hospital: Hospital Comarcal de Figueres, Ronda Rector Arolas s/n (☎972 50 14 00), behind and to the left of the Dalí museum.

Internet Access: Biblioteca Fages de Climent, Pl. Sol, 11 (☎972 67 70 84) Offers free 15min. internet access. Open M-F 10am-8:30pm, Sa 10am-1:30pm. **Café de Nit** offers free **Wi-Fi** to customers (see **Nightlife**).

Post Office: C. Santa Llogaia, 60-62 (☎972 50 54 31). Open M-F 8:30am-8:30pm, Sa 9:30am-1:30pm. **Postal Code:** 17600.

CATALUÑA

ACCOMMODATIONS

Many visitors to Figueres make the journey a daytrip from Barcelona, but quality, affordable accommodations in Figueres are easy to find. Many hostels are on upper floors above bars or restaurants. Others are closer to La Rambla and Carrer Pep Ventura. Inquire at the tourist office about hostels and pensions.

Hostal La Barretina, C. Lasauca, 13 (☎972 67 64 12; www.hostalbarretina.com). From the train station, walk up La Rambla to its end; take a left on C. Lasauca; the hostel is a block up on the left. Hotel-like luxury—each room has TV, A/C, heat, and bath. Reception in the restaurant downstairs. Breakfast €3, other meals €10. Wheelchair-accessible. Reservations recommended. Singles €30; doubles €45. AmEx/MC/V. ❸

Hostal San Mar, C. Rec Arnau, 31 (☎972 50 98 13). From the beginning of La Rambla, follow C. Girona and continue as it becomes C. Jonquera; take the 5th right onto C. Isabel II (the plaza with trees after Museu Dalí), then the 2nd left on C. Cadaqués. Follow to end of street. Clean rooms with bath and TV, but removed from city center in an area that is not well trafficked. Singles €17; doubles €34; triples €51; quads €68. Cash only. ❶

FOOD

The restaurants surrounding La Rambla on the small side streets tend to be of higher quality than those near the Teatre-Museu Dalí that serve *paella* to the masses. The extensive outdoor **market,** at Pl. del Gra, has an amazing fruit and vegetable selection. (Open Tu, Th, Sa 5am-2pm.) Another option is to buy groceries at **Bonpreu,** Pl. Sol. (☎972 51 00 19. Open M-Sa 9am-9pm. MC/V.)

Cafè Hotel París, La Rambla, 10 (☎972 50 07 13). This chic, thoroughly modern spot is a great deal if you opt for the combination plates (€8-14). Chicken with sesame salad (€8.70), salmon with ratatouille, and spaghetti with clams (€8.20). All natural and homemade, down to the coffee ice cubes for iced coffee. Desserts €3.10. By day, the outdoor patio's wicker chairs attract those seeking the breeze and a chat, while by night red leather chairs lend the establishment a low-key but sophisticated feel. Open daily 8am-midnight. MC/V. ❷

Restaurant Hotel Duran, C. Lasauca, 5 (☎972 50 12 50; www.hotelduran.com). Walk up La Rambla to the end and look for C. Lasauca on the left. One of Dalí's haunts; you can eat in the dining room—complete with arches and green chandeliers—where he once held court. Delicious *canelones* (cannelloni; €9.75). Most meat and seafood entrees €10.50-26. *Menú* €17. Open daily 12:45-4pm and 8:30-11pm. AmEx/MC/V. ❸

SIGHTS

TEATRE-MUSEU DALÍ. Welcome to the world of the definitive Surrealist master. This site, home of the self-proclaimed "largest surrealistic object in the world," held the municipal theater for the town of Figueres before it was destroyed at the end of the Spanish Civil War. Dalí's personal mausoleum/museum/monument is ego worship at its finest. Naughty cartoons, trippy sculptures, a dramatic, traditional tomb, and a pantheon of paintings of Gala, his wife and muse, immerse the audience in his world. The collection includes *Soft Self-Portrait with a Slice of Bacon*, *Poetry of America*, *Galarina*, *Meditating Rose*, and *Galatea of the Spheres*. A small number of hand-selected works by other artists, including El Greco, Marcel Duchamp, and architect Peres Piñero, round out the collection. The museum is large and takes at least an hour to see regardless of your chosen route. *(Pl. Gala i Salvador Dalí, 5. ☎972 67 75 00; www.salvador-dali.org. From La Rambla, take C. Sant Pere 3 blocks up. Or just follow the crowds and signs at every street corner. Open July-Sept. daily 9am-7:45pm; Oct.. and March-May Tu-Su 9:30am-5:45pm; Nov.-Feb. 10:30am-7:45pm; June daily 9:30am-5:45pm. Last entry 30min. before close. €11, students and seniors €8, groups over 25 €7 per person, under 8 free.)*

NIGHTLIFE

A bit removed from touristy Rambla, **Plaça del Sol,** behind the tourist office, contains nearly all of the town's nightlife. **Cafè de Nit,** Pl. del Sol, n/a, offers pool in the back (€2 per game) and mixed drinks for €5.50. Crowd onto the terrace out front or enjoy your sweet *caipirinha* under the artistic lights inside. (☎972 50 12 25. Free Wi-Fi. Open daily 5pm-3am. Cash only.) The popular dance club **La Serradora,** Pl. del Sol, 6, features a disco ball, long twisting bar, and maze-like dance floor. (Open W-Su 11pm-3:30am. Cash only.)

NAVARRA (NAVARRE)

Navarra is a historically independent kingdom that formed in the Middle Ages from eastern segments of the Basque country as a wedge against aggressive neighbors. The religiously and politically conservative region sided with the fiercely Catholic Nationalist forces in the Spanish Civil War, but Navarrans also throw the country's wildest parties—Pamplona's **Fiestas de San Fermín** (July 6-14) are undoubtedly the most (in)famous. Aside from summer partying, Navarra is the entry point to Spain on the **Camino de Santiago** and home to pastoral mountain villages famed for cheese-making and quality hiking and cycling.

HIGHLIGHTS OF NAVARRA

PLAY Hemingway and travel through the region he popularized in his fiction.

ABANDON your sanity and run with the bulls in **Pamplona** (p. 315).

PAMPLONA (IRUÑA) ☎948

El encierro, la Fiesta de San Fermín, the Running of the Bulls, utter debauchery—call it what you will, the outrageous festival of the city's patron saint is the principal attraction that gained Pamplona (pop. 200,000) international notoriety. *San Fermín* is rightly touted as the biggest and craziest festival in all of Europe. The famous *encierro*, the daily running of the bulls from July 7 to 14, draws visitors from around the world. Ever since Ernest Hemingway immortalized the chaos of *San Fermín* in *The Sun Also Rises*, visitors have come to experience the legendary spectacle, and drink themselves silly while they're at it. At the bull ring, Hemingway's bust welcomes fans to the eight-day extravaganza of dancing, dashing, and drinking—no sleeping allowed.

Although *San Fermín* may be the city's most irresistible attraction, Pamplona's lush parks, Gothic cathedral, massive citadel, and winding *casco antiguo* merit a visit at any time of the year. However, beware of the post-*San Fermín* recovery period, when many establishments close for one to two weeks. Despite being the capital of Navarra, Pamplona has Basque roots; the area was settled by the early shepherds and nomads of this distinct culture long before the Roman "founders" arrived and named the city after Pompey.

TRANSPORTATION

Flights: Aeropuerto de Noaín (☎948 16 87 00; www.aena.es), 6km from town. Accessible only by **taxi** (€10-12). **Iberia** (☎948 31 71 82) to **Barcelona** and **Madrid. Spanair** (☎902 13 14 15; www.spanair.com) flies to **Palma** and **Tenerife. TAP-Air Portugal** (☎902 10 01 45; www.flytap.com) flies to **Lisboa.**

Trains: Estación **RENFE,** Av. de San Jorge (☎902 24 02 02). Bus #9 from Po. Sarasate (20min., every 15 min., €1). Info daily 6am-10pm. **Ticket office,** C. Estella, 8 (☎948 24 02 02). Open M-F 9am-1:30pm and 4:30-7:30pm, Sa 9:30am-1pm. Trains are not the best option, as Pamplona is not well connected by rail and the station is far from the city center. To: **Barcelona** (6-8hr., 3 per day 12:31pm-12:57am, €33-45); **Madrid** (3hr., 4 per day 6:45am-7:34pm, €50.20); **Olite** (35min.; M-Sa 4 per day 9:22am-8:10pm, Su 7:05pm; €2.50); **San Sebastián** (1hr.; 5 per day 5:36am-6:42pm,

Su 3 per day 10:55am-6:42pm; €14.20-19.65); **Vitoria-Gasteiz** (1hr., M-Sa 3 per day 8:45am-7:40pm, €4-11); **Zaragoza** (2hr., 2 direct per day 4:45 pm and 7:03pm; 3 others connect through Castejon de Ebro).

Buses: Estación de Autobuses on C. Yangüas y Mirandaby the Ciudadela. **La Burundesa** (☎948 22 17 66; www.laburundesa.com) to **Bilbao** (2hr.; M-Sa 6 per day 7am-8:30pm, Su 5 per day 9am-8pm; €12.85) and **Vitoria-Gasteiz** (1.5hr.; M-F 11 per day 7am-9pm, Sa 8 per day 7am-8:30pm, Su 6 per day 9am-9pm; €6.85-7.50). **Conda** (☎948 22 10 26; www.conda.es) to **Madrid** (5hr.; M-Sa 6 per day 1:30am-6:30pm, Falso midnight-9:30pm, Su 10 per day 1:30am-9:30pm; €25.24) and **Zaragoza** (2-3hr., M-Sa9-12 per day 7am-10pm, €11-12). **La Estellesa** (☎948 22 22 23; www.laestellesa.com) to **Estella** (1hr.; M-Sa 12 per day 7:30am-8:30pm, Su 4 per day 10am-7pm; €3.69) and **Logroño** (1hr.; M-Sa 5 per day 7:30am-7pm, Su 4 per day 10am-7pm; €7.69). **La Tafallesa** (☎948 22 28 86) to **Olite** (50min.; M-F 3 per day 8:15am-9pm, Sa 6 per day 9:30am-8:30pm, Su 1 and 8:30pm; €2.84) and **Roncal** (leaves 5pm, returns 7am, €7.67). **La Veloz Sangüesina** (☎948 87 02 09) to **Sangüesa** (M-Sa 3 per day 1-8pm, Su 8:15pm; €3.30). **Vibasa** (☎948 10 13 63) to **Barcelona** (6-8hr., 4-5 per day 8:05am-5:15pm, €26). **La Roncalesa** (☎948 22 10 26) to **San Sebastián** (M-F 14 per day 7am-10:45pm, Sa-Su 11 per day 8:15am-10:45pm; €6.50).

Taxis: Teletaxi (☎948 23 23 00) or **Radiotaxi** (☎948 22 12 12). Taxi stand at Parque de la Taconera at the intersection of C. Navas de Tolosa and C. Taconera; another at C. Conde Olivio and C. Tudela near the bus station.

Car Rental: Europcar, Hotel Blanca Navarra, Av. de Pío XII, 43 (☎948 17 25 23). Take bus #4-1, 4-2, or 15 from Po. Sarasate and get off after the traffic circle past the Ciudadela. 21+. Open M-F 8:30am-1pm and 4-7:30pm, Sa 9am-1pm. Airport office open M-F 8:30am-3:30pm and 4-10pm, Sa 10am-1pm, Su 5-10pm. (☎948 31 27 98). AmEx/MC/V. **AVIS,** C. Monasterio de la Oliva, 29 (☎948 17 00 36) and at airport (☎948 16 87 63). Open M-F 8am-1pm and 4-7pm, Sa 9am-1pm. Airport hours coincide with arrivals (M-F morning and evening, Sa morning, Su evening). AmEx/MC/V. **Hertz** at airport (☎948 31 15 95) open M-F 8am-12pm and 3-10pm, Sa 10am-1pm, Su 5:10-8:10pm.

ORIENTATION AND PRACTICAL INFORMATION

Pamplona is a relatively small city, and most sites are generally accessible on foot. The **casco antiguo,** in the northeast quarter of the city, contains most major attractions. The wide-open **Plaza del Castillo** is Pamplona's center. To reach it from the **bus station,** take Av. Conde Oliveto, then turn left after two blocks at Pl. Príncipe de Viana onto Av. de San Ignacio (second from the left), which runs into the plaza. From the **train station,** take bus #9 to Pl. de las Merindades and head up Av. Carlos III until the plaza at the end. North of Pl. del Castillo, the Baroque **Ayuntamiento** is a helpful marker in the swirl of medieval streets, but it is still easy to get lost—pick up a free map at the tourist office. The **ciudadela** is outside of the *casco antiguo*, just 5min. up Av. del Ejercito from the bus stop. The **Río Arga** runs along the high northern walls of the casco antiguo.

Tourist Office: C. Hilarión Eslava, on Pl. San Francisco (☎848 420 420; www.turismo.navarra.es). Aside from maps and info on the region, accommodations, food, and culture, the staff offers a crucial minute-by-minute **San Fermín Fiesta Programme** guide that lists every event and another guide to the encierro with relevant bank schedules in addition to info on transportation, internet access, laundry, showers, and luggage storage. Info also available at www.pamplona.net. Ask about private guided tours. English and French spoken. Open during San Fermín daily 8am-8pm; July-Aug. M-F 9am-8pm,Sa 10am-8pm, Su 10am-2pm; Sept.-June M-Sa 10am-2pm and 4-7pm, Su 10am-2pm.

Currency Exchange: Banco Santander Central Hispano, Pl. del Castillo, 21 (☎948 20 86 00), has a 24hr. **ATM** and will exchange American Express travelers checks commis-

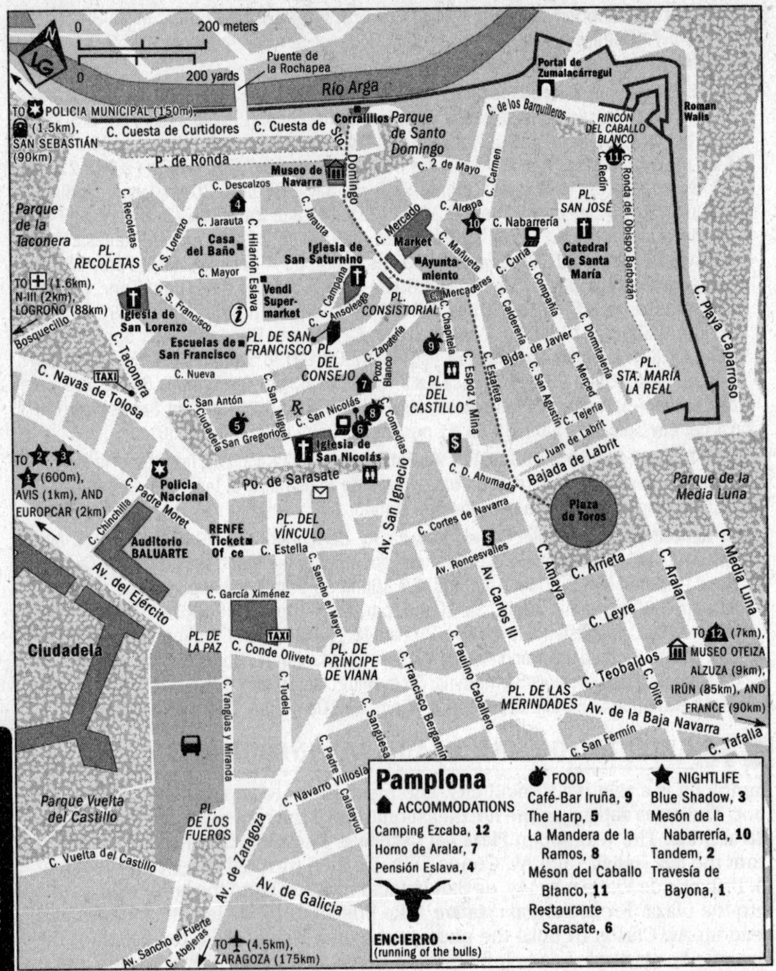

sion-free. During *San Fermín* open M-F 9:30am-noon; April-Sept. M-F 8:30am-2pm; Oct.-Apr. M-F 8:30am-2pm, Sa 8:30am-1pm. Note that hours are reduced right after *San Fermín*—make sure to get money before the weekend.

Luggage Storage: At the **bus station.** Bags €5.10 per day, large packs €3 per day. Open M-Sa 6:15am-9:30pm, Su 6:30am-1:30pm and 2-9:30pm. Closes for *San Fermín*, when the **Escuelas de San Francisco,** the stone building at the end of Pl. San Francisco, opens instead from July 4 at 8am to July 16 at 2pm. Lines are long, and you must have passport or ID. €3.40 per day and each time you check on luggage. Open 24hr.

Laundromat and Public Baths: Casa del Baño, C. Eslava, 9, (☎948 22 17 38). Drop-off laundry service (€10.60 wash and dry). Open M-Sa 8:30am-8pm and Sunday 9am-2pm. Showers €1.05, full bath €3.10. No laundry service during *San Fermín*. Showers open daily 8am-9pm.

Municipal Police: C. Monasterio de Irache, 2 (☎092 or 948 42 06 40). **National Police,** C. General Chinchilla, 3 (☎091).

Pharmacy: FarPlus, C. San Nicolás, 74 (☎948 21 07 04). Open M-F 9am-1:30pm and 4:30-7:30pm, Sa 9:30am-1:30pm. Late-night pharmacy on some nights, rotates daily. All pharmacies post location for that evening.

Medical Services: Hospital de Navarra, C. Irunlarrea 3 (☎848 42 22 22, medical emergencies 112), at the corner with Av. de Pío XII. The **Red Cross** sets up stands at the bus station and along the *corrida* during *San Fermín.*

Internet Access: At the **library** on Pl. San Francisco. Free **internet** access for up to an hour with a sign-up sheet, and free Wi-Fi, accessible in parts of the plaza close to library. Open Sept.-June M-F 8:30am-8:45pm, Sa 8:30am-1:45pm; July-Aug. M-F 8:30am-2:45pm. **Kuria.net,** C. Curia, 15 (☎948 22 30 77). Look for the big yellow sign. First 10min. €0.50, 1hr. €2.50. During *San Fermín* €4.50 per hr. English-speaking staff. Open July-Aug. daily 10am-10pm; Sept.-June 10am-2:30pm and 4-10pm closed Su. **Locutorio San Nicolás,** C. San Nicolás, 37. €2 per hr. Open daily 11am-11pm (☎948 21 24 61).

Post Office: Po. de Sarasate, 9 (☎948 20 68 40). Open M-F 8:30am-8:30pm, Sa 9:30am-2pm; July 6th 9am-2pm; closed July 7th. **Postal Code:** 31001.

ACCOMMODATIONS AND CAMPING

If you think you're going to get a good night's sleep on a budget during *San Fermín*, think again. Unless you've booked a hotel room at least five months in advance, start fluffing up your sweatshirt: it's going be your pillow on the park grass or a *pensión* floor. Some early birds may be lucky enough to secure space at campgrounds or the few hostels that don't take reservations. Expect to pay rates up to four times the listed prices in most budget hotels. Many who can't find rooms (or never planned on finding them at all) sleep outside on the lawns of the park around the Ciudadela, Pl. de los Fueros, and Pl. del Castillo, or along the banks of the river. Those who choose this risky option should store their luggage, or, at the very least, sleep on top of it. Try to stay in a large group or near other tourists.

HOSTEL HASSLES? During *San Fermín*, the tourist office offers a real-time list of available official accommodations in the city, but don't expect to find much during the first 2 or 3 days. Check the newspaper *Diario de Navarra* for unofficial *casas particulares* (guest homes), though some advertisers are hesitant to let non-Spanish speakers into their home; look for advertisements posted on the streets in the days leading up to the festival.

During the rest of the year, finding a room in Pamplona is no problem. Hostels line busy C. San Nicolás and C. San Gregorio, off Pl. del Castillo, as well as the parallel C. Zapatería and C. Nueva, off Pl. de San Francisco. On weekends, expect plenty of noise on these streets; rabble-rousing (and open drinking) in Pl. del Castillo and the surrounding streets may make it difficult to sleep. Most hostels have different prices for *temporada alta* (before, after, and during *San Fermín*), *temporada media* (usually only July and Aug., but sometimes June or Sept.), and *temporada baja* (the rest of the year). The price icons below reflect *temporada media* prices.

Pensión Eslava, C. Hilarión Eslava, 13, 2nd fl. (☎948 22 15 58). Although inside the *casco antiguo*, it is not as crowded as other *pensiónes* and relatively quiet. Big, very basic rooms, some with balconies. Shared baths. Doubles for *San Fermín* €100. Otherwise singles €15; doubles €20-30. Cash only. ❶

Horno de Aralar, C. San Nicolás, 12 (☎948 22 11 16). Five fresh, sunny, spotless rooms with TV, fan, and full bath above an upscale, homey restaurant. During *San Fermín* all rooms €200-300. Otherwise singles €40; doubles €50; triples €55. MC/V. ❹

Camping Ezcaba (☎948 33 03 15; www.campingezcaba.com), in Eusa, 7km down the road to Irún. Take city bus line 4-V (dir.: Oricaín) from Pl. de las Merindades (4 per day, during *San Fermín* 26 per day). Hop off at the final stop; ask the driver or follow other backpackers on the moderate walk (500m) to the campground. The taxi ride costs around €15. Fills fast during *San Fermín*. *San Fermín* prices €10.59 per person, €11.68 per tent, €10.59 per car and €9.31 for electricity. Otherwise €4.90 per person, €5.35 per tent, and €4.90 per car; electricity €4.28. MC/V. ❶

FOOD

Tiny neighborhood cafe-bars advertise their hearty *menús* on their doors or on placards outside: try the side streets near C. Jarauta, C. Descalzos, near Po. de Ronda, and the area above Pl. San Francisco. C. Navarrería and Po. de Sarasate are lined with numerous *bocadillo* bars. Many cafes and restaurants raise their prices during *San Fermín* and then close for one to two weeks to recover. The nicely renovated city market, **Mercado de Santo Domingo,** C. Mercado, is to the right of the Casa Consistorial, down the stairs, and hosts hordes of the butchers and produce-sellers. (Open M-Th 8am-2pm, F 8am-2:30pm and 4:30-7:30pm, Sa 8am-2:30pm.) **Vendi Supermarket** is at the corner of C. Hilarión Eslava and C. Mayor. (☎948 22 15 55. Open during *San Fermín* M-Sa 9am-2pm; otherwise M-F 9am-2pm and 5:30-7:30pm, Sa 9am-2pm. MC/V.)

Café-Bar Iruña, Pl. del Castillo (☎948 22 20 64). This former casino that Hemingway made famous in *The Sun Also Rises* serves up typical Navarran dishes in classic form. From the antique decor of the elegant interior and the bust of Hemingway at the attached bar, you'll be reminded that this cafe (dating back to 1888) is fully conscious of its robust history. Reasonably-priced *menú* (€13). Otherwise tranquil interior becomes a roaring banquet hall around 10pm. Drinks and *bocadillos* at the bar, terrace seating on the famed plaza. During *San Fermín* bar only. Open M-Th and Su 8am-11pm, F 8am-2am, Sa 9am-2am. MC/V. ❸

The Harp, C. San Gregorio. Come for a lively dose of English language and Irish breakfasts, along with moderately priced imported beers and a welcoming atmosphere. The only authentic (i.e. owned by an Irishman) Irish bar in Pamplona. Often open late nights when everything else is closed. *Menú* €9-13.Sandwiches €5. Open M-Th and Su 10am-1am, F-Sa 10am-3am. MC/V. ❷

Mesón del Caballo Blanco, C. del Redín, at the Ricón del Caballo Blanco along the Roman walls past the cathedral. (☎948 21 15 04). Take a break for a few drinks and *pinchos*, like *tostadas* (toasted bread with various toppings, €5), or salads (€5.50-7). Grab a seat on the old stone terrace along the high northeast corner of the city. A local favorite on summer afternoons. Open daily noon-midnight, weekends until 1:30. ❶

Restaurante Sarasate, C. San Nicolás, 19 (☎948 22 57 27), above a seafood store. Mellow atmosphere. Organic, flavorful vegetarian dishes, both typical and innovative options. Vegan and gluten-free dishes available. Try one of the delicious mixed fresh fruit juices (€1.30). Lunchtime *menú* €10.50, F-Sa night and Su *menú* €16. During *San Fermín*, pure capitalism and culinary tradition prevail, and the restaurant serves typical meat and fish dishes. Open M-Th and Su 1-4pm, F-Sa 1-4pm and 8:30-11pm. V. ❸

La Mandera de la Ramos, C. San Nicolás, 9, is a mark of the new, hip, modern Pamplona. Subdued purple lounge lighting reveals original stone walls, dark wood beams, and a glass-covered stone wine vat beneath the floor. Gleaming legs of pork for *Jamón Ibérica* (a traditional Spanish snack) hang over a bar bearing images of Pamplona's storied past. Serves *pinchos* (tapas) and *tostadas* (€5-8), as well as a selection of *bocadillos* (€5). On weekend nights, tables are put away to make way for a dance floor. ❷

SIGHTS

CATHEDRAL AND CHURCHES. Carlos III and his wife Queen Leonor are entombed here, in an alabaster mausoleum in the recently restored 16th to 18th-century Gothic **Catedral de Santa María.** *(Pl. San José. ☎948 22 29 90. Open during San Fermín 10am-2pm; closed July 7 and 11; otherwise M-F 10am-2pm and 4-7pm, Sa 10am-2pm. Guided tours, including church, cloister, and Museo Diocesano; for groups, call ahead. €4.40, groups €3.35 per person, children €2.60.)* The 13th-century Gothic **Iglesia de San Saturnino,** C. Ansoleaga, 4, which served both religious and defensive purposes in the city's past, is near the *Ayuntamiento.* *(☎948 22 11 94. Open 9:30am-12:30pm and 6-8pm; July 6, 7, and 13 9:30am-1:30pm and 6:30-8pm. Free.)* The Romanesque 12th-century **Iglesia de San Nicolás,** in Pl. San Nicolás, is also close by. It too once served as a fortress; its turrets were removed after the Castilian conquest of Navarra. *(C. San Miguel, 15. ☎948 22 12 81. Open daily 9am-12:30pm and 6-8:30pm. Free.)* For a peek at *San Fermín,* head to **Iglesia de San Lorenzo,** also known as Capilla San Fermín, and follow the C. San Francisco past the tourist office. *(C. Mayor, 74. ☎948 22 87 90. Open M-F 8am-12:30pm and 6:30-8pm, Sa 8am-1pm. Free.)* All churches in Pamplona have modified visiting hours during *San Fermín.* Check with tourist office for more information.

NIGHTLIFE

There is (night)life after *San Fermín,* and it is not difficult to find. **Plaza del Castillo** is the social heart of Pamplona, with outdoor seating all around the beautifully lit plaza. Revelers of all ages gather at bars in the *casco antiguo* to demonstrate their vocal abilities: singing, shouting, and any other type of loud carousing are the norm. Barhopping down C. San Nicolás and C. San Gregorio is a favorite nighttime activity (check out The Harp and La Mandarra de la Ramos on p. 314), as is drinking at the bars on C. Calderería, C. San Agustín, and C. Jarauta. On summer weekend nights, the drinking and partying pours out onto the streets and sidewalks. **Mesón de la Nabarrería,** C. Nabarrería, 15, a down-to-earth establishment near the cathedral, draws crowds day and night to dance to a funky mix of Spanish and American music and enjoy cheap beer. (☎948 21 31 63. Open July-Aug. M-Th and Su 10am-2am, F-Sa noon-4pm and 6:30pm-2:30am; Sept.-June M-Th and Su noon-4pm and 6:30pm-midnight, F-Sa noon-4pm and 6:30pm-2:30am. Open all night during *San Fermín.*)

If you don't mind the trek, follow the example of claustrophobes and college students who escape the cramped streets of the *casco antiguo* to the bars in Barrio San Juan on Av. de Bayona. You'll find more dancing and partying at **Travesía de Bayona,** a small plaza of bars and discotecas off Av. de Bayona, just before it forks into Monasterio de Velate. The most popular clubs are **Blue Shadow** (☎948 27 51 09) and **Tandem** (☎948 26 92 85), Tr. de Bayona, 3 and 4, both of which have good dancing, big crowds, and friendly bartenders. (Beer €3.50. Mixed drinks €6. Both open Th-Sa 10pm-4am.) Av. de Bayona also boasts a great number of stylish and pricey nightspots.

FIESTA DE SAN FERMÍN (JULY 6-14)

No limits, no lethargy, and no liability make Pamplona's **Fiesta de San Fermín**—known to English-speakers as "The Running of the Bulls"—Europe's premier party. At no other festival will you witness mayhem quite like this 9-day frenzy of parades, bullfights, dancing, fireworks, concerts, champagne-spraying, and wine. *Pamploneses*, clad in white with *fajas* (red sashes, about €5) and *pañuelos* (handkerchiefs, €1.50-5) display impossible levels of physical stamina and alcohol tolerance envied by even the hardiest of partiers. From the moment the fiesta starts on July 6th until the moment it ends on July 14th, the party doesn't let up for even a second.

FERMÍN FAUX PAS. Don't commit the faux pas of wearing your *pañuelo* before the first *chupinazo* (rocket blast); tie it around your wrist to keep it safe. The plaza gets unbearably packed; wear closed-toed shoes and prepare to get up close and personal with fellow revelers; be wary of pickpckets. Other potential dangers include suffocation and injury from broken glass. Claustrophobics and agoraphobics should avoid the square.

Around 10am on July 6th, the whole city crowds around the **Casa Ayuntamiento** and the adjacent streets in anticipation of the mayor's noontime appearance. If you plan to get in to the square, arrive no later than 10:45am. While they wait, the people in the square spray each other with various alcoholic drinks, sing fiesta chants, and have massive food fights. The residents who live in the buildings above the square also join in the fun, throwing down buckets of water and other goodies, like giant beach balls, on the masses below. If you're planning to be in the plaza, don't expect to remain dry or clean by the end. As the midday hour approaches, the crowd sings and chants *"San Fermín!"* raising *pañuelos* high above their heads. As the mayor emerges, he fires the awaited rocket blast from the balcony and screams, "People of Pamplona! Long live *San Fermín!*" in Spanish and *Euskera* (Basque), a roar erupts from the sea of waving red triangles in the plaza below. Champagne and corks rain down along with eggs, ketchup, mustard, wine, flour, and yellow *pimiento.* Within minutes, the streets of the *casco antiguo* flood with improvised singing and dancing troupes, and the streets stay crowded for the remainder of the fiesta. The *peñas*, Pamplona's celebrated social clubs, lead the hysteria. Several times throughout the festival, they are joined by the *Comparsa de Gigantes y Cabezudos*, a troupe of beloved *gigantes* (giant wooden monarchs) and *zaldikos* (courtiers on horseback). *Kilikis* (swollen-headed buffoons) run around chasing little children and hitting them with fake clubs. These misfits, together with the city band and church and town officials, escort a 15th-century statue of *San Fermín* on his triumphant procession through the *casco antiguo*, serenading him with the *jota*, a local folk song. The statue is brought from the Iglesia de San Lorenzo at 10am on July 7, the actual *Día de San Fermín;* in exchange for this promenade, he is asked to protect the runners of the *encierro*, who sing to him before their fateful sprint.

THE RUNNING OF THE BULLS

The *encierro* (running of the bulls) is the highlight of *San Fermín.* The ritual dates back to the 14th century. It served the practical function of getting the bulls from their corrals to the bullring until someone decided it would be fun to run in front of—not behind—the bulls. The city authorities originally tried to ban the dangerous practice, but eventually decided that if they couldn't beat the masses, they should join them, and made the *encierro* an official part of *San Fermín.* These days, the first and grandest *encierro* of the festival is at 8am on July 7 and is repeated every day for the next week. Hundreds of bleary-eyed, adrenaline-charged runners flee from large, horned bulls, as bystanders cheer from barricades, windows, and balconies.

One rocket marks the release of the bulls; another announces that all the bulls have left the enclosure into the course. Both the bulls and the mob scurrying ahead of them are dangerous: in recent years, overcrowding has resulted in the bulls getting blockaded by the masses. The course has three sharp turns, which the bulls often have difficulty navigating; when their legs slide out from under them, they falter, creating a heaping pile of bull. Avoid outside corners to prevent getting crushed under said pile, and be especially careful at the Mercaderes-Estafeta corner. Bulls that are separated from the herd tend to be more nervous and aggressive, often turning against the flow of the crowd and attacking runners. After the final, dangerous, downward-sloping stretch, the run cascades through a perilously narrow opening (where a large proportion of injuries occur) and pours into the bullring amid shouts and cries from spectators. After the bulls have been rounded into their pens inside the Pl. de Toros, young bulls with protective padding on their horns are released into the ring to "play" with the mass of people.

NO BULL. Some of the more sober participants walk the course the night before. If you're planning to run, don't bring anything except for your rolled-up newspaper. Those with backpacks, cameras, or anything of the sort will be thrown out of the course by the police.

The safer alternative is to watch the *encierro* from the bullring or the sidelines. Music, waves, chanting, and dancing pump up spectators until the headline entertainment arrives. Bullring spectators should arrive at 6:45am at the latest. Tickets for the *grada* (free) section are available at 7am in the bullring box office (July 7, 8, and 14, €5.50; July 9-13, €4.50). You can watch for free, but the free section is overcrowded, and it can be hard to see and breathe. To watch from the sidelines, arrive by 6:15am or earlier, as the fences get unbearably packed. One of the best places to sit is the wall over C. Santo Domingo, right near the beginning of the run.

Tickets to the daily **bullfights,** every evening at 6:30pm, are incredibly hard to get, as over 90% of the tickets belong to season ticket-holders. The remaining few are sold every evening for the next day's fight. You can try your luck by lining up at the bullring ticket office before 8:30pm every evening, from the 7th of July onwards, or just buy scalped tickets (€40 and up). For prices of face-value tickets, if you're lucky enough to get them, check www.feriadeltoro.com.

TICKET TIP. Don't get ripped off by the scalpers outside the bull ring! Your best bet is to wait until right before the fight starts and then bargain tough with them. You may be able to cut the asking price in half.

THE PARTYING OF THE PARTICIPANTS

Right after the first rocket goes up on July 6th, the insanity spills over to the streets, gathering steam until nightfall, when it explodes with singing in bars, dancing in alleys, spontaneous parades, and a no-holds-barred party in **Pl. del Castillo,** which quickly becomes a huge open-air dance floor. If you don't want to stick out like a sore thumb, the attire for this dance-a-thon includes sturdy, closed-toed shoes (there's glass everywhere), a white T-shirt and pants or skirt (soon to be wine-soaked), a red *pañuelo* (handkerchief), and a cheap bottle of champagne (to spray—don't pay more than €3). Cheap white clothes are available at countless stands throughout the city.

After each night's hedonistic carnival, the new day's party begins (or ends) each day at 6am, when bands with shrill trumpets march down the streets. The city eases the transition with tamer concerts, outdoor dances, a mule-and-horse procession, a rural sports festival, fun fairs, bull leaping and swerving demonstrations in the bullring, and other such performances. To catch an important event that doesn't involve binge drinking, check out the Pamplona Cathedral Choir's performance of the Vespers, a religious song for the occasion, at 8pm on July 6 in the chapel of *San Fermín.* Also, don't miss the fireworks competition that takes place every night at 11pm over the *Ciudadela.* After the first few days of *San Fermín,* crowds thin out, and the atmosphere goes from Olympic-level citywide debauchery to a more distilled, experts and locals-only flavor of insanity. The festivities culminate at midnight on July 14 with the singing of *Pobre de mí: "Pobre de mí, pobre de mí, que se han acabado las Fiestas de San Fermín."* (Poor me, poor me, the festivals of *San Fermín* have ended.)

PAÍS VASCO (EUSKADI)

As the Basque saying goes, "Before God was God and the rocks were rocks, the Basques were Basques." The País Vasco is officially composed of the provinces Gipuzkoa, Álava, and Vizcaya, but the Basque homeland, *Euskal Herria*, extends into Navarra and southwestern France. The region boasts one of the most varied landscapes in Spain, from verdant hills to industrial wastelands and quaint fishing villages to the glittering coastal cities of Bilbao and San Sebastián. The people are marked by their deep attachment to the land and immense cultural and national pride. However, it is *euskera*, a language unrelated to any other in Europe, that binds and literally defines them. Even the Basque name for themselves, *Euskaldinuak*, means "speakers of *euskera*."

The Basques are thought to have descended from the first Europeans, whose arrival predated that of the Indo-European tribes. Their culture and genes have gone relatively undiluted despite Roman incursions, medieval interference, and finally the Spanish abolition of the *fueros*, medieval grants of semi-autonomy. The Basques enjoyed a brief return to independence under the Second Spanish Republic, but the Republican defeat in the Spanish Civil War ushered in the Fascist rule of General Francisco Franco, who oppressed the Basques and banned *euskera* and other forms of cultural self-expression. In 1968, in response to such injustices, the organization *Euskadi ta Askatasuna* (ETA; "Basque Country and Freedom") began a terrorist movement that persists today. Anti-ETA sentiment is now quite strong among Basques, but many also argue that the methods employed to suppress ETA undermine free speech and disregard human rights either way. Street protests and graffiti continue to call for amnesty for political prisoners.

Today, most Basques share a desire to preserve their cultural identity. Although *castellano* is the predominant language, *euskera* has enjoyed a resurgence since Franco's death. Traditions like *cesta punta* or *pelota vasca* (known outside Spain as the deathly fast sport of *jai alai*) continue to thrive. Basque cuisine is some of Iberia's finest, including *bacalao a la vizcaína* (salt cod in tomato sauce) and dishes *a la vasca* (in parsley steeped white wine sauce). Tapas, considered a regional specialty, are called *pintxos* (PEEN-chos); locals wash them down with *sidra* (cider) and the local white sparkling wine, *txakoli*. Several famous chefs, including Juan Mari Arzak, hail from this region.

HIGHLIGHTS OF PAÍS VASCO

BASQUE in the seaside splendor of **San Sebastián** (p. 320).

ADMIRE your reflection (and the art) at the **Museo Guggenheim** in Bilbao (p. 333).

SAN SEBASTIÁN (DONOSTIA) ☎943

San Sebastián (pop. 180,000) glitters on the shores of the Bay of Biscay. An elaborate, Romantic-style boardwalk, elegant waterfront palaces, and wide golden beaches give the city an air of gentility masking the 21st-century edge found in its boutiques, surf shops, and nightclubs. Ever since Queen Isabel II made Playa de la Concha popular in the mid-19th century, the city has been a fashionable vacation venue for much of Europe's aristocracy. Still, its cosmopolitan air doesn't interfere with its strong sense of regional culture.

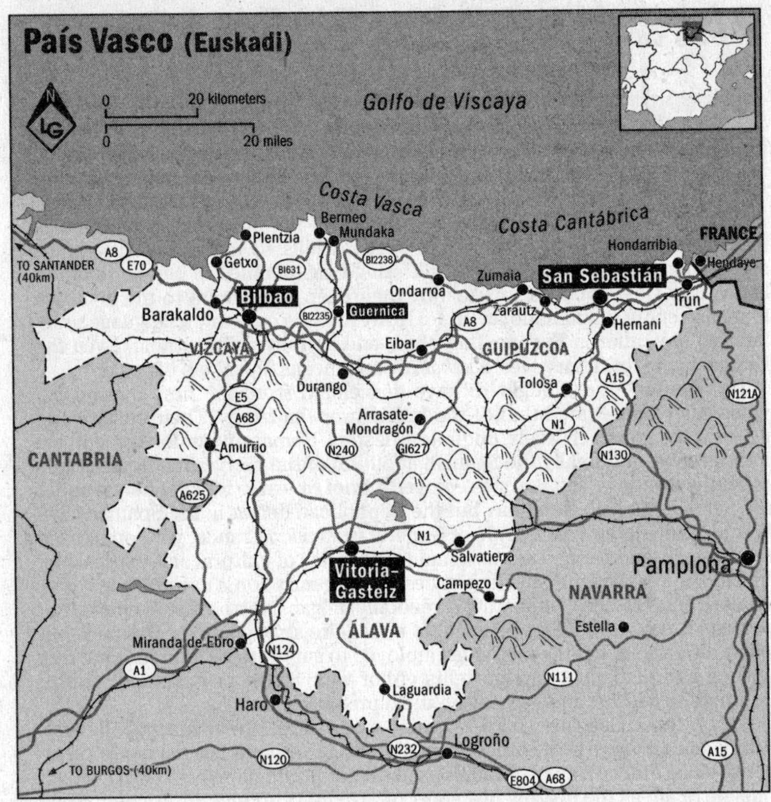

San Sebastián once stood as one of Spain's great ports, but much of it was destroyed during the 1813 Peninsular War, when an invading Anglo-Portuguese force dislodged Napoleon in the process of setting fire to the city. The ruined walls were finally torn down in 1864, amid the construction of a more modern city replete with French architectural influences. Today, San Sebastián draws tourists old and young to bathe and surf along its beaches, hike its mountains, and enjoy its lively and friendly atmosphere.

TRANSPORTATION

Flights: Airport in Hondarribia (☎943 66 85 00; www.aena.es), 22km east of the city. **Iberia** (☎943 66 85 21; www.iberia.es) flies to **Madrid. Air Nostrum** (☎902 40 05 00; www.airnostrum.es) flies to **Barcelona, Málaga, Palma di Mallorca,** and **Sevilla. Interbus** service to Hondarribia stops at airport (45min.; every 20-30min. M-Sa 7:35am-9:45pm, July-Aug. also Su 8:45am-9:45pm; €1.75). A new airport shuttle goes to and from the bus platform at Pio XIII with each flight (€2). A **taxi** to the airport costs €27.

Trains: San Sebastián has 2 train stations.

Estación de Amara, Euskotren (www.euskotren.es), runs to: **Bilbao** (2hr., hourly 5:47am-8:47pm, €6); and **Hendaye, France** (every 30min., €1.35).

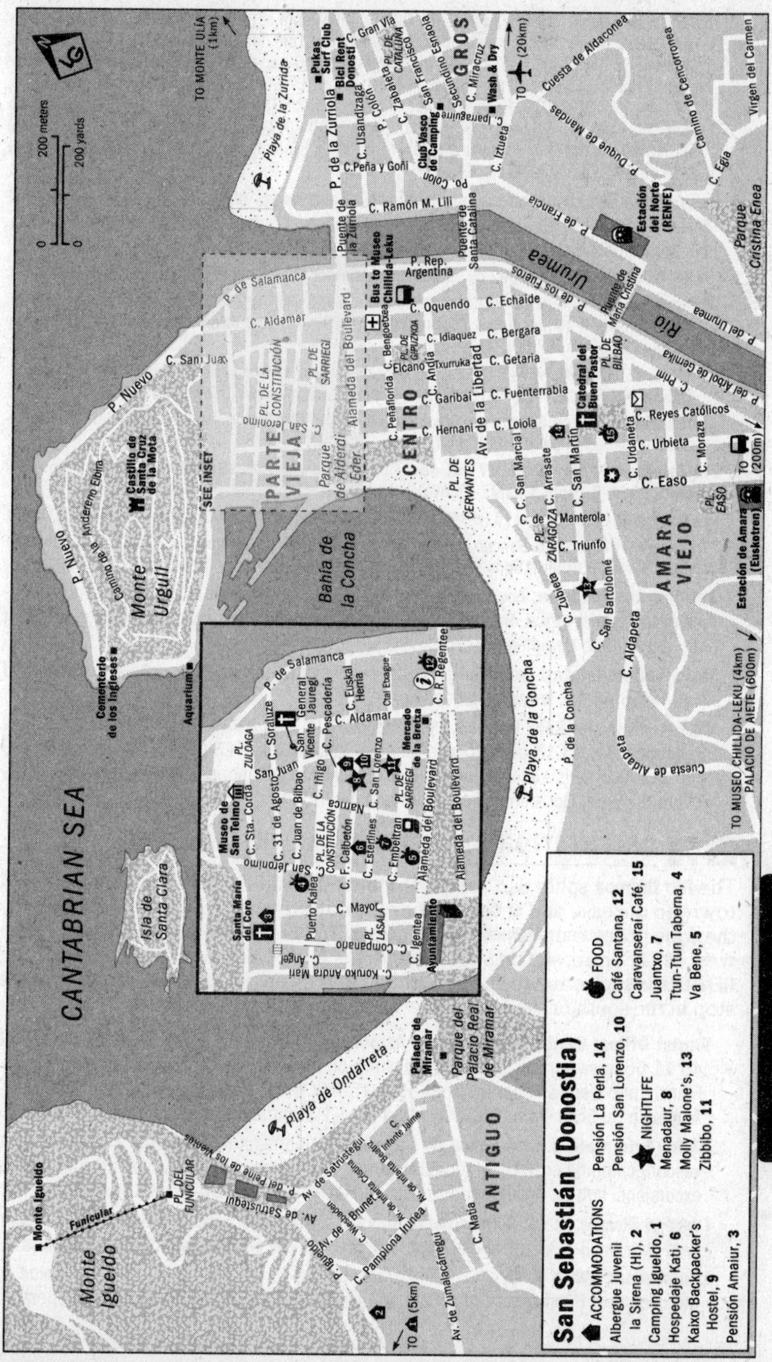

San Sebastián (Donostia)

ACCOMMODATIONS
- Albergue Juvenil la Sirena (HI), 2
- Camping Igueldo, 1
- Hospedaje Kati, 6
- Kaixo Backpacker's Hostel, 9
- Pensión Amaiur, 3
- Pensión La Perla, 14
- Pensión San Lorenzo, 10

NIGHTLIFE
- Menadaur, 8
- Molly Malone's, 13
- Zibbibo, 11

FOOD
- Café Santana, 12
- Caravanserai Café, 15
- Juantxo, 7
- Ttun-Ttun Taberna, 4
- Va Bene, 5

PAÍS VASCO

Estación del Norte, RENFE (☎902 24 02 02; www.renfe.es), Po. de Francia. across the river over Puente María Christina. Info open daily 7:30am-11pm. To: **Barcelona** (8hr.; daily 10:45am, M-F and Su 10:59pm; €37.10-48.70); **Burgos** (3hr., 6 per day 8:32am-10:20pm, €21); **Hendaye, France** (45min., 4 per day 6:34am-8:43pm, €9.90-11.20); **Madrid** (7-8hr.; 8:32am, 2:37pm; €37.20-56.70. Express train 5hr., 8:32am, 2:37pm and 5:51pm; €55); **Salamanca** (6hr.; M-F and Su 8:32am, 1:37pm, 10:20pm; €30.70-39.90); **Tarragona** (7½hr.; 10:45am and 10:59 pm, €47) and **Vitoria-Gasteiz** (1hr.; M-Sa 8 per day 6:57am-10:20pm, Su 7 per day 8:32am-10:37pm; €8.85-17.20).

Buses: San Sebastián has a bus platform and a series of ticket windows around the corner, though not all under 1 roof. Av. de Sancho el Sabio, 31-33, and Po. de Vizcaya, 16. Most open June-Aug. daily 8am-9pm.

ALSA, Po. de Vizcaya, 16 (☎902 42 22 42), to **Santander** (3hr., 8 per day 8:10am-12:20am, €12.48).

Continental Auto, Av. de Sancho el Sabio, 31 (☎943 46 90 74; www.continental-auto.es) to: **Madrid** (6hr., 7-10 per day 7:15am-12:30am, €30-42) and **Vitoria-Gasteiz** (1hr., 8 per day 7:15am-12:30am, €7.50).

Interbus, Pl. Gipuzkoa (☎943 64 13 02; www.interbus.es) to **Hondarribia** (45min.; every 20-30min. 7:45am-10:05pm, July-Aug. also Su 8:45am-10pm; €1.75.) and **Irún** (35min., every 15-30min., €1.60).

La Burundesa, Av. de Sancho el Sabio, 31 (☎943 46 23 60; www.laburundesa.com), to **Vitoria-Gasteiz** (1hr., 7-8 per day 8:30am-8:30pm, €7.50).

La Estellesa, Po. de Vizcaya, 17 (☎943 47 01 15; www.laestellesa.com), to **Logroño** (2hr., 4 per day 8:30am-8:15pm, €11.97-13.66).

La Roncalesa, Po. de Vizcaya, 16 (☎943 46 10 64), to **Pamplona** (1hr., 6-10 per day 7am-9:15pm, €6.50).

Transportes PESA, Av. de Sancho el Sabio, 33 (☎902 10 12 10; www.pesa.net), to **Bilbao** (1hr.; M-F every 30min. 6:30am-10pm, Sa every hr. 7:30am-10pm, Su every hr. 8:30am-10pm; €9.20).

Public Transportation: Local buses (☎943 00 02 00; www.dbus.es). Maps and schedule at the tourist office. **Bus #16** goes from Alameda del Boulevard to campground past Mt. Igueldo and beaches (€1.25).

Taxis: Vallina Teletaxi (☎943 40 40 40; www.vallinagrupo.com) and **Radiotaxi Donosti** (☎943 46 46 46; www.taxidonosti.com).

Bike Rental: Bici Rent Donosti, Po. de la Zurriola, 22 (☎639 01 60 39). Provides bike trail maps. Bikes €13 per 4hr., €17 per day. Tandem bikes €6 per hr., €20 per 4hr., €30 per day. Also sells second-hand bikes. Call ahead for mopeds. Open July-Sept. daily 10am-8:30pm; Oct.-June 10am-2pm and 4-8:30pm.

ORIENTATION AND PRACTICAL INFORMATION

The **Río Urumea** splits San Sebastián down the middle, with the **parte vieja** (old town) to the east, and **El Centro** (the new downtown) to the west, separated by the wide pedestrian **Alameda del Boulevard.** The famed **Playa de la Concha** is to the west of El Centro, starting just beneath the end of Alameda del Boulevard. The **RENFE train station** and the neighborhood **Gros** lie on the east side. Intercity **buses** stop in the south of the city on the west side of the river.

Tourist Office: Centro Municipal de Atracción y Turismo, C. Reina Regente, 3 (☎943 48 11 66; www.sansebastianturismo.com), on the river edge of the *parte vieja*. English, French, and German spoken. Open June 15-Aug. M-Sa 9am-8pm, Su 10am-2pm; July-Aug. also Su 3:30-7pm; Oct.-May M-Sa 9am-1:30pm and 3:30-7pm, Su 10am-2pm.

Hiking Information: Club Vasco de Camping, C. Iparraguirre, 8 (☎943 27 18 66; www.vascodecamping.org). Local mountaineering and hiking club organizes and coordinates excursions. Info on hiking opportunities in País Vasco. Open M-F 6-8:30pm.

Luggage Storage: At the **Continental Auto** ticket office, Av. de Sancho el Sabio, 31 (€2, open 7am-2pm and 3-8:30pm); also at **Wash & Dry** (€3 per day, free with drop-off and pickup wash.)

Laundromat: Wash & Dry, C. Iparraguirre, 6 (☎943 29 31 50). On the east side of the river, over Puente de Santa Catalina. Lines are long in high season. Coin-operated washer and dryer available daily 8am-10pm. €6 wash, €6 dry, €0.50 detergent. Drop-off and pickup service available M-F 9:30am-1pm and 4-8pm, €20.

Police: Policia Municipal, C. Easo, 41 (☎092).

Medical Services: Casa de Socorro, C. Bengoetxea, 4 (☎943 44 06 33). Provides services to EU citizens only, but will redirect others to a private clinic.

English-Language Book Store: Elkar, C. Fermín Calbetón, 30, (☎943 42 26 96, www.elkar.com). Sells a wide selection of novels, as well as travel guides, maps, and Spanish-English dictionaries. (Open M-Sa 10am-2pm and 4-8pm, July and Aug. until 9pm)

Internet Access: You can find a *locutorio* offering internet access, phones, and calling cards all over the place in the *parte vieja,* though prices tend to be better outside of the busy center. Also at the **Biblioteca Central,** Pl. Ayuntamiento, at the front of the huge Casa Consistorial. Free Wi-Fi; free internet access up to 45min.; sign up at front desk. Open M-F 10am-8:30pm, Sa 10am-2pm and 4:30-8pm.

Post Office: C. Urdaneta (☎902 19 71 97), behind the cathedral. Open M-F 8:30am-8:30pm, Sa 9:30am-2pm. **Postal Code:** 20006.

ACCOMMODATIONS AND CAMPING

Small *pensiones* are scattered throughout the noisy *parte vieja.* For a more restful night's sleep farther from the action, look for *hostales* and *pensiones* on the outskirts of El Centro. Many *pensiones* and *hostales* in San Sebastian offer great low prices during the off-season, but when the high season hits in early-mid June (depending on the establishment), prices jump way up, some as much as double the low season cost. In July and August, *completo* (no vacancy) signs appear in many doorways. Particularly tight times are during *San Fermín* (July 6-14), the International Jazz Festival (July 22-27), and *Semana Grande* (week of Aug. 15); September's film festival is not much better. To make matters worse, many *pensiones* don't take reservations in summer. Come early in the day and be prepared to shop around, as finding a room may take some time. Solo travelers should be prepared to barter for a double; single rooms are virtually impossible to come by. The tourist office has a list of all registered accommodations in the city and a booking service for a charge, though many of the cheapest *pensiones* are not registered with the office.

PARTE VIEJA

Brimming with reasonably priced *pensiones* and restaurants, the *parte vieja* is where backpackers go for a night's rest (or more accurately, a night's partying). Its proximity to Playa de la Concha and the port makes this area a prime night-spot; scores of places offer a night's sleep above loud *pintxos* (tapas) bars. Call in advance for reservations, and expect to deal with some noise.

Pensión Amaiur, C. 31 de Agosto, 44, 2nd fl. (☎943 42 96 54; www.pensionamaiur.com). Facing the Iglesia de Santa María, look for the flower-filled balconies to your right. The owners are passionate about operating this beautiful *pensión.* After Virginia, the owner, greets you like a family member, choose from 13 bright rooms in a historic, warmly decorated house. 7 common baths and 2 tidy kitchens with microwave and toaster. Study room with travel info, public phone, and internet access (€1 per 18min.) Free Wi-Fi. English spoken. Singles €24-37; doubles €35-50, with balcony €42-60; triples €54-80; quads €65-95. AmEx/MC/V. ❷

Pensión San Lorenzo, C. San Lorenzo, 2 (☎627 34 32 06; www.pensionsanlorenzo.com), off C. San Juan by the *mercado.* This hostel's helpful owner offers rooms with kettle, toaster, fridge, TV, and private bath. Internet access €1.50 per hr. Free Wi-Fi. Doubles June €40, July-Sept. €55, Oct.-May €28. Cash only. ❷

Kaixo Backpacker's Hostel, C. San Juan, 9, 2nd fl. (☎659 39 38 42; reservations ☎943 42 06 51). This hostel is ideal for the budget traveler. Dorms and shared baths with free laundry, free internet, and kitchen access. Insider tapas tours of the city on weekend nights, as well as hiking and surfing. Bike rentals €2 per hr. and surfboard rentals €20 per day for guests. Dorms €25, Sept.-May €20. ❷

Hospedaje Kati, C. Fermín Calbetón 21, (☎943 43 04 87 or 677 06 69 00; www.hospedajekati.com). This *hostal* lets beds in homey shared rooms on the 5th fl. of their building in the heart of the *parte vieja.* Owners treat guests like beloved grandchildren. Elevator and outdoor terrace. Shared bathrooms with shower. Beds €20, July €25, Aug. €30. Also offers a private double and single (€50, Aug. €60). Cash only. ❷

OUTSIDE THE PARTE VIEJA

These accommodations tend to be quieter than those in the *parte vieja*, but are still close to the port, beach, bus, and train stations, with most accommodations no more than 10min. from the old city by foot. This area is also home to some of the city's most elegant boulevards and buildings.

Pensión La Perla, C. Loiola, 10, 2nd fl. (☎943 42 81 23; www.pensionlaperla.com), on the street directly in front of the cathedral. English spoken. Rooms come with private bath with bathtub, beautiful wooden floor, and balcony. Free internet and Wi-Fi. Quiet, central location. Singles €25-35; doubles €35-55. Cash only. ❷

Albergue Juvenil la Sirena (HI), Po. Igueldo, 25 (☎943 31 02 68), 3min. from the beach. Bus #16 runs to Po. Igueldo, right in front of the albergue, from Alameda del Boulevard (every hr. 7:30am-10pm, €1). Clean, large dorms as well as 2- to 4-person rooms. Multilingual staff. Laundry and kitchen available. Library and free internet. Breakfast included. Sheets €3. Max. 3-night stay if full. Curfew 2am, 4am on weekends. May-Sept. €16-19, 26+ €18-20. €2 extra without HI or ISIC card. MC/V. ❶

Camping Igueldo, (☎943 21 45 02; www.campingigueldo.com), 5km west of town atop Monte Igueldo. Bus #16 ("Barrio de Igueldo-Camping") runs between site and Alameda del Boulevard (every hr. 7:30am-10pm, €1). *Parcelas* (spot for 2 people with room for car and tent, includes water and electricity) June 16-Sept. 15 and *Semana Santa* €29.10, extra person €4.60; electricity €3.60. Sept. 16-June 15 *parcelas* €19-26. Fully equipped family-size bungalows €69-101. Min. 5-night stay in high season. MC/V. ❷

FOOD

Pintxos (tapas), chased down with local *sidra*, are a religion here. Bars line the streets in the *parte vieja*, where arrays of enticing tidbits on toothpicks cover countertops everywhere. The modern **Mercado de la Bretxa,** in an underground shopping center, sells everything from fresh produce and meat to *pintxos.* The huge supermarket inside offers a choice of groceries (open M-Sa 8am-9pm, though most vendors take lunch 3-5pm).

PARTE VIEJA

Juantxo, C. Esterlines, 6 (☎943 42 74 05), main entrance off C. Embeltran, 6. An authentic *pintxos* experience in a warm, friendly setting (some local *pintxos* bars can be surprisingly intimidating). Juantxo serves up the delicious little snacks (€1.35) in larger *ración* portions (€3.25-4.50) too, as well as sandwiches (€3-3.50) and *tortillas* (€3-3.50). Open daily 9am-11:30pm. Cash only. ❶

Ttun-Ttun Taberna, C. San Jeronimo, 25. (☎943 68 82). Painted with the red, green, and blue of the Basque flag and decorated with photographs of local festivals and *pelota* *vasca*. For lunch, they offer one choice: a superb and inexpensive *menú* (€9) with an assortment of authentic Basque options. Open daily 1-4pm. ❷

Café Santana, C. Reina Regente, half a block toward the river from the tourist office. *Pintxos* (€1.40-2.40) all nicely labeled. *Bocadillos* €4-6. Open July-Sept. daily 7am-10pm; Oct.-June M-Sa 7am-10pm, Su 7am-3pm. MC/V. ❶

Va Bene, Alameda del Boulevard, 14 (☎943 42 24 16). Frequented by tourists and locals alike for high-quality, low-price hamburgers and hot dogs served in the tradition of the best American diners. Norman Rockwell prints and an English-speaking staff lay on the Americana unoppressively. Burgers €2.95-4.95, sandwiches (ham, chicken, etc.) €3.15-4.95. Open daily June-Sept. 11:30am-1am, F-Sa until 2:15; Oct.-May 11am-12:15am, F-Sa 11:30am-1:45am. Cash only. ❶

OUTSIDE THE PARTE VIEJA

C. Reyes Católicos, outside the *parte vieja* just below the cathedral, is lined with popular bars and restaurants. If you wish to have a nice, quiet restaurant meal either out on a terrace or inside, this is the place to go.

Caravanserai Café, Pl. del Buen Pastor (☎943 47 54 18), near the cathedral. Chic and artsy, without pretentious prices. Fabulous vegetarian appetizers and entrees (€4-10). Entrees €6-10. €0.60 surcharge for patio dining. Open M-Th 8am-midnight, Sa-Su 10:30am-11:30pm. AmEx/MC/V. ❷

SIGHTS

San Sebastián has enough sights and attractions to keep you running from one end of the bay to the other for days. After enjoying them one by one, the best way to absorb it all is an evening stroll along *Playa de la Concha*, which has breathtaking views of both mountains. Santa Clara, the Estatua del Sagrado Corazón, and the city's skyline are all within view from here.

MUSEO CHILLIDA-LEKU. The Museo Chillida-Leku houses a large collection of the works of Eduardo Chillida, San Sebastián's contemporary art guru and former Harvard University professor. His stone and steel sculptures are spread over peaceful, spacious outdoor lawns; pieces are hidden around every turn of the path. The 16th-century farmhouse at the center, a spectacular construction of huge wood beams and arching stone restored by the sculptor himself (and considered a work of art on its own), now houses some of Chillida's earliest pieces. *(Bo. Jau-*

A PEACE POSTPONED

After nearly 40 years of violence and 8000 deaths, the Basque separatist movement, ETA ("Basque Homeland and Freedom" in *euskara*), announced a permanent ceasefire in early 2006 and began negotiations with the Spanish government. As discussions progressed, there was hope that the organization's bloody campaign for an independent Basque state was nearing an end.

That optimism vanished in December 2006, when ETA claimed responsibility for a bombing in Madrid's Barajas Airport. Though the organization announced that it was still committed to the ceasefire, the Spanish government announced that ETA had clearly violated the terms of the truce, and declared the peace process as unquestionably over. In June 2007, the ceasefire officially came to an end. In an interview with El País in June of 2008, Prime Minister Jose Luis Rodriguez Zapatero stated that he was no longer willing to negotiate with ETA, noting that dialogue had thus far proven useless.

Meanwhile, in the Plaza de España in Vitoria-Gasteiz, a banner bears the message "No to ETA," while the *Ayuntamiento* in San Sebastian proclaims: "No to ETA; Human Rights and Co-Existence in Peace." The sight of such slogans is a powerful sign that political dialogue has its place. Though ETA continues to be a significant force, not all advocates of Basque liberation are with them.

regui, 66. 15min. from the town center. Autobuses Garayar, line G2, leave from C. Oquendo every 30min. daily 7am-10pm, €1.25. By car, take N-1 out of San Sebastián south toward Vitoria-Gasteiz. Turn toward Hernani on GI-131. Museum is on the left. ☎943 33 60 06; www.museochillidaleku.com. Open July-Aug. M-Sa 10:30am-8pm, Su 10:30am-3pm; Sept.-June Tu-Su 10:30am-3pm. Daily tours and audioguides. €8.50, students and retired €6.50, under 12 free.)

MONTE IGUELDO. San Sebastián's mountains afford spectacular views, but those from Monte Igueldo win hands down if you can bear (or if you seek) the noise of the amusement park atop the mountain. Monte Igueldo is located across the bay from the *parte vieja*. The sidewalk toward the mountain ends just before the base of Monte Igueldo, next to Eduardo Chillida's spectacular sculpture, *El Peine de los Vientos* (Wind Comb) by the raging sea. The best way to the summit is the #16 bus, then the funicular to the top. If you choose to walk, be careful; the only way up is along a narrow *carretera* (road/highway) with no sidewalks. On top of the hill you'll find an 18th-century tower with a dazzling **panoramic view** of the sea, mountains, and city. *(☎943 21 02 11. Open July-Sept. daily 10am-10pm; Oct. and Jan.-May M-F 11am-6pm, Sa-Su 11am-8pm; Apr.-June M-F 11am-8pm, Sa 11am-10pm, Su 10am-10pm. €2, children €1. Funicular runs every 15min. €1.30, round-trip €2.30. Tower open daily 10am-9pm. €2. Mar.-Oct. opening hours depend on weather.)*

MONTE URGULL. Across the bay from Monte Igueldo and just above the *parte vieja*, the paths on Monte Urgull wind through shady woods and monuments, providing stunning vistas of the old town and fishing port below. The fortified hills served as a major defense base for the city until the 19th century; today, visitors can absorb its history, as well as some local art, at the **Castillo de Santa Cruz de la Mota,** which tops the summit with 12 cannons, a chapel, a museum of San Sebastian's military and maritime history, and the statue of the **Sagrado Corazón de Jesús** that towers, watchful, over the city. *(Paths lead to the summit from Po. Nuevo; the official Subido al Castillo (Ascent to the Castle) starts at the end of Pl. de Kaimingaintxo, past the Iglesia de Santa María toward Santa Clara. Entire park open May-Sept. 8am-9pm; Oct.-Apr. 8am-7pm. Castillo and exhibitions open daily in summer 8am-8pm, in winter 8am-6pm. Free.)*

MUSEO DE SAN TELMO. The Museo de San Telmo resides in a former Dominican monastery and houses magnificent collections of Basque art, funerary relics, prehistoric Basque artifacts, dinosaur skeletons, and more recent anthropological exhibits. Especially impressive is the converted church, hung with monumental tapestries of Basque traditions like whaling and navigation in Republican style. *(Pl. Zuloaga, 1. ☎943 48 15 80; www.donostiakultura.com. Currently under renovations, expected to reopen in 2010.)*

PALACES. When Queen Isabel II started vacationing here in the mid-19th century, fancy buildings sprang up like wildflowers. The **Palacio de Miramar** has passed through the hands of the Spanish court, Napoleon III, and Bismarck. *(Between Playa de la Concha and Playa de Ondarreta. Open daily June-Aug. 8am-9pm; Sept.-May 8am-7pm. Free.)* The other royal residence, Palacio de Aiete, is also closed to the public, but surrounding trails in the adjacent garden are not. *(Follow Cuesta de Aldapeta or take bus #19 or 31. Grounds open daily June-Sept. 8am-9pm, Oct.-May 8am-7pm. Free.)*

AQUARIUM. If you can't stand to eat any more of your finned friends, come see thousands of them on display. The second floor holds a coral and conch collection. Come Monday, Thursday, or Sunday at noon to see the feeding. *(Po. del Muelle, 34, on Pl. de Carlos Blasco de Imaz. Arrows point the way from the port. Look for the big "Aquarium" sign. ☎943 44 00 99; www.aquariumss.com. Open July-Aug. daily 10am-9pm; Apr. 8-June 30 and Sept. M-F 10am-8pm, Sa-Su 10am-9pm; Mar. 1-Apr. 7 M-F 10am-7pm, Sa-Su 10am-8pm. €10, students and seniors €8, children €6.)*

BEACHES

The gorgeous **Playa de la Concha** curves from the port to **Pico del Loro,** the promontory home of the **Palacio de Miramar.** The flat beach, popular among families with children, virtually disappears during high tide. Sunbathers jam onto the smaller and steeper **Playa de Ondarreta,** beyond Miramar, and surfers flock to the bigger waves of more exposed **Playa de la Zurrida,** across the river from Mt. Urgull. Picnickers head for the alluring **Isla de Santa Clara** in the bay. (☎943 00 04 50. Motorboat ferry (5min.) departs from docks behind the *Ayuntamiento* June-Sept. every 30min. Round-trip €3.25.)

Several sports-related groups offer a variety of activities and lessons. For kayaking, call the **Federación Gipuzkoaka de Piragüismo,** Po. de la Concha, 18. (☎943 44 51 03. €7 per hr. Open July-Aug. M-F 10am-1pm and 4-7pm.) Surfers should check out the **Pukas Surf Club,** Av. de la Zurriola, 24, or the hut on the beach, for expert info, lessons, and rentals. The store manufactures its own surfboards and offers 5hr. courses at various levels for €65. (☎943 32 00 68; www.pukassurfeskola.com and www.pukassurf.com. Surfboard rental €25 per day, fins €3 per hour, wetsuits €20 per 2 days. Guided surfing €49 per hr. Open M-Sa 9am-9pm. MC/V.) For general information on all sports, pick up a copy of the **UDA-Actividades Deportivas** brochure at the tourist office.

NIGHTLIFE AND FESTIVALS

The *parte vieja* pulls out all the stops in July and August, particularly on C. Fermín Calbetón, three blocks in from Alameda del Boulevard. During the year, when students outnumber backpackers, nightlife tends to move beyond the *parte vieja.* Keep an eye out for coupons, but beware—some deals are phony.

San Sebastián is a great city for cultural events and festivals. Highlights of the year are the renowned, week-long **Jazzaldia** jazz festival in late July and the equally prestigious San Sebastián **International Film Festival** in late September. During both, ticketed events take place alongside free street performances. For more traditional celebrations, come for **Semana Grande,** held annually the week around August 15th, when the entire city heads to the streets for shows, parades, concerts, and a nightly international fireworks competition over the Concha beach. Reserve ahead if you plan to visit during any of these events.

Molly Malone's, C. San Martin, 55, (☎943 46 98 22). San Sebastian's popular Irish bar fills with a crowd of Spaniards and travelers. A popular pregame spot before hitting the discotecas, the bar also draws the college-age crowd on Thursdays for international music night. Open 4pm-4am, weekends until 5am.

Mendaur, C. Fermín Calbetón, 8, (☎943 42 22 68; www.mendaur.es). Mendaur pumps dance music until the wee hours of the morning. Drink deals for the night posted on the chalkboard outside. Beer €3. Mixed drinks €6. Open 5pm-3:30am.

Zibbibo, Pl. de Sarriegi, 8, (☎943 42 53 34). In the *parte vieja* and packed with young tourists, Zibbibo is practically a disco, just on a smaller scale. Blend of Top 40 and Euro-techno. "Grande" sangria €5.50. 2-pint Heineken €5.50. Happy hour daily 7-9pm and 10:30-11:30pm. Open M-W 4pm-2:30am, Th-Sa 4pm-3:30am. AmEx/MC/V.

BILBAO (BILBO) ☎944

Over the last decade, Bilbao (pop. 354,000) has made a technological, cultural, and aesthetic turnaround. The economic engine of the Basque country and a major shipbuilding center since the 1700s, Bilbao, known as "Botxo" to Basques, was an important trade link between Castilla and Flanders. Bilbao has

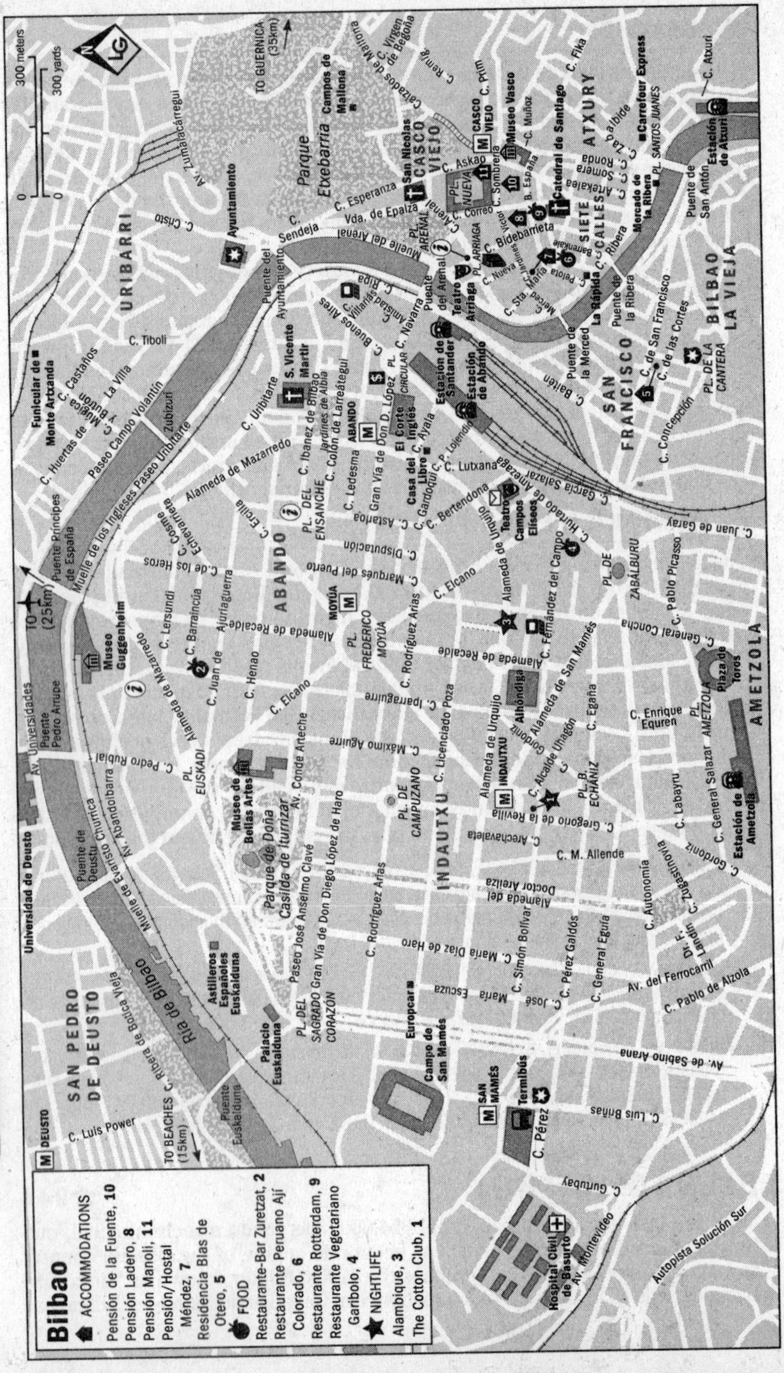
Bilbao
ACCOMMODATIONS
Pensión de la Fuente, 10
Pensión Ladero, 8
Pensión Manoli, 11
Pensión/Hostal Méndez, 7
Residencia Blas de Otero, 5
FOOD
Restaurante-Bar Zuretzat, 2
Restaurante Peruano Ají Colorado, 6
Restaurante Rotterdam, 9
Restaurante Vegetariano Garibolo, 4
NIGHTLIFE
Alambique, 3
The Cotton Club, 1
300 meters
300 yards
URIBARRI
ABANDO
INDAUTXU
SAN PEDRO DE DEUSTO
CASCO VIEJO
SIETE CALLES
ATXURY
SAN FRANCISCO
BILBAO LA VIEJA
AMETZOLA
Ría de Bilbao
Museo Guggenheim
Museo de Bellas Artes
Parque de Doña Casilda de Iturrizar
Parque Etxebarria
Campos de Mallona
Ayuntamiento
Universidad de Deusto
Campo de San Mamés
Termibús
Hospital Civil de Basurto
Estación de Santander
Estación de Abando
Estación de Atxuri
Estación de Ametzola
Plaza de Toros
Alhóndiga
Teatro Arriaga
Teatro Campos Elíseos
Catedral de Santiago
Museo Vasco
Mercado de la Ribera
El Corte Inglés
Casa del Libro
Carrefour Express
Palacio Euskalduna
Astilleros Españoles Euskalduna
Funicular de Monte Artxanda
TO GUERNICA (35km)
TO BEACHES (15km)
TO (25km)
Autopista Solución Sur

diversified from its industrial roots by appealing to tourists with its forward-thinking architecture, busy shopping streets in the *casco viejo*, and pleasant green spaces. Its incredibly efficient public transportation, built around a futuristic subway system and the recently overhauled international airport, remains the envy of other big cities. Frank Gehry's Guggenheim Museum, whose graceful gleaming curves embody the spirit of the new Bilbao, has powerfully fueled the city's rise to international cultural prominence. Enjoy Basque cuisine, summer festivals, and unforgettable art in this booming tourist destination.

TRANSPORTATION

Flights: Airport (☎944 86 96 64; www.aena.es), 12km from Bilbao. Serviced by many European budget airlines flying to different cities in Spain and Europe. To reach the airport take **BizkaiBus** (☎902 22 22 65) marked *Aeropuerto* from Termibus, or Pl. Moyúa in front of the Hacienda building (line A-3247; 25min., every 30min. 5:25am-9:55pm; €1.10). Buses return from airport to Pl. Moyúa (2 per hr. 6:15am-midnight). **Taxis** from airport to Pl. Moyúa cost approx. €18-20.

Trains: Bilbao has 3 train stations.

Ferrocarriles Vascongados/Eusko Trenbideak (FV/ET): Estación de Atxuri, Cl. Atxuri, 8 (☎902 54 32 10; www.euskotren.es). Trains to **San Sebastián** (2hr.; 17-18 per day M-F 5:57am-8:34pm, Sa-Su 6:57am-8:34pm; €6.20), **Guernica** (every 15 min., 5:57am-10:27pm, €2.40). Also connects to Hendaye, France.

FEVE: Estación de Santander, C. Bailén, 2 (☎944 25 06 15; www.feve.es). To: **León** (7hr., 2:30pm, €20.55) and **Santander** (3hr.; 8am, 1, 7:30pm; €7.25). Also offers extensive local service.

RENFE: Estación de Abando, Pl. Circular, 2 (☎902 24 02 02). M: Abando. To: **Barcelona** (9-10hr.; July-Aug. daily 10:05am, 10:25pm; Sept.-June daily 10:05am, M-F 10:25pm; €38.40-50.50); **Madrid** (5-6hr., daily 8:55am and 5:10pm, €40.10-45.20); **Salamanca** (5hr., 2pm, €28.20); **Burgos** (2½ hr.; 6 per day, 8:55am-11pm; €17-30). Info booth open in summer daily 7:30am-10:30pm; in winter 9:30am-1:30pm and 4:30-8pm.

Buses: The following companies are based at the **Termibús terminal,** C. Gurtubay, 1 (☎944 39 52 05). M: San Mamés. **Info booth** open M-F 7am-10pm, Sa 8am-9pm, Su 9am-10pm.

ALSA: (☎902 42 22 42; www.alsa.es). To: **Barcelona** (7hr.; 4 per day 7:15am-10:30pm, F and Su also 11:30pm; €40.59); **Santander** (1hr.; every 30-60min. 6am-11:30pm, also 1:45am; €6.44-11.80); **Zaragoza** (4hr.; 7 per day 6:30am-8:45pm, F and Su also 4:30 and 9:30pm; €19.10).

Continental Auto: (☎944 27 42 00). To: **Burgos** (2hr.; M-Sa 7-10 per day 6:30am-8:30pm, Su 7 per day 8:30am-10:30pm; €10.49) and **Madrid** (4-5hr.; M-F 10-18 per day 7am-1:30am, Su hourly 8am-1:30am; €26.11).

PESA: (☎902 10 12 10; www.pesa.net). To **San Sebastián** (1hr.; M-F every 30-60 min. 6:30am-10pm, Sa-Su 7:30am-10pm; €9.20).

La Unión: (☎944 27 11 11). To: **Haro** (1hr.; M-F 5 per day 7:30am-8pm, Sa 4 per day 8:30am-8pm, Su 3 per day 8:30am-7:30pm; €8.55); **Logroño** (1hr.; M-F 6 per day 7:30am-8pm Sa 4 per day 8:30am-10pm, Su 4 per day 8:30am-11pm; €11.05); **Pamplona** (2hr.; July-Sept. M-Sa 6 per day 7am-8:30pm, Su 5 per day 8:30am-8pm; Oct.-June M-Th and Sa 7:30am-7pm, F 7:30am-8pm, Su 11am-8pm; €12.85); **Vitoria-Gasteiz** (1hr.; M-F every 30min. 6am-10pm, Sa hourly 7am-10pm, Su hourly 7:45am-9:30pm except 9:30am; €5.45).

Public Transportation: There is an office with information on public transportation in the San Mames metro stop just below Termibus. (☎944 76 61 50; open 8:30am-7:30pm). If you'll be in Bilbao for a few days, buy a pre-paid Creditrans pass for €5, €10, or €15 at metro ticket machines, ONCE booths, or most kiosks. The card is a convenient way to pay for all Bilbao public transportation on Bilbobús, BizkaiBus, EuskoTran, the metro, and the funicular. All fares on these lines discounted with the card.

Bilbobús runs 23 lines across the city (daily 6am-11:30pm; M-F €0.90, Sa-Su €1). Signs at most stops have extensive lists of bus schedules.

BizkaiBus (☎902 22 22 65) connects Bilbao to the suburbs and the airport. 20% discount on fares with Creditrans. Leaves daily from in front of Estación de Abando to **Guernica** (lines A-3514 and

A3515; 45min.; M-F every 15min. 6:15am-10pm, Sa every 30min. 6:30am-10:30pm, Su every 30min. 7:30am-10:30pm.)

EuskoTran, C. Buenos Aires, 9 (☎902 54 32 10), runs brand-new, fast, comfortable tram-trains on a circuit in Bilbao. When walking in the city, make sure to avoid the tracks, which often run next to the sidewalk. Service now reaches from the Termibus station to Atxuri (€1; Creditrans €0.40).

Metro (☎944 25 40 00 or 944 25 40 25; www.metrobilbao.net). Ultra-modern. Though it only has 2 lines, one on each side of Bilbao's river, it will quickly get you just about anywhere you need to go in and around the city. Look for 3 interlocking red circles to find entrances, and **hang on to your ticket** after entering—you'll need it again to exit. Travel within 1 zone €1.30, 2 zones €1.45, 3 zones €1.55 (Creditrans €.68/€.81, €.91). Trains run daily every 15min. 6am-10:30pm, also every 30min. F 10:30pm-2am, Sa 10:30pm-6am hourly, in winter 8:30am-7pm.

Taxis: Teletaxi (☎944 10 21 21). **Radio Taxi Bilbao** (☎944 44 88 88).

Car Rental: Europcar, C. Licenciado Poza, 56 (☎944 42 22 26; www.europcar.es). 21+ with passport and valid driver's license. Open M-F 8am-1pm and 4-7:30pm, Sa 9am-1pm. Airport branch (☎944 71 01 33). Open daily 7:30am-11:30pm.

ORIENTATION AND PRACTICAL INFORMATION

The Ría de Bilbao runs through the city, separating the historic **casco viejo** to the east from the newer parts of town to the west. The train stations are directly across the river from the **casco viejo,** while the bus station is considerably farther west. **Gran Vía de Don Diego López de Haro** connects three of Bilbao's main plazas, heading east from **Pl. del Sagrado Corazón,** through central **Pl. Federico Moyúa,** and ending at **Plaza Circular.** The **Guggenheim Museum** is in the mid-northern part of the newer, western bank, about a 20min. walk from the *casco viejo*.

Tourist Office: Oficina de Turismo de Bilbao, central branch at Pl. Ensanche, 11 (☎944 79 57 60; www.bilbao.net/bilbaoturismo). Provides information on city transportation, accommodations, museums, and restaurants. Open M-F 9am-2pm and 4-7:30pm; Semana Grande (mid-Aug.), Sa-Su 9am-2pm and 4-7:30pm. **Branch** at **Teatro Arriaga** (open July-Aug. M-Sa 9:30am-2pm and 4-7:30pm, Su 9:30am-2pm; Sept.-June Tu-F 11am-6pm, Sa 11am-7pm, Su 11am-2pm), and another near the **Guggenheim,** Abandoibarra Etorbidea, 2. English spoken. Open Tu-F 11am-6pm, Sa 11am-7pm, Su 11am-2pm; July-Sept. M-Sa 10am-7pm, Su 10am-6pm. All 3 offices offer guided walking tours of the old quarter and of the newer Ensanche-Abandoibarra (Sa-Su 10am for old quarter, noon for newer neighborhood, €4.) The tourist office also runs an accommodations booking service for a fee, call for information.

Currency Exchange: Caja Laboral, Pl. Circular. 24hr. ATM. Open M-F 8:30am-2:15pm and 4:15-7:45pm; Oct-Mar. Sa 8:30am-1:15pm; June 15-Sept. 30 closed F afternoons.

Luggage Storage: In **Termibús terminal** by information booth, lockers €1; inside €1 per bag. Open M-F 7am-10pm, Sa-Su 8am-9pm.

English-Language Bookstore: Casa del Libro, Alameda de Urquijo, 9 (☎944 15 32 00), next to New Inn Urrestarazu. English, French, and Italian best-sellers and classics; find Grisham next to Gogol. Open M-Sa 9:30am-9pm. AmEx/MC/V.

Municipal Police: C. Luis Briñas, 14 (☎092).

Medical Services: Hospital de Basurto, Av. Montevideo, 18 (☎944 00 60 00). For **emergencies** call ☎112.

Internet Access: Biblioteca Municipal, C. Bidebarrieta, 4 (☎944 15 09 15) has part-time free Wi-Fi, internet access, and library card with sign-up. Open Sept. 16-May 31 M 2:30-8pm, Tu-F 8:30am-8:30pm, Sa 10am-1pm; June Tu-F 8:30am-7:30pm, Sa 10am-2pm.; July M-F 8:30am-7:30pm; Aug. M-F 8:30am-1:45pm.

Post Office: Alameda de Urquijo, 19 (☎944 70 93 38). Open M-F 8:30am-8:30pm, Sa 9:30am-2pm. **Postal Code:** 48008.

ACCOMMODATIONS

During **Semana Grande** (Aug. 17-25), rates are higher than those listed below. **Plaza de Arriaga** and **Calle Arenal,** near the *casco viejo*, have budget accommodations, while upscale options pepper the river and new city off **Gran Vía.**

Pensión Méndez, C. Sta. María, 13, 4th fl.(☎944 16 03 64). Bright, very cheerful rooms with firm beds and spacious balconies. Singles €25; doubles €35; triples €50. MC/V. ❷. The affiliated **Hostal Méndez,** 1st. fl. is pricier, but has newly renovated rooms with windows, full bath, and TV. Many have balconies. Singles €38-40; doubles €50-55; triples €65-70. MC/V. ❹

Residencia Blas de Otero, C. de las Cortes, 38 (☎944 34 32 00). A university dorm that rents out rooms in summer. All rooms come with desk, full kitchenette and private bathroom. Free internet in lobby and connection in rooms, and 24hr. guard. Laundry machines (€3 wash and dry) and game room in basement. Location can be somewhat dangerous at night; travel in a group. Singles €31.50-38; doubles €46-55.50. MC/V. ❸

Pensión Ladero, C. Lotería, 1, 4th fl. (☎944 15 09 32). Recently renovated shared baths, rooms with TV, some with balcony. Two extremely large triples, and several considerably smaller doubles, though all well-appointed. Singles €24; doubles €36; triples €53. No reservations. Cash only. ❷

Pensión Manoli, C. Libertad, 2, 4th fl. (☎944 15 56 36). Tucked on the tiny C. Libertad just outside the Pl. Nueva by the *casco viejo* metro stop with small but tidy rooms and shared baths. Rooms with balconies over the street. Free Wi-Fi. Singles €25; doubles €30. ❷

Pensión de la Fuente, C. Sombrerería, 2 (☎944 16 99 89). Quiet, comfortable rooms with basic amenities. Doubles differ in size, some include porches. TV €2. Wi-Fi available. Singles €24; doubles €33-36, with private bath €45. Extra bed €12. Cash only. ❷

FOOD

Restaurants and bars in the *casco viejo* offer a wide selection of local dishes, *pintxos*, and *bocadillos*. The new city has even more variety. **Mercado de la Ribera,** on the riverbank at the end of C. Somera and C. Ronda, is the biggest indoor market in Spain; it's worth a trip just to see the endless counters of freshly caught fish and the rows of equally fresh vegetables (open M-Th and Sa 8am-2pm, F 8am-2:30pm and 4:30-7:30pm). **Carrefour Express,** Pl. Santos Juanes, has groceries and is just past Mercado de la Ribera. (Open M-Sa 9am-9pm. AmEx/MC/V.) **El Corte Inglés,** Gran Vía, 7-9, in Pl. Circular, has a supermarket on the sixth floor. (☎944 25 35 00. Open M-Sa 10am-9pm. AmEx/MC/V.)

Restaurante Peruano Ají Colorado, C. Barrenkale, 5 (☎944 15 22 09). This intimate restaurant specializes in traditional Andean ceviche (marinated raw fish salad; €9.95-12.75), and serves up a full menu of excellent, filling Peruvian mountain dishes. M-F lunch *menú* €12. Open Tu-Sa 1:30-4pm and 9-11pm, Su 1:30-4pm. MC/V. ❷

Restaurante Vegetariano Garibolo, C. Fernández del Campo, 7 (☎944 22 32 55). Bright white walls and delicious, creative vegetarian fare, but get here early; seating is limited and the line is long. *Menú* M-F and Su €12; Sa €15, F and Sa night €25. Open M-Th 1-4pm, F-Sa 1-4pm and 9-11pm. MC/V. ❸

Restaurante Rotterdam, C. del Perro, 6 (☎944 16 21 65). The first owner opened this restaurant after retiring from the sea, naming it after his favorite city abroad. Serves authentic Basque dishes (entrees €9-14) in a cozy restaurant decorated with pictures of Bilbao's historic past. For dessert, don't miss the *Goxua*, a local dessert layering whipped cream, cake, and *crema catalana* (€3). Menu in *euskera*, Spanish, English, and French. Open 11am-4pm and 7-10:30pm. ❷

Restaurante-Bar Zuretzat, C. Iparraguirre, 7 (☎944 24 85 05), near the Guggenheim. The walls are lined with helmets signed by the workmen who built the Guggenheim from 1993 to 1997. High-quality seafood. Don't miss the incredibly sweet cinnamon rice pudding (€3.20). *Menú* €10-12. Open daily 7:30am-11:30pm. MC/V. ❷

SIGHTS

MUSEO GUGGENHEIM BILBAO. Lauded in the international press with every superlative imaginable, Frank Gehry's Guggenheim, opened in 1997, has catapulted Bilbao straight into cultural stardom. Visitors are greeted by Jeff Koons's *Puppy*, a dog composed of 70,000 live flowers standing almost as tall as the museum. The undulating shapes and flowing forms of the building itself are undoubtedly its main attraction. Sheathed in mute titanium, tan limestone, and fluid glass, the US$122 million building is said to resemble an iridescent fish, ship, or a blossoming flower. The dramatically spacious interior features a towering atrium and a series of unconventional exhibition spaces, including a colossal 130m by 30m hall with *The Matter of Time*, a massive permanent installation of curving steel plates by Richard Serra. Especially endearing is the mammoth 30 ft. high metal spider lovingly called *"Maman,"* (mommy) on the walkway by the river. Don't be surprised if you are asked to take your shoes off, lie on the floor, walk through mazes, or even sing during your visit to the eccentric exhibits. For those who find modern art hard to swallow, a handy (and free) multilingual audioguide provides good commentary and explanations, some by the artists themselves. *(Av. Abandoibarra, 2. Easily reached by Euskotran, Guggenheim stop. ☎944 35 90 80; www.guggenheim-bilbao.es. Open July-Aug. daily 10am-8pm; Sept.-June Tu-Su 10am-8pm. Free guided tours Tu-Su 11am, 12:30, 4:30, 6:30pm. Sign up 30min. before tour at the info desk. Restaurant open Tu-Su 1-3:15pm, W and Sa also 9-10:30pm. Menú €19-24. Adjacent cafeteria open Tu-Su 9am-9pm, July-Aug. also M. First-floor cafe open Tu-Su 9am-9pm. Wheelchair-accessible. Museum €12.50, students and seniors €7.50, under 12 accompanied by adult free. Audio tour included in admission price.)*

MUSEO DE BELLAS ARTES. Although it can't boast the name recognition of the Guggenheim, the Museo de Bellas Artes wins the favor of locals. The museum has an impressive collection of 12th- to 20th-century art, featuring excellent 15th- to 17th-century Flemish paintings and works by El Greco, Zurbarán, Goya, Gauguin, Francis Bacon, Velázquez, and Mary Cassatt, as well as canvases by Basque artists. A separate section showcases contemporary art, with works by Basque sculptors Chillida and Oteiza. *(Pl. del Museo, 2. Take C. Elcano to Pl. del Museo or bus #10 from Pte. del Arenal. ☎944 39 60 60. Guided visit every Sunday at noon with reservations; call ahead ☎944 39 61 47. Open Tu-Sa 10am-8pm, Su 10am-2pm. €5.50, students and seniors €4, under 12 free. W free. Guided visit €4.)*

NIGHTLIFE AND ENTERTAINMENT

Bilbao has a thriving bar scene. In the *casco viejo*, revelers spill out into the streets to sip their *txikitos* (chee-KEE-tos; small glasses of wine), especially off of Barrenkale, one of the seven original streets from which the city of Bilbao has grown. The action in the *casco viejo* tends to die down around 2am. Then, teenagers and 20-somethings fill C. Licenciado Poza on the west side of town, especially between C. General Concha and Alameda de Recalde, where a covered alleyway connecting C. Licenciado Poza and Alameda de Urquijo teems with bars and loud, flashy discotecas. Laid-back **Alambique,** Alda. Urquijo, 37, provides elegant seating and chance for conversation under chandeliers and photos of old Bilbao. (☎944 43 41 88. Beer €2-3. Open M-Th 8am-2am, F-Sa 8am-3am, Su 5pm-3am.) **The Cotton Club,** C. Gregorio de la Revilla, 25 (entrance on C. Simón Bolívar, around the corner from the metro stop), decorated with over 30,000 beer bottle caps, draws a huge crowd on Friday and Saturday nights, while the rest of the week draws a more lowkey 30-something crowd. A DJ spins Friday and Saturday at 1am; occasional live concerts with notable Spanish artists. (☎944 10 49 51. Beer €3. Over 100 choices of whiskey; mixed drinks €6. Rum €6. Open M-Th 5pm-3:30am, F-Sa 5pm-6am, Su 6:30pm-3:30am.)

FESTIVALS

The massive fiesta in honor of *Nuestra Señora de Begoña* takes place during **Aste Nagusia,** a nine-day party in late August, with fireworks, concerts, theater, bullfighting—you name it. Pick up a *Bilbao Guide* from the tourist office for event listings. Street theater takes over the Pl. Arriaga in mid-July. Documentary and fantasy filmmakers from all over the world gather for a week in December for the **Festival Internacional de Cine Documental y Cortometraje de Bilbao.** Contact the tourist office for specific information and ticket sales, or visit www.zinebi.com/fant. Each January, Bilbao hosts **Zinegoak,** an international festival of gay, lesbian, and transgender film (www.zinegoak.com). During the summer, the municipal band offers free **concerts** every other Sunday morning at the bandstand in Pl. Arriaga, Parque del Arenal in winter. Bilbao is also the home of a world-class opera season (www.abao.org, tickets range from €53-169). Catch some *fútbol* at an Athletic de Bilbao match at **Campo de San Mamés.**

ASTURIAS AND CANTABRIA

Asturias and Cantabria are a far cry from familiar sun-and-tapas Spain. These tiny northern regions, tucked between País Vasco and Galicia, are distinguished by endless greenery, precipitous ravines, and jagged cliffs. The impassable peaks of the Cordillera Cantábrica halted the advance of the Moors, making Asturias and Cantabria the stronghold of the Visigoth Christians, who left behind a trail of pre-Romanesque churches. Cut off from the rest of Spain during Moorish rule of the country, today the Asturians and Cantabrians take pride in their states' preservation of "true Spain." It was the Asturian hero Don Pelayo who officially launched the *Reconquista* in AD 722 from the Picos hamlet of Covadonga, a campaign that lasted until the fall of Granada in 1492. Today the heir to the Spanish throne is titled the Príncipe de Asturias. Asturias and Cantabria remain somewhat isolated from Spain proper—the endless, rough terrain has limited the number of rail lines through the regions, leaving lone roads to wind along the steep mountain sides and scalloped shore. These two little territories also maintain cultures that differ from the rest of Spain—they have their own dialects, drinking customs, and way of life.

Despite their shared landscape and location, Asturias and Cantabria have distinct personalities from one another as well. Asturias draws hearty mountaineers looking to reach new heights in its national parks, while Cantabria—with the world-class resort towns of Santander and Comillas—appeals to Spain's vacationing elite. Cuisine also distinguishes the two regions. Asturias is famous for its apples, strong cheeses, wholesome fresh fruit, and *arroz con leche* (rice pudding); true Asturians can be recognized by the way they take their cider, poured from several feet above and downed immediately. Cantabrian cuisine comes from the mountains and the sea, with *cocido montanés* (bean stew) and *marmita* (tuna, potato, and green pepper stew) as popular delicacies. No matter what's on the menu, portions are always hearty and filling.

HIGHLIGHTS OF ASTURIAS AND CANTABRIA

RELAX on the renowned Península de Magdalena in **Santander** (p. 340).

SWIG some of Asturias's famous cidra in **Oviedo** (p. 335).

BURY your feet in the silky sand of **Comillas** (p. 347).

ASTURIAS

Mountain ranges and dense alpine forests define the Asturian landscape. Though Asturias never fell to the marauding Moors, today visitors invade to take advantage of the booming adventure tourism industry in the Parque Nacional Picos de Europa. The wide swaths of sand and lively waves of Gijón draw swarms of beachgoers, but plenty of quiet, cliff-lined coves lie just off the beaten path, where tropical and alpine vegetation mingle.

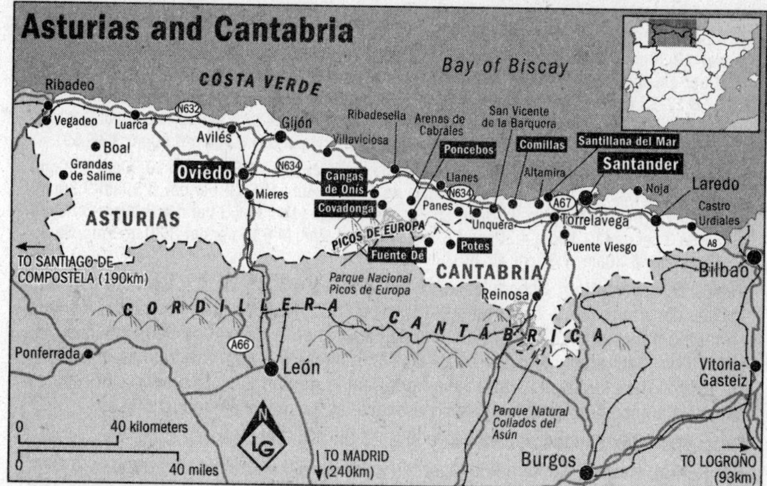

OVIEDO

☎958

Although the city of Oviedo (pop. 200,000) has faded into the background of Spanish political life, its bustling old quarter, immense park, spectacular art museum, and endless shopping are more than enough to keep visitors busy for several days. Oviedo's name comes from the Latin *urbis* (city), and for a few centuries, it was the most important city in Spain. As a haven from Moorish attacks, Oviedo became the epicenter of the *Reconquista* and was made the capital of the Kingdom of Asturias around AD 810. If the urban scene isn't for you, the mountains on the horizon, with majestic Monte Naranco minutes away and the Picos de Europa beyond, allow you to explore the countryside.

TRANSPORTATION

Flights: Aeropuerto de Ranón/Aeropuerto Nacional de Asturias (☎985 12 75 00), in Avilés, 28km from Oviedo. **ALSA** runs buses from the station to the airport M-F every hour 6am-11pm, €5.80. **Aviaco** (☎985 12 76 03) and **Iberia** (☎985 12 76 07) fly to **Barcelona, London,** and **Madrid.**

Trains: Both **RENFE** and **FEVE** serve Oviedo from **Estación del Norte,** Av. de Santander.

FEVE (☎985 29 76 56), 3rd fl. Info open daily 7am-9:30pm. To: **Bilbao** (7-8hr.; 9am, 3:35pm €20.55); **El Ferrol** (6hr.; 7:47am, 2:47pm; €19.35) via **Ribadeo** (4hr., €10); **Llanes** (2hr., 5 per day 9:05am-6:55pm, €6.95); **Santander** (4hr.; 9:05am, 3:35pm; €13.20).

RENFE (☎902 24 02 02), 1st fl. Pay attention to the type of train; a slow local train through the mountains can double your travel time. Info open daily 8am-9pm. To: **Barcelona** (12-13hr.; daily 10:57am, 7:34pm; €48-56) via **Burgos** (5-6hr., €25-29); **Gijón** (30min.; daily 3-4 11:10am-10:05pm, Sa-Su also at 10:29pm; €2.60-10.80); **León** (2hr.; M-F 7 per day 7:29am-7:24pm, Sa-Su 7 per day 7:43am-8:50pm; €7-18); **Madrid** (6-9hr., 3 per day 7:43am-6:43pm, €45.30) via **Valladolid** (4hr., €28).

Buses: Information open daily 7am-10:30pm. **ALSA** (national) and **Económicos/EASA** (regional) buses run out of the station on C. Pepe Cosmen (☎902 49 99 49). Open daily 6:30am-12:30am.

ALSA (☎902 422 242). To: **Barcelona** (12hr.; 8:30am, 7:30pm; €51); **Burgos** (3hr.; 8:30am, 7:30pm; €16.67); **La Coruña** (4-6hr.; M-Sa 6 per day 6:30am-6:30pm, Su 6 per day

6:30am-7pm; €21-35); **León** (1½hr., 9-12 per day 12:30am-10:30pm, €8.30); **Logroño** (6hr.; 8:30am, 7:30pm; €23-25). **Madrid** (5hr.; M-Sa 11-13 per day 12:30am-7:30pm, Su 14 per day 12:30am-7:30pm; €31-49); **San Sebastián** (6-8hr.; M-Sa 6-8 per day 1am-5:45pm, Su 8 per day 1am-9:45pm; €25-45); **Santander** (3-4hr.; M-Th, Sa 10-12 per day 1am-8:45pm, F, Su 12-13 per day 1am-9:45pm; €13-22); **Santiago de Compostela** (5-7hr.; 6 per day M-Sa 6:30am-6:30pm, Su until 7pm; €26-38); **Valladolid** (3-4hr.; M-Sa 5 per day 12:30am-6:30pm, Su 6 per day 12:30am-7:30pm; €17.63); **Vigo** (7-9hr.; 4 per day 6:30am-6:30pm; €36-59).

Económicos/EASA (☎985 29 00 39). To: **Arenas de Cabrales** (2hr.; M-F 3 per day 10:30am-6:30pm, Sa-Su 10:30am, 6:30pm; €8.10); **Cangas de Onís** (1½hr.; M-F 12 per day 6:30am-9:30pm, Sa-Su 7-8 per day 8:30am-9:30pm; €5.70); **Covadonga** (1hr.; M-F 3 per day 8:30am-3:30pm, Sa-Su 3 per day 12:15pm-4:30pm; €6.70); **Llanes** (1-2hr.; M-F 14 per day 8:30am-9pm, Sa-Su 11 per day 8:30am- 7:30pm; €8.80).

Public Transportation: Schedules vary, but **TUA** (☎985 22 24 22, www.tua.es) runs buses daily between 6-7am until 10-11pm (€0.85). All stops have bus maps. #4 runs from the train station down C. Uría, turning off just before Campo de San Francisco. #2 goes from both stations to the hospital. #2, 5, and 7 run from the train station along C. Uría to the old city. #10 also runs from Campo de San Francisco and C. Uría up to Monte Naranco. Bus schedule usually available at the municipal tourist office.

Taxis: Radio Taxi Ciudad de Oviedo (☎985 25 00 00). 24hr. service.

Car Rental: Hertz, C. Ventura Rodríguez, 4 (☎985 26 39 05). From €45 per day. 200km limit. 23+, must have had license for 2 years; under 25 €8 extra per day. Open M-F 9am-1pm and 4-7:30pm, Sa 9:30am-noon. AmEx/MC/V.

ORIENTATION AND PRACTICAL INFORMATION

The train station is at the top of **Calle Uría,** the city's main passage. Follow it downhill from the station to the city center and *casco viejo*, with the park, **Campo de San Francisco,** on your right. The cathedral is down C. San Francisco from C. Uría. From the bus station, turn right out of the main entrance and walk up the road, which will bring you C. Uria in front of the train station.

Tourist Office: Regional Office, C. Cimadevilla, 4 (☎985 21 33 85). Open Sept.-June daily 10am-7pm, July-Aug. 1am-8pm. **Municipal Office,** C. Marqués de Santa Cruz, 1 (☎985 22 75 86). Open Sept.-June daily 10am-2pm and 4:30-7pm, July-Aug. 9:30am-2pm and 4:30-7:30pm. Branch in *Ayuntamiento* stays open through siesta.

Currency Exchange: Banco Santander Central Hispano, C. Pelayo Esq. Alonso Quintanilla (☎985 24 24 24). Branch, C. Uría, 1 (☎985 10 60 00), across the street from the park. Both open Apr.-Sept. M-F 8:30am-2pm; Oct.-Mar. M-F 8:30am-2pm, Sa 8:30am-1pm.

Luggage Storage: Lockers at the train station (open daily 7am-11pm; medium bags €3 per day, large €4.50) and the bus station (open daily 6:30-12:30am; €2 per day).

English-Language Bookstore: Librería Cervantes, C. Dr. Casal, 9 (☎985 20 77 61). The English-language book section is on the 2nd floor. Open M-Sa 10am-1:30pm and 4:15-8:15pm. Closed the last two Sa of July and the first two Sa of Aug. MC/V.

Laundromat: C. Emilio Alarcos Llorach, 1. (☎985 08 88 66). Open daily 9am-10pm.

Police: Municipal, C. General Yague (☎985 11 34 77), across the street from Hotel Reconquista. Main office located on the Carretera del Rubín. **Guardia Civil** (☎985 28 02 04), also located on the Carreterra del Rubín, next door to the municipal office.

Pharmacy: Farmacia Dr. Luis Gómez Prado, C. Magdalena, 17 (☎985 20 30 84).

Medical Services: Hospital Central de Asturias, C. Calvo Sotelo. (☎985 10 61 00) **Emergencies:** ☎112.

Internet Access: Free internet at **Biblioteca de Asturias Ramon Perez Ayala,** Pl. Daoíz y Velarde, 11. Max. 30min. Open M-F 8:30am-8:50pm, Sa 10pm-1am and 4-8:50pm, Su

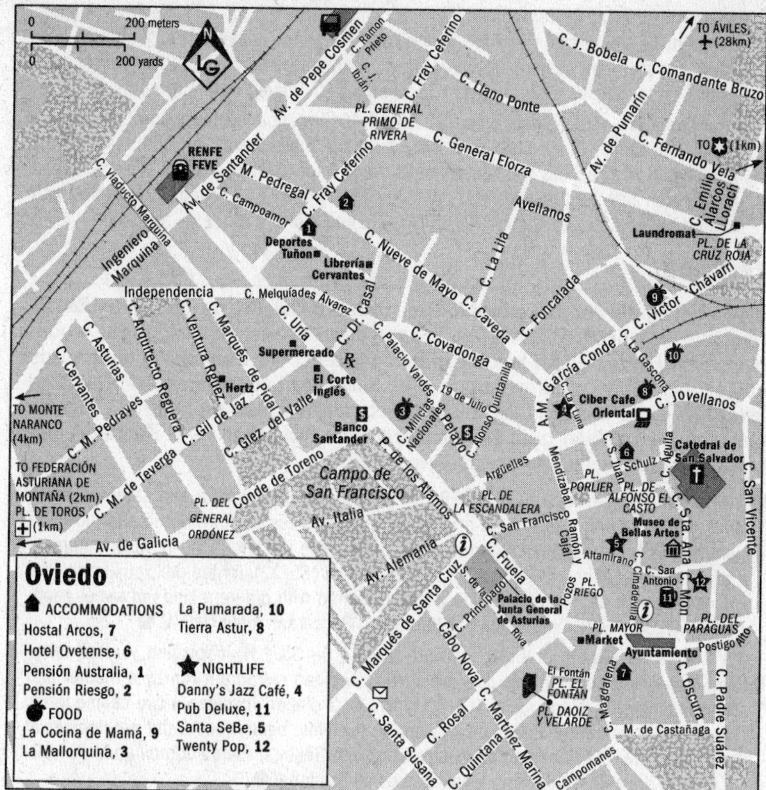

10am-1pm. **Ciber Cafe Oriental,** C. Jovellanos, 8 (☎985 20 28 97). €1.50 per 30min., €2.20 per hr., €3.90 per 2hr. Free Wi-Fi. Open M-F 8am-1am, Sa-Su 9am-3am.

Post Office: C. Santa Susana, 18 (☎985 20 88 62). **Lista de Correos,** fax, and photocopying. Open M-F 8:30am-8:30pm, Sa 9:30am-2pm. **Postal Code:** 33007.

ACCOMMODATIONS

Although *pensiones*, *hostales*, and hotels pack the new city on C. Uría, C. Campoamor, and C. Nueve de Mayo, cheap accommodations can be scarce in July and August. Most rooms are clean and many are in restored buildings, offering comfort and convenience at a higher price than nearby cities.

Hostal Arcos, C. Magdalena, 3, 2nd fl. (☎985 21 47 73). Minutes away from the grand cathedral. Vibrant paint colors and photos of Oviedo at its finest adorn the walls of this romantic, friendly hostel. All rooms have TVs and free Wi-Fi, and a few come with chandeliers. Singles €30-35; doubles €40-55, depending on the season. Cash only. ❸

Pensión Riesgo, C. Nueve de Mayo, 16 (☎985 21 89 45). Doilies, heavy curtains, and mismatched bedspreads decorate this *pensión*. Wheelchair-accessible. Singles €15; doubles €26-28, with shower €28-30; summer prices average €3 more. Cash only. ❶

Pensión Australia, C. Campoamor, 14, 2nd fl. (☎985 22 22 67). Centrally located between the train station and the park. Expansive rooms come with a TV and big windows, but they can seem a bit bare. Clean, common bathroom and cozy living room. Laundry free. Singles €22; doubles €35; triples €40. Shared bath. Cash only. ❷

Hotel Ovetense, C. San Juan, 6 (☎985 22 08 40; www.hotelovetense.com). Well-maintained but small rooms just steps away from the main plaza. Full bath, satellite TV, phone, and Wi-Fi access. Restaurant and *sidrería* (cider bar) downstairs. Reserve ahead in summer. July-Sept. singles €37, doubles €53, triples €63, quads (2 doubles with shared bath.) €85. Oct.-June €30/45/57/75. AmEx/MC/V. ❹

FOOD

If you have only enough euros for one drink in Oviedo, be sure to try **sidra** (cider) by the bottle (€1.50-3.60). For the best experience, head to the wood-beamed *sidrerías* (cider houses), where waiters pour from above their heads and expect you to swallow in one gulp. *Sidrerías* line **C. Gaconga**—"The Boulevard of Cider"—and cheap restaurants can be found on C. Fray Ceferino between the bus and train stations. The **indoor market** at Pl. el Fontán (open M-Sa 8am-8pm) sells produce and groceries.

Tierra Astur, C. La Gascona, 1 (☎985 20 25 02). Wooden *terraza* and cavernous interior, complete with a faux meat market. The perfect place to down bottle after bottle of *sidra* (€5) with traditional Asturian meat and cheese platters (€5-14). Also features a wide selection of salads and generous fish entrees (€5-22). Try the delicious traditional desserts, such as *frixuelos,* a type of crepe stuffed with different kinds of sweet goodness (€3.30-4.80). Open daily 1-4:30pm and 8pm-1am. AmEx/MC/V. ❸

La Cocina de Mamá, C. Victor Chavarri, 9 (984 08 35 13). If you find yourself missing home, head over to this cozy, welcoming Asturian restaurant run by a mother and her daughter. Delicious *menú* (€8.50 lunch, €10 dinner) includes a two-course meal, wine and bread, and homemade dessert. Try the white bean *fabada,* the *escalopines al cabrales,* and the decadent chocolate cake with Bailey's. *Platos combinados* (€4.50-7). Open daily 8am-midnight. Meals served all day long. ❷

La Mallorquina, C. Milicias Nacionales, 5 (☎985 22 40 75; www.la-mallorquina.net). This restaurant has a glass terrace and the feel of a Parisian cafe. Magnificent range of cakes, pastries, and chocolates. Salads (€8-14), sandwiches (€3-7), and entrees (€10-18). Open M-F 7am-11pm, Sa 7:30am-11pm, Su 8am-11pm. AmEx/MC/V. ❷

La Pumarada, C. Gascona, 8 (☎985 20 02 79). Down the street from Tierra Astur. Popular for its Asturian entrees and *sidra*-soaked atmosphere. Waiters pour cider from bottles high over their heads, and every table has a bucket to catch the spills. Tapas €6-15. Entrees €8-22. Sidra €2.50. Open daily 9am-1:30am. MC/V. ❸

SIGHTS

MUSEO DE BELLAS ARTES. The three beautifully maintained buildings of the Museo de Bellas Artes in the Palacio de Velarde display one of the best public art collections in Spain. In addition to the Klimt-esque work of Hermen Anglada Camarasa, highlights include 18 pieces of the original *Retablo de Santa Marina* and works by Goya, Velázquez, Sorolla, Dalí and Picasso—there is also an entire room on the first floor full of saint portraits by El Greco. *(C. Santa Ana, 1, just up from Pl. de Alfonso II. ☎985 21 30 61. Open July-Aug. Tu-Sa 10:30am-2pm and 4-8pm, Su 10:30am-2:30pm; Sept.-June Tu-F 10:30am-2pm and 4:30-8:30pm, Sa 11:30am-2pm and 5-8pm, Su 11:30am-2:30pm. Free.)*

CATEDRAL DE SAN SALVADOR. A recent renovation restored Oviedo's 14th-century Gothic cathedral to its original splendor. The **Capilla de Santa María del Rey Casto,** which contains the royal pantheon, was chosen by Alfonso II el Casto in AD 802 to house the remains of Asturian monarchs and Christian relics rescued from the Moors. In this chapel, also look for the statue of San Pedro holding a metal key in his hand. According to legend, if you make three wishes and turn the key around three times, one of the wishes will come true. The cathedral complex includes pristine cloisters, the famous crypt of **Santa Leocadia,** which holds the remains of the martyrs Eulogio and Leocadia, and a *cámara santa* (holy chamber) containing several enormous golden and jeweled crosses. The highlights of the church museum, a Bible from the 12th century and a modern painting of Mother Teresa, warrant the entrance fee. *(Pl. de Alfonso II. ☎985 22 10 33. Open July-Sept. daily 10:15am-8pm. Last entry 7:15. Oct.-June 10:15am-1pm and 4-6pm. Cathedral free. Cámara Santa €1.50. Museum, including cloisters and crypt, €3; children €1.50. Th evening free.)*

MONTE NARANCO. Take an afternoon away from the hustle and bustle of Oviedo and venture into the Picos by way of Monte Naranco. Not only does the mountain make for a pleasant half-day hike, but it also showcases some of Asturias' oldest sites. The recreational palace **Santa María del Naranco** and the royal church of **San Miguel de Lillo,** located on the side of Monte Naranco, both built in the 9th century, represent some of the first European attempts to blend architecture, sculpture, and murals after the fall of the Roman Empire. A guided tour around the two ancient buildings will tell you all about how the two buildings were utilized when Asturias was the last defense against the Moors. The top of Monte Naranco is approximately a 4km hike from the center of Oviedo. Bus #10 takes you near the top, but the walk up the mountain should take no more than two hours; the municipal tourist office has maps. Although the main trail is a bit steep, the path brings you through some of the beautiful greenery around Oviedo and allows you a glimpse of the majestic mountains surrounding the city. *(From C. Uría, take bus #10 toward the train station. Daily 7:50am, then hourly 8:30am-7:30pm, 8:15pm, 9:40pm.; €0.75. ☎676 03 20 87. Both structures open Apr.-Sept. Tu-Sa 9:30am-1pm; 3:30-7pm, M-Su 9:30am-1pm; Oct.-March M 10am-1pm, Tu-Sa 10am-12:30pm, 3-4:30pm, Su 10am-12:30pm. €3, children €2. M free, but no guide.)*

NIGHTLIFE

The streets south of the cathedral, especially C. Mon and around Pl. Riego, Pl. el Fontán, and Pl. el Paraguas, teem with noisy *sidrerías* and clubs. Mid-week nightlife in Oviedo is pretty tame, and some clubs and pubs close despite official weekday hours. But from Thursday to Saturday, the discotecas and bars keep the music pumping all night long. **Pub Deluxe,** C. Mon 15, has both a laid-back bar and disco-dance club feel, and is popular with younger crowd. (Beer €2.50-3. Drinks €4.50. Open M-W and Su 11pm-3:30am, Th 11pm-4:30am, F-Sa 11pm-5:30am.) After a few *chupitos* (shots) and *copas* (mixed drinks), most students head to one of the clubs near the Pl. Riesgo. **Twenty Pop,** C. Mon, 12, features pop music and 70s decor, while **Santa SeBe,** C. Altamirano, 6, has a vaguely psychedelic feel. Both clubs pick up after 2am and are popular with locals. (Beer €2.20-2.50. Mixed drinks €3.50-5. Open weekends 11pm-5:30am.) At **Danny's Jazz Café,** C. La Luna, 11, between C. Alcalde M. García Conde and C. Jovellanos, Nat King Cole and Miles Davis LPs fill the walls. A lively spot even mid-week. Live music is an occasional treat. (☎985 21 14 83. Beer €2.80. Mixed drinks €5.50. Open M-Th, Su 11pm-3:30am, F-Sa 11pm-4:30am.) Wine connoisseurs follow *la ruta de los vinos* (the wine route) from bar to bar along **C. El**

Rosal. For about 10 days around Sept. 21, Oviedo throws a fiesta with concerts and processions in honor of its patron saint, San Mateo.

OUTDOOR ACTIVITIES

If you're headed to the **Parque Nacional Picos de Europa,** Oviedo is definitely the place to stock up on gear and supplies, as shops within the park and in gateway towns can be prohibitively expensive. A good first stop is the **Federación Asturiana de Montaña,** Av. de Julián Clavería, 11, near the bullring and university, a 30min. walk from the city center, or take bus #2 (dir.: Hospital) from C. Uría. From the bus stop, go into green gate for the **Federación Deportivos del Principado de Asturia,** enter the building through the second door on the right, and go up to the second floor. This office is in charge of all outdoor activities in the national park and can direct visitors to branches throughout the area. It organizes excursions and provides guides and advice on weather and the best hiking routes. Instructors for everything from paragliding to kayaking are available, and the office also provides guidance on gear suppliers in Oviedo. (☎985 25 23 62; www.fempa.net. Open M-Th 10am-2pm.)

SALUD! The quality of an establishment's *sidra* can be measured by the server's style of pouring. Generally, the higher they hold the bottle over their heads and the farther down and more horizontally they hold the glass, the better the *sidra* is. Remember to down your glass quickly, in true Asturian style, to get all the good fizz at the top. Watch your shoes, as servers often care more about the height of their pour than the amount they spill.

CANTABRIA

From the spectacle of Santander's El Sardinero beaches to the provincial park of Oyambre, it's the coast that makes Cantabria famous. Though it has yet to see the resort build-up of Spain's southern shores, the region's beach towns, declared by some to have the world's cleanest surfing water, are by no means untouched or secluded. Cantabria also has hiking in the Picos de Europa, Paleolithic cave drawings, and renowned architecture, including Gaudí's **El Capricho** and the 12th-century **Colegiata de Santa Juliana** in Santillana del Mar.

SANTANDER ☎942

Every summer in Santander (pop. 185,000), beautiful coastline and miles of spotless, sandy beaches play host to thousands of tourists looking to catch up on their tans. Palm trees rub shoulders with pines, pasty Brits bake next to bronzed Spaniards, and the hustle and bustle of the city center is easily forgotten on a stroll down El Sardinero's vine-filled boardwalks. Santander became fashionable thanks to royal attention; King Alfonso XIII summered in the early 20th century on Peninsula La Magdalena, and hotels now occupy the summer palaces of his court in El Sardinero. Santander is well-visited, yet far more relaxed than the frenetic beaches in the Costa del Sol, and in the weeks between its big summer festivals, the crowds thin a little. With a mountainous horizon and cliff-top lighthouses, Santander is the Bay of Biscay at its best.

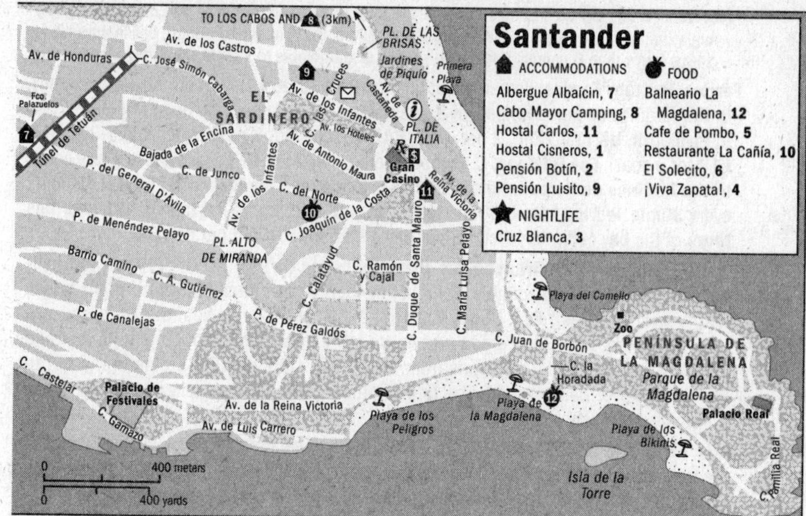

TRANSPORTATION

Flights: Aeropuerto de Santander, Av. de Parayas (☎942 20 21 00; www.aena.es), in nearby Camargo (5km away). Serviced by many European budget airlines, including **Ryanair.** Accessible by taxi (€15-17); buses run from bus station to airport every 15-30min. 6:30am-10:45pm (€1.50).

Trains: FEVE (☎942 20 95 22; www.feve.es) and **RENFE** (☎902 24 02 02; www.renfe.es), Pl. de las Estaciones. RENFE serves distant destinations to the south, as Santander is the terminus of a national rail line; take a regional FEVE train to cities east or west of Santander. RENFE info open daily 8:30am-1pm and 3:30-9pm; station open 5am-12:30am. RENFE goes to **Madrid** (5-6hr.; M-F 3 per day 7:05am-7:20pm, Sa 2 per day 7:05am, 2:05pm, Su 4 per day 7:05-7:20pm; €31.75-44.20), **Valladolid** (3-4hr., 5-8 per day 7:05am-8:10pm, €14.90-26.40) and **Palencia** (2-3hr.; 5-7 per day 7:05am-7:20pm, Su 7:05am-8:10pm; €11.75-23.20) as well as **Barcelona** to the west (9-10hr.; daily 10:05am, Su-F 12:25pm; €40-52.90, overnight bunk €50.90. FEVE goes to: **Bilbao** (2¾hr., 3 per day 8am- 2pm,7pm, €7.35) and **Oviedo** (4hr.; 9:10am, 4:10pm; €13.50), as well as several local destinations.

Buses: C. Navas de Tolosa directly in front of train stations (☎942 21 19 95; www.santandereabus.com). Info open daily 8am-10pm.

ALSA (☎902 42 22 02; www.alsa.es) goes to: **Barcelona** (8-9hr.; 9am, 9pm; €47.31) via Lleida (8hr., 9pm only, €36.86); **Bilbao** (1hr., every 30min.-1hr. 3:45am-11:59pm, €6.44-11.80); **Oviedo** (3hr.; 8-12 per day 7:15am-8pm and 3:30am, F, Su also 10:15pm; €12.59-21.70); **San Sebastián** (2-3hr.; 9-11 per day 3:45am-8:30pm, Su also 11:55pm; €12.48-23.71); **Salamanca** (6hr.; 8:30am, 5pm.; €16.05) and **Vitoria-Gasteiz** (2½hr., 4-5 per day 8am-9pm, €10.33).

Continental Auto (☎902 33 04 00; www.continental-auto.es) goes to: **Madrid** (6hr.; M-Sa 6 per day 12:30am-7pm, Su 8 per day 12:30am-11:59pm; €26.43-39); and **Burgos** (4hr.; M-Sa 6 per day 8am-12:30am, Su 8 per day 12:30am-8pm; €10.12-18.50).

La Cantabrica (☎942 72 08 22) runs buses to **Comillas** (1hr., €3.40) through **Santillana del Mar** (40min., €2.15; Sept.-June M-F 4 per day 10:30am-7:15pm, Sa-Su 3 per day 11:30am-8:30pm; July-Aug. M-F 7 per day 8:30am-9:30pm, Sa-Su 5 per day 10:30am-9:30pm). Buy tickets onboard.

Palomera (☎942 88 06 11) runs buses to the town of **Potes** in the **Picos de Europa** during July-Aug. (2hr.; M-F 3 per day 10:30am-5pm, Sa 10:30am, 3:15pm, Su 10:30am). Call in advance for groups larger than 6 people. Continuing service also available to **Fuente Dé** during July and Aug.

Ferries: Brittany Ferries, Estación Marítima (☎942 36 06 11; www.brittany-ferries.com), by the Jardines de Pereda. Reserve 2 weeks ahead in summer. Info open M-F 9am-7pm. To **Plymouth, UK** (18-22hr., 2 per week, €45-73, car with 2 passengers €225-363 plus €10 for a seat). **Los Reginas,** C. Embarcadero (☎942 21 67 53; www.losreginas.com), by the **Jardines de Pereda,** runs to **Pedreña, Somo,** and the **Playas del Puntal** (15min., every 30min. leaving from 8:30am, returning until 8:25pm, round-trip €3.90), and runs **tours** of the bay (1hr., July-Oct. 13 per day 11:15am-8:30pm per day, €8).

Public Transportation: Transportes Urbanos buses (☎942 20 07 71) run throughout the city (July-Aug. roughly 6am-11pm, Sept.-June 6am-10:30pm; night buses hourly midnight-6am; €1). Buses #1, 4, 7, 9, 13, and 14 run from the *Ayuntamiento* to El Sardinero on Po. de Pereda and Av. de la Reina Victoria, stopping at Pl. de Italia and Jardines de Piquío. #15 runs from the RENFE station to El Sardinero and out to the Cabo Mayor campground. The tourist office gives out free schedules, and maps are posted at every stop.

Taxis: (☎942 33 33 33 or 36 91 91). 24hr. service to greater Santander. Taxis wait outside the train and bus stations, on C. Vargas, and near the *Ayuntamiento* as well as by the Gran Casino in El Sardinero. The tourist office has a map with all taxi stops throughout the city.

Car Rental: Avis (☎942 22 0 25), in the RENFE parking lot, Pl. de los Estaciones. 21+, must have had license for 1 year. Open M-F 8:30am-1pm and 4-7:30pm, Sa 9am-1pm. **National** (☎942 22 29 26), right next to Avis. Open M-F 9am-1pm and 4-7pm, Sa 9am-1pm, Su 10am-1pm.

ORIENTATION AND PRACTICAL INFORMATION

Santander sits on a peninsula in the Bay of Biscay, and its southern shores form the Bahía de Santander. There are two main sections of the city: **El Centro,** around the train and bus stations and the Jardines de Pereda, and **El Sardinero,** along the beach to the east. El Centro and El Sardinero are separated by a hill. The main roads connecting them are the **Túnel de Tetuán** and the main thoroughfare, which starts at the *Ayuntamiento* as **Avenida Calvo Sotelo** and runs along the shore to the Jardines de Piquío in El Sardinero, changing its name to **Paseo de Pereda** and **Avenida de la Reina Victoria** along the way. Santander's famed park, **La Península de la Magdalena,** sits at the eastern tip of Santander. The best way to get around is by bus on one of the free bikes loaned out by the tourist office.

Tourist Office: Regional office inside Mercado del Este (☎942 31 07 08; www.turismocantabria.com), open July-Sept. daily 9am-9pm; Oct.-June daily 9:30am-1:30pm and 4-7pm. Santander tourism office in Jardines de Pereda (☎942 20 30 00; www.ayto-santander.es). Open daily July-Aug. 9am-9pm; Sept.-June M-F 8:30am-7pm, Sa 10am-2pm. **Branch** in El Sardinero, across from the grand casino, open July-Aug. daily 10am-9pm; June M-F 10am-7pm, Sa-Su 10am-2pm. Both branches, as well as a booth on the Península de La Magdalena, rent out **free bicycles** for 4hr. Open daily July-Aug. 10am-7pm; Sept.-June 10am-2pm and 4-6pm. Closed Nov.-Jan.

Currency Exchange: Banco Santander Central Hispano, on Av. Calvo Sotelo. **Branch** at Pl. de Italia. Open May-Sept. M-F 8:30am-2pm, Oct.-Apr. also Sa 8:30am-1pm. 24hr.

Luggage Storage: Lockers at the **bus station** on the bottom level. Open daily 6am-midnight. Consignment for large items (€2.40 per item per day) M-F 7am-10pm, Sa 7am-1am. Passport or local ID required.

Police: Pl. Canadio (☎092).

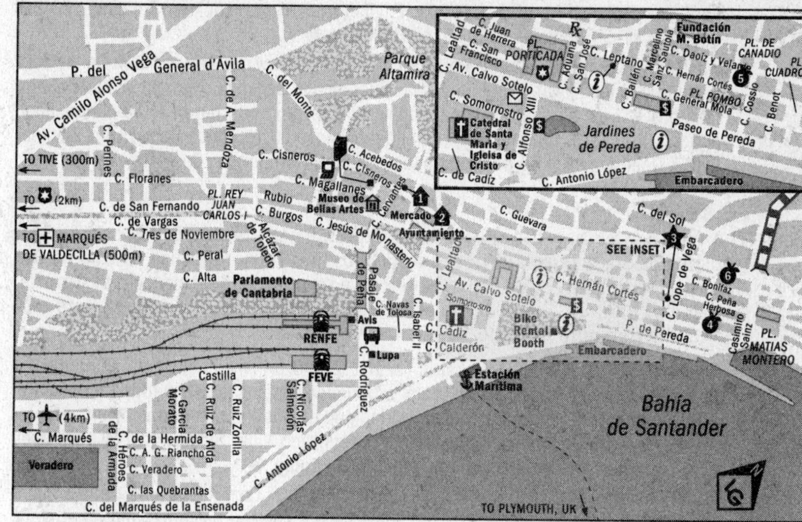

Hospital: Hospital Universitario Marqués de Valdecilla, Av. de Valdecilla, 25 (☎942 20 25 20). For **emergencies** call ☎061.

Pharmacy: Farmacia Calvo Sotelo on Av. Calvo Sotelo (☎942 22 43 15). 24hr. In El Sardinero, **Somacarrera,** Pl. de Italia, 1 (☎942 27 05 96), underneath the Gran Casino. Open daily 9:30am-1:30pm and 4:30-8pm. For locations of late-night pharmacies, check the schedule at any pharmacy.

Internet: Free at the **Biblioteca Pública,** C. Gravina 4 (☎942 24 15 50) July-Aug. M-F 8:15am-1:45pm, Sept.-June daily 8:15am-1:45pm and 4-9:30pm. Also at **Divernet Informática,** C. Cisneros, 29 (☎942 24 14 25). English spoken. €2 per hour. Open M-Sa 9:30am-2pm and 3:30-8:30pm, Su 4-9:30pm.

Post Office: Av. Alfonso XIII (☎942 36 55 19). Open M-F 8:30am-8:30pm, Sa 9:30am-2pm. **Branch** in El Sardinero on Av. Castaneda. Open M-F 8:30am-8:30pm, Sa 9:30am-1pm. **Lista de Correos** and fax. **Postal Code:** 39080.

ACCOMMODATIONS AND CAMPING

Accommodations fill quickly in July and August, especially during the big festivals, so reserve ahead. For a complete list of *pensiones* and *hostales* along with their prices, contact the tourist office or visit its website.

EL SARDINERO

Lodging in El Sardinero is available along the busy Reina Victoria, overlooking the bay and close to the beaches and promenade. There are also a few quieter *pensiones* along Av. de las Castros. From the *Ayuntamiento* in El Centro, ask bus drivers to drop you off at El Piquío (Hotel Colón).

Pensión Luisito, Av. de los Castros, 11 (☎942 27 19 71). Well-kept rooms and an incredibly friendly owner will make you feel right at home. Many have spacious balconies, and some overlook the garden and a slice of the sea. Room sinks, hall baths. Breakfast €2.82 Open July-mid-Sept. Singles €26; doubles €44. Cash only. ❷

Hostal Carlos, Av. de la Reina Victoria, 135 (☎942 27 16 16). Stay in the wood-floored and marble-sculptured palace where King Alfonso XIII put up his favorite barons at the beginning of the 1900s. English and French spoken. Breakfast €3.60. Singles €37-56; doubles €53-76. AmEx/MC/V. ❹

Cabo Mayor Camping, Av. del Faro (☎942 39 15 42; www.cabomayor.com). On the scenic bluff of Cabo Mayor, 3km from Playas Primera and Segunda. From the *Ayuntamiento,* take bus #15 to "Camping." By car, follow Av. del Faro north out of El Sardinero. Pool, currency exchange, supermarket, bar, and tennis courts. Reception 8am-11pm. Electricity €3. Open Apr.-Oct. €5 per adult and per tent, €4.50 per car. Cash only. ❶

EL CENTRO

The city center has the advantage of being near cheap food, convenient transportation, a pleasant portside *paseo,* and busy nightlife. North of the *Ayuntamiento* and Av. de Calvo Sotelo is a tranquil collection of restaurants, shops, and bars. Pl. Santa Lucia is the nucleus of several blocks of bars and nightclubs that spill into the streets on weekends.

Pensión Botín, C. Isabel II, 1, 1st fl. (☎942 21 00 94; www.pensionbotin.com). The committed owners have over 20 years' experience keeping guests happy. Immaculate, homey rooms, some with balconies overlooking the market behind the *Ayuntamiento*. All rooms have TV, brand-new private showers, and sink. Singles €27-40; doubles €36-58; ask about rates for rooms of up to 5 people. ❸

Hostal Cisneros, C. Cisneros, 8, 1st fl. (☎942 21 16 13). Cozy rooms have clean wooden floors overlooking the nearby streets. Some have a covered balcony. Shared baths, TV, free Wi-Fi. Sept-June singles €25; doubles €35. July-Aug. all rooms €51. Cash only. ❷

Albergue Albaícin, C. Francisco Palazuelos 21-23, (☎942 21 77 53). A school that converts classrooms into dorm-style rooms in the summer; probably your only chance to write on a blackboard from your bed. On the hill above El Centro, it has stunning views of the bay, but be prepared for a steep climb. Coin-operated laundry machines. Breakfast included. Open July-Aug. Bunks in 10-bed mixed or single-sex dorm €18. ❶

FOOD

EL SARDINERO

El Sardinero is packed with ice cream stands and expensive restaurants, though the better values may be found in El Centro. One of the best grocery options is **Diferente,** C. Joaquín de la Costa, 28, in the Hotel Santemar shopping complex. (☎942 281 782. Open M-F 9am-2:30pm and 5:30-9:30pm, Sa 9am-2:45pm and 5:45-9:30pm, Su 9:30am-3pm. AmEx/MC/V.)

Balneario La Magdalena, C. la Horadada (☎942 03 21 07), on Playa de la Magdalena. Bar and restaurant perched above the beach, with a delectable menu of meat (€12-17) and fish (€13-17). Lunch *menú* €15.50. Open daily 9am-midnight. MC/V. ❸

Restaurante La Cañla, Joaquín Costa, 45 (☎942 27 04 91). Popular among tourists and reasonably priced. A variety of seafood and helpful waitstaff. *Pintxos* €1-1.50. Fish €7.50-15. Su *menú* €13. Open daily 1-4pm and 8pm-midnight. ❸

EL CENTRO

Many restaurants in and on the streets surrounding Pl. Cañadio serve entrees until drinks and dancing take over. In the Barrio Pesquero (Fisherman's Neighborhood), the day's catch is grilled within sight of the docks. For fresh meat and vegetables, roam the aisles of the **Mercado de la Esperanza** behind the *Ayuntamiento.* (Open Su-F 8am-2pm, Sa 8am-2pm and 5-7:30pm.)

El Solecito, C. Bonifaz, 19 (☎942 36 06 33, takeout 32 51 18). The plates are the only square things in this artsy hole-in-the-wall bistro. Autumn leaves, African masks, and intimate booths make for a unique dining experience. Try the incredibly tender *croquetas de solomillo* (sirloin croquettes; €7.50) or their large selection of pastas (€8.50-10). Pizzas €6.50-10. Reservations recommended for weekend dinner. Open M-Th and Su 1-4pm and 8-11:30pm, F-Sa 1-4pm and 8pm-12:30am. MC/V. ❷

Café de Pombo, C. Hernán Cortés, 21 (☎942 22 32 24). On Pl. de Pombó, behind the central Banco de Santander, in a building once home to Cuban national hero José Martí. Coffee, pastries, ice cream, crepes, sandwiches—all delicious, all huge, all between €1-5, served out on the square or in an elegant dining area that conjures up the feel of a literary haunt. Open daily 8am-1am. Cash only. ❶

¡Viva Zapata!, C. Hernán Cortés, 47 (☎942 21 20 31). Dine to the tune of Mexican *corridos* alongside Diego Rivera prints and indigenous tapestries. Mexican entrees (€9.75-12.75) made from authentic ingredients are served with true Mexican beers and a selection of delicious tequilas. Open daily 12-4pm and 8pm-12:30am. ❷

SIGHTS

Assuming you're not fast asleep on the beach, the best way to experience Santander is to wander the beaches and peninsulas. The tourist office has a list of 1-2hr. walking tours; they are definitely a good way to get to know the city itself. On a rainy day, head indoors to the free museums and churches.

PENÍNSULA DE LA MAGDALENA. Although more like an amusement park than a palace grounds, La Magdalena is Santander's prime attraction and one of the most beautiful parts of the city. The entire peninsula is filled with palms and pines, and is ringed by bluffs plunging into the sea. **Playa de la Bikini** is, according to local lore, the first place where the two-piece bathing suit was ever worn in Spain. Crowds of people line the main walkways, but you can find peace and quiet among the paths or in a secluded, romantic cliffside nook. The park's crowning landmark is the **palacio,** a neo-Gothic mansion that Alfonso XIII used as a summer home. Today, the palace hosts the elite Universidad Internacional Menéndez Pelayo's summer sessions on oceanography. You may find tourists exchanging grunts with the sea lions at the mini-zoo, which also houses penguins and seals. A **tourist train** runs past the zoo, an adjacent display of historic ships, and through the rest of the peninsula. *(☎942 29 10 44 or 639 51 36 72. Open 9:15am-9:15pm. €2.10, children €1.40)* You can also rent Segway scooters at a booth near the park entrance. *(☎630 32 32 30. Open 11am-2:30pm and 4-9pm. Peninsula tours €8-15, 2hr. city tour €35.)* Walking, however, is the best way to explore, and the 2km path ends with tasty incentives: snack stands and bars flank the park's entrance. *(☎942 27 25 04. Park open daily June-Sept. 8am-10pm; Oct.-May 9am-8:30pm. The palace has no scheduled visiting hours, during winter months inquire at tourist office.)*

LOS CABOS. More peninsular parks lie just north of the El Sardinero beaches. While Cabos Menor and Mayor lack the manmade attractions and action of La Magdalena, their bluffs and secluded beaches make for a more peaceful setting. Cabo Menor, the southernmost of the two, houses Santander's golf course and another mini-zoo; it also has postcard-worthy views of Cabo Mayor's 19th-century lighthouse. From Pl. de Italia, walk up Av. de Castañeda past Glorieta del Dr. Fleming, and turn right onto Av. de Pontejos, which turns into Av. del Faro and takes you toward the capes. There are great views from the path around the cliffs encircling the Cabos. To reach it, follow Av. García Lago to the end of Playa la Segunda and look for stairs that lead up to the top of the peninsula. *(Parque Municipal de Mataleñas on Cabo Menor open 9am-9pm.)*

BEACHES

In Santander, every day is a beach day: rain or shine, locals flock to the beach as soon as work gets out and spend the late afternoon and evening soaking up the sun. Whichever beach you choose, it is hard to go wrong in Santander, where the sand is always silky, soft, and clean. The waves, however, can get very rough, and with the raging wind, it is not uncommon for five-foot breakers to crash onto the beach. Calmer water and rockier beaches can be found on the bay side. The best and most popular beaches are undoubtedly **Playas Primera y Segunda** in El Sardinero. Not only does the sand go on forever, but the EU has declared these one of its "blue flag" cleanest beaches. Primera and Segunda are also hangouts for Santander's surfing crowd, which emerges during and after rain. Crowds rush to the calmer waters on the southern shore of La Magdalena. Rock-framed **Playa de Bikinis** is the secluded haunt of Santander's guitar-strumming teens. To escape the beach-going hordes, either head across the bay by ferry to **Playas Puntal, Somo,** and **Loredo,** which line a narrow peninsula of dunes, or hike up to the remote beaches of Los Cabos where **Playa de Mataleñas** and **Playa de los Molinucos** await you without throngs of people (or lifeguards).

NIGHTLIFE AND FESTIVALS

Santander's nightlife revolves around multiple epicenters and has a definite schedule. Dinner lasts roughly from 10pm until midnight or 1am at places like **Cruz Blanca,** C. Lope de Vega, 5, where you can have a table with its own beer tap (€6 per liter) to warm up for the evening. (☎942 08 47 00. Open M-Th and Su 9am-11:30pm, F-Sa 9am-1:30am. MC/V.) After that, people begin to carry drinks from bars into outdoor spaces like the **Pl. Santa Lucia.** Pl. Cañadio fills to the brim with drink-bearing locals. Try nearby Australian-themed **El Dorado,** C. Hernan Cortes, 18 (open daily noon-5am). In El Sardinero, visit Pl. de Italia, which also hosts the **Gran Casino** (18 to gamble, long pants and shoes required). By 2am on a weekend, Pl. Santa Lucia, C. Rio de la Pila, and C. Casimior Sainz are filled with waiters desperately trying to recover glasses before patrons flock to nightclubs for the last stops of the night. The night isn't dead until you've had **chocolate con churros** (€3), a traditional Spanish breakfast of hot chocolate so thick, that it's more of a dipping sauce than a drink. Treat that early morning hangover at **Chocolateria Aliva ❶, C.** Daoiz y Velarde, 7, which starts serving churros at 5am on weekends. (☎942 22 20 49. Open M-F 7am-12:30pm and 5:30-10pm, Sa-Su 5am-12:30pm and 5:30-10pm. Cash only.)

The huge, month-long **Festival Internacional de Santander** in August brings crowds of people and myriad classical music and dance performances to town, many held in the city's historic churches. For more info, contact the office in the Mercado del Este (☎942 22 34 34. Open M-F 11am-2pm and 5-8pm, Sa 11am-1pm in the months leading up to the festival.) For a younger, more contemporary scene, try the **Santander Summer Festival** (mid-August), which brings rock, pop and techno to the beaches (www.santandersummerfestival.com). The **Semana Grande** festival takes place the third week of July on the El Sardinero promenades, with bathers clad in swimsuits. That same week, the *barrio pesquero* celebrates the **Virgen del Carmen,** patron saint of men of the sea.

DAYTRIPS FROM SANTANDER

SANTILLANA DEL MAR

La Cantábrica (☎942 72 08 22) buses depart from the main bus station in Santander. (45min.; July-Aug. M-F 7 per day 8:30am-9:30pm, Sa-Su 5 per day 10:30am-9:30pm;

Oct.-June M-F 4 per day 10:30am-7:15pm, Sa-Su 3 per day 11:30am-8:30pm; €2.15. Return to Santander July-Aug. M-F 7 per day 7:30am-8:15pm, Sa-Su 5 per day Sa-Su 10:20am-8:15pm; Oct.-June M-F 4 per day 7:30am-6pm, Sa-Su 3 per day 10:20am-7:30pm.) The bus stop is at the foot of the town near the park.

The layout of the stone streets and medieval palaces in Santillana del Mar remain practically unchanged since the 16th century. Some say the city's name contains three lies; the town was never home to a saint (*sant*), is not flat (*llana*) and it does not lie on the sea (*mar*). In fact, the name is derived from the name of Saint Juliana, whose relics were housed in the *Colegiata* there. Beyond striking architecture, the town has several worthwhile museums and lies within walking distance of the famed Altamira cave drawings.

Although the caves housing the Altamira cave drawings are closed indefinitely to preserve the prehistoric artwork, the **Museo de Altamira** (2km from Santillana) seeks to bring information about the **caves** and Spanish prehistory to the public. The museum includes a reproduction of the caves modeled using precise digital topographical surveys. Call ☎942 84 01 57 to inquire about seeing the real thing; a limited number of people who book ahead are allowed to see the caves on designated days. (☎942 81 80 05. Open June-Sept. Tu-Sa 9am-8pm, Su 9:30am-3pm; Oct.-May Tu-Sa 9:30am-6pm, Su 9:30am-3pm. €2.40, students with ID €1.20, under 18 and retired free. Su free. Follow purple signs off of the highway as it enters town from the south. 25min. walking; ALSA buses run to the museum on the way to Torrelavega, 12 per day 8am-10:15pm.) The **Museo de la Inquisición** does not limit its catalog of torture instruments to Spain but covers all of Europe's gruesome past (and present). Sardonic notes in English explain the uses of lovely tools such as the rack, the iron maiden, and the bull of Phalaris. (C. Jesus Otero, 1. Open daily in summer 10am-9pm, winter 10:30am-8pm. €3.60, students €2.40.) The **Museo de Jesus Otero** is located at the upper end of C. Jesus Otero, and contains many of the famous local sculptor's works in the yard and in the building, which also contains a library (Open Tu-Sa 10am-1:30pm and 4-8pm. Free.) The town's religious centerpiece is the **Colegiata de Santa Juliana,** whose 12th-century ivy and moss-covered **cloister** leads to a Romanesque **church.** (Follow C. de la Carrera as it becomes C. Canton and then C. Rio to the top of the town. Open daily 10am-1:30pm and 4-7:30pm. €3.) The **Museo Diocesano** has its own cloister, as well as exhibits from local archaelogical digs and a display of religious art from former Spanish holdings in the Americas and Philipines. (Corner of C. Jesus de Tagle and Av. le Dorat, just up from the bus stop. Open in summer 10am-1:30pm, 4-7:30pm; in winter 10am-1:30pm and 4-6:30pm. €3.) The tourist office gives out a pamphlet with a guide to the town's historic architecture. Many of these centuries-old buildings are closed to the public, but their outer grandeur is on display to all.

Santillana is small, so orientation is simple with the help of the tourist office's map. From the bus stop, head uphill across Av. le Dorat to entier the city. C. Santo Domingo branches into C. Juan Infanta (which leads into the Pl. Mayor) and C. de la Carrerea which becomes C. Canton and leads up towards the Colegiata at the northern end of town. Parallel to that runs C. Jesus Otero. The **tourist office** is located at C. Jesus Otero, 20. From the bus stop, walk up to Av. le Dorat, take a right and then your first left onto C. Jesus Otero. (☎942 81 82 5. Open in summer 9am-9pm; winter closes at midday for siesta.) The **post office** is at Pl. Mayor, 3. (☎942 81 80 40. Open M-F 8:30am-2:30pm, Sa 9:30am-1pm.)

COMILLAS

Note that Santillana del Mar and Comillas are on the same bus line. La Cantábrica (☎942 72 08 22) buses depart from the main bus station in Santander. (1hr.; July-Aug. M-F 7 per day 8:30am-9:30pm, Sa-Su 5 per day 10:30am-9:30pm; Oct.-June M-F 4 per day

10:30am-7:15pm, Sa-Su 3 per day 11:30am-8:30pm; €3.40. Return to Santander July-Aug. M-F 7 per day 7:15am-8pm, Sa-Su 5 per day Sa-Su 10am-8pm; Oct.-June M-F 4 per day 7am-5:30pm, Sa-Su 3 per day 10am-7:15pm.) The bus stop is at the bottom of the hill across from the Palacio de Sobrellano.

The coast of Comillas (pop. 2500), with gorgeous green hills rolling into the sea, boasts an intoxicating landscape. Whether you choose the tranquil inlets or the wind-swept swaths of sand on the Bay of Biscay, the beaches of Comillas are the main attraction, drawing everyone from Spanish nobles to foreign visitors to its shores. This small resort town's central beach, **Playa Comillas,** is an expanse of silky sand; on windy days, 10-foot breakers pound the shores.

Comillas is also known for its architectural attractions. Most notable, and amusing, is **El Capricho,** Gaudí's summer palace, built between 1883-1885. While it is not open to tourists, most visitors are content to see the swirling turrets, sunflower facades, and gingerbread-esque windows from outside. Behind the palace, a quiet corner contains a statue of a sitting Gaudí, looking up and admiring his whimsical work. From the bus stop, you can see the colorful palace on the hill; follow the footpath across the street for a closer view. One way to get a look inside El Capricho is to eat in its **restaurant ❹.** (Reservations ☎924 72 03 65. Entrees €16-20. *Menú* €21-25. Open Tu-Sa 1-3:30pm and 9-11pm, Su 1-3:30pm; in August 1-4pm and 9-11:30pm. MC/V). Next to it on the same hill are the neo-Gothic **Palacio de Sobrellano,** designed by Catalan architect Joan Martorell, and the **Capilla-Panteón,** containing furniture designed by Gaudí. (Open May-Sept. daily 10:30am-8:30pm; Oct.-Apr. 10:30am-2pm, 4-7:30pm. Entrance to both only by guided tours. Tickets sold 5min. before each tour; €3 each for the *capilla* and *palacio.* Tours run every 30min., *palacio* lasts 20min., *capilla* lasts 15min.) From the lawn of the *palacio*, you can see the impressive facade of the **Universidad Pontificia** (closed to the public). Comillas goes up in a blaze of fireworks, goose-chasing, and dancing during the town's **Fiesta de Cristo del Amparo** in the days surrounding July 15th.

Comillas Aventura's booth by the bus stop will take care of all your active sporting needs, with bike rentals, surf rentals and lessons, canyoning, and horseback riding. (☎625 61 14 49. Open daily 9:30am-1:30pm and 6-9pm). The **tourist office** is at Pl. Joaquín de Piélago, 1, two blocks from main bus stop. (☎942 72 25 91. Open July-Aug. daily 9am-9pm; Sept.-June daily 9am-2pm and 4-6pm.)

GALICIA (GALIZA)

If, as the Galician saying goes, "rain is art," then there is no area more artistic than northwestern Spain. Often veiled in a silvery mist, this province of fern-laden woods, slate-roofed fishing villages, and endless beaches has earned a reputation as a land of magic with tales filled with witches, fairies, and buried treasure. The Celts stopped by during their voyage to Ireland around 900 BC, and ancient *castros* (fortress-villages), inscriptions, and *gaitas* (bagpipes) attest to this Celtiberian past. The rough terrain has historically hampered trade, but ship building, auto manufacturing, and even renowned fashion labels are contributing to the region's gradual modernization and development. Tourists have begun to visit even Galicia's smallest towns, and Santiago de Compostela, the terminus of the Camino de Santiago, continues to be one of the world's most popular destinations for backpackers and religious pilgrims.

Galicians speak *gallego*, the linguistic link between Castilian Spanish and Portuguese. Newspapers and street signs alternate *gallego* and *castellano*, but most conversations are conducted in the latter. Regional cuisine features *caldo gallego* (a vegetable broth), *vieiras* (scallops), *empanadas* (stuffed turnovers), and *pulpo a gallego* (boiled octopus). While regionalism in Galicia certainly doesn't cause the well-publicized political stir that it does in the País Vasco or Cataluña, you still may see graffiti calling for *"liberdade"* (liberty).

HIGHLIGHTS OF GALICIA

PROGRESS with other pilgrims on the way to **Santiago de Compostela** (p. 349).

WATCH your step at the edge of the world, **Cabo Finisterre** (p. 355).

SANTIAGO DE COMPOSTELA ☎981

For hundreds of years, visitors to Santiago de Compostela (pop. 94,000) have arrived with sore feet, aching shoulders, and tears of joy. As the final stop on the Camino de Santiago, an 800km pilgrimage through northern Spain that ends in the cathedral housing the remains of St. James, this bewitching city brims with life. The city, which developed parallel to the Camino, is rich with symbols honoring the pilgrims' presence, from cross-emblazoned pastries to scallop-shell jewelry. But the city is not merely a pilgrims' post—Santiago is a rich and rewarding destination for all who pass through its streets. The contagious excitement of pilgrims and students gathering in countless tapas bars, the smell of sweet almond cakes, and the eerie strains of Celtic bagpipes and flutes fill the city's crooked Baroque streets from night 'til the dawn light.

TRANSPORTATION

Flights: Aeropuerto Lavacolla (☎981 54 75 00), 10km toward Lugo. Buses leave for the airport from the bus station and the C. Doutor Teixeiro (6:40am-10:30pm, €1.55). Schedule in the daily *El Correo Gallego* (€0.75) and at the tourist office. **Iberia,** R. do Xeneral Pardiñas, 36 (☎981 57 20 24). Open M-F 9:30am-2pm and 4-7pm.

Trains: R. do Hórreo (☎902 24 02 02). Info open daily 7am-11pm. To: **Bilbao** (10hr., 9:04am, €41) via **León** (6hr., €29) and **Burgos** (8hr., €36); **A Coruña** (1hr.; M-F 20 per day 6:55am-10:54pm, Sa 18 per day 6:55am-10:34pm, Su 17 per day

7:23am-10:34pm; €3.90-13.80); **Madrid** (8hr.; M-F and Su 1:57, 10:35pm, Sa 9:54am, 10:35pm; €45); **Vigo** (2hr., M-F 17 per day 5:35am-9:22pm, €5.90-8) via **Pontevedra** (1hr., €3.90-5.25).

Buses: Estación Central de Autobuses, R. de Rodríguez (☎981 54 24 16), 20min. walk from downtown. **Bus #5** goes to Pr. de Galicia (10min.; M-F every 20 min. 6:40am-10:40pm, Sa every 20min. 7am-3pm, every 30min. 3-10:30pm, Su every 30min. 7:30am-10:30pm; €0.90). Info open daily 6am-10pm. **ALSA** (☎981 58 61 33, reservations 902 42 22 42, www.alsa.es). Open daily 6:30am-9pm. To **Madrid** (8-9hr.; M-Sa 4-5 per day 7am-9:30pm, Su 4 per day 9:45am-9:30pm; €40-57, round-trip €67-108), **San Sebastián** (13hr.; 8:30am, 4pm on Fr, 6pm; €55.66, round-trip €102), and **Bilbao** (11hr.; 8:30am, Fr and Su at 4pm, 6, 11:15pm; €48.79, round-trip €67). **Castromil** (☎981 58 97 00). To: **Finisterre** (2hr.; M-F 4 per day 8am-7:30pm, Sa 4 per day 9am-3:20pm, Su 3 per day 9am and 10am; €11.75); **A Coruña** (1hr.; M-F 6:50am, hourly 8am-10:30pm, Sa 12 per day 9am-10:30pm, Su 11 per day 10am-10:30pm; €5.75); **El Ferrol** (2hr.; M-F 7 per day 9:15am-9pm, Sa-Su 6 per day 9:15am-9pm, Su until 10pm; €9.60); **Noia** (1hr.; M-F 12 per day 9am-9:30pm, Sa 8 per day 10am-10pm, Su 6 per day 10am-8pm; €3.20); **Vigo** (2hr.; M-F hourly 9am-10pm, Sa hourly 9am-1pm and 5-9pm, Su 9 per day 10am-9pm; €8) via **Pontevedra** (1hr., €5.50).

Public Transportation: Local buses (☎981 58 18 15). **Bus #6** goes to the train station (7:20am-11pm), **#4** to the campgrounds (7am-10:30pm), and **#5** to the bus station.

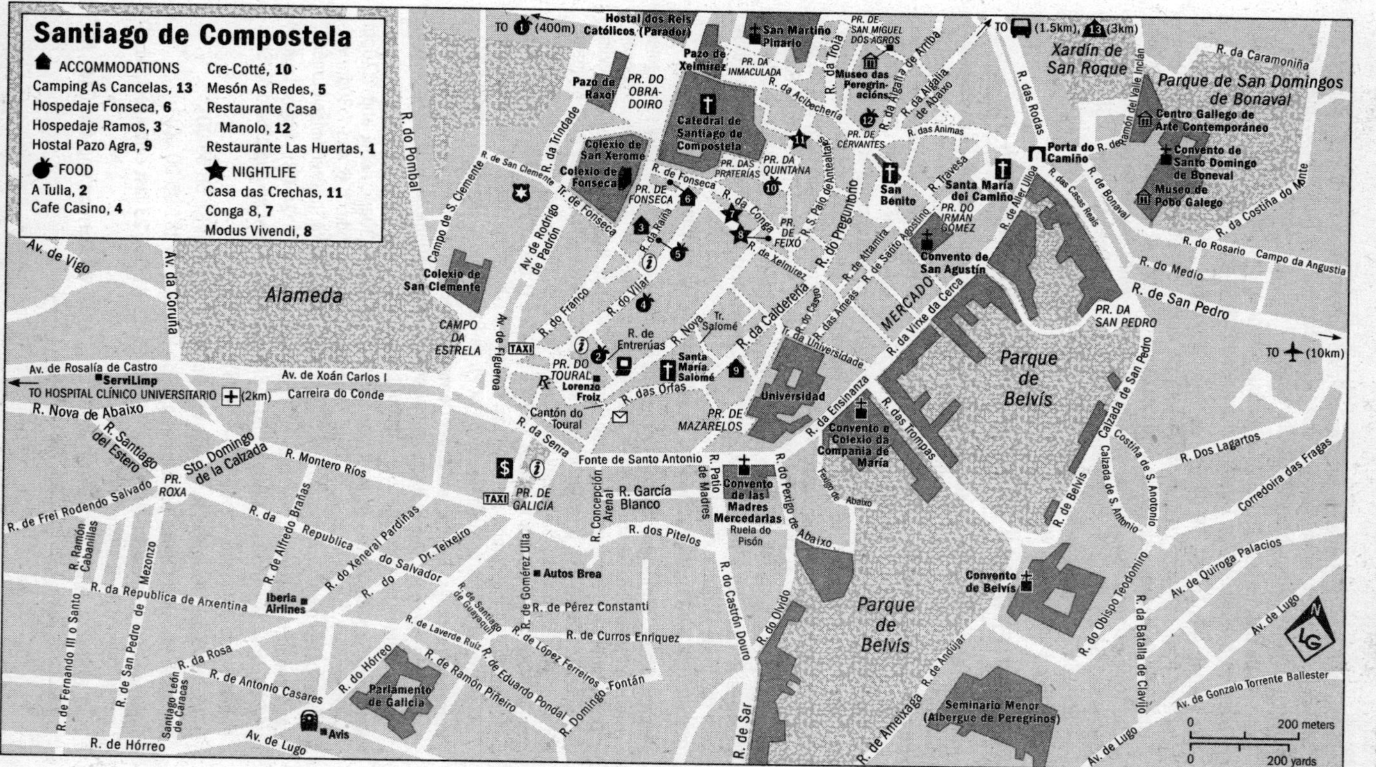

Santiago de Compostela
ACCOMMODATIONS
Camping As Cancelas, 13
Hospedaje Fonseca, 6
Hospedaje Ramos, 3
Hostal Pazo Agra, 9
FOOD
A Tulla, 2
Cafe Casino, 4
Cre-Cotté, 10
Mesón As Redes, 5
Restaurante Casa Manolo, 12
Restaurante Las Huertas, 1
NIGHTLIFE
Casa das Crechas, 11
Conga 8, 7
Modus Vivendi, 8
TO (400m)
Hostal dos Reis Católicos (Parador)
San Martiño Pinario
PR. DE SAN MIGUEL DOS AGROS
TO (1.5km), (3km)
Xardín de San Roque
Parque de San Domingos de Bonaval
Centro Gallego de Arte Contemporáneo
Convento de Santo Domingo de Boneval
Museo de Pobo Galego
Porta do Camiño
Pazo de Xelmírez
PR. DA INMACULADA
Museo das Peregrinacións
Pazo de Raxoi
PR. DO OBRADOIRO
Catedral de Santiago de Compostela
Colexio de San Xerome
Colexio de Fonseca
PR. DE FONSECA
PR. DAS PRATERÍAS
PR. DA QUINTANA
PR. DE CERVANTES
San Benito
Santa María del Camiño
PR. DO IRMÁN GÓMEZ
Convento de San Agustín
MERCADO
Parque de Belvís
PR. DA SAN PEDRO
TO (10km)
Alameda
Colexio de San Clemente
CAMPO DA ESTRELA
PR. DO TOURAL
Lorenzo Froiz
Cantón do Toural
Santa María Salomé
Universidad
PR. DE MAZARELOS
Convento e Colexio da Compañía de María
Convento de las Madres Mercedarias
Ruela do Pisón
PR. DE GALICIA
PR. ROXA
Autos Brea
Iberia Airlines
Parlamento de Galicia
Avis
Convento de Belvís
Seminario Menor (Albergue de Peregrinos)
Av. de Rosalía de Castro
ServiLimp
TO HOSPITAL CLÍNICO UNIVERSITARIO (2km)
Av. de Xoán Carlos I
Carreira do Conde
R. Nova de Abaixo
Av. de Vigo
Av. da Coruña
R. do Pombal
Av. de Figueroa
Fonte de Santo Antonio
R. da Senra
R. Montero Ríos
R. de San Pedro
R. do Rosario
R. do Medio
Campo da Angustia
R. da Caramoniña
R. das Rodas
R. de Bonaval
R. de Belvís
R. Dos Lagartos
Corredoira das Fragas
Av. de Lugo
R. de Hórreo
R. de Sar
R. do Castrón Douro
R. dos Pitelos
R. García Blanco
Av. de Gonzalo Torrente Ballester
0 200 meters
0 200 yards

In the city center, almost all buses stop at Pr. de Galicia, where there are 2 stops, one on the R. do Dr. Teixeiro side and one along R. de Montero Ríos. Except for #6, buses run daily 7:30am-10:30pm every 20-30min. €0.90.

Taxis: Radio Taxi, (☎981 569 292) at the bus station and Pr. de Galicia. Stand outside Zara in Pr. de Galicia. 24hr. Late-night service near clubs in Pl. Roxa.

Car Rental: Avis (☎981 59 04 09), at the train station. 23+, must have had license for 1 yr. Open M-F 9am-1:15pm and 4-7pm, Sa 9am-12:45pm, Su 9:30am-12:30pm. From €47.86 per day, plus €0.19 extra per kilometer, €396.41 per week, 25 and under €12 extra per day. Discounts are available for longer rentals. **Autos Brea,** Gomez Ulla, 8 (☎981 56 26 70), 23+, must have had license for 2 yr. Open M-F 9am-1:30pm and 4-8pm, Sa 9am-1pm and 4-7pm, Su 10am-1pm. Cars from €63 per day, with insurance included. Deposit required for all rentals.

ORIENTATION AND PRACTICAL INFORMATION

Santiago centers around **Pr. de Obradoiro** and the **Catedral de Santiago de Compostela.** The cathedral marks the center of the old city, on a hill above the new city. The train station is at the southern end of town. To reach the old city from the station, take bus #6 to **Praza de Galicia** or walk up the stairs across the parking lot from the main entrance, cross the street, bear right onto R. do Hórreo, and continue uphill for 10min. The **bus station** is at the town's northern end, a 20min. walk; exit the bus station, walk up R. de Anxel Casal and turn left at the roundabout onto R. da Pastoriza, which becomes R. dos Basquinos, R. de Santa Clara, and then R. de San Roque. Follow the road left on R. das Rodas, which becomes R. de Aller Ulloa, R. da Virxe da Cerca, and R. da Ensinanza, which leads to Pr. de Galicia; or take bus #5 to Pr. de Galicia (5min.). In the old city, three streets lead to the cathedral: **Rúa do Franco, Rúa do Vilar,** and **Rúa Nova.**

Tourist Office: Municipal Office, R. do Vilar, 63 (☎981 55 51 29; www.santiagoturismo.com). English, French, German, Portuguese, Italian, and other languages spoken. Open June-Sept. 9am-9pm; Oct.-May 9am-2pm, 4-7pm. **Regional Office,** R. do Vilar, 30 (☎981 58 40 81), provides information about Galicia and daytrips from Santiago. Open M-F 10am-8pm, Sa 11am-2pm and 5-7pm, Su 11am-2pm. Info about guided tours of Santiago. **Oficina Xacobeo,** (☎981 58 40 81) also at R. do Vilar, 30, provides information on the Camino de Santiago. Open M-F 10am-8pm. There is another tourist office located closer to the train station at Pr. de Galicia. Open M-F 10:30am-1:30pm.

Currency Exchange: Banco Santander Central Hispano, Pr. de Galicia, 1 (☎981 58 61 11). Open Apr.-Sept. M-F 8:30am-2pm; Oct.-Mar. M-F 8:30am-2pm, Sa 8:30am-1pm. **Western Union** services and 24hr. **ATM** outside.

Religious Services: Mass in the cathedral (p. 354) M-F 9:30am, noon, and 7:30pm vespers; Sa 9:30am, noon, 6, 6:30pm (vespers) Su 10am, noon, 1, 6, and 7:30pm vespers. Special pilgrim's mass at noon featuring the *botafumeiro* (huge incense burner).

Laundromat: ServiLimp, C. Rosalía de Castro, 33 (☎981 59 24 08). 4kg of laundry €7.80. Open M-F 9:30am-1:30pm and 4-8pm, Sa 10am-2pm. Jul-Aug closed on Sa.

Police: Pr. do Obradoiro, 1 (☎981 54 23 23).

24hr. Pharmacy: Farmacia R. Bescanses, Pr. do Toural, 1 (☎981 58 59 90).

Hospital: Hospital Clínico Universitario, Tr. da Chupana (☎981 95 00 00).

Internet Access: CyberNova, R. Nova, 50 (☎981 56 41 33). 23 fast computers. €1.90 per hr. Open daily 8:30am-1am.

Post Office: R. Orfas, 17. (☎981 58 12 52). **Lista de Correos** and fax. Open M-F 8:30am-8:30pm, Sa 9am-2pm. **Postal Code:** 15703.

ACCOMMODATIONS AND CAMPING

The liveliest and most popular rooms are on R. do Vilar and R. da Raíña. Youthful celebration may filter up into your room if you are staying in the old city, so consider staying in another part of the city if you need quiet.

Hospedaje Ramos, R. da Raíña, 18, 2nd fl. (☎981 58 18 59), above **O Papa Una** restaurant. In the center of the old city, these well-lit, modern rooms have private baths and sound-proof windows. Some rooms have views of the cathedral. Reserve 2 weeks ahead in summer. Singles €23; doubles €36. Cash only. ❷

Hospedaje Fonseca, R. de Fonseca, 1, 2nd fl. (☎646 937 765). Colorful rooms with floor-to-ceiling windows that let in lots of sun. Shared baths. Sept. 16-June singles, doubles; and triples €15 per person. July-Aug. singles €20, doubles €30. Cash only. ❷

Hostal Pazo Agra, R. da Calderería, 37 (☎981 58 35 17). Rich colors, beautiful fixtures, and an old-fashioned feel, as well as an extremely friendly family ownership, characterize this *hostal*. Rooms have high ceilings and glass doors opening onto balconies. Exterior bathrooms are private. Reception in *hostal* or in **Restaurante Zingara,** Cardenal Payá, 2, just around the block. Grandma cooks breakfast everyday for €4. May-Oct. singles €28; doubles €38. Nov.-Apr. €25/36. MC/V. ❸

Camping As Cancelas, R. 25 de Xullo, 35 (☎981 58 02 66). 3km north of the cathedral. Take #4 from R. da Senra, 1 block off Pr. de Galicia as you head toward it. Laundry, supermarket, and pool. Reception 8am-11pm. July-Aug. €5.90 per person, €6.15 per car and tent; Sept.-June €4.50 per person, car, and tent. Electricity €4.10. MC/V. ❶

FOOD

Santiago's restaurants are worth the trek, but be wary of exorbitant prices. **Rúa da Raíña** is the best street for delicious, affordable meals, and **Rúa do Franco** has excellent tapas bars. **Rúa do Vilar** and **Rúa Nova** are also good options. In the new city, look near Pr. Roxa. Santiago is famous for its seafood, so be sure to try *paella* or *mejillones* (mussels) before you leave. End your meal with a *tarta de Santiago*, a rich almond cake emblazoned with a sugary St. James cross. The best bakery in town, **Confitería El Coral,** R. Dr. Teixeiro, 32, has a tantalizing selection of homemade chocolate, ice cream, and pastries. (☎981 56 20 10. Open M-Sa 9:30am-2:30pm and 4:30-9pm, Su 9:30am-3pm and 5-10:30pm, Jun-Sept closed during Su afternoons.) The **market** near the **Convento de San Agustín** is a sight in its own right. (Open M-Sa 8am-2pm.) **Supermercado Lorenzo Froiz,** Pr. do Toural, is one block from Pr. de Galicia. (Open M-Sa 9am-10pm. MC/V.)

Restaurante Casa Manolo, Pl. Cervantes, s/n (981 58 29 50). Extremely popular among pilgrims and locals alike, this restaurant becomes packed with hungry voyagers who come for the hearty portions and great prices. Delight in the sizable *menú* (€8), while lounging to laid-back music. Open M-Sa 1pm-4pm and 8-11:30pm, Su open only during early afternoon. MC/V. ❷

A Tulla, R. de Entrerúas, 1 (☎981 58 08 89). This family restaurant is hidden behind a tiny, easy-to-miss alley between R. do Vilar and R. Nova. To get there from R. do Vilar, look for the alley to the right of Consorcio de Santiago, underneath the overhang labeled "Casa del Doctor." Entrees €6.50-8.50. *Menú* €11.80, vegetarian *menú* €9.50. Open M-Sa 1-4pm and 8:30pm-midnight. MC/V. ❷

Restaurante Las Huertas, R. das Hortas, 16 (☎981 561 979). Right down the street from the cathedral, Las Huertas is an intimate, elegant nook that offers delicious food at reasonable prices. Excellent *paella* for 2 with a bottle of *albariño* (a local white wine) €26. *Menú del día* €9. Entrees €9-12. Open daily 1-4pm and 9-11:30pm. MC/V. ❷

Café Casino, Rúa de Vilar, 35 (☎981 57 75 03). With deep armchairs, dark wood, and stained glass, this coffee shop wouldn't be out of place on a Parisian boulevard. Delicious coffees (€2.50-4) and rich desserts (€3.20-5). Open daily 8:30am-1:30am. ❶

Cre-Cotté, Pr. de Quintana, 1 (☎981 57 76 43). Rich crepes (€5.80-8.50) and an extensive selection of salads (€7.80-8.80) served on the beautiful terrace next to the cathedral or in the lemon-colored, welcoming dining room. *Menú* €11. Open July-Aug. 1pm-midnight; Sept.-June 1-4:30pm and 8:30pm-midnight. AmEx/MC/V. ❷

Mesón As Redes, R. da Raiña, 17 (☎981 576 822). Over half the options at this laid-back restaurant are under €6 and can serve as a full meal—Spanish tortillas, pastas, seafood, hamburgers, sandwiches, and even heaping *platos combinados.* Open M-Th noon-4:30pm and 8pm-midnight, F-Su noon-4:30pm and 7pm-1am. Cash only. ❶

SIGHTS

CATEDRAL DE SANTIAGO DE COMPOSTELA. This Romanesque masterpiece has been the terminus Christian pilgrimages for close to a millenium. The 9th-century discovery of James the Apostle's relics gave rise to a small chapel, then two pre-Romanesque churches, followed by the development and flourishing of the entire city. The current cathedral, which faces east into Pr. do Obradoiro, was erected in 1075. Pilgrims unburdened of their backpacks fill the plaza, gazing for hours upon the cathedral's magnificent moss-covered walls and ornate spires. The Baroque **Obradoiro Facade** dominates the square of the same name, which means "workshop" in *gallego;* it was here that stonemasons worked during its construction. Many consider Maestro Mateo's **Pórtico de la Gloria,** set in the Obradoiro facade, the crowning work of Spanish Romanesque sculpture. This apocalyptic 12th-century amalgam of angels, prophets, saints, sinners, demons, and monsters is a veritable compendium of Christian theology.

From the southern **Praza das Praterías,** recognizable by the sea horse, enter the cathedral through the Romanesque arched double doors. To the west of the cathedral, the **Pórtico Real** and **Porta Santa** face **Praza da Quintana.** To the north, a blend of Doric and Ionic columns, rebuilt after a fire in the 18th century, grace **Praza da Inmaculada,** which mixes Romanesque and Neoclassical styles. Inside the cathedral, the revered remains of **Saint James** (Santiago) lie beneath the high altar in a silver coffer, while his bejeweled bust, polished by the embraces of thousands of pilgrims, rests above it. The **botafumeiro,** a silver censer used in religious rituals, swings during High Mass and liturgical ceremonies. Older than the towers that house them, the bells of Santiago were stolen in 997 by Moorish invaders and transported to Córdoba. When Spaniards later conquered Córdoba, they had their revenge when they forced Moors to carry the bells back. *(☎981 58 35 48. Open daily 7am-9pm. Free.)*

MUSEO DAS PEREGRINACIÓNS. This three-story 14th-century Gothic building is full of creatively displayed historical tidbits about the Camino and other worldwide pilgrimages. It also includes statues of the Virgin as a pilgrim carrying the baby Jesus, illustrations of the different routes to Santiago, and exhibits on the rituals of pilgrimage and the iconography of Santiago. *(R. de San Miguel, 4. ☎981 58 15 58; www.mdperegrinacions.com. Open Tu-F 10am-8pm, Sa 10:30am-1:30pm and 5-8pm, Su 10:30am-1:30pm. €2.40, students, seniors and children €1.20, pilgrims free. Special expositions and most of the summer free.)*

NIGHTLIFE

Many begin the night by hopping from one tapas bar to another. The best street for tapas is **Rúa do Franco,** with popular options including **A Taberna do Bispo**

(Franco, 37), **Casa Rosalía** (Franco, 10), and **Xantares** (Franco, 40). If you'd rather boogie with local students, try the bars and clubs off **Pr. Roxa.**

Casa das Crechas, Vía Sacra, 3 (☎981 57 61 08). A cavernous, witchcraft-themed drinking hole, alive with good cheer and bonhomie. Renowned for its live jazz and Galician folk concerts, as well as the spontaneous *foliadas* that erupt when celebrants arrive with instruments to improvise raucous music and dance unrestrainedly. Call ahead for schedule. Beer €2. Open daily in summer noon-4am; in winter 4pm-3am.

Modus Vivendi, Pr. Feixóo, 1 (☎981 57 61 09; www.pubmodusvivendi.net). Welcome to bohemia. A hot spot on the Santiago scene, with a darkened interior and psychedelic decoration. Indie music and cool art set the tone at this pub, as locals and foreigners chat in the cramped but cozy interior. Events listed on the website and cultural magazine, *Revista Move.* Beer €2. Mixed drinks €4.50. Open Jul-Sept M-W 6:30pm-3am, Th-Su until 4:30am; Oct.-June M-W 4:30pm-3am, Th-Su 6:30pm-4:30am.

Conga 8, R. da Conga, 8 (☎981 58 34 07). Salsa, merengue, and Spanish pop music mix keep the basement dance floor crowded. Popular hangout for locals around 3am. Beer €2. Mixed drinks €4.50. Open daily 10pm-5am.

ENTERTAINMENT AND FESTIVALS

The local newspaper *El Correo Gallego* (€0.75) and the free monthly *Compostela Capital* list art exhibits and concert information. Consult any of three local monthlies, *Santiago Días Guía Imprescindible*, *Compostelán*, or *Modus Vivendi*, for updates on the live music scene. One of the city's biggest festivals, **Fiestas de la Ascensión,** 40 days after Easter Sunday, features concerts, a famous cattle market, and the consumption of many an octopi in the *Santa Susana* oak grove. The city celebrates the **Día de Santiago** (July 25, 2009) for a full two weeks (July 15-31, 2009), in a celebration called **Apóstolo;** on the night of the 24th, a Pontifical Mass is held in the cathedral during **Las Vísperas de Santiago.**

DAYTRIPS FROM SANTIAGO DE COMPOSTELA

The northern part of the Rías Baixas hides undiscovered hamlets frequented only by pilgrims. These small towns make good daytrips from Santiago, although buses in this area tend to make frequent stops, so travel can be slow.

CABO FINISTERRE (CABO FISTERRA)

Arriva/Finisterre buses run from Santiago to Fisterra (2½hr.; M-F 9am, 10am, 12pm and 7pm, Sa 9 and 10am, 12 and 3:20pm, Su 9 and 10am; €11.75, round-trip €21.40) and back (M-F 8:20 and 11:45am, 2:45, 4:45 and 7pm; Sa 11:45am, 1:45, 4:45 and 7pm; Su 11:45am, 4:45 and 7pm.). The bus stop is near the Albergue de Peregrinos, 50m uphill from the water.

After arriving in Santiago, many pilgrims decide to continue as far as their feet and the land will take them; the windswept shores of Fisterra, once believed to be the end of the world, are their final stop. Jutting out precariously from the infamously rocky **Costa de la Muerte** ("Coast of Death"; Costa da Morte in Gallego), **Cabo Fisterra** was, for centuries, a crucial port for all naval trade along the Atlantic. Today, the isolated town, Spain's last stop before the "New World," still feels like the end of the earth. The 45min. trail up to the lighthouse from the center of town reveals a truly breathtaking view. The best beach in the town is on the flat isthmus that connects the peninsula with the mainland. The beaches are powdery and wide, the waters calm but frigid. To get there, either walk 4km along the road to Santiago or take the bus and ask to stop. The 1hr. hike from the port up **Monte San Guillermo** cuts through heather-covered mountainside and commands incredible views of the sea. At the top of the cliffs, pilgrims burn their clothes and throw the ashes into the wind, as a ritual for cleansing their souls after the long journey. The mountain also hosts Fisterra's famous bed-shaped fertility rocks. Couples having problems conceiving are advised to make a go of it on the rocks under a full moon (harvest moons give best results). On another hill on San Guillermo are **As Pedras Santas,** two large boulders that slide effortlessly side-to-side when you press the right spot.

If you miss the last bus back to Santiago, you can stay at **Hospedaje López ❷,** R. de Carrasqueira, 4. The clean, inexpensive rooms with shared baths all have views of the coast, and some have balconies. From the bus stop, cross the street and walk uphill; when you reach the post office turn left onto the narrow street, C. Carrasqueira; you'll be greeted by welcoming lawn gnomes. (☎981 74 04 49. Singles €20; doubles €25.) For delicious and inexpensive seafood, try the numerous cafes and restaurants lining the Paseo del Puerto, right on the ocean. **Bodegón O Casón ❷,** Paseo del Puerto s/n, is the cheapest of the restaurants along the Paseo Marítimo, offering fresh seafood on fantastic terraces, with views of the harbor and cove. (☎981 74 02 86. *Menú del día* €8 Open daily noon-4:30pm and 7:30-11pm.) The **Albergue de Peregrinos,** C. Real, 2, has brochures and tourist info. From the bus stop, facing the water, turn right. (☎981 74 07 81. Open Sept.-May M-F 11am-2pm and 5-10pm; June-Aug. 1-10pm.) Nearby, **Bazar de Artesanía da Costa da Morte** has maps and information on bike rentals and tours. (☎981 74 00 74. Bikes €4 per hr., €12 per day. Open daily 10am-1:30pm and 5-9pm.)

O CASTRO DE BAROÑA AND PORTO DO SON

To reach these two towns, you'll need to make a connection in Noia. Castromil (☎981 58 90 90) runs buses from Santiago to Noia (1hr.; M-F 13 per day 8:15am-10pm, Sa 8 per day 10am-10pm, Su every 2hr. 10am-8pm; €3). From Noia, Hefsel buses stop at Porto do Son and O Castro de Baroña (in front of Café-Bar O Castro) en route to Riveira (30min.; M-F 14 per day 6:50am-9:30pm, Sa 7 per day 8am-9pm, Su 10 per day 9am-10pm; €1.60). Be sure to tell the bus driver where you're going, as the stop for Castro is easy to miss. From the bus stop at Castro, follow signs to the fortress, downhill toward the water. Catch the bus home across the road from Café-Bar O Castro.

One of Galicia's best-preserved coastal Celtic villages, **O Castro de Baroña** lies 19km south of Noia. The remains of a fifth-century Celtic fortress cover the neck of the isthmus, ascending to a rocky promontory above the sea; circular foundations are all that remain of the 1500-year old structures, but they make for a tangled, snaky vista from the area's highest point. Waves crash against the sides of the little peninsula, giving the remains of the fortress a lonely, peaceful feeling. The bluff descends to the soft sands of an excellent crescent beach, where clothing is "*prohibido*," but don't be intimidated by the hostile graffiti denouncing those who don swimsuits; beachgoers are friendly and some cover their bodies as well. **Hotel Villa del Sol ❷,** Tr. 13 de Septiembre, 4, has clean rooms with white-curtained windows, closet, bath, and TV. (☎981 85 30 49. Singles €25; doubles €30.)Stop for coffee or a bite at **Café-Bar O Castro ❶,** Lugar Castro de Baroña, 18, in the Castro de Baroña bus stop. Neighboring Porto do Son has inexpensive accommodations scattered around the bus stop.

PORTUGAL

Portugal wears the ornaments of modernity and the artifacts of the past with equal elegance. With the oldest established borders in Europe, Portugal broke free from Moorish rule to reach great heights as a superpower during the Golden Age of discovery and imperial expansion, but plummeted to lows as a vassal under Spanish and French dominion. These extremes of fortune have contributed to the Portuguese concept of *saudade*, a yearning for people, places, and times that are gone, an idea that finds its greatest expression in the musical style *fado*. *Saudade* may be stitched into the soul of the nation, but Portugal is a vibrant country with pulsing cities, animated festivals, and a fervent passion for soccer. From the quiet forests of Douro and Minho to the rollicking coastal scene of the Algarve, cosmopolitan Lisboa to the sun-drenched, castle-dotted interior towns, the country is a treasure trove of landscapes, art, and architecture. Portugal has something to offer every traveler, including a sense of *saudade* when it comes time to leave.

HISTORY

In the 14th and 15th centuries, Portugal ruled a wealthy empire that stretched from America to Asia, and was one of the most powerful nations in the world. While the country's international prestige diminished with the Spanish invasion in 1580, the Portuguese people's pride did not, and they regained independence in 1640. Today national pride is as strong as ever: one need look no further than the emotional fanfare surrounding the 2008 European Football Championship and the 2006 World Cup semifinals for evidence. Modern Portugal, a country with a stable democracy, a growing economy, and a vibrant culture, has proven the strength of its national character.

EARLY HISTORY (8000 BC-AD 469). Settlement of Portugal began around 8000 BC when neolithic tribes arrived from Andalucía. The traditions of these hunters and fishermen evolved into the Megalithic culture that emerged in 2000 BC and left its mark in the necropolises scattered across the Beira Alta. During the first millennium BC, several tribes began to enter the Iberian Peninsula, including the **Celts,** who settled in northern Portugal and Galicia in the 9th century BC, and the **Phoenicians,** who founded fishing villages in the Algarve. The **Greeks** and **Carthaginians** soon followed in 600 BC, settling the southern and western coasts. The Romans gained control of Portugal in 140 BC and integrated the region into the Iberian province of Lusitania, which included the whole of Portugal and parts of western Spain. Six centuries of Roman rule ensued.

GIMME MOORS (469-1139). Rome's decline in the AD 3rd and 4th centuries had a heavy impact on the Iberian Peninsula. In the wake of diminished Roman power, the **Visigoths,** a wandering Germanic tribe, crossed the Pyrenees in 469 and dominated the peninsula for the next two centuries. In 711, Muslims (also known as **Moors**) invaded Iberia, toppling the Visigoth monarchy and establishing a foothold along the southern coast, which they called the *al-Gharb* (Algarve). Their 400-year rule left a legacy of agricultural advances, architectural landmarks, and linguistic and cultural trends.

8000 BC
Neolithic tribes settle in Portugal.

1000 BC
Portugal's love affair with *bacalhau* (cod) officially begins with the arrival of Phoenician fishermen.

200 BC
Romans invade the Iberian Peninsula, gaining control of Portugal half a century later.

AD 469
Visigoths cross the Pyrenees and invade Iberia.

711
The Moors settle in the area they called the al-Gharb (Algarve).

718
The *Reconquista* begins.

1139
Dom Afonso Henriques declares Portuguese independence from Spain and crowns himself king.

1279-1325
Dinis I reigns and writes copious amounts of poetry in the Portuguese language.

1386
The Treaty of Windsor is signed, assuring centuries of cooperation between Britain and Portugal.

THE RECONQUISTA AND THE BIRTH OF PORTUGAL (1139-1415). Though the Christian *Reconquista* officially began in 718, it didn't pick up steam until the 11th century, when Fernando I united Castilla and León, providing a strong base from which to reclaim territory for the Christians. At the same time, Portugal was fighting for its own sovereignty. The groundwork for this sovereignty was laid in the Battle of São Mamede in 1128, when **Dom Afonso Henriques (Afonso I)** declared independence from Castilla and León. The following year, after the victory over the Muslims in Ourique, Afonso named himself the first king of Portugal. Dom Afonso Henriques' legacy, the boundary between Spain and Portugal, is the oldest established border in Europe.

With the help of Christian military groups like the Knights Templar, the new monarchy battled Muslim forces, capturing Lisboa in 1147. By 1249, the forces of the *Reconquista* under **Afonso III** had defeated the last remnants of Muslim power with campaigns in the Alentejo and the Algarve. The Christian kings, led by **Dinis I** (1279-1325), promoted the Portuguese language above Spanish, and, with the **Treaty of Alcañices** (1297), settled border disputes with neighboring Castilla, asserting Portugal's identity as the first unified and independent nation in Europe.

João I (1385-1433), the first king of the House of Aviz, ushered in a period of unity and prosperity. Dom João increased the power of the crown, establishing a strong base for future Portuguese expansion and economic success. The Anglo-Portuguese alliance, secured with the **Treaty of Windsor** (1386) and João's marriage to Phillipa of Lancaster, influenced Portugal's foreign policy well into the 19th century.

PORTUGAL SAILS THE OCEAN BLUE (1415-1580). The 15th century was one of the greatest eras of imperial expansion in Portuguese history. Under the leadership of João's son, **Prince Henry the Navigator,** Portugal became a world leader in exploration and trade. Portuguese adventurers captured the Moroccan city of Ceuta in 1415, discovered Madeira (and scurvy) in 1419, happened upon the uninhabited Açores in 1427, and began to exploit the African coast for riches. Lagos became Europe's first slave market in 1441. In 1488, **Bartolomeu Dias** opened the route to the East and paved the way for Portuguese entry into the spice trade when he rounded Africa's Cape of Storms, later renamed the Cape of Good Hope.

The Portuguese monarchs may have rejected **Christopher Columbus,** but they funded many other momentous voyages. In 1497, they supported **Vasco da Gama,** who led the first European naval expedition to India. Successive expeditions put numerous East African and Indian colonies under Portuguese control. (The colonies were less than thrilled about this, as revolts would often prove.) Three years after da Gama's voyage, **Pedro Álvares Cabral** claimed Brazil for Portugal, establishing a far-flung empire. Portugal's international power peaked during the reign of **Dom Manuel I the Fortunate** (1495-1521). Under Manuel, known as "the King of Gold,"

Portugal
ATLANTIC OCEAN
SPAIN
MINHO
TRÁS-OS-MONTES
DOURO LITORAL
DOURO ALTO
BEIRA ALTA
BEIRA LITORAL
BEIRA BAIXA
ESTREMADURA
RIBATEJO
ALTO ALENTEJO
BAIXO ALENTEJO
ALGARVE
SERRA DO GERÊS
SERRA DO MARÃO
SERRA DA ESTRÊLA
SERRA DA GARDUNHA
SERRA DE AIRE
SERRA DE SÃO MAMEDE
SERRA DE OSSA
SERRA DE ADIÇA
SERRA DE MONCHIQUE
Parque Nacional da Peneda-Gerês
Parque Natural de Montesinho
Parque Natural do Alvão
Parque Natural do Douro Internacional
Parque Natural da Serra da Estrêla
Parque Natural de Arrábida
Vila Nova de Cerveira
Valença do Minho
Caminha
Viana do Castelo
Caldas de Gerês
Bragança
Barcelos
Braga
Guimarães
Mirandela
Miranda do Douro
Amarante
Vila Real
Porto
Espinho
Ovar
Aveiro
Viseu
Luso
Buçaco
Guarda
Manteigas
Coimbra
Sabugal
Sortelha
Figueira da Foz
Conímbriga
Monsanto
Leiria
Batalha
Nazaré
São Martinho do Porto
Alcobaça
Fátima
Tomar
Castelo Branco
Ilhas Berlengas
Cabo Carvoeiro
Peniche
Caldas da Rainha
Óbidos
Santarém
Castelo de Vide
Marvão
Crato
Portalegre
Ericeira
Vila Franca de Xira
Mafra
Sintra
Queluz
Cascais
Estoril
Lisboa
Elvas
Estremoz
Évora Monte
Évora
Setúbal
Cabo Espichel
Tróia Peninsula
Sesimbra
Alcácer do Sal
Baía de Setúbal
Sines
Santiago do Cacém
Beja
Mértola
Lagos
Silves
Portimão
Albufeira
Tavira
Cabo de São Vicente
Sagres
Faro
Olhão
Vila Real de Santo António
Golfo de Cádiz
Costa Verde
Costa Da Prata
Costa Azul
Costa Dourada
Minho
Lima
Cávado
Tamega
Douro
Mondego
Zêzere
Tejo
Mira
Guadiana
0
50 kilometers
0
50 miles
LG
N

PORTUGAL

1415
Ceuta conquered; Prince Henry the Navigator fosters Portuguese overseas expansion.

1495-1521
Dom Manuel I the Fortunate reigns.

1498
Vasco da Gama lands in India.

1500
Pedro Alvares Cabral claims Brazil for Portugal.

1519
Portuguese-born explorer Magellan sets sail around the globe on Spain's dime.

1580-1598
Spaniard Felipe II reigns as King of Portugal.

1588
Portugal is dragged into Spain's conflict with England; the Iberian armadas are crushed.

1640
The House of Bragança leads the reassertion of independence from Spain.

1706-1750
João V, bolstered by gold extracted from Brazil, builds new palaces and academies in Portugal.

1755
A massive earthquake shakes Portugal, destroying Lisboa and killing up to 100,000.

Portugal controlled vast tracts of land and the riches these lands contained. One of the greatest feats of Portuguese navigation occurred at the end of Manuel's rule, when Fernão de Magalhães, known as **Magellan,** completed the first circumnavigation of the globe in 1521.

BRING ON THE BRAGANÇA (1580-1801). Competition from other commercial powers with alternative routes to the east eventually took its toll, and the House of Aviz lost its predominance in 1580. After a succession crisis, the Habsburg King of Spain, **Felipe II,** claimed the Portuguese throne, and the Iberian Peninsula was briefly ruled by one monarch. Over the course of the next 60 years, the Habsburgs dragged Portugal into several ill-fated wars, including the Spanish Armada's crushing loss to England in 1588. After initial good relations, King Felipe began to neglect his smaller domain, and Portugal quickly lost much of its once-vast empire. In 1640, however, the **House of Bragança** engineered a nationalist rebellion against the unfortunate monarch. After a brief struggle, the House of Bragança assumed control, asserting Portuguese independence from Spain. To secure sovereignty, the Bragança dynasty went to great lengths to reestablish ties with England. In 1661, Portugal ceded Bombay to England, and the marriage of Catherine of Bragança to England's Charles II cemented the Portuguese-British alliance. Nearly half a century later, **João V** (1706-1750) restored a measure of prosperity for Portugal, if not Brazil, using newly mined gold and diamonds from the colony to finance massive building projects in the mother country, including the construction of extravagant palaces. The bulk of the architecture did not survive the momentous **earthquake of 1755,** which struck during Mass, devastating Lisboa and southern Portugal, not to mention rattling the clergy and intellectuals of Europe. Fires, started by the overturned votive candles in churches, raged throughout the city, ultimately killing over 60,000 people. Dictatorial minister **Marquês de Pombal** was able to rebuild Lisboa, repairing widespread damage and reshaping the royal government while he was at it.

BACK AND FORTH (1807-1910). Napoleon took control of France in 1801 and set his sights on the rest of Europe. When he reached Portugal six years later, his army encountered little resistance. The Portuguese royal family opted for flight over fight and escaped to Brazil. **Dom João VI** returned to Lisboa in 1821, only to face an extremely unstable political climate. Amidst turmoil within the royal family, João's son **Pedro** declared Brazil's independence, becoming the country's first ruler. The Constitution of 1822, drawn up in Portugal during the royal family's absence, severely limited the power of the monarchy. After 1826, the **War of the Two Brothers** (1828-1834) between constitutionalists (supporting Pedro, the new king of Brazil) and monarchists (supporting Miguel, Pedro's younger brother) divided the country over the question of the Portuguese throne. Six gory years later, Pedro's daughter **María II** (1834-1853) ascended the throne at the tender age of 15. The next 75 years were marked by continued tension between liberals and monarchists.

SUPER SALAZAR (1910-1970). Portugal spent the early years of the 20th century trying to recover from the political discord of the 19th century. On October 5, 1910, the king, 20-year-old **Dom Manuel II,** fled to England in search of amnesty; the military officers and middle classes that overthrew him soon set up the **First Republic.** Their aim of a stable, bourgeois democracy was soon derailed by tensions with the Church, and the republic gained worldwide disapproval for its expulsion of the Jesuits and other religious orders. Additionally, conflict between the government and labor movements undermined domestic stability. Portugal's decision to enter **World War I** on the side of the Allies proved economically fatal and internally divisive, despite the eventual victory. The weak republic teetered and eventually fell in a 1926 military coup. General **António Carmona** took over as leader of the provisional military government and, in the face of financial crisis, appointed **António de Oliveira Salazar,** a prominent economics professor, as minister of finance. In 1932, Salazar became prime minister, but soon devolved into a dictator. His *Estado Novo* (New State) granted suffrage to women, but was otherwise rigidly traditionalist and authoritarian. During this period, society was frozen around the ideal of "God, Fatherland, and Family," only opening to the outside world and economic growth near the regime's end. A terrifying secret police, *Polícia Internacional e de Defesa do Estado* (PIDE) crushed all opposition to Salazar's rule, and rebellions in the African colonies were quelled in bloody battles.

YOU SAY YOU WANT A REVOLUTION (1974-2000). The slightly more liberal prime minister **Marcelo Caetano** continued the unpopular African wars after Salazar's death in 1970. In just a few years, international disapproval of Portuguese imperialism and the army's dissatisfaction with colonial entanglements led **General António de Spinola** to call for decolonization. On April 25, 1974, a left-wing military coalition calling itself the Armed Forces Movement overthrew Caetano in a quick coup. This **Carnation Revolution** sent citizens dancing into the streets, and put a "Rua 25 de Abril" in nearly every town in Portugal. The Marxist-dominated armed forces granted civil and political liberties and withdrew claims on the country's African colonies by 1975, resulting in the immigration of over 500,000 refugees.

The socialist government nationalized several industries and seized large estates in the face of substantial opposition, but would soon back off from outright Marxism. The country's first elections, in 1976, put the charismatic socialist prime minister **Mario Soares** into power. When a severe economic crisis hit, Soares instituted "100 measures in 100 days" to shock Portugal into shape. In 1986, Portugal was admitted into the European Community, bringing it into the European fold. Despite losing the premiership to the center-right Social Democratic Party (PSD) in the previous year, Soares then became the nation's first civilian president in 60 years. Soares was eventually replaced by the Socialist former mayor of Lisboa, **Jorge Sampaio,** in 1996.

1807
The royal family flees for Brazil as Napoleon's forces approach the border.

1828-1834
Sibling rivalry and political strife collide in the War of the Two Brothers.

1839
Construction begins on Sintra's Palacio da Pena.

1869
Portugal abolishes slavery.

1916
Portugal joins the Allies in World War I.

1917
Three children claim to see the Virgin Mary in Fatima and receive her secret message.

1932
António de Oliveira Salazar begins his 36-year regime as prime minister and dictator.

1974
Caetano is overthrown in the Carnation Revolution.

1976
Free and open elections are held in Portugal for the first time in history. Mario Soares becomes prime minister.

1986
Portugal joins the European Community.

1988
Marathoner Rosa Mota takes the gold for Portugal in the 1988 Olympic Games.

CURRENT EVENTS

The **European Union** declared Portugal a full member of the EU Economic and Monetary Union (EMU) in 1999, and the nation continues its quest to close the economic gap with the rest of Western Europe. Political integration was furthered during Portugal's tenure as President of the Council of the European Union in 2007. In 1999, Portugal ceded **Macau,** its last overseas territory, to the Chinese. Portugal and Indonesia have agreed to cooperate over the reconstruction of East Timor, formerly a Portuguese colony.

2002
Jose Manuel Durao Barroso becomes prime minister only to leave two years later to become President of the European Commission.

Jorge Sampaio returned to the presidency after the January 2001 parliamentary elections, but Socialist prime minister **António Guterres** resigned in December of 2001, just after overseeing Portugal's successful transition to the euro. President Sampaio then appointed Social Democrat **Jose Manuel Durão Barroso** as prime minister. Barroso resigned the post in July 2004 to accept the Presidency of the European Commission. **Pedro Santana Lopez,** of the same party, took his place but lost the post to **José Sócrates,** the leader of the Socialist party, in March 2005. The presidential elections of 2006 named **Aníbal Cavaco Silva,** who had lost to President Sampaio in the 1996 presidential elections, as the next head of state.

2004
Portugal hosts the European Football Championship; much drunken cheering ensues.

2007
The Africa-EU Summit takes place in Lisboa.

In 2004, Portugal hosted the **European Football Championship.** In preparation, local transportation, such as the Lisboa metro system and national rail lines, was vastly improved. On the other hand, Portugal has encountered challenges to its economy. In 2005, a severe drought hit the Algarve region, hampering agriculture and tourism, which together account for more than 60% of Portugal's employment. The drought also resulted in uncontrollable wildfires.

FURTHER READING.

A Concise History of Portugal, by David Birmingham (1993). An amazing amount of historical and cultural information in one volume.

Prince Henry 'the Navigator,' by Peter Russell (2000). A debunking of numerous myths about one of Portugal's most misunderstood leaders.

Journey to Portugal, by José Saramago (1990). A literary examination of Portugal from the Nobel Prize-winning author.

PEOPLE AND CULTURE

LANGUAGE

Although this softer sister of Spanish is closely related to the other Romance languages, modern Portuguese is an amalgamation of diverse influences. The majority of Portuguese is derived from Latin, but the Moorish occupation also left behind Arabic echoes. A close listener will also find hints of English,

Italian, French, and even Slavic languages. Portugal's global escapades spread the language to other regions, from Brazil in South America to Macau in China. Today, Portuguese (the world's sixth most-spoken language) unites over 200 million people worldwide, most of them in Portugal, Brazil, Mozambique, and Angola. Some travelers may be heartened to know that English, Spanish, and French are widely spoken throughout Portugal, especially in tourist-oriented locales. The *Let's Go* **Phrasebook** (p. 500) contains useful phrases in Portuguese, and the **Glossary** (p. 503) lists terms used in this guide.

RELIGION

Though the constitution mandates that there be no state religion in Portugal, roughly 85% of the Portuguese population identifies as Roman Catholic, though a large number are non-practicing. A major force in shaping Portugal's history, the Catholic Church still influences present-day Portugal; cathedrals dot the cities and *romarias (*festivals honoring patron saints), are celebrated everywhere. Portugal is also home to communities of Protestants, Jehovah's Witnesses, and Mormons, as well as 40,000 Muslims and a few hundred Jews.

FOOD AND DRINK

The Portuguese season their dishes with the basics of Mediterranean cuisine: olive oil, garlic, herbs, and sea salt. Cumin and coriander are especially popular, and dishes can be quite spicy. Pork, potatoes, and pastries are the omnipresent Holy Trinity of Portuguese cuisine, although each region has its own distinctive culinary traditions.

LOCAL FARE

LISBOA AND THE NORTH. The cuisine of Northern Portugal reflects its geography. Open ocean and lush forests provide for delicious seafood, game, and produce. Small farms produce succulent sausages, as well as distinctive *queijos* (cheeses) like Serra da Estrela, which is made in the region of the same name. This cheese is so soft that it is typically eaten with a spoon. Excellent produce means that *sopas* (soups) are usually made from local vegetables. Common varieties include *caldo de ovos* (bean soup with hard-boiled eggs), *caldo de verdura* (vegetable soup), and the famous *caldo verde* (a potato and kale mixture with a slice of

LOOKING BACK

Portugal emerged from Antonio de Oliveira Salazar's dictatorship (1932-1974) far behind much of Europe. Although physical results of the dictatorship remain evident in broken windows, unpaved roads, worn-down buildings, and murals of political slogans, the effects on the people are not as easy to see or understand.

Chatting with a senior citizen gave me insight into how life has changed for older generations. Sitting at an oak table in a century-old house with my octogenarian friend, Maria, I was shocked to learn that a mere 15 years ago her town, only an hour's drive from Lisboa, had no running water, no electricity, and no paved roads. Living in the grasp of a harsh dictatorship, she said, was like living in another universe.

Before democracy, many citizens, including Maria, did not realize other religions besides Catholicism existed. The opening of the political sphere has allowed for more religious freedom, but progress has been slow. Even though it has been decades since Salazar ruled, marriages sanctioned by non-Catholic churches were only recently recognized by the state. The process of understanding and accepting others is in many ways just beginning in Portugal. Older generations are curious about how younger generations understand the world and about where they will guide it.

—Illiana Quimbaya

sausage and olive oil). Portugal's delectable *broa* (cornbread) is at its best in this region. For dessert, dine on *pasteis de nata* (custard tarts) in Belém (p. 398), *queijadas da Sapa* (cheese tarts) in Sintra (p. 400), and egg yolk-based sweets just about everywhere.

ALGARVE. Miles of coastline have established fresh seafood as the core of the cuisine in this area. While *bacalhau* (cod) is undoubtedly the fish of choice for most Portuguese, *choco grelhado* (grilled cuttlefish) and *peixe espada* (swordfish) are also excellent. More adventurous diners should try the *polvo* (boiled or grilled octopus) and *lulas grelhadas* (grilled squid). In Lagos (p. 406), dishes served *em cataplana* (in a clam-shaped steaming dish) are an expensive treat. For the more economically savvy, *caldierada* is a fish stew that is sure to satisfy any traveler. Marzipan made with almonds from local groves are reminders of the region's Moorish legacy. The Algarve is also known for its oranges and figs. For something different, try *pêras* (pears) drenched in sweet port wine and served with raisins and hazelnuts on top. *Pastelarias* (bakeries) are in most towns, and provide a cheap and tasty breakfast.

ALENTEJO. The arid plains of central Portugal lend themselves to ranching rather than farming. Pork, chicken, and beef appear on most menus, often combined in *cozida à portuguesa* (boiled beef, pork, sausage, and vegetables), or served with heavy sauces and other embellishments. True connoisseurs add a drop of *piri-piri* (chili pepper sauce) to their *cozida* (meat and vegetable stew). This sauce also adds a kick to *frango assado* (roast chicken), which competes with *bacalhau* (cod) for the title of Portugal's favorite dish. A more expensive delicacy is roasted *cabrito* (goat). Hearty bread-based soups like *açorda à alentejana* (Alentejan stew) round out the menu, or could be a meal in themselves. No matter what you order, leave room for the *batatas* (potatoes), prepared countless ways, that accompany every meal.

DRINKS

The exact birth date of Portuguese wine is unknown, although 5000 BC is a good estimate. It may not be an international star, but the quality and low cost of Portuguese *vinho* (wine) is truly astounding. The best of them all, *vinho do porto* (port), pressed by foot from the red grapes of the **Douro Valley** (p. 432) and fermented with a touch of brandy, is a dessert in itself. When chilled, white port can be a snappy aperitif, while ruby or tawny port is an after-dinner classic. The island of Madeira produces its own popular wine, heated for six months before bottling. Sparkling *vinho verde* comes in either red or white—its name refers to the wine's age, rather than the color. Excellent local table wines include *Colares, Dão, Borba, Bairrada, Bucelas,* and *Periquita.* If you can't decide, experiment with the *vinho de casa* (house wine), either the *tinto* (red) or the *branco* (white). Tangy *sangria* comes filled with fresh orange slices and makes a meal festive at minimal expense. Your Portuguese drinking vocabulary should contain the terms: *claro* (new wine), *espumante* (sparkling wine), *rosado* (rose wine), *vinho de mesa* (table wine), and *vinho verde* (young wine).

Bottled Sagres, Cristal, and Super Bock are excellent beers. If you don't ask for it *fresco* (cool), it may come *natural* (room temperature). A tall, slim glass of draft beer is called a *fino* or an *imperial*, while a larger stein is a *caneca.* To sober up, order a *bica* (espresso), a *galão* (coffee with milk, served in a glass), or a *café com leite* (coffee with milk, served in a cup).

MEALS AND DINING HOURS

Portuguese eat their hearty midday meal—*almoço* (lunch)—between noon and 2pm, and *jantar* (dinner) between 8pm and midnight. Breakfast in Portugal is typically a small affair—a pastry from a *pastelaria* (bakery) and *cafezinho* (espresso) from a cafe usually suffice for *pequeno almoço* (literally, "small lunch"). If you get the munchies between 4 and 7pm, snack bars sell *sandes* (sandwiches) and sweet cakes. It is advisable to make reservations when dining in some of the more upscale city restaurants. A full meal costs €6-15, depending on the restaurant's location and quality. *Meia dose* (half-portions) cost more than half-price but are often more than adequate. The ubiquitous *prato do dia* (special of the day) or *ementa* (menu) of appetizer, bread, entree, dessert, and beverage will satisfy even the largest appetite. Standard pre-meal bread, butter, cheese, and *pâté* may be served without your asking, but these pre-meal munchies are not free (€1-3 per person). You may appreciate them, however, since chefs start cooking only after you order, so be prepared to wait. Smoking is somewhat accepted in most establishments, although signs stating "*proibido fumar*" (no smoking) are more and more common. A ban on public smoking was enacted in May 2007 but was revised shortly after and came into effect in January 2008.

A SWEET GUIDE

You've probably found yourself ogling the glass display case of Portugal's many *pastelarias* wondering which tempting treat to pick. Wonder no more with this quick guide to sugar heaven:

Altreia: a sweet and simple treat from Northern Portugal made of pasta cooked with eggs and sugar topped with cinnamon.

Arroz-doce: sweet rice. There are an infinite number of variations on this simple rice pudding, so try it wherever you go!

Bolinhos: balls of cake filled with cream and/or dried fruit.

Bolinhos de Jerimu: pumpkin, egg, and Port wine fried to sweet perfection. Yum.

Dolce de Ovos: Aveiro's sweet made of egg yolk and sugar.

Pão-de-ló: the Portuguese version of sponge cake.

Pastel de Natas: petit pastries filled with cinnamon cream, also known as *pastel de Belém.*

Pastel de Santa Clara: star-shaped puffs filled with almond cream from the northeast.

Rabanadas: thick slices of bread soaked in milk (or wine), tossed in sugar, and fried.

Pão de Deus: sweet bread topped with a pineapple and coconut concoction. Add butter and the bread melts in your mouth while the shredded coconut gives a slight crunch. God's bread indeed.

CUSTOMS AND ETIQUETTE

The Portuguese are generally friendly, easygoing, and receptive to foreign travelers. Even if your Portuguese is a little rusty, a wholehearted attempt at speaking the native tongue will be appreciated.

TABOOS. Shorts and flip-flops may be seen as disrespectful in some public establishments and rural areas, even during a heat wave. Though dress in Portugal is more casual in the hot summer months than in the cold of winter, strapless tops on women and collarless t-shirts on men are generally unacceptable. Skimpy clothes are always a taboo in churches, as are tourist visits during masses or services. Do not automatically assume that Spanish will be understood by the Portuguese; while many Portuguese do speak Spanish, one of the best ways to offend a local is to tacitly suggest that Portugal is part of Spain.

PUBLIC BEHAVIOR. On any list of Portuguese values, politeness would be at the top. Be sure to address a Portuguese as *senhor* (Mr.), *senhora* (Ms.), or *senhora dona* (Mrs.), followed by the first name. To blend in, it's a good idea to be as formal as possible at first meeting. Introduce yourself in detail, giving more than just your name. You'll be welcomed openly and made to feel at home if you mention who you are, where you're from, and what you are doing in Portugal. Don't be surprised if you get pecked on both cheeks by younger Portuguese, but handshakes are generally the standard introductory gesture.

TIPPING. In restaurants, a service charge *(serviço)* of 10% is usually included in the bill. When service is not included, it is customary to leave 5-10% as a tip. It is also common to barter in markets.

THE ARTS

ARCHITECTURE

PREHISTORIC ARCHITECTURE. The largest prehistoric remains in Portugal are at Valverde, near Évora. These **dolmens,** or ancient tombs, complement the town's later architectural styles manifest in the Celtic round stone houses, Roman forums, and the temple of Diana. Romanesque cathedrals can also be found in Lisboa (p. 388), Porto (p. 437), and Coimbra (p. 441), while Alcobaça (p. 426) and Batalha (p. 429) feature Gothic-style monasteries.

MANUELINE STYLE. Portugal's signature **Manueline** style celebrates the prosperity and imperial expansion of Dom Manuel I's reign (p. 358). Manueline works merge Christian images and maritime motifs, such as shells, coral, waves, fish, anchors, and ropes, with lavish Gothic, Plateresque, and Moorish-influenced ornaments. The **Torre de Belém** (p. 399), an elaborate expression of Manueline style, was built by King João II as a defense fortress. Close seconds are the **Mosteiro dos Jerónimos** (p. 398) in Belém and the **Mosteiro Santa Maria de Vitória** (p. 429) in Batalha, both grand testaments to Portugal's imperial success.

AZULEJOS. Few Moorish structures survived the *Reconquista*, but the style influenced later Portuguese architecture. One of these most beautiful traditions is that of the colorfully painted ceramic tiles **(azulejos)** that grace walls and ceilings. These ornate tiles, originally carved in relief by the Moors, later took on Flemish designs. Contrary to popular belief, their name comes not from the color, *azul* (blue), but rather from the Arabic word *azulayj* (little stone). Lisboa's **Museu Nacional do Azulejo** (p. 391) showcases *azulejo* collections.

PAINTING AND SCULPTURE

THE AGE OF DISCOVERY. The 15th and 16th centuries saw vast cultural exchange with Renaissance Europe and beyond. Flemish masters like **Jan van Eyck** brought their talent to Portugal, and many Portuguese artists polished their skills in Antwerp, Belgium. One result of this exchange was the emergence of a group of painters known as the **Lisboa School,** which included Gregorio Lopes, Garcia Fernandes, and Dom Manuel's favorite artist, **Jorge Afonso.** Afonso stood out for his realistic portrayals of human anatomy, and today his best works hang at the **Convento da Madre de Deus** in Lisboa (p. 391). In the late 15th century, the talented **Nuno Gonçalves** led a revival of the primitivist school, which is characterized by simple forms rendered in bold, primary colors.

THE BAROQUE ERA. Portuguese Baroque art featured even more diverse styles and themes. Wood-carving became extremely popular in Portugal during the Baroque period. **Joachim Machado** carved elaborate *crèches* (figurines of the nativity) in the early 1700s. On canvas, portraiture became a hallmark of Portuguese painting. The prolific 19th-century artist **Domingos António de Sequeira** depicted historical, religious, and allegorical subjects using a technique that would later inspire French Impressionists. Many of Sequeira's works can be found throughout palaces and churches in Lisboa. Portugal has also seen its share of sculptors as well as carvers and painters. Porto's prominent **António Soares dos Reis** brought his Romantic sensibility to 19th-century Portuguese sculpture. His work went largely unappreciated in his lifetime, however, and the sculptor ultimately committed suicide.

PRESENT DAY. In the 20th century, Cubism, Expressionism, and Futurism trickled into Portugal despite Salazar-instituted censorship. More recently, the late **Maria Helena Vieira da Silva** won international recognition for her abstract works, and the master **Carlos Botelho** gained international renown for his wonderful vignettes of Lisboa life before his death in 1982.

LITERATURE

THE RENAISSANCE. Portuguese literature blossomed during the Renaissance, most notably in the letters of **Francisco de Sá de Miranda** (1481-1558) and the poetry of **António Ferreira** (1528-1569). **Luís de Camões** (1524-1580) celebrated Vasco da Gama's sea voyages to India in Portugal's greatest epic, *Os Lusíadas (The Lusiads;* 1572), modeled on the *Aeneid.*

NINETEENTH-CENTURY REBIRTH. Portugal's imperial decline was paralleled in the literature of the 17th and 18th centuries. The 19th century, however, saw a dramatic rebirth led by poet **João Baptista de Almeida Garrett** (1799-1854), the leader of the romantic movement in Portugal and a twice-exiled political liberal. Political thinkers dominated the crop of literary intelligentsia in the **Generation of 1870,** shifting the focus literature from the romantic to the realist. The most visible influence on this shift was novelist and life-long diplomat **José Maria Eça de Queiroz.** He conceived a distinctly Portuguese social realism often critical of the bourgeois elements of 19th-century Portugal. His most famous work was *O Crime do Padre Amaro* (*The Sin of Father Amaro;* 1876).

PESSOA AND THE MODERN TRADITION. **Fernando Pessoa** (1888-1935), Portugal's most famous writer and poet of the late 19th and early 20th centuries, wrote in English and Portuguese under four different names: Pessoa, Alberto Caeiro, Ricardo Reis, and Alvaro de Campos; each alias is associated with a different writing style. His semi-autobiography, *Livro do Desassossego* (*The Book of Disquiet;* 1982) his only prose work, was posthumously compiled and is viewed today as a modernist classic.

RECENT WORKS. Portugal's literary tradition continues to thrive in the contemporary era, as writers like Miguel Torga have gained international fame for their satirical novels. **José Saramago,** winner of the 1998 Nobel Prize for Literature, is Portugal's most important living writer. His work, written in a realist style and laced with irony, has achieved new acclaim in the post-Salazar era, dominating in all genres from the dystopian parable of *Blindness* (1998) to the historical fiction of *Baltasar and Blimunda* (1987). The end of the dictatorship also saw the emergence of female writers. In *Novas Cartas Portuguesas* (1972), collectively written by Maria Barreno, Maria Horta, and Maria Velho da Costa, the three female protagonists expose the mistreatment of women in a patriarchal society. Other acclaimed post-Salazar authors include **António Lobo Antunes** and **José Cardoso Pires.** Antunes is known for his scattered style and psychoanalytic themes. Pires, known for his 'cinematic' style, often commented on the repression of the Salazar regime.

FURTHER READING. For Portuguese classics, check out Literature (p. 367). The more famous works have been translated into English.

Ballad of Dogs' Beach, by Jose Cardoso Pires (1986). Examines the terror of Salazar's secret police.

The Last Kabbalist of Lisboa, by Richard Zimler (1998). A murder mystery that explores the world of Portugal's 16th-century Jewish mystics.

The History of the Siege of Lisboa, by José Saramago (1989). A subversive and allegorical perspective on Portuguese history by the Nobel Laureate.

PORTUGAL

MUSIC

FADO. Fado (FAH-doo) is a musical tradition unique to Portugal, identified by a sense of *saudade*, meaning pining or nostalgia. Literally translated as "fate," *fado* is characterized by tragic, romantic lyrics and mournful melodies. Supposedly, these songs of longing were originally sung by fishwives whose husbands were at sea. Lisboa and Coimbra are now the most active centers for this tradition, but the two regional styles differ sharply. Lisboa's singers tend to be female, and the songs are up-tempo, while almost all *fado* singers in Coimbra are male and the tunes are more tearful. Solo ballads, accompanied by the *guitarra portuguesa* (a flat-backed guitar similar to a mandolin), appeal to the romantic side of Portuguese culture. **Amália Rodrigues** (1920-1999) gained international renown as a singer of *fado* and Portuguese folk music. **Mariza,** Portugal's answer to Madonna, continues the tradition today, alongside more conventional pop artists of Portuguese descent, like Nelly Furtado.

CLASSICAL. Apart from its folk tradition, the music of Portugal has yet to achieve international fame. Portuguese opera peaked with **António José da Silva** (1705-1739), a victim of the 1739 Inquisition. The Renaissance in Portugal led to the development of pieces geared for solo instrumentalists and vocals. Coimbra's **Carlos Seixas** thrilled 18th-century Lisboa with his genius, and contributed to the development of the sonata. **João Domingos Bomtempo** (1775-1842) introduced symphonic innovations from abroad and established the *Sociedade Filarmónica*, modeled on the London Philharmonic, in Lisboa in 1822.

In the late 19th century, **Joly Braga Santo** led a modern revival of Portuguese classical music. The Calouste Gulbenkian Foundation in Lisboa has also kept Portuguese music alive, sponsoring a symphony orchestra since 1962 and hosting local folk singers (including Fausto and Sérgio Godinho), ballets, operas, and jazz festivals. The **Teatro Nacional de São Carlos,** with its own orchestra and ballet company, has further bolstered Portuguese music. The Teatro has spawned a group of talented young composers, including **Filipe Pires, Antonio Vitorino d'Almeida,** and **Jorge Peixinho,** all of whom have begun to make their mark in international competitions.

THE MEDIA

Portugal's most widely read daily newspapers are *Público* (www.publico.pt), *Diário de Notícas* (www.dn.sapo.pt), and *Jornal de Notícas* (www.jn.sapo.pt). If you haven't mastered Portuguese, check out *The News* (www.the-news.net), Portugal's only online English-language newspaper. Those interested in international news can also pick up day-old foreign papers at larger newsstands.

Portuguese TV offers four main channels: the state-run Canal 1 and TV2, and the private SIC (Sociedade Independente de Communicação) and TVI (TV Independente). Couch potatoes can also enjoy numerous cable channels, most airing Brazilian and Portuguese soap operas and subtitled foreign sitcoms.

SPORTS

Futebol is the game of choice for just about all Portuguese sports fans. Team Portugal has had its moments in the sun—the national team took second in the 2004 European Championships and garnered a third-place finish in 2000 at the European Championship with the help of Luis Figo and goldenboy Cristiano Ronaldo. However, the team has also fallen short at crucial moments, like at the World Cup 1998 qualifications, the semifinals of the World Cup in 2006, and the 2008 European Championship quarterfinals. Portugal hosted the 2004 European Championship, in which Greece emerged victorious over Portugal in the final match. Lisboa's **Benfica,** with some of the world's best players, including American sensation Freddy Adu, has not only an avid Portuguese fan base but also a substantial international following.

Portuguese athletes have also made names for themselves in long-distance running. Marathon queen **Rosa Mota** dominated her event during the 1980s, and runner **Carlos Lopes** brought home Portugal's first Olympic gold medal at the 1984 games. Besides jogging and pick-up soccer, the Portuguese often turn to the sea. Wind, body, and conventional **surfers** make waves along the northern coast, while **snorkelers** and **scuba divers** set out to the south and west.

NATIONAL HOLIDAYS

The following table lists the national holidays for 2009.

DATE	FESTIVAL
January 1	Dia do Ano Novo (New Year's Day)
January 6	Dia do Reis (Epiphany)
February 24	Carnaval (Carnival)
April 3-12	Semana Santa (Holy Week)
April 9	Senhor Ecce Homo (Maundy Thursday)
April 10	Sexta-feira Santa (Good Friday)
April 12	Páscoa (Easter)
April 25	Dia de 25 Abril (Liberation Day)
May 1	Dia do Trabalhador (Labor Day)
June 10	Dia de Camões (Portugal Day)
June 11	Corpo de Deus (Corpus Christi)
August 15	Assunção (Feast of the Assumption)
October 5	Dia da República (Republic Day)
November 1	Dia de Todos Santos (All Saints' Day)
December 8	A Conceição Imaculada (Feast of the Immaculate Conception)
December 25	Festa de Natal (Christmas)
December 31	Noite Velha (New Year's Eve)

LISBOA (LISBON)

At sunset, the scarlet glow cast over the Rio Tejo is matched by the ruby red shimmer inside your glass of *vinho do porto*. Welcome to Lisboa. A magnificent history has left its mark upon this ancient city: illustrious bronze figures stand proud in open plazas, Roman arches and columns inspire reverence in visitors, and a towering 12th-century castle keeps watch from atop one of the city's infamous seven hills. Lisboa is quickly becoming one of the most talked-about capitals in Europe, driven by cutting-edge fashion, flourishing art and music scenes, and enthusiastic nightlife. Graffiti adorns the time-worn walls of Bairro Alto, and at night the cobblestone sidewalks echo with the modern rhythms of local clubs. A monumental past may loom over every corner of the city, but Lisboa is thriving in the present. Immigrants and visitors from all around the world give Lisboa an international feel that is hard to come by anywhere else in Portugal. Crowds of unique people—street performers, break dancers, and peddlers of various sorts—line the streets of Baixa and Bairro Alto, giving the city its diverse and distinctive flavor.

Complexity is not new to Lisboa. Half a dozen civilizations claim parenthood of the city, beginning with the Phoenicians, Greeks, and Carthaginians. The Romans arrived in 205 BC and ruled for 600 years. Under Julius Caesar, Lisboa became one of the most important port cities in Lusitania, and in 1255, Lisboa was made the capital of Portugal. The city, along with the empire, reached its zenith at the end of the 15th century, when Portuguese navigators pioneered the exploration of Asia, Africa, and South America during the Age of Discovery. A catastrophic earthquake on November 1, 1755 catalyzed the nation's fall from glory—close to one-fifth of the population died, and two-thirds of Lisboa was destroyed in the resulting fires. Immediately, the Prime Minister Marquês de Pombal began a massive reconstruction effort, an overhaul that explains the contrast between the neat, grid-like layout of Baixa (entirely destroyed in the earthquake) and the hilly mazes of the surrounding areas that at least partially survived. Twentieth-century Lisboa saw plenty of change, as new technologies complemented the traditions of the past. Temples, castles, and cathedrals stand next to crowded plazas, buzzing cafes, and blaring *discotecas*, giving Lisboa a life of its own.

INTERCITY TRANSPORTATION

BY PLANE

All flights land at **Aeroporto de Lisboa** (☎218 41 35 00 or 41 37 00 for departures and arrivals) near the city's northern edge. Major **airlines** have offices at Pr. Marquês de Pombal and along Av. da Liberdade. The cheapest way into town is by bus: walk out of the terminal, turn right, and go straight across the street to the bus stop, marked by yellow metal posts with arrival times of incoming buses. Take bus #44, 45, or 745 (15-20min., every 12-25min. 6am-12:15am, €1.40) to Pr. dos Restauradores; the bus stops in front of the tourist office, located inside the Palácio da Foz. The express AeroBus #91 runs to the same locations (15min.; every 20min. 7am-11pm; €3.50, TAP passengers free); it's

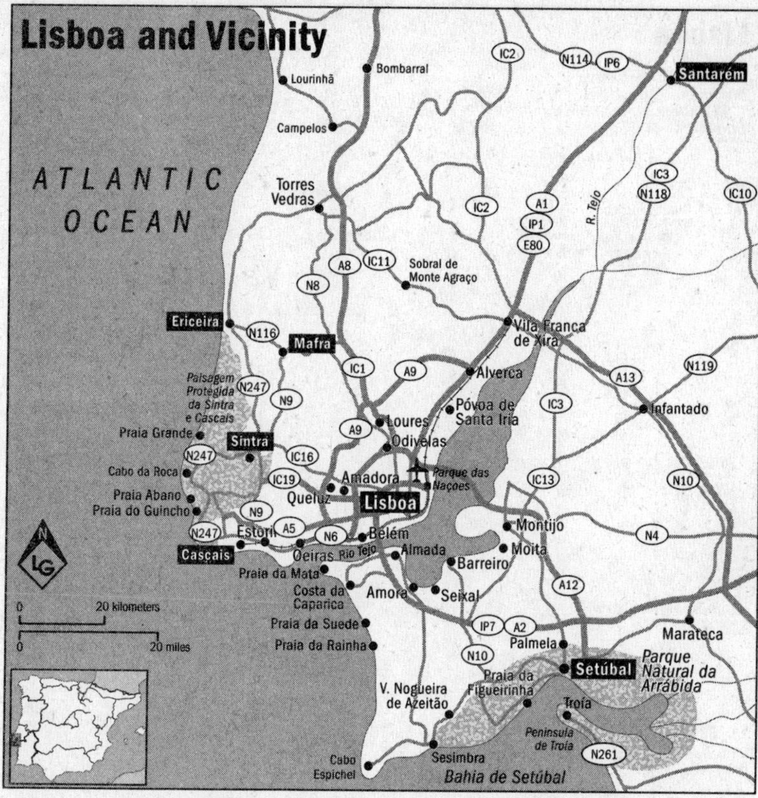

Lisboa and Vicinity

a good option during rush hour. The bus stop is in front of the terminal exit. A **taxi** downtown costs about €10-15 (plus a €1.60 baggage fee) at low traffic, but you're billed by time, not distance. Beware that some drivers may keep your change or take a longer route.

PRE-PAY YOUR WAY. Ask at the airport tourist office (☎218 450 660; open 7am-midnight) about the voucher program, which allows visitors to pre-pay for cab rides from the airport (€21).

BY TRAIN

Train service in and out of Lisbon routinely confuses newcomers, as there are four stations in Lisbon and one across the river in Barreiro, each serving different destinations. Portugal's affordable, express **Alfa Pendular** line offers the easiest connections between Lisbon and Braga, Porto, Coimbra, and Faro. Regional trains make frequent stops; buses, although more expensive and lacking toilets, are faster and more comfortable. Suburban train lines, which offer service to Cascais and Sintra (and stops along the way), are efficient and reliable. Contact **Caminhos de Ferro Portugueses** for further info. (☎808 20 82 08; www.cp.pt.)

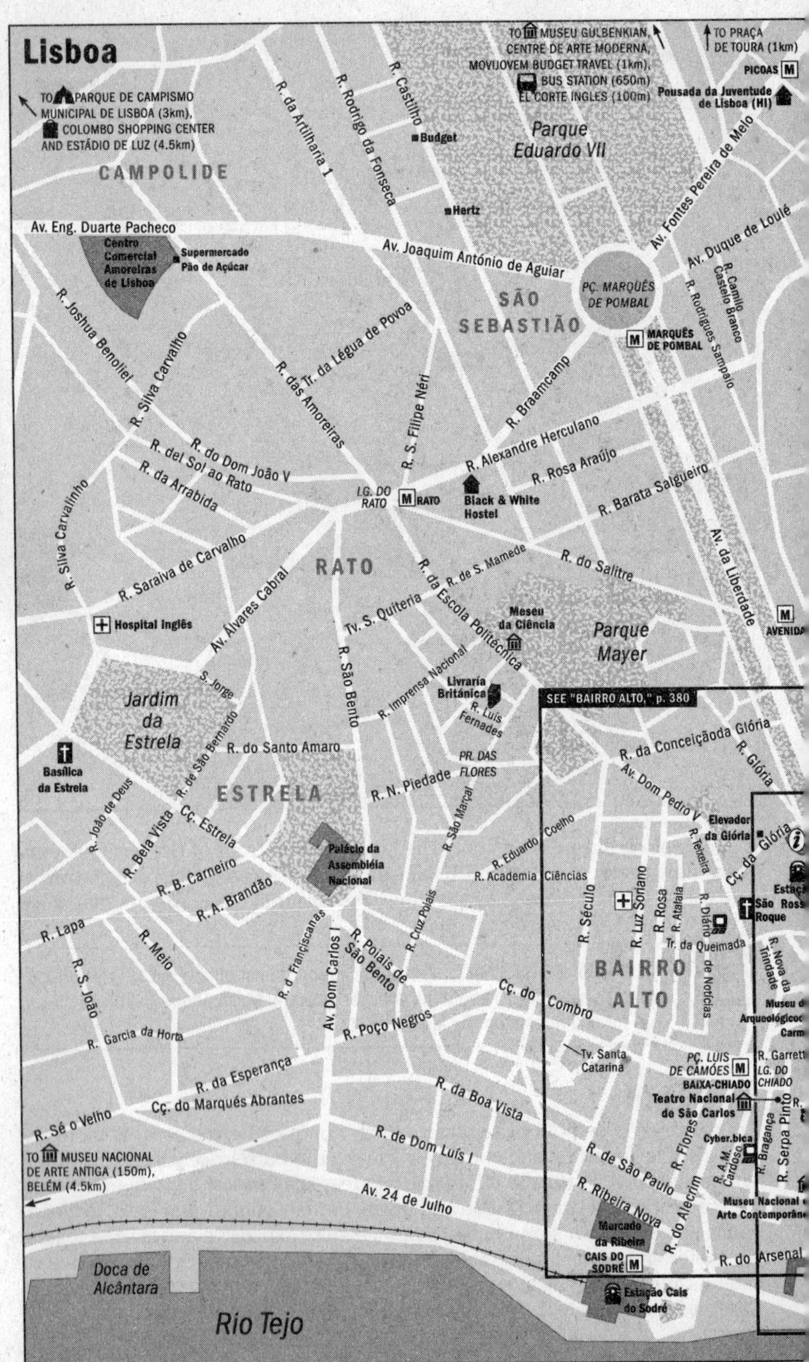
Lisboa
TO PARQUE DE CAMPISMO MUNICIPAL DE LISBOA (3km), COLOMBO SHOPPING CENTER AND ESTÁDIO DE LUZ (4.5km)
TO MUSEU GULBENKIAN, CENTRE DE ARTE MODERNA, MOVIJOVEM BUDGET TRAVEL (1km), BUS STATION (650m) EL CORTE INGLES (100m)
TO PRAÇA DE TOURA (1km)
PICOAS
Pousada da Juventude de Lisboa (HI)
CAMPOLIDE
Parque Eduardo VII
Budget
Hertz
Av. Eng. Duarte Pacheco
Centro Comercial Amoreiras de Lisboa
Supermercado Pão de Açúcar
Av. Joaquim António de Aguiar
PÇ. MARQUÊS DE POMBAL
SÃO SEBASTIÃO
MARQUÊS DE POMBAL
Av. Fontes Pereira de Melo
Av. Duque de Loulé
R. Camilo Castelo Branco
R. Rodrigues Sampaio
R. da Artilharia 1
R. Rodrigo da Fonseca
R. Castilho
R. Joshua Benoliel
R. Silva Carvalho
Tr. da Légua de Povoa
R. das Amoreiras
R. S. Filipe Néri
R. Braamcamp
R. Alexandre Herculano
R. Rosa Araújo
R. Barata Salgueiro
R. do Dom João V
R. del Sol ao Rato
R. da Arrabida
LG. DO RATO
RATO
Black & White Hostel
R. Silva Carvalinho
R. Saraiva de Carvalho
RATO
R. da Escola Politécnica
R. de S. Mamede
R. do Salitre
Av. da Liberdade
Av. Álvares Cabral
Tv. S. Quitéria
Museu da Ciência
Parque Mayer
AVENIDA
Hospital Inglês
R. São Bento
R. Imprensa Nacional
Livraria Británica
R. Luís Fernades
SEE "BAIRRO ALTO," p. 380
Jardim da Estrela
S. Jorge
R. de São Bernardo
R. do Santo Amaro
PR. DAS FLORES
R. da Conceiçãoda Glória
R. Glória
Av. Dom Pedro V
Basílica da Estrela
ESTRELA
R. N. Piedade
R. João de Deus
R. Bela Vista
Cç. Estrela
R. São Marçal
R. Eduardo Coelho
Elevador da Glória
Cç. da Glória
R. Teixeira
Palácio da Assembléia Nacional
R. Academia Ciências
R. B. Carneiro
R. A. Brandão
R. Século
R. Luz Soriano
R. Rosa
R. Atalaia
R. Diário de Notícias
Estação Rossio
São Roque
R. Lapa
R. Meio
R. d Franciscanas
Av. Dom Carlos I
R. Poiais de São Bento
R. Cruz Polais
Tr. da Queimada
R. Nova da Trindade
BAIRRO ALTO
R. S. João
Cç. do Combro
Museu Arqueológico Carm
R. Garcia da Horta
R. Poço Negros
Tv. Santa Catarina
PÇ. LUIS DE CAMÕES
BAIXA-CHIADO
R. Garrett
LG. DO CHIADO
R. da Esperança
Cç. do Marqués Abrantes
R. da Boa Vista
Teatro Nacional de São Carlos
R. Sé o Velho
R. de Dom Luís I
Cyber.bica
R. Flores
R. A. M. Cardoso
R. Bragança
R. Serpa Pinto
TO MUSEU NACIONAL DE ARTE ANTIGA (150m), BELÉM (4.5km)
R. de São Paulo
R. Ribeira Nova
R. do Alecrim
Museu Nacional Arte Contemporân
Av. 24 de Julho
Mercado da Ribeira
CAIS DO SODRÉ
R. do Arsenal
Doca de Alcântara
Estação Cais do Sodré
Rio Tejo

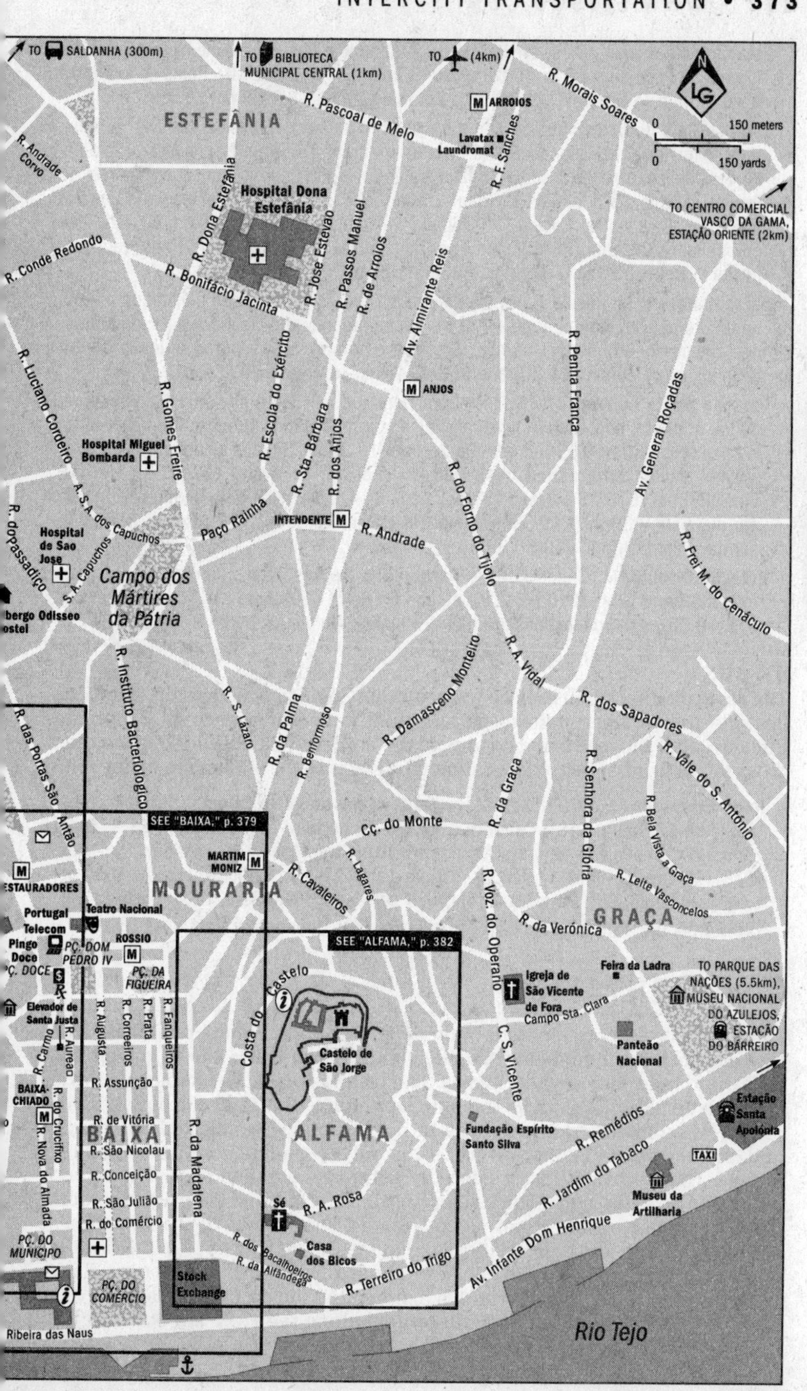

TO SALDANHA (300m)
TO BIBLIOTECA MUNICIPAL CENTRAL (1km)
TO (4km)
ESTEFÂNIA
ARROIOS
Lavatax Laundromat
150 meters
150 yards
TO CENTRO COMERCIAL VASCO DA GAMA, ESTAÇÃO ORIENTE (2km)
Hospital Dona Estefânia
ANJOS
Hospital Miguel Bombarda
INTENDENTE
Hospital de Sao Jose
Campo dos Mártires da Pátria
Albergo Odisseo Hostel
SEE "BAIXA," p. 379
MARTIM MONIZ
MOURARIA
RESTAURADORES
Portugal Telecom
Teatro Nacional
ROSSIO
Pingo Doce
PÇ. DOM PEDRO IV
PÇ. DA FIGUEIRA
Elevador de Santa Justa
BAIXA-CHIADO
BAIXA
PÇ. DO MUNICIPO
PÇ. DO COMÉRCIO
Stock Exchange
Ribeira das Naus
SEE "ALFAMA," p. 382
Castelo de São Jorge
ALFAMA
Sé
Casa dos Bicos
GRAÇA
Igreja de São Vicente de Fora
Feira da Ladra
Panteão Nacional
TO PARQUE DAS NAÇÕES (5.5km), MUSEU NACIONAL DO AZULEJOS, ESTACÃO DO BÁRREIRO
Fundação Espírito Santo Silva
Estação Santa Apolónia
TAXI
Museu da Artilharia
Rio Tejo
LISBOA

Estação do Barreiro, across the Rio Tejo. Southbound trains. Accessible by ferry from the Terreiro do Paço dock off Pr. do Comércio (30min., 2 per hr., €2.10). Trains go to **Pinhal Novo** (25min., 1-2 per hr., €1.30) and **Setúbal** (20min., 1-2 per hr., €1.70).

Estação Cais do Sodré, just beyond the end of R. do Alecrim, beside the river; a 5min. walk from Baixa. M: Cais do Sodré or take any tram 28E from Bairro Alto or Alfama. Serves the southwestern suburbs. Take trains labeled "Cascais Todos" or "Oeiras" to **Belém** (10min., 3-4 per hr. 5:30am-1:30am, €1.20). Take trains labeled "Cascais Todos" or "Cascais" to **Estoril** (30-35min., 3-4 per hr. 5:30am-1:30am, €1.70). Take any trains to **Cascais** (35-40min., 6 per hour 5:30am-1:30am, €1.70) and the youth hostel in **Oeiras** (20min., 6 per hr. 5:30am-1:30am, €1.30).

Estação Rossio, M: Rossio. Cross the *praça* for 2 blocks until you see the station on your right. Alternatively, you can get off at M: Restauradores and walk down Av. da Liberdage; the station will be on your right. Serves the northwestern suburbs. Trains to **Queluz** (20min., every 20min., €1.20) and **Sintra** (40min., every 20min., €1.70).

Estação Santa Apolónia, Av. Infante Dom Henrique. M: Santa Apolónia. Runs international, northern, and eastern lines. All trains stop at **Estação Oriente.** The ticket office is open M-F 5:30am-1030pm and Sa-Su 6am-10:30pm. There is a **currency exchange** station and an **information desk** (English spoken). To: **Aveiro** (2½hr., 16 per day 6am-9:30pm, €16-35); **Braga** (3½hr.; 7am, 1, 4, 7pm; €22-43); **Coimbra** (2hr., 19 per day 6am-9:30pm, €19.50-30); **Madrid** (10hr., 10:30pm, €59); **Porto** (3-4hr., 16 per day 6am-9:30pm, €19.50-39.50).

Estação Oriente, M: Oriente, by the **Parque das Nações.** Offers service to the south. Trains to **Évora** (2hr.; 8:10am, 2:10pm, and 6:10pm; €10); **Faro** (3¼-3¾hr., 6 per day, €18-19.50), with connections to other destinations in the Algarve.

BY BUS

The **bus station** in Lisbon is close to the Jardim Zoológico metro stop, but it can be tricky to find. Once at the metro stop, follow the exit signs to Av. C. Bordalo Pinheiro. Exit the metro and go around the corner. Walk ahead 100m and then cross left in front of Sete Rios station. The stairs to the station are on the left.

Rede Expressos (☎707 22 33 44; www.rede-expressos.pt). To: **Braga** (5hr., 14-16 per day 7am-12:15am, €18); **Coimbra** (2hr., 24-32 per day 7am-12:15am, €13); **Évora** (2hr., 20-25 per day 7am-10:30pm, €11.50); **Faro** (4hr., 9-11 per day 7am-1am, €18-19); **Lagos** (4hr., 9-14 per day 7:30am-1am, €18-19); **Peniche** (1½-2hr., 9-10 per day 7am-10pm, €8); **Portalegre** (4hr., 7-8 per day 7:30am-8pm, €13); **Porto** (3½hr., 20-24 per day 7am-12:15am, €17.50); **Tavira** (5hr., 9 per day 7am-1am, €18-19).

ORIENTATION

Lisboa's historic core has four main neighborhoods: commercial **Baixa** (the low district), museum-heavy **Chiado,** nightlife-rich **Bairro Alto** (the high district), and hilly, labyrinthine **Alfama.** The last, Lisboaâ€™s famous medieval Moorish neighborhood, was the lone survivor of the 1755 earthquake. The cityâ€™s oldest district is a maze of narrow alleys, unmarked alleyways, and *escandinhas*â€"stairways that seem only to lead to more unidentifiable streets. Expect to get lost repeatedly without a detailed map. The street-indexed *For Ways* maps (including Sintra, Cascais, and Estoril) are good, though expensive (sold at newsstands; â,¬5). The maps at the tourist offices are also reliable and free. Visitors exhausted from treks up and down the historic center's many hills can hop aboard tram 28E, which runs East-West through these neighborhoods, connecting most of their major sights. The *bairros* extending in both directions along the river are some of the fastest-growing sections of the city, offering pulsing nightlife and stunning architectural beauty, both ancient and contemporary.

THE BAIRROS OF LISBOA

BAIXA

Baixa, Lisboa's old business hub, is the city's historic center, with restaurants and trendy apparel stores lining its streets. The neighborhood grid begins at **Praça Dom Pedro IV** (better known as **Rossio**) and ends at **Praça do Comércio** on the Rio Tejo. The *praças* (squares) function as decorative bookends to the new Lisboa that took shape following the earthquake of 1755, which destroyed most of the city. (If Mr. Richter's scale had been available at the time, the quake would probably have reached an 8.9.) Pr. do Comércio was built on the site of the former Royal Palace, which toppled in the quake, and hence bears the nickname Terreiro do Paço (Palace Lot). Expect to meet many travelers in Baixa: the tourist offices, cheap *pensões*, and stylish hostels concentrated here make Rossio the city's tourist hub. Linked to Rossio is **Praça dos Restauradores,** an urban transit hub and the main drop-off for airport buses. Pr. dos Restauradores lies just above Baixa; Avenida da Liberdade runs uphill from it to the modern business district surrounding **Praça do Marquês de Pombal.**

BAIRRO ALTO AND CHIADO

As Lisboa's most famous neighborhood, Bairro Alto means something different to everyone. To thousands of natives, the upper floors and laundry-covered balconies of the neighborhood's many colorful buildings are home. To music lovers, it's a must-see for *fado*. And to night owls, it's the best place to party. Cobblestone sidewalks lead to inexpensive cafes filled with locals enjoying *bacalhau assado* (grilled codfish), and graffiti-covered walls separate the quirky shops selling shoes and T-shirts from bars that bustle every night of the week. Bairro Alto has budget delights as well, such as the bargain-filled shopping center at the end of **Rua Garrett,** and better yet, the beautiful churches and museums around cultured **Chiado,** which abuts Baixa below. At night, *fado* singers perform traditional Portuguese songs of longing as the well-to-do enjoy fine meals and red wine. Meanwhile, hip young *Lisboetas* grab drinks at the bars between **Rua do Norte** and **Rua da Atalaia** before taking the party to the hilly streets. Get your beer or caipirinha in a plastic cup so you can take it with you as you wander from place to place; the night never ends in Bairro Alto.

ALFAMA

Hilly Alfama, Lisboa's medieval quarter, was the lone neighborhood to survive the infamous 1755 earthquake. The **Castelo de São Jorge,** with its commanding view of Baixa and Bairro Alto, sits at the neighborhood's peak. Around and below it, layers of houses, shops, and restaurants descend to the Rio Tejo. Between Alfama and Baixa is the **Mouraria** (Moorish quarter), ironically established by Dom Afonso Henriques after the expulsion of the Moors in 1147. This labyrinth of alleys, small stairways, and unmarked streets is a challenge to navigate and poorly lit after dark, so be careful at night.

GRAÇA

If the climb to Graça doesn't take your breath away, the incredible *miradouros* (lookout points) you'll find there will. The neighborhood is one of the oldest in Lisboa, and in addition to great views of the city and river, Graça offers several impressive historical sights that keep tourists trekking up its hilly streets day after day. Graça is a mainly residential area and is easily accessible by tram 28E, making it a quick and convenient trip from Baixa or Bairro Alto.

AROUND PRAÇA DO MARQUÊS DE POMBAL

Lisboa's modern business center, the area around Pç. do Marquês de Pombal abounds in department stores, shopping centers, and office complexes. Amid this sea of commerce, peaceful **São Sebastião** houses two of the finest museums in all of Portugal, legacies of oil tycoon Calouste Gulbenkian.

FARTHER AFIELD

Lisboa calms down as you move west from Bairro Alto into **Estrela** and **Prazeres,** where cobblestone streets give way to leafy parks and peaceful manicured cemeteries. South of these neighborhoods, the docks of riverfront **Alcântara** house Lisboa's most vibrant club scene. Several kilometers downriver, architecturally stunning **Belém** (p. 398) celebrates the glory of Portugal's imperial past. Northeast of the historic core, the **Parque das Nações** (p. 397), built to host the 1998 World Exposition, is home to a fantastic oceanarium and Santiago Calatrava's soaring Gare do Oriente.

LOCAL TRANSPORTATION

CARRIS, Lisboa's efficient public transportation system, runs subways, buses, trams, funiculars throughout Lisboa and its surroundings (☎213 61 30 00; www.carris.pt). Short-term visitors should consider a 24-hour **bilhete combinado** (€3.50), good for unlimited travel on all CARRIS transports. Those planning a longer stay, or who intend to take the metro, should acquire a rechargeable **viva viagem** card. The pass itself costs €0.50 and can be purchased and charged in all metro stations. When entering buses, trams, or the metro, hold the card against the magnetic reader; your trip will cost only €0.79. CARRIS booths, located in most train and major metro stations (including Baixa-Chiado, Restauradores, and Marquês de Pombal), sell day passes and dispense information. (Open daily 6:30am-1pm.)

Buses: €1.40 within the city, or €0.79 with a viva viagem card. Pay on the bus; exact change not required.

Metro: (☎213 50 01 00; www.metroLisboa.pt). €0.79 with a viva viagem card (required for travel on the metro). 4 lines traverse downtown and the business district. A red "M" marks metro stops. Trains run daily 6:30am-1am, though some stations close earlier.

Trams: €1.40, or €0.79 with a viva viagem card. Many vehicles date from before WWI. Line 28E runs through Graça, Alfama, Baixa, Chiado, and Bairro Alto. Line 15E heads from Pr. do Comércio and Pr. da Figueira to Belém, passing the clubs of Alcântara along the way.

Funiculars and Elevators: €1.40, or €0.79 with a viva viagem card. Funiculars link the lower city with the residential areas in the hills. The Elevador da Glória goes from Pr. dos Restauradores to Bairro Alto, while the Elevador de Santa Justa links Chiado to Baixa.

Taxis: Cabs can be hailed on the street throughout the historic center. Restaurateurs and club bouncers will gladly call you a cab after dark. **Rádio Táxis de Lisboa** (☎218 11 90 00), **Autocoope** (☎217 93 27 56), and **Teletáxis** (☎218 11 11 00). Luggage €1.60.

Car Rental: Lisboa's narrow streets are hardly ideal for driving, but those who insist can rent cars at agencies located at the airport, train stations, and downtown. **Avis,** Av. D. Duarte 4 (☎213 17 42 31; www.avis.com.pt); **Budget,** R. Castilho, 167B (☎213 86 05 16; www.budgetportugal.com); **Hertz,** R. Castilho, 72A (☎213 81 24 30; www.hertz.pt).

PRACTICAL INFORMATION

TOURIST AND FINANCIAL SERVICES

Tourist Office: Palácio da Foz, Pr. dos Restauradores (Portugal info ☎213 46 63 07, Lisboa info ☎213 46 33 14). M: Restauradores. The largest tourist office, with info for all of Portugal. Open daily 9am-8pm. The **Welcome Center,** Pr. do Comércio (☎210 31 28 10), is the main office for the city. Sells tickets for sightseeing buses and the **Lisboa Card,** which includes transportation and entrance to most sights, as well as discounts at various shops, for a flat fee (1-day €16, 2-day €27, 3-day €33.50; children age 5-11 €9.50/14/17). Open daily 9am-8pm. **Airport branch** (☎218 45 06 60) near the terminal exit. Open daily 7am-midnight. For info, check "Ask Me Lisboa" kiosks in Santa Apolónia, Belém, and on R. Augusta.

Tours:

CARRiSTur (☎213 58 23 34; www.carristur.pt), a subsidiary of the city's public transit provider, runs 1½hr. tours of Lisboa's historic center in pre-WWI tram cars. Tours depart every 30min. from the Pç. do Comércio 10am-8pm. €18, children 4-10 €9, under 4 free.

GoCar Tours R. Douradores, 16 (☎210 96 50 30; www.gocartours.pt). Reserve a yellow mini-car online for a GPS-guided self-tour along 1 of 4 Lisboa routes. A bit pricey, but a novel way to see the city and focus on sites of individual interest. Cars accommodate 2 people. €25 1st hr., €20 2nd hr., €18 each additional hr.

Inside Lisboa (☎968 41 26 12; www.insideLisboa.com). A wide range of walking tours throughout Lisboa; some tours include tram rides and food tastings. Tours depart from the Rossio daily at 10am. Tours €14-18, under 26 €10-14. Also offers daytrips to Cascais, Sintra, and elsewhere; check website for details.

Budget Travel: Tagus Travel, Pç. de Londres, 9C (☎218 49 15 31; www.taguseasy.pt).

Embassies: See **Embassies and Consulates,** p. 8.

Currency Exchange: Banks are open M-F 8:30am-3pm. Exchange money at **Nova Câmbios,** Praça D. Pedro IV, 42 (☎213 24 25 53). **Western Union,** Pr. Dom Pedro IV, 41 (☎213 22 04 80), inside **Cota Câmbios,** performs money transfers. Open daily 8pm-10pm. The main post office, most banks, and travel agencies also change money, and exchanges line the streets of Baixa. Ask about fees first—they can be exorbitant.

LOCAL SERVICES

English-Language Bookstore: FNAC, Armazéns do Chiado, 4th fl., R. do Carmo, 2 (☎213 22 18 00). Large section just for English books, but they can be found throughout the store in the regular sections as well. Open daily 10am-10pm.

Libraries: Biblioteca Municipal Central, Palácio Galveias (☎217 80 30 20). M: Campo Pequeno. Open M and Sa 1-7pm, Tu-F 10am-7pm. **Biblioteca Municipal Camões,** Largo do Calhariz 17 (☎213 42 21 57). Free internet. Open M and W-F 10:30am-6pm, 2nd and 4th M and Sa of every month 10:30am-6pm.

Shopping Centers:

Armazéns do Chiado, R. do Carmo 2 (☎213 21 06 00; www.armazensdochiado.com). Food court at the top. Open daily 10am-10pm, restaurants close at 11pm.

El Corte Inglés (☎213 71 17 00; www.elcorteingles.pt), between Av. António Augusto de Agular and Marquês da Fronteira e Sidónio Pais. M: São Sebastião. Portugal's 1st branch of the Spanish department store. Open M-Th 10am-10pm, F-Sa 10am-11:30pm, Su 10am-1pm. MC/V.

Colombo, Av. Lusíada (☎217 11 36 00; www.colombo.pt), in front of Benfica stadium. M: Colégio Militar-Luz. Over 400 shops, a 10-screen cinema (adult ticket €5), and a small amusement park. Open daily 9am-midnight.

Centro Comercial Amoreiras de Lisboa, Av. Eng. Duarte Pacheco (☎213 81 02 00; www.amoreiras.com), near R. Carlos Alberto da Mota Pinto. M: Marquês de Pombal. Towers house 383 shops, including a huge **Pão de Açúcar** supermarket and cinema. Open daily 10am-11pm.

Centro Comercial Vasco da Gama, Av. Dom João II (☎218 93 06 01; www.centrovascodagama.pt). M: Oriente. Open daily 10am-midnight.

EMERGENCY AND COMMUNICATIONS

Police: Tourism Police Station, Palácio Foz in Restauradores (☎213 42 16 24), and at R. Capelo, 13 (☎213 46 61 41 or 42 16 34). English spoken.

Late-Night Pharmacy: 24hr. pharmacy rotates, check the listings in the window of any pharmacy. Look for a lighted green cross, or check listings at **Farmácia Azevedos,** Pr. Dom Pedro IV, 31 (☎213 43 04 82), at the base of Rossio in front of the metro. Regular hours 8:30am-7:40pm.

Medical Services: ☎112 in case of emergency. **Hospital de Saint Louis,** R. Luz Soriano, 182 (☎213 21 65 00) in Bairro Alto. Open daily 9am-8pm. **Hospital de São José,** R. José António Serrano (☎218 84 10 00 or 261 31 28 57).

Telephones: Portugal Telecom, Pr. Dom Pedro IV, 68 (☎808 21 11 56). M: Rossio. Pay the cashier after your call or use a phone card. Also has pre-paid internet (€2 per hr.). Office open daily 8am-11pm. Portugal Telecom phone cards (50 units €3) available at the office or at bookstores and stationers. Local calls cost at least 2 units. Minutes per unit vary. PT cards should only be purchased for local use; better deals on non-local calls can be found elsewhere.

Internet Access: Portugal Telecom (see above). **The Instituto Portuges da Juventude,** Av. Liberdade 194 (☎213 17 92 00; juventude.gov.pt). 30min. of free internet and assistance for students. Open Tu-Sa 9am-8pm. **Web C@fé,** R. Diário de Notícias 126 (☎213 421 181) in Bairro Alto. Doubles as a bar. €0.75 per 15min. Open daily 7pm-2am.

Post Office: Main office, Pr. dos Restauradores (☎213 23 89 71). Open M-F 8am-10pm, Sa-Su 9am-6pm. To avoid the lines, go to the branch at Pr. do Comércio (☎213 22 09 20). Open M-F 8:30am-6:30pm. Cash only. **Postal Code:** 1100.

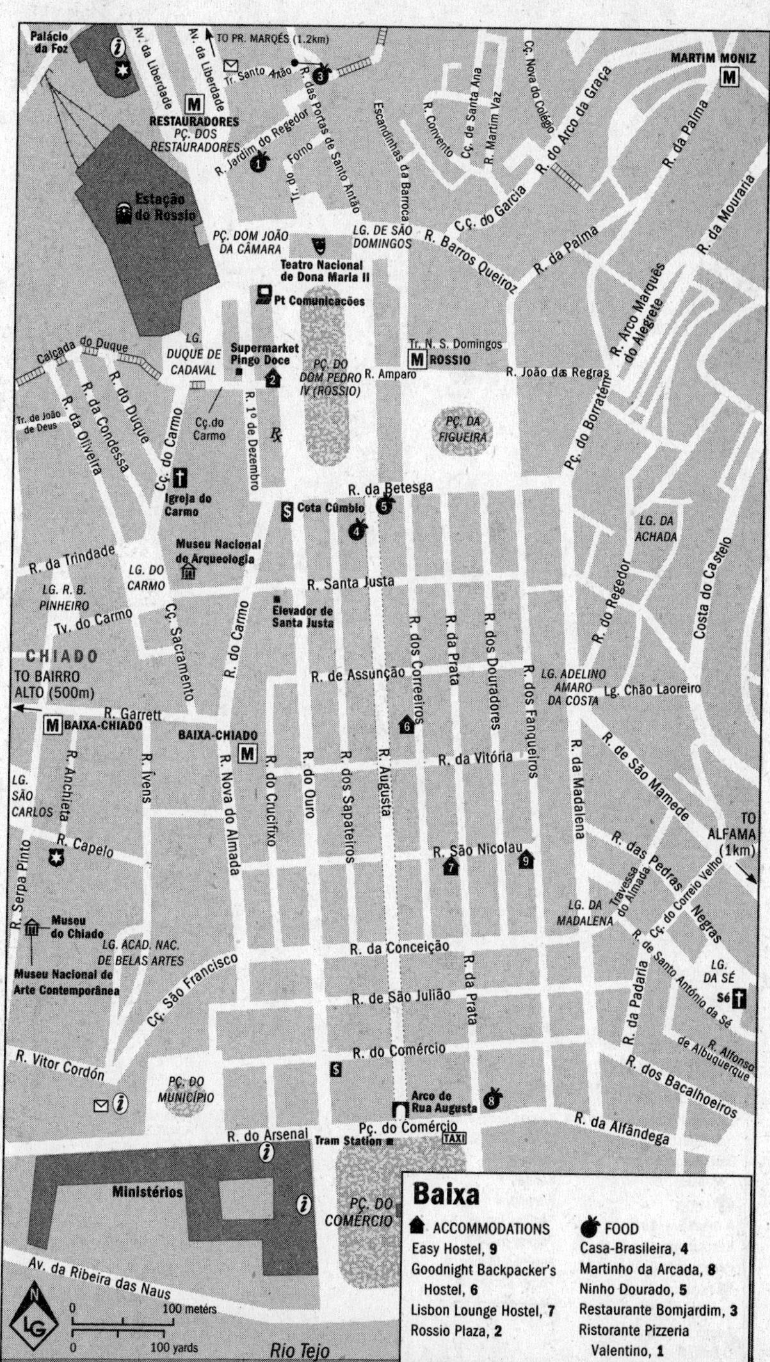
Palácio da Foz
Av. da Liberdade
TO PR. MARQÉS (1.2km)
Tr. Santo Antão
MARTIM MONIZ
RESTAURADORES
PÇ. DOS RESTAURADORES
R. Jardim do Regedor
R. das Portas de Santo Antão
Escandinhas da Barroca
R. Convento
Cç. de Santa Ana
R. Martim Vaz
Cç. Nova do Colégio
R. do Arco da Graça
R. da Palma
R. da Mouraria
Forno
Tr. do
Estação do Rossio
Cç. do Garcia
PÇ. DOM JOÃO DA CÂMARA
LG. DE SÃO DOMINGOS
R. Barros Queiroz
Teatro Nacional de Dona Maria II
Pt Comunicacões
R. Arco Marquês do Alegrete
Calçada do Duque
LG. DUQUE DE CADAVAL
Supermarket Pingo Doce
PÇ. DO DOM PEDRO IV (ROSSIO)
Tr. N. S. Domingos
ROSSIO
R. Amparo
R. João das Regras
Tr. de João de Deus
R. da Oliveira
R. da Condessa
R. do Duque
Cç. do Carmo
R. 1º de Dezembro
PÇ. DA FIGUEIRA
Pç. do Borratém
Igreja do Carmo
R. da Betesga
Cota Câmbio
LG. DA ACHADA
Museu Nacional de Arqueologia
R. da Trindade
LG. DO CARMO
LG. R. B. PINHEIRO
R. Santa Justa
Elevador de Santa Justa
Tv. do Carmo
Cç. Sacramento
R. do Carmo
R. dos Correeiros
R. da Prata
R. dos Douradores
R. dos Fanqueiros
R. do Regedor
Costa do Castelo
CHIADO
TO BAIRRO ALTO (500m)
R. de Assunção
LG. ADELINO AMARO DA COSTA
Lg. Chão Laoreiro
R. Garrett
BAIXA-CHIADO
R. Anchieta
R. Ivens
R. Nova do Almada
R. do Crucifixo
R. do Ouro
R. dos Sapateiros
R. Augusta
R. da Vitória
R. da Madalena
R. de São Mamede
LG. SÃO CARLOS
R. Capelo
R. Serpa Pinto
R. São Nicolau
TO ALFAMA (1km)
R. das Pedras Negras
Travessa do Almada
Cç. do Correio Velho
LG. DA MADALENA
Museu do Chiado
LG. ACAD. NAC. DE BELAS ARTES
Museu Nacional de Arte Contemporânea
Cç. São Francisco
R. da Conceição
R. de Santo António da Sé
LG. DA SÉ
Sé
R. de São Julião
R. da Padaria
R. Alfonso de Albuquerque
R. do Comércio
R. Vitor Cordón
R. dos Bacalhoeiros
PÇ. DO MUNICÍPIO
Arco de Rua Augusta
R. da Alfândega
R. do Arsenal
Pç. do Comércio
Tram Station
TAXI
Ministérios
PÇ. DO COMÉRCIO
Av. da Ribeira das Naus
0
100 meters
100 yards
Rio Tejo
LG
Baixa
ACCOMMODATIONS
Easy Hostel, 9
Goodnight Backpacker's Hostel, 6
Lisbon Lounge Hostel, 7
Rossio Plaza, 2
FOOD
Casa-Brasileira, 4
Martinho da Arcada, 8
Ninho Dourado, 5
Restaurante Bomjardim, 3
Ristorante Pizzeria Valentino, 1

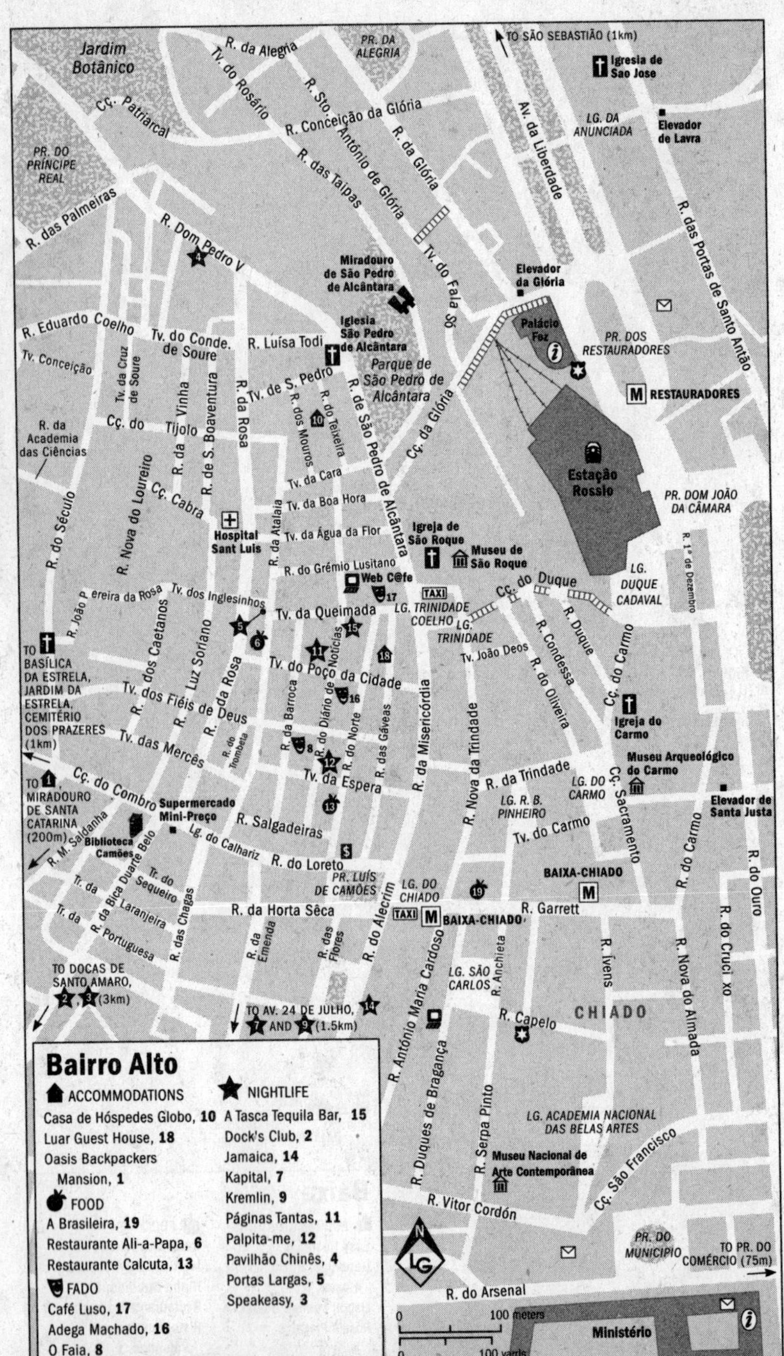
Bairro Alto
ACCOMMODATIONS
Casa de Hóspedes Globo, 10
Luar Guest House, 18
Oasis Backpackers Mansion, 1
FOOD
A Brasileira, 19
Restaurante Ali-a-Papa, 6
Restaurante Calcuta, 13
FADO
Café Luso, 17
Adega Machado, 16
O Faia, 8
NIGHTLIFE
A Tasca Tequila Bar, 15
Dock's Club, 2
Jamaica, 14
Kapital, 7
Kremlin, 9
Páginas Tantas, 11
Palpita-me, 12
Pavilhão Chinês, 4
Portas Largas, 5
Speakeasy, 3
Jardim Botânico
R. da Alegria
PR. DA ALEGRIA
TO SÃO SEBASTIÃO (1km)
Igresia de Sao Jose
Tv. do Rosário
R. Sto. Antônio de Glória
R. Conceição da Glória
Cç. Patriarcal
R. da Glória
LG. DA ANUNCIADA
Elevador de Lavra
PR. DO PRÍNCIPE REAL
R. das Taipas
Av. da Liberdade
R. das Palmeiras
R. Dom Pedro V
Tv. do Fala Só
R. das Portas de Santo Antão
Miradouro de São Pedro de Alcântara
Elevador da Glória
Palácio Foz
PR. DOS RESTAURADORES
R. Eduardo Coelho
Tv. do Conde. de Soure
R. Luísa Todi
Igiesia São Pedro de Alcântara
Parque de São Pedro de Alcântara
RESTAURADORES
Tv. Conceição
Tv. da Cruz de Soure
Tv. de S. Pedro
R. da Rosa
Cç. da Glória
R. da Academia das Ciências
Cç. do Tijolo
R. da Vinha
R. de S. Boaventura
R. dos Mouros
R. do Teixeira
R. de São Pedro de Alcântara
Estação Rossio
R. Nova do Loureiro
Cç. Cabra
Tv. da Cara
Tv. da Boa Hora
PR. DOM JOÃO DA CÂMARA
R. do Século
Hospital Sant Luis
R. da Atalaia
Tv. da Água da Flor
Igreja de São Roque
Museu de São Roque
R. 1º de Dezembro
R. do Grémio Lusitano
Web C@fe
Cç. do Duque
LG. DUQUE CADAVAL
R. João Pereira da Rosa
Tv. dos Inglesinhos
Tv. da Queimada
LG. TRINIDADE COELHO
LG. TRINIDADE
R. Duque
TO BASÍLICA DA ESTRELA, JARDIM DA ESTRELA, CEMITÉRIO DOS PRAZERES (1km)
R. dos Caetanos
R. Luz Soriano
Tv. do Poço da Cidade
Tv. João Deos
R. Condessa
Cç. do Carmo
Tv. dos Fiéis de Deus
R. da Barroca
R. do Diário de Notícias
R. do Oliveira
Igreja do Carmo
Tv. das Mercês
R. do Trombeta
R. do Norte
R. das Gáveas
R. da Misericórdia
R. Nova da Trindade
Museu Arqueológico do Carmo
TO MIRADOURO DE SANTA CATARINA (200m)
Cç. do Combro
Supermercado Mini-Preço
Tv. da Espera
R. da Trindade
LG. DO CARMO
Cç. Sacramento
Elevador de Santa Justa
R. Salgadeiras
LG. R. B. PINHEIRO
Biblioteca Camões
R. M. Saldanha
Lg. do Calhariz
Tv. do Carmo
R. do Carmo
R. do Ouro
R. Duarte Belo
Tr. do Sequeiro
R. do Loreto
BAIXA-CHIADO
Tr. da Laranjeira
R. da Bica
PR. LUÍS DE CAMÕES
LG. DO CHIADO
R. Garrett
Tr. da Portuguesa
R. das Chagas
R. da Horta Sêca
R. do Alecrim
R. Ivens
R. do Cruci xo
R. da Emenda
R. das Flores
R. António Maria Cardoso
LG. SÃO CARLOS
R. Anchieta
R. Nova do Almada
TO DOCAS DE SANTO AMARO, 2, 3 (3km)
TO AV. 24 DE JULHO, 7 AND 9 (1.5km)
R. Capelo
CHIADO
R. Duques de Bragança
R. Serpa Pinto
LG. ACADEMIA NACIONAL DAS BELAS ARTES
Museu Nacional de Arte Contemporânea
Cç. São Francisco
R. Vitor Cordón
PR. DO MUNICIPIO
TO PR. DO COMÉRCIO (75m)
R. do Arsenal
Ministério
0
100 meters
100 yards
TAXI

ACCOMMODATIONS AND CAMPING

Lisboa has seen an explosion of tourism in recent years, and with it, a rapid growth in accommodations catering to student travelers on a budget. The result is a remarkable selection of fresh, funky, comfortable, and even occasionally elegant hostels, all at prices travelers to Paris or Madrid could only dream of. These hostels are concentrated in Baixa and Bairro Alto and tend to be very similar in setup: mixed four- to eight-person dorms, shared bathrooms, a common living room, and free internet. They do differ slightly in amenities, but most are comfortable and run €18-20 in the summer. Thanks to online booking, they fill up fast, so reserve ahead. Unless otherwise stated, assume that linens and towels are included but that internet is not.

Pensões and budget hotels abound in Lisboa, but room quality varies significantly—ask to see the room before paying. During the summer, expect to pay €20-30 for a single and €35-45 for a double, depending on amenities. You can usually find a room in the summer with little or no notice, but you may want to book in advance during mid-June for the Festa de Santo Antonio. In the low season (Oct.-Apr.), prices generally drop €5 or more, so try bargaining. Many establishments only have rooms with double beds and charge per person. Several hotels can be found in the center of town on Av. da Liberdade, while cheaper *pensões* cluster in Baixa and Bairro Alto. Avoid those surrounding Rossio: while they're very convenient, they're usually around €10 more than the norm. Look around Baixa's **Rua da Prata, Rua dos Correiros,** and **Rua do Ouro** for cheaper accommodations. Lodgings near **Castelo de São Jorge** are quieter and closer to the sights, but more difficult to reach. Be careful at night thoughout the historic center and be particularly mindful walking alone through the poorly lit, winding streets of Alfama and in Bairro Alto.

Camping is reasonably popular in Portugal, but campers can be prime targets for thieves. Stay at an enclosed campsite and ask ahead about security. There are 30 campgrounds within a 45min. radius of the capital. The most popular, **Lisboa Camping,** is inside the 900-acre *parque florestal*, and has a four-star rating. (☎217 62 82 00; www.Lisboacamping.com. €6, children under 12 €3, tents €6-7, cars €4. Prices fall in winter. Bungalows available.)

BAIXA

Baixa may not offer much in the way of fine dining or nightlife, but its prime location between Alfama and Bairro Alto makes the neighborhood an excellent home base. Hostels here are among the best designed and most inviting in the city; as a result, they fill quickly in the summer, so book well ahead. The neighborhood's many *pensões*—less luxurious and more expensive than its hostels—may have last-minute availability, even during the high season. Prices tend to be a bit higher than in surrounding neighborhoods. Be advised that most accommodations are located on upper floors, a hassle for travelers with heavy luggage.

Kitsch Hostel, Pr. Dos Restauradores 65 (☎213 46 73 32; www.kitschhostel.com). M: Restauradores. Opened in March 2009, this centrally located hostel is every bit as quirky as the name would suggest. Enter through the Tabacaria Restauradores into an energetic world of reflective ceilings, celebrity collages, and delightfully tacky furniture. All rooms with shared bath. Breakfast included. Towels €1. Free internet and Wi-Fi. Key deposit €10. 4- to 12-bed dorms M-Th and Su €14-16, F-Sa €16-18; doubles from €50; triples from €60. AmEx/MC/V. ❶

Living Lounge Hostel, R. do Crucifixo 116 (☎213 46 10 78; www.Lisboaloungehostel.com), and **Lisboa Lounge Hostel,** R. de São Nicolau 41 (213 462 061; www.Lisboaloungehostel.com). M: Baixa-Chiado (Baixa exit). Under joint ownership, both of these hostels feature excellent contemporary design, with bold colors and cool

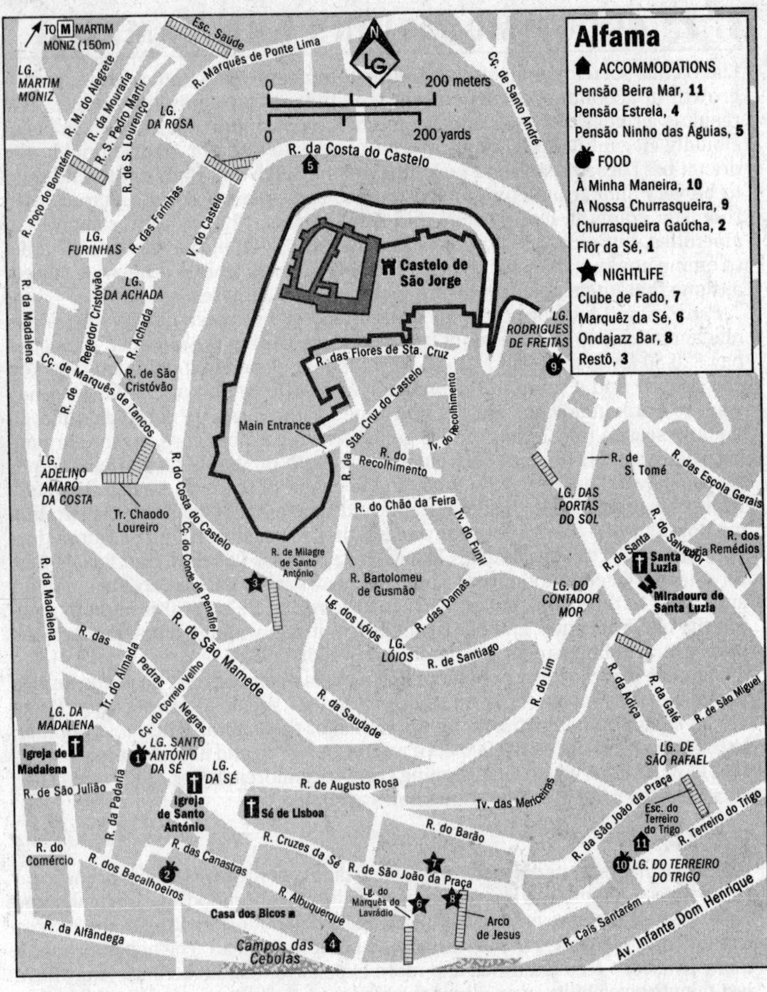

touches like chandeliers made from teacups. Free city tours Tu and F. Nightly dinners (€8) include wine and dessert. All rooms with shared bath; singles at Living Lounge only. Breakfast included. Laundry €7. Free internet and Wi-Fi. Key deposit €5. 4- to 8-bed dorms Oct. 15-Apr. 14 €18, Apr. 15-May 31 and Sept. 16-Oct. 14 €20, June 1-Sept. 15 €22; singles €30/35/35; doubles €50/60/60. AmEx/MC/V. ❶

Goodnight Backpacker's Hostel, R. dos Correeiros, 113, 2nd fl. (☎213 43 01 39; www.goodnighthostel.com). M: Baixa-Chiado (Baixa exit). Exposed stone, offbeat wallpaper, and dozens of little black birds adorn this lively hostel spread over 4 fl. (no elevator). Breakfast included. Towels €1. Free internet and Wi-Fi. Key deposit €5. Dorms €16-20; doubles with shared bath €50. Cash only. ❶

Rossio Hostel, Cç. do Carmo 6 (☎213 42 60 04). M: Rossio. This hostel's prime location on the Rossio and gorgeous doubles set it apart. Exposed wooden beams, well-chosen furniture, and bright, bold colors befit a boutique hotel with twice the price. Request a Rossio view. All rooms with shared bath. Breakfast included. Laundry €5. Free internet. 4- and 6-bed dorms €20-24; doubles €57-65. MC/V. ❷

Travellers House, R. Augusta 89 (☎210 11 59 22; www.travellershouse.com). M: Baixa-Chiado (Baixa exit). Book well in advance—this popular hostel fills quickly. Centrally located. Breakfast included. Free internet. Laundry €4. 4- and 6-bed dorms €23-25; doubles with shared bath €30-35. MC/V. ❷

Home Hostel, R. de São Nicolau 13 (☎218 88 53 12). M: Baixa-Chiado (Baixa exit). Formerly Easy Hostel. Basic dorms in the heart of Baixa. Breakfast included. Free internet and laundry. Key deposit €5. 4- and 6-bed dorms June-Sept. €20-22, Oct.-May €16-18. Cash only. ❷

BAIRRO ALTO AND CHIADO

Although less central than Baixa, the many budget accommodations in Bairro Alto and Chiado offer the most direct access to nightlife and museums.

Oasis Backpackers Mansion, R. de Santa Catarina, 24 (☎213 47 80 44; www.oasisLisboa.com). From M: Baixa-Chiado, follow directions to the Miradouro de Santa Catarina (p. 390). Facing the river, turn to your right; the hostel is the yellow house at the bottom of the hill. True to its name, funky Oasis is a backpacker's haven. A diverse range of travelers gather for home-cooked dinners in the classy dining room (M-Sa, €5) or for drinks in the patio bar (open daily 6pm-midnight). Breakfast included. Laundry €7. Free internet and Wi-Fi. Key deposit €5. Co-ed dorms €18-20; doubles with private bath €44. AmEx/MC/V. ❶

Lisboa Poets Hostel, R. Nova da Trinidade 2 (☎213 46 10 58; www.Lisboapoetshostel.com), on the 5th fl. Decked out in soothing earth tones and beanbag chairs, this ideally located newcomer to Lisboa's hostel scene features a small book exchange and spacious 2- to 6-bed dorms named for famous writers. Breakfast included. Laundry €7. Free internet and Wi-Fi. Key deposit €5. Co-ed dorms mid-Oct. to mid-Apr. €18, mid-Apr. to June €20, Jul. to mid-Oct. €22; doubles mid-Oct to mid-Apr. €42-65, mid-Apr. to mid-Oct. €45-70. MC/V over €50. ❷

Pensão Globo, R. Teixeira 37 (☎213 46 22 79; www.cb2web.com/globo). Simple but comfortably appointed rooms with TV and bath, some with patio. Convenient location. Laundry €10. Singles and doubles €20-60; triples €75; quads €85. Low-season discounts. Cash only. ❷

Pensão Luar, R. das Gáveas 101 (☎213 46 09 49; www.pensaoluar.com). Touches like the beautiful *azulejo* tiling on the staircase distinguish this affordable and excellently located but otherwise unremarkable *pensão.* Rooms are small and basic but very clean. Use of safe €1. Laundry €10 for 6kg. Singles €15-50; doubles €55-65; quads €60-85 (more expensive rooms include shower). Low-season discounts. Cash only. ❷

ALFAMA

Alfama has few lodging options and they're generally a bit more expensive, but staying here is a nice change of pace (especially after hectic Baixa). The steep, unmarked streets can make each trip back to the *pensão* a grueling workout, but hikes frequently pay off with postcard views of downtown Lisboa.

Pensão Ninho das Águias, Costa do Castelo, 74 (☎218 85 40 70). Perched at the top of Alfama, Ninho das Águias towers above Lisboa's other *pensões,* literally and metaphorically. Beautiful common spaces, garden patio, family vibe, and fantastic views, especially from rooms 5, 6, 12-14, and the small tower at the top of the stairs. English and French spoken. Reserve ahead in summer. Singles €30; doubles €45, with bath €50; triples (some with bath) €60. Sept.-Apr. prices drop by €10. Cash only; prices may be flexible with bargaining. ❸

Pensão Beira Mar, Largo Terreiro do Trigo, 16 (☎218 86 99 33; www.guesthousebeiramar.com), near the Sta. Apolonia train station. Avoid the 4-story climb by entering through the back where there are only 2 flights of stairs. 7 brightly decorated rooms with showers and sinks, some with TVs. Living room and kitchen for guest use. Breakfast included. Free internet. Singles €20-25; doubles €35-45; triples €60; quads €70. Oct.-May prices drop by €5. Cash only. ❷

Pensão Estrela, R. dos Bacalhoeiros, 8 (☎218 86 95 06; estrela-arganil.planetaclix.pt). Don't be put off by the ancient, dilapidated staircase; the rooms to which it leads are quite nice and have basic amenities like TVs. Some look out onto the water. The proprietress is extremely helpful. Spanish spoken, no English. Laundry €5. Singles €25-35; doubles €30-45; triple €45-60. ❷

AROUND MARQUÊS DE POMBAL

Black and White Hostel, R. Alexandre Herculano, 39, 1st fl. (☎213 46 22 12; www.costta.com). M: Marquês de Pombal. From the station, walk away from the statue down Av. da Liberdade and turn right on R. Alexandre Herculano; the hostel is 3 blocks down on your left. 15min. walk to both Baixa and Bairro Alto. One of the most artistic hostels in town—rooms are boldly painted with murals of psychedelic spirals and Andy Warhol prints. Breakfast included. Free internet. Key deposit €10. 4-, 6-, and 14-person dorms €15-20. Sa-Su all rooms €17. Cash only. ❶

Pousada de Juventude de Lisboa (HI), R. Andrade Corvo, 46 (☎213 53 26 96). M: Picoas. Exit the metro station onto R. Andrade Corvo; the hostel is marked by a large banner directly in front of you. A large hostel worth looking into if others are booked. Breakfast included; lunch and dinner €6 each. Reserve ahead. 4- and 6-bed dorms €16-18; doubles with bath and TVs €43-45. MC/V. ❶

FOOD

Calorie-counters beware: Lisboa has some of the cheapest, most irresistible restaurants of the western European capitals, not to mention the best wine. A full dinner costs about €9-11 per person and the *prato do dia* (daily special) is often only €5-7. Between lunch and dinner, snack on cheap, filling, and addictive Portuguese pastries. Lisboa boasts almost as many *pastelarias* as Spain has tapas bars, and the city abounds with seafood specialties such as *pratos de caracois* (snail dishes), *creme de mariscos* (seafood chowder with tomatoes), and *bacalhau cozido com grão e batatas* (cod with chickpeas and boiled potatoes, doused in olive oil). For a more diverse selection, head up to the winding streets of Bairro Alto where you'll find many international restaurants.

FOOD BY TYPE

International	
Restaurante Ali-a-Papa (p. 384)	BA ❸
Restaurante Calcuta (p. 386)	BA ❷
Ristorante-Pizzeria Valentino (p. 385)	B ❷
Ali-a-Papa (p. 386)	BA❷
Portuguese	
A Nossa Churrasqueira (p. 388)	A ❶
Churrasqueira Gaúcha (p. 386)	A ❷
Martinho da Arcada (p. 385)	B ❹
Restaurante Vegetariano Jardim das Cerejas (p. 386)	BA❷
Restaurante Bomjardim (p. 385)	B❷
Cafes	
A Brasileira (p. 386)	BA ❷
Kaffeehaus (p. 386)	BA ❷
Bar Cerca Moura (p. 397)	G ❶
Casa-Brasileira (p. 385)	B ❶
Esplanada Igreja da Graça (p. 388)	G ❶
Flôr da Sé (p. 386)	A ❶
noo bai café (p. 385)	B ❷
O Pitéu (p. 388)	G ❷
Pastelaria Estrela da Graça (p. 388)	G ❶
Pastelaria Rigoleto (p. 386)	BA ❷

A Alfama **B** Baixa **BA** Bairro Alto and Chiado **G** Graça

MARKETS

Pingo Doce and **Mini-Preço supermarkets** have locations throughout the city; most locations are open 9am-8pm. Check www.clubeminipreco.website.pt for specific locations. Two convenient locations are R. 1 de Dezembro, 81-83, just outside Pr. do Dom Pedro IV, and R. do Loreto.

Supermercado Pão de Açúcar, Av. Duarte Pacheco (☎213 82 66 80), in the Amoreiras Shopping Center de Lisboa. Take bus #11 from Pr. dos Restauradores or Pr. da Figueira. A large supermarket with a wide selection. Open daily 9am-11pm.

Mercado da Ribeira, Av. 24 de Julho (☎213 46 29 66). M: Cais de Sodré. Accessible by bus #40 or tram #15. This vast, century-old, picturesque market complex is located inside a warehouse just outside Estação Cais do Sodré. Go early for the freshest selection of fruit, fish, and a variety of other foods. Prices on produce can't be beat. Produce market open Tu-Sa 5am-2pm. Flower market open M-Sa 5am-7pm. Cash only.

BAIXA

Baixa is not a gourmand's paradise. **Rua das Portas, Rua Augusta,** and **Rua dos Correeiros** are lined with restaurants promising authentic Portuguese cuisine, although the menus in nine languages posted outside tell a different story. To eat affordably, look for restaurants offering appealing *pratos do dia* or set *menus.*

Ristorante-Pizzaria Valentino, R. Jardim do Regedor 37-45 (☎213 46 17 27). A slice of Italy on the Pr. Dos Restauradores. Watch chefs prepare Italian classics in the open kitchen, and keep your eyes peeled for the Portuguese soccer stars known to swing by. Try the crunchy-crusted Pizza Caprese (€8.50). Homemade pasta €7-15. Pizzas €4-9. Open daily noon-midnight. MC/V. ❷

Casa Brasileira, R. Augusta 267-269. A great place to grab a pastry and a drink while sightseeing. Huge selection of baked goods €1-3.50. Large salads and basic entrees (hamburgers, omelettes, etc.) all €8. Open M-Sa 7am-1am, Su 8am-1am. Cash only. ❷

Martinho da Arcada, Pr. do Comércio 3 (☎218 87 92 59). Enjoy the one-of-a-kind ambience at the oldest restaurant in Lisboa, founded in 1782. Guests can read poems on the walls by Portuguese poet Fernando Pessoa, a regular during his lifetime. Outside seating available. Fish options less expensive than grilled meats or chicken, though still pricey. Entrees €17-38. Open M-Sa noon-4pm and 7-11pm. AmEx/MC/V. ❸

Restaurante Bonjardim, Tr. Santo Antão 10 (☎213 42 74 24). The self-proclaimed "king of chicken" serves up hearty portions of scrumptious fried, baked, and roast chicken (€9.20) both indoors and under the umbrellas outside. Other grilled meats €9-12. Open daily noon-11pm. AmEx/MC/V. ❷

BAIRRO ALTO AND CHIADO

The narrow streets of Bairro Alto are lined with cozy international restaurants and *fado* houses, while Chiado is home to trendy date spots and sleek cafes. Those in search of cheap, traditional places should not lose hope—although not immediately apparent, Portuguese holes-in-the-wall can be found on the side streets off Cç. do Combro.

noo bai café, Miradouro de Santa Catarina (☎213 46 50 14; www.noobaicafe.com). Follow directions to the Miradouro de Santa Catarina (p. 390). Its sandwiches (€3-5) may be excellent and its coffee (€1-2.50) and beer (€2-4) surprisingly affordable, but it's the patio's commanding view of the Tagus and the dramatic, burnt-orange 25 de Abril bridge that draws a crowd. If you see an open table by the railing, spring for it—and stay the whole day. Internet €3 per hr., free with €5 purchase. Open M-Sa noon-midnight, Su noon-10pm. MC/V over €5. ❶

A Brasileira, R. Garrett 120-22 (☎213 46 95 41). This beautiful wood- and marble-filled cafe has been a Lisboa institution since poet Fernando Pessoa started coming here in the early 20th century. (He's still hanging around—that's his statue planted on the patio.) Light sandwiches and croissants €2-4; entrees €8-20. Open daily 8am-2am. Kitchen open noon-3pm and 7-11pm. AmEx/MC/V. ❷

Kaffeehaus, R. Anchieta 3 (☎210 95 68 28). A calm, sleekly designed slice of Austria beside the Lg. São Carlos. Grab a design magazine in Portuguese, English, or German and settle in for coffee and a sandwich (€4-7). Austrian brunch (€3.50-9) served Sa-Su 11am-8pm. Open Tu-Sa 11am-midnight, Su 11am-8pm. MC/V. ❷

Restaurante Vegetariano Jardim das Cerejas, Cç. Do Sacramento 34-36 (☎213 46 93 08). An island of vegetarian bliss amid a sea of fish and meat. All-you-can-eat lunch buffet €6.90, dinner €8.90. Open daily 8am-10:30pm. AmEx/MC/V. ❷

Txakoli, R. de São Pedro de Alcântara 65 (☎213 43 00 39). Dimly lit and decorated with deep reds and dark woods, this seductive tapas bar is ideal for a late-evening date. Portions are pricey (meat entrees from €14) but shareable, better for a light meal than a full dinner. Open daily 7pm-1am or later. MC/V. ❸

Pastelaria Rigoleto, R. Capelo 12 (☎213 47 04 62). A typical and always-packed Portuguese lunch spot with prices well below the Chiado average. Daily fish and meat specials (€5-6.50) are simple but delicious. Open daily 7:30am-8pm. MC over €5. ❷

Restaurante Calcuta, R. do Norte 17 (☎213 42 82 95; www.restaurantcalcuta.com). Listen to soothing Indian music while you enjoy favorites like *saag paneer* (€8) and prawn masala (€9.50) in this intimate restaurant. Many vegetarian options. Open M-Sa noon-midnight, Su 6pm-midnight. MC/V. ❷

Ali-a-Papa, R. da Atalaia 95 (☎213 47 41 43). Tucked away on a picturesque street, this tiny, owner-operated Morrocan place is more notable for its excellent decor and cozy ambience than for the complexity of its food. Simple but pleasant dishes include Tagine with eggplant and couscous (€10). Open daily 7pm-4am. AmEx/MC/V. ❷

ALFAMA

The winding streets of Alfama conceal a number of small and simple restaurants, often packed with locals. The **Rua da Padaria** and the area around its intersection with **Rua dos Bacalhoeiros** offers the cheapest options in Lisboa.

Flôr da Sé, Largo Santo António da Sé, 9-11 (☎218 87 57 42), next to the Santo Antonio church. This *pastelaria* is clean, brightly lit, and serves quality food at notably low prices. The lunchtime *prato do dia* (€4.50) is scrumptious, and homemade desserts and candies taste as good as they look. Open M-F and Su 7am-8pm. Cash only. ❶

À Minha Maneira, Largo do Terreiro do Trigo 1 (☎218 86 11 12; www.a-minha-maneira.pt). Once a bank, the old vault has been revamped into a wine closet. Various meat and fish dishes with little choice for vegetarians. Free Wi-Fi. Entrees €8-15. Open daily noon-3pm and 7-11:30pm. Cash only. ❷

Churrasqueira Gaúcha, R. dos Bacalhoeiros, 26C-D (☎218 87 06 09). Portuguese food cooked to perfection in a comfortable, cavernous setting. Incredibly fresh meat, poultry, and fish. No vegetarian options. Entrees €8-12. Open M-Sa 10am-midnight. AmEx/MC/V. ❷

Pois, R. São João da Praça, 93-95 (☎218 86 24 97; www.poiscafe.com). A relaxed, contemporary cafe in a traditional neighborhood. Airy dining room with giant stone arches and comfy couches. Menu with snacks, tapas, and lunch foods. Open Tu-Su 11am-8pm. Cash only. ❶

Costa do Castelo, Cç. Marquês de Tancos, 1 (☎218 88 46 36). Colorful tables and chairs fill this intimate restaurant just beyond the walls of the Castelo. Excellent wine selection. Open Tu-Sa 11am-2am, Su 3-11pm. AmEx/MC/V.

DISTANCE: 1 mi.

DURATION: 2hr.

WHEN TO GO: Tu or Sa for the Feira da Ladra.

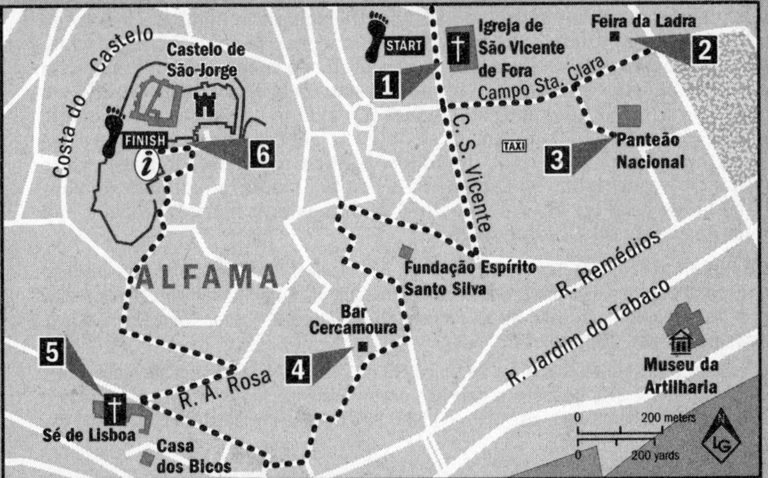

Much of Lisboa was destroyed in the 18th century by a massive earthquake. The most interesting and well-preserved structures are located in the areas of Alfama and Graça. To save yourself the grief of a 2+ hr. hike uphill, start this walking tour of Lisboa with a ride in one of the city's trams. From Praça do Comércio take tram #28 (€1.30) up to the Igreja de São Vicente de Fora.

1. IGREJA DE SÃO VICENTE DE FORA. Built between 1582 and 1629, the Igreja, like many in Portugal, is ornately decorated with gold leafing, large archways, and stained-glass windows. The sacristas, covered with beautiful Sintra marble, are a sight to see. This house of worship is particularly interesting because it's dedicated to Lisboa's real patron saint, St. Vincent.

2. FEIRA DA LADRA. If you happen to be strolling along on a Tuesday or a Saturday between 7am and 4pm you will find a pleasant surprise behind the large church structure: the Feira da Ladra, a flea-market style fair that sells everything from used shoes to African necklaces.

3. PANTEÃO NACIONAL. Around the corner from the feira is the stunning Panteão Nacional. The Panteão was intended to be a church but the town ran out of money before it could be completed. Seized by the government, it was turned into a monument documenting and honoring the forefathers of Portugal.

4. BAR CERCAMOURA. From the Panteão Nacional follow the tram tracks downhill. Window shop or stop at variety of unique antique stores on either side of the street. About ½ mi. downhill there is a great viewpoint from which the skyline of Lisboa, from Alfama, to Baixa, and to the Tejo, can be viewed. Take a break at the Bar Cercamoura before heading onward.

5. SÉ DE LISBOA. The small but impressive Sé lacks the splendor of Lisboa's grander cathedrals, but its sheer age and wonderful location make for an enjoyable visit.

6. CASTELO DE SÃO JORGE. Follow the signs to the castle. At the top of the small hill you'll find the entrance to the Castelo de São Jorge. Constructed during the 5th century by Visigoths, the castle was later dominated by the Moors and finally by the royal family of Portugal. Today, it stands as a series of stone walls with amazing views of Lisboa.

A Nossa Churrasqueira, Lg. Rodrigues de Freitas, 2 (☎218 86 66 02). Chickens rotate over flaming coals behind the counter of this quality budget restaurant in the heart of Alfama. Hearty portions. Entrees €7-9. Open Tu-Su noon-10pm. Cash only. ❷

GRAÇA

Good, cheap eats are easy to find in the area around the Lg. da Graça; stop by a view of the many *pastelarias* lining the square to compare *pratos do dia* (€4-6). To get there, take any tram 15E one stop beyond the large white Igreja de São Vicente de Fora. Those in search of a snack or light lunch with an incredible view should head to the **Esplanada Igreja de Graça,** where two kiosks serve tea (€1.50) and sandwiches (€2-4) atop Lisboa's most dramatic hills. (Open daily 11:30am-2am. Cash only.) To get there from the tram stop, climb the stairs to your right and follow Lg. de Graça past the large, white building to your right; the Esplanada is just behind the small park on your left. Things heat up after dark, when churches and markets recede and thumping beats take center stage.

O Pitéu, Lg. da Graça, 95-6 (☎218 87 10 67). *Azulejo*-lined walls and wine-inspired decorations. Serves a few Brazilian dishes in addition to traditional Portuguese dishes of fish, chicken, pork, and steak. Entrees €8-12. Open M-F noon-3pm and 7-10pm, Sa noon-3pm. Cash only. ❷

Pastelaria Estrela da Graça, Lg. da Graça, 98 (☎218 87 24 38). Try an affordable *prato do dia* (€4-6) or a delicious homemade pastry, accompanied by a large glass of jaw-droppingly underpriced house wine (€0.50-0.90). Open daily 7am-10pm. Cash only. ❶

SIGHTS

With 3000 years of history, Lisboa is constantly gesturing to the past. Moorish *azulejos* (painted tiles) adorn the Alfama district; the 12th-century Sé cathedral maintains a tough Romanesque stone facade; the elaborate Manueline monastery in Belém features excessive ornamentation reflective of Portugal's glory during the Age of Discovery. The Neoclassical design of Praça do Comércio's triumphal Roman arch marks a return to the simpler forms favored by the Marquês de Pombal's post-earthquake rebuilding. But Lisboa's beauty speaks of the present as well, from the sleek, modern Parque das Nações to the expressive, graffitied streets of Bairro Alto. Those planning to do a lot of sightseeing in a few days should consider purchasing the Welcome Center's **Lisboa Card** for a flat fee (p. 377). Many museums and sites are closed on Mondays and free on Sundays before 2pm.

BAIXA

Although Baixa claims few historical sights, the lively pedestrian traffic and dramatic history surrounding the neighborhood's three main *praças* make it a monument on its own. Beware Baixa's softly cooing pigeons, well-trained by countless statues of distinguished leaders on which they've made their mark.

AROUND ROSSIO. Begin your historical tour of 18th-century Lisboa at its heart: **Rossio,** or **Praça Dom Pedro IV** as it is more formally known. The city's main square was once a cattle market, public execution stage, bullring, and carnival ground. Today, it is the fast-paced domain of tourists and ruthless local drivers circling Pedro's enormous statue, and shadier characters by night. Another statue, this one of Gil Vicente, Portugal's first great dramatist, peers from atop the **Teatro Nacional de Dona Maria II** (easily recognized by its large, Parthenon-esque columns) at one end of the *praça.*

AROUND PRAÇA DOS RESTAURADORES. In Praça dos Restauradores, a giant obelisk celebrates Portugal's hard-earned independence from Spain, achieved in 1640 after 60 years of Spanish rule. The obelisk stands by a bronze sculpture of the "Spirit of Independence," a reminder of the centuries-old Spanish-Portuguese rivalry. The tourist office is housed at Palácio da Foz, and shops line the *praça* and C. da Glória, the hill that leads to Bairro Alto. Pr. dos Restauradores is also the start of **Avenida da Liberdade,** one of Lisboa's most elegant promenades. Modeled after the boulevards of 19th-century Paris, this mile-long thoroughfare ends at **Praça do Marquês de Pombal.** There, an 18th-century statue of the Marquês still watches over the city he whipped into shape 250 years ago.

AROUND PRAÇA DO COMÉRCIO. After the earthquake of 1755 leveled this section of Lisboa, the Marquês de Pombal designed the new streets to serve as a conduit for goods from the ports on the Rio Tejo to the city center. The grid formed perfect blocks, with streets designated for specific trades: *sapateiros* (shoemakers), *douradores* (gold workers), and *bacalhoeiros* (cod merchants) each had their own avenue. The roads lead to Praça do Comércio, on the banks of the Tejo. Today the *praça*, watched over by a 9400 lb. statue of **Dom João I,** serves as a tourist hub, providing a wide and inviting space between the Tejo's many boats and the city's buzzing crowds.

BAIRRO ALTO AND CHIADO

Cultured Chiado is home to many of Lisboa's finest museums, while Bairro Alto offers some of the best views in the city. Lively **Praça Luís de Camões,** where the two meet, is a prime spot for people watching.

MUSEU ARQUELÓGICO DO CARMO. Built around the ruins of a medieval church destroyed in the 1755 earthquake, this museum features archeological remains from four millennia. Strengths of the small collection include mummies from 16th-century Peru and ancient Egypt, but the highlight is undoubtedly the museum building itself. At its heart is a stunning open-air courtyard framed by the soaring stone arches of the collapsed church, and its galleries occupy a set of beautifully restored gothic rooms. *(On Lg. do Carmo. ☎213 47 86 29. Open M-Sa Oct.-May 10am-6pm, Apr.-Feb. 10am-7pm. €2.50, students and seniors €1.50, under 14 free.)*

IGREJA E MUSEU DE SÃO ROQUE. When the Plague descended on Lisboa in 1505, King Manuel I begged the residents of Venice to send him a relic of São Roque, to whom legend assigned miraculous healing powers. The plague went on to kill thousands in Portugal, but the Jesuits nonetheless began to construct a splendid church in São Roque's honor in 1555. The church, under construction for more then two centuries, reflects a diverse range of architectural and decorative styles. Particularly notable are the dozens of creepy wooden angel-children emerging from the gilded walls of the **Chapel of Our Lady of Piety** (third on the left) and the Italianate **Chapel of Saint John the Baptist** (fourth on the left), considered a masterpiece of neoclassical art. Astounding **gold candlesticks** and other accoutrements originally displayed in this chapel have been moved to the adjacent museum, which also includes permanent exhibits on Jesuit history and Eastern art. *(On Lg. Trinidade Coelho. ☎213 23 53 80. Church open M 2-6pm; Tu-W, and F-Su 9am-6pm; Th 9am-9pm. Museum open T, W, and F-Su 10am-6pm; Th 2-9pm. Church free. Museum €2.50; students, seniors, and under 14 free; free Su until 2pm.)*

MUSEU DO CHIADO. With just a small permanent collection of Portuguese art from the late 19th century to the present, the recently rebuilt Museu do Chiado, home of the National Museum of Contemporary Art, welcomes large new temporary exhibitions every three months. As a result, the art filling its sleek, soaring galleries can range from Romanian avant-garde painting to recent Portuguese photography. *(R. Serpa Pinto 4. ☎213 43 21 48; www.museudochiado-ipmuseus.pt. Open Tu 2-6pm, W-Su 10am-6pm. €4, under 25 and over 65 €2, under 14 free; free Su until 2pm.)*

VIEWS. With a name like "High Neighborhood," it's no surprise that Bairro Alto deals in dramatic vistas. The **Parque São Pedro de Alcântara,** located two blocks behind the Igreja de São Roque, offers a beautifully maintained garden terrace along with a panorama of Baixa and Alfama. Behind the Museo do Carmo on R. Santa Justa, the towering Victorian **Elevador de Santa Justa,** part of the CARRIS network, whisks tourists and commuters alike between Bairro Alto and Baixa. The **Miradouro de Santa Catarina** overflows with locals drinking cheap beer (available at a nearby kiosk) as they take in the Taugus below. To get there from Pr. Luís de Camões, walk down R. do Loreto (it changes name twice after leaving the *praça*), turn left on R. Marechal Saldanha, and follow it to the end.

WEST OF BAIRRO ALTO

Lisboa grows substantially greener as you head west from Bairro Alto. The area's most notable attractions are in the pleasant residential neighborhoods of Estrela and Prazeres.

CEMITÁRIO DOS PRAZERES. Lisboa's most famous cemetery is not only the final resting place of some of Lisboa society's biggest names, but one of the most pleasant places to spend a peaceful afternoon. Thousands of elaborate mausoleums constitute a veritable city of the dead, replete with tree-lined "avenues" and its own small chapel and museum of death-related artifacts. *(Pr. S. João Bosco. ☎213 96 15 11. Take tram 28E (but only cars labeled "Prazeres") from Pr. Do Comércio or Pr. Luís de Camões to the end of the line; the large granite structure in front of you is the entrance. Cemetery open daily May-Sept. 9am-6pm, Oct.-Apr. 9am-5pm. Museum open Tu-Su 10am-4:30pm. Free.)*

BASÍLICA DA ESTRELA. Queen Dona Maria I in 1796 promised God anything for a son. When she finally gave birth to a baby boy, she built this church as a small token of her gratitude. After taking in the baroque interior rich in pink and green marble, check out the ancient *presépio*, or crib, at the center of the beautiful nativity scene to the right of the main altar. If you're visiting on a Wednesday or Friday afternoon, ask in the vestry for permission to ascend to the rooftop terrace; you'll be rewarded with a fantastic view. *(Pr. da Estrela. ☎213 96 09 15. Take any tram 28E from Pr. Do Comércio or Pr. Luís de Camões to Estrela, where you'll see a large white church on your left and a park on your right. Open daily 7:45am-8pm. Presépio open M-Sa 10-11:45am and 1:30-5pm, Su 2-5pm. Terrace open W and F 2-5pm. Free.)*

JARDIM DA ESTRELA. Across from the Basílica, the wide paths of the soothing Jardim da Estrela wind through duck ponds, tropical plantings, and blossoming jacarandas. The park contains a large children's playground and climbing net, an ice cream shop, and even a small library. *(Pr. da Estrela. Follow directions to the Basílica, above. Open daily 6am-midnight.)*

SÃO SEBASTIÃO

MUSEU DO ORIENTE. Just opened in 2008, this new museum documents Portugal's more than five centuries of involvement in the East with detailed permanent exhibitions of artifacts from across Asia. Not to be missed are the room-sized Indian Altar to Durga and the dramatic Indonesian Barong, included in the "Gods of Asia" exhibit. *(Av. Brasilia at the Doca de Alcântara. ☎213 58 52 00; www.museudooriente.pt. Take tram 15E in the direction of Belém; get off when you see a* *large warehouse covered in black cloth on your left. Open M, W-Th, Sa-Su 10am-6pm; F 10am-10pm. €4, seniors €2.50, ages 6-12 and students €2, under 6 free. Free F 6-10pm.)*

FUNDACION CALOUSTE GULBENKIAN. Perhaps Portugal's biggest fan ever, native Armenian Calouste Gulbenkian was so charmed when he visited in 1942 that he stayed in the same hotel in Lisboa for 13 years, until his death in 1955. In his will, the millionaire left his extensive art collection (some of it purchased from the Hermitage in St. Petersburg, Russia) to Portugal. The collection, which offers a survey of Western art from ancient Egypt through the early 20th century, forms the core of the Museu Calouest Gulbenkian. Although it lacks any true blockbusters, the worthwhile museum's highlights include excellent French Neoclassical decorative arts, intricate Art Nouveau jewelry, and paintings by Monet, Rodin, and Fantin-Latour. Across a lush sculpture garden from the Museu stands the Fundacion's second project, the smaller **Centro de Arte Moderno José de Azeredo Perdigão.** The Centro hosts temporary exhibitions of contemporary art and houses a small permanent collection focused on artists from Portugal and its former colonies. *(Av. Berna, 45A. ☎217 82 30 00; www.gulbenkian.pt. M: São Sebastião. From the main entrance of El Corte Inglés, follow the main road, Av. Augusto Antonio de Aguiar, downhill until you see the sign for the "Fundação Calouste Gulbenkian." Take a right up the staircase, climb another set of stairs, and the Museu is across the parking lot. Open Tu-Su 10am-6pm. Museums €4 each, €7 together. Students, teachers, and seniors 50% discount. Free Su until 2pm.)*

MUSEU NACIONAL DO AZULEJO. Housed within the 16th-century Convento da Madre de Deus, this museum is devoted to the art of the *azulejo* (see Architecture, p. 366). A Manueline doorway leads into a Baroque interior embellished with oil paintings and *azulejos*. Don't miss the chorus room on the second floor, with royal skulls on both sides of the room. *(R. Madre de Deus, 4. East of Alfama in Xabregas. From Pr. do Comércio, just next to the giant arch, take bus #104 or 105. From M: Santa Apolonia cross the street and take bus #28 or 754. The museum is next to the Igreja Madre de Deus. ☎218 10 03 40; www.mnazulejo-ipmuseus.pt. Open Tu 2-6pm, W-Su 10am-6pm. Last entry 5:30pm. €4; under 25, seniors, and teachers €2. Free Su before 2pm.)*

ALFAMA

CASTELO DE SÃO JORGE. Built by the Moors in the 11th century, the castle was conquered by Don Alfonso Enriquez, first king of Portugal, then converted into a playground for the royal family between the 14th and 16th centuries. The towers and castle walls allow for a spectacular panoramic view of Lisboa and the Rio Tejo. Also inside the walls are a small museum, cafe, and gallery. *(☎218 80 06 20; www.egeac.pt. Open daily Mar.-Oct. 9am-9pm; Nov.-Feb. 9am-6pm. Last entry 30min before closing. €5, students €2.50, with Lisboa card €3.50, under 10 or over 65 free.)*

LOWER ALFAMA. The small white **Igreja de Santo António** was built in 1812 over the saint's alleged birthplace. The construction was funded with money collected by the city's children, who fashioned altars bearing saintly images to place on doorsteps. The custom is reenacted annually on June 13, the saint's feast day and Lisboa's biggest holiday, which draws out thousands and involves a debaucherous festival the night before. The church is located on R. da Alfândeo, which begins two blocks away from Pr. do Comércio and connects Baixa and lower Alfama. *(Veer right when you see Igreja da Madalena in Lg. da Madalena on the right. Take R. de Santo António da Sé and follow the tram tracks. ☎218 86 91 45. Open daily 8am-7pm. Mass daily 11am, 5, and 7pm.)* In the square beyond the church is the 12th-century **Sé de Lisboa.** The cathedral's interior lacks the ornamentation of the city's other churches, but its age, treasury (containing

LISBOA

a small collection of religious objects and manuscripts), and cloister (an archeological site and small museum) make for a worthwhile visit. *(☎218 86 67 52. Open daily 9am-7pm except during mass, held Tu-Sa 6:30pm, Su 11:30am and 7pm. Free. Treasury open M-Sa 10am-1pm and 2-5pm. €2.50, students €1.50. Cloister open M-Sa 10am-6:30pm, Su 2-6:30pm. €2.50, students €1.25.)*

GRAÇA

PANTEÃO NACIONAL. The National Pantheon was originally meant to be the Igreja da Santa Engrácia; the citizens of Graça started building the church in 1680 to honor their patron saint. Their ambitions outstripped their finances, however, and they abandoned the project before completing the dome, leaving a massive hole in the top. General Salazar's military regime eventually took over construction, dedicating it as the National Pantheon, a burial ground for important statesmen, in 1966. In a twist of irony, when democracy was restored in 1975, the new government relocated the remains of prominent anti-Fascist opponents to the building and prohibited those who had worked with Salazar from entering. The dome juts out above the Graça skyline, providing an amazing view of Lisboa from its outdoor terrace. Highlights include the tombs of presidents as well as cenotaphs (honorary tombs for people buried elsewhere) for explorers. The Pantheon houses the remains of Amália Rodrigues, the queen of *fado*, and the cenotaphs of Vasco da Gama, the famous Portuguese explorer, and Luis de Camoes, the 17th-century poet. *(To reach the Panteão, take any #28E tram from R. Do Loreto or R. Garrett. ☎218 85 48 20. Open Tu-Su 10am-5pm. €2.50, seniors €1.25, under 14 free. Free Su and holidays until 2pm.)*

IGREJA AND MOSTEIRO DE SÃO VICENTE DE FORA. Built between 1582 and 1629, the Igreja is dedicated to St. Vincent, Lisboa's official patron saint, though Lisboa tends to celebrate its adopted patron saint, St. Antony, much more. The church sanctuary is closed indefinitely for restoration, but in the meantime, the attached Mosteiro offers a small museum detailing the history of the church, offering access to the beautiful chapel inlaid with four colors of marble and displaying some of the church's excellent collection of *azulejo* tile. *(From the bottom of R. dos Correeiros in Baixa, take bus #12 or any tram #28E in the direction of the castle; hop off when you see the large white church on your right. ☎218 85 56 52. Mosteiro open Tu-Su 10am-6pm; last entry 5pm. €4, students and seniors €2, under 13 free.)*

FEIRA DA LADRA. Every Tuesday and Saturday between the Panteão and Igreja de São Vicente, local vendors hit the streets in the early morning for the Graça "thieves market." Merchants bring piles of goods, from Beatles paraphernalia to African sculptures, and passersby are encouraged to bargain. Get steals on old wristwatches and cameras, dig through piles of jewelry, or admire handmade chandeliers and crucifixes. *(Tu and Sa 8am-late afternoon.)*

FESTIVALS AND ENTERTAINMENT

Those who love to mingle with locals will want to visit Lisboa in June. Open-air *feiras*—festivals of eating, drinking, live music, and dancing—fill the streets. After savoring *farturas* (huge Portuguese pastries whose name means "abundance") and Sagres beer, join in traditional Portuguese dancing. On the night of June 12, the streets explode into song and dance in honor of St. Anthony during the **Festa de Santo António.** Banners are strung between streetlights and confetti falls in buckets during a parade along Av. da Liberdade. Young crowds pack the streets of Alfama and the neighborhoods of Bairro Alto and Santa Catarina, and grilled *sardinhas* (sardines) and *ginja* (wild cherry liqueur) are sold everywhere. Lisboa also has a number of commercial *feiras*. From late May to early June, bookworms burrow for three weeks in the outdoor **Feira do Livro** in Parque Eduardo VII, behind Pr. Marquês de Pombal. The **Feira Internacional de Lisboa** occurs every few months in the Parque das Nações; in July and August, the **Feira de Mar de Cascais** and **Feira de Artesanato de Estoril** (celebrating famous Portuguese pottery) take place near the casino. Year-round *feiras* include the **Feira de Oeiras** (sells antiques on the fourth Sunday of each month) and the **Feira de Carcanelos** (sells clothes Th 8am-2pm) in Rato. Packrats should catch the **Feira da Ladra,** a large flea market held every Tuesday and Sunday.

Agenda Cultural and *Follow Me Lisboa*, free at the tourist office and at kiosks in the Rossio on R. Portas de Santo Antão, have information on concerts, *fado*, movies, plays, and bullfights as well as lists of museums, gardens, and libraries.

FADO

A mandatory experience for visitors, Lisboa's trademark entertainment is the traditional *fado*, an expressive art combining elements of singing and narrative poetry (see **Music,** p. 368). *Cantadeiras de fado*, cloaked in black dresses and shawls, relate emotional tales of lost loves and faded glory. Numerous *fado* houses lie in the small streets of Bairro Alto and near R. de São João da Praça in Alfama. Some have both *fado* and folk dance performances. To avoid making a tragedy of your budget, explore nearby streets; various bars and small venues often offer free shows with less notable performers. Those in town during the **Festa do Fado** (June 5-27) should check out the free evening performances at the Castelo de São Jorge (details at www.egeac.pt). Book in advance for dinner performances, especially on weekends, and arrive at *fado* houses 30-45min. early. Minimum consumption requirements tend to run €10-20, but ask ahead of time as they may only apply to the second show, which starts around 11pm and typically does not require reservations. The following places are quite touristy and tend to draw and older crowd, but they do feature Portugal's biggest names.

Café Luso, Travessa da Queimada, 10 (☎213 42 22 81; www.cafeluso.pt). Pass below the club's glowing neon-blue sign to reach *fado* nirvana. Open since 1927, Lisboa's premier *fado* club combines the best in Portuguese music, cuisine, and atmosphere. Fixed menu €25. Entrees €22-39. Min. €25. *Fado* and folkloric dance 8:30-10pm; the *fado* continues until 2am. Make reservations for F and Sa nights. Open daily 7:30pm-2am. AmEx/MC/V.

O Faia, R. Barroca, 54-56 (☎213 42 67 42; www.ofaia.com). Performances by famous *fadistas* like Anita Guerreiro and Lenita Gentil, as well as very fine Portuguese cuisine, make O Faia worth your time and money. 4 singers. Entrees €20-35. Min. €20, includes 2 drinks. *Fado* starts at 9:30pm. 2nd show starts at 11:45pm. Open M-Sa 8pm-2am. AmEx/MC/V.

Clube de Fado, R. S. João da Praça, 92/94 (☎218 85 27 04; www.clube-de-fado.com). A relaxed alternative to the *fado* scene in Bairro Alto, Clube de Fado's rustic wood and stone parlor takes you back to the days of a less hectic Lisboa. Entrees €20-50. Reserve ahead. Show €7.50. Open daily 8pm-2am; *fado* starts at 9:30pm. AmEx/MC/V.

Adega Machado, R. do Norte, 91 (☎213 22 46 40; fax 46 75 07). Founded in 1937, Machado is one of the larger *fado* restaurants and features some of the best known *cantadeiras* and guitarists. The many portraits and wall decorations make this cavernous bar covered in traditional yellow tiles warm and inviting. A typical meal with drinks, is €35. Min. drink charge €16. Open Tu-Su 8pm-2am; *fado* starts at 8:45pm. AmEx/MC/V.

THEATER, MUSIC, AND FILM

Teatro Nacional de Dona Maria II, Pr. Dom Pedro IV, stages performances of classical and foreign plays. (☎213 25 08 00; www.teatro-dmaria.pt. €5-20.) At Lisboa's largest theater, **Teatro Nacional de São Carlos,** R. Serpa Pinto, 9, near the Museu do Chiado in Bairro Alto, opera reigns from late December to mid-June, and the **Orquestra Sinfonica Portuguesa** plays from December to July. (☎213 25 30 45; www.saocarlos.pt. Tickets €7-60. Open M-F 1-7pm, performance days from 1pm until 30min. prior to shows.)

The **São Jorge movie theater,** Av. da Liberdade, 175 (☎213 10 34 00; www.egeac.pt) is one of the oldest in Portugal. Daily shows are held between 2:30 and 9:30pm. Ten-screen cinemas are also located in the **Amoreiras** (☎213 81 02 00; M: Marquês de Pombal), the **Colombo** shopping center (☎217 11 36 00; M: Colegio Militar Luz), and on the top floor of the **Centro Vasco da Gama** (☎218 93 06 01; M: Oriente). The largest theater, with 14 screens, is part of the **El Corte Inglés** shopping complex (☎213 71 17 00; M: São Sebastião). American films are shown with Portuguese subtitles. Movies cost about €7; matinee shows are slightly cheaper.

LISBOA

BULLFIGHTING

Portuguese bullfighting differs from the Spanish variety in that the bull is typically not killed in the ring, but butchered afterwards, a tradition that dates back to the 18th century. These spectacles take place most Thursdays from late June to late September at **Praça de Touros de Lisboa,** Campo Pequeno. (☎217 93 21 43; www.campopequeno.com.) The newly renovated *praça* doubles as a shopping center during the day and also features the distinctly Portuguese *toureio equestre*, or horseback bullfighting at night. Aficionados should include **Santarém** (p. 419) in their travel plans—it's the capital of Portuguese bullfighting and hosts the most celebrated *cavaleiros.*

FUTEBOL

Futebol is the lifeblood of many a Portuguese citizen. *Futebol* fever became an epidemic during the 2006 World Cup, and after a month of nail-biting, shop-closing, crowd-gathering soccer mania, the Portuguese team returned from Germany national heroes after reaching the semifinal round for the first time in 40 years. These days, the Portuguese get riled up for the popular Euro Cup and regional games. If you are in Lisboa when Portugal is playing, go to **Marques de Pombal** (M: Marques de Pombal), where you will see hundreds of fans screaming at a giant TV screen. If they win, follow the fans to the main *praça*, where they will stop traffic, clamber onto random cars, and sometimes flip them over. Lisboa's two main teams are **Benfica** and **Sporting,** both of which feature some of the world's finest players. (Benfica at Estádio da Luz. ☎707 200 100; www.slbenfica.pt. M: Colégio Militar-Luz. Ticket office open daily 10am-7pm. Sporting at Alvalade Stadium. ☎707 20 44 44; www.sporting.pt. M: Campo Grande. Ticket office open M-F 10am-7pm.) Benfica made headlines with its magical rise to the semifinal round of the 2006 UEFA Champions League, the most prestigious club tournament in Europe, for the first time in over a decade. Benfica and Sporting are bitter rivals—be careful whom you support, since both have diehard fans who won't care that you're "just a tourist." Check the newspaper *A Bola* for games.

NIGHTLIFE

Bairro Alto is one giant street party every night until 2am, and is a good first stop for nightlife. **Rua do Norte, Rua do Diário de Notícias, Rua da Rosa,** and **Rua Atalaia**, which run parallel to each other, pack many small bars and clubs into three short blocks, making bar-hopping as easy as crossing the street. Several gay and lesbian establishments lie in this area; there are also some in **Rato** near the edge of Bairro Alto, past Pr. Príncipe Real. The options south of Bairro Alto near the water are larger, flashier, and generally more diverse. The **Docas de Santo Amaro** host a strip of waterfront bars, clubs, and restaurants, while the **Avenida 24 de Julho** and the parallel **Rua das Janelas Verdes** (Street of Green Windows), in the **Santos** area, have some of the most popular clubs and discotecas. Beneath the bridge stands the new **LX Factory,** a hipster haven featuring trendy restaurants, design shops, cafes, bars, and performance spaces. Check out www.lxfactory.com for details. Newer expansions include the area along the river across from the Santa Apolónia train station, home to glitzy club Lux. The Bairro Alto bar scene is very casual, but sandals, sneakers, and jeans (excepting the highest-end designer pairs) are generally not allowed in clubs—some places have uptight fashion police at the door. Inside, beer runs €3-5, and it gets more expensive as the night wears on. Some clubs also charge a cover (generally €5-13), which usually includes two to four free drinks. Entrance is often free for women. There's no reason to show up before midnight; crowds flow in around 2am and stay past dawn.

BAIRRO ALTO

From tiny bars to punk clubs to posh *fado* restaurants, the Bairro Alto and nearby districts can't be beat for nightlife and entertainment.

BAIRRO ALTO AND NORTH TO THE JARDIM BOTANICO

Pavilhão Chinês, R. Dom Pedro V 89 (☎213 424 729). Ring the doorbell and a red-vested waiter will usher you into this delightful cross between classic and kitsch. Sip a drink or play pool in lounges dripping with Chinese paper fans, model airplanes, and anything else that happened to strike the owner's eclectic fancy. Huge range of teas (€4) and throwback mixed drinks like the Tom Collins and Sidecar (€7.50 each) presented in a 50+ page menu-cum-graphic novel. Open M-Sa 6pm-2am, Su 9pm-2am. AmEx/MC/V.

Portas Largas, R. da Atalaia 105 (☎213 46 63 79). Thanks to daily live music, this Bairro Alto classic is a safe bet any night of the week, even during the low-season. Gay-friendly with a mixed, welcoming crowd. Beer €2-4. *Caipirinhas* €4. Open daily July-Sept. 7pm-2am, Oct.-June 8pm-2am. Cash only.

Friends Bairro Alto, R. da Rosa 99A. Bar and book exchange rolled into one; bring a book and trade it for another or for a mojito or beer. Coffee, cheap drinks, and free internet attract a lively crowd of teens and 20-somethings. Live music Tu, W, and F nights. Beer €1.50. *Caipirinhas* €3. Open daily 3pm-2am. Cash only.

Discoteca Trumps, R. da Imprensa Nacional 104 (☎213 97 10 59; www.trumps.pt). This always-packed "hetero-friendly" club is ideal for anyone in search of an unpretentious place to dance. 2 underground dance floors (one plays pop, the other house) lined with black-and-white photographs of buff male and female torsos. More relaxed upstairs lounge. Mostly male clientele, but all are welcome. €10 cover buys equivalent drink credit. Open F-Sa 11:45pm-6am. AmEx/MC/V.

Palpita-me, R. Diário de Notícias 40B. Sing out-of-tune Portuguese and American hits at this no-frills karaoke bar popular with local 20-somethings. Live music nightly in the dancier room next door. Shots €1-2. Mixed drinks €4-5. Karaoke begins 11:30pm. Open M-Sa 8pm-2am. Cash only.

Páginas Tantas, R. Diário de Notícias 85 (☎213 46 54 95). A calm, jazz-themed sanctuary from the wild street parties of Bairro Alto. Young professionals sip beer (€2-4) and mixed drinks (€5.50) beneath portraits of jazz greats. Live jazz some weekend nights. Open daily 8pm-2am. Cash only.

SOUTH OF BAIRRO ALTO: ALCÂNTARA AND THE RIVERFRONT

A visit to any of these clubs will most likely involve a cab ride (about €6 from Rossio or Bairro Alto). Tram 15E runs the length of the Rio Tejo but stops at 1am; the area along the river is not ideal for a late-night stroll.

op art, Doca de Santo Amaro (☎213 95 67 87; www.opartcafe.com). During the week, trendy op art is a relaxed spot to grab a light meal or a drink; on F and Sa, it morphs from cafe to club as guest DJs pack the small all-glass structure to capacity. Beer €2.50, mixed drinks €5. Cover typically €5-10, includes 1 drink, €10-20 for special events. Open Tu-Th 3pm-2am, F 3pm-6am, Sa 1pm-6am, Su 1pm-2am. AmEx/MC/V.

Dock's Club, R. da Cintura do Porto de Lisboa 226 (☎213 95 08 56). This large club plays great hip hop, latino, and house music, and starts to fill up around 2am. 2 bars inside, with a pleasant patio-bar out back. €14 buys equivalent drink credit. Girls' night Tu: women pay no cover and get €14 in free drinks. Open Tu, F-Sa midnight-6am. AmEx/MC/V.

Kapital, Av. 24 de Julho 68 (☎213 95 71 01). One of the classiest clubs in Lisboa, Kapital's ruthless door policy makes admission a competitive sport. Dress nicely; this is definitely the time to break out your designer duds. Don't expect to get in, especially if you're an unaccompanied male or if it's clear you're a tourist. Those who make it past the door earn access to a sleek, multi-level space with a panoramic view of the Rio Tejo. Drinks €5. Cover €12-20; includes 2 drinks. Open M-Sa 11:30pm-6am. MC/V.

Kremlin, Escadinhasda Praia, 5 (☎213 957 101), off Av. 24 de Julho. During the 80s, this discotheque somewhat mystifyingly claimed to be the 3rd best in the world. Run by the same management as Kapital, but with a more mixed crowd, including Kapital rejects and Lisboa newcomers. Come nicely dressed. Rave music amid unusual paintings and marble statuary. Cover €6 for women, €12-18 for men; includes drink credits. Open F-Sa midnight-8:30am. MC/V.

Jamaica, R. Nova do Carvalho, 6 (☎213 42 18 59). M: Cais do Sodre. This small 40-year-old club is famous for playing 80s music, alternative rock, and protest songs prohibited during the Salazar era. A long line forms around 2am and the place stays packed 'til early morning. Cover €6 for men, with drink credits; no cover for women. Open Tu-Sa midnight-6am. Cash only.

ALFAMA AND GRAÇA

Restô, R. Costa do Castelo, 7 (☎218 86 73 34). Don't be surprised to see a flying trapeze or tightrope act—Restô is on the grounds of a government-funded clown school, Chapitô. Upstairs serves Argentine steaks (€17-30) and Spanish tapas (€4-8). Huge, colorful patio with a carnival atmosphere. Downstairs bar open W-Su 10pm-2am. Shows most evenings; check the schedule online. Open M-F noon-3pm and 7:30pm-1:30am, Sa-Su noon-1:30am. Cash only.

Lux, Av. Infante D. Henrique A, (☎218 82 08 90; www.luxfragil.com). Across from the Sta. Apolónia train station; take a taxi (€5-6 from Baixa or Bairro Alto). One-of-a-kind view from the roof of this enormous 3-story complex, which many deem the best club in Lisboa. Lounge at the bar upstairs or descend into the maelstrom of light, sound, and dancing downstairs. Bouncers are very selective and tend not to look kindly on pushy tourists, so smile, be very polite, speak in Portuguese if possible, and dress well—the stylish hipster look works better than suiting up. Arrive after 2am. Cover is typically €12, though you get an equivalent amount in free drinks. Open Tu-Sa 11pm-6am. AmEx/MC/V.

Ondajazz Bar, Arco de Jesus, 7 (☎ 218 87 30 64, www.ondajazz.com). Visit the Ondajazz Bar for a wide selection of performances including jazz, blues, world music, and poetry readings. Relaxed coffee shop atmosphere. Open mic W. Cover €5-7 most nights; no cover W. Dinner and concert package (€30-37) includes starter, entree and a drink. Open M-Th and Su 8pm-2am, F-Sa 8pm-3am. Kitchen open until 11pm. MC/V.

Bar Cerca Moura, Largo das Portas do Sol, 4 (☎218 87 48 59). Take tram 28E toward Graça from Baixa. Hop off when you see the statue and the gorgeous view on the right; the bar is on your left. Cozy, leather-covered interior and airy outdoor seating are perfect for kicking off the night. Snacks €2-4. Beer and wine €2-3. Mixed drinks €5. Open daily noon-2am. Cash only.

OUTER DISTRICTS

PARQUE DAS NAÇÕES

Take the metro to M: Oriente at the end of the red line. The station has escalators to the park's main entrance, through the Centro Vasco da Gama shopping center. (☎218 93 06 01; www.centrovascodagama.pt. Open daily 10am-midnight.) Parque das Nações (☎218 919 333; www.portaldasnacoes.pt). If you are planing to visit many attractions, consider the Cartâo do Parque, a pass granting admission to the park's major ones (€17.50, under 13 or over 65 €9).

Until the mid-1990s, this area was a muddy mess consisting of a few rundown factories and warehouses along the banks of the Tejo. Today, after millions spent preparing for the 1998 World Exposition, the Parque das Nações (Park of Nations) is a masterpiece in civil planning and engineering. Much more than a park, the region is becoming a small city, with residential areas to the north and south. Inside the park, visitors will find museums, exhibition spaces, cafes, and one of Lisboa's finest attractions, the **Oceanário de Lisboa.** Visitors can find maps and buy tickets at the information center across the street from the **Centro Vasco da Gama** shopping mall, at the park's main entrance. On the way in, turn around to take in contemporary architect Santiago Calatrava's soaring **Estação Oriente** behind you.

OCEANÁRIO. The park's biggest attraction, this enormous oceanarium has interactive sections showcasing the four major oceans, recreating everything about them down to their sounds, smells, and climates. Visitors can get within arm's length of playful sea otters and penguins. These sections surround the gigantic main tank, home to over 470 different species of fish, sharks, and other sea creatures. Although pricey, it's worth the splurge. *(☎218 91 70 02; www.oceanario.pt. Open daily Apr.-Oct. 10am-7pm; Nov.-Mar. 10am-6pm. €11, ages 4-12 €5.50, over 65 €6, under 4 free. Family pass €26.50. Audio guides €2.)*

OTHER ATTRACTIONS. The **Pavilhão do Conhecimento,** an interactive science museum, features exhibits on mathematics and technology that cater primarily to children. *(☎218 91 71 00; www.pavconhecimento.pt. €7, ages 7-17 and over 65 €4, ages 3-6 €3, under 3 free. Family pass €15.)* Older visitors can experience a less benign side of math at the **Casino Lisboa** *(☎218 92 90 00; www.casino-Lisboa.pt. Open Su-Th 3pm-3am, F-Sa 4pm-4am.)* **Telecabinas,** or cable cars, run between the Ocenário and Torre Vasco de Gama (Portugal's tallest building), offering a bird's eye view of the park and the Rio Tejo. *(☎218 95 61 43. 8min.; M-F 11am-7pm, Sa-Su 10am-7pm. One-way*

€3.90, round-trip €6; ages 5-14 and over 65 €2/3.30; under 5 free.) **Bike rentals** are also available; ask at the Information Center for details.

BELÉM

Visitors can reach Belém by tram, bus, or train. By tram, take 15E (dir: Algés) and get off at the Mosteiro dos Jerónimos stop, 1 stop beyond the stop labeled Belém. You can also take bus #28 or #714 from Pr. Figueira, Pr. do Comércio, or Cais do Sodré. Both of these options will deposit you along the area's commercial spine, R. de Belém. Alternatively, take the train from Estação Cais do Sodré. To start at the Padrão dos Descobrimentos, exit the station by the overpass toward the water. To begin at Mosteiro dos Jerónimos, exit the overpass to the right, then go through the public gardens to R. de Belém.

The Age of Discovery began in Portugal, and there is no greater tribute to its pioneering spirit than the seafront of Belém. Explorers like Vasco da Gama and Prince Henry the Navigator launched their famous 15th-century voyages from its sands. Today, visitors come from around the world to see the architectural embodiments of Portugal's past glories of exploration and faith. But it is not just a rich history that makes Belém worth your while. The town is also famous for its delicious custard-filled pastries, *pasteis de nata*, sometimes called *pasteis de Belém*. These desserts, with a recipe perfected at the nearby monastery, have been served in their original form at the famous **Pasteis de Belém ❶**, R. de Belém, 84-92, since the restaurant's 1837 opening. (☎213 63 74 23; www.pasteisdebelem.pt. Additional seating in back. *Pasteis* €0.90 apiece. Open daily 9am-11pm.) If wandering the shores has left you with an empty stomach, stop in at **Pão Pão Queijo Queijo ❶**, R. de Belém, 124. This small, quaint locale is perfect for a quick bite. It serves delicious pitas (€3-4), sandwiches (€3-4), and entrees (€6.75), though it is exceptionally crowded 1-3pm. (☎213 62 33 69. Additional seating upstairs. Open M-Sa 10am-midnight, Su 10am-8pm.)

MOSTEIRO DOS JERÓNIMOS. Established in 1502 in honor of Vasco da Gama's ground-breaking expedition to India, the Mosteiro dos Jerónimos is a gorgeous church and cloister designed with minute Renaissance detail and ornate Gothic construction; it is perhaps the finest example of Manueline architecture in Portugal. The Mosteiro was recognized for its beauty in the 1980s, when it was granted UNESCO World Heritage status. Note the anachronism on the main church door: Prince Henry the Navigator mingles with the Twelve Apostles on both sides of the central column. The symbolic tombs of poet Luís de Camões and explorer Vasco da Gama lie in opposing transepts. The peaceful cloister houses an exhibit on the history of Belém. *(☎213 62 00 34. Open Tu-Su May-Sept. 10am-6:30pm; Oct.-Apr. 10am-5:30pm. Last entry 30min. before closing. Church free. Cloister €6, seniors over 65 €2, students with ID free.)* Directly across from the church lies the **Museu Nacional de Arqueologia,** an archaeology museum appealing primarily to those with an academic interest in the subject. The five-room museum mounts temporary exhibitions exploring Portugal's ancient past and houses a permanent collection of Bronze Age jewelry and artifacts from ancient Egypt. *(☎213 62 00 00. Open Tu-Su 10am-6pm. €4; students, teachers, and seniors €2, LisboaCard holders free. Free Su before 2pm. Cash only.)* At the far side of the Mosteiro complex, the **Museu de Marinha** bursts with boats—both historical models and a collection of dozens of full-size royal yachts—that tell a visual history of Portugal's maritime past. *(☎213 62 00 19; www.museu.marinha.pt. €3; ages 6-17 and students €1.50, under 6 free.)*

CENTRO CULTURAL DE BELÉM. Contemporary art buffs will bask in the glow of this luminous complex, a monolithic modern counterpart to the Mosteiro across the street. Three pavilions hold rotating world-class exhibitions and a huge auditorium hosts concerts and performances, ranging from puppet shows to plays, orchestral music, and even Indonesian music and dance. Within the complex, the new **Museu Colecção Berardo** displays an eclectic and extensive exhibition of modern and contemporary art; its exhibits change regularly. Jackson Pollock, Cindy Sherman, and Francis Bacon are just three of the many blockbuster artists represented in the collection. *(☎213 61 24 00; www.ccb.pt. Ticket office open daily 1-7:30pm. Museu Colecção Berardo ☎213 61 28 78. Open M-Th 10am-7pm. F-Sa 10am-10pm. Last entry 30min. before closing. Free.)*

TORRE DE BELÉM. The best-known tower in all of Portugal, the Torre de Belém is a stone fortress sitting on the banks of the Rio Tejo. Built under Manuel I from 1514-1519 as a military stronghold, the Torre served during the Spanish occupation as Portugal's most famous political prison. The tower is a powerful symbol of Portuguese grandeur and has majestic views in every direction. Images of this UNESCO World Heritage site can be found in just about every postcard stand in Lisboa. *(A 15min. walk from the monastery, with the water on your left. Take the first pedestrian overpass you reach to cross the highway; the tower is at the back corner of the park. Open Tu-Su May-Sept. 10am-6:30pm; Oct.-Apr. 10am-5:30pm. Last entry 30min. before closing. €4, 15-25 and seniors €2, under 15 or with LisboaCard free. Free Su until 2pm.)*

PADRÃO DOS DESCOBRIMENTOS. Along the river and directly across the highway from the Mosteiro is the Padrão dos Descobrimentos, built in 1960 to celebrate the 500th anniversary of Prince Henry the Navigator's death. The view is better than from the Torre, and there's an elevator that transports visitors 50m up to the narrow roof top. You can see the 25 de Abril bridge, Lisboa, and the Cristo Redentor monument on your left; the Atlantic Ocean is to your right. The Padrão is also home to the **Lisboa Experience,** a 25min. audovisual presentation about the history of Lisboa narrated in English, Spanish, German, and French. *(Across the highway from the garden in front of the Mosteiro, acessible by pedestrian underpass. ☎213 03 19 50; www.egeac.pt. Open May-Sept. M-Su 10am-7pm; Oct.-Apr. Tu-Su 10am-6pm. Last entry 30min. before closing. Tower €2.50; students and seniors €1.50. Lisboa Experience presentation runs every 30min. 10:30am-5pm; €4, students and seniors €3, Lisboa Card holders €2.80. Both together €5/4/3.50.)*

BEYOND LISBOA

CASCAIS

Cascais is a beautiful beach town, serene during the low-season, and brimming with vacationers in the summer. Surfers and beach lovers will find everything they need in this tight-knit community.

TRANSPORTATION. Trains from Lisboa's **Estação Cais do Sodré** (☎213 42 48 93; M: Cais do Sodré) head to **Cascais** (30min., 3 per hr. 5:30am-1:30am, €1.65). **Scott URB** has a bus terminal in downtown Cascais, to the left side of the blue glass tower of the shopping center behind the train station. Buses #418 (40min., every 50min. 6:30am-7:50pm) and the more scenic #403 via Cabo da Roca (60-80min.; every 75min. M-Sa 6:30am-8:40pm, Su 9:10am-8:40pm) go from Cascais to **Sintra** for €3.35. To visit **Praia de Guincho,** a popular windsurfing beach considered by many to be best on the coast, take the circular route bus #405/415 to the Guincho stop (22min., every 1-2hr. 7:15am-7:40pm, €2.60).

PRACTICAL INFORMATION. To get to the **tourist office,** Av. dos Combatentes de Grande Guerra, 25, exit the train station through the ticket office and look for the McDonald's arches across Lg. da Estação. To the right of McDonald's is Av. Valbom; the office is a yellow building with "*turismo*" in big letters at the end of the street. The staff has English, Spanish, French, German, and Russian speakers. (☎214 86 82 04. Open in summer M-Sa 9am-7pm, Su 10am-6pm; in winter M-Sa 9am-7pm, Su 10am-6pm.)

ACCOMMODATIONS AND FOOD. Sleeping in Cascais; most stay in Lisboa or at nearby Oeiras, which has a *pousada da juventude* (HI youth hostel). If you do stay, the best place to crash is **Cascais Beach Hostel ❷,** R. da Vista Alegre, 10, located five blocks away from the beach, and relatively well-located. Green co-ed dorms with 4-8 beds are very clean. Offers shared kitchen, free internet, luxurious common room with TV, swimming pool, and sunbathing deck. (☎309 90 64 21; www.cascaisbeachostel.com. Dorms Apr. 15-Nov. 15 €20; Nov. 16-Apr. 14 €18; doubles €49, with bath €69. Cash only.)

There are several restaurants on Av. dos Combatentes de Grande Guerra. The best is **Restaurante Dom Manolo ❷,** one of the only restaurants that cooks with a charcoal oven. Try their *sardinhas assadas*, mussels, and grilled chicken. (☎214 83 11 26. Entrees €6.5-11. Open daily 10am-midnight. Cash only.) For a rawer taste of the sea, head to **Sushi eXpress ❸,** R. Dra. Iracy Doile, 9A. Located 1 block from the train station, it serves up Japanese favorites to go. (☎214 86 74 28. Rolls €5-10. Sushi/sashimi boxes €7-16. Open daily noon-9pm. Cash only.)

OUTDOOR ACTIVITIES AND ENTERTAINMENT. **Praia da Ribeira, Praia da Rainha,** and **Praia da Conceição** are especially popular with sunbathers. To reach Praia da Ribeira, take a right upon leaving the tourist office and walk down Av. dos Combatentes de Grande Guerra until you see the water. Facing the water, Praia da Rainha and Praia da Conceição are to your left. Or take advantage of the **free bike rentals** offered at two kiosks in Cascais (one is in front of the train station, by the McDonald's, the other is in the parking lot of the Cidadela fortress, up Av. dos Carlos I). With a passport or driver's license and your hotel information, and you can use the bikes from 8am to 6:30pm. Ride along the coast (to your right if facing the water) and check out the **Boca de Inferno** (Mouth of Hell), a stunning open cave where the crashing waves supposedly whisper the devil's words. Go on a rainy day to really hear the cave roar. (About 1km outside Cascais, a 20min. walk up Av. Rei Humberto de Itália.) Devilry of a different sort starts as the sun sets, as nightlife picks up on **Largo Luís de Camões,** the main pedestrian square.

SINTRA ☎219

Deep in the misty Serra mountains lies the enchanting city of Sintra, home to ancient castles, fairy-tale palaces, and verdant gardens. For centuries, sultans, kings, and wealthy noblemen were drawn by the area's haunting beauty, and they left a trail of opulence and grandeur behind them. Today, Sintra is Portugal's dreamland. Tourists from around the world explore the mysterious city, eager to absorb every detail and uncover every secret.

TRANSPORTATION

Horse-drawn Carriages: Sintratur, Largo Rainha D. Amélia (☎219 24 12 38; www.sintratur.com). Fixed routes or pay by the hr. Carriages, drivers, and horses for hire wait in the Praça da República. To **Quinta da Regaleira** and back (30min., €30) or **Monserrate**

LISBOA

and back, including a 30min. stop on the grounds for a quick picnic (1hr., €70). Prices are for up to 4 people per ride. Carriages available daily Apr.-Sept. 10am-6pm.

Trains: Estação de Caminhos de Ferro, Av. Dr. Miguel Bombarda (☎219 23 26 05). To Estação Sete Rios in **Lisboa** (40min., daily every 20min. 5:06am-12:56am, €1.65). From the train station, take the subway to downtown Lisboa.

Buses: ScottURB buses (☎214 69 91 25; www.scotturb.com), on Av. Dr. Miguel Bombarda. Buses run to **Cascais** (#417; 40min., every hr. M-F 6:30am-9:15pm, Sa 7:20am-7:50 pm, Su 8:10am-7:50pm, €3.25; or #403 Via Cabo da Roca; every hr. M-Sa 6:35am-8:40pm, Su 9:10am-8:40pm). **Mafrense** buses, 500m up the street away from Vila on Av. Dr. D. Cambournac, go to **Ericeira** (50min., daily every hr. 7:15am-8:25pm, €2.60).

ORIENTATION AND PRACTICAL INFORMATION

Situated in the mountains 25km northwest of Lisboa and 12km north of Cascais, Sintra has three main neighborhoods. Excursions to the area by bus or train begin in the modern **Estefânia,** where several banks and budget accommodations can be found. **São Pedro de Sintra,** farther uphill, has more shops and municipal offices. Sintra, famous for its heart, **Sintra-Vila,** better known as the **Historic Center** and home to most of the town's fantastic sights. The 15min. walk from Estefânia is scattered with statues and fountains like bread crumbs for sight-hungry tourists. To get to the Historic Center, take a left out of the train station onto Av. Dr. M. Bombarda and follow it for 150m. At the intersection, take the curving road to the left, **Volta do Duche,** which passes the **Parque da Liberdade** and leads to the edge of the Historic Center, where shops begin to appear again. Stay to the right, and the **Palácio Nacional de Sintra** should be visible on the right. The tourist office is straight ahead. Sintra is navigable by foot, but a few sights lie outside (and uphill from) the town center. The ScottURB bus #434 sells day tickets to most of these sights (€4). Pay on the bus, which departs from in front of the main train station (every 15min. 9:35am-7:05pm) and stops in the Historic Centre. From there, the bus will head to the **Castelo dos Mouros** and then **Palácio da Pena.** On the way back down the mountain, the bus stops in front of the **Museu Brinquedo** (Toy Museum).

Tourist Office: Pr. da República, 23 (☎219 23 11 57; fax 210 23 87 87), in the Historic Center. Open daily June-Sept. 9am-8pm; Oct.-May 9am-7pm. **Branch** in the train station (☎219 24 16 23) with the same hours. English, French, and Spanish spoken.

Police: Guarda Nacional Republicana, R. João de Deus, 6 (☎219 24 78 50), next to the train station.

Pharmacy: Pharmazul, Av. Dr. Miguel Bombarda, 37 (☎/fax 219 24 38 77). Open M-F 10am-7pm, Sa 10:30am-7:30pm, Su 10am-2pm.

Medical Services: Centro de Saúde, R. Dr. Alfredo Costa, 34, 1st fl. (☎219 23 62 00). Open M-F 8am-8pm, Sa-Su and holidays 10am-7pm.

Internet Access: Sabot, R. Dr. Alfredo Costa, 74 (☎219 23 08 02), across the street from the main train station, to the right of the Chinese restaurant. €1 per 15min., €1.60 per 30min., €2.50 per hr. CD burning €1.80 (CD included). Open M-Sa 1pm-midnight, Su 7pm-midnight.

Post Office: Pr. da República, 26 (☎219 10 67 91). Open M-F 9:30am-12:30pm and 2:30-6pm. **Postal Code:** 2710.

SAVE YOUR STAMPS. Many post offices in Portugal sell pre-stamped postcards for international postage, saving you up to €0.75 per card.

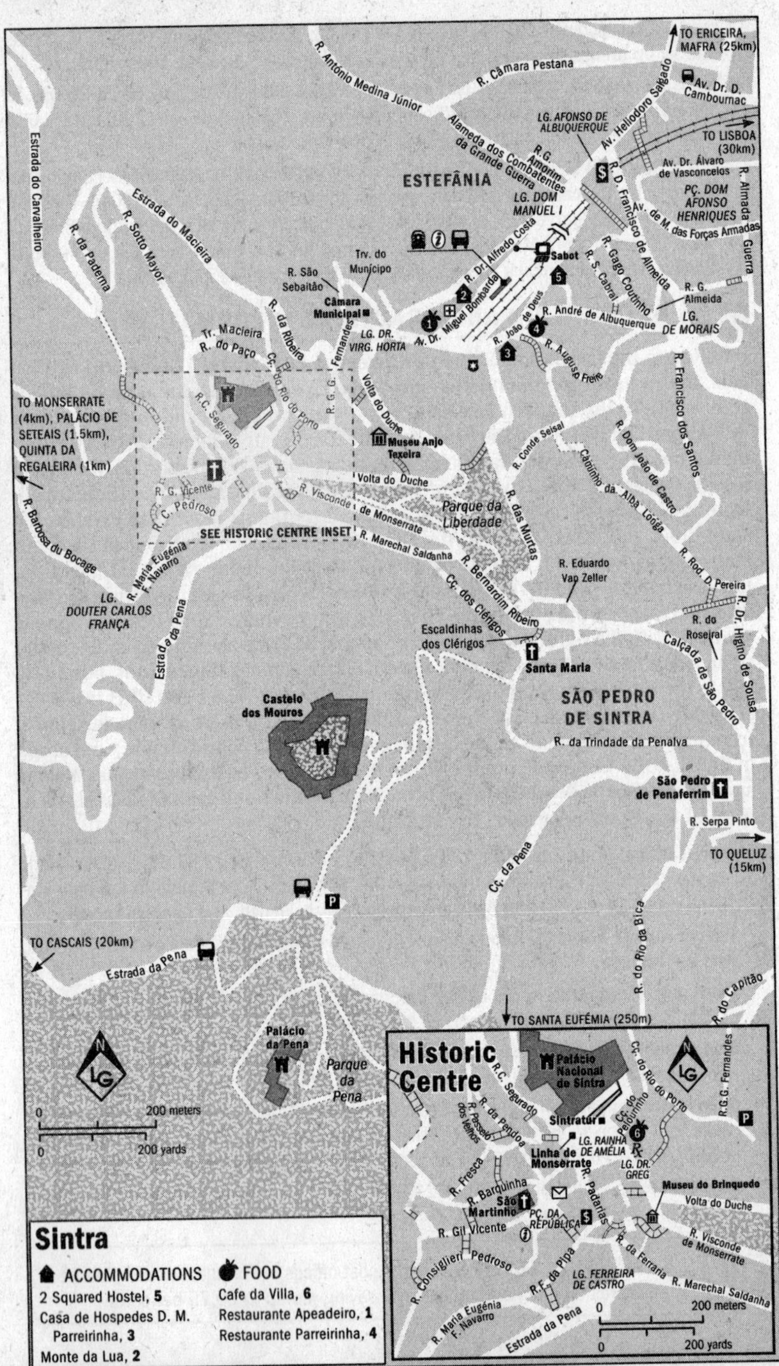

Sintra
ACCOMMODATIONS
2 Squared Hostel, 5
Casa de Hospedes D. M. Parreirinha, 3
Monte da Lua, 2
FOOD
Cafe da Villa, 6
Restaurante Apeadeiro, 1
Restaurante Parreirinha, 4
Historic Centre
ESTEFÂNIA
SÃO PEDRO DE SINTRA
TO ERICEIRA, MAFRA (25km)
TO LISBOA (30km)
TO MONSERRATE (4km), PALÁCIO DE SETEAIS (1.5km), QUINTA DA REGALEIRA (1km)
TO QUELUZ (15km)
TO CASCAIS (20km)
TO SANTA EUFÉMIA (250m)
SEE HISTORIC CENTRE INSET
Castelo dos Mouros
Palácio da Pena
Parque da Pena
Parque da Liberdade
Museu Anjo Texeira
Câmara Municipal
Santa Maria
São Pedro de Penaferrim
Escaldinhas dos Clérigos
Sabot
Palácio Nacional de Sintra
Sintratur
Linha de Monserrate
São Martinho
Museu do Brinquedo
LG. AFONSO DE ALBUQUERQUE
LG. DOM MANUEL I
LG. DR. VIRG. HORTA
LG. DE MORAIS
LG. DOUTER CARLOS FRANÇA
PÇ. DOM AFONSO HENRIQUES
LG. RAINHA DE AMÉLIA
LG. DR. GREG
PC. DA REPÚBLICA
LG. FERREIRA DE CASTRO
R. Câmara Pestana
R. António Medina Júnior
Av. Heliodoro Salgado
Av. Dr. D. Cambournac
Alameda dos Combatentes da Grande Guerra
R. G. Amorim
R. D. Francisco de Almeida
Av. Dr. Álvaro de Vasconcelos
Av. de M. das Forças Armadas
R. Almada Guerra
R. Dr. Alfredo Costa
Av. Dr. Miguel Bombarda
R. Gago Coutinho
R. S. Cabral
R. G. Almeida
R. André de Albuquerque
R. João de Deus
R. Augusto Freire
R. Francisco dos Santos
R. Dom João de Castro
Caminho da Alba Longa
R. Conde Seisal
R. das Murtas
R. Rod. D. Pereira
R. Eduardo Van Zeller
R. do Roseiral
R. Dr. Higino de Sousa
Calçada de São Pedro
R. da Trindade da Penalva
R. Serpa Pinto
Cç. da Pena
R. do Rio da Bica
R. do Capitão
Estrada do Carvalheiro
R. da Paderna
R. Sotto Mayor
Estrada do Macieira
R. São Sebaitão
Trv. do Munícipo
Tr. Macieira
R. do Paço
R. da Ribeira
Cç. do Rio do Porto
R. G. G. Fernandes
Volta do Duche
R. C. Segurado
R. G. Vicente
R. C. Pedroso
R. Visconde de Monserrate
R. Marechal Saldanha
R. Bernardim Ribeiro
Cç. dos Clérigos
R. Barbosa du Bocage
R. Maria Eugénia F. Navarro
Estrada da Pena
R. da Pendoa
R. Passeio dos Velhos
Cç. do Pelourinho
R. Fresca
R. Barquinha
R. Gil Vicente
R. Consiglieri Pedroso
R. Padarias
R. da Ferraria
R. F. da Pipa
200 meters
200 yards

ACCOMMODATIONS

In Sintra, you can stay at the oldest hotel in Iberia or in a 19th-century palace, but grandeur is matched by price. Most hotels in Sintra are more expensive than in nearby towns or Lisboa, a 45min. train ride away. For those on a budget, the central tourist office has a list of private accommodations, but prices are similar to the *residenciais* (singles €25-60; doubles €40-70).

2 Squared Hostel, R. João de Deus, 68 (☎219 24 61 60). The best budget accommodation in Sintra, this hostel also has a cafe downstairs. Brightly painted rooms are spacious and open, though some face the train station and can be loud. 30min. free internet access and Wi-Fi. Private lockers in each room. Reserve ahead by phone. English spoken. Dorms €15; double with shared bath €20. Cash only. ❶

Casa de Hóspedes Dona Maria Parreirinha, R. João de Deus, 12/14 (☎219 23 24 90; www.dmariaparreirinha.com). Exit the train station and go left around the tracks. *Azulejo*-decorated hallways, immaculate tile floors, and cable TV. Most rooms have private baths. Free parking available. Some English spoken. Singles €30, with bath €35; doubles €35/40; triples €45; quints €70. €5-10 less in winter. Cash only. ❸

Monte da Lua, Av. Miguel Bombarda, 51 (☎219 24 10 29). Across the street from the train station. Excellent location. Offers rooms with heat, TV, and telephone. Singles €25, with private bath €30; high-season doubles €40, low-season €35. Cash only. ❷

FOOD

Pastelarias and restaurants crowd the end of Rua João de Deus and Avenida Heliodoro Salgado. In the old town, Rua das Padarias (near the **Palácio Nacional**) is lined with lunch spots. On the second and fourth Sundays of every month, take bus #433 from the train station to São Pedro (15min.) for the **Feira de São Pedro,** which features local cuisine, music, clothes, flowers, and antiques.

Café da Villa, Calçada do Pelourinho, 8 (☎967 09 13 96), in the main square in front of the Palácio Nacional. Decorated with colorful flags and paintings of famous faces, like the Dalai Lama's. Offers internationally themed meals (€8-15), which include 3 courses and a drink. Great late-night hangout. Open daily noon-2am. AmEx/MC/V. ❷

Restaurante Parreirinha, Rua João de Deus, 43 (☎219 23 12 07), behind the train station. A welcome change from the dark, antiquated café-bars of the city. Stainless-steel appliances, a flat-screen TV, and cinnamon-colored tablecloths make for a modern vibe. Variety of fish and wine. Daily special €6.50. Entrees €7-10. No vegetarian entrees. Open M-Su 10am-4pm and 7-10pm. MC/V. ❷

Restaurante Apeadeiro, Av. Miguel Bombarda, 3A (☎219 23 18 05). From the flag on the wall to the *futebol* (soccer ball) over the bar, this is a classic Portuguese cafe. Entrees €7-13. Open M-W and F-Su 11am-3pm and 7-10pm. AmEx/MC/V. ❷

SIGHTS

QUINTA DA REGALEIRA. A UNESCO World Heritage sight, this turret-studded palace was built in the early 1900s by Brazilian Antonio Monteira and flamboyant Italian architect Luigi Manini. Quinta's gardens, wells, grottoes, and towers form one of the oldest occult gardens of Europe, a true dreamland in fairy tale Sintra. Its design follows mythological and historical themes, rendered in a fascinating amalgam of Manueline (Portuguese late-Gothic) and Renaissance styles. The **Poço Iniciatico** (Initiation Well) was inspired by the secret rituals performed by the famous Knights Templar. Beneath the castle you can explore a fantastic tunnel system. *(To get to the Quinta da Regaleira, turn right out of the tourist* *office and follow R. Consiglieri Pedroso as it turns into Rua M. E. F. Navarro, a 15min. walk. ☎219 10 66 50. Open daily Oct. and Feb.-Apr. 10am-6:30pm, last entrance 6pm; Apr.-Sept. 10am-8pm, last entrance 7pm; Nov.-Jan. 10am-5:30pm, last entrance 5pm. Unguided visits €6, students and seniors €4. Guided tours at 10:30, 11am, noon, 2:30, 3:30pm; €10, students and seniors €8.)*

PALÁCIO DA PENA. Built in the 1840s by Prince Ferdinand of Bavaria, husband of Portugal's Dona Maria II, this royal retreat embraces romantic and fantastic styles with meticulous detail. The prince, nostalgic for his native country, rebuilt and embellished the ruined monastery with the assistance of a Prussian engineer, combining the artistic heritages of Germany and Portugal. The result is magical: a colorful Bavarian castle decorated with Arabic minarets, Gothic turrets, Manueline windows, and a Renaissance dome. *(Bus #434 runs to the palace from outside the tourist office every 15min. All-day bus pass €4. ☎219 10 53 40; www.parquesdesintra.pt. The area surrounding the palace, Parque da Pena, is open daily June-Aug. 9:30am-8pm, Sept.-May 9am-7pm. €7.50, children and seniors €5.50. Palacio admission Sept.-Apr. €8, children and seniors €6. May-Aug. €11, children and seniors €9. Open daily 9:45 am-5:30pm. Tickets for both attractions are sold until 1hr. before closing. Guided tours in English, Portuguese, and Spanish; €5, €3.50 per person for groups of 10 or more.)*

LISBOA

CASTELO DOS MOUROS. Built in the 8th century by the Moors, this ancient castle rests on the slopes of the Serra mountains. It was abandoned during the Moorish retreat to the south in 1147, but Dom Fernando II made some much-needed repairs in the 19th century. On a clear day, a long, steep climb up the walls will be rewarded with unmatched views of the Ribatejo plains and the clashing natural rock formations and manmade walls. *(1km below the Palácio da Pena. Bus #434 departs from outside the tourist office and stops at the castle. All-day bus pass €4. ☎219 23 73 00; www.parquesdasintra.pt. Open daily June-Sept. 9am-8pm, last entrance 7pm; Oct.-May 10am-6pm, last entrance 5pm. €5, seniors and under 17 €3, family price for 2 children and 2 adults €12. Guided tours €5, €3.50 per person for groups of 10 or more.)*

MONSERRATE. Located 4km from the center of Sintra, Monserrate is well worth a visit for those staying in town for more than a day. This sprawling estate is known for its quiet botanical gardens shaded by towering sequoias and tropical ferns. The garden has more than 3500 species of plants, and its lawn is watered by the oldest irrigation system in Portugal. The Moghul-style mansion, with its burnt-orange roof modeled on Brunelleschi's Dome in Florence, is a classic example of Portuguese Romanticism. Designed by the English architect John T. Knowles in 1858, the estate became a refuge for eccentric English aristocrat William Beckford following scandals regarding his homosexual affairs. *(To get to Monserrate, catch the small green train/roofless bus line, Linha de Monserrate, ☎214 66 26 03, beside the Palácio Nacional in Pr. da República. 20 min., every hr., €6 round trip. Monserrate ☎219 23 73 00 or 10 78 06. Open daily summer 10am-1pm, 2pm-7pm; winter 10:30am-1pm, 2pm-5pm. Last entrance 30min. before closing. €5, children and seniors €3, families of 2 adults and 2 children €12. Guided tours €5, €3.50 for groups of 10 or more.)*

PALÁCIO NACIONAL DE SINTRA. The palace, also known as the Paço Real or Palácio da Vila, dominates Pr. da República. Once a summer residence for Moorish sultans and their harems, the Palácio da Vila was taken over by the Portuguese following the Muslim defeat. The conquest is illustrated in the paintings of Portuguese noblemen gunning down Moorish soldiers. The palace and gardens were built in two stages: Dom João I built the main structure in the 15th century, and Dom Manuel I made it home to the best collection of *azulejos* (glazed tiles) in the world a century later. The palace has over 20 rooms, including the *azulejo*-covered **Sala dos Árabes** and the gilded **Sala dos Brasões.** Some of the palace's greatest treasures are overhead: look up at the ceiling to see the royal coat of arms surrounded by the armorial bearings of 72 noble families, elaborately painted animals, and various other artistic flourishes. The palace is marked by a bird theme: doves symbolizing the Holy Spirit line the walls of the **Capela,** swans grace the **Sala dos Cisnes,** and on the ceiling of the **Sala das Pegas** magpies representing ladies-in-waiting hold a piece of paper proclaiming D. João I's motto—*"por bem,"* or "for good." *(Lg. da Rainha Dona Amélia. ☎ 219 10 68 40; www.ippar.pt. Open M-Tu and Th-Su 10am-5:30pm. Last entrance 5pm. €5, seniors and students €2.50; Su and holidays before 2pm free.)*

ALGARVE AND ALENTEJO

The Algarve and the Alentejo form a striking contrast. The Alentejo's small villages, seemingly stuck in another time, provide an escape from the Algarve's heavily touristed beaches and wild nightlife. Nearly 3000hr. of annual sunshine have transformed the Algarve from a fishermen's backwater town into one of Europe's favorite vacation spots. In July and August, visitors mob its resorts, packing bars and discos from sunset until long after sunrise. Still, the Algarve isn't all about excess. The region between Faro and the Spanish border remains relatively untouched, and, to the west of Lagos, towering cliffs shelter pristine beaches. Life slows down even more as you enter the Alentejo, where arid plains punctuated by olive trees, two-toned cork trees, and fields of wheat and sunflowers stretch to the horizon in a display of endless shades of yellow. This vast region appeals to those in search of relaxation, history, and plenty of wine. The Algarve and Alentejo provide visitors with the best of both worlds.

HIGHLIGHTS OF ALGARVE AND ALENTEJO

SPELUNK among the grottoes and sea cliffs of **Lagos** (p. 406).

CHANNEL the spirit of Prince Henry the Navigator at his outpost in **Sagres** (p. 412).

FEEL it in your bones at Évora's **Capela dos Ossos** (p. 417).

ALGARVE

Behold the Algarve: a land where happy campers come to bask in the sun. Off the sands, the geometric designs and minaret-style chimneys of Algarve's old houses reveal a strong Arab influence. While regional crafts specialize in basket-weaving, the Algarve's most perfect craft is its delicious seafood—local favorites include flavorful *sardinhas assadas* (grilled sardines) and the creamy *caldeirada* (seafood chowder). Almonds and figs also make their way into most regional cooking, especially in divine desserts like *figos cheios*. In the winter, the resorts empty and wildlife of a different sort arrives, as roughly one-third of Europe's flamingos migrate to the wetlands surrounding Olhão.

LAGOS ☎282

Lagos (pop. 17,500) has a way of making visitors want to stay forever; just ask any one of city's expatriate bartenders, surf guides, or restaurant owners. As the Algarve's capital for almost 200 years, Lagos launched many of the caravels that brought Portugal power and fortune in the 15th and 16th centuries. Today, the city is immersed in another, equally profitable golden age—tourism. While the 20-somethings recuperate from the previous night, the 40-plus crowd comes out in the morning and lingers until dinner time, perusing storefronts, taking dolphin tours, and relaxing in the sunny plazas.

TRANSPORTATION

To reach Lagos from northern Portugal, you must go through Lisboa; trips originating in the east generally transfer in Faro.

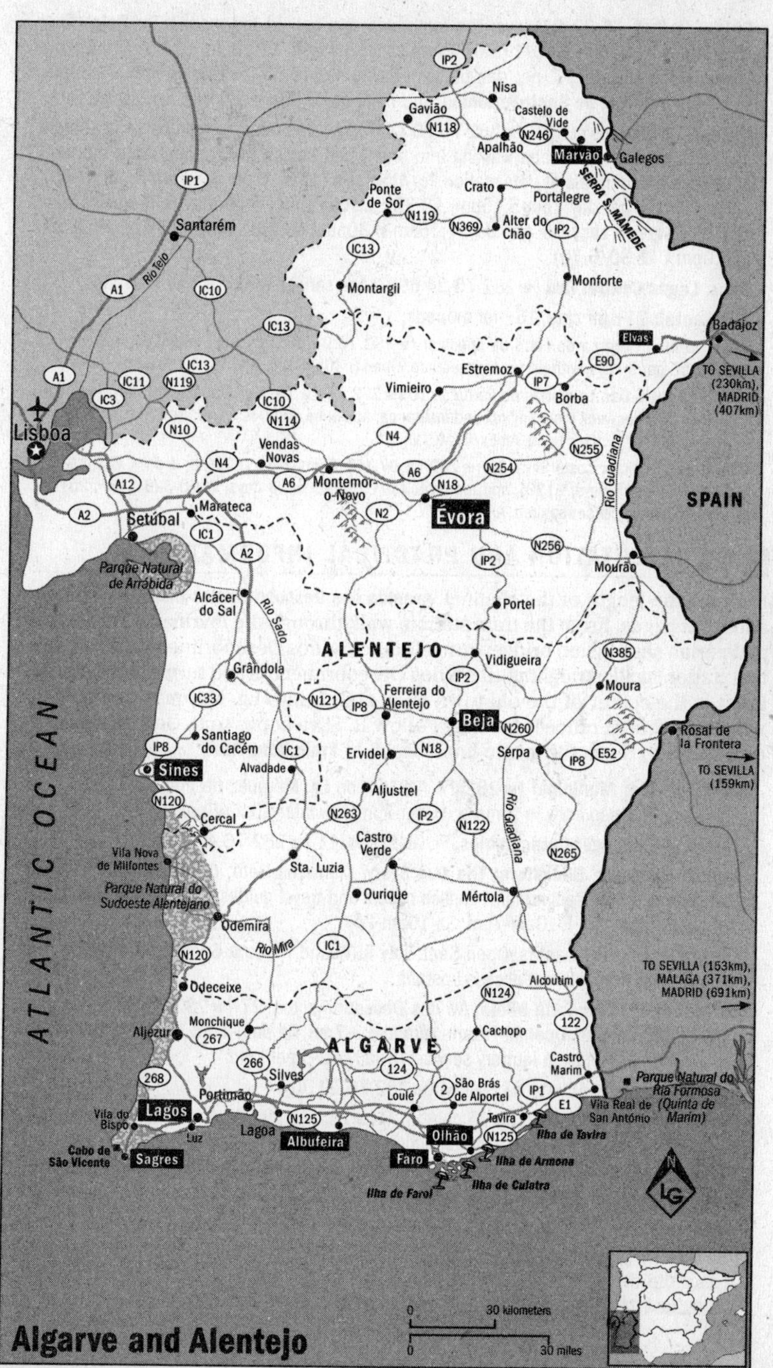
ATLANTIC OCEAN
SPAIN
ALENTEJO
ALGARVE
Lisboa
Santarém
Setúbal
Marateca
Parque Natural de Arrábida
Alcácer do Sal
Grândola
Santiago do Cacém
Sines
Cercal
Vila Nova de Milfontes
Parque Natural do Sudoeste Alentejano
Odemira
Odeceixe
Aljezur
Monchique
Silves
Portimão
Lagos
Luz
Vila do Bispo
Cabo de São Vicente
Sagres
Lagoa
Albufeira
Loulé
São Brás de Alportel
Faro
Olhão
Tavira
Ilha de Tavira
Ilha de Armona
Ilha de Culatra
Ilha de Farol
Vila Real de San António
Castro Marim
Parque Natural do Ria Formosa (Quinta de Marim)
Cachopo
Alcoutim
Mértola
Ourique
Castro Verde
Sta. Luzia
Aljustrel
Alvadade
Ervidel
Ferreira do Alentejo
Beja
Serpa
Moura
Vidigueira
Portel
Mourão
Évora
Montemor-o-Novo
Vendas Novas
Vimieiro
Estremoz
Borba
Elvas
Badajoz
Monforte
Alter do Chão
Crato
Portalegre
Marvão
Galegos
Castelo de Vide
Apalhão
Nisa
Gavião
Ponte de Sor
Montargil
Rosal de la Frontera
SERRA S. MAMEDE
Rio Tejo
Rio Sado
Rio Mira
Rio Guadiana
TO SEVILLA (230km), MADRID (407km)
TO SEVILLA (159km)
TO SEVILLA (153km), MALAGA (371km), MADRID (691km)
0 30 kilometers
0 30 miles
Algarve and Alentejo

Trains: (☎282 76 29 87), over the footbridge and behind the marina. To: **Beja** (4hr.; 8:19am, 12:19pm; €9.80/17.30); **Évora** (5hr.; 8:19am, 12:19pm; €14.50/21.60) via **Faro; Lisboa** (3-4hr., 7 per day 6:11am-6:12pm, €15.50); **Silves** (40min., 1:39pm, €1.70); **Vila Real de Santo António** (3hr., 7 per day 7:03am-7:04pm, €6.50) via Faro.

Buses: The **EVA** bus station (☎282 76 29 44), off Av. dos Descobrimentos, is just before R. Porta de Portugal (when walking into town) and across the channel from the footbridge to the marina and train station. To: **Albufeira** (13hr., 6 per day 7am-5:15pm, €5); **Faro** (2hr., 6 per day 7am-5:15pm, €5.35); **Lisboa** (5hr., 6 per day 5:30am-6:15pm, €19); **Sagres** (1hr., 16 per day 7:15am-8:30pm, €3.40); **Sines** (2-4hr.; 3:20pm, 4:30pm;€12.30/6.70).

Taxis: Lagos Central Taxi (☎282 76 24 69). 24hr. service to Lagos and environs.

Car Rental: 21+ for cars, 16+ for mopeds.

Auto Jardim, Travessa do Ferro de Engomar (☎282 76 94 86; www.auto-jardim.com). Cars from €91.50 per 3 days, without tax or insurance. Open 8:30am-1pm and 2:30-7pm. AmEx/MC/V.

Luzcar Rent-a-Car, Lg. Portas de Portugal, 10 (☎282 76 10 16; www.luzcar.com). July-Sept. cars from €200 per week including tax and insurance; Apr.-June and Oct. €150; Nov.-Mar. €130. Baby seat and roof rack included. AmEx/D/MC/V.

Motorent, R. Victor Costa Silva, 8B (☎282 76 97 16). Rents bikes (€20 per 3 days, €37), scooters (€63 per 3 days, €120), and motorcycles (€55-110 per 3 days, €100-320). 18+, 25+ for motorcycles; license required. AmEx/MC/V.

ORIENTATION AND PRACTICAL INFORMATION

Running the length of the channel, **Avenida dos Descobrimentos** carries traffic to and from Lagos. From the train station, walk through the marina and cross the pedestrian suspension bridge; turn left onto Av. dos Descobrimentos. From the bus station, walk straight until Av. dos Descobrimentos and turn right. **Praça Gil Eanes** is the center of the old town and extends into Lg. Marquêz de Pombal, where the tourist office is located. Follow R. Silva Lopes to R. General Alberto da Silveira to reach the grotto-lined beach of **Praia Dona Ana.**

Tourist Office: Municipal (☎282 76 41 11), on Lg. Marquêz de Pombal. Open M-Sa 10am-6pm. Open daily in summer 10am-7pm, in winter 10am-6pm.

Currency Exchange: Cotacâmbios, Pr. Gil Eanes, 11 (☎282 76 44 52).

English-Language Bookstore: The Owl Story, Marreiros Neto, 67 (☎282 79 22 89). Large selection of secondhand English novels and travel guides. Comfy chairs available for clients. Open M-F 10am-7pm, Sa 10am-2pm.

Library: R. Dr. Julio Dantas. Open Sept.-July Tu-W and F 10am-6pm, Th 10am-8pm, Sa 10am-1pm. Free internet access upstairs.

Laundromat: Lavanderia Míele, Av. dos Descobrimentos, 27 (☎282 76 39 69). Wash and dry €7 per 5kg. Open M-F 9am-1pm and 3-7pm, Sa 9am-1pm. Some youth hostels and apartments have a laundry service, usually €2-5 per load.

Police: R. General Alberto da Silveira (☎282 76 29 30).

Pharmacy: Farmácia Silva, R. 25 de Abril, 9 (☎282 76 28 59). Ask at any pharmacy for a pamphlet listing the hours and locations of all the pharmacies in Lagos.

Medical Services: Hospital Distrital de Lagos, R. Castelo dos Governadores (☎282 77 01 00).

Internet Access: Snack Bar Ganha Pouco, 1st right after the footbridge coming from the bus station. Internet access and munchies. €2.50 per hr.; €0.50 per fax. Open M-Sa 8am-7:30pm, Su 9am-7:30pm. Several bars in Lagos have computers; check along R. Lançarote de Freitas. Free access also found in the **library** and the **Cultural Center** lobby, just minutes down from all the listed hostels. Open daily 1pm-midnight.

Post Office: R. da Porta de Portugal (☎282 77 02 50), between Pr. Gil Eanes and the river. Fax €4.25 per 2 pages. Open M-F 9am-6pm. **Postal Code:** 8600.

ACCOMMODATIONS AND CAMPING

In July and August, budget spots fill quickly; reserve more than a week in advance. Some places, like the Rising Cock, set aside a limited number of last-minute rooms. Locals trying to rent rooms in their homes will probably greet you at the station or in the streets. Though these rooms may be a little out of the way, they can be the best deals in town at €10-15 per person in summer.

Pousada da Juventude de Lagos (HI), R. Lançarote de Freitas, 50 (☎282 76 19 70. July-Aug; book through Movijovem at ☎217 23 21 00). Social staff and lodgers congregate in the courtyard and barhop at night. Kitchen and TV room with billiards and foosball. Breakfast included. Internet €1 per 15 min. From mid-June to mid-Sept. dorms €16; doubles with bath €43. From mid-Sept. to mid-June €11/32. Cash only. ❶

Rising Cock, Travessa do Forno, 14 (☎968 75 87 85; www.risingcock.com). Legendary among backpackers and spring-breakers. Youthful, gregarious atmosphere. Mrs. Ribeiro, referred to by guests as "Mama," makes breakfast (included). Upstairs patio, kitchen, huge common room with big-screen TV, DVD library, and free internet access and Wi-Fi. Co-ed rooms with lockers; most have baths. Reserve ahead. Prices vary by season. In summer mixed dorms €22-25. AmEx/MC/V. ❷

The Monkey House, R. Gil da Vicente, 23. (☎282 76 03 89; www.themonkeyhouse.eu). Not quite a zoo. 4-room dorms and clean, tiled bathrooms open into a spacious common room with big-screen TV, terrace, kitchen, and free internet. Mountain-bike rental €10 per day. Laundry €5. Breakfast included in the One Fat Monkey Diner (next door). Call for bus/train station pickups. €22-25. AmEx/MC/V. ❷

Camping Trindade (☎282 76 38 93), just outside town. Follow Av. dos Descobrimentos toward Sagres. €3.50 per person; €4.50 per tent; €4.80 per car. ❶

FOOD

The cheapest dining options in Lagos are the local indoor produce **market** on Av. dos Descobrimentos and **Supermercado São Roque,** R. da Porta de Portugal, 61 (☎282 76 28 55; open July-Sept. M-F 9am-8pm, Sa 9am-7pm; Oct.-June M-F 9am-7:30pm, Sa 9am-7pm). Eateries on R. de Silva Lopes and R. 25 de Abril tend to be more expensive.

Casa Rosa, R. do Ferrador, 22 (☎282 18 02 38). The friendly staff at this Australian/American restaurant will engage the daring in an intense game of Connect Four. Various vegetarian options. Entrees €5-7.50. All-you-can-eat spaghetti or vegetarian bolognese €5 daily. The strawberry daiquiris (€4.50) are a sweet start or finish to any meal. Free internet access for diners. Open daily 5pm-midnight. ❶

A Forja, R. dos Ferreiros, 17 (☎282 76 85 88). Few traditional Portuguese restaurants exist in Lagos but locals swear by A Forja, known affectionately as "Blue Door." Serves Algarvian seafood; look for a placard outside listing specials, like the tremendous plate of *pato* (duck). Entrees €7-15. Open daily noon-3pm and 6:30-10pm. Cash only. ❷

Mediterraneo, R. Senhora da Graça, 2 (☎282 18 31 00). Mediterranean and Thai cuisine, including enticing tapas (€2-7.50). Great seafood, and some of the town's most enticing options for vegetarians. Salads €6-8. Pizza €7-8. Entrees €8.50-14.50. Open Tu-Sa 7pm-late. Cash only. ❷

Mullen's, R. Cândido dos Reis, 86 (☎963 50 16 58). A unique combination of great Portuguese and international cuisine, stereotypical Irish pub atmosphere, and live jazz. Try the duck in orange sauce and the spicy *frango grelhado* (grilled chicken). Live music

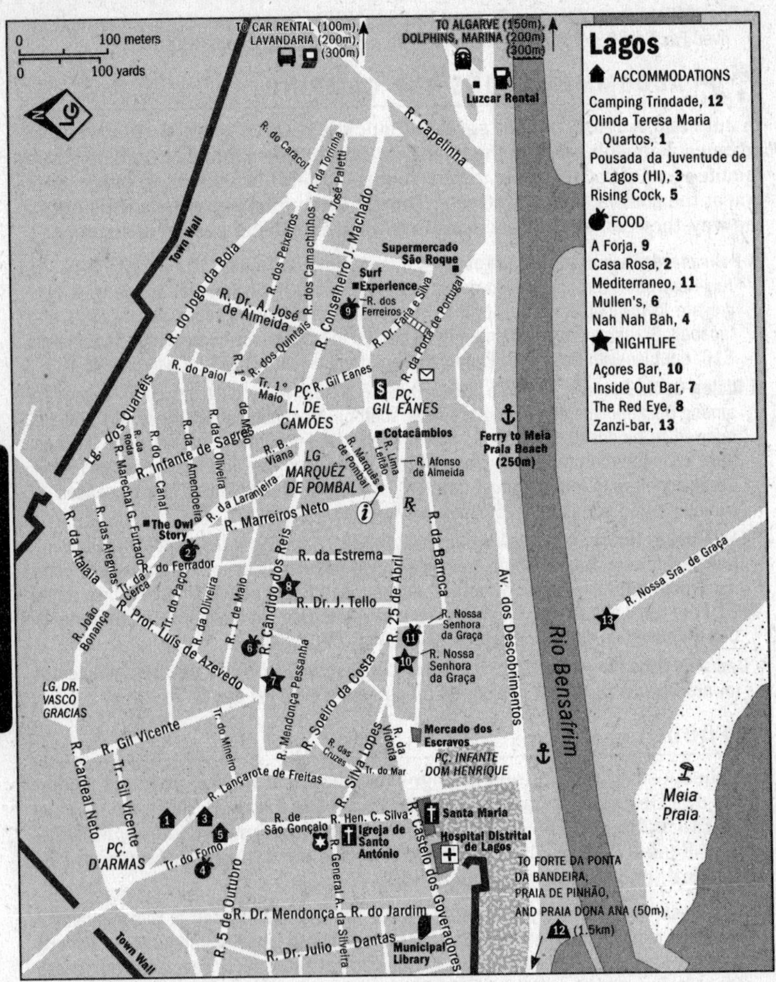

Tu. Tapas €2.50-6. Entrees €8-14. Beer €3.50. Mixed drinks €5. Restaurant open daily 6-10:30pm; bar open daily 11pm-2am. ❷

Nah Nah Bah, Travessa do Forno, 11. Owner personally prepares dishes and chats with customers nightly. Try The Nah Nah Bird (seasoned with Algarvian spices, fresh oranges, and strawberries) with the "legendary" Nah Nah chips (€8.50). Reggae beats (sometimes with live DJ) and cabana-feel keep the relaxed vibe alive well into the night. Entrees €6.50-10. Open 6pm-late. ❷

SIGHTS AND BEACHES

The few sights that Lagos has to offer can be seen on a lazy afternoon walk back from the beach. The **Forte da Ponta da Bandeira,** a 17th-century fortress with maritime exhibitions and tiled chapel, overlooks the marina. It is the site of Lagos's traditional **Banho 29** (Bath 29) festivities; in ancient times, locals traveled to the waters of Lagos and purified themselves in the sea at midnight on August 29. The date has been transformed to an annual celebratory rave. (☎282 76 14 10. Open Tu-Su 9:30am-12:30pm and 2-5pm. €2, students €1, under 13 free.) Also near the waterfront is the former **Mercado dos Escravos** (slave market). Legend has it that the first sale of African slaves in Portugal took place here in 1444. It is currently an art gallery, although one wall bears the arms of the 17th-century Marquis de Nisa. The second floor housed the Lagos Customs Office until 1820. One block from Pr. Infânte Dom Henrique is **Igreja de Santo António.** The church is home to a museum containing artifacts ranging from the Neolithic age to the present, along with a magnificient guilded vault and *retablo mayor.* (Open Tu-Su 9:30am-12:30pm and 2-5pm. €2.20; seniors, students, and under 18 €1.) Lagos's beaches are undeniably seductive. A 4km blanket of flat, smooth sands (crowded in summer but bare in the sunny low season) lines the well-known Meia Praia, across the river from town. To get there, hop on the quick ferry near Pr. Infante Dom Henrique (€0.50). For plunging cliffs and smaller coves, follow Av. dos Descobrimentos toward Sagres to **Praia de Pinhão** (20min.). Five minutes farther down the coast lies **Praia Dona Ana,** with sculpted ochre cliffs and grottoes that appear on half of all Algarve postcards.

WATER ACTIVITIES

If you're up for more than lounging, Lagos offers a wide variety of watersports, from scuba diving to surfing to (booze) cruising. For **grotto boat tours,** stroll the various companies on Av. dos Descobrimentos, on the marina side. Most tours last 45min. and start from €10. **Bom Dia** offers a 2hr. tour for €17-21.

The Booze Cruise (☎969 41 11 31). A 4hr. afternoon boat ride around Lagos's coast. You're certain to get vertigo, whether from looking up at the dizzying heights of the cliffs or the all-you-can-drink bar. Not for those looking for a tour—anchor drops about an hour in. €35, all inclusive. Booking available through The Rising Cock and Joe's Garage.

Algarve Dolphins, Marina de Lagos, 10 (☎282 76 46 70; www.bomdia-boattrips.com). 1hr. of dolphin-watching in the ocean in high-speed rescue boats. Tours leave from the Lagos Marina. €30, €35 for guaranteed sightings.

Surf Experience, R. dos Ferreiros, 21 (☎282 76 19 43; www.surf-experience.com). 1- to 2-week surfing trips with lessons, transportation, and accommodations in a Lagos surf house. All levels welcome. Daytrips when space available. Board and wetsuit rental €75/114. Apr.-Nov. 1 week with board €525, 2 weeks €881; Dec.-Mar. €473/836.

NIGHTLIFE

Lagos's young crowd flocks from the beaches to the bars as the sun dips below the horizon. In town, the area between **Praça Gil Eanes** and **Praça Luis de Camões** is filled with cafes. **Rua Cândido dos Reis, Rua do Ferrador,** and the intersection of **Rua 25 de Abril, Rua de Silva Lopes,** and **Rua Soeiro da Costa** are the bar and club scene mecca. The streets get busy around 10pm, and serious pedestrian traffic hits at midnight. Bars boast an abundance of drink specials.

Inside Out Bar, R. Cândido dos Reis, 119 (www.insideoutbar.com). Inside Out is an insomniac's dream come true; things don't pick up until a little after 2am, when most of the other bars close. The house specialty is the barely legal Fishbowl (€25), mixed by feisty bartenders. Outfitted with a pool table, an extensive drink menu, and entertaining staff, it's a shame this bar ever has to close. Beer €3-4.50. Shots €3-3.50. Mixed drinks €5-6.50. Open daily 8pm-4am.

Zanzi-bar, R. 25 de Abril, 93. Another "2 o'clock" stop, Zanzi-bar is always packed. The back room has a few tables for a more intimate setting. Scan the crowd for waiters and waitresses from local restaurants. Beer €3. Shots €2.50-3. Try house specials such as the *morangsca* (with fresh strawberries, 0.5L €8, 1L €15), sangria (€5/9), frozen margarita (€9/18), and kamikazi (€9/12.50). Open daily 7pm-4am.

The Red Eye, R. Cândido dos Reis, 63. Brits and Aussies flood in around midnight for the classic rock, cheap liquor, and casual pool games. Mostly a pickup scene. Free shot with 1st drink. Beer €2-3. Mixed drinks €3.50-5. Shots €2.50. Jug of sangria €10. Happy hour with €5 2-pint mixed drinks 8-10pm. Open daily 8pm-2am.

Açores Bar, R. Sra. da Graça, 12. A Portuguese twist on the mainly Anglophone-run bar scene, owned by a couple from the Açores. Multi-level bar allows for more breathing room than most surrounding establishments can claim, although the population explodes around 1am. Reggae music nightly. €8 for L of sangria. Open daily 6pm-2am.

DAYTRIP FROM LAGOS

PRAIA DA ROCHA

To reach Praia da Rocha from Lagos, take the bus to Portimão (40min., 10 per day 6:11am-8:19pm, €3.75) and get off at the Praia da Rocha stop.

A short jaunt from Lagos, locals and tourists agree that Praia da Rocha is the best beach that the Algarve has to offer. With vast expanses of big surf, red cliffs, and secluded coves, Praia da Rocha's reputation is well deserved, and the crowds attest to this fact. The tourist office at the end of R. Tomás Cabrieira offers maps and lists of accommodations and restaurants. (☎282 41 91 32. Open May-Sept. daily 9:30-7pm; Oct.-Apr. M-F 9:30am-12:30pm and 2-5:30pm, Sa-Su 9:30am-12:30pm.)

SAGRES ☎282

Marooned atop a windy plateau at the southwesternmost point in Europe, Sagres (pop. 3000) was considered the end of the world for centuries and its name ("Sacrum" or "Sacred Place") bears witness to that mystical impact as world's end. It was here that Prince Henry's famous school of navigation organized exploratory voyages to the far reaches of the globe. While large tour groups and upscale vacationers are discouraged by its desolate location and relative lack of recreation, Sagres's picturesque beaches, friendly locals, and lively nightlife make it a perfect destination for travelers in search of a stress-free day. Sagres, with access to both southern and western coasts, is rapidly becoming one of Europe's prime surfing grounds.

TRANSPORTATION AND PRACTICAL INFORMATION. EVA **buses** (☎282 76 29 44) run from Lagos (1hr.; 14 per day M-F 6:10am-7:35pm, Sa 9 per day 6:10am-7:10pm, Su 7 per day 7:15am-7:10pm; €3.40). Buses also run to Lisboa (5hr., July-Sept. daily 4pm, €18). When arriving in Sagres use the **tourist office** on Av. Comandante Matoso as a signpost for when to get off. Schedules are posted to the left of the tourist office door. The office offers practical and recreational pamphlets in English, including maps, regional information, and suggestions for golfing and enjoying the surf. (☎808 78 12 12; www.visitalgarve.pt. Open Tu-Sa 9:30am-12:30pm and 1:30-5:30pm.) The **police** are in Vila do Bispo (☎282 63 91 12). Other local services include: **banks** and **ATMs** along Av. Comandante

Matoso and across from the post office and at the supermarket; a **pharmacy** all the way down on R. Comandante Matoso, at the corner of R. Jaime Conde (☎282 62 48 50; open M-F 9am-2pm and 3-7pm, Sa 9am-1pm and 5-7pm, Su 11am-1pm and 5-7pm); and a **post office** on the right-hand side of Av. Comandante Matoso as you walk toward Praia da Baleeira (☎707 26 26 26; open M-F 9am-12:30pm and 2-5:30pm). **Freeride Surfcamp,** or Casa Azul, with a blue-tiled hub on Pr. da República, offers surf lessons and packages from €45 per day (including free pickup from Lagos bus and train stations) for surfers of all levels. (☎282 62 42 45; www.freeridesurfcamp.com). Other bookings are available at **Surf Planet,** Est. Nacional, 268 (☎282 62 48 15; www.surfplanet-pt.com; from €45 per day; open M and Th-Su 9am-8pm, W 9a,-7:30pm; AmEx/MC/V) and **Sagres Natura,** R. Mestre Antonio Galhardo (☎282 62 40 72; www.sagresnatura.com; from €45 per day; open daily 9:30am-8pm, AmEx/MC/V). **Bike rentals** at **Surf Planet** (€5/10/15 for 1/4/8hr.) and **Sagres Natura** (€15 per day). Free internet at Água Salgada and neighbor O Dromedário (see **Entertainment, p. 414**).

ACCOMMODATIONS AND CAMPING. Finding a bed in Sagres is not hard; windows everywhere display multilingual signs advertising rooms. Singles and doubles range €20-30 and triples €30-40, with lower rates in winter. Use caution if considering offers at the bus station; prices tend to run a little higher than those on Av. Comandate Matoso, and rooms could be outside the main city. To stay within city limits, try **Atalaia Apartamentos ❷,** on R. Patrão António Faustino, just off the main drag. The spacious beach-themed rooms match the blue and yellow painted tiles adorning the hallway. The apartments boast full kitchen, bath, living room, and terrace. (☎282 62 46 81. Prices vary; call ahead.) The shop owner at **Oceanus ❷,** R. Comandante Matoso near the pharmacy, offers clean, colorful and mostly spacious rooms with complete bath above the store. (☎282 62 45 58. Small singles €20; doubles €25; triples €30. Larger rooms €30/35/40. Reception open daily 9am-8pm.) Sagres strictly forbids open-air **camping** due to its strong winds. Campers can get their fix at **Orbitur Campground ❶,** 2.5km toward Cabo de São Vicente, just off ER 268 and about a 25min. walk to the lesser-known Praia do Belixe. (☎282 62 43 71. Reception 8am-10pm. June-Aug. €4.30 per person; €4.60 per tent; €3.80 per car. Sept.-May prices €0.20 less.)

FOOD. For groceries, try **Alisuper,** a supermarket on R. Comandante Matoso. (☎282 62 44 87. Open daily 9am-8pm.) **O Dromedário Bistro ❷,** on R. Comandante Matoso, is a Moroccan-inspired haven with an extensive bar, constant stream of American pop/rock, and free internet (ask the bartender for the code). Try the hearty crepes (€2.40-5.30), colorful salads (€3.90-6.80), inventive sandwiches (€2.10-6.70), and fresh fruit juices and shakes (€2-3.50). The bar is a hot nightspot, especially on Karaoke Thursdays. (☎282 62 42 19; www.dromedariosagres.com. Restaurant open daily 10am-midnight. Bar open daily in summer until 3am; in winter until 2am.) The colorful, minimalist decor of **Com Alma Caffé ❷,** right across Atalaia Apartamentos, is inviting. (☎282 62 48 56. Pasta and pizza €6.80-9.30. Beer €1-2.60. Mixed drinks €3.50-5.)

SIGHTS AND BEACHES. Near town, the **Fortaleza de Sagres** divides the famed Ponta de Sagres that grips both coasts of the jutting peninsula with its far-reaching walls. The fort, once home to Prince Henry the Navigator, is an integral part of every visit to Sagres, if only for its sweeping ocean views. (Open daily May-Sept. 9:30am-8pm; Oct.-Apr. 9:30am-5:30pm. Closed May 1 and Dec. 25. €3, under 25 or retired €1.50. Youth cardholders

€1.20. Free 30min. guided tours at noon, 4, 5pm. Max. 20 people. Meet near compass.) Several swimmer-friendly **beaches** fringe the peninsula, the most prominent of which is **Mareta,** at the bottom of the road from the town center. Craggy rock formations bookend this sandy crescent. Mareta is popular for its length and isolation, but this beach is not immune to Sagres's infamous wind. Less than a mile up the coast from **Praia da Baleeira** is **Praia de Martinhal,** widely acclaimed for its windsurfing. Less windy **Praia da Belixe** is located 3km outside of town on the way to Cabo de São Vicente.

ENTERTAINMENT. With the last traces of sunlight snuffed out, rock music and crowds fill the lively **Rosa dos Ventos** in Pr. da República. (☎282 62 44 80. Beer €1-2. Mixed drinks €3-5. Famous sangria €6.50. Happy hour 5-8pm, sangria €4. Open M-Tu and Th-Su 10am-2am.) Another hot spot is **Água Salgada,** on R. Comandante Matoso, pulsing with mixes spun by a live DJ. Free Wi-Fi and PC access, card games, and foosball provide entertainment off the dance floor. (☎282 62 42 97. Beer from €1.70. Mixed drinks €5. Shots €2. Sandwiches, pizza, and salads available. Open June-Aug. daily 10am-4am. Sept.-May M abd W-Su 10am-4am.) Next door is **O Dromedário** (see **Food,** p. 413), where trendy young locals let loose. A projector screen plays surf movies while the DJ keeps the party moving with the likes of Lynyrd Skynyrd and REM. (☎282 62 42 97. Beer €1.70-4. Daiquiris and coladas €4.50-7. Open in summer daily 10pm-3am; in winter Th and Su 10am-2am, F-Sa 10am-4am.)

ALENTEJO

Vast golden plains dotted with giant stone castles and tiny red-roofed villages cover the region between the Tagus and the Algarve. A sharp contrast to the commotion of Lisboa or the wilds of the Algarve, the Alentejo graces travelers with a more stately, historical setting. Évora, Elvas, and other remarkably well-preserved towns lie in the Alto Alentejo, while Beja remains the only major town on the seemingly endless Baixo Alentejo plain. The region is known primarily for its cork; more than two-thirds of the world's supply comes from here, and the local villages specialize in cork handicrafts. The area is best in the spring; fiery temperatures can turn the Alentejo into an oven in summer.

ÉVORA ☎266

Évora (pop. 55,000) is the capital and largest city of the Alentejo region, with a wall-enclosed old city of palaces, churches, and Roman ruins at its center. The city is also famous for its unusual medieval approach to recycling (see **Capela dos Ossos,** p. 417). Across the city, mock burials decorate the sidewalks in lieu of benches. During the school year, university students enliven the town, especially during the Queima das Fitas (Burning of the Ribbons), a week-long graduation celebration the last week of May with live music, dancing, and drunken merriment. The town remains surprisingly active in the summer, despite the absence of students and the locals' inclinations to vacation on the coast.

TRANSPORTATION

Trains: Lg. da Estação de CP, at Av. dos Combatentes de Grande Guerra (☎266 70 21 25 or 808 20 82 08; www.cp.pt). Service to: **Beja** (1hr., 5 per day 6:22am-6:44pm,

€6.40-11.40), **Faro** (5hr.; 6:22am, 12:44pm; €12.80-19.80), and **Lisboa** (2hr., 3 per day 6:44am-6:44pm, €11.10).

Buses: Av. São Sebastião (☎266 76 94 10), 300m outside the town wall. More frequent schedules than trains. Buses go to: **Beja** (1hr., 7 per day 8:45am-8pm, €7); **Braga** (8-10hr.; M-Sa 8 per day 6am-8:45pm, Su 9 per day 6am-9:30pm; €20) via **Porto** (6-8hr., 6 per day 8:30am-8pm, €16); **Castelo Branco** (2-3hr., 6 per day 6am-5pm, €11.90); **Elvas** (1hr.; 12:15, 1:45, 5pm; €9.50); **Faro** (4hr.; 8:45am, 2:30, 5:15pm; €13.50); **Lisboa** (2hr., 9 per day 7am-8pm, €10.80); **Portalegre** (1hr.; 10:25am, 2, 5:15pm; €10); **Setúbal** (1hr.; 8:30, 10:15am, 2pm; €8.70).

Taxis: ☎266 73 47 34. 24hr. taxis wait in Pr. do Giraldo and Pr. do Sertorio.

ORIENTATION AND PRACTICAL INFORMATION

To reach **Praça do Giraldo** from the **bus station** (15min. walk), turn right up Av. São Sebastião, keeping the small white wall to the right, and continue straight when it turns into R. Serpa Pinto at the city wall. Follow this road into Pr. do Giraldo, the center of the city. All major sights are a short walk from this square. No direct bus connects the train station to the center of town. By foot, go up Av. Dr. Baronha and continue straight as it turns into R. da República at the city wall. To avoid either walk, hail a taxi (€3).

Tourist Office: Pr. do Giraldo, 73 (☎266 77 70 71; www.cm-evora.pt/guiaturistico). Staff speaks English, French, and Spanish and provides maps, lists of restaurants, and public phones. Self-guided audio tours of the city €2, due back before 5:30pm. Wheelchair-accessible. Open daily May-Oct. 9am-7pm; Nov.-Apr. 9am-6pm.

Currency Exchange: 24hr. **ATM** outside the tourist office. Several banks line Pr. do Giraldo, all open M-F 8:30am-3pm.

Police: R. Francisco Soares Lusitano (☎266 70 20 22).

Pharmacy: Farmácia Galeno, R. da República, 34 (☎266 70 32 77). Open M-F 9am-1pm and 3-7pm.

Hospital: Hospital do Espírito Santo, Lg. Senhor Jesus da Pobreza (☎266 74 01 00 or 266 75 84 24), near city wall and the intersection with R. Dr. Augusto Eduardo Nunes.

Internet Access: CyberCenter, R. dos Mercadores, 42 (☎266 74 69 23). 20 high-speed computers. €1.50 per hr. Open M-F 10:30am-11pm, Sa-Su 2-10pm. **Bar Oficin@,** R. Moeda, 27 (☎266 70 73 12). Only 1 computer, so expect to wait. €0.50 per 10min., €2.50 per hour. Open Tu-F 8pm-2am, Sa 9pm-2am.

Post Office: R. de Olivença (☎266 74 54 80; fax 74 54 86). **Poste Restante** and fax. Open M-F 8:30am-6pm. Main office on Largo Portas de Moura (☎266 74 98 40).**Postal Code:** 7999.

ACCOMMODATIONS AND CAMPING

Most accommodations cluster on side streets off Pr. do Giraldo and are well advertised. They're crowded in the summer, especially during graduation in May and the Feira de São João, the June celebration of Évora's patron saint. Private *quartos*, about €25-30 per double, are pleasant summer alternatives to the crowded *pensões;* check with the tourist office for listings.

Casa dos Teles, R. Romão Ramalho, 27 (☎266 70 24 53, casadosteles@planetaelix.pt). 1 block off Pr. do Giraldo. The friendly dog gives this 200-year-old private home a welcoming feel. Spacious, private rooms are decorated with pictures from around town. All with TV, 4 rooms with A/C. The top room serves as a double, triple, or quint with private bath and fridge. Reserve ahead. June-Sept. singles €20-25; doubles €30-35, with bath €40; triple/quad €40. Oct.-May €5 less. Cash only. ❷

Casa Palma, R. Bernardo Matos, 29A (☎266 70 35 60). Located right off Pr. da República. The house is over 100 years old and looks like an antiques market. Its grandmotherly owner keeps it in excellent shape and charges reasonable prices for petite rooms on the top floor. She'll meet you at the door every time you return, as well. All rooms have TV, some a small balcony. Singles €20-25; doubles €30-35. Cash only. ❷

Pensão Residencial Giraldo, R. dos Mercadores, 27 (☎266 70 58 33). Spacious, comfortable rooms have TV and carpeting. Clean rooms with A/C make for a refuge from the streets outside. Reserve ahead. In summer singles €30, with bath €35; doubles €35/45; triples €55. In winter €5-15 less. Cash only. ❸

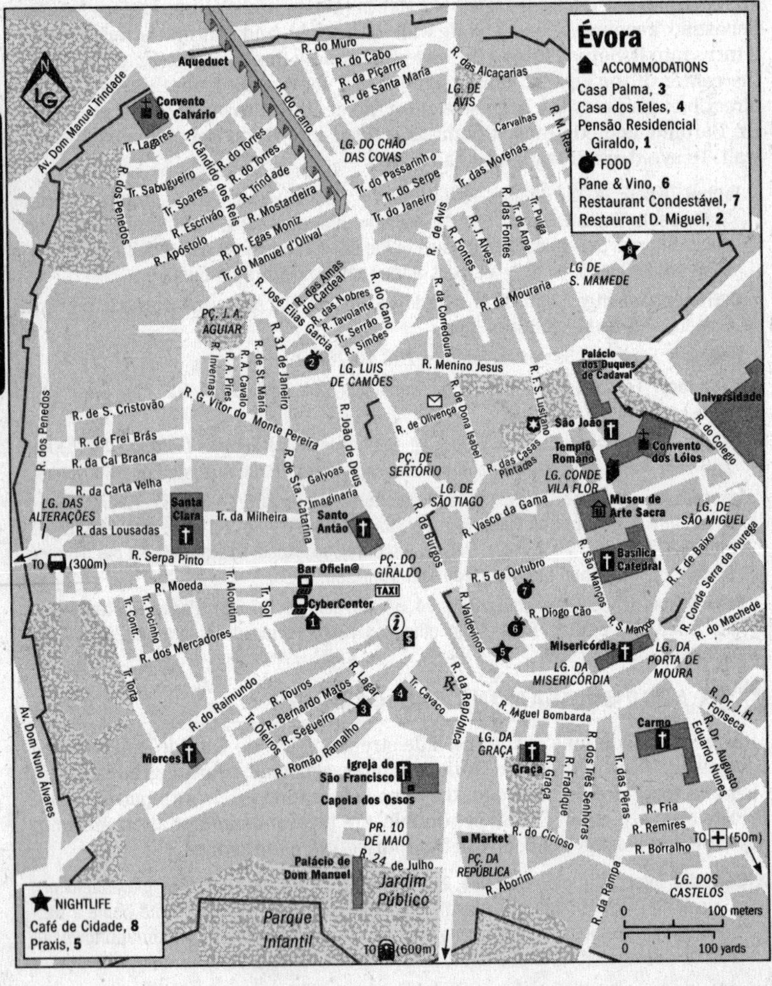

FOOD

Restaurants are scattered near Pr. do Giraldo, especially along **Rua dos Mercadores** and the small streets off **Rua 5 de Outubro,** but many are tourist-oriented; to find inexpensive local favorites, wander away from the center and the main sights. The **market,** near Pr. da República, sells crafts and regional goods as well as cheese and produce. (Open Tu-Su 7am-1pm.)

Condestável, R. Diogo Cão, 3 (☎266 70 20 08; www.softline.pt/residencial-diana). Cheap, simple, but delicious. Enjoy a two-course meal with soup, fish or meat, drink and coffee for €5.90-7. Also nice for a drink at night. Open daily 8am-midnight. MC/V. ❶

Pane & Vino, R. Diogo Cão, 22 (☎266 74 69 60). This popular corner restaurant's classic, thin-crust pizzas are too good to be missed. Pizzas and pasta €6-9. Open Tu-Su noon-3pm and 7-11pm. AmEx/MC/V. ❷

D. Miguel, Trav. de Cavella (☎ 266 74 14 42) The cheapest Portuguese meal you can find in Évora. The food has a homemade feel with several meat and fish options. Entrees €5-7. Open M-F 8am-10pm. Cash only. ❶

SIGHTS

CAPELA DOS OSSOS. Few places on earth rival the Capela dos Ossos in spookiness. The "Chapel of Bones" warmly welcomes visitors: "*Nós ossos que aqui estamos, pelos vossos esperamos*" ("We bones that are here are waiting for yours"). In order to provide a hallowed space to reflect on the profundity of life and death, three Franciscan monks built this chapel from the remains of over 5000 anonymous bodies buried in surrounding churches. The walls are covered in neatly piled bones and skulls, while the three founders lie enclosed in stone sarcophagi. For thrills and chills, check out the preserved corpse hanging from one of the chapel's walls, then go give Mom a call: legend has it that the body is a son cursed by his mother for disobedience and cruelty. *(Pr. 1 de Maio. Follow R. da República from Pr. do Giraldo, then take a right into Pr. 1 de Maio; next to the Convento de São Francisco to the right of the church steps. ☎266 70 45 21. Open M-Sa May-Sept. 9am-12:50pm and 2:30-5:45pm; Oct.-Apr. 9am-12:50pm and 2:30-5:15pm. Last entrance 5min. before closing. An audio tour plays in several languages inside the chapel. €1.50, students €1, €0.50 more for camera use—well worth it.)*

BASÍLICA CATEDRAL. Built during the 12th century, the Basílica Catedral, also known as the Sé, looms over Évora with its two giant asymmetrical towers like a mad scientist's castle. Inside, however, its ornate carvings and splendid architecture are similar to those of other European cathedrals. Climb the cloisters' stairs to see the view of Évora from the terrace or tour the **Museu de Arte Sacra,** which displays religious ornaments and sculptures from the 17th and 18th centuries. *(From the center of Pr. do Giraldo, head to the end of R. 5 de Outubro. Cathedral open M 9am-12:45pm and 2-4:45pm, Tu-Su 9am-4:45pm. Cloisters open daily 9am-noon and 2-4:30pm. Museum open Tu-Su in summer 9am-4:30pm; in winter 9am-12:30pm and 2-4:30pm. Cloisters and museum €3, students €2.50; cloisters and cathedral €1.50, cathedral only €1.)*

TEMPLO ROMANO. Enormous and well-preserved columns of an ancient Roman temple sit in a spacious square at the highest point of the city, perpetual reminders of Évora's long history. The small temple was built in the AD first century from local granite but walled up in the Middle Ages and used as a slaughter house. It is widely believed, despite scarce historical evidence, that the small temple was built in honor of the goddess Diana.

IGREJA DE SÃO JOÃO DE EVANGELISTA AND PALÁCIO DE DUQUES DE CADAVAL. Also known as the Convento dos Loíos, the Igreja faces the Templo Romano. The church and ducal palace are owned by the Cadaval family, who restored the buildings with their personal fortunes in 1957-58. The interior of the church is covered with dazzling *azulejos*, and a beautiful cloister with an outdoor cafe is open to tourists. The main part of the convent is now used as a luxury *pousada* for guests looking for a unique overnight experience. *(Lg. Conde do Vila Flor. Spring-fall Tu-Su open 10am-12:30pm and 2-6pm; winter 10am-12:30pm and 2-5pm. €3, €5 for church and next-door exhibition hall.)*

NIGHTLIFE

Évora's nightlife is fueled largely by the students from the university, who fill the bars after midnight and then move on to the clubs. Wednesday nights are student nights at most establishments, so expect larger crowds. The cafes in Pr. do Giraldo are great for socializing and stay busy until around midnight. The infamous **Praxis,** R. Valdevinos, is the only nightclub in town, boasting four different bars and two floors for dancing. (☎266 70 81 77. Beer €1.50. Mixed drinks €4-6. Min. consumption €7 for men, €5 for women. Open W-Su until 6am.) A warehouse-like bar/cafe, **Café de Cidade,** R. das Alca Carias, 1, swarms with local crowds. (☎266 78 51 63. Open M-Sa 11am-2am. AmEx/MC/V.)

RIBATEJO AND ESTREMADURA

Some of the greatest treasures of Portugal can be found in the region just north of Lisboa. Home to festivals of food, bullfighting, and crafts, the old provinces still maintain a regional character. The Ribatejo is often referred to as the "Heart of Portugal" for its central location and bountiful agricultural production. With the ornate monasteries in Alcobaça and Batalha, the fairy-tale town of Óbidos, and the hallowed sanctuary at Fátima, one of the largest Catholic pilgrimage destinations in the world, Ribatejo boasts some of the country's finest sights. Its beaches are exquisite too: serrated cliffs and whitewashed fishing villages line Estremadura's Costa de Prata (Silver Coast), where majestic palaces overlook the oceanic expanse and the undiscovered alleys of charming villages.

HIGHLIGHTS OF RIBATEJO AND ESTREMADURA

RECHARGE with a short trip to beautiful and relaxing **Nazaré** (p. 423).

WORSHIP the mysterious ways of the Virgin Mary at **Fátima** (p. 429).

SANTARÉM ☎243

Nicknamed the "balcony over the Tagus," Santarém (pop. 60,000) is a 3000-year-old city known for its ancient churches connected to the Knights Templar, traditional farming festivals, and the best view of the Tejo in all of Portugal. From religious *festas* in the winter months, to bike festivals in the fall, to a celebration of national theatre in the spring, this small city is in constant motion. The prime time to visit Santarém is in the first days of June, when the city holds its Feira Nacional de Agricultura, a renowned festival featuring bullfighting, good food, and wild, yet traditional, celebration.

TRANSPORTATION

Trains: The **station,** Estrada da Estação (☎243 32 11 99), 2km outside of town. **Bus** service between the station and town (10min.; M-F every 45min. 6:50am-7:45pm, Sa 4 per day 8am-1:30pm; €1.30). Taxi service from town to the station Su, €4.30. Trains run to: **Faro** via **Lisboa's Estação do Barreiro** (4hr., 5 per day 9:16am-6:09pm, €27); **Lisboa's Sta. Apolónia** (1hr., 15 per day 9:16am-10:16pm, 6.40); **Porto** (2½ hrs., 12 per day 8:14am-10:14pm, €22); **Tomar** (1hr., 17 per day 6:15am-10:20pm, €6.40); **Coimbra** (1½ hr., 12 per day 8:15am-10:15 pm, €11).

Buses: Rodoviária do Tejo, on Av. do Brasil (☎243 33 32 00). To: **Braga** (4 hr., 3 per day 10:45am-6:45pm, €16.10); **Caldas da Rainha** (1hr., 2-3 per day 7:20am-6:20pm, €5.25); **Coimbra** (2hr., 3 per day 10:45am-6:45pm, €11.80); **Faro** (7hr.; M-F 10 per day 7:45am-7pm, Sa 10:30am-4:30pm, Su 10:30am-7pm; €18.50); **Leiria** (1hr., 4 per day 10:45am-6:45pm, €10.50); **Lisboa** (1hr.; M-F and Su 7 per day 10:45am-7pm, Sa 7:45am-7pm; €6.70); **Óbidos** (1hr., 4 per day 7:20am-2:45pm, €5.75) via **Caldas Rainha; Porto** (4hr., 5 per day 10:45am-6:45pm, €15); **Nazaré** (2hr., M-F 7:30am, €6.40).

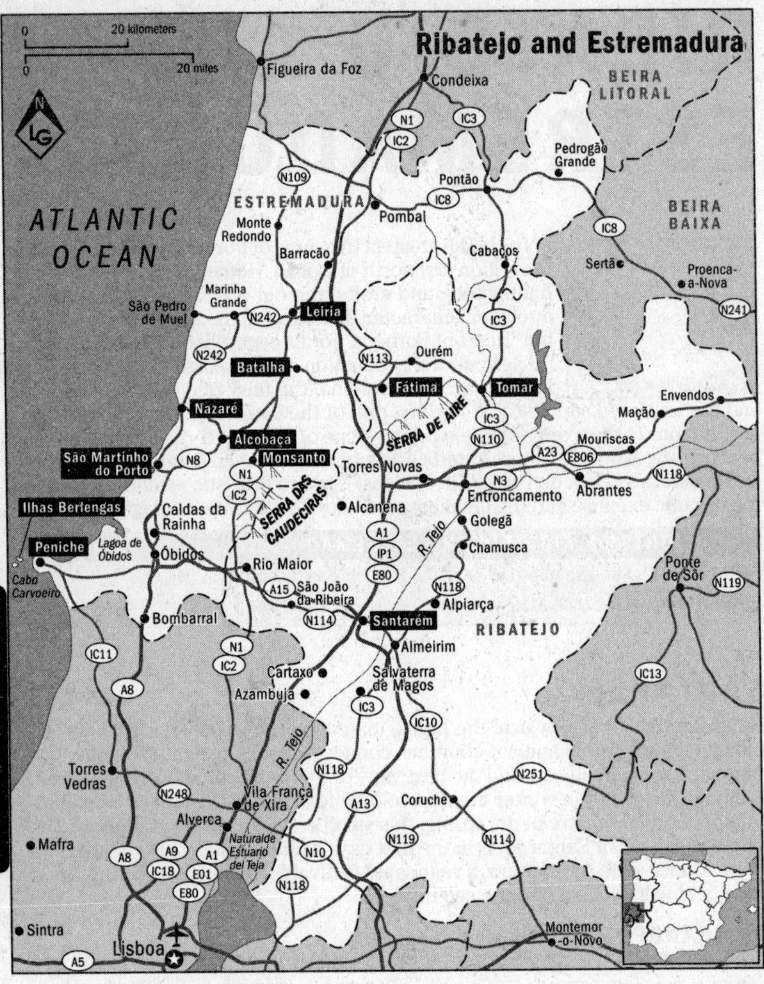

Taxis: Scaltaxis (☎243 33 29 19) has a stand across the park from the bus station. 24hr. service.

ORIENTATION AND PRACTICAL INFORMATION

The historic center consists of narrow grid-like streets typical of old Portuguese cities. The main square is **Praça Sá da Bandeira.** From there, Rua Serpa Pinto and Rua Capelo e Ivans run through the core of old Santarém. Avenida Sá da Bandeira marks the outer edge of the historic center and meets Avenida Afonso Henriques at the "W" shopping center. Av. Afonso Henriques runs to the newer part of the city, and passes the bullfighting stadium in Praça de Touros.

Tourist Office: R. Capelo e Ivens, 63 (☎243 30 44 37). Maps and informative brochures on accommodations and transportation. Helpful, friendly staff speaks English, French, and Spanish. Open M 9am-12:30pm and 2-5:30pm, Tu-F 9am-7pm, Sa-Su and holidays 10am-12:30pm and 2:30-5:30pm.

Currency Exchange: Caixa Geral de Depósitos (☎243 33 30 07), at R. Dr. Texeira Guedes and R. Capelo e Ivens. Open M-F 8:30am-3pm.

Police: Av. do Brasil (☎243 32 20 22), down the street from the bus station.

Pharmacy: Farmácia Veríssimo, R. Capelo e Ivens, 72 (☎243 33 02 30). Open M-F 9am-7:30pm, Sa 9am-1pm.

Hospital: Av. Bernardo Santareno (☎243 30 02 00). Take R. Alexandre Herculano until it becomes Av. Bernardo Santareno. English spoken.

Internet Access: Esp@ço Net (☎243 32 53 11), in the Sala de Leitura Bernardo Santa Reno, a public library by the park between the bus station and the police station. 9 computers, max. 40min. Free. Library open M-F 9am-8pm, Sa 9:30am-1pm, internet access M-F 10am-6:30pm.

Post Office: (☎243 30 97 00), on the corner of Lg. Cândido dos Reis and R. Dr. Texeira Guedes. Open M-F 8:30am-6:30pm, Sa 9am-12:30pm. **Postal Code:** 2000.

ACCOMMODATIONS

Accommodation prices, while never rock-bottom in Santarém, increase during the **Ribatejo** fair in early June.

Residencial Muralha, R. Pedro Canavarro, 12 (☎243 32 23 99, fax 32 94 77). Simple, comfortable, and charming rooms, all with TV and large *azulejo*-covered private bath. Centrally located. Reserve a week ahead in summer. Singles with bath €30; doubles €35-40; quads €50. Cash only. ❸

Residencial Beirante, R. Alexandre Herculano, 5 (☎243 32 25 47, fax 33 38 45). This 42-room mini-hotel has tidy rooms with all the perks: phone, blow-dryers, A/C, TV, breakfast, and a restaurant downstairs. Call ahead in summer. Singles €30; doubles €40. Cash only. ❸

Pensão José Rodrigues, Tr. Do Froes, 14 (☎ 962 83 79 09), marked by a small hanging "Dormidas" sign. Half the price of everything around it. Gigantic footprint rugs mark the way to spotless rooms decorated with pastel-flowered bedspreads. Some doubles are a combined bedroom and bathroom. Singles €15, with shower €20; doubles with shower €25. During the 1st 2 weeks of June, prices might increase by €5. Cash only. ❶

RIBATEJO AND ESTREMADURA

FOOD

Many small eateries reside in the narrow streets around R. Capelo e Ivens and R. Serpa Pinto. The municipal **market,** in the pagoda on Lg. Infante Santo near Jardim da República, sells fresh produce. (Open M-Sa 6am-2pm.) The somewhat pricey **Supermercado Minipreço,** R. Pedro Canavarro, 31, is on the street leading from the bus station to R. Capelo e Ivens. (Open M-Sa 9am-8pm.)

Adiafa, Campo E. Infante da Câmara (☎243 32 40 86), out by the bullfighting stadium. A giant restaurant that looks like a barn on the inside. Try their *sopa de legumes* (€1.50) or pork *portuguesa.* Ask for a half, or *meia,* portion; it is more than enough. Entrees €6-13. Open daily 10am-9:30pm. AmEx/MC/V. ❷

A Caravana, R. Capelo e Ivens, 28. A great place for lunch, with cafeteria-style entrees cooked fresh for takeout. Also a sit-down restaurant, with glass-covered tables showcasing a variety of seeds and beans. Entrees €6-10. Open M-Sa 10am-7pm. Cash only. ❷

O Saloio, Tr. do Montalvo, 11 (☎243 32 76 56), off R. Capelo e Ivens. This local favorite serves a variety of meat and a mean *caldeirada* (monster fish stew). No vegetarian options. Entrees €5-10. Open M-Sa 10am-7pm. Cash only. ❷

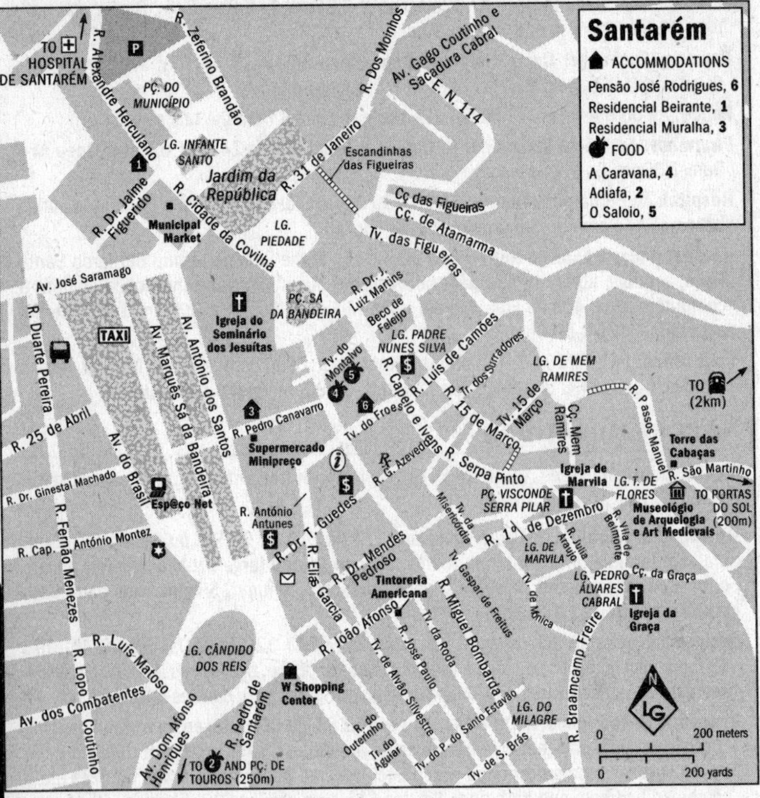

SIGHTS

PORTAS DO SOL. Imposing Moorish walls surround this tranquil park of flowers and fountains, high above the Rio Tejo and the Alentejo plains. Climb the stone steps to the top and take in the timeless beauty of the surrounding countryside. Don't be surprised if you're the only one noticing the spectacular view, though; the park serves as Santarém's prime spot for lovers' rendezvous. A quiet cafe, a large birdcage, and a playground are enclosed by the ancient castle walls. *(Take R. Serpa Pinto to R. São Martinho, past the Torre das Cabaças, and stay right as the road becomes Av. 5 de Outubro after the abandoned Art Deco theater. Open daily June-Aug. 9am-10pm, Sept.-May 9am-6:30pm. Free.)*

PRAÇA VISCONDE DE SERRA PILAR. Centuries ago, Christians, Moors, and Jews gathered for social and business affairs in this small *praça*. *(Take R. Serpa Pinto from Pr. Sá da Bandeira.)* The 12th-century **Igreja de Marvila,** off the *praça*, was revamped in the late 17th century with traditional ornamentation of the era, and is undergoing another renovation in 2008. Don't be fooled by the simplicity of the exterior; the *azulejo*-covered interior is dazzling, as is the Manueline entrance. *(Open Tu-Su 9am-12:30pm and 2-5:30pm. Free.)* The early Gothic minimalism of nearby **Igreja da Graça** contrasts with Marvila's exuberance; construction began in 1380 on the orders of the first earls of Ourém, and the cloister dates back to the 16th century. Inside, in the **Capela de São João Evangelista,** lies Pedro Cabral, the explorer who "discovered" Brazil, and one of the few of his crew to live long enough to return home. *(Open Tu-Su 9am-12:30pm and 2pm-5:30pm. Free.)*

TORRE DAS CABAÇAS. The medieval Torre das Cabaças (Tower of the Gourds) was named after the eight earthen bowls installed in the 16th century to amplify the sound of the bell's ring. Today the tower serves as the **Museu de Tempo.** The interior walls of the tower are peppered with clocks and sundials from different eras and civilizations. Buy tickets across the street at the small **Museológio de Arqueologia e Arte Medievais,** which has a hearty collection of medieval cookware and an exhibit comparing Christian and Muslim influences on Santarém. *(Take R. Serpa Pinto to São Martinho, past Pr. Visconde de Serra Pilar. Open W-Su 9am-12:30pm and 2-5:30pm. Tower €1, Archaeology Museum €2, both €2.50; under 25 €0.50/1/1.25.)*

NIGHTLIFE AND FESTIVALS

Most of the fun in Santarém takes place outside the historic center. Every other Sunday, bargain hunters flock to the large market in front of the bullfighting stadium, where they sift through mounds of goods, from clothes to furniture to pets. (Open 7am-2pm.) This is also the location of the annual **Festival Nacional de Gastronomia,** a giant celebration of Portuguese cuisine in late October or early November. Better known is the **Feira Nacional de Agricultura** (a.k.a. Feira do Ribatejo), a 10-day extravaganza of markets, bullfighting, and farmers racing tiny horses. The party starts the first week of June and continues until the 11th or 13th. When there is no BBQing or horseback riding to be done, however, Santarém is a little lethargic, especially in comparison with Lisboa. A few sleepy pubs can be found beside the shopping center, along R. Pedro de Santarém, the road that leads to the bullfighting stadium in Pr. de Touros.

NAZARÉ

☎262

Home to a beautiful stretch of golden sand and calm turquoise water, Nazaré (pop. 16,000) has become one of the Ribatejo's main tourist attractions. In true postcard fashion, the beaches are lined with hundreds of small colorful tents that help visitors escape the hot summer sun. In Nazaré, tourism is a big business dominated by women dressed in traditional black scarves and aprons who sell snacks and souvenirs and rent rooms or beach tents to tourists. Still, the town's relaxed feel begs tourists to return year after year for a peaceful vacation under the warm Portuguese sun. At night, Nazaré is just as busy as it is during the day. Local bars and cafes stay crowded all night, and the beach comes alive again in the early morning.

TRANSPORTATION

Buses: Av. Vieira Guimarães (☎967 44 98 68), perpendicular to Av. da República. More convenient than trains (6km away). To: **Alcobaça** (20min.; M-F 12 per day 7:10am-7:10pm, Sa 8 per day 7:10am-6:45pm; €1.75); **Batalha** (50min., 6 per day 7:10am-6:50pm, €3.30); **Caldas da Rainha** (1hr.; M-F 10 per day 6:30am-7:25pm, Sa-Su 2-3 per day 8:30am-2:45pm; €3.10); **Coimbra** (2hr.; 4 per day M-Sa 6:25am-7:25pm, Su 8:25am-7:25pm; €10.20); **Fátima** (1hr., 3 per day 7:10am-5:10pm, €4.50); **Leiria** (1hr., 5 per day 7:10am-6:45pm, €3.30); **Lisboa** (2hr.; M-Th 6 per day 6:50am-6:40pm, F and Su 9 per day 6:50am-7:40pm, Sa 5 per day 6:50am-4:40pm; €8.30); **Porto** (3hr.; M-Sa 4 per day 6:25am-7:25pm, Su 7 per day 8:25am-7:25pm; €12.50).

Taxis: Praça de Taxi (☎262 55 13 63).

ORIENTATION AND PRACTICAL INFORMATION

All of the action in Nazaré takes place near the beach, mainly along **Avenida da República,** which follows the coastline. The avenue runs past the two main squares, **Praça Dr. Manuel de Arriaga** and then **Praça Sousa Oliveira,** before ending at the cliffs. From there, the funicular runs up the side of the mountain, connecting the two levels of Nazaré. **Sítio,** the old town, forms the second story of the city, and its position 100m above the water has kept it calmer and more traditional than the beach area below. The downtown area is grid-like and easily navigable by foot. To get to the tourist office from the bus stop, take a right out of the station toward the beach and then another onto Av. da República; the office is a 5min. walk along the shore and lies between the two plazas.

Tourist Office: (☎262 56 11 94), beachside on Av. da República. Provides maps and info. English, French, and Spanish spoken. Open daily July-Aug. 9am-9pm, Sept. and Apr.-June 9:30am-1pm and 2:30-7pm, Oct.-Mar. 9:30am-1pm and 2:30-6pm.

Bank: Major banks lie on and around Av. da República. **Millennium BCP,** Av. Manuel Remígio (☎262 00 11 70), is right on the beach. Open M-F 7:30am-3:30pm.

Laundromat: Lavandaria da Nazaré, Rua Branco Martins, 19 (☎262 55 27 61). Walk away from the cliffs on Av. da Republiça, turn left on R. das Traneiras and then take a right on R. Branco Martins. The laundromat will be the 2nd door on your left. Dry-cleaning and laundry available. English spoken. Wash and dry (€3 per kg), ironing (€0.15 per kg). Open M-Sa 9am-1pm 3-7pm. Cash Only.

Police: (☎262 55 00 70) at the corner of R. Sub-Vila and Av. Vieira Guimarães near the bus station.

Pharmacy: Farmácia Sousa on R. Mouzinho de Albuquerque, 30 (☎262 56 12 21). Up the street from Pr. Sousa Oliveira. Open M-Th 9am-7pm, F 9am-8pm, Sa 9am-1pm.

Medical Services: Hospital da Confraria da Nossa Senhora de Nazaré (☎262 55 23 23), in the Sítio district on the cliffs above the town center. **Centro de Saúde** (☎262 56 91 20), Urbanização Caixins, in the new part of town. Go down Av. da República, which becomes Av. Manuel Remígio. Turn left on R. das Hortas, and go almost to the end. Open M-F 9am-1pm and 2-6pm.

Internet Access: Centro Cultural, Av. Manuel Remígio (☎262 56 23 88), on Av. da República. Max. 30min. Free. Open Sept.-July 14 M-F 9:30am-1pm and 2-7pm, Sa 3-7pm. July 15-Aug. M-F 10am-1pm, 3-7pm, and 9pm-midnight, Sa 3pm-7pm and 9pm-midnight.

Post Office: Av. da Independência Nacional, 2 (☎262 56 91 00). From Pr. Sousa Oliveira, walk up R. Mouzinho de Albuquerque. **Posta Restante** and **fax.** Open M-F 9:30am-12:30pm and 2:30-6pm. **Postal Code:** 2450.

ACCOMMODATIONS AND CAMPING

Nazaré is inhabited by the most aggressive room-hawkers in Portugal. They swarm arriving buses at the station and line Av. da República offering their homes to tourists and locals alike. Bargain with the same aggressive attention they use to court you. Agree on a price before seeing the room, but don't settle the deal until afterward. In summer, don't pay over €30 for a rented room.

Hospedaria Ideal, R. Adrião Batalha, 98 (☎262 55 13 79), a block away from Pr. Dr. Manuel. 6 rooms with high ceilings, mirrors, and comfortable beds. Clean shared bathroom with retro linoleum. During the summer, rooms include 3 meals per day without beverages. July-Aug. singles €35-40, doubles €75, triples €100-110; Sept.-June €15/20/25-30 Cash only. ❸

Vila Turística Conde Fidalgo, Av. da Independência Nacional, 21-A (☎262 55 23 61). Choice of rooms with private bathroom TV and mini-fridge or private apartments with TV, kitchen, refrigerator, microwave, and bath. Laundry €5. July-Aug doubles €40-50, apartments for 5 €90; Sept-Jun €30-35/75-80. Cash only. ❹

Vale Paraíso, Estrada Nacional, 242 (☎262 56 18 00; www.valeparaiso.com), 2.5km out of town in a wooded area. Take the buses to Alcobaça or Leiria (10min., 12 per day 7am-7pm, €1.70). This camping complex includes swimming pools, restaurant, supermarket, showers, internet access (€2 per 30min., €3 per hr.), and laundry (€7). June-Sept. 14 €4.50 per person, €4-5.50 per tent, €3.50 per car; Sept. 15-May €3.20/3-4.50/2.90. Bungalows Oct.-Mar. €15.50 for 2 people, €20.50 for 3-4 people; Apr.-May and Sept. €23/31; June-July 14 €33/41; July 15-Aug. €56/65. AmEx/MC/V for purchases over €150. ❶

FOOD

For groceries, check out the municipal market in the huge warehouse across from the bus station. (Open daily 7am-2pm.) Supermarkets, like **Minipreço,** line R. Sub-Vila which is parallel to Av. da República. (Open daily 9am-9pm.)

Pastelaria Batel, R. Mouzinho de Albuquerque, 2 (☎262 55 11 47), and on Av. Vieira Guimarães. The best-known pastry shop in Nazaré, and the place to try sweet local specialties. All pastries €0.80-1.20. Try the *tamares* (little boats with custard filling capped in chocolate), *sardinhas* (flaky pastry, not fish), or the *nazarenos* (almond pastry). Open daily June-Aug. 7am-2am, Sept.-May closed W. Cash only. ❶

O Borgas, R. Mouzinho de Albuquerque, 4 (☎262 56 20 02), near Pr. Sousa Oliveira. *Bife na lage,* seasoned steak grilled on a heated rock at the diner's table, is the house specialty (€10). Complete tourist menu for €11.50 (plate of the day, bread, a drink, dessert, and coffee). Vegetarian options include grilled vegetables, various soups, and salad. Entrees €6-12.50. Open M-W and F-Su noon-4pm and 6pm-2am. MC/V. ❷

BEACHES AND ENTERTAINMENT

Nazaré's main attraction is its beautiful beach, where locals spend their days playing volleyball, racquetball, and, of course, soccer. The colorful tents ornamenting it can be rented from the women sitting in front of them along Av. da República (€6 per day, €35 per week). After catching some rays, take the **funicular** (3min.; every 15min. 7:15am-9:30pm, every 30min. 9:30pm-midnight; €0.90), which runs from R. Elevador off Av. da República, to the **Sítio,** the cliff top area of Nazaré. For centuries, all of Nazaré stood on the Sítio, well above the dangerous tide below. The charming cobbled streets, weathered buildings, and breathtaking views are perfect for a picnic. Consider making the 20min. trip to **São Martinho do Porto,** whose tranquil waters, red-roofed houses and palm-studded hillside give this lagoon a Mediterranean charm unsullied by the hordes of tourists seen in Nazaré. Bus schedules are posted at the tourist office.

On Saturday afternoons in May and June, locals dress in traditional outfits and haul fishing nets out of the water, using an old-fashioned technique in an event known as **Arte Xávega,** named after the style of boat used. An exciting fish auction, open to the public, follows. During the summer, look for late-night **folk music** gatherings on the beach. **Bullfights** are also popular and Nazaré features *corridas* on various summer weekends (usually Sa 10pm; tickets from €10). Bullfights occur the first three Saturdays in July and August and the first week of September. Inquire at the tourist office for exact times, dates, and prices.

DAYTRIPS FROM NAZARÉ

ALCOBAÇA

Buses are the best way to reach Alcobaça. The bus station on Av. Manuel da Silva Carolino (☎262 58 22 21) offers service to: Batalha (30min., 7 per day 7:30am-7:10pm, €2.60); Leiria (1hr., 6 per day 7:30am-7:10pm, €3.25); Lisboa (2hr.; M-F 2 per day, Sa-Su 1 per day 6:30am-3pm; €8.30); and Nazaré (25min.; M-F 11 per day 7:30am-7:40pm, Sa-Su 7-9 per day 8:10am-7:25pm; €1.70).

Visitors from around the world travel to this tranquil hillside town to stand inside the **Mosteiro de Santa Maria de Alcobaça,** the largest church in Portugal. This enormous abbey was founded in 1153 by Portugal's first king, Dom Afonso Henriques, following his removal of the Moors from Santarém. In an attempt to secure Christianity in the region, the king granted the land to Cistercian monks. In gratitude, the monks built a monastery spanning over 200m in length, the largest building of the Cistercian order in all of Europe. It was also the first Portuguese structure constructed using Gothic techniques. Today, all that remains of the original facade are the pointed-arched doorway and the rose window above it. In the sanctuary of the church lie the tombs of Portugal's most famous star-crossed lovers, Dom Pedro I and his wife, Inês de Castro. Note the engravings, which draw a close comparison between the life of Christ and that of Dona Inês. Surrounding the monastery's cloisters are numerous Gothic rooms, most notably the **Sala dos Monges** (Monks' Hall), and the immense *azulejo*-covered kitchen and refectory, where the monks could roast more than six oxen at a time. If you can manage it, time your visit to coincide with the religious opera concerts held M-F at 11am and 3pm, or just wander the halls to their somber accompaniment. *(☎262 50 51 20. Open daily Apr.-Sept. 9am-7pm, Oct.-Mar. 9am-5pm. Last entrance 30min. before closing. €5, seniors over 65 €2.25, students free. Su before 2pm free.)*

To escape the international swarm flowing in and out of the monastery, take a 5min. hike to the **Castelo de Alcobaça** and check out the ruins of a 12th-century castle. The remaining stone walls provide a serene retreat for crowd-weary travelers and an incredible panoramic view of the surrounding area. Be careful, as the climb up the walls is easier than the descent. From R. D. Pedro V, turn right on R. Alexandre Herculano. At the end of the street, go left, following the "*castelo*" sign. Continue through the intersection as the road becomes R. do Castelo, passing Igreja da Misericórdia on the left. About 200m up the hill the road splits, and there will be a dirt trail to the left, marked by a "*castelo*" sign.

Alcobaça makes a great daytrip, but should you spend the night, **Pensão Corações Unidos ❶,** R. Frei António Brandão, 39, off Pr. 25 de Abril, has 35 rooms decorated in a rustic style with private bathrooms. Buffet breakfast is included. (☎262 58 21 42. Reception 8am-midnight in the restaurant below. July-Sept. €17 per person, Oct-June €12.50. AmEx/MC/V.) The **tourist office** is on the corner of Pr. 25 de Abril, across from the hulking monastery. Turn right out of the bus station and right again onto Av. dos Combatentes de Grande Guerra, following the road as it becomes R. D. Pedro V and curves around the monastery. The tourist office is at the end of the strip of shops, across from the monastery. (☎262 58 23 77. English, Spanish, and French spoken. 15min. free internet access provided. Open daily May-July and Sept. 10am-1pm and 3-7pm; Aug. 10am-7pm, Oct.-Apr. 10am-1pm and 2-6pm.)

LEIRIA ☎244

An ancient castle towers over this city of 120,000, while a *futebol* stadium glistens below. In Leiria, Portugal's two great passions, history and soccer, rival one another for veneration. Situated between Lisboa and Coimbra, Leiria was a strategic point during Dom Afonso Henriques's campaign against the Moors, culminating in its recapture in 1135. Today, the city is one of Portugal's most important economic centers, and it is bedecked with trendy boutiques and cozy restaurants. Leiria has not lost its historic feel, and its population, hailing from across Portugal, makes for a diverse urban center basking in a regal past.

TRANSPORTATION

Trains: The train station is 3km outside town (☎244 88 20 27). Buses run to train station from stop on Av. 25 Abril, the street beside the garden connecting the tourist office and the bus station. The stop is a green post marked "*urbana*." (15min.; every 45min. M-F 7:22am-7:32pm, Sa 7:22am-4:42pm; €1. Ask the tourist office for an exact schedule.) To: **Coimbra** (1-3hr., 5 per day 7:10am-7:59pm, €5-8); **Figueira da Foz** (1hr., 3 per day 9:51am-8pm, €4.90); **Lisboa** (2-4hr., 4 per day 7:11am-8:22pm, €6-14).

Buses: The bus station (☎244 81 57 17), off Pr. Paulo VI, is across the park from the tourist office. Ticket office in back. Most convenient transport out of Leiria. Express buses are usually twice the price of regional buses. To: **Alcobaça** (50min., M-F 10:30am and 5:15pm, €2.60); **Batalha** (20min., 8 per day 7:30-4:50pm, €1.57-2.60); **Coimbra** (1hr., 11 per day 7:15am-2am, €8.50); **Fátima** (1hr., 10 per day 8am-7:25pm, €2.73-5); **Figueira da Foz** (1hr., 12 per day 7:45am-7:25pm, €5); **Lisboa** (2hr., 13 per day M-F 6am-11pm, Sa 7am-11pm, Su 7:45am-11pm; €11); **Nazaré** (1hr., 12 per day 8am-9:30pm, €2.60-6.60); **Porto** (3hr., 10 per day 7:15am-2am, €13.50); **Santarém** (2hr., 3 per day 10:30am-5:15pm, €4.50-11); **Tomar** (1hr., 4:30pm, €8.50).

Taxis: Many gather at the Jardim Luís de Camões (☎244 81 59 00 or 88 15 50).

ORIENTATION AND PRACTICAL INFORMATION

The **Jardim Luís de Camões** is at the center of Leiria, surrounded by *pensões* and restaurants. Just off the garden is **Praça Rodrigues Lobo,** the heart of the historical center, between the Jardim Luís de Camões and the castle. The *praça* is full of cozy cafes and student bars, and the castle is a 10min. climb from here.

Tourist Office: (☎244 84 87 70), in the Jardim Luís de Camões, across the park from the bus station. Has maps, accommodations lists, and a **model of Batalha's monastery** made entirely of sugar, egg whites, and water. Free short-term luggage storage, **internet** access (15min. limit), maps, and other goodies on occasion. English, French, and Spanish spoken. Open daily May-Sept. 10am-1pm and 3-7pm, Oct.-Apr. 10am-1pm and 2-6pm.

Laundromat: Ecosec Lavanderia (☎244 83 36 38), on Beco de São Francisco. From the bus station, walk away from the tourist office on Av. Heróis de Angola, take a left at the theater on Cor. T. Sampaio, and take a right on Beco de São Francisco. €4 per kg, shirts and pants €3.80 per kg. Open M-F 9am-6pm.

Police: Lg. São Pedro (☎244 82 43 00), by the castle.

Hospital: Hospital de Santo André (☎244 81 70 00), on R. Olhalvas, on the way to Fátima. For non-emergencies, go to the closer **Centro Saúde Dr. Arn. Sampaio** (☎244 81 78 20), R. Dr. Egas Moniz, a 10min. walk from the tourist office.

Internet Access: Convenient (and free) service at **Espaço Internet,** Lg. de Santana (☎244 81 50 91), in the Mercado Sant'Ana. 12 computers with fast connections. 1hr. time limit when people are waiting. Gets crowded in the afternoon. Identification (passport, driver's license) required to use a computer. Open M-F 9am-7pm, Sa 2-7pm. Access also free at **Biblioteca Municipal Afonso Lopes Vierira,** Lg. Cândido dos Reis, 6, beside the Pousada de Juventude. Open M 1-6pm, Tu-F 10am-6pm.

Post Office: Downtown office, **Estaçâo Santana** (☎800 20 68 68), Av. dos Combatentes da Grande Guerra, between the tourist office and the youth hostel. Open M-F

8:30am-12:30pm and 2-6pm. **Main office,** Av. Heróis de Angola, 99 (☎244 84 94 00), past the bus station toward the mall. Open M-F 8:30am-12:30pm and 2-6:30pm, Sa 9am-12:30pm. **Postal Code:** 2400.

ACCOMMODATIONS

Pousada da Juventude de Leiria (HI), Lg. Cândido dos Reis, 7 (☎244 83 18 68). From the bus station, walk across the garden and cross the street to the plaza with fountains. Take a right after the Caixa Geral de Depósitos building, and follow to the end. If there is construction going on, follow the metal wall down the street. Take a left on Lg. Cândido dos Reis. The *pousada* is on the left. An old bishop's residence, now with guest kitchen, TV room, and library. Wi-Fi (€5/hr.) Breakfast included. Single-sex dorms €11; doubles €26, with bath €28. HI card required (get it there for €2). AmEx/MC/V. ❶

Pensão Residencial Leiriense, R. Afonso de Albuquerque, 6 (☎244 82 30 54; fax 82 30 73). Off Pr. R. Lobo. Bright, slightly undersized rooms with private bath, A/C, cable TV and phone. Great location for hitting up the bars around the area. Check-out noon. Singles €25; doubles €40. MC. ❷

FOOD

The **Mercado Municipal,** on Av. Cidade de Maringá, near the stadium and beside the river, sells fresh fish and produce. (Open Tu and Sa 8am-1pm.) Groceries and fresh bread are available at Leiria's convenient **Pingo Doce,** Av. Heróis de Angola, 69, just past the bus station. (Open daily 9am-9pm.)

O Tamoeiro, Rua Barão Viamonte, 48 (☎). Right off Rua Direita. Dine like a king, with the whole *menú* served to your table. Cheese, ham, gourmet seafood, and vegetarian dishes (€1.50-3), and the signature meat plate (€6) come in small plates, and you choose what to eat once everything is served. Add a cup of wine for €1.50. Open M-Sa 7:30pm-2am. Reserve ahead on F. AmEx/MC/V. ❷

Cervejaria Camões, Jardim Luís de Camões (☎961 94 77 08) behind the tourist office. French-inspired steaks, served in a pan with a delicious array of sauces, are the house specialty. Vegetarians can chow down on one of many creative salads. Budget friendly lunch specials for €6. Entrees €5-16. Open daily 10am-2am. MC/V. ❷

SIGHTS AND BEACHES

Leiria's most significant monument is the giant **Castelo de Leiria,** visible throughout the city and particularly stunning late at night, when it is completely lit up against the dark mountainside. Built by Dom Afonso Henriques after he snatched the town from the Moors, this granite fort presides atop the crest of a volcanic hill on the north edge of town. One of the *castelo's* highlights is the **Torre de Menagem** (Homage Tower), which houses rusty swords, chain mail armor, and artifacts found on-site. The **Sala dos Namorados** (Lovers' Hall) sets the stage for medieval courting—don't miss the beautiful view of the town and river from the terrace, as well as the gigantic, colorful **Estádio Doutor Magalhães Pessoa,** built especially for two Euro Cup 2004 soccer games. From the main square, walk toward the bus station on Lg. 5 de Outubro. Turn left on Lg. das Forças Armadas, just after the Banco de Portugal. Follow the signs past the austere, Sé (cathedral) and zigzag up to the castle. *(☎244 81 39 82. Castle open Apr.-Sept. M-F 9am-6:30pm, Sa-Su 10am-6:30pm; Oct.-Mar. M-F 9am-5:30pm, Sa-Su 10am-5:30pm. Tower open Tu and Su 10am-noon and 1-5pm. €2.50; students, children, and seniors €1.25.)*

Nearby beaches are accessible via buses running from the station to **Praia de Viera** (45min.; 9 per day 7am-7:30pm, last return 6:30pm; July-Sept. 14; €2.60). **Praia Pedrógão,** popular with locals and lined with stately residences (1hr.; 5 per day 9:15am-6pm, last return 7:30pm; €2.60) and the more secluded **São Pedro de Muel** (45min.; 4 per day 8:50am-4:30pm, last return 7:15pm; €2). Check for the exact schedules at the bus station in Leiria, as they are subject to change.

DAYTRIP FROM LEIRIA

BATALHA

Buses run from Leiria to Batalha (20min., 8 per day 7:30-4:50pm, €1.57-2.60), and return to Leiria (20min. M-F 16 per day 7:15am-7:43pm. Sa-Su 3 per day 8:03am-7:43pm, €1.65). The easiest way to get to the caves is by taxi (€30-40 round-trip including waiting time). Be sure to set the price with the taxi driver before you head out. It is possible to take a bus, but the bus schedules from Batalha require careful planning and involve several hours of layover. Check with the tourist office to confirm schedules.

The **Mosteiro Santa Maria da Vitória,** a UNESCO World Heritage site, puts Batalha on the map. Its flamboyant facade soars upward in Gothic and Manueline style, opulently decorated and crowned in dozens of spires. Construction began in 1386 to fulfill Dom João I's covenant to the Virgin Mary: he promised to build a monument in her honor if the Portuguese defeated the Castilian invaders at the Battle of Aljubarrota. The **Capela do Fundador,** the pantheon of João I and the Avis dynasty, lies immediately to the right of the church, housing the sarcophagi of Dom João I, his English-born queen Philippa of Lancaster, and their famous son Prince Henry the Navigator. Just outside the pantheon entrance rests the simpler tomb of Martin Gonçalves, the man who saved Dom João I's life at Aljubarrota. Though the 15th-century **Claustro de Dom Afonso V** is the *mosteiro's* highlight, the **Capelas Imperfeitas** (Unfinished Chapels) are also impressive. Jealous of his predecessor's impressive pantheon, Dom Duarte commissioned the construction of an equally impressive pantheon to house his remains and those of his progeny; unfortunately, construction of the Mosteiro dos Jerónimos in Belém drained resources and interest, leaving the elegant Renaissance chapel roofless. Today the *mosteiro* houses a tomb of unknown soldiers from WWI, and is under constant guard by military officials. There is also a professional school of stone carving that demonstrates how some of the mosteiro's ornate sculptures were made. (Open daily Apr.-Sept. 9am-6pm, Oct.-Mar. 9am-5pm. €5, seniors €2.5, under 14 and students free. Su before 2pm free.)

A 20min. drive outside town brings you to a spelunker's paradise: a series of spectacular underground *grutas* (caves) in Estremadura's natural park. The **Grutas de Mira de Aire,** with a river 110m below ground level, are the deepest and the largest in all of Portugal. They are so popular that 3 million people visited them within the first 10 years of their opening. The nearby **Grutas de Santo António and Alvados,** with their caverns and sandcastle-like limestone formations, are equally impressive. (☎244 44 03 22 or 249 84 18 76. Grutas de Mira de Aire open daily June-Sept. 9:30am-6pm, Oct-May 9:30am-5pm, €5 per person. Grutas de Santo António and Alvados open daily Sept.-May 10am-5pm, June-Aug. 10am-6pm. €5. Last tickets sold 30min. before closing.)

FÁTIMA

☎249

Until May 13, 1917, when the Virgin Mary appeared to three local peasant children, Fátima (pop. 8,000) was just a quiet sheep pasture. Now, every year, over 4 million Catholics make the pilgrimage here to see the stunning Santuário built to honor the miracle. A sign at the entrance of the Santuário complex states, in several languages, "Fátima is a place for adoration; enter as a pilgrim." Only France's Lourdes rivals this site in popularity with Catholic pilgrims; the miracles believed to have occurred here attract an endless international procession of religious groups. The plaza in front of the church, larger than St. Peter's Square in the Vatican, floods with pilgrims on the 12th and 13th of each month. These pilgrims have created a large tourism industry in Fátima—there are over 10,000 beds for visitors in the various hotels and *residenciais*.

TRANSPORTATION

Trains: The **Caxarias** station (☎808 208 208; www.cp.pt), 20km out of town, is closer than the **Fátima** station, 25km away. Caxarias to: **Coimbra** (1hr., 17 per day 5:10am-10:01pm, €6.40-10.10); **Lisboa** (2hr., 12 per day 3:56am-9:43pm, €10-17); **Porto** (2-3hr., 15 per day 5:15am-10:52pm, €13.40-24); **Santarém** (1hr., 16 per day 3:56am-9:43pm, €4.90-7.60). Buses run between Caxarias and Fátima stations (30min., 5 per day 7:40am-5:20pm, €2) and the Fátima train and bus stations (45min., 7 per day 7:40am-6:45pm, €2.67).

Buses: Av. D. José Alves Correia da Silva (☎249 53 16 11). To: **Batalha** (30min., 3 per day 8:07-5:40pm, €1.1.65); **Coimbra** (1hr., 16 per day 7:45am-9:30pm, €8); **Leiria** (35min., 13 per day 7:45am-8pm, €2.67-5); **Lisboa** (1-2hr., 11-19 per day 7am-8pm, €8.70); **Nazaré** (1hr., 8:45am-7:45pm, €3.50-8.70); **Porto** (2-3hr., 4 per day 7:45am-7:40pm, €12); **Santarém** (1hr., 5 per day 7:30am-5:45pm, €10); **Tomar** (1hr.; M-Sa 9:15am and 7:23 pm, Su 8:58pm; €3.20).

Taxis: Next to the bus station (☎49 53 11 93 or 249 53 38 16).

ORIENTATION AND PRACTICAL INFORMATION

Fátima is essentially a religious monument surrounded by souvenir shops, and all activity centers around the basilica complex. The **Santuário de Fátima** is the huge, open *praça* in the middle of everything, which fills with visitors on special occasions and on the 12th and 13th of each month. Directly below it, the new 9000-seat church, inagurated in 2007, stands as the fourth largest church in the world. **Av. Dom José Alves Correia da Silva** is below the Santuário, beginning near the bus station. It runs past the lower end of the complex to the tourist office, which is situated in a stone building with a wooden roof. From the bus station, go right and walk approximately 10min.; the office is on the right.

Tourist Office: The Santuário has its own information **office** (on the left side when facing the basilica; ☎249 53 96 23) with temporary **luggage storage.** Every day at 6:30am it posts the day's schedule of masses. English, French, and Spanish spoken. Open M-Sa 9am-6pm, Su 9am-5pm. The **town office** is at Av. D. José Alves Correia da Silva (☎249 53 11 39). Free **internet** access (15min. limit). English, French, and Spanish are spoken. Open daily June-July and Sept. 10am-1pm and 3-7pm, Aug. 10am-7pm; Oct.-April 10am-1pm and 2-6pm.

Banks: Several major banks have branches along the commercial center of R. Jacinta Marto. Most open 8:30am-3pm.

Police: Av. D. José Alves Correia da Silva (☎249 53 05 80), past the bus station.

Medical: Centro de Saúde (☎249 53 18 36) on R. Jacinta Marto, near bus station.

Internet: Space Net on the 3rd fl. of the Museu da Vida do Cristo complex has self-service coin-operated internet access. €0.50 per 15min. Open daily 9am-11pm.

Post Office: R. Dr. Jose A Formigão (☎249 53 90 81). Open M-F 8:30am-6pm. **Postal Code:** 2495.

ACCOMMODATIONS AND FOOD

Scores of *residenciais* and hotels surround the basilica complex. Prices vary greatly. Saturday stays are usually €5-10 more than weekday stays, and it's best to reserve a month ahead on summer weekends and holidays and a week ahead otherwise. **Residencial Aleluia ❷**, Av. D. José A. C. Silva, 120, down the street from the bus stop on the lower corner of the complex, has chic rooms with A/C, TV, hardwood floors, suede bedspreads, and leather couches. (☎249 53 15 40; www.residencialaleluia.com. Breakfast €3. Lunch/dinner buffets €11. Singles €25-30, doubles €30-35, triples €42-48. Prices go up €5 on summer weekends and during all of Aug. AmEx/MC/V.) Another option is the new **St. Brigid Hotel ❸**, R. Francisco Marto, 100, two blocks away from the *santuario*. The hotel just opened in 2008 and all rooms have TV, A/C, and private bathrooms. (☎249 53 31 11, fax 249 53 20 28. Singles €30, doubles €40, triples €50. MC/V.)

Restaurants and snack bars cluster between souvenir shops along R. Francisco Marto, R. Santa Isabela, and R. Jacinta Marto. Close to the wax museum on the left side of the Santuário, the upstairs **O Terminal ❷**, R. Jacinta Marto, 24, offers the biggest portions of traditional Portuguese food for the best prices in town. Entrees €5-9. (☎249 53 19 77. Open daily 10am-3:30pm and 6-9:30pm. Cash only.) On the other side of the Santuário, well-established **Restaurant Alfredo ❷**, R. Francisco Marto, 159 CV, serves huge plates and is always filled with locals. Their *bacalhau no forno* (oven-broiled cod) is a house specialty. Limited vegetarian options. (Down the stairs past the corner Millennium BCP bank. Entrees €6-10. Open daily noon-3pm and 7-10pm. MC/V.) Rock-bottom prices can be found at the **Pingo Doce** supermarket on Av. D. José A. C. da Silva. (From the bus station, go to the left. Open daily 8:30am-9pm.)

SIGHTS

SANTUÁRIO DE FÁTIMA. As soon as you walk into the main *praça*, you'll feel Fátima's overwhelming presence. Many of the devout travel the length of the gigantic plaza on their knees, all the way from the cross to the *capelinha*, praying for divine assistance or giving thanks to the Virgin Mary. During the grand pilgrimages on the 12th and 13th from May to October, the crowds fill the entire plaza.

Uphill, overlooking the plaza, rises the **Basílica do Rosário** (erected in 1928), featuring a crystal cruciform beacon atop the tower's seven-ton bronze crown. Inside are the tombs of the three "seers," or witnesses of the apparitions. Francisco and Jacinta died as children, and lie in opposite naves. Lúcia, the third and oldest child, died in 2005 at the age of 97 after serving as a devout nun for over 70 years. Her tomb was placed beside Jacinta's in February 2006. *(Open daily 7:30am-10:30pm. Mass daily at 7:30, 9, 11am, 3, 4:30, and 6:30pm. Free.)* To the left is the **Capelinha das Aparições**, the first of the buildings to be constructed, where a statue of the Virgin now stands in the exact location where the miracles are said to have taken place. Sheltered beneath a metal and glass canopy, the *capelinha* was built in 1919 and continues to house "Perpetual Adoration," which consists of several masses in various languages during the day and a fire continuously fueled by the candles of visitors. *(International mass Th 9am. Candlelight procession daily Apr.-Oct. 9:30pm.)*

GRUTAS DA MOEDA (MOEDA CAVES). Fátima's caves offer a refreshing change from the religious sites and are easily accessible. Discovered in 1971 by two hunters chasing a fox, the caves lie 45m below the surface and conceal several stunning limestone formations and an underground waterfall. Bring a rain jacket if you go in the winter, as cave showers are frequent. *(☎244 70 43 02 or 244 70 38 38. www.grutasmoeda.com. Call ☎800 20 56 18 from the tourist office to schedule a free pick-up. The number does not work outside of the tourist office. Caves open daily July-Sept. 9am-7pm, April-June. 9am-6pm, Oct.-Mar. 9am-5pm; last tickets sold 30min. before closing. €5, cartão jovem €3.50, children 6-12 €2.50.)*

THE NORTH

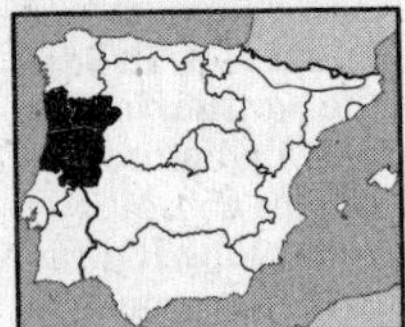

As new buildings and modern flair come to Europe, many lament the loss of the "old country," as if the last century's big cities and big governments squashed the soul of the continent. This march of progress must have lost its beat when it neared the north of Portugal, where ancient narrow streets, ornately decorated buildings, green mountains, and peaceful vineyards stretch for miles, unaltered by time. The region is not just famous for its sweet wine; history buffs go to the North to retrace the steps of Lusitania's ancestors. With ample opportunities for hiking, camping, and relatively untamed forestry, the region is also paradise for nature-lovers. A visit to the North is indispensable. After all, though wine can be shipped, Portugal's finest countryside cannot.

HIGHLIGHTS OF THE NORTH

MARVEL at the elaborate **Capela de São Miguel** in Coimbra (p. 445).

SAVOR the brilliant flavors in a glass of port wine at a vineyard in **Porto** (p. 432).

DOURO AND MINHO

The region of the Douro and Minho rivers is wine country—the purples, blues, and greens of the stretching vineyards and *quintas* (wine estates) are worthy of a Keats ode. The major cities of this region, Porto and Braga, are enchanting as well. With lively festivals, tall medieval towers, and amazing shopping, these metropolises provide numerous opportunities for adventure.

PORTO (OPORTO) ☎22

Stunning edifices rise up from the bustling city squares of Oporto (pop. 263,000) with an elegance reminiscent of Paris or Prague. Portugal's second largest city, commonly referred to as Porto, is brimming with small shops and residences that seem to be on the brink of toppling into the Rio Douro. Once a magnificent Roman trade center, Porto still retains its thriving commercial industry, focusing predominantly on the production, sale, and most importantly, consumption, of port wine. Visitors to Porto usually come to admire the monuments of its medieval glory days, but it's the warmth of the city that makes them fall in love with it. The charm of its friendly bars and cafes by day, and the yellow lights reflected in the Rio Douro by night, lend Porto an unforgettable romance.

TRANSPORTATION

Flights: Aeroporto Francisco de Sá Carneiro (☎229 43 24 00), 13km from downtown. The recently completed **metro E** (violet line) goes to the airport and is the fastest and cheapest option (25min., €1.35). Buses #601 and 87 run to the airport from R. do Carmo, but make multiple stops (1hr., €1.50). The **aerobus** (☎225 07 10 54) from Av. dos Aliados near Pr. da Liberdade is more efficient (40min., every 30min. 7am-7pm, €4, free for TAP passengers). Buy tickets on board. **Taxis** are even quicker (15-20min.,

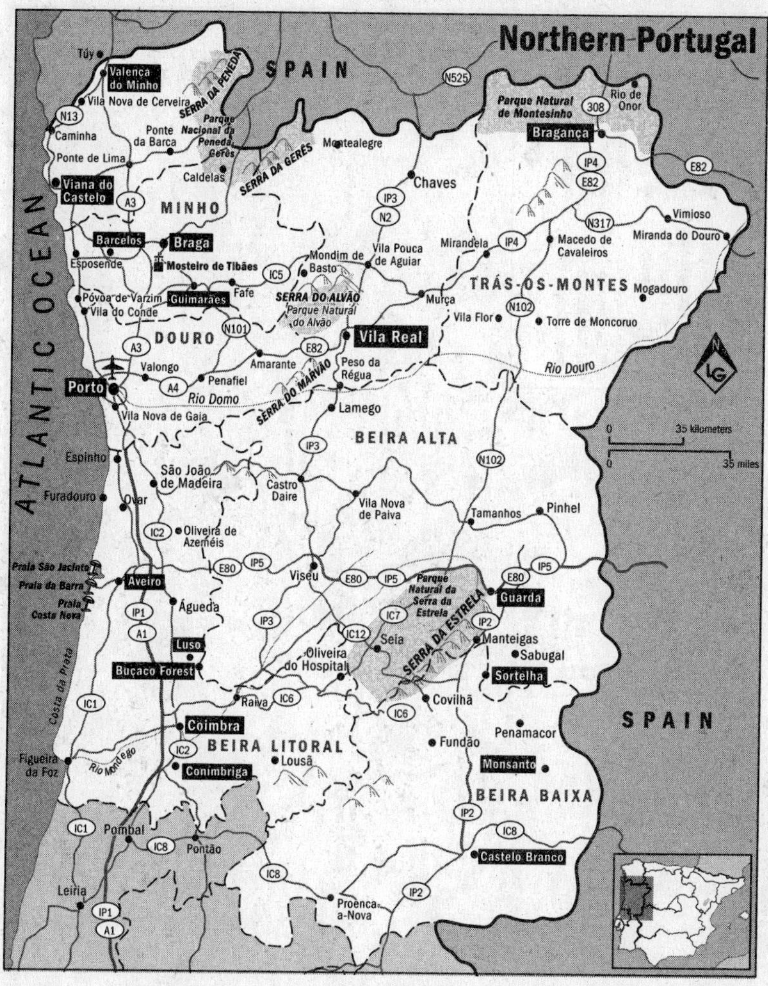

€18-20). **TAP Air Portugal,** Pr. Mouzinho de Albuquerque, 105 (☎226 08 02 31), flies to major European cities, with 6 daily shuttles to Lisboa (35min., €100-150).

Trains: Trains arriving in Porto stop at **Estação de Campanhã** (☎808 20 82 08; www.cp.pt), on R. da Estação, before entering the station in the town center, **Estação de São Bento** (☎808 20 82 08), Pr. Almeida Garrett. Trains leaving S. Bento will run to Campanhã first (5min., every 5-10min. 5:35am-12:40am, €1). From Estação de Campanhã trains run to: **Aveiro** (1hr., 47 per day 5:09am-1:23am, €2.10-12.50); **Braga** (1hr., 30 per day 5:55am-10:50pm, €2-12.50); **Coimbra** (1-2hr., 17 per day 6:05am-1:35am, €12-16.10); **Lisboa** (3-4hr., 18 per day 6:15am-1:35am, €15.60-28.60); **Madrid** (11-12hr., 10pm, €64; change at Entroncamento); **Viana do Castelo** (1-2hr., 11 per day 6am-8:35pm, €4.75-7); **Vigo,** Spain (4hr.; 8:05am, 6:05pm; €12.80).

Buses: Several companies operate in the downtown area.

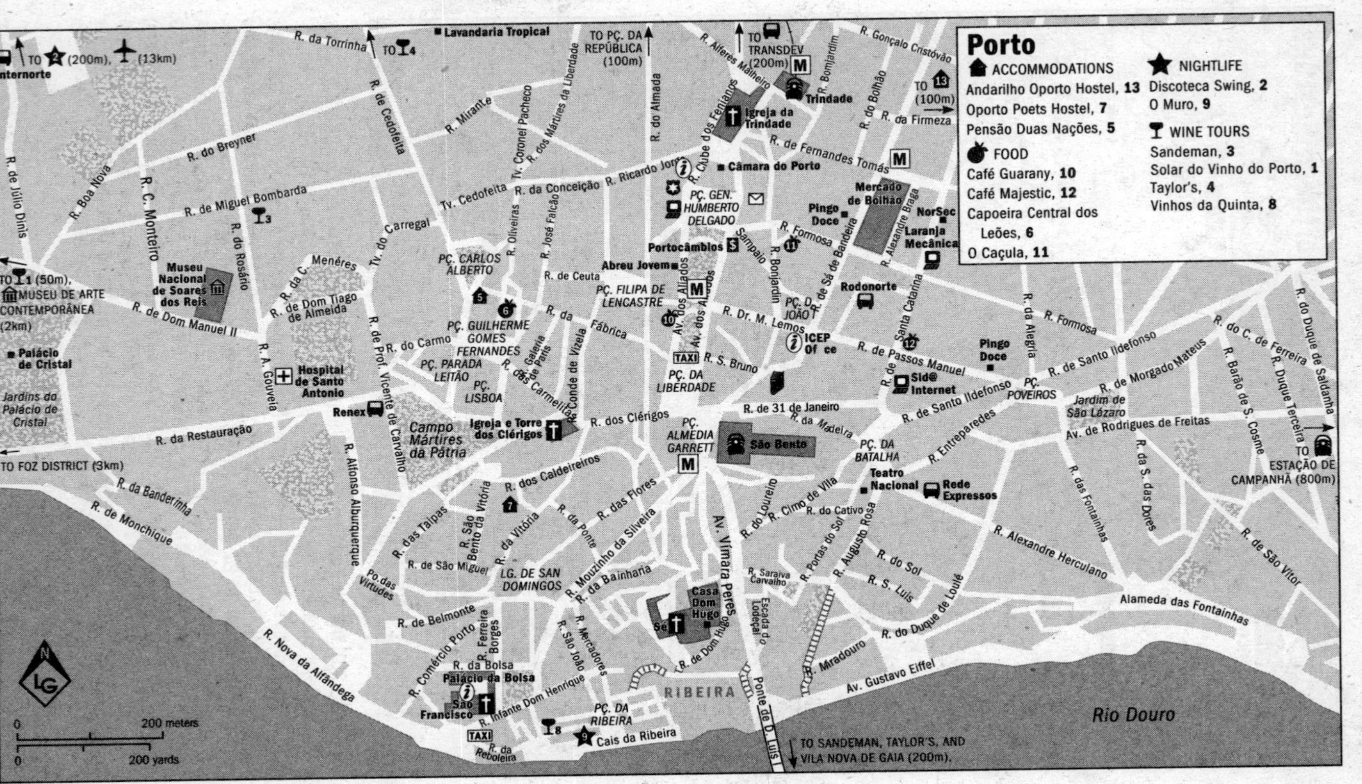
Porto
ACCOMMODATIONS
Andarilho Oporto Hostel, 13
Oporto Poets Hostel, 7
Pensão Duas Nações, 5
FOOD
Café Guarany, 10
Café Majestic, 12
Capoeira Central dos Leões, 6
O Caçula, 11
NIGHTLIFE
Discoteca Swing, 2
O Muro, 9
WINE TOURS
Sandeman, 3
Solar do Vinho do Porto, 1
Taylor's, 4
Vinhos da Quinta, 8
Rio Douro
Ponte de D. Luís I
Av. Vímara Peres
RIBEIRA
São Bento
Igreja e Torre dos Clérigos
Campo Mártires da Pátria
Palácio da Bolsa
São Francisco
Sé
Casa Dom Hugo
Teatro Nacional
Mercado de Bolhão
Câmara do Porto
Igreja da Trindade
Trindade
Hospital de Santo Antonio
Museu Nacional de Soares dos Reis
Palácio de Cristal
Jardins do Palácio de Cristal
TO ESTAÇÃO DE CAMPANHÃ (800m)
TO SANDEMAN, TAYLOR'S, AND VILA NOVA DE GAIA (200m).
TO FOZ DISTRICT (3km)
TO PÇ. DA REPÚBLICA (100m)
TO TRANSDEV (200m)
TO 1 (50m), MUSEU DE ARTE CONTEMPORÂNEA (2km)
TO 2 (200m), (13km)
Internorte
TO 4
TO 13 (100m)
R. de Júlio Dinis
R. Boa Nova
R. C. Monteiro
R. de Dom Manuel II
R. da Restauração
R. de Monchique
R. da Banderinha
R. Nova da Alfândega
R. Alfonso Alburquerque
R. de Prof. Vicente de Carvalho
R. de Cedofeita
R. da Torrinha
R. do Rosário
R. de Miguel Bombarda
R. do Breyner
R. A. Gouveia
R. dos Clérigos
R. de 31 de Janeiro
R. de Santa Catarina
R. de Passos Manuel
R. de Sá da Bandeira
R. Formosa
R. da Alegria
R. do Almada
R. das Flores
R. Mouzinho da Silveira
R. de Belmonte
R. das Taipas
R. da Vitória
R. dos Caldeireiros
R. Alexandre Herculano
R. das Fontainhas
Alameda das Fontainhas
R. de São Vitor
R. Duque Terceira
R. do Duque de Saldanha
R. Barão de S. Cosme
R. de Santo Ildefonso
R. de Fernandes Tomás
R. Gonçalo Cristóvão
R. do Bolhão
R. da Firmeza
R. Bonjardim
Av. dos Aliados
PÇ. DA LIBERDADE
PÇ. DA BATALHA
PÇ. DA RIBEIRA
PÇ. CARLOS ALBERTO
PÇ. LISBOA
PÇ. FILIPA DE LENCASTRE
PÇ. ALMEDIA GARRETT
PÇ. POVEIROS
PÇ. GEN. HUMBERTO DELGADO
PÇ. GUILHERME GOMES FERNANDES
PÇ. PARADA LEITÃO
PÇ. D. JOÃO I
LG. DE SAN DOMINGOS
Cais da Ribeira
Av. Gustavo Eiffel
Rede Expressos
Renex
Rodonorte
Portocâmbios
Abreu Jovem
ICEP Of ce
Pingo Doce
Lavandaria Tropical
Laranja Mecânica
NorSec
Sid@ Internet
200 meters
200 yards

Internorte, Pr. Galiza, 96 (☎226 05 24 20) has service to **Madrid** (10hr., daily 9am and 9:45am,and 8:30pm, €48), as well as other international cities. Book 3 days ahead. Open M-F 9am-12:30pm and 2-6:30pm, Sa 9am-12:30pm and 2-4pm, Su 9am-12:30pm and 2-5:30pm.

Rede Expressos, R. Alexandre Herculano, 366 (☎222 00 69 54; www.rede-expressos.pt). To **Braga** (1hr., 10 per day 10am-4:30am, €5.70); **Bragança** (3-5hr., 7 per day 9:15am-11pm, €12); **Coimbra** (1hr., 11 per day 6:45am-12:45am, €11); **Lisboa** (4hr., 11 per day 6:45am-12:45am, €16); **Viana do Castelo** (1hr., 4 per day 11am-11pm, €7.20).

Renex, Campo Mártires da Pátria, 37 (☎222 00 33 95), has express service to **Lagos** (8hr., 6 per day 7:30am-1:15am, €24) via **Lisboa** (3hr., 12 per day 7:30am-1:15am, €29) and **Vila Real de Santo António** (9hr., 3 per day 9am-5pm, €44).

Rodonorte, R. Ateneu Comercial do Porto, 25 (☎222 00 56 37 or 00 43 98), to **Vila Real** (1hr.; M-F 16 per day 7am-9:20pm, Sa-Su 7 per day 7am-9:20pm; €6.50-7) via **Amarante** (1hr., €5.20).

Transdev, R. Dr. Alfredo Magalhães, 94 (☎222 00 26 60), 2 blocks from Pr. da República, has buses to **Braga** (1hr.; M-F 17 per day 7:30am-8pm, Sa-Su 5-6 per day 10am-6pm; €4.20).

Public Transportation: A €0.50 rechargeable **Andante** card must be purchased before using the metro, trams, and some buses. It can be purchased with an individual ticket or beforehand at the tourist office, at many small kiosks throughout the city, or at the **STCP** office, Pr. Almeida Garrett, 27 (open M-F 8am-7:30pm, Sa 8am-1pm). Transportation ticket prices are determined by a zone system; each zone is an additional fare. Most of Porto is in 1 zone, and 2 trips on the metro or tram are €1.80; €9.50 for 11 trips. A single bus fare is €1.40. The best option for those planning on significant travel is an unlimited Andante tour ticket (1-day €5, 3-day €11; available on board or at the tourist office), which is valid for all STCP buses and trams, the Aerobus, and the metro. All buses operate between 6am-9pm, half operate until 1am, and a handful run 1-5am. Tram operates 8am-8pm every 30 min. Metro 6am-1am.

Taxis: Av. dos Aliados and along the river in Ribeira. Ask for a quote, and only use metered taxis. Luggage €1.60 extra. **Radiotáxis,** R. de Alegria, 1802 (☎225 07 39 00).

ORIENTATION AND PRACTICAL INFORMATION

Porto's heavy traffic and chaotic maze of one-way streets fluster travelers who come by car. The city center is easy to navigate, however: hillside **Praça da Liberdade** is joined to **Praça General Humberto Delgado** by **Avenida dos Aliados,** forming a long, open, and easily recognizable main square. The liveliest part of the city during the day is located around the gigantic **Mercado do Bolhão** and includes the main pedestrian thoroughfare, **R. de Santa Catarina,** packed with stores and cafes as well as a large shopping center. Along the Río Douro, directly below the city center, lies the **Ribeira** district, where much of Porto's sights and nightlife are located on steep sidestreets. The two-level **Ponte de Dom Luís I** spans the river, connecting Ribeira to **Vila Nova de Gaia** and its many port wine cellars. Down the river from Ribeira (5km), the **Foz** district has many popular beaches and venerable nightclubs, but the **industrial area,** 4-5km northwest of the city center, has the best discotecas in Porto.

Tourist Office: Main office, R. Clube dos Fenianos, 25 (☎223 39 34 70; www.portoturismo.pt). Staff speaks English, French, German, Italian, and Spanish. Offers maps and general info about Porto. Open M-F 9am-6:30pm, Sa-Su 9:30am-6:30pm. Ribeira branch, R. Infante Dom Henrique, 63 (☎222 06 04 12); same hours and services. **Turismo de Portugal** office, Pr. Dom João I, 43 (☎222 05 75 14). Open Nov.-Mar. M-F 9am-7pm, Sa-Su 9:30am-3:30pm; Apr.-Oct. M-F 9am-7:30pm, Sa-Su 9:30am-3:30pm. Airport **branch** (☎229 41 25 34). Open daily Jan.-Mar. 8am-11pm; Apr.-Dec. 8am-11:30pm.

Budget Travel: Abreu Jovem, Av. dos Aliados, 221 (☎222 04 35 80). Between Pr. da Liberdade and the main tourist office. English-speaking staff offers advice and student rates. Open M-F 9am-12:30pm and 2:30-6:30pm.

Currency Exchange: Portocâmbios, R. Rodrigues Sampaio, 193 (☎222 00 02 38). Open M-F 9am-noon and 1-6pm, Sa 9am-12:30pm. ATM on Av. dos Aliados.

Laundromat: NorSec, Via Catarina, 115, 1st fl. (☎222 00 31 32), in the shopping center on R. de Santa Catarina. Go down the stairs, and NorSec is in the back on the left. €5 per kg wash and dry. Open daily 10am-10pm.

Police: R. Clube dos Fenianos, 11 (☎222 08 18 33).

Pharmacy: Farmácia Souza Soares, R. de S. Catarina, 141 (☎222 00 21 45). 3 blocks from Pr. G. H. Delgado at R. Formosa. Posts 24hr. pharmacy schedule. Open M-F 9am-8pm, Sa 9am-7pm.

Hospital: Hospital de Santo António (☎222 07 75 00), on R. Alberto Aires Gouveia.

Internet Access: Laranja Mecânica, in a small shopping center on R. de Santa Catarina, 274; €0.50 per 15min., €1.30 per hr. Open M-Sa 10am-midnight, Su 3pm-8pm. **Sid@Internet,** R. Santa Catarina, 72. 2nd fl. €0.90 per hr. 10am-7pm, €0.50 per hr. 7pm-1am. Open M-F 10am-1am, Sa-Su 2pm-midnight.

Post Office: Pr. Gen. Humberto Delgado (☎223 40 02 00). Fax, phone, and **Poste Restante.** Financial services closed after 6pm. Open M-F 8:30am-7:30pm, Sa 9:30am-3pm. **Postal Code:** 4000.

ACCOMMODATIONS

Expensive *pensões* congregate around Av. dos Aliados. The best deals are around Pr. Filipa de Lancastre or near the *mercado* on R. de Fernandes Tomás and R. Formosa. Prices dip in the low season (Oct-May), so try bargaining.

Oporto Poets Hostel, Tv. do Ferraz, 13 (☎223 32 42 09). The hippest place to stay in Porto, with colorful, 6-to 8-bed co-ed dorm rooms. Check out the nighttime view from the patio with a beer and grilled sausage from the barbecue. Laundry €5, with dry €7. High season dorms €20, doubles €44; low season €18/40. Cash only. ❷

Andarilho Oporto Hostel, R. da Firmeza, 364 (☎222 01 20 73; www.andarilhohostel.com). No sign; look for a red door right on the street. Co-ed rooms of 6, 8, or 10 beds are large enough to do cartwheels in. Bright, huge living area just off the patio garden. Laundry €4, with dry €6. Free breakfast, Wi-Fi and internet access. High season €20 per person; low season €18. Cash only. ❷

Pensão Duas Nações, Pr. Guilherme Gomes Fernandes, 59 (☎222 08 16 16). Bedroom walls painted brightly for an upbeat feel. Well-furnished rooms, though modestly decorated. Reception until 2am. Laundry €7. Internet access €1 per 30min. Singles €14, with bath €22.50-25; doubles €23-25; triples €36; quads €46-53. Cash only. ❶

THE NORTH

FOOD

Quality budget meals can be found near Pr. da Batalha on R. Cimo de Vila and R. do Cativo. Try the delicious *bifanas* (small pork sandwiches) on R. Bomjardim and the wide selection of olives in the local *azeitarias* (olive houses). Ribeira is popular for affordable riverside dinners, but for something even cheaper you can try the local *francisinhas* (bread, cheese, ham and meat covered in a secret sauce) at many of the local cafes. **Supermarket Pingo Doce** is on R. de Sa de Bandeira, 387, two blocks from Pr. G. H. Delgado. (Open M-Sa 8:30am-8:30pm, Su 9am-8pm.) The **Mercado de Bolhão** has an enormous selection of fresh bread, cheese, meat, and olives. (Open M-F 7am-5pm, Sa 7am-1pm.)

O Caçula, R. do Bonjardim, 20 (☎222 05 59 37; www.ocacula.com). The only place in town where a fancy 3-course meal goes for €6.50. Drinks not included. Delicious vegetarian options. Free Wi-Fi. Open M-Sa noon-3pm and 7pm-last customer. MC/V. ❶

Café Majestic, R. de Santa Catarina, 112 (☎222 00 38 87). One of the best replicas of 19th-century bourgeois opulence—it was originally called Elite Café—this Titanic-inspired restaurant is the oldest and best known in the city. Entrees €9-16. Sandwiches €5-13. Elaborate pastries €4-6. Open M-Sa 9:30am-midnight. AmEx/MC/V. ❷

Capoeira Central dos Leões, Pç. Guilherme Gomes Fernandes, 16 (☎222 05 11 85). Large portions for a small budget. Chicken with a generous side of fries goes for €2.30, and a whole chicken is €7.20. Save room for the creative and yummy desserts (layered strawberry ice cream cake €2.50). Delivery available. Open 9am-9pm. Cash only. ❶

Café Guarany, Av. dos Aliados, 85 (☎223 32 12 72; www.cafeguarany.com). On Pr. da Liberdade. Features live weekend entertainment, from *fado* to Cuban music. Best for coffee and dessert (€2-3). Duck with port wine €15. Sandwiches €3.50-9. Salads €6-10, entrees €6-14. Wi-Fi (15min. €1.25). Open daily 9am-midnight. AmEx/MC/V. ❷

SIGHTS

For most travelers, the first brush with Porto's fine artwork is the Estação de São Bento, a monastery-turned-*azulejo* collection, which displays ancient forms of transportation. Up Av. dos Aliados in Pr. Gen. Humberto Delgado, the **Câmara do Porto** (City Hall) attests to Porto's late 19th-century prosperity.

PALÁCIO DA BOLSA. The elegant Palácio da Bolsa (Stock Exchange) is one of Porto's most visited sites, as it is essentially one tremendous work of art. It was built over the ruins of the Convento de São Francisco, after the convent was destroyed by fire in 1832. The construction took 60 years longer than expected due to the painstaking task of making the enormous granite staircase. The pinnacle of embellishment is the golden **Sala Árabe** (Arabian Hall), designed by Portuguese artists with the sole intention of impressing potential foreign investors. The green crests on the ceiling proclaim "Allah above all," and its gold and silver walls are covered with the oddly juxtaposed inscriptions "Glory to Allah" and "Glory to Dona Maria II," the Catholic queen. Only guided tours are allowed, since the building still houses the Commerce Association of Porto. *(R. Ferreira Borges. ☎223 39 90 00. Open daily Apr.-Oct. 9am-7pm, Nov.-Mar. 9am-1pm and 2-6pm. Last tour 30min. before closing. Multilingual tours every 30min. €5, students €3. Tour of palace and wine cellars across the river €6/4. Palace and a bus tour of Porto €12. Palace and a Port wine cruise €12. Palace tour, bus tour, and wine cruise for €20.)*

IGREJA DE SÃO FRANCISCO. The Gothic and Baroque eras of ecclesiastical architecture were known for gilded wood, but they outdid themselves here. At one point, there was between 400-600kg of gold on the chapel's walls and altar, all donated by rich families trying to buy their way into paradise. Check out the giant family tree tracing Christ's genealogy, starting from the loins (literally) of a statue of Jesse of Bethlehem, father of King David. Next door, a museum showcases religious art from the 16th-18th centuries; in the basement of the museum lies the Ossário, the mass burial grounds for Porto's poor. The cavernous catacombs have several individual graves belonging to the benefactors. *(R. Infante Dom Henrique. ☎222 06 21 00. Open daily Feb.-May 9am,-6pm June-Oct. 9am-7pm, Jul.-Aug. 9am-8pm. €3, students €2.50.)*

MUSEU NACIONAL DE SOARES DOS REIS. A former royal residence and Portugal's first art museum (founded in 1833), Soares dos Reis houses a collection of 19th-century Portuguese painting and sculpture, much of it by Soares dos Reis, often called Portugal's Michelangelo. It features works by other greats as well, like Marquês de Oliveira. *(R. Dom Manuel II, 44. ☎223 39 37 70. Open Tu 2-6pm, W-Su 10am-6pm. Last entrance 5:30pm. €3, seniors and students €1.50. Su until 2pm free.)*

IGREJA E TORRE DOS CLÉRIGOS. The 18th-century **Igreja dos Clérigos** is decorated with Baroque and Rococo carvings. The highlight of the church is its **Torre dos Clérigos,** the city's tallest landmark and the tallest tower in Portugal, topping out at over 75m. The spectacular view of the Rio Douro valley doesn't come easily, though: it involves 225 spiraling steps. *(R. S. Filipe de Nery. ☎222 00 17 29. Church open M-Sa 8:45am-12:30pm and 3:30-7pm, Su 10am-1pm and 8:30-10:30pm. Tower open daily Apr.-July and Sept.-Oct. 9:30am-1pm and 2:30-7pm; Aug. 9:30am-7pm; Nov.-Mar. 10am-noon and 2-5pm. Tower €2, church free.)*

JARDINS DO PALÁCIO DE CRISTAL. Beautiful gardens lie outside the Palácio do Cristal (Glass Palace), which is not, in fact, made out of glass. Take a gander at the geese, swans, ducks, peacocks, and fountains, while enjoying a stroll through the lush vegetation. Walk toward the side opposite to the entrance, and you'll get an unmatched view of the Douro and its picturesque bridges. *(R. Dom Manuel II. ☎226 05 70 80. Open daily until dark.)*

SÉ. On the hilltop south of the train station stands Porto's imposing Romanesque Sé (cathedral). The Sé was built in the 12th-13th centuries, and the Gothic, *azulejo*-covered cloister was added in the 14th century. The gold and silver **Capela do Santíssimo Sacramento,** to the left of the altar, was used as the bishop's study. During the Napoleonic invasion, townspeople whitewashed the altar to prevent vandalism. *(Terreiro da Sé. ☎222 05 90 28. Open M-Sa 9am-12:30pm and 2:30-7pm, Su 2:30-6pm. Nov.-Mar closes 1hr. earlier. Cloister €2.)*

MUSEU DE ARTE CONTEMPORÂNEA. This museum houses rotating exhibits of contemporary international paintings, architecture, photography, and sculpture. Its 44 colossal acres of manicured gardens, fountains, and old farmland, tumbling down toward the Douro River, are also easy on the eyes. *(R. D. João de Castro, 210. ☎226 15 65 00. Several kilometers out of town, on the way to the beach. Bus #207 leaves from Av. dos Aliados; ask the driver to stop at the museum. 30min., return buses run until midnight. Museum open Apr.-Sept. Tu-F 10am-7pm, Sa-Su 10am-8pm; Oct.-Mar. Tu-Su 10am-7pm. Park Tu-Su 10am-7pm. Museum and park €5, park only €2.50. Su before 2pm free.)*

NIGHTLIFE

The heart of Porto's nightlife is **Ribeira.** Summer crowds leave outdoor cafes at 2am and head to neighboring bars or more distant clubs. The Ribeira's narrow, poorly lit streets can be unsafe at night, so don't go alone. Nightlife in Porto is tough without a car, as most clubs are along the river in **Foz** and in the industrial zones. Bus #500 runs until 1am from the São Bento train station to the beach at Matosinhos, passing Foz along the way. Bus #200 also runs past Foz to the beach until 1am, but begins at Pr. da Liberdade. A taxi to Foz from downtown costs €4-5. To get to the clubs in the **industrial center,** take the metro to Viso, which runs until 1am, as does bus #201 from Pr. da Liberdade to Viso. A taxi ride will cost €5-6. **Gaia,** on the other side of the Douro River, is safer and better lit. Here, numerous bars, discotheques, wineries, and arcades line up with a beautiful view of Porto's lights. You can cross the D. Luis bridge by foot to get back to Porto and catch a bus or taxi from there.

Discoteca Swing, R. Julio Dinis, 766 (☎226 09 00 19). A staple of Porto's nightlife for over 25 years, Swing is at its most swinging at around 2 or 3am. Beer €2-3. Mixed drinks €6-8. Su ladies' night includes 2 free drinks. W-Th no cover, F-Su €2.50-10, usually €5. Open W-Su midnight-6am. AmEx/MC/V.

O Muro, Muro dos Bacalhoeiros, 87-88 (☎222 08 34 26), upstairs from a pedestrian street along the water off Pr. de Ribeira. A tiny yet remarkable restaurant during the day, O Muro attracts night owls with a great view of the river and complimentary snacks with a beer (€1-4.50) or a glass of port (€2.50). Entrees €7.50-12. Kitchen closes at midnight. Open Tu-Su noon-2am.

WINERIES

No visit to Porto is complete without one of the city's famous wine-tasting tours. They are incredibly cheap (€1-3), if not free, and take about 30min. Wine tasting is most prevalent across the river, in Vila Nova de Gaia and its 17 large port lodges reside. Tours there often include visits to the wine caves below. To get there, walk across the bottom level of the Ponte de D. Luiz I in Ribeira. It's best to visit the wineries from noon-2pm when most tourists head away from the tours for lunch.

Solar do Vinho do Porto, R. Entre Quintas, 220 (☎226 09 47 49). Go around the Palácio de Cristal to the end of R. de Entre Quintas. Enjoy a fine glass of port on the swanky outdoor terrace of a former manor house. Limited snack menu includes cheesecake (€3). Port €1-25. Open M-Sa 4pm-midnight. AmEx/MC/V.

Vinhos de Quinta, R. Fonte Taurina, 89 (☎222 08 92 57). A small, humble, non-profit wine shop dedicated to small, lesser-known port wine producers. The owners serve samples for a fee of €2.50-10. Prices are rock bottom (about half off retail, €2.50-70) and all proceeds go to farmers in the Douro. Open Tu-Su 11am-8pm.

Sandeman, Lg. Miguel Bombarda, 3 (☎233 74 05 00, fax 233 74 05 94), just off Av. Diogo Leite. Founded by a Scottish merchant 2 centuries ago, Sandeman now offers a tourist-friendly dive into the world of port. Lively tours every 20min. €3. Open Mar.-Oct. daily 10am-12:30pm and 2-6pm; Nov.-Feb. M-F 9:30am-12:30pm and 2-5:30pm.

Taylor's, R. do Choupelo, 250 (☎223 74 28 00; www.taylor.pt). Walk along the river and make a left on R. Afonso III. Go right as it splits and take the stairs to R. do Choupelo. Taylor's will be on the left. Offers expert wine knowledge, outdoor gardens (complete with peacocks), and free tours and tasting. Tours every 20-30min., last tour 5pm. Open July-Aug. M-Sa 10am-6pm, Sept.-June M-F 10am-6pm. AmEx/MC/V.

FESTIVALS

For two weeks in February, Porto hosts the **Fantasporto Film Festival,** screening international fantasy, sci-fi, and horror flicks for crowds of film enthusiasts. Early June brings the **Festival Internacional de Teatro de Expressão Ibérica,** which stages free performances of Portuguese and Spanish drama. Porto's biggest party, however, is the **Festa de São João** (June 23-24), when locals storm the streets for free concerts, folklore, *fado*, and (of course) wine. After the fireworks on the first night of the festival, people go to the beach to fulfill superstitious traditions including jumping over bonfires three times for good luck, and for the women, rolling around in the morning dew to ensure fertility.

PARQUE NACIONAL DA PENEDA-GERÊS

Portugal's northern border with Spain is a sight to behold: a dark, quiet forest spread over rugged mountains and winding rivers, punctuated by faint hiking trails. A crescent-shaped nature reserve, the **Parque Nacional da Peneda-Gerês,** became Portugal's first protected area in 1971. The park consists of the northern Serra da Peneda and the southern Serra do Gerês, and it provides refuge for the endangered Iberian wolf. Most travelers base themselves in Vila do Gerês (also called Caldas do Gerês), a spa town that draws hordes in late summer. From here, visitors can explore the park's many relaxing villages, turquoise waters, tree-covered mountains, and Iron Age ruins. Activities range from hikes past abandoned monasteries to adrenaline-powered water sports to pampering in the thermal waters.

TRANSPORTATION AND PRACTICAL INFORMATION. **Empresa Hoteleira do Gerês** (☎253 26 20 33) runs buses between **Braga** and **Gerês,** from terminal #18 in Braga's **bus station.** (to Gerês 1hr.; M-F 11 per day 7:05am-8pm, Sa 7 per day 8am-7:10pm, Su 6 per day 8am-7:10pm; return 1hr.; M-F 11 per day 6:30am-6:30pm, Sa 6 per day, Su 5 per day 7:15am-6:30pm. €3.80.) Gerês is essentially a 500m one-way street loop, running beside the water. The tourist office is at the far end of the loop, uphill from the bus stop. Next to the tourist office is a two-lane highway which continues 13km to Spain. To catch the bus back to Braga, you must be on the side of the loop that leads traffic away from the tourist office downhill.

To get to the **tourist office** from the bus stop, walk uphill along Av. Manuel Francisco da Costa; the office is off the rotary at the end of the mini-shopping center. The staff speaks English, French, Italian, and Spanish and provides information on activities in the park as well as **luggage storage.** (☎253 39 11 33. Open M-W and F-Sa 9am-12:30pm and 2:30-6pm.) The **police** (☎253 39 11 37) are off Av. Manuel Francisco da Costa, and the **Red Cross** (☎253 39 16 60) is on Cha de Ermida. **Espaço Internet** in the Biblioteca Municipal on Av. Manuel Francisco da Costa, across from the spa, has free **Internet.** (☎253 39 17 97. Open M-F 9:30am-1pm and 2-5:30pm, Sa 9am-12:30pm.) The **post office** is off the rotary that leads to the center. (☎253 39 00 10. Open M-F 9am-12:30pm and 2-5:30pm.)

ACCOMMODATIONS AND FOOD. There are plenty of accommodations in Gerês, from fancy hotels to budget *pensões*. Try **Residencial Ribeiro ❷,** R. Miguel Torga, 101, where the kindly owner offers beautiful rooms with private bathrooms and free breakfast. From the bus stop, head down the street until the road splits off at the ice cream shop and goes downhill. Follow the road to the bottom of the hill, then follow the signs left. (☎253 39 19 09. Singles €25, doubles €35, triples €45. Cash only.) A comparable option is **Pensão Residencial o Horizonte de Gerês ❷,** R. de Arnaçó, 19. Go around the loop past the tourist office until the road splits. Take a right uphill for two blocks and the *pensâo* will be on the left. Simply decorated rooms come with a TV and private bath. More expensive rooms have a view of the valley. (☎253 391 260. Breakfast included. Singles €25-30, doubles €35-40, triples €45-50. Cash only.) For camping, try **Camping Vidoeiro ❶,** 1km up the road from the tourist office and 250m beyond the park office. (☎253 39 12 89. Reception 8am-noon and 3-7pm. Open May 15-Oct. 15. €2.20 per person, €3.10-4.20 per tent, €3.10 per car.) Meals are served at the *pensões* throughout town. A small **supermarket** is on the way into town, across from the post office. (Open M-Sa 8am-12:30pm and 2:30-7pm, Su 8am-noon.) Restaurants line Av. Manuel Francisco da Costa, near the bus stop where the buses from Braga arrive. For a filling meal, try **Vai-Vai ❷,** located just down the street from the tourist office, across from the spa. The *menú* (€8) includes a choice of fish, chicken, or pork served with soup, a drink, and dessert. Entrees run €7-12. Cheaper snack menus are available at the cafe next door. Come early for lunch; the place is small and gets packed from 1-2pm. (☎253 39 12 26. Open M-Sa 10am-10pm. Cash only.)

HIKING AND OUTDOOR ACTIVITIES. The main **park office** is in **Braga,** on Av. António Macedo. (☎253 20 34 80. Open M-F 9:30am-12:30pm and 2:30-5:30pm.) The Gerês **branch,** on Av. Manuel Francisco da Costa, is a white building 1km uphill from the tourist office, near the campgrounds. (☎253 39 01 10. Open in summer daily 9am-noon and 2-5:30pm; in winter M-F 9am-noon and 2-5:30pm.) Casual visitors tend to stick to the gentle, scenic southern trails, while dedicated hikers head north. The popular **Trilha da Preguiça** (Lazy Trail; 5km) begins 3km north of Gerês proper, on the right side of the highway, and follows the Rio Gerês. Another hike follows the road from the tourist office to Spain 10km farther toward **Portela do Homem,** a town with a river pool in the **Minas dos Carris** valley. Other popular longer trails are Trilho da Aguia do Sarilhâo, Trilho dos Currais, and Trilho da Cidade da Calcedonia. The tourist and park offices can recommend additional hikes.

As the name suggests, the main attraction of **Caldas do Gerês** (Gerês hot springs) is its spa, owned by **Empresa das Águas do Gerês,** on Av. Manuel Francisco da Costa, 133, as are the hotel, restaurant, and park by the tourist office. The spa complex (the pink building in the center of town) contains therapeutic waters. (☎253 39 11 13; www.aguasdogeres.com. Open May-Oct. M-Sa 8am-noon and 4-6:40pm.) For a bewildering array of spa services, go to the office, a yellow building across from Hotel das Águas do Gerês. (30min. full-body massage €20. Sauna €7.50. Whirlpool €6. Open M-Sa 8am-noon and 2:30-5:30pm.) To the left of the tourist office, the beautiful **Parque das Termas** has mineral waters, jogging trails, three pools, and canoe rentals. Purchase tickets at the booth inside. (☎253 39 11 13. Park open 9am-7pm. Entrance €1, under 12 €0.50. Free if at hotel. Pool open daily July-Sept. 10am-7pm; M-F €4, Sa-Su €6; May-June 9am-6pm; €4, under 12 €2. Tennis €3 per hr. Canoeing €3 per 30min.)

Geresmont, R. de Arnaçó, 43, has a variety of outdoor activities, including paintballing, rope climbing, canoeing, and off-roading. (☎919 61 77 73; www.geresmont.com.) South of Gerês, the **Miradouro do Gerês** overlooks the **Caniçada** reservoir—beware the mass migrations of weekend picnickers. The village of **Rio Caldo,** at the base of Caniçada reservoir just 8km south of Gerês, is a base for canoeing and waterskiing through **Água Montanha Lazer.** (☎253 39 17 79; www.aguamontanha.com. Single canoe €4.50 per hr, €14 per ½-day, €22 per day. Double canoe €7.50/23/25. 5-person motorboat €35/95/125. Waterskiing boat with driver and equipment included €40 per 20min., €100 per hr.

THE THREE BEIRAS

The Three Beiras region offers a versatile sampling of the best of Portugal: the pristine beaches of the coast, the rich greenery of the interior, and the ragged peaks of the Serra da Estrela. The Costa da Prata (Silver Coast) lines the shore, passing through Aveiro on the way to Porto. Its countryside is dotted with red-roofed farmhouses surrounded by expanses of corn, sunflowers, and wheat. A mecca for youth since the days in which it boasted the only university in Portugal, Coimbra hosts an opinionated, lively population; its nightlife, folklore and gorgeous architecture continue to attract young people. Only recently discovered by tourists, the region retains a wealth of Portuguese traditions.

COIMBRA ☎239

The crown jewel of the three Beiras, Coimbra is a rollicking city of 200,000, but it possesses the vibe of a metropolis many times its size. Backpackers and local college students roam graffiti-lined streets, providing a youthful exuberance rare in the Portuguese interior. For centuries, the Universidade de Coimbra was the only university in Portugal, attracting young men from the country's elite. Though universities now abound in Portugal, Coimbra's university district maintains its historical appeal. Visitors may be surprised to see the outer facade of the university in a state of disrepair; the city's preservation efforts are aimed at the buildings' interior, so be sure to see the indoor splendor.

TRANSPORTATION

Trains: (Info ☎808 20 82 08; www.cp.pt). **Estação Coimbra-A (Nova)** is 2 blocks from the lower town center, on the river. **Estação Coimbra-B (Velha)** is 3km northwest of town. Regional trains stop first in Coimbra-B, then some continue to Coimbra-A, departing in reverse order. Long-distance trains stop in Coimbra-B only; take a connecting train to Coimbra-A to reach the city (4min., right after trains arrive, €1.08 or free if transfer). To: **Braga** (2-3hr., 16 per day 5:45am-8:40pm, €10-20); **Figueira da Foz** (1hr., 20 per day 5:35am-12:10am, €2); **Lisboa's Sta. Apolonia** (2-3hr., 17 per day 5:30am-8:46pm, €12-30); **Porto** (1-2hr., 14 per day 5:45am-11:45pm, €6.90-20).

Buses: Joalto (formerly AVIC), R. João de Ruão, 18 (☎239 82 01 41; www.joalto.pt). Bus stops are in front of the Coimbra-A train station. To: **Condeixa** (25min., 6-15 per day 7:05am-11:30pm, €1.79) and **Conímbriga** (30min.; departs M-F 9:05, 9:35am, returns 1, 6pm; Sa-Su departs 9:35am, returns 6pm; €2.20). **RBL** (☎239 85 52 70; www.rede-expressos.pt), at the end of Av. Fernão de Magalhães and a 15min. walk past Coimbra-A. To: **Évora** (4-6hr., 9 per day 6:15am-2:15am, €15.80); **Faro** (8-9hr., 14 per day 6:15am-2:10am, €23); **Lisboa** (2hr., 18 per day 6:15am-2:15am, €13); **Luso** and **Buçaco** (45min., M-F 5 per day 7:35am-7:30pm, Sa 9am; €2.90); **Porto** (1hr., 14 per day 7am-3am, €11).

Public Transportation: SMTUC buses and street cars (☎239 81 02 47; www.smtuc.pt). 1-way on the bus €1.60, 3-trip ticket €2, 1-day pass €3, book of 11 €6. Sold at vending machines in Lg. da Portagem, Pr. da República, and in local shops like mini-markets and bookstores.

Taxis: Politaxis (☎239 49 90 90), outside Coimbra-A and the bus station.

Car Rental: Avis (☎239 83 47 86, reservations toll-free 800 20 10 02; www.avis.com), in Coimbra-A train station. 21+. From €80 per day. Manual transmission only. Open M-F 8:30am-12:30pm and 3-7pm. AmEx/MC/V.

THE NORTH

ORIENTATION AND PRACTICAL INFORMATION

Coimbra's steep, cobbled streets rise in tiers above the Río Mondego. The main pedestrian thoroughfare runs from **Praça 8 de Maio** to **Largo da Portagem** by the river and the tourist office. It starts as **Rua Visconde da Luz** and becomes **Rua Ferreira Borges** as it nears the water. This road forms a triangle region with the **Rio Mondego** called **Baixa,** which is the most central of the three major parts of town and the location of the Coimbra-A train station, as well as dozens of great restaurants and accommodations. The historic **university district** looms atop the steep hill overlooking Baixa. On the other side of the university, the **Praça da República** area is home to cafes, a shopping district, and the youth hostel.

Tourist Office: Regional, Lg. da Portagem (☎239 48 81 20; www.turismo-centro.pt). English, French, and Spanish spoken. Open June 16-Sept. 14 M-F 9am-8pm Sa-Su 9:30am-1pm and 2:30-6pm; Sept. 15-June 15 M-F 9-5pm, Sa-Su 10am-1pm and 2:30-5pm. **Municipal,** Praça da Porta Férrea (☎239 85 98 84). Open M-F 9am-6pm, Sa-Su 9am-12:30pm and 2-5:30pm.

Budget Travel: Tagus (☎239 83 62 05) inside the A.A.C. building on R. Padre António Vieira. Sells ISIC cards. Open M-F 9:30am-6pm.

Currency Exchange: Montepio Geral, Lg. da Portagem (☎239 85 17 00 or 82 80 31). €5 commission above €50. Open M-F 8:30am-3pm.

Laundromat: Lavandaria Lucira, Av. Sá da Bandeira, 86. Wash and dry €5.90 per 6kg (full machine), €2 for 1kg. Specify if you don't want your clothing ironed (*passada*). Open M-Sa 9am-1pm and 3-7pm, Su 9am-1pm.

Police: Local, Av. Elisio de Moura, 155 (☎239 79 76 40). **Serviço de Estrangeiros e Fronteiras** (tourist), Loja do Cidadão, Av. Fernão de Magalhães (☎239 85 35 00).

Pharmacy: Farmácia Universal, Pr. 8 de Maio, 32 (☎239 82 37 44), in the center of town. Open M-F 8am-7pm, Sa 8am-1pm.

Hospital: Hospital da Universidade de Coimbra (☎239 40 04 00), at Pr. Professor Mota Pinto and Av. Dr. Bissaya Barreto. Take bus #6, 7, 7t, 29, 35, 36 or 37.

Internet Access: Casa Aninhas, Pr. 8 de Maio, 38. This free, city-run service is popular, so expect a 15-30min. wait. Passport or driver's license required. Open M-F 10am-8pm, Sa-Su 10am-10pm. **Sp@cenet,** Av. Sá da Bandeira, 67 (☎239 83 98 44). €2 per hr. Open M-Sa 10am-midnight, Su 1pm-midnight. **Web@aventura,** Rua Quebra Costas 63 (☎239 10 81 89). €2 per hr. Open M-F 10am-10:30pm, Sa noon-10:30pm.

Post Office: Estação Central, Av. Fernão de Magalhães, 223 (☎239 85 07 70). **Poste Restante** and **fax.** Open M-F 8:30am-6:30pm, Sa-Su 9am-noon. **Municipal Office,** Lg. D. Dinis (☎239 85 17 60). Open M-F 9am-6pm, Sa 9am-noon. **Branch office,** Pr. da República (☎239 85 18 20). Open M-F 9am-6pm. **Postal Code:** 3000.

ACCOMMODATIONS

Accommodations are packed on Av. Fernão de Magalhães. Their bright flashing signs make the area between the Largo das Olarias and the Coimbra-A train station seem like a mini Vegas strip. The youth hostel is a 20min. walk or short bus ride away from the city center.

Residencial Vitória, R. da Sota, 11-19 (☎239 82 40 49; fax 84 28 97). Convenient location next to the train station. Friendly staff, and newer rooms with bath, phone, cable TV, breakfast, and A/C. In summer singles €30, doubles €45, triples €60. In winter €25/40/50. Older rooms without amenities are acceptably comfortable, with shower, sink, and TV. Breakfast €2.50. Singles €20, doubles €30. AmEx/MC/V. ❷

Residência Solar Navarro, Av. Emídio Navarro, 60-A, 2nd fl. (☎239 82 79 99). Rock-bottom prices, large rooms, and high ceilings. Ensuite bathrooms. Singles €15; doubles, triples, and quints €12.50 per person. Cash only. ❶

Pousada da Juventude de Coimbra (HI), R. Henrique Seco, 14 (☎239 82 29 55). Off R. Lourenço Azevedo, to the left of Parque de Santa Cruz. At the end of the road, take the 2nd right, or take the #6,7 or 29 bus from in front of the train station. Get off 2 stops after Pr. da República, on Bysseia Barreto. Kitchen, TV room (with pool table and foosball), impeccable bathrooms. Breakfast included. 24hr. bag drop-off. Dorms €11; singles with bath €16; doubles €26, with bath €28. AmEx/MC/V. ❶

FOOD

The side streets below Pr. do Comércio, the areas around R. Direita off Pr. 8 de Maio, and the university side of Pr. da República are a good bet for bargain eats. Restaurants offer local favorites: steamy portions of *arroz de lampreia* (rice with eel) and *cabrito* (young goat). The cheapest meals are at the **UC Cantinas** (full meal for under €2), the university student cafeterias, on the right side of R. Oliveiro Matos and up the stairs near Lg. Dom Dinis. You'll need an ISIC card, and you may want to leave your backpack at home. For groceries, stock up at **Mercado Dom Pedro V** on R. Olímpio Nicolau Rui Fernandes (open M-Sa 8am-1pm). The supermarket **Pingo Doce,** is on R. João de Ruão, 14, a 3min. walk up R. da Sofia from Pr. 8 de Maio (☎239 85 29 30; open daily 8:30am-9pm).

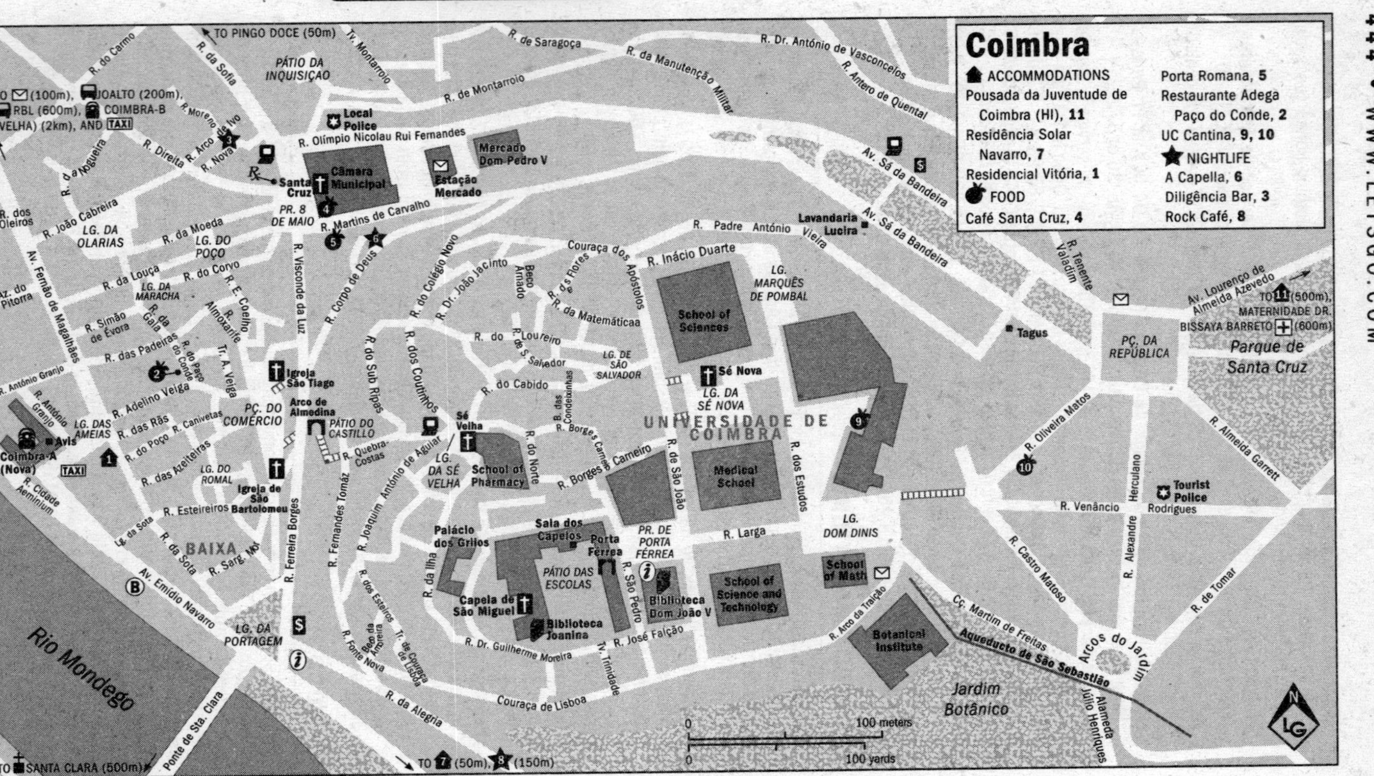
Coimbra
ACCOMMODATIONS
Pousada da Juventude de Coimbra (HI), 11
Residência Solar Navarro, 7
Residencial Vitória, 1
FOOD
Café Santa Cruz, 4
Porta Romana, 5
Restaurante Adega Paço do Conde, 2
UC Cantina, 9, 10
NIGHTLIFE
A Capella, 6
Diligência Bar, 3
Rock Café, 8
TO PINGO DOCE (50m)
TO (100m), JOALTO (200m), RBL (600m), COIMBRA-B (VELHA) (2km), AND TAXI
PÁTIO DA INQUISIÇAO
Local Police
Câmara Municipal
Estação Mercado
Mercado Dom Pedro V
Santa Cruz
PR. 8 DE MAIO
LG. DA OLARIAS
LG. DO POÇO
LG. DA MARACHA
Igreja São Tiago
Arco de Almedina
PÇ. DO COMÉRCIO
PÁTIO DO CASTILLO
LG. DAS AMEIAS
Coimbra-A (Nova)
Avis
LG. DO ROMAL
Igreja de São Bartolomeu
BAIXA
LG. DA PORTAGEM
Rio Mondego
Ponte de Sta. Clara
TO SANTA CLARA (500m)
TO (50m), (150m)
Sé Velha
LG. DA SÉ VELHA
School of Pharmacy
Palácio dos Grilos
Sala dos Capelos
Porta Férrea
PÁTIO DAS ESCOLAS
Capela de São Miguel
Biblioteca Joanina
PR. DE PORTA FÉRREA
Biblioteca Dom João V
Sé Nova
LG. DA SÉ NOVA
LG. DE SÃO SALVADOR
School of Sciences
LG. MARQUÊS DE POMBAL
UNIVERSIDADE DE COIMBRA
Medical School
LG. DOM DINIS
School of Science and Technology
School of Math
Botanical Institute
Jardim Botânico
Aqueducto de São Sebastião
Arcos do Jardim
Lavandaria Lucira
Tagus
PÇ. DA REPÚBLICA
Parque de Santa Cruz
TO (500m), MATERNIDADE DR. BISSAYA BARRETO (600m)
Tourist Police
R. de Saragoça
R. da Manutenção Militar
R. Dr. António de Vasconcelos
R. Antero de Quental
R. de Montarroio
Tv. Montarroio
R. da Sofia
R. do Carmo
R. Olímpio Nicolau Rui Fernandes
Av. Sá da Bandeira
R. Martins de Carvalho
R. Visconde da Luz
R. Ferreira Borges
Av. Fernão de Magalhães
Av. Emídio Navarro
R. Padre António Vieira
Couraça dos Apóstolos
R. Inácio Duarte
R. da Matemática
R. do Loureiro
R. do Cabido
R. dos Coutinhos
R. do Sub Ripas
R. Corpo de Deus
R. do Colégio Novo
R. Dr. João Jacinto
R. Borges Carneiro
R. de São João
R. dos Estudos
R. Larga
R. São Pedro
R. José Falcão
R. Dr. Guilherme Moreira
Tv. Trinidade
Couraça de Lisboa
R. da Alegria
R. Fonte Nova
R. Fernandes Tomáz
R. Joaquim António de Aguiar
R. do Norte
R. da Ilha
R. Arco da Traição
Cç. Martim de Freitas
R. Castro Matoso
R. Oliveira Matos
R. Venâncio Rodrigues
R. Alexandre Herculano
R. Almeida Garrett
R. de Tomar
Alameda Júlio Henriques
R. Tenente Valadim
Av. Lourenço de Almeida Azevedo
100 meters
100 yards

Restaurante Adega Paço do Conde, R. do Paço do Conde (☎239 82 56 05). Adored by locals. Abundant grilled meat and fish dishes for only €5-6. The giant restaurant is partly indoors, partly outdoors, and covered by a tin roof, and the entrance is marked by a large archway. Entrees €4-13. Open M-Sa 11am-10pm. MC/V. ❶

Café Santa Cruz, Pr. 8 de Maio, 5 (☎239 83 36 17; www.cafesantacruz.com). Formerly part of a church, this is the city's most famous cafe. A vaulted ceiling and carved wooden chairs distinguish the dining space. Outdoor seating is available with a view of the plaza and the Igreja de Santa Cruz. Sandwiches €1.60-3. Summer, open M-Sa 7:30am-2am, winter M-Sa 7:30am-midnight. Cash only. ❶

Porta Romana, R. Martins de Carvalho, 8/10 (☎239 82 84 58), tucked away behind Café Santa Cruz. A wide variety of pasta entrees for €6-8 and pizzas for €4-7. Half portions of local cuisine from €4.50. Try the *Fettucine Fantasia,* with Roquefort cheese, cream sauce, and ham (€6.50). Open Tu-Su 10am-2am. Cash only. ❶

SIGHTS

OLD TOWN. Take in Coimbra's old town sights by making the steep 15min. climb from the river up to the university. Begin at Pr. 8 de Maio, often a scene for folk music and dance, and the **Igreja de Santa Cruz.** The 16th-century church boasts an enormous center dome and *azulejo*-lined walls, though the centerpiece is the tomb of Dom Afonso Henriques, Portugal's first king. *(☎239 82 29 41. Open M-F 7:30am 6:30pm, Sa 7:30am-12:30pm and 2pm-7:30pm, Su 8:30am-12:30pm and 4pm-7:30pm. Check the schedule at the main door for mass times. Sacristia with royal tombs €2.50, students and seniors €1.50.)* The ascent continues to the ancient **Arco de Almedina,** a remnant of the Moorish town wall, one block uphill from Lg. da Portagem. The gate leads past several university bookstores to the steep, twisted, and aptly named R. Quebra-Costas (Back-Breaker Street). Up a narrow stone stairway looms the 12th-century Romanesque **Sé Velha** (Old Cathedral). *(☎239 82 52 73. Open M-Th 10am-1pm and 2pm-6pm, F 10am-1pm, Sa 10am-5pm. Cathedral free. Cloister €1, students €0.80).* Follow the signs to the 16th-century **Sé Nova** (New Cathedral), whose mixed classical- and Baroque-style exterior was finished for the resident Jesuit community. Bring sunglasses: the gilded main altar can be blinding at certain times of day. *(☎239 82 31 38. Open Tu-Sa 8:30am-noon and 2pm-6pm. Free.)*

UNIVERSIDADE DE COIMBRA. Though many buildings have since been constructed from reinforced concrete, the original law school retains its spot on the architectural dean's list. Enter through the **Porta Férrea** (Iron Gate), off R. São Pedro, to the **Pátio das Escolas,** which sports an excellent view of the city. The staircase to the right leads up to the **Sala Grande dos Actos** or **Sala dos Capelos** (Graduates' Hall), where portraits of Portugal's kings (6 of whom were born in Coimbra) hang below a 17th-century ceiling; this is where graduates receive their diplomas. The magnificent **Capela de São Miguel,** adorned with intricate *talha dourada* carvings (especially the organ), is a sight to behold. *Azulejos*, gold, silver, paintings, or carved wood line every surface; almost no floor, wall, or ceiling space is left uncovered. At the end of the row of buildings is the oldest library in Portugal, the **Biblioteca Joanina,** which overwhelms visitors with gold-trimmed extravagance. The portrait of Louis XV stares at viewers from every angle, making sure they don't snatch any of the library's 300,000 ancient books. A small army of bats keeps the books bug free. The library's oldest book, a marriage guide for young men, dates back to 1523. *(☎239 85 98 84. www.uc.pt. Open daily Mar. 13-Oct. 8:30am-7pm; Nov.-Mar. M-F 9am-5pm, Sa-Su 10am-4pm. Tickets to all of the university sights can be purchased outside the Porta Férrea, in the Biblioteca Dom João V. General ticket €6, seniors and students €4.20. The Sala dos*

Capelos and Biblioteca Joanina are each €3.50, seniors and students €2.45. There is a limit to how many people can be in the library at a time, so expect a 15-20min. wait.)

NIGHTLIFE

After dinner, the outdoor cafes surrounding Praça da República buzz until 2am, after which crowds move on to the bars and clubs farther afield. The scene is best October through July, when the students are around Figueira da Foz, an hour away, which offers more options and makes a popular night trip. Many take the train, party all night, and return in the morning.

A Capella, R. Corpo de Deus on Lgo. Victoria (☎239 833 985). From Pr. 8 de Maio, take R. V. da Luz for about 100m and make a sharp U-turn to the left on R. Corpo de Deus. A Capella is tucked off the road to the left. Built in 1364, A Capella is now a small late-night cafe and the best place to hear *fado.* Very touristy, so don't expect to see many locals around. The professional *fadistas* play *fado* classics with historic scenes from Coimbra projected on the background wall. Mixed drinks €4-5. Performances at 9:30, 10:30, and 11:30pm. Cover €10, includes 1 drink. Open daily 9pm-3am.

Diligência Bar, R. Nova, 30 (☎239 82 76 67). Touristy during the summer, yet still intimate and pleasant. Original *fado* performed by students and regulars after 10pm. Entrees €9-11. Sangria €9.50 per jug. Min. consumption €5. Open daily 7pm-2am. V.

Rock Cafe, Parque Verde do Mondego (☎239 63 60 38, fax 239 84 21 38). On the riverside in the park, about 500m from the Ponte de Santa Clara towards the white bridge. You can go for a snack or salad (€2-6) during the day or rock during the night. The place often gets packed, specially during the weekends, when live bands play popular hits in English and Portuguese. Open M-Th noon-3am, F-Sa noon-4am. Live music Th-Sa starting at midnight. AmEx/MC/V.

FESTIVALS

Students run wild during the **Queima das Fitas** (Burning of the Ribbons), Coimbra's infamous week-long festival in the first or second week of May. The festivities begin when graduating seniors set fire to narrow ribbons, gifts from friends and family to commemorate their graduation; they then receive wide, ornamental replacement ribbons. The fun continues with nights of music and food in the streets of Coimbra. The **Festas da Rainha Santa,** in the first week of July, brings live choral music to the streets and the city's largest fireworks display to the sky. During even-numbered years, there are two processions of the statue of Rainha Santa (one at the beginning, one at the end), which reflect the festival's religious roots. Elderly ladies line the streets hours before the event to claim their spot on the sidewalk. During this time, folklore dance groups sometimes organize shows in front of Igreja de Santa Cruz, where participants are dressed in traditional costumes that remember the city's rural past. The firework-punctuated **Feira Popular** in the second week of July involves a giant fair full of games and carnival rides that keep the people across the river laughing and screaming all night. (€1, rides €2.)

MOROCCO

Morocco, the hazy spit of land across the Strait of Gibraltar, is 13km and worlds away from Europe. The nation contains unparalleled raw beauty, with lush valleys, enormous desert dunes, ancient imperial cities, and North Africa's highest mountains. While you may reach Morocco today by high-speed ferry rather than brigantine ship, your path has been well worn by years of cultural exchange. Moorish rule in southern Spain is manifest across the old land of *al-Andalus* in a legacy of breathtaking art, architecture, and technology, while even the Spanish language, with thousands of words derived from Arabic, testifies to centuries of fluidity between Iberia and northern Africa. Arab, African, and European influences come together gracefully in modern Morocco. Locals hawk *thuya* wood from the beaches of Essaouira next to Fez's famed blue pottery, along with movies from America and sandals from China. Donkeys hurtle down alleys past women who accessorize headscarves with Gucci shades. Today, the "Western Kingdom" continues to balance its ancient heritage with a contemporary struggle for national sovereignty, stability, and prosperity.

Let's Go coverage of Morocco is meant to feature selected highlights of the country as a side trip from Spain or Portugal, accessible from the most common travel hubs of Tangier, Casablanca, and Marrakesh. As you journey south through Iberia, skim across the strait to discover the roots of *al-Andalus* in this flourishing modern nation. It might just be the highlight of your trip.

LIFE AND TIMES

HISTORY

ANCIENT TIMES. Archaeological evidence along Morocco's Atlantic coast suggests that regions of the country have been inhabited since at least 125,000 BC. The **Berber** people arrived between 4000 and 2000 BC, and traces of their early civilization, particularly their tool use, can be seen in the High Atlas Mountains. Though the **Phoenicians** developed colonies along the coast in the ninth century BC, they exerted little control or influence over the area. After the sack of Carthage, near modern Tunis in Tunisia, the **Romans** came to control North Africa's agricultural supply. When the Pax Romana deteriorated in the AD fourth century, the Romans abandoned Morocco. By 420 the country was ruled by the **Vandals,** followed by a period of brief **Byzantine** rule. Each of these civilizations faced a similar problem: it was impossible to exert any control over the land without a reliable overland route. As a result, much of the country remained unexplored for centuries.

IMPERIAL ISLAM (AD 669-1554). Morocco achieved stability in the late seventh and early eighth centuries when **Muslim** armies invaded North Africa. Less than 50 years after the death of the prophet **Muhammed** in 632, Uqba bin Nafi al-Fihri had spread the religion and the rule of the Umayyad Dynasty across the Maghreb to Morocco. The native Berbers could not hold off the Muslim troops, making peace with Islamic governor **Musa ibn Nusayr.** Many converted to Islam, setting the stage for the invasion of Spain in 711. Arab rule

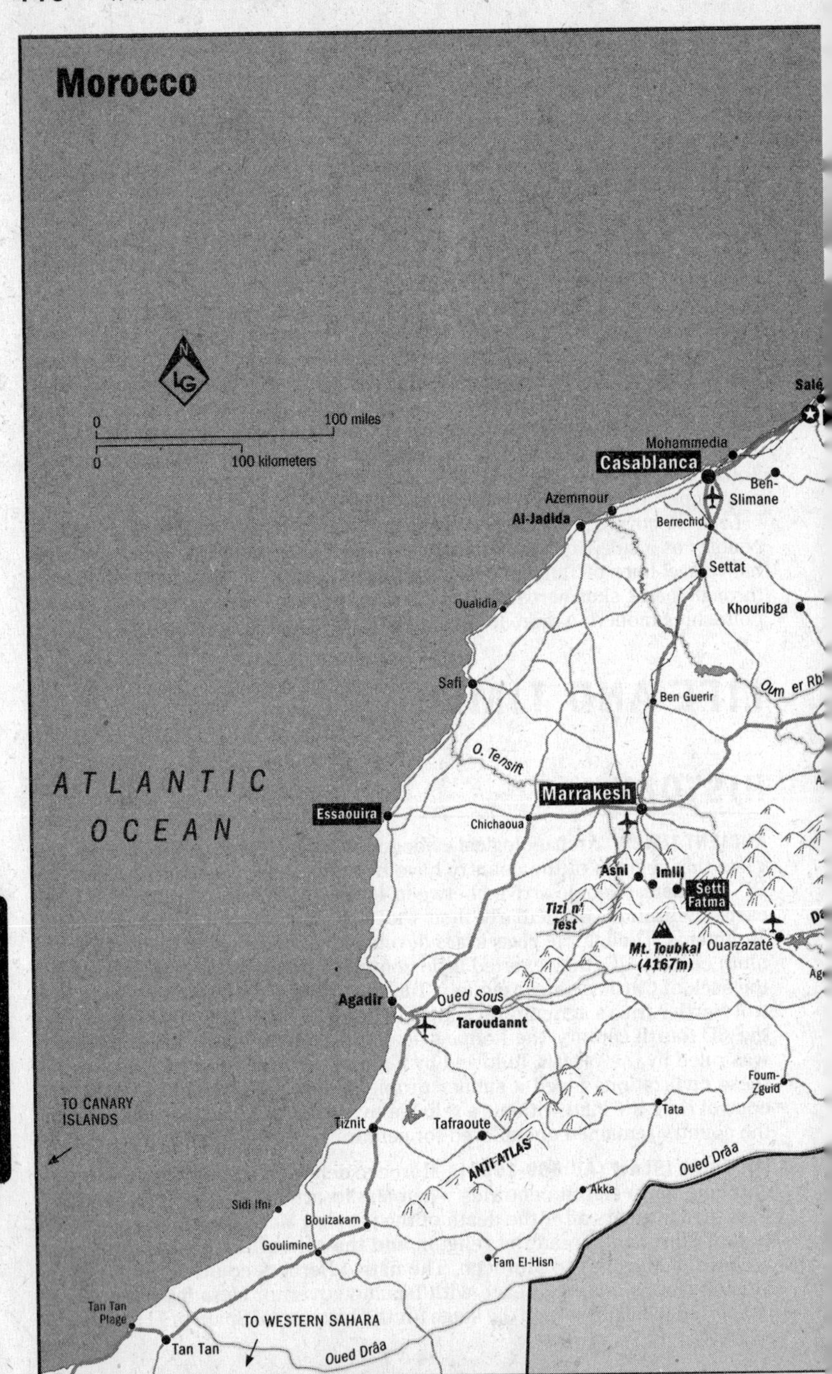
Morocco
0
100 miles
0
100 kilometers
ATLANTIC OCEAN
Casablanca
Mohammedia
Ben-Slimane
Azemmour
Al-Jadida
Berrechid
Settat
Khouribga
Oualidia
Safi
Ben Guerir
Oum er Rb
O. Tensift
Marrakesh
Essaouira
Chichaoua
Asni
Imlil
Setti Fatma
Tizi n' Test
Mt. Toubkal (4167m)
Ouarzazate
Agadir
Oued Sous
Taroudannt
Foum-Zguid
Tata
TO CANARY ISLANDS
Tiznit
Tafraoute
ANTI-ATLAS
Oued Drâa
Akka
Sidi Ifni
Bouizakarn
Goulimine
Fam El-Hisn
Tan Tan Plage
Tan Tan
TO WESTERN SAHARA
Oued Drâa
Salé

MOROCCO

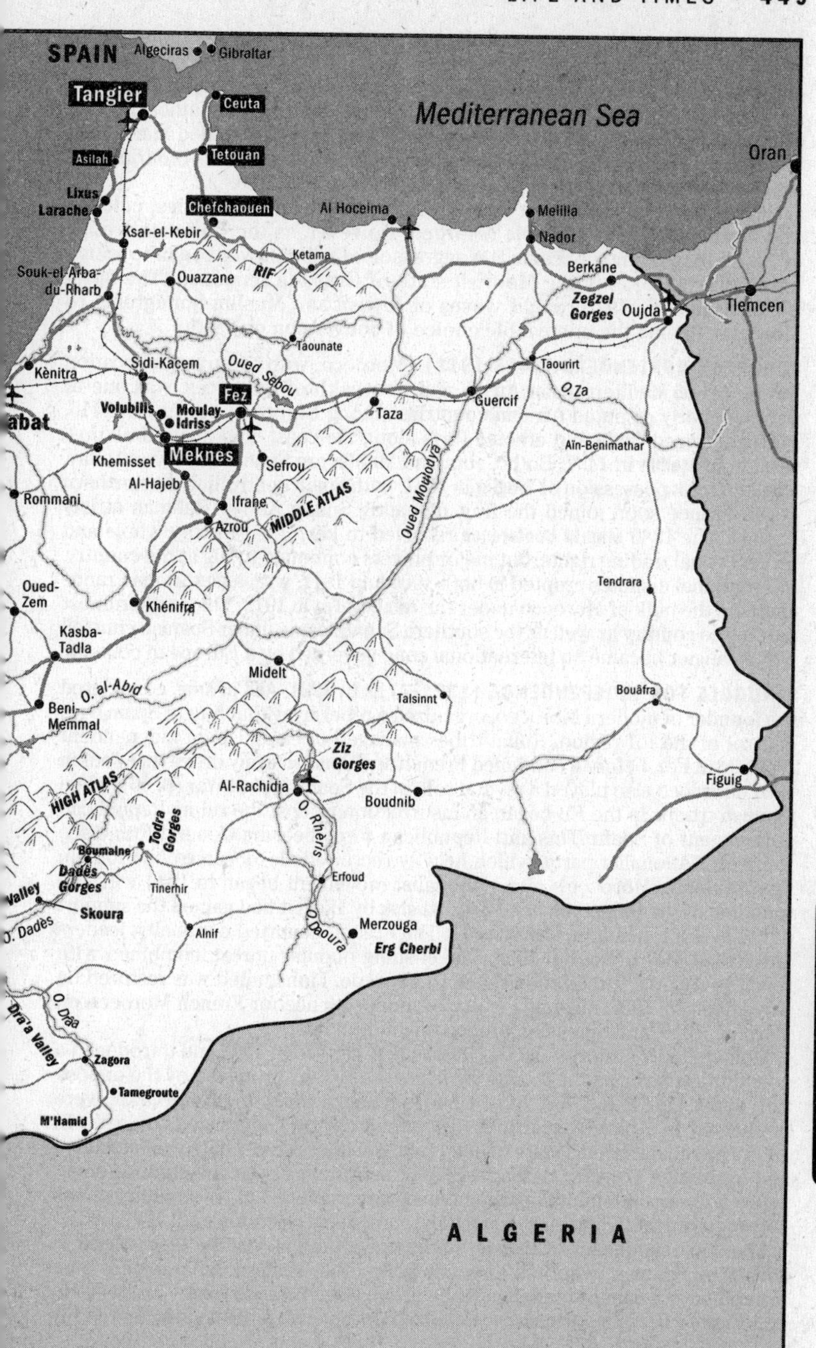
SPAIN
Algeciras
Gibraltar
Tangier
Ceuta
Mediterranean Sea
Oran
Asilah
Tetouan
Lixus
Larache
Chefchaouen
Al Hoceima
Melilla
Nador
Ksar-el-Kebir
Ketama
RIF
Berkane
Souk-el-Arba-du-Rharb
Ouazzane
Zegzel Gorges
Oujda
Tlemcen
Taounate
Sidi-Kacem
Oued Sebou
Taourirt
Kènitra
Fez
O. Za
Guercif
Taza
Volubilis
Moulay-Idriss
abat
Meknes
Aïn-Benimathar
Khemisset
Sefrou
Al-Hajeb
Oued Moulouya
Rommani
Ifrane
MIDDLE ATLAS
Azrou
Tendrara
Oued-Zem
Khénifra
Kasba-Tadla
Midelt
O. al-Abid
Bouâfra
Beni-Memmal
Talsinnt
Ziz Gorges
Figuig
HIGH ATLAS
Al-Rachidia
Boudnib
Todra Gorges
O. Rhèris
Boumaine
Dadès Gorges
Erfoud
Tinerhir
Valley
Skoura
O. Dadès
Merzouga
Alnif
O. Daoura
Erg Cherbi
O. Drâa
Dra'a Valley
Zagora
Tamegroute
M'Hamid
ALGERIA

MOROCCO

was short-lived in Morocco. A series of local Muslim dynasties took control of the area, claiming descent from Muhammed to legitimize their rule. **Idris ibn Abd Allah,** after fleeing Arabia, founded the first Moroccan state in 789. Over the next few hundred years, Morocco was conquered by one minor dynasty after another, most notably the **Almoravid Dynasty,** which founded Marrakesh in 1070 and fought to repel the Christian advance in Iberian *al-Andalus*, and the **Almohad Dynasty,** which defeated the Almoravids in 1160.

During the reign of Berber dynasties in the 13th-16th centuries, cultural and intellectual links to **Iberia** resurged. However, as the Christian troops of Iberia increasingly became the aggressor, Muslim power began to wane, until, after 1248, only the Moorish state of Granada remained. The **Spanish Inquisition** in 1492 brought waves of Jewish and Muslim immigrants to Morocco, fleeing the unenviable choice of conversion or death.

EUROPEAN CONTENDERS (1415-1912). Morocco, with its strategic location on the tip of Mediterranean Africa and its wealth of resources, was one of the most hotly disputed African countries among European powers. In 1415, Portugal seized **Ceuta** and erected forts along the coast, and Spain took possession of **Melilla** in 1497. Both Ceuta and Melilla are Spanish exclaves today. England took possession of **Tangier** in 1661, with Spain controlling the northern coast. France soon joined the fray, defeating Sultan Abd-ar Rahman at Isly in 1844. The 1880 **Madrid Conference** resolved to keep the territory whole and protect equal trading rights, but major powers continued to tug at the country. International disputes erupted in both 1905 and 1911, with a victorious France claiming the bulk of Morocco under the **Treaty of Fez** in 1912. The northernmost part of the country as well as the southern Sahara came under Spanish control, while Tangier became an international zone governed by a European council.

STRUGGLE FOR INDEPENDENCE (1921-77). In 1921, **Abd al-Krim,** considered the founder of modern Morocco, organized a rebel army that fought Spain over control of the Rif region. Rifian tribes managed to establish an independent republic in Fez, before a combined French and Spanish army drove them out in 1927. Morocco also played a pivotal role in the Spanish Civil War (p. 60), when Spanish troops in the Rif began an insurrection against the ruling Republican government of Spain. This anti-Republican force became General Francisco Franco's Nationalist party, which heavily recruited Moroccan troops to help fight in Spain. Morocco's own nationalist movement began in 1944 with the founding of the Independence Party, **Istiqlal;** by 1947, it had gained the support of the Moroccan sultan, **Mohammed V.** The French deported nationalist leaders and exiled Mohammad in 1953. The ensuing popular unrest, combined with revolt in Algeria, forced the French to concede. Mohammed was restored on November 18, 1955, signing a treaty of independence for French Morocco on March 2, 1956, and Spanish Morocco one month later.

Mohammed V's successor, **King Hassan II,** ascended in 1961 and introduced a constitution favoring the monarchy. This was heavily protested by the opposition party, UNFP. In 1963, 10 of UNFP's leaders, including Ben Barka, were implicated in a plot to overthrow the monarchy and sentenced to death. In 1965, Hassan declared a state of emergency, seizing direct control of executive and legislative powers. Hassan's 1970 constitution ended the state of emergency and restored limited parliamentary government, but two military coups and governmental divisions delayed parliamentary elections until 1977.

The most significant of Hassan's political triumphs was the **Green March** in 1975. The Spanish, who had long controlled the Western Sahara, were confronted with a Saharan independence group—the **Polisario Front**—just as General Franco lay dying. Hassan capitalized on Spanish weakness to march his troops into the Sahara. He was victorious, partially due to the disorganization of the Polisario Front and the Spanish unwillingness to fight over the impoverished region. Unfortunately, a resolution to the Western Sahara dispute is still being sought. The Polisario Front gained support from Algeria, but war ravaged the Sahara until the UN declared a ceasefire in 1989.

MODERN MOROCCO (1977-2008). Today, Morocco is a constitutional monarchy. There is a parliament and Chamber of Representatives, but the king and his advisers make most important decisions. Under Hassan II, censorship squelched opposition from such groups as trade union activists and university radicals. Sluggish industrial growth, riots, drought, and the drain of war in the Western Sahara further sapped support for the government, but Morocco began to recover in the 90s. **Islamist** movements in North Africa caused concern, although Hassan's regime remained stable in comparison to those in neighboring countries. Morocco's relations with its neighbors were strained, particularly with Algeria, where illegal arms shuttling resulted in the closing of the Morocco-Algeria border in 1994. Southern Europe began to take a greater interest in Morocco, advocating tighter border controls in light of increased illegal **immigration** through Morocco.

The reign of current king **Mohammed VI** is considered to have brought progress and reform to Morocco. Not only did he release thousands of political prisoners, but in March 2002 Mohammed made waves with his semi-public marriage to a computer engineer. Traditionally, royal marriages were strictly kept secrets, and the public release of the name and photograph of the king's bride was widely seen as heralding an era of openness and modernity. Most notably, the king introduced a family code in 2004, the **Mudawana,** meant to give women more power and to equalize laws on divorce, custody, and consent. In the same year, Mohammed opened a commission investigating the human rights abuses of Hassan II, **Instance Equité et Réconciliation (IER).** Despite recent advances, a significant percentage of the Moroccan population lives below the poverty line, sometimes on less than a dollar a day. Morocco's social problems—unemployment, illiteracy, high infant mortality—remain deeply entrenched, but modernization and reform are the keywords today.

CURRENT EVENTS

The terrorist attacks of September 11, 2001, dealt a sharp blow to tourism in Morocco, as a public fear of flying and of visiting Muslim countries set in. Local authorities cracked down on suspected agents and affiliates of al-Qaeda, and in June 2002 the government arrested three Saudis on Moroccan soil, announcing that it had foiled an al-Qaeda plot to attack American and British ships in the Strait of Gibraltar. The spate of global terrorist activity since then, like the Madrid and London bombings, has not spared Morocco. Suicide bombings took place in Casablanca in 2003 and 2007, but, given the random and unpredictable nature of terrorism, travelers to Morocco face little elevated risk.

The dispute over control of the **Western Sahara** continues. In 2002, the European Union moved to send $13.3 million in aid to refugees from the Western Sahara, now displaced to southwestern Algeria. In 2007 and 2008, Morocco and the native Polisario Front undertook negotations over the future of the region. Unfortunately, little progress has been made, with Saharan refugees facing an uncertain future and the disputed status of the territory likely to persist.

Border disputes have strained relations between Morocco and Spain, causing clashes over immigration, fishing rights, and oil exploration in disputed waters. The island of Perejil was occupied by Moroccan soldiers in late July

2002 before being retaken in a peaceful operation by an elite team of Spanish commandos. Morocco, which claims sovereignty over the island, justified sending troops there by establishing an observation post to tackle illegal immigration and drug smuggling across the Strait of Gibraltar, issues that continue to be salient for both countries.

PEOPLE AND CULTURE

LANGUAGE

Morocco is a paradise for polyglots. Although Classical Arabic is the official language of Morocco, it is rarely spoken and has become almost exclusively a written language. Most Moroccans speak French and the modern dialect of Arabic called **darija,** a compacted Arabic peppered with Spanish and French. In this book, city names appear first in English, then in Arabic. (Fèz is written neither as Fès, the French spelling, nor Faas, the Arabic spelling.) A massive naming shift from French to Arabic is underway on street signs, so some of the streets mentioned in this book may go by a different title (here they are listed in both French and Arabic when necessary).

RELIGION

The religion of Islam was founded by the Arab prophet **Muhammed** in AD 622. Informed of his prophetic calling by the angel Gabriel, Muhammed is believed by Muslims to be the last of a long chain of visionaries that includes Abraham, Moses, Elijah, and Jesus. During his life, Muhammed's words and deeds were recorded in *hadith* (sayings) that make up the **Sunna,** or the "way of Muhammed." Following his death, the Muslim community split into two branches: the **Sunni** and the **Shi'a.** The Sunni wanted Muhammed's successor chosen by the Islamic community, while the Shi'ites insisted on a blood relative of the prophet. More than 99% of Moroccans are Sunni Muslim, though Morocco also has a small Jewish minority and an even smaller Christian one. Islam is the official state religion.

At the heart of the Islamic faith is the Arabic word islam, meaning submission. The believer accepts submission to the will of Allah (God) as embodied in the **Qur'an** (book of recitation). This Arabic text is considered by Muslims to be a miracle—perfect, immutable, and untranslatable. All practicing Muslims adhere to the **five pillars** of Islam: the formal profession of faith, prayer toward Mecca five times per day, alms-giving, fasting during the month of Ramadan, and, if possible, a pilgrimage to Mecca. While there is a difference between popular and orthodox Islam, Morocco is marked by a smaller theological gap between religious intellectuals and the general public than in other Arab countries. Another twist is the sect of **Sufism,** traditionally popular in Morocco. It takes a mystical approach to Islam that is based on the belief that Muslims will find the truth of God's love and knowledge through a personal experience with God. Sufis have seen a spiritual revival since the 1980s. Morocco has also had its share of Islamic **fundamentalist movements,** but the country faces substantially less religious unrest than other North African and Middle Eastern countries.

FOOD AND DRINK

EATING OUT

Moroccan chefs lavish aromatic and colorful spices on their dishes—ginger, cumin, saffron, honey, and sugar. Staples of Moroccan cuisine are couscous, tajine, and soups, with a blend of spices known as *ras al-hanut* lending the cuisine its distinctive flavor. **Tajine** is a stew of meat, vegetables, olives, and prunes named after the cone-shaped clay dish in which it is cooked. Vegetarian tajines are common as well. **Couscous** is a semolina-grain pasta about the size of sesame seeds, usually served with stewed meat or vegetables. Most Moroccan entrees include meat, but *couscous aux légumes* (couscous with vegetables) is a great vegetarian option. **Harira,** a chickpea soup, is very popular, and **baguettes, Moroccan breads,** and **honey-soaked pastries** are everywhere.

Common dishes include *poulet* (chicken), which can be prepared either *rôti* (roasted on a spit with olives) or *limon* (with lemon). Look for *kefta* (ground beef cooked in an array of herbs and spices), often served on a baguette. Other specialties include **mechoui,** whole lamb spitted over an open fire, and **pastilla,** a combination of pigeon or chicken, onions, almonds, eggs, butter, cinnamon, and sugar under a pastry shell. For a lighter treat, slurp sweet natural **yogurt** with mounds of peaches, nectarines, or strawberries, or try an oily Moroccan **salad** with finely chopped tomatoes, cucumbers, and onions. Snackers can munch on briny olives, roasted almonds, dried chickpeas, and cactus buds. **Lunchtime** runs from noon to 2pm, **dinner** from 7 to 9pm. If a service charge isn't automatically included, a 10% **tip** should suffice.

DRINKING

Despite the Islamic prohibition against **alcohol,** Moroccan, French, and Spanish wines can be found in supermarkets and restaurants. Moroccan bars are entirely male and often frequented largely by foreigners. More pleasant are the many **coffee houses** where you can relax with inexpensive Moroccan and French-pressed coffee and espresso. **Moroccan mint tea,** green tea steeped with mint leaves and saturated with sugar, defines the rhythm of the day in Morocco. Whether it is a steaming glass in the *kasbah* or a shared pot in an Atlas village, savor the ritual and the company. When you leave, you may discover you have become as addicted as most Moroccans.

CUSTOMS AND ETIQUETTE

TABOOS. Avoid clothing that exposes too much flesh. Modest clothing for both men and women is recommended, particularly in more rural areas. Even properly dressed non-Muslims are barred from entering many of Morocco's active mosques. Taboo topics to avoid in conversation with Moroccans include sex, Israel and Palestine, the royal family, and the Western Sahara.

PUBLIC BEHAVIOR. Tourists in larger areas are susceptible to the advances of Moroccans offering to guide them. If you refuse, be polite but insistent. Western women tend to attract attention from Moroccan men. In general, the best way to react is not at all. Toning down public visibility is always smart.

TABLE MANNERS. A traditional Moroccan meal begins with handwashing. Dinner may be served from a communal dish at a low, round table. Avoid directly using your left hand when eating, as this hand is traditionally reserved for personal hygiene. In more personal settings, such as in a Moroccan home, vocally praising the food is important.

THE ARTS

Art is a constant presence in Morocco. The traditional and contemporary art scene in Morocco has an undeniable vibrancy, whether through architecture, handicrafts, literature, dance, or song. Foreign fascination with Morocco is nothing new, as the country has entranced Western painters, writers, and travelers for centuries. Painters like Eugene Delacroix helped spread the idea of Orientalism with his exoticized, 19th century images of souks and sultans, but today's scene is one of hybrid literature, bursting colors, and thumping beats.

ART AND ARCHITECTURE

Moroccan **mosques** (sometimes called *djemma* or *masjid*) unite Islamic culture and devotion in elegant and functional places of worship. The *qibla* (wall) contains the *mihrab* (prayer niche) and faces Mecca. Attached to most mosques, Qur'anic *medersas* (schools, also *madrasas*) have classrooms, libraries, and a prayer hall around a central courtyard and fountain. **Islamic art** avoids portraying people, animals, and plants, and as a result it is rich in colorful geometric designs on tiles, woodwork, stone, and ceramics. **Calligraphy,** particularly elegant illuminations of Qur'anic verses, melds religious imagery with high art. Sultans reserved their most dazzling designs for imperial **palaces,** with long, symmetrical reception and dwelling rooms studded with decorative gates, hidden gardens, and tiny pools and fountains. **Berber architecture** in the Atlas Mountains and the southern desert, in contrast, is stark and enclosed. Kasbahs, monumental fortress-like structures, feature plain facades, thick walls, central courtyards, narrow passageways, and simple high towers. Walled Berber villages, known as *qsour* (or a *qsar*), house densely packed mud-brick houses.

R-E-S-P-E-C-T. Non-Muslims are usually prohibited from entering Moroccan mosques, although visitors may glimpse the splendor of interior courtyards from doorways. Non-Muslim guests should keep a respectful distance during prayers, which occur five times per day.

CRAFTS

Morocco is a paradise for **carpet** connoisseurs, with astounding regional patterns, colors, and materials, while the leather industry is equally renowned. The glazed tiles that make up a *zellij*, or **mosaic,** can be found on everything from mirrors to tables, but Moroccan **ceramics** are just as ubiquitous and just as striking. Vibrant swirls of blue, green, yellow, and turquoise mark dishes of all shapes and sizes, and Fez is particularly famous for its blue-and-white designs. Saharan and Berber **terra cotta** ware is also common. The south is known for **silver** jewelry, often inlaid with colorful stones or glass. Moroccan **woodwork,** too, is impressive; craftsmen transform blocks of cedar into delicate, intricately carved objets d'art. Moroccan *souqs* (markets) are filled with these local handicrafts. **Bargaining** is serious business, as much a cultural art form as an everyday activity. Engage with vigor: a reasonable final price should be about 50% of your seller's original quote. If you hit a standstill, walk out the door: the owner may just chase after you with a better offer.

MUSIC

In the north, a hybrid genre known as **Andaloussi** is played on instruments like the *bendir* (tambourine), *oud* (lute), and *darbuqa* (hand drum), setting classical poetry against complex musical structures. Developed in Granada in the ninth century, Arab-Andalusian music took hold in Morocco after the Muslim expulsion from Spain in 1492. **Berber** folk music is a communal, emotive celebration of life and art, often incorporating dance in village performances and rituals. **Gnaoua,** a style of hypnotic trance music with roots in sub-Saharan Africa, makes its mark with an annual festival in **Essaouira** (p. 485). Moroccan popular music is heavily influenced by **Rai,** a rebellious, polyglot pop born in urban Algeria. International superstars in the Maghreb canon include **Cheb Mami, Rachid Taha,** and **Cheb Khaled.**

LITERATURE

IN TRANSLATION. Moroccan intellectuals in the 1930s were instrumental precursors of the writers who are active today. Moroccan writers work in Arabic, French, and Spanish, and much of this work can be found in translation. Paul Bowles published the tales of storyteller **Mohammad Mrabet** in the 60s and 70s in books such as *The Lemon* and *M'hashis.* In *Dreams of Trespass: Tales of a Moroccan Girlhood*, **Fatima Mernissi** writes about the constraints facing women in a Fez harem in the 1950s. Contemporary, internationally acclaimed writers include **Mohamed Choukri, Driss Chraïbi, Mohamed Zafzaf,** and **Driss El Khouri.**

ON MOROCCO. Most foreign literature focuses on the country's intoxicating culture and landscape. *In Morocco*, by **Edith Wharton,** describes her travels through Rabat, Salé, Fez, and Meknes in the early 20th century. *The Voices of Marrakech*, by Bulgarian Nobel laureate **Elias Canetti,** eloquently records a European Jew's encounter with the Jewish community of Morocco in the 50s. In these same years, Morocco was a haven for expatriates and foreign writers like **Paul Bowles, Tennessee Williams, Jack Kerouac,** and **William S. Burroughs.** No reading list would be complete without *The Sheltering Sky*, *The Spider's House*, and *Days: Tangier Journal*, all by Bowles. For insight into the country's social history, pick up *The House of Si Abd Allah*, edited by noted scholar **Henry Munson,** which recounts an oral history of a Moroccan family.

SPORTS AND RECREATION

Moroccans are passionate about **soccer. Basketball** is a distant runner-up but has widespread appeal. The country also has a history of Olympic medalist track stars, and annual marathons in the Atlas Mountains and in Marrakesh make Morocco a prime destination for **runners. Skiing** is common in the Atlas Mountains (from late December to early March), and breathtaking **walking** and **trekking** can be undertaken across the country, particularly in the Rif and Atlas ranges. **Watersports** are popular on the Atlantic coast, and Morocco is also a popular destination for **cyclists** and **mountain bikers.**

NATIONAL HOLIDAYS

The following table lists national holidays. The dates of all Muslim holidays, which begin at sundown before the day listed, are based on the lunar calendar and are valid for 2009.

DATE	HOLIDAYS
January 1	New Year's Day
January 11	Independence Manifest
May 1	Labor Day
August 14	Reunification Day
August 20	Anniversary of the King's and People's Revolution
August 21	Young People's Day—celebrates the king's birthday
November 6	Anniversary of the Green March on Western Sahara
November 18	Independence Day
August 21-September 19	Ramadan
September 20	Eid al-Fitr
November 27	Eid al-Adha
December 18	Islamic New Year

ESSENTIALS

The information in this section is designed to help travelers get their bearings once they are in Morocco. For info about general travel preparations (including passports and permits, money, health, packing, international transportation, and more), consult the Essentials section at the beginning of this guide.

ENTRANCE REQUIREMENTS

Passport: Required for all citizens of United Kingdom, Canada, Australia, New Zealand, South Africa, Ireland, and the United States.

Visa: Required in addition to passport for citizens of South Africa.

International Driving Permit (p. 30). Required for all those planning to drive in Morocco, although foreign licenses with photo ID may be accepted.

EMBASSIES AND CONSULATES

In Morocco, most embassies and consulates are open Monday through Friday from around 8am to noon; some reopen after lunch until 6pm.

British Embassy: 28 Av. SAR Sidi Mohammed, Souissi, Rabat (☎+212 37 63 33 33). **Consulates:** Villa Les Sallurges, 36 Rue de la Loire, Polo, Casablanca (☎+212 022 85 74 00); Trafalgar House, 9 Rue Amerique du Sud, Tangier (☎+212 39 93 69 39).

Canadian Embassy: 13 bis, Jaafar As-Saddik, BP 709, Agdal, Rabat (☎+212 37 68 74 00; www.dfait-maeci.gc.ca/morocco).

Irish Honorary Consulate: COPRAGRI Bldg., Bd. Moulay Ismail km 6300, Route de Rabat, Aïn Sebaâ, Casablanca (☎+ 212 22 66 03 06).

Australian Embassy: Refer to the Canadian Embassy in Rabat (above). In case of emergency, contact any Commonwealth embassy.

New Zealand Embassy: Refer to the New Zealand Embassy in Spain (p. 8). In case of emergency, contact any Commonwealth embassy.

South African Embassy: 34 Rue de Saadiens, Rabat (☎+212 37 70 67 60).

US Embassy: 2 Av. de Mohammed El Fassi, Rabat (☎+212 037 76 22 65, after-hours 76 96 39). Consulate: 8 Bd. Moulay Youssef, Casablanca (☎+212 22 22 14 60).

TRANSPORTATION

BY PLANE

If you hope to see a lot of Morocco in a short time, flying may be your best option. **Royal Air Maroc** (www.royalairmaroc.com), Morocco's national airline, flies to and from most major cities in Europe, including Madrid and Lisboa. Domestically, a network of flights radiates from the Mohammed V Airport outside Casablanca. Flights connect Marrakesh, Rabat, Tangier, Fez, Agadir, and other Moroccan cities at least once per day. **Regional Airlines** (www.regionalmaroc.com) flies from Barcelona, Las Palmas, Lisboa, Madrid, and Málaga and offers many domestic routes, including Agadir, Casablanca, and Tangier. Some of the cheapest flights between Europe and Morocco, however, can be found on smaller budget carriers. For last-minute deals and internet specials, compare routes on airlines like **easyJet, Ryanair, Click Air,** and **Atlas Blue.**

BY FERRY

One of the most popular modes of travel between Spain and Morocco is by crossing the Strait of Gibraltar by ferry. Spanish government-run **Trasmediterránea** (☎902 16 01 80; www.balearia.net); leaves Algeciras's Estación Marítima for Ceuta and Tangier. Other companies include **EuroFerries, BuqueBus, Comanov, Comarit, FRS,** and **Limadet,** which operate upwards of sixteen weekly crossings per route. Crossing times vary from 30min. to 1½hr. depending on the ship. Passengers should expect to fill out a customs form and present their passport for an entry stamp before disembarking for Morocco.

BY TRAIN

Trains in Morocco are faster than buses, more comfortable, fairly reliable, and prompt. Second-class train tickets are slightly more expensive than corresponding CTM bus fares; first-class tickets cost around 20% more than those second-class. The main line runs from Tangier via Rabat and Casablanca to Marrakesh. A spur connects Fez, Meknes, and points east. Tickets bought on board cost at least 10% more and may cause trouble with the conductor.

BY BUS

Plan well ahead if you plan to use buses as your method of transport. They're not all that fast or comfortable, but they are extremely cheap and travel to nearly every corner of the country. **Compagnie de Transports du Maroc (CTM),** the state-owned line, has the fastest, most luxurious, most reliable, and generally most expensive buses. In many cities, CTM has a station separate from other lines; reservations are usually not necessary. *Let's Go* lists CTM stations in each city. Several dozen private companies operate as well. Other private companies, called *cars publiques* (a.k.a. *souq* buses), have more departures but are slower and much less comfortable. In bus stations, each company has its own info window; window-hop for information on destinations and schedules. The baggage check at CTM bus depots is usually safe. Your bags, however, may not be accepted for storage if you don't have padlocks on the zippers. Private bus companies also have baggage checkrooms.

BY TAXI

Two separate hordes of taxis prowl Moroccan streets: intra-urban *petit taxis* and inter-urban *grand taxis,* both dirt cheap by European standards. *Petit taxis* hold a maximum of three passengers and are all painted in one color depending on the municipality. Make sure the driver turns the meter on; they are required to do so by law. Otherwise, agree on the price before you go (around 50% of what the driver asks is fair). There is a 50% surcharge after 8pm in most localities. Don't be surprised if the driver stops for other passengers or picks you up with other passengers in the car, but, if you are picked up after the meter has been started, note the initial price. *Grand taxis* are the most expensive way to travel but go just about everywhere. Unlike their *petit* cousins, they don't usually cruise for passengers, congregating instead at a central area in town. They hold up to six passengers, but, if you're planning a long ride, you might buy two spaces to allow for extra room. A taxi won't go until it is filled, and ask other passengers what they are paying to avoid being ripped off.

BY CAR AND BY THUMB

There are two reasons to rent a car in Morocco: large group travel and destinations not reached by Morocco's public transportation system. Otherwise, rental is unnecessary. Roads can be very dangerous; reckless passing maneuvers, excessive speed, shoddy maintenance, and poorly equipped vehicles are all common. Multinational car rental chains **Hertz, Avis,** and **Europcar** all have branches in Morocco. Large local firms such as **Afric Car, Moroloc,** and **Locoto** offer cars for considerably less money but may also be less reliable. Both international and local firms are easy to find in all major cities. Before you leave the lot, make sure that you have a full spare, a complete toolkit, and a good map. Once on the road, you face a myriad of complications, the most serious being **security checks.** Virtually any trip will bring you to at least one checkpoint. Expect to be pulled over and asked to produce your passport and proof of rental. You also may be stopped for traffic violations, real or not. The fine is payable on the spot in dirhams. Whatever you do, do not travel with drugs in your car. **Hitchhiking** is very rare among travelers in Morocco, as transportation is already dirt cheap by European and North American standards. If Moroccans do pick up a foreigner, they will most likely expect payment. Hitching is more frequent in the south and in the mountains, where transportation is irregular. *Let's Go* does not recommend hitchhiking.

MONEY

In Morocco, banking hours are Monday through Friday 8:30 to 11:30am and 2:30 to 4:30pm, during Ramadan from 9:30am to 2pm. In the summer, certain banks close at 1pm and do not re-open in the afternoon. As in Europe, ATMs are the best way to change money. When changing large sums, keep in mind that it is very difficult to change currencies back upon departure. Taxes are generally included in prices, though in malls and *grandes surfaces* (larger superstores) you will find a 7% value added tax on food and a 20% tax on luxury goods.

SAFETY AND SECURITY

EMERGENCY ☎	Police: ☎19. Highway services: ☎177.

Morocco has received a bad rap, for the most part undeserved, among travelers. While the crime rate is higher than in Spain or Portugal, there is far more to Morocco than hustlers and drugs. Nevertheless, visitors should be careful. Large cities like Tangier and Fez are filled with fake guides offering tours of the city for a small price; they should be avoided. And as in all big cities, travelers should be wary of pickpocketers and aggressive panhandlers.

GLBT acceptance simply does not exist in the same way that it does in many Western countries. Travelers to Morocco should remember that homosexuality is technically a criminal offense in this country, and public displays of affection are not recommended. However, the cautious traveler will face little harassment or persecution. **Female travelers** will probably have extra difficulties traveling through Morocco without a male companion. At the very least, they should never travel alone. Visitors will feel safer and more comfortable (and will avoid offending local sensibilities) by not wearing short skirts, sleeveless tops, and shorts; moreover, females should always wear bras. Regardless, non-Moroccan women may be gawked at, commented upon, approached by hustlers, followed, or even groped. Moroccan woman may "hiss" at indecently clad female travelers. The best response to male harassers may be silence, but yelling *"shuma"* (meaning shame) may well embarrass them. If an uncomfortable situation persists, look out for a policeman.

Debates between the Moroccan government and the Algerian-based Polisario Front over possession of the **Western Sahara** resulted in a guerrilla war until the late 1980s. The UN called a cease-fire in 1991, but there are still unexploded landmines in the area. Travel to the Sahara is difficult and not recommended; clearance information can be obtained from Moroccan embassies.

HEALTH

All travelers in Morocco face a different set of health issues than in Spain and Portugal; food and waterborne diseases in particular are a common cause of illness. The CDC recommends that travelers drink only bottled or boiled water, avoiding tap water, fountain drinks, and ice cubes. It is also advisable to only eat only fruit and vegetables that are cooked and that you have peeled yourself. Stay away from food sold by street vendors and check to make sure that dairy products have been pasteurized. There is only a slight malaria risk in Morocco, but consult your doctor before leaving about the possibility of a vaccine.

While there is a public health system in Morocco, travelers should seek out private clinics, which offer the most dependent and affordable care. There are few English-speaking doctors, though French is widespread; learn a few basic words of medical vocabulary in French in case of an emergency. Private clinics are found in large cities and university towns with medical schools, such as Casablanca and Rabat. Travelers with significant medical problems that might need sudden and immediate attention are advised to stay in larger cities.

ACCOMMODATIONS

YOUTH HOSTELS

The Federation Royale des Auberges de Jeunesse (FRMAJ) is the Moroccan Hosteling International (HI) affiliate. Beds cost 45-60dh per night, and there is a surcharge for nonmembers everywhere but in Casablanca. Some hostels sell HI memberships on the spot. Call ahead for reservations. You'll probably need to bring your own sleepsack and towel, and there are usually curfew and lockout times. For hostel addresses, contact FRMAJ, Parc de la Ligue Arabe, BP 15998, Casa Principale, Casablanca 21000 (☎022 47 09 52). For more info on national youth hostel associations, see **Accommodations,** p. 35.

HOTELS

Although there is an official star system for rating hotels in Morocco, the rating reflects little more than price. Hotels that are not part of the system are not necessarily worse—standards vary greatly—but they are usually cheaper. Rooms can vary widely even within a particular hotel, so ask to see another room if you don't like the first. Cheap hotels in Morocco are extremely inexpensive—as little as 80dh per night. Listings are generally divided between medina and ville nouvelle establishments. Medina hotels are usually cheaper, but less comfortable and with fewer amenities. Hot showers, when available, may cost extra (usually less than 10dh). Many hotels offer laundry services.

CAMPING

Camping is popular and cheap (about 20dh per person), especially in the desert, mountains, and beaches. Like hotels, conditions vary widely. You can usually expect to find restrooms, but electricity is not as readily available. Use caution if camping unofficially, especially on the beaches, as theft is a problem.

KEEPING IN TOUCH

Useful communication information (including international access codes, calling card numbers, country codes, operator and directory assistance, and emergency numbers) is listed on the inside back cover of this book.

TELEPHONES. Morocco has invested hundreds of millions of dollars into modernizing its telephone system, markedly improving services. Phone offices (téléboutiques) are located in most cities. If you can't find one, head to the post office—they always have at least one phone for international calls. Remember that the initial zero (0) in city codes is dialed only when calling from another area within Morocco; from outside of Morocco the number is omitted. Local calls do not require dialing any portion of the city code. The most economical way to make international calls is with a calling card (see **By Telephone,** p. 33). To call home with a calling card, contact the operator for your service provider in Morocco by dialing the appropriate toll-free access number.

MAIL. Sending via airmail *(par avion)* can take a week to a month to reach the US or Canada. Less reliable surface mail *(par terre)* takes up to two months. Express mail *(recommandé* or *exprès postaux)*, is faster than regular airmail and more reliable. Post offices and tabacs sell stamps. For fast service (2 days to the US), your best bet is **DHL** (www.dhl.com), which has drop-off locations in major cities, or **FedEx** (www.fedex.com).

EMAIL. Cybercafes are common in major cities and more touristed towns. *Let's Go* lists internet access wherever possible.

EXPLORING MOROCCO

Northern Morocco is punctuated by ports and the occasional beach and bounded on the south by the high Rif mountains. Its valuable coastal cities, fought over by Moroccans, Berbers, Spaniards, and other European powers for centuries, have traditionally been the most common ports of entry to Morocco. This political back-and-forth, which continues today with Spanish exclaves Ceuta and Melilla, gives the north a strange flavor of a Morocco mingled with a touristed Europe. The aftertaste is not always the most pleasant, so for a better experience of an older, unadulterated Morocco, keep on pushing south.

TANGIER ☎039

For travelers venturing out of Europe for the first time, Tangier (pop. 600,000) can be overwhelming. The heat and the hustlers often leave uninspiring first impressions, but the energy and history, as well as the novelty for daytrippers, keep travelers coming. For centuries, the region bounced from one imperial power to the next, resulting in the 1923 with the declaration of Tangier as an "international zone" loosely governed by the US and eight European powers. Law enforcement dwindled, and the city began to attract rich heiresses, drug users, spies, and Beat Generation poets. When Morocco declared its independence in 1956, the new government tried to change Tangier's image, closing down most of the brothels and increasing police presence. Nowadays, the city has been reclaimed by Moroccans, and continues to thrive—its position as a gateway to Africa will keep the city moving, no matter who's in charge.

TRANSPORTATION

Flights: Royal Air Maroc, Pl. France (☎039 37 95 08). Domestic and international flights. **Iberia,** at the airport (☎039 39 34 33), flies daily to Madrid. A taxi to the airport, 16km from Tangier, costs 80-100dh for up to 6 people.

Trains: Trains leave from **Tanger Ville,** 4km south of the town center (not the old station on Av. d'Espagne). A *petit taxi* there costs around 10dh. To: **Asilah** (1hr., 4 per day, 8am-5:15pm, 15dh); **Casablanca** (7hr., 4 per day 8am-9pm, 118dh); **Fez** (5hr., 1 per day, 97dh) via **Meknes** (5hr., 81dh); and **Marrakesh** (11hr., 9:05pm, 275dh).

Buses: Non-CTM buses leave from Av. Yacoub al-Mansour at Pl. Jamia al-Arabia, 2km from the port entrance. Ask blue-coated personnel or check the boards for ticket information. The standard price for luggage is 5dh. A *petit taxi* from the port to the terminal costs around 8dh. From window #11 to: **Asilah** (11am, 4:30pm); from window #2 to **Casablanca** (6hr., every hr. 5am-1am) via **Rabat** (4-5hr.); **Marrakesh** (10hr., 6 per day, 6:45am-1am); from window #3 to: **Chefchaouen** (6 per day 5:45am-5:45pm); **Ceuta** (40min., 7 per day 6:15am-2:45pm); **Fez** (6hr., 5:30am, 6pm); **Tetouan** (21 per day, 5:30am-9:15 pm). The **CTM station** (☎039 93 11 72) near the port entrance offers pricier, less frequent service to the same destinations. To: **Casablanca** (6hr., 5 per day 5:30am-midnight, 140dh); **Chefchaouen** (3hr., 12:15, 8pm, 40dh); **Fez** (6hr., 5 per day 9:15am-9:15pm, 115dh) via **Meknes** (5hr., 100dh; **Marrakesh** (10hr.; 3 per day 11:15am, 2:45, 5:30pm; 220dh); and **Tetouan** (1hr.; 12:15, 8pm; 20dh).

Ferries: The cheapest and most convenient option is to buy a ticket at the very end of the ferry terminal, where company offices are located, though ticket agencies are

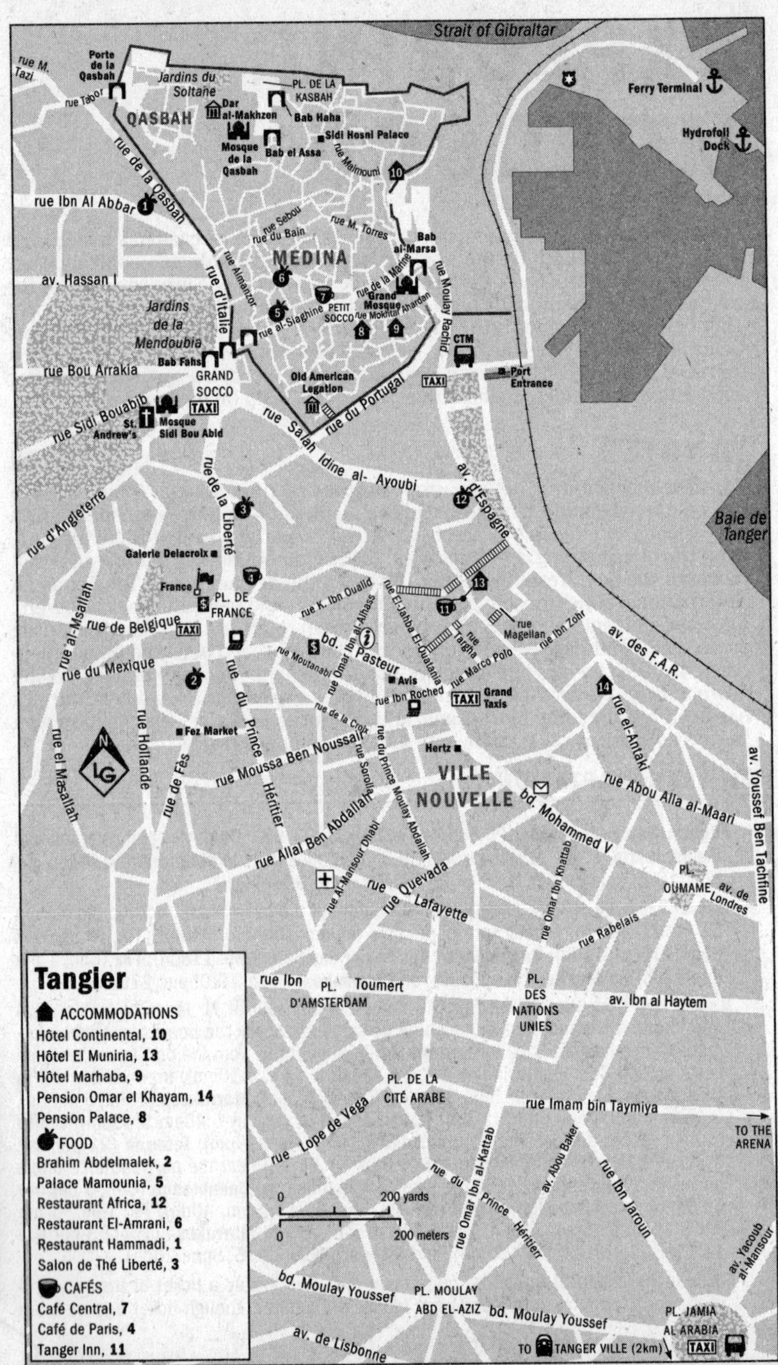

Tangier
ACCOMMODATIONS
Hôtel Continental, 10
Hôtel El Muniria, 13
Hôtel Marhaba, 9
Pension Omar el Khayam, 14
Pension Palace, 8
FOOD
Brahim Abdelmalek, 2
Palace Mamounia, 5
Restaurant Africa, 12
Restaurant El-Amrani, 6
Restaurant Hammadi, 1
Salon de Thé Liberté, 3
CAFÉS
Café Central, 7
Café de Paris, 4
Tanger Inn, 11
Strait of Gibraltar
Ferry Terminal
Hydrofoil Dock
Porte de la Qasbah
Jardins du Soltane
QASBAH
Dar al-Makhzen
Mosque de la Qasbah
Bab el Assa
Bab Haha
PL. DE LA KASBAH
Sidi Hosni Palace
MEDINA
Bab al-Marsa
Grand Mosque
PETIT SOCCO
Old American Legation
GRAND SOCCO
Bab Fahs
Jardins de la Mendoubia
St. Andrew's
Mosque Sidi Bou Abid
CTM
Port Entrance
Galerie Delacroix
France
PL. DE FRANCE
Avis
Grand Taxis
Fez Market
Hertz
VILLE NOUVELLE
Baie de Tanger
PL. OUMAME
PL. D'AMSTERDAM
PL. DES NATIONS UNIES
PL. DE LA CITÉ ARABE
PL. MOULAY ABD EL-AZIZ
PL. JAMIA AL ARABIA
TO THE ARENA
TO TANGER VILLE (2km)
0 200 yards
0 200 meters

located throughout the city. You'll need a boarding pass (available at any ticket desk) and a customs form (ask uniformed agents). Near the terminal, pushy men with ID cards will try to arrange your ticket and fill out your customs card for 10dh; just do it yourself. **FRS** (☎039 94 76 12) sends fast ferries to **Tarifa** (every 2hr. 8am-10pm; passenger 372 dh, car 920dh). **Euroferrys** (☎039 94 81 990) goes to **Algeciras** (7am and 4pm. Single ticket 526dh; car 1923dh).

Taxis: *Grand taxis* to nearby locations. Prices subject to bargaining; a fair price for 6 passengers is 20dh per person. Found everywhere, especially by the main bus stop, the Grand Socco, and the intersection of Blvd. Pasteur and Blvd. Mohammed V.

Car Rental: Avis, 54 Blvd. Pasteur (☎039 93 46 46). English spoken. Cars from 650dh per day with tax and insurance included. AmEx/MC/V. Min. age 25 for all cars. A special international license is not required. Open daily 8am-7pm.

ORIENTATION

Av. d'Espagne, a large boulevard that runs from the port along the waterfront to the train station 6km away, makes Tangier easy to navigate. Many of the *ville nouvelle* hotels are located about 1.5km down Av. d'Espagne away from the ferry terminal (a *petit taxi* should cost 5dh, but if you don't have a lot of baggage and you have your wits about you, just walk). Hustlers tend to swoop in here. Adjacent to the ferry terminal area on Ave. d'Espagne is the CTM station. **Rue du Portugal** heads uphill here and forms the border between the *ville nouvelle* and the medina. You can enter the medina and easily find some of its accommodations by turning right above the CTM station, continuing uphill on **Rue de la Plage.** You will reach the large, busy rotary known as the **Grand Socco,** which is the center of activity directly above the medina. From the Grand Socco, you can head down into the medina via **Rue al-Siaghin,** which leads to the **Petit Socco,** or walk down the bustling **Rue d'Italie** (if facing the medina, the street on the left through the large archway), which skirts the medina's western wall. The *ville nouvelle's* main commercial road is the **Blvd. Pasteur,** which connects the main square, **Pl. de France,** with **Blvd. Mohammed V.** Banks, the post office, and cafes can all be found on Blvd. Mohammed V.

PRACTICAL INFORMATION

Tourist Office: 29 Blvd. Pasteur (☎039 94 80 50). Some English, French, and Spanish spoken. Glossy brochures and basic map of the city, but nothing to get excited about. List of accommodations available. Open M-F 8:30am-noon and 2-7:20pm.

Currency Exchange: There is a branch of **BMCE** on most ferries and one in the port complex, although these only change cash. BMCE's main office in Tangier is located at 21 Blvd. Pasteur (☎039 93 11 25). No commission here, but other Moroccan banks charge fees for exchanging traveler's checks. Open M-F 9am-1pm and 3-7pm. Major banks line Blvd. Pasteur and Blvd. Mohammed V, several of which have **ATMs.** Travel agencies near the port are required to change money at official rates. There are **Western Union** locations at Pl. de France and the main post office.

Luggage Storage: At the train station (10dh per bag). Open 24hr. Also at the bus station (7dh per bag). Both open daily 6am-1am.

Police: ☎19. At the port and main train station. At the port, ask for the **Brigade Touristique,** which deal with issues and complaints from travelers.

Medical Services: Red Crescent, 6 Rue al-Mansour Dahbi (☎039 94 25 17), runs a 24hr. medical service. **Ambulance:** ☎039 31 27 27.

Internet Access: Several cafes in the *ville nouvelle,* including **Cyber Café Adam,** 2 Rue Ibn Roched, off Blvd. Pasteur and Blvd. Mohammed V. 10dh per hr. Open daily 8:30am-2am. **Espace Net** is on Ave. de Mexique, 1 block from Pl. de Paris.

Laundry: Pressing Jemelas, 20 Rue de las Once (☎063 22 21 98), off the Petit Socco and around the corner. 6-7dh per garment.

Post Office: 33 Blvd. Mohammed V (☎039 93 25 18), on the downhill continuation of Blvd. Pasteur. Poste Restante. Open M-Th 8:30am-6:30pm, Sa 8:30am-12:15pm. Parcels received around the corner from main entrance, on the back side of the building.

ACCOMMODATIONS

Whether you stay in the *ville nouvelle* or medina, you are bound to meet some hustlers "welcoming" you to Morocco. Your best bet is to ignore them and look like you know where you're going, even if you don't. In late summer, reservations are a good idea, as hotels fill up. Accommodations in the *ville nouvelle* generally offer more comfort and cleanliness, which is definitely worth the extra dirhams. Singles run from 50-80dh. In many places you'll have to pay for a hot shower, and you will definitely have to bring your own toilet paper.

MEDINA

The most convenient hostels are near Rue Mokhtar Ahardan, off the Petit Socco. From the Grand Socco, take the first right down Rue al-Siaghin to the Petit Socco, which is really a small intersection. Rue Mokhtar Ahardan begins at the end of the Petit Socco closest to the port. At night, the smaller streets off the medina can be unsafe.

Pension Palace, 2 Rue Mokhtar Ahardan (☎039 93 61 28). Downhill, on the alley exiting the Petit Socco to the right. The gorgeous courtyard, full of plants and tilework, starred in Bertolucci's adaptation of *The Sheltering Sky.* Clean, soft beds and one stark lightbulb. Communal toilets could use lids. Singles 50dh; doubles 100dh, with bath 150dh; triples 150/200dh; quads 200/260dh. ❶

Hotel Marhaba, 14 Rue de la Poste (☎039 93 88 02), to the left off of Mokhtar Ahardan. Set back off the madness of the medina, it's clean and not crumbling—a relief from some of the other budget options in the neighborhood. Big beds and sinks in all the rooms, and the showers are clean. Hot showers 7dh. Singles 80dh, doubles 100dh. ❷

Hôtel Continental, 36 Dar Baroud (☎039 93 10 24), overlooking the port. From the ferry terminal, bear right around the CTM station, and follow the many signs. A splurge for comfort and ambience. A grand hotel furnished with a mix of Moroccan ornament and Art Deco. Nice terrace overlooks less appealing port and warehouses. Wi-Fi available. Breakfast included. Showers hot only in the mornings. Reservations recommended. Singles 426dh, doubles 552dh, triples 668dh. MC/V. ❺

VILLE NOUVELLE

Hotels line Av. d'Espagne heading away from the port. The best values lie a few blocks uphill toward Blvd. Pasteur and Blvd. Mohammed V.

Hôtel El Muniria, Rue Magellan (☎039 93 53 37). From the port, walk south along the tree-lined pedestrian walkway. Take 1st right after Hôtel Biarritz on Av. d'Espagne walking away from the medina, and follow as it winds uphill. William Burroughs wrote *Naked Lunch* in room #9, and Jack Kerouac and Allen Ginsberg stayed in room #4. A great deal for Tangier, with spacious rooms, hot showers, and towels. Attached bar (**Tanger Inn,** see p. 467) is the hippest place in town. Singles 150dh, doubles 180dh. ❷

Pensión Omar El Khayam, 26 Ave. Antaki (☎063 71 84 60), up the hill from Av. d'Epagne past the port. In a distinctive yellow-brick imitation Moorish house, this *pensión* offers clean, neat, tiled rooms. Communal baths old, but clean and serviceable. Hot showers included—a plus. Singles 80dh, with bath 120dh; doubles 120/150dh. ❶

FOOD

MEDINA

The **Grand Socco** is home to fruit stalls, sandwich joints, and juice stands galore, so pick and choose before heading down to the **Petit Socco,** where there are cheap eateries on all sides. **La Rue d'Italie** is the place to go for a sit-down meal, with Moroccan and European fare side by side.

Restaurant Hammadi, 2 Rue de la Kasbah (☎039 93 45 14), the continuation of Rue d'Italie just outside the medina walls. Moroccan carpets, plush booths, and a group of local musicians set the ambience and attract tourists in droves. Specialties are *tajine* (40dh) and couscous (45dh). Beer and wine served. Entrees 40-60dh. 10% tax added to each meal. Open daily 11am-3pm and 7pm-midnight. MC/V. ❷

Restaurant El-Amrani, at the end of Rue Smihi. From the Grand Socco, walk down Rue d'Italie and head through the first gate (Bab Rahbat Zraa), and follow Smihi to the end. A hole-in-the-wall joint where old Moroccan men come to get heaping plates of beans and meat or fish (15-25dh) or the delicious **watermelon** (8dh). Unless you speak Arabic, ordering will involve a bit of charades, but it's worth it. ❶

Palace Mamounia, 4 Rue al-Siaghine (☎039 93 50 99), towards the Petit Socco. Elegant dining upstairs among wicker chairs, shady arbor, and huge Moroccan vases. Take note of the 15% service charge before you sit down. Massive Moroccan set menu 100dh. Open daily 8am-10pm. ❸

VILLE NOUVELLE

The restaurants along **Av. d'Espagne** tout unspectacular and overpriced *menus touristiques* for 50dh and up. Beachfront restaurants run by high-end hotels are what you might expect—expensive and boring. You're better off scouting around **Pl. France** or grabbing a hot sandwich along **Blvd. Pasteur.**

Salon de Thé Liberté, 47 Rue de la Liberté. The cafe on the street is excellent for people-watching, but the secret garden, niftily hidden in the back, offers a better and quieter place to chow down on Moroccan favorites (meat dishes 35-45dh) and Western dishes alike. Spaghetti 15-35dh. Couscous 45dh. Open 8am-10:30pm. ❷

Brahim Abdelmalek, 14 Rue de Mexique (☎039 93 17 96), under an off-white awning. Cheap sandwiches in a hurry. King Hassan II allegedly lunched here; you can too, for less than 15dh. Open daily 10:30am-3am. ❶

Restaurant Africa, 83 Rue Salah Eddine al-Ayoubi (☎039 93 54 36), just off Av. d'Espagne near Pension Miami, opposite the old train station. A quiet, unassuming place with small tables sticks to international favorites (spaghetti, hamburgers) and Moroccan staples. Beer and wine served. Big 4-course *menu du jour* 50dh. Entrees 35-45dh. Open daily 9am-12:30am. ❷

SIGHTS

IN AND NEAR THE MEDINA

OLD AMERICAN LEGATION. The old legation is quirky and fascinating look at early American history. In 1821, this became the first foreign property acquired by the United States. The museum contains correspondence between George Washington and his "great and magnanimous friend" **Sultan Moulay ben Abdallah**—Morocco was the first nation to recognize America's independence. The legation displays a hilarious letter from the consul detailing his attempts to (unsuccessfully) refuse a gift of lions from the sultan. Visit the room dedicated to famous expat writer **Paul Bowles,** featuring photographs from Tangier's storied "interzone" days. The friendly curators will give excellent tours on request, but calling first is recommended. *(8 Rue d'America. Enter the medina via the large white steps on Rue du Portugal and look for the yellow archway emblazoned with the US seal. ☎039 93 53 17. Open M-F 10am-1pm and 3-5pm. Donation suggested.)*

ST. ANDREW'S CHURCH. In 1883 Moulay Hassan I granted this parcel of land to Great Britain to build an Anglican church. Out of respect for local architecture, it was built in a fusion of English and Moorish styles, with the roof above the altarpiece composed of intricately carved wood. A highlight is the Lord's Prayer inscribed in Arabic around the chancel arch. The cemetery outside is quiet and holds some English notables in North Africa. The church is kept locked but if you can find Mustapha, the happy, friendly caretaker, he will let you in and tell you a little about the church. *(At the end of Rue d'Angleterre. Open daily 9:30am-12:30pm and 2:30-4:30pm. Services Su at 8:30 and 11am. Donations recommended.)*

DAR AL-MAKHZEN. An opulent palace with handwoven tapestries, inlaid ceilings, and foliated archways, the Dar al-Makhzen was once home to the ruling pasha of Tangier and is now the **Museum of Moroccan Art.** The museum highlights the societies of Tangier from pre-Roman times to the Romans and Moors, with lead sarcophagi, funerary urns, pottery and musical instruments, and a gorgeous Roman mosaic depicting the voyage of Venus. It is all set around a lovely courtyard with a fountain and *zellij* tilework. The gardens in the middle are nicely shaded and a good place to hide from the heat. *(The easiest way to reach the museum and the Pl. de la Kasbah grounds is to enter the medina from Porte de la Kasbah gate and stick to the rampart wall until you reach the wide open space of Pl. de la Kasbah. The museum is to the right. ☎039 93 20 97. Open M and W-Su 9am-12:30pm and 3-5:30pm. 10dh.)*

MARKETS. The medina's commercial center is the **Grand Socco.** This busy square and traffic circle is cluttered with fruit vendors, parsley stands, and kebab and fish stalls. Off of Rue de Fez is the small, colorful **Fez Market,** where local merchants cater to Tangier's Europeans. *(Uphill on Rue de la Liberté, across Pl. France, and 2 blocks down Rue de Fez on the right.)* More pungent are the market stalls south of the Grand Socco, where saffron and a hundred other spices are on sale along with watermelons, dates, figs, olives, parsley, mint, melon, mango, and of course, tangerines—they originally came from Tangier, or, in French, Tanger. *(South of the Grand Socco along Rue Ayoubi and the streets off of it.)*

OTHER SIGHTS. Rue Riad Sultan runs alongside the Jardins du Soltane and continues to Pl. de la Kasbah, a sunny courtyard with a promontory offering spectacular views of Spain and the Atlantic Ocean. With your back to the water, walk toward the far right corner of the plaza. Just around the corner, to the right, the **Mosque de la Kasbah** rears its octagonal minaret. Outside the medina, 17th- and 18th-century bronze cannons hide in the **Jardins de la Mendoubia,** a welcome escape from the excitement of the Soccos. *(Opposite Rue de la Liberté, where Rue Bou Arrakia joins the Grand Socco, through the white gate marked #50.)* To laze about with a cold drink and stare across the glinting strait to Spain, head to the **Terrace des Parrasseux** (Idler's Terrace), which has benches with a clear view across to Europe. *(Off Pl. de France down Pasteur.)*

ENTERTAINMENT

The most popular evening activity in Tangier is sipping mint tea in front of a cafe on Pl. de France, in Blvd. Pasteur, or in Ville Nouvelle, which does have its share of small bars. The **Café de Paris,** 1 Pl. de France, hosted countless meetings between spies during WWII. Coming from the Grand Socco, look to the left. (☎039 93 84 44. Tea and coffee 5-6dh. Open daily 7am-11:30pm.) Inside the medina, **Café Central** was a favorite of William S. Burroughs, but today is mostly a hangout for middle-aged Moroccan men. (Off the Petit Socco; same hours and prices as Café de Paris). **Café Hafa,** an old Paul Bowles haunt, has a great view of Spain on a clear day. Sipping a mint tea (5dh) on one of the cafe's many terraces is a great way to clear your head of the city's bustle, and worth getting lost on the way there. (From the Kasbah, follow Rue Tabor for 10 minutes. When you can see the water through the buildings to the right, head toward it; it's down a street to the left. You may have to ask around to find it. Open daily 10am-8pm.) Cafes tend to attract a male crowd, but female tourists should not be afraid to grab a table and an orange juice, as it is perfectly acceptable. For a harder drink, there are few spots with ambience that attracts both genders in equal number. The hippest place in town is **Tanger Inn,** Rue Magellan, next to Hotel Muniria. Subdued house music attracts men and women, both local and foreign, for a nice cosmopolitan mix. A good place to sit back and nurse a drink (beer 20dh) at the end of the day. (Open daily 10pm-1am, until late Th-Sa.)

CEUTA (SEBTA) ☎039

Travelers hoping to avoid Tangier altogether may opt to ferry to the Spanish enclave Ceuta (pop. 75,000; called Sebta within Morocco) and from there cross the Moroccan border, only 5km away. There isn't much to keep you in Ceuta, and little to see besides some old walls and a monument to Franco. It is advisable to keep moving on immediately to Tetouan (35min.) or Chefchaouen (allow 4hr.), but if you're stuck in Ceuta, try the helpful **tourist booth** (☎956 50 62 75) in the ferry terminal, which has a map. Ceuta doesn't have much in the way of budget options, but if you're here overnight, try **Pensión la Bohemia ❸,** Paseo de la Revellín, 16. To get here, follow the water to Pl. de la Constitución and then head half a block down Po. de la Revellín. A dark hallway leads up to clean, small rooms. (Singles and doubles €35. Cash only.)

BORDER CROSSING. To reach the Moroccan border from Ceuta, grab a taxi from the town center (€6-7) or take bus #7 (€0.70); to reach the bus stand from the ferry (5min.), exit the terminal and take a left onto the main street. At the end of the street, near a roundabout with a fountain in the middle (and near the water), take a right up the hill, and then another right to the stand. Taxis and buses stop short of the border; you must cross on foot and have your passport stamped. Expect to be accosted by guides wanting to escort you to their cousin's rug emporium. Head straight to the parking lot, where *grand taxis* await (p. 457). Cash exchange is available at the border; do it here rather than in Ceuta. From the border, full *grand taxis* to Tetouan are 15-20dh per person. From there you can connect to the more mellow Chefchaouen by catching a bus or taxi. If you are heading to **Algeciras** from Ceuta, you can use one of several ferry companies (**Balearia** and **Acciona Trasmediterranea** among them) that offer fast service (35min., every hr. 7am-9pm, €40-45). Don't forget about the **time difference** between Spain and Morocco—Spain is 1hr. ahead, and 2hr. during daylight savings time.

CHEFCHAOUEN (CHAOUEN) ☎039

Tucked high in the Rif is the small, gleaming town of Chefchaouen (pop. 50,000). The town's laid-back ambience, excellent location for gorgeous hiking and mountain treks, and ready availability of *kif* (hashish) have lured backpackers for decades, but the breeze and blinding blue of its enchanting medina are more than worth a few days' rest.

TRANSPORTATION

The **bus station** (☎039 98 95 73) is a long hike downhill from town; **taxis** (10-15dh) pass along the road next to the station. Most buses are just passing through, and they fill up, so get tickets as early as possible. **CTM** and other buses go to: **Fez** (5hr.; 1, 3:15, 6pm; 65 dh); via **Ouzzane,** the best bet for connections (1hr.; 25dh); **Marrakesh** (8-9hr., 4 per day 1:30-8pm); **Casablanca** (8hr., 7pm) via **Rabat** (7hr.); **Tangier** (3:15pm, 40dh); and **Tetouan** (1hr., noon, 3:15pm, 25dh). To get to **Ceuta,** you must go through **Tetouan.** Private companies also have daily buses to **Fez** and **Meknes. Grand taxis** are the easiest way to get to **Tetouan** (30dh) and **Ceuta,** although they often take a while to fill. Taxis leave a block downhill from Pl. Mohammed V on **Av. al-Massira al-Khadra.**

PRACTICAL INFORMATION

From the bus stations, head up the steep hill and turn right after several blocks onto **Av. Mohammed V,** which leads to the tree-filled, circular **Pl. Mohammed V;** the center of town is a 20min. walk (or 10-15dh cab ride). Cross the plaza and continue east on Av. Hassan II, the main road of the *ville nouvelle.* Here you'll find **currency exchange** at the **BMCE** (open M-F 8:15am-2:15pm), the **post office** with telephones (open M-F 8am-4:30pm, Sa 8am-noon) and **internet** at **IRIC,** 10 av. Hassan II. (☎039 98 97 15. 10dh per hr. Open daily 9am-midnight.) Chefchaouen has no tourist office. Down Av. Hassan II is the **Bab al-Ain,** the main gate into the medina. From Bab al-Ain, the main street twists uphill to place **Uta al-Hammam,** the plaza at the heart of the medina. Just east of Uta al-Hammam is **Place el-Majzen,** the end of Av. Hassan II, which runs past Bab al-Ain and skirts the southern edge of the medina. **Hospital Mohammed V** (☎039 18 62 28) is a block west from Pl. Mohammed V on Av. al-Massira al-Khadra, down a flight of stairs from the plaza and on the left, and **police** can be reached at ☎19.

ACCOMMODATIONS

Chefchaouen has a slew of colorful budget hotels. Inside the medina, head uphill from **Bab al-Ain.** Lodgings are clustered along these streets and around **Pl. Uta al-Hammam.** Firmly a backpackers town, Chefchaouen is full of establishments that have social common rooms and rooftop terraces.

Hotel Andaluz, 1 Rue Sidi Salem (☎039 98 60 34). Directly behind Credit Agricola on Pl. Uta al-Hammam, in the medina. Small but comfortable rooms are set around a beautiful central courtyard filled with handcrafted Moroccan furniture. Friendly owners know a great deal about the town and good local hikes. Excellent roof terrace and free book exchange. Room includes hot showers. Singles 30dh; doubles 100dh; triples 150dh. Ask to sleep on the terrace for 30dh. ❶

Pension la Castellana, 4 Sidi Ahmad Bouhali (☎039 98 62 95). Walk to the end of Pl. Uta al-Hammam. Next to a *hamman,* this place caters to backpackers and encourages long stays. Communal kitchen and common room with stereo. Free hot showers. Singles 30dh; doubles 60dh; triples 90dh; quads 120dh. ❶

Pension Anaia (☎039 88 30 19). Along Hassan II, just below Place el-Majden. Common rooms on each floor feel like hip hookah dens, with funky couches and plush cushions everywhere. Rooms vary from spacious to cramped, but all are clean. Hot water in communal showers. Singles 60dh; doubles 120dh. ❶

Hotel Rif, Rue Hassan II (☎039 98 69 82). Just outside the medina walls. Follow Rue Hassan II to the right around the medina; Hotel Rif will be on your left. American kitsch meets Moroccan vistas at Hotel Rif. The terrace offers great views, especially of the mountains to the south. Rooms are standard but clean. Staff can help with hikes. Singles 160dh, with shower 200dh; doubles 190/240dh. Breakfast included. MC/V. ❶

FOOD

Inside the medina, outdoor seating is available in Pl. Uta al-Hammam at various restaurants, which have largely identical menus but good ambience.

Chez Aziz, just outside Bab al-Ain, the medina's gate. For a quick bite, stop by for a hearty egg and meat sandwich (10-15dh). Open daily noon-midnight. ❶

Al Kasaba, just off the plaza. Al Kasaba's secluded booths are candle-lit and decked out in Berber finery. The excellent three-course menu (60dh) provides a great way to while away the evening. The savory kebabs are a good bet for dinner. ❶

Restaurant Fuentes, in Pl. Uta al-Hammam, but set back from the hustle of the plaza. Get lost in the patterned intricacies of the ceiling as hip music plays, complementing the blue light at this quiet spot. Serves up traditional Moroccan fare and pasta dishes. Plates 35-50dh. Open daily 6-10:30pm. ❶

SIGHTS

Chefchaouen's steep **medina** is one of Morocco's best to explore, perhaps because it is less crowded and more relaxed than those of larger cities. Enter through Bab al-Ain and walk uphill toward **Pl. Uta al-Hammam,** the center of the medina. The side streets are worth a look, too, as some are drenched in exquisite bright blue paint, giving the town a fresh, Mediterranean feel unlike any other in Morocco. Also worth seeing is the 17th-century **kasbah** built by Moulay Ismail, Morocco's famous rogue. Inside is a **museum** with traditional Berber garments and pictures of Chefchaouen during the Rif War. The old jail cells, with rusty leg irons on the walls, are open, as is the tower. The view of the city is worth all the stairs. (Open M and W-Su 9am-1pm and 3-6:30pm. 10dh.)

HIKING

For information on maps, trails, or contacting guides, see Ahmed at **Hotel Andaluz** or the reception at **Hotel Rif.** Follow the **Ras al-Ma River** (still known as Hippie River from the days Chefchaouen attracted many) upstream into the hills for just a few kilometers for spectacular results. For a view of the city, hike to the **Hotel Asmaq** (follow signs for the *ville nouvelle*). Behind the hotel, there's a path that winds up the peak to the left, then runs down into the valley. Try reaching the "Spanish mosque," the ruins of a mosque built by the Spanish but abandoned in the Rif War. It's about 3km up the path on a hill overlooking the town. **Jebel el-Kalaa** (1616m), the peak that towers over Chefchaouen, is a reasonable one-day hike for anyone in decent shape. To get to the trailhead, head out **Bab el-Majarrol** at the end of the medina and walk up to **Hotel Atlas Chaouen.** Alternatively, you can walk up **Moulay Ali ben Rachid** (outside Bab al-Ain) and hike through the cemetary. Walk past the hotel along the road until you reach the entrance to **Talassemtane National Park.** The gravel path (marked with a sign reading "El-Kalaa and Izelan") is the start of the trail. The

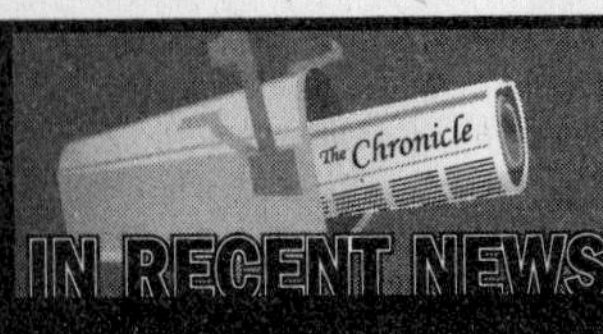

KIF IN THE RIF

With an army of backpackers passing through and something called the "Hippie River" in Chefchaouen, you might expect a little hash to be passed around in the Rif. How about as much as one-third of the world's supply?

The hills in the Rif are excellent for growing kif, the bright green shoot-like plant that can be refined into hashish. Kif has long been smoked by locals, as a milder form of hash mixed with tobacco, but it wasn't until the 60s that local farmers began to realize that the plant could be concentrated into hash and sold for enormous profit to recreational drug users all around the world.

Since then, kif has become the dominant force in the economy of the Rif, despite the fact that it's technically illegal. The ramifications have gotten more serious due to increased pressure from the US and the European Union, Morocco's primary trading partners. Nevertheless, authorities have largely turned a blind eye to the massive production and export of kif that goes on in the mountains. Perhaps, some suggest, it is a tacit acknowledgement of the crop's importance to what is otherwise a struggling and very limited local economy.

Still, when you're dealing with kif, you're playing with fire. Penalties for kif possession include up to 10 years in jail. While the locals might all be selling, kif is a risky game to play in the Rif.

first hour is a series of switchbacks through pine groves. Once you clear them, it's scrub and flowers, along with lots of grazing goats. After 2-2½hr., the trail cuts sharply to the left (almost 180°) while the 4WD track continues past the mountain. You may pass *kif* plantations along the way (look for the short, densely growing bright green shoots, the only plants being watered), but farmers generally ignore you. The final 2-3hr. to the summit follow small switchbacks through large boulders and arid scrub. The path falls apart toward the top and some scrambling may be required, but the way is clear. The hike to the summit should take 5-6hr. at a moderate pace, and the descent is obviously much quicker. Berbers frequent and live along the lower trails, and a *"la bes"* or friendly wave will be warmly reciprocated. If you do continue straight and miss the turn (you are far from alone in this club), the hiking is still gorgeous, leading though several Berber villages and past the **Sfiha Telj,** huge rocky crags that stick out of the mountains. There are a few campsites but no large settlements for at least another day's hike, so plan accordingly.

THE MIDDLE ATLAS

The Middle Atlas is Morocco's heartland, an arid stretch where empires grew and political dynasties rose and fell. The region sees ancient medinas traversed by donkeys and modern cities growing side-by-side.

FEZ ☎055, 035

The colorful, chaotic medina of Fez beats at its own crazy pace. Donkeys rush by with refrigerators on their backs, old men weave carpets and dance around dye pits with huge stacks of leather, children lead lost tourists out of alleyways, and everyone is selling something. Since UNESCO designated Fez a World Heritage Site in 1981, the city's walls have been largely restored, rebuilding a link with its long and illustrious past. Founded in the 8th century by Moulay Idriss I, Fez rose to prominence with the construction of the Qaraouiyine, one of the world's first universities, in the 9th century. Fez emerged as the Maghreb's pre-eminent city, nurturing political dynasties and handing down legal rulings to the rest of the region. Fez reconciles its identity as the oldest town in Morocco with the demands of a modern city in the *ville nouvelle,* all while managing to remain at the artistic, intellectual, and spiritual helm of the nation.

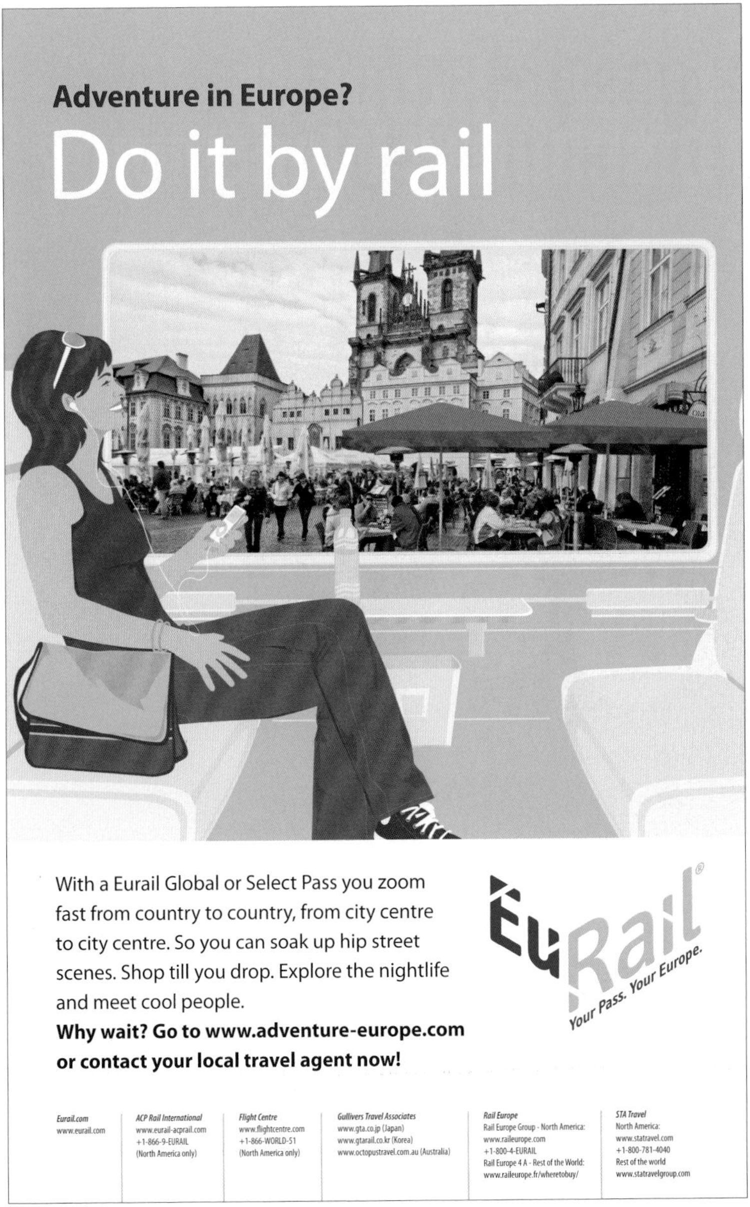
Adventure in Europe?
Do it by rail
With a Eurail Global or Select Pass you zoom fast from country to country, from city centre to city centre. So you can soak up hip street scenes. Shop till you drop. Explore the nightlife and meet cool people.
Why wait? Go to www.adventure-europe.com or contact your local travel agent now!
EuRail®
Your Pass. Your Europe.
Eurail.com
www.eurail.com
ACP Rail International
www.eurail-acprail.com
+1-866-9-EURAIL
(North America only)
Flight Centre
www.flightcentre.com
+1-866-WORLD-51
(North America only)
Gullivers Travel Associates
www.gta.co.jp (Japan)
www.gtarail.co.kr (Korea)
www.octopustravel.com.au (Australia)
Rail Europe
Rail Europe Group - North America:
www.raileurope.com
+1-800-4-EURAIL
Rail Europe 4 A - Rest of the World:
www.raileurope.fr/wheretobuy/
STA Travel
North America:
www.statravel.com
+1-800-781-4040
Rest of the world
www.statravelgroup.com

TRANSPORTATION

Flights: Aérodrome de Fès-Saïs (☎035 62 48 00), 12km out of town on the road to Immouzzèr. Bus #16 leaves from Pl. Mohammed V (3dh). *Grand taxis* (120dh) also run there. **Royal Air Maroc,** 54 Av. Hassan II (☎035 62 55 16), flies daily to **Casablanca**. Also services **Tangier, Marrakesh, Marseilles, London,** and **Paris.** Open daily 8:15am-12:30pm and 3:30-7:30pm.

Trains: Av. Almohades, at Rue Chenguit (☎055 93 03 33), a 5min. taxi ride to the ville nouvelle (5dh) or a 10min. ride to the medina's **Bab Boujeloud** (10dh). 2nd-class trains are a little pricier than buses but more than worth it. To: **Casablanca** (4hr., 15 per day, 2:10am-6:50pm); **Marrakesh** (7-8hr., 9 per day, 2:30am-6:50pm) via **Rabat** (3hr.); **Meknes** (1hr., 11 per day 2:10am-6:50pm). For **Tangier,** take a westbound train and change at Sidi Kacem junction.

Buses: CTM (☎055 73 29 92) stops near Pl. d'Atlas, at the far end of the *ville nouvelle.* From Pl. Florence, walk down Blvd. Mohammed V for 15min. and turn left onto Av. Youssef ben Tachfine. At Pl. d'Atlas, take the 1st right. To: **Casablanca** (5hr., 8 per day 6am-2am, 105dh) via **Rabat** (3hr., 75-80dh); **Chefchaouen** and **Tetouan** (4hr.; 8, 11:15am, 11:45pm; 75-90dh); **Meknes** (1hr., 9 and 11pm, 25dh); **Tangier** (6hr., 4 per day 11am-1:30am, 115dh). The **private bus station** in Fez is just outside the medina near **Bab Boujeloud,** and seems like it was designed to cause maximum confusion, with a huge number of windows for different destinations. To: **Casablanca** (25 per day 4:30am-1pm, 76dh) via **Rabat** (54dh); **Marrakesh** (5 per day 5am-9pm); **Meknes** (every 2hr. 6am-8pm).

Public Transportation: Pl. Mohammed V and Pl. de la Résistance are the major hubs for city buses. Important routes include: bus **#9** and **11** from the Syndicat d'Initiative to **Bab Boujeloud** and **Dar Batha; #19** from the train station to **Pl. Rcif** in the middle of Fez al-Bali; **#47** from the train station to **Bab Boujeloud.** City buses cost 2.50dh; fares increase 20% July-Sept. 15 after 8:30pm, Sept. 16-June after 8pm.

Car Rental: Hertz, 1 Ave. Lalla Meryem (☎035 62 28 12). Open M-Sa 8:30am-noon and 2-6:30pm, Su 9am-noon. Cars start at around 500dh per day, 20% tax not included. Minimum age 25. Domestic drivers' license required.

Taxis: *Grand taxis* go to the airport (120dh), **Meknes** (20dh per person), and **Rabat** (60-70dh per person) along with other local destinations. Stands are at the train station, the bus station, Place de la Resistance, and Bab Guissa. **Petit taxi** drivers are generally good about using the meter. Fares increase 50% after 8pm.

ORIENTATION AND PRACTICAL INFORMATION

Fez is large and spread-out but still manageable. It is essentially three cities in one: the fashionable, French-built *ville nouvelle,* 1.5km from the medina; the Arab **Fez al-Jdid** ("New Fez"), containing the Jewish cemetery and the palace of Hassan II, next to the medina; and the enormous medina of **Fez al-Bali** ("Old Fez") housing nearly 500,000 residents. The *ville nouvelle* is most convenient for services, with the quietest accommodations, and is based on **Av. Hassan II** and **Blvd. Mohammed V,** which intersect at the more central **Pl. Florence,** the center of activity. Walking down Av. Moulay Youssef from the *ville nouvelle* brings you to **Pl. Alaouites** in Fez al-Jdid, directly in front of the king's palace, **Dar al-Makhzen.** After passing through Bab Smarine on the left, Rue Fez al-Jdid follows the length of the palace. At the end, a right through Bab Dakakeen leads to Fez al-Bali and its main gate Bab Boujeloud. The two main streets of Fez al-Bali heading down from the gate are **Tala'a Kebira** and **Tala'a Seghira,** although they are barely wide enough for its shops, a donkey, and your backpack.

Tourist Office: Syndicat d'Initiative, Pl. Mohammed V (☎055 62 34 60). You may need more guidance than their maps give, but luckily the staff is helpful and can answer most questions. Hire official guides for 150dh for half-day, 250dh for full day. Open M-F 8:30am-noon and 2:30-6:30pm, Sa 8:30am-noon.

Currency Exchange: BMCE, Pl. Mohammed V, opposite the Syndicat d'Initiative and to the right of main bank entrance. Handles MC/V and travelers check transactions. Has **ATMs.** Open M-F 8:15am-2:15pm. Pl. Florence has branches of most Moroccan banks.

Luggage Storage: At the train station. 10dh per bag, 6am-9pm. Also at the private bus station, 5 dh per bag. Open 6am-11pm.

Police: ☎19. Corner of Av. Mohammed V and Rue Allal Laoudiyi, next to the post office.

Late-night Pharmacy: Municipalité de Fès, Av. Moulay Youssef (☎035 62 34 93), off Pl. de la Résistance, 5min. uphill from royal palace. Open daily 9pm-6am.

Hospital: al-Ghassani (☎035 62 27 77), in the Dhar al-Mahrez district east of town. From Pl. Mohammed V, walk down Ave. Mohammed Slaoui as it becomes Ben Arbi Alaoui for 15 mins., and then turn left on Ave. al-Ghassani.

Internet Access: There are several internet cafes in the *ville nouvelle;* just look for a "Cyber" sign. **Cyber Club** is one block south of Pl. Mohammed V, on a corner on the left, above the teleboutique. 10dh per hour. Open daily 10am-8pm.

Post Office: At the corner of Av. Hassan II and Blvd. Mohammed V in the *ville nouvelle.* Branch offices at Pl. d'Atlas and in the medina at Pl. Batha. All branches open July-Sept. 15 M-F 8:30am-2:30pm, Sa 8-11:45am; Sept. 16-June M-F 8:30am-12:15pm and 2:30-6:30pm.

ACCOMMODATIONS

VILLE NOUVELLE

Accommodations in the *ville nouvelle* offer an escape from the madness of the medina and generally offer a little more value for your money. Pl. Florence and the southern end of Av. Mohammed V have good options for a cheap room.

Hotel Royal, 36 Rue de Soudan (☎035 62 46 56), off Pl. Florence. Perfect location in the center of the *ville nouvelle.* Good value—simple rooms are big and airy, all with showers and some with balconies over the street. Hot water in the morning only. Singles 100dh; doubles 140dh; triples 190dh; quads 230dh. ❶

Auberge de Jeunes (HI), 18 Rue de Abdeslam Serghini (☎035 62 40 85; www.fesyouth-hostel.com). High walls hide the shady, tree-filled courtyard. Rooms are small but well-maintained. Communal showers are sparkling, but cold. Single-sex dorms 55dh. Doubles 130dh. HI members pay 5dh less. ❶

Hôtel Amor, 31 Rue Arabie Saoudite (☎055 62 27 24), off pl. Florence. Quiet lobby leads to clean, well-furnished rooms with pretty beds. Private showers with hot water. Attached restaurant and bar is a convenient plus. Singles 170dh; doubles 192dh. ❷

Hotel El Fath, 107 Rue Mohammed El Hayani (☎035 94 46 50), on the corner of Blvd. Mohammed V. Higher floors are a hike and furniture is a little banged up, but years of scribbles add personality. Balconies offer nice views over the bustle of the *ville nouvelle.* Hot water all day long. Singles 100dh; doubles 150dh. ❶

FEZ AL-BALI

Just inside the Bab Boujeloud are a slew of budget hotels. They may be lacking in luxury (or hot water, even), and you'll be hassled as soon as you step out the door, but it is the place to stay if you want to be close to the action.

Hôtel Cascade, 26 Serrajine Boujeloud (☎055 63 84 42), just inside Bab Boujeloud and to the right. Hugely popular with backpackers and tourists, Cascade is a social place with friendly staff and simple, pretty rooms. Bathrooms are sparkling and showers are hot. The terrace, full of people playing cards and chatting around the snack bar, provides a bird's-eye view of Bab Boujeloud and the medina. Fills up quickly, so come early. Singles 80dh; double with shower 180dh; terrace 40 dh. ❶

Hôtel Mauritania, 20 Serrajine Boujeloud (☎055 63 35 18), to the right after the Bab Boujeloud. Whole place is a little battered, including the tiled rooms and shower, but it's right there in the medina. Beds are big with a strangely generous amount of bedding for the Fassi summer. Hot showers 10dh. Singles 80dh; doubles 150dh. ❶

Pension Talaa, 14 Talaa Seghira (☎035 63 33 59), right off the street. Rooms are absolutely minuscule but clean and newly-tiled, and management is friendly. Showers and modern toilet in wooden stalls, but clean and come with hot water. Watch yourself on the stairs to the top—they are unimaginably steep. Singles 75dh; doubles 150dh. ❶

Hotel National, Pl. Boujeloud, just before the gate on the left. Cracks in the floor and spare rooms are made up for by friendly owner and colorful tile and paintings on the way up. Shower could use a little more light. Singles 100dh; doubles 120dh. ❶

FOOD

VILLE NOUVELLE

Cheap sandwich shops and rotisserie places are the order of the day in the *ville nouvelle*, along with Italian spots, all of which offer a guilty getaway from Moroccan food. Pastry places and juice shops along Blvd. Mohammed V are top-notch, and perfect spots for a sweet breakfast. Or simply poke through stalls of fresh food at the central market on **Blvd. Mohammed V,** two blocks up from Pl. Mohammed V. (Open daily 8am-2pm.)

Pizzeria Chez Vittorio, 21 Rue Brahim Roudania (☎055 62 47 30), just down from Hotel Central. Does a convincing job of capturing the ambience of a small Italian joint—wine, conversation, red tablecloths, and a family feel. Beer (25-35dh), wine, and spirits served. 10% service charge. Pizza and spaghetti 60-75dh. Open daily noon-4pm and 7-11pm. MC/V. ❷

Restaurant Bajalloul, 22 Rue Arabie Saoudite, on the inside corner of Pl. Florence. Locals, families, and chatty women come for heaping meat plates (30-40dh), most served with salad. Open daily noon-midnight. ❷

Cremerie Skali, Blvd. Mohammed V, 3 blocks up from Pl. Mohammed V. A shaded breakfast spot on the corner that with pastries (5-10dh) and huge plates of fried eggs (15dh). The tropical juices (8-11dh) alone make a stop worthwhile. Open daily 7am-10pm. ❶

Snack Chez Hamza, 25 rue Brahim Roudani (☎055 93 02 14), across the street from Hotel Central. A no-frills sandwich shop. Good for a bite on the run. Sandwiches 15dh. *Tajines* and couscous 25-35dh. ❶

FEZ AL-BALI

Stalls line **Tala'a Kebira** and **Tala'a Seghira,** near the **Bab Boujeloud** and are scattered further down toward the sights. *Harira* (spicy lentil soup; 10dh) typically comes with potatoes and bread. Sandwiches will run you 15dh. Fresh-squeezed and cheap orange juice (3-4dh) is plentiful outside Bab Boujeloud. For some of the cheapest eateries in Morocco, go left from Tala'a Kebira at **Madrasa al-Atarrine,** and head into the medina toward **Pl. Achabine.** Other than the relatively cheap fare just inside the gate, sit-down dining in the medina consists of pricey "palace" restaurants done up in extreme Moroccan decor.

La Kasbah, Rue Serrajine just inside Bab Boujeloud. A sweet set of terraces overlooking the entrance to the medina offer shade, a breeze, and a beautiful view. Big helpings of standard Moroccan food. Plates 40dh, menu 70dh. Open daily 10am-11pm. ❷

Restaurant des Jeunes, 16 Rue Serrajine (☎055 63 49 75), next to Hotel Cascade. Quick and reliable Moroccan staples, right there by the Bab. Breakfasts (20dh) include omelette and crepe delights. Proximity to hotels guarantees more than a few tourists. Plates 40dh, menu 70dh. Open daily 9am-midnight. ❶

Restaurant Dar Jamai, 14 Foundouk Lihoudi (☎035 63 56 85), 100m from the Palais Jamai. Take a left past the hotel, then a right. Hang a left and follow the signs. Elegantly decked out with pillows and Berber rugs, a traditional restaurant without the excess of the other "palace" spots. Huge 4-course menu 100dh. Open daily noon-11pm. ❸

Café Noria, Boujeloud Gardens. Technically in Fez al-Jdid. At the end of Rue de Fez al-Jdid, head down the stairs; it's just inside the Boujeloud gardens. Known as the "Lover's Café," come here with or without your love to sip an orange juice or mint tea under the huge shady canopy of the trees. A getaway from the noise of the medina. Light menu available. Drinks 8-10dh. Salads 20dh. Open 8am-10pm. ❶

SIGHTS

FEZ AL-BALI

The medina here is a world of its own, a nest of 9000 unmarked streets packed with millennia-old *medersas*, *souqs*, and mosques, all withstanding the carnival of donkeys, artisans, and shopkeepers that own the narrow streets. While there are sights to be seen, wandering off down narrow alleys and taking a random turn can lead to colorful scenes just as worthwhile. The madness abates a little under the midday sun, so if you want to poke around when it is least crowded, come between noon and 3pm.

WITH A GUIDE. The easiest way to get to know the medina is with a guide. Official guides, speaking many languages, are available at the **Syndicat d'Initiative.** They'll save you time, discourage hustlers, and provide detailed explanations. (Don't assume that they'll help you bargain for goods, though.) You can hire a guide for half a day (3hr., 150dh) or a full day (5-6hr., 250dh). Though much cheaper, unofficial guides are illegal, often lack historical knowledge, and usually take travelers only to shops from which they will get a hefty commission. Whoever you hire, nail down an itinerary and price right off the bat.

WITHOUT A GUIDE. The bold and independent will find that with a little effort and research, the medina can be conquered (well, explored) without a guide. To keep hustlers and merchants at bay, ignore calls or hisses and simply say *"non, merci"* or *"la shokran"* to those who approach you directly. Remember: walking downhill will take you farther into the medina, while trekking uphill will lead you out to Bab Boujeloud. Without a guide, there are two classic approaches to exploring the medina. The first is to head to the main gateway **Bab Boujeloud** and wander down **Tala'a Kebira** from there. Virtually all of the sights in Fez's medina lie along the Tala'a Kebira (or the Grand Tala'a), old Fez's main street and an essential reference point for anyone attempting to navigate the medina. The Tala'a Kebira heads downhill from Bab Boujeloud to the **Qaraouiyine Mosque** area. The Bab Boujeloud is the main entrance to the medina; faux guides tend to gather here. Built in 1912 by the Frenchman Maréchal Lauyote, the *bab* is tiled in blue on one side (the color of Fez) and green on the other (the color of Islam). The square just inside the *bab* is where the Moroccan revolution against the French occupation began. Down to the right is the **Tala'a Seghira,** Fez's other main street, lined mostly by shops catering to locals. The second approach is to taxi inside the medina to the more centrally located **Place Rcif** nearby the Qaraouiyine Mosque. This choice puts you right near the center of the sights described below. The final option, for those with lots of time and even more patience, is simply to get lost in the magnificent atmosphere that is Fez's medina. You'll be vulnerable to hustlers, but you'll get to know the city on your own. When you're done, ask merchants or women how to get to Tala'a Kebira and follow it back uphill to Bab Boujeloud.

BOU INANIA MEDERSA. When Sultan Abu Inan was given the bill for the construction, he tore it up and threw it in the river that crossed the courtyard, claiming that no price could be put on beauty. And indeed, this *medersa* (a.k.a., madrasa, or religious school), built between 1350 and 1356, is Morocco's finest. Stunning stucco and cedar craftsmanship cover the walls of the recently renovated courtyard, and intricate *zellij* tilework complements the plasterwork. Once home to several hundred students who studied and prayed here, it is still used as a mosque, one of the few open to non-Muslims. The prayer room is off-limits, however. *(Open daily 9am-5:30pm. 10dh.)*

TANNERIES. Leather is dyed by hand here in huge earthen vats, with men treading the leather by foot. It is first washed in a greenish-blue liquid, then moved to a washing machine before being soaked in a mixture of pigeon excrement and cow urine to soften it up. The process takes up to a week, except for yellow garments, which are colored by hand with expensive saffron in two days. Red coloring comes from poppy flowers, blue from indigo, and brown from the henna plant. Feel free to take pictures of the men nimbly walking between the huge palette of dye pits below. With any luck, they will give you a sprig of mint to ward off the incredible stench of the dye pits—otherwise you'll have to stomach the smell, which intensifies on hot days. As you try to leave, they'll try to sell you something leather—jackets, pouffes (round footstools), or slippers. Unless you're armed for a bargaining battle, find the exit. *(Turn left at the end of Tala'a Kebira and follow the winding road until you reach a T-junction; turn right and follow the signs to Chouara tanneries, or wait to be accosted by a tannery "guardien", who will lead you up (20dh) to the terraces of a leather store to see Fez's iconic tanneries.)*

NEJJARINE MUSEUM OF ART. Dedicated to wood craftsmanship, the museum showcases an extensive collection of tools, massive wedding chairs, musical instruments, Qu'ranic tablets, and doors. There is no shortage of finery on display—one entire room is dedicated to beautiful shelving. The tiled bathrooms are worth a visit, as they're the nicest around. The building itself is a beautifully restored warehouse originally built by Moulay Ismail. The rooftop terrace, affording a gorgeous view from the middle of the city, is perfect for a break and a bit of mint tea. *(The easiest way to get to the Place Nejjarine, with its tiled fountain, is to go all the way down Tala'a Seghira until it turns into Tala'a Kebira. Turn around, facing the direction you just came from, and go down the steps that are about 10m in front of you. At the bottom of the steps, follow the path to the small square; the museum is just off this small courtyard. Open daily 10am-5pm. 20dh, tea 10dh.)*

SPICE SOUQ AND OTHER MARKETS. Back on the Tala'a Kebira, the Attarine (Spice) Souq stretches several hundred meters to the end of the street. Now the domain of merchants hawking knock-off watches and personal hygiene items, it used to be a collection of shops, 150-170 in total, selling medicinal herbs and spices. Most were sold to physicians at the Maristan Sidi Frej, located in the Henna Souq (at the beginning of the Attarine Souq), where the depressed were treated with music, spices, and sex. The first psychiatric hospital in the Western world, opened in Valencia in 1410, was modeled on it. The Henna Souq, which is named for the dye that local women wear on their hands and feet for weddings, still sells a little of its namesake, but the *souq* is largely dominated by pottery shops today.

QAIRAOUINE MOSQUE. Exiting the *medersa*, turn left, and then left again; a few meters down is a little opening into the mosque, one of its 14 gates. The mosque also holds six fountains (3 for men and 3 for women), 300+ pillars, and can hold up to 20,000 worshippers (second only to the mosque of Hassan II in Casablanca). Founded in 857 by Fatima al-Fihri, a woman, the mosque is one of the oldest universities in the world. It trained students in logic, math, rhetoric, and the Qur'an while Europe stumbled through the Dark Ages. The Saadian pavilions are modeled on the Lion Court at the Alhambra in Granada, and the Almoravid *minbar* (pulpit) is made from ivory from Córdoba. What started as a small *medersa* grew in size and grandeur to encompass a huge plot of land in the medina. It is all off-limits to tourists, who must be satisfied by taking pictures through the archways.

THE DAR BATHA MUSEUM. The beautiful Dar Batha Museum, located by Hotel Batha, with its well-kept garden, makes an excellent diversion for those tired of endless, winding medina streets. The building itself, a 19th-century palace, may be turn out to be the highlight of the visit. The spacious Andalusian mansion hosted Sultan Hassan I and his son, Moulay Abd al-Aziz, during the last years of decadence before the French occupation. The museum, which hosts Moroccan music concerts in September, chronicles Fez's artistic history. The collection's centerpiece is the display of ceramics with the signature cobalt "Fez blue" adorning white enamel. *(Start at Bab Boujeloud, head straight down the Tala'a Seghira, take the right just before the next arch and follow the road to Pl. l'Istiqlal, home to the museum. Open W-Th and Sa-M 8:30am-noon and 2:30-6pm, F 8:30-11:30am and 3-6pm. 10dh.)*

FEZ AL-JDID

Fez al-Jdid, squarely between the medina and the *ville nouvelle*, was built in the 13th century by the Merenid sultan Youssef Yacoub to fortify himself against the world. The enormous **Dar al-Mahkzen,** his royal palace, is his gargantuan legacy to the city. The palace is not open to the public, and is in fact heavily guarded, but you can take a look at the gorgeous brass doors in front, at the end of the plaza. Just south of the plaza is the **mellah,** or Jewish quarter. In the 14th century the city's Jews were relocated here to offer them greater protection—and to more easily tax them. While there are few Jewish families remaining in the city, the architecture and neighborhood testify to their once significant presence. On the right as you head into Fez al-Jdid is an enormous **Jewish cemetery,** the final resting place for over 2,000 people. *(Open dawn-dusk; donations requested).* **Rue de Fez al-Jdid** is a sight in and of itself, a street absolutely choked with garment stalls. Locals flood in during the evening and it becomes an almost impassable mass of old women bargaining for clothing and young men calling out their wares like auctioneers. Bear left at the end of Rue de Fez al-Jdid into the **Petit Méchouar;** on the left is Bab Dakakeen, the back entrance to the Dar al-Makhzen. Bab al-Seba, an imperial gate, opens onto the **Grand Méchouar,** a roomy plaza lined with street lamps. From here it's an easy walk to Bab Boujeloud—turn through the opening to the right of Bab al-Seba, continue straight for 250m, veer to the right, and pass through a large arch at the end of the road. The entrance to the refreshing **Boujeloud Gardens,** a refuge from the midday sun, is on the right. *(Open Tu-Su. Free.)*

OUTSIDE THE MEDINA

There isn't much to see in Fez outside of the medina, but there are glorious views of the medina itself from the hills north of the city. The ramparts of

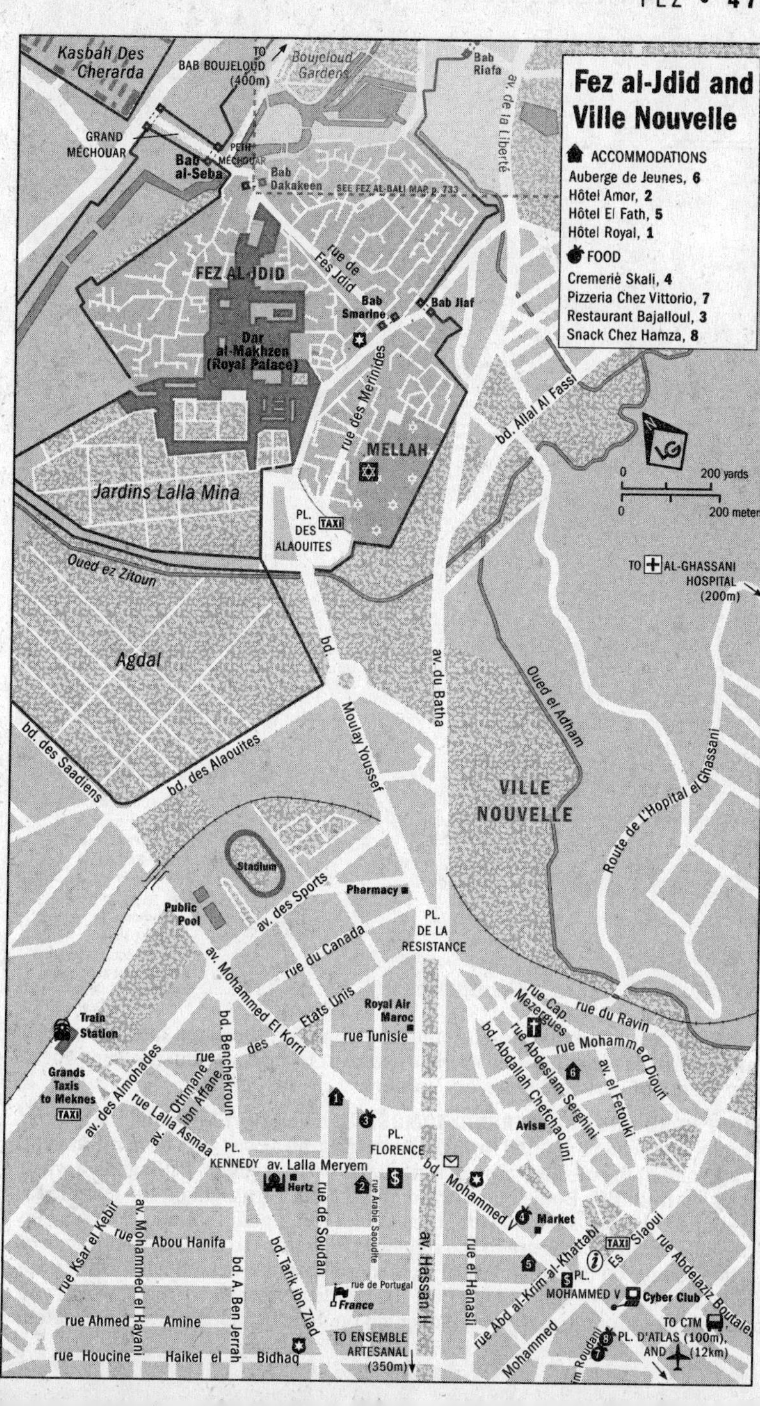
Fez al-Jdid and Ville Nouvelle
ACCOMMODATIONS
Auberge de Jeunes, 6
Hôtel Amor, 2
Hôtel El Fath, 5
Hôtel Royal, 1
FOOD
Cremeriè Skali, 4
Pizzeria Chez Vittorio, 7
Restaurant Bajalloul, 3
Snack Chez Hamza, 8
Kasbah Des Cherarda
TO BAB BOUJELOUD (400m)
Boujeloud Gardens
Bab Riafa
av. de la Liberté
GRAND MÉCHOUAR
PETIT MÉCHOUAR
Bab al-Seba
Bab Dakakeen
SEE FEZ AL-BALI MAP, p. 733
FEZ AL-JDID
rue de Fes Jdid
Bab Smarine
Bab Jiaf
Dar al-Makhzen (Royal Palace)
rue des Merinides
MELLAH
bd. Allal Al Fassi
Jardins Lalla Mina
PL. DES ALAOUITES
TAXI
0
200 yards
200 meters
TO AL-GHASSANI HOSPITAL (200m)
Oued ez Zitoun
Agdal
bd. Moulay Youssef
av. du Batha
Oued el Adham
bd. des Saadiens
bd. des Alaouites
VILLE NOUVELLE
Route de L'Hopital el Ghassani
Stadium
Public Pool
av. des Sports
Pharmacy
PL. DE LA RESISTANCE
rue du Canada
av. Mohammed El Korri
rue des Etats Unis
Royal Air Maroc
rue Tunisie
rue Cap. Mezergues
rue du Ravin
rue Mohammed Diouri
rue Abdeslam Serghini
bd. Abdallah Chefchaouni
av. el Fetouki
Train Station
Grands Taxis to Meknes
bd. Benchekroun
rue Othmane ibn Affane
av. des Almohades
rue Lalla Asmaa
Avis
PL. FLORENCE
PL. KENNEDY
av. Lalla Meryem
Hertz
rue Arabie Saoudite
rue de Soudan
bd. Mohammed V
Market
av. Mohammed el Hayani
rue Abou Hanifa
rue Ksar el Kebir
bd. A. Ben Jerrah
bd. Tarik ibn Ziad
av. Hassan II
rue el Hanasli
rue Abd al-Krim al-Khattabi
Es Slaoui
rue Abdelaziz Boutaleb
PL. MOHAMMED V
Cyber Club
rue de Portugal
France
rue Ahmed Amine
rue Houcine Haikel el Bidhaq
TO ENSEMBLE ARTESANAL (350m)
Mohammed
rue Roudani
TO CTM PL. D'ATLAS (100m), AND (12km)

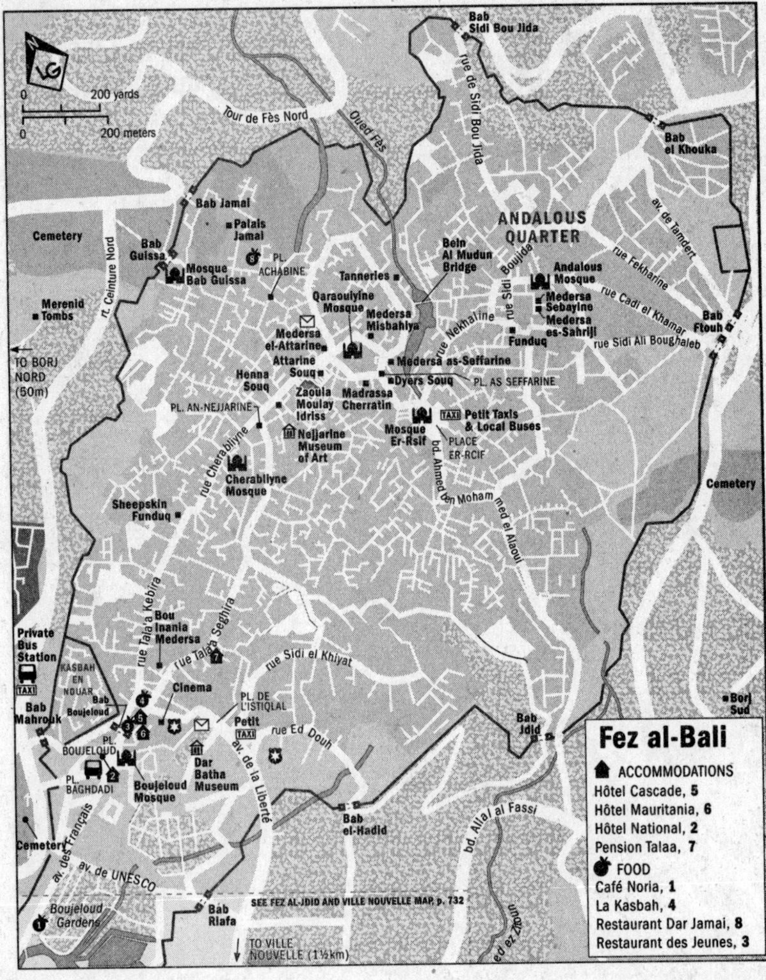

the Borj Nord and the old Merenid tombs are on the same hill. Be careful after dark, as aggressive hustlers are known to frequent the area and there are plenty of dark and unsavory corners.

BORJ NORD AND THE MERENID TOMBS. To reach Borj Nord and the nearby tombs (they can be spotted from the ground), grab a *petit taxi* from the medina (5dh) or exit the medina through a small gate to the right on Pl. Baghdadi when walking from Bab Boujeloud toward Fez al-Jdid. Turn right on the main road, walk past the bus station 200m, then take a small path that winds its way up the hillside; the tombs are to the right and Borj Nord to the left. Thousands of white tombs, on the other side of Hotel des Merinides from Borj Nord, dot the hillside. Equally old and derelict are the **fortress ruins** above them, which you can wander around, marvel at, and climb on. Spectacularly old and neglected, they're amazingly accessible and worth a look. From the hills the panorama of the city, sprawled out in all its capricious sandstone antiquity, is especially impressive in the half-light of dawn or dusk; during calls to prayer, when over a hundred *muezzin* summon the faithful, the experience is almost mystical.

SHOPPING AND CRAFTS

As anyone hawking goods in the medina will tell you, Fez is the artisanal capital of Morocco. Notable goods include the blue pottery, made with cobalt; the selection of rugs and carpets; and the leather, made in the famous tanneries (see above). But really, everything is on offer: henna, herbal remedies for aging and impotence, daggers, brass tea services and sheepskins. Quality ranges from the handmade artisanry to shoddy, mass-produced stuff, but discerning the difference can be difficult for an untrained eye. In general, the stores along **Tala'a Kebira** offer cheaper but lower-quality items, while the *funduqs* and specialty stores will sell much better goods at significantly higher prices. If you do want to buy, bargain at a few stores first to get an idea of what something is worth. The first offer is always too much, often by twice, and only until the price is lowered for a third or fourth time are you usually getting a good deal. Do not let a middleman selling hats lead you to buy a *djellaba* or any other good—when he says he's negotiating the price, he's probably negotiating his commission. Lastly, a lot of the tannery and carpet showrooms are built in maze-like houses with many passageways, making it difficult to escape gracefully. But be firm; there's never an obligation to buy, no matter how many red carpets have been rolled out for you. Waiting until the end of the day, when shopkeepers are more inclined to make a sale rather than lose money, is a good time to try and buy.

THE ATLANTIC COAST

The towns along Morocco's Atlantic coast are more laid-back than their conservative cousins in the interior. Men and women alike sunbathe, swim, and surf. The west coast contains Morocco's industrial boom towns—Casablanca, the country's commercial center, and Rabat, its political capital—which, while very much part of the modern country, are best avoided by travelers with limited itineraries. If you're looking to relax by the sea, your best bets are smaller, more tranquil coastal cities, like Essaouira and Asilah.

CASABLANCA ☎022

Though sprawling Casablanca (a.k.a. "Casa") has a famous name, there is little to see here other than the awe-inspiring Hassan II Mosque. Unfortunately, no one's looking at you, kid, except the hustlers who prowl the port and medina. A small city at the turn of the 20th century, the French built the wide boulevards and now-crumbling Art Deco buildings and made it into the booming commercial center it is today. A clash of desperately poor shantytowns and urban high-rises which dominate the skyline, Africa's largest port has little time for tourists and feels a little faded. Hidden on the western edge, though, is the Hassan II Mosque, the third-largest mosque in the world and a spectacular modern wonder.

TRANSPORTATION

The **Casa Port train station** is near the youth hostel and the city center; the **Casa Voyageurs** train station is a 50min. walk from Casa Port or a 25-30dh *petit taxi* ride. The private bus station is even farther away. To get from Casa Port to the convenient downtown **CTM bus station,** cross the street, and follow Blvd. Houphouet-Boigny to the head of Pl. Nations Unies. At the rotary, take a sharp left onto the wide **Av. des Forces Armées Royales** (known as Av. des F.A.R.), and turn on to the side street just before Hotel Farah; the station is right there. **Taxi** drivers at the station will often "forget" about the meter and ask for a ridiculous price upon dropping you off, so demand that they turn it on or settle for a price beforehand, despite their protests. Alternatively, walk a few blocks from the station for a taxi. Accommodations are almost all within walking distance, but be careful at night. Most of the major airlines and countless travel agencies are located on Av. des F.A.R. as you walk east from Pl. des Nations Unies.

Flights: Aéroport Mohammed V (☎022 53 90 40) handles all flights. Trains run between the airport terminal and the Casa Port train station (45min., 1 per hr., 6am-10pm, 30dh), stopping at Casa Voyageurs en route. You may have to change trains at Ain Sebaa, so check your ticket. Make sure to get on a train that runs to Casa Port. **Royal Air Maroc** (☎022 31 41 41), at the airport and 44 Av. des F.A.R. (☎022 31 11 12). Open M-F 8:30am-12:15pm and 2:30-7pm, Sa 8:30am-noon and 3-6pm.

Trains: There are 2 main train stations: **Casa Port** (☎022 27 18 37), undergoing massive construction, on the waterfront close to the heart of the city, and **Casa Voyageurs** (☎022 24 38 18), 4km outside the city center on Blvd. Ba Hammed. Casa Port has northbound service to **Rabat** (1hr., every 30min. 6:30am-9:30pm, 31dh). Casa Voyageurs has southbound service to **Fez** (5hr., 12 per day, 6:15am-10:30pm, 101dh) via **Meknes** (4hr., 86dh), **Marrakesh** (3hr., 9 per day, 4:50am-8:50pm, 84dh); **Tangier** (6hr., 4 per day 6:15am-12:15am, 124dh; transfer at **Sidi Kacem**).

Buses: Using CTM rather than a private company is worth the extra money and effort; the private bus station is a long taxi ride away from the city center. **CTM,** 23 Rue Léon L'Africain (☎022 45 80 00), off Blvd. Hassan Seghir. To: **Essaouira** (6hr.; 7, 7:30am, 5pm; 135dh); **Fez** (6hr., 12 per day 7am-9pm, 100dh); **Marrakesh** (4hr., 9 per day, 8am-11pm, 85dh); **Meknes** (5hr., 11 per day 7am-7:30pm, 80dh); **Tetouan** (7hr. 6am, 4, 11:30pm; 125dh); **Tangier** (6hr., 6 per day 6am-11:45pm, 105dh).

Car Rental: Though travelers don't need a car in Casa, the city has dozens of rental companies. **Avis,** 19 Av. des F.A.R. (☎022 31 24 24). Open M-F 8am-7pm, Sa 8am-noon and 2-7pm, Su 8am-noon. AmEx/MC/V. **Hertz,** 25 Rue de Arabi Jilali (☎022 84 09 39), same hours. Min. age 25 for all cars at all dealerships.

METER MADNESS. In Casablanca, *petit taxi* drivers are particularly flagrant in taking "scenic routes" and failing to turn on the meter. Start with a sense of the route, and double-check the meter. The daytime rate should start at 1.40dh, the nighttime rate at 2.10dh. Taxi drivers are required by law to use their meter, and the surcharge by night is 50% of fare, not double.

ORIENTATION AND PRACTICAL INFORMATION

The city has two main squares, **Pl. Nations Unies,** below the landmark clock tower and a 5min. walk from Casa Port, and **Pl. Mohammed V.** Pl. Nations Unies spreads out in front of the Hyatt Regency. All the main arteries radiate from it; **Av. Hassan II** heads to Pl. Mohammed V six blocks south, **Blvd. Mohammed V** heads east toward Casa-Voyageurs, and just above it is **Rue Allal ben Abdallah,** around which lie many of the city's cheap lodgings and eateries. Along the top of Pl. Nations Unies runs **Av. Forces Armées Royales (F.A.R.),** which has all of the city's travel agencies and airlines. Turning right as you leave Casa Port will lead you along the medina walls and eventually bring you to **Hassan II Mosque.**

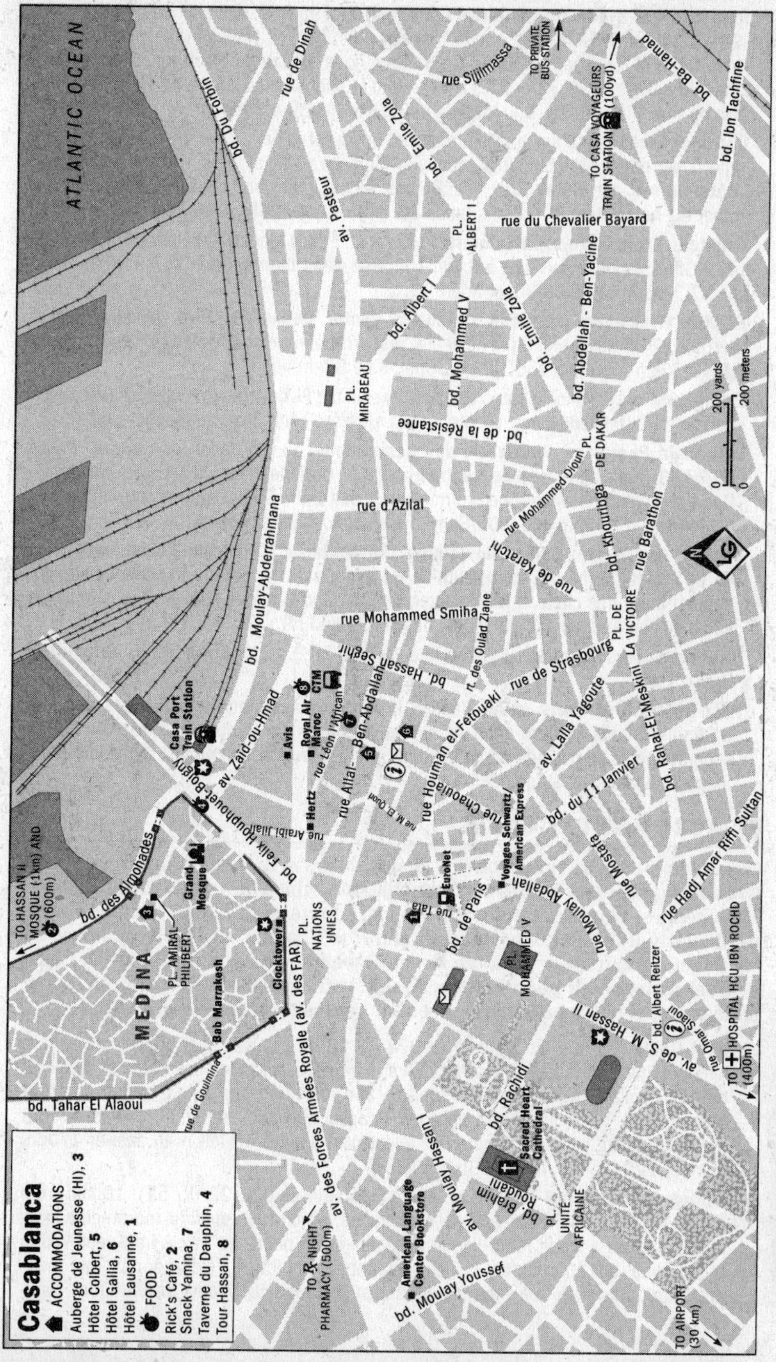

Casablanca
ACCOMMODATIONS
Auberge de Jeunesse (HI), 3
Hôtel Colbert, 5
Hôtel Gallia, 6
Hôtel Lausanne, 1
FOOD
Rick's Café, 2
Snack Yamina, 7
Taverne du Dauphin, 4
Tour Hassan, 8
ATLANTIC OCEAN
TO HASSAN II MOSQUE (1km) AND (600m)
bd. des Almohades
MEDINA
PL. AMIRAL PHILIBERT
Grand Mosque
Bab Marrakesh
Clocktower
bd. Tahar El Alaoui
rue de Goulmina
Casa Port Train Station
bd. Du Forbin
bd. Felix Houphouet-Boigny
av. Zaïd-ou-Hmad
bd. Moulay-Abderrahmana
PL. NATIONS UNIES
av. des Forces Armées Royale (av. des FAR)
TO NIGHT PHARMACY (500m)
Avis
Royal Air Maroc
CTM
Hertz
rue Araibi Jilali
rue Léon l'Africain
rue Allal-Ben-Abdallah
bd. Hassan Seghir
rue Mohammed Smiha
rue d'Azilal
PL. MIRABEAU
av. Pasteur
rue de Dinah
bd. Emile Zola
rue Sijilmassa
TO PRIVATE BUS STATION
TO CASA VOYAGEURS TRAIN STATION (100yd)
bd. Ba-Hamad
bd. Ibn Tachfine
rue du Chevalier Bayard
PL. ALBERT I
bd. Albert I
bd. Mohammed V
bd. Emile Zola
bd. Abdellah - Ben-Yacine
bd. de la Résistance
PL. DE DAKAR
rue Mohammed Diouri
rue de Karatchi
bd. Khouribga
rue Barathon
rt. des Oulad Ziane
rue de Strasbourg
PL. DE LA VICTOIRE
rue Houman el-Fetouaki
av. Lalla Yagoute
rue M. El Quori
rue Chaouia
Voyages Schwartz/ American Express
bd. du 11 Janvier
bd. Rahal-El-Meskini
rue Mostafa
rue Hadj Amar Riffi Sultan
EuroNet
rue Tata
bd. de Paris
rue Moulay Abdallah
PL. MOHAMMED V
av. de S. M. Hassan II
bd. Albert Reitzer
rue Omar Slaoui
TO HOSPITAL HCU IBN ROCHD (400m)
bd. Rachidi
Sacred Heart Cathedral
bd. Brahim Roudani
PL. UNITÉ AFRICAINE
av. Moulay Hassan I
American Language Center Bookstore
bd. Moulay Youssef
TO AIRPORT (30 km)
200 yards
200 meters

Tourist Office: Syndicat d'Initiative et de Tourisme, 98 Blvd. Mohammed V (☎/fax 022 22 15 24), at Rue Chaouia, about 4 blocks down from Pl. Nations Unies. English spoken. Open M-F 8:30am-6:30pm, Sa 8:30am-noon. **Office de Tourisme,** 55 rue Omar Slaoui (☎022 27 95 33 or 27 11 77). From Pl. Mohammed V, take Av. Hassan II, turn left on Rue Allal al-Fassi, and then right. Open M-F 8:30-4:30pm.

Currency Exchange: Many banks are closed on weekends and after 4pm; try the airport and larger hotels, which change money at Morocco's official rates. The **Hyatt Regency, Hôtel Suisse,** and **Hôtel Safir,** near Pl. des Nations Unies and the bus station, and the other big hotels near Pl. Nations Unies are all safe bets. **24hr. ATMs** are everywhere.

American Express: Voyages Schwartz, 112 Av. du Prince Moulay Abdallah (☎022 22 29 47). Offer standard services, but won't receive wired money. Open M-F 8:30am-noon and 2:30-6:30pm, Sa 8:30am-noon.

English Bookstore: American Language Center Bookstore, Blvd. Moulay Youssef (☎022 27 95 59), at Pl. Unité Africaine. Vast array of novels and reference books. Open M-F 9:30am-12:30pm and 3:30-6:30pm, Sa 9:30am-noon.

Emergency: ☎19. Police located by clock tower in the Pl. des Nations Unies. Tourist police handle travel-related issues. Located on Av. Hassan II and Blvd. Houphouet-Boigny.

Late-Night Pharmacy: Pharmacie des Generations, 53 Rue Jaber ibn Hayane (☎022 20 73 33). Walk down Hassan II and turn right on blvd. de Paris. It's a 15min. walk to Pl. Oued al-Makhazine, where the pharmacy is. Open 24hr. Other pharmacies with normal hours (8am-12:30pm and 2:30-8pm) are on almost any city block.

Medical Assistance: Centre Hospitalier Universitarire (CHU) Ibn Rochd (☎022 22 41 09), south of the city. Walk south on Hassan II past the parks and continue straight through the traffic circle. 4 blocks later, turn left and continue straight; the complex is one block up on the right. Served by buses #29 and 59.

Internet Access: EuroNet, 51 Rue Tata (☎022 26 57 21). 10dh per hr. Open daily 8am-11pm.

Post Office: Blvd. Paris, at Av. Hassan II. Poste Restante and telephones. Open M-F 8:30am-4:30pm, Sa 9am-noon. As always, packages are shipped and received from a separate office on the side of the building. Another **branch** located just to the left of the Syndicat d'Initiative. Same hours.

ACCOMMODATIONS

Casa's glory days are long gone by, and it shows in the crumbling façades and worn feel of all of its budget accommodations, which have seen grander times. The cheapest places are in the streets just southeast of Pl. des Nations Unies, particularly Rue Allal ben Abdallah and Rue Chaouia. Casa is very noisy, so try to get a room away from the street. Depending on where you are in Casa, a street name could be in French, Arabic with transliteration, or both; some listings below note particularly recent or confusing changes.

Hotel Gallia, 19 Rue ibn Batouta (☎022 48 16 94). Casa's best budget option is a hilarious mix-and-match of leather doors, pink walls, and Moroccan staples (look for the 6ft. hookah). Management is friendly, and rooms are big, bright affairs with faux flowers, large beds, and clean showers. Popular with backpackers. Breakfast (25dh) available, along with a computer for guest use. Singles 150dh, with shower 170dh; doubles 220/250dh; triples 295/330dh. ❶

Auberge de Jeunesse (HI), 6 pl. Ahmed Bidaoui (☎022 22 05 51). 10min. from Casa Port. Head right along Blvd. Almohades, which runs outside the medina wall, and go left up a small ramp-like street; blue signs point the way. A little removed in the medina, but an excellent value. Pleasant central lounge, clean dorms, and modern bathrooms with hot showers. Breakfast included (8-10am) and internet available. Reception open daily 8-10am and noon-11pm. Lock-out 10am-noon. Check-out 10am. Dorms 60dh doubles 130dh, triples 190dh. ❶

Hôtel Lausanne, 24 Rue Tata, formerly Rue Poincaré (☎022 26 86 90). A step up from similar small hotels, a sparkling and well-maintained place with excellent service. Catch up on Egyptian soap operas and Arab news in modern rooms with TV and hot showers. Singles 225dh, doubles 270dh, triples 350dh. ❷

Hôtel Colbert, 38 Rue Chaouia, formerly Rue Colbert (☎022 31 42 41). Comfy couches in reception and a leafy central courtyard lead up to spacious, spotless rooms. Communal showers are immaculate. Usually booked, so arrive early. Singles 115dh, with shower 150dh; doubles 150/185dh; each additional person 36dh. ❶

FOOD

Casa offers every cuisine under the sun, from McDonald's to Mexican, for those willing to look. But it can be strangely difficult to find Moroccan food in Morocco's largest city, with the center dominated by sandwich joints, *patisseries*, and pizzerias. The cheap eats capital is **Pl. de 16 de Novembre,** 2 blocks southeast of Pl. des Nations Unies. Glaring neon signs light the streets around it with snack places and cheap *tajine* restaurants. **Rue Chaouia** has a slew of rotisserie chicken places, always good bets. For fresh meats and produce, try haggling at the **central market,** 7 Rue Chaouia (open daily 8am-1pm).

Rick's Café, 248 Blvd. Sour Jdid (☎022 27 42 07). Follow the port road away from the center until the end of the medina walls; signs point to Rick's on the left. Fez-topped waiters serve pricey dishes to a largely tourist crowd in this nod to American cinema. The cheesecake alone (45dh) is worth a visit. Live jazz piano seals the deal. Roof terrace has nice views and expensive drinks. Wi-Fi hot spot. T-shirts and mugs for sale. Entrees 120-150dh. Open daily 1-3pm and 6pm-1am. AmEx/MC/V. ❹

Taverne au Dauphin, 115 Blvd. Felix Houphouet-Boigny (☎022 22 12 00), up the road from the port. A classy seafood place where fine wine mingles with the smell of briny oysters. Small fried dishes (40-60dh) are tasty but the Oualidia oysters (from 51dh) are the way to go. Serves wine and beer. Open M-Sa noon-3pm and 7-11pm. V. ❸

Tour Hassan, 136 Av. des F.A.R. (☎022 31 03 50). Glossy wood panelling, curves, and plants nod to the city's Art Deco past, compensating for the linoleum tables and soft rock. Sit inside, as the road is noisy. Good selection of alcohol, including the namesake Casablanca beer (35dh). Pizzas 40-50dh. Meat 70-90dh. Open 8am-12:30am. ❷

Snack Yamina, 35 Rue Chaouia. Not to be confused with the nearby Snack Amine. This king of roadside rotisseries serves up chicken plates (25dh) and fried fish specials (30-40dh) in a jiffy. Can't beat it for price or convenience. Open daily 9am-11pm. ❶

SIGHTS

HASSAN II MOSQUE. Taking the Qu'ranic verse literally that "the throne of God is built upon the water," former King Hassan II built his mosque, the third largest in the world, to hang dramatically over the Atlantic. It was designed by Frenchman Michel Pinseau, and construction began in 1986, with 10,000 workers and 2500 master craftsmen working in shifts nonstop (all day, every day) until 1993; it was opened the next year. The construction came to a total of US$800 million, much of it collected through public taxes. Guided tours let visitors into Pinseau's masterpiece, one of the few places in the country open to non-Muslims. Inside is the **prayer hall,** which accommodates 25,000 worshippers. Fabulously intricate stucco patterning covers the walls, and the hand-

LES MUSIQUES DU MONDE

Every year in early June, people from all over the world pour into the ancient city of Fez to hear Sufi chants in Arabic, requiems in Latin, and popular songs in African patois and Hindi. This confusion of tongues has one common purpose—to share the world's sacred heritages through music.

The World Sacred Music Festival brings together performing artists from around the world in an effort to promote interfaith and intercultural dialogue. In the past, stars like Ravi Shankar of India have performed, but more traditionally smaller local groups are the headliners. Concerts are free to the public and take place in Dar Batha, outside Bab Boujeloud, and in the Bab Makina.

In addition, the Festival hosts Fez Encounters, a series of talks bringing together journalists, academics, and politicians to discuss global issues ranging from climate change to cultural identity in the face of globalization. The role of moral belief in the modern world is central here, but the art and music are what draw crowds and truly bring them together.

The World Sacred Music festival 2009 will take place May 29-June 6, 2009. While concerts and talks are free, finding accommodations during the festival can be difficult, so booking ahead is advisable. Visit www.fesfestival.com for more information on dates and events.

carved cedar roof, an engineering marvel, opens to the sky when the mosque is full and the weather is good. In winter, the floor is electrically heated. All of the materials to build the mosque came from Morocco, except the Italian glass for the 57 chandeliers and the Carrera marble that surrounds the *mihrab*, the prayer niche that points to Mecca. At one end of the prayer hall, silver electric gates weighing over 34 tons open only once a year—during the birthday celebration for the Prophet—for a grand entrance by his living descendant, the King himself. Downstairs are the ablution rooms for men and women, each containing 41 fountains, and the *hammams*, which one day (so they say) will be open for Muslims and non-Muslims alike. The plaza outside, blinding in midday, accommodates another 80,000 and offers the best views of the **minaret** (210m), the tallest in the world. Dominating the skyline during the day, the mosque glows brighter by night, shooting a 20 mi. long laser beam toward Mecca. *(Walk past the medina along the coastal road for about 15min., or take a petit taxi—should be no more than 10-15dh, though drivers will often ask for an unmetered 20dh. Tickets are sold to the left of the minaret, down the stairs. Guests must be modestly attired; women should cover their legs and shoulders. You'll have to take your shoes off before entering the prayer hall. Tours take 1hr. and are given M-Th and Sa 9, 10, 11am, noon, and 3pm, F 9, 10am, and 3pm. Tours in Arabic, English, French, and Spanish. 120dh, students 60dh.)*

NIGHTLIFE

Casa's Western feel might leave you hoping for a club scene, and the city doesn't disappoint. Avoid the center, full of slightly seedy, male-dominated bars. The real action is in **Aïn Diab,** a relatively wealthy neighborhood on the beach 4km west of the city center. The main drag, **Blvd. de la Corniche,** is lined with discos, upscale bars, and dance clubs. The young and sexy flock here on the weekends to flirt, drink, and show a little skin (or a lot). Most places get going after 1am and are open until the very early hours. Cover will probably run from 75-100dh, and up to 150dh at the *très chic* places. Dress codes require something more than shorts and sandals, so put on some nice shoes and a collar, or a skirt for women. While most places are fairly low-key, women will probably feel more comfortable in groups. Be wary of overly friendly Moroccan women, who might be out strolling for more than just a drink. Expect to pay 40-50dh each way for a cab from the center to Aïn Diab.

ESSAOUIRA

☎044

The siren song of Essaouira is inescapable. Its cool ocean breeze, sprawling beaches, local art and laid-back lifestyle are enough to make anyone want to go native. Notable as a dye-producing colony since Phoenician times, it was an important port throughout the ages, first for its secure ramparts, later and up to today for its sardines. The Gnaoua World Music Festival, held every year in June, and the city's numerous galleries all flaunt its artistic riches, but for most of the year its a quietly hip place. Jimi Hendrix and Cat Stevens liked the vibe in '69, and it hasn't changed much. Give yourself more than a day and you might find your visit slipping into weeks, months, and even years.

TRANSPORTATION

Buses: CTM runs from the station outside the medina, a 15min. walk from Pl. Moulay Hassan. Ticket window open 6:30am-10:30pm. To: **Agadir** (2hr., 2:30pm, 65dh), **Marrakesh** (3hr., 12:30 and 5pm, 55dh), and **Casablanca** (6hr.; 7:45, 11:10am, 4pm; 115dh). **Pullman du Sud** offers one overnight bus to **Casablanca** (7hr., midnight, 90dh). **Supratours** (☎024 47 53 17) buses leave from near **Bab Marrakesh;** to get to the ticket office and bus lot, walk past the post office from the beach and take the next left. In summer, it's best to buy a day or two in advance. Buses go to **Agadir** (2hr., 1:15pm, 65dh), **Marrakesh** (2hr., 5 per day 6am-6pm, 65dh), and **Safi** (3hr., 12:30pm, 40dh). Buy tickets at the office (open daily 5:30-6:30am, 9am-noon, and 3-6:45pm). Smaller companies offer frequent services to the cities above.

ORIENTATION AND PRACTICAL INFORMATION

The **bus station** is about 1km from the medina along Blvd. Industrie. Exit the rear of the station (where the buses park) and walk to the right, passing two *souqs* (or deserted wastelands, depending on the hour), to reach the medina gate, **Bab Doukkala** (10min.). The gate opens onto **Av. Mohammed Zerktouni,** one of two main arteries; the other is the parallel **Rue Mohammed ben Abdallah.** To reach the city center from Bab Doukkala, continue on Av. Mohammed Zerktouni as it becomes Av. l'Istiqlal (at an intersection surrounded by *souqs*). Walk until you see a clock tower and gate on the right. Go through the gate, pass through the square, and follow the road as it winds to Pl. Moulay Hassan, the heart of Essaouira. The ramparts line the streets of the plaza. To get to the beach, head left at the plaza and walk for 5min.

Tourist Office: Delegation Regionale de Tourisme, Rue de Caire (☎024 47 50 80). From the clocktower, walk 2 blocks toward the port and turn left on to Rue Caire. Some English spoken. Open M-F 9am-noon and 2:30-6:30pm.

Currency Exchange: Banks cluster around Pl. Moulay Hassan. **Bank Credit du Maroc,** Pl. Moulay Hassan (☎024 47 58 19), cashes traveler's checks and has an **ATM.** Open M-F 8:30am-3:45pm. **BMCE** (same hours as above) with an **ATM** is at the end of Pl. Moulay Hassan, near Ben Abdallah.

Luggage Storage: Available for 24hr. at the bus station (5dh per bag).

Police: ☎19. Station is on the same street as the tourist office.

Hospital: Hopital Sidi Mohammed ben Abdellah, Av. de l'Hopital (☎024 47 27 16), just past the post office away from the beach. Also **Croissant Rouge** (☎062 63 79 18), next to the tourist office. Open daily 9am-8pm.

Bookstore: Galerie Aida, 2 Rue de la Skala (☎024 47 62 90), off Pl. Moulay Hassan. Crafts, used books (in English and French), and art. Open daily 10am-8pm.

Internet Access: The area just above Pl. Moulay Hassan has a few *teleboutiques.* **Mogador Informatique** (☎024 47 50 65), on Av. l'Istiqlal to the right of the clocktower. 10dh per hour. Open daily 9am-midnight. **Internet Club,** right next to the tourist office, has Wi-Fi. 10dh per hour. Open daily 1am-11pm.

Post Office: Av. al-Moqamah at Lalla Aicha, the 1st left after Hôtel les Isles walking away from the medina by the shore. Poste Restante. Open 8:30am-noon and 2:30-6:30pm. **Branch** office on Rue Laalouj. **Postal Code:** 44000.

ACCOMMODATIONS

Hotels in Essaouira are a little pricier than elsewhere in Morocco but generally better, most with pretty rooms, reliable hot water, and breezy roof terraces.

Hostel Essaouira, Derb Laghrissi. Walking away from the port on Av. de l'Istiqlal, turn right after the big mosque. Walk until you see signs for Dar Nafoura and turn left. Follow this to the big blue phone sign, turn right, and then take your first left. Grab a beer and make yourself at home with Bob Marley and a surfing crowd. Super friendly staff and guests chill out together in the kitchen/lounge downstairs, feasting and chatting on the couches and swings well into the night. Beautiful courtyard. Rooms clean and comfortable. Ask about working at the hostel or long-term stays. Beds 120dh. ❶

Hotel Cap Sim, 11 Ibu Rochd (☎024 78 58 34). Standing in pl. Moulay Hassam facing Credit du Maroc, make a left on rue Skala, the street along the ramparts right next to Banque Populaire. Make a right just before the archway and follow the street around to the hotel. Tall windows, a bright courtyard, and colorful rooms, along with a smiling staff, make it bright and cheerful. Attached bathrooms have clean tile and hot showers. Breakfast included. Singles and doubles 230dh, with shower 360dh. MC/V. ❸

Hôtel Tafraout, 7 rue Marrakesh (☎024 47 62 76). In pl. Moulay Hassan, walk past the restaurants and cafes and take a left onto the busy rue Sidi Mohammed ben Abdallah. Look for the sign a few blocks up. Lovely little brass sinks, traditional lamps, and Berber blankets on the beds lend great personality. Clean and well-maintained. Standard shower. Singles 180dh, with shower 280dh, doubles 280/400dh. Extra bed 100dh. ❸

Hôtel Smara, 26 rue Skala (☎024 47 56 55). Standing in Pl. Moulay Hassan, facing Credit du Maroc, make a left on rue Skala, right next to Banque Populaire (3min.). Arrive early—this is the most popular hotel among backpackers. Rooms are simple but adequate, with the perk of ocean waves crashing 100m away. Breakfast 10dh, served on an ocean terrace. Laundry 2dh per garment. Some English spoken. Singles 76dh; 1-bed doubles 104dh, 2-bed doubles 134dh; terrace suite with ocean views 196dh. ❷

FOOD

Some of the cheapest dining, as well as the best place to score some of Essaouira's daily catch, are the stalls at the port end of Pl. Moulay Hassan. Tasting menus (60dh) offer up 3 kinds of fish, squid, and shrimp. Sardines, the city's lifeblood, are cheapest (10h), while the rest of the catch (sea urchins, anyone?) will run you 30-40dh. Prices and selection are identical wherever you choose to eat, so just grab a table and dig in.

Taros Café, 2 Rue de Skala (☎024 47 64 07), right off of Pl. Moulay Hassan. Elegant fish and fowl are served among local art displays in this wonderful restaurant/café/gallery. The night isn't finished without a drink on the terrace, the hippest night spot in Essaouira (mixed drinks 50-70dh). Gaze over the railing to the ocean below, or just lounge and watch the live music and belly dancing. Plates 90-120dh. Desserts 50-60dh. Open daily 11am-4pm and 6pm-late. AmEx/MC/V for purchases over 300dh. ❸

Crêperie Mogador, Rue Laalouj, near the museum. A refreshing change from *tajines* and pizza; grab a *crêpe salée* (savory crepe; 45dh), huge affairs stuffed with meat, tomato, and egg. For dessert or a lighter snack, the sweet crepes (20-40dh) come in a glorious spectrum of sweetness, from honey or chocolate (30dh) to the enormous specialty peach melba (50dh). Open Sa-Th noon-3pm and 7-10pm. ❶

Restaurant Laayoune (☎024 47 46 43). From the top of Pl. Moulay Hassan (away from the port), take a right and continue past rue Sidi ben Mohammed Abdallah. Follow the road as it turns right; the restaurant is ahead on the left. Conversation and candlelight fill the air in this elegant but affordable local spot for Moroccan fare. All 4 set menus (58-78dh) are an excellent value. Fills up at night; be prepared to wait. Plates 50-70dh. Open daily noon-4pm and 7-11pm. ❷

SIGHTS

While it is possible to spend days lolling in cafes or napping away in the city's breezy air, Essaouira's ramparts, beaches, and galleries give the town its graceful beauty and should not be missed.

RAMPARTS AND PORT. The town's two *skalas* (forts) sit dramatically over the violent Atlantic, offering spectacular views of the ocean and the isles. The strange mixture of European and Moroccan military architecure, built by a Frenchman in the 18th century, is so picturesque that Orson Welles used it in his adaptation of Othello. **Skala de la Ville,** the more accessible of the two and free to the public, is down Rue de Skala from Pl. Moulay Hassan. The brass cannons, given to the city by European traders, are fun to climb and offer gorgeous views of the Atlantic crashing on the rocks below. The unoccupied nooks are popular with canoodling Moroccan couples, and it is easy to see why. The other, **Skala du Port,** offers incredible oblique shots of the old medina walls—don't forget your camera. On the other side are the colorful old fishing boats and the beach melting away into the horizon. *(Open M-Th and Sa-Su 9am-5:30pm, Fri 9am-12:30pm and 3-6pm. 10dh.)*

MEDINA SHOPS AND MUSEUMS. Under the ramparts are the cave-like woodshops that produce some of Morocco's finest crafts. The lovely, deep aroma of *thuya* wood wafts along the street, where all sorts of hand crafted finery are on display. the artisans inlay the *thuya* with cedar and ebony to produce the usual cups, chess sets, and drums, along with statues and masks, which make for incredible keepsakes. In addition to the wood, there's a great local painting scene in Essaouira, and galleries line the streets around the rampart. Quality is variable, but as most artists take their cues from the gorgeous landscapes, you can't go too wrong. For silver jewelry, head to the *souq* located just outside the medina walls on Av. Oqba ben Nafil. Look for the sign that says *"bijoux"* above the entrance on the right, about a block from rue de Caire on the right. **Museum Mohammed ben Abdallah,** near the Hôtel Majestic on Rue Derb Laalouj, is in the former residence of a pasha. It features antique woodwork and important manuscripts, including a 13th-century Qur'an. *(☎024 47 53 00. Currently closed for restorations, so call ahead. Open M and W-Su 9am-noon and 3-6:30pm. 10dh.)*

BEACHES. Essaouira's soft sand stretches for miles to the south, but the same lovely winds that keep the town cool make sunbathing difficult. That said, it's still one of Morocco's best, and offers up a slew of activities. Kitesurfing, beach soccer, and swimming are all excellent. The beach is crowded but unguarded, so be careful if you do take a dip. To reach the sand, head to the port and veer left; you can't miss it. You'll have to walk past the crowds near the port to get a decent spot in the sand. Windsurfing clubs cluster on the beach and rent boards. **UCPA Maroc,** right along the boardwalk, offers rentals and lessons. (☎061 34 33 04. Surfboards 50dh per hr., 200dh per day. Windsurfing 250dh per hr., 600dh per day. Surfing lessons 125dh per hr. Windsurfing lessons 220dh per hr. Kitesurfing lessons start at 1600dh for 6hr. of instruction.)

PURPLE ISLES. The dramatic, rocky islets visible from the ramparts, despite their modest appearance, have been a valuable commodity for several millennia. A Berber king from Mauritania, Juba II, set up dye factories here around 100 BC, producing the purple dye used to color Julius Caesar's cape, among other things, and giving the Isles their name. In 1506, the Portuguese, under King Manuel, built a fortress, and Moulay Hassan added a prison. Nowadays they are home to the rare Eleonora's falcons. Visiting them is possible but discouraged during breeding season (roughly Mar.-Oct.). You must first receive a free permit from the Port Office, which can take several days to process. Then you must arrange transportation with a fisherman or someone who owns a boat. Try to bargain for 400-500dh.

THE HIGH ATLAS

The High Atlas is among the most striking and varied landscapes in the world, embracing snow-capped mountains, unearthly pink rock fortresses, and gargantuan waterfalls alike. So diverse is this region that movies set in locales as disparate as Tibet and Arabia have been filmed here. At the feet of the High Atlas lies Marrakesh, a city overflowing with unique architecture, exotic bazaars, and magical energy. Falling southeast from the Atlas ranges and stretching through Ouarzazate to the sand-dune seas of the Sahara is Morocco's own desert. Mountainous and desolate, its deep reds and oranges are softened only by the rare, green veins of oases that creep through the valley floors. Set into this landscape are fantastic Berber towns and *kasbahs*, where *pizid* (mud and straw) castles tower over the road. Excursions are possible by local transportation, but a rental car is best for exploring this region.

MARRAKESH ☎044

In a world gradually losing its magic and mystery, old Marrakesh has both in abundance. It all centers around Djema'a al-Fna, an incredible outdoor spectacle with snake charmers, charlatans, mystics, and healers, apparent holdouts from an earlier age. The Red City was founded in 1062 by the Almoravids and with its mosques and *medersas* quickly became an important center of culture and learning in North Africa. The Almohads destroyed much of the city upon succeeding them, hiring Andalusian artisans to rebuild it and giving the city its distinctive Moroccan-Spanish flavor. The city served as capital under various dynasties and remains the the tourism capital to this day, attracting droves of foreigners to its medina and *souqs*. The city's absurd heat leaves many begging for an escape, but the region doesn't disappoint. Hikes into the nearby Atlas mountains and camel treks into the desert are both a short drive away. Its location in the heart of Morocco, along with its old world allure, has made Marrakesh the hotspot it is today. And if you believe the clairvoyants in the square, the city will remain so for many years to come.

TRANSPORTATION

Flights: Aéroport de Marrakesh Menara (☎024 44 79 10 or 024 44 78 65), 5km south of town. Taxi from town 80-90dh, but they'll ask for 100dh. Bus #11 from the Koutoubia Mosque to the airport (about 7am-10pm, 3dh). Domestic and international flights on **Royal Air Maroc,** 197 Av. Mohammed V (☎024 42 55 00). Open M-F 8:30am-12:15pm and 2:30-7pm.

Trains: Av. Hassan II (☎024 44 65 69). Going away from the medina on Av. Mohammed V, turn left on Av. Hassan II (40min.). A taxi to or from pl. Djema'a al-Fna costs 10dh. To: **Rabat** (5hr., 9 per day 5am-9pm, 100-120dh) via **Casablanca** (4hr., 84dh); **Fez** (8hr., 8 per day 5am-7pm, 180dh) via **Meknes** (7hr., 160-170dh); **Tangier** via **Sidi Kacem** (6hr., 8 per day 5am-7pm, 200dh). 2nd class is often overbooked; pay attention when boarding so that you don't end up in an unnecessarily overcrowded car.

Buses: (☎024 43 39 33), a 25min. walk outside the medina walls by Bab Doukkala. To get there, walk out of the medina on Av. Mohammed V, pass through Bab Larissa, and then turn right, continuing along the walls to Bab Doukkala. The station is to the left. Arrive 30-60min. early, as seats fill quickly. Ignore the vagrants who want a tip for leading you to the right window; they will be fairly easy to find. **CTM** is window #10. To: **Casablanca** (4hr.; 4 per day 6:30am-6:30pm, 80dh); **Fez** (10hr.; 7am, 12, 11:45pm; 150dh); **Essaouira** (3hr.; 8am, 12:30pm; 65dh); **Ouarzazate** (4hr., 4 per day 7am-12:30am, 75dh); **Rabat** (5hr.; 2:30, 6:30am, 12:30pm; 65dh); **Tangier** (11hr., 2:30am) via **Tetouan** (9hr.). Private companies run frequently to destinations throughout Morocco, including **Essaouira** (window #7; 3hr., 13 per day, 4am-5pm, 35dh), **Rabat** (window #2; 5-6hr., 15 per day, 80-90dh), **Fez** (window #1; 10hr., 20 per day 4am-5pm, 125dh), and **Azilal** (window #18; 3hr., 8:30am, 12:30, 3:30pm, 60dh)

Grand Taxis: It's best to start from Bab al-Rob, where you can share a taxi to **Asni** (15dh) or **Setti Fatma** (20dh). There is another *grand taxi* stand on Av. Houmane el-Fetouaki; walk down Rue Bab Agnaou, turn left on Houmane el-Fetouaki, and walk for 2min. As always, you have to wait for the taxi to fill up. If you already have a group assembled, there's no need to head to Bab al-Rob; take one of the *grand taxis* at Djema'a al-Fna.

Car Rental: Hertz, 154 Blvd. Mohammed V (☎024 43 99 84). Open M-Sa 8am-noon and 2:30-6:30pm, Su 9am-noon. AmEx. **Avis,** 137 Blvd. Mohammed V (☎024 43 37 27). Same hours. AmEx/MC/V. Rentals at both agencies start at about 300dh per day for a Fiat Uno, plus 2.50dh per km. Min. age 25 for all cars, though many offices don't require proof of age. No special license required. Many hotels arrange rentals.

Moped/Scooter Rental: Rental stands dot the sidewalks around Pl. de 16 Novembre and back towards the medina. Rental fees are approx. 150dh per 6hr., or 300dh for the whole day. The only requirement is knowing generally how to drive one, so there's no insurance. Moped traffic in the city is always a little crazy, so drive at your own risk.

ORIENTATION AND PRACTICAL INFORMATION

Marrakesh and its medina are less crowded and maze-like than Morocco's other imperial cities, but just as crowded and noisy. Most of the excitement, as well as budget food and accommodation, centers around **Djema'a al-Fna** and the medina streets directly off of it. The *souqs* are on the streets leading north off of Djema'a al-Fna, and past them are several of the city's sights. The bus and train stations, administrative buildings, and luxury hotels are in **Guéliz,** the central neighborhood in the *ville nouvelle,* down **Av. Mohammed V;** from Djema'a al-Fna, walk to the towering **Koutoubia Minaret,** turn right, and walk for 20min. to reach **Pl. de 16 Novembre,** the central plaza. Also in Guéliz are most of the car rentals, newsstands, banks, and travel agencies. Bus #1 runs between the minaret and the heart of Guéliz (3dh). Or, take one of the many *petits taxis* (10dh) or horse-drawn carriages (15dh within the medina walls, 25dh to locations outside, sometimes more at night).

Tourist Office: Delegation Regionale de Tourisme, Av. Mohammed V (☎024 43 61 79), at Pl. Abdel Moumen ben Ali, a 30min. walk from Djema'a al-Fna. Take a *petit taxi* for about 15dh. Most helpful if you speak French; but all visitors can pick up glossy maps. (There is a better map on sale for 15dh at many tobacco shops and hotels.) Official guides, worthwhile in Marrakesh, can be booked here (½-day 150dh, full day 250dh). Visit a travel agency for Atlas or other excursions. Open daily 8:30am-noon and 2:30-6:30pm, summer 7:30am-3pm, Ramadan 9am-3pm.

Currency Exchange: Banks with 24hr. **ATMs** line Av. Mohammed V and Av. Hassan II in Guéliz. **Banque Populaire,** Av. Mohammed V, changes money. Open M-F 8:15am-3:45pm. In the medina, Rue Bab Agnaou, left of the post office, has plenty of banks and 24hr ATMs. Many hotels will change money 24hr. Try **Hôtel Ali** or **Hôtel Essaouira.**

Police: ☎19, off Djema'a al-Fna. In the *ville nouvelle,* the station is on Rue Ouadi al-Makhazine, off Pl. de 16 Novembre.

Late-Night Pharmacy: ☎024 44 54 26, off Djema'a al-Fna, on the way to Av. Mohammed V, on the right. Open Tu-Su 9pm-6am.

Medical Emergency: Doctor on call until 10pm at the late-night pharmacy. For more extensive service and 24hr. emergency service, try **Polyclinique du Sud,** 2 Rue Yougoslavie (☎024 44 79 99 or 024 42 57 51), in the *ville nouvelle.* From Pl. de 16 Novembre, walk 3 blocks down Av. Mohammed V away from the medina. Bear right onto Rue de Yougoslavie; it's 2 blocks down on the right. Private clinic with a range of specialists.

Internet Access: Many good internet cafes with A/C are on Bab Agnaou, the pedestrian mall off Djema'a al-Fna. **Hassan Internet,** just off Bab Agnaou, has a fast connection. 8dh per hr. Open 8am-midnight.

Post Office: Pl. 16 Novembre (☎024 43 09 77), off Av. Mohammed V. A madhouse. Unreliable Poste Restante. Open M-F 7:30am-3pm. Branch offices (☎024 44 09 77) in Djema'a al-Fna and near Bab er-Rob. Open M-F 7:30am-3pm. **DHL** and **FedEx** locations at Residence Al Mouhandiz, 113 Av. Abdel Karim El Kahattabi. **Postal Code:** 40000.

ACCOMMODATIONS

Marrakesh's inexpensive accommodations are in abundant supply near Djema'a al-Fna. Budget hotels clump along the *derbs* (side streets) just south of the place, as do *riads,* which are palatial, opulent restored medina homes with gorgeous terraces and home-cooked meals. Staying at a *riad* doesn't come cheap, but if you have a few extra dirhams, consider treating yourself to a night in one. On the far other end of the spectrum, many hotels allow you to sleep on the terrace for 30-40dh, a good option if you can't find a room, are desperately broke, or simply can't stand the ridiculous summer heat.

Hotel CTM, Djema'a al-Fna (☎024 44 23 25). Location, location, location: steps from the monkeys and mystics of the square, Hotel CTM offers elegant rooms in the front courtyard and less expensive, simpler rooms in the back. Communal shower is cold, but good for midday salvation from the heat. Terrace cafe and parking (30dh) to boot. Singles 120dh, with shower 160dh; doubles 190/230dh; triples 350dh. Newer rooms with A/C and shower 320/430/650dh. ❶

Hôtel Ali, Rue Moulay Ismail (☎044 44 49 79), past the post office off Djema'a al-Fna. A small mall of tourist services available here—currency exchange, Atlas excursions, two restaurants, massage services and shiatsu (150-200dh), and the good old-fashioned *hammam* (120dh) on the 2nd fl. Rooms are furnished with big, comfy beds, many with A/C. Showers are clean. The common areas are social, and the hotel is always bustling. English spoken. Call ahead or get here early. Singles 200dh, doubles 300dh, triples 400dh, quads 500dh. Terrace 40dh. ❶

Hôtel Sindi Sud, 109 Riad Zitoun al-Qedim (☎024 44 33 37), down Derb Sidi Bouloukat. From Djema'a al-Fna, face Hotel CTM and walk down the street to the left of it. Sindi Sud is down the first alley to the right. Psychedelic doors guard neat little rooms around a central courtyard. Reception arranges trips to Ouzoud and the desert; prices

Marrakesh

ACCOMMODATIONS
- Hôtel Ali, 3
- Hôtel CTM, 8
- Hôtel Sindi Sud, 9
- Riad Hôtel Assia, 7

FOOD
- Chez Chegrouni, 10
- Hotel Ali, 2
- Hôtel Restaurant Islane, 1
- La Maison du Couscous, 5
- Restaurant El Bahja, 4

NIGHTLIFE
- Café Argana, 6
- Café Paris, 11

TO BAB EL KHEMIS (500 m)
Ben Youssef Mosque
Medersa ben Youssef
Museum of Marrakesh
SOUQS
Koubba al-ba'Adiyn
Babouche Souq
PL. RAHBA KEDIMA
Spice Souq
Souq Smarine
rue Souq Smarine
PLACE BEN SALAH
rue Issebtiyne
TO TANNERIES (300m)
rue Dabachi
rue Douar Graoua
Dar Si Said Museum of Moroccan Art
TO BAB AGHNAT (500m)
Al-Bahia Palace
The Mellah
rue Riad Zitoun al-Jdid
rue riad Zitoun Qedim
PLACE DES FERBLANTIERS
al-Badi Palace
Dar al-Makhzen
Fountain
Mouassin Mosque
rue Mouassine
DJEMA'A AL-FNA
Pharmacy
PLACE DE FOUCAULD
rue Bab Agnaou
rue Moulay Ismail
MEDINA
Bab Agnaou
Kasbah Mosque & Saadian Tombs
TO AGDAL GARDENS (1.2km)
rue Oqba ban Nafaa
avenue Houmane el-Fetouaki
rue Sidi Mimoun
Koutoubia Mosque
Bab er-Rob
rue Dar al-Glaoui
rue de Bab Doukkala
rue Fatima Zohra
Sidi
avenue Mohammed V
Bab Doukkala
rue al-Adaia
Bab Larissa
rue Abou el Abbes Sebti
Bab Jedid
boulevard al-Yarmouk
TO AIRPORT
TO MAJORELLE GARDENS (800 m)
rue Mohammed al-Mellakh
avenue Ahmed Oaqueila
PLACE DE LA LIBERTE
rue Temple
rue Haroun Errachid
Olive Grove de Bab Jdid
avenue Des Nations Unies
rue Echchouada
rue Hafid Ibrahim
PLACE DU XVI NOVEMBRE
avenue Yacoubel Marini
rue Chaouki
rue el Chafi
avenue Paris
avenue al-Qadissia
avenue al-Menara
TO MENARA GARDENS (600m)
rue Moulay Hassan
rue Ouadi al-Makhazine
VILLE NOUVELLE
Jardin Harti
avenue du President Kennedy
TO (100m)
boulevard Moulay Rachid
avenue Hassan II
TO TRAIN STATION (100m)
rue al-Qadi Ayad
avenue de France
rue Mohamed al-Hansali
rue al-Jahed
0 300 yards
0 300 meters

EXPLORING MOROCCO

vary based on duration and group size. Breakfast 20dh. Singles 60dh, doubles 100dh, triples 150, with shower 300dh, quads 200/400dh. Terrace 30dh. ❶

Riad Hôtel Assia, 32 Rue de la Recette (☎024 39 12 85; www.hotel-assia-marrakech.com). Walk down Rue Bab Agnaou (left of the post office) and turn left when you see the signs. Modern convenience meets traditional Moroccan style in this lovely *riad.* Hand-worked *zellij* adorns the bathroom floor in simple but elegant air-conditioned rooms, all around a leafy central courtyard. The terrace has stunning views of the Koutoubia mosque. Shower, toilet, TV, and phone in rooms. Singles 250dh, doubles 380dh, triples 550dh, quads 650dh. ❷

FOOD

A small city of food stalls sprouts up in the early evening at Djema'a al-Fna, dishing up cheap fare from nightfall until well after midnight. Follow the crowds to the best *harira* (spicy bean and chickpea soup), served with dates and *chabakia* (a gooey honey-coated pastry), all for 3dh. The snails (5dh) are for the truly intrepid. Kebabs and sausages (25-30dh) are also on offer, but beware hidden garnish charges. You can't miss the orange juice (3dh), available all day and night, as the juicemen jockey for your business. On the other end of the price spectrum, Marrakesh also boasts many "palace restaurants" where music, outrageous portions, and liquor combine for a memorable, if expensive, evening (usually 300-600dh per person). The usual rotisserie places and snack bars, popular lunch stops, line Bab Agnaou.

Chez Chegrouni, 4 Pl. Djema'a al-Fna (☎024 47 46 15). Top *tajines* come at decent prices in this unobtrusive plaza-corner joint. The excellent chicken *tajine* with lemon and onion (50dh) is best taken on the terrace as you watch the action unfold. Salads 15dh. *Tajines* 50-60dh. Terrace prices slightly higher. Open daily 9am-late. ❶

Hôtel Restaurant Islane, Av. Mohammed V (☎024 44 00 81), on the roof of Hôtel Islane across from the Koutoubia Mosque. Wicker chairs and quality Italian food, with a stunning wide-angle view of the mosque. Pizzas (55-70dh) are spectacular. *Tajines* 80-90dh. F-Sa buffet 140dh. Open daily noon-3pm and 7-11pm. MC/V. ❷

Restaurant El Bahja, 41 Rue Bani Marine (☎024 44 03 43), to the right of the post office. Their motto is *"Le meilleur de la rue"* (the best of the street), and they serve up Moroccan staples at unbeatable prices. Sit down and grab a *tajine* or *grillade* (meat plate 25-30dh). 3-course menus 55-65dh. Open daily noon-11pm. ❶

Hôtel Ali (see **Accommodations,** p. 492). A tasty all-you-can-eat Moroccan buffet dinner situated 4 floors above the bustle of Djema'a al-Fna on the rooftop of Hôtel Ali, with a good variety of couscous, meat, salads, and fruit. A good place for women traveling alone. 70dh for hotel guests, 80dh for all others. Served daily 6:30-10pm. ❷

La Maison du Couscous, 53 Rue Bab Agnaou (☎024 38 68 92; www.couscousmarrakech.com), just off the plaza. Caters largely to tourists, but a very reliable option for couscous. Try the exotic *couscous du Sahara,* served with dried figs, dates, and camel meat. Dishes 70-100dh. Open daily 11am-11pm. AmEx/MC/V, min. 100dh. ❷

SIGHTS

DJEMA'A AL-FNA. Welcome to Djema'a al-Fna (Assembly of the Dead), arguably the most fantastic open-air spectacle in the world. Once the sight of public executions, it has been given over to a loose fraternity of storytellers, dancers, and entertainers. By day, old women will tattoo you with henna, while Barbary apes dance on chains next to men charming snakes. But the real entertainment comes at night, when food stalls come out and smoke fills the air, lending a mystical quality to the men muttering stories and women chanting over tarot cards. Sit down and listen to a story, watch a boxing match, or just stand amidst the commotion, marveling at the ebb and flow of the menagerie around you.

MEDINA AND SOUQS. Marrakesh's medina is less overwhelming than that of Fez, but almost as big and brash, stuffed with tanneries, *babouche* stalls, carpet bazaars, sheepskin vendors, and all manner of crafts. A survey of the medina (primetime for crowds is 5-8pm) begins at the *souqs*. From Djema'a al-Fna, enter the medina directly across from the **Café-Restaurant-Hôtel de France**. Walk past the first line of touristy places and take a quick left through the archway, which marks the beginning of **Rue Souq Smarine,** the main thoroughfare through the markets. This street is home to the **fabric souq,** with gorgeous silky woven blankets, and their owners, calling out to you to buy them. There's also the usual range of lamps, hookahs, and leather stores. A few minutes later you'll come to a large alley to the right heading into the **Rahba Kedima.** You might smell it first: the square is full of stalls selling herbs, spices, and soaps for all variety of cuisines and illnesses. Deeper in the square is **La Criée Berbère,** once home to a slave auction and now full of friendly men using impressive skills of persuasion to sell you carpets. Back on **Rue Souq Smarine** the road quickly forks. The right fork leads past more of the same shops, and eventually to the **Medersa ben Youssef.** The left fork is the *babouche souq*, a small universe of stalls selling traditional Moroccan slippers. When you reach a huge, sharp left turn, head down it to find the dyers' *souq*, full of huge bubbling vats. Pushing through them will lead you to the 16th-century **Mouassine Fountain,** a grimy but character-laden sight. Those with strong stomachs can visit the tanneries: continue through the *souqs* and take a right after the Medersa ben Youssef. Head straight for 10min. through a run-down stretch of the medina, and the tanneries are on your right. If you get lost in the medina, ask a merchant for directions, or ask a child to lead you out of the maze for a few dirhams.

AL-BAHIA PALACE. The grandest palace in all of Marrakesh was built by the vizier Si Ahmed ibn Musa, better known as Bou Ahmed, who named it Al-Bahia ("the Brilliance"). Indeed, this seemingly never-ending network of courtyards, rooms, and sleeping quarters is a masterpiece. Every cedar-wood ceiling is spectacularly carved, making it easily one of the best displays of such craftsmanship in the country. Look for the five-piece ceiling in the side annex. From time to time it also holds contemporary art exhibits. *(From Djema'a al-Fna, walk down rue Riad Zitoun al-Qedim to its end at pl. Ferbiantiers, then turn left and follow the road as it curves to a red archway, which opens onto a long, tree-lined avenue leading to the palace door. Open M-Th and Sa-Su 8:30-11:45am and 2:30-5:45pm, F 8:30-11:30am and 3-5:45pm. 10dh.)*

MEDERSA BEN YOUSSEF. In 1565, Sultan Moulay Abdallah al-Ghalib raised the Medersa ben Youssef in the medina center; it was the largest Qur'anic school in the Maghreb until its closing in 1960. The *medersa* is a glorious example of the Merenid style, with *zellij* tile, stucco work, and carved cedar in layers on the courtyard walls. A huge arch opens on to the *mihrab* (prayer niche) and the prayer room. Upstairs are 132 cells, which they claim once accommodated all 900 of the students. *(Walk down the main souq street, Rue Souq Smarine, and bear right onto Rue Souq al-Kebir. Follow it to its end. Open Tu-Su, June-Aug. 9am-1pm and 2:30-6pm; Sept.-May 9am-6:30pm. 20dh, children 10dh. Combined admission for medersa, Museum of Marrakesh, and Koubba al-Ba'adiyn 60dh.)*

DAR SI SAID. This 19th-century palace, built by the younger brother of Bou Ahmed, houses the Museum of Moroccan Arts, a superb collection of traditional handicrafts from around the country. The highlight of the collection is a 10th-century marble basin dating from the year 1000, brought to Marrakesh from Córdoba by Ali ben Youssef—it is the oldest preserved object in the city.

Rugs, leatherwork, pottery, and weapons are all on display here as well. If you tire, head out to the courtyard's cool gazebo-covered fountain. *(Go toward al-Bahia, and continue on Rue Zitoun al-Jadid, taking the 2nd right heading toward Djema'a al-Fna and the 1st left down the alley where the museum resides. ☎ 024 38 95 64. Open M, W-Th, and Sa-Su 9-11:45am and 2:30-5:45pm, F 9-11:30am and 3-5:45pm. 10dh.)*

MUSEUM OF MARRAKESH. Collections of daggers, Fassi ceramic, and Berber clothing complement a contemporary art gallery showcasing work by Moroccan painters. The building itself, a 19th-century palace, is lavish and contains a traditional *hammam* to explore. *(Off the open plaza at the end of Rue Souq Smarine in the back of the medina, around the corner from the medersa and Koubba al-Ba'adiyn. ☎ 024 39 09 11. Open daily 9am-6pm. 40dh, students 20dh. Combined admission for 3 monuments 60dh.)*

KOUTOUBIA MOSQUE. Dominating the medina's skyline is the finest and best-preserved remnant of the Almohad dynasty, which ruled from 1130 to 1213. The 70m-tall minaret, built by the sultan Yacoub al-Mansour, is topped by four golden lanterns; legend has it that the sultan's wife melted her gold jewelry to gild the fourth. The mosque was the model for its sisters, one in Rabat and the other—the Giralda—in Sevilla (see p. 152). *(Entrance is forbidden to non-Muslims.)*

KOUBBA AL-BA'ADIYN MONUMENT. Next to the *medersa* is the bizarrely protruding cupola of the 12h-century Koubba al-Ba'adiyn, Marrakesh's oldest monument. Despite the destruction of all other Almoravid relics by the succeeding Almohads, their influence is undeniable here—this is the structure on which much of Morocco's architecture is modeled. It was excavated in the 20th century, and much remains hidden underground or by other structures. While the exterior of the cupola is unpainted, the curves and interior decoration are definitely distinct from later architecture and are worth a look. *(Walk down the main souq street, Rue Souq Smarine, bear right onto Rue Souq al-Kebir, and turn left at the madrasa. Open daily 9am-5:30pm. Bang on the door if it's closed. 10dh. 60dh for all 3 monuments.)*

SAADIAN TOMBS. Modeled after the interior of Granada's Alhambra, the Saadian Tombs served as the royal Saadian necropolis during the 16th and 17th centuries, and three halls of tombs have been preserved in much of their splendor. The first room is home to the children of Sultan Ahmed al-Mansour, followed by the **Hall of the Twelve Columns,** covered in marble, a gold-inlaid dome, and stucco work. The sultan, along with his descendants, are buried here. The last and smallest room is home to his mother and father. The unmarked tombs in the garden belong to women, while those of men are covered in Arabic calligraphy. The minaret of the Mosque of the Kasbah, al-Mansour's personal mosque, towers above the complex. *(From Djema'a al-Fna, walk down rue Bab Agnaou 5min. to Bab er-Rob, take a left through Bab Agnaou, and follow the signs into an alley just past the mosque. English tours (15-20dh) available from the guides near the entrance. Open daily 8:30-11:30am and 2:30-5:45pm. 10dh.)*

GARDENS. Since the 12th century, rulers have dealt with the sun by constructing massive gardens irrigated with water from the Atlas. The **Majorelle Gardens** were designed by French painter Jacques Majorelle in the 1920s, and are owned and maintained today by the Yves Saint-Laurent Foundation. Buried in the back is a lone column fragment, a memorial to the famous French designer, born in North Africa in 1936. On the same site is the small **Museum of Islamic Art.** *(From Djema'a al-Fna, walk toward Koutoubia Mosque and take a right on av. Mohammed V. After exiting the medina, take a right and follow the walls to the bus station. Bear left onto Blvd. Safi and turn right onto Av. Yacoub al-Mansour; the gardens are on the left. Better yet, take a petit taxi for 15dh (drivers will ask for 30). Open daily June-Aug. 8am-noon and 3-7pm, Sept.-May 8am-noon and 2-5pm. Gardens 30dh, museum 15dh.)* Winston Churchill and King Mohammed VI have both enjoyed the gardens of **La Mamounia,** perhaps the poshest hotel in the city, and you can too. The hotel allows the public to visit the gardens, but you'll have to dress appropriately and act the part. *(The hotel is 5min. from Djema'a al-Fna on Av. Houman el Fetouaki just before exiting through Bab Jedid. Open to the public until 2pm, although the doormen will often turn you away even earlier.)*

NIGHTLIFE

Most travelers hang around Djema'a al-Fna or in one of the terrace cafes that overlooks it for most of the night. **Café Argana** is a quiet spot with amazing views. Drinks 10dh. **Café Paris** is another pleasant option. Not much distinguishes the terrace bars: they all have great views. For a hard drink, try the bars at the **Tazi** (☎024 44 27 87) and **Foucauld** (☎024 44 54 99) hotels, where locals and tourists mix with the help of 25dh Spéciale Flag. (Both bars open at 9pm. To find the Tazi, head away from Djema'a al-Fna 200m down the street to the left of the Banque du Maroc. For Foucauld, turn right by the Tazi onto the road that becomes Av. Mohammed V and walk two blocks.) Young, pretty Marrakeshis like to party, and they support a thriving club scene. Most clubs pick up on the weekends after 1 or 2am. **Diamant Noir,** in **Hôtel Marrakech** on Av. Mohammed V, is a fairly popular, playing a good mix of current house and hip-hop jams. (Open 10pm-late. Cover 90-120dh.) **Pacha,** the famous Ibiza club, now rages through the night in Morocco, too. Features famous DJs and epically large dance floors. (☎024 38 84 05. Cover 150dh, weekends 300dh. Open 9pm-dawn.) Both are an expensive cab ride away from the medina in Guéliz.

NO WORK, ALL PLAY

THE BEAT GOES ON

Essaouira sacrifices a little of it famous laid-back beach feel ever June when musicians and music afi cionados descend on the town fo the four-day **Gnaoua World Musi Festival.** Gnaoua (pronounced guh now-a) is a North African fusior genre of spiritual music, formec as slaves from West Africa brough their musical traditions to Nortl Africa and fused them with Moroc can and North African rhythms anc instrumentation. Traditionally, the musical groups, each of which was a spiritual brotherhood, would go through rituals to honor the sever saints of Islam or to invoke djinns and spirits, as the performers woulc enter a trance-like state.

The spiritual aspect of the music remains, but has lost it overtly religious rituals. The fes tival in Essaouira is famous fo the creative interpretations o gnaoua, adding elements of jaz reggae, and world music for 4 days of public performances. The most famous *maalems* (maste musicians) perform at Bab Sba and Place Moulay Hassan. As i the town's relaxed attitude didn' already encourage brotherhood the gnaoua brings together every one present together for severa days of musical and spiritual com munion. The hippies felt the love here when they stopped by in the 70s, and it hasn't left yet.

(The concert lasts 4 days anc takes place in late June every year. Visit the website, www.festi val-gnaoua.net, for details.)

APPENDIX

CLIMATE

Climate on the Iberian Peninsula varies hugely by both region and season. While Asturians mull cider to keep warm as the cold rain falls, Sevilla's patios fill with sangria drinkers trying to stay cool under the sweltering afternoon sun. Like Spain, Portugal has both warm inland plains and a temperate coast. That coastal Mediterranean climate that blesses Spain and Portugal extends south to Morocco, which, although generally regarded as a desert, has a wealth of green mountains and fertile expanses. The following table contains average temperature ranges and rainfall for selected cities.

SPAIN	JANUARY			APRIL			JULY			OCTOBER		
	°C	°F	mm	°C	°F	mm	°C	°F	mm	°C	°F	mm
Barcelona	6-13	43-55	31	11-18	52-64	43	21-28	70-82	27	15-21	59-70	86
Madrid	2-9	36-48	39	7-18	45-64	48	17-31	63-88	11	10-19	50-66	53
Santander	7-12	45-54	119	10-15	50-59	83	16-22	61-72	54	12-18	54-64	133
Sevilla	6-15	43-59	66	11-24	52-75	57	20-36	68-97	1	14-26	57-79	70
PORTUGAL												
	°C	°F	mm	°C	°F	mm	°C	°F	mm	°C	°F	mm
Faro	9-15	48-59	70	13-20	55-68	31	20-28	68-82	1	16-22	61-72	51
Lisboa	8-14	46-57	111	12-20	52-68	54	15-25	59-77	3	14-22	57-72	62
Porto	5-13	41-55	159	9-18	48-64	86	15-25	59-77	20	11-21	52-70	105
MOROCCO												
	°C	°F	mm	°C	°F	mm	°C	°F	mm	°C	°F	mm
Marrakesh	4-18	39-64	25	11-26	52-79	31	19-38	66-100	3	14-28	57-82	23
Rabat	8-17	46-63	66	11-22	52-72	43	17-28	63-82	0	14-25	57-77	48

To convert from degrees Fahrenheit to degrees Celsius, subtract 32 and multiply by 5/9. To convert from Celsius to Fahrenheit, multiply by 9/5 and add 32.

CELSIUS	-5	0	5	10	15	20	25	30	35	40
FAHRENHEIT	23	32	41	50	59	68	77	86	95	104

MEASUREMENTS

Like the rest of the rational world, Spain, Portugal, and Morocco use the metric system. The basic unit of length is the meter (m), which is divided into 100 centimeters (cm) or 1000 millimeters (mm). One thousand meters make up one kilometer (km). Fluids are measured in liters (L), each divided into 1000 milliliters (mL). A liter of pure water weighs one kilogram (kg), which is divided into 1000 grams (g). One metric ton is 1000kg.

MEASUREMENT CONVERSIONS	
1 inch (in.) = 25.4mm	1 millimeter (mm) = 0.039 in.
1 foot (ft.) = 0.305m	1 meter (m) = 3.28 ft.
1 yard (yd.) = 0.914m	1 meter (m) = 1.094 yd.
1 mile (mi.) = 1.609km	1 kilometer (km) = 0.621 mi.
1 ounce (oz.) = 28.35g	1 gram (g) = 0.035 oz.
1 pound (lb.) = 0.454kg	1 kilogram (kg) = 2.205 lb.
1 fluid ounce (fl. oz.) = 29.57mL	1 milliliter (mL) = 0.034 fl. oz.
1 gallon (gal.) = 3.785L	1 liter (L) = 0.264 gal.

SPANISH PHRASEBOOK

Each vowel has only one pronunciation: *a* ("ah" in "father"); *e* ("eh" in "pet"); *i* ("ee" in "eat"); *o* ("oh" in "oat"); *u* ("oo" in "boot"); *y*, by itself, is pronounced the same as the Spanish i ("ee"). Most consonants are the same as in English. Important exceptions are: *j* ("h" in "hello"); *ll* ("y" in "yes"); *ñ* ("ny" in "canyon"); and *r* at the beginning of a word or *rr* anywhere in a word (trilled). *H* is always silent. *G* before *e* or *i* is pronounced like the "h" in "hen;" elsewhere it is pronounced like the "g" in "gate." *X* has a bewildering variety of pronunciations: depending on dialect and word position, it can sound like the English "h," "s," "sh," or "x." *B* and *v* have similar pronunciations. Spanish words receive stress on the syllable marked with an accent. In the absence of an accent mark, words that end in vowels, *n*, or *s* receive stress on the penultimate syllable. For words ending in all other consonants, stress falls on the last syllable. The Spanish language has masculine and feminine nouns, and gives a gender to all adjectives. Masculine words generally end with an *o*, feminine words generally end with an *a*. Pay close attention—slight changes in word ending can have drastic changes in meaning. For instance, when receiving directions, mind the distinction between *derecho* (straight; more commonly *recto*) and *derecha* (right). Sentences that end in ? or ! are also preceded by the same punctuation upside-down: *¿Cómo estás? ¡Muy bien, gracias!*

ESSENTIAL PHRASES

ENGLISH	SPANISH	PRONUNCIATION
Hello.	Hola.	OH-la
How are you?	¿Cómo está?	KOH-mo es-TA
Good, thanks.	Muy bien, gracias.	MWEE bee-en, GRA-see-ahs
Goodbye.	Adiós.	ah-dee-OHS
Yes/No	Sí/No	SEE/NO
Please.	Por favor.	POHR fa-VOHR
Thank you.	Gracias.	GRA-see-ahs
You're welcome.	De nada.	DAY NAH-dah
Do you speak English?	¿Habla inglés?	AH-blah een-GLAYCE
I don't speak Spanish.	No hablo español.	NO AH-bloh ehs-pahn-YOHL
Excuse me.	Perdón.	pehr-DOHN
I don't know.	No sé.	NO SAY
Can you repeat that?	¿Puede repetirlo?	PWEH-day reh-peh-TEER-lo
Let's dance.	Bailamos.	by-lah-MOHS

ON ARRIVAL

ENGLISH	SPANISH	ENGLISH	SPANISH
I am from (the US/ Europe).	Soy de (los Estados Unidos/Europa).	What's the problem, sir/ madam?	¿Cuál es el problema, señor/señora?
Here is my passport.	Aquí está mi pasaporte.	I lost my passport.	Perdí mi pasaporte.
I will be here for less than six months.	Estaré aquí por menos de seis meses.	I have nothing to declare.	No tengo nada para declarar.
Where is customs?	¿Dónde está la aduana?	Where do I claim my luggage?	¿Dónde puedo reclamar mi equipaje?
I don't know where that came from.	No sé de donde vino eso.	Please do not detain me.	Por favor no me detenga.

DIRECTIONS

ENGLISH	SPANISH	ENGLISH	SPANISH
(to the) right/left	(a la) derecha/izquierda	across from	enfrente de/frente a
next to	al lado de/junto a	near/far	cerca/lejos
straight ahead	derecho	turn (command)	doble
on top of/above	encima de/arriba	beneath/below	bajo de/abajo
traffic light	semáforo	corner	esquina
street	calle/avenida	block	cuadra

SURVIVAL SPANISH

ENGLISH	SPANISH	ENGLISH	SPANISH
How can you get to...?	¿Cómo se puede llegar a...?	Is there anything cheaper?	¿Hay algo más barato/ económico?
Does this bus go to (Italy)?	¿Va este autobús a (Italia)?	I'm in a hurry!	¡Tengo prisa!
Where is (Azorín) street?	¿Dónde está la calle (Azorín)?	What bus line goes to..?	¿Qué línea de buses tiene servicio a...?
When does the bus leave?	¿Cuándo sale el bús?	From where does the bus leave?	¿De dónde sale el bús?
I'm getting off at...	Bajo en...	I have to go now.	Tengo que ir ahora.
Can I buy a ticket?	¿Podría comprar un boleto?	How far is...?	¿Qué tan lejos está...?
How long does the trip take?	¿Cuántas horas dura el viaje?	Please let me off at the zoo/hostel.	Por favor, déjeme en el zoológico/hostal
I am going to the airport.	Voy al aeropuerto.	The flight is delayed/ cancelled.	El vuelo está atrasado/ cancelado.
Where is the bathroom?	¿Dónde está el baño?	Is it safe to hitchhike?	¿Es seguro pedir aventón?
I lost my baggage.	Perdí mi equipaje.	I'm lost.	Estoy perdido(a).
How much does it cost per day/week?	¿Cuánto cuesta por día/ semana?	Does it have (heating/air-conditioning)?	¿Tiene (calefacción/aire acondicionado)?
Where can I buy a cell-phone?	¿Dónde puedo comprar un teléfono celular?	Where can I check e-mail?	¿Dónde se puede chequear el email?
Could you tell me what time it is?	¿Podría decirme qué hora es?	Are there student discounts available?	¿Hay descuentos para estudiantes?

ACCOMMODATIONS

ENGLISH	SPANISH	ENGLISH	SPANISH
Is there a cheap hotel around here?	¿Hay un hotel económico por aquí?	Are there rooms with windows?	¿Hay habitaciones con ventanas?
Do you have rooms available?	¿Tiene habitaciones libres?	I am going to stay for (four) days.	Me voy a quedar (cuatro) días.

ENGLISH	SPANISH	ENGLISH	SPANISH
I would like to reserve a room.	Quisiera reservar una habitación.	Are there cheaper rooms?	¿Hay habitaciones más baratas?
Can I see a room?	¿Podría ver una habitación?	Do they come with private baths?	¿Vienen con baño privado?
Do you have any singles/doubles?	¿Tiene habitaciones sencillas/dobles?	Does it have (heating/A/C)?	¿Tiene (calefacción/aire acondicionado)?
I'll take it.	Lo tomo.	Who's there?	¿Quién es?
I need another key/towel/pillow.	Necesito otra llave/toalla/almohada.	The shower/sink/toilet is broken.	La ducha/pila/el servicio no funciona.

EMERGENCY

ENGLISH	SPANISH	ENGLISH	SPANISH
Help!	¡Socorro!/¡Ayúdeme!	Call the police!	¡Llame a la policía!
I am hurt.	Estoy herido(a).	Leave me alone!	¡Déjame en paz!
It's an emergency!	¡Es una emergencia!	They robbed me!	¡Me han robado!
Fire!	¡Fuego!/¡Incendio!	They went that way!	¡Fueron en esa dirección!
Call a clinic/ambulance/doctor/priest!	¡Llame a una clínica/una ambulancia/un médico/un padre!	I will only speak in the presence of a lawyer.	Sólo hablaré en presencia de un abogado(a).
I need to contact my embassy.	Necesito contactar mi embajada.	Don't touch me!	¡No me toque!

MEDICAL

ENGLISH	SPANISH	ENGLISH	SPANISH
I feel bad/better/fine/worse.	Me siento mal/mejor/bien/peor.	What is this medicine for?	¿Para qué es esta medicina?
I'm sick/ill.	Estoy enfermo(a).	Where is the nearest hospital/doctor?	¿Dónde está el hospital/doctor más cercano?
I'm allergic to...	Soy alérgico(a) a...	Here is my prescription.	Aquí está la receta médica.
I have a cold/a fever/diarrhea/nausea	Tengo gripe/una calentura/diarrea/náusea.	Call a doctor, please.	Llame a un médico, por favor

OUTDOORS/RECREATION

ENGLISH	SPANISH	ENGLISH	SPANISH
Is it safe to swim here?	¿Es seguro nadar aquí?	Do you have sunscreen?	¿Tiene crema solar?
What time is high/low tide?	¿A qué hora es marea alta/baja?	Is there a strong current?	¿Hay una corriente fuerte?
Where can I rent a surfboard/bike?	¿Dónde puedo alquilar un planeador de mar/bicicleta?.	Where is the trail?	¿Dónde está el rastro?
Do I need a guide?	¿Necesito una guía?	Can I camp here?	¿Puedo acampar aquí?

EATING OUT

ENGLISH	SPANISH	ENGLISH	SPANISH
Do you have anything vegetarian/without meat?	¿Hay algún plato vegetariano/sin carne?	Can I see the menu?	¿Podría ver la carta/el menú?
I would like to order (the eel).	Quisiera (el congrio).	Table for (one), please.	Mesa para (uno), por favor.
Check, please.	¡La cuenta, por favor!	Do you take credit cards?	¿Aceptan tarjetas de crédito?
Where is a good restaurant?	¿Dónde está un restaurante bueno?	Delicious!	¡Qué rico!

APPENDIX

NUMBERS, DAYS, AND MONTHS

ENGLISH	SPANISH	ENGLISH	SPANISH	ENGLISH	SPANISH
0	cero	20	veinte	last night	anoche
1	uno	21	veintiuno	weekend	(el) fin de semana
2	dos	22	veintidos	morning	(la) mañana
3	tres	30	treinta	afternoon	(la) tarde
4	cuatro	40	cuarenta	night	(la) noche
5	cinco	50	cincuenta	month	(el) mes
6	seis	100	cien	year	(el) año
7	siete	1000	mil	early/late	temprano/tarde
8	ocho	1 million	un millón	January	enero
9	nueve	Monday	lunes	February	febrero
10	diez	Tuesday	martes	March	marzo
11	once	Wednesday	miércoles	April	abril
12	doce	Thursday	jueves	May	mayo
13	trece	Friday	viernes	June	junio
14	catorce	Saturday	sábado	July	julio
15	quince	Sunday	domingo	August	agosto
16	dieciseis	today	hoy	September	septiembre
17	diecisiete	tomorrow	mañana	October	octubre
18	dieciocho	day after tomorrow	pasado mañana	November	noviembre
19	diecinueve	yesterday	ayer	December	diciembre

PORTUGUESE PHRASEBOOK

Portuguese words are often spelled like their Spanish equivalents, although the pronunciation is different. In addition to regular vowels, Portuguese, like French, has nasal vowels: those with a *tilde* (*ã*, *õ*, etc.) or before an *m* or *n* are pronounced with a nasal twang. At the end of a word, *o* is pronounced "oo" as in "room," and *e* is sometimes silent (usually after a *t* or *d*). The consonant *s* is pronounced "sh" or "zh" when it occurs before another consonant. The consonants *ch* and *x* are pronounced "sh," although the latter is sometimes pronounced as in English; *j* and *g* (before *e* or *i*) are pronounced "zh"; *ç* sounds like "es." The combinations *nh* and *lh* are pronounced "ny" as in "canyon" and "ly" as in "billion." The masculine singular definite article is "o" and the feminine singular definite article is "a."

ESSENTIAL PHRASES

ENGLISH	PORTUGUESE	PRONUNCIATION
Yes/No.	Sim/Não.	see/now
Hello.	Olá.	oh-LAH
Good day/afternoon/night.	Bom dia/tarde/noite.	bom DEE-ah/TARD/NOYT
Goodbye.	Até logo.	ah-TEH low-go
Please.	Por favor.	pohr fa-VOHR
Thank you.	Obrigado/a.	oh-bree-GAH-doh/dah
Sorry/excuse me.	Desculpe.	dish-KOOLP-eh
Do you speak English?	Fala inglês?	FAH-lah een-GLAYSH?
I don't understand.	Não entendo	now ehn-TEHN-doh
Where is...?	Onde é...?	OHN-deh eh...?
How do you get to...?	Como chego à...?	COH-moo SHEH-go ah...?

How much does this cost?	Quanto custa?	KWAHN-too KOOST-ah?
Do you have a single/double room?	Tem um quarto individual/duplo?	tem oom KWAR-too EEN-dee-vee-doo-WAHL/DOO-ploh?
That is very cheap/expensive.	É muito caro/barato.	eh MUY-toh CAH-roh/bah-RAH-toh
Help!	Socorro!	soh-HOH-roh!
Who/what	quem/que	KEHM/KEH
When/why	quando/porque	KWAN-doh/pohr-KAY
I want/would like...	Eu quero/gostaria...	EH-oo KER-oh/gost-ar-EE-uh
What is your name? My name is...	Como se chama? O meu nome é...	COH-mo seh SHAH-mah? oh MEH-oo NO-meh eh...
I am (twenty) years old.	Eu tenho (vente) anos.	Eh-oo TEN-yo (VIN-teh) anyos.

NUMBERS, DAYS, AND MONTHS

ENGLISH	PORTUGUESE	ENGLISH	PORTUGUESE	ENGLISH	PORTUGUESE
0	zero	20	vinte	last night	ontem à noite
1	um/uma	21	vinte-um/uma	weekend	(o) fim-de-semana
2	dois/duas	22	vinte-dois/duas	morning	(a) manhã
3	três	30	trinta	afternoon	(a) tarde
4	quatro	40	quarenta	night	(a) noite
5	cinco	50	cinquenta	month	(o) mês
6	seis	100	cem	year	(o) ano
7	sete	1000	um mil	early/late	cedo/tarde
8	oito	1 million	um milhão	January	Janeiro
9	nove	Monday	segunda-feira	February	Fevereiro
10	dez	Tuesday	terça-feira	March	Março
11	onze	Wednesday	quarta-feira	April	Abril
12	doze	Thursday	quinta-feira	May	Maio
13	treze	Friday	sexta-feira	June	Junho
14	catorze	Saturday	sábado	July	Julho
15	quinze	Sunday	domingo	August	Agosto
16	dezasseis	today	hoje	September	Setembro
17	dezassete	tomorrow	amanhã	October	Outubro
18	dezoito	day after tomorrow	depois de amanhã	November	Novembro
19	dezanove	yesterday	ontem	December	Dezembro

MOROCCO PHRASEBOOK

While Moroccan Arabic *(darija)* is historically related to standard Arabic, the dialect has evolved to such an extent that it could almost be considered a separate language. Berber, French, and even Spanish have had deep influences on the vocabulary and pronunciation of the language. Though Arabic is the official language and by far the most commonly spoken tongue, French remains widely understood, particularly in the governmental and tourist domain. Try out some Arabic—making the effort goes a long way towards being a respectful and engaged visitor—but speakers of English, Spanish, and other romance languages might have more luck sticking with French. Moroccan Arabic spellings are transliterated and should be pronounced phonetically.

ARABIC ESSENTIALS

ENGLISH	MOROCCAN ARABIC
Hello (polite).	es salaam alaykum
Hi/How are you?	la bas?
Fine, thanks.	la bas, barak
Yes/No	eeyeh/la
Please.	'afak (m)/'afik (f)
Thank you (very much).	shukran (bezzef)
You're welcome.	la shukran 'la wejb
Excuse me.	smeh leeyah
My name is...	esmee...
Goodbye	bessalama
God willing	ensha'llaah
I'm from...	ana men...
I don't speak Arabic.	makan'refsh l'arbeeyah
Do you speak English?	wash kat'ref negleezeeya?
Is this bus going to...?	wash had lkar ghaadee l...?
I'm looking for...	kanqellab 'la...
Get away from me!	ba'd mennee!
Help!	'teqnee!
I am sick.	ana mreed
I want (I would like)...	bgheet...
Where is the (train station)?	feen kayn (lagaar)?
What time does the...leave?	wufuqash kaykhrej...?
bus/train	otubees/tran
We like Morocco!	'azhebatna lmagreeb!

FRENCH ESSENTIALS

THE BASICS		
Hello (Good day)/Hi.	Bonjour/Salut	bohn-ZHOOR/sah-LU
Good evening.	Bon soir	bohn-SWAH
How are you?	Ça va?	sa-VA?
Goodbye	Au revoir	oh ruh-VWAH
Yes/No/Maybe	Oui/Non/Peut-être	wee/nohn/p'TET-ruh
Please	S'il vous plaît	see voo PLAY
Thank you	Merci	mehr-SEE
You're welcome	De rien/Je vous en prie	duh rhee-ehn/jh'VOOS on PREE
Pardon me	Excusez-moi/Pardon	ex-KU-zay-MWAH/pahr-DOHN
Help!	Au secours!	oh sek-OOR!
I'm lost	Je suis perdu(e)	jh'SWEE pehr-DU
I'm sorry	Je suis désolé(e)	jh'SWEE day-zoh-LAY
Do you speak English?	Parlez-vous anglais?	par-lay-voo ahn-GLAY?
I don't speak French.	Je ne parle pas français.	jh'ne parl pah frahn-SAY
I don't understand.	Je ne comprends pas.	jh'ne KOHM-prahn pas
I would like...	Je voudrais...	jh'voo-DRAY
How much does this cost?	Combien ça coûte?	comb-YEN sa coot?
Leave me alone.	Laissez-moi tranquille	LESS-say-mwah trahn-KEEL
I need help.	J'ai besoin d'assistance.	jhay bezz-WEHN dah-SEE-stahnss
My name is ( ). What's your name?	Je m'appelle ( ). Comment vous appelez-vous?	JH'ma-PELL ( ). kuh-MAHN voo-za-pell-ay-VOO?
Stop!	Arrêtez!	ahr-eh-TAY
It's just one step from the sublime to the ridiculous.	"Du sublime au ridicule il n'y a qu'un pas." (Napoléon)	doo soo-BLEEM oh ree-dee-CULE eel nee ah KHUN pah

GLOSSARY

SPAIN: TRAVELING

abadía: abbey
abierto: open
ayuntamiento/ajuntament (C): city hall
albergue: youth hostel
alcazaba: Muslim citadel
alcázar: Muslim palace
arena: sand
autobús/autocar: bus
avenida/avinguda (C): avenue
bahía: bay
bakalao: Spanish techno
bandera azul: blue flag, EU award for clean beaches
baños: baths
barcelonés: of Barcelona
barrio viejo: old quarter
biblioteca: library
billete/boleto: ticket
buceo: scuba diving
cabo: cape
cajero automático: ATM
calle/carrer (C): street
cambio: currency exchange
capilla: chapel
castillo/castell (C): castle
catedral: cathedral
cerrado: closed
carretera: highway
casco antiguo/viejo: old city
chocolate: chocolate or hash
ciudad vieja/ciutat vella (C): old city
colegio: high school
consigna: luggage storage
Correos: post office
corrida: bullfight
cripta: crypt
cuarto: room
encierro: running of the bulls
entrada: entrance
ermita/ermida (C): hermitage
escuela: (elementary) school
estación: station
estanco: tobacco shop
estanque: pond
estany (C): lake
extremeño: of Extremadura
fachada: facade
feria: outdoor market, fair
ferrocarriles: trains
fiesta: holiday or festival
fuente/font (C): fountain
gallego: of Galicia
gitano: gypsy
glorieta: rotary
iglesia/església (C)/igrexa (G): church
IVA: value-added tax
jardín público: public garden
judería: Jewish quarter
librería: bookstore
lista de correos: poste restante
litera: sleeping car (in trains)
llegada: arrival
madrileño: Madrid resident
madrugada: early morning
manchego: from La Mancha
mercado/mercat (C): market
mezquita: mosque
mirador: lookout point
monestir (C): monastery
monte: mountain
mosteiro (G): monastery
mozárabe: Christian art style
mudéjar: Muslim architectural style
muelle/moll (C): wharf, pier
murallas: walls
museo/museu (C): museum
oficina: office
palacio/palau (C): palace
parador nacional: state-owned hotel
parte viejo: old town
paseo, Po./passeig, Pg. (C): promenade
pico: peak
playa/platja (C): beach
plaza/plaça, Pl. (C)/praza, Pr. (G): square, plaza
puente: bridge
quiosco: newsstand
rastro: flea market
real: royal
REAJ: Spanish youth hostel network
Reconquista: Christian reconquest of the Iberian peninsula from the Moors
refugio: shelter, refuge
reina/rey: queen/king
retablo: altarpiece
ría (G): estuary
río/riu (C): river
rua (G): street
sacristía: part of the church where sacred objects are kept
sala: room, hall

salida: exit, departure
selva: forest
Semana Santa: Holy Week, leading up to Easter Sunday
sepulcro: tomb
seu (C): cathedral
Sevillana: type of flamenco
SIDA: AIDS
sierra/serra (C): mountain range
Siglo de Oro: Golden Age
sillería: choir stalls
tienda: shop, tent
tesoro: treasury
torre: tower
universidad: university
v.o.: versión original, a foreign-language film subtitled in Spanish
valle: valley
zarzuela: Spanish light opera

SPAIN: FOOD AND DRINK

a la plancha/a brasa: grilled
aceite: oil
aceituna: olive
adabo: battered
agua: water
aguacate: avocado
aguardiente: firewater
ahumado/a: smoked
ajo: garlic
al horno: baked
albóndigas: meatballs
alioli: Catalan garlic sauce
almejas: clams
almendras: almonds
almuerzo: midday meal
anchoas: anchovies
anguila: eel
arroz: rice
arroz con leche: rice pudding
asado: roasted
atún: tuna
bacalao: salted cod
bistec: steak
bocadillo: sandwich
bodega: wine cellar
bollo: bread roll
boquerones: anchovies
brasa: chargrilled
cacahuete: peanut
café con leche: coffee w/milk
café solo: black coffee
calabacín: zucchini
calamares: calamari, squid
caldereta: stew
calimocho: red wine and cola
callos: tripe
camarones: shrimp
caña: beer in a small glass
canelones: cannelloni
cangrejo: crab
caracoles: snails
carne: meat
cava (C): sparkling white wine
cebolla: onion
cena: dinner
cerdo: pig, pork
cereza: cherry
cervecería: beer bar
cerveza: beer
champiñones: mushrooms
choco: cuttlefish
chorizo: spicy red sausage
chuleta: chop, cutlet
chupito: shot
churros: fried dough sticks
cocido: cooked, stew
conejo: rabbit
coñac: brandy
copas: drinks
cordero: lamb
cortado: coffee with little milk
croquetas: fried croquettes
crudo: raw
cuchara: spoon
cuchillo: knife
cuenta: the bill
desayuno: breakfast
dorada: sea bass
empanada: meat/fish pastry
ensaladilla rusa: vegetable salad with mayonnaise
entremeses: hors d'oeuvres
escabeche: pickled fish
espagueti: spaghetti
espárragos: asparagus
espinacas: spinach
fabada asturiana: bean soup with sausage and ham
flan: crème caramel
frambuesa: raspberry
fresa: strawberry
frito/a: fried
galleta: cookie
gambas: prawns
garbanzos: chickpeas
gazpacho: cold tomato soup with garlic and cucumber

ginebra: gin
guisantes: peas
helado: ice cream
hielo: ice
horchata: sweet almond drink
horneado: baked
huevo: egg
jamón serrano: cured ham
jatetxea (B): restaurant
jerez: sherry
langosta: lobster
langostino: large prawn
leche: milk
lechuga: lettuce
lenguado: sole
lomo: pork loin
manzana: apple
manzanilla: dry, light sherry
mayonesa: mayonnaise
mejillones: mussels
melocotón: peach
menestra de verduras: vegetable mix/ pottage
menú: full meal with bread, drink, and side dish
merienda: tea/snack
merluza: hake
migas: fried breadcrumb dish
mojito: white rum and club soda with mint and sugar
morcilla: blood sausage
muy hecho: well-done (steak)
naranja: orange
natillas: creamy milk dessert
navajas: razor clams
paella: rice and seafood dish
pan: bread
pasa: raisin
pastas: small sweet cakes
pastel: pastry
patatas bravas: potatoes w/spicy tomato sauce and mayo
patatas fritas: French fries
pato: duck
pavo: turkey
pechuga: chicken breast
pepino: cucumber
picante: spicy
pimienta (negra): (black) pepper
pimiento (rojo): (red) pepper
piña: pineapple
pintxo (B): Basque for tapa
plancha: grill
plátano: banana
plato del día: daily special plato combinado: entree and side dish
poco hecho: rare (steak)
pollo: chicken
pulpo: octopus
queso: cheese
rabo de toro: bull's tail
ración: small dish
rebozado: battered and fried
refrescos: soft drinks
relleno/a: stuffed
sal: salt
salchicha: pork sausage
sangría: red wine punch
seco: dried
servilleta: napkin
sesos: brains
setas: wild mushrooms
sidra: (alcoholic) cider
solomillo: sirloin
sopa: soup
taberna: tapas bar
tapa: bite-sized snack
tenedor: fork
ternera: beef, veal
terraza: patio seating
tinto: red (wine)
tocino: (Canadian) bacon
tomate: tomato
tortilla española: potato fritatta
tortilla francesa: omelette
tostada: toast
trucha: trout
trufas: truffles
tubo: tall glass of beer
txakoli (B): fizzy white wine
uva: grape
vaca, carne de: beef
vaso: glass
verduras: green vegetables
vino: wine
vino blanco: white wine
vino tinto: red wine
xampanyería (C): champagne bar
yema: candied egg yolk
zanahoria: carrot
zarzuela de marisco: shellfish stew
zumo: fruit juice

PORTUGAL: TRAVELING

alto/a: upper
autocarro: bus
bairro: neighborhood, district
baixo/a: lower

berrões: stone pigs found in Trás-Os-Montes
bicicleta de montanha: mountain bike
bilhete: ticket
bilheteria: ticket office
câmara municipal: town hall
camioneta: long-distance bus
capela: chapel
casa de abrigo: shelter-house, usually in parks
castelo: castle
centro de saúde: state-run medical center
chegadas: arrivals
cidade: city
claustro: cloister
construção: construction
conta: bill
coro alto: choir stall
Correios: post office
cruzeiro: large stone cross; cruise
Dom, Dona: courtesy titles, usually for kings and queens
domingo: Sunday
entrada: entrance
esquerda: left (abbr. E, Esqa)
estação rodoviária: bus station
estrada: road
feriado: holiday
floresta: forest
fortaleza: fort
grutas: caves
horario: timetable
igreja: church
ilha: island
intercidade: inter-city train
lago: lake
largo: small square
ligação: connecting bus/train
livraria: bookstore
miradouro: lookout
mosteiro: monastery
mouraria: Moorish quarter
mudança: switch/change
palácio: palace
paragem: stop
partidas: departures
pelourinho: stone pillory
pensão (s.), pensões (pl.): pension(s)/guesthouse(s)
ponte: bridge
porta: gate/door
posto de informações turísticas: tourist office
pousada da juventude: youth hostel
pousada: guest house
praça: square
praça de touros: bullring
praia: beach
PSP: Polícia de Seguranca Pública, the local police force
quarta-feira: Wednesday
quarto de casal: room with double bed
quinta-feira: Thursday
quiosque: kiosk; newsstand
rés do chão (R/C): ground floor
residencial: guesthouse, more expensive than pensões
retábulo: altarpiece
ribeira: stream
ria: narrow lagoon
rio: river
romaria: pilgrimage-festival
rua: street
sábado: Saturday
saída: exit
sé: cathedral
segunda-feira: Monday
selos: stamps
sexta-feira: Friday
terça-feira: Tuesday
termas: spa
tesouraria: treasury
tourada: bullfight
velho/a: old
vila: town

PORTUGAL: FOOD AND DRINK

açorda: soup with bread and garlic
adega: wine cellar, bar
alface: lettuce
alho: garlic
almoço: lunch
ameijoas: clams
arroz: rice
arrufada de Coimbra: raised dough cake with cinnamon
assado: roasted
azeitonas: olives
bacalhau: cod
bacalhau à transmontana: cod braised with cured pork
balcão: balcony, or a counter in a bar or café
batata: potato
batido: milkshake
bem passado: well done (steak)
bica: espresso

bitoque de porco: pork chops
bitoque de vaca: steak
bolachas: cookies
branco: white (wine)
cabrito: kid (goat)
café com leite: coffee with milk
café da manhã: breakfast
caldeirada: shellfish stew
caldo: broth/soup
camarões: shrimp
caneca: pint-size beer mug
caracóis: snails
carioca: coffee with hot water; like American coffee
carne: meat
carne de vaca: beef
cebola: onion
cerveja: beer
chocos: cuttlefish
chouriço: sausage
churrasco: BBQ
churrasqueira: BBQ house
cogumelos: mushrooms
conta: bill
couvert: charge added to bill for bread
cozido: boiled
cozido no forno: baked
doce: sweet
ementa: menu
ervilhas: green peas
esacalfado: poached
espadarte: swordfish
espetadas: skewered meat served with melted butter
esturjão: sturgeon
fatia: slice
feijão: bean
frango: chicken
frito: fried
galão: coffee with hot milk
gasosa: soda
gelado: ice cream
grão: chickpeas
grelhado: grilled
guisado: stewed
hambúrguer no prato: hamburger patty with fried egg
imperial: draft beer
jantar: dinner
lagosta: lobster
lampreia: lamprey
laranja: orange
legumes: vegetables
leitão: suckling pig
linguado: sole
linguiça: very thin sausage
lula: squid
maçã: apple
manteiga: butter
mariscos: shellfish
massapão: marzipan
mexilhões: mussels
ovo: egg
padaria: bakery
pão: bread
pastelaria: pastry shop
peru: turkey
pimentos: peppers
polvo: octopus
porco: pork
posta: slice of fish or meat
prato do dia: dish of the day
presunto: ham
queijo: cheese
recheado: stuffed
salmão: salmon
sande/sanduíche: sandwich
seco: dry
sobremesa: dessert
suco: juice
tasca: bistro/cafe
tigelada: egg custard
tinto: red wine
toucinho do ceu: cake made with pumpkin, egg-yolk, and bacon-drippings
uva passa: raisin
vinho de casa: house wine
vinho verde: sparkling wine
vitela: veal

MOROCCO

adhan (A): call to prayer
agneau (F): lamb
aguelmane (A): lake
alcazaba (A): citadel
alcázar (A): palace
al-kebir (A): leather
aourir (A): small mountain
attarine (A): perfume
aujourd'hui (F): today
azrour (A): rock
auberge de jeunesse (F): youth hostel
azib (A): shepherd's hut
bab (A): gate
beurre (F): butter
bière (F), birra (A): beer
billet (F): ticket
blanc (F): white

boeuf (F): beef
boulettes de viande (F): meatballs
brochette (F): shish-kebab
borj (A): tower
bus (F): bus
chambre (F): room
chameau (F): camel
chaud (F): hot
compris (F): included
consigne (F): left luggage
couscous (F): semolina grain
coûter (F): to cost
crevettes (F): shrimp
dar: palace
demain (F): tomorrow
djebel (A): mountain peak
djellaba (A): long Moroccan garment
djoutia (A): flea market
douche (F): shower
droite (F): right
erg (A): sand dune
fassi (A): resident of Fes
fermé (F): closed
froid (F): cold
gare (F): train station
gare routière (F): bus station
gauche (F): left
gite (F): gov't approved Berber houses used as shelters
haj (A): Mecca pilgrimage
hammam (A): public bath
kasbah (A): fort, citadel, medina
kif (A): marijuana
litham (A): veil
louer (F): to rent
madrasa (A): school
makhzen (A): government
medina (A): old Arabic city
mellah (A): Jewish quarter
mihrab (A): prayer niche
msalla (A): prayer area
mosquée (F): mosque
moussem (A): festival
muezzin (A): calls Muslims to prayer
musée (F): museum
nouveau/nouvelle (F): new
oued (A): river
ouvert (F): open
palais (F): palace
pastilla (A): pigeon pie
piscine (F): pool
poisson (F): fish
poste (F): post office
qsar, qsour (pl.) (A): fortified village with curved, white-washed houses
rue (F): street
salle de bain (F): bathroom
smarine (A): textiles
souq (A): market
tagine (A): Moroccan stew
timbre (F): stamp
tmer (A): dates
toilette (F): toilet
train (F): train
vieux/vielle (F): old
ville (F): city
voiture (F): car
zellij (A): decorative tiles

INDEX

INDEX

MAP INDEX

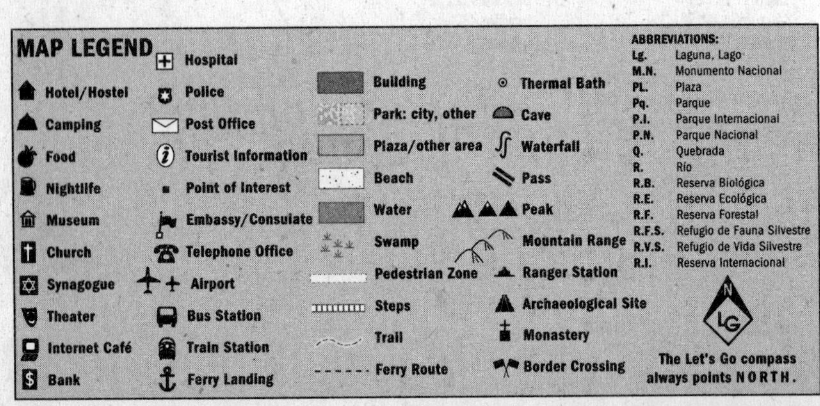

MAP LEGEND
Hotel/Hostel
Camping
Food
Nightlife
Museum
Church
Synagogue
Theater
Internet Café
Bank
Hospital
Police
Post Office
Tourist Information
Point of Interest
Embassy/Consulate
Telephone Office
Airport
Bus Station
Train Station
Ferry Landing
Building
Park: city, other
Plaza/other area
Beach
Water
Swamp
Pedestrian Zone
Steps
Trail
Ferry Route
Thermal Bath
Cave
Waterfall
Pass
Peak
Mountain Range
Ranger Station
Archaeological Site
Monastery
Border Crossing
ABBREVIATIONS:
Lg. Laguna, Lago
M.N. Monumento Nacional
PL. Plaza
Pq. Parque
P.I. Parque Internacional
P.N. Parque Nacional
Q. Quebrada
R. Río
R.B. Reserva Biológica
R.E. Reserva Ecológica
R.F. Reserva Forestal
R.F.S. Refugio de Fauna Silvestre
R.V.S. Refugio de Vida Silvestre
R.I. Reserva Internacional
N
LG
The Let's Go compass always points NORTH.

ABOUT LET'S GO

THE STUDENT TRAVEL GUIDE

Let's Go publishes the world's favorite student travel guides, written entirely by Harvard students. Armed with pens, notebooks, and a few changes of clothes stuffed into their backpacks, our student researchers go across continents, through time zones, and above expectations to seek out invaluable travel experiences for our readers. Because we are a completely student-run company, we have a unique perspective on how students travel, where they want to go, and what they're looking to do when they get there. If your dream is to grab a machete and forge through the jungles of Costa Rica, we can take you there. If you'd rather bask in the Riviera sun at a beachside cafe, we'll set you a table. In short, we write for readers who know that there's more to travel than tour buses. To keep up, visit our website, www.letsgo.com, where you can sign up to blog, post photos from your trips, and connect with the Let's Go community.

TRAVELING BEYOND TOURISM

We're on a mission to provide our readers with sharp, fresh coverage packed with socially responsible opportunities to go beyond tourism. Each guide's Beyond Tourism chapter shares ideas about responsible travel, study abroad, and how to give back to the places you visit while on the road. To help you gain a deeper connection with the places you travel, our fearless researchers scour the globe to give you the heads-up on both world-renowned and off-the-beaten-track opportunities. We've also opened our pages to respected writers and scholars to hear their takes on the countries and regions we cover, and asked travelers who have worked, studied, or volunteered abroad to contribute first-person accounts of their experiences.

FIFTY YEARS OF WISDOM

Let's Go has been on the road for 50 years and counting. We've grown a lot since publishing our first 20-page pamphlet to Europe in 1960, but five decades and 54 titles later our witty, candid guides are still researched and written entirely by students on shoestring budgets who know that train strikes, stolen luggage, food poisoning, and marriage proposals are all part of a day's work. This year, for our 50th anniversary, we're publishing 26 titles—including 6 brand new guides—brimming with editorial honesty, a commitment to students, and our irreverent style. Here's to the next 50!

THE LET'S GO COMMUNITY

More than just a travel guide company, Let's Go is a community that reaches from our headquarters in Cambridge, MA all across the globe. Our small staff of dedicated student editors, writers, and tech nerds comes together because of our shared passion for travel and our desire to help other travelers get the most out of their experience. We love it when our readers become part of the Let's Go community as well—when you travel, drop us a postcard (67 Mt. Auburn St., Cambridge, MA 02138, USA), send us an e-mail (feedback@letsgo.com), or sign up on our website (www.letsgo.com) to tell us about your adventures and discoveries.

For more information, updated travel coverage, and news from our researcher team, visit us online at www.letsgo.com.

HELPING LET'S GO. If you want to share your discoveries, suggestions, or corrections, please drop us a line. We appreciate every piece of correspondence, whether a postcard, a 10-page email, or a coconut. Visit Let's Go at **http://www.letsgo.com,** or send email to:

feedback@letsgo.com, subject: "Let's Go Spain & Portugal with Morocco"

Address mail to:

Let's Go Spain & Portugal with Morocco, 67 Mount Auburn St., Cambridge, MA 02138, USA

In addition to the invaluable travel advice our readers share with us, many are kind enough to offer their services as researchers or editors. Unfortunately, our charter enables us to employ only currently enrolled Harvard students.

Distributed by Publishers Group West.
Printed in Canada by Friesens Corp.

ISBN-13: 978-1-59880-317-4
ISBN-10:1-59880-317-4
Twenty-fifth edition
10 9 8 7 6 5 4 3 2 1

Let's Go Spain & Portugal with Morocco is written by Let's Go Publications, 67 Mount Auburn St., Cambridge, MA 02138, USA.